10th International Symposium on Practical Design of Ships and Other Floating Structures

2007 PRADS
10th TRIENNIAL

Editors:
Roger I. Basu • Vadim Belenky • Ge (George) Wang • Qing Yu

Volume 2

This publication contains the papers presented at the 10th International Symposium on Practical Design of Ships and Other Floating Structures held on 30 September to 5 October 2007 at Hotel Zaza in Houston, Texas, USA.

Editors: Roger I. Basu, Vadim Belenky, Ge (George) Wang and Qing Yu
Copy Editor: Donna Browning
Managing Editor: Carole McElroy
Production Editor: Joan Hauff

© Copyright 2007 ABS

ISBN 0-943870-04-6 PRADS 2007 – Volume 1
ISBN 0-943870-05-4 PRADS 2007 – Volume 2

All rights reserved. No part of this publication may be reproduced, stored in a retrieval system, or transmitted in any form or by any means, electronic, mechanical, photocopying, recording, or otherwise, without the prior written permission of ABS, 16855 Northchase Drive, Houston, TX 77060 USA.

Printed in the United States of America by Alcom Printing Group, Harleysville, Pennsylvania.

Preface

This PRADS Symposium is being held during a period of tremendous world economic activity. As the large Asian and other economies experience rapid growth, the demand for energy, raw materials and finished goods has increased correspondingly. As a result, our industry is experiencing a sustained boom in the construction of ships and offshore structures.

In this environment, symposia such as PRADS take on an added importance as forums where advances in the design, construction and operation of ships and other floating structures can be discussed. The demands on designers are ever increasing as competition drives the industry towards systems that are more optimized and have better performance, while also satisfying safety requirements. The symposium provides an opportunity for naval architects and engineers in industry and academia to interact and exchange ideas on a whole range of topics pertinent to the marine and offshore industries.

The first PRADS symposium was held in 1977 in Tokyo and subsequently in other venues in the Far East and Europe. This is the 10th such symposium and is the first to be held in the Americas. As such ABS and its cosponsors are particularly proud to be the hosts and organizers. In this regard we are fortunate that the Ship Structure Committee is associated with the organization of this symposium.

A little over 300 abstracts were submitted for consideration from which about 160 papers were finally approved to appear as part of the Proceedings of the 10th International Symposium on the Practical Design of Ships and Other Floating Structures held in Houston, Texas from 30 September to 5 October 2007. A broad range of subjects are represented in these symposium volumes including traditional subjects such as hydrodynamics, loads, strength and fatigue, topical subjects such as ice, and advanced areas such as computational fluid dynamics.

On behalf of the Standing Committee of PRADS and the local organizers we thank the authors for their contribution to these proceedings. We also thank the delegates for their participation in the symposium. The success of a symposium such as this relies on the efforts of many individuals. We take this opportunity to thank them for their dedication in making this event a success.

Roger I. Basu
Ge (George) Wang

PRADS Standing Committee

Prof. S. Motora (Honorary Chairman), Ship and Ocean Foundation, Japan
Dr. R.I. Basu (Chairman), ABS, USA
Prof. R. Birmingham, University of Newcastle, United Kingdom
Dr. T. Borzecki, Technical University of Gdansk, Poland
Prof. W. Cui, China Ship Scientific Research Center, China
Prof. J.J. Jensen, Technical University of Denmark, Denmark
Dr. Jan O. de Kat, A.P. Moller-Maersk A/S, Denmark
Prof. T. Kinoshita, University of Tokyo, Japan
Prof. Chang-Sup Lee, Chungnam National University, Korea
Prof. E. Lehmann, Hamburg University of Technology, Germany
Prof. T. Moan, Norwegian University of Science and Technology, Norway
Dr. R. Porcari, CETENA, s.p.a., Italy
Prof. Sergio Sphaier, Federal University of Rio de Janeiro, Brazil
Dr. G. Wang (Secretary), ABS, USA

Honorary Committee

Mr. C.B. Choo, Chairman and CEO, Keppel Offshore & Marine Ltd., Singapore
Adm. R. Kramek, SNAME President, USA
Dr. D. Liu, Member, ABS Board of Directors, USA
Prof. A. Mansour, University of California at Berkeley, USA
RAdm B. M. Salerno, USCG, USA
Mr. R. Somerville, Chairman and CEO, ABS, USA
Dr. J. S. Spencer, National Transportation Safety Board, USA
VAdm. P. E. Sullivan, Commander, NAVSEA, USA

Program Committee

Mr. P. Cojeen, SSC/ US Coast Guard
Prof. C. Dalton, University of Houston
Mr. J. Gallagher, Chief Executive, BMT International
Prof. D. Karr, University of Michigan
Mr. P. Noble, Manager, ConocoPhillips Marine
Mr. F. Puskar, President, Energo Engineering
Prof. R. Randall, Texas A & M University
Dr. P. Stanton, Vice President, Technip USA
Mr. D. Wisch, Fellow, ChevronTexaco

Organizing Committee

Dr. R. I. Basu, ABS
Dr. V. Belenky, ABS
Lt. B. Gates, SSC / US Coast Guard
Ms. C. Nordstrom, ExxonMobil
Dr. G. Wang, ABS
Dr. Q. Yu, ABS

Sponsors

ABS
Ship Structure Committee
Herbert Engineering Corp.
Society of Naval Architects and Marine Engineering
Altair Engineering, Inc./Altair Hyperworks
Greater Houston Convention and Visitors Bureau

Table of Contents

Volume 1

Navy 1

3-D Potential Flow Simulation of Multiple Ships in Waves for Ship-to-Ship Transfer at Sea 1
Kenneth M. Weems, SAIC, Sheguang Zhang, SAIC, Woei-Min Lin, SAIC, and Sean M. Kery, Oceaneering Intternational Inc.

Assessing the Effectiveness of Dynamic Deck Motion Limit Systems 10
Brook Sherman, USCG and Virginia Polytechnic Institute & State University, Leigh McCue, Virginia Polytechnic Institute & State University, Naipei P. Bi, Naval Surface Warfare Center, and Judah Milgram, Naval Surface Warfare Center

On Naval Classification 19
Derek Novak, ABS, and Glenn Ashe, ABS

Sloshing and Hydroelasticity

The Influence of Nonlinearities on Wave-induced Motions and Loads Predicted by Two-dimensional Hydroelasticity Analysis 27
J.H. Park, University of Southampton, and P. Temarel, University of Southampton

Hydro-Elastic Criterion for Practical Design 35
Hannes Bogaert, MARIN, and Mirek Kaminski, MARIN

Prediction of Pressure variation in the tank of LNG Carrier 44
Joong Nam Lee, Samsung Heavy Industries, Ho Byung Yoon, Samsung Heavy Industries, K. Kawabata, Samsung Heavy Industries, Ki Hun Joh, Samsung Heavy Industries, Moon Keun Ha, Samsung Heavy Industries, Tai Yong Lee, KAIST, and Sung Hyun Hong, KAIST

Vibration

Finite Element Modeling for Superstructure Vibration of a VLCC - Structural Modeling and Damping Ratio 50
Yu Takeda, Ishikawajima-Harima Heavy Industries, Isao Neki, Ishikawajima-Harima Heavy Industries, and Hiroki Kusumoto, IHI Marine United Inc.

Propeller Broad Band Excitation and Associated Ship Structure Response 57
N. Buannic, Principia R.D, F. Besnier, Principia R.D, L. Jian, Principia R.D, A. Blanchet, AKER Yards, and S. Branchereau, AKER Yards

Measurements of Wave Induced Vibrations Onboard a Large Container Vessel Operating in Harsh Environment 64
Gaute Storhaug, Det Norske Veritas, and Erlend Moe, Det Norske Veritas

Safety 1

Risk Based Strength Calculation of Inland Navigation Vessels 73
Gennadiy V. Egorov, Marine Engineering Bureau, Odessa, Ukraine

Formal Safety Assessment of LNG Tankers 82
Erik Vanem, Det Norske Veritas, Pedro Antão, Instituto SuperiorTécnico, Francisco Del Castillo deComas, Navantia and Rolf Skjong, Det Norske Veritas

Consideration on Response Time Distribution for Evacuation Analyses 91
Keiko Miyazaki, National Maritime Research, and Susumu Ota, National Maritime Research Institute

Navy 2

Controllability of High-Speed Craft   97
Jessica Calix St. Pierre, Northrop Grumman Ship Systems, John. P. Hackett, Northrop Grumman Ship Systems, Christopher Bigler, Northrop Grumman Ship Systems, and Frans H.H.A. Quadvlieg, MARIN

Automated Long-Term Motions and Loads Analysis for the Design of Novel Vessels   105
Matthew Collette, SAIC, Woei-Min Lin, SAIC, Jun Li, SAIC, Han Yu, ABS, and Allen Engle, Naval Surface Warfare Center Carderock

A Numerical Approach to Predict the Cavitation Performance of Semi-balanced Rudders   114
Heinrich Streckwall, Hamburg Ship Model Basin, Je-Jun Park, Daewoo Shipbuilding & Marine Eng, and Young-Hun Jang, Daewoo Shipbuilding & Marine Eng

Loads 1 (Wave Induced)

Long Duration Simulation of Wave-Structure Interactions in a Numerical Wave Tank   122
Debabrata Sen, Indian Institute of Technology Kharagpur, and Nagan Srinivasan, National Oilwell Varco Houston

A Study on Nonlinear Wave Loads of a Large Container Carrier in Rough Seas   132
Yoshitaka Ogawa, National Maritime Research Institute

Influence of FPSO Length on the Global Loads Induced by Abnormal Waves   141
N. Fonseca, Technical University of Lisbon, C. Guedes Soares, Technical University of Lisbon, and R. Pascoa, Technical University of Lisbon

Shafting and Speed Trials

Analysis of Asymmetrical Shaft Power Increase During Tight Maneuvers   149
M. Viviani, Genoa University, C. Podenzana Bonvino, Genoa University, S. Mauro, INSEAN, M. Cerruti, Fincantieri C.N.I. Spa, D. Guadalupi, SPMM MARISTAT, and A. Menna, SPMM MARISTAT

Pont Aven, an Advanced Approach to the Design of a Fast Ferry Shaftline and Bearing Arrangement   158
Rik Roemen, Wärtsilä Propulsion Netherlands BV, and Jasper Grevink, Wärtsilä Propulsion Netherlands BV

Practical Aspects of Conducting Speed Trials in the Open Ocean   165
Frederick H. Ashcroft, General Dynamics NASSCO, and Andrew Davidson, General Dynamics NASSCO

Safety 2

Development of a Probabilistic Methodology for Damage Stability Regarding Bottom Damages   174
Felix-Ingo Kehren, Hamburg University of Technology, and Stefan Krüger, Hamburg University of Technology

Improving FSA as a Prerequisite for Risk-Based GBS   182
Christos A. Kontovas, National Technical University of Athens, Harilaos N. Psaraftis, National Technical University of Athens, and PanosZachariadis, Atlantic Bulk Carrier Management Ltd, Piraeus, Greece

Fuel Tank Protection: Implications for Container Ship Designs   191
Hendrik Bruhns, Germanischer Lloyd

Navy 3

Numerical Analyses on Hydrodynamic Characteristics of High Speed Catamarans in Waves ... 196
Yoshiyuki Inoue, Yokohama National University, and Md. Kamruzzaman, Nippon Kaiji Kyokai, Class NK

Hydrodynamic Assessment and Optimization of New Fast Foil Assisted SWAMH ... 205
Stefano Brizzolara, University of Genoa, and Dario Bruzzone, University of Genoa

Global Hull Girder Loads on High-Speed Monohulls ... 212
Balji Menon, ABS, Ahmed Ibrahim, ABS, and Derek Novak, ABS

Loads 2 (Hydrodynamics)

Efficient Estimation Method for Design Wave-induced Load and Consideration of the Limited Wave Height Effect ... 217
Hiroshi Kawabe, Tokai University, and Torgeir Moan, Norwegian University of Science and Technology

Advanced Hydrodynamic Analysis of LNG Terminals ... 224
X.B. Chen, Bureau Veritas, F. Rezende, Bureau Veritas, S. Malenica, Bureau Veritas, and J.R. Fournier, Single Buoy Moorings, Inc.

Passenger Submersible Hydrostatic and Hydrodynamic Numerical Surface Stability Analysis ... 234
Lin Li, ABS, and Ravinder Tanwar, ABS

Fabrication and Fatigue

Statistical B-Spline FEM for Predicting Effects of Geometric Covariance ... 242
Hyun Chung, University of Michigan, and Jae-Seon Yum, Mokpo National

Development of Automatic Computer-Aided Engineering System for Weld Distortion Analysis in Ship Production ... 250
Jung-Goo Park, Samsung Heavy Industries, Hee-Young Heo, Samsung Heavy Industries, Yun-Sok Ha, Samsung Heavy Industries, Tae-Won Jang, Samsung Heavy Industries, Kyeong-Hee Han, Altair Engineering, Sang-Heon Lee, Altair Engineering, Song-Soo Moon, Altair Engineering, and T.K. Narayan, Altair Engineering

Simulation of Behavior of Fatigue Cracks: A Complete Industrial Process on a Ship Deck Beam ... 257
M. Serror, Bureau Veritas, D. Lebaillif, Giat Industries, and I. Huther, CETIM

Safety 3

CATS - Cost-effectiveness in Designing for Oil Spill Prevention ... 266
Erik Vanem, Det Norske Veritas, Øyvind Endresen, DNV Research & Innovation, and Rolf Skjong, Det Norske Veritas

Passenger Ferry Accidents in Bangladesh: Design and Socio-economic Aspects ... 275
Kho Shahriar Iqbal, Osaka University, Kazuhiko Hasegawa, Osaka University, Gabriele

Bayesian Estimation of Wave Spectra - Proper Formulation of ABIC ... 284
Ulrik Dam Nielsen, Technical University of Denmark

Stability: Framework and Methodology 1

Risk-based Frameworks for Ship Design and Approval ... 293
Pierre C. Sames, Germanischer Lloyd AG

Safe Return to Port A Framework for Passenger Ship Safety ... 299
Dracos Vassalos, Universities of Glasgow and Strathclyde

On Performance-Based Criteria for Intact Stability ... 309
Vadim Belenky, ABS, Jan Otto de Kat, A.P. Møller - Mærsk A/S, and Naoya Umeda, Osaka University

Loads 3

Experimental Investigation of the Application of Response Conditioned Waves for Long-Term Nonlinear Analyses   322
Ingo Drummen, Norwegian University of Science and Technology, and Torgeir Moan, Norwegian University of Science and Technology

Development of Measurement System in Sea Trial Using VDR   330
Hyun-Soo Kim, Samsung Heavy Industries, Gun-Il Park, Samsung Heavy Industries, Ki-Jung Kim, Samsung Heavy Industries, Hyun-Sook Jang, Samsung Heavy Industries, Jae-Woong Choi, Samsung Heavy Industries, and Mun-Keun Ha, Samsung Heavy Industries

Ultimate Strength 1

Ultimate Strength of Trapezoidal-Profile Stiffened Aluminum Panels Subjected to Transverse Compression, Considering HAZ Effects   336
Qiaofeng Chen, Norwegian University of Science and Technology, and Torgeir Moan, Norwegian University of Science and Technology

A Method for Estimating the Uncertainties in Ultimate Longitudinal Strength of Cross Section of Ship's Hull Based on Nonlinear FEM   345
Minoru Harada, Nippon Kaiji Kyokai, and Toshiyuki Shigemi, Nippon Kaiji Kyokai

On the Effect of Damage to the Ultimate Longitudinal Strength of Double Hull Tankers   354
Rui M. Luis, Technical University of Lisbon, Arwa W. Hussein, Technical University of Lisbon, and C. Guedes Soares Technical University of Lisbon

Design 1 (CNG Carriers)

Development of a Guide Using Guidance for Novel Concepts   363
Phillip G. Rynn, ABS, Harish N. Patel, ABS, and Chris Serratella, ABS

Features of CNG Carrier Design   373
Scott C. McClure, A. C. McClure Associates Inc., Hien T. Djie, A. C. McClure Associates Inc., and Charles N. White, EnerSea Transport LLC

Feasibility Study of Combined Carriage of CNG and Crude Oil   379
I. Rana, Technip UK, and R. S. Dow, University of Newcastle upon Tyne

Stability: Framework and Methodology 2

Principle and Application of Continuation Methods for Ship Design and Operability Analysis   388
Kostas J. Spyrou, National Technical University of Athens, and Ioannis G. Tigkas, National Technical University of Athens

Dynamic Stability Criteria Based on the Simulation of Full Scale Accidents   396
Stefan Krueger, Hamburg University of Technology, and Florian Kluwe, Hamburg University of Technology

A Capsizing Probability under Dead Ship Condition Taking Account of an Effect of a Correlation of Winds with Waves   404
Yoshitaka Ogawa, National Maritime Research Institute

Slamming/Spring/Whipping 1

Hybrid Approach to Compute Ship Slamming ... 412
S. P. Singh, Indian Register of Shipping, and Manoj Kumar, Indian Register of Shipping

Springing/Whipping Response of a Large Ocean-Going Vessel - Investigated by an Experimental Method ... 419
Gaute Storhaug, Det Norske Veritas, and Torgeir Moan, Norwegian University of Science and Technology

Assessment of Whipping Effects Induced by Stern/Bow-flare Slamming ... 428
Giovanni Cusano, CETENA SpA, Luca Sebastiani, CETENA SpA, and Giorgio Bacicchi, Fincantieri

Ultimate Strength 2

Ultimate Strength of Open Corrugated Panels ... 437
J. Kippenes, Det Norske Veritas, E. Byklum, Det Norske Veritas, and E. Steen, Det Norske Veritas

Ultimate Limit State Design of Stiffened Plate Structures under Combined Biaxial Compression and Lateral Pressure Loads ... 445
Jeom Kee Paik, Pusan National University, Jung Kwan Seo, Pusan National University, Bong Ju Kim, Pusan National University, and Owen F. Hughes, Virginia Tech

Experimental and Numerical Investigations on the Ultimate Strength of Curved Stiffened Plates ... 453
S.-R. Cho, University of Ulsan, H.-Z. Park, Hyundai MipoDockyard, H.-S. Kim, University of Ulsan, and J.-S. Seo, University of Ulsan

Design 2

A Contribution to Knowledge Based Engineering Methods in Ship Structural Design ... 461
Robert Bronsart, University of Rostock, and Michael Zimmermann, University of Rostock

Decision Support Methodology for Concept Design of Multi-Deck Ship Structures ... 468
Vedran Zanic, University of Zagreb, Jerolim Andric, University of Zagreb, and Pero Prebeg, University of Zagreb

A Methodology for Creating Design Ship Responses ... 477
Laura K. Alford, University of Michigan, Muhammed S. Khalid, University of Michigan, DaeHyun Kim, University of Michigan, Kevin Maki, University of Michigan, and Armin W. Troesch, University of Michigan

Stability: State-of-the-Art 1

Intact Stability of Ships - Recent Developments and Trends ... 487
Alberto Francescutto, University of Trieste

Review of Damage Stability of Ships - Recent Developments and Trends ... 497
Apostolos D. Papanikolaou, National Technical University of Athens

Intact and Damage Stability of Ships and Offshore Structures - Bridging the Gap ... 510
Vadim Belenky, ABS, and Andrew Breuer, ABS

Slamming/Spring/Whipping 2

Experimental and Numerical Study on the Water Entry of Symmetric Wedges and a Stern Section of Modern Containership — 518
S. H. Yang, HHI, H. H. Lee, HHI, T. H. Park, HHI, I. H. Lee, HHI, and Y. W., HHI

Analysis of the Ship Response to Stern Slamming Loads — 527
Daniele Dessi, INSEAN, Michele De Luca, INSEAN, Riccardo Mariani, INSEAN, and Daniele Carapellotti, INSEAN

Experimental Study of Whipping Responses Induced by Stern Slamming Loads — 535
Hanbing Luo, China Ship Scientific Research Center, Qiang Qiu, China Ship Scientific Research Center, and Zheng-quan Wan, China Ship Scientific Research Center

Structural Reliability

Structural Reliability of Ship Hull Subjected to Nonlinear Time Dependent Deterioration, Inspection and Repair — 543
Yordan Garbatov, Technical University of Lisbon, and Carlos Guedes Soares, Technical University of Lisbon

Calibration of the Hull Girder Ultimate Capacity Criterion for Double Hull Tankers — 553
Torfinn Hørte, Det Norske Veritas, Ge Wang, ABS, and Nigel White, Lloyd's Register

Approximate Method for Probabilistic Presentation of the Cross-Sectional Properties of Shipbuilding Structural Profiles and Hull Girder — 565
Lyuben D Ivanov, ABS, Ge Wang, ABS, and Ai-Kuo Lee, ABS

Design 3 (Container Carrier)

Practical Initial Design Optimization of Large Container Ships — 574
T. Okada, IHI, M. Toyoda, IHI, and E. Kobayashi, IHI

Container Vessels - Potential for Improvements in Hydrodynamic Performance — 580
Uwe Hollenbach, HSVA GmbH, Hilmar Klug, HSVA GmbH, and Friedrich Mewis, HSVA GmbH

Stability: State-of-the-Art 2

Stability of Floating Offshore Structures — 588
Dracos Vassalos, Universities of Glasgow and Strathclyde, Dimitris Konovessis, Universities of Glasgow and Strathclyde, Kie Hian Chua, Universities of Glasgow and Strathclyde, and Zafer Ayaz, Universities of Glasgow and Strathclyde

Stability of Deep Water Drilling Semi Submersibles — 595
Arjan Voogt, MARIN, and Julian Soles, GlobalSantaFe

Fatigue 1

Effect of Toe Grinding on Fatigue Strength of Ship Structure — 601
Hong Ryeul Ryu, HHI, Wha Soo Kim, HHI,, Woo Il Ha, HHI, Sung Won Kang, Pusan National University, and Myung Hyun Kim, Pusan National University

Fatigue Strength between Arc and Laser Hybrid Welded Joints — 609
H. Remes, Helsinki University of Technology, and P. Varsta, Helsinki University of Technology

Fatigue Crack Control in Structural Details Using Surface Peening — 617
Shi Song Ngiam, Bureau Veritas Consulting, and Feargal P Brennan, Cranfield University

Collision and Grounding

Damage Assessment and Impact Resistant Design of FPSOs with Respect to Supply Vessel Collisions ... 622
  Lin Hong, MARINTEK, Jørgen Amdahl, MARINTEK, Hagbart S. Alsos, MARINTEK, and Frank Klæbo, MARINTEK

Static and Dynamic Analysis of a Tanker During Grounding ... 631
  H. S. Alsos, Norwegian University of Science and Technology, and J. Amdahl, Norwegian University of Science and Technology

Structural Integrity of Column of Semi-Submersible Platform, Subjected to Supply Boat Collisions ... 639
  Alexandre P. Saraiva, CENPES Petrobras, and Julio C. R. Cyrino, COPPE/UFRJ

Design 4

Product Platform-Based Development of Engineered-to-Order Ships ... 650
  Jan Jaap Nieuwenhuis, Schelde Naval Shipbuilding, and Ubald Nienhuis, Delft University of Technology

A New Weighted Support Vector Regression and its Application in Freight Capacity Prediction of Fleets ... 661
  Dongqin Li, Wuhan University of Technology, Lizheng Wang, Wuhan University of Technology, Chengfang Wang, Wuhan University of Technology, and Shunhuai Chen, Wuhan University of Technology

Fuzzy Optimal Arrangement of Spaces within a Zone-deck Region of a Ship ... 666
  Eleanor Nick, University of Michigan, and Michael G. Parson, University of Michigan

Volume 2

CSR 1

A Study on Design Modification of a VLCC Based on CSR Requirements ... 674
Minsu Cho, Daewoo, SeongKi Kim, Daewoo, ManSoo Kim, Daewoo, and SungKon Han, Daewoo

Common Structural Rules for Tankers: From Design Situations to Rule Requirements ... 677
Liv Hovem, Det Norske Veritas, Ragnar Thunes, Sevan Marine AS, Torfinn Hørte, Det Norske Veritas, and Åge Bøe, Det Norske Veritas

A Study on Thickness Effect on Welded Joint of Longitudinal Stiffeners ... 687
Tetsuya Nakamura, Universal Shipbuilding Corporation, and Satoshi Yamamoto, Universal Shipbuilding Corporation

Dynamics 1 (Parametric Roll)

Preventing Parametric Roll with Use of Devices and their Practical Impact ... 693
Naoya Umeda, Osaka University, Hirotada Hashimoto, Osaka University, Shohei Minegaki, Osaka University, and Akihiko Matsuda, National Research Institute of Fisheries Eng

Nonlinear Aspects of Coupled Parametric Rolling in Head Seas ... 699
Marcelo A S Neves, LabOceano COPPE/UFRJ, and Claudio A Rodríguez, LabOceano COPPE/UFRJ

On Parametric Rolling of Ships ... 707
J. Randolph Paulling, University of California, Berkeley

Strength 1

Estimation of Maximum Stress of a Container Ship by Means of Design Irregular Wave and Direct Loading Analysis Method ... 716
Toichi Fukasawa, Kanazawa Institute of Technology, and Satoshi Miyazaki, Mitsubishi Heavy Industries

Structural Analysis of Asphalt Carriers ... 724
Joško Parunov, University of Zagreb, Ivo Senjanovic, University of Zagreb, and Ivica Donkov, Iceberg Ltd.

Structural Behavior of Suezmax Tanker Under Extreme Bending Moment ... 731
Tiago P. Estefen, COPPE/UFRJ, Leandro C. Trovoado, COPPE/UFRJ, and Segen F. Estefen, COPPE/UFRJ

Design 5

Product Lifecycle Management and Business Transformation: Concepts for the Marine and Offshore Industries ... 741
Robert G. Beadling, Dassault Systemes Americas Corporation

Habitability: Setting Criteria Fit for Humans ... 749
Clifford C. Baker, ABS, Kevin P. McSweeney, ABS, Denise B.McCafferty, ABS, and E. Johan Hendrikse, Jr., ABS

Multicriterion Scantling Optimization of the Midship Section of a Passenger Vessel Considering IACS Requirements ... 758
T. Richir, University of Liege, J.-D. Caprace, University of Liege, N. Losseau, University of Liege, M. Bay, University of Liege, M. G. Parsons, University of Michigan, S. Patay, Aker Yards, and P. Rigo University of Liege

CSR 2

Progressive Hull Collapse Characteristics of Tanker Structures Designed by IACS Pre-CSR and CSR Methods ... 764
   Jeom Kee Paik, Pusan National University, Jung Kwan Seo, Pusan National University, Bong Ju Kim, Pusan National University, and Owen F. Hughes, Virginia Tech

The Application of CSR for Design of Bulk Carriers with CSR Notation ... 776
   Yingqiu Chen, China Classification Society, and Zhihu Zhan, China Classification Society

Optimal Design of Longitudinal Scantlings Amidships for Oil Tanker Based on JTP Rule ... 784
   Chunyan Ji, Jiangsu University of Science and Technology

Dynamics 2

Large Scale Seakeeping Experiments in the New, Large Towing Tank B600 ... 790
   Jean-François Leguen, Bassin d'essais des careens, and D. Fréchou, Bassin d'essais des careens

Improvement of Safety in a Seaway for Large Container Ships by Reducing the Risk of Parametric Rolling Utilizing Rudder Control ... 799
   Yojiro Wada, Samsung Heavy Industries, Sam Kwon Hong, Samsung Heavy Industries, Dong Yeon Lee, Samsung Heavy Industries, Yun We Choi, Samsung Heavy Industries, and Young Jin Lee, Samsung Heavy Industries

Numerical Modeling of Roll Dynamics and Virtual Instrumentation Based Ship Fin Control ... 808
   V. Anantha Subramanian, Indian Institute of Technology, G.Dhinesh, Indian Institute of Technology, and G. Asokuma, Indian Institute of Technology

Strength 2

Mesh Size Effects in Simulating Ductile Fracture of Metals ... 815
   Y. N. Li, University of Michigan, D. G. Karr, University of Michigan, and G. Wang, ABS

Simulation of Response of Steel Plates under Pressure Pulses ... 823
   M.S. Samuelides, National Technical University of Athens, D. Daliakopoulos, National Technical University of Athens, and J.K. Paik, Pusan National University

Finite Element Analysis of a 1.2 Tonnes WIG Craft under Water Impact Loads ... 831
   Bok Won Lee, Korea Advanced Inst. of Science and Technology, Chun-Gon Kim, Korea Advanced Inst. of Science and Technology, Mi Young Park, Hankuk Fiber Glass Co., Ltd., Han Koo Jeong, Maritime and Ocean Engineering Research Institute, and Kuk Jin Kang, Maritime and Ocean Engineering Research Institute

Materials

Design Optimization of Steel Sandwich Hoistable Car-Decks Applying Homogenized Plate Theory ... 839
   Jani Romanoff, Helsinki University of Technology, and Alan Klana, Helsinki University of Technology

The Problem of Fatigue on Large High Speed Craft and the Comparison between the Behavior of High Tensile Steel Structures and Aluminum Alloy Ones: The View of an International Shipbuilder ... 847
   S. Ferraris, Fincantieri C.N.I., and V. Farinetti, Fincantieri C.N.I.

Application of Sandwich Panels in Design and Building of Dredging Ships ... 855
   A Jeroen Kortenoeven, IHC HOLLAND Dredgers BV, Bart Boon, Bart Boon Research and Consultancy, and Arnold de Bruijn, IHC Holland Dredgers BV

SSC 1

Mechanical Collapse Testing on Aluminum Stiffened Plate Structures for Marine Applications ... 865
Jeom Kee Paik, Pusan National University, Celine Andrieu, Alcan Marine France, and H. Paul Cojeen, US Coast Guard

Improving Fatigue Life for Aluminum Cruciform Joints by Weld Toe Grinding ... 881
Naiquan Ye, Norwegian University of Science & Technology, and Torgeir Moan, Norwegian University of Science & Technology

Welding Distortion Analysis of Hull Blocks Using Equivalent Load Method Based on Inherent Strain ... 889
Chang Doo Jang, Seoul National University, Yong Tae Kim, Seoul National University, Young Chun Jo, Seoul National University, and Hyun Su Ryu, Seoul National University

CFD 1

A CIP-based Cartesian Grid Method for Nonlinear Wave-body Interactions ... 894
Masashi Kashiwagi, Kyushu University, Changhong Hu, Kyushu University, Ryuji Miyake, Nippon Kaiji Kyokai, and Tingyao Zhu, Nippon Kaiji Kyokai

CFD Hull Form Optimization of a 12,000 cu. yd. (9175 m3) Dredge ... 903
Bruce L. Hutchison, The Glosten Associates, and Karsten Hochkirch, Friendship Systems GmbH

Hydrodynamic Performance and Structural Design of a SWATH Ship ... 911
You-Sheng Wu, China Ship Scientific Research Center, Qi-Jun Ni, China Ship Scientific Research Center, Wei Xie, China Ship Design and Development Center, Sa-Ya Zhou, China Ship Design and Development Center, Guo-Hong You, China Ship Scientific Research Center, Chao Tian, Shanghai Jiao Tong University, Yan Zhang, Dalian Scientific Test and Control Technology Institute, and Qiang Wu, China Shipbuilding Industry Corporation

Corrosion

Development of New Applied Models for Steel Corrosion in Marine Applications Including Shipping ... 919
Robert E Melchers, The University of Newcastle

Strength and Deformability of Corroded Steel Plates Estimated by Replicated Specimens ... 928
Yoichi Sumi, Yokohama National University

Simulation of Inspections on Ship Plates with Random Corrosion Patterns ... 935
A.P. Teixeira, Technical University of Lisbon, and C. Guedes Soares, Technical University of Lisbon

SSC 2

The Impact of Fusion Welds on the Ultimate Strength of Aluminum Structures ... 944
Matthew D. Collette, SAIC

Ultimate Strength of Frames and Grillages Subject to Lateral Loads - an Experimental Study ... 953
Claude Daley, Memorial University Newfoundland, Greg Hermanski, Institute for Ocean Technology NRC, and Mihailo Pavic, BMT Fleet Technology Ltd.

Research Needs in Aluminum Structure ... 960
Robert A. Sielski, Naval Architect - Structures, California

CFD 2

Significance of the EFFORT Project for the Design of Complicated Sterns   968
A. de Jager, IHC, M. Visonneau, Fluid Mechanics Laboratory, P. Queutey, Fluid Mechanics Laboratory, J. Windt, MARIN, and A. Thoresson, Berg Propulsion

Stern Flow Analysis and Design Practice for the Improvement of Self-propulsion Performance of Twin-skeg Ships   981
D. W. Park, HHI, M. G. Kim, HHI, S. H. Chung, HHI, and Y. K. Chung, HHI

Ship Hull Simulations with a Coupled Solution Algorithm   989
Philip J. Zwart, ANSYS Canada, Philippe G. Godin, ANSYS Canada, Justin Penrose, ANSYS Europe, and Shin Hyung Rhee, Seoul National University

Fatigue 2

Experimental Investigation on Fatigue Behavior of Side Longitudinals of Tanker under Periodic Storm Loading   997
Kukbin Kim, HHI, Jinsoo Park, HHI, Pan Young Kim, HHI, and Wha Soo Kim, HHI

Fatigue Design of Web Stiffened Cruciform Connections   1003
Inge Lotsberg, Det Norske Veritas, Trond A. Rundhaug, Det Norske Veritas, Harald Thorkildsen, Det Norske Veritas, Åge Bøe, Det Norske Veritas, and Torbjørn Lindemar, Det Norske Veritas

On Corrosion Fatigue Crack Propagation of TMCP Steel in Seawater Ballast Tanks   1012
Won Beom Kim, Pusan National University, and Jeom Kee Paik, Pusan National University

SSC 3

New Directions in Ship Structural Regulations   1016
Claude Daley, Memorial University Newfoundland, Andrew Kendrick, BMT Fleet Technology Ltd., and Mikhail Pavic, BMT Fleet Technology Ltd.

A Method for the Quantitative Assessment of Performance of Alternative Designs in the Accidental Condition   1025
Jonathan Downes, Newcastle University, Colin Moore, Herbert Engineering Corporation, Atilla Incecik, Newcastle University, Estelle Stumpf, Bureau Veritas, and Jon McGregor, Bureau Veritas

Extreme Waves and Ship Design   1033
Craig B. Smith, Dockside Consultants, Inc.

Hydrodynamics 1

An Integrated Approach for Hydrodynamic Optimization of SWATH Hull Forms   1041
Claus Abt, Friendship Systems GmbH, and Gregor Schellenberger, Nordseewerke GmbH

Study on Reduction of Wave-making Resistance in Multiple Load Conditions using Real-coded Genetic Algorithm   1050
Akihito Hirayama, Akishima Laboratories (Mitsui Zosen), and Jun Ando, Kyushu University

Investigations into the Effect of Bulb Shape on Wave Resistance of Ro Ro Vessel   1057
Rahul Subramanian, Indian Institute of Technology, G. Dhinesh, Indian Institute of Technology, and K. Murali, Indian Institute of Technology

Fatique Analysis 1

Application of the Two-parameter Unified Approach for Fatigue Life Prediction of Marine Structures — 1064
Weicheng Cui, China Ship Scientific Research Center, Rugang Bian, China Ship Scientific Research Center, and Xiangchun Liu, Harbin Engineering University

Local Stress Analysis of Welded Ship Structural Details under Consideration of the Real Weld Profile — 1071
Wolfgang Fricke, Hamburg University of Technology, and Adrian Kahl, Germanischer Lloyd

Estimate Method of Hotspot Stress for Ship Structural Members Based on FE Analysis — 1080
Norio Yamamoto, Nippon Kaiji Kyokai, Research Institute, Naoki Osawa, Osaka University, and Koji Terai, Nippon Kaiji Kyokai Research Institute

SSC 4

Design of X-joints in Sandwich Structures for Naval Vessels — 1086
Brian Hayman, Det Norske Veritas, Christian Berggreen, Technical University of Denmark, Christian Lundsgaard-Larsen, Technical University of Denmark, Kasper Karlsen, Technical University of Denmark, and Claus Jenstrup, Technical University of Denmark

Hydrodynamic Pressure and Structural Loading of High-Speed Catamaran and SES — 1096
William S. Vorus, University of New Orleans, and Robert D. Sedat, US Coast Guard

Recent Hydrodynamic Tool Development and Validation for Motions and Slam Loads on Ocean-Going High-Speed Vessels — 1107
Woei-Min Lin, SAIC, Matthew Collete, SAIC, David Lavis, CDI Marine, Stuart Jessup, Naval Surface Warfare Center, and John Kuhn, SAIC

Hydrodynamics 2

Speed Power Prediction Using Potential Flow Codes — 1117
Uwe Hollenbach, HSVA GmbH, and Henning Grashorn, HSVA GmbH

Application of Artificial Neural Networks for the Prediction of Inland Water Units Resistance — 1126
Maged M Abdel Naby, Alexandria University, Heba W Leheta, Alexandria University, Adel A Banawan, Alexandria University, and Ahmed A Elhewy, Alexandria University

Fatigue Analysis 2

A Comparative Study for the Fatigue Assessment of Typical Ship Structures using Hot Spot Stress and Structural Stress Approaches — 1134
Myung Hyun Kim, Pusan National University, Sung Won Kang, Pusan National University, Seong Min Kim, Pusan National University, Jae Myung Lee, Pusan National University, Young Nam Kim, Hanjin Heavy Industries & Construction Co., Sung Geun Kim, Hanjin Heavy Industries & Construction Co., Kyoung Eon Lee, Hanjin Heavy Industries & Construction Co., and Gyeong Rae Kim, Hanjin Heavy Industries & Construction Co.

Study on the Relationship between Shell Stress and Solid Stress in Fatigue Assessment of Ship Structure — 1142
Myung Hyun Kim, Pusan National University, Sung Won Kang, Pusan National University, Seong Min Kim, Pusan National University, Jae Myung Lee, Pusan National University, Young Nam Kim, HHI, Sung Geun Kim, HHI, Kyoung Eon Lee, HHI, and Gyeong Rae Kim, HHI

A Study on the Fatigue under Combined Tensile and Compressive Mean Stresses in Ship Structure — 1150
Naoki Osawa, Osaka University, Kiyoshi Hashimoto, Osaka University, Junji Sawamura, Osaka University, Tohei Nakai, Osaka University, and Shota Suzuki, Osaka University

Offshore 1

Extreme Value Predictions for Wave- and Wind-induced Loads on Floating Offshore Wind Turbines using FORM — 1158
Sunvard Joensen, Technical University of Denmark, Jørgen J. Jensen, Technical University of Denmark, and Alaa E. Mansour, University of California

Hydrodynamic Design of a Monocolumn Platform Avoiding Excessive Heave and Pitch Motions — 1167
Fernando G. S. Torres, CENPES/PETROBRAS, Sergio H. Sphaier, LabOceano/COPPE/UFRJ, Isaias Q. Masetti, CENPES/PETROBRAS, Ana Paula dos Santos Costa, CENPES/PETROBRAS, and Joel S. Sales Jr., LabOceano/COPPE/UFRJ

Comparative Analysis of Design Criteria for Rigid Risers — 1175
Leile M. Froufe, ABS, and Theodoro A. Netto, COPPE /UFRJ

Propellers

Development of Overlapping Propellers for a Large LNG Carrier — 1186
Kazuyuki Ebira, Kawasaki Shipbuilding Corporation, Christian Johannsen, HSVA GmbH, and Yasunori Iwasaki, Kawasaki Shipbuilding Corporation

Design of Marine Propellers Using Genetic Algorithm — 1193
Jaekwon Jung, Samsung Heavy Industries, Jae-Moon Han, Samsung Heavy Industries, Kyung Jun Lee, Samsung Heavy Industries, and In-Haeng Song, Samsung Heavy Industries

Numerical Modeling of Propeller Tip Flow with Wake Sheet Roll-up by B-spline Higher-order Panel Method — 1200
G.-D. Kim, MOERI, B.-K. Ahn, Chungnam National University, B.-G. Paik, MOERI, W.-S. Lee, Chungnam National University, and C.-S. Lee, Chungnam National University

Ice 1

Measuring of Ice Induced Pressures and Loads on Ships in Model Scale — 1206
Janne Valkonen, Helsinki University of Technology, Koh Izumiyama, National Maritime Research Institute Japan, and Pentti Kujala, Helsinki University of Technology

On Connection between Mesoscale Stress of Geophysical Sea Ice Models and Local Ship Load — 1214
Tarmo Kõuts, Tallinn University of Technology, Kequang Wang, University of Helsinki, and Matti Leppäranta, University of Helsinki

A Comparison of Local Ice Pressure and Line Load Distributions from Ships Studied in the SAFEICE Project — 1221
Robert Frederking, NRC Canadian Hydraulics Centre, and Ivana Kubat, NRC Canadian Hydraulics Centre

Offshore 2

Recent Design Advances in Ship-shaped Offshore Installations — 1230
Jeom Kee Paik, Pusan National University

Engineering Challenges in Offshore Construction Work in Conjunction with Offshore Fixed and Floating Platforms — 1238
Gengshen Liu, Aker Marine Contractors US Inc.

Extreme Load and Fatigue Damage on FPSO in Combined Waves and Swells — 1247
Booki Kim, ABS, Xiaozhi Wang, ABS, and Yung-Sup Shin, ABS

Cavitation of Rudder and Propulsors

Numerical Study on Horn Rudder Section to Reduce Gap Cavitation — 1255
Sunho Park, Hanjin Heavy Industries & Construction Co., Jaekyung Heo, Hanjin Heavy Industries & Construction Co., and Byeongseok Yu, Hanjin Heavy Industries & Construction Co.

Development of Rudder Cavitation Suppression Devices and Its Concept Verification through Experimental and Numerical Studies — 1261
Shin Hyung Rhee, Seoul National University, Jung-Keun Oh, Seoul National University, Seung-Hee Lee, Inha University, and Hyochul Kim, Inha University

Performance Prediction of Single or Multi-Component Propulsors using Coupled Viscous/Inviscid Methods — 1269
Spyros A. Kinnas, University of Texas, Hanseong Lee, FloaTec, Hong Sun, University of Texas, and Lei He, University of Texas

Ice 2

Maximum Ice-Induced Loads on Ships in the Baltic Sea — 1278
Pentti Kujala, Helsinki University of Technology, Janne Valkonen, Helsinki University of Technology, and Mikko Suominen, Helsinki University of Technology

Length of Ice Load Patch on a Ship Bow in Level Ice — 1287
Koh Izumiyama, National Maritime Research Institute Mitaka, Tadanori Takimoto, National Maritime Research Institute Mitaka, and Shotaro Uto, National Maritime Research Institute Mitaka

Strength and Vibration Multimode Control for Ship, Moving in Ice Condition — 1295
V. Alexandrov, Admiralty Shipyards, A. Matlakh, State Marine Technical University St. Petersburg, Yu Nechaev, State Marine Technical University St. Petersburg, and V. Polyakov, State Marine Technical University St. Petersburg

Offshore 3 (FPSO)

Structural Analysis and Modifications - Two Tankers for Offshore FPSO and FSO Service — 1303
Lars Henriksen, Viking Systems, Arata Kamishohara, MODEC, and Hiroyuki

Damping and Stiffness from the Taut-Leg Mooring Lines in FPSOs Model Testing — 1311
Antonio C. Fernandes, LabOceano COPPE/UFRJ, Fabio P. S. Mineiro, Petrobras, André L.Rosa, LabOceano COPPE/UFRJ, Joel S. Sales, LabOceano COPPE/UFRJ, and André Ramiro, LabOceano COPPE/UFRJ

Maneuvering and Control

The Propulsion and Maneuvering Concept of the BCF- Super C- Class Double End Ferries — 1317
Stefan Krüger, Hamburg University of Technology, Heike Billerbeck, Flensburger Schiffbau GmbH, and Tobias Haack, Flensburger Schiffbau GmbH

Correction of Current Effects from Maneuvering Trials — 1324
Young Jae Sung, HHI, Kyoung-soo Ahn, HHI, and Tae-il Lee, HHI

Concept Basis of On-board Intelligent Systems Development — 1331
Alexander B. Degtyarev, St. Petersburg State University, and Yury I. Nechaev, St. Petersburg State University

Ice 3

Engineering Practice on Ice Propeller Strength Assessment Based on IACS Polar Ice Rule - URI3 — 1337
Sing-Kwan Lee, ABS

Structural Risk Analysis of a NO96 Membrane Type LNG Carrier in the Baltic Ice Operation — 1346
Sungkon Han, Daewoo, Jae-Yeol Lee, Daewoo, Young-Il Park, Daewoo, and Jungsin Che, Innoqual Co. Ltd.

A Study on Design Modification of a VLCC Based on CSR Requirements

Minsu Cho [1], SeongKi Kim [1], ManSoo Kim [1] SungKon Han [2]

[1] Hull Basic Design Team, Daewoo Shipbuilding & Marine Engineering Co. Ltd.
Seoul, Korea
[2] New Product R&D Team, Daewoo Shipbuilding & Marine Engineering Co. Ltd.
Koje, Kyungnam, Korea

Abstract

A VLCC was designed based on CSR (Common Structural Rules) by DSME (Daewoo Shipbuilding and Marine Engineering Co., LTD), and it is found that the new design based on the CSR requirements is quite different from that based on the previous Class Rules.

The present study addresses the main causes and results of scantling increase, structural modifications, and final change in hull weight of the VLCC design based on the CSR requirements.

Keywords

VLCC; CSR; DSME; Weight; Structural design.

Introduction

There have been dramatic changes in structural design for double hull oil tankers since the issue of Common Structural Rules (CSR) for the double hull oil tanker in April 2006. The CSR is now gaining support from ship structure engineers, since many unclear regulations became rather specific through the unification of various rules of Classification Societies.

Longer design periods and more design resources, however, are to be taken due to the increase in design criteria, such as local scantling of multi-section due to dynamic pressure, prescriptive requirement for primary supporting members, and increased load cases for FEM.

In addition, the hull weight increase from the requirement becomes burdensome to shipowners and shipbuilders at the same time.

A VLCC design has been developed according to the CSR requirement and discussion has been made for scantling changes, modifications of structural design details, and resultant increase in hull weight in the present paper.

Design Concept of CSR

The CSR development committee reported the objectives of the development of the new unified rules as follows:

(1) To eliminate competition between class societies with regard to structural requirements and standards.

(2) To employ the combined experience and resources of all IACS societies to develop a set of unified Rules.

(3) To ensure that a vessel meeting these new standards will be recognized by industry as being at least as safe and robust as would have been required by any of the existing Rules.

(4) To fully embrace the intentions of the anticipated IMO requirements for goal based new construction standards.

The following design concepts characterize the CSR in line with the proposed objectives mentioned above:

- North Atlantic environment as basis for loads and fatigue standard
- 25 years design life
- Net Thickness Approach
- Enhanced Strength Assessment
- Hull Girder Ultimate Strength
- Advanced Buckling Analysis
- Local Fine Mesh Analysis to check Repeated Yield
- Slamming Draft based on Ballast Water Exchange

These concepts are found to summarize the common understanding prevailing among naval architects and to exclude optimisms underlying uncertainties in requirements especially on maintenance.

Governing Design Factors to Weight Increase

A number of critical design factors are noticed during the development of a VLCC by the authors from DSME. Details are as follows:

25 years design life based on north Atlantic environment

The previous Class rules were based on design life of 20 years and World-Wide wave condition, but the CSR changed the design life requirement to 25 years with North Atlantic wave condition. Thus, these modified, more severe design concepts are found to give significant effects on the weight increase of longitudinal members in order to satisfy fatigue and local strength requirements.

Net Thickness Approach

Some of the previous class rules had no corrosion addition (e.g. LR) or were found to have a different corrosion addition concept from the wastage allowance that is referred to by shipowners during operation. There was much confusion and many complaints reported from the shipowners for the unclear definitions.

A new net thickness approach is adopted in the CSR and the resulting corrosion additions of the CSR are found to be quite larger than those on the previous rules shown in Table 1. However, since the design concept has been changed, a direct comparison should not be made.

Table 1: Corrosion Addition (unit: mm)

Structural Member		ABS	DNV	CSR
Upper Deck in WBT		2.0	2.0	4.0
Upper Deck in COT		1.0	1.0	4.0
Internal in WBT	Within 3m below top of tank	2.0	3.0	4.0
	Elsewhere	1./2.	1.5	3.0
Internal in COT	Within 3m below top of tank	1.5	2.0	4.0
	Elsewhere	1./1.5	0./1.	2.5
Side Shell		1.5	1.0	3.5
Inner Hull Longi. BHD & Hopper		1.5	1.0	3.0
Inner Bottom		1.5	1.5	4.0
Bottom Shell		1.0	1.0	3.0

For all the locations listed in Table 1, the CSR gives larger corrosion additions. All CSR requirements are thought to be properly modified / compromised from previous rules due to the modified corrosion additions. However, the weight increase due to the enhanced corrosion additions is found to be demanding considering the experiences of the authors from the detailed calculations for local requirements and F.E. analysis results.

Extreme loading for FEM

An F.E. analysis for the VLCC with the CSR loading conditions reveals very high stresses or buckling factors as compared to those by the previous Rules at some details. Design modification or increases in plate thickness, which are not expected from the previous design experiences, have to be implemented to satisfy CSR.

There are about 30 load cases for the F.E. analysis for a VLCC; therefore, it is difficult to specify which load case governs required reinforcement of each structural member. However, the load case shown in Fig. 1 would be one of the extreme load cases because this load case causes the design of deck transverse web was modified and bottom and side shell plate thickness was increased to a considerable extent.

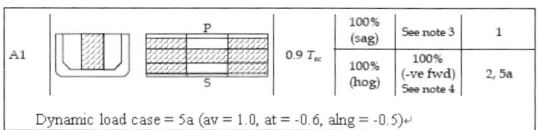

Fig. 1: Load Case A1, Dynamic LC=5a

Bottom Slamming

Specially, the CSR requirement for bottom slamming is estimated to be much more severe than the previous rules. Thus, heavy reinforcements are necessary in the bottom area subjected to slamming pressure.

Design Modification Result

Weight increases for each structural member due to the CSR requirements are calculated using a reference VLCC – a VLCC with DNV Class by DSME design.

Longitudinal Members

Hull weight increase of longitudinal members is mainly due to local scantling, fatigue life, and the advanced buckling requirements. The weight increases of the longitudinal members are summarized in Table 2.

Table 2: Weight Increase for Longi. Members

Structural Member		Increase
Plating (mm)	Side Shell	1.0~2.0
	Inner Hull Longitudinal BHD	1.0~2.0
	Longitudinal BHD	1.0~3.0
Stiffener (Weight Increase)	Side Shell	3%
	Inner Hull Longitudinal BHD	4%
	Upper Deck	-7%
	Hopper	3%
	Longitudinal BHD	5%
	Inner Bottom	10%
	Bottom	13%

Transverse Members

Scantlings of transverse members were increased mainly because of yielding and advanced buckling requirements. In addition, deck transverse web was enlarged to satisfy yielding criteria as shown in Fig.2. The weight increases are summarized in Fig.2 and 3.

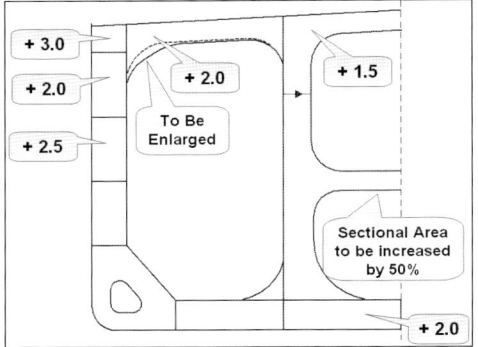

Fig. 2:   Transverse Web

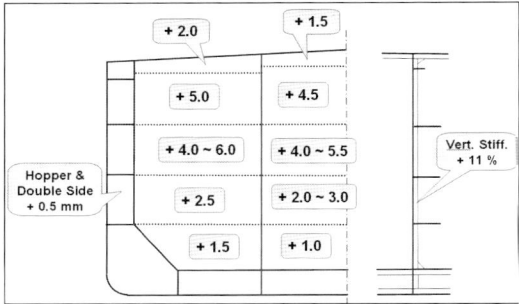

Fig. 3:   Transverse Bulkhead

Bottom slamming

The CSR requirements for bottom slamming were found to cause the scantling increases shown in Table 3.

Table 3:   Summary of Bottom Slamming Evaluation

ITEM	DNV	CSR
Slamming Draft	6.6 m	6.6 m
Slamming Pressure	926 kPa	947 kPa
Net Shear Area of Bottom Longitudinal	92.1 cm2	128.4 cm2
Corrosion Addition	1.5 mm	3.0 mm
Web Size of Bottom Longitudinal	635*15.0 "AH"	700*20.5 "AH"
Floor Thickness	18.0 MILD	25.5 "AH"

Conclusions

The new CSR requirements are found to demand large scantlings in general compared to the previous Classification Rules. The present study investigates the required reinforcements using a DSME-developed VLCC design with DNV Class.

The investigation has been made for longitudinal members, transverse members and fore bottom area separately comparing the new scantlings with the reference vessel.

It can be concluded in general that the CSR specifies high standard requirements in terms of loading and corrosion addition, which turn out to require heavy scantlings and result in a significant hull weight increase. The total weight increase was summarized in Table 4.

Table 4:   Summary of Weight Increase

Structural Member		Weight Increase (Ton)
Cargo Area	Longi. Member	700
	Trans. Member	650
	Slamming, sloshing, etc.	300
Outside Cargo Area		300
Total		1950

The above hull weight increase is found to be quite a burden to shipowners and shipbuilders as well. However, some owners and builders began to accept the weight increase on condition that the new ship with CSR should become more robust and reliable.

In addition, the design period and labor costs for the design increased almost 3 times as much as the previous because of the increased design criteria, such as local scantling of multi-section due to dynamic pressure, prescriptive requirements for primary supporting members, and the increased load cases and fine mesh models for FEM. However, as single design can be used for any class vessel, engineering work can be reduced for consecutive projects even with a different class. Thus, more engineering work for design optimization or further development can be performed at the next projects. Consequently the CSR will contribute to the development of shipbuilding in the long run.

References

International Association of Classification Society LTD (IACS) (2006), "Common Structural Rules (CSR) for Double Hull Oil Tankers."

10th International Symposium on Practical Design of Ships and Other Floating Structures
Houston, Texas, United States of America
© 2007 American Bureau of Shipping

Common Structural Rules for Tankers:
From Design Situations to Rule Requirements

Liv Hovem[1], Ragnar Thunes[2], Torfinn Hørte[1], Åge Bøe[1]

[1] Det Norske Veritas,
[2] Sevan Marine AS

Abstract

The systematics behind the development of the Common Structural Rules for Tankers is described. It is shown how identified design situations encountered by the ship during its life are described by load scenarios and how these are addressed by corresponding rule requirements. It is shown that for the requirements for the assessment of the scantling's ultimate and serviceability limit states, each load scenario is represented by two combinations of static and dynamic loads to achieve a consistent rule set with respect to safety level. Some simplifications are made during the rule development including omission of load scenarios or load combinations justified never to be governing. The background for choosing the two load combinations and the justification and process of elimination of the non-governing load scenarios is also covered.

The applied systematic process is generic and the motivation for describing the methodology is to show how a risk based approach can be beneficial also for structural rule development, and that such methodology can be useful for future rule development projects and for assessment of ships of novel design.

Keywords

Risk based rule development; Load scenarios; Design format; Uniform safety level; Common Structural Rules.

Introduction

The development process of the Common Structural Rules (CSR) for Tankers was based on a defined risk-based framework to ensure that ships built in compliance with these Rules meet the goals and objectives of the Rules.

The objectives of the Rules are to mitigate the risks of structural failure in relation to safety of life, environment and property and to ensure adequate durability of the hull structure for its intended life. To meet the objectives all design situations and corresponding hazards as identified in a systematic review (hazard identification) must be addressed during the rule development. For strength requirements the relevant hazards to address are the load scenarios that may occur during the operation of the ship. Such load scenarios can be represented as load combinations, and it is important that a consistent safety level for all load combinations is achieved in the final Rules. The rule developers must also aim at developing Rules that are user friendly (as simple as possible) and at the same time transparent. However, it can be difficult to understand what hazards or load scenarios are considered during the development because only the potential dimensioning or governing cases are included in the final rule set as illustrated in Figure 1 below.

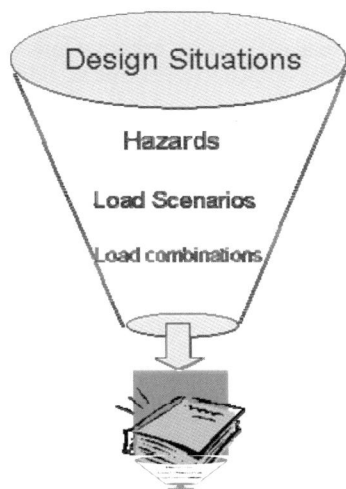

Fig. 1: From Design Situations to Rule Requirements

The purpose of this paper is thus three-fold; (i) to describe the methodology for how the intended design situations and load scenarios are included in the Rules, (ii) to describe how a consistent safety level is achieved and (iii) to describe the process of eliminating load scenarios that are not dimensioning for the ship structure. The paper touches upon the following issues:

- Identification of design situations and load scenarios

- Alternative approaches to achieve a consistent safety level for the identified load scenarios and combinations of loads
- Application of the selected approach
- Elimination of redundant load combinations.

Because this paper focuses on how the dimensioning loads are identified and included in the Rules, discussion and description of important topics such as e.g. the applied capacity models, dynamic load formulations, alternative design formats or rule calibration are not included.

Identification of Design Situations and Load Scenarios

A systematic review (hazard identification) should cover the structural configurations and arrangements that are intended covered by the Rules and all phases of the life of a ship. The following phases or design situations were identified during the rule development of Common Ship Rules for Tankers:

- Design
- Construction
- Operation
- Repair
- Scrapping

The hazards identified for the operational phase are the most significant hazards to address by structural requirements and cover load scenarios both at sea (loaded and ballast voyages between ports) and in harbor conditions (sheltered waters, ports and terminals)

The load scenarios cover operations such as transit conditions, loading and unloading, tank testing conditions, ballast water exchange situations and special operation in harbor such as e.g. propeller afloat. In addition accidental flooding is covered.

The identified load scenarios can be represented by combinations of both static and dynamic local loads, which are usually pressure load components and static and dynamic global loads which are usually hull girder bending moments. Given the broad range of operations that are covered by the Rules the number of load combinations is significant. To reduce the number of combinations it is a principle in the Rules that the most unfavourable combination of static and dynamic loads should be addressed and that the combinations should be sufficiently severe and varied so as to encompass all conditions that can reasonably occur during operation. However, even when this principle is applied the number of combinations of static and dynamic loads is considerable and a process of eliminating load scenarios and load combinations which are not governing was needed to meet the aim of as simple as possible Rules. The elimination process is described later.

A Consistent Safety Level

The following describes a systematic and transparent approach to the ultimate and serviceability limit states (ULS/SLS) requirements that provides a consistent safety level for the load scenarios covered by the Rules. Alternative approaches to obtain an acceptable safety level for all combinations of static and dynamic loading are discussed.

The approaches discussed here are based on the working stress design format, which is the most commonly applied design format in the Common Structural Rules for Tankers (one exception is the hull girder strength criteria where the partial safety factor design format is applied). Consistency in safety level following different approaches is evaluated versus results from a simplified structural reliability analysis.

From a probabilistic point of view, one would aim for a consistent safety level in terms of the same target annual probability of failure for different structural elements where the consequences of failures are considered similar. How well a rule requirement meets this aim, depends on its ability to properly account for different combinations of uncertainties for the various structural elements it is intended to cover; e.g. some elements may be dominated by static loads, other by dynamic loads.

The wave loads, ship motions and accelerations are based on North Atlantic environment considering 25 years return period. This implies that the wave bending moments and shear forces acting on the hull girder, sea pressure acting on the shell and dynamic loads on internal structure caused by ship acceleration are consistent and correspond approximately to 10^{-8} probability of occurrence (per wave cycle).

Assessment of structural strength based on the working stress format can in principle be described as:

$$S + D \leq \eta R \qquad (1)$$

where
S   is the characteristic static loads (or load effects in terms of stresses), local and global
D   is the characteristic dynamic loads based on 10^{-8} probability of occurrence. The dynamic loads are normally a combination of local and global load components
R   is the characteristic structural resistance (e.g. yield/buckling etc)
η is the permissible utilization factor (resistance factor)

In such a rule format, the definition of the characteristic values and the value selected for the utilization factor are the means of providing a desired level of safety. However, it can be difficult to achieve the aim of consistent probability of failure if the same equation is intended to cover a large span of cases (e.g. structural elements experiencing significantly different combinations of static and dynamic loads). The reason is that with the utilization factor on the resistance only, the ratio between static and dynamic loading has to be approximately similar for two structural components in order to achieve a consistent safety level.

A simplified structural reliability analysis has been performed with basis in the rule requirement given in equation (1). Probability distributions, representing typical cases, have been assigned to the static and dynamic load effects as well as to the resistance. The purpose is to illustrate how the probability of failure varies depending on the ratio of static versus dynamic load, and for various utilization factors. A factor k_D has been defined as the ratio between dynamic and total load. From the reliability analysis results it is possible to find the total safety factor, defined as $1/\eta$, as a function of k_D at constant annual probability of failure. This is illustrated in Figure 2, and exemplifies the challenge of obtaining a consistent safety level by a simple rule formulation.

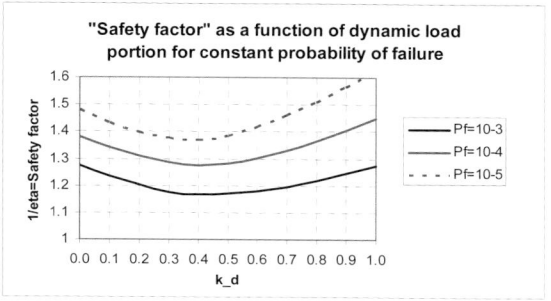

Figure 2 Safety factor as a function of k_D (dynamic portion of the load) at constant annual probability of failure.

Referring to Figure 2 the working stress format as expressed in equation (1) will be a horizontal line since there are no load factors on static and dynamic loads. For a selected probability of failure, the utilization factor can be tailored to a certain value of k_D. A utilization factor based on an equal ratio of static and dynamic load would be unacceptable for cases where either the static or the dynamic load is strongly dominant. It can thus be concluded that a consistent safety level can not be obtained by means of equation (1) alone and a constant utilization factor.

Note that the presented example is simplified and made for illustration purposes only. It should not be used as basis for setting actual requirements. Other assumptions would yield different results, but the principle is valid.

Criteria for selection of approach

In order to define a methodology that complies with the objectives, the following criteria for selection should be considered:

- Provide, as far as practically possible, a constant probability of failure for all combinations and relevant ratios of static and dynamic load effects.
- Applicable to all types of capacity models (longitudinal strength, local strength, Finite Element) and failure modes (yield, buckling etc)
- Applicable to all relevant structural elements

- Feasible to develop and calibrate
- Simple to use and maintain
- Transparent development

Alternative approaches

Alternative approaches to obtain an acceptable consistency in safety level for all combinations of static and dynamic loading are discussed below. As mentioned earlier, the alternatives are based on the working stress format. Assume the solid line in Figure 3 and Figure 4 represents the target safety level for the rules; i.e. constant probability of failure for different structural elements where failure is associated with similar consequences. All dynamic loads are assumed to be derived at 10^{-8} probability of occurrence. It is further assumed that most structural elements within the hull has a certain static load portion of the total load implying that dynamic load portions above 0.7 is not considered relevant concerning the ultimate and serviceability limit states requirements because fatigue is likely to be governing for structural elements where the dynamic load is strongly dominant. For the cases where the dynamic load is dominant for ULS/SLS requirements (e.g. bottom slamming and bow impact) alternative approaches applies. Note that the numbers given for the safety factors below are fictitious and have no explicit relevance other than illustrating the principle.

Alternative I

The design loads are given in terms of one combination of static and dynamic loads, i.e.

$$S + D \leq \eta R$$

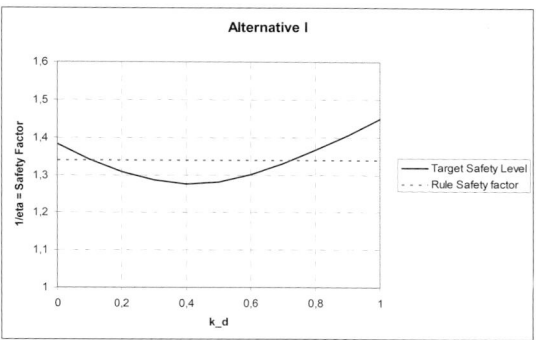

Figure 3 Rule safety factor and target safety level for alternative I.

The rule safety factor is illustrated by the horizontal line in Figure 3, and it can be seen that it is impossible to achieve a constant safety level with only one rule requirement for all combinations and ratios of dynamic and static loads.

A modified version of this alternative will be to develop acceptance criteria as a function of the level of dynamic loading. This will facilitate a constant safety level for all combinations of static and dynamic loading, but a variable safety factor may not be feasible to use in rule requirements.

Alternative II

The design loads are given in terms of two combinations of static and dynamic loads, i.e.

Combination A) $S \leq \eta_1 R$

Combination B) $S + D \leq \eta_2 R$

The b) combination is identical to alternative I and the a) combination considers static loading only (and the associated line in Figure 4 goes to zero for pure dynamic loading, $k_d=1$). It can be seen from the figure that two different assessment combinations improves the ability to obtain a consistent safety level within the range of dynamic loading. A second benefit of having two assessment conditions is that a second degree of freedom is introduced for calibration of the rule requirement.

This alternative may be modified and expanded to make it fit the target curve better than presented in Figure 4.

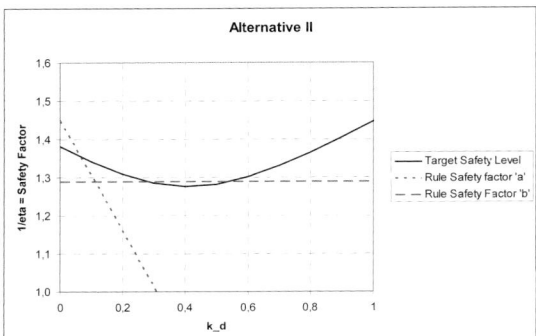

Figure 4. Rule safety factors and target safety level for alternative II.

Alternative III

The third option could be to select the characteristic values for the static loads, dynamic loads and the resistance to make the target safety level curve flat (horizontal). A constant safety level would be achieved for all combinations of static and dynamic loading with one Rule combination of static and dynamic loads as alternative I. This approach would however require very complex functions for describing the characteristic values for the loads as they would have to include information about and variation based on the ratio of static versus dynamic loading also taking into account the probability level of the dynamic load.

The Selected Approach

The requirements for the assessment of the scantlings for the ultimate and serviceability limit state categories in principle considers two combinations of static and dynamic loads. The purpose of the two is to provide a reasonably consistent safety level for relevant combinations and ratios of static and dynamic loads, while yet keeping a simple and practical approach.

For the working stress design method, which is the design format applied in the scantling requirements in Section 8 of the Common Ship Rules, the following format is thus applied;

Combination A) $S \leq \eta_1 R$

Combination B) $S + D \leq \eta_2 R$

Loads

The static loads are normally a combination of local and global components and are operational loads grouped into lightship weight, buoyancy loads, variable loads and other loads. The operational loads occur as a consequence of the operation and handling of the ship.

The dynamic loads are also normally a combination of local and global load components and are environmental loads due to external influences. The environmental loads covered by the Rules are loads due to wave action.

Accidental loads include loads that result as a consequence of an accident or operational mishandling of the ship. The accidental loads covered by the Rules are pressures on watertight boundaries due to flooding of compartments.

The characteristic values of the load components applied in the Rules are dependent on the design load combination being considered. The characteristic loads are typical values and are:

- for operational loads the 'expected' or specified values which may occur frequent
- for environmental loads typically a load at a given low probability of occurrence, i.e. an 'extreme' value which occur seldom

Capacity models

The failure modes are yield and buckling failure and the capacity models for the ULS/SLS requirement are

- first yield and buckling elastic capacity models
- plastic capacity and buckling slenderness

The first yield and buckling elastic capacity models are in general applied, but for specific issues such as design against impact pressures, the plastic capacity and buckling slenderness models are used. For more information about the capacity models reference is made to the Common Ship Rules for Tankers.

Acceptance criteria

The utilization factor (or acceptance criteria) are categorized into three sets and the specific acceptance criteria set that is applied for the different rule requirements depends on the probability level of the characteristic load, the criticality of the considered structural item and the applied capacity model. The acceptance criteria sets are denoted AC1, AC2 and AC3 and are conceptually shown in Table 1 and further described below.

Table 1: The acceptance criteria sets

Acceptance criteria set	Yield	Buckling
AC1 = η_1	70-80% of yield stress	Usage factor typically 0.8
AC2 = η_2	90-100 % of yield stress	Usage factor typically 1.0
AC3 = η_3	Plastic criteria	Slenderness criteria to achieve stocky design

The acceptance criteria set AC1 is applied when the combined characteristic loads are at a probability level close to the expected value. In practise this means that the loads occur often or frequent. The allowable stress for a frequent load is lower than for an extreme load to take into account effects of:

- Repeated yield (may cause low cycle fatigue)
- Allowance for some dynamic loading not explicitly included in the assessment.
- Margins for operational mistakes inducing increased operational loads, e.g. overfilling of tanks, increased hull girder bending moments etc.

The relative contribution from the static load varies for the different structural items and therefore the acceptance criteria may vary slightly dependent on the structure being considered.

The acceptance criteria set AC2 is applied when the combined characteristic loads are extreme values. High utilization is allowed because the considered loads are extreme loads with a low probability of occurrence. In practise this means that the loads occur seldom.

The acceptance criteria set AC3 is applied for capacity formulations based on plastic collapse models.

The Process of Eliminating Redundant Load Combinations – Operation at Sea

The following describes how the identified load scenarios are included in the Rules. Loads are combined with capacity models and acceptance criteria within the chosen approach. In principle all load scenarios should be addressed by both the A) and B) load combination as described earlier, however some simplifications are made during the rule development. When it can be justified that some of the load scenarios never govern they are not included explicitly in the Rules.

In Table A1 in the Appendix, the sea going load scenarios are listed. A discussion of each load scenario and how it is included in the Rules are given below. In Table A1 the redundant load scenarios and load combinations are identified by a strike through.

Load Scenario 1:
Seagoing – Transit - Operational and environmental loads

The load scenario applies to all structure and the load that the vessel has to withstand is the most unfavourable combination of static and cyclic dynamic loads.

The static loads consist of the global (S_{G1}) and local (S_{L1}) load components that are relevant for the structure being considered. The static global loads are associated by the permissible still water loads in sea-going conditions. The local static loads are given by the considered loading pattern and drafts and the loading patterns that in combination with the dynamic loads give the most onerous load on the structure are considered.

The dynamic loads consist of the global (D_{G25}) and local (D_{L25}) load components that that are relevant for the structure being considered. For the load scenario at sea in heavy weather, the rule applies loads with the 25 year return period as the characteristic load value. This value corresponds to the 10^{-8} probability level.

The applied capacity models (R_1) are first yield and buckling. The acceptance criteria set for design format **1A)** is AC1 because the combined characteristic loads are given at the probability level close to the expected value. The acceptance criteria set for design format **1B)** is AC2 (high utilization) because the considered loads are extreme loads with a low probability of occurrence. In practise this means that the loads occur seldom.

Combination **1A)** is not included in the Rules because it is covered by the operations in harbor and sheltered water, (Table A2). The reason is that the permissible static loads are higher in harbor and sheltered sea due to loading and unloading operations which give the need for increased permissible limits. Combination **1B)** is included in the Rules.

Load Scenario 2:
Seagoing – Transit - Impact Loads

The load scenario applies to the structure in the fore-body and the loads are impact loads in heavy weather, i.e. bottom slamming and bow impact pressure loads. Internal impact loads are not covered by the CSR for Tankers because such loads only occur in long tanks which are not typical for large tankers. Internal impact loads are covered by the individual class societies' rules for tanks exceeding limitations given in CSR for Tankers. The static loads (S_2) only include a local load component which in general is 0 because there is no or little local static pressure acting where and when impact pressures occur. The exception is counter pressure from ballast which is considered with bottom slamming pressure.

The dynamic load (D_i) is the external impact local load with short duration and a 25 year return period. This is considered an extreme load.

The capacity model is a plastic capacity model. The slenderness criteria are applied to achieve a stocky design. The applied acceptance criteria set is AC3 due to the plastic capacity model and extreme load.

Design format combination **2A)** is not included in the rules because the static load (S_2) is 0 or if present counteracting the impact pressure and hence reducing the net pressure, ref. remark on bottom slamming above. Combination **2B)** is included in the Rules.

Load Scenario 3:
Seagoing – Transit – Internal sloshing loads
The load scenarios apply to the structure forming the cargo tank boundaries and the load is internal sloshing pressures.

The static load includes both the global (S_{G3}) and the local (S_{L3}) static component, however the local static component is 0 in way of sloshing exposed areas or counteracting if the neighbouring tank is filled in which case using a value of 0 is conservatively chosen. The global static load is equal to the global static load considered in combination **1A)** and **1B)**.

The dynamic load (D_{slh}) is the local sloshing pressure load. The characteristic sloshing load is given at the 10^{-4} probability level, which is a load that may occur in moderate seas and is therefore considered frequent loads, where the chosen probability level is regarded as an expected value. Global dynamic loads are not relevant because it can be shown that these are out of phase with the dynamic local loads.

The applied capacity models are first yield and buckling and the applied acceptance criteria set is AC1 due to the probability level of the characteristic load which is close to the expected value.

3A) is not included in the rules because the local static load (S_{L3}) is 0 in way of sloshing exposed areas. **3B)** is included in the Rules.

Load Scenario 4:
Seagoing – Transit - Cyclic dynamic wave loads
This load scenario applies to all structure and is covered by the fatigue requirement and therefore not discussed further in this paper.

Load Scenario 5:
Seagoing - Ballast Water Exchange (by flow through and sequential method)
This load scenario applies to ballast tanks only, and the load that the structure must withstand is the most unfavorable combination of static and cyclic dynamic loads.

The static loads consist of the global (S_{G5}) and local (S_{L5}) load components that are relevant for the structure being considered. The static global load is similar to the static global load in combinations **1A and 1B)**. The static local loads reflect the tank pressures arising from the operation.

The dynamic loads are similar as for the seagoing – transit operation as in combination **1B)** as the design principle for the actual loading scenario is that the Rules should base the design criteria on ballast water exchange without weather restrictions.

The acceptance criteria set for the two design formats are AC1 and AC2 for the same reasons as described in combinations **1A and 1B)** above.

Combination **5A)** is not included explicitly in the rules because it is covered by the ballasting and tank testing operations in harbor and sheltered water. The permissible static global loads are typically higher in harbor and sheltered sea, and the static tank pressures are equal to or lower than the tank pressures from ballasting and tank testing operations in harbor and sheltered water. Combination **5B)** is included in the Rules.

Load scenario 6:
Sea-going - Ballasting
This load scenario applies to ballast tanks only and consists of the global (S_{G6}) and local (S_{L6}) load components that are relevant for the structure being considered. The static local load includes tank overfilling pressure. It is assumed that the operation takes place in sheltered areas or in calm weather indicated by the reduction factor k in **6B)**.

The static global load is equal to the static global load in combination **1A)** and **1B)**, but is less then for the operations in harbor and sheltered waters because the permissible still water bending and shear is typically higher in harbor/sheltered waters than in sea-going

The static local loads (S_{L6}) include the overfilling tank pressures arising from the operation. The overfilling tank pressure is considered being an extreme operational load because the overfilling tank pressure is a short duration situation that occurs relatively seldom and that has limited uncertainty related to it, i.e. not a significant chance for experiencing a higher overfilling pressure than the specified design value. Careful operation is however also a basic assumption for this categorisation of the load.

The dynamic loads are in principle of the same magnitude as in combination **1B)**, however it can be argued that the dynamic loads can be reduced significantly (illustrated by $k \cdot D_{G25} + k \cdot D_{L25}$, in the Table A1 where k is a reduction factor) because the probability of the joint occurrence of the overfilling pressure (short duration) and extreme dynamic loads are small (not likely that the operation will take place in severe wave conditions).

Combination **6A)** is not included in the rules because it is covered by the load scenario ballasting in harbor sheltered waters. Combination **6B)** is not explicitly included in the rules due to the assumption of reduced dynamic load.

Load Scenario 7:
Seagoing – Tank testing
This load scenario applies to ballast tanks only.

Combination **7A)** is covered by the tank testing scenario in harbor and sheltered waters because the permissible still water bending and shear is higher in harbor/sheltered waters. Combination **7B)** is not covered explicitly due to a simplification which assumes that the magnitude of dynamic loads that occurs simultaneously with the tank testing pressure is lower than what occurs during ballast water exchange. This assumption can be justified by considering the joint probability of occurrence of dynamic and static loads during the tank testing operation.

The Process of Eliminating Redundant Load Combinations – Operation in Harbor

The following discusses the load scenarios that occur in harbor and sheltered water. A general assumption is that these operations occur in moderate environmental wave loads. The discussion refers to Table A2 in Appendix.

Load scenario 8:
Offshore loading and unloading
The load scenario is not explicitly covered by the CSR for Tankers. Offshore loading and unloading is implicitly covered by the assumption that the dynamic loads are reduced compared to the at sea in transit load scenario.

Load scenario 9:
Harbor and sheltered waters - Loading /unloading
The load scenario applies to all structure and the structure must withstand the most unfavorable combination of static and cyclic dynamic loads.

The static loads consist of the global (S_{G9}) and local (S_{L9}) load components that are relevant for the structure being considered. The static global loads are given by the permissible loads in harbor conditions which are higher than in seagoing conditions. The local static loads are given by the considered loading pattern and loading drafts. The loading patterns that in combination with the dynamic loads give the most onerous load on the structure are considered.

The dynamic loads consists of the global (D_{Gred}) and local (D_{Lred}) load components that that are relevant for the structure being considered. For the load scenarios in harbor and sheltered waters, the dynamic load is assumed significantly reduced compared to the load level at 25 year return period.

The applied capacity models (R_9) are elastic yield and buckling equal to in combination **1A)** and **1B)**.

Combination **9A)** is included in the rule requirements. Combination **9B)** is not included as it is assumed that it is covered by the **9A)** condition and the seagoing transit condition described in combination **1B)**.

Load Scenario 10:
Harbor and sheltered waters – Transit
The static loads are equal to or lower than the static loads in other load scenarios in harbor and sheltered waters. The dynamic loads are assumed significantly reduced relative to the load level at 25 year return period. This load scenario is thus covered by other load scenarios (e.g. load scenarios 1, 9, 11 and 12)

Load Scenario 11:
Harbor and sheltered waters – Ballasting
This load scenario applies only to ballast tanks.

The static global loads are given by the permissible loads in harbor conditions which are higher than in seagoing conditions. The static local loads ($S_{L11} = S_{L6}$) is the overfilling tank pressures arising from the operation, and is considered an extreme operational load because the overfilling tank pressure is a short duration situation that occurs seldom. Careful operation is a basic assumption for this categorisation of the load.

The dynamic loads ($D_{Gred} + D_{Lred}$) are reduced compared to the load scenarios in sea going conditions. In addition the probability of joint occurrence between a severe dynamic load and S_{L11} is assumed small, and thus the dynamic load is neglected.

The applied capacity models (R_{11}) are elastic yield and buckling equal to in combination **1A)** and **1B)**.

The applied acceptance criteria for combination A) are AC1. AC1 is usually applied in conjunction with frequent loads and it is thus a conservative approach to apply AC1 in this situation with a load categorized as extreme. However, the application of AC1 can also justify the neglecting of the dynamic loads in this load scenario.

Combination **11 A)** is included in the rules, while combination **11 B)** is not included explicitly in the rules, but assumed covered by combination **11A)**.

Load scenario 12:
In harbor and sheltered waters - Tank testing
This load scenario applies only to ballast tanks.

The static global loads are given by the permissible loads in harbor conditions which are higher than in seagoing conditions. The static local loads ($S_{L12} = S_{L7}$) is the tank testing pressures arising from the operation.

The dynamic loads ($D_{Gred} + D_{Lred}$) are reduced in sheltered waters compared to the load scenarios in sea going conditions. In addition the joint probability of occurrence of severe dynamic and static loads during the tank testing operation is assumed low.

The applied capacity models (R_{12}) are elastic yield and buckling equal to in combination **1A)** and **1B)**.

Combination **12A)** is included in the rules with AC1 for expected loads. Combination **12B)** is not included explicitly but assumed covered by combination **12A)**.

Load scenario 13:
In harbor - Special conditions in harbor (e.g. propeller afloat or dry docking)
These conditions are only checked if they are included in the loading manual.

Static loads are taken from the loading manual. The dynamic loads are not relevant because the operations are normally done in flat water. The applied capacity models (R_{13}) are elastic yield and buckling equal to combinations **1A)** and **1B)**.

Combination **13A)** is included in the rules with AC1.

Load scenario 14.
Accidental Flooding in Seagoing condition
The discussion refers to Table A3 in Appendix and the load scenario applies to watertight boundaries and the collision bulkhead. The collision bulkhead is more critical then the water tight boundaries because the consequence of failure is higher.

The static local load (S_{L14}) is due to flooding to the water line in damaged condition and is considered an extreme load. Global loads are neglected for this case. The dynamic loads are assumed reduced relative to the 25 year return period because the joint probability of accidental flooding and 25 year storm is considered low.

The applied capacity models (R_{14}) are elastic yield and buckling.

The applied acceptance criteria set is AC2 for the water tight bulkhead since the load is considered extreme, however for the collision bulkhead some additional safety margin is included due to the high consequence of failure and AC1 is applied.

Combination **14 A**) is included in the rules while combination **14 B**) is not included in the rules. The reason is that the rule criterion that controls the accidental flooding scenario is a simplified criterion. The simplification refers to that combination B) is not applied, instead there is allowance for some environmental load in A) by plasticity above the given elastic capacity model. Permanent deformation is allowed to occur in this load scenario or the water tight boundaries.

Conclusions

The paper describes a systematic approach that goes from identifying design situations and load scenarios to the final Rule requirements. It is shown how a consistent safety level is achieved through a simple approach. The systematics is risk based and generic, and even though there are rooms for improvements, the concept should be applicable also to structural rule development for other ship types and for assessment of novel designs.

Acknowledgement

The authors would like to thank colleagues in American Bureau of Shipping, Lloyd's Register and Det Norske Veritas who have actively contributed to the discussions regarding the above during the development of the Common Structural Rule for Tankers.

The views represent those of the authors and do not necessarily reflect the views of Det Norske Veritas and Sevan Marine AS.

References

IACS (2006a). "Common Structural Rules for Double Hull Tankers", Rules, January 2006. http://www.iacs.org.uk/csr/double_hull_oil_tankers/index.html

Mathiesen, Jan (2003) "Pilot Reliability Analysis Using Ship Rules Format for Local Design with Varying Static and Dynamic Load Content", DNV Memo TNCNO713/JMAT/71300000-J-920

IMO (2002). "Guidelines for the Use of Formal Safety Assessment (FSA) in the IMO Rule Making Process," MSC Circ 1023/MEPC Circ. 392, April 2002

Appendix

Table A1: Sea-going load scenarios

Load Scenarios - Sea going cases			Load Combination			Rule requirements	
Operation	Loads that the vessel is exposed to and has to withstand:		No.	Design methods	'Probability' of load	Rule Format Ref Sect 8, CSR for Tankers	Accept Criteria Set
Transit	Operational loads and environmental wave loads	Most unfavourable combination of static and cyclic dynamic loads	1A)	$S_{G1} + S_{L1} \leq \eta_{1a} R_1$	Expected-value	-	-
			1B)	$S_{G1} + S_{L1} + D_{G25} + D_{L25} \leq \eta_{1b} R_1$	Extreme value	$S_{G1} + S_{L1} + D_{G25} + D_{L25} \leq \eta_{1b} R_1$	AC2
		Impact Loads in heavy weather (bottom slamming and bow impact pressure)	2A)	$S_2 \leq \eta_{1a} R_2$	-	-	-
			2B)	$S_2 + D_i \leq \eta_{2b} R_2$	Extreme value	$S_{L2} + D_{25,i} \leq \eta_{2b} R_2$	AC3
		Internal Impact	-	-	-	-	-
	Operational loads and environmental wave loads	Internal sloshing loads	3A)	$S_{G3} + S_{L3} \leq \eta_{3a} R_3$	-	-	-
			3B)	$S_{G3} + S_{L3} + D_{slh} \leq \eta_{3b} R_3$	Expected	$S_{G3} + D_{slh} \leq \eta_{1a} R_1$	AC1
		Cyclic wave loads	4)	$D_{fatigue-range} \leq \eta_4 R_4$	Expected	$D_{fatigue-range} \leq \eta_4 R_4$	-
BWE by flow through and sequential	Operational loads and environmental wave loads	Most unfavourable combination of static and cyclic dynamic loads	5A)	$S_{G5} + S_{L5} \leq \eta_{5a} R_5$	Expected-value	-	-
			5B)	$S_{G3} + S_{L5} + D_{G25} + D_{L25} \leq \eta_{5b} R_5$	Extreme value	$S_{G5} + S_{L5} + D_{G25} + D_{L25} \leq \eta_{1b} R_1$	AC2
Ballasting	Operational loads (incl. overfilling pressure) and wave loads.	Most unfavourable combination of static and cyclic dynamic loads	6A)	$S_{G6} + S_{L6} \leq \eta_{6a} R_6$	Extreme-value	-	-
			6B)	$S_{G6} + S_{L6} + k \cdot D_{G25} + k \cdot D_{L25} \leq \eta_{6b} R_6$	Extreme-value	-	-
Tank Testing	Operational loads and environmental wave loads.	Most unfavourable combination of static and cyclic wave loads.	7A)	$S_{G7} + S_{L7} \leq \eta_{7a} R_7$	Expected-value	-	-
			7B)	$S_{G7} + S_{L7} + k \cdot D_{G25} + k \cdot D_{L25} \leq \eta_{7b} R_7$	Extreme-value	-	-

Table A2 Harbor and sheltered water load scenarios

Load Scenarios - Harbor and sheltered water

Operation	Loads that the vessel is exposed to and has to withstand:		No.	Load Combination Design Method	'Probability' of load	Rule Format Ref Sect 8, CSR for Tankers	Accept Criteria Set
Offshore loading/ unloading	Operational loads and moderate environmental wave loads	Most unfavourable combination of static and cyclic wave load	~~8A)~~	~~$S_{G8} + S_{L8} \leq \eta_{8a} R_8$~~			
			~~8B)~~	~~$S_{G8} + S_{L8} + D_{Gred} + D_{Lred} \leq \eta_{8a} R_8$~~			
Loading /unloading	Operational loads and moderate environmental wave loads	Most unfavourable combination of static and cyclic wave load	9A)	$S_{G9} + S_{L9} \leq \eta_{9a} R_9$	Expected value	$S_{G9} + S_{L9} \leq \eta_{1a} R_1$	AC1
			~~9B)~~	~~$S_{G9} + S_{L9} + D_{Gred} + D_{Lred} \leq \eta_{9a} R_9$~~	~~Extreme Value~~	-	-
Transit	Operational loads and sea loads and inertia loads due to moderate waves	Most unfavourable combination of static and cyclic wave load	~~10A)~~	~~$S_{G10} + S_{L10} \leq \eta_{10a} R_{10}$~~	-	-	-
			~~10B)~~	~~$S_{G10} + S_{L10} + D_{Gred} + D_{Lred} \leq R_{10}/\eta_{10b}$~~			
Ballasting	Operational loads (incl. overfilling pressure) and moderate environmental wave loads	Most unfavourable combination of static and cyclic wave load	11A)	$S_{G11} + S_{L11} \leq \eta_{11a} R_{11}$	Extreme value	$S_{G11} + S_{L11} \leq R_1/\eta_{1a}$	AC1
			~~11B)~~	~~$S_{G11} + S_{L11} + D_{Gred} + D_{Lred} \leq \eta_{11b} R_{11}$~~	-	-	-
Tank testing	Operational loads and sea loads and inertia loads due to moderate waves	Most unfavourable combination of static and cyclic wave load	12A)	$S_{G12} + S_{L12} \leq \eta_{12a} R_{12}$	Expected value	$S_{G12} + S_{L12} \leq R_1/\eta_{1a}$	AC1
			~~12B)~~	~~$S_{G12} + S_{L12} + D_{Gred} + D_{Lred} \leq \eta_{12a} R_{12}$~~			
Special conditions in harbor	Operational loads e.g propeller afloat or dry dock	Most unfavourable combination of static load	13A)	$S_{G13} + S_{L13} \leq \eta_{13a} R$	Expected value	$S_{G13} + S_{L13} \leq R_1/\eta_{1a}$	AC1
			~~13B)~~				

Table A3: Accidental Loads

Load Scenarios - Sea going cases

Operation	Loads that the vessel is exposed to and has to withstand:			Load Combination Design methods	'Probability' of load	Rule check Rule Format Ref Sect 8	Accept Criteria Set
Accidental flooding	Operational loads and environmental wave loads	Static load due to flooding and environmental loads		14A)	$S_{L14} \leq \eta_{14a} R_{14}$	Extreme value	$S_{L14} \leq \eta_{1b} R_1$	AC2 for water tight boundaries AC1 for collision bulkhead
				~~14B)~~	~~$S_{L14} + D_{Lred} \leq \eta_{14b} R_{14}$~~	-	-	-

A Study on Thickness Effect on Welded Joint of Longitudinal Stiffeners

Tetsuya Nakamura [1], Satoshi Yamamoto [2]

[1] Technical Research Center, Universal Shipbuilding Corporation
Tsu, Mie, Japan
[2] Initial Design Department, Universal Shipbuilding Corporation
Kawasaki, Kanagawa, Japan

Abstract

In the fatigue strength assessment using the Common Structural Rules for Tankers and Bulk Carriers (CSR) developed by the International Association of Classification Societies (IACS), the thickness effect was applied to the welded joints between the longitudinal stiffeners and the web stiffeners. However, it is not clear whether the thickness effect influences welded joints of large-scale components such as the longitudinal stiffeners, since the thickness effect is in general derived from only small-scale fatigue tests and various analyses. In this paper, therefore, the thickness effect on the welded joints between the longitudinal stiffeners and the web stiffeners has been examined mainly from the viewpoint of the stress concentration at the weld toe. First, in order to clarify the factors influencing the thickness effect, the relationship between the stress concentration and the thickness is summarized on the basis of the fatigue tests and the calculation data of the cruciform joints. Second, the thickness effect on the boxing welded joint is examined using the results of the fatigue test data and the FE analyses. Last, in order to confirm the thickness effect on the welded joints between the longitudinal stiffeners and the web stiffeners, the FE analyses have been carried out to determine the stress concentration at the weld toe of the joints. These results confirm that the thickness effect on the welded joints between the longitudinal stiffeners and the web stiffeners is not dependent upon the faceplate thickness.

Keywords

Fatigue; Thickness effect; Longitudinal stiffeners; Welded joint; Stress concentration; FE analysis; Weld toe.

Introduction

The effect of the thickness is an important factor in the evaluation of the fatigue strength of the steel structures and has been adopted in various fatigue design standards and design rules.

The thickness effect usually adopts the m power law, which means that the fatigue strength decreases in inverse proportion to m power of the thickness. The fatigue strength calculation considering the thickness effect is given in Eq1.

$$\sigma(t) = \sigma(t_0)\left(\frac{t_0}{t}\right)^m \quad (1)$$

$\sigma(t_0)$; fatigue strength for t_0

t_0; reference thickness

m; exponent

The thickness effect expressed as Eq.1 is applied to the welded joints in cases where the plate thickness is greater than the reference thickness.

In the "Fatigue design of welded joints and components" published by the International Institute of Welding (IIW), a thickness effect was applied to welded joints such as the cruciform joints and the T joints, which was verified by the experiments using the fundamental specimens and/or some analyses. The thickness effect proposed by the IIW varies according to the types of the welded joints.

Recently, the Common Structural Rules for Tankers and Bulk Carriers (CSR) developed by the International Association of Classification Societies (IACS) entered into force, in which a thickness effect is taken into account in the fatigue strength assessments. The thickness effect in the CSR adopts $m=0.25$, regardless of the types of the welded joints.

The thickness effects in the CSR and the IIW standard are shown in Table 1. The exponent m, the reference thickness t_0 and the types of welded joints are changed according to the base plate thickness in the CSR and the IIW standard respectively.

Table 1: Thickness Effect in CSR and IIW Standard.

design standards and rules	exponent m	reference thickness t0	types of welded joints
IIW	0.3	25mm *gross	cruciform joint, T joint, plate with an attachment (as weld)
	0.2		cruciform joint, T joint, plate with an attachment (ground) butt joint
	0.1		butt joint removed reinforcement, base metal, etc.
CSR	0.25	22mm *net	all joints including the longitudinal stiffners

The fatigue strength by the thickness effect in the CSR and the IIW standard is shown in Fig. 1. As can be seen in Fig. 1, the fatigue strength evaluated by using the CSR is lower than in cases using the IIW standard in the range of 22 - 40 mm in thickness.

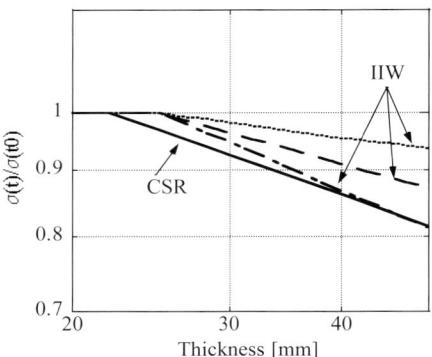

Fig. 1: Comparison of the Thickness Effect in CSR and IIW Standard

As mentioned above, the thickness effect is applied to all types of the welded joints in the CSR. However, it has not been confirmed whether the thickness effect influences the welded joints of the longitudinal stiffeners and the web stiffeners differing from these fundamental specimens.

In this paper, therefore, the thickness effect on the welded joints between the longitudinal stiffeners and the web stiffeners has been examined mainly from the viewpoint of the stress concentration at the weld toe.

Influence Factors of the Thickness Effect

The thickness effect is essentially affected by the following factors:

(1) The stress concentration at the weld toe is mainly determined by the local welded geometry, in spite of the plate thickness (Fig. 2).

(2) The stress gradient in the plane of the crack growth depends on the plate thickness as shown in Fig. 3.

(3) The residual welding stress, which acts as the mean stress, increases concomitantly with any increase in the material thickness.

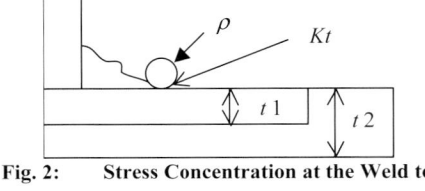

Fig. 2: Stress Concentration at the Weld toe

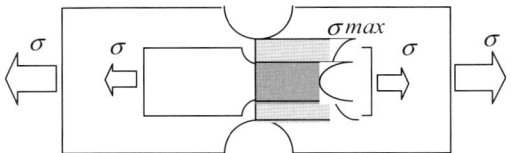

Fig. 3: A Schematic of the Stress Gradient as to Plate Thickness Direction

Thickness Effect on Cruciform Joints

The fatigue tests and the FE analyses for the cruciform and T joints have been performed to examine the thickness effect (Yagi, 1991). The following significant results of the thickness effect on the cruciform and T joints have been obtained from the previous study.

(1) The thickness effect for the crack initiation is greater than the one for the crack propagation. This fact indicates that the stress gradient in the plate thickness affects the thickness effect.

(2) The thickness effect on the cruciform joints depends not only upon the plate thickness but also the size of the attachments.

(3) The exponent m is distributed roughly between 1/10 and 1/3 depending on the types of the welded joints and the loading patterns.

(4) The thickness effect on the welded joints can be evaluated by using the stress concentration factor at the weld toe.

Fig.4 shows the relationship between the plate thickness and the stress concentration factors at the weld toe on the cruciform joints.

The stress concentration factor (SCF) is defined as follows.

$$SCF = \frac{\sigma_{max}}{\sigma_n} \quad (2)$$

Where σ_n is a nominal stress and σ_{max} is a maximum stress at the weld toe.

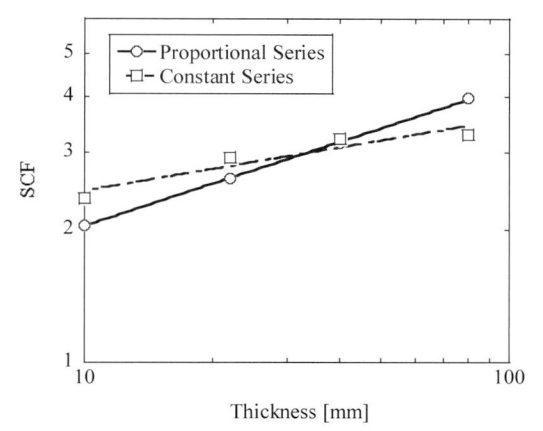

Fig. 4: Effect of the Base Plate Thickness on the Stress Concentration Factors at the Weld toe of Cruciform Joints

These stresses have been obtained from the FE analyses of the cruciform joints. The analyses have been carried out for two series of the joint proportion, i.e. the proportional series and the constant series.

The "proportional series" are those in which the ratio of the thickness of the base plate and the attachment is constant. The "constant series" are those in which attachments are constant thickness and the base plate thickness varies.

The stress concentration factors at the weld toe are raised with increases in the base plate thickness in both series. Exponent m is equal to 0.322 in the "proportional series" and 0.165 in the "constant series".

From these results, the thickness effect on the cruciform joints is clearly shown. Furthermore it can be pointed out that there is a high correlation between the stress concentration factor and the thickness effect.

Thickness Effect on Boxing Welded Joints

Review of Fatigue Tests Results

The fatigue tests of the boxing welded joints for the steel bridge structures in a range of the base plate thickness 10-30mm have been performed by Anami (1997).

Relations between the base plate thickness and the fatigue strength at 2 million cycles are shown in Fig. 5.

In the boxing welded joints, the fatigue strength tends to decrease with an increase in the base plate thickness. This fact means that a thickness effect appears on the boxing welded joints as well as the cruciform joints.

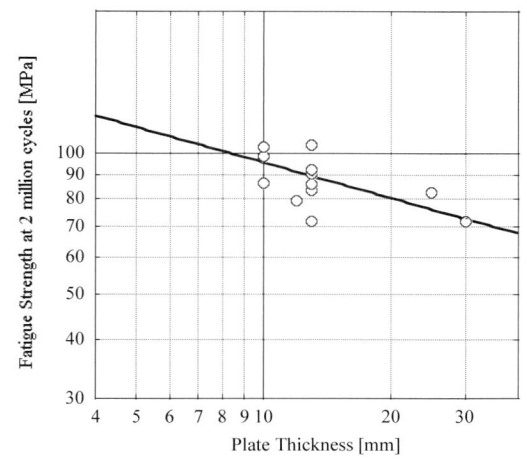

Fig. 5: Effect of the Base Plate Thickness on the Fatigue Strength of Boxing Welded Joints

FE Analyses of the Boxing Welded Joints

The FE analyses have been carried out to ascertain the stress concentration factors at the weld toe of the boxing welded joints. The analyses have been performed using the I-DEAS. FE models of the boxing welded joints are modeled using 8- node solid elements and some 6- node as well. The modeling area is 1/8 part of the joint considering a symmetrical shape. The minimum mesh size around the weld toe is set to 0.5mm. The weld root is modeled by using double nodes without consideration of the influence of contact between the base plate and the attachment. The FE model is illustrated in Fig. 6. The dimensions are defined as shown in Fig. 6.

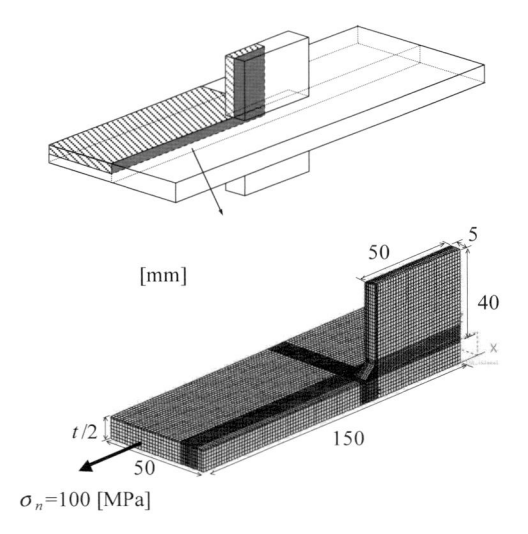

Fig. 6: FE Model and the Dimensions of Boxing Welded Joints used in This Study

The axial load 100MPa is enacted at the end of the base plate. The FE analyses have been carried out using 3 FE models, in which the base plate thickness is different.

The stress distribution is shown in Fig. 7. It was found that the stress concentration appeared within a limited area close to the weld toe of the attachment.

Fig. 8 shows the relationship between the base plate thickness of the boxing welded joints and the stress concentration at the weld toe.

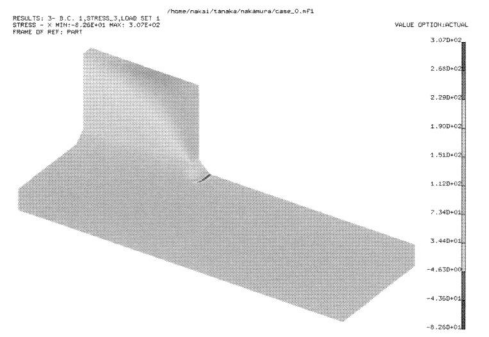

Fig. 7: Results of the FE Analysis in the Case of the Base Plate Thickness =20mm

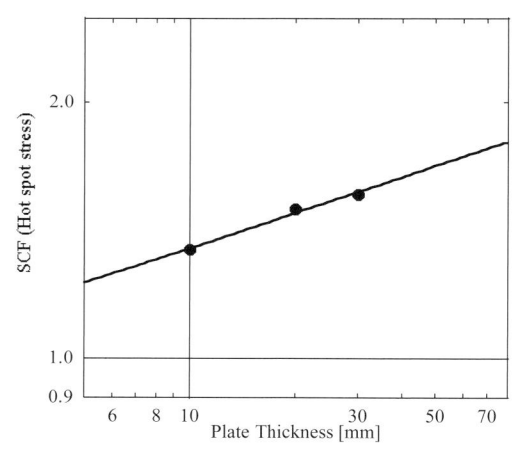

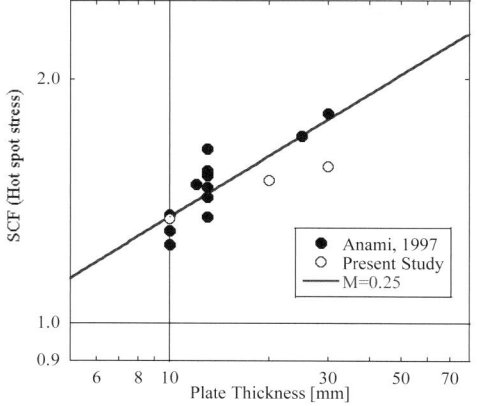

Fig. 8: Effect of the Base Plate Thickness on the Stress Concentration Factors at the Weld toe of Boxing Welded Joints

As seen in Fig. 8, as in the cruciform joints, the stress concentration at the weld toe of the boxing welding joints increases with increasing base plate thickness. From the calculation data, the exponent m of the boxing welding joint is about 0.136, which is close to the value of the cruciform joint (m=0.165).

Anami performed the FE analyses for the boxing welded specimens that were used for the fatigue tests. The stress concentration factors are calculated. The calculation results indicate that the stress concentrations of the boxing welded joints are thickness dependant. The stress concentrations derived from the present study are plotted together with those from Anami's study in Fig. 9.

Thickness Effect of Longitudinal Stiffeners

FE Analyses of the Longitudinal Stiffeners

In case of the fatigue assessment in the CSR, the thickness effect is adopted to all welded joints including the intersection between the longitudinal stiffeners and the web stiffeners. However the fatigue test data on the longitudinal stiffeners are insufficient to confirm the thickness effect.

Fig. 9: Effect of the Base Plate Thickness on the Stress Concentration Factors at the Weld toe of Boxing Welded Joints

Therefore the FE analyses have been performed to ascertain the stress concentration at the weld toe of the welded joints between the longitudinal stiffeners and the web stiffeners.

A simplified FE model consisting of an I-beam with an attachment is used in this study as a longitudinal stiffener and a web stiffener. The analysis was preformed using the NASTRAN. The FE model of an I-beam is modeled by using 8- node solid elements and some of 6- nodes. The modeling area is 1/8 part of the joint considering a symmetrical shape. The minimum mesh size around the weld toe is set to 0.5mm. The FE model of an I-beam with an attachment is shown Fig. 10.

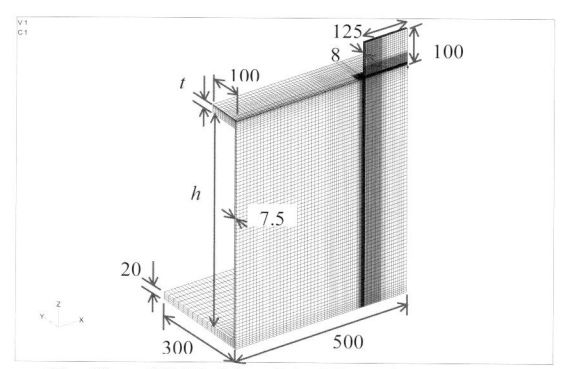

Fig. 10: FE Model and the Dimensions of I-beam Section with an Attachment used in This Study

The dimensions of the models are defined according to Fig.10. The thickness of the face plates are 10, 20, 25, 30, 40 mm, and the depths of the web plates have been changed to retain the same section modulus as shown in Table 2. The axial and bending loads are respectively enacted on the end of the beam.

Table 2: The Faceplate Thickness and the Depth of the Web.

(mm)

Face Plate Thickness	10	20	25	30	40
Depth of Web	817	662	600	546	460

Calculation Results of I-beam models

In Figures. 11 and 12, the deformations and the stress distributions of the I-beam models with 25mm in the faceplate thickness are presented for each load case.

Fig. 11: FE Analysis Result under the Axial Loading (t=25mm)

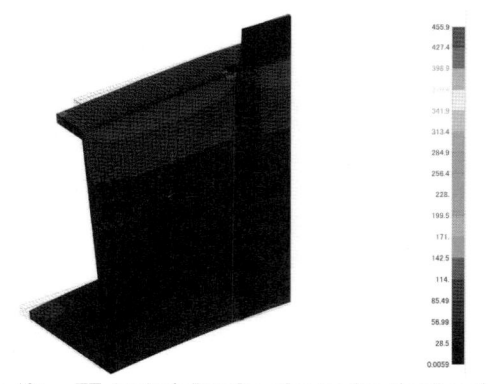

Fig. 12: FE Analysis Result under the Bending Loading (t=25mm)

Fig. 13 shows the relationship between the faceplate thickness of the I-beams and the stress concentration at the weld toe.

As can be seen in Fig. 13, the stress concentrations are constant regardless of the faceplate thickness under the axial loading cases, and are slightly raised with increasing faceplate thickness under the bending loading cases. The exponent m derived from the calculated results is 0.004 for the axial loads, and is 0.042 for the bending loads. These values are negligible.

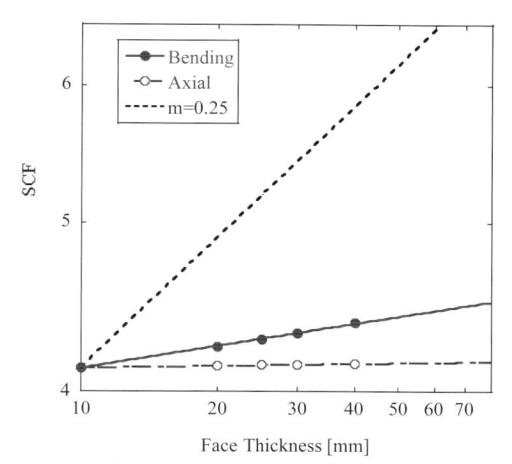

Fig. 13: Effect of the Faceplate Thickness on the Stress Concentration Factors at the Weld toe of I-beam Sections with attachments

Therefore the thickness effect has not been observed under both the axial and the bending load cases. As the results show, it is not necessary to take into account the thickness effect in the fatigue strength assessment on the longitudinal stiffeners.

In order to examine the difference between the boxing welded joints and the longitudinal stiffeners, the stress distribution in the faceplates are compared.

The stress distribution in the faceplate of the I-beam acting under the axial load is shown in Fig. 14.

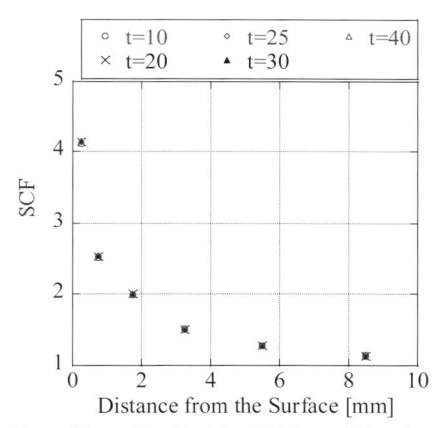

Fig. 14: Stress Gradient for Thickness Direction of the I-beam Section Models under the Axial Load

The stress distribution in the faceplate remains almost the same regardless of the faceplate thickness. The stress distribution in the faceplate of the I-beam under the bending load is shown in Fig. 15.

The stress distribution in the faceplate is slightly different near the surface of the faceplate. The stress distribution in the base plate of the boxing welded joint under the axial load is shown in Fig. 16.

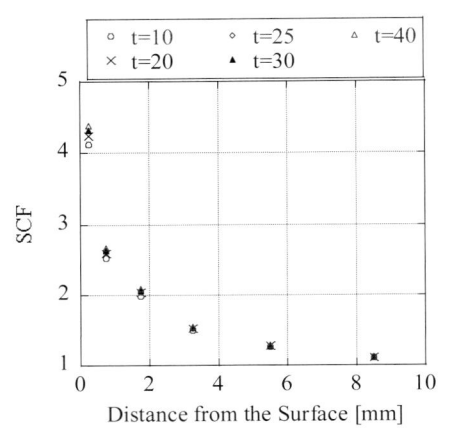

Fig. 15: Stress Gradient for Thickness Direction of the I-beam Section Models under the Bending Load

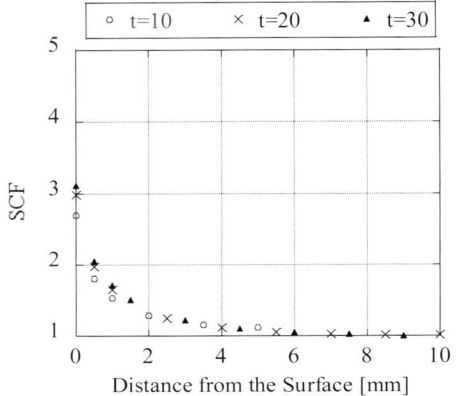

Fig. 16: Stress Gradient for Thickness Direction of the Boxing Welded Joint Models under the Axial Load

The stress distribution in the base plate is relatively more divergent near the surface of the base plate of the boxing welded joint than the I-beam joint.

Conclusions

Through the analytic research focusing on the stress concentration, an examination related to the thickness effect on the welded joints has been carried out. From these results, the following is concluded:

(1) In the simplified welded joints such as the cruciform joints and the boxing joints, the thickness effect was observed. From the examination results, it is thought that 1/4 lower power can be applied for the fatigue assessment of these types of the welded joints.

(2) In the welded joint of the longitudinal stiffeners and the web stiffeners, the thickness effect was negligible. The thickness effect on the longitudinal stiffeners differs from that of the simplified cruciform and boxing welded joints.

References

Anami, K. and Miki, C. (1997). "A Study on Size Effect of Fatigue Strength at Weld Joint Toe," J. Steel Construction Engineering, Vol.4, No.14, pp. 9-17.

IACS. (2006). "Common Structural Rules for Double Hull Oil Tankers".

IACS. (2006). "Common Structural Rules for Bulk Carriers".

Hobbacher, A. (1996), "Fatigue design of welded joints and components," International Institute of Welding (IIW).

Yagi, J., Machida, S., Tomita, Y., Matoba, M. and Soya, I. (1991). "Influencing Factors on Thickness Effect of Fatigue Strength in As-welded Joints for Steel Structures," J. Society of Naval Architects, Japan, pp. 289-2.

Preventing Parametric Roll with Use of Devices and Their Practical Impact

Naoya Umeda[1], Hirotada Hashimoto[1], Shohei Minegaki[1], Akihiko Matsuda[2]

[1] Department of Naval Architecture and Ocean Engineering, Osaka University, Suita, Osaka, JAPAN
[2] National Research Institute of Fisheries Engineering, Hasaki, Kamisu, Ibaraki, JAPAN

Abstract

For preventing parametric rolling of a post-Panamax containership in head seas, the effects of two different devices are investigated. One device is a sponson for decreasing restoring variation, and the other is an anti-rolling tank for increasing roll damping. Model experiment indicates that the sponson can reduce the amplitude of parametric rolling, and the anti-rolling tank can exclude parametric rolling. By executing a cost-benefit analysis based on numerical simulation, the ART with its size of 1.65 percent of the ship displacement is a cost-effective risk control option for protecting onboard containers during the 20 years trans-Pacific service.

Keywords

Parametric roll; Anti-rolling tank; Sponson; Risk control option; Container; Life cycle value.

Introduction

Recently parametric roll is identified as one of the major threats to onboard containers. The accident of the C11 class post-Panamax containership is well known (France et al. 2003) and similar accidents of containerships follow it. A large containership having larger metacentric height could suffer parametric rolling in head seas at low speed. Here the roll period is twice as long as the encounter period, and is nearly equal to its natural roll period. The amplitude of such parametric roll can be much larger than that of harmonic roll in beam seas and could result in loss or damage of onboard containers together with shorter natural roll period. In case of the C11 class it was documented that about 800 onboard containers were lost or damaged.

Although parametric rolling in following seas has been investigated from the ship stability viewpoint (Umeda et al., 1995) so far, parametric rolling in head seas attracts current practical interests. For preventing the parametric roll in head seas, several guidelines for predicting the occurrence and magnitude of parametric rolling were published. The International Maritime Organization (IMO, 2006) extended its operational guidance as MSC.1/Circ. 1228, and the American Bureau of Shipping (ABS, 2004) developed a design guideline. The International Towing Tank Conference (ITTC, 2005) recommended a guideline for model basins. Thus, to some extent, it is possible to avoid parametric rolling by designers or operators.

Given a ship, however, it is desirable to provide a cost-effective risk control option for preventing parametric rolling without replacement of the ship, such as additional devices preventing parametric rolling. Parametric roll could occur when the restoring variation in waves is sufficiently large and the roll damping is relatively small. (Kerwin, 1955) Therefore, it seems to be possible to develop devices preventing parametric rolling by decreasing the restoring variation or increasing the roll damping. For this purpose the authors investigated two different devices; one is a sponson for decreasing the restoring variation and the other is an anti-rolling tank (ART) for increasing the roll damping. It is noteworthy here that fin stabilizers are not effective because parametric roll often occurs at low speed. This paper summarizes recent experimental works on the sponsons and the anti-rolling tanks for preventing parametric rolling (Umeda et al., 2005) and attempts to examine whether or not the ART is a cost-effective risk control option by calculating its life cycle value.

Subject ship

Throughout this paper, a 6600 TEU post-Panamax containership designed by the National Maritime Research Institute (NMRI) is used. As shown in Table 1 and Fig. 1, this ship has an exaggerated bow flare and transom stern. As a result, significant restoring variation in longitudinal waves can occur as shown in Fig. 2. Here the wavelength, λ, is equal to L_{PP} and the wave steepness, H/λ, is 1/20. For the cost benefit analysis, we assume that the ship engages in trans-Pacific route during twenty years. The number of containers on deck is assumed to be 2070.

Table. 1 Principle particulars of the containership

Items	Ship	model
Length: L_{pp}	283.8 m	2.838 m
Breadth: B	42.8 m	0.428 m
Depth: D	24.4 m	0.244 m
Draught at FP: T_f	14.0 m	0.014 m
Mean draught: T	14.0 m	0.014 m
Draught at AP: T_a	14.0 m	14.0 m
Block coefficient: C_b	0.629	0.629
Pitch radius of gyration: κ_{yy}/L_{pp}	0.244	0.258
Longitudinal position of centre of gravity from the amidships: x_{CG}	5.7 m aft	0.057 m aft
Metacentric height: GM	1.06 m	0.0106 m
Natural roll period: T_ϕ	30.3 s	3.2 s

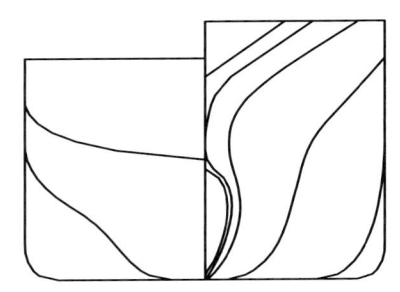

Fig.1 Body plan of the containership.

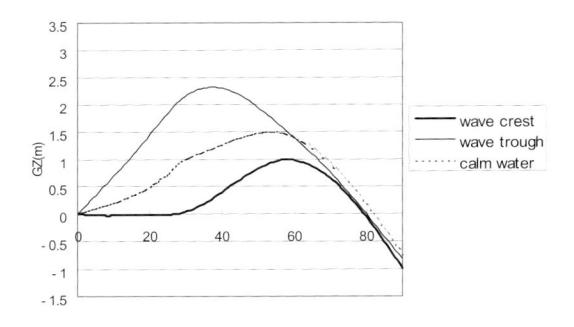

Fig. 2 GZ curves of the containership with $H/\lambda=0.05$ and $\lambda/L_{PP}=1.0$.

As mentioned later, model experiments of the ship were carried out with a scaled model at a seakeeping and maneuvering basin of the National Research Institute of Fisheries Engineering. The model was self-propelled and steered by an autopilot. The details of the experimental set-ups and procedures were described in Hashimoto et al. (2006).

Effectiveness of sponsons

The restoring variation in longitudinal waves can be significant if the wavelength is comparable to the ship length. When the ship center situates at a wave crest, the water plane area of the ship can be smaller because of bow flare and transom stern, and then the metacentric height can be smaller. For preventing this reduction, additional buoyancy at the ship centre could be a solution. Thus, the authors designed sponsons as shown in Fig. 3. The breadth of the sponson is 11.7% of the original ship breadth. Since the sponson is added above the calm water plane, no increase of calm water resistance exists.

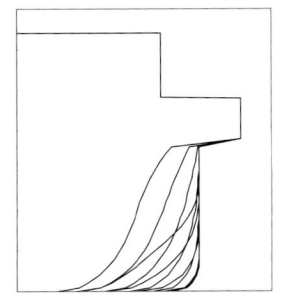

Fig. 3 Sponson attached to the containership for preventing parametric roll.

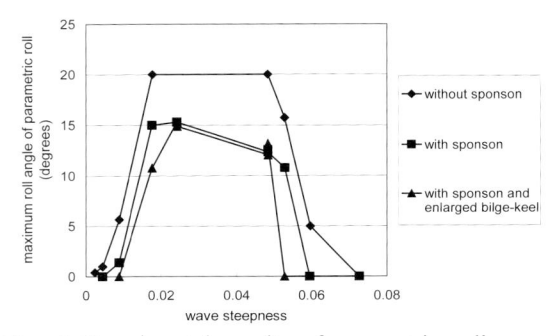

Fig. 4 Experimental results of parametric roll as a function of wave steepness with $\lambda/L_{pp}=1.6$. (Umeda et al., 2005)

With the aid of these sponsons, almost no restoring reduction at a wave crest occurs. For examining the effectiveness for preventing parametric roll, free-running model experiments were executed. The results of the experiment with and without the sponsons are shown in Fig. 4. The propeller RPM was adjusted to realise the relationship of parametric rolling that natural roll frequency is the half of encounter frequency. In all conditions tested the sponsons reduced maximum roll angles. The ABS guide (ABS, 2004) regarding the prevention of accidents due to parametric rolling states that a maximum roll angle is to be less than 15 degrees. (Therefore, the experiment confirms that the sponsons tested reduce the maximum roll angle to less than 15 degrees. The result also indicates that by further increasing the roll damping by 76 percent increasing the size of the bilge-keel is less effective in preventing parametric rolling and can only reduce the occurrence. This result indicates that the sponson is effective in reducing severe parametric rolling, but additional enlargement of the bilge keel has minimal effect.

Effectiveness of ART in regular waves

An ART has the effect of additional damping by using the phase lag of tank water to ship roll motion. In this investigation, the design of the tank has three water ducts, connecting both port and starboard tanks, to alter the natural period of the tank water flow. In addition, each tank has a plate with a slit on the bottom to increase the vortex-generating damping effect. Both side tanks are also connected with an air pipe. The ART model is shown in Fig.5, and its dimensions and definitions are shown in Table. 2 and Figure 6, respectively.

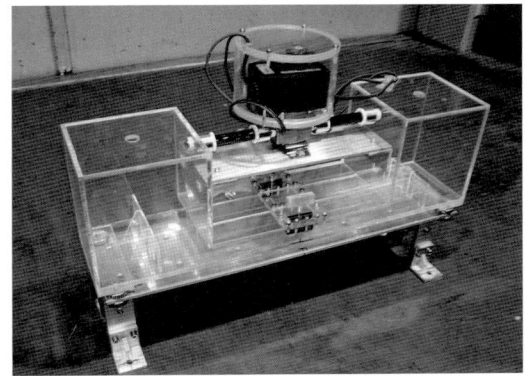

Fig.5 the ART model.

Table.2 Dimensions of the ART model.

H_t	0.125 m
D_t	0.09 m
B_{tt}	0.107 m
B_t	0.428 m
H_{tt}	0.018 m
W_t	0.045 m

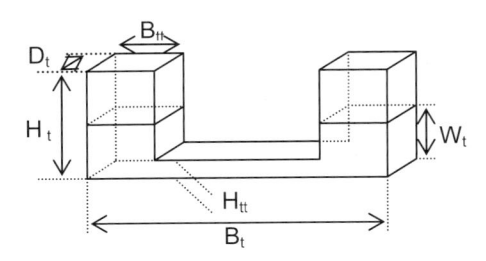

Fig. 6 Definitions of ART dimensions.

In reference to Belenky et al.(2003) the effectiveness of an ART has been examined with a numerical experiment by Belenky. In the present paper it is examined by a model experiment. Here the ART model was attached above the main deck near the amidships. The procedure of the experiment is the same as the case of the sponsons. Metacentric height with free water effect of the ART was corrected to be the same as that without the ART by shifting the ballast weight position, but the natural roll period can be different between the cases with and without the ART. Thus, propeller RPM was adjusted to realise the typical parametric roll condition for both cases.

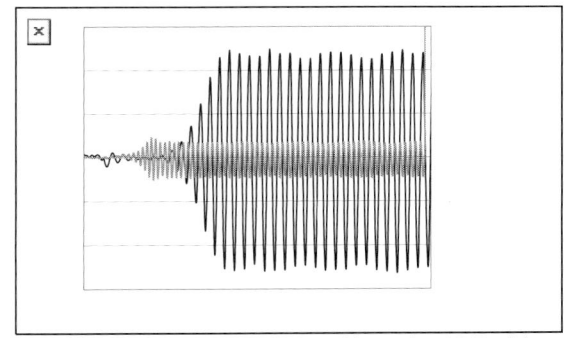

Fig. 7 Time series of model run without the ART with λ/L_{PP}=1.3 and H/λ=0.03. (Umeda et al., 2005)

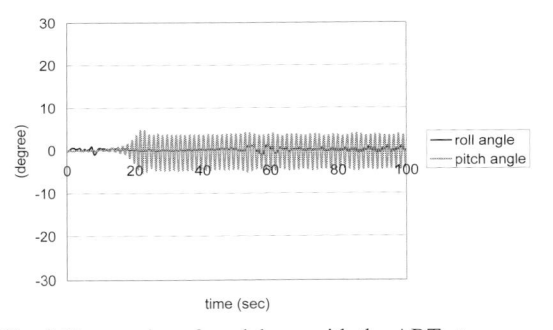

Fig. 8 Time series of model run with the ART at λ/L_{PP}=1.3 and H/λ=0.03. (Umeda et al., 2005)

In the model run without the ART, parametric rolling with a maximum amplitude of 23 degrees, with a roll period twice as long as the wave encounter period was clearly observed, shown in Fig.7. On the contrary, in the model run with the ART the parametric rolling has completely disappeared. Therefore, we can conclude the use of the ART is very effective in avoiding parametric rolling.

It is important to optimize the size of the ART by utilizing systematic numerical simulation. For this purpose, a mathematical model of the water tank effect (Taguchi et al., 2003) is combined with an uncoupled ship roll model (Umeda et al., 2004). Wave exciting roll moment is zero because the condition is based upon head seas.

Ship:
$$(I_{xx} + J_{xx})\ddot{\phi} - K_{\dot\phi}\dot\phi - K_{\dot\phi\dot\phi\dot\phi}\dot\phi^3 + mg(GM\phi + C_3\phi^3 + C_5\phi^5)$$
$$+ mg\{(a_1\zeta_{ae} + a_2\zeta_{ae}^2 + a_3\zeta_{ae}^3) + (b_1\zeta_{ae} + b_2\zeta_{ae}^2 + b_3\zeta_{ae}^3)\cos 2\pi(\xi_G/\lambda)\}$$
$$\{\phi - (1/\pi^2)\phi^3\} + J_{st}\ddot\eta + K_{st}\eta = 0 \qquad (1)$$

where

ϕ	: ship roll angle
η	: inclination of tank water surface
I_{XX}	: moment of inertia in roll
J_{XX}	: added moment of inertia in roll
$K_{\dot\phi}$	: linear roll damping coefficient
$K_{\dot\phi\dot\phi\dot\phi}$	: cubic roll damping coefficient
m	: ship mass
g	: gravitational acceleration
GM	: metacentric height
C_3, C_5	: constant coefficients of restoring moment in still water
a_1, a_2, a_3	: coefficients of average of variation of roll restoring moment
b_1, b_2, b_3	: coefficients of amplitude of variation of roll restoring moment
ξ_G	: longitudinal position of center of gravity from a wave trough
λ	: wave amplitude
J_{st}	: coefficient of inertia coupling of tank water and ship
K_{st}	: coefficient of static coupling of tank water and ship
ζ_{ae}	: amplitude of Grim's effective wave (Grim, 1961)

Tank water:
$$J_{st}\ddot\phi + K_{st}\phi + J_t\ddot\eta + B_t\dot\eta + K_{st}\eta = 0 \qquad (2)$$

where

J_t	: inertia coefficient of tank water
B_t	: tank water damping coefficient
K_{st}	: restoring coefficient of tank water

The variation of roll restoring moment is considered as a function of wave amplitude with the Froude-Krylov assumption. The damping coefficient of the ship is estimated from the roll decay test in calm water with no forward velocity. The damping of the tank water, B_t, is numerically estimated to fit the measured time history of the roll decay within the first half cycle.

Comparisons between the free running model experiment and the numerical simulation were conducted, shown in Fig.9. In the case of a 100 percent water level in the ART, numerical simulation can predict experimental results, i.e. no parametric rolling occurs. In the case of 11% of water level in the ART, the numerical result agrees with the experiment in steady amplitude and developing rate of parametric roll. The difference in the start of the parametric rolling is due to that in initial disturbance between the experiment and the simulation. The comparisons demonstrate that the mathematical model can qualitatively predict parametric rolling of a ship with the ART.

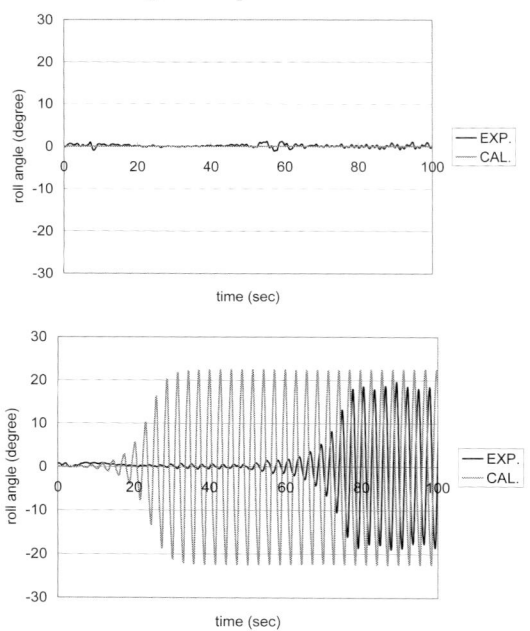

Fig. 9 Comparison of roll angle between experiment and calculation with ART at 100% water level (above) and 11% water level (below) for $\lambda/L_{PP}=1.3$ and $H/\lambda=0.03$. (Umeda et al., 2005)

Cost-benefit analysis of ART during life cycle

Since exaggerated bow flare and transom stern are designed for maximizing the container number for a modern containership, the use of the ART, which could reduce the container number, can be allowed only as a cost-effective measure for risk of loss of containers due to parametric rolling. Thus a cost-benefit analysis of the ART during its life cycle was executed.

First, the size of the ART is determined by numerical simulation in irregular waves with the significant wave height of 14.2 meters and mean wave period of 10.2 seconds, which can be a worst condition for parametric rolling in the North Pacific. Here the Dt are systematically changed by keeping the transverse section shape constant so that the tank water damping can be estimated with the fore-mentioned model experiment. This is because the tank water damping can be assumed to be proportional to the Dt. In the numerical simulation the restoring variation in irregular waves is estimated with the Grim effective wave concept. The results are presented in Fig. 10. If the parametric rolling amplitude is required to be 10 degrees or less, the size of ART should be 1.65 percent of the ship displacement or larger. Thus, the size of ART investigated here is determined as 1.65 percent of the ship displacement.

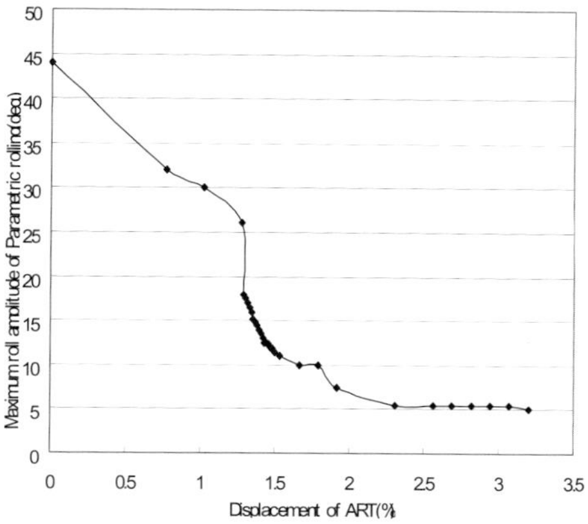

Fig. 10: Relationship between the ART size and parametric roll angle in irregular waves. Here the ART size is indicated by the ratio of its water weight to the ship displacement.

Second, the numerical simulation was carried out for all possible combinations of significant wave heights and mean wave periods in the North Pacific. To realize the worst situations, the ship speed is assumed to satisfy the natural roll period to the encounter period ratio of 2 and ship heading is head waves. Because of non-ergordicity of parametric rolling, the average in the maximum parametric roll angles of ten realizations per one stationary sea state was calculated as shown in Table 3. Each realization has the simulation duration of 30 minutes.

Third, consequence of parametric rolling is estimated with the following formula for the transverse load acting on the containers, W_T, in the guide for Certification of Container Securing System (ABS, 1988).

Table 3 Maximum parametric roll angle in irregular head waves

Significant wave height(m)	~4	4~5	5~6	6~7	7~8	8~9	9~10	10~11	11~12	12~13	14~
14	×	×	×	×	×	33	41	41	40	36	36
13~14	×	×	×	×	×	×	41	41	41	×	×
12~13	×	×	×	×	22	23	35	39	41	17	29
11~12	×	×	×	×	23	36	29	33	35	32	27
10~11	×	×	×	24	18	24	32	32	32	32	26
9~10	×	×	×	24	18	24	31	32	22	26	16.7
8~9	×	×	27	18	2.5	24	1.2	28	18	26	3.7
7~8	×	×	23	0.1	2.2	1.3	0	27	18	0.6	0.7
6~7	×	1.5	18	0.2	0	1.5	0	1.2	0.8	1	0.05
5~6	×	1.5	0.2	0.3	0	0	0	0.5	0.2	0.06	0.06
4~5	0	0	0.2	0.6	0	0	0	0	0	0	0
3~4	0	0	0	0	0	0	0	0	0	0	0
2~3	0	0	0	0	0	0	0	0	0	0	0
1~2	0	0	0	0	0	0	0	0	0	0	0
0~1	0	0	0	0	0	0	0	0	0	0	0

Wave zero crossing period (sec.)

Third, consequence of parametric rolling is estimated with the following formula for the transverse load acting on the containers, W_T, in the guide for Certification of Container Securing System (ABS, 1988).

$$W_T = W_{container}(\sin\phi_{max} + 0.0026\frac{\pi^3\phi_{max}}{T_\phi^2}z_{container} + 0.0051\frac{\pi^2 L_{PP}}{T_H^2}\sin\phi_{max}) \quad (3)$$

where ϕ_{max}: maximum roll amplitude, T_ϕ: natural roll period, T_{heave}: natural heave period and $z_{container}$: height of container from ship roll centre. We assume that the tiered containers will fall down if W_T exceeds the breaking load, say 60 tons. As a result, the critical angle, ϕ_c, can be estimated as a function of tier number and then the probability of damage of containers with the i-th tier set during the simulation can be calculated with the following equation:

$$p_i = \int_0^\infty \int_0^\infty H(\phi_{max}(H_{1/3}, T_{01}) - \phi_c) f(H_{1/3}, T_{01}) dH_{1/3} dT_{01} \quad (4)$$

where

$$H(x) = 1 \quad when \quad x \geq 0$$
$$= 0 \quad when \quad x < 0$$

and the $f(H_{1/3}, T_{01})$ is a joint probability function of the significant wave height and mean wave period (Shinkai and Wan, 1995).

Fourth, the number of damaged containers per trip, $L_{container}$, was estimated with the following formula:

$$L_{containers} = \sum_{i=1}^{M} m_i \left\{1 - (1 - p_i)^{\frac{t_{trip}}{t_{simulation}}}\right\} \quad (5)$$

where $t_{simulation}$: simulation duration, t_{trip}: trip hours, m_i: number of containers with the i-th tier set and M: number of container tier sets. Then, the economic loss of the case with the ART can be calculated as follows.

$$R_{ART} = 20N\left(C_{container}L_{containers} + \frac{W_{ART}}{W_{container}}F_{container}\right) + C_{ART} \quad (6)$$

where $C_{container}$: value of one container, $W_{container}$: weight of one container, W_{ART}: water weight of the ART, $F_{container}$: freight rate of one container, C_{ART}: cost of the ART and N: number of trips per year. Since no damage occurs, the loss of the case without the ART can be obtained as follows:

$$R_{noART} = 20NC_{container}L_{containers} \quad (7)$$

Based on the above method and the assumed parameters shown in Table 4, the economic losses of the cases with and without the ART during 20 years are estimated as follows:

$R_{ART} = 16.5 million$ USD

$R_{noART} = 40.5 million$ USD

As a result, the balance is 24 million USD. Therefore, the use of ART is a cost-effective risk control option for the containership for the trans-Pacific service.

Table 4 System parameters used for the cost-benefit analysis

M	5
m_1 (3tier)	54
m_2 (4tier)	288
m_3 (5tier)	270
m_4 (6tier)	324
m_5 (7tier)	1134
$C_{container}$	5.4×10^4 (USD)
W_{ART}	5.01×10^5 (kg)
$W_{container}$	3.0×10^4 (kg)
$F_{container}$	2.5×10^4 (USD)
C_{ART}	3.8×10^5 (USD)

Conclusions

For the prevention of parametric rolling in head seas of the 6600 TEU containership, the effect of the devices was investigated noting the following:

1. The model experiments demonstrate that installing a sponson with its width of 11.7% of the ship breadth, the maximum roll amplitude of parametric rolling decreases from 20 degrees to 15 degrees, with a wavelength to ship length ratio of 1.6.
2. The model experiments demonstrate that installing an ART, parametric rolling can disappear completely with a wavelength to ship length ratio of 1.3.
3. Numerical simulation with the tank water damping obtained from a roll decay test can qualitatively predict the occurrence and magnitude of parametric rolling.
4. The numerical study shows that installing an ART with its size of 1.65 percent of the ship displacement is a cost-effective risk control option for protection of onboard containers during the 20 years trans-Pacific service.

Acknowledgements

This work was supported by the Grants-in-Aid for Scientific Research of the Japan Society for Promotion of Science (No. 18360415). The information of the ART was provided by JFE SOLDEC Corporation. The National Maritime Research Institute provided the data of the subject ship. The authors express their sincere gratitude to these organizations.

References

ABS (2004). "Guide for the Assessment of Parametric Roll Resonance in the Design of Container Carriers ".

ABS (1988). "Guide for Certification of Container Securing Systems".

Belenky, VL, Weems, KM, Lin, WM, Paulling JR, Berkeley, UC (2003). "Probabilistic Analysis of Roll Parametric Resonance in Head Sea", Proceedings of the 8th International Conference on the Stability of Ships and Ocean Vehicles, Madrid, pp.337-339.

France, WN, Levadou M, Treakle TW, Paulling, JR, Michel RK and Moore C (2003). "An Investiation of Head-Sea Parametric Roll and Its Influence on Eontainer Lashing System", Marine Technology, Vol 40 (1), pp 1-19.

Grim, O (1961). "Beitrag zu dem Problem der Sicherheit des Schiffes im Seegang" , Schiff und Hafen , 66 , pp.490 – 497 (in German).

Hashimoto, H, Umeda, N, Matsuda, A and Nakamura, S (2006). "Experimental and Numerical Studies of Parametric Roll of a Post-Panamax Container Ship in Irregular Waves", Proceedings of the 9th International Conference on Stability of Ships and Ocean Vehicles, Rio de Janeiro, Vol. 1, pp. 181-190.

ITTC (2005) "Guideline on Predicting the Occurrence and Magnitude of Parametric Rolling", ITTC Recommended Procedures and Guidelines 7.5-02 07-04.3.

IMO (2006) "Revised Guidance to the Master for Avoiding Dangerous Situations in Adverse Weather and Sea Conditions", MSC.1/Circ. 1228.

Kerwin, JE (1995). "Note on Rolling in Longitudinal Waves", International Shipbuilding Progress, Vol 2(16), pp. 597-614.

Shinkai, A and Wan, S (1995) "The Statistical Characteristics of Wave Data in the North Pacific and Long-Term Predictions", Transactions of the West-Japan Society of Naval Architects, No. 90, pp. 127-136 (in Japanese).

Taguchi, H, Sawada, H and Tanizawa, K (2003). "A Study on Complicated Roll Motion of a Ship Equipped with an Anti-Rolling Tank", Proceedings of the 8th International Conference on Stability of Ships and Ocean Vehicles, Madrid, pp.611-612.

Umeda, N, Hamamoto, M, Takaishi, Y, Chiba, Y, Matsuda, A, Sera, W, Suzuki, S, Spyrou, KJ and Watanabe, K (1995) "Model Experiments of Ship Capsize in Astern Seas", Journal of the Society of Naval Architects of Japan, Vol.177, pp.207-217.

Umeda, N, Hashimoto, H, Minegaki, S and Matsuda, A (2005) "Investigation on Anti-Parametric Rolling Devices (in Japanese)", Conference Proceedings of the Kansai Society of Naval Architects, No. 24, pp. 21-24.

Umeda, N, Hashimoto, H, Vassalos, D, Urano, S and Okou, K (2004). "Non-linear Dynamics on Parametric Roll Resonance with Realistic Numerical Modelling", International Shipbuilding Progress, 51, 2/3, pp.205-220.

Nonlinear Aspects of Coupled Parametric Rolling in Head Seas

Marcelo A S Neves, Claudio A Rodríguez

LabOceano, COPPE/UFRJ
Rio de Janeiro, Brazil

Abstract

Parametric rolling in head seas is a kind of nonlinear phenomenon that has attracted much attention recently. A third order nonlinear mathematical model that couples heave, roll and pitch motions has been proposed by the Authors. This new model has succeeded in reproducing strong parametric resonance conditions. However, there are some important nonlinear characteristics that have not been completely understood yet. This paper explores the influence of third order nonlinearities as well as the relevance of coupling between the vertical modes and the roll motion in the modeling of parametric resonance in head seas. New derived limits of stability are introduced and discussed. Some relevant dynamical aspects are clarified. The influence of initial conditions on the development of roll amplifications is investigated and the effect of coupled or uncoupled modeling of the roll motion is addressed. Analytical and numerical limits are discussed.

Keywords

Parametric resonance; Roll motions; Limits of stability; Fishing vessels; Stability in waves; Coupled motions.

Introduction

In longitudinal waves a ship may be forced to roll heavily. This is not due to direct wave excitation. Instead, an internal excitation is the mechanism responsible for the so-called parametric excitation.

Occurrences of head seas parametric resonance with different ship types have been reported by, among others, France et al. (2003), Luth and Dallinga (1999), Hua et al. (2006). In the case of fishing vessels, head-sea parametric rolling has been discussed in Neves et al. (2002). Two small vessels were tested at different speeds, various wave amplitudes, and two metacentric height conditions for each hull. The two vessels have very similar characteristics but their sterns are different. The present study focuses on analyzing, both analytically and numerically, some of the situations in which parametric resonance was strongly developed during the experiments. This will be performed making use of the coupled third-order mathematical model introduced by Neves and Rodríguez (2005, 2006).

Considering that limits of stability are a practical and direct way of assessing the safety of a design, the paper is focused on the comparison of the limits of stability derived from second and third order models. Considering that analyticity is an important tool when handling complex stability issues, the new stability limits of the corresponding Hill's equation have been derived and compared to the Mathieu-type stability limits. It is important to realize that a more complete description of the stability diagram shall provide the designer with a more reliable and precise basis for assessing the limits of stability, particularly in the case of ship designs in which large amplifications associated with parametric rolling are expected to occur.

Neves and Rodríguez (2004) showed a comparison of the limits of stability for the second and third order models based on Hsu's approach (Hsu, 1963) for the roll variational equation. The present paper explores in depth the influence of third order nonlinearities as well as the relevance of coupling between the vertical modes and the roll motion in the limits of stability. The above effects are investigated through the analysis of the time domain numerical responses obtained by systematic variation of encounter frequency and wave amplitude. This new way of obtaining the limits of stability is a more realistic procedure of assessing parametric resonance and also has an additional feature: a color map that identifies the magnitude of the steady roll parametric amplitude.

Other nonlinear characteristics of parametric roll behavior, such as dependence on initial conditions are investigated.

Equations of Motion

Two right-handed co-ordinate systems are employed to describe the motions. An inertial reference frame (C,x,y,z) is assumed to be fixed at the mean ship motion, defined by the ship speed U. Regular waves are assumed to travel forming an angle χ with ship course. Another reference frame $(O,\overline{x},\overline{y},\overline{z})$ is fixed at the ship having the $\overline{xy}$ plane coinciding, for the ship at rest, with the undisturbed sea surface, $\overline{z}$-axis passing through the vertical that contains the centre of gravity. The two systems coincide when excitations are absent. See Fig. 1.

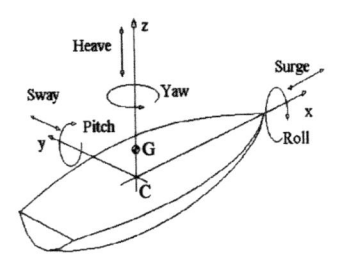

Fig. 1: Co-ordinate axis

Nonlinear equations of motion considering the three restoring degrees of freedom may be expressed in matrix form using a displacement vector:

$$\vec{s}(t) = \begin{bmatrix} z(t) & \phi(t) & \theta(t) \end{bmatrix}^T$$

defining the heave translational motion and the roll and pitch angular modes, indicated in Figure 1:

$$(\tilde{M}+\tilde{A})\ddot{\vec{s}} + \tilde{B}(\dot{\phi})\dot{\vec{s}} + \vec{C}_{res}(\vec{s},\zeta) = \vec{C}_{ext}(\zeta,\dot{\zeta},\ddot{\zeta}) =$$
$$\vec{C}_{ext(FK)}(\zeta) + \vec{C}_{ext(Dif)}(\dot{\zeta},\ddot{\zeta}) =$$
$$\begin{bmatrix} Z_W(t) & K_W(t) & M_W(t) \end{bmatrix}^T \quad (1)$$

Hull inertia $\tilde{M}$ is a diagonal 3x3 matrix. Its elements are: m, the ship mass, J_{xx}, J_{yy} the mass moments of inertia in the roll and pitch modes, respectively, taken with reference to the chosen origin. Elements in matrix $\tilde{A}$ represent hydrodynamic generalized added masses. These hydrodynamic reactions are assumed to be linear. Damping terms $\tilde{B}(\dot{\phi})$ describe hydrodynamic reactions dependent on ship velocities, and may incorporate nonlinear terms in the roll equation. Vector $\vec{C}_{res}(\vec{s},\zeta)$ describes nonlinear restoring forces and moments dependent on the relative motions between ship hull and wave elevation $\zeta(t)$. On the right hand side of equation (1), the generalized vector $\vec{C}_{ext}(\zeta,\dot{\zeta},\ddot{\zeta})$ represents wave external excitation, usually referred to in the literature as the Froude-Krilov plus diffraction wave forcing terms, dependent on wave heading χ, encounter frequency ω_e, wave amplitude A_w and time t.

Wave effects due to incident waves of arbitrary direction along the hull are modeled as a change of the hull average submerged shape defined by the instantaneous position of the wave. Contributions independent of the ship motions, contained in the $\vec{C}_{ext}(\zeta,\dot{\zeta},\ddot{\zeta})$ forcing term, as is usually adopted, appear on the right hand side of equation (1). It is observed that for longitudinal waves, there is no roll external excitation: $K_W(t) = 0$. Derivation of nonlinear restoring terms up to third order is discussed in Appendix A.

$$(m+Z_{\ddot{z}})\ddot{z} + Z_{\dot{z}}\dot{z} + Z_{\ddot{\theta}}\ddot{\theta} + Z_{\dot{\theta}}\dot{\theta} + Z_z z + Z_\theta \theta +$$
$$\frac{1}{2}Z_{zz}z^2 + \frac{1}{2}Z_{\phi\phi}\phi^2 + \frac{1}{2}Z_{\theta\theta}\theta^2 + Z_{z\theta}z\theta + \frac{1}{6}Z_{zzz}z^3$$
$$+\frac{1}{2}Z_{zz\theta}z^2\theta + \frac{1}{2}Z_{\phi\phi z}\phi^2 z + \frac{1}{2}Z_{\phi\phi\theta}\phi^2\theta + \frac{1}{2}Z_{\theta\theta z}\theta^2 z$$
$$+\frac{1}{6}Z_{\theta\theta\theta}\theta^3 + Z_{\zeta z}(t)z + Z_{\zeta\theta}(t)\theta + Z_{\zeta\zeta}(t)z + Z_{\zeta zz}(t)z^2$$
$$+Z_{\zeta\zeta\theta}(t)\theta + Z_{\zeta z\theta}(t)z\theta + Z_{\phi\phi\zeta}(t)\phi^2 + Z_{\theta\theta\zeta}(t)\theta^2 = Z_w(t)$$
(2a)

$$(J_{xx}+K_{\ddot{\phi}})\ddot{\phi} + K_{\dot{\phi}}\dot{\phi} + K_{\dot{\phi}|\dot{\phi}|}\dot{\phi}|\dot{\phi}| + K_\phi\phi + K_{z\phi}z\phi + K_{\theta\phi}\theta\phi$$
$$+\frac{1}{2}K_{zz\phi}z^2\phi + \frac{1}{6}K_{\phi\phi\phi}\phi^3 + \frac{1}{2}K_{\theta\theta\phi}\theta^2\phi + K_{z\theta\phi}z\theta\phi$$
$$+K_{\zeta\phi}(t)\phi + K_{\zeta\zeta\phi}(t)\phi + K_{\zeta z\phi}(t)z\phi + K_{\zeta\theta\phi}(t)\phi\theta = K_w(t)$$
(2b)

$$(J_{yy}+M_{\ddot{\theta}})\ddot{\theta} + M_{\dot{\theta}}\dot{\theta} + M_{\ddot{z}}\ddot{z} + M_{\dot{z}}\dot{z} + M_z z + M_\theta \theta +$$
$$\frac{1}{2}M_{zz}z^2 + \frac{1}{2}M_{\phi\phi}\phi^2 + \frac{1}{2}M_{\theta\theta}\theta^2 + M_{z\theta}z\theta + \frac{1}{6}M_{zzz}z^3$$
$$+\frac{1}{2}M_{zz\theta}z^2\theta + \frac{1}{2}M_{\phi\phi z}\phi^2 z + \frac{1}{2}M_{\phi\phi\theta}\phi^2\theta + \frac{1}{2}M_{\theta\theta z}\theta^2 z$$
$$+\frac{1}{6}M_{\theta\theta\theta}\theta^3 + M_{\zeta z}(t)z + M_{\zeta\theta}(t)\theta + M_{\zeta\zeta}(t)z + M_{\zeta zz}(t)z^2$$
$$+M_{\zeta\zeta\theta}(t)\theta + M_{\zeta z\theta}(t)z\theta + M_{\phi\phi\zeta}(t)\phi^2 + M_{\theta\theta\zeta}(t)\theta^2 = M_w(t)$$
(2c)

Neves and Rodríguez (2006) have shown that the mathematical model introduced above has good capabilities to reproduce strong roll parametric amplifications of fishing vessels. In this paper numerical results will be obtained for a transom stern fishing vessel denominated TS, described in detail in Neves et al. (2002).

Limits of Stability -Analytical Approach

The linear variational equation in roll is has been derived by Neves and Rodríguez (2004) as:

$$(J_{xx}+K_{\ddot{\phi}})\ddot{\varphi} + B_e\dot{\varphi} + [K_\phi + R_0 \quad (3)$$

$$+R_1 Cos(\omega_e t + \tau_1) + R_2 Cos(2\omega_e t + \tau_2)]\varphi = 0$$

where R_0, R_1, and R_2 are time-independent restoring coefficients, and τ_1 and τ_2, are the phases of the periodic restoring moments relative to the wave. In contrast to the second order model, where the resultant roll variational equation is a Mathieu type, in the third order model we obtain a Hill type equation. As can be seen from Eq. (3), in addition to the Mathieu terms two additional contributions appear. These new terms, as explained in Authors' previous works, rise interesting nonlinear features in the stability analysis of roll variational equation: nonlinear stiffness and biharmonic parametric excitation.

The limits of stability corresponding to the linear variational equation, equation (3), have been derived by Hsu (1963). More details of Hsu's algorithm are presented in Appendix B at the end of the paper. Figures 2 and 3 show the computed limits for two forward speeds. This type of result allows some qualitative analysis with interesting results and conclusions about the dynamic characteristics of the roll motion described by third order mathematical models.

First zone of instability ($\omega_e/\omega_{n4} = 2$) is the wider, therefore, potentially more dangerous than the subsequent one, as had already been observed by Blocki (1980), Skomedal (1982), and others in the analysis of Mathieu-type equations.

In a second order model, rigidity is directly proportional to the GM value. In the third order model, there is an additional contribution of nonlinear origin (R_0) having a quadratic dependence on the wave amplitude.

This non-periodic contribution is caused by parametric changes due to the vertical motions and wave passage along the hull. These effects may be evaluated by means of hydrostatics in waves (Paulling, 1961, Neves et al., 2005, 2006).

A more rigid system means less percentage of change of the instantaneous restoring moment with respect to the calm water restoring moment (initial rigidity), thus reducing the sensitivity of the dynamic system to parametric resonance. This tendency had been observed by Skomedal (1982) in numerical analyses.

Additionally, relevant characteristics intrinsic to the third order model are:

a) Bending to the right of the stability curves in the third order model, not observed in lower order models. This is due to the nonlinear stiffening of the system. As expected, it is more significant for higher waves.

b) *Exact* tuning in the first region of instability, which in the second order model is defined by $\omega_e/\omega_{n4} = 2$, is represented by a vertical backbone line, whereas in the third order model this is given by a backbone curve defined by $\omega_e/\omega_4 = 2$, where ω_4 is the nonlinear frequency of oscillation of the system in waves. For waves with higher amplitudes, the curve of *exact* tuning bends to the right introducing a detuning to the system, as a function of wave amplitude squared.

c) Reduced areas of instability in comparison with the areas obtained in the second order model, as a direct consequence of the higher rigidity (nonlinear). It should be observed that in some cases, as in Figs. 2 and 3, the areas of instability display upper frontiers, as a consequence of the bending to the right of the stability curves. That implies that at a given frequency, above a certain level of wave amplitude, the increase in rigidity defuses the increase in the amplitude of parametric excitation.

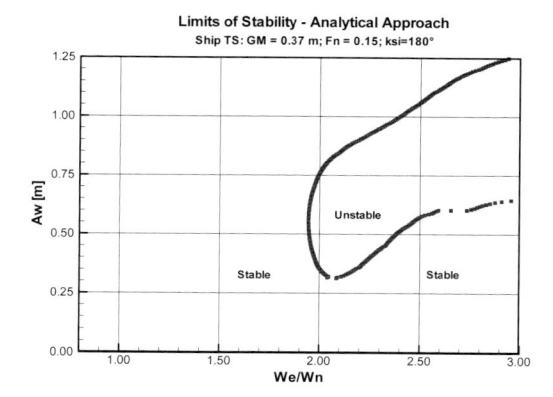

Fig. 2: Analytical approach, Fn=0.15

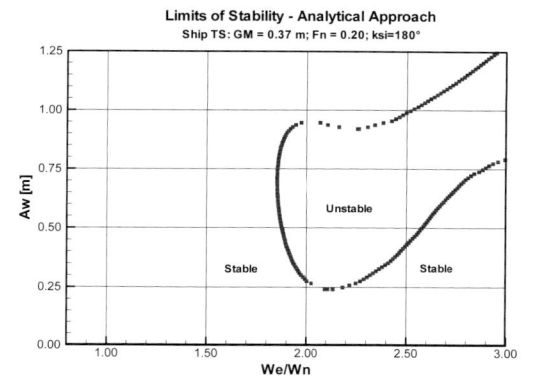

Fig. 3: Analytical approach, Fn=0.20

Limits of Stability - Numerical Approach

An alternative way of computing the instability regions is by solving the equations of motion- Eqs. 2, for a large set of wave amplitudes and tuning factors (encounter frequency/natural roll frequency)-, which may be varied systematically. Then, at each time that instabilization takes place (roll amplification), a point may be plotted in the corresponding plane (A_w vs. tuning factor). Depending on the magnitude of the steady roll amplitude, these points will have an identifying color.

In spite of the aspect that this procedure is much more time consuming for computation, it has the advantage of letting us know the instability regions not only qualitative, but also quantitatively.

Under this alternative method, two different numerical approaches could be used: one assuming an uncoupled nonlinear roll motion equation, and the other using the 3 DOF motion equations coupling the heave, roll and pitch modes.

Uncoupled Roll Motion

Suppose that parametric rolling is modeled as an uncoupled mode from the vertical motions. Numerical results may be obtained for the roll motion amplitude assuming that the heave and pitch motions are linear harmonic functions in Equation (2b). It is observed that the numerical results are quite similar to the analytical values in terms of the area of instabilities.

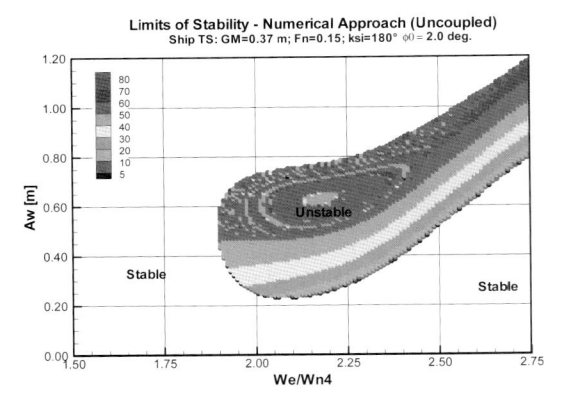

Fig. 4: Numerical uncoupled approach, Fn=0.15

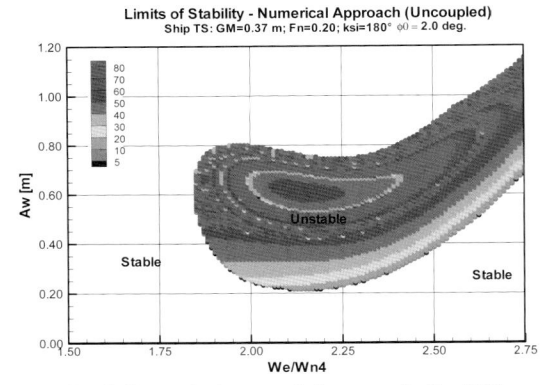

Fig. 5: Numerical uncoupled approach, Fn=0.20

As can be noted from figures 4 and 5, the shape and location of the regions of stability agree well with the analytical approach. This would indicate that pure roll nonlinearities have little or NO influence on these characteristics of the limits. On the other hand, roll results inside the unstable area are relevant information made available in this numerical procedure.

Coupled Roll Motion (3 DOF)

A more refined and reliable way of getting the limits of stability for parametric resonance is to solve numerically the three-degrees-of freedom (DOF) ship motion equations (2), and plot the responses, as explained in the previous section. This more complete approach when applied to the same conditions tested above for TS ship resulted in the limits of stability shown in Figures 6 and 7.

In general, the shape and location of first instability regions ($\omega_e = 2.0\omega_{n4}$) obtained with the 3 DOF numerical approach agrees well with the previous approaches. However, when comparing the limits of Figures 6 and 7 with the corresponding ones of Figures 4 and 5, relevant differences can be observed in the mapping of amplitudes of parametric rolling for the two forward speeds. Such differences reflect the influence of nonlinearities of heave and pitch, which in general tend to control the magnitude of roll amplifications.

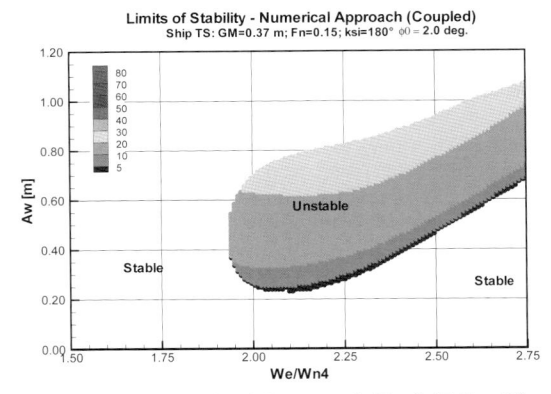

Fig. 6: Numerical 3 DOF approach, Fn=0.15 ($\phi_0 = 2°$)

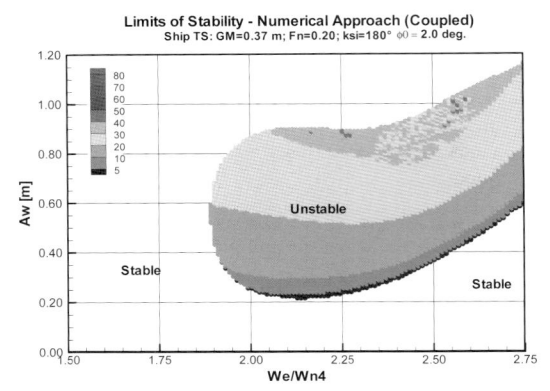

Fig. 7: Numerical 3 DOF approach, Fn=0.20 ($\phi_0 = 2°$)

Concerning the concavity of the instability regions at Fn=0.20 that had been observed in Figure 3, we confirm here its existence and also call the attention of the readers for the risk of getting more critical responses at frequencies higher than the Mathieu tunings, even for quite low wave amplitudes.

Analysis of coupling on the roll restoring moment

Figure 8 shows the (a) heave, (b) roll and (c) pitch motions that contribute to the (d) time-variation of the roll restoring moment corresponding to a point of the mapping of Figure 7. It is pointed out that typically for this ship condition parametric resonance is not only produced by pitch motion. Heave motion is also very strong, such that the prevailing dynamic response comes from a complete heave-roll-pitch problem.

Due to the 3rd order terms, super-harmonics will appear in the roll restoring moment time series, as shown in Figure 8d.

It is interesting to observe that for this large wave amplitude the heave and pitch motions are clearly non-symmetrical.

702

Also interesting is the reduction in pitch amplitude that occurs as the parametrically excited roll motion develops.

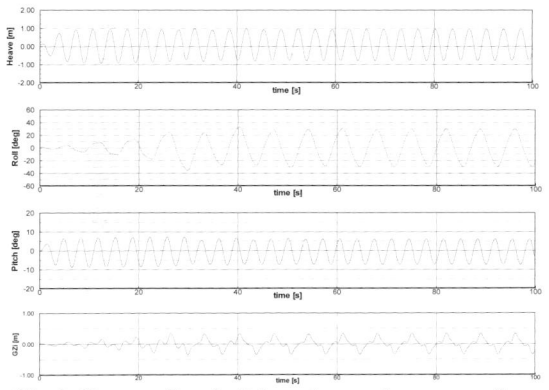

Fig. 8: Heave, roll and pitch motions and corresponding roll restoring moment of ship TS for GM=0.37 m; Fn=0.20; Aw=0.85 m; We = 2.106Wn4

This is indicative of the ability of the coupled model to capture the complex exchange of energy between the modes: roll motion develops due to the vertical modes and with the roll development, vertical motions are reduced, thus indicating that a global level of energy is maintained.

Influence of wave amplitude

Figure 9 shows the roll amplitudes against wave amplitude for three tunings around the *exact* Mathieu tuning $\omega_e = 2.0\ \omega_{n4}$ corresponding to conditions described in the mapping of Figure 7. Again, for high amplitudes (extreme right of the graph) abrupt changes in roll response are observed, indicating the occurrence of a bifurcation for high wave amplitudes. The lower and upper limits of stability are thus regions of substantially distinct behavior, what had not been made clear in the analytical approach discussed earlier.

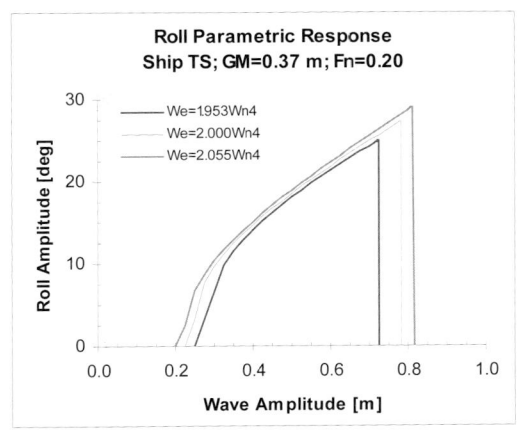

Fig. 9: Jump in roll response at high wave amplitudes, Fn=0.20.

Influence of initial conditions

It is possible to compute the limits of stability for different initial conditions, and identify the conditions that bring different steady parametric roll amplitudes. This phenomenon would indicate the possibility of occurrence of jump effect, bifurcation or even chaos. Figure 10 illustrates the limits of stability for the same conditions showed in Figure 7, but considering an initial condition for roll of 20°.

It is clear that the first influence of initial conditions is to modify the size of the instability regions. In the case illustrated in Figure 10, the first region of instability became greater (growing upwards and to the left side). This additional instability region denotes a zone of initial condition susceptibility. Then, a good beginning for the study of typical nonlinear behavior would be the exploration of this zone.

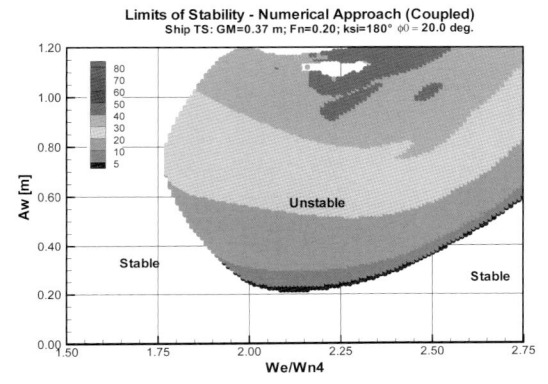

Fig. 10: Numerical 3 DOF approach, Fn=0.20 (ϕ_0 = 20°)

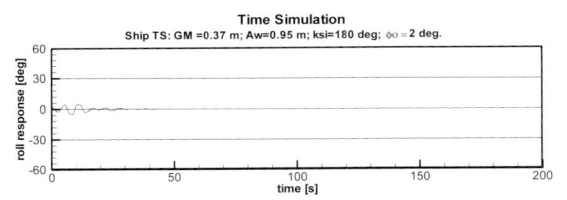

Fig. 11: Time series, Fn=0.20; ϕ_0 = 2°

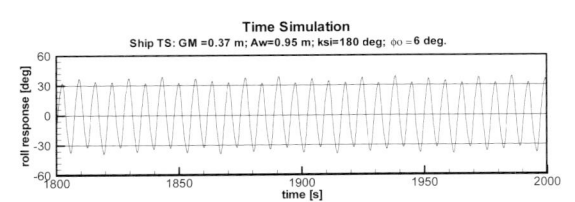

Fig. 12: Time series, Fn=0.20; ϕ_0 = 6°

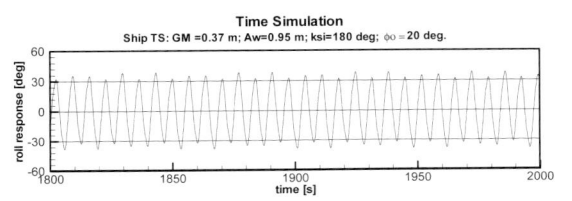

Fig. 13: Time series, Fn=0.20; ϕ_0 = 20°

We consider in Figures 11 ~13 the time series for three different initial conditions in roll for the case of TS ship at Fn=0.20, A_w=0.95 m and ω_e = 2.158 ω_{n4}. As expected, for this set of parameters different initial conditions resulted in substantially different roll responses. For the smaller initial conditions no parametric resonance was developed, as had been noted in the stability map of Figure 7 (2° of roll initial condition). For the roll initial condition of 6°, parametric rolling develops in an erratic way, no single amplitude is observed. Then, it becomes necessary to look at phase diagrams in order to identify if there is a multiperiod response or the possibility of occurrence of chaos. Figures 14 to 16 show the phase diagrams for the respective conditions shown in the time series, initial conditions $\phi_0 = 2°$, $\phi_0 = 6°$ and $\phi_0 = 20°$.

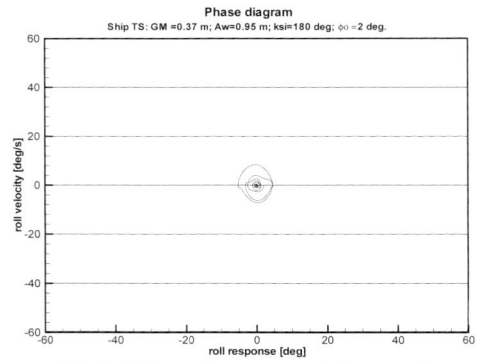

Fig. 14: Phase diagram, Fn=0.20; $\phi_0 = 2°$

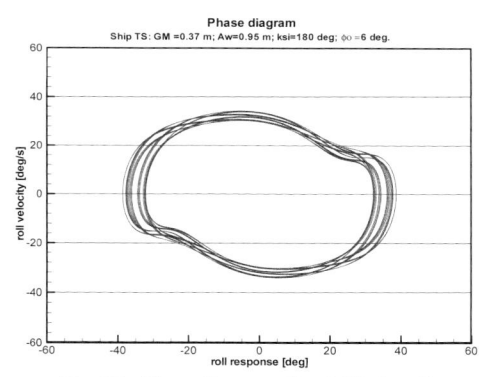

Fig. 15: Phase diagram, Fn=0.20; $\phi_0 = 6°$

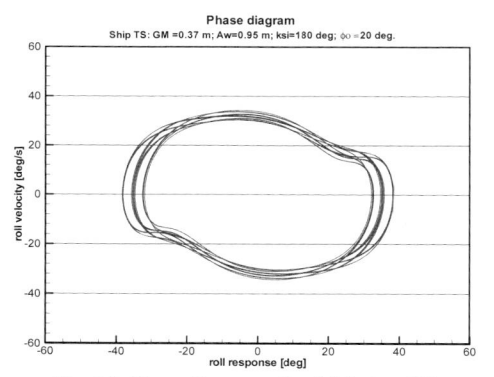

Fig. 16: Phase diagram, Fn=0.20; $\phi_0 = 20°$

Clearly, it is noted that the small initial condition response is stable and does NOT develop parametric rolling. In other words, the response is attracted by a single attractor, which in this case corresponds to the null parametric rolling attractor. For the larger initial conditions, the responses are attracted by a "not-easy-to-identify attractor". We can just say that it is not a single point or a limit cycle attractor. Maybe a strange attractor or even a chaotic attractor, but a definite answer to this question should be given based on more specific nonlinear analysis tools such as bifurcation analysis, Poincaré mapping, Lyapunov exponents, etc. (Guckenheimer & Holmes, 1983, Seydel, 1988, Liaw et al., 1993).

Conclusions

Based on a third order mathematical model for parametric rolling, three approaches for computing the limits of stability have been presented.

The analytical approach has shown good agreement with the numerical responses, and due to its relatively easy implementation, should find good applicability in the ship preliminary design stage. One limitation of the analytical approach is that it does not provide information on the magnitude and distribution of parametric rolling. To overcome this inconvenience, two numerical approaches have been proposed. One using the uncoupled roll equation, and the other applying the full nonlinear equations coupling heave, roll and pitch. Comparing the two latter approaches, a relevant conclusion can be drawn, i.e., the extreme importance of nonlinear couplings between the vertical modes and roll in the determination of parametric roll amplitudes. As can be noted in the respective figures, the uncoupled numerical approach can induce us to wrong predictions of parametric amplitudes.

Another contribution of the present investigation is the identification of initial conditions susceptibility zones within the instability regions, so that the analysis of typical nonlinear phenomena can be focused on these zones. Preliminary analysis of these zones has shown great influence of initial conditions on the development of parametric rolling.

Appendix A

Nonlinear restoring actions

We consider in this appendix the force and moments dependent on position. To third order, positional terms (relative displacements) due to the combined actions of ship motions in calm water and wave elevation along the hull may be formally expressed in terms of a Taylor series expansion about the average position. For this purpose, it is convenient to define a generalized vector $\vec{q} = [\vec{s}, \zeta]^T$ such that the positional actions are:

$$\vec{C}_{pos} = \sum_{i=1}^{4} \frac{\partial \vec{C}_{pos}}{\partial q_i}\bigg|_0 q_i + \frac{1}{2}\sum_{i=1}^{4}\sum_{j=1}^{4} \frac{\partial^2 \vec{C}_{pos}}{\partial q_i \partial q_j}\bigg|_0 q_i q_j +$$

$$\frac{1}{6}\sum_{i=1}^{4}\sum_{j=1}^{4}\sum_{k=1}^{4} \frac{\partial^3 \vec{C}_{pos}}{\partial q_i \partial q_j \partial q_k}\bigg|_0 q_i q_j q_k \quad \text{(A-1)}$$

Undisturbed wave elevation, according to the Airy linear theory may be defined as:

$$\zeta(x,y,t;\chi) = A_w Cos[kxCos(\chi) + kySin(\chi) - \omega_e t]$$

where A_w is wave amplitude, k is wave number, defined as $k = 2\pi/\lambda$ where λ is the wave length, χ is wave heading (incidence) and ω_e is the encounter frequency, defined as $\omega_e = \omega_w - kU\cos\chi$. In longitudinal waves the equation of wave surface elevation is:

$$\zeta(x,t) = A_w Cos[kx + \omega_e t]$$

It is important to note in Equation (A-1) that the first, second and third order terms independent of $\vec{s} = [z \ \phi \ \theta]^T$ may be more appropriately accommodated on the right hand side of Equation (1) of the main text. Following the formalism of Equation (A-1):

$$\vec{C}_{ext(FK)}(\zeta) =$$

$$\frac{\partial \vec{C}_{pos}}{\partial \zeta}\bigg|_0 \zeta + \frac{1}{2}\frac{\partial^2 \vec{C}_{pos}}{\partial \zeta^2}\bigg|_0 \zeta^2 + \frac{1}{6}\frac{\partial^3 \vec{C}_{pos}}{\partial \zeta^3}\bigg|_0 \zeta^3 \quad \text{(A-2)}$$

These terms represent linear and nonlinear Froude-Krilov force/moments excitations that appear in the forcing vector $\vec{C}_{ext}(\zeta,\dot{\zeta},\ddot{\zeta})$ on the right hand side of Equation (1) (main text), in which are cast all the terms independent of the ship bodily motions, vector $\vec{s}$.

Vector $\vec{C}_{res}$, representing nonlinear restoring actions, corresponds to:

$$\vec{C}_{res} = \vec{C}_{pos}(z,\phi,\theta,\zeta) - \vec{C}_{ext(FK)}(\zeta) = \quad \text{(A-3)}$$
$$[Z(t) \ K(t) \ M(t)]^T$$

It is clear that the heave, roll and pitch motions will be completely coupled to each other.

Higher order diffraction force and moments are assumed not to be relevant; for this reason, in the present mathematical model, diffraction forces/moments are defined as being proportional to the first order wave motion.

It is observed that nonlinear effects due to body-wave interactions proportional to second and third order hull-wave relative displacements, due to their mathematical affinity with the purely hydrostatic terms, are considered on the left hand side of the equations of motion, Equation (3) (main text), being named wave passage effects (on the parametric excitation).

Appendix B

Limits of stability

The stability analysis of a Hill equation is presented by Hsu (1963), and when applied to Equation (3) of the main text, two instability regions appear, defined by:

- **First Region of Stability (s = 1):**

$$2\omega_4 + \frac{A_w}{2\omega_4}\Big[(d_{44}^{(1)})^2 + (e_{44}^{(1)})^2 - \quad \text{(B-1)}$$

$$4\omega_4^2(f_{44}^{(0)})^2\Big]^{\frac{1}{2}} > \omega_e$$

$$> 2\omega_4 - \frac{A_w}{2\omega_4}\Big[(d_{44}^{(1)})^2 + (e_{44}^{(1)})^2$$

$$-4\omega_4^2(f_{44}^{(0)})^2\Big]^{\frac{1}{2}}$$

- **Second Region of Stability (s = 2):**

$$\omega_4 + \frac{A_w}{4\omega_4}\Big[(d_{44}^{(1)})^2 + (e_{44}^{(1)})^2 \quad \text{(B-2)}$$

$$-4\omega_4^2(f_{44}^{(0)})^2\Big]^{\frac{1}{2}} > \omega_e$$

$$> \omega_4 - \frac{A_w}{4\omega_4}\Big[(d_{44}^{(1)})^2 + (e_{44}^{(1)})^2$$

$$-4\omega_4^2(f_{44}^{(0)})^2\Big]^{\frac{1}{2}}$$

where:

$$d_{44}^{(1)} = \frac{[K_{z\phi}\eta_3 Cos(\alpha_z) + K_{\phi\theta}\eta_5 Cos(\alpha_\theta) + K_{\zeta\phi c}]}{(J_{xx} + K_{\ddot{\phi}})}$$

$$e_{44}^{(1)} = \frac{[-K_{z\phi}\eta_3 Sin(\alpha_z) - K_{\phi\theta}\eta_5 Sin(\alpha_\theta) + K_{\zeta\phi s}]}{(J_{xx} + K_{\ddot{\phi}})}$$

$$d_{44}^{(2)} = \frac{A_w}{(J_{xx} + K_{\ddot{\phi}})}\Big[\frac{1}{4}K_{zz\phi}\eta_3^2 Cos(2\alpha_z)$$

$$+ \frac{1}{4}K_{\theta\theta\phi}\eta_5^2 Cos(2\alpha_\theta)$$

$$+ \frac{1}{2}K_{z\phi\theta}\eta_3\eta_5 Cos(\alpha_z + \alpha_\theta)$$

$$+ \frac{\eta_3}{2}\left[K_{\zeta z \phi c} Cos(\alpha_z) + K_{\zeta z \phi s} Sin(\alpha_z)\right]$$
$$+ \frac{\eta_5}{2}\left[K_{\zeta \theta \phi c} Cos(\alpha_\theta) + K_{\zeta \theta \phi s} Sin(\alpha_\theta)\right]$$
$$+ K_{\zeta \zeta \phi c} \Bigg]$$

$$e_{44}^{(2)} = \frac{A_w}{(J_{xx} + K_{\ddot\phi})}\Bigg[-\frac{1}{4}K_{zz\phi}\eta_3^2 Sin(2\alpha_z)$$
$$-\frac{1}{4}K_{\theta\theta\phi}\eta_5^2 Sin(2\alpha_\theta)$$
$$-\frac{1}{2}K_{z\theta\phi}\eta_3\eta_5 Sin(\alpha_z + \alpha_\theta)$$
$$+\frac{\eta_3}{2}\left[-K_{\zeta z \phi c} Sin(\alpha_z) + K_{\zeta z \phi s} Cos(\alpha_z)\right]$$
$$+\frac{\eta_5}{2}\left[-K_{\zeta \theta \phi c} Sin(\alpha_\theta) + K_{\zeta \theta \phi s} Cos(\alpha_\theta)\right]$$
$$+ K_{\zeta \zeta \phi s}\Bigg]$$

$$f_{44}^{(0)} = \frac{K_\phi}{A_w(J_{xx} + K_{\ddot\phi})}$$

$$\omega_4 = \left[\omega_{n4}^2 + \omega_{m4}^2\right]^{1/2}$$

$$\omega_{n4}^2 = \frac{K_\phi}{(J_{xx} + K_{\ddot\phi})}$$

$$\omega_{m4}^2 = \frac{A_w^2}{(J_{xx} + K_{\ddot\phi})}\Bigg[\frac{1}{4}K_{zz\phi}\eta_3^2 + \frac{1}{4}K_{\theta\theta\phi}\eta_5^2$$
$$+\frac{1}{2}K_{z\theta\phi}\eta_3\eta_5 Cos(\alpha_z - \alpha_\theta)$$
$$+\frac{\eta_3}{2}\left[K_{\zeta z \phi c} Cos(\alpha_z) - K_{\zeta z \phi s} Sin(\alpha_z)\right]$$
$$+\frac{\eta_5}{2}\left[K_{\zeta \theta \phi c} Cos(\alpha_\theta) - K_{\zeta \theta \phi s} Sin(\alpha_\theta)\right]$$
$$+ K_{\zeta \zeta \phi 0}\Bigg]$$

In the above expressions $\eta_3, \eta_5, \alpha_z, \alpha_\theta$ represent the heave and pitch linear amplitude and phase response operators.

Acknowledgements

The present investigation is supported by CNPq within the STAB project (Nonlinear Stability of Ships). The authors also acknowledge financial support from LabOceano-COPPE/UFRJ and CAPES.

References

Blocki, W. (1980), "Ship Safety in Connection with Parametric Resonance of the Roll". International Shipbuilding Progress, vol. 27, no. 306, pp. 36-53.

France, W.N., Levadou, M., Treakle, T.W., Paulling, J.R., Michel, R.K., and Moore, C., 2003, "An Investigation of Head-Sea Parametric Rolling and its Influence on Container Lashing Systems", Marine Technology, vol. 40, no. 1, pp. 1-19.

Guckenheimer, J., and Holmes, P., 1983, Nonlinear Oscillations, "Dynamical Systems, and Bifurcations of Vector Fields", Applied Mathematical Sciences, vol. 42, Springer-Verlag.

Hua, J. Palmquist, M. and G. Lindgren "On Analysis of the Parametric Roll Events Measured Onboard the PCTC AIDA", 9th International Conference on Stability of Ships and Ocean Vehicles, Rio de Janeiro, Sep. 2006 (Vol. 1), p 109.

Hsu, C.S., 1963, "On the Parametric Excitation of a Dynamic System Having Multiple Degrees of Freedom", Transactions of the ASME Journal of Applied Mechanics, vol. 30, no. 3, pp. 367-372.

Liaw, C.Y., Bishop, S.R., and Thompson, J.M.T., 1993, "Heave-Excited Rolling Motion of a Rectangular Vessel in Head Seas", International Journal of Offshore and Polar Engineering, ISOPE, vol. 3, no. 1, pp. 26-31.

Luth, H.R., and Dallinga, R.P., 1999, "Prediction of Excessive Rolling of Cruise Vessels in Head and Following Waves", PRADS Conference.

Neves, M.A.S., Pérez, N., and Lorca, O., 2002, "Experimental Analysis on Parametric Resonance for Two Fishing Vessels in Head Seas", Proceedings of 6th International Ship Stability Workshop, Webb Institute, NY.

Neves, M.A.S. and Rodríguez, C., 2004, "Limits of Stability of Ships Subjected to Strong Parametric Excitation in Longitudinal Waves", Proceedings of International Maritime Conference on Design for Safety, Osaka, pp. 139-145.

Neves, M.A.S. and Rodríguez, C., 2005, "A Nonlinear Mathematical Model of Higher Order for Strong Parametric Resonance of the Roll Motion of Ships in Waves", Marine Systems & Ocean Technology - Journal of SOBENA, Vol. 1 No. 2, pp. 69-81.

Neves, M.A.S. and Rodríguez, C., 2006, "On Unstable Ship Motions Resulting from Strong Nonlinear Coupling", Ocean Engineering, Vol. 33, pp. 1853-1883.

Paulling, J. R. (1961), "The Transverse Stability of a Ship in a Longitudinal Seaway". Journal of Ship Research, vol. 4, no. 4 (Mar.), pp. 37-49.

Seydel R., 1988, From Equilibrium to Chaos: Practical Bifurcation and Stability Analysis, Elsevier Science Publishing Co., Inc., NY.

Skomedal, N. (1982), "Parametric Excitation of Roll Motion and its Influence on Stability", In: Proceedings of the 2nd International Conference on Stability of Ships and Ocean Vehicles (STAB'82), Tokyo, Japan, pp. 113-125.

On Parametric Rolling of Ships

J. Randolph Paulling

Professor Emeritus
Department of Naval Architecture and Offshore Engineering
University of California, Berkeley, California

Abstract

Modern research on parametric rolling of ships was first conducted in Germany in the late 1930s in an effort to explain the capsizing of some small ships such as coasters and fishing vessels in severe following seas. The work included experiments with models in open water as well as numerical and theoretical computations. The principal objective was to explain capsizing and observations of parametric rolling were, in effect, a byproduct. The phenomenon was thought to be of concern principally in following seas and for small, low freeboard ships. In the 1990s, however, there were reports of containerships and even some cruise ships experiencing heavy rolling in head seas. The APL CHINA casualty in October 1998 focused attention on parametric rolling in head seas. Results of the investigation of this casualty received wide dissemination in the technical press. Since that time much theoretical and experimental work has been focused on head seas parametric roll and today IMO and the Class Societies have recommendations to designers and masters for its avoidance.

Introduction

Parametric roll has been recognized by naval architects for more than fifty years. It may be described as a spontaneous rolling motion of the ship moving in head or following seas that is not directly excited by the waves but comes about as a result of a dynamic instability of the motion. In pure head or following seas transverse symmetry of the ship implies that no wave-induced roll exciting moment exists. Nevertheless, for certain frequencies of wave encounter, it is found that a small initial disturbance in roll can trigger an oscillatory rolling motion that grows to appreciable amplitude after only a few cycles. This is explained in terms of a dynamic instability or bifurcation in the motion characteristics. In 1863, William Froude identified a ship roll-heave coupling phenomenon akin to parametric roll consisting of heave oscillations at the heave natural frequency excited by the small roll induced variations in the buoyant force which occur at twice the roll frequency.

The occurrence of parametric roll is directly related to variations in the transverse stability of the ship as it moves through head or following waves. As the ship encounters successive waves, the geometry of the immersed portion of the hull varies as the waves move along the ship length. This results in a time varying transverse stability as measured by both GM for small angles of heel and by GZ at large angles. Fig. 1 illustrates a ship in head or following seas with wave crest amidships and wave trough amidships. If the hull form is flared above the mean waterline fore and aft, as is normally the case, it is clear from this illustration that the mean width of the waterplane is greater for trough amidships than for crest amidships. Elementary stability considerations indicate that these variations in waterplane characteristics result in increased initial transverse stability for the ship in the trough and diminished stability in the crest. Further considerations demonstrate that these variations in stability exist at large angles of heel as well, thus the entire range of GZ versus angle is affected.

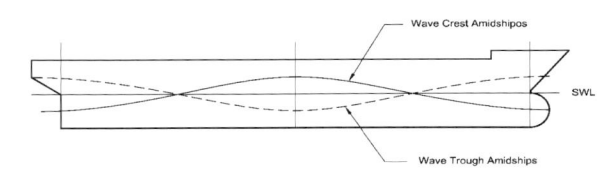

Fig. 1. Ship on wave crest and trough respectively

Fig. 2 contains the large angle righting arm curves computed for two ships in the crest amidships, trough amidships positions. The first is a general cargo ship of 1960s vintage and the second a modern post-Panamax container ship. As the ship moves through head or following seas and the wave crest moves along the length of the ship, the GZ curve varies in time between the two extremes. Therefore GZ is to be represented as a surface with wave crest location and angle of heel as independent variables.

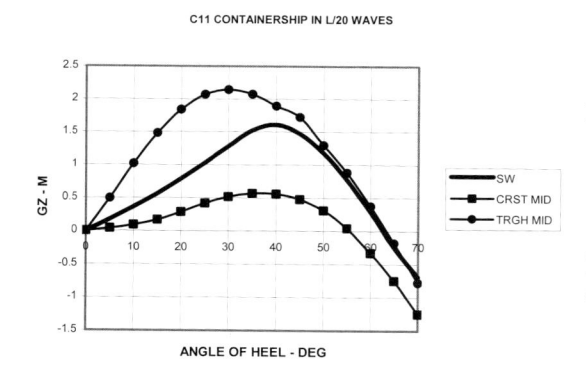

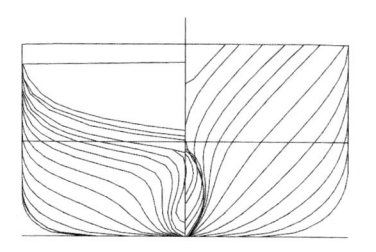

Fig. 2b. C11 Post-Panamax Containership

A simple dynamic model of parametric roll

The dynamic rolling motion of a ship undergoing these stability variations in head or following seas is analogous to that of a spring-mass system in which the spring constant varies sinusoidally in time. For the ship the frequency of variation equals the frequency of wave encounter. We can examine the small amplitude roll dynamics of a ship with periodic stability variations using a simplified model as follows. As the ship moves through head or following seas the time-varying GM is approximated by a sinusoidal function of time, Equation (1).

$$GM(t) = GM_o(1 + C\cos\omega t) \qquad (1)$$

Here, GM_o = still water GM,

C = fractional variation of GM

ω = encounter frequency

If we neglect damping, the equation of motion for uncoupled roll without excitation will be given by Equation (2).

$$I_x \frac{d^2\phi}{dt^2} + \Delta\phi(GM_o + CGM_o \cos\omega t) = 0 \qquad (2)$$

Here, ϕ = angle of roll,
Δ = ship displacement,
I_x = mass moment of inertia in roll, including added mass.

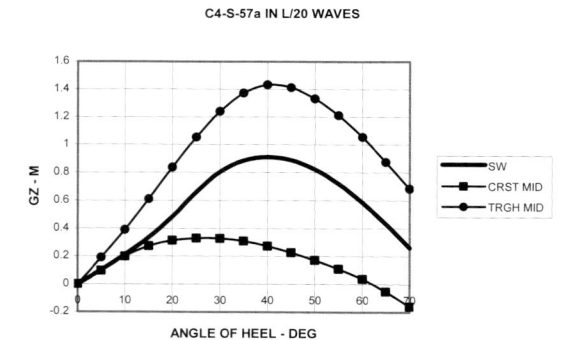

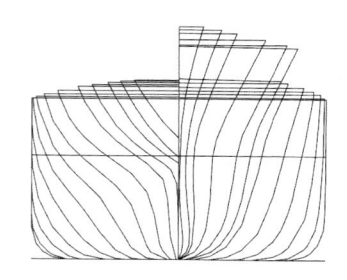

Fig. 2a. C4-S-57a AMERICAN CHALLENGER Dry Cargo Ship of 1960s Vintage

Now divide both sides of (2) by I_x and make the change of variable,

$$\tau = \omega t \qquad \text{for which} \qquad \frac{d^2}{dt^2} = \omega^2 \frac{d^2}{d\tau^2}.$$

We note that $\omega_n^2 = \frac{\Delta GM_o}{I_x}$,

where ω_n = natural frequency of roll,

We define

$$\delta = \frac{\Delta GM_o}{\omega^2 I_x} = \frac{\omega_n^2}{\omega^2},$$

$$\varepsilon = \frac{C\Delta GM_o}{I_x \omega^2} = C\frac{\omega_n^2}{\omega^2}.$$

The equation of roll motion now becomes,

$$\frac{d^2\phi}{d\tau^2} + (\delta + \varepsilon\cos\tau)\phi = 0. \quad (3)$$

This ordinary differential equation with sinusoidally varying spring constant is known as the *Mathieu* equation. The behavior of its solutions has been determined and is illustrated in Fig. 3, known as the Ince-Strutt diagram. Here the shaded regions represent stable solutions to the equation and unshaded regions correspond to unstable solutions. Thus, if the two parameters (δ,ε) for the system lie in a stable region, an arbitrarily small initial disturbance will die out with increasing time, while if they lie in an unstable region, the disturbance will grow with time. We see that δ is equal to the square of the ratio of the natural frequency of roll to the frequency of variation of GM and ε is proportional to the fractional change in GM.

The first unstable region is centered on a value $\delta=1/4$ or a ratio of natural frequency to frequency of GM variation of ½. If, in a given situation, the frequency ratio does not exactly satisfy this value, unstable motion can still occur for a sufficiently large value of C, *i.e.*, if the amplitude of the variation in GM is sufficiently large. The effect of linear damping is to merely raise the instability threshold at a given δ with the result that unstable motion can still occur if C is sufficiently large. In order for a limit on the ultimate amplitude to exist, there must be nonlinear damping in the system, for example, quadratic roll damping.

From the foregoing simplified analysis we can expect that, if the ship encounters regular head or following seas at a frequency near one-half the natural frequency of roll, a small disturbance in roll will grow to appreciable amplitude. The ultimate amplitude will depend on the amplitude of the stability variation, i.e., a function of wave amplitude, and the roll damping. In real situations, the initial disturbance is always present and supplied by some external effect such as wind or oblique wave components.

Fig. 3. Ince-Strutt diagram illustrating stability of solutions of the Mathieu Equation

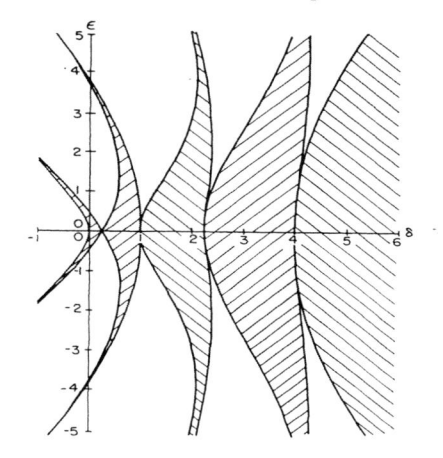

Early parametric roll research

Much of the earliest work on parametric roll was conducted in Germany starting in the late 1930s and focused on smaller working ships such as fishing boats, seagoing tugs and small coastal cargo craft which had experienced a number of casualties. Some of the research involved experiments with free running models, and the main objective was to investigate the cause of capsize of a specific ship. In some following sea experiments, several cycles of parametric rolling prior to the model capsize were observed and in others, the model capsized without any preliminaries. The discovery of parametric roll may, therefore, have been a byproduct of the capsizing work.

Observations from these experiments and later ones resulted in terms such as "pure loss of stability" and "low cycle resonance" being coined to describe the capsizing behavior. The first term describes a situation in which the ship, moving at a speed near the phase speed of a high and steep wave, remains on the crest of the wave for sufficient time that capsize occurs without any oscillatory rolling motion. The wave, of course, must be sufficiently steep and high so that GZ becomes very small or negative over the entire range of heel angles in the crest amidships condition. The second describes a parametric rolling situation in which the rolling motion of the ship in head or following seas builds up to capsize in a small number of cycles. In this case, the wave may or may not be so high as to result in vanishing

GZ but the ship must encounter a sufficient number of nearly regular waves for the motion to increase to capsizing.

Experimental determination of GZ in following seas

In 1961 Paulling published some results of towing tank model experiments designed to measure the GZ of a ship in following seas. In these experiments, a model was towed in regular following waves using a device that constrained the model to a fixed angle of heel while allowing freedom to heave and pitch. The restraining moment was continually recorded during the experiment and was observed to vary periodically as successive waves overtook the model. A series of experiments were conducted at different model speeds, angles of heel and wave proportions. Several different models were tested representing variations in beam and freeboard on the DTMB Series 60 hull forms.

Results from experiments conducted at various model speeds in following seas revealed very little dependence of GZ on speed in the normal speed range for seagoing ships. Since the experiments were conducted in following seas only they did not explore the possible effects that might come from the greater pitch-heave motions in head seas.

Some results obtained in these experiments, compared with computed values are shown in Fig. 4. The computations assumed pitch-heave static equilibrium of the ship on wave and were performed with mechanical integrator and desk calculator as was the state of the art at the time. The agreement is seen to be good for the following seas used in the experiments.

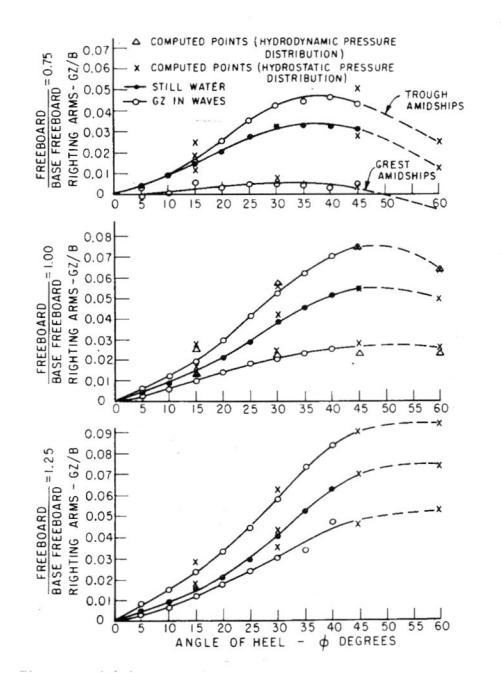

Fig. 4 Model measurements of GZ in following seas. Series 60 C_b=0.60, Varied freeboard.

Some early numerical studies of the rolling motion of a ship in following seas (Kerwin 1955) suggested that the transient behavior of the roll motion was rather gradual, i.e., a large number of cycles would be required in order for the rolling motion to grow to appreciable amplitude. This slow transient growth was interpreted to imply that a large number of nearly regular waves would have to be encountered in order for the rolling motion to grow to appreciable amplitude. For this reason the significance of parametric roll in real irregular waves was discounted.

Nevertheless, although the waves in a real ocean are random, from time to time, groups of several successive waves will be encountered that appear to be almost regular. Furthermore, the waves as observed from a moving ship have a different character than the waves at a fixed location. Following waves appear to have distinctly different characteristics than head or beam seas. This is a consequence of the dispersion relation, i.e., the dependence of wave velocity on wave length. When observed from a point moving in the same direction as the waves, as in following seas, the wave spectrum is compressed into a narrower band

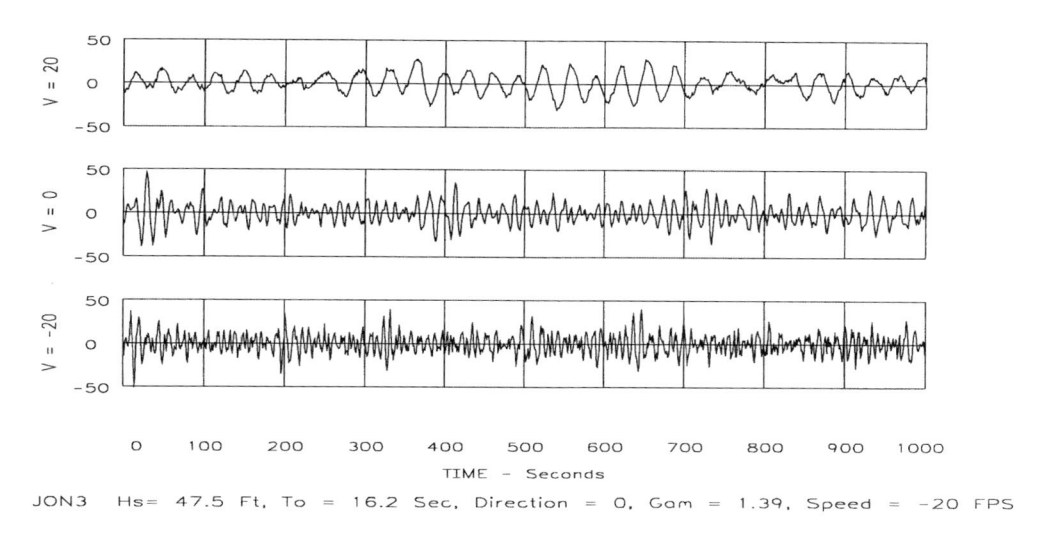

Fig. 5 Unidirectional random waves observed from moving and stationary points

of lower frequencies than that for a fixed point, while head seas result in a spreading of the spectrum over a wider band of higher frequencies. The resulting appearance of the wave time history is shown in Fig. 5. Here, the upper graph contains the wave profile observed from a point moving in the same direction as the waves, the center graph is the profile observed from a fixed point and the lower graph corresponds to a point moving opposite to the wave motion. Clearly, following seas appear much more regular than head or beam seas.

The San Francisco Bay Experiments

In the 1970s experiments were conducted using large radio controlled free running models in San Francisco Bay and reported by (Oakley, et., al. 1974). Models of the C4-S-57a cargo ship and the SL-7 container ship were used in these experiments that were conducted in wave conditions ranging from moderately severe up to a mild hurricane. The model was propelled at constant RPM on a predetermined heading and steered by an internal autopilot. A nearby wave buoy was arranged to sense and record wave amplitude and directionality in the test area. Fig. 6 shows a model being launched from the test support vessel, a catamaran named Froude-Krylov,

Fig. 6 Launching the model from the Froude-Krylov

and Fig. 7 illustrates part of a typical test record.

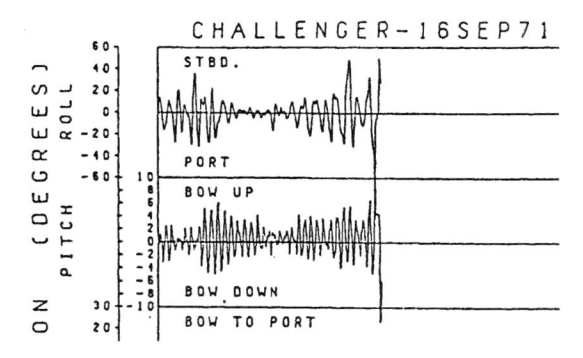

Fig. 7. Example of recorded pitch and heave motions

In Fig. 7, the lower trace contains the pitch motion of the model, occurring at the wave encounter frequency, while the upper trace is the roll motion, occurring at one-half the encounter frequency. This is an illustration of parametric roll in the first resonance band, i.e., at a frequency of encounter equal to twice the roll frequency. This record, which almost certainly represents the encounter of a well formed group consisting of several nearly regular waves, comes from a following sea experiment showing capsize due to low cycle resonance.

The APL CHINA Casualty

In the early 1990s several containerships reported the occurrence of heavy rolling in head seas and the description of the incidents indicated the possibility of parametric rolling. Some of the reports indicated that the rolling motion built very quickly, during the encounter of only three or four waves. These containerships were built with hull forms having great flare forward and wide flaring stern sections in order to maximize container space on deck while keeping a fine underwater form for low resistance. These are features, however, that lead to large stability changes as the ship moves through waves. Also the typical metacentric height of such a ship results in a natural roll frequency near one-half the head sea encounter frequency if the ship moves at low speed in a wave length approximately equal to the ship length. This may lead to parametric roll if the master must reduce speed in head seas to reduce large pitch motions and slamming.

The effect on stability of the flared form can be seen in Fig. 2. At the smaller angles of heel, the righting arm curves, trough versus crest amidships, diverge to a greater extent for the C11 containership than for the older, more wall-sided dry cargo ship of traditional form. This action results in a larger value for C, the coefficient of variation of GM in Equation (1), and leads to increased susceptibility to parametric roll.

The APL CHINA casualty in October 1998 focused worldwide attention on head seas parametric roll. While eastbound in the North Pacific Ocean, the ship found itself in a rapidly moving weather system that was formed by the convergence of two low pressure systems and, despite weather routing advice, was unable to avoid the rapidly changing situation. The resulting combined system was described as an "explosively intensifying low" or meteorological 'bomb" and referred to by some as a Pacific version of the "perfect storm". At the height of the storm, the ship's deck log recorded estimated wind of Beaufort force 11 (50-63 kts.) and sea state 9 (Hs>14m). A weather and sea state hindcast performed after the incident gave peak sustained winds of 30.8 m/s or 60 knots and a significant wave height of 14.9 m

During the height of the storm, the master attempted to maintain a heading into the seas at a speed just sufficient to retain control. The ship reported rolls of over 40 degrees and violent pitching in the very high and confused seas. As a result of the violent motions combined with boarding seas, severe damage to- and loss of a large number of containers was sustained as illustrated in Figs. 8a-b.

Fig. 8a APL CHINA Container Damage

Fig. 8b APL CHINA Container Damage

After the casualty, extensive studies including weather analyses, model experiments, numerical simulations, and theoretical analyses were undertaken. These pointed to head seas parametric roll as a major cause. A significant outcome of this and related work is the development by classification societies and IMO of rules and guidelines for the avoidance of parametric roll both in the design and operation of ships.

A somewhat more sophisticated model

In order to illustrate some additional characteristics of parametric rolling, we shall now consider a slightly modified form of Equation (2) as follows,

$$I_x \frac{d^2\phi}{dt^2} + B(\frac{d\phi}{dt}) + \Delta GZ(\phi,t) = 0 \qquad (4)$$

Here, $B(\frac{d\phi}{dt})$ is a general roll damping term that may include linear and more complex damping such as quadratic, cubic or other functions of roll velocity.

$\Delta GZ(\phi,t)$ is the generalized time varying restoring moment function.

The usual method of solving equation (4) is a stepwise numerical integration in the time domain and the forth order Runge-Kutta method was used in the present examples. The surface $GZ(\phi,t)$ is represented by a tabulated family of GZ curves similar to those in Fig. 2, computed for a number of successive closely spaced positions of the wave along the ship length. A simple interpolation scheme gives the value of GZ for the instantaneous angle of heel and wave position at each time step. The damping may be estimated using any of several methods found in the literature on ship rolling.

Initial condition sensitivity

Having coded this numerical integrator, it is easy to play "what if" games that may lead to understanding of some of the basic features of parametric roll response. We shall look at the sensitivity of roll response to the initial disturbance using the C11 containership as an example. The GZ curves were constructed for 20 equally spaced positions of the wave crest along the ship length and the nonlinear roll damping was estimated using the method embedded in the US Navy's SMP code. The natural undamped roll period of the ship was estimated to be about 23 seconds assuming a mass radius of gyration in roll of 0.4B and GM of 0.05B. In head seas of length equal to the ship length, the critical frequency ratio of ½ occurs at a speed of about 5.5 knots.

Fig. 9 presents results in regular head seas for initial roll angles of 0.1, 1.0 and 5.0 degrees. As expected this figure shows a transient behavior strongly dependent on the initial disturbance. Reported cases of unexpected head seas parametric roll have indicated that the motion built up rapidly over the occurrence of four to six large rolls. In heavy head seas some component waves from directions other than dead ahead will always exist and these could very likely set up roll motions of five degrees or more.

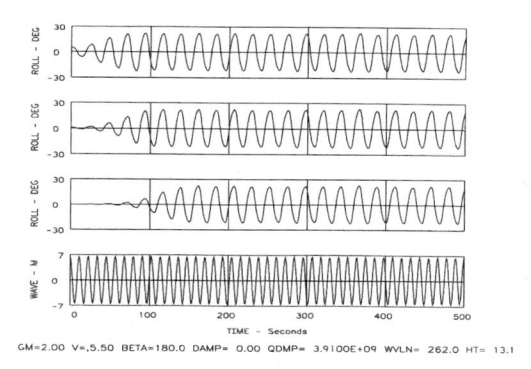

Fig. 9 Sensitivity of transient response to initial disturbance for initial roll angle = 0.1, 1.0, 5.0 deg.

GZ variation in head seas

The computation of the GZ curves for a ship poised in static equilibrium on the wave is felt to be satisfactory for moderate speeds in following seas as demonstrated in Fig. 4. In head seas static equilibrium of pitch and heave is probably not as good an assumption as in following seas. This is especially true at higher speeds for which the encounter frequencies may approach resonance in pitch and heave.

In order to test the sensitivity of the GZ curve to forward speed, we make the assumption that the pitch-heave motion in head seas of the heeled ship differs only slightly from the corresponding

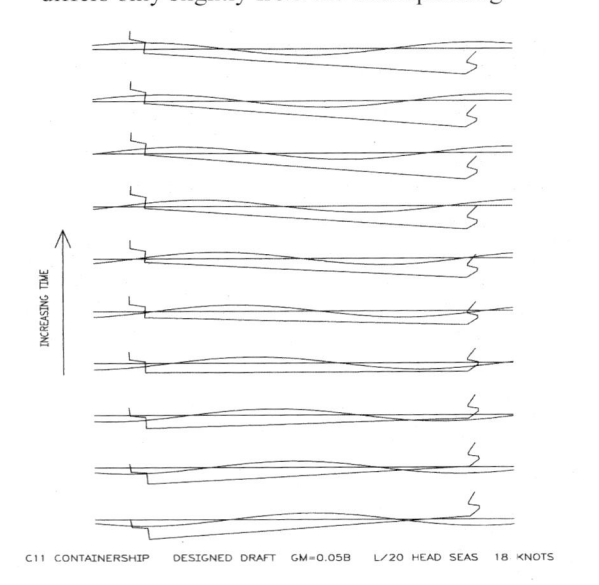

Fig.10. C11 Containership in L/20 head seas at 18 knots.

motion of the upright ship. We may then use a standard linear ship motions code to determine the dynamic pitch-heave attitude at successive positions of the wave along the ship length, after which we perform the GZ computation as in the static case. This neglects the dynamic pressure distribution on the ship due to the motions as well as the effect of heel on the pitch-heave motion. Since the Froude-Krylov pressure terms usually predominate, this procedure can be thought of as providing a first order correction for head seas. An example of the ship's varying attitude with passage of the waves is shown in Fig. 10.

Fig. 11 contains results of such stability computations in the form of maximum and minimum GZ curves for the wave trough, - wave crest amidships positions. The ship speed is 18 knots in both head and following seas. Also shown are GZ curves for the static pitch-heave attitude that simulates following seas. The dynamic motion curves are labeled "F" for following and "H" for head seas. From these results we conclude that the effect of pitch-heave dynamics is to reduce somewhat the variation of the GZ curves about the still water curve in head seas. As expected, we see that the assumed static pitch-heave attitude is quite close to the dynamic attitude in following seas.

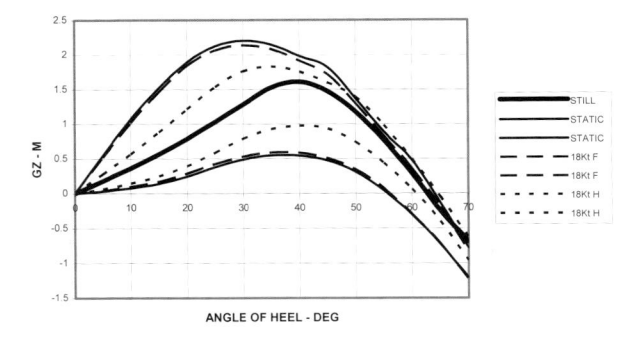

Fig. 11. Max – min GZ curves for C11 containership – dynamic pitch-heave at 18 kts

Conclusions

A very brief survey is given of some of the practical implications of parametric roll for ships in following and head seas. Early works on the phenomenon was concentrated on rolling and capsize in following seas. In 1998, the APL CHINA casualty brought out quite dramatically the possibility and consequences of head seas parametric roll. Much research has come about as a result and both the regulatory bodies and ship owners are now taking steps both in the ship design process and in the operation of ships to avoid parametric roll.

Acknowledgement

The work reported upon here has been supported over a period of many years principally by the US Coast Guard, the American Bureau of Shipping and the Society of Naval Architects and Marine Engineers

References

Arndt, B. and Rodin, S. "Stabilität bei vor-und-achterlichem Seegang", *Schiffstechnik*, vol. 5, no. 29, Nov. 1958, 192-199.

DeKat, J. O. and Paulling, J. R., "The Simulation of Ship Motions and Capsizing in Severe Seas", *Transactions*, The Society of Naval Architects and Marine Engineers, vol. 97, 1989

France, William N., Levadou, M., Treakle, T. W., Paulling, J. R., Michel, R. K., Moore, C., "An Investigation of Head-Sea Parametric Rolling and its Influence on Container Lashing Systems", *Marine Technology*, vol 40, no. 1 Jan 2003, 1-19.

Froude, W., "Remarks on Mr. Scott-Russell's Paper on Rolling", *Transactions*, The Institution of Naval Architects, 1863

Graff, W. and Heckscher, E., "Widerstands und Stabilitäts versuche mit drei Fischdampfermodellen", *Werft-Reederei-Hafen*, vol. 22, 1941, 115-120 (also DTMB Translation No.75, June 1942).

Grim, O., "Rollschwingungen, Stabilität und Sicherheit im Seegang", *Schiffstechnik*, vol. 1, 1952, 10-21.

IMO, "Guidance to the Master for Avoiding Dangerous Situations in Following and Quartering Seas", MSC Circ. 707 dated 19 October 1995.

Kempf, G, "Die Stabilitätsbeanspruchung der Schiffe durch Wellen und Schwingungen", *Werft-Reederei-Hafen,* vol. 19, 1938,. 200-202.

Kerwin, J. E., "Notes on Rolling in Longitudinal Waves", *International Shipbuilding Progress*, vol 2, 1955, 597-614.

Oakley, O. H., Paulling, J. R. and Wood, P. D. , "Ship Motions and Capsizing in Astern Seas", *Proceedings,* Tenth ONR Symposium on Naval Hydrodynamics, ONR, ACR 204, 1974.

Paulling, J. R. and Rosenberg, R. M., "On Unstable Ship Motions Resulting from Nonlinear Coupling", *Journal of Ship Research,* vol. 3, no.1, 1959.

Paulling, J. R. , "The Transverse Stability of a Ship in a Longitudinal Seaway", *Journal of Ship Research,* vol. 4, no. 4, 1961.

Shin, Y. S., Belenky, V. S., Paulling, J. R., Weems, K. M., Lin, W. M., "Criteria for Parametric Roll of Large Containerships in Longitudinal Seas", *Transactions,* SNAME, vol 112, 2004, 14-47.

Tikka, Kirsi K., and Paulling, J. R., "Prediction of Critical Wave Conditions for Extreme Vessel Response in Random Seas", *Proceedings,* Stab90, Naples, 1990.

Wendel, K., "Stabilitätseinbussen im Seegang und durch Koksdeckslast", *Hansa* 1954, pp 2016-2022.

Wendel, K., "Safety from Capsizing", *Fishing Boats of the World 2*, (J. O. Traung Ed)., Fishing News Books, Ltd., London, 1960, 496-504.

Estimation of Maximum Stress of a Container Ship by Means of Design Irregular Wave and Direct Loading Analysis Method

Toichi Fukasawa [1], Satoshi Miyazaki [2]

[1] Kanazawa Institute of Technology,
Nonoichi, Ishikawa, Japan
[2] Mitsubishi Heavy Industries, LTD
Nagasaki, Nagasaki, Japan

Abstract

Design Irregular Wave is a phase-controlled irregular wave train in which a maximum of a certain ship response can be realized in a given short-term sea state. On the other hand, Direct Loading Analysis Method is a calculation method of time-varying stresses in a whole ship structure by using FEM. In this paper, a methodology to estimate the maximum of local stress by means of the Design Irregular Wave and the Direct Loading Analysis Method is presented, and the design short-term sea state in ship structural design is discussed. Sample calculations were performed on a 6,200 TEU Post-Panamax size container ship, and the maximum stress and the short-term sea state for the maximum stress were clarified. Significant wave height and the mean wave period of the design short-term sea state and the encounter angle of ship to wave in ship structural design were discussed based on the calculated maximum stresses.

Keywords

Ship structural design; Design irregular wave; Direct loading analysis method; Maximum stress; Container ship; Design short-term sea state.

Introduction

In order to estimate the extreme value of ship response, a "Design Wave" concept has been often adopted in recent ship structural design. The extreme value can be calculated taking account of nonlinearity of ship response with less effort in the Design Wave method. A regular wave train is usually assumed as the Design Wave, and a time domain simulation of ship response is carried out by using a linear or nonlinear computational program of ship response. Actual sea state, however, is random and the ocean wave is irregular. The regular wave hypothesis may cause erroneous results but may be avoided if the regular wave is properly calibrated by a stochastic analysis.

On the other hand, random irregular wave trains can be used in time domain simulations. Although the nonlinearity in ship response can be taken into account in this method, it will take considerably longer to obtain statistically significant extreme values of ship response.

A phase-controlled irregular wave has recently been proposed in order to compensate the defects of above two methods. Tromans, Anaturk and Hagemeijer (1991) proposed a "New Wave", and Hansen and Nielsen (1995) proposed a "Most Likely Wave (MLW)". The most likely wave profile was estimated in these methods assuming that the maximum response occurs near the largest wave elevation, and the response to the concentrated wave was analyzed. These methods, however, lack the consideration on the response characteristics of a ship or an offshore structure. Fukasawa (1995) proposed a "Design Irregular Wave (DIW)", where the ship response characteristics are taken into account, resulting in some application results reported (Fukasawa, 1998; Fukasawa and Cho, 2001; Fukasawa, 2005a; Fukasawa, 2005b; Fukaswa, Kawabe and Moan, 2007). The Design Irregular Wave is an irregular wave train of which phase angles of regular wave components are controlled to realize a maximum response of a ship. On the other hand, Adegeest, Braathen and Lseth (1998) and Adegeest, Braathen and Vada (1998) proposed a "Most Likely Extreme Response (MLER)" method, whereby the extreme response can be estimated by using a response spectrum. A time domain simulation can also be carried out with the use of the phase-controlled irregular wave, of which regular wave components are obtained by an inverse transformation of response spectrum by using the transfer function. It was verified by Pastoor (2002), Pastoor, Helmers and Bitner-Gregersen (2003), Dietz, Hansen and Jensen (2004), and Soares and Pascoal (2005) that the extreme response by MLER method almost agrees with the values obtained from model experiments and statistical considerations. Although the DIW method and the MLER method are different in the process of calculation, the basic concept to get the Design Wave by using phase of response is the same.

The phase-controlled irregular wave can be considered to be the most promising approach in the Design Wave concept. Thus far, extreme wave bending moment was estimated in a given short-term sea state by using DIW and MLER methods with nonlinearities in ship response were appropriately taken into account. It is, however, difficult to estimate the extreme value of local stress even in the phase-controlled irregular wave. In DIW or MLER methods, phase information of stress transfer function is necessary to superimpose the regular wave components. However, it is rather difficult to calculate the phase angle of local stress. A number of FE analyses with a structural model of the ship is necessary to be conducted in time domain to get the phase information of stress transfer function.

Recently, the Direct Loading Analysis Method (DILAM) has been proposed, and calculating the stress transfer function with powerful computer resources makes the process easier. The Direct Loading Analysis Method is a calculation method of time-varying stress in a whole ship structure by using a complete FEM model of ship structure with direct load transfer from wave load analysis.

In this paper, the estimation method of extreme stress of a container ship is investigated by combining the Design Irregular Wave and the Direct Loading Analysis Method. Sample calculations are performed on the local stress of a 6,200 TEU Post-Panamax size container ship. Maximum stress in each short-term sea state in the Walden's wave scatter diagram in North Atlantic is estimated. Significant wave height and the mean wave period of design short-term sea state and the ship encounter angle to wave in ship structural design are discussed based on the estimated maximum stresses.

Design Irregular Wave Method

The Design Irregular Wave (DIW) is an irregular wave train in a given short-term sea state, which causes a maximum response of a ship by adjusting the phase angle of each regular wave component. The regular wave components of DIW are generated from a restricted frequency range of the wave spectrum in the short-term sea state. The phase angle of each regular wave component of DIW is determined according to the phase information of transfer function of response of the ship.

An irregular wave train can be generated from the wave spectrum $S(\omega)$ by dividing the frequency range of wave spectrum into N components. In the DIW method, regular wave components are generated from a restricted frequency range of the wave spectrum. Fig.1 shows the normalized wave spectrum and a typical stress spectrum normalized by the maximum value. It is noted in the figure that the stress spectrum is a narrower band than the wave spectrum. This observation means that wave components in higher frequency range do not affect stress response. In other words, only the regular wave components in the restricted frequency range, as shown by the vertical lines in Fig.1, would contribute to the stress response. Therefore, only the regular wave components in this frequency range are used in producing DIW. The frequency range of DIW is chosen so as to include the normalized stress spectrum that exceeds α as indicated in Fig.1. It was confirmed that the maximum stress calculated in DIW barely changes for an α in the range of $0.1 < \alpha < 0.5$, and $\alpha = 0.2$ is taken in the present paper for simplicity.

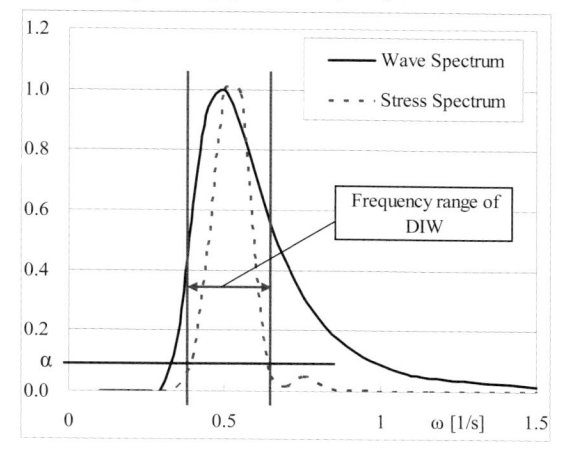

Fig. 1: Normalized wave and stress spectra

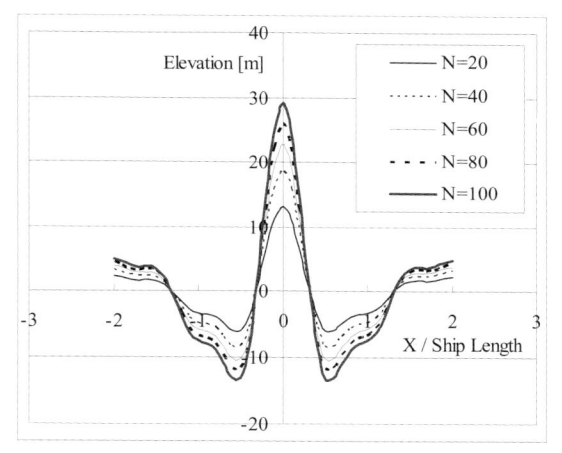

Fig. 2: Superposed wave profile

The elevation of superposed irregular wave train $\zeta(t)$ is represented by Eq.(1).

$$\zeta(t) = \sum_{i=1}^{N} \sqrt{2 S(\omega_i) \Delta \omega} \cos(\kappa_i X + \omega_i t - \varepsilon_i) \quad (1)$$

whereby κ_i, ω_i and ε_i are the wave number, frequency, and phase angle of i-th regular wave component. The frequency interval $\Delta\omega$, or the number of division of wave spectrum N, is usually chosen empirically, and is not uniquely fixed in general. The amplitude of each regular wave component depends on the frequency interval as is shown in Eq.(1), and the elevation of superposed regular wave components increases in proportion to $\sqrt{N}$. Superimposed wave profile of regular wave components is shown in Fig.2 in case of N=20, 40, 60, 80 and 100, where the phase angle in Eq.(1) is taken as $\varepsilon_i = 0$. It can be seen that the wave steepness increases with the increase of the number of division, N, of wave spectrum, and the wave may break in case of large number of N. In order to fix the number of division of wave spectrum uniquely, the following wave breaking criteria is adopted in the DIW method.

Maximum wave steepness is less than 1/10.

The observed maximum wave steepness is around 1/10 in ocean waves, thereby supporting this fact. The number of division of wave spectrum can be fixed uniquely with this restriction.

The phase angles of regular wave component in Eq.(1) are fixed intentionally in the DIW method so that the local stress attains its maximum at time t=0. Let the i-th regular wave component and the resulting stress to be,

$$\zeta_i(t) = \overline{\zeta}_i \cos(\kappa_i X + \omega_i t') \quad (2)$$

$$\sigma_i(t) = \overline{\sigma}_i \cos(\omega_i t' - \varepsilon_{\sigma i}) \quad (3)$$

whereby the maximum stress occurs at $t' = \varepsilon_{\sigma i}/\omega_i$.

Converting the time scale as

$$t' = t + \frac{\varepsilon_{\sigma i}}{\omega_i} \quad (4)$$

we have

$$\zeta_i(t) = \overline{\zeta}_i \cos(\kappa_i X + \omega_i t + \varepsilon_{\sigma i}) \quad (5)$$

$$\sigma_i(t) = \overline{\sigma}_i \cos(\omega_i t) \quad (6)$$

Comparing Eqs.(1) and (5), it is found that if the phase angle of a regular wave component is taken to be ($\varepsilon_i = -\varepsilon_{\sigma i}$), the maximum stress occurs at time t=0. If all the phase angle of regular wave component of DIW is determined in this manner, the maximum value of superposed stress in the irregular wave train occurs at time t=0, in case where the ship response is assumed to be linear.

Moreover, in the DIW method, the following restriction is also imposed.

Maximum wave height is less than 1.934 H_V.

Since the equivalent response to the 1/1000 highest value in short-term sea state is usually estimated by using DIW, the maximum wave height should also be equivalent to the 1/1000 highest value (Fukasawa, Kawabe and Moan, 2007).

It should be noted here that the basic concept of the DIW method is that the wave components that contribute to the maximum response could be estimated by a linear theory, even the ship response is nonlinear. Moreover, the DIW method is to be changed according to the target response of the ship, that is, vertical bending moment, local stress, and so on.

Direct Loading Analysis Method (DILAM)

Structural analysis using FEM is essential to investigate the local stress in hull structure of a ship. It is the usual practice to use a FE model of partial structure of the ship, which represents the typical cargo hold area. In order to estimate the stresses associated with the global response of the ship in waves, it is preferable to carry out a global structural analysis by using a complete FE model of ship structure.

DIScrete Analysis Method (DISAM) has been proposed as a global structural analysis method thus far (Kuramoto, Tozawa, Shirokibara, Inoue and Fushimi, 1991; Smith, Kawagoe and Shirakihara, 2001). In DISAM, a linear superposition method is adopted to calculate the local stress assuming that the structural response is linear. By dividing the surface of ship's hull into several panels, a load-stress influence matrix is calculated by applying a unit load on each panel one by one in FEM calculations. Superposing the hydrodynamic pressure on the load-stress influence matrix according to the pressure distribution pattern, and interpolating the obtained stresses in time, the stress fluctuation is obtained. Although DISAM is an efficient method for applying nonlinear wave loads to ship structure with reduced number of load cases in FE analysis, it is difficult for designers to grasp overall deformations and stress distribution in ship structure together with the hydrodynamic pressure or load distribution on the hull.

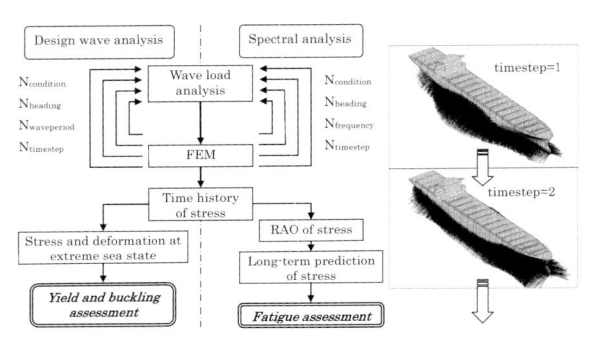

Fig. 3: Concept of DILAM

To compensate the weakness in DISAM, the DIrect Loading Analysis Method (DILAM) was recently proposed (Inoue, Sato and Otsuka, 2005). In DILAM, load data obtained in wave load analyses are transferred to FE model in time-domain. Higher computational power is necessary in DILAM in comparison with DISAM, yet highly accurate analysis can be carried out in DILAM. The concept of DILAM is shown in Fig.3, which was developed for both spectral analysis in fatigue assessment and design wave analysis for stress and buckling assessment with extreme load.

As a great deal of calculation is required for DILAM, efficient data processing is of primary importance in order to carry out the analysis, especially with the consideration of the following important three components.

(1) External and internal pressures are automatically applied to FE model by an automatic load transfer module, which has been developed for the interface between wave load analysis program and FEM program.

(2) Local pressures acting on the hull are summed up and the global load balance is checked by a global

load balance check module, so that any imbalance of total load will not occur due to the difference of numerical model of wave load analysis to FEA model.

(3) Maximum and minimum stress values are automatically picked up from the stress history by a post-processing module, and the stress RAO is calculated.

As for the spectral analysis, FE analysis should be carried out at all necessary load cases as follows.

$$N_{loadcase} = N_{timestep} \cdot N_{frequency} \cdot N_{heading} \cdot N_{condition} \quad (7)$$

In the design wave analysis, the automatic load transfer module and the global load balance check module are both necessary. In the post-processing stage, commercial post-processing software is usually used for checking stress distributions and deformations at extreme wave case. Since DILAM can be applied to the design wave approach while taking account of nonlinear stress response in arbitrary design wave including irregular wave, it can be expected that the stress response analysis in more realistic extreme wave is carried out by combining DILAM with DIW.

Example calculations

Maximum stress of a 6,200 TEU Post-Panamax size container ship (L x B x D - d=287.0m x 40.0m x 23.9m - 13.0m) was investigated in the present paper. Stress evaluation points are shown in Fig.4; that is, 19 points in each side of near midship section (at Frame 186) and 7 points in each side of the section in front of engine room bulkhead (at Frame 86). Longitudinal stress (X-direction), transverse stress (Y-direction), and vertical stress (Z-direction) were investigated according to the element direction of the stress point.

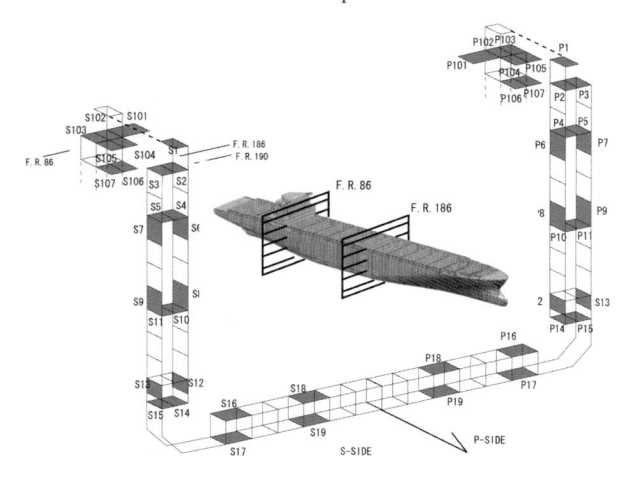

Fig. 4: Evaluation points of stress

In order to calculate the local stress of the container ship, ship motions (surge, heave, pitch, sway, yaw and roll) and hydrodynamic pressures acting on the ship's hull were first calculated with the use of a linear strip method. The obtained ship motion and hydrodynamic pressure data were converted to the time-varying series data for DILAM input, which are the acceleration and the hydrodynamic pressures on the whole hull structure. FE analyses were then carried out for each time step with the use of a FE model of complete hull structure of the ship shown in Fig.4. Obtained stresses in each time step, which is the output of DILAM, were interpolated as a sinusoidal function in time, and the amplitude and the phase angle of each stress component were assembled as the stress transfer function.

The stress spectra were then calculated with the use of wave spectra. The ISSC wave spectrum was used in the calculations given by

$$S(\omega)/H_V^2 = 0.11 \frac{T_V}{2\pi} \left(\frac{T_V}{2\pi}\omega\right)^{-5} \exp\left\{-0.44\left(\frac{T_V}{2\pi}\omega\right)^{-4}\right\} \quad (8)$$

whereby H_V and T_V are the observed significant wave height and the observed mean wave period. Significant wave height was taken as 0.25, 1.25, 2.25, 3.25, 4.25, 5.25, 6.25, 7.25, 8.25, 9.25, 10.25, 11.25, 12.25, 13.25, 14.25 and 15.25[m], while the mean wave period was 4, 6, 8, 10, 12, 14, 16, and 18[s], respectively, according to the Walden's wave scatter diagram in North Atlantic. Encounter angles between ship and wave, χ, were taken as 0, 30, 60, 90, 120, 150, 180[deg], where 180[deg] is the right head sea.

Once the stress spectrum is obtained, the frequency range of DIW can be determined. From the restricted frequency range, the regular wave components were generated with the restriction of wave breaking and maximum wave height for each short-term sea state. With the use of the phase information of stress transfer function, the DIW was determined.

Results and Considerations

Nonlinearity of response

It is possible to conduct a nonlinear simulation of ship response in DIW, because the DIW is a time-varying irregular wave. Once the nonlinear ship motion and hydrodynamic pressure in DIW are obtained with the use of an appropriate nonlinear computational code of ship response, the resulting nonlinear stress can be calculated with the use of DILAM, because the input data of DILAM is the time histories of ship motion and hydrodynamic pressure as aforementioned. The aim of this paper, however, is to clarify the dominant short-term sea state for ship structural design and the possible maximum stress systematically, thereby making a linear calculation suitable in the outcome. On the other hand, as the DIW method is used to estimate the extreme response of a ship in a short-term sea state, the maximum wave height is rather large and the nonlinearity of ship response cannot be ignored. Therefore, a linear calculation is adopted in this paper and the nonlinearity of response is introduced as a correction factor for the stress value.

The nonlinearity correction factor is estimated in the vertical bending moment calculation, because the vertical bending moment is dominant to the longitudinal stress of the ship. Example time history of nonlinear vertical bending moment at midship in DIW is shown in Fig.5, where the significant wave height is H_V=14.5[m] and mean wave period is T_V=12[s]. The nonlinear computational code used in the calculation is TSLAM (Yamamoto, Fujino and Fukasawa, 1980), and the ship's hull is assumed to be rigid. It can be seen from the figure that the impulsive sagging bending moment is caused by slamming. Fig.6 shows the variation of maximum/minimum values of vertical wave bending moment with the significant wave height. The slamming effect appears in the sagging side, which may be largely influenced by ship speed or other factors. Therefore, in order to evaluate the nonlinearity correction factor systematically, the slamming effects are neglected to estimate the nonlinear correction factor in the present paper.

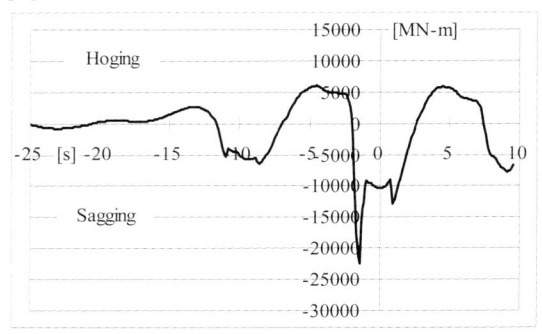

Fig. 5: Time history of VBM at midship (Fn= 0.1561, T_V=12s, H_V=14.5m)

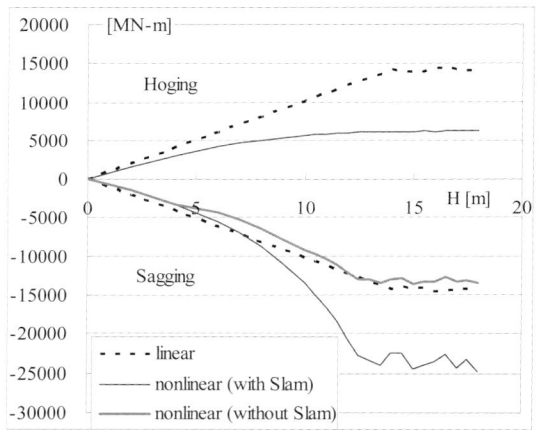

Fig. 6: Maximum/Minimum values of VBM in short-term sea state (Fn=0.1561, T_V=12s)

In Fig.6, there is very little difference in the sagging moment between linear and nonlinear calculation results without slamming case, while the nonlinear hogging moment is almost half of the linear one. The ratio of linear and nonlinear bending moment is 0.52 in hogging side and 0.89 in sagging side, respectively. Actual stress is caused by superposition of still water bending moment and wave bending moment, whereas the still water bending moment depends on the loading condition of each ship. Taking account of this fact, the nonlinearity correction factor is considered in the double amplitude of bending moment, roughly calculated as 0.7. This correction factor will be used to estimate the nonlinear local stresses. It is noted here that the double amplitude of the nonlinear bending moment with slamming case is almost the same as that of linear one. It is well known that still water bending moment is in hogging side in case of container ship, and this leads to the maximum value of nonlinear bending moment is showing little difference from that estimated by linear theory even when the slamming impact is taken into account.

Estimated Maximum Stress

In case of linear response, maximum stress in a short-term sea state can be obtained from the regular wave components of DIW and the stress transfer function for various encounter angle of ship to wave. The maximum stress among the various wave encounter angle is taken as the maximum stress in the short-term sea state, and the maximum value of each stress point among all the short-term sea state is assembled. Obtained maximum values of each stress point are shown in Figs.7 and 8. The horizontal axis shows the stress point, where X, Y and Z stand for the stress direction and the number indicates the stress point shown in Fig.4.

It can be seen from the figures that the obtained stresses are relevant to the structural design value of the ship, and the horizontal or vertical stresses are rather small comparing to the longitudinal ones. This statement means that the combination of DIW and DILAM is effective in order to examine the maximum stress in ship structure.

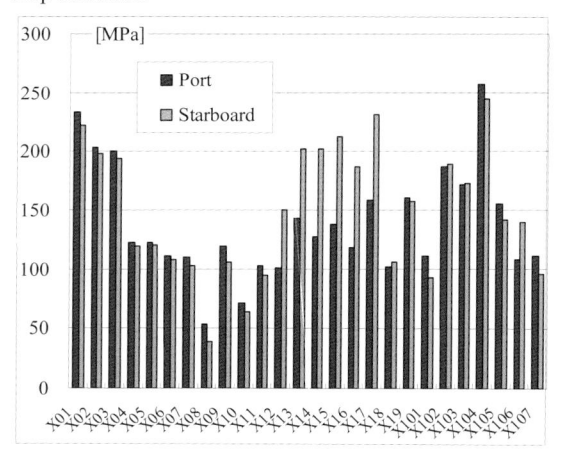

Fig. 7: Maximum longitudinal stress

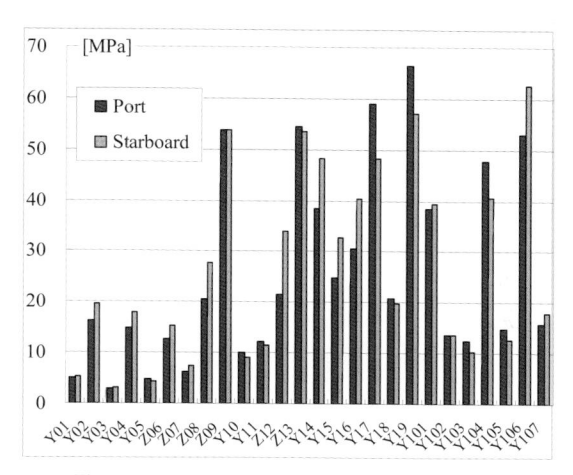

Fig. 8: Maximum transverse/vertical stress

Consideration on Design Short-Term Sea State

Comparing the stresses in port and starboard sides, the short-term sea state and the heading angle of ship to wave where the maximum value occurs at the stress point are summarized in Table 1. The wave direction is considered to be starboard tack in the table, and the cases written in boldface with hatching are the stress point of starboard side (weather side).

Table 1: Short-term sea state and ship heading angle to wave for maximum stress

	T[s]	H[m]	χ[deg]		T[s]	H[m]	χ[deg]
X01	16	15.25	180	**Y01**	18	15.25	150
X02	16	15.25	180	**Y02**	12	13.25	60
X03	16	15.25	180	**Y03**	12	13.25	60
X04	16	15.25	180	**Y04**	12	13.25	60
X05	16	15.25	180	Y05	16	15.25	180
X06	16	15.25	180	Z06	14	15.25	30
X07	18	15.25	150	Z07	14	15.25	30
X08	12	13.25	60	Z08	16	15.25	60
X09	14	15.25	60	Z09	14	15.25	60
X10	12	15.25	60	Y10	14	15.25	60
X11	14	15.25	60	Y11	14	15.25	60
X12	12	13.25	60	**Z12**	14	15.25	30
X13	14	15.25	60	Z13	14	15.25	30
X14	14	15.25	60	**Y14**	14	15.25	60
X15	14	15.25	60	**Y15**	14	15.25	60
X16	16	15.25	30	**Y16**	14	15.25	30
X17	16	15.25	30	Y17	14	15.25	30
X18	12	13.25	60	Y18	8	15.25	30
X19	16	15.25	180	Y19	14	15.25	30
X101	14	15.25	60	**Y101**	14	14.25	60
X102	16	14.25	150	**Y102**	14	14.25	60
X103	16	15.25	180	Y103	14	15.25	60
X104	14	15.25	60	Y104	14	15.25	60
X105	16	15.25	180	Y105	14	15.25	60
X106	14	15.25	180	**Y106**	12	15.25	60
X107	12	14.25	150	**Y107**	12	15.25	60

It was found from Table 1 that the maximum stress occurs in the short-term sea state of the mean wave period T_V =12 - 16[s] and the significant wave height H_V = 15.25[m] in many cases. This means that a certain short-term sea state can be taken as the design short-term sea state. Firstly, the mean wave period of the design short-term sea state is investigated. The standard deviation of vertical bending moment (VBM) and torsional moment (TM) are shown in Figs. 9 and 10, which were derived from the short-term prediction of stress response. It can be seen from the figures that the maximum value occurs at the wave period of 12 [s] (χ =180[deg]) for VBM, while at the period of 8[s] (χ =60[deg]) for TM. These wave periods are a little bit shorter than that appeared in Table 1. Consider the following: The wave elevation in a short-term sea state of shorter mean wave period cannot be large enough because of the wave breaking restriction in DIW. In other words, the maximum wave elevation can be larger in the short-term sea state of longer mean wave period. Non-dimensional stress is largest at the peak wave period of standard deviation of stress, but the stress amplitude increases with the wave elevation. This fact leads to the shift of mean wave period to the longer side where maximum stress occurs.

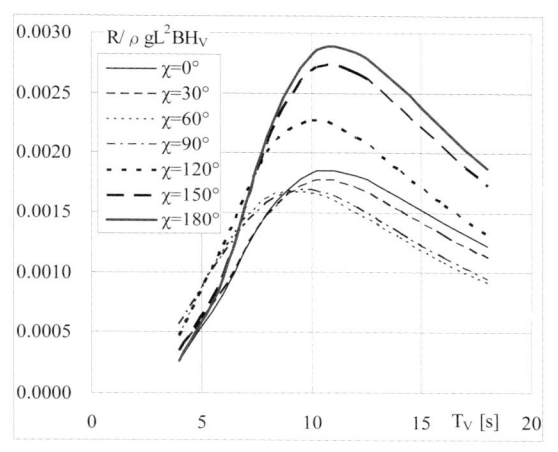

Fig. 9: Standard deviation of VBM at midship

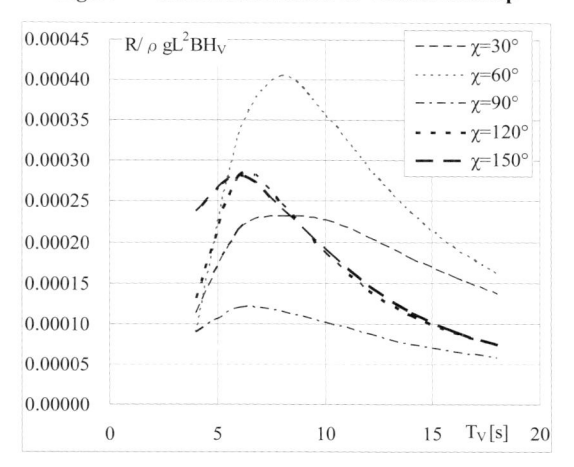

Fig. 10: Standard deviation of TM at midship

Next, the significant wave height of the design short-term sea state is investigated. The significant wave heights appearing in Table 1 are those of the largest value in the calculation, 15.25[m]. It seems from the results that the short-term sea state of largest significant wave height is important to ship strength. However, this critical wave height depends on the ship length. It can be seen from Fig.6 that the wave breaking in DIW is remarkable above the wave height of 13-14[m] in case of the mean wave period of 12[s]. This statement means that the critical wave height decreases in case of the shorter mean wave period, and the smaller value should be adopted for the significant wave height of design short-term sea state in smaller ship cases (Fukasawa, Kawabe and Moan, 2007).

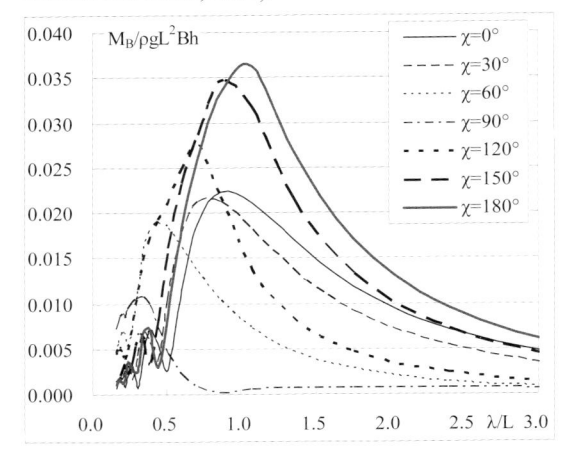

Fig. 11: Non-dimensional VBM at midship

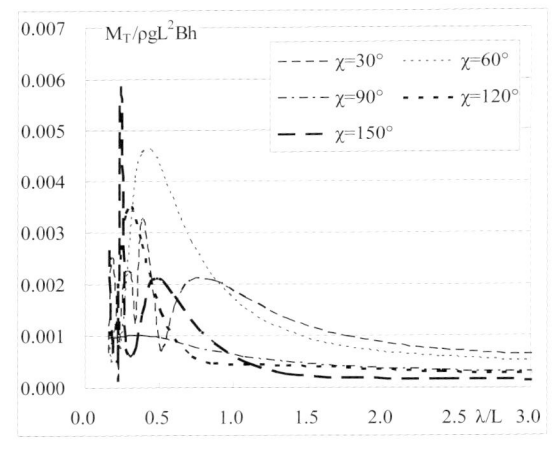

Fig. 12: Non-dimensional TM at midship

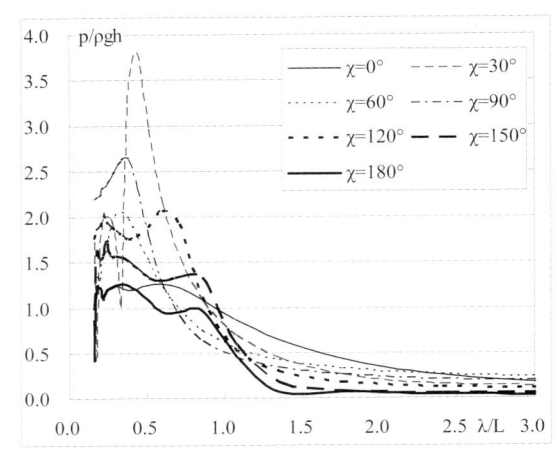

Fig. 13: Non-dimensional pressure at midship

Lastly, the wave direction is investigated. It can be found in Table 1 that wave directions of 180, 60 and 30[deg] are important to the maximum stresses. The transfer function of VBM, TM and the hydrodynamic pressure at weather side water line at midship are shown in Figs. 11-13. It can be seen from Figs.9 to 13 that VBM is significant at the wave direction of χ =180[deg], TM is significant at the wave direction of χ =60[deg], and the hydrodynamic pressure is significant at the wave direction of χ =30[deg], respectively. It can be concluded here that the important wave direction can be predicted from the transfer function or the standard deviation of VBM, TM and hydrodynamic pressures.

Conclusions

The estimation method of maximum local stress of a container ship was investigated by combining the Design Irregular Wave and the Direct Loading Analysis Method. The design short-term sea state was discussed based on the obtained maximum stress. The conclusions are as follows:

1. Maximum stresses obtained by DIW and DILAM were revealed to be relevant to the structural design values of the ship with the use of the nonlinearity correction factor.

2. Mean wave period of design short-term sea state for maximum local stress is a little bit larger than that of the peak period of standard deviation of vertical bending moment and torsional moment.

3. Significant wave height of design short-term sea state for maximum local stress is the largest value of the Walden's wave scatter diagram in this container ship. However, the smaller wave height may be important for smaller ships.

4. The wave encounter angles in which the maximum stress occurs are 180[deg], 60[deg] and 30[deg], whereby vertical bending moment, torsional moment and hydrodynamic pressures are significant, respectively.

References

Adegeest, LJM, Braathen, A and Loseth, RM. (1998). "Use of Non-Linear Sea-Loads Simulations in Design of Ships," 7th PRADS, pp.53-58.

Adegeest, L, Braathen, A and Vada T (1998). "Evaluation of Methods for Estimation of Extreme Nonlinear Ship Responses Based on Numerical Simulations and Model Test," 22nd Symp. on Naval Hydrodynamics, pp.84-99.

Dietz, JS, Hansen, PF and Jensen, JJ (2004). "Design Wave Episodes for Extreme Values Ship Responses," Proc 9th Symp. on Practical Design of Ship and Other Structures, 1, pp.286-293.

Fukasawa, T (1995). "On the Design Wave for Collapse Strength of a Ship," 9th Technical Exchange and Advisory Meeting (TEAM 95), pp.187-201.

Fukasawa, T (1998). "Behavior of 20,000 DWT Tanker in Japan Sea," Proc. International Conference on Shipbuilding and Ocean Engineering, Problems and Perspectives, SOPP-98, pp.187-191.

Fukasawa, T and Cho, SR (2001). "On the Design Criteria for Ultimate Longitudinal Strength of a Ship," 15th Asian Technical Exchange and Advisory Meeting on Marine Structures, TEAM2001, pp.144-151.

Fukasawa, T (2005a). "Consideration on the Design Irregular Wave in Comparison with the Long-Term Prediction Results," 19th Asian Technical Exchange and Advisory Meeting on Marine Structures, TEAM 2005, pp.160-167

Fukasawa, T (2005b). "Maximum Response Estimation by means of Design Irregular Wave -1st Report-: Estimation of Vertical Bending Moment-," J. Japan Soc. Naval Architecture and Ocean Engineering., Vol.2, pp.123-129. (in Japanese)

Fukasawa, T, Kanehira, Y and Miyazaki, S (2006). "Maximum Response Estimation by means of Design Irregular Wave -2nd Report-: Estimation of Local Stress of a Container Ship-", J. Japan Soc. Naval Architecture and Ocean Engineering., Vol.4, pp.221-227. (in Japanese)

Fukasawa, T, Kawabe, H and Moan, T (2007). "On extreme ship response in severe short-term sea state," Advancements in Marine Structures, Proc. of MARSTRUCT 2007, pp.33-40.

Hansen, PF and Nielsen, LP (1995). "On the New Wave Model for the Kinematics of Large Ocean Waves," Proc. OMAE, Offshore Technology, 1A, pp.17-24.

Inoue, S, Sato, K and Otsuka, H (2005). "DILAM-Latest technology for full spectral ship structural analysis," 12th International Conference on Computer Applications in Shipbuilding, Conference Proceedings, Vol.1, pp.265-274.

Kuramoto, Y, Tozawa, S, Shirokibara, H, Inoue, S, and Fushimi, A (1991). "Study on the Load-Stress Simulation Method for Ship Structure in Waves," J. Soc. Naval Architects of Japan, Vol.170, pp 425-436. (in Japanese)

Pastoor, LW (2002). "On the Assessment of Nonlinear Ship Motions and Loads," Ph.D. Thesis, Delft Univ. of Tech.

Pastoor, W, Helmers, JB and Bitner-Gregersen, E (2003). "Time Simulation of Ocean-Going Structures in Extreme Waves," Proc. OMAE2003, OMAE2003-37490.

Smith, JF, Kawagoe, Y and Shirakihara, H (2001). "A Structural Longevity Study on the NWS LNG carriers," LNG13, PO-24.1-PO-24.9.

Soares, CG and Pascoal R (2005). "On the Pfofile of Large Ocean Waves," Trans. ASME, Vol.127, pp.306-314.

Tromans, PS, Anaturk, AR and Hagemeijer, P (1991). "A New Model for the Kinematics of Large Ocean Waves, -Application as a Design Wave-," Proc. 1st Int. Offshore Polar Eng. Conf., ISOPE, pp.64-71.

Yamamoto, Y, Fujino, M, and Fukasawa, T (1980). "Motion and Longitudinal Strength of a Ship in Head Sea and the Effects of Non-Linearities," Naval Architecture and Ocean Engineering, SNAJ, Vol 18, pp 91-100.

Structural Analysis of Asphalt Carriers

Joško Parunov[1], Ivo Senjanović[1] and Ivica Donkov[2]

[1] University of Zagreb, Faculty of Mechanical Engineering and Naval Architecture
[2] Iceberg Ltd
Zagreb, Croatia

Abstract

The aim of the paper is to describe extensive finite element analysis carried out in the design phase of asphalt carriers that are presently under construction in Croatia. The structural analysis of these ships is more demanding than that of ordinary oil tankers since heated cargo is carried in non-structural tanks, connected with ship hull by a large number of supports and keys. The 3-hold methodology is used for finite element structural analysis with an iterative procedure to properly account for non-linear stiffness of vertical supports at high temperatures. Based on the experience gained during the analysis, some general conclusions are drawn that may be useful in the future design of this type of ship.

Keywords

Asphalt carrier; Structural analysis; Finite element method.

Introduction

At present, the world fleet of asphalt carriers' numbers 92 ships, thus accounting for 0.2% of the world's tanker fleet, with the average age of 17.3 years. Today's market trends of these vessels are marked by the increasing demand for new buildings, increasing transport fees, and the need for the replacement of the old fleet. Thus, over the last 5 years the construction of 22 new asphalt carriers has been ordered, while among them are 4 in Croatia, bringing the total to about 26% all the number of ordered asphalt carriers.

Since they are intended for the carriage of dense cargo stored at rather high temperature (up to 250°C), asphalt carriers are quite sophisticated vessels having a complex hull structure, cargo space and cargo survey and control equipment. Therefore, designers and shipyards producing these ships are faced with many difficult challenges.

Cargo with temperatures above 200°C is generally carried in non-structural self-supporting insulated tanks that must be free to elongate in all directions. This specification is achieved by means of suitable vertical supports, anti-rolling, anti-pitching and anti-flotation keys. Since forces in supports and keys are quite unequally redistributed, they have to be determined by the ship structural analysis.

The vertical tank supports are usually dimensioned-based on uni-directional compressive loads. However, load component tangential to the supports may be developed by either of the following cases:

1) during simultaneous tank filling and cargo heating,

2) non-parallelism of tank bottom surface and support structure caused by the fabrication procedure.

To account for these phenomena, supports need to be analyzed by very fine mesh of the finite elements using solid elements.

The ship designer also needs to find answers to other specific problems caused by the presence of non-structural tanks. For example, it is necessary to account for relative deformations occurring between tank and the ship hull in order to better design a safe piping system as well as avoid undesired contacts and collisions between the tank and the hull. These relative deformations may be particularly important for large non-structural tanks and for single bottom ships with low stiffness, undergoing large deflections.

The aim of the present paper is to describe the case study of the structural analysis of asphalt carriers that are presently under construction in Croatia. The results of the presented structural analysis largely influenced the design development of the ship and associated time schedule, since some of the results were quite unexpected. For that reason, based on the experience gained in this study, general conclusions are drawn that may be useful as guidelines for designers in order to anticipate and account for expensive and time-consuming modifications already in the early design phase. It should be noted that according to the author's knowledge, similar studies have not been published thus far. Some available articles on asphalt carriers deal with general design of these vessels (HSB, 1997; Fairplay Solutions, 1997).

Ship description

The analyzed ship and the entire equipment are designed for unrestricted navigation and transportation of the crude oil products, asphalt, bitumen, coal-tar pitch and other similar cargoes. The maximum specific gravity of the cargo is 1.25t/m^3, while the maximum cargo temperature is 250°C. The main characteristics of the ship are listed in Table 1.

Table 1: Main characteristics

Length overall	L_{OA}	108.5m
Length btw. perpendiculars	L_{PP}	99.9m
Breadth molded	B	18.6m
Depth to main deck	D	10.6m
Draught	T_{max}	8.34m
Deadweight	DWT	9233m
Cargo tank capacity	∇	7748m^3
Ship speed	V_S	13.42 knots

The ship has a single bottom and a single side shell in the cargo tank area and a raised continuous deck ("trunk deck"). The cargo space consists of three non-structural blocks of tanks:

- Block I – Tank no.1 placed in the front area of the cargo space;
- Block II – placed forward of the pump room, consists of Tank no.2 (C), Tanks no.3 (SB&PS) and Tank no.4 (C);
- Block III – placed afterwards of the pump room, consists of Tanks no. 5 (SB&PS) and Tank no. 6 (C).

The pump room is a structural space situated between Tank blocks II and III in the middle of the cargo space. The general arrangement of the ship is shown in Figure 1.

The focus of the present paper is on the extensive structural analysis carried out in the design stage. The main assignments of the analysis are as follows:

a) Strength evaluation of the primary structural members of ship hull and non-structural tanks (e.g. web frames, longitudinal girders, stringers);
b) Calculation of reaction forces in vertical cargo tank supports, anti-rolling, anti-pitching and anti-floating keys;
c) Analysis of relative hull and cargo tank deformation;
d) Assessment of combined stresses in the vertical supports by very fine mesh analysis.

The design development process as well as some constructional and technological features of this ship that were particularly prominent during building of the vessel have been recently described (Grubišić, 2006a, 2006b).

Principles of structural analysis

The model, calculations and post-treatments of the structural analysis are carried out using software VeriSTAR Hull, developed by classification society Bureau Veritas (2005). Guidelines for analysis of asphalt carriers are those of the Bureau Veritas for asphalt carriers and LPG carriers that are familiar structures from the aspect of structural analysis (Bureau Veritas, 1995, 2001).

The applied methodology is the so-called 3-hold methodology, where 3 cargo holds are modeled by the finite element method. The finite element model is fixed at its fore end, while vertical and horizontal shear forces and bending moments are imposed at its aft end in order to ensure equilibrium of the model. The aft end section remains free as the transverse primary members ensure rigid constraints in such a way that the section remains flat after deformation. In addition to global bending moments and shear forces, the model is loaded by external/internal and static/dynamic pressures according to BV Rules. The results of the analysis in the aft and fore holds are assumed to be unrealistic because of the influence of boundary conditions, while results in the middle hold are considered as relevant.

In the actual example, part of the engine room, tank-block III (with the adjacent hull) and pump room are modeled for the analysis of the tank-block III. For the analysis of the tank-block II, pump room and tank-blocks II and I (with the adjacent hull) are used. The whole structural model is shown in Figure 2, where part of the engine room, tank-block III, pump room, tank-block II and tank-block I may be seen from the left to the right, respectively. It should be noted that both portside and starboard are modeled, but for the clarity of presentation only the portside is shown in Figure 2.

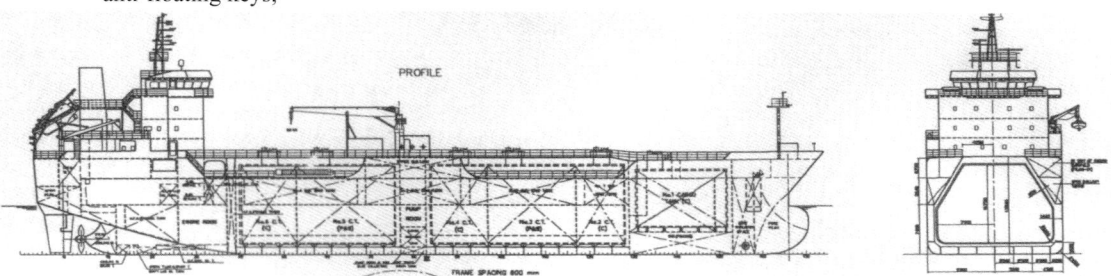

Fig. 1: General arrangement of the asphalt carrier

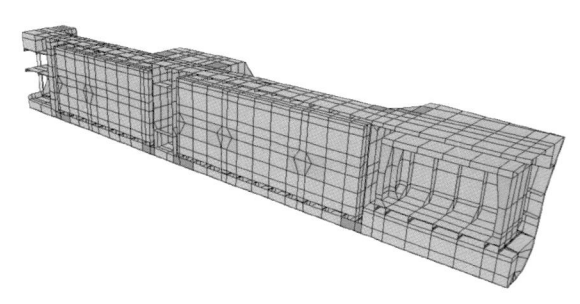

Fig. 2: Structural model of the cargo hold area

"Net thickness" approach is employed in the study, which means that all calculations are performed using scantlings reduced by corrosion deduction thickness proposed by BV rules (BV, 2005).

A specific feature of asphalt carriers is that cargo tank-blocks are not welded to the hull forming thus separating part of the hull structure. In order to reduce stresses induced by thermal expansion and contraction, cargo tank-blocks are insulated and separated from the hull, lying on vertical supports that are mounted on the hull bottom structure. Furthermore, the motion of cargo blocks in transverse and horizontal directions is prevented by the use of anti-rolling and anti-pitching keys respectively. In order to ensure ship survivability in a damaged condition, there are also anti-floating keys designed in such a way as to provide sufficient support for cargo block floating inside the damaged hull.

Vertical supports impose a principal difficulty in structural analysis of asphalt carriers. The supports are normally modeled by linear-elastic spring elements having equal stiffness in tension and compression. However, such linear model is unrealistic, as the stiffness of support in tension is zero, i.e. the cargo block and ship hull are free to separate. Thus, for each loading case, it is necessary to establish a list of supports in tension, to leave them out of the model and to perform the analysis again. This implies that an iterative procedure is necessary in order to appropriately account for different compression-tension behaviors of elastic supports. Deformation of the cargo block in ballast on the crest of the wave is shown in Figure 3, where the importance of correct modeling of vertical support stiffness can be clearly noticed.

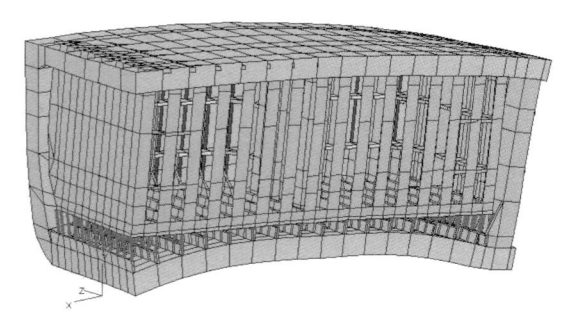

Fig. 3: Deformation of cargo tank-block and ship hull in ballast in crest of the wave

Since vertical supports are designed to reduce the temperature from 250°C at the tank bottom to 70-80°C at the ship hull floors, it is not necessary to take into account in the strength assessment the influence of the temperature on mechanical properties of the hull steel. However, it is crucial to reduce mechanical properties, both yield stress and modulus of elasticity, of the steel used for the tank construction. This process may be done by using expressions provided in the documentary notes (BV, 1995), for 250°C, reduction of mechanical properties read approximately 15% for both yield stress and modulus of elasticity.

The stiffness of supports is derived from the component stiffness of layers forming the support, assuming that layers act as serially connected elastic springs. For the actual ship, stiffness of vertical supports is calculated to be 3.73MN/mm. Therefore, a deformation of only 0.27mm is sufficient to reach 1MNm, which is the load carrying capacity of the vertical support installed on the ship. This fact leads to quite an important conclusion that supports are almost completely rigid as compared to the stiffness of the ship hull, as deformation of the ship bottom is about two orders of magnitude larger than maximum permissible deformation of vertical supports. In other words, the designer should not consider that there would be any load redistribution among supports because of their elasticity.

Loading conditions to be applied in structural analysis are the most unfavorable conditions according to the ship loading manual. Typically, the following loading conditions are to be considered:

- Full load resulting in design sagging still water bending moment;
- Ballast condition resulting in design hogging still water bending moment;
- Alternate condition with maximum cargo density (ρ=1.25 t/m^3);
- Flooded condition (damaged ship);
- Asymmetric filling (the most frequent, this loading condition is only applicable in harbor, i.e. during loading/unloading operations).

Still water loading conditions are then combined with dynamic wave-induced loads according to BV Rules. The most severe combinations of loading conditions and wave loads are to be found for each analyzed primary structural member.

Strength evaluation of the hull and cargo tanks

One of the most important results of the strength analysis is the thickness increase of the hull bottom and side shell plating. This increase reads up to 3.5mm above "rule" requirements for plate thickness, as shown in Figure 4.

Thickness increase is a consequence of plate buckling because of the bending of primary members. In the bottom shell plating, buckling occurs in ballast in the crest of wave, when the hogging bending moment reaches the maximum value. At the side shell, it occurs in the full load condition, in the crest of wave, when sea pressure on the side shell reaches the maximum value.

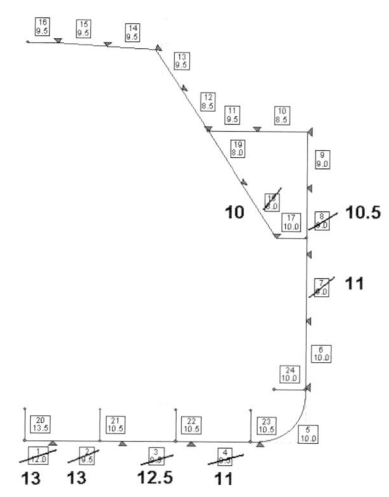

Fig. 4: Thickness increase of the hull bottom and side shell plating

Fine mesh analysis is necessary for detailed structural verification in the heavily loaded area. Typically, the detail where fine mesh analysis is necessary is in the bilge area, in particular if large openings such as manholes reduce the shear area of the primary members. This fine mesh model is shown in Figure 5, together with "master nodes" from the coarse mesh model and concentrated forces representing support reactions.

Concerning primary structure of independent tanks, the ends of the bottom grillage and the end connections of the longitudinal and transverse stringers represent the most loaded area making large local reinforcements necessary. The principal reason for these large local reinforcements is the very high design cargo density and the reduced mechanical properties of cargo tank material.

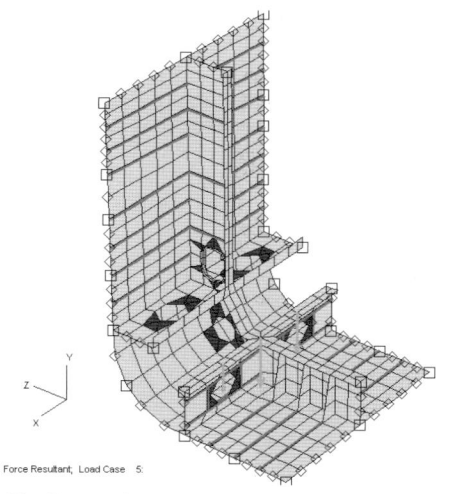

Fig. 5: Fine mesh model of the connection of typical web floor and vertical side web

Reaction forces in vertical supports and anti-rolling keys

Vertical supports have several functions:
- to support loads induced by cargo and tank mass imposed on acceleration generated by the ship's motion in rough sea,
- to absorb the temperature difference,
- to control expansion and contraction of the cargo tank.

There are different types of supports available on the market capable of carrying load between 300 and 1000kN and having dimensions of approximately 250x250mm (length x breadth) with a height of about 65mm. In the actual example, altogether 308 vertical supports with load-carrying capacity of 1000kN each are installed: small cargo block I is placed on 34 supports, cargo block II on 148 supports, while cargo block III on 126 supports. Each vertical support has a sandwich structure that consists of two basic layers. The upper layer is a kind of textilite with good insulation and sliding properties, while the lower layer is a two-component epoxy resin for casting, which serves as a distance washer. Such supports are already installed on some asphalt carriers having tanks much smaller than those analyzed in the present study. Experience showed that the capacity of supports is not much affected by the aging.

Supports are generally placed at the intersection of primary members (girders and floors) and also on specific locations where found necessary due to the findings of structural analysis. Disposition of vertical support below cargo block II is shown in Figure 6.

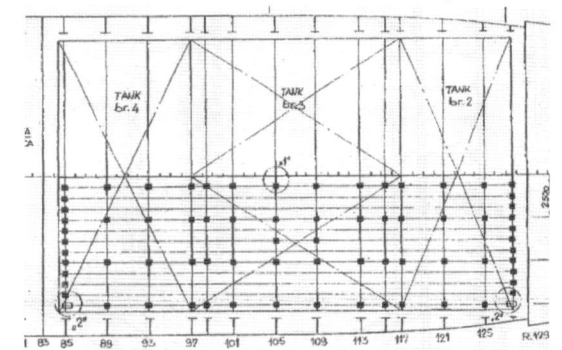

Fig. 6: Disposition of vertical supports below tank-block II

Based on the results of the analysis, five zones with principally different behaviors of support reactions are identified. These zones are characterized by different relative stiffness of the cargo tank and the ship bottom, and are described in paragraphs (i-v) below. Support reactions in different characteristic zones are presented in Figures 7-9, showing the distribution of reaction forces along floors, from PS to SB.

i. Zone of cargo tank-block ends – this is the stiffest area because of rigid transverse bulkheads of both the hull and tank-blocks. This area carries great amount of support reactions in full load. For that reason, at the tank-block end bulkheads, supports are placed at each stiffener, as seen in Figure 6. Typical support reactions below the tank-block end bulkheads in full load are presented in Figure 7.

ii. Bilge zone - a very stiff area with almost absolute rigidity of both the tank and the hull because of the tank longitudinal bulkhead and the ship side. This area also carries a great amount of support reactions in full load condition. In Figure 8, two large support reactions at the PS and SB belong to this zone.

iii. Centerline zone in the interior of the cargo hold – this is zone with the lowest stiffness of the hull because floors are rather soft in their center and the very high rigidity of the tank because of rigid CL bulkhead. Generally, reaction forces in the support will be here the lowest in full load condition and the largest in ballast. For the full load condition, reactions in supports near the centerline are at zero, as may be seen in Figure 8.

iv. Transverse bulkheads of cargo tanks inside cargo tank-blocks. Here, relatively large tank stiffness and hull stiffness are met, decreasing from the bilge to the centerline. Therefore, reaction forces will be very high in the bilge area and very low in the remaining part of the bulkhead. Typical distribution of reaction forces in the vertical supports below the transverse bulkhead in the interior of the tank-block is presented in Figure 9.

v. Other areas – relatively soft tank bottom and more rigid hull bottom will lead to reaction forces uniformly distributed. This scenario is the ideal situation that would be preferred in the entire ship bottom. Such support reactions are presented in Figure 8 around stiffener 6 (SB and PS).

Anti-rolling keys are normally fitted at every floor in a line at the center of the bottom. Anti-rolling keys at the top of the tank may be necessary for narrow and high tanks that may capsize at rolling which is not the case for the design being presented. Therefore, only the bottom keys were installed. Forces in the anti-rolling keys are non-uniformly distributed along the tank-block, depending upon the relative stiffness between the tank-block and ship hull. Generally, the highest forces are induced in the anti-rolling keys at the ends of the tank-block, with the magnitude more than 4 times larger compared to the average forces in the mid-length of the cargo block. Typical distribution of the forces in the anti-rolling keys is presented in Figure 10, where it may be seen that forces are very sensitive to a local variation of the stiffness as well.

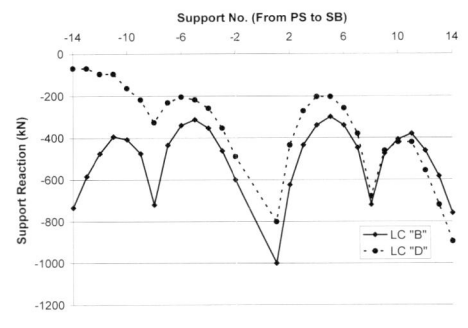

Fig. 7: Typical support reactions below tank-block end bulkhead in full load (B and D load cases from BV Rules)

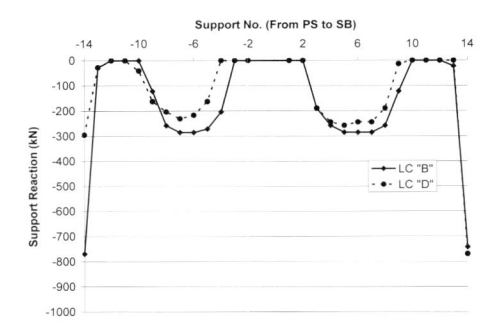

Fig. 8: Typical support reactions at the typical floor in the middle of the tank-block in full load (B and D load cases from BV Rules)

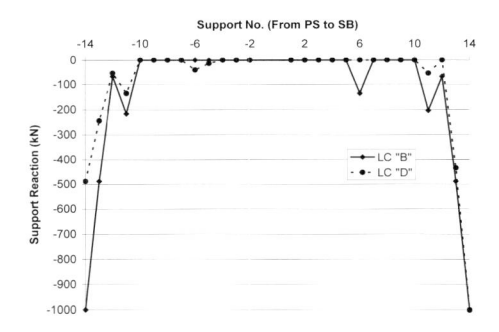

Fig. 9: Typical support reactions below transverse bulkhead in the middle of the cargo block in full load (B and D load cases from BV Rules)

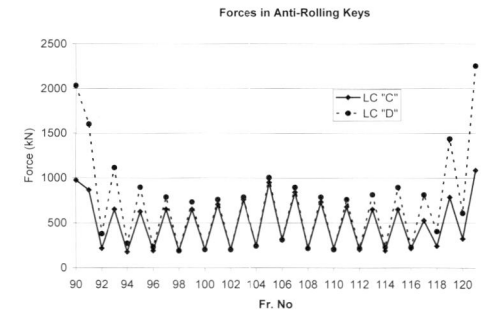

Fig. 10: Typical distribution of forces in anti-rolling keys along the tank-block length in full load (C and D load cases from BV Rules)

Assessment of combined stresses in vertical supports

Vertical supports are designed for pure vertical forces, neglecting thus combined stresses induced by the following:

- the frictional forces between tank bottom and sliding pads,
- the misalignment between tank bottom and the top of the floors, as shown in Figure 11.

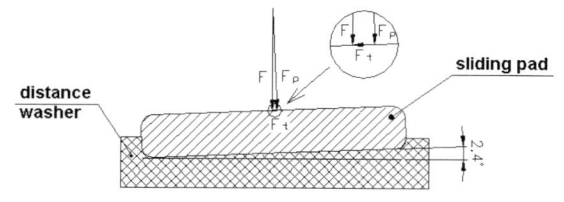

Fig. 11: Horizontal force induced by misalignment between the tank bottom and the top of the floors

Horizontal frictional forces and horizontal components of misalignment forces tend to increase locally the maximum compressive forces in the distance washer, whose permissible compressive stress is much lower compared to that of the sliding pad. To investigate the level of maximum compressive stresses, additional very fine mesh analysis of vertical supports is performed. The fine mesh model of the structure around the most loaded support is shown in Figure 12. The support is modeled by 3D solid elements taking into account the actual material properties (Young's modulus and Poisson coefficient) at the design temperature of 250°C. The maximum compressive stresses calculated in the analysis are 23MPa, while the permissible compressive stress of the epoxy resin reads 25MPa. Therefore, the supports are found to be acceptable, even with the misalignments.

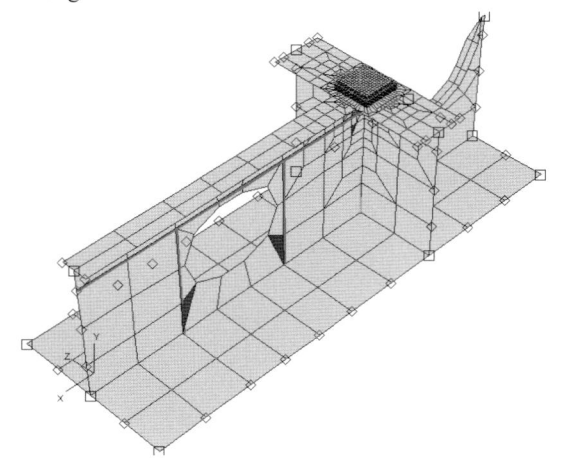

Fig. 12: Fine mesh model of the vertical support and adjacent structure

Relative deformation between the cargo tank-block and the ship hull

Relative deformation between the cargo tank and ship hull are important in the design of asphalt carriers for several reasons:

- for the design of the cargo piping system, since pipes are connected to the hull and tanks, which are in permanent relative motion,
- to avoid structural contacts between the tank-block and the hull, that may prevent free deformation and induce additional stresses in the structure,
- to avoid damage of the insulation of the cargo tank, as a consequence of possible contacts.

Therefore, the analysis of relative deformation is an integral part of the analysis of these vessels. For the actual ship, the most critical detail for the relative deformation is the anti-floating key, placed at the intersection of the vertical and sloped sides of the tank and the hull. The maximum relative transverse deformation is induced for full load condition, in beam seas and reads 41mm, as shown in Figure 13. Maximum transverse deformation occurs in web frames at the mid-length of the tank block. The maximum relative vertical deformation occurs for the ship in ballast loading condition, on the crest of the wave, when hogging deformation is the largest. This deformation reads 45mm, as shown in Figure 14, and occurs in the web frames near the tank-block ends.

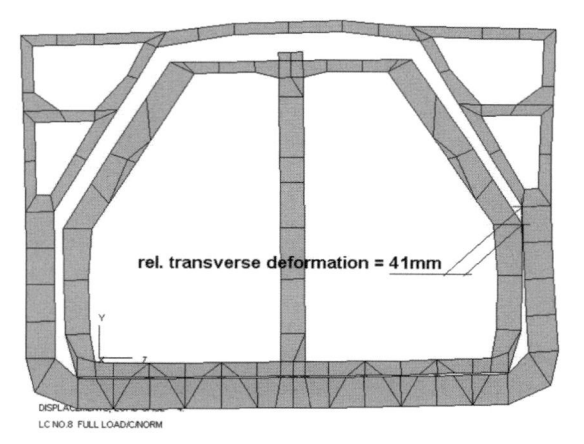

Fig. 13: Relative transverse deformation between the web frame of the cargo tank and the web frame of the ship hull

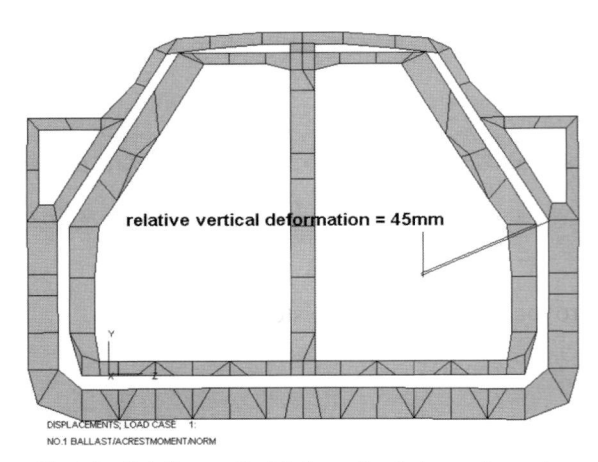

Fig. 14: Relative vertical deformation between the web frame of the cargo tank and the web frame of the ship hull

Conclusions

Asphalt carriers are sophisticated ships imposing numerous design and technological challenges for shipyards. Due to the lack of earlier experience in the building of such ships, the problems encountered may cause delay in delivery and serious financial penalties. This paper deals with specific issues related to structural analysis of asphalt carriers aiming to clarify the analysis procedure and to enable anticipating specific problems already in the early design phase. Among such problems, non-uniform distribution of reaction forces in vertical supports and anti-rolling keys are of particular relevance. Also, the designer should bear in mind from the beginning of the design process the fact that relative deformations of the tank and hull structure may influence the design of the cargo piping system and that the clearance between tank and hull should be sufficiently large to avoid their collision. Finally, imperfections caused by the technology of the ship building, such as misalignments between the tank bottom and the vertical supports, need to be accounted for in order to have safe and appropriate design of supports.

General conclusions elaborated in the paper are successfully applied to other asphalt carriers and it was found that the findings and recommendations presented in the paper are fairly insensitive to moderate changes in structural configurations and may be safely applied by the designers of different types of asphalt carriers.

Acknowledgement

The authors express their thanks to the management and engineers of *Kraljevica Shipyard* and to the ship designer Mr. Nenad Flesh, N.A. from *Brodotrogir Shipyard* for their support during the study and for their permission to use the technical documentation and to publish the article.

The opinions presented herein are those of the authors and should not be construed as reflecting the views of any institution involved.

References

HSB International (1997). "RATHBOYNE Handy Size Bitumen Tanker for Irish Owners", June, pp. 29-35

Fairplay Solutions (1997). "Hot Cargo Meets Cold Steel", June, p. 38

Grubišić, R (2006a). "Asphalt Carriers from *Kraljevica Shipyard*", Brodogradnja, Vol 57, No 1, pp. 23-31

Grubišić, R (2006b). "Asphalt Carriers from *Kraljevica Shipyard* – Constructional and Technological Aspects", Brodogradnja, Vol 57, No. 2, pp. 137-143

Bureau Veritas, "Rules for Classification of Steel Ships", 2005

Bureau Veritas, "Documentary Note: Asphalt Carriers", October 1995

Bureau Veritas, "Guidelines Notes for Structural Analysis of LPG Carriers", June 2001

Structural Behavior of Suezmax Tanker Under Extreme Bending Moment

Tiago P. Estefen, Leandro C. Trovoado and Segen F. Estefen

Ocean Engineering Department – COPPE/UFRJ
Rio de Janeiro, Brazil

Abstract

Structural failure of Suezmax tanker due to extreme bending moment is analyzed. The paper describes both numerical and experimental structural simulations. Small scale panels representative of the double hull tanker bottom under axial compressive loading are analyzed in order to perform correlation studies to adjust the numerical model for further use in full scale structures. The small scale steel models are manufactured using appropriate techniques to maintain the scaled distortion magnitudes within recommended tolerances. The models have all the stiffened panels mapped before testing and instrumented with strain-gages and load cells in order to provide realistic data for the numerical modeling as well as results for the correlation studies. The numerical model is represented by shell elements assuming finite membrane strains and large rotations. Both geometric and material nonlinearities in addition to the geometric imperfection distribution are taken into account. Full scale numerical analyses for a model representative of a Suezmax tanker compartment between web frames is submitted to sagging and hogging loading conditions to evaluate the influence of geometric initial imperfections on both moment-curvature relationship and panels buckling behavior.

Keywords

Ultimate strength; Stiffened panels; Ultimate bending moment; Buckling analysis.

Introduction

Structural failure of a Suezmax tanker due to extreme bending moment is analyzed. The paper describes both numerical and experimental structural simulations. Small scale panels representative of the double hull tanker bottom under compressive loading are analyzed in order to perform correlation studies to adjust the numerical model for further use in full scale structures.

The small scale steel models are manufactured using appropriate techniques to maintain the scaled distortion magnitudes within recommended tolerances. The models have all the stiffened panels mapped before testing and instrumented with strain-gages and load cells in order to provide realistic data for the numerical modeling as well as results for the correlation studies. Full scale numerical analyses are then performed for a Suezmax tanker compartment to evaluate the influence of geometric initial imperfections on both moment-curvature relationship and panels buckling behavior.

The small scale models are mapped using laser tracker equipment with sub-millimeter accuracy. Point clouds then obtained are processed by a specialist software to generate the actual panel surface to be exported to a finite element program which performs the ultimate structural analyses. The numerical model is discretized by shell elements assuming finite membrane strains and large rotations. Both geometric and material nonlinearities in addition to the actual imperfection distribution are taken into account. The full scale model representative of a Suezmax tanker compartment between web frames is submitted to sagging and hogging loading conditions through controlled incremental rotations applied to the loaded edge. Special attention is focused on the buckling failure mode associated with upper deck and bottom respectively. The material stress-strain curves for small and full scale models are obtained from uniaxial tensile tests.

Finally, the stiffened panels are analyzed to identify the buckling initiation on a particular panel and the influence on the progressive failure of the whole compartment. Interaction between panels and stiffeners are identified to better describe the global failure mode.

Studies on numerical-experimental correlation were performed by Estefen (2006) in order to adjust the numerical models to be used for ultimate strength evaluation of full scale panels. Small scale steel models representatives of panels from semi-submersible platform columns were fabricated. Equivalent dimensional tolerances as prescribed for the prototype were obtained for the small scale models. The theoretical model was based on the finite element method, incorporating both geometric and material nonlinearities.

Sun and Wang (2005) describe a procedure for calculating the ultimate strength of ship structures, considering failure modes of plating, stiffened panels and the hull girder.

Rigo et al. (2001) performed an assessment of the sensitivity of the strain-stress curves on the ultimate hull bending moment and the moment-curvature relationship.

Ikeda et al. (2001) studied the influence of the thickness decrease due to corrosion on the ultimate longitudinal strength of aged single hull tankers. The decrease ratio of the section modulus of hull girder is approximately the same as that of the flange area of the deck and/or bottom plating with longitudinal stiffeners and girders. Linear relationship is observed between the diminution ratios of the ultimate longitudinal strength and the section modulus. In relation of the ultimate longitudinal strength the decrease of 15% is allowable at the deck and the bottom plating.

Estefen et al. (2007) studied the influence of different geometric imperfection distributions on the buckling behavior of a semisubmersible platform column segment represented by the structural arrangement between web frames, based on nonlinear finite element analyses. The magnitude of the initial geometric imperfections confirmed the influence of this parameter on the axial buckling load. However, the greater influence on the ultimate strength and on the plates' failure sequence is due to the initial imperfection mode.

Numerical-Experimental Correlation

Studies on numerical-experimental correlation were performed in order to adjust the numerical models to be used for ultimate strength of ship structures of a Suezmax tanker compartment. Initially small scale steel models representatives of panels from the double hull tanker bottom were fabricated scale 1:19. Equivalent dimensional tolerances as prescribed for the prototype were obtained for the small scale models. The theoretical model was based on the finite element method, incorporating both geometric and material nonlinearities. In order to perform the correlation study a small scale model of stiffened flat panels were fabricated. Fabrication techniques and geometric characteristics are described below.

Longitudinal tee stiffeners have been used in a model representative of stiffened panels between web frames. Initially the longitudinal tee stiffeners are manufactured using a special jig, Fig. 1.

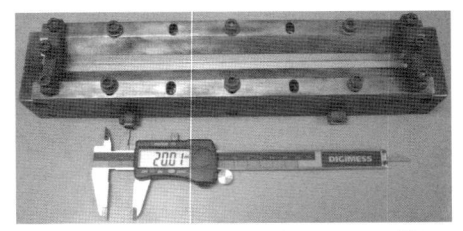

Fig. 1: Jig employed to manufacture tee stiffener

The welding process employed for the manufacture of the stiffeners was the electric arc with tungsten wire and inert gas protection (TIG), amperage of 30 A, without material addition, Fig. 2. Before the welding, pre-heating is applied up to 250°C.

Fig. 2: Welding process using TIG

Fig. 3 shows the stiffener being removed from the jig.

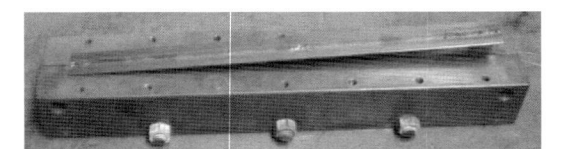

Fig. 3: Tee stiffener being removed from the jig

Concluded the fabrication of the tee stiffeners it is initialized the assembly of the model. For each model the independent pieces for plates between stiffeners are cut within prescribed dimensional tolerances. The model is then mounted using a special designed jig to facilitate the welding process and to minimize distortions, Fig. 4.

Fig. 4: Special designed jig for the panel welding

The fabrication sequence of the small scale models are detailed in the following description.

Step 1 - The individual plates are cleaned to remove rust.

Step 2 - Positioning of the stiffener plates in the jig, Fig. 5.

Fig. 5: Positioning of the stiffener in the jig

Step 3 – Positioning of the plate pieces between the stiffeners in the jig, Fig. 6.

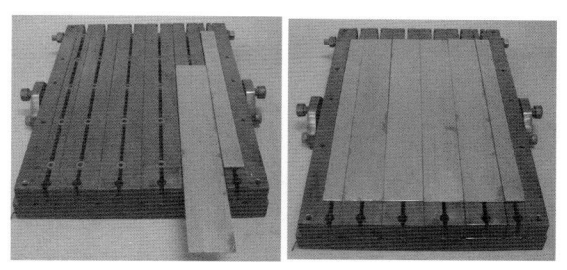

Fig. 6: Positioning of the plate pieces between the stiffeners

Step 4 – Jig fixture to minimize distortions during welding, Fig. 7.

Fig. 7: Jig fixture to minimize the distortions

Step 5 – Four additional plate pieces are positioned externally to the borders to provide the adequate boundary conditions during the welding. These four pieces will be used only to absorb weld heating and then discarded.

Step 6 - Pre-heating up to 250°C.

Step 8 – Welding process to join each stiffener with the neighbor pair of plates. As for the manufacture of the tee stiffener it has been employed the electric arc with tungsten wire and inert gas protection (TIG), amperage of 30 A, without material addition.

Step 9 – After concluding the welding procedure for the whole panel, the model is submitted to a uniform heating and then to ambient temperature for 24 hours to relieve residual stresses before being taken away from the jig.

Step 10 – Remove the fixture from the model, Fig. 8.

Fig. 8: Removing the fixture from the model

Step 11 - Fabricated panel model with length (a) of 240.50 mm, spacing between stiffeners (b) of 43.70 mm and plate thickness (t) of 1 mm. Stiffener dimensions: thickness web (t_w) of 0.67 mm, web height (h_w) of 21.60 mm, flange width (b_f) of 7.60 mm and flange thickness (t_f) of 1 mm. The borders plates present half space between stiffeners to obtain adequate boundary conditions. Fig. 9 shows the small scale steel model of the stiffened panel.

Fig. 9: Small scale steel model of the stiffened panel

The initial imperfection distributions were measured using the equipment Laser Tracker acquired by the COPPE - Submarine Technology Laboratory. It is a portable contact measurement system that uses laser technology presenting sub-millimeter accuracy. Portable measurement arm linked to the equipment was employed to measure the small scale models, Fig. 10.

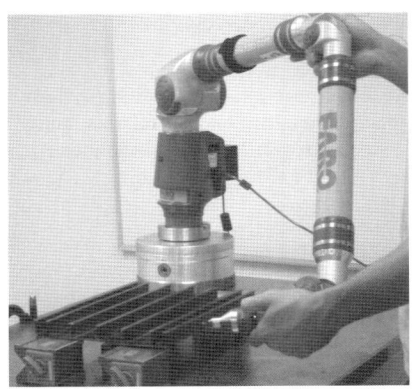

Fig. 10: Measurement of the small scale model using the portable arm with sub-millimeter accuracy

The obtained data are used to generate the actual surface using the software Verisurf (2006). The computer model is then exported to ABAQUS, Hibbitt et al. (2006), for the numerical simulation of the panel ultimate strength under in-plane compression.

Instrumentation of the models was performed using strain-gages. One biaxial strain-gage (longitudinal and transversal directions) and uniaxial strain-gages (longitudinal direction) were used. Strain-gage positions are shown in Fig. 11. The compression tests were performed in an Instron machine, model 8802.

Fig. 11: Location of the strain-gages on the model

A mesh sensitivity study was performed in order to define the most appropriate mesh refinement for the subsequent ultimate strength analyses. The mesh refinement was defined with 45 elements along the length and 15 elements between longitudinal stiffeners. Along the stiffener web height and flange width it was adopted 8 and 2 elements, respectively. The panels have been represented by ABAQUS shell element S4. It is able to analyze thin and thick shells, taking into account finite membrane deformations and large rotations. Material stress-strain curve was obtained by uniaxial tensile tests of specimens cut from the plates employed in the model fabrication. Yield stress (σ_o) and Young modulus (E) are 365 N/mm^2 and 207,863 N/mm^2, respectively.

Results for Numerical-Experimental Correlation

Fig. 12 shows the curves applied force versus axial displacement for both experimental test and numerical analysis. The highest buckling load was obtained for the experimental model with 1.03% higher than the numerical value. At post-buckling regime, the experimental curve is practically identical with the numerical up to the displacement of 1 mm. Afterwards the experimental values are slightly lower than the numerical ones.

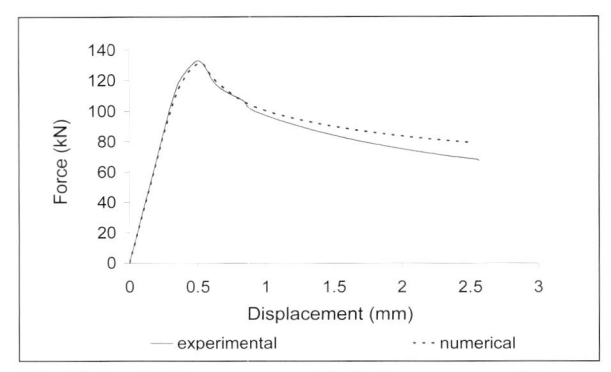

Fig. 12: Applied force versus axial displacement – model 1

Figs. 13 and 14 present the post-buckling modes for experimental test and numerical simulation, respectively.

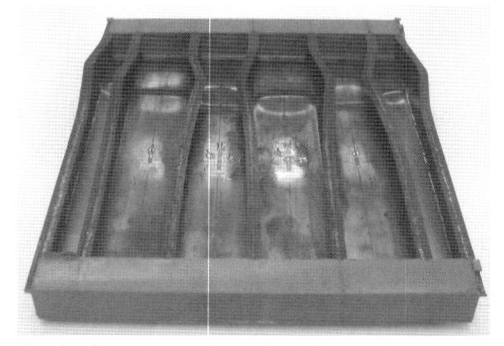

Fig. 13: Experimental post-buckling mode – model 1

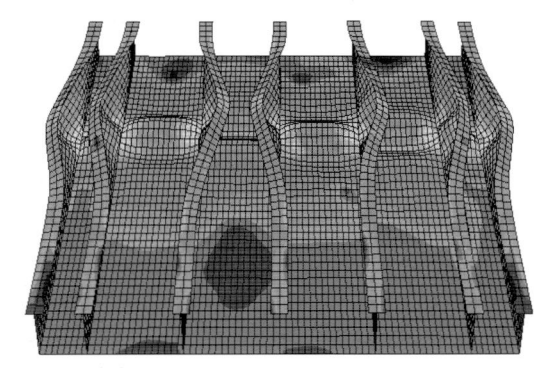

Fig. 14: Numerical post-buckling mode – model 1

Structural Behavior of Ships under Bending

The position of the wave in relation to the ship hull girder has a considerable influence on the distribution of the buoyancy along the ship length. A wave of length equal to the length of the ship moving along the ship can occupy a variety of positions. Two conditions will be considered in the analyses. The first one considers the crests at the perpendiculars. In this condition the ship will sag, with the deck in compression and the bottom in tension, as shown in Fig. 15. The other condition considers the crest midship. In this condition the ship will hog, the deck being in tension and the bottom in compression, as shown in Fig. 16.

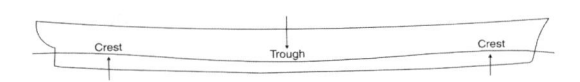

Fig. 15: Sagging condition (Eyres, 2001)

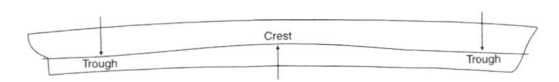

Fig. 16: Hogging condition (Eyres, 2001)

In this paper the structural behavior under vertical bending is studied based on the ultimate limit state, in which it is determined the maximum bending moment that the ship can absorbed.

Distortions generated by the fabrication process, the initial geometrical imperfections, are quantitatively represented by the distance of the actual surface from the idealized one assumed for design purposes. This type of imperfection, characterized by the shape and amplitude of the distribution, is the main cause of different buckling loads in nominally identical panels.

Numerical Model of a Suezmax Tanker – Midship Compartment Between Web Frames

The Suezmax tanker ship chosen for this study has the following principle geometric characteristics.

- Length Overall (LOA.) = 254.00 m
- Length between perpendiculars (LBP) = 244.00 m
- Breadth (B) = 42.00 m
- Depth (D) = 21.00
- Draft (T) = 15.00 m
- Displacement = 126,000 ton

Based in this information the modeled region was a typical compartment between web frames positioned at the midship. The dimensions are:
- compartment length: 31.36 m
- space between web frames: 4.48 m
- double hull bottom spacing: 2.3 m
- double hull side spacing: 2.5 m

Fig. 17 illustrates the longitudinal elements of the midship section.

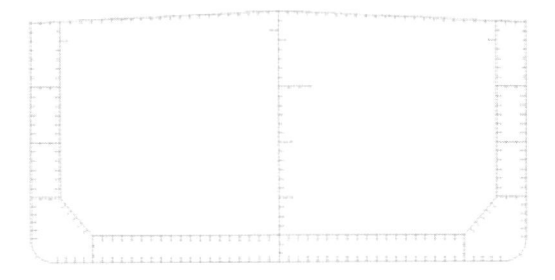

Fig. 17: Midship section

The analysis is restricted to the midship stiffened panels between web frames. To minimize the boundary effects two neighbor spacings between web frames, forward and aft midship spacing were considered. Therefore, the model is composed by three spacings between web frames. A longitudinal symmetry condition was utilized to minimize both computer time and output file. Fig. 18 illustrates the position of the analyzed ship region.

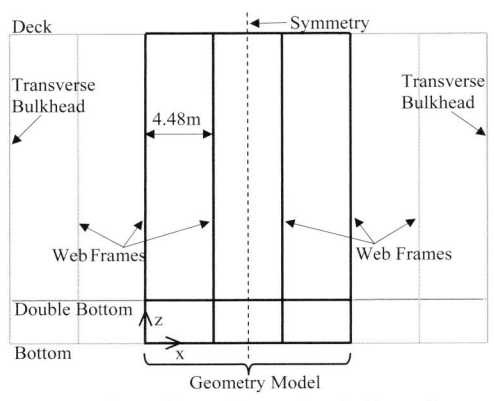

Fig. 18: Position of the analyzed ship region

In order to model a Suezmax tanker compartment between web frames it was necessary to create an automatic way to implement and vary the initial geometric imperfections on the plates between stiffeners. It was done using CAD. The initial geometric imperfection is represented by eq. 1.

$$w(x,y) = w_{max} \cdot \sin\left(\frac{m \cdot x \cdot \pi}{a}\right) \cdot \sin\left(\frac{n \cdot y \cdot \pi}{b}\right) \quad (1)$$

where:

w - out-of-plane displacement at the control point;

w_{max} - maximum panel out-of-plane displacement;

x - longitudinal position of the control point;

y - transverse position of the control point;

m - number of longitudinal half-waves;

n - number of transverse half-waves;

a - longitudinal plate length;

b - transverse plate length.

The midship section has the geometry composed of a variety of structural components which are summarized in flat and curved stiffened panels. Both tee and angle bar stiffeners have been employed.

Fig. 19 shows a typical flat panel between longitudinal stiffeners with amplified out-of-plane displacements. It is possible to insert up to seven half-waves in the longitudinal direction and one in the transverse direction.

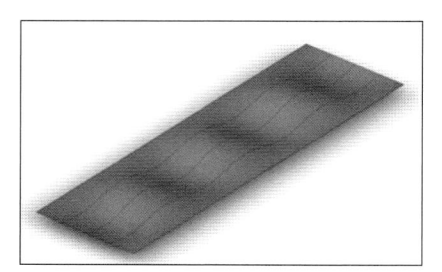

Fig. 19: CAD constructed panel

Those panels were used to generate all the elements of the Suezmax tanker compartment presented in Fig. 20.

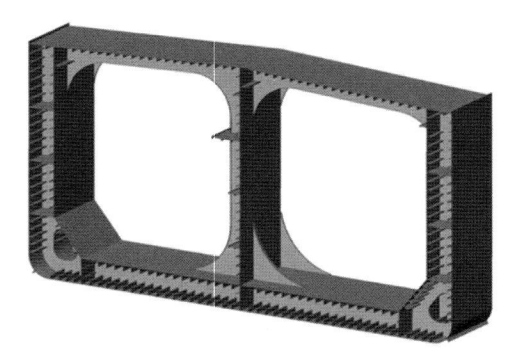

Fig. 20: Geometry model with longitudinal symmetry

By doing this it is possible to insert imperfection on any panel or longitudinal stiffener. Once the numerical model is finalized it is easy to change imperfections because it is only necessary to change the values on the panel model, rebuilding the geometry. The computer model is then exported to ABAQUS, Hibbitt et al. (2006) software for finite element analysis.

The numerical-experimental study initially employed the ABAQUS shell element S4 (with four integration points) and the mesh refinement with 45 elements along the length between web frames and 15 elements between longitudinal stiffeners. Due to the high number of elements of the Suezmax compartment section studies on the small scale model was done to verify the possibility of using the element S4R (with one integration point) and a less refinement mesh. The best results were obtained using the element S4R with 36 elements along the length and 12 elements between longitudinal stiffeners. This combination decreases the computer time for the analysis and also the size of the output file. Results using either S4 (mesh 45x15) or S4R (mesh 36x12) elements for the plates between longitudinal stiffeners were practically identical as shown in the curve average longitudinal compressive stress (σ_L) versus average compressive strain (ε_L), Fig. 21, where σ_o and ε_o are the yield stress and strain, respectively. For the web frames it was utilized the triangular shell element S3R.

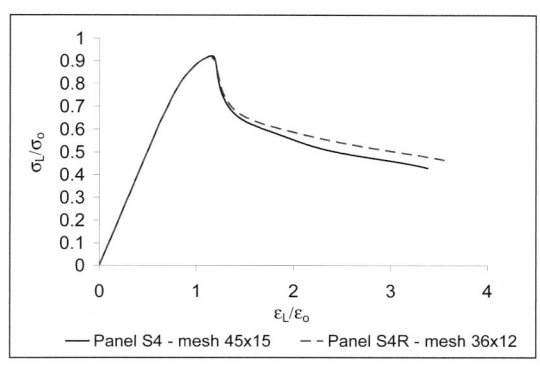

Fig. 21: Comparison of results using either S4 or S4R element to represent the plates

The Suezmax tanker compartment between web frames is submitted to sagging and hogging loading conditions through controlled incremental rotations applied to all nodes of model edge. It was used the coupling constraints available in ABAQUS, Hibbit et al. (2006). Therefore, the incremental rotations are applied at reference node and then transmit the movement to all the loaded edge. The reference node was positioned in the initial neutral axle. It is assumed that this plane remains flat and normal to the neutral line during the loading.

The following boundary conditions were assumed for the reference node: displacement along the y and z axle equal to zero ($U_y = U_z = 0$) and rotational along the x axle equal to zero ($\theta_x = 0$).

Material stress-strain curve was employed in the analysis presented values for yield stress (σ_o) and Young modulus (E) of 235 N/mm² and 210,000 N/mm², respectively.

The panel geometry assumed in the numerical models has the following characteristics. The upper deck, inner bottom and the bottom have the plate length of 4480 mm, space between longitudinal stiffeners (b) of 830 mm and plate thickness (t) of 16.5, 16 and 19 mm, respectively. Stiffener dimensions of the upper deck: thickness web (t_w) of 13 mm, web height (h_w) of 300 mm, flange width (b_f) of 90 mm and flange thickness (t_f) of 17 mm. Stiffener dimensions of the inner bottom: thickness web (t_w) of 11.5 mm, web height (h_w) of 475 mm, flange width (b_f) of 150 mm and flange thickness (t_f) of 18 mm. Stiffener dimensions of the bottom: thickness web (t_w) of 11 mm, web height (h_w) of 425 mm, flange width (b_f) of 150 mm and flange thickness (t_f) of 18 mm. It was considered the thickness of 19 mm for the web frame.

Four analyses were carried out to study the Suezmax tanker compartment behavior under extreme bending moment. Two models were developed and submitted to sagging and hogging. The plate initial geometric imperfection was represented by the sinusoidal distribution given by eq. 1. All models have the magnitude imperfection based on the maximum allowable imperfection amplitude recommended by DNV (2004), eq. 2. For these models both stiffeners and web frames were assumed without geometric imperfections.

$$w_{\max} = 0.005\,b \qquad (2)$$

The first model has the imperfection mode with one half-wave on both directions (m=1, n=1). The second model has the imperfection mode coincident with the natural buckling mode (m=4, n=1). The natural buckling mode of the panels of the double hull tanker bottom has been determined using a reduced size of the stiffened panel.

Ultimate Bending Strength

Fig. 22 shows the moment-curvature relationships obtained for models 1(m=1) and 2 (m=4) for the conditions of hogging and sagging. In hogging, the ultimate bending moment for model 1 and 2 were 9.67 and 8.15 E+09 N.m, respectively. The drop of the ultimate bending moment for the imperfection mode coincident with the natural buckling mode (model 2) compared with the result for the one half-wave imperfection mode (model 1) is about 15.72%. In sagging, the ultimate bending moment for model 1 and 2 were 7.92 and 6.34 E+09 N.m, respectively. The drop of the ultimate bending moment for the imperfection mode coincident with the natural buckling mode (model 2) compared with the result for the one half-wave imperfection mode (model 1) is about 19.95%.

In relation to the curvature (1/m) corresponding to the ultimate bending moment the results obtained for the hogging condition for model 1 and 2 were 3.13 and 1.77 E-04, respectively. The values obtained for the sagging conditions were less than those for hogging condition, with the corresponding values for model 1 and 2 of 1.42 and 1.06 E-04, respectively. Curvature decreases for hogging and sagging conditions from model 1 to model 2 at collapse were 43.45 and 25.35%, respectively.

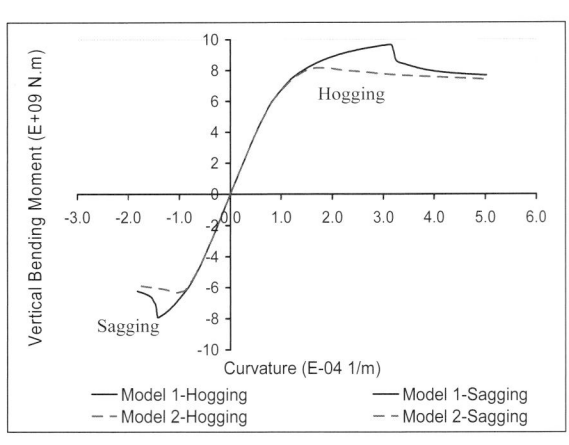

Fig. 22: Moment-curvature relationships

Failure Sequence

Fig. 23 shown at the appendix illustrates the panels, stiffeners and longitudinal girders for the analyzed numerical model in order to improve the results understanding.

The results obtained for model 1 (m=1) in the hogging condition show that the symmetric stiffeners from the longitudinal girder GS2 and GS6 are the first to collapse with an average longitudinal compressive stress value of 188 N/mm². The failure sequence then propagates to the other two symmetric stiffeners from the longitudinal girder (GS1 and GS5). The subsequent elements to failure are the plates of the longitudinal girder (GP2/GP8 and GP3/GP9). Before the collapse of the bottom plates some longitudinal bottom stiffeners had already collapsed. The last components to collapse were the plate and the stiffener of the central longitudinal girder (GP6 and GS4). Fig. 24 shows the double hull bottom post-buckling modes for model 1.

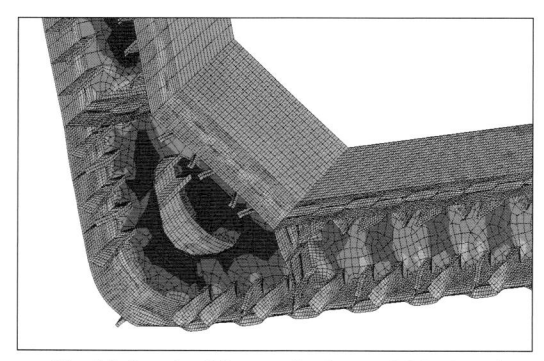

Fig. 24: Post-buckling modes for model 1 – hogging

The results obtained for model 2 (m=4) in the hogging condition indicates that the first plate to collapse is the plate of the central longitudinal girder (GP5) with an average longitudinal compressive stress value of the 143.6 N/mm². In model 1 analysis this plate was one of the last to collapse with the stress value of 232.6 N/mm². Those differences imply in a decrease of 38.26% for ultimate compressive stress. In model 2 almost all the plates collapse before the stiffeners. The only exceptions are the longitudinal bottom stiffener BS22 that collapses before the bottom plates BP3, 4, 43 and 44 and the stiffener BS23 that collapses before the bottom plates BP1, 2, 45 and 46. The last plate to collapse, after all the stiffeners, is the plate GP4.

Model 1 and 2 have the post-buckling mode of the plates with 5 half-waves, as can be seen in Fig. 25. This figure has a longitudinal symmetry. The natural buckling mode of the panels of the double hull tanker bottom was determined using a small section of a stiffened panel and 4 half-waves were obtained. This difference from post-buckling mode (5 half-waves) to the natural buckling mode (4 half-waves) occurs because the conditions of loading are different between small scale and full scale models. In the small scale the applied load is uniaxial compressive and in the full scale rotation along the neutral axle.

Model 2 has the initial imperfection mode with 4 half-waves and a slight transition occurs to reach the post-buckling mode (5 half-waves). However, for model 1 the plates collapse almost with the same displacement of the stiffeners. This happens because of the severe transition from the initial imperfection geometry (1 half-wave) to reach the post buckling mode (5 half-waves).

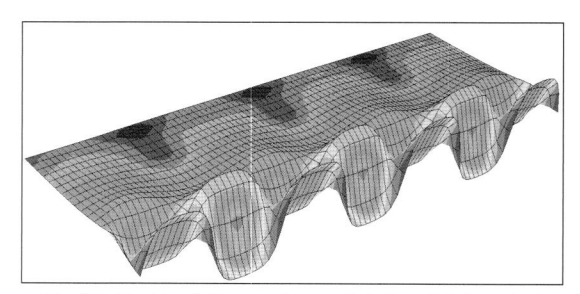

Fig. 25: Post-buckling mode - models 1 and 2 (hogging)

Analyzing the results for the sagging conditions, similar behavior as observed in the hogging analysis is obtained for the failure sequence and the post-buckling mode. The first plate to collapse for model 1 was LBP2 with an average longitudinal compressive stress value of the 220 N/mm². Then the failure sequence presents the almost simultaneous failures of plates and stiffeners. The last elements to collapse were the side plates and stiffeners with the stress value close to 225 N/mm².

In relation to the model 2 almost the plates have collapsed before the stiffeners. The only exception is longitudinal bulkhead stiffener LBS1 that collapses before the deck plates DP1 and 50 and symmetry double side plates DSP2 and 4. The first plate to collapse was the deck plate DP18 with the stress value of 189 N/mm².

In model 1 this plate collapses with the value of 241 N/mm². Those differences imply in decrease of 21.6%. The last elements to collapse were the side stiffeners SS1 and 2.

Conclusions

The paper studied the influence of different geometric imperfection distributions on the buckling behavior of a Suezmax tanker compartment between web frames submitted to bending in both sagging and hogging conditions.

A correlation study has been performed using the results from small scale experiments and numerical simulations in order to establish the numerical model, mesh refinement and finite element formulation, to be used in the full scale simulations.

Initial distortion mode coincident with the natural buckling mode of a particular plate generates lower bound buckling load. On the other hand, some imperfection modes can difficult the buckling failure, therefore generating upper bound values for the respective buckling loads.

Results obtained for the ultimate bending strength in hogging and sagging from model 1 (one half-wave in both directions) to model 2 (natural buckling mode) indicated a decrease of 15.72 and 19.95%, respectively. Considering the results from both vertical bending moment and curvature at the collapse it is confirmed that the bending mode in sagging dominates the ultimate strength of tankers.

Full scale measurements of the geometric imperfection distributions on actual marine structures during the construction could contribute to a better understanding of buckling failure mechanism. The next phase of the research work in progress will consider actual geometric imperfection distributions from measurements during ship construction.

Acknowledgements

The authors acknowledge the support from FINEP and PETROBRAS in the context of the agreement between the Ministry of Science & Technology and TRANSPETRO for the technology development of the Brazilian shipbuilding industry. Special thanks to Mr. Marcelo Pinheiro and Mr. Marcelo Oliveira who fabricated the small scale models.

References

Estefen, T. P. and Estefen, S. F. (2006) "Semisub column ultimate strength under compressive loading", World Maritime Technology Conference, March 6-10, London, UK.

Estefen, T. P., Werneck, D. S. and Estefen, S. F. (2007) "Influence of the geometric imperfection on the buckling behavior of floating platform column under axial load". Proceedings of the 26th International Conference on Offshore Mechanics and Arctic Engineering, June 10-15, San Diego, USA.

Eyres, D. J. (2001). " Ship Construction". Fifth Edition, Elsevier Butterworth Heinemann, Oxford.

Ikeda, A., Yao, T., Kitamura, O., Yamamoto, N., Yoneda, M. and Ohtsubo, H. (2001) "Assessment of ultimate longitudinal strength of aged tankers". Proceedings of the 8th International Symposium on Practical Design of Ships and Other Floating Structures, September 16-21, Shanghai, China, Vol. II, pp 997-1003.

Hibbitt, Karlsson and Sorensen (2006) "ABAQUS User`s and Theory Manuals". Version 6.5.

Offshore Standard Det Norske Veritas (2004) "DNV-OS-C401, Fabrication and testing of offshore structures".

Rigo, Ph., Toderan, C., Yao, T. (2001) "Sensitivity analysis on ultimate hull bending moment". Proceedings of the 8th International Symposium on Practical Design of Ships and Other Floating Structures, September 16-21, Shanghai, China, Vol. II, pp 987-995.

Sun, Haihong and Wang, Xiaozhi. (2005). "Procedure for calculating hull girder ultimate strength of ship structures". Journal of Marine Systems and Ocean Technology, Vol. 1, No. 3, pp 137-143.

Appendix

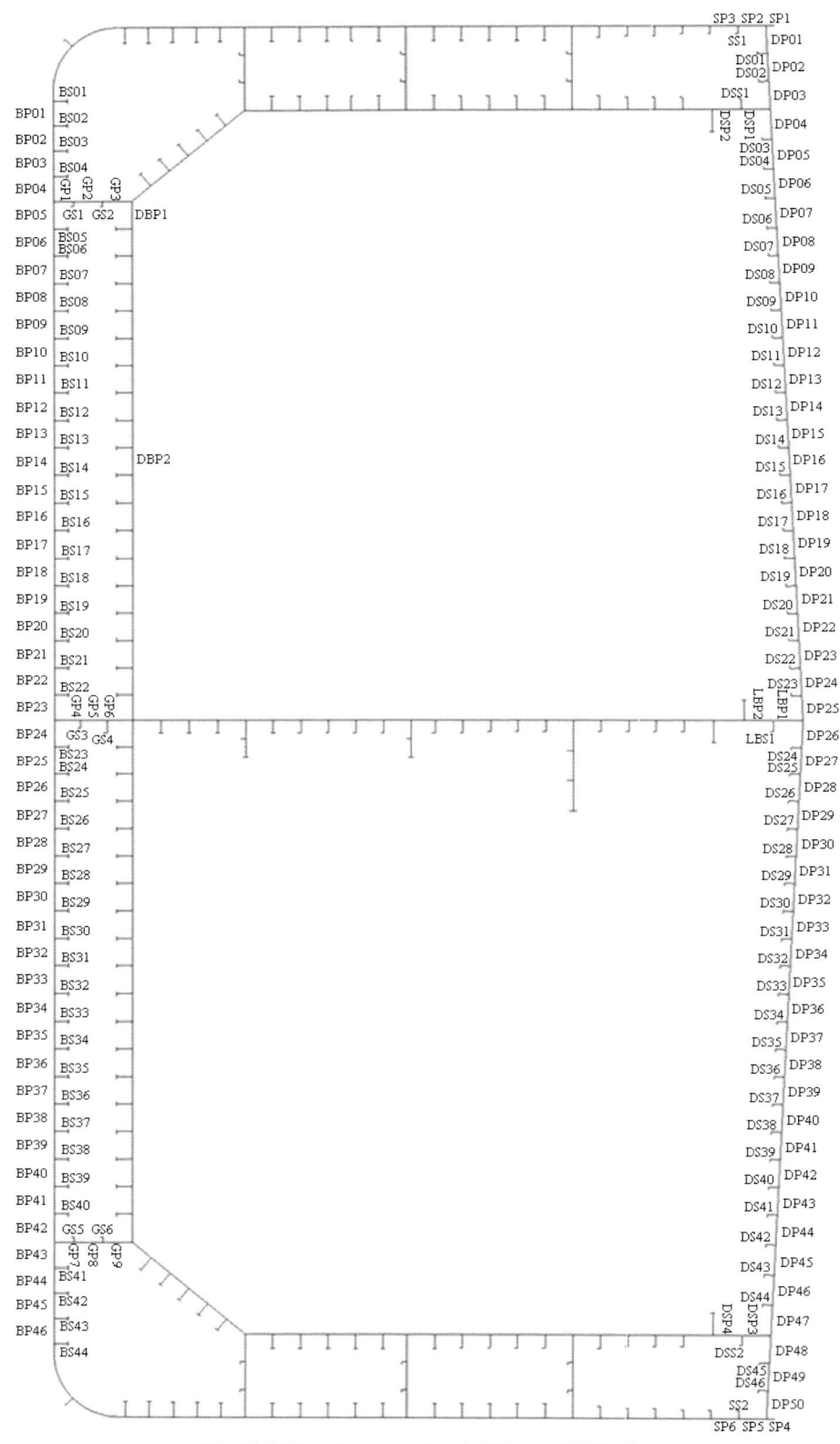

Fig. 23: Mid section – panel and stiffeners distribution

Product Lifecycle Management and Business Transformation: Concepts for the Marine and Offshore Industries

Author: Robert G. Beadling

Dassault Systemes Americas Corporation
Yorktown, Virginia

Abstract:

There is a clear opportunity to advance the state of US Mid-tier shipyards and similar operations through the adoption of Product Lifecycle Management (PLM). application software developed specifically for ship design and production can be used in concert with solutions for collaboration, digital mockup and product data management developed for aerospace to bring about business transformation across all phases of a single ship or a class of ship's lifecycle. This notion has already been proven by foreign engineering and construction companies in Europe and Asia. Business Transformation concepts will be explored along with examples of advanced solutions currently in use.

Keywords

Product lifecycle management; PLM; Business transformation; CAD; Digital manufacturing; Shipbuilding; Offshore; Product data management.

Introduction

In the US Shipbuilding and Offshore Industries, we face a general deficit of skilled human resources relative to the current level of opportunities and challenges. This deficit exists at all levels from the organizations that perform design and engineering to the shipyard production workers There is sufficient production capacity, but increased pressure to reduce costs as operating expenses and material prices rise. At the same time, new technologies have been developed that are specifically targeted for shipbuilding which can also be augmented by more generic PLM technologies to address current business challenges. These technologies have already been adopted for use in the DDG-1000 Program. The success experienced by the Yantai Raffles shipyard in collaboration with Sevan Marine to build the Sevan Stabilized Platform (SSP-300) suggests that this same technology can also bring benefits to the next tier of shipbuilders.

This paper will explore recent developments in information technology for Product Lifecycle Management that are demonstrating the potential to alleviate the adverse conditions affecting US mid-tier shipbuilders today.

Background

Studies were recently released by the Office of the Deputy Under Secretary of Defense for Industrial Policy (ODUSD (IP)), the Office of Naval Research (ONR) – Navy MANTECH and the Center for Naval Shipbuilding Technology (CNST) on the current viability of our mid-tier shipyards to build 400 foot long or smaller surface combatants. They provide some insight to more global problems at the next level of detail. It could also be expected that the same issues identified by the studies would come to bear in the design and construction of a sophisticated offshore platform for deepwater exploration.

The ONR study points out a number of conditions that are prevalent in today's mid-tier yards. A few of the more critical elements are as follows:

1. Insufficient process modeling that leads to:

- Poor production planning and scheduling

- Poor outfit parts marshalling, block assembly and materials handling

- More corrective man-hours needed at each assembly stage

2. Better human resource enabling is needed.

- Difficulties arise in bringing skilled labor up to speed on naval shipbuilding design and construction practices
- Further challenges arise with the added complexity of naval ships.

3. Lack of sufficient capacity within the primary yard leading to the need for more outsourcing.

- This is leading to major rework and manual checking in integrating subassemblies and other sub-products being developed and built remotely, coming from outside resources.

4. There is a general need to accelerate communications and engineering change decisions with the customer in design reviews.

- In some cases, critical design changes were accepted before cost and schedule impacts were well understood.

5. Difficulty in maintaining an accurate/current representation of the ship configuration and follow-on configurations (hull effectivity of changes).

- Manual processes are being employed for extracting data and updating/maintaining configurations must be employed adding delays and cost.

The conclusion of the studies is that, for the smaller combatant, the work should still be kept at the larger US shipyards. The studies give some recognition to the fact that a level of automation has taken place to varying degrees throughout the survey sample. However, none of these yards appear to have adopted a Product Lifecycle Management (PLM) strategy. The automation efforts have brought some efficiency to the execution of existing processes such as the generation of drawings and plate nesting and burning operations, but, (based on the outcome of the ODUSD/ONR studies) they have not significantly transformed these shipyards to the point where overall turnaround times can be substantially reduced or throughput capacities have been significantly expanded.

While this assessment was targeted at the shipyard's abilities to perform naval ship construction, it also gives a strong indication of overall US industry status relative to global shipbuilding capabilities. The intent of this paper is to suggest that we would have much to gain by adopting the same PLM technologies that are being deployed at our larger shipyards and in the aerospace and defense industry at large in the mid-tier yards. This would hold true even if it is to perform work on smaller naval vessels, Coast Guard cutters, commercial ships or offshore platform production.

Concepts – PLM and Transformation

As the relative costs of goods and services go ever higher, the cost of software and computing resource to address them becomes a lesser factor in the development equation. Among others, the aerospace and automotive industries have continued to evolve and fully exploit emerging technologies. They have generally progressed from using digital mockup to adopt the widespread use of Product Lifecycle Management (PLM) where a product is fully developed and managed PLM combines a modern IT toolset, IT infrastructure and company engineering and manufacturing workflow and practices to the full lifecycle of a product per figure 1.

The implementation of PLM led to the next logical step of enabling collaborative environments that are supported by high speed networking and the use of the Internet. The use of Global Collaborative Environments (GCEs) has gone hand in glove with the globalization of business models. It is important to know that GCEs can be made available to both the major original equipment manufacturers and their suppliers at the lower tiers.

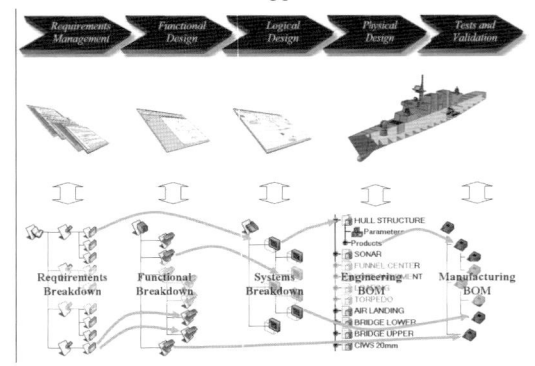

Figure 1: A graphical view of how the IBM PLM Shipbuilding Solution supports the complete deve lopment of complex vessels

At the same time, considerable investment has been made to provide advancements that have been specifically targeted for the shipbuilding and offshore industries. In January 2001, the DD-21 Alliance announced a strategic partnership to accelerate the development of V5 PLM Solutions for shipbuilding with Dassault Systemes. Working with the Alliance and other shipbuilders around the globe, considerable advances have been made in arrangements, structural design, fluid and electrical systems design as well as steel production and production planning. Some of this investment has even brought benefits to the aerospace industry to enable the design of tubing systems and manufacturing fixtures that use heavy structures. In October, 2004, Northrop Grumman, leading a development consortium of six companies and more than one hundred suppliers, announced that they had selected a PLM Solution developed by Dassault Systèmes, as the collaborative product development environment for the project. The group would use CATIA V5, as the 3D product-development and authoring application; and ENOVIA Life Cycle Applications (LCA), for product data lifecycle management and decision support

The components of the system that forms the basis of Dassault Systemes' PLM solution for shipbuilding and offshore design and engineering include:

CATIA for Design & Authoring – addressing the full range of disciplines/functionalities from mechanical to structural to fluid systems design.

ENOVIA product data management – supporting Digital 3D Mock-up, Concurrent design, collaboration and Virtual Product Modeling. ENOVIA can manage, millions of part instances and supports searches based on systems, disciplines and physical locations.

ENOVIA brings Life-cycle, change management, revision management and hull effectivity and provides the central interface to CATIA, DELMIA & other systems (SAP, non-CAD data bases…)

DELMIA delivers the applications for digital manufacturing, construction and maintenance planning as well as human simulation capabilities. DELMIA's Manufacturing Hub maintains a connection to the engineering database in ENOVIA to eliminate data duplication and enable change management between the engineering product data and the manufacturing process and resource information.

Now, through the application of these technologies, business transformation can be realized by consciously working to improve in the following areas:
1. Global Collaboration
2. Product Excellence
3. Production Performance
4. Collaborative Lifecycle Workflow
5. Knowledge and Know How Capture and Sharing

The remainder of this paper will expand on each of these areas to develop a clearer vision of where improvements can be made in the shipbuilding and offshore industries today:

1. Global Collaboration

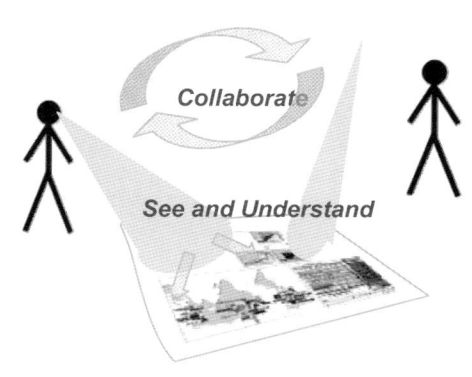

Fig. 2

The nature of business is changing rapidly throughout the world. US leading market indicators that track capital investment within this country are no longer meaningful as businesses develop new facilities and partnerships throughout the world. Enabling the seamless exchange of data has become essential to support new development of complex products. The shipbuilding industry can leverage the technological advances in this area through several Product Data Management capabilities that are now available.

Multi-site collaboration is now supported both through product data replication, as well as web-client tools that allow collaboration on single project with as many different connections as needed. Work and action flow can be controlled across a global enterprise and the solution can be customized to support the lifecycle of engineering changes as needed, from working on a "best-so-far" philosophy in early stages to a more controlled approach systematically incorporating revisions as the detail design converges.

For light collaboration with markups and similar functions, the solution includes applications that allow access through a standard Internet connection. This can be used to provide direct access to clients and ship owners, allowing them to view progress and make comments. The solution requires no installation of software; code is supplied through the Internet. This permits direct usage of the data without a need for specialist knowledge or access to a client site.

Global collaboration was recently employed in the development of Sevan Marine's Sevan Stabilized Platform the SSP 300 an innovative FPSO vessel with a cylindrical rather than conventional ship-shaped design. Using Dassault Systemes shipbuilding solutions that are built upon ENOVIA for product data management to perform concurrent design, engineering and production planning and simulation, Norway's Sevan Marine worked with Yantai Raffles Shipyard in Yantai, China to develop the platform and plan its construction. PLM technology enabled real time validation of the FPSO design against analysis requirements and construction processes. This simultaneous validation minimized the revision common in the energy market, ensuring significant time gains for the Sevan/Yantai team.

Yantai Raffles utilized the same design, data exchange and digital manufacturing components. This facilitated a collaborative design and manufacturing environment for the SSP 300. Chief Executive Officer Brian Chang has since presented in several venues about the advantages PLM has brought to this project and the benefits that they expect to realize in all of their projects going forward.

The SSP 300 project is an example of an innovative response to market conditions. In this case, the deployment of PLM has fundamentally altered the design-manufacturing business equation, enabling innovation and rapid adaptation to changing customer requirements. In the future, the FPSO manufacturer will continue to implement PLM solutions that will enable the company to capture, manage and exploit intellectual property created during product development, providing companywide 3-D collaborative workspaces that will connect its teams with the suppliers and customers.

Yantai Raffles is certainly not one of the larger shipyards in the world, but, as its recent financial reports would suggest, it is now among the most profitable. This same approach to collaboration could be employed by the US Mid-tier to the same effect - addressing the need to accelerate communication and share in development process with partners and suppliers.

2. Product Excellence

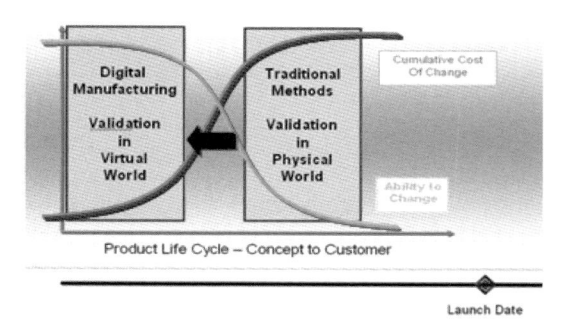

Fig. 3

The notion is well known and understood that the earlier a change is made in product development, the less costly it is to do so. Initially, major gains can be realized just through the use of 3D mockup and the elimination of physical prototypes. Figure 3 also points out that 3D design development sets a virtual stage for manufacturing. For Yantai Raffles and Sevan Marine, the integrated mechanical and structural design tools - working in a configuration-managed digital mock-up, enabled the optimization of the multi-discipline design process behind the SSP-300. Not only did this integrated environment bring efficiency to the development process and minimize rework, but it improved the overall quality of information that would be available to support sourcing and production.

With a PLM shipbuilding solution, it is now possible to design a complete 3D product model before production commences, and to use that model as the basis for detail design, purchasing, build strategy, production planning, workshop documentation, installation and even maintenance. The system supports online collaboration through the product data management system and its portal, which gives everyone on the team, from owners to purchasing, the means to view and markup 3D models using a simple web browser.

The product data management system stores individual ship parts, process templates and manufacturing resources as intelligent and interconnected components that know about themselves and their relationship to one another by attaching information about their real-world industrial characteristics and behaviors. The system actually uses the design context to pick the most appropriate part from the project catalogue. Designers only need to engage with engineering to resolve conflicts – when no part is available or when multiple parts fulfill the same requirements. When the time comes to order parts, integration of the design solution with the corporate ERP and procurement systems through an enterprise-level integration framework ensures that shipyard buyers purchase the correct materials at the right time.

The product data management system facilitates design development by enabling the packaging of engineering change orders (ECOs) that include links to all relevant information about the change. It also determines all objects within the design that will be effected by the change. The product data management system manages the workflow through the review cycle for each ECO and tracks the status from in-work through to approval or rejection. Users can apply a "hull effectivity" to clearly identify which ships of a class will be changed. The user can then use the product data management system to filter the database in setting up her design session to find the correct configuration for the hull number or numbers of interest. The filtering process can, at the same time show revisions in work and past revision levels that have been approved. Highlighting can also be used to show when a component or set of components is being considered for change.

Every 3D model is continually associated with the 2D drawings that are made from it. Deleting an object in 3D removes it from each 2D drawing, and vice versa. Every change automatically updates every drawing, eliminating many sources of error. The authoring system is also integrated with engineering analysis tools and offers the opportunity to perform Finite Element Modeling directly from a 3D model where both heavy structure and mechanical parts can be joined together to test designs for the rigorous duty to be experienced at sea.

System intelligence also provides interference clash detection. Today's interference analysis can distinguish between true penetrations and subtle contacts, eliminating the false positives that burn designers' time. It also analyzes soft interferences – modules that don't touch or bump but interfere with each other when maintenance or operation is required, from leaving enough room for worker access to providing clearance around light fixtures to ensure their illumination is not blocked by nearby objects.

Product excellence sets the stage for production performance. With collaboration from the customer and all disciplines to reach the point of release to manufacturing, we have a level of assurance of producibility as well as a clearer confidence that the ship or platform will function as intended.

3. Production Performance

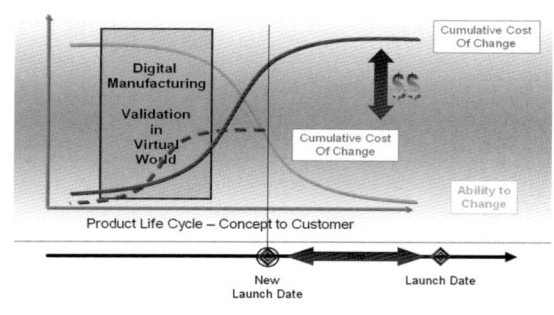

Fig. 4

Production performance is about a shift of focus from **Product** to **Process.** Figure 4 illustrates that Digital Manufacturing brings the ability to validate production processes in the virtual world. As a result, there is strong potential to optimize and reduce the overall cost of production by shortening cycle time. Once again, the need for change can be discovered much sooner to avoid higher costs of change later in the lifecycle.

The implementation of digital manufacturing – the ability to simulate and fully plan production by exploiting the 3D model is clearly gaining ground. US shipbuilders are taking note of the success of this technology in aerospace. Aircraft and ships share a major similarity in the way that they are constructed in a modular fashion. Pre-outfitting of modules is a key to efficiency in both industries. There is great value in visualizing assembly of more complex modules to ensure that conflicts and interferences are resolved in advance. At the same time, details about process steps and resource requirements (human, facilities, tooling, and equipment) can be captured and applied to planning and scheduling for the plant floor.

The Digital Manufacturing environment enables the manufacturing team to influence the design to reduce the cost of manufacturing and eliminate engineering change orders caused by previously undetected problems with manufacturability. High-level Process Planning by the Advance Planners during the conceptual design phase ensures that the units of construction can be efficiently manufactured in yards and in supplier facilities. After the design is released to production planning, any changes in the engineering bill of material are automatically flagged in effected production plans that are stored in the manufacturing hub so that the engineering bill of materials and the manufacturing bill can be synchronized. Changes to the design that have already had manufacturing plans established in the manufacturing hub can then be brought up to date to represent the most current state of the ship design.

Digital manufacturing includes the creation of the production system, the planning of the production process and verification of the sequence of operations using simulation to support design for manufacturing. During the detail design phase, detailed planning and process design is finalized and verified in a 3D environment. The product model and producibility studies can be used as the basis for creation of 3D work instructions for the shop floor.

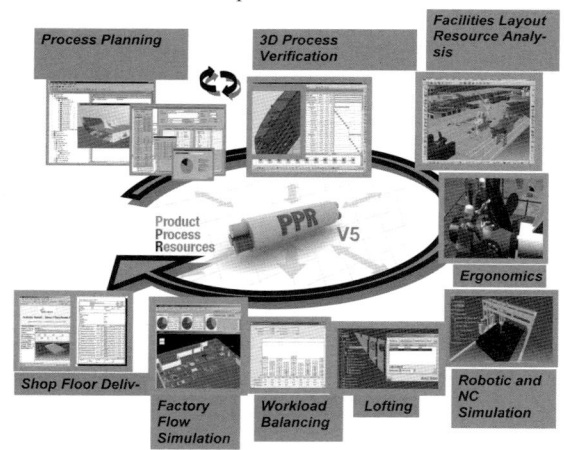

Fig. 5: Digital Manufacturing Applications

The general functions supported include process planning, process verification, time measurement, layout planning, ergonomics, robotics, NC simulation, yard material flow simulation, production management and 3D Electronic Work Instructions. (see Figure 5) The use of 3D images in work instructions will substantially help less experienced production workers to perform new tasks correctly the first time – helping to address the skills deficit.

As the PLM Shipbuilding Solution is based on a global PPR (Product-Process-Resource) data model architecture with embedded product data management functionality, it is possible to keep track of data extracted for production. Once data is delivered for cutting or burning, this is tracked in the system. In this way, production data can be traced, accommodating late design modifications.

Many yards have pre-existing IT systems to store and manage production data. These systems can be fed through integration with the PLM system, if this is needed to maintain synchronization with the legacy systems.. To ensure a consistent data set, however, it is important that the PLM system remain the master, with other systems serving as clients of that data. Post delivery, data in the manufacturing hub also provides a rich resource for Maintenance Planning and the creation of 3D Maintenance and Repair Instructions.

To summarize, Process Excellence functions on several levels:

- Ensuring that there is a high fidelity understanding of the steps needed and their sequence.

- Delivering the detailed production information in sufficient detail (using 3D images wherever it helps).

- Ensuring that the steps and their sequence are efficient and the necessary resources (human, tools, equipment and facilities) are assigned to each process.

- Maintaining strong agreement between the engineering bill of materials (EBOM) and the planning and manufacturing BOMs. (PBOM/MBOM) so that the most up to date and accurate version of the design is what is delivered.

4. Collaborative Lifecycle Workflow

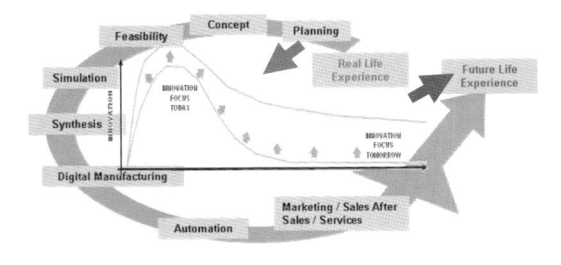

Fig. 6

Today, much more investment is being made in the use of the most advanced forms of simulation. The use of physics-based simulation is on the rise to more accurately predict both product and process performance. A paradigm shift is moving the way we think about innovation away from being product-oriented at the feature-function level and instead is moving toward enhancing the user experience, process automation or the sales/service experience. Another way of saying it is that we move the innovation focus to later stages of product lifecycle.

Fig. 7

Can this be applied to shipbuilding? In fact, we see more and more simulation of shipboard activities from machinery maintenance to weapons and cargo handling. Human models are being used in simulation more widely and immersive technologies are appearing in daily use in the naval ship design community. Figure 7 is a frame grab from a complete simulation showing human models performing maintenance on a controllable pitch propeller Figure 8 illustrates the results of a complex simulation showing how lighting and fabric colors and textures will appear in a cruise liner cabin.

Experiencing the ship before it is committed to steel is bringing a heightened sense of anticipation about what a new ship can be and how it can be used in the future. Through the use of advanced simulation, the experiences of builders, maintainers, operators and passengers will be enhanced.

5. Capturing and Reusing Corporate Knowledge and Know-how

Another way to meet the demand for faster design and manufacturing is to manage and re-use knowledge accumulated from previous projects. A step-wise approach will allow yards to gradually build up a database of captured knowledge to achieve the benefit of re-using it. How do we place a value on this with an ageing workforce?

The Dassault Systemes PLM solution is built on a knowledge engine technology whose foundation is to capture and reuse best practices and automate procedures at the highest level possible. Within the design, engineers can create, store and manage rules that help perform standard checks. These checks are performed not just once, but continuously as the rules are inserted into the design. This ensures that once the rules have been embedded in the design data, any modifications will be checked against the rule.

System intelligence also enhances interference clash detection processes. But, unlike most systems, which only identify hard interferences, knowledge rules can distinguish between true collisions and light contacts, eliminating the false positives that burn designers' time. It also analyzes soft interferences – components that don't touch, but interfere with each other when maintenance or operation is required, leaving enough room for worker access. Checks can also be made on clearance around light fixtures to ensure their illumination is not blocked by nearby objects.

Knowledge engineering rules analyze design intent. For example, in a piping diagram, the distance between pipes and heat sources is automatically calculated, and the rules can be programmed to assign the proper level of insulation to the pipes and neighboring structural elements based on an analysis of the fluids to be transported.

To ensure compliance with classification society rules, catalogued knowledge rules can be embedded in the structural design. This can include rules that check or drive the correct plate thickness, based on the scantling, define the type of connection for detailing based on whether the panel encloses a water-tight compartment, etc. The basic design is used to produce a weight estimate, both an overall estimate and an estimate for each section. Applying the block schema on top of the design provides preliminary report by section.

As the design progresses, information on how the panels and other major structural parts are to be assembled can be embedded within the design. This information is taken into account when the block split is performed. The blocks will contain a starting hierarchy for different subassemblies (Interim products see Figure 7), based on the defined rules set.

Yards can define their own rules to be used when organizing the parts. These rules can be catalogued and re-used as part of the action flow in the detailing phase. During the basic design, where the overall panels and stiffening were defined, logical connections are captured wherever possible. Where automatic connection definition is not possible, connections can be defined manually. This logical connection information is maintained in the data that results after the structural block is split.

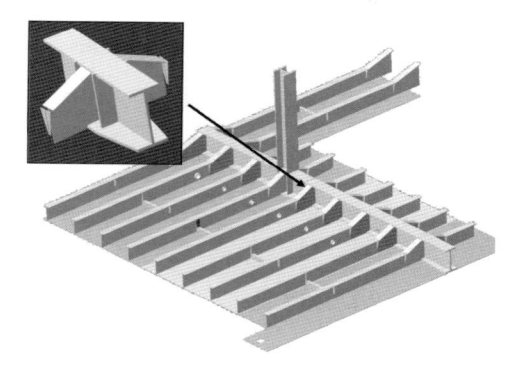

Fig. 8

By utilizing the knowledge engine in the design tool, rules are defined for realizing a given connection (see Figure 8). In cases where the connection detailing is unambiguous, detailing can be automatically realized by the software. During the realization of a connection, the piece part is automatically assigned to the right location in the interim product to which it belongs, from an assembly point of view, again using the defined rules.

As the shipbuilding industry started with very few systems, if any, it is natural that the ship hull structure was the first discipline to adopt a PLM approach with close integration between design and manufacturing. Nevertheless the same design progression is supported for the systems, outfitting and electrical disciplines.

Many yards follow the tradition of "schematic diagramming," defining systems drawn on top of the original general arrangement drawings. This practice can be supported in the solution and can be further used to automatically deliver the basic layout of major equipment. Using information carried by the logical view of the equipment object (the 2D schematic symbol), and the "in scale" position on the active deck level, automatic space reservations can be generated, as well as auto-routed fluid systems, based on the diagrams' defined network. This can be used, for example, to derive early bills of material for pipe length. The generated layout is then modified to solve the obstacles, which can only be seen in the 3D design when combined with the basic design of the hull structure.

To accommodate flexibility in the design progression the PLM Shipbuilding Solution allows the user to size and manage the data in the most optimized way. At the start of engineering, it is important to work with all of the nearby systems of the ship in context. This helps the designer to deliver the most optimized layout.

Conclusions

The technologies discussed are not visions or statements of direction, but are, in fact, capabilities in use today in shipbuilding, offshore and aerospace industries. Mid-tier shipyards and other similar enterprises can investigate PLM and the benefits of 3D-based applications for the marine industry and develop strategies to address the business challenges that they face in an incremental fashion. Hopefully, the following conclusions can be reached:

- Problems of insufficient process modeling and production planning can be addressed by 3D-enabled DELMIA production planning and manufacturing simulation.
- The need for more outsourcing to augment capacity can be enabled by use of a Global Collaborative Environment and the use of ENOVIA to manage change and maintain the product configuration.
- Corrective man-hours at each assembly stage can be reduced through the use of CATIA for 3D Design, Interference checking, accurate and more detailed planning and the use of thorough 3D work packages
- Difficulties in bringing skilled labor up to speed in the use of design standards and construction practices for complex ship and offshore products can be alleviated by embedding standards and rules in CATIA application execution, developing more detailed work packages including 3D, and the use of simulations to help understand the assembly process.
- Major rework and manual checking in integrating subassemblies and other sub-products coming from outside resources can be minimized by the higher accuracy from 3D models with more attribute information available and the use of collaborative capabilities.
- Collaborative capabilities can also be used to accelerate communications and make more informed decisions along with customers in design reviews
- ENOVIA change management and the tight integration between CATIA and ENOVIA can make the processes of maintaining an accurate/current representation of the ship configuration and follow-on configurations (hull effectivity of changes) more automatic.

All of these potential improvements can go straight to the bottom line of a mid-tier shipyard. Overall labor and rework costs can diminish while the ability to maintain cost and schedule targets is enhanced. The return on investment for implementing an enterprise PLM strategy has been proven time and again by the world's best companies. We can see that in the case of Yantai Raffles, the effect of PLM has been transformational – allowing this young company to expand rapidly with an innovative new product in a global marketplace.

References

First Marine International (Nov. 2006). "Capabilities Study of Mid-tier US Shipyards ", published by the Office of Naval Research (ONR) – Navy MANTECH and the Center for Naval Shipbuilding Technology (CNST)

First Marine International (2007). " Findings for the Global Shipbuilding Industrial Base Benchmarking Study – Part 2: Mid-tier Shipyards ", published by the Office of the Deputy Under Secretary of Defense for Industrial Policy (ODUSD(IP)) and the Center for Naval Shipbuilding Technology (CNST)

Major, Fredrik, Sevan Marine ASA and Gibbels, Rolf Dassault Systemes (2006), "Collaboration Aids Innovation Offshore", 2006 Global Offshore Report • www.eandpnet.com, Hart Publications, 1616 S. Voss, Suite 1000, Houston, TX 77057 USA

Popko, Ed, IBM and Barlach, Christian, Dassault Systemes (2004). "From Innovation to Reality - Managing ship process and resources for competitive advantages ", An IBM / Dassault Systèmes Thought Leadership Paper

Popko, Ed, IBM and Barlach, Christian, Dassault Systemes (2004). "Digital Manufacturing: The Virtual Shipyard ", An IBM / Dassault Systèmes Thought Leadership Paper

10th International Symposium on Practical Design of Ships and Other Floating Structures
Houston, Texas, United States of America
© 2007 American Bureau of Shipping

Habitability: Setting Criteria Fit for Humans

Clifford C. Baker, Kevin P. McSweeney, Denise B. McCafferty, and E. Johan Hendrikse, Jr.

American Bureau of Shipping
Houston, Texas, United States

Abstract

The American Bureau of Shipping (ABS) has published a series of Guides for habitability and comfort at sea that not only includes the crew and offshore habitability but also passenger comfort (ABS, 2001 and 2002). The Guides represent a significant step forward in the development of classification standards that will help improve maritime safety by reducing crew fatigue. One aspect of the Guides development process refers to activities to verify and validate the content of the Guides in terms of (1) criteria imposed, (2) data collection processes and methods, and (3) interpretation of the findings important to rendering decisions to grant habitability notations (a sort of declaration of likely comfort). While it has been established that the requirements in the various Guides perform well with regard to being consistent with environmental conditions noted at sea, the larger question remains as to whether or not established standards (International Organization for Standardization (ISO), Classification Societies, etc.) are suitable for promoting human comfort. This paper discusses:

- the current criteria and guidance,
- experience gathered from validating those criteria aboard vessels and offshore structures,
- assessment of the validity and the utility of the criteria to facilitate comfort.

The paper later focuses on the human experience of vibration, human performance, and comfort.

Keywords

Ergonomics; Whole-body vibration; Noise; Temperature; Humidity; Task lighting; Habitability; Mariner comfort; Human fatigue management.

Introduction

The ABS Habitability Guides are provided to help improve maritime safety by reducing crew fatigue facilitating crew performance and enhancing the quality of life at sea. One aspect of the Guide's development process involves activities to verify and validate the content of the Guides in terms of (1) criteria stated, (2) data collection processes and methods, and (3) interpretation of findings in rendering decisions to grant habitability notations. In the process of this verification and validation activity, ABS representatives have visited numerous vessels and offshore structures to measure the accommodations and the ambient environmental characteristics of the crews' working and living spaces. The ambient environmental characteristics measured are human whole-body vibration (WBV), noise, indoor climate, and lighting. The objectives of validation trials were to:

- Measure the ambient environmental conditions on-board using the procedures and guidance provided in the Guides

- Evaluate the measurement procedures and methods as expressed in the Guide

- Identify any difficulty in executing measurement procedures and recommend improvements for future revisions of the Guide

- Validate criteria contained within the Guide

- Provide an indication to the owners/operators of the structures visited of the level of compliance with the requirements of the Guides.

Guides currently offering notations for compliance exist for passenger comfort and crew habitability on ships and offshore installations. The current Guides are not specific to any particular vessel size.

Criteria and requirements for all sections in the Guides were culled from a wide range of industry and international standards. Weight and preference were applied to standards and guidance documents specifically related to maritime applications. Every requirement in each Guide has a source in industry or international standards.

In the course of assessment and validation, accommodations checklists were applied and direct measurements carried out for each environmental requirement contained in the ABS Guides. Measurements were carried out on passenger ferries, tankers, Mobile Offshore Drilling Units (MODUs), and offshore crew boats. With a view to expanding the applicability of the Guides, measurements have recently been taken aboard offshore supply vessels (OSVs), crew boats, and yachts (McSweeney and Craig, 2007; Baker, 2007; McSweeney and Craig, 2003; McSweeney and Baker 2004).

Measurement data collected was then compared to the criteria contained in the various Guides. The following are summaries of the findings for accommodations and for each environmental characteristic.

Accommodations

One of the more influential factors for supporting human performance and reducing human error is suitable facility design. The quality of the accommodations where the vessel's crew sleep, eat and relax will influence job performance. It will also influence each individual's overall sense of comfort and well-being. Suitable facility design should be targeted to support reliable seafarer performance and comfort (ILO, 1970; McCafferty, et.al., 2000).

Based on vessel visits and the conduct of accommodations assessments using the Guides, vessel accommodations are generally achievable and suitable to facilitate comfort, sleep, and mariner provisions. It was noted that available space considerations for smaller vessels may require some of the size/space related accommodations criteria to be modified.

Indoor Climate

Measurements of the vessels' thermal environments generally met the Guide's criteria related to temperature and humidity. In no case, however, were vessels visited under extreme thermal conditions.

For all vessels and installations visited, it was deemed that the indoor climate criteria and methodologies within each Guide are reasonable and achievable.

Lighting

Deviations from the Guide's lighting criteria were identified in all vessels visited, and noncompliances occurred on a space-by-space basis. Some deviations were the result of the crew intentionally removing elements from the lighting fixtures, or by not turning on all the lights in that space, due to glare or personal preference. In other cases, inadequate light levels were evident as a result of design, for example; deviations in some galleys were attributed to the design of galley lighting fixtures, placement, and light emitted.

For all vessels and offshore installations visited, it was deemed that the criteria and methodologies within each Guide are reasonable and achievable. Some minor modifications to lighting criteria are being considered based on additional guidance recently published (NORSOK, 2004, ISO 8998, 2005).

Based on visits to Offshore Supply Vessels (OSVs), lighting criteria were added related to OSV deck and cargo handling areas.

Noise

Numerous exceptions from the criteria in the Guides were noted on all vessels visited. Generally, the magnitude of these exceptions was only at a few decibels. There were, however, cases of large deviations. A main contributor to noise levels leading to exceeding criteria tended to be ventilation system design at the point of ducting into a space.

For all vessels and offshore installations visited, it was deemed that the criteria and methodologies within each Guide are generally achievable. However, recommendations from the International Maritime Organization (IMO) are being reviewed, and the noise criteria in each Guide are under reconsideration. The IMO recommendations for noise are slightly inconsistent from those required within the existing ABS Guides, and the ABS Guides will be selectively modified according to IMO guidance (IMO, 1981).

Whole-Body Vibration

Measurements taken on large vessels showed vibration levels in manned crew spaces were generally within the limits stated in the Guides. Most of the required sea and operating conditions in the Guide for the measurement of human whole-body vibration were met with the exception of typical Sea State levels for floating structures on a MODU visit.

While exceptions to the ABS criteria were found for noise, lighting, and indoor climate, these generally were not significant departures and many cases seemed potentially remediable. With respect to whole-body vibration, the larger vessels visited were generally found to meet the ABS requirements for human whole-body vibration. For smaller vessels (OSVs, crew vessels), there was a reduced level of compliance with vibration criteria.

There is also some disagreement within the ergonomics community as to what constitutes a suitable measurement of human comfort and exposure to human whole-body vibration (WBV). One contentious area is the selection of the frequency weightings to be used to compute a value of human WBV experience and exposure.

Given the above, the remainder of this paper discusses human performance and comfort in the presence of vibration and motion.

What are Comfortable and Tolerable Levels of Vibration?

Vibration and Human Expectations

Two significant factors that influence comfort in the presence of vibration are individual differences and expectations. To illustrate individual differences, the levels of tolerable or comfortable vibration to a ten year old will be much different compared to that of a senior citizen. Similarly, tolerances will vary among normally healthy 30 year-olds. People simply have different tolerances, and in the setting of standards related to comfort, allowing any level of vibration will not be satisfactory to all people. Setting of vibration standards is usually directed at satisfying a percentage of people, and that often depends on the population of people to be satisfied. For the ABS passenger comfort Guide, the criterion is set allowing for approximately 10% of males and 15% of females to experience some level of motion sickness (females are slightly more susceptible than males) while still being compliant with the Guide. The case of paying passengers on a cruise liner requires that a significant majority of passengers deem their environment to be comfortable, and justifies more restrictive vibration criteria.

Regarding expectations, tolerance to varying levels of vibration will differ by occupation and experience to vibration through exposure. The expectations as to what level of vibration to expect on the job depend on the work environment. For example, school teachers, office workers, or hospital workers expect a level of on-the-job vibration that is lower than the expectations of those who operate machinery, aircraft, or ships. It is expected that the vibration expectations of mariners are somewhat higher than those of a general land-based population, and therefore tolerance to higher levels of vibration may be deemed acceptable. In support of this statement, there is also the consideration that mariners selected this career knowing the environmental characteristics of living aboard ship, including exposure to vibration and other environmental characteristics addressed in the comfort and habitability Guides. Still, more must be done to attract mariners to the profession.

The population of experimental subjects involved in vibration and comfort research are typically land based and diverse in occupational background. This population likely possesses an "average" tolerance to exposure to vibration in terms of perceived comfort. It is from these data that frequency weighting curves, frequency band limits, and limiting amplitudes for comfort are derived. These are good predictors of general population response to vibration in terms of comfort. These are fair predictors for mariners.

Human WBV, Comfort, and Performance

The immediate question is simply, "What are comfortable and tolerable levels of vibration?" Comfort can be defined as "a condition of ease or satisfaction of human needs," or "the freedom from pain and concern." Given this, "comfort" is not directly observable. It must be inferred by use of operational definitions and subjective assessment.

In studying comfort and in establishing its characteristics with regard to human WBV (as well a vibration of parts of the human body, such as the arms, hands, eyes, and so on), an historic approach is to assemble a group of human research participants, arm them with definitions of comfort and discomfort (a "semantic scale"), expose them to different levels of vibrations of differing frequencies and amplitudes, and then ask each to rate each level. A sample semantic scale for vibration comfort/discomfort follows:

- Very unpleasant
- Unpleasant
- Mildly unpleasant
- Not unpleasant
- Just Noticeable
- Not Noticeable

A participant would rate each vibration exposure according to the scale provided. After making subjective judgments, norms are identified when, for example, half of the participants state that a particular level of vibration is comfortable vs. an adjacent level.

Where there is a high consistency of responding to a particular frequency, for example, where all the participants respond in just about the same way (as, for example "Unpleasant"), it can be stated that the participants are sensitive to that frequency. Where there is consistency at a frequency (for many levels of amplitude) that is "Just Noticeable" or "Not noticeable," then it can be stated that the subjects are not susceptible to those frequencies of vibration. From this, distributions of comfort susceptibility can be derived and used in the development of human WBV frequency weighting distributions. Analytic approaches that examine part-body vibrations (e.g., hand, arm, etc.) can also be used when vibration and their resonances are demonstrated to be moving and torsioning those body parts (Griffin, 1990, 1997).

Vibrations in the frequency range of 0.5 Hz to 80 Hz have significant comfort and performance effects on the human body. Table 1 presents a sample of the results of several of these vibration and comfort research studies. Table 2 provides examples of the effects of several levels of body discomfort and vibration frequency. Table 3 identifies some human performance issues related to exposure to vibration.

When considering human WBV, every organ or segment of a body has a resonant frequency such that when an arm (for example) is vibrated at its resonance frequency, the vibration is amplified – sometimes to as much as four times the source, or input, vibration level (Griffin, 1990). Figure 1 presents the susceptibility of various body parts with regard to vibration frequency in terms of both human performance (ability to reliably do productive work) and human comfort.

In the ABS Guides for Habitability and Comfort, the collective vibration tolerances are considered in establishing limits for human WBV.

Low Frequency Vibration and Motion Sickness

Low frequency vibration, usually involving the vertical (z) axis, is associated with motion sickness at sea (Lawther and Griffin, 1986, 1988a, 1988b). Motion sickness is characterized by feelings of any combination of nausea, dizziness, pallor, cold sweats, vomiting, headache, salivation, and fatigue. In extreme cases, vertigo can be experienced.

The mechanism of motion sickness is a disassociation of the senses integrated to form a perception of motion and body orientation. In other words, the primary sense of balance and orientation (formed mainly in the inner ear) and other senses, principally vision, are in "disagreement" as to body orientation, acceleration, and the direction of gravity. A main source of these disparate sensory reports (termed "vection") resulted from being on a moving or unstable platform.

Table 1: Comparison of Results from Four Experiments using Semantic Scales
(Adapted from Griffin, 1990)

Study	Scale	Mean magnitude (m/sec² RMS)	Situation
Fothergill (1972)	• Very unpleasant • Unpleasant • Mildly unpleasant • Not unpleasant • Noticeable	2.5 1.7 1.1 0.7 0.3	Seated subjects Magnitudes of 8 Hz sinusoidal vibration
Jones and Saunders (1974)	• Very unpleasant • Very uncomfortable • Uncomfortable • Mean threshold of vibration discomfort • Not uncomfortable	3.7 2.2 1.2 0.7 0.33	Seated subjects Magnitudes of 10 Hz sinusoidal vibration
Oborne and Clarke (1974)	• Very uncomfortable • Uncomfortable • Fairly uncomfortable • [to] Fairly comfortable • Comfortable • Very comfortable	More than 2.3 1.2 to 2.3 0.5 to 1.2 0.5 to 1.2 0.23 to 0.5 Less than 0.23	Standing subjects Magnitudes of 10 Hz sinusoidal vibration
Fothergill and Griffin (1977c)	• Very uncomfortable • Uncomfortable • Mildly uncomfortable • Noticeable, but not uncomfortable	2.7 1.8 1.1 0.4	Seated subjects Magnitudes of 10 Hz sinusoidal vibration

Table 2: Discomfort complaints and Vibration Frequency (Hz).

2.5 to 5	• Neck pain • Back pain
4 to 8	• General feeling of discomfort • Influences on breathing • Abdominal pains • Muscle contractions
5 to 7	• Chest pains
6 to 8	• Lower jaw symptoms
10 to 18	• Urge to urinate
12 to 16	• Lump in the throat
13 to 20+	• Head symptoms • Sensory • Increased muscle tone

Table 3: Human Performance and Vibration Frequency (Hz)

0.1 Hz to 0.5 Hz	• Motion sickness • Motion Induced Instability • Decreased coordination • Fatigue
0.5 Hz to 15 Hz	• Motion Induced Instability • Decreased coordination • Fatigue • Abdominal discomfort
15 Hz to 25 Hz	• Motion Induced Instability • Much discomfort • Fatigue • Difficult hand/arm control • Vibrato, undulating speech
25 Hz +	• Sensations and perceptions influenced • Blurred vision • Task performance decay

Sopite syndrome occurs in frequencies similar to those inducing motion sickness. Sopite syndrome is characterized by drowsiness, fatigue, difficulty in concentrating, and disturbed sleep. It seems to be a form of motion sickness without nausea.

In the general population:

- About 25% of people are generally susceptible
- Habituate (get over it) in less than a week
- Learn to habituate
- Susceptibility increased with age, up to about 10 years of age, then decreases
- A small number never habituate.

Frequencies of vertical oscillation/vibration to which people seem to be susceptible to motion sickness are in the 0.1 to 0.6 Hz range, with the middle values being the most strongly inducing of motion sickness.

Vibration Criteria and Guidance

The question remains as to what levels of human WBV and the associated characteristics of that vibration (band limitations and frequency weighting) are appropriate for marine systems.

In order to help answer the questions as to what are reasonable, comfortable, and achievable levels of WBV for mariners, a comparison was made of several requirements documents that impose limits on vibration to which humans are exposed. These include (Lewis, et al., 2007):

- ISO Standard 2631-1. Mechanical vibration and shock-evaluation of human exposure to whole-body vibration-Part 1: General requirements, 1997.
- British Standard 6841. Measurement and evaluation of human exposure to whole-body mechanical vibration and repeated shock. British Standards Institution, 1987.
- ISO Standard 6954-1984. Mechanical Vibration and Shock – Guidelines for the overall evaluation of vibration in merchant ships, 1984.
- ISO Standard 6954-2000. Mechanical vibration – Guidelines for the measurement, reporting and evaluation of vibration with regard to habitability on passenger and merchant ships, 2000.

Of these, none actually impose limits on acceptable levels of vibration. Rather, they merely present typically reported levels of human comfort as a function of human WBV level, and it is left to the users of these guidance documents to specify limits.

Translating guidance of this sort to recommended or required limits requires consideration of the environments under which vibration exposure will occur and the expectations of those exposed. As stated in ISO 2631 (1997), ". . . the reactions of various magnitudes depend on passenger expectations with regard to trip duration and the types of activities passengers expect to accomplish (e.g., reading, eating, writing, etc.)." ISO

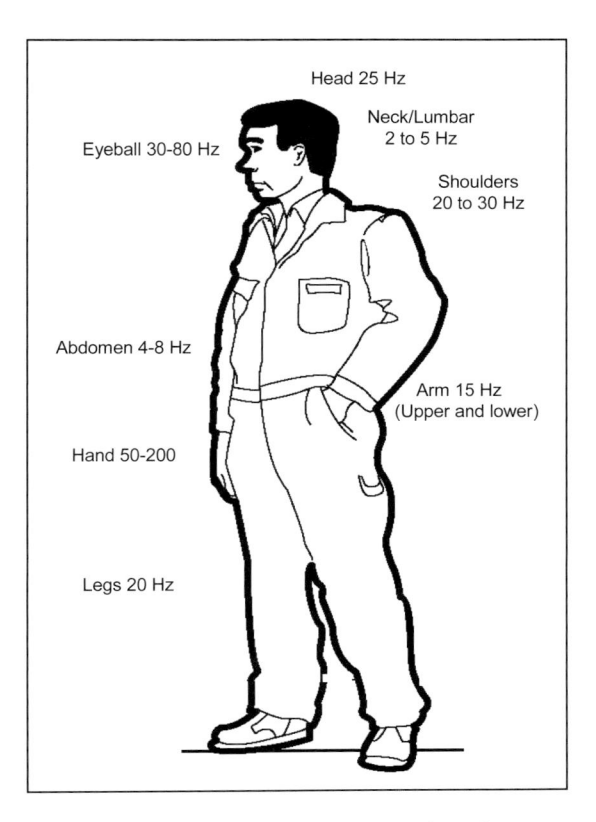

Fig. 1: Body Part Resonance as a Function of Vibration Frequency

2631 and BS 6841 present the following human WBV limits as guidance:

- Less than 0.315 m/s^2 - Not uncomfortable
- 0.315 m/s^2 to 0.63 m/s^2 - A little uncomfortable
- 0.5 m/s^2 to 1.0 m/s^2 - Fairly uncomfortable
- 1.25 m/s^2 to 2.5 m/s^2 - Very uncomfortable
- Greater than 2.0 m/s^2 - Extremely uncomfortable

ISO 6954 (2000) is consistent with ISO 2631 (1997) regarding provision of guidance rather than prescribing limits. According to ISO 6954 (2000): "It is recommended that the classification to be applied to the various areas of a vessel be agreed between the interested parties (e.g., shipbuilder and vessel owner), prior to any assessment of the habitability." Three levels of human WBV guidance are provided, for passengers, crew, and work areas, in the frequency range of 1 Hz to 80 Hz, as follows:

	Values above which adverse comments are probable	Values below which adverse comments are not probable
Passenger:	0.143 m/s^2	0.0715 m/s^2
Crew:	0.214 m/s^2	0.107 m/s^2
Work Area:	0.286 m/s^2	0.143 m/s^2

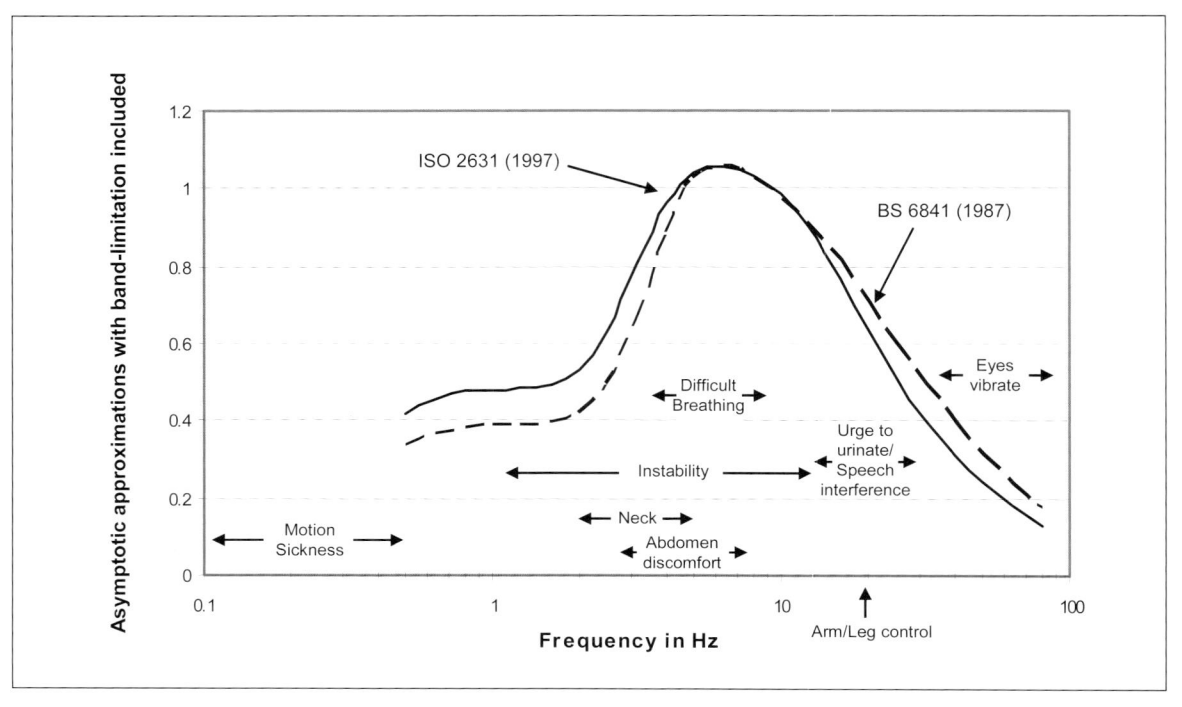

Fig. 2: Relative Frequency Weighting Distributions for ISO 2631 and British Standard 6841.

Comparing this guidance to the empirical data in Table 1, the guidance (if conformed to) would provide a very comfortable WBV environment. In fact, 0.143 m/s² is very near the threshold of perception, and some people would not sense any WBV.

Figure 2 presents the relative frequency weighting distributions for ISO Standard 2631 and British Standard 6841. Annotated on this figure are the associated frequencies of human WBV where discomfort or performance degradations are noted. Compelling (but by no means by accident) in this figure are the coincidences of highly valued/weighted frequencies with associated human susceptibility: the more significant frequencies/spectra (significant to comfort and performance) are more heavily weighted.

Table 4 presents a comparison of the required or recommended levels of vibration over which mariners should not be exposed based on four different sources of recommendations or requirements: ABS habitability and comfort guides (2001), ISO Standard 6954 (2000), ISO Standard 6954 (1984), and ISO Standard 2631:1997.

The values in Table 4 are expressed at five different frequencies to allow a comparison of recommendations/requirements among those documents that express acceleration as an RMS velocity vs. as observed peak values. Comparisons are presented as velocities.

Comparison of the values in Table 4 with Tables 1 through 3 reveals that all sources of recommended vibration limits for human exposure provide for a level of human comfort and performance and are also consistent with human research attempting to establish vibration comfort limits.

With regard to vibration band limitations, varying requirements are as follows.

- ISO 6954 (1984): 1 to 100 Hz
- ISO 6954 (2000): 1 to 80 Hz
- BS 6841 WBV (1987): 0.5 to 80 Hz
- BS 6841 Motion Sickness (1987): 0.1 to 0.5 Hz
- ISO 2631: Motion Sickness (1987): 0.1 to 0.5 Hz

Given the consideration of contiguous band limitations for WBV and motion sickness of BS 6841, ABS resolved to base habitability and comfort WBV requirements on those weighting distributions, band limitations, and WBV guidance of BS 6841. These are consistent with regard to weighting of ISO 6954 (which states "the results of each measurement shall be the overall frequency-weighted r.m.s. value as defined for acceleration in ISO 2631-1: 1997.")

Table 5 presents a summary of the ABS limiting vibration requirements. Note that there are impending notations in the table suitable for smaller ships and vessels. This is in acknowledgment of the measured vibration characteristics of these vessels.

The limiting values in Table 5 are based on the recommendations of BS 6841 since it provides for a continuous measurement of vibration (WBV and Motion sickness related) from 0.1 Hz to 80 Hz – the frequencies of interest in terms of human comfort and performance.

Table 4: Comparison of the required or recommended levels of vibration over which mariners should not be exposed

Source	Application	Application area	Criterion	Overall weighted	1 Hz	5 Hz	10 Hz	20 Hz	30 Hz	Comments
American Bureau of Shipping (2001)	Passenger & cargo vessels	Crew Performance (**HAB**)	Maximum acceptable levels (z-axis)	0.400	1.000	0.400	0.400	0.500	0.750	Equivalent RMS acceleration magnitudes assuming all the energy occurs at a single frequency.
		Crew Comfort (**HAB+**)		0.315	0.788	0.315	0.315	0.394	0.591	
	Passenger vessels	Passenger Comfort (**COMF**)	Maximum acceptable levels (z-axis)	0.315	0.788	0.315	0.315	0.394	0.591	
		Optimum Comfort (**COMF+**)		0.200	0.500	0.200	0.200	0.250	0.375	
ISO 6954:2000	Merchant ships	Working Areas, Crew Accommodation, Passenger Cabins	Adverse comments probable (worst axis)	0.343	0.381	0.579	1.044	1.546	0.343	Weighting based on BS 6841 for ABS Guides and Appendix A of ISO 6954: 2000.
				0.257	0.285	0.433	0.781	1.157	0.257	Weighting scale for 30 HZ calculated per ISO 8041:2005 using W_m weighting.
				0.172	0.191	0.289	0.522	0.773	0.172	
		Working Areas, Crew Accommodation, Passenger Cabins	Adverse comments not probable (worst axis)	0.172	0.191	0.289	0.522	0.773	0.172	
				0.128	0.143	0.217	0.391	0.578	0.128	
				0.086	0.096	0.146	0.263	0.389	0.086	
ISO 6954:1984	Merchant ships	All Areas	Adverse comments probable	n/a	0.112	0.112	0.224	0.448	0.672	Equivalent RMS acceleration calculated from (peak acceleration)/(1.8*1.4142) as suggested in ISO 6954:1984.
			Adverse comments not probable (worst axis)		0.049	0.049	0.099	0.198	0.297	Weighting based on ISO 6954:1984
ISO 2631:1997	General	All Areas	Not uncomfortable	< 0.315	0.312	0.77	1.49	3.15	4.77	Highest values used in each range to compute unweighted single frequency magnitude.
			A little uncomfortable	0.315 to 0.63	0.623	1.54	2.97	6.30	9.54	
			Fairly uncomfortable	0.5 to 1.0	0.989	2.44	4.72	10.0	15.2	Frequency weighting per ISO 2631 using W_d scale.
			Uncomfortable	0.8 to 1.6	1.583	3.91	7.57	16.0	24.2	
			Very uncomfortable	1.25 to 2.5	2.473	6.11	11.8	25.0	37.9	
			Extremely uncomfortable	Over 2.0	1.987	4.89	9.43	20.0	30.3	

COMF+ is a higher level of passenger Comfort Notation that includes restrictions on low frequency oscillation/vibration associated with motion sickness, and also requires a lower acceptable level of human WBV. HAB+ is a higher Comfort Notation that includes measurements of low frequency oscillations associated with motion sickness.

Table 5: ABS Vibration Requirements (m/s²)

Ship and Offshore **HAB** notation:	0.4
Ship and Offshore **HAB+** notation:	0.315
Passenger **COMF**	0.315
Passenger **COMF+**	0.20
Passenger **COMF+** (MSDV)	30 m/s$^{1.5}$
OSV HAB Notation (Pending)	0.5
OSV HAB+ Notation (Pending)	0.4
Yacht **COMF(Y)** and **COMF(Y) +** (Pending)	TBD
Other Work Boats and Vessels	TBD

Notes:

Motion Sickness Dose Value (MSDv) units are exposure units, expressed as m/s$^{1.5}$ which is acceleration over time of exposure.

No motion sickness criteria for **HAB.**

Motion sickness (Passenger **COMF+**) 0.1 to 0.5 Hz.

0.5 to 80 Hz for **COMF** and **HAB** notations

Frequency weightings in accordance with BS 6841.

HAB+ Notation directed and crew comfort and human (job) performance.

HAB Notation directed at human (job) performance.

The acceptable levels of human WBV from Table 5 are based on those discussed in both BS 6841 and ISO 2631 as they influence the factors of human comfort and performance. Given that the guidance allows for flexibility, depending on the environment and user expectations, and that the weighting distributions are more or less coincident, the ABS criteria are consistent with the intent of both documents.

Further, comparing the ABS requirements with the data presented in Table 1, the ABS **HAB** and **HAB+** requirements are squarely within the bounds of "not uncomfortable" according to all standards and the research efforts presented by Griffin. Noting those research efforts, perceived discomfort is observed at around 0.7 meter/second². The ABS requirements for a vessel or offshore **HAB** notation of less than 0.4 meter/second² is well under this boundary.

Pending requirements for smaller craft (OSVs, yachts) are under review and development. The human WBV requirements to be imposed (if any) will continue to be consistent with the research literature related to comfort and performance, and within the intent and guidance of the British, ISO, and related standards.

Discussion and Conclusion

Based on review of human tolerances to potential environmental stressors, a broad range of environmental guidance, requirements, and criteria related to human comfort and performance, and recognition of the special environment the sea imposes on humans and machines, ABS has developed a series of habitability criteria for the marine industry. Validation of requirements related to temperature, humidity, noise, lighting, human WBV and motion sickness revealed that the only contentious and difficult requirement is related to human vibration. Requirements for the areas of noise vibration and atmospherics were found to be sound, pragmatic, and achievable with little modification.

Human WBV levels observed on vessels and offshore structures were quite variable, and in most cases bordered the ABS requirements. Larger vessels, ferries, and offshore structures generally met the human WBV requirements of the Guides, however; smaller craft such as OSVs and crew boats did not fare as well, and many would not be considered for a habitability notation.

Review of studies of human perception of comfort in the presence of whole-body vibration revealed significant latitude between the recommendations of current vibration standards specific to the maritime industry and human tolerance to vibration. Furthermore, considering the different expectations as to acceptable levels of vibration comfort, it is anticipated that the expectations of mariners will be quite different from that of land-based occupations.

With regard to human whole-body vibration, the objectives of the ABS Habitability and Comfort Guides have been to specify levels of vibration that afford crew and passenger comfort while also facilitating job performance (or better put, limiting interference with job performance due to the presence of vibration), while recognizing the constraints imposed by working on an unstable platform at sea.

Direct measurement of vibration aboard a number of vessels has helped to characterize the typical, and attainable, vibration environment. Happily, the levels of human whole-body vibration that are reported as comfortable are within these levels. To be sure, some vibration will be sensed and perceived, but not typically to the level of distraction or discomfort.

The issues related to vessel motion and experiences of motion sickness are under review and assessment.

It is considered that the ABS standards afford a more than adequate level of comfort and human performance without imposing an excessively strident demand on vessel design.

References

American Bureau of Shipping. (2001). *Guide for Passenger Comfort on Ships*. Houston, TX: Author.

American Bureau of Shipping. (2002). *ABS Guide to Crew Habitability on Offshore Installations.* Houston, TX: Author.

American Bureau of Shipping. *Rules for Building and Classing Steel Vessels Under 90 meters in Length*. Houston, TX: Author.

Baker, C.C. (2007). Comfort / Habitability Measurements of Offshore Supply Vessels. American Bureau of Shipping

British Standards Institution. (1987). *Guide to measurement and evaluation of human exposure to whole-body mechanical vibration and repeated shock* (BS 6841: 1987). London: Author.

Griffin M.J, in Salvendy (ed.), 1997. *Handbook of human Factors and Ergonomics*. Chapter 25, Vibration and Motion. New York: John Wiley and Sons.

Griffin M.J. (1990). *Handbook of human vibration*. London: Academic Press.

IMO Resolution A.468 (XII), Code on Noise Levels on Board Ships, 19 November 1981.

International Labor Office. (1970). *Accommodation of Crews (Supplementary Provisions Convention) (*Convention C133). Geneva: Author.

ISO 2631-1. (1997). *Mechanical vibration and shock – Evaluation of human exposure to whole body vibration* (ISO 2631-1: 1997, Part 1: General Requirements). Geneva: Author.

ISO 6954. (1984). Mechanical vibration and Shock – Guidelines for the overall evaluation of vibration in merchant ships. Geneva: Author.

ISO 6954. (2000). Mechanical vibration – Guidelines for the measurement, reporting and evaluation of vibration with regard to habitability on passenger and merchant ships. Geneva: Author.

ISO 8998. (2005). Lighting of Indoor Work Places. Geneva: Author.

Lawther, A. and Griffin, M. J. (1986). The Motion of A Ship at Sea and the Consequent Motion Sickness Amongst Passengers. *Ergonomics,* 29, 535-552.

Lawther, A. and Griffin, M. J. (1988a). *A survey of the Occurrence of Motion Sickness Amongst Passengers at Sea.* Aviation, Space, and Environmental Medicine. 59 Number 5. 399-406.

Lawther, A. and Griffin, M. J. (1988b). Motion Sickness and Motion Characteristics of Vessels at Sea. *Ergonomics,* 31, 1373-1394.

Lewis, C., Lawton, B., and Griffin, M. (2007). *Suggestions for Modification of ABS Guides for Crew Habitability, for Application to Offshore Supply Vessels.* University of Southampton.

McCafferty, D., McSweeney, K., Hendrikse, J., and McKinney (2000). *Habitability and Human Performance.* The Human Factors in Ship Design and Operation 2000 Proceedings. RINA International Conference. London.

McSweeney, K. and Craig, B., (2003). Assessment of the Habitability and Ambient Environmental Characteristics of the Genesis and Typhoon Offshore Installations - American Bureau of Shipping, Houston, TX

McSweeney, K. and Craig, B., (2007). OSV Habitability Measurements on the L&M Chermamie Botruc #39 - American Bureau of Shipping, Houston, TX

McSweeney, K., and Baker, C.C. (2004). Comfort / Habitability Measurements of British Columbia Ferries. American Bureau of Shipping.

NORSOK-002. (2004) Working environment (Rev. 4)

Multicriterion Scantling Optimization of the Midship Section of a Passenger Vessel Considering IACS Requirements

T. Richir [1) 2)], J.-D. Caprace [1) 3)], N. Losseau [1) 2)], M. Bay [4)],
M. G. Parsons [5)], S. Patay [6)] and P. Rigo [1) 3)]

[1)] ANAST, University of Liege, Belgium
[2)] Fund for Training in Research in Industry and Agriculture of Belgium (F.R.I.A.)
[3)] National Fund of Scientific Research of Belgium (F.N.R.S.)
[4)] HEC Management School, University of Liege, Belgium
[5)] NA&ME, University of Michigan, USA
[6)] AKER YARDS SA, France

Abstract

In the scantling design of a passenger ship, minimum production cost, minimum weight and maximum moment of inertia (stiffness) are conflicting objectives. For that purpose, recent improvements were made to the LBR-5 software (French acronym of "Stiffened Panels Software", version 5.0) to optimize the scantling of ship sections by considering production cost, weight and moment of inertia in the optimization objective function. Moreover, IACS requirements regarding bending, shearing and buckling strength are currently available in LBR-5. Until now, only raw scantling optimizations were performed with LBR-5. Thanks to new developments using heuristics, it is now possible to realize discrete optimization so that a standardized and "ready to use" set of optimum scantlings can be obtained.

Keywords

Multicriterion optimization; Scantling design; IACS requirements; Passenger vessel; LBR-5 software.

Introduction

Scantling design involves multiple conflicting criteria, objectives or goals. It is, thus, a multicriterion optimization problem. The traditional approach to solve this type of problem is to use a weighted-sum of the multiple criteria as the optimization objective function. The conventional scalar numerical optimization methods can then be used to solve the problem. In this paper, the authors employed the LBR-5 software which uses the optimization algorithm CONLIN, based on convex linearization and a dual approach (Fleury, 1989; Rigo and Fleury, 2001). The most common definition of the multicriterion optimum is the Pareto front, which results in a set of solutions. In a design situation, one specific solution must be sought for implementation. Useful specific compromise solutions can then be defined, e.g. weighted sum, min-max and nearest to the utopian solutions.

The longitudinal scantlings of the midship section of a passenger ship were optimized with LBR-5. This section is characterized by 14 decks, a 40 m breadth and a 45 m height. IACS common structural requirements were imposed, while production cost and moment of inertia were both considered in the objective function. A maximum weight constraint was applied. The entire Pareto front was calculated, and the scantlings of the equal weights nearest to the utopian solution are shown in this paper.

Overview of Multicriterion Optimization

The following overview is adapted directly from Parsons and Scott (2004).

Single Criterion Problem

The single criterion optimization problem is usually formulated as:

$$\min_x F(x) = F_1(x), \qquad x = [x_1, x_2, ..., x_N]^T$$

subject to the equality and inequality constraints

$$h_i(x) = 0, i = 1, ..., I$$
$$g_j(x) \geq 0, j = 1, ..., J \qquad (1)$$

where there is a single optimization criterion or objective function $F_1(x)$ that depends on the N unknown design independent variables in the vector x. For a practical engineering solution, the problem is usually subject to I equality constraints and J inequality constraints $h_i(x)$ and $g_j(x)$, respectively, that also depend on the design variables in the vector x. The minimization form is general because a maximization problem can be solved by minimizing the negative or the inverse of the cost function.

Multicriterion Optimization

The multicriterion optimization problem involves K > 1 criteria and can be formulated as:

$$\min_x F(x) = [F_1(x), F_2(x), \ldots, F_K(x)],$$

$$x = [x_1, x_2, \ldots, x_N]^T$$

subject to equality and inequality constraints

$$h_i(x) = 0, i = 1, \ldots, I$$
$$g_j(x) \geq 0, j = 1, \ldots, J \quad (2)$$

where there are now K multiple optimization criteria $F_1(x)$ through $F_K(x)$ and each depends on the N unknown design variables in the vector x. The overall objective function F is now a vector. In general, this problem has no single solution due to conflicts that exist among the K criteria.

Pareto Optimum Front

When there are multiple conflicting criteria present, the most common definition of an optimum is Pareto optimality. This term was first articulated by the Italian-French economist V. Pareto in 1906. Also referred to today as Edgeworth-Pareto optimality: *A solution is Pareto optimal if it satisfies the constraints and is such that no criterion can be further improved without causing at least one of the other criteria to decline.* Note that this emphasizes the conflicting or competitive interaction among the criteria. These definitions typically result in a set of optimal solutions rather than a single unique solution. A design team, of course, typically seeks a single result that can be implemented in the design. This result should be an effective compromise or trade-off among the conflicting criteria. Often this result can be reached by considering factors not able to be included in the optimization model.

Global Criterion Optima

As noted, engineering design requires a specific result for implementation, not a set of solutions as provided by the Pareto optimal set. The more intuitive ways to achieve an effective compromise among competing criteria are, among others, the weighted sum, the min-max and the nearest to the utopian solutions.

These solutions can be found through the global criteria:

$$P[F_k(x)] = \left\{ \sum_{k=1}^{K} \left[w_k \left| (F_k(x) - F_k^0) / F_k^0 \right| \right]^\rho \right\}^{1/\rho},$$

$$\sum_{k=1}^{K} w_k = 1 \quad (3)$$

where F_k^0 is the value of the criterion F_k obtained when that criterion is the single criterion used in the optimization - the best that can be achieved with that criterion considered alone. The scalar preference function $P[F_k(x)]$ replaces $F(x)$ in Eq. 1 for numerical solution.

The weighted sum solution results from Eq. 3 when $\rho = 1$, whereas the nearest to the utopian solution results when $\rho = 2$ and the min-max solution when $\rho = \infty$. The numerical implementation for the min-max solution uses the equivalent of Eq. 3 with $\rho = \infty$,

$$P[F_k(x)] = \max_k \left[w_k \left| (F_k(x) - F_k^0) / F_k^0 \right| \right] \quad (4)$$

Moreover, a solution could be obtained for a number of values of ρ and then the design team could decide which solution best represents the design intent.

Mapping the Entire Pareto Front

In dealing with multicriterion problems, it is highly desirable to be able to study the entire Pareto front. This action allows the design team to consider all options that meet the Pareto optimality definition. The final design decision can then be based on the considerations modeled in the optimization formulation as well as the many additional considerations, factors, and constraints that are not included in the model. This is practical when there are two criteria, but rapidly becomes impractical, for computational time and visualization reasons when the number of criteria increases beyond two.

To map the entire Pareto front, the three following methods can be used:

- *Repeated weighted sum solutions.* If the feasible object function space is convex, weighted sum solutions can be obtained for systematically varied weights.

- *Repeated weighted min-max solutions.* If the feasible object function space does not have a slope that exceeds w_1/w_2, weighted min-max solutions can be obtained for systematically varied weights.

- *Multicriterion optimization methods.* Multicriterion implementations of Generic Algorithms (MOGA), Evolutionary Algorithms, Particle Swarm Optimization, etc. can obtain the entire Pareto front in one optimization run.

LBR-5 Software

The scantling design of ships is always defined during the earliest phases of the project. That is, the preliminary design stage or the first draft that corresponds in most cases to the offer. At this time, few parameters (dimensions) have been definitively fixed, and standard finite element modeling is often unusable, particularly for design offices and modest-sized shipyards. An optimization tool at this stage can, thus, provide precious help to designers. This is precisely the way the LBR-5 optimization software for stiffened structures was conceptualized (Rigo, 2001).

Scantling Design Variables

In LBR-5, a structure is modeled with stiffened plate elements (Fig. 1). For each element, nine design variables are available:

- Plate thickness.
- For longitudinal members (stiffeners, crossbars, longitudinals, girders, etc.),
  o web height and thickness,
  o flange width,
  o spacing between two longitudinal members.
- For transverse members (frames, transverse stiffeners, etc.),
  o web height and thickness,
  o flange width,
  o spacing between two transverse members (frames).

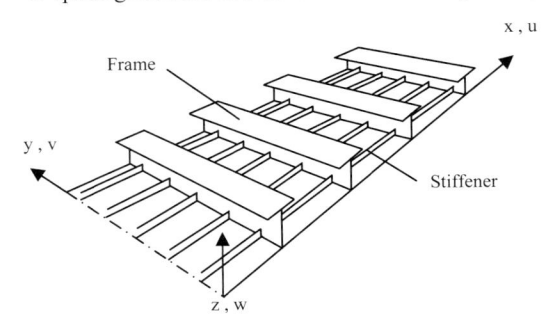

Fig. 1: LBR-5 Stiffened Plate Element

Rule-Based Structural Constraints

Structural constraints from IACS requirements and Bureau Veritas rules are now available in LBR-5. They are listed below:

- Hull girder strength (IACS requirements)
  o Bending/shear strength
    - $\sigma_a \leq 175/k$
    - $\tau_a \leq 110/k$
    with k = material factor
    σ_a = hull girder bending stress (N/mm²)
    τ_a = hull girder shear stress (N/mm²)
  o Buckling strength
    - Compressive buckling of plates
    - Shear buckling of plates
    - Compressive buckling of stiffeners
- Local strength (BV rules)
  o Stiffener bending strength

Multicriterion Optimization

Production cost, weight and moment of inertia can be used as objective function in LBR-5. They are considered simultaneously through Eq. 3 in a multicriterion problem. The Pareto Front can be mapped in LBR-5 by using the *Repeated weighted sum solutions* method described above.

Discrete Optimization

The scantling design variables are discrete by nature. The objective functions are nonlinear functions. As the objective and the constraints are nonlinear functions the scantling optimization of a ship belongs to the class of mixed-integer non linear problems (MINLP).

A heuristic is used to solve this problem (Bay et al., 2007). The method is a two-stage local search heuristic.

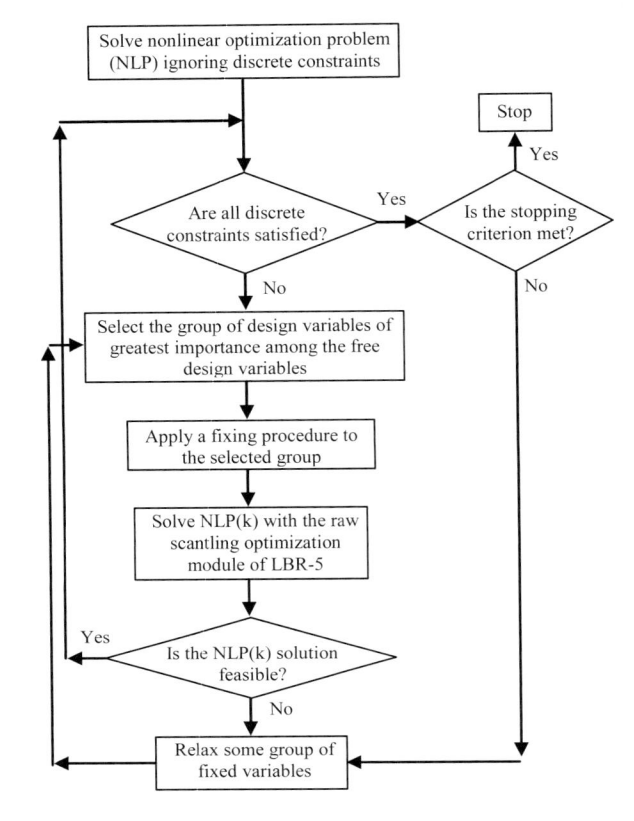

Fig. 2: Heuristic Flowchart

At a strategic level, a *dive and fix* method controls the definition of nonlinear sub-problems. The generation of the explicit sub-problems and their optimization are performed at a tactical level by using the raw scantling optimization module of LBR-5 based on CONLIN algorithm (Fig. 2).

An initial scantling is given by the designer. This solution may be feasible or not, discrete or not. Given an initial scantling the heuristic starts computing an optimal solution of the NLP problem, i.e. the problem where all discretization constraints have been removed and all the variables are free (no variable has its value rounded and fixed).

At each iteration k, the heuristic starts with the solution of the previous iteration k-1. The group of design variables (for instance, plate thickness of all stiffened panel elements) of greatest importance among the free design variables is selected and the values are fixed according to a rounding procedure. This operation leads to a NLP(k) sub-problem which is solved with the raw scantling optimization module of LBR-5. If the NLP(k) problem appears to have no feasible solution, a relax procedure is applied to free the design variables that have been fixed at the previous iteration and the algorithm moves to the next iteration. If a feasible solution for NLP(k) is obtained, the algorithm moves to the next iteration (*diving*). This iterative scheme is repeated until all discretization constraints are satisfied.

The round and the relax procedures are the core of the *dive and fix* heuristic. They act jointly to define which regions of the solution space will be explored. They control the creation of the nonlinear sub-problems NLP(k) at each iteration by defining how the values for the design variables are rounded and fixed, taking into account the results of the previous iterations.

Application

Geometry and Load Cases

The midshi section of a passenger vessel was imported into LBR-5 from Mars2000 (scantling verification software based on Bureau Veritas rules). Indeed LBR-5 allows the direct importation of Mars2000 geometry and loads. The Mars2000 model was initially prepared by Aker Yards, France. The section is characterized by 14 decks, a 40 m breadth and a 45 m height. Fig. 3 shows the imported midship section (transversal members and pillars were added manually). A total of 118 LBR-5 stiffened plate elements were used to define the model including 19 pillars. Based on structure symmetry, only the half structure was modelled.

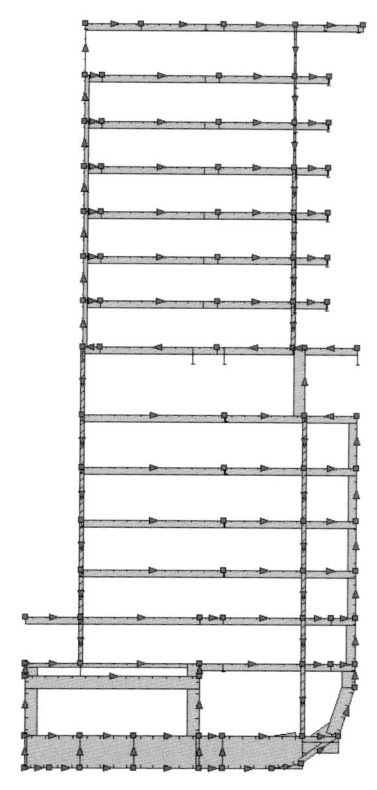

Fig. 3: LBR-5 Model of the Midship Section

Ten load cases were considered in the calculation:
- Two "IACS load cases" (hogging and sagging): still water bending plus wave bending with a probability of exceedance = 10^{-8}
- Eight "BV load cases" (hogging and sagging)
  o Load case "a": still water bending plus wave bending with a probability of exceedance = 10^{-5} plus sea pressure (scantling draft and ballast draft)
  o Load case "b": still water bending plus wave bending with a probability of exceedance = 10^{-5} plus sea pressure (scantling draft and ballast draft) plus inertial pressure

Design Variables

Five scantling design variables were activated in each LBR-5 stiffened plate element:
- Plate thickness
- For longitudinal stiffeners,
  o web height and thickness,
  o flange width,
  o spacing between two longitudinal stiffeners.

Discrete Optimization

The solution space for the discrete design variables was defined with a step of 1 mm for the thicknesses and 10 mm for the web height and flange width. The spacing remains a continuous design variable.

Objective function

Production cost and moment of inertia (stiffness) were the two objectives considered in this application. The production cost was calculated with an advanced cost module that takes into account the detailed shipyard database of Aker Yards, France. About 60 different fabrication operations are considered, covering the different construction stages, such as girders and web-frames prefabrication, plate panels assembling, blocks pre-assembling and assembling, as well as 30 types of welding and their unitary costs (Richir et al., 2007).

Constraints

In each LBR-5 stiffened plate element, structural constraints were applied according to IACS requirements and BV rules (Table 1).

Table 1: Structural Constraints

	Load case		
	"IACS"	BV "a"	BV "b"
$\sigma_a \leq 175/k$	X		
$\tau_a \leq 110/k$	X		
Compressive buckling of plates	X		
Shear buckling of plates	X		
Compressive buckling of stiffeners	X		
Local stiffener bending strength		X	X

Equality constraints were also imposed between the longitudinal stiffener spacing of any two LBR-5 stiffened plate elements that are vertically aligned.

Global constraints regarding the hull girder minimum section modulus and moment of inertia were considered. These constraints were taken from IACS requirements. A maximum weight constraint was also applied. Moreover, the structural vertical center of gravity was not permitted to rise during the optimization process to avoid stability problems.

The problem can thus be summarized as follow:

- 118 LBR-5 stiffened plate elements,
- 10 load cases,
- 383 scantling design variables,
- 4 global constraints,
- 1418 structural constraints,
- 56 equality constraints.

Pareto Front

The entire Pareto front was obtained using a process that randomly altered the weights in the weighted sum solution and solved the optimization problem for each of these problems. The resulting convex Pareto front is shown in Fig. 4. More than 200 points were calculated. To avoid large computing time only raw scantling optimizations were performed. The Pareto front was generated in about 100 minutes with a Pentium 2.40 GHz and 512 Mo of RAM desktop. The equal weights min-max and nearest to the utopian solutions are also shown in Fig. 4.

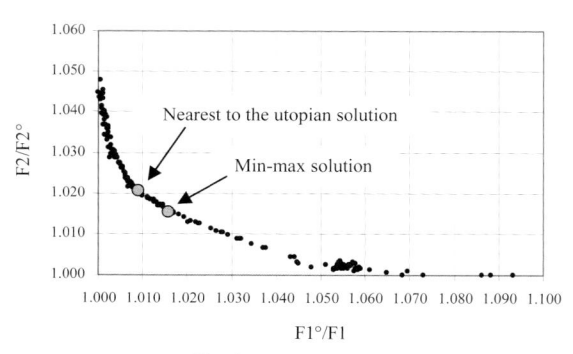

Fig. 4: Pareto Front
(F1 = Moment of Inertia and F2 = Production Cost)

Using Fig. 4, the design team is now able to choose a compromise solution from the Pareto front, by considering additional factors and constraints that are not included in the optimization problem.

Equal Weights Nearest to the Utopian Solution

The equal weights nearest to the utopian solution were also calculated by performing a discrete optimization. The cost and stiffness savings, obtained by comparison with the initial scantling, are given in Table 2.

Table 2: Cost and Stiffness Savings

	Saving (%)
Production cost	1.758
Moment of inertia (stiffness)	14.992

Note that the initial scantlings did not satisfy some structural constraints; otherwise the cost savings would have been higher. Moreover, the associated weight to the cost objective could be increased to improve the cost saving, if desired.

The scantlings of the equal weights nearest to the utopian solution are shown in Figs. 5~6. For confidentiality reasons, the scantlings are expressed in percent of change from the initial design.

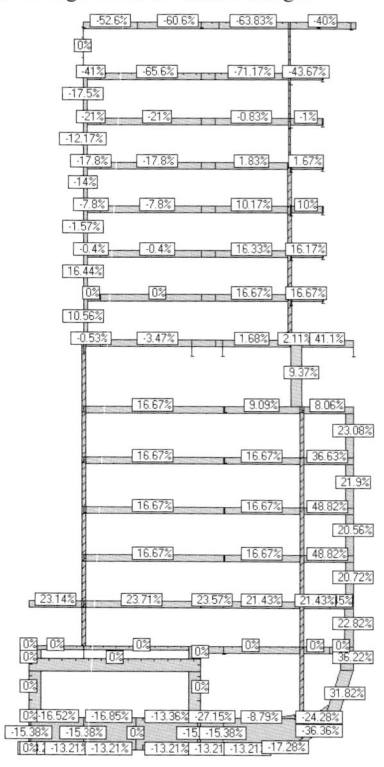

Fig. 5: Change in Plate Thickness (%)
(plus = decrease; minus = increase)

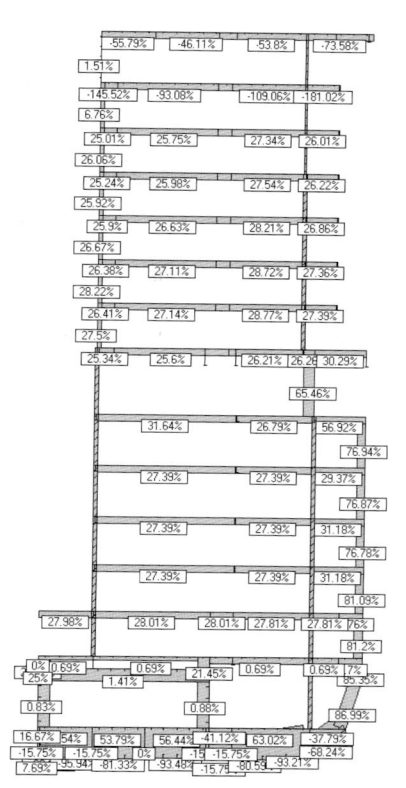

Fig. 6: Change in Stiffener Section Modulus (%)
(plus = decrease; minus = increase)

Conclusions

Thanks to the recent developments outlined here, the LBR-5 software allows performing multicriterion optimization by considering production cost, weight and moment of inertia in the optimization objective functions. The entire Pareto front can be mapped by using a process that randomly alters the weights in the weighted sum solution and solves the optimization problem for each of these problems. Useful specific compromise solutions from the Pareto front, e.g. the nearest to the utopian and min-max solutions, can be easily calculated.

Moreover, it is now possible to perform discrete optimization with LBR-5 so that a standardized and "ready to use" set of optimum scantlings can be obtained.

Finally, IACS requirements, regarding bending, shearing and buckling strength are now available in LBR-5.

Acknowledgement

The present research was achieved with the funding and support of MARSTRUCT Network of Excellence (FP6 project funded by EU), IMPROVE (FP6 project funded by EU) and AKER YARDS SA, France.

References

Bay, M., Crama, Y., Richir, T., and Rigo, P. (2007). "A Mixed-Integer Heuristic for the Structural Optimization of a Cruise Ship", Proc COMPIT'07, Cortona, pp 212-224

Fleury, C. (1989). "CONLIN, An Efficient Dual Optimizer Based on Convex Approximation Concepts", Structural Optimization, Vol 1, pp 81-89

Parsons, M. G., and Scott, R. L. (2004). "Formulation of Multicriterion Design Optimization Problems for Solution with Scalar Numerical Optimization Methods", Journal of Ship Research, Vol 48, No 1, pp 61-76

Richir, T., Losseau, N., Pircalabu, E., Toderan, C., and Rigo, P. (2007). "Least Cost Optimization of Large Passenger Vessels", Proc MARSTRUCT Conference, Glasgow, pp 483-488

Rigo, P. (2001). "A Module-Oriented Tool for Optimum Design of Stiffened Structures", Marine Structures, Vol 14, No 6, pp 611-629

Rigo, P., and Fleury, C. (2001). "Scantling Optimization Based on Convex Linearizations and a Dual Approach", Marine Structures, Vol 14, No 6, pp 631-649

Progressive Hull Collapse Characteristics of Tanker Structures Designed by IACS Pre-CSR and CSR Methods

Jeom Kee Paik[1], Jung Kwan Seo[1], Bong Ju Kim[1], and Owen F. Hughes[2]

[1] Department of Naval Architecture and Ocean Engineering, Pusan National University, Busan, Korea
[2] Department of Aerospace and Ocean Engineering, Virginia Tech., Blacksburg, VA, USA

Abstract

The present paper addresses the progressive collapse strength characteristics of a hypothetical AFRAMAX-class double hull oil tanker structure under vertical bending moments. IACS CSR (Common Structural Rules) and Pre-CSR methods are applied for the determination of scantlings of the same class tanker structures, and the resulting two designs are compared in terms of plate thickness and structural weight. The progressive collapse behavior of the hull structure is carried out by ANSYS nonlinear FEA and ALPS/HULL methods. The effects of initial imperfections on the progressive hull collapse behavior are investigated. The ultimate bending strength of the tanker hull designed by the CSR method is compared with that of the same class tanker hull designed by pre-CSR method, together with the IACS CSR requirements of the ultimate bending moment capacity.

Keywords

IACS CSR (Common Structural Rules); Ultimate limit states (ULS); Progressive collapse analysis; Double hull oil tanker; Nonlinear finite element method.

Introduction

It is desirable to perform the progressive collapse analysis to determine the ultimate load-carrying capacity of a system structure that is composed of various individual structural components. This is because the progressive failures of individual structural components and their interacting effects with increase in the applied actions usually significantly affect the collapse strength behavior of the system structure.

In the present paper, the progressive collapse analysis under vertical bending moments is undertaken for AFRAMAX class double hull oil tanker structures, designed by IACS CSR (Common Structural Rules) method (IACS 2006) and by IACS pre-CSR method. ANSYS (2006) nonlinear FEA and ALPS/HULL (2006) methods are employed for the progressive collapse analysis, and their resulting solutions are compared to identify the differences of the two designs in terms of the ultimate bending moment capacity. The effects of initial imperfections on the progressive hull collapse behavior are also studied.

IACS CSR design versus IACS pre-CSR design

In the present study, a hypothetical AFRAMAX-class double hull tanker structure was designed, with the principal dimensions as indicated in Table 1. The material yield stress (c_Y) of hull structures used for the present study is 315MPa, and elastic modulus (E) is 205.8GPa.

Table 1: Principal dimensions of the object ship

Length O.A.	250.000 m
Length B.P.	239.000 m
Length Scantling	236.292 m
Breadth	43.800 m
Depth	21.000 m
Designed draught	13.600 m
Scantling draught	14.900 m
Block coefficient	0.87

Two design methods, namely IACS CSR and pre-CSR methods are applied for the structural scantling of the same class double hull oil tanker. The basic properties of the hull structures designed by IACS CSR and pre-CSR methods are compared in Table 2.

It was found that the plate thickness of the hull structure designed by IACS CSR method is greater than that by IACS pre-CSR method, as follows (Paik et al. 2007)

- 2.5~4.0mm increase of bottom plate thickness considering ultimate limit states (ULS);
- 0.5mm increase of lower side shell plate thickness considering lateral pressure actions;
- 1~2mm increase of upper side shell plate thickness considering lateral pressure actions;
- 2~5mm increase of upper deck plate thickness considering section modulus and fatigue requirements;
- 1mm increase of inner bottom plate thickness considering local pressure actions;

- 2~3mm increase of inner side shell plate thickness considering ULS and shearing forces;
- 2mm increase of center longitudinal bulkhead plate thickness considering ULS.

Table 2: Comparison of basic hull properties for the CSR versus pre-CSR designs

Property		CSR design	Pre-CSR design
Cross sectional area (m^2)		5.4982	5.0156
Moment of inertia (m^4)		378.4787	343.1075
Section modulus (m^3)	Bottom	40.7442	36.7955
	Deck	29.9172	27.1978
Full plastic moment (MNm)		12742.76	11670.64

It is to be noted that the larger scantling of the CSR design structure is also due to larger corrosion margin values specified by the CSR than those by the pre-CSR. For 6 cargo hold areas in between 180.6m length of the hull structure amidship, the structural weight of the CSR design structure was greater than the pre-CSR design structure by some 1,000 ton.

The slenderness ratio of plates surrounded by support members $\beta = (b/t)\sqrt{\sigma_Y/E}$ is in the range of 1.99~2.45 for bottom plates, 2.36~2.55 for deck plates, and 2.66 for side shell plates. This implies that the plate thickness is likely to be thin, and the plates may be prone to buckle at least in the elastic-plastic regime before the ultimate limit state is reached.

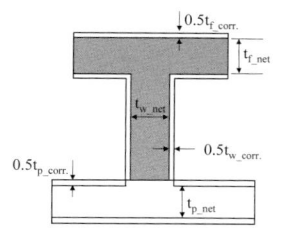

Fig.1: Deduction of corrosion margin values applied for the ULS assessment

The approach of net scantlings is typically applied for the ULS assessment of stiffened plate structures, i.e., by deducing 100 percent corrosion margin values (i.e., 50 percent deduction from each side of plating and stiffener), as illustrated in Fig.1.

For the progressive hull collapse analysis against vertical bending moment, on the other hand, 50 percent corrosion margin values (i.e., 25 percent for each side) are typically deduced for the IACS CSR hull structure, although 100 percent corrosion margin values are deduced for the IACS pre-CSR hull structure, according to the corresponding rule requirements.

Progressive hull collapse analysis

Analysis methods and structural modeling

ANSYS nonlinear FEA and ALPS/HULL methods are used for the progressive collapse analysis. A sliced-hull section model between two transverse frames amidship is adopted for the purpose of the analysis.

Figure 2 shows the ANSYS FEA and the ALPS/HULL models that are used for the progressive collapse analysis under either sagging or hogging.

Before the hull girder reaches the ULS, the deck structures typically buckle under sagging condition, while the bottom structures buckles under hogging condition. Upper part of vertical structures is likely to buckle under sagging condition, and lower part of vertical structures is prone to buckle under hogging condition. For ANSYS finite element modeling, therefore, very fine meshes are employed to reflect buckling collapse behavior of plating and support members over the entire hull section, including deck structures, bottom structures and vertical structures (e.g., side-shell structures, longitudinal bulkhead structures).

On the other hand, ALPS/HULL employs idealized structural unit method (ISUM) using very large size elements (Paik and Thayamballi 2003, 2007); Plating surrounded by support members is modeled as one ISUM rectangular plate element, and any support member (e.g., longitudinal stiffeners) without attached plating is modeled as one ISUM beam-column element.

Initial imperfections

For the present study, the effects of initial imperfections in the form of initial deflection and residual stress are also evaluated in association with the progressive collapse behavior of the hull structures under vertical bending moment. In the case, the same level of initial deflections of plating and stiffeners are assumed for all individual plates surrounded by support members (e.g., longitudinal stiffeners and transverse frames), as follows

$$w_{opl} = \frac{b}{200} \quad (1)$$

$$w_{oc} = w_{os} = \frac{a}{1000} \quad (2)$$

where w_{opl} = plate initial deflection, w_{oc} = column type initial deflection of stiffeners, w_{os} = sideways initial deflection of stiffeners, b = plate breadth or longitudinal stiffener spacing, a = plate length or transverse frame spacing.

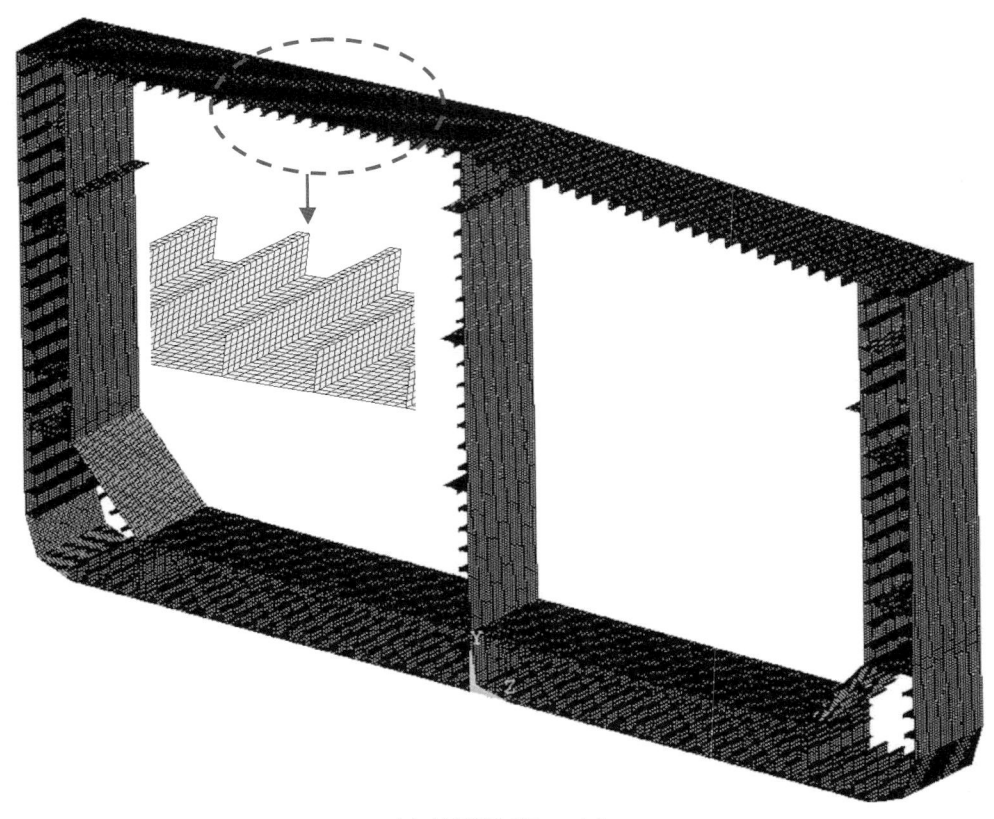

(a) ANSYS FE model

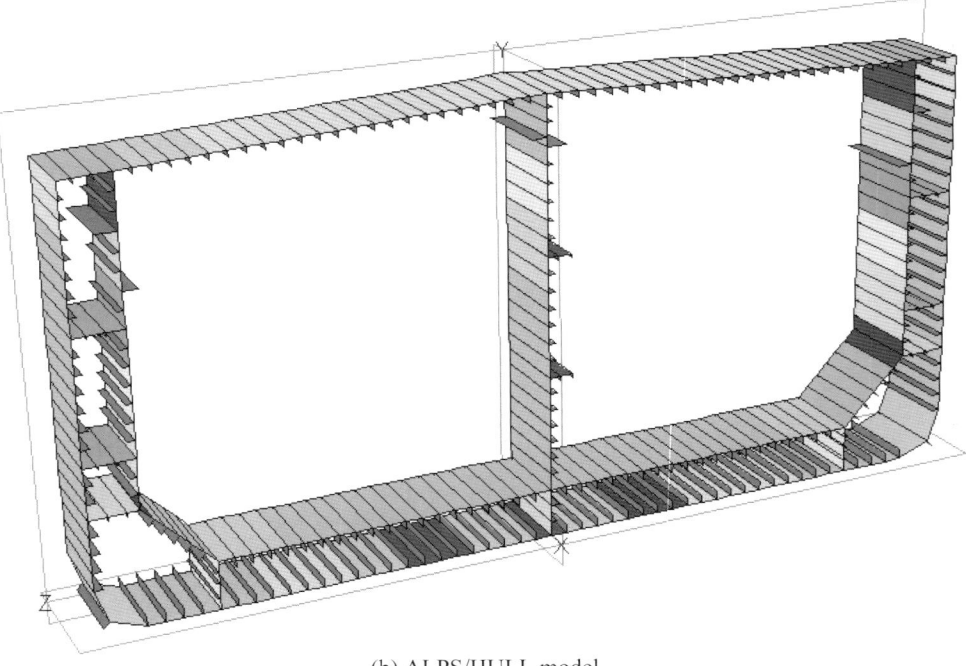

(b) ALPS/HULL model

Fig.2: Progressive collapse analysis models for the double hull oil tanker under vertical bending moment

(a) Buckling mode shape

(b) Hungry horse mode shape

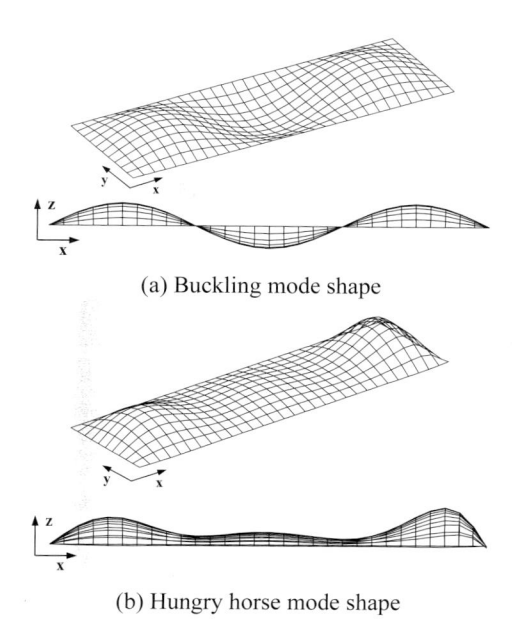

Fig.3: A schematic of two shapes of plate initial deflection considered in the present study

While the plate initial deflection primarily affects the buckling collapse of plating, column type initial deflection of stiffeners significantly affects the column type collapse of stiffeners, and sideways initial deflection of stiffeners affect flexural-torsional buckling or tripping of stiffeners.

Two types of plate initial deflection shape are considered, namely buckling mode shape and hungry horse mode shape, as shown in Fig.3. It is to be noted that the actual number of plate buckling half-waves can be determined as a function of plate aspect ratio, and it can be different from the schematic representation of Fig.3.

On the other hand, it is assumed that the shape of either column type initial deflection or sideways initial deflection of stiffeners corresponds to the buckling mode of the stiffener, that gives the smallest buckling strength to the corresponding buckling mode.

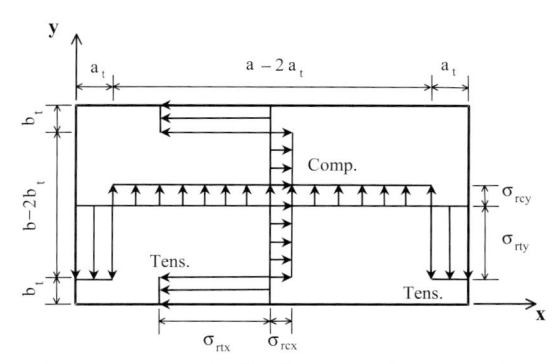

Fig.4: Assumed distribution of residual stress in a plate

Welding residual stresses can develop in plates and stiffeners. Figure 4 illustrates the welding induced residual stress distribution in a plate surrounded by support members, showing that the residual stress distribution in a direction consists of tensile stress block and compressive stress block, and also the residual stresses can developed in both longitudinal and transverse directions as long as welding is performed along all (four) edges of plating (Paik and Thayamballi 2003).

In the present study, however, it is assumed that welding residual stress exists in the ship length direction only, because the hull girder action considered in the present study is vertical bending moment and the effect of welding residual stress in the transverse direction may be small.

Three different levels of residual stress are considered in a plate as follows

$$\sigma_{rcx} = 0.0, \quad \sigma_{rcx} = -0.05\sigma_Y, \quad \sigma_{rcx} = -0.15\sigma_Y \quad (3)$$

where σ_{rcx} = compressive residual stress in the longitudinal direction, σ_Y = material yield stress that is considered to equal σ_{rtx} (tensile residual stress in the longitudinal direction).

It is assumed that all plates have the same level of residual stress. Also, all stiffeners have the same level of residual stress.

Progressive hull collapse behavior

ANSYS FEA analysis was undertaken for IACS CSR structure only. Figure 5 shows the collapse mode of individual structural components over the hull cross section at ULS, under sagging or hogging, obtained by ANSYS FEA when residual stresses do not exist, while initial distortions of plating and stiffeners exist with the buckling mode shape.

It is interesting to note that plate elements and stiffeners in a large part of vertical structures as well as in deck structures have failed under sagging before ULS, although outer bottom panels and very lower part of vertical structures have collapsed by stiffener web buckling mode under hogging.

Figures 6 and 7 respectively show the vertical bending moment versus curvature curves of the CSR and pre-CSR design hull structures under sagging or hogging with varying the levels of initial imperfections, obtained by ANSYS and ALPS/HULL methods. Figure 8 compares the progressive collapse behavior of CSR and pre-CSR design hull structures obtained by ALPS/HULL method, when the magnitude of welding residual stress is 5% of the material yield stress.

Tables 3 and 4 summarize the ultimate hull girder strength computations by ANSYS nonlinear FEA and ALPS/HULL methods for various cases of initial imperfections. The IACS CSR solutions obtained by the so-called multi-step methods (IACS 2006) are also compared, together with the IACS CSR requirements of ultimate hull girder strength.

(a) Sagging

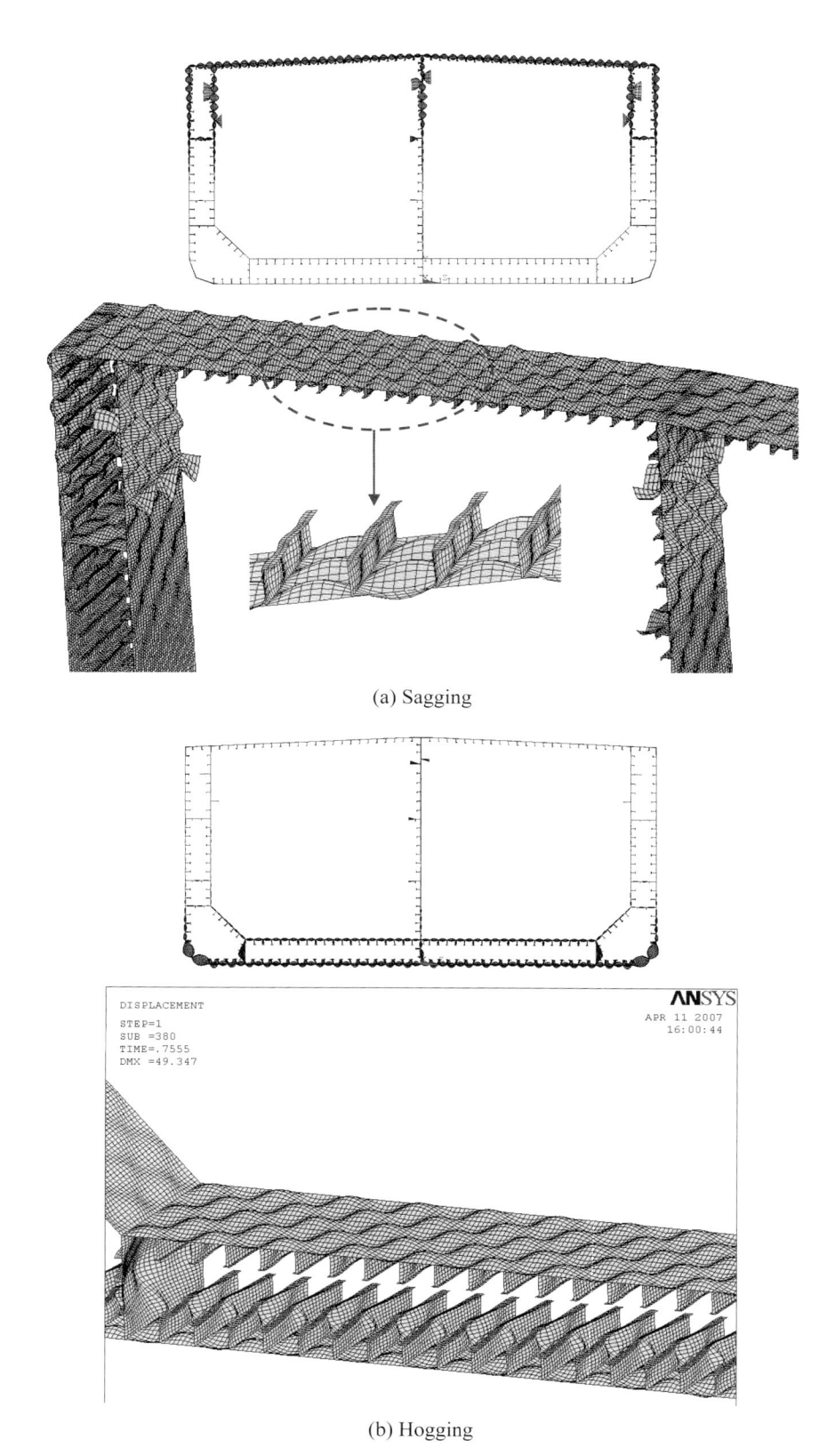

(b) Hogging

Fig.5: Collapsed structural components of CSR design hull structure at ULS under sagging or hogging, obtained by ANSYS nonlinear FEA

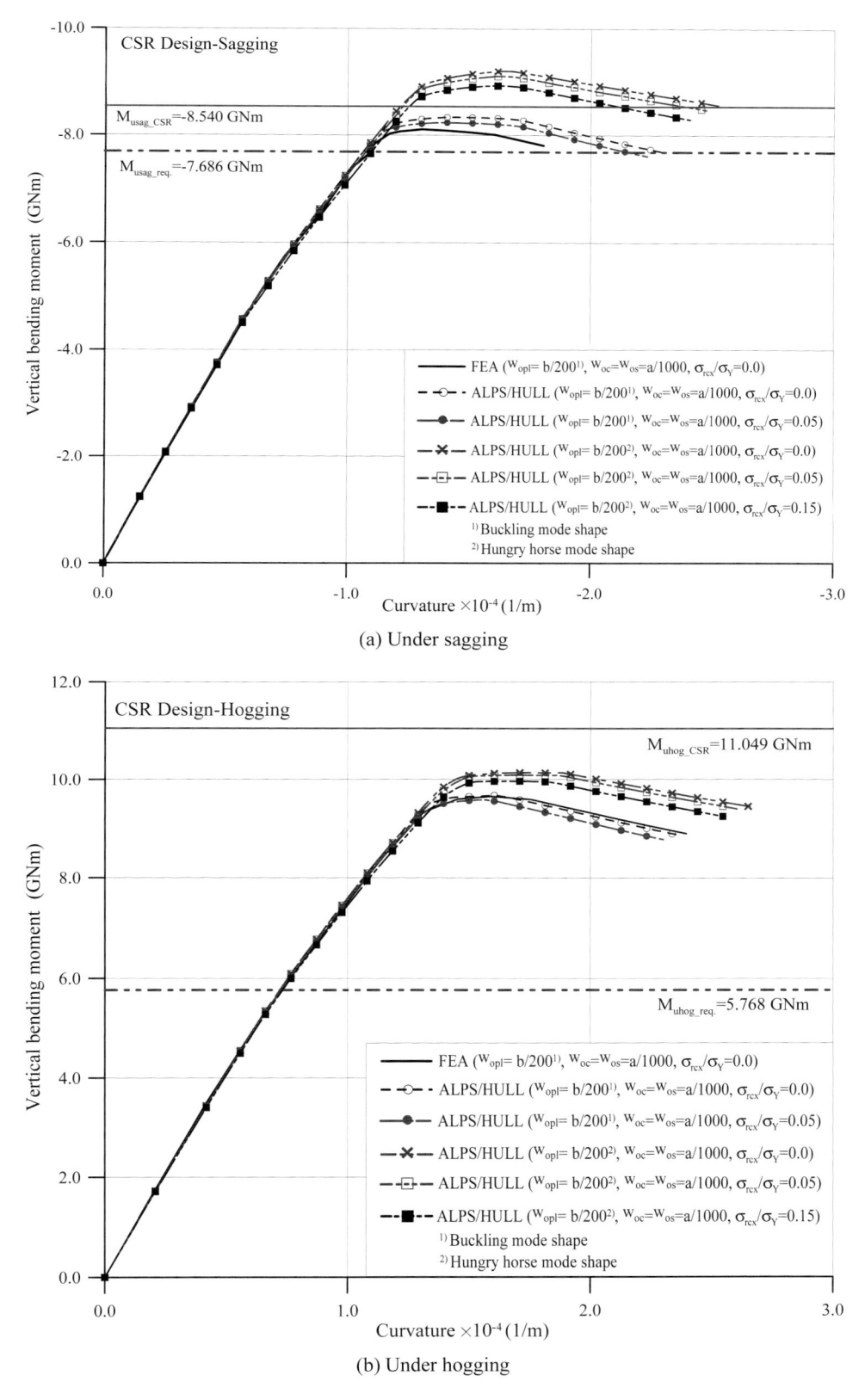

Fig.6: Vertical bending moment versus curvature curves for CSR design hull structure with varying the levels of initial imperfections, obtained by ANSYS and ALPS/HULL methods

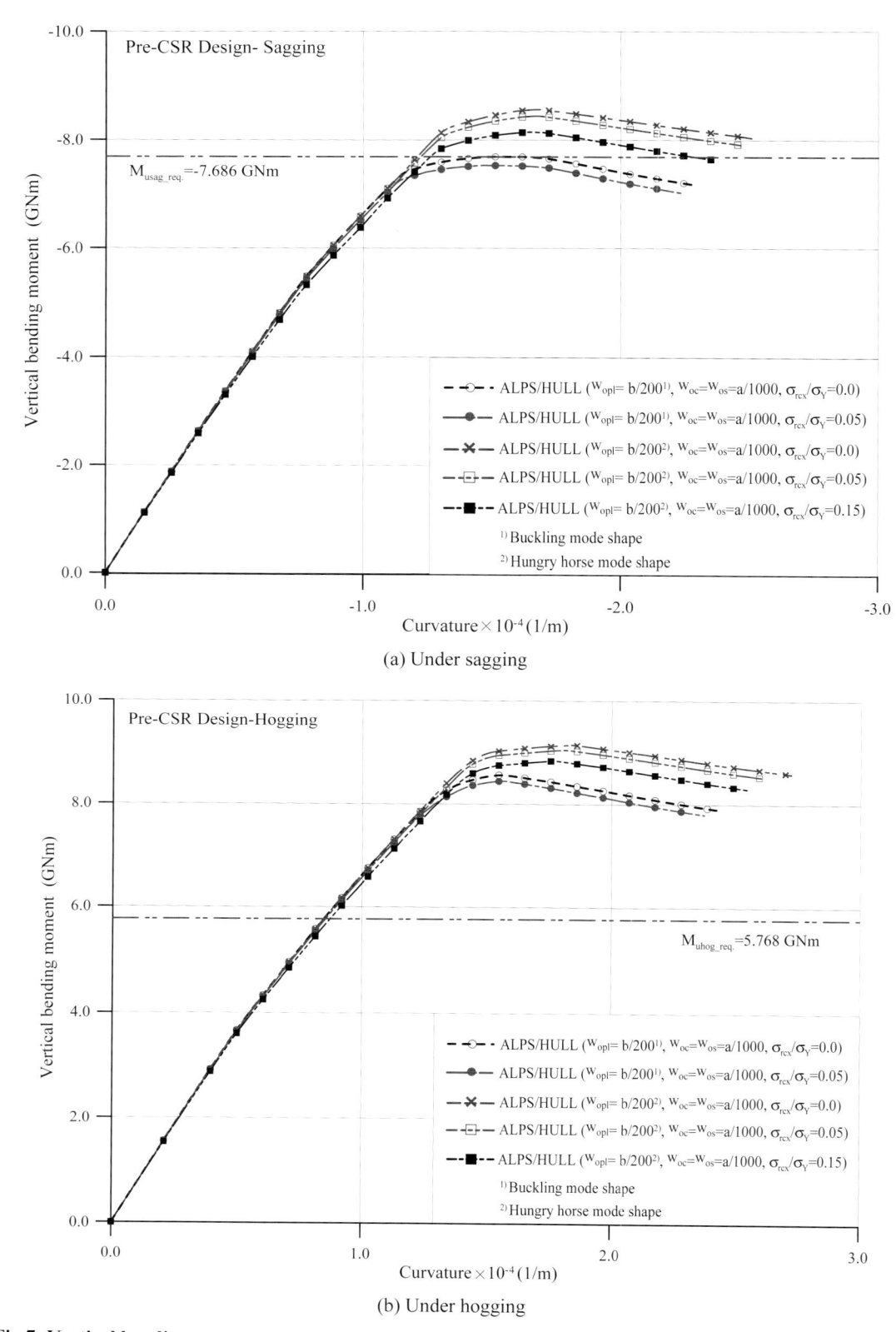

Fig.7: Vertical bending moment versus curvature curves for pre-CSR design hull structure with varying the levels of initial imperfections, obtained by ANSYS and ALPS/HULL methods

(a) Buckling mode shape

(b) Hungry horse mode shape with residual stress of 5% yield stress

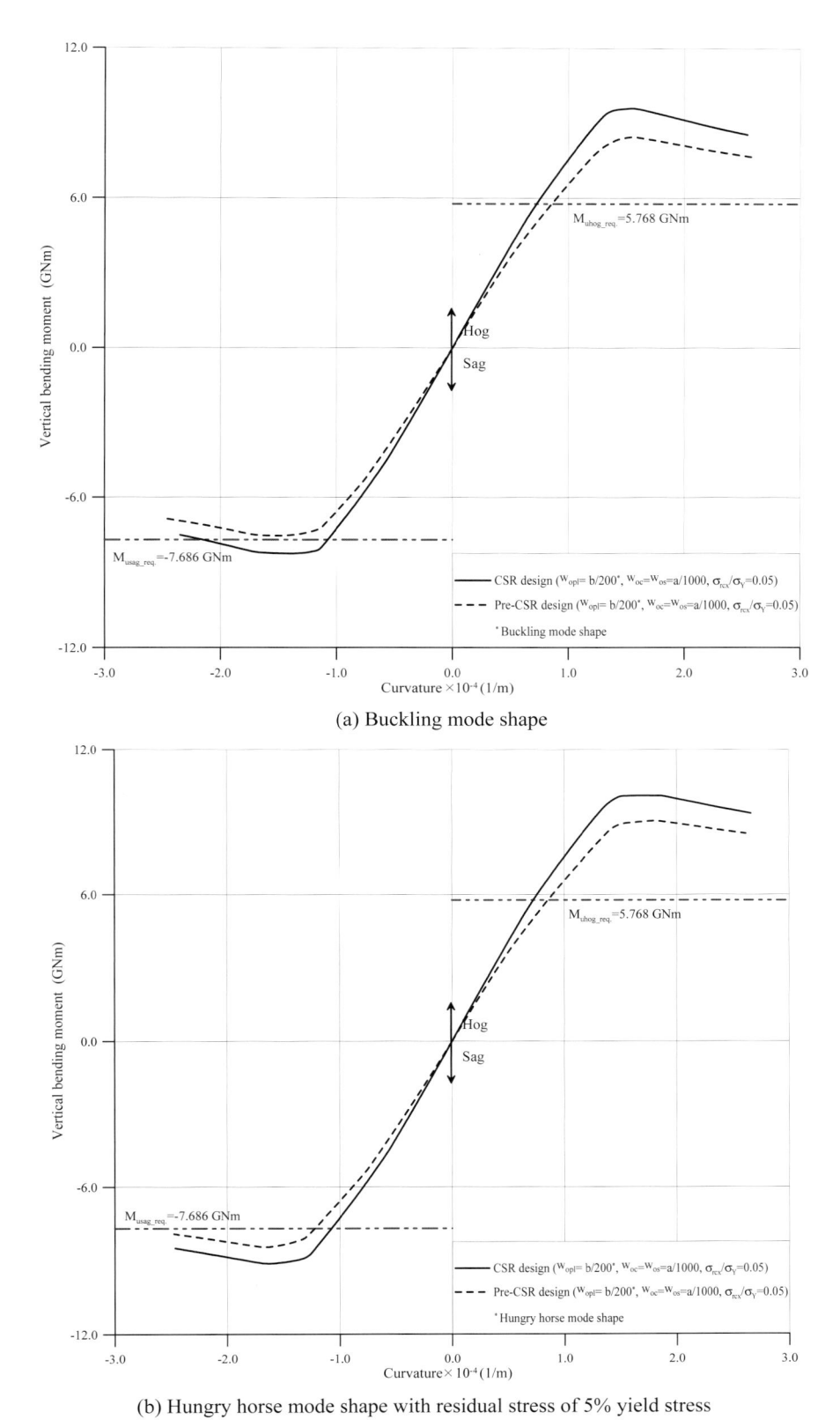

Fig.8: Comparison of hull collapse behavior for CSR and pre-CSR designs, obtained by ALPS/HULL method

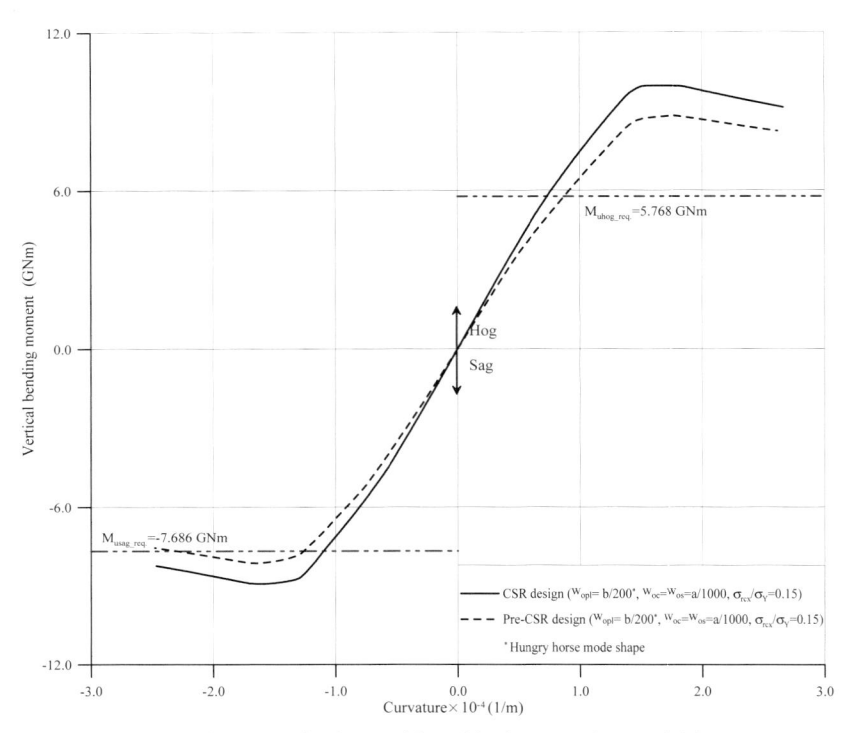

(c) Hungry horse mode shape with residual stress of 15% yield stress

Fig.8 (*Continued*): Comparison of hull collapse behavior for CSR and pre-CSR designs, obtained by ALPS/HULL method

Discussions and concluding remarks

Based on the results of the progressive hull collapse analyses for CSR and pre-CSR designs of an AFRAMAX class double hull oil tanker, the following conclusions can be drawn:

1) Most upper part of vertical structures above the neutral axis position of the hull structure as well as deck structures have collapsed under sagging condition before the hull girder collapse is reached, although outer bottom panels and very lower part of vertical structures have failed under hogging condition.
2) For both CSR and pre-CSR design hull structures, both deck and outer bottom panels collapsed by stiffener web buckling mode under sagging or hogging conditions, respectively.
3) For CSR design hull structures without welding residual stress but with initial distortions, the difference of ultimate hull girder strength computations between ANSYS nonlinear FEA and ALPS/HULL methods is less than 2.8%, indicating that ALPS/HULL method solutions are in very good agreement with more refined nonlinear FEA results.
4) ALPS/HULL method can deal with initial imperfections in terms of the magnitude and the shape as parameters of influence on progressive hull collapse analysis. The ultimate bending moments of the CSR hull structures with initial distortion of hungry horse mode shape were increased by 10.4% for sagging and 4.8% for hogging, compared to those with buckling mode shape keeping the same magnitude of initial deflection.
5) It is considered that the most realistic situation of initial imperfections is the hungry horse mode shape with an average level of welding residual stress (15% of yield stress). The ultimate strength of the structure with hungry horse mode shape of plate initial deflection can be greater than that with buckling mode shape as well. The ultimate bending moment for CSR design hull structure under the most realistic situation noted above is still greater than the structure with buckling mode shape of plate initial deflection but without residual stress, by 7.1% for sagging and 3.0% for hogging.
6) In terms of the most realistic situation of initial imperfections noted above, the ultimate bending moment of CSR design hull structure is greater than pre-CSR design hull structure, by 9.6% for sagging and 12.8% for hogging.
7) The safety margin of CSR design hull structure with the most realistic situation of initial imperfections noted above is 16.1% for sagging and 72.7% for hogging, against the IACS CSR requirement, that is considered to be sufficient enough. It is interesting to note that the safety margin of the hull structure with buckling mode shape of plate initial deflection but without residual stress is 8.4% for sagging and 67.7% for hogging.
8) It is convinced that the ALPS/HULL method can be very useful for the progressive hull collapse

analysis and enter in daily-design practice since the computing time used for ALPS/HULL analysis is about 5 minutes by personal computer (while ANSYS nonlinear FEA required some 8 days for the computations only, i.e., except for the structural modeling times).

Acknowledgements

The present study was undertaken at the Ship and Offshore Structural Mechanics Laboratory, Pusan National University, which is a National Research Laboratory funded by the Korea Science and Engineering Foundation (Grant No. ROA-2006-000-10239-0). The authors are pleased to acknowledge the support of Samsung Heavy Industries.

References

ALPS/HULL (2006). "A computer program for progressive collapse analysis of ship hulls" (version 2006.3), Proteus Engineering, Stevensville, MD, USA.

ANSYS (2006). User's manual (version 10.0), Swanson Analysis Systems Inc., Houston.

IACS (2006). "Common structural rules for double hull oil tankers", International Association of Classification Societies, London.

Paik, J.K., Kim, B.J., and Seo, J.K. (2007). "Evaluation of IACS common structural rules in terms of ultimate limit state design and assessment of ship structures", Proceedings of OMAE 2007 – 26th International Conference on Offshore Mechanics and Arctic Engineering, OMAE2007-29187, 10-15 June 2007, San Diego, California.

Paik, J.K., and Thayamballi, A.K. (2003). "Ultimate limit state design of steel-plated structures", John Wiley & Sons, Chichester, UK.

Paik, J.K., and Thayamballi, A.K. (2007). "Ship-shaped offshore installations: Design, building, and operation", Cambridge University Press, Cambridge, UK.

Table 3(a): Ultimate hull girder strength computations for IACS CSR design hull structure under sagging

Analysis method		Initial imperfections				
		$w_{opl} = b/200$, $w_{oc} = w_{os} = 0.001a$ (Buckling mode shape)		$w_{opl} = b/200$, $w_{oc} = w_{os} = 0.001a$ (Hungry horse mode shape)		
		$\frac{\sigma_{rcx}}{\sigma_Y} = 0.0$	$\frac{\sigma_{rcx}}{\sigma_Y} = 0.05$	$\frac{\sigma_{rcx}}{\sigma_Y} = 0.0$	$\frac{\sigma_{rcx}}{\sigma_Y} = 0.05$	$\frac{\sigma_{rcx}}{\sigma_Y} = 0.15$
IACS CSR requirement	$M_{usag\_req.}$ (GNm)	-7.686				
CSR method	M_{usag_CSR} (GNm)	-8.540				
	$M_{usag\_CSR} / M_{usag\_req.}$	1.111				
ALPS/HULL method	M_{usag_HULL} (GNm)	-8.338	-8.235	-9.208	-9.112	-8.931
	$M_{usag\_HULL} / M_{usag\_req.}$	1.084	1.071	1.198	1.185	1.161
ANSYS FEA method	M_{usag_FEA} (GNm)	-8.107	-	-	-	-
	$M_{usag\_FEA} / M_{uhog\_req.}$	1.054	-	-	-	-
Comparison	$M_{usag\_CSR} / M_{usag\_FEA}$	1.053	-	-	-	-
	$M_{usag\_HULL} / M_{usag\_FEA}$	1.028	-	-	-	-

Table 3(b): Ultimate hull girder strength computations for IACS CSR design hull structure under hogging

Analysis method		Initial imperfections				
		$w_{opl} = b/200$ $w_{oc} = w_{os} = 0.001a$ (Buckling mode shape)		$w_{opl} = b/200$ $w_{oc} = w_{os} = 0.001a$ (Hungry horse mode shape)		
		$\frac{\sigma_{rcx}}{\sigma_Y} = 0.0$	$\frac{\sigma_{rcx}}{\sigma_Y} = 0.05$	$\frac{\sigma_{rcx}}{\sigma_Y} = 0.0$	$\frac{\sigma_{rcx}}{\sigma_Y} = 0.05$	$\frac{\sigma_{rcx}}{\sigma_Y} = 0.15$
IACS CSR requirement	$M_{uhog\_req.}$ (GNm)	5.768				
CSR method	M_{uhog_CSR} (GNm)	11.049				
	$M_{uhog\_CSR} / M_{uhog\_req.}$	1.915				
ALPS/HULL method	M_{uhog_HULL} (GNm)	9.675	9.584	10.141	10.090	9.962
	$M_{uhog\_HULL} / M_{uhog\_req.}$	1.677	1.661	1.758	1.749	1.727
ANSYS FEA method	M_{uhog_FEA} (GNm)	9.654	-	-	-	-
	$M_{uhog\_FEA} / M_{uhog\_req.}$	1.674	-	-	-	-
Comparison	$M_{uhog\_CSR} / M_{uhog\_FEA}$	1.144	-	-	-	-
	$M_{uhog\_HULL} / M_{uhog\_FEA}$	1.002	-	-	-	-

Table 4(a): Ultimate hull girder strength computations for pre-CSR design hull structure under sagging

IACS requirement versus ALPS/HULL method		Initial imperfections				
		$w_{opl} = b/200$ $w_{oc} = w_{os} = 0.001a$ (Buckling mode shape)		$w_{opl} = b/200$ $w_{oc} = w_{os} = 0.001a$ (Hungry horse mode shape)		
		$\frac{\sigma_{rcx}}{\sigma_Y} = 0.0$	$\frac{\sigma_{rcx}}{\sigma_Y} = 0.05$	$\frac{\sigma_{rcx}}{\sigma_Y} = 0.0$	$\frac{\sigma_{rcx}}{\sigma_Y} = 0.05$	$\frac{\sigma_{rcx}}{\sigma_Y} = 0.15$
IACS CSR requirement	$M_{uhog\_req.}$ (GNm)	-7.686				
ALPS/HULL method	M_{uhog_HULL} (GNm)	-7.690	-7.528	-8.564	-8.442	-8.147
	$M_{uhog\_HULL} / M_{uhog\_req.}$	1.001	0.979	1.114	1.098	1.060

Table 4(b): Ultimate hull girder strength computations for pre-CSR design hull structure under hogging

IACS requirement versus ALPS/HULL method		Initial imperfections				
^	^	$w_{opl} = b/200$ $w_{oc} = w_{os}= 0.001a$ (Buckling mode shape)		$w_{opl} = b/200$ $w_{oc} = w_{os}= 0.001a$ (Hungry horse mode shape)		
^	^	$\frac{\sigma_{rcx}}{\sigma_Y} = 0.0$	$\frac{\sigma_{rcx}}{\sigma_Y} = 0.05$	$\frac{\sigma_{rcx}}{\sigma_Y} = 0.0$	$\frac{\sigma_{rcx}}{\sigma_Y} = 0.05$	$\frac{\sigma_{rcx}}{\sigma_Y} = 0.15$
IACS CSR requirement	$M_{uhog\_req.}$ (GNm)	5.768				
ALPS/HULL method	M_{uhog_HULL} (GNm)	8.557	8.444	9.139	9.039	8.832
^	$M_{uhog\_HULL} / M_{uhog\_req.}$	1.483	1.464	1.584	1.567	1.531

The Application of CSR for Design of Bulk Carriers with CSR Notation

Yingqiu Chen[1], Zhihu Zhan[2]

[1] China Classification Society, Beijing, China
[2] Shanghai Rule Research Institute of China Classification Society, Shanghai, China

Abstract:

In this paper, the differences between IACS CSR on bulkers and traditional design rules for bulk carriers are presented. The purpose of the paper is to make ship designers know further clearly the basic design demands of the IACS CSR on bulkers. The characteristics of the principle dimension distribution of IACS CSR for bulk carriers and some questions arisen from the design stage are discussed based on the first bulk carrier with CSR Notation in China.

Key words:

Common Structural Rules (CSR); Yield strength; Buckling strength; Fatigue strength.

1 Introduction

Ships have always been regarded as the safest transportation means since long time ago. However, the costly accidents, especially for bulk carriers and oil tankers, have frequently occurred since the nineteen nineties. IMO, IACS and industrial departments are all devoted to solve these problems. The standard of IMO based on goals and CSR of IACS should be regarded as the active responses for improving safety and protecting environment.

In June, 2003, the forty seventh council of IACS decided to develop the common structural rules for double hull oil tankers and bulk carriers. The aim of CSR is to develop a set of common Rules and procedures for the determination of the structural requirements for oil tankers and bulk carriers

Objectives of the above CSR should be:

(1) To eliminate competition between class societies on scantlings

(2) To embrace the intentions of the anticipated IMO requirements for Goal-Based Standards for new buildings

(3) To ensure that a ship meeting these new Rules will be recognized by industry as being safe, robust and fit for purpose as would have been required by any of the existing Rules

(4) To employ the combined experience of all class societies to develop an agreed set of Rules

On April 1st, 2006, the CSR of IACS takes entry into force.

The paper will introduce the practice of CSR for the bulk carriers design in Chinese shipyard using CCS software and under CCS indication. Meanwhile, the some technical details of the 1st bulk carrier with CSR notation and classed with CCS will be introduced to discuss some problems in the process of the ship design.

2 New characteristics of CSR for bulk carriers

Comparing with traditional design rules, the application of CSR for bulk carriers has the following three characteristics, which influenced the design of bulk carriers a lot.

2.1 The concept of net scantling

The most important characteristic of CSR is the concept of net scantling. It provides the same inspection standard for the construction and operation, which can make the inspection of classification clearer and fairer. That means net scantling has to be retained during the ship's whole life since it is built as to meet the structure safety requirement.

In order to carry out this concept, the scantling marks should include the following contents:

(1) as built

(2) renewal

(3) voluntary addition required from ship owners

The following draw marking has been used by CCS:

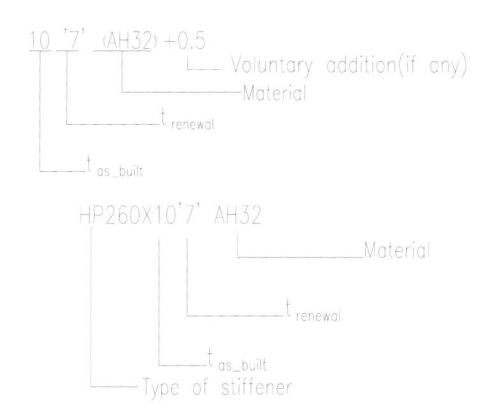

Fig.1 An marking example for plate and stiffener

Net scantling has been used in the strength calculation, the corrosion addition are listed in Table 1.

Table 1 Corrosion addition in the strength calculations

the evaluation content	corrosion addition
hull girder strength	$0.5t_c$
yield strength	$0.5t_c$
buckling strength	t_c
fatigue strength	$0.5t_c$

Note: t_c is the total corrosion addition.

2.2 The addition of new class notations

If the ship length is over 150 m, a mark of grab is added in CSR for bulk carriers. The mark is denoted as:

GRAB [X]

where, x describes the weight of grab.

This additional mark comes from the requirement of protection for the cargo holds in SOLAS. According to the requirement, the thickness, t_{GR}, of inner bottom and hopper plate of bottom side tank are calculated by the following formula:

$$t_{GR} = 0.28(M_{GR}+50)\sqrt{sk} \quad \text{mm}$$

In the area from the bottom to 3 meters above of sloping plate of bottom side tank and transverse bulkhead stool, the net thickness, t_{GR}, is calculated by the following formula:

$$t_{GR} = 0.28(M_{GR} + 42)\sqrt{sk}$$

The additional notation shows the requirement of protection for cargo holds. It leads to the rise of the thickness of inner bottom, as shown in the following:

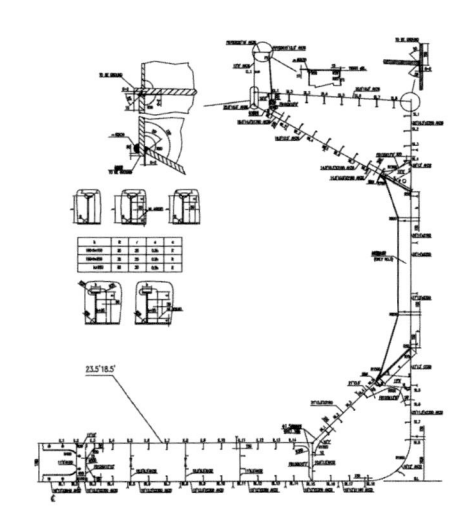

Fig. 2 the thickness increase by Grab notation

2.3 Equivalent design wave and combination of load cases

Regular waves that generate response values equivalent to the long-term response values of the load components considered being predominant to the structural members are set as Equivalent Design Waves (EDW). They consist of:

- regular waves when the vertical wave bending moment becomes maximum in head sea (EDW "H")
- regular waves when the vertical wave bending moment becomes maximum in following sea (EDW "F")
- regular waves when the roll motion becomes maximum (EDW "R")
- regular waves when the hydrodynamic pressure at the waterline becomes maximum (EDW "P")

The definitions of wave crest and wave trough in the EDW "H" and EDW "F" are given in Fig.3. The definitions of weather side down and weather side up for the EDW "R" and EDW "P" are given in Fig .4

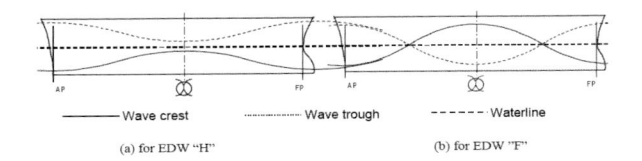

Fig.3 Definition of wave crest and wave trough in EDW

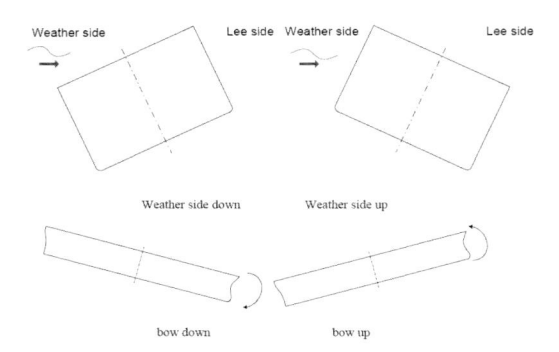

Fig.4 Definitions of ship motion

CSR is based on the first principle that all the scantlings are determined by load. load cases factors are list in table2:

Table2 Load combination factor LCF

	LCF	H1	H2	F1	F2	R1	R2	P1	P2
M_{WV}	C_{BV}	-1	1	-1	1	0	0	$0.4 - \frac{T_{LC}}{T_S}$	$\frac{T_{LC}}{T_S} - 0.4$
Q_{WV}	$C_{QW}^{(1)}$	-1	1	-1	1	0	0	$0.4 - \frac{T_{LC}}{T_S}$	$\frac{T_{LC}}{T_S} - 0.4$
M_{WH}	C_{WH}	0	0	0	0	$1.2 - \frac{T_{LC}}{T_S}$	$\frac{T_{LC}}{T_S} - 1.2$	0	0
a_{surge}	C_{XS}	-0.8	0.8	0	0	0	0	0	0
$a_{pitch\,x}$	C_{XP}	1	-1	0	0	0	0	0	0
$g\sin\Phi$	C_{XG}	1	-1	0	0	0	0	0	0
a_{sway}	C_{YS}	0	0	0	0	0	0	1	-1
$a_{roll\,y}$	C_{YR}	0	0	0	0	1	-1	0.3	-0.3
$g\sin\theta$	C_{YG}	0	0	0	0	1	-1	0.3	-0.3
a_{heave}	C_{ZH}	$0.6\frac{T_{LC}}{T_S}$	$-0.6\frac{T_{LC}}{T_S}$	0	0	$\frac{\sqrt{L}}{40}$	$-\frac{\sqrt{L}}{40}$	1	-1
$a_{roll\,z}$	C_{ZR}	0	0	0	0	1	-1	0.3	-0.3
$a_{pitch\,z}$	C_{ZP}	1	-1	0	0	0	0	0	0

(1) The LCF for C_{QW} is only used for the aft part of midship section. The inverse value of it should be used for the forward part of the midship section.

Note: LCF in the first row only apply to the aft part, the reverse values should be used in the fore part.

The design load determined by the equivalent design wave method, shows the concept of first design principle. Therefore, the scantling is more reasonable and safer. However, it is more complicated for the designer to determine the scantling. One convenient method to solve this problem is to utilize the software programmed by the ship classification society. CCS developed the COMPASS-SDA/SDP program system, aiming at making both design and review efficient.

2.4 The ultimate strength of hull girder

The ultimate strength of hull girder of current vessel whose length is 150 meters and above should be assessed.

The ultimate bending moment capabilities of hull girder are defined as the maximum values of the curve of bending moment capacity M versus the curvature χ of the transverse section considered (see Fig 5).

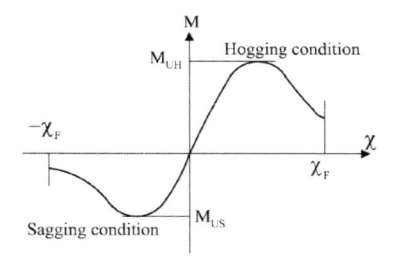

Fig.5 moment capacity M contrasted to curvature χ

In CSR bulk rules, The curve M-χ is to be obtained through an incremental-iterative procedure, Fig. 6 show the solve procedure.

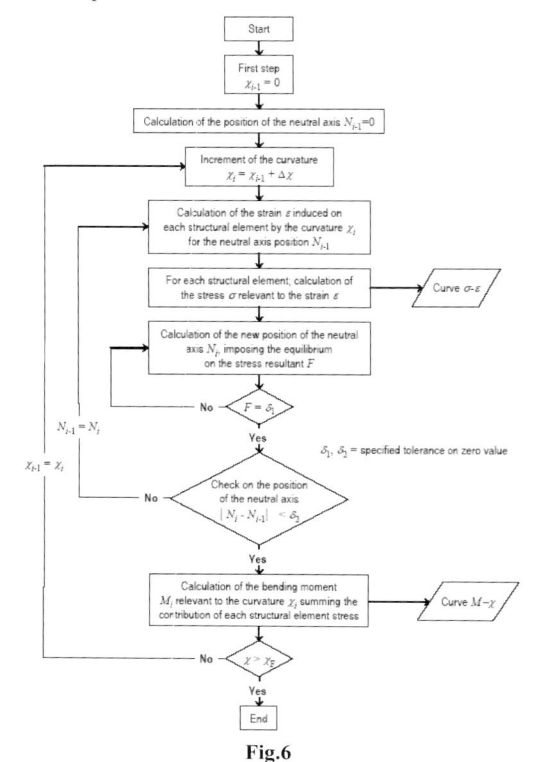

Fig.6

Ultimate bending strength should be satisfied with the following formula in any transverse section.

$$M \leq \frac{M_U}{\gamma_R}$$

where, M_U — ultimate bending moment capacity at the specified section, KN·m, based on the net scantling.

$M_U = M_{UH}$, hogging condition

$M_U = M_{US}$, sagging condition

M_{UH} – Ultimate bending moment capacity under hogging condition, defined in [2.2.1] of reference [2]

M_{US} – Ultimate bending moment capacity under sagging condition, defined in [2.2.1] of reference [2]

M – The moment applied to vessel which is intact or flooding or port.

γ_R – safety factor, 1.0 for given.

For the bulk carriers above 150m, the demand of ultimate strength leads to the increase of deck scantling.

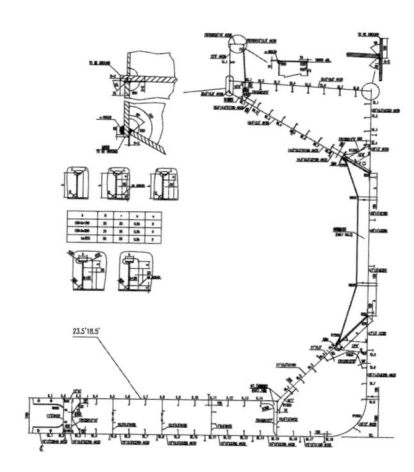

Fig.6 Example of increment of scantling in deck

3 Software system of CCS for CSR bulk carriers

In order to make both the design and approval efficient, CCS developed the software program system named Compass-Structure Design Program (SDP) and Compass-Structure Direct Assessment (SDA).

Compass SDP can determine all the rule structure scantling for CSR, including fore part and the after part of the ship, The most convenient characteristic is the SDP include some useful tools, e.g. rule calculator, shear flow calculation tool.

Compass SDA aim at the direct calculation, which is developed based on commercial Finite element software system MSC Patran/Nastran using PCL language. It can carry out yielding strength, buckling strength, fatigue strength and fine mesh finite element analysis. It also includes some useful tools, especially, the automatically buckling assessment tool and the automatically fine mesh analysis tool.

Buckling assessment tool can carry out the buckling calculation automatically, and give the evaluate result.

Fine mesh analysis tool is developed using PCL language too, it can mesh the element automatically based on the coarse mesh analysis result, Fig.7 is an example of fine mesh using fine mesh analysis tool.

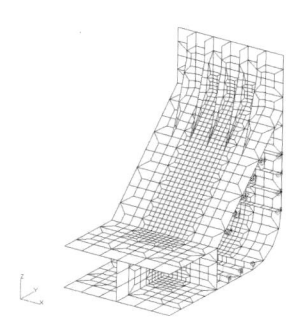

Fig.7 is an example of fine mesh using fine mesh analysis tool.

4 Application

Based on CSR for bulk carriers, the first bulk carrier designed by Chinese ship designers and approved by CCS, has been marked the notation of 'CCS CSR BC'. All the drawings have been approved, and the ship is under construction in China since Nov.28th, 2006.

The principle dimensions are listed in Table 10.

Table 10 Principle dimensions

LENGTH	O.A	189.90	M
LENGTH	SCANTLING	179.45	M
LENGTH	B.P	182.00	M
BREADTH	(MLD)	32.26	M
DEPTH	(MLD)	17.60	M
DRAFT	DESIGN	11.00	M

Fig.8~Fig.12 show the typical scantling distribution

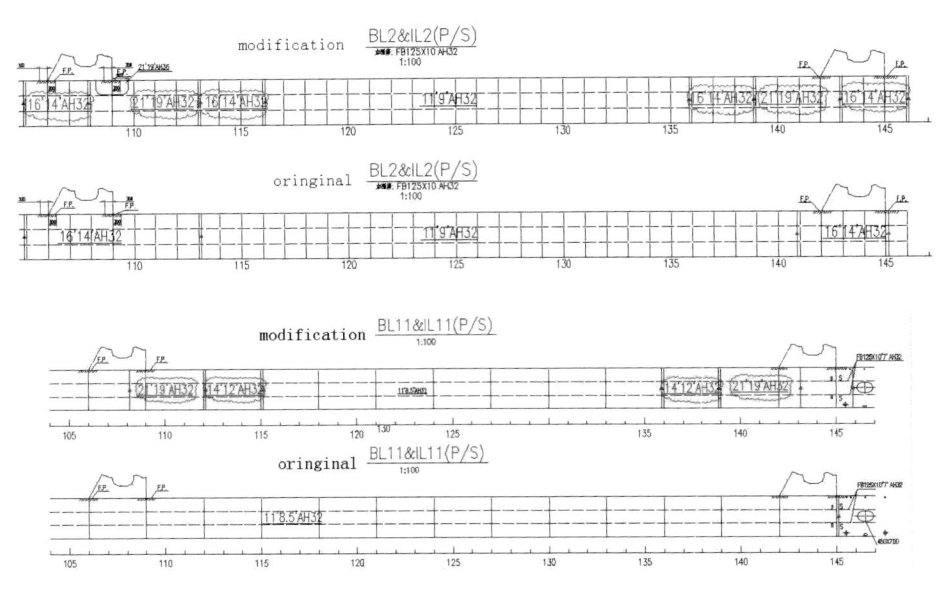

Fig.7 Typical scantling distribution Side girder

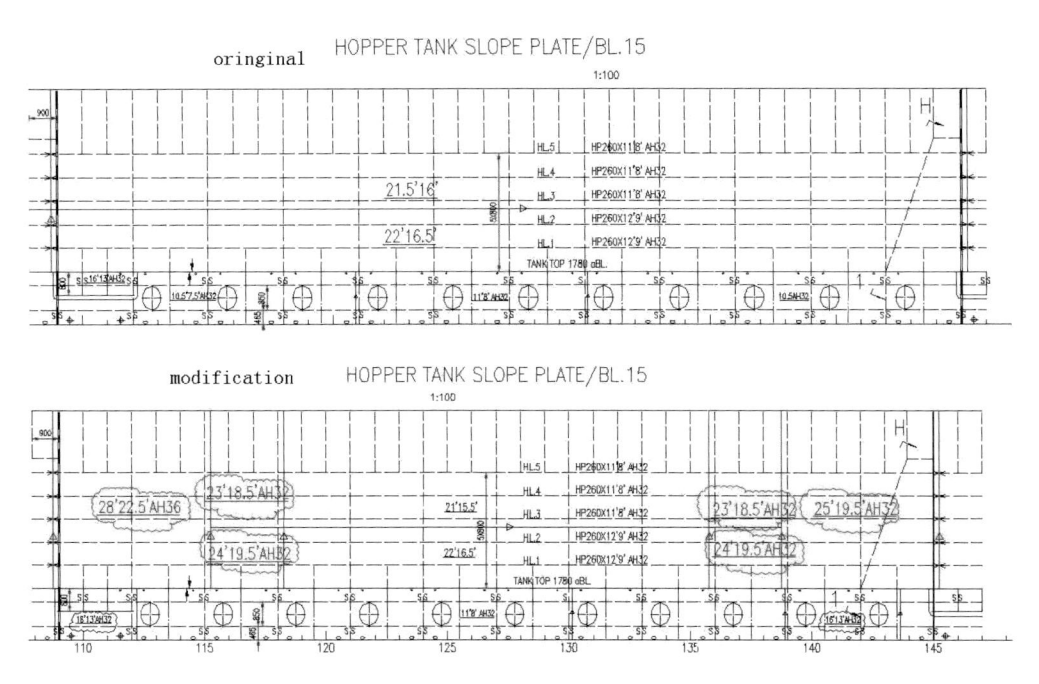

Fig.8 Typical scantling distribution of hopper tank slope plate

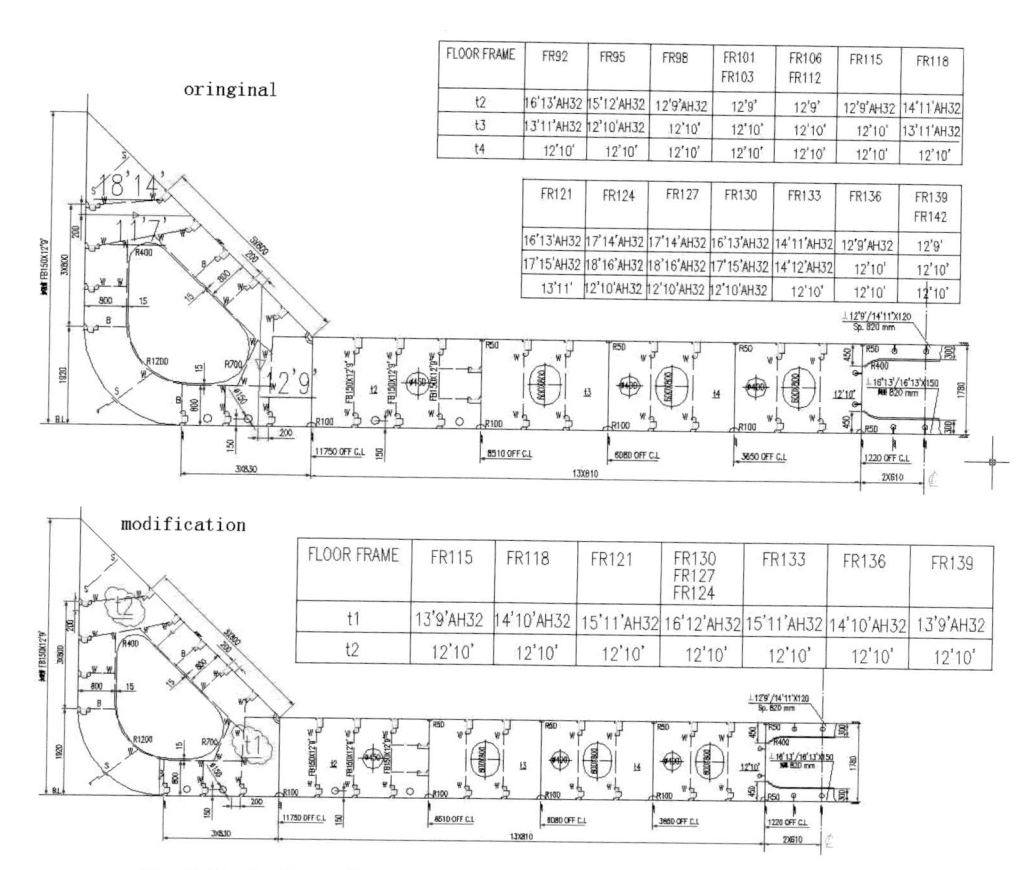

Fig. 9: Typical scantling distribution of transverse frame in hopper tank

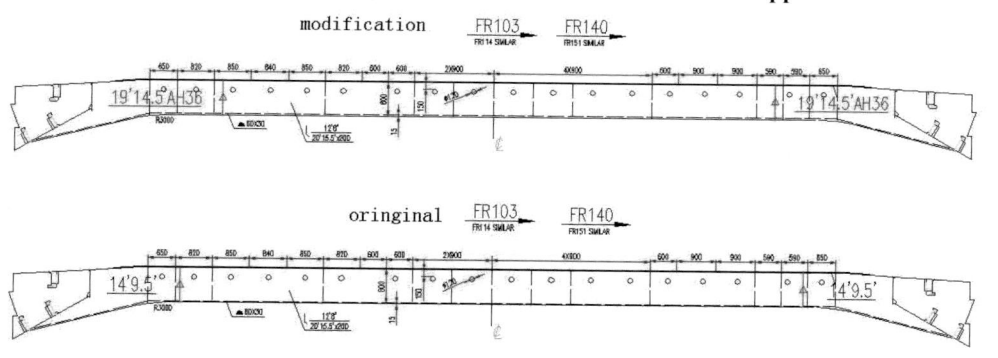

Fig. 10: Typical scantling distribution hatch end beam

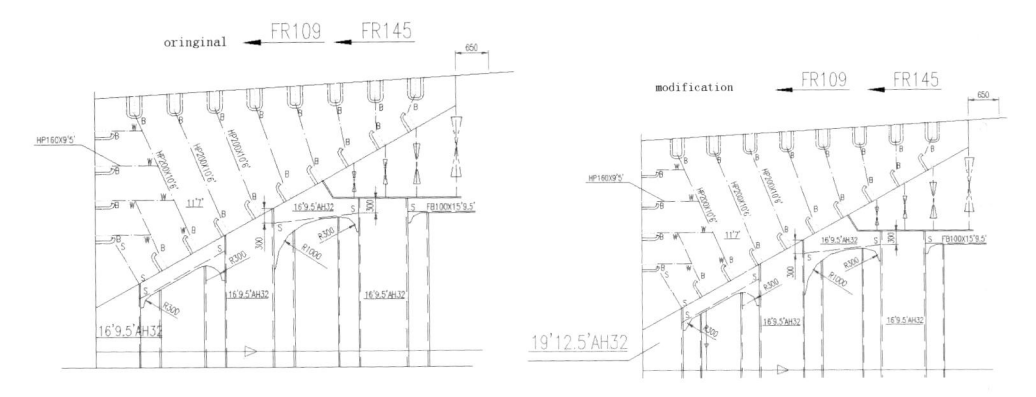

Fig. 11: Typical scantling distribution of transverse bulkhead

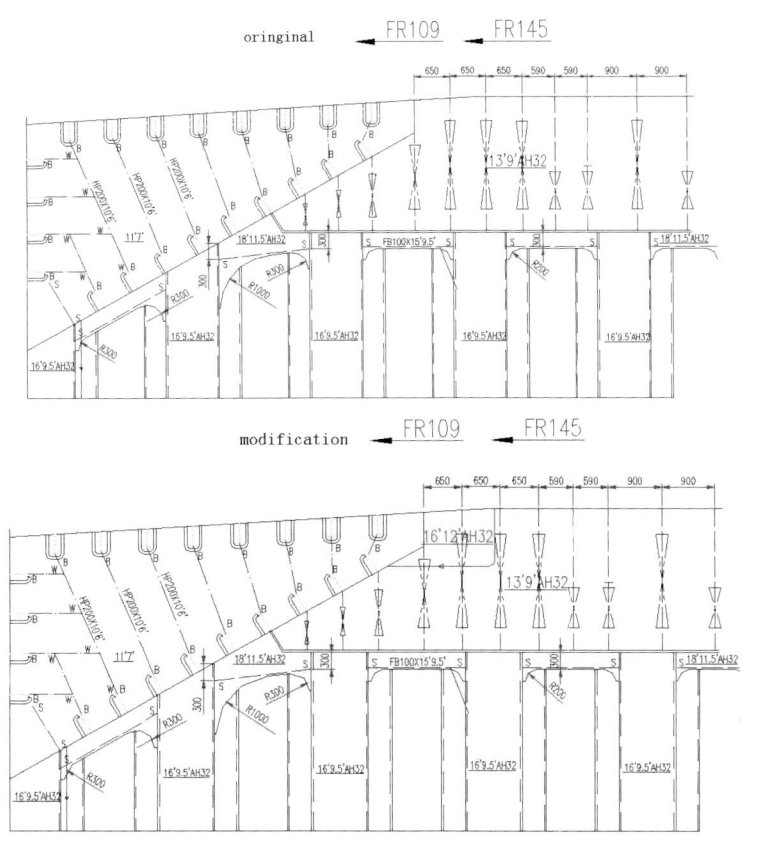

Fig. 12: Typical scantling distribution of vertical plate in upper stool

In using CSR to the design of bulk carrier, Some problems are met. An example is the Thickness increase of inner bottom caused by steel coils.

It was found that the plate thickness would be 33 mm for those ships, which carry steel coils structures if the formula provided by CSR was adopted in design.

$$t = K_1 \sqrt{\frac{(g + a_z)F}{\lambda_P R_Y}}$$

The formula above is based on the assumption that the method to fix steels showed in fig.6-2 of reference [2] is the standard one. If the steel were arranged in 2 or more rows, the formula in [2.7.2] and [2.7.3] of reference [2] will be adopted for only the bottom row of steel reach the hopper tank slope plate, while the direct strength analysis or approved methods will be adopted for the other cases.

Thus plate thickness was determined according to the result of finite element method. Through direct calculation, it can be found that the steel can be loaded even on bulk carriers with timber inner bottom as long as the formula of steel structure strength was satisfied.

It also points out that some modifications and explanations of the formula of steel structure strength should be made for the sake of better design.

5 Summary

(1) The thickness of inner bottom plate and hopper plate with CSR notation will be increased comparing traditional bulk carriers, the cause is the Grab[X] notation;

(2) The structure scantling will be increased with CSR notation comparing traditional bulk carriers, the cause is the ultimate strength requirement;

(3) The thickness formula of inner bottom plate should be modified;

(4) The weight increase of the ship is about 5% comparing to traditional bulk carriers.

References

[1] CCS, rules for construction of sea-going steel ship, 2006, china communications press;

[2] IACS, Common Structural Rules for Bulk Carriers, 2006, china communications press;

Optimal Design of Longitudinal Scantlings Amidships for Oil Tanker Based on JTP Rule

Chunyan Ji

Jiangsu University of Science and Technology

Zhenjiang, Jiangsu, China

Abstract

The paper takes the minimization of weight of large crude oil carrier midship section structure as the object of optimal design. The optimization model is built, which has 21 design variables and 34 constraint conditions about longitudinal strength and local strength, etc based on JTP rules. Correspondingly, the Relative Difference Quotient Algorithm (RDQA) model is built for the optimal design. A 76,000 DWT Large Crude Oil Carrier (LCC) is adopted as an example. The optimal design results show that the value of objective function decreases of more than 9.7% without including corrosion additions, and increases of 6.38% with corrosion additions compared to the original design based on ABS rule. Finally, optimal design results based on different rules (JTP and CCS) are compared. It shows that the weight of large crude oil carrier amidships section structure optimally designed on JTP rule increase 5.6% than on CCS rule with the same optimal algorithm.

Keywords: Optimal design; Oil tanker; JTP rule.

Introduction

In present oil is still the main energy, about 50 percent of the demanding oil amount comes from sea transport. So oil tanker has an important role in the sea transport. In order to satisfy the MARPOL73/78 rule-appendx-I13F and 13G, oil tanker usually adopted the double shell structure type, which induced the weight increasing. According to statistics, the steel weight of 30,000 ~ 150,000 oil tanker is 70-85 percent of the deadweight, and it will be more than 78 percent for more than 150,000 oil tankers. Therefore how to reduce the weight of the oil tanker is a very important problem for ship designers. The optimization design of ship structure is a good choice, which was first put forward by D.Kav and J.Moe in 1966. Until now there has been a great development for optimal design method for ship structures. Arai and Shimizu proposed response surface methodology to optimally design of ship structures (Arai and Shimizu, 2000). Genetic algorithm was studied on application to the optimal structural design of a ship's (Kitamura, Nobukawa, and Yang, 2000; Kyu-Yeul and Roh, 2001). It is noted that Xu studied fuzzy optimum design of ship structures (Xu Changwen,1988). In addition intellectual method was induced to design ship structural (Zeng Guangwu, 1992).

Among many factors which affect the design weight, improved design rule is very important. In order to mitigate the risks of structural failure in relation to the safety of life, environment and property and to ensure adequate durability of the hull structure for its intended life, IACS developed the Common Structural Rules for Oil Tankers (JTP) and Bulk Carrier (JBP). The common rules have been in operation since April.1, 2006. Compared to the former rules, the common rule takes on bigger changes on corrosion addition and structural strength assessment. So a great interest developed with designers and researchers as to how much weight change the common rule would take.

This paper studied optimization design method for the large crude oil carrier midship section structure based on JTP rule (Common Structural Rules for Double Hull Oil Tankers, 2005). A 76,000 DWT LCC is adopted as an example to illustrate the weight change trend due to the common rule.

Discrete Optimization Model of Oil Tanker Structure

Objective Function

A panama oil tanker is taken as an analysis example. The object is to optimally design the midship structures of the tanker.

In the process of optimum design of ship structures, the structural weight of unit length midship is adopted as objective function to be minimized:

$$F(X) = \sum_{j=1}^{m} \rho_j A_{Fj} + \sum_{i=1}^{n} \rho_i A_{Vi} \quad (1)$$

where $F(X)$ represents the structural weight of unit length midship, X is the design variable vector, n is the number of the design variables, m is the number of the unchanged structural member, ρ_j and ρ_i represent respectively material density of the ith or jth member (kg/m^3), A_{Fj} is the cross section area of jth unchanged member, A_{Vi} is the cross section area of ith variable member.

Design Variables

In order to reduce the dimensions of the optimum design problem, the paper regards the structural members near the neutralized axis as the determined ones, which should be consistent with the requirement of the JTP rule, while, for those members and their space as design variables, which contributes much to the hull girder strength. As shown in Fig.1, 21 design variables are selected for the panama ship. In this paper, the longitudinal spaces of the deck, inner bottom and outer bottom are described with the same variable, and the type of inner longitudinal and side longitudinal are also the same at the same vertical location. There are six variables to define types of inner longitudinal along the height of the ship:

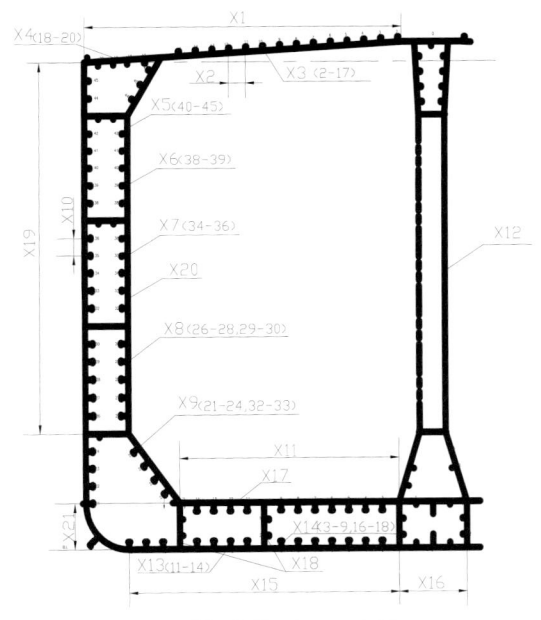

Fig.1: Design variables

Note:
X1: thickness of the deck plating (mm);
X2: longitudinal space of the deck, inner bottom and outer bottom (mm)
X3: type of deck longitudinal; X4: type of deck longitudinal at deck stringer;
X5-X9: type of inner longitudinal and side longitudinal
X10: longitudinal space of inner and outerside (mm)
X11: thickness of the floor plating (mm)
X12: thickness of longitudinal bulkhead plate (mm)
X13-X14: type of bottom longitudinal
X15: thickness of bottom shell plating (mm)
X16: thickness of box-shape beam plating (mm)
X17: type of bottom longitudinal
X18: thickness of outboard girder plating (mm)
X19: thickness of bottom shell plating
X20: thickness of inner side plating near the neutralized axis (mm)
X21: height of double bottom (mm)

The Determination of Discrete Variables

All these design variables are handled as discrete parameters. In this paper there are three types of variables: longitudinal space, thickness of the plating and types of longitudinal. These variables are dispersed with the following algorithm:
(1) For longitudinal space, the JTP rule has no specific requirements to its minimum and maximum limits. According to design experience, the minimum and maximum limits are respectively 700mm and 800mm. The discrete space values are selected as 50mm.
(2) The discrete value of the plating thickness is 0.5mm.
(3) Types of longitudinal are selected in sort ascending among the profiled bar assembles provided by CCS rule.

Design Constraints

During the summarizing of the design constraints, the corrosion additions should be considered based on JTP rule described in 3.3.2 to 3.3.7 unless otherwise specified in the specific rule requirements. The required net thickness of steel structures is to be calculated as the following equation:

$$t_{net} = t_{gross} - \alpha t_{corr} \quad (2)$$

Where t_{net} is the net thickness, t_{gross} is the gross thickness, t_{corr} is corrosion additions which are given in detail in 3.2 of JTP rule for individual structural members, α is the coefficient of corrosion.

(1) Hull Girder Bending Strength Constraints

Within $0.4L$ amidships the net hull girder section moment of inertia about the transverse neutral axis, $I_{v\text{-}net50}$, is not to be less than the rule minimum hull girder section modulus of inertia, $Iv\text{-}min$, defined as:

$$I_{v-\min} = 2.7 C_{wv} L^3 B(C_b + 0.7) \quad cm^4 \quad (3)$$

Where C_{wv} is the wave coefficient, L is the rule length, B is the molded breadth, C_b is the block coefficient but is not to be taken as less than 0.60.

Within $0.4L$ midship the net vertical hull girder section modulus, $Z_{v\text{-}min}$, at the deck and keel is not to be less than the rule minimum hull girder section modulus.

$$Z_{v-\min} = 0.9 k\, C_{wv}\, L^2 B(C_b + 0.7) \quad cm^3 \quad (4)$$

Where k is a higher strength steel factor.

The net hull girder section modulus about the horizontal neutral axis, $Z_{v\text{-}net50}$, is not to be less than the rule required hull girder section modulus, $Z_{v\text{-}req}$, based on the permissible still-water bending moment and design wave bending moment defined below:

$$Zv - reg = \frac{|M_{sw-perm} + M_{wv-v}|}{\sigma_{perm}} 10^{-3} \quad m^3 \quad (5)$$

Where $M_{sw-perm}$ is permissible hull girder hogging or sagging still water bending moment, M_{wv-v} is hogging or sagging vertical wave bending moment, σ_{perm} is allowable hull girder bending stress in N/mm².

(2) Hull Girder Shear Strength Constraints

Net hull girder shear strength capacity, $Q_{v-net50}$, is not to be less than the required vertical shear force Q_{v-req} as indicated in the following:

$$Q_{v-req} = Q_{sw-perm} + Q_{wv} \quad kN \quad (6)$$

Where $Q_{sw-perm}$ is permissible hull girder positive or negative still water shear force, Q_{wv} is vertical wave positive or negative shear force.

(3) Local strength constraints

Thickness of plating constraints:
The thickness of plating and stiffeners in the cargo tank region is to comply with the appropriate minimum thickness requirements given in Table 1.

Table 1 Minimum net thickness for plating and local support members

Scantling location			Net thickness(mm)
plating	Hull envelope up to $T_{sc}+4.6m$	Keel plating	5.5+0.03L_2
		Bottom shell/bilge/side shell	3.5+0.03L_2
	Hull envelope above $T_{sc}+4.6m$	Side shell /upper deck	4.5+0.02L_2
	Hull internal structure	Hull internal tank boundaries	4.5+0.02L_2
		Non-tight bulkheads, bulkheads between dry space and other plates in general	4.5+0.01L_2
Double bottom centerline girder			5.5+0.025L_2
Other double bottom girders			5.5+0.02L_2
Web and flanges of vertical web frames on longitudinal bulkheads, horizontal stringers on transverse bulkhead and deck transverses(above and below upper deck)			5.5+0.015L_2

Note: L_2 is the rule length

In addition the required net thickness, t_{net}, is to be taken as the greatest value calculated for all applicable design load sets, given by:

$$t_{net} = 0.0158 \alpha_p s \sqrt{\frac{|P|}{C_a \sigma_{yd}}} \quad mm \quad (7)$$

Where P is design pressure for the design load set being considered, in kN/m², C_a is permissible bending stress coefficient, σ_{yd} is specified minimum yield stress of the material, in N/mm², α_p is the plate element revised coefficient, s is the effective spacing of curved plating.

Longitudinal constraints:
The required net section modulus of longitudinal, Z_{net}, is to be taken as the greatest value calculated for all applicable design load sets, given by:

$$Z_{net} = \frac{|P|sl^2_{bdg}}{f_{bdg} C_s \sigma_{yd}} \quad cm^3 \quad (8)$$

Where f_{bdg} is bending moment factor, l_{bdg} is effective bending span, in m, C_s is permissible bending stress coefficient for the design load set being considered, and other symbols are same as Eq.7.

The required net web thickness, t_{w-net}, is to be taken as the greatest value calculated for all applicable design load sets and given by:

$$t_{w-net} = \frac{f_{shr}|P|sl_{shr}}{d_{shr} C_t \tau_{yd}} \quad mm \quad (9)$$

C_t permissible shear stress coefficient for the design load set being considered, $\tau_{yd} = \frac{\sigma_{yd}}{\sqrt{3}}$ N/mm^2, l_{shr} is effective shear span, in m, d_{shr} is the effective web depth of stiffeners.

Double bottom depth constraint:
The minimum double bottom depth, d_{bb}, is to be taken as the lesser of:

$$d_{db} = \frac{B}{15} \quad m, \quad \text{but not less than 1.0m} \quad (10)$$
$$d_{db} = 2.0 \quad m$$

Relative Difference Quotient Algorithm

A general mixed discrete-continuous variable nonlinear optimization problem (MD-NLP) is defined as follows:

$$\min f(X)$$
$$\text{s.t.} \quad g_j(X) \leq 0, \quad j=1,2,\ldots,m \quad (11)$$
$$x_i \in S_i; \; S_i \in S; \; i=1,2,\ldots,n$$

During the optimum search, the changes of design variables will induce the changes of the objective value. The Relative Difference of the objective function is defined as:

$$\frac{\Delta f}{\Delta x_i} = \frac{f(x_{i,j+1}) - f(x_{ij})}{x_{i,j+1} - x_{ij}} \quad (12)$$

Where Δf represents the changed value of the objective function, Δx is the varational value of the design variable x_i changing from the current value x_{ij} to the next discrete $x_{i,j+1}$.

The Relative Difference of the constraints is defined as:

$$\frac{\Delta g}{\Delta x_i} = \frac{g(x_{i,j+1}) - g(x_{ij})}{x_{i,j+1} - x_{ij}} \quad (13)$$

Where $\Delta g = g_{(x_i,j+1)} - g(x_{ij})$ is the variational value of constraint.

The Relative Difference is defined as
$$\beta_i = \frac{\Delta g/\Delta x_i}{\Delta f/\Delta x_i} = \frac{\Delta g}{\Delta f} = \frac{g(x_{i,j+1}) - g(x_{ij})}{f(x_{i,j+1}) - f(x_{ij})} \quad (14)$$

For optimum design problem with multiple constraints conditions, the constraints condition should be normalized.
$$g_j(X) \leq 0 \quad (j=1,2,3,\ldots,m) \quad (15)$$

At the design point the constraints assemble $G\{g_j(X)\}$ is divided into two sub-assembles:
$$G_1 = \{g_j(X) | g_j(X) > 0\} \quad (16)$$
$$G_2 = \{g_j(X) | g_j(X) \leq 0\}, \text{ set to be zero} \quad (17)$$

So
$$Z(X) = \|G_1\|_2 = \left(\sum g_j^2(X)\right)^{1/2} \quad (18)$$

The relative difference in multiple constraints problem is defined as:
$$\beta_i = \frac{\Delta Z/\Delta x_i}{\Delta f/\Delta x_i} = \frac{\Delta Z}{\Delta f} = \frac{Z(x_{i,j+1}) - Z(x_{ij})}{f(x_{i,j+1}) - f(x_{ij})} \quad (19)$$

The relative difference vector is:
$$B = \{\beta_1, \beta_2, \ldots, \beta_n\} \quad (20)$$

Then the superimposition equation is expressed as:
$$X^{(Q+1)} = X^{(Q)} + D \cdot \Delta X^{(Q)} \quad (21)$$

Where $\Delta X^{(Q)}$ is the changed value vector, whose elements is variational value of every current value x_{ij} to the next $x_{i,j+1}$, D is coefficient vector, which is defined as follows:
$$\begin{aligned} D_i &= 1, \quad \beta_i = \min\{\beta_1, \beta_2, \cdots, \beta_n\} \\ &= 0, \quad \beta_i \neq \min\{\beta_1, \beta_2, \cdots, \beta_n\} \end{aligned} \quad (22)$$

Numerical Analysis and Discussion

Main Parameters of the Oil Tanker
The principle dimensions of the oil tank used in the numerical analysis are:
Length B.P=220m; Breadth(mld.)=32.26m;
Depth(mld.)=21.20m, Draught=12.50m; Scantling Draught=14.7m; Block coefficient=0.89;
Deadweight=760000ton.
The material is Q235-steel and AH32- steel.

The Constraints Conditions
Table 2 lists the constraints conditions for 21 design variables, which are calculated based on JTP rule. Table 2 is the bound limits of design variables.

Table 2 the bound limits of design variables

Variable symbol	definition	Minimum value	Maximum value
X1	Thickness(mm)	8.75	20
X2	Longitudinal space(mm)	600	800
X3	section modulus(cm^3)	20.92	The maximum value
X4	Thickness(mm)	7.16	20
X4	section modulus(cm^3)	20.92	----
X5	section modulus(cm^3)	206.55	The maximum value
X6	section modulus(cm^3)	239.96	The maximum value
X7	Thickness of faceplate(mm)	13.58	25
X7	Thickness of web plate(mm)	10	20
X7	section modulus(cm^3)	305.39	----
X8	Thickness of faceplate(mm)	13.73	25
X8	Thickness of web plate	10	20
X8	section modulus(cm^3)	430.02	----
X9	Thickness of faceplate(mm)	13.36	25
X9	Thickness of web plate(mm)	10	20
X9	section modulus(cm^3)	928.7	----
X10	Longitudinal space(mm)	600	800
X11	Thickness(mm)	11.06	20
X12	Thickness(mm)	13.83	25
X13	Thickness of faceplate(mm)	13.46	25
X13	Thickness of web plate(mm)	10	20
X13	section modulus(cm^3)	546.16	----
X14	Thickness of faceplate(mm)	13.24	25
X14	Thickness of web plate(mm)	10	20
X14	section modulus(cm^3)	546.16	----
X15	thickness(mm)	10.18	20
X16	thickness(mm)	11.87	20
X17	Thickness of faceplate(mm)	13.87	25
X17	Thickness of web plate(mm)	10	20

X17	section modulus(cm³)	946.56	———
X18	Thickness(mm)	11.06	20
X19	thickness(mm)	11.06	20
X20	thickness(mm)	9.13	20
X21	Height(m)	2000	2500

Optimization Results

The original structure of the tanker was designed by ABS rule. Table 3 gives the original size and optimal design results based on JTP rule.

The optimization results shows that the structural weight using optimum design method based on JTP rule will induce a weight increase of 6.3847% when including the corrosion addition, and weight decrease of 9.7353% without the corrosion addition compared to the original design based on ABS rule. In addition, in order to analyze the difference on structural weight of large crude oil carrier midship section structure optimally designed based on JTP rule and CCS rule for the same type ship, this paper also carries out optimization design for the oil tanker based on CCS rule using the same optimum method and the same design variables. The optimization results demonstrate that the structural weight will increase by 5.6109% based on JTP rule considering corrosion addition compared to CCS rule.

Conclusions

This paper takes the minimization of weight of a large crude oil carrier midship section structure as the object to optimally design a panama oil tank based on JTP rule requirement. The Relative Difference Quotient Algorithm (RDQA) is adopted to search the optimum design. A 76,000 DWT LCC is carried out as an analysis example. The optimal design results show that the value of objective function decreases by more than 9.7% without considering corrosion additions, and increases 6.38% with corrosion additions. Finally, optimal design results based on different rules (JTP and CCS) are compared. It shows that the weight of large crude oil carrier midship section structure optimally designed on JTP rule increase 5.6% rather than on CCS rule with the same optimal algorithm.

Table 3 Comparison of optimization results

Design variable	Original value	Optimal design value without corrosion addition	Optimal design value with corrosion addition
X1	14.5	12	16
X2	785	700	700
X3	220×11.5	240×14	240×14
X4	200×14	200×9	200×11
X5	240×12	240×14	240×14
X6	280×11	240×14	240×14
X7	T260×12+90×20	T260×11+90×15	T260×13+90×18.5
X8	T330×12+90×20	T330×11+90×15	T330×13+90×18.5
X9	T310×12+90×20	T310×11+90×15	T310×13+90×18.5
X10	770	700	700
X11	15.5	12	16
X12	21	19	21.5
X13	T330×12+90×20	T330×11+90×15	T330×13+90×18.5
X14	T310×12+90×20	T310×11+90×15	T310×13+90×18.5
X15	14.5	11	14
X16	17.5	12	16
X17	T350×12+90×20	T350×11+90×15	T350×13+90×18.5
X18	12	12	14.5
X19	15	12	14.5
X20	14	10	13
X21	2000	2300	2300
Weight of the unit length(kg)	35590.23	32125.4	37862.57
Changed weight percent	—	-9.7353%	+6.3847%

References

Arai, M., Shimizu,Y (2000). "On the application of response surface methodology to the optimization of ship structural design", Journal of the society of Naval Architects of Japan,Vol 188, pp 545-552.

Common Structural Rules for Double Hull Oil Tankers. March, 2005.

Kitamura, M, Nobukawa, H, and Yang, F (2000). "Application of a Genetic Algorithm to the Optimal Structural Design of a Ship's Engine Room Taking Dynamic Constraints into Consideration", Journal of Marine Science and Technology-SNAJ,Vol 5,pp 131-146.

Kyu-Yeul Lee, Myung-II, Roh (2001). "An Efficient Genetic Algorithm Using Gradient Information for Ship Structural Design Optimization", Ship Technology Research,Vol 48,pp 161-170.

Xu Changwen (1986). "On fuzzy optimization of ship structure", International shipbuilding progress, Vol 33,No 337, pp 154-158.

Zeng Guangwu.(1992). "A New Method of Engineering Optimization Design-pattern Transposition Method", Proc. Of Conf. On Optimization Techniques and Application, World Scientific, Singapore, pp 827-832.

Large Scale Seakeeping Experiments in the New, Large Towing Tank B600

Jean-François Leguen, Didier Fréchou,

Bassin d'essais des carènes
Val de Reuil, France

Abstract

In early 2000, the French marine institute, Bassin d'essais des carènes (BEC), built a new towing tank facility which is dedicated to physical simulation on large scale model and high sea state. This paper presents the main characteristics of this new facility and very peculiar seakeeping tests performed with a 1/5th scaled frigate model (called AMANDA), the hull structure of which, is in mechanical similarity to full scale. The main objective of this test is to validate numerical design tools, including the prediction code for the induced waves motion and the prediction code for the structural response at wave frequency and above; i.e. whipping effect.

Keywords

Towing tank; Seakeeping; Stress; Hydroelasticity; Modal Analysis.

Introduction

BA is part of the French MoD. More specifically, it is part of the systems evaluation and test directorate that provides analysis evaluation and testing for the French military procurement agency, the DGA. Technical expertise, numerical simulation capability, and test facilities are available to customers in all sectors of naval industry, including procurement agencies, ship owners, design offices, shipyards, and companies specializing in underwater systems, weapon or combat systems.

BEC is in charge of the expertise for hydrodynamics, hydroacoustics and structure. In order to answer different issues, several types of studies are undertaken:

Tests on scale models

Segmented model hulls with rigid girder are used in order to obtain bending moment or segmented model hulls with elastic girder are used to directly obtain the stress responses (see Dupau, Leguen and Darquier 2007).

Sea trials

BEC is involved in the set-up of hull monitoring of several French military vessels (Leguen, Bourdon and Dispa, 2007).

Computer simulations

Usually, 3D linear frequency seakeeping codes are used in order to obtain bending moments or pressure in order to be used as input data of structural linear codes such as ABAQUS.

Tests on ship model in complete mechanical structure similarity to full scale

Experiments on the frigate model "AMANDA" in complete mechanical structure similarity to full scale were exceptional and possible, due to the characteristics of the new large towing tank, the B600. The main objective of BEC was to validate tools and design methodologies used by yards. Due to her similarity with a real ship, experiments on AMANDA allow for checking tools, from the excitation forces (the waves) to the stress response on a naval structure. The strong advantage to perform experiments in a towing tank, compared to sea trials, is the ability to control the wave environment.

The large towing tank B600

The most imposing test facility at BEC located at Val de reuil, the one that justifies the qualification of testing station and the surface area of a military terrain, is the large towing tank B600. The B600 is one of the most recent and the longest towing tank in Europe. Its size and capacity allow the simulation of sea conditions above sea state 8 for high speed ships, experimentation on immersed submarine models, and even towing of large scale models.

Most of the world's towing tanks are designed according to traditional dimensions: lengths are generally between 100 and 400 meters, depending on the size of the testing station with, at one end, a test preparation zone and, sometimes, a wave generator at the other end. The model tested is connected to a platform that translates between these two extremities. Although this type of design works for conventional vessels, it is complicated for testing high speed vessels due to insufficient useful test durations once the vessel has reached a stable speed, i.e. taking into account the distances required for the acceleration and deceleration of the platform. In calm waters a longer useful distance in a towing tank allows a full series of measurements in different experimental conditions (variations of speed, of the position of a mobile appendage or of the frequency of propeller rotation) to be taken during a single test run. In irregular swell in similarity to full scale, a longer tank also facilitates a realistic statistical analysis of the behavior of a ship: it is essential, in a minimum number of test runs, to be sure to have encountered enough waves for the test to be judged representative of a realistic mixture of all wavelength components of the wave spectrum.

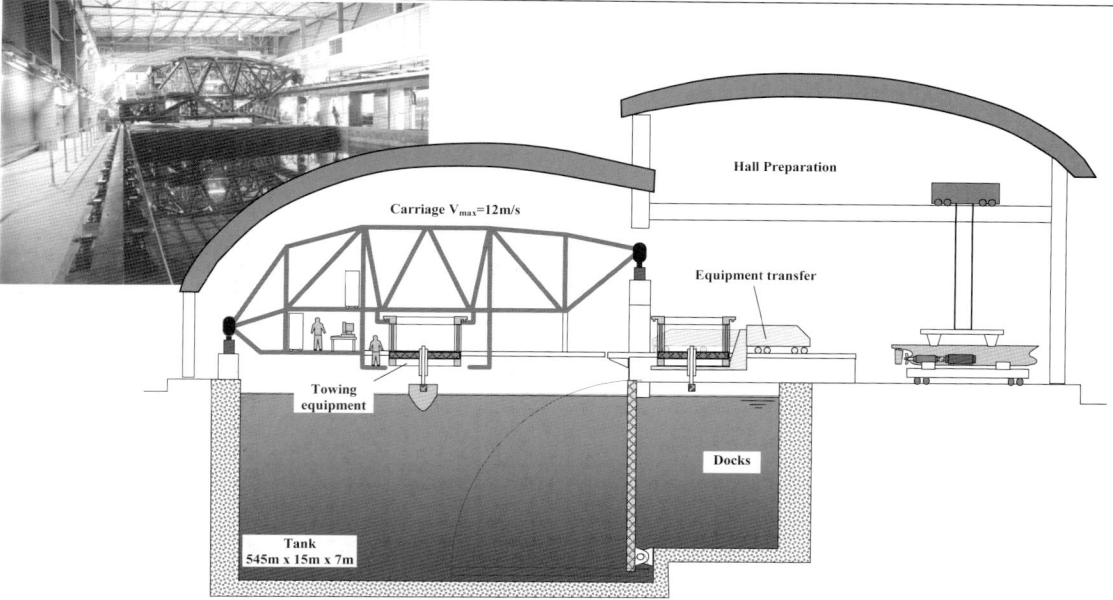

Fig. 1: B600 Large towing tank section

Housed in a six hundred meters long building, which explains its name, the B600 has almost 545 m of useful length, for a width of 15 m and a depth of 7 m. Powered by extremely rapid and precise electric motors, its 120 ton carriage is propelled at speeds of between 0.1 and 12 m/s, which allows simulations of the behavior of two types of ship, including the most rapid, with sufficiently large model sizes to obtain measurements that can be projected to represent real situations, following accepted practices. The size of the tank also allows large-scale testing. The models can reach 11 to 14 m and weigh between 4000kg and 7000kg. This possibility is in particular useful for ships with complex propellers like pump-jet on Pod (Bellevre, Copeaux. and Gaudin 2006) that must be particularly representative to improve the reliability of performance predictions. It also makes it possible to significantly increase the Reynolds number while respecting the Froude similarity so as to better guarantee the local wake in critical cases (bulbous bows, ballasted sterns, etc.).

The B600 is also equipped with a generator of monodirectional regular and irregular waves of a crest to trough height of up to 1 m. This generator can produce waves of 20 m for a traditional model scale of 1/20th and 30 m for a scale (also very traditional) of 1/30th. This enables the study of the dynamic stability of a following wave (notably via evaluations of the risk of broaching: under the effect of a following wave the ship loses its course and is positioned perpendicular to the wave, which increases the risk of capsize). The B600 could also be used for the study of rogue waves capable of overturning a ship.

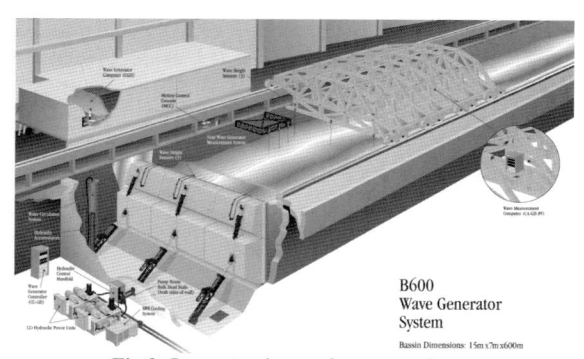

**Fig 2: Large towing tank wave maker
Regular wave of 1m crest to trough amplitude
(with the courtesy of MTS)**

The wave generator is a dual flap-type wavemaker of 15m wide and a dynamic stoke of +/-12°. The upper board is 1.5m immersed in water and the lower board is 3.5m high. The system is able not only to control independently the lower board and the upper board, but also to have both the upper board and the lower board acting as a single board (mono flap mode). The water behind a wet back wavemaker is always a source of possible chaotic forces imposed to the board. That is the main reason of the choice of a dry back.

The wave maker capacity (maximum crest to trough height versus wave period) is presented on figure 3 for the mono flap mode.

Wave maker capacity (regular wave) in mono flap (both upper and lower flaps)

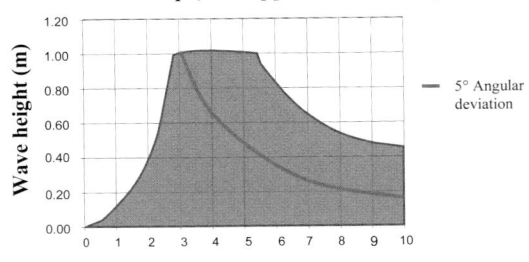

Fig. 3: B600 wave maker capability

The main challenge on that very long tank was to be able to limit as much as possible the wave energy dissipation while the wave is propagating in the tank. As pointed out by B. Molin (2001), "Even if it looks simple, generating a stokes regular wave in a tank is impossible : as the wave maker gets started, a transient stage ensues when all natural modes of the tank participate; the long modes damp out slowly and last throughout the test and beyond; as the wave travels down the tank a return current is established; if no proper control is applied to the wave maker motion, free wave at harmonics of the fundamental wave frequency are emitted ; reflections occur from the beach, back to wave maker, etc. When a model is introduced the situation gets worse with the diffracted and radiated waves being re-reflected from the side walls back to the model.". In order to limit those effects, the specifications for the wave board were oriented on the flatness of the front faces, its alignment, tight manufacturing tolerances, wave board assembly resonant frequencies, and accuracy in the board motion (position, speed and acceleration). In practice, we obtained a stability of the wave over distance from the wave board larger than 40 times the wavelength of the generated wave.

The control command of the wave board allows the generation of different types of waves: Airy wave, second order and third order Stokes wave, irregular wave (Bretschneider, Jonswap, OCHI…) as well as transient wave packet as described by Klaus and Kühnlein (1995). The next figures show some results on irregular wave and transient wave packet generations.

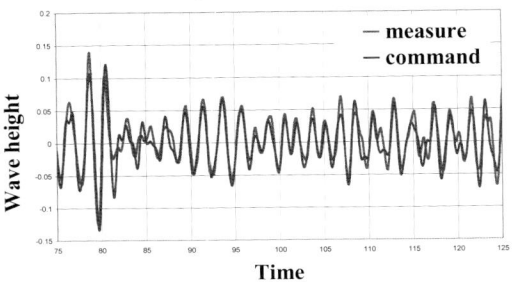

Fig. 4: Time trace of an irregular wave generation

The transient wave packet is constructed on the basis of a classical spectrum (Bretschneider) where the phase of each component is not randomly chosen, but determined in order to be in phase at one moment in one position of the tank. (Klaus and Kühnlein, 1995). As shown further this transient wave packet wave generation is used to determine the RAO of a ship. Regarding the test time duration, it is more effective to use this type of wave generation than performing the tests at different wave periods to build the spectral response.

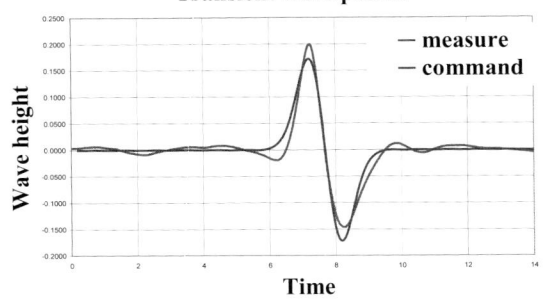

Fig. 5 : Time trace of transient wave packet at one location in the tank

Another special feature in the control command is to take into account in the wave generation process of the phenomena related to the propagation and reflection of waves in the tank. As shown in figure 6, in order to guarantee that all the wave components are present together when the model reaches its test speed, the wavelength components of the irregular wave are generated successively, i.e. the short wavelengths are generated first, then the medium ones, then the large ones. The main benefit of this type of generation is a longer test time for the measurements because the effect of reflection from the absorber is then delayed compared to a generation in which all the wavelength components started at the same time.

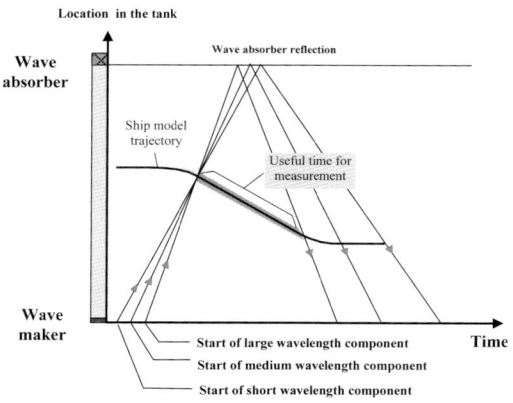

Fig. 6: Time trace of an irregular wave generation

A large wave absorber of 20 m long acting like a beach of a parabolic shape dissipates the wave energy by breaking waves. The performances are quite satisfactory with wave reflection coefficient about 5% for all the wave periods less than 5 sec and about 10% for wave periods higher than 5 seconds.

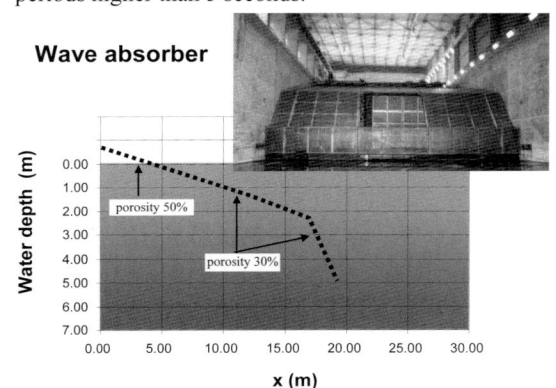

Fig. 7: B600 wave absorber

For seakeeping tests in the tank, it is of relevance to measure the wave encountered by the ship model during the runs. Due to the high wave height and high carriage speed, all the techniques for wave measurement are not useable for they are more appropriate to measurement at a fixed position. The wire probes (capacity and resistance types) are rapidly inefficient at speeds higher than 2m/s and for wave heights larger than 0.5m due to water flowing along the wire. The servo type probes (ORCA, KENEK) are limited in vertical motion speed i.e. not more than 3m/s and are very sensitive to dust particles on the water surface. Although acoustic probes present the advantage of being a non intrusive technique, their dynamics of 40 Hz max limits their use. That is the reason why, BEC developed a Laser based wave measurement device. The technique is based on the image processing of the Laser beam spot at the water surface. The motion of the spot is directly related to the water height which then gives the wave height measurement. Figure 7 shows the basic principle of the technique.

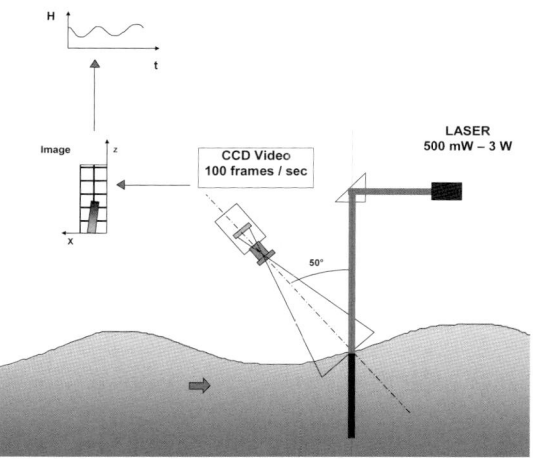

Fig. 7 : Laser probe for encountered wave measurement

Large scale model

The dimensions of the B600 also allow the towing of a large scale model, built in similarity of a full scale mechanical structure. For a traditional model (scale of about 1/20), such a model would have a hull as thick as cigarette paper and would collapse on the lightest touch. The very first test with a large scale model in the B600 tank was conducted on the model called 'AMANDA', 23 m long, i.e. 1/5th of the La Fayette frigate, in order to validate calculations of wave induced loads and of the structural response of the vessel (stress). The first tests were in stationary conditions (at the end of 2000), then with forward motion (in 2004), the model was equipped with deformation and accelerometer gauges, and the measurements were collected by a computer. The characteristics of the B600 wave generator and platform enabled the simulation, for a real speed of 17 knots, of (Beaufort scale) sea states of 3 to 5.

AMANDA main characteristics

AMANDA model main characteristics during experiments which are not representative of a real case are given in table 1. The objective was not to obtain results for a real displacement of the full scale frigate but to validate tools. As a matter of fact, we decided to use a light displacement in order to facilitate the 12 tons mass handling operations and also to induce more whipping effects in the aft part of the ship.

Table 1: Main characteristics of AMANDA

Displacement	18 t
Overall Length	25 m
Height (including superstructures)	3.2 m
Light mass	11 t
Draught	0.7
Beam	3.1
Material	Steel

AMANDA has some special particularity with regards to the models usually used at BEC. She was built in the late eighties for a study about acoustics discretion. The purpose was to estimate the structural induced noise of the future frigates and to calibrate some solutions to reduce it. For that study, it was necessary to choose a model not only in geometric similarity with the real frigate but also in similarity for vibration and noise. That is the reason why the structural arrangement of the real ship has been reproduced in order to have a direct scaling relationship between the modes of resonance of the real ship and the model.

The model was refit in order to be used for seakeeping / structural experiments in the B600 in 2003.

The objective was to make the test with a ship model with a complete mechanical structure that takes into account the elasticity of the structure like on real ships. The similarity is not only true for global geometric characteristics, but also for the mechanical internal structure: bulkheads, stiffeners and plates have sizes and thickness reduced by a factor 1/5. But all parameters are not in scale with the real vessel as the hull material. The same material, steel, was used to build AMANDA as the full scale frigate.

Fig. 8: Handling process of AMANDA

Non dimensional analysis

First step is to verify the similarity conditions, for natural frequency of the ship structure which can be represented by a simple girder.

Natural frequencies in air are related to:
- The length of the girder, L, expressed in meters [m]
- Inertia of the girder's section, I [m^4].
- The total mass of the girder, M [kg].
- The added mass in heave, M [kg].
- The material characterized by Young's Modulus E [N/m²].

The natural frequency f of the first mode of girder response is related to:

$$f \approx \sqrt{\frac{EI}{(M + M_a)L^3}} \quad (1)$$

Because the model is built with a geometrical scale λ and because the Young's modulus doesn't change, the factor between the natural frequency of the model and the natural frequency of the full scale vessel will be equal to the geometrical scale $1/\lambda$. Because wave frequency in the towing tank and at sea are related with the scaling factor $1/\sqrt{\lambda}$ (following Froude similarity laws), some phenomena, as whipping, which mix frequency of waves and natural frequency, could be affected by the non respect of hydroelastics similitude laws. However, the numerical tools can easily take into account this fact.

Modal analysis in air

The final purpose of the experiments was the modal analysis in water, but a modal analysis in air was performed in order to characterize the model. Those experiments, as the modal analysis in water, were performed by ETAS which is another establishment of the French DGA, more focused on ground vehicles (Lelan and Lagadec, 2003). The model was supported by two pneumatic cushions in order to have a free / free condition. Pneumatic cushions were controlled at very low frequency to avoid any interference at the natural frequency of the model. The excitation was performed by two excitators (random signal) elastically suspended and linked to the structure by a needle. Responses in term of 3D accelerations were measured all over the model at about 463 points (i.e. 1389 degrees of freedom). Most of the points were located on main frame, but some were measured on the superstructure to detect some local modes.

Fig. 9: Modal analysis in air

Fig. 10: Modal analysis in water

Modal analysis in water

The same apparatus was used in water as for the modal analysis in air, except the air cushions which are not needed in this case. To avoid reflection on the tank wall, AMANDA was located near the middle of the tank. Some tests along the wall show that effects could be neglected as soon as the distance between the wall and the model is greater than the beam of the model. Location of measurement points was the same as in air. Frequency range studied was 8 Hz -90 Hz.

Operational analysis

The modal analysis in water was performed without waves and without forward speed (as for the analysis in air!). To validate a methodology which could be applied at full scale and to estimate the influence of the natural frequency due to forward speed, some extra tests were done. With forward speed, it was impossible to use the same apparatus, so operational analysis was used by ETAS. In this case, the excitation is only due to the forward speed. In this case transfer functions from the excitations to the response were impossible to obtain as the previous modal analysis, but natural frequencies of identified modes were achievable.

Table 2: Natural Frequencies (in Hertz)

Modes	In air	In water
1st. Bending in vertical plane	12.4	8.7
2nd Bending in vertical plane	26.5	18.1
3rd Bending in vertical plane	55.7	27.4
4th Bending in vertical plane	78.4	33.2

Seakeeping experiments in the B600: set-up & instrumentation

Large scaled models, such as AMANDA, are towed at the back of the carriage using a cable. A second cable fixed on the stern of the model is attached to a winch located on the ground at one end of the basin. This winch is controlled to act as a brake for the deceleration phase of the run and for the return phase of the run. It also helps the course keeping during the run of the model in the basin axis. The junction between the model and the two cables is arranged not to perturb the pitch and heave motion of the model.

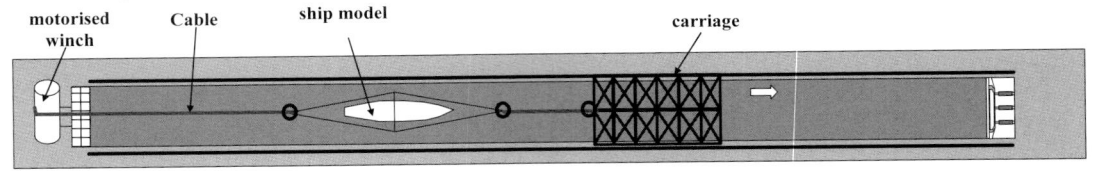

Fig. 11: Towing set-up for high scaled model

About 30 strain gauges were fixed on the structure of the model, mainly on longitudinal stiffeners in order to obtain the global deformation of the girder on waves. Then, experiments in waves were performed without and with forward speed. Regular waves at various periods and with heights up to 1m crest to trough were performed. Transfer functions (RAO) of rigid body motion were measured with and without sidewall effects, using a transient wave packet. Records of local and global deformations of the girder at the encountered frequency of waves, as well as at the natural frequency of the girder, were then analysed.

Fig. 12: AMANDA in B600, 4m/s head waves

The most impressive tests were performed in head waves with forward speed up to 4 m/s (Figure 5).

To obtain RAOs, not only were usual tests in regular waves performed but also tests using a transient wave packet technique. The comparison of RAOs from those two techniques is very good even for amplitude (Figure 13) and phases (Figure 14) of stress.

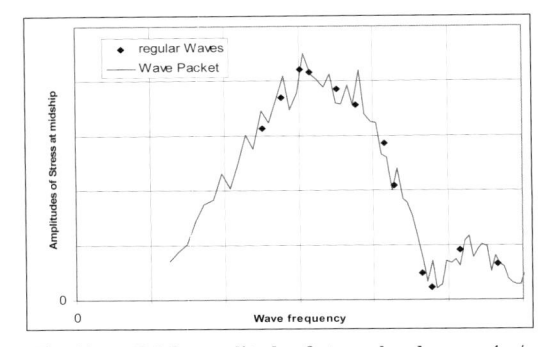

Fig. 13: RAO, amplitude of stress, head waves 4m/s

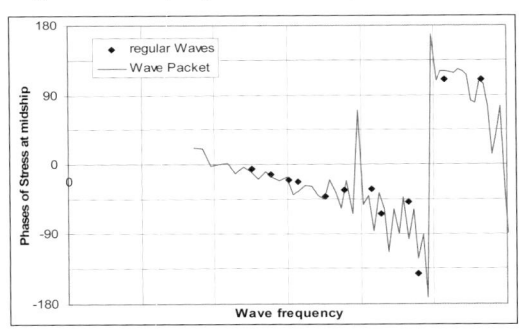

Fig. 14: RAO, phase of stress, head waves 4m/s

Extra experiments

Due to the unique opportunity of AMANDA in the B600, some extra experiments were done to obtain data in very different domains as acoustics (wake noise) and about scale effects in general. For example roll damping was estimated at different forward speeds by extinction tests, in order to compare these results to small scale model and full scale measurements.

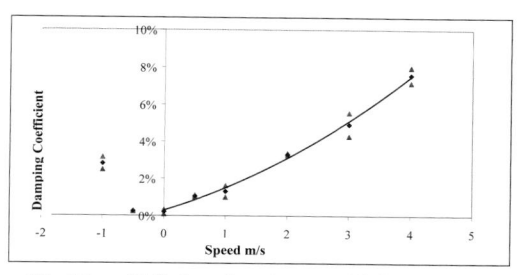

Fig. 15: Roll damping change with forward speed

Whipping phenomena were observed for the most severe wave heights, particularly in following waves without forward speed. In these wave and speed conditions, strong slamming occurs systematically under the aft part of the model. This part was particularly exposed to slamming because it was just above the water level, due to the light displacement.

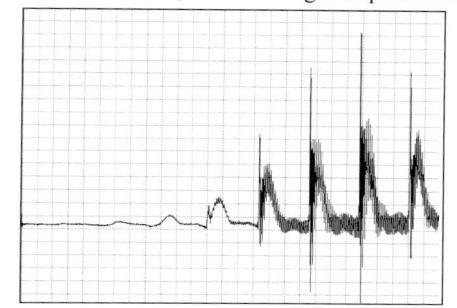

Fig. 16: Time trace of Stress response with whipping effects on increasing regular waves

Numerical simulations

The first step, for the numerical simulations, is a classical seakeeping code. In this case, we used a three-dimensional linear code, working in the frequency domain. Pitch RAOs are validated against experiments. Due to the size of the model, the side wall effect and finite depth effect are important. With the wave packet techniques it is possible to process raw signals with or without the confined effects. Seakeeping codes can take these kinds of effects and can be validated (see figure 17). There is still a shift in frequency which is not yet fully explained.

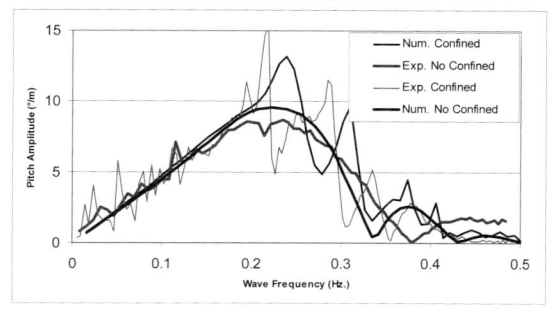

Fig. 17: Amplitude of Stress along the girder

Modal analysis calculations using the numerical code ABAQUS were done on a full mesh of the model (figure 18).

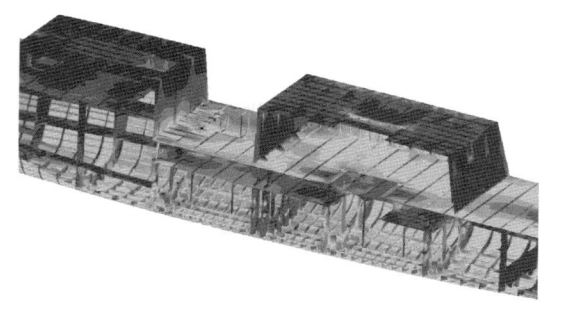

Fig. 18: Finite Element Mesh and stress responses

Calculations of natural modes in air and in water were done and compared to the measurements. Two methods were tested. The first one is based on a simple 2D section approximation of the girder; the second one used the full FEM model.

Table 2: Natural frequencies (in Hertz) in water

modes	2D	3D	Exp.
1st Bending in vertical plane	7.9	8.0	8.7
1st Bending in horizontal plane.	11.0	14.6	14.7
1st Torsion along beam axis.	46.4	24	23.1

The 2D method calculation was judged too simple to obtain accurate results in particular for AMANDA which has a complex structure including large openings and long superstructures.

Numerical calculations to simulate the stress response in waves were made with a set of numerical codes in use at BEC. From the seakeeping code, outputs in term of transfer functions of pressure on each wetted panel are selected. These pressures are then used as an input of the structural FEM code ABAQUS. Linear structure calculations were done by the modal superposition method that gives local stresses.

For each run the numerical simulations are compared to the experiments. For example figure 19 shows the comparison of the stress repartition along the girder in regular waves (no forward speed, following waves). Comparisons are globally good.

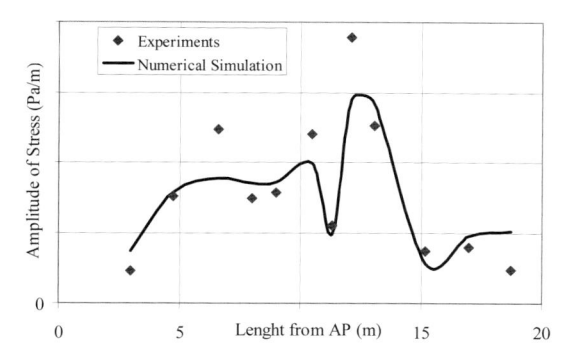

Fig. 19: Amplitude of Stress along the girder

Conclusions

The complete set of numerical tools for motions, stress and local accelerations predictions, was validated using this very special experiment. Those tools could be used to predict the behavior of a naval platform on heavy seas, including the structural response.

Acknowledgements

The study was funded by the French Navy through the SPN (Service des Programme Navals) which supports the Bassin d'essais des carènes in its research activities. Many thanks also to ETAS which participated actively in the experimental tasks. We also wish to thank the whole staff of Bassin d'essais des carènes. Without them, this very complete project would not have been possible. In particular we would like to thank V. Robic in charge of the project at this time and B. Hamelin who took charge of the huge handling problems.

References

Bellevre D, Copeaux P and Gaudin C. (2006), "Pump-jet Pod : an ideal mean to propel large military and merchant ship", T-Pod Conference , Brest, France.

Dupau T., Leguen J-F, and Darquier M (2007), "Comparison of experimental methods to assess internal loadings applied to a naval structure". Journées de l'Hydrodynamique, Brest, France

Klaus, G F and Kühnlein, W L(1995). "A new approach to seakeeping in oblique waves with transient waves packets". ASME, volume 1-A, Offshore Technology

Leguen J-F, Bourdon O and Dispa H (2007). "Hull Monitoring of a French Frigate, Description, Treatments and Applications", ISOPE, Lisbon.

Lelan P. and Lagadec, M (2003) "Measuring inertia properties of heavy vehicle using modal analysis", ASTELAB.

Molin B, (2001) "Numerical and physical wavetanks: making them fit", Ship Technolgy Research, Vol 48, 2-22.

ental investigations on a possibility of prevention

Improvement of Safety in a Seaway for Large Container Ships by Reducing the Risk of Parametric Rolling Utilizing Rudder Control

Yojiro Wada, Sam Kwon Hong, Dong Yeon Lee, Yun We Choi, Young Jin Lee

Samsung Ship Model Basin, Samsung Heavy Industries, Ltd.
Daejeon-city, South Korea

Abstract

The effectiveness of rudder control to prevent the parametric rolling is discussed experimentally and theoretically for large container ships. Free running model experiments for a 9,000 TEU class container ship were carried out in various wave conditions to investigate the effect of rudder control on this instability phenomenon. Rudder was utilized to control both ship heading and rolling. Theoretical investigations were also carried out by stability analysis and numerical simulations. From these investigations, it was shown that the risk of parametric rolling can be eliminated by only rudder control within the rudder rate given in the SOLAS regulation and that it is very important not to amplify the disturbance of rolling in the earlier stage of the phenomenon. Rudder action could be a disturbance to the occurrence of parametric rolling, but, on the other hand, rudder control plays a good role to improve the safety in a seaway by reducing the risk of parametric rolling.

Keywords

Container ship; Safety; Parametric rolling; Motion control; Rudder; Longitudinal waves.

Introduction

Recent rapid-growth of Chinese economy has been playing an important role in the activation of global sea-transportation in the world, especially in the Asian region. With this trend as a result of remarkable increase of the needs for container transportation by seaway, many large container ships, so-called Post-Panamax type, were thrown into services aiming at the scale merit by enlargement. And recently, further enlargement of container ships has been increasingly accelerated as shown in the fact that mega-container ships exceeding 10,000 TEU class are now on order. (Lee, 2006)

However, enlargement of hull form resulted in a new problem in the design of these ships. Hull form characterized by extensive flare at bow and stern part yields large fluctuation of transverse stability in longitudinal waves and induces large roll motion due to parametric resonance.

Photo 1 : Damage on Large Container Ship (Porter, 2000)

The extreme roll response of ships in a seaway due to parametric resonance is the serious problem for the ship owner and ship yards. Recently, taking the opportunity of the accident of extensive cargo loss and hull damage on a Post-Panamax container ship, various studies have been performed to understand the physics of this unstable phenomenon in large container ships, to establish susceptibility criteria of danger due to parametric rolling, and to evaluate the influences of induced large rolling on the design and operation of these ships.(France, 2003; Shin, 2004; ABS, 2004) One of the most effective operations in a seaway to avoid parametric rolling is to change the relations with encounter waves outside a susceptible region by changing speed or heading, because this phenomenon occurs when certain requirements on the relations between a ship and encounter waves are satisfied.

On the other hand, roll control by anti-rolling devices using fin, water tank (Shin, 2004) or rudder etc. seems to be another effective solution. These devices generate anti-rolling moment against the excitation and improve the instability in parametric rolling. Among these devices, rudder seems to be more attractive compared with other devices, because it does not cause a large cost-up and reduction of cargo capacity, and it is also applicable to the ships after delivery through a small modification of steering system.

This paper shows the results of the experimental and theoretical investigations on a possibility of prevention of parametric rolling by rudder control for 9,000 TEU class container ships. Free running experiments were carried out in various longitudinal waves for two kinds of transverse meta-centric height. Both movable rudder and anti-rolling fin were installed on the model and used to control ship heading and rolling by applying the simple feed-back law. Theoretical investigations were carried out by stability analysis based on the 1 DOF-equation of rolling, and by numerical simulations with the coupling equations of 6-DOF motions (Hamamoto, 1993), taking account of the fluctuation of meta-centric height in waves. From these investigations, it is shown that rudder control is effective to eliminate the risk of parametric rolling and that it is very important to restrain the roll disturbance in the earlier stage before the roll amplitude has been developed.

Experimental Investigations

Particulars of Subject Ship

Free running model experiments were carried out for 9,000 TEU class container ship in the towing tank of Samsung Ship Model Basin (SSMB). The towing tank has the size of 400 m × 14m × 7 m in length, breadth and depth, respectively. A set of plunger-type wave generator system is installed on one shorter side.

Principal particulars of the subject ship at design load condition are shown in Table 1. A wooden model of scale ratio 1/60 was used. The model was equipped with a propeller, a rudder, bilge keels and a pair of movable anti-rolling fin. The rudder was normally designed and it was not specially designed for the roll control. The fin was designed to have similar heel-capacity as the rudder.

Procedures of Experiments

The model was installed under the carriage and self-propelled. Power for the instruments on the model was supplied from the carriage. Procedures of experiments are summarized in Table2. Propeller revolution was automatically controlled to keep average speed of the model at the carriage speed, referring the relative longitudinal position to the carriage. Rudder and anti-rolling fin were connected to servo-motors. Heading angle of the model was kept by control of rudder angle. Lateral drifting was also controlled simultaneously by rudder, because the towing carriage can not compensate the large displacement of the model in lateral direction. Rolling was controlled by either rudder or fin, or both rudder and fin. Command signal to control the actuator is calculated by feed-back controller. Ship motions of 6 DOF were measured by a non-contact optical sensor system with 3 CCD cameras. Angular velocity of rolling and yawing was measured by a 3-axis rate-gyro. Over view of the model is shown in Photo 2.

Table 1 : Principal Particulars

Length	[m]	321.0
Breadth	[m]	45.6
Draft	[m]	13.0

Table 2: Control of Actuator

Actuator	Feed-back Signal	Controlled Variable
Propeller	Surging	Ship Speed
Rudder	Swaying	Lateral Drifting
	Yawing (Angle, Rate)	Heading Angle
	Rolling (Angle, Rate)	Roll Angle
Fin	Rolling (Angle, Rate)	Roll Angle

Experimental Conditions

Experiments were carried out for two kinds of transverse meta-centric height GM_T. Conditions of meta-centric height and natural roll period are shown in Table 3. The value of GM_T 3.0 m is the highest condition and that of 1.2 m is the most frequent condition in the operation in a seaway.

Combinations between ship speed and wave frequency in longitudinal waves which satisfy the frequency condition of the parametric rolling were examined to decide the experimental condition, in which the wave encounter frequency is about twice of the natural roll frequency. According to these examinations, susceptibility of parametric rolling is higher in head wave for GM_T 3.0 m and so in following wave for GM_T 1.2 m. Therefore, head and following waves were selected as the wave direction for GM_T 3.0 m and 1.2 m, respectively.

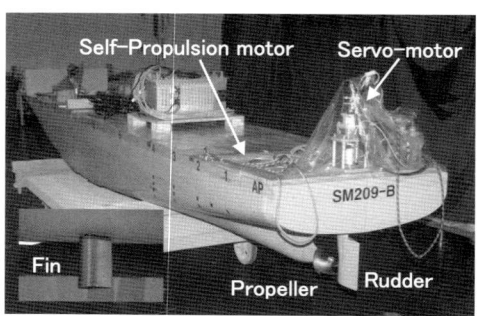

Photo 2 : Ship Model for Free Running Test

Table 3 : Transverse Meta-centric Height

GM_T	Natural Roll Period T_φ
3.0 m	21.0 sec
1.2 m	30.0 sec

Table 4 : Experimental Condition for Regular Wave

GM_T [m]	Speed [kn]	λ/Lpp	Hw [m]	Rudder Rate [deg/sec]
3.0	9 ~ 17	0.7, 0.8, 0.9	4.3, 8.6	2.3, 4.6, 10.0
1.2	10 ~ 12	0.3 ~ 1.0		2.3, 4.6

Table 5 : Experimental Condition for Irregular Wave

GM_T [m]	Speed [kn]	Tv [sec]	H_s	Rudder Rate [deg/sec]
3.0	15	11.6	7.5	2.3, 4.6
1.2	10, 11	8.6, 9.6, 11.6		

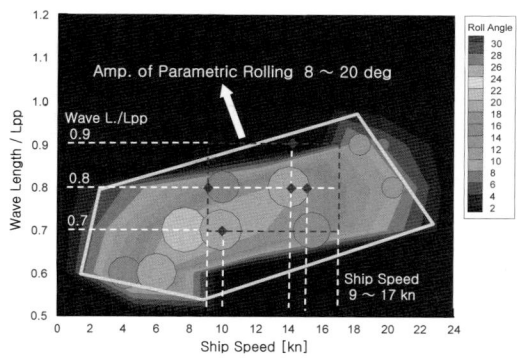

Fig.1 : Magnitude of Parametric Rolling in Head Waves

Experimental conditions in regular wave are shown in Table 4, where λ/Lpp and Hw shows the wave length ratio and wave height, respectively. Experiments were carried out for two kinds of wave amplitudes because the occurrence of the parametric rolling depends on the magnitude of the fluctuation of GM_T due to waves. Fig.1 shows an example of the magnitude of parametric rolling of the subject ship in regular head waves of 8.6 m height for the case of GM_T 3.0 m (Lee, 2005). Horizontal and vertical axis shows the ship speed and the wave length, respectively. The maximum roll amplitude in this condition is about 20 deg. Among theses conditions, 6 combinations of ship speed and wave length were selected for the verification of the controllability. Further, the effect of rudder rate was also investigated because the controllability is much affected by the rudder rate. Conditions for the following wave were decided by the same manner as in head wave.

Experimental conditions for the irregular waves are shown in Table 5. The three kinds of average wave period defined by sea-state 5, 6 and 7 were combined with the significant wave height of 7.5 m. And the ship speed was decided so as to approximately satisfy the encounter frequency condition for the parametric rolling.

Experimental Results

In this section, the experimental results on the effectiveness of rudder control are shown.

Fig.2 shows the time history of roll angle in regular head waves of λ/Lpp 0.8 and Hw 8.6 m without roll control. Ship speed is 15.0 kn and GM_T is 3.0 m. Heading angle of the model was kept constant by the auto-pilot system. Typical process of the parametric rolling is well observed in the figure. The roll amplitude is gradually developed up to the steady value of about 18 deg, and the amplitude of the rudder angle is 20 deg in the steady condition, which is the limit angle set in the experiments, as shown later.

The result of the case with roll control by rudder is shown in Fig.3. The experimental condition is same as in Fig.2. Rudder rate is 2.3 deg/sec in full scale which corresponds to the rate in the SOLAS regulation. Roll control was started at the same time as heading control from the initial stage just after the carriage started. The control gains were adjusted through some runs to obtain the favorable controllability, but not optimized.

Significant rolling doesn't occur at all. It shows that the rudder control even by the simple feed-back law plays a good role to prevent the parametric rolling and that it is very important to restrain the roll disturbance in the earlier stage, because the rolling amplitude is amplified due to the instability.

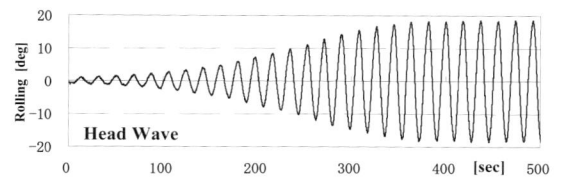

Fig.2 : Typical Process of Parametric Rolling

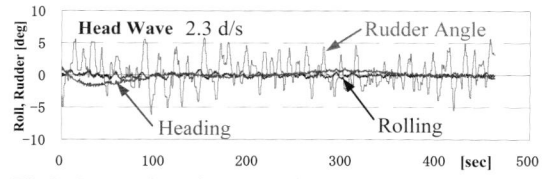

Fig.3 : Prevention of parametric rolling by rudder control

Photo 3 : Large Rolling due to the Parametric Rolling

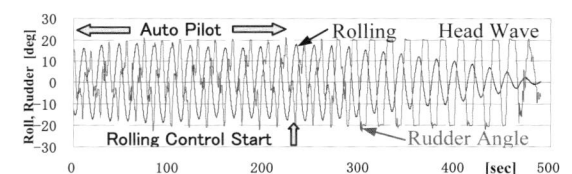

Fig.4 : Stopping Parametric Rolling by Rudder Control

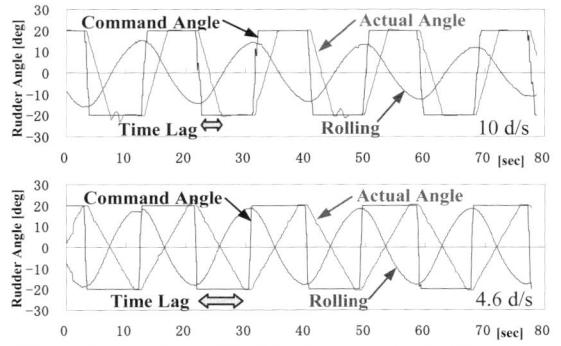

Fig.5 : Comparison of Rudder Response to the Command

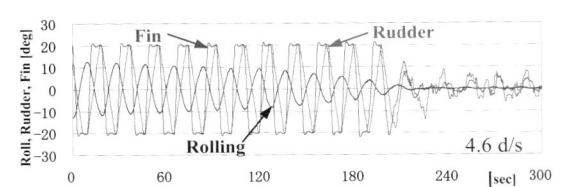

Fig.6 : Effect of Combined Control with Rudder and Fin

Fig.4 shows the case in which rudder control was started after the steady rolling has been obtained. The experimental condition is same as in Fig.2 and Fig.3. The rudder rate is 10.0 d/s in full scale. If the rudder rate is high enough, even the large parametric rolling can be stopped by the rudder control, while it could not be stopped in the case of the rudder rate 4.6 d/s. And there were no significant effects on the ship's heading. The model kept straight course.

The actual rudder response to the control command is compared in Fig.5 for the rate 10.0 d/s and 4.6 d/s. It is clearly shown that the phase lag of rudder response at the rate 4.6 d/s is much larger than that at 10.0 d/s. This is the reason why the parametric rolling could not be stopped in the case of the rate 4.6 d/s. Roll amplitude is gradually reduced in the case of the rate 10.0 d/s.

However, as shown in Fig.6, in case that the fin is controlled together with the rudder, the parametric rolling could be stopped even if the rudder rate is 4.6 d/s, while it was not possible to stop the rolling only by the fin of the present area. In this case, both devices were controlled independently without any consideration of interference. Rate of the fin is about 15 d/s.

Fig.7 shows an example in which the amplitude of parametric rolling is not so large as in the above condition. Wave condition is regular head waves of λ/Lpp 0.9 and Hw 8.6 m. Ship speed is 14.0 kn and GM_T is 3.0 m. Rudder control was started after the steady rolling of about 8 deg with the rudder rate 4.6 d/s. Rolling can be stopped within the realistic rudder rate obtained by use of the reserved pump.

As shown in these figures, even in the case in which the parametric rolling has been developed, rolling can be stopped by the rudder control. However, the controllability is affected by the rudder rate, the natural roll period and the magnitude of rolling. The relation between the natural roll period and the rudder rate is the important parameter as well as the hydrostatic capacity of the rudder to heel the ship hull.

Fig.8 shows the results in irregular following waves. The significant wave height is 7.5 m and the average period is 11.6 sec. Ship speed is 10.0 kn and GM_T is 1.2 m. Roll control was started at the same time as the heading control just after the carriage started. The parametric rolling with the maximum angle of 22 deg could be completely stopped by rudder control with the rate 2.3 d/s. And the rudder angle is also within the range of ± 5 deg. Fig.9 shows the comparison of the maximum roll angle in the case without and with rudder control. Three kinds of average wave period and two kinds of the rudder rate were examined for the wave of significant height 7.5 m. Roll amplitude is reduced by more than 80 % in all cases. The effect of the rudder

rate seems to be small because the time constant of the rudder is much smaller than the natural roll period.

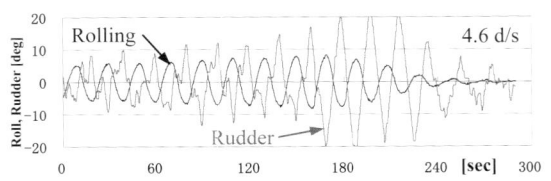

Fig.7 : Stopping Parametric Rolling by Rudder Control

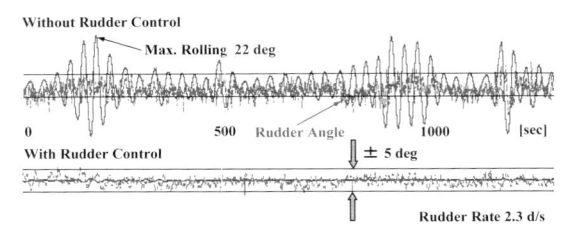

Fig.8 : Prevention of the Parametric Rolling in Irregular Following Waves

Theoretical Investigations

In this section, the effect of roll control by rudder and fin on the improvement of instability phenomenon is shown theoretically by stability analysis and numerical simulations.

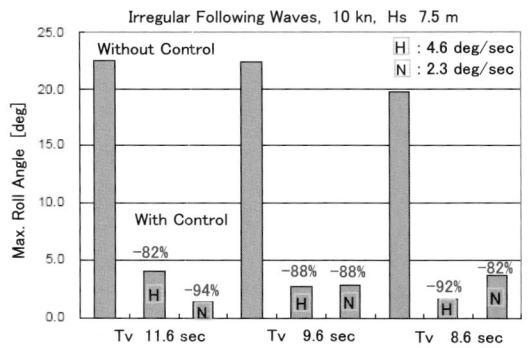

Fig.9 : Comparison of the Maximum Amplitude of Rolling in Various Irregular Following Waves

Stability Analysis on Parametric Rolling

Equation of Motion

To analyze the stability of parametric rolling, 1-DOF equation of rolling is assumed as Eq.(1).

$$(I_{xx} + A_{44}) \cdot \ddot{\phi} + B_{44} \cdot \dot{\phi} + D_{44} \cdot \dot{\phi} \cdot |\dot{\phi}| + C_{44} \cdot \phi = M_R + M_F \quad (1)$$

$$M_R = \frac{1}{2} \cdot (1 + a_H) \cdot \rho \cdot U_R^2 \cdot A_R \cdot (z_R - z_G) \cdot f_\delta \cdot \delta_c \quad (2)$$

$$M_F = 2 \times \frac{1}{2} \cdot \rho \cdot U^2 \cdot A_F \cdot R \cdot f_\alpha \cdot \alpha_c \quad (3)$$

$$\delta_c = \delta_C = -K_{PR} \cdot \phi - K_{DR} \cdot \dot{\phi} \quad (4)$$

$$\alpha_c = \alpha_\phi + \alpha_c = -\frac{R}{U} \cdot \dot{\phi} - K_{PF} \cdot \phi - K_{DF} \cdot \dot{\phi} \quad (5)$$

I_{xx} and A_{44} is the moment of inertia of mass and added mass, B_{44} and D_{44} is the linear and nonlinear damping coefficient, respectively. C_{44} is the restoring moment coefficient. M_R and M_F are the roll moment due to the rudder and the fin. The wave exciting moment is assumed zero in longitudinal waves.

A_R, A_F, (z_R-z_G) and R are the area and the moment lever of the rudder and the fin, respectively. a_H is the hydrodynamic interaction coefficient between the hull and the rudder. U_R is the rudder inflow velocity, U is the ship speed. f_δ and f_α are the derivative of rudder normal force coefficient C_N and that of fin lift coefficient C_L, respectively. δ_e is the rudder angle based on the roll control. α_e is the effective fin angle, which includes the damping effect due to the inflow induced by rolling. As for δ_e, it is assumed that the effect of induced flow due to rolling is included in the linear damping coefficient B_{44}. K_{PR}, K_{DR}, K_{PF} and K_{DF} are the control gains. Here, the following expression is assumed for the coefficients in Eq.(1).

$$B_{44} = B_{440} = 2 \cdot \zeta_0 \cdot (I_{xx} + A_{44}) \qquad (6)$$

$$D_{44} = \frac{2}{\pi} \cdot N \cdot (I_{xx} + A_{44}) \qquad (7)$$

$$C_{44} = W \cdot [GM_{T0} + \Delta GM_T \cdot \cos(\omega_e \cdot t)] \qquad (8)$$

ζ_0 and N are linear and nonlinear roll damping coefficient of the hull with bilge keel. W is the displacement. GM_{T0} is the meta-centric height in still water and ΔGM_T is the amplitude of the fluctuation of GM_T in waves. ω_e is the encounter frequency.

By substituting Eq.(2)~(8) into Eq.(1) and assuming that the rudder inflow velocity U_R is equal to the ship speed, the equation of rolling is expressed as follows.

$$\ddot{\phi} + 2 \cdot \zeta_0 \cdot \dot{\phi} + \frac{2N}{\pi} \cdot \dot{\phi} \cdot |\dot{\phi}| + [\frac{W \cdot GM_{T0}}{(I_{xx}+A_{44})} + \frac{W \cdot \Delta GM_T}{(I_{xx}+A_{44})} \cdot \cos(\omega_e \cdot t)] \cdot \phi =$$
$$-\frac{(1+a_H) \cdot \rho \cdot U^2 \cdot A_R \cdot (z_R-z_G) \cdot f_\delta}{2 \cdot (I_{xx}+A_{44})} \cdot [K_{DR} \cdot \dot{\phi} + K_{PR} \cdot \phi]$$
$$-\frac{\rho \cdot U^2 \cdot A_F \cdot f_\alpha}{(I_{xx}+A_{44})} \cdot [\{\frac{R}{U}+K_{DF}\} \cdot \dot{\phi}+K_{PF} \cdot \phi] \qquad (9)$$

Further, the following new parameters ω_o, ω_a, ν_R, ν_F are introduced and the nonlinear damping term is linearized. Finally, Eq.(12) is obtained as the equation of rolling.

$$\frac{W \cdot GM_{T0}}{(I_{xx}+A_{44})} = \omega_0^2 \quad , \quad \frac{W \cdot \Delta GM_T}{(I_{xx}+A_{44})} = \omega_a^2 \qquad (10)$$

$$\frac{(1+a_H)\cdot \rho \cdot U_R^2 \cdot A_R \cdot (z_R-z_G) \cdot f_\delta}{2 \cdot W \cdot GM_{T0}} = \nu_R^2 \quad , \quad \frac{\rho \cdot U^2 \cdot A_F \cdot R \cdot f_\alpha}{W \cdot GM_{T0}} = \nu_F^2 \qquad (11)$$

$$\ddot{\phi} + 2 \cdot \{\zeta_0 + \frac{\omega_e \cdot N \cdot \phi_m}{\pi} + \frac{\omega_0^2}{2 \cdot U} \cdot \nu_F^2 \cdot R + \frac{\omega_0^2}{2} \cdot [\nu_R^2 \cdot K_{DR} + \nu_F^2 \cdot K_{DF}]\} \cdot \dot{\phi}$$
$$+ \{\omega_0^2 \cdot [1 + \nu_R^2 \cdot K_{PR} + \nu_F^2 \cdot K_{PF}] + \omega_a^2 \cdot \cos(\omega_e \cdot t)\} \cdot \phi = 0 \qquad (12)$$

Here, let $\omega_e \cdot t = \tau$ and $\phi(\tau) = x(\tau) \cdot e^{-\mu \cdot \tau}$. The well-known Mathieu Equation is obtained.

$$\frac{d^2 x}{d\tau^2} + (p + q \cdot \cos \tau) \cdot x = 0 \qquad (13)$$

$$p = \frac{\omega_{0m}^2}{\omega_e^2} - \mu^2 \quad , \quad q = \frac{\omega_a^2}{\omega_e^2} \qquad (14)$$

$$\omega_{0m}^2 = \omega_0^2 \cdot [1 + \nu_R^2 \cdot K_{PR} + \nu_F^2 \cdot K_{PF}] \qquad (15)$$

$$\mu = \frac{\zeta}{\omega_e} = \frac{1}{\omega_e} \cdot (\zeta_0 + \frac{\omega_e \cdot N \cdot \phi_m}{\pi} + \Delta \zeta) \qquad (16)$$

$$\Delta \zeta = \frac{\omega_0^2}{2 \cdot U} \cdot \nu_F^2 \cdot R + \frac{\omega_0^2}{2} \cdot [\nu_R^2 \cdot K_{DR} + \nu_F^2 \cdot K_{DF}] \qquad (17)$$

Eq.(12) and (13) include the effect of control of the rudder and the fin. The effect of roll control on the instability of parametric rolling can be evaluated by applying this equation.

As shown in the above equation, roll damping seems to be a very important parameter for the improvement of stability in parametric rolling. Threshold value of damping coefficient μ_T for the various combinations of "p" and "q" is given by the following equation by ABS Guidance. (Shin, 2004; ABS, 2004)

$$\mu_T = \frac{q}{2} \cdot (1 - \frac{3}{16} \cdot q^2) \cdot (1.002 \cdot p + 0.16 \cdot q + 0.759) \times$$
$$\sqrt{1 - \{\frac{q^2 - 16 + \sqrt{q^4 + 352 \cdot q^2 + 1024 \cdot p}}{16 \cdot q}\}^2} \qquad (18)$$

From this result, threshold value of non-dimensional roll damping is given as follows.

$$\zeta_T' = \frac{\zeta_T}{\omega_o} = \mu_T \cdot \frac{\omega_e}{\omega_o} \quad (\quad \zeta' = \frac{\zeta}{\omega_o} = \mu \cdot \frac{\omega_e}{\omega_o} \quad) \qquad (19)$$

Effect of Roll-Control on Stability

In this section, an example of stability analysis is shown. The equivalent linear roll damping of the hull with bilge keel used in the analysis was obtained from the free decay test in calm water. The non-dimensional damping at 15 kn is 3.2 % of the critical damping. As shown in Eq.(12), the effective lift induced on the fixed fin due to rolling acts as the additional damping. The damping of the hull with fixed fin was estimated from Eq.(11) and (16) using the derivative f_α obtained by the static heeling test. The estimated value of damping is 5.3 % and agreed well with the measured results of the free decay test with fixed fin. Based on these pre-investigations, stability analysis was carried out.

The threshold damping ζ_T' by Eq.(18) and the obtained damping ζ' are compared in Table 6 for 4 cases, "W/O Control", "Rudder Control", "Fin Control" and "Rudder+Fin Control". And Fig.10 shows the relation between the roll damping and the stability region for the various combination of parameter "p" and "q" in Eq.(14). Conditions of the calculation are same as those in Fig.2, 3 and 4. ΔGM_T is 2.5 m. The values of ν_R and ν_F are 0.193 and 0.184, respectively. In the case with roll control, the values of control gain are K_{PR} 1.0 and K_{DR} 23.2 for rudder, K_{PF} 1.0 and K_{DF} 23.2 for fin in full scale, respectively. These are the values used in the experiments. The results of rudder angle test were used for f_δ. In the analysis, actuator dynamics is not taken into account. So, the results are equivalent to the case with enough actuator power. The upper region above ζ' curves in the figure shows unstable region in which there exists a susceptibility of parametric rolling.

This figure clearly shows that if the roll damping becomes larger, the stable region also becomes larger. If ζ' is larger than ζ_T' which is decided by p and q, the state of rolling is stable.

Table 6 : Increase of Damping by Roll Control

	W/O Con※	Rudder※	Fin	Rudder + Fin
p	0.191	0.193	0.193	0.189
q	0.160			
ζ_T'	0.135	0.138	0.139	0.129
ζ'	0.053	0.181	0.170	0.298

※ model is equipped with fixed fin

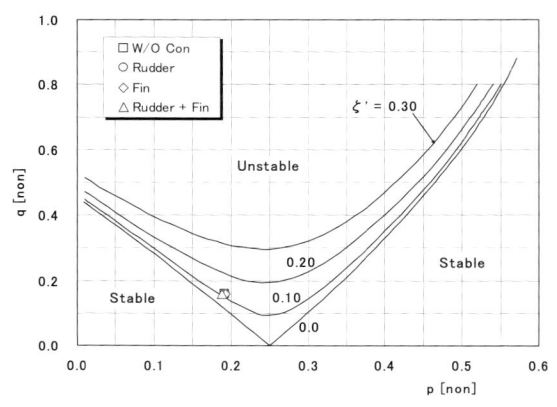

Fig.10 : Improvement of Susceptibility of Parametric Rolling by Roll-Control

As shown in Table 6, the relations between ζ' and ζ_T' except "Fin Control" condition well explain the results of free running test in waves. However the estimated state of rolling in "Fin Control" condition is stable, while the state in the experiments is unstable. One of the reasons of this difference is considered to be the decrease of fin lift due to the stall and the free surface effect induced by the fluctuation of relative water depth at fin position through large rolling and wave. Indeed, if it is assumed that the fin lift is decreased by 30 %, the value of ζ' decreases to 0.128, the smaller value than ζ_T'. This means that the state of rolling falls into the unstable condition as in the experiments.

Judging from these investigations, the procedures of stability analysis presented above seems effective for the evaluation of the effect of roll control on the parametric rolling by correctly evaluating the hydrodynamic characteristics of rudder and fin.

Investigations by Numerical Simulations

Equations of Motion

Equations of 6-DOF motion (Hamamoto, 1993) are applied for the numerical simulation. Coupled equations between these components are taken into account to evaluate the large rolling in waves. For sway, roll and yaw, coupled equations are given as follows.

$$(m+m_y) \cdot \dot{v} + (m+m_x) \cdot u \cdot r + Y_v \cdot v - Y_r \cdot r + m_y \cdot x_G \cdot \dot{r}$$
$$- m_y \cdot (z_R - z_G) \cdot \ddot{\phi} = -(1+a_H) \cdot F_{NR} \cdot \cos(\delta_a) + 2 \cdot F_{LF} \cdot \sin \beta \quad (20)$$

$$(I_{zz} + J_{zz}) \cdot \dot{r} + m_y \cdot x_G \cdot \dot{v} + N_v \cdot v - m_y \cdot (z_R - z_G) \cdot u \cdot \dot{\phi}$$
$$-(I_{xx} + J_{xx}) \cdot \dot{\phi} \cdot \dot{\theta} + (N_r + m_y \cdot x_G \cdot u) \cdot r =$$
$$-(1+a_H) \cdot (x_R - x_G) \cdot F_{NR} \cdot \cos(\delta_a) + 2 \cdot (x_F - x_G) \cdot F_{LF} \cdot \sin \beta \quad (21)$$

$$(I_{xx} + J_{xx}) \cdot \ddot{\phi} + K_\phi \cdot \dot{\phi} + m \cdot g \cdot GM_T(t) \cdot \phi$$
$$-\{m_y \cdot \dot{v} + Y_v \cdot v - (Y_r - m_x \cdot u) \cdot r\} \cdot (z_R - z_G) - (I_{xx} + J_{xx}) \cdot \dot{\theta} \cdot r =$$
$$(1+a_H) \cdot (z_R - z_G) \cdot F_{NR} \cdot \cos(\delta_a) - 2 \cdot R \cdot F_{LF} \quad (22)$$

Here, u, v and r are the longitudinal velocity, lateral velocity and yaw rate. φ and θ are the roll angle and pitch angle. m, I_{xx} and I_{zz} are the mass and the mass moment of inertia around x and z-axis. m_x, m_y, J_{xx} and J_{zz} are the added mass and added mass moment of inertia. Y_v, Y_r, N_v and N_r are the maneuvering derivatives which express the damping force and moment due to lateral drifting and rotating of the ship. For the roll motion, equivalent linear damping coefficient is taken into account.

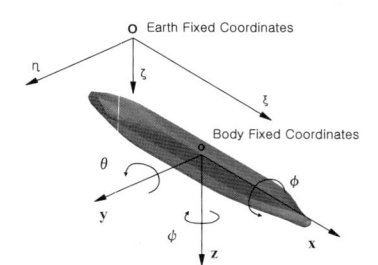

Fig. 11 : Coordinate Systems

F_{NR} and F_{LF} are the rudder normal force and the fin lift, respectively. δ_a is the actual rudder angle in which the steering gear dynamics is taken into account as shown later. β is the angle between horizontal axis and fin axis in the vertical plane. z_R and z_G are the z-coordinate of the acting point of rudder normal force and the center of gravity. z_R is assumed to be a half of the rudder height. x_R, x_F and x_G are the x-coordinates of the position of rudder, fin and the center of gravity.

The value of GM_T changes due to the fluctuation of relative wave height at each section including the effect of the frame line and vertical motions. Wave exciting force and moment for the lateral motion are assumed to be zero in the longitudinal waves.

In the above equations, rudder normal force and fin lift are given using effective inflow angle δ_e and α_e, which include the effect of the lateral motions.

$$F_{NR} = \frac{1}{2} \cdot \rho \cdot U_R^2 \cdot A_R \cdot C_N(\delta_e) \quad (23)$$

$$F_{LF} = \frac{1}{2} \cdot \rho \cdot U^2 \cdot A_F \cdot C_L(\alpha_e) \quad (24)$$

$$\delta_e = \delta_a + \frac{1}{U_R} \cdot [\gamma \cdot v + \ell_R \cdot r - (z_R - z_G) \cdot \dot{\phi}] \quad (25)$$

$$\alpha_e = \alpha_a + \frac{1}{U} \cdot [-\{v + (x_F - x_G) \cdot r\} \cdot \sin \beta + R \cdot \dot{\phi}] \quad (26)$$

C_N and C_L are the function of δ_e and α_e. The effect of the vertical motion and the wave orbital motion on α_e was not taken into account due to the symmetry in longitudinal waves. γ and ℓ_R are the coefficients for the effect of lateral motions on the rudder inflow angle. Dynamics of steering gear to get the actual rudder angle

δ_a is modeled by the first-order dynamical system. Rudder is controlled for both heading and rolling using feed-back law.

$$T_R \cdot \dot{\delta}_a + \delta_a = \delta_c \quad (27)$$

$$\delta_c = K_{PR\text{-}YAW} \cdot (\psi^* - \psi) + K_{DR\text{-}YAW} \cdot r + K_{PR\text{-}ROLL} \cdot \phi + K_{DR\text{-}ROLL} \cdot \dot{\phi} \quad (28)$$

T_R is the time-constant. δ_C is the command rudder angle. $K_{PR\text{-}YAW}$, $K_{DR\text{-}YAW}$, $K_{PR\text{-}ROLL}$ and $K_{DR\text{-}ROLL}$ are the PD gains of the rudder control.

The same model as Eq.(27) or the higher order model can be assumed for the dynamics of the fin actuator.(Sgobbo, 1999) But, the dynamics of the fin actuator was not taken into account in this paper ($\alpha_a = \alpha_c$), because the operating rate of fin is much higher than that of rudder and so, the actuator dynamics has much less influence in real situation. Command fin angle α_c is given by Eq.(29)

$$\alpha_c = K_{PF\text{-}ROLL} \cdot \phi + K_{DF\text{-}ROLL} \cdot \dot{\phi} \quad (29)$$

Substituting Eq.(23) ~ (26) into Eq.(20) ~ (22), the equations of lateral motion are derived as follows.

$$(m+m_y) \cdot \dot{v} + (m+m_x) \cdot u \cdot r + Y_v \cdot v - Y_r \cdot r + m_y \cdot x_G \cdot \dot{r}$$
$$-m_y \cdot (z_R - z_G) \cdot \ddot{\phi} = -(1+a_H) \cdot \frac{1}{2} \cdot \rho \cdot U_R^2 \cdot A_R \cdot C_N(\delta_e) \cdot \cos\delta_a$$
$$+\rho \cdot U^2 \cdot A_F \cdot C_L(\alpha_e) \cdot \sin\beta \quad (30)$$

$$(I_{zz} + J_{zz}) \cdot \dot{r} + m_y \cdot x_G \cdot \dot{v} + N_v \cdot v - m_y \cdot (z_R - z_G) \cdot u \cdot \dot{\phi} - (I_{xx} + J_{xx}) \cdot \dot{\phi} \cdot \dot{\theta}$$
$$+(N_r + m_y \cdot x_G \cdot u) \cdot r = -(1+a_H) \cdot \frac{1}{2} \cdot \rho \cdot U_R^2 \cdot A_R \cdot (x_R - x_G)$$
$$\cdot C_N(\delta_e) \cdot \cos\delta_a + \rho \cdot U^2 \cdot A_F \cdot (x_F - x_G) \cdot C_L(\alpha_e) \cdot \sin\beta \quad (31)$$

$$(I_{xx} + J_{xx}) \cdot \ddot{\phi} + K_\phi \cdot \dot{\phi} + m \cdot g \cdot GM_T \cdot \phi - \{m_y \cdot \dot{v} + Y_v \cdot v - (Y_r - m_x \cdot u) \cdot r\}$$
$$\cdot (z_R - z_G) - (I_{xx} + J_{xx}) \cdot \dot{\theta} \cdot r = (1+a_H) \cdot \frac{1}{2} \cdot \rho \cdot U_R^2 \cdot A_R \cdot (z_R - z_G) \cdot C_N(\delta_e) \cdot \cos\delta_a$$
$$-\rho \cdot U^2 \cdot A_F \cdot R \cdot C_L(\alpha_e) \quad (32)$$

Generally, feed-back gains can be designed using linear quadratic regulator theory. To apply this method, these coupled equations and actuator dynamics are transformed into the following linear state equations assuming that the effect of the coupling with the vertical motion is negligible.

$$\dot{\mathbf{x}} = \mathbf{G} \cdot \mathbf{x} + \mathbf{H} \cdot \mathbf{u} \quad (33)$$

$$\mathbf{x} = [\phi, \ \psi, \ v, \ \dot{\phi}, \ r, \ \delta_a, \ \alpha_a, \ \dot{\alpha}_a]^T \quad (34)$$

$$\mathbf{u} = [\delta_C, \ \alpha_C]^T \quad (35)$$

$\mathbf{x}$ and $\mathbf{u}$ are the state variable matrix and control variable vector, respectively. Superscript T means transpose. $\mathbf{G}$ and $\mathbf{H}$ are the coefficient matrices. The rudder normal force and the fin lift are linearized as follows.

$$F_{NR} = \frac{1}{2} \cdot \rho \cdot U_R^2 \cdot A_R \cdot f_\delta \cdot \delta_e \quad (f_\delta = \frac{dC_N}{d\delta}) \quad (36)$$

$$F_{LF} = \frac{1}{2} \cdot \rho \cdot U^2 \cdot A_F \cdot f_\alpha \cdot \alpha_e \quad (f_\alpha = \frac{dC_L}{d\alpha}) \quad (37)$$

$$\delta_e = \delta_a + \frac{1}{U_R} \cdot [\gamma \cdot v + \ell_R \cdot r - (z_R - z_G) \cdot \dot{\phi}] \quad (38)$$

$$\alpha_e = \alpha_a + \frac{1}{U} \cdot [R \cdot \dot{\phi} - \{v + (x_F - x_G) \cdot r\} \cdot \sin\beta] \quad (39)$$

Defining the cost function J using the weighting matrices $\mathbf{Q}$ and $\mathbf{R}$, the optimal feed-back gain matrix $\mathbf{K}$ is given by Eq.(41).

$$J = \int [\mathbf{x}^T \cdot \mathbf{Q} \cdot \mathbf{x} + \mathbf{u}^T \cdot \mathbf{R} \cdot \mathbf{u}] \ dt \quad (40)$$

$$\mathbf{K} = \mathbf{R}^{-1} \cdot \mathbf{H}^T \cdot \mathbf{P} \quad (41)$$

The matrix $\mathbf{P}$ is the unique positive semi-definite solution given by solving the following Riccati Equation.

$$\mathbf{G}^T \cdot \mathbf{P} + \mathbf{P} \cdot \mathbf{G} + \mathbf{Q} - \mathbf{P} \cdot \mathbf{H} \cdot \mathbf{R}^{-1} \cdot \mathbf{H}^T \cdot \mathbf{P} = 0 \quad (42)$$

The control variable vector $\mathbf{u}$ is given as the optimal feed-back of state variable.

$$\mathbf{u} = -\mathbf{K} \cdot \mathbf{x} \quad (43)$$

Simulation of Parametric Rolling

Based on the theoretical formulations above, a few simulations were carried out for the subject ship to verify the theoretical model which takes account of the effect of roll control by rudder and fin. In these simulations, results of the roll decay test for bare hull and the captive model test for the subject ship were used.

Fig.12 shows the simulated result on the rolling in the same condition as Fig.2. Though the period to get the steady condition is a little longer in the experiment than in the simulation, the amplitude of rolling agrees well between the both results. Fig.13 shows an example of the rolling control by rudder in the same condition as the experimental result shown in Fig.4. And Fig.14 shows the comparison of the heading angle between the simulation and the experiment in this condition. It is said that the theoretical simulations well estimate the effect of the rudder control on the response of the ship. As shown above, theoretical simulation also seems to be the useful tool to evaluate the parametric rolling and the effect of rudder control as the stability analysis.

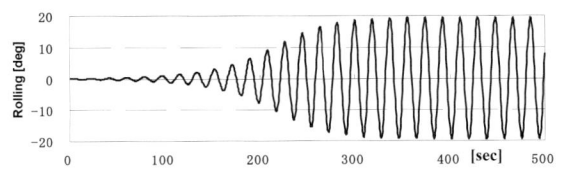

Fig.12 : Simulated Result on the Parametric Rolling

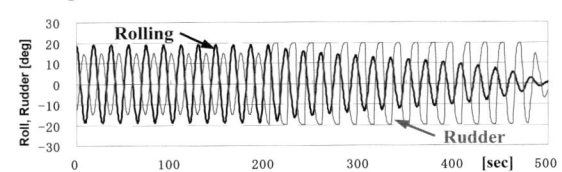

Fig.13 : Simulated Result on the Effect of Rudder Control

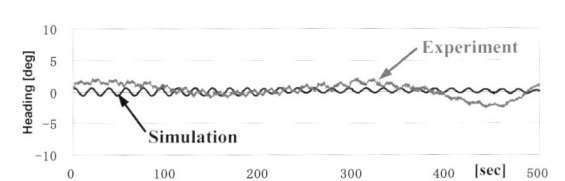

Fig.14 : Comparison of Heading between Simulation and Experiment (With Rudder Control)

Application to the Real Operation

As shown above, parametric rolling is the instability phenomenon which occurs when the particular condition is satisfied. Therefore, the system to prevent such rolling is not always required to be operated. In the application to the real operation, it is practical to be combined with the monitoring system which forecasts the occurrence of parametric rolling.

Fig.15 shows an example of the application to the real system. (SIRUS System ; **S**amsung **I**ntelligent **RU**dder **R**oll **S**tabilizer System) This system consists of a controller, wave monitoring system, sensors and data-base to forecast the parametric rolling. The controller is connected to the auto-pilot system which is inevitably on board for the navigation. In case that there is a certain susceptibility of parametric rolling, the rudder command for roll control is superposed on those from the auto-pilot system by the controller and returned again to the line to the steering gear. Such a system can be combined with Integrated Navigation System as one of optional functions, or it can be simply realized only by the controller and sensors without wave monitoring system. Further researches to put this system into practical use have been in progress.

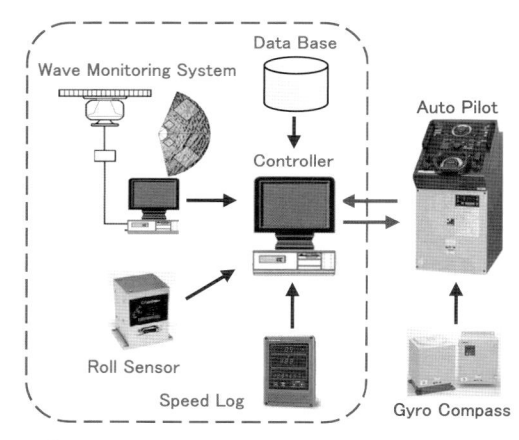

Fig.15 Example of the Application to the Real System   (SIRUS System)

Conclusions

With the progress of recent enlargement of the ships, improvement of the safety in a seaway has been discussed from various view points as the hull structures, the sea-keeping quality and the maneuverability, etc. In this paper, the effectiveness of rudder control to prevent the parametric rolling phenomenon was investigated experimentally and theoretically. From these investigations, it was concluded as follows.

(1) The risk of parametric rolling can be prevented by only rudder control within the rudder rate given in the SOLAS regulation. Rudder action could be a disturbance, but, on the other hand, rudder control based on a simple feed-back law plays a good role to this objective.

(2) On this occasion, it is very important to control rolling while the amplitude of parametric rolling has not been developed yet.

(3) Even in the case in which the roll amplitude has been developed, roll motion can be stopped by rudder control. However, the effectiveness of control is affected by the relations between the rudder rate and the natural period and magnitude of rolling.

(4) The relation between the natural roll period and the rudder rate is an important parameter as well as the hydrodynamic capacity of rudder to heel ship's hull.

(5) The same tendency as in rudder is applicable to the anti-rolling fin. And combined control by rudder and fin is more effective to avoid parametric rolling.

(6) Stability analysis which takes account of the effect of rolling control seems a useful method to evaluate the effect of rudder control on the susceptibility of parametric rolling. It was verified that the instability of parametric rolling phenomenon can be much improved by rudder control which induces the significant increase of roll damping.

(7) Some examples of the simulated results on the parametric rolling including rudder control were shown. The simulation model used in this paper also seems to be applicable to the evaluation of the controllability of the parametric rolling. Further study will be required to put this method into practice.

(8) An example of the practical system to prevent the parametric rolling by utilizing rudder control was presented. Effective operation in a seaway will be expected in combination with the monitoring system which forecasts the occurrence of parametric rolling.

References

ABS (2004), "GUIDE FOR THE ASSESSMENT OF PARAMETRIC ROLL RESONANCE IN THE DESIGN OF CONTAINER CARRIERS"

France W.N. (2003), "An Investigation of Head-Sea Parametric Rolling and its Influence on Container Lashing System", Marine Technology, Vol.40, No.1

Hamamoto M. (1993), "A New Coordinate System and the Equations Describing Manoeuvring Motion of a Ship in Waves" (in Japanese), Journal of The Society of Naval Architects of Japan, No.173

Lee D.Y. (2005), "On the Study of Parametric Oscillation in Seaway", Journal of the Society of Naval Architects of Korea, Vol.43

Lee J.T. (2006), "Current Issues and Inter-related Development of Shipping and Shipbuilding Industries in Korea", Proc. of the 2nd Pan Asian Association of Maritime Engineering Societies (PAAMES) and Advanced Maritime Engineering Conference (AMEC) 2006

Porter J. (2000), "Hundreds of boxes lost in Pacific storm", Lloyd's List, 8th Feb. 2000

Sgobbo J.N. (1999), " Rudder/Fin Roll Stabilization of the USCG WMEC 901 Class Vessel ", Marine Technology, Vol.36, No.3

Shin Y.S. (2004), "Criteria for Parametric Roll of Large Containerships in Longitudinal Seas",

SNAME Annual Meeting 2004, Washington D.C.

Crossbow Technology Catalogue, Gyro System AHRS400CD

FURUNO Catalogue, Doppler Speed Log DS-50

TOKIMEC Catalogue, Auto-Pilot PR-6000, Gyro Compass TG-8000

Numerical Modeling of Roll Dynamics and Virtual Instrumentation Based Ship Fin Control

V. Anantha Subramanian, G. Dhinesh, G. Asokumar

Department of Ocean Engineering,
Indian Institute of Technology, Madras, India.

Abstract

Virtual instrumentation platforms are available today to design and implement refined algorithms for precision control of fin stabilizers. While on the one hand this non-traditional strategy obviates the need for cumbersome hardware involved in controllers and instrumentation panels, it also facilitates compact computation of the feedback control data and precise control signal on the actuators. This paper reports the implementation of a virtual instrumentation algorithm for fin control. It combines the analysis of fin lift dynamic characteristics taking into account the hull in its proximity using computational fluid dynamics (CFD). The frequency dependent hydrodynamic coefficients of the ship hull and stabilizer fin are represented in a polynomial function form. A harmonic distortion analyzer function is used to detect fundamental frequency in the error signal (roll), and using this in a feedback control loop, the control signal for the actuator is generated. The algorithm is generalized for coupled sway, roll and yaw conditions, and can be employed for single or multiple input systems. It is demonstrated in a laboratory model for induced roll disturbances. The robustness and stability of the system is brought out through numerical and experimental simulations for regular and random excitation conditions. By combining numerical hydrodynamics with virtual instrumentation, a modern control strategy is presented.

Key words

CFD; Roll stabilization; Active fin control; Virtual instrumentation.

Introduction

Ride control systems are used in small as well as large crafts. They play a significant role in reducing motions and in minimizing motion sickness incidence. The theory of active motion control is well documented in literature (Fossen, 1994). Designers rely on experimental data to obtain the kinematics as well as the dynamics of fin behavior when subjected to an angle of attack. Under dynamic forward speed conditions, fins are also subjected to the influence of cavitation, aeration, and ground board effect due to the presence of the hull in the proximity. Exact quantification of fin behavior can be obtained using Computational Fluid Dynamics (CFD) tools to model the flow kinematics with regard to the fin in the above conditions.

With regard to the control system, traditional instrumentation and hardware control represent well-established technologies for controlling the fins for optimum ride control and comfort. In recent times, the tool of virtual instrumentation has been increasingly projected to obtain radically simple but very effective control of a variety of processes and tasks both in the laboratory environment as well as in field conditions. The advantage of virtual instrumentation is obvious because it substitutes cumbersome hardware based circuits and processing, with software based circuits which are programmed in a virtual environment on the computer screen. Therefore, this work reports combining the above two technologies and demonstrates the functioning of an effective feedback control system for reducing the motions of a hull form in laboratory conditions. The motion equations incorporating fin characteristics described by Sgobbo and Parsons (1999) have been used in the control algorithm. Numerical simulations obtain the fin lift capacity, and these data are incorporated in the fin control loop along with the hydrodynamic characteristics (in terms of the coefficients) of the vessel in a virtual environment. The method works on the principle of equilibrium stabilization with active stabilizer fins using virtual instrumentation based control. Virtual instrumentation also has the intrinsic advantage of a great deal of flexibility and effectiveness.

Numerical solution for obtaining the fin kinematics and lift

The governing equations are solved using a commercial RANS solver Comet. The solver uses a cell centered finite volume approach, and the interface is captured using the Volume of Fluid (VOF) method with the High Resolution Interface Capturing (HRIC) scheme for convective flux. The solution domain is subdivided into a finite number of control volumes that may be of arbitrary shape. The integrals are numerically approximated using the midpoint rule. The mass flux through each cell face is taken from the previous iteration, following a simple Picard iteration approach. The remaining unknown variables at the center of the cell face are determined by combining a central differencing scheme (CDS) with an upwind differencing scheme (UDS).

Coupling body motion with fluid flow

Coupling of fluid flow with body motion has been carried out using a body motion module. Initially the RANS and turbulence closure equations are solved to obtain the pressure and velocity field. The forces and moments acting on the body are then calculated by integrating the normal (pressure) and tangential (friction) stresses over the body surface. Computed force moments from the flow solver are used as input to the body motion module which solves the equations of motions of the rigid body.

Grid system and Boundary condition

The computational domain used is a rectangular block bounded by $-0.5<x/Lpp<1$, $-5<y/B<5$, $-5<z/T<1$. Grid independence study has been performed and an optimum grid size of 0.34 million cells in the domain is chosen for the simulations. The co-ordinate system and the Boundary Conditions (BC) used are shown in Fig. 1. Velocity inlet BC is used at the inlet, port and starboard sides, bottom and top boundaries with inlet velocity equal to the vessel speed. Wall with no slip condition is used over the hull surface and on the fins, and zero gradient boundary of known pressure (hydrostatic pressure) distribution is used at the outlet boundary. The simulations are performed for a known condition of center of gravity. The above simulations shown are for a 10-degree angle of attack for the fins. The figures mentioned above are demonstrative of typical results obtained from the CFD studies, and are for vessel speed at Froude number 0.31.

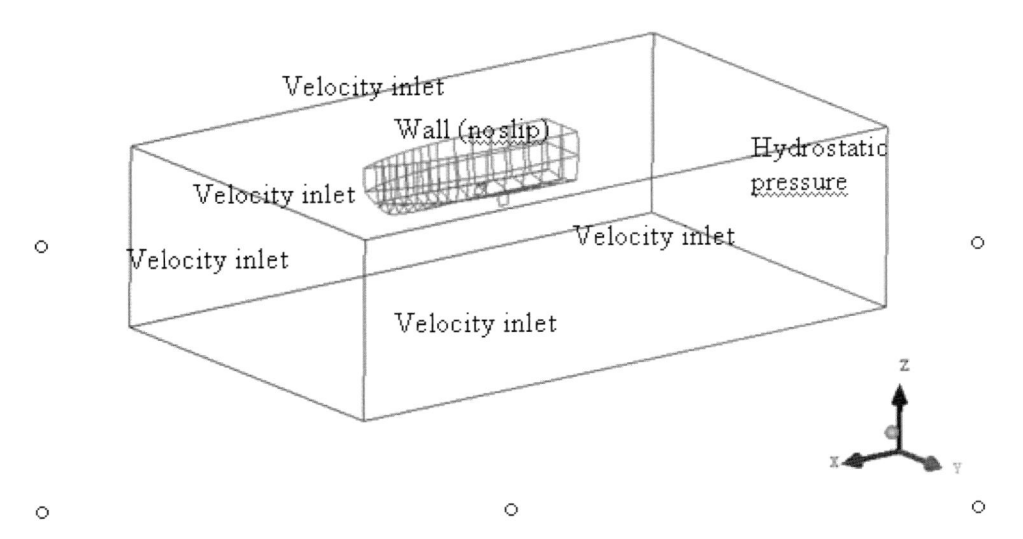

Fig. 1 Boundary conditions

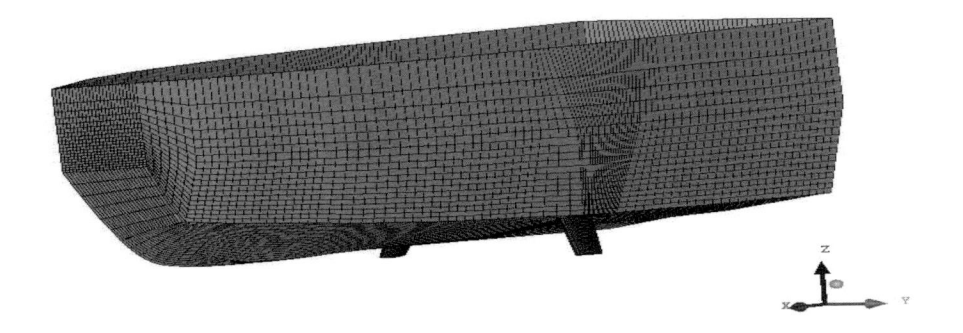

Fig. 2 Mesh on the hull and fin surface

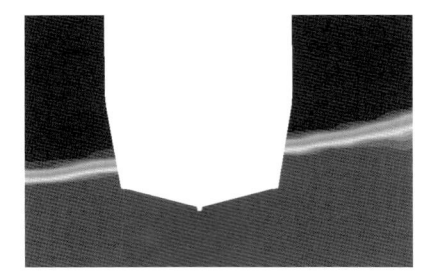

Fig. 3 Fin induced roll showing fin lift capacity

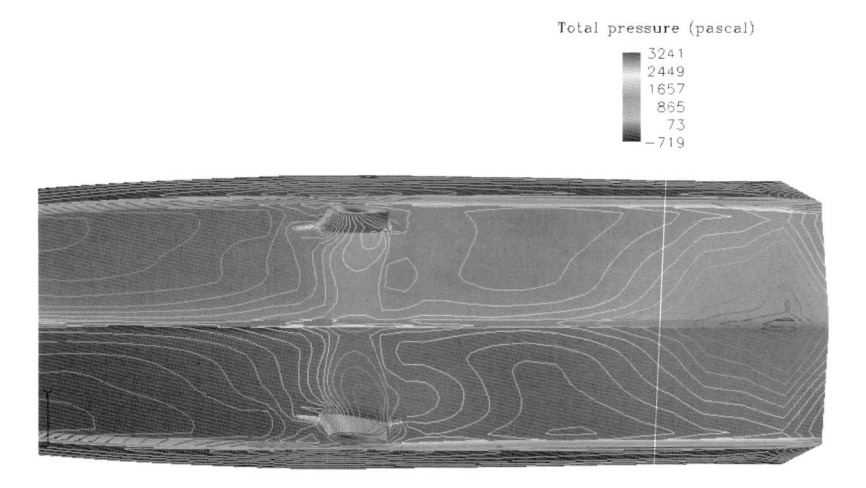

Fig. 4: Pressure contours around the fin in dynamic condition

Formulation of motion control equation using fins

The general roll motion equation in single degree of freedom (SDOF) can be written as

$$I_{xx}\ddot{\theta} + B\dot{\theta} + C\theta = E(t) \quad (1)$$

Where $\ddot{\theta}$ = roll acceleration (rad/s²)

$\dot{\theta}$ = roll velocity (rad/s)

θ = roll displacement (rad)

I_{xx} = virtual mass moment of inertia (t-m²)
B = damping coefficient (t-m²/s)
C = restoring moment (kN-m)
E(t) = wave exciting moment (kN-m).

In linear theory, the harmonic responses of the vessel $\eta_j(t)$ [Lewis, 1989] is directly proportional to the amplitude of exciting moment/force at the same frequency with some phase shift. Consequently the ship motions will have the form

$\eta_j(t) = |\eta_j| \cos(\omega_e t+\sigma_j) \Rightarrow |\eta_j| e^{i\omega_e t}$ and

$E(t) = |E_j| \cos(\omega_e t+\sigma_j) \Rightarrow |E_j| e^{i\omega_e t}$

Differentiation with respect to time (t) gives

$\dot{\eta}_j(t) = i\omega_e |\eta_j| e^{i\omega_e t}$ and $\ddot{\eta}_j(t) = -\omega_e^2 |\eta_j| e^{i\omega_e t}$, j is the motion mode.

Assuming $\theta = \eta_4$, m_{44} = mass moment of inertia for roll, ω_e = encounter frequency (rad/s) and E_4 = wave exciting moment, Eq. (1) gets modified as follows.

$[-(a_{44}+m_{44})\omega_e^2 + iB_{44}\omega_e + C_{44}]\eta_4 = E_4$ This is rewritten as

$[-\omega_e^2(a_{44}+m_{44}) + i\omega_e B_{44} + C_{44}]\eta_4 = E_4$

$\Rightarrow [C_{44} - \omega_e^2 m_{44} - b_1 - ib_2]\eta_4 = E_4$

where $b_1 = \omega_e^2 * a_{44}$, $b_2 = -\omega_e * B_{44}$ and $S_{44} = C_{44}$ restoring coefficient.

Introducing $b_{44} = b_1 + ib_2$, the roll motion is

$(S_{44} - b_{44} - \omega_e^2 * m_{44})\eta_4 = E_4 \quad (2)$

If we consider the 3-degree of freedom (3DOF) model (sway, roll, yaw), the above equation can be written in matrix form as follows:

$$([S]-[b]-\omega_e^2*[m])[\eta_j] = [E_j] \quad (3)$$

Where j=2, 4, 6;
Equation (3) represents the 3-DOF model for sway, roll and yaw in coupled condition (without fin). By incorporating the fin effect into the motion equation (3) [Sgobbo and Parsons, 1999], the above equation gets modified as follows:

$$\{S-[(b_1+\omega_e^2*m_f)+i(b_2-\omega_e*B_f)]-\omega_e^2*m\}$$
$$[\eta_j] = [E_j+E_f] \quad (4)$$

In which, m_f, B_f and E_f are fin induced mass, damping and moment/force matrices respectively. It is given in matrix form as follows.

$$m_f = \begin{bmatrix} A_{22f} & A_{24f} & A_{26f} \\ A_{42f} & A_{44f} & A_{46f} \\ A_{62f} & A_{64f} & A_{66f} \end{bmatrix}$$

$A_{22f} = (-2)M_f$, $A_{24f} = (-2)M_f R_f$, $A_{26f} = (-2)M_f l_f$;
$A_{42f} = (-2)M_f R_f$, $A_{44f} = (-2)M_f R_f^2$,
$A_{46f} = (-2)M_f R_f l_f$, $A_{62f} = (-2) M_f l_f$,
$A_{64f} = (-2) M_f R_f l_f$, $A_{66f} = (-2) M_f l_f^2$

Where $M_f = (b/2)* c_m *\rho* (2*\pi)/4$.

$$B_f = \begin{bmatrix} B_{22f} & B_{24f} & B_{26f} \\ B_{42f} & B_{44f} & B_{46f} \\ B_{62f} & B_{64f} & B_{66f} \end{bmatrix} \quad E_f = \begin{bmatrix} Y_\alpha \\ K_\alpha \\ N_\alpha \end{bmatrix}$$

$B_{22f} = (-\rho)S_f VC_{L\alpha} \cos(\theta)$,
$B_{24f} = (-\rho)S_f VC_{L\alpha} \cos(\theta) R_{vf}$
$B_{26f} = (-\rho)S_f VC_{L\alpha} \cos(\theta) l_f$
$B_{42f} = (-\rho)S_f VC_{L\alpha} \cos(\theta) R_{vf}$
$B_{44f} = (-\rho)S_f VC_{L\alpha} R_f^2$
$B_{46f} = (-\rho)S_f VC_{L\alpha} \cos(\theta) l_f R_{vf}$
$B_{62f} = (-\rho)S_f VC_{L\alpha} \cos(\theta) l_f$
$B_{64f} = (-\rho)S_f VC_{L\alpha} \cos(\theta) l_f R_{vf}$
$B_{66f} = (-\rho)S_f VC_{L\alpha} \cos(\theta) l_f^2$
$Y_\alpha = (-\rho)S_f V^2 C_{L\alpha} \cos(\theta)$; $K_\alpha = (-\rho)S_f V^2 R_f C_{L\alpha}$;
$N_\alpha = (-\rho)S_f V^2 C_{L\alpha} \cos(\theta) l_f$

Where

S_f = profile area of the pair of fin (m^2), V = ship speed (m/s), $C_{L\alpha}$ = slope of coefficient of lift. (lift coefficient/rad), ρ = water density (t/m^3),

θ = angle between hull vertical plane and fin, Rvf = vertical component of lever arm. i.e. the vertical distance from the ship center of gravity to the center of pressure on the fin, R_f = lever arm, i.e. the distance from the ship center of gravity to the center of pressure on the fin, α_t =Fin angle of attack, l_f = longitudinal distance between roll center to fin center of pressure. See Fig.5. The damping coefficient as a polynomial is shown in Fig. 6.

The above equations represent the sway, roll, and yaw coupled equations with fin related terms. The equations can also be simplified to represent single degree of freedom solution equation. The obtained lift values for the fin were applied to a laboratory simulated fin based control system on board a yacht model. The particulars of the vessel as well as those of the fins are given in Tables 1,2.

Table 1 Main particulars of ship for simulation studies

Particulars	Prototype	Model (Scale 1:20)
LBP	38m	1.9m
Beam	8.2m	0.41m
Draft (T)	1.7m	0.085m
Depth (D)	5.36m	0.268m
K_{xx}	3.28m	0.164m
K_{yy} and K_{zz}	11.4m	0.57m
Displacement	183.5t	23kg
Design speed	13knots	1.5m/s

Table 2 Main particulars of fin

Particulars	Prototype	Model (Scale 1:20)
Type	NACA 0015	NACA 0015
Aspect ratio	1.0	1.0
Mean span	1.87m	0.0935m
Mean chord	1.87m	0.0935m
Profile area	3.5m^2	0.0087m^2

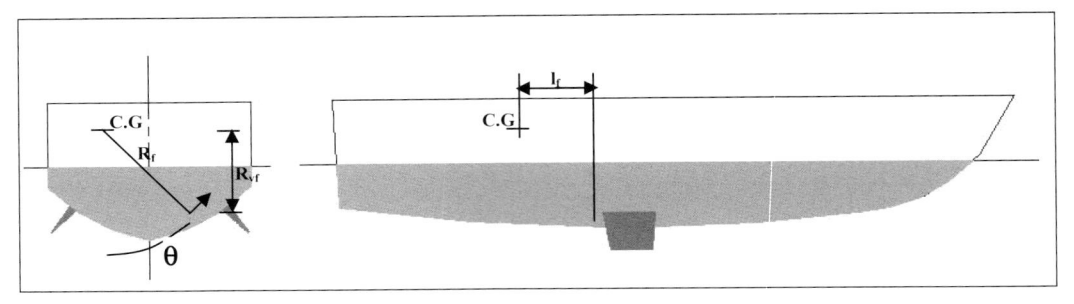

Fig. 5 Fin location

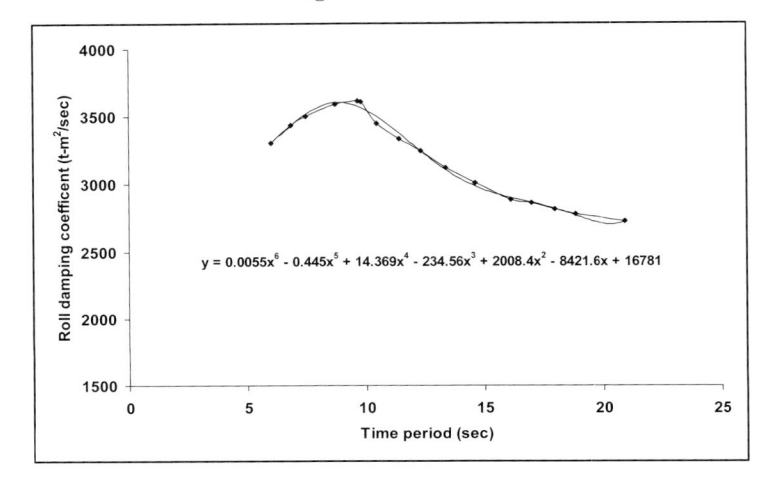

Fig. 6 Roll damping coefficient for the yacht

Control algorithm using Harmonic Distortion Analyzer for frequency based coefficients

The essential components of the control system are (i) clinometer (ii) virtual instrumentation which generates the control signal (iii) servo amplifier (iv) actuator (v) mechanical linkage The fin control system block diagram is shown in Fig.9 and has 5 modules namely,: 1) Sensor 2) Signal conditioner 3) Control signal generator 4) Comparator 5) Actuator. The control algorithm is described in Subramanian et al (2007). Using an inbuilt function namely, the Harmonic Distortion Analyzer in LabVIEW, the dominant frequency for a short-term measured response signal (roll) is obtained. The program uses stored polynomial equations formulated for representing the virtual mass moment of inertia and the damping coefficient. The ideal lift moment is then calculated and there from the required fin angle which would produce this lift. The control algorithm gives instantaneous control for fin operation.

Experimental investigations and results

The fin lift was estimated from numerical simulations as given in the first section. (See Fig. 7, 8.) The fin lift capacity is shown in Fig. 10. The obtained values were incorporated in the control algorithm along with the vessel hydrodynamic coefficients in the virtual instrumentation environment. Tests were conducted in the towing tank with simulated roll oscillation at different speeds and the reduction in roll was estimated. The fin performance is shown in Fig. 11, 12, 13. The percentage of roll reduction varies with the range of 20% at a ship speed of 5.6 knots to 66% at a ship speed of 13 knots. In conclusion, the work demonstrates an effective control algorithm for roll stabilization combining numerical hydrodynamics with virtual instrumentation.

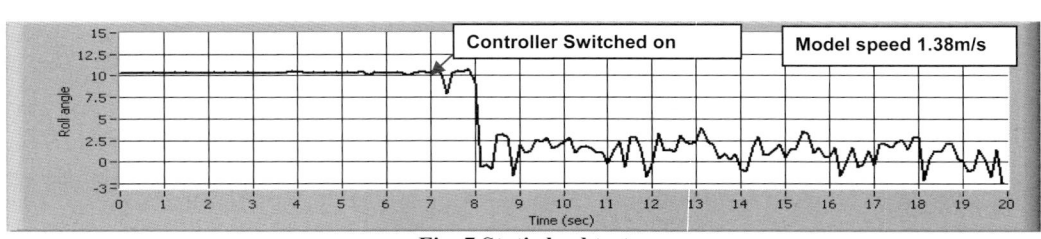

Fig. 7 Static heel test

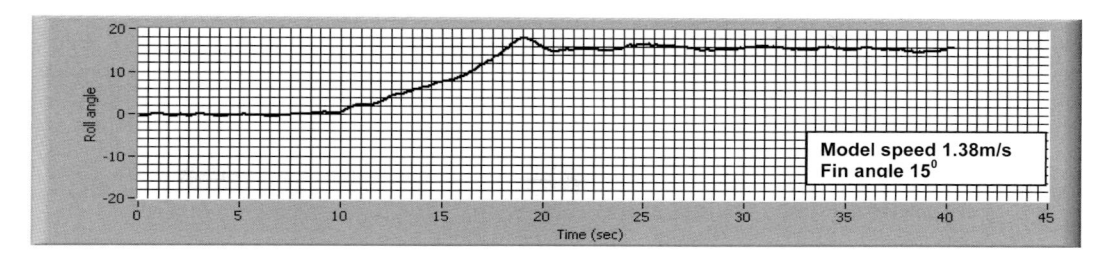

Fig. 8 Fin lift capacity test

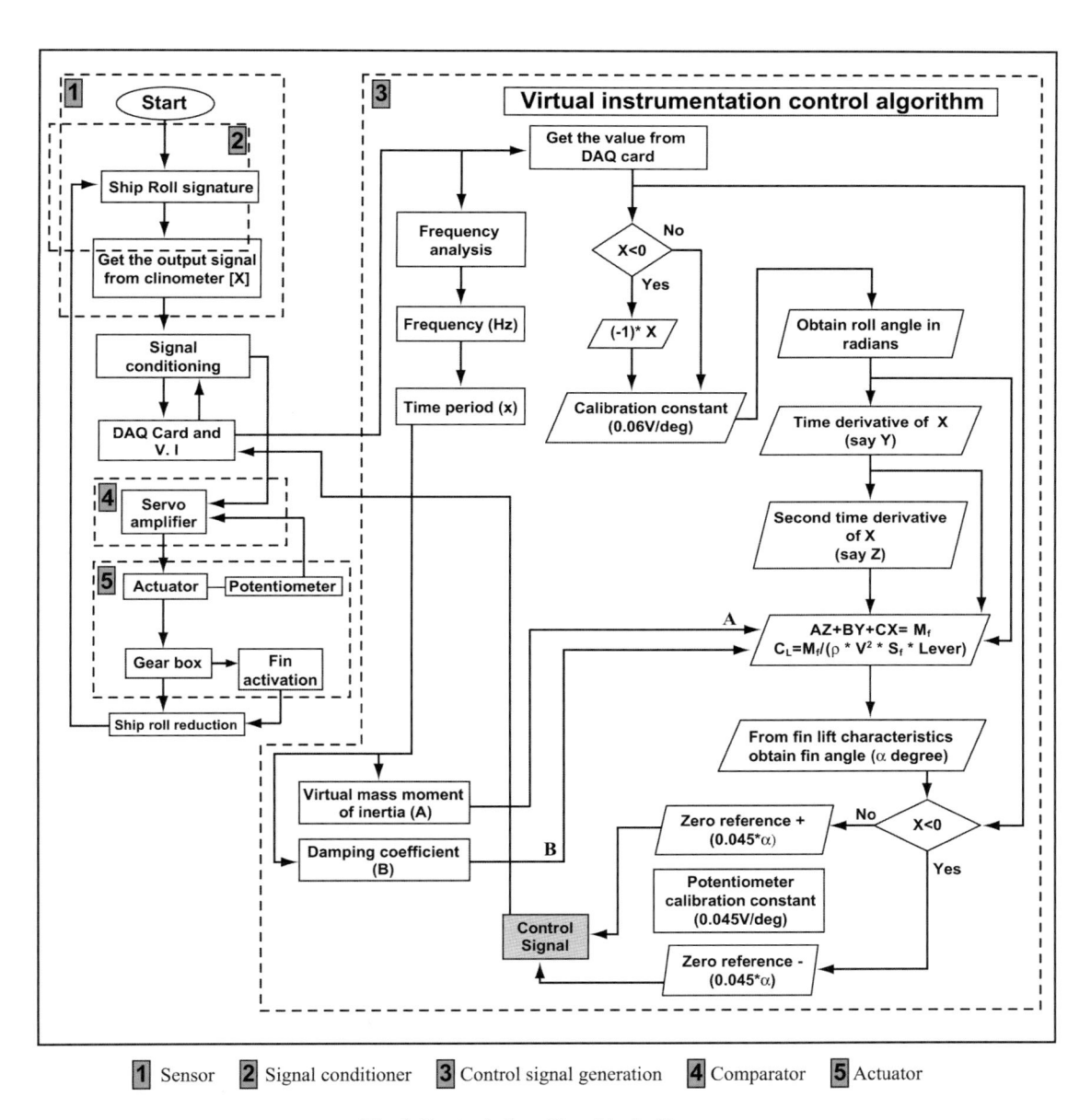

Fig. 9 Control algorithm block diagram

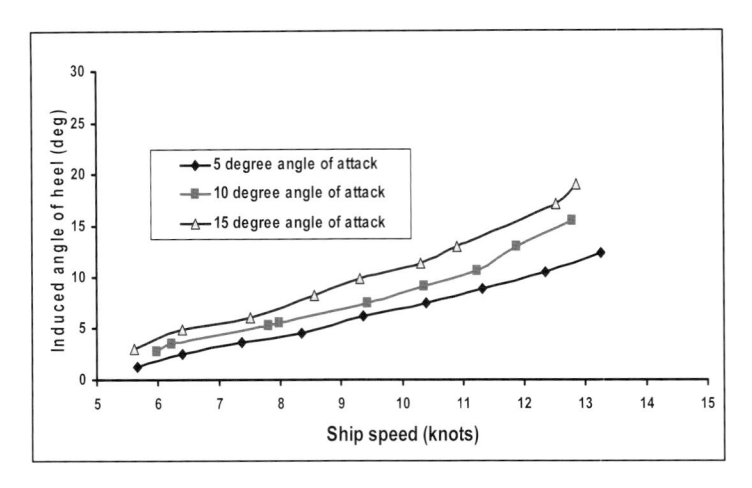

Fig. 10 Fin lift capacity with angle of attack

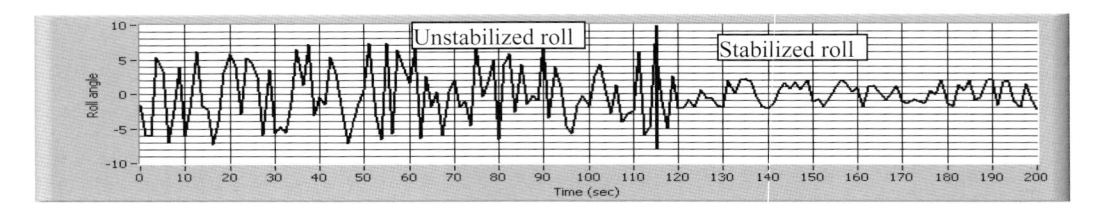

Fig. 11 Simulated roll motion stabilization (ship speed 12knots)

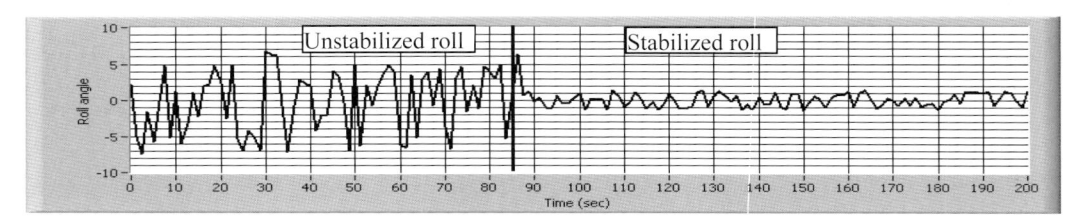

Fig. 12 Simulated roll motion stabilization (ship speed 16knots)

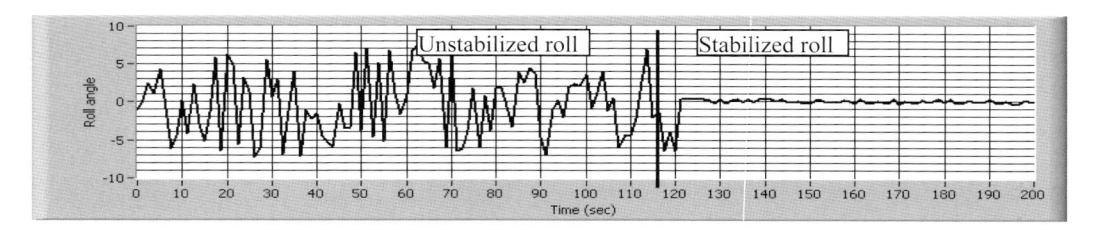

Fig. 13 Simulated roll motion stabilization (ship speed 20knots)

References

Fossen, I. T. Guidance and control of ocean vehicles, John Wiley & Sons

Lewis, E. V. *Principles of Naval Architecture Second revision Vol. III Motions in waves and Controllability*, The Society of Naval Architecture and Marine Engineers, Jersey City, NJ, 1989

Sgobbo, J.N. and Parsons, M.G. (1999) Rudder/Fin Roll Stabilization of the USCG WMEC 901 Class vessel. *Marine Technology*, 36(3), 157-170

Subramanian V. A, Asok kumar G., Jagdeeshkumar V., (2007) Active fin control for yacht using virtual instrumentation , *Ocean Engineering vol. 34, 390-402*

Mesh Size Effects in Simulating Ductile Fracture of Metals

Y. N. Li [1], D. G. Karr [1], G. Wang [2]

[1] University of Michigan, 2600 Draper Rd., Ann Arbor MI, 48109-2145
[2] American Bureau of Shipping, 16855 Northchase Drive, Houston TX, 77060-6008

Abstract

Physical scale and size effects influence the failure of structures and structural components. This can be especially true when failure is due to brittle, quasi-brittle, or ductile fracture. When simulating ductile fracture using the finite element method, mesh size effects are also encountered. A common approach for analyzing the response of hull structures due to grounding and impact, for example, is to eliminate elements or to allow elements to split when a critical strain to failure is achieved. However, an important complication arises because of the observed mesh size sensitivity whereby strain to failure generally increases with finer finite element meshes. In this paper we explore the relation between the critical strain to failure, ε_f, and the size of the "unit cell" or finite element. Our study focuses on applications for marine structures involving fracture of metals including, for example, aluminum, magnesium, and steel alloys. Extensions to two and three dimensional stress states are also discussed.

Keywords

Size effects; Ductile fracture; Bifurcation; Simulation.

Introduction

The study of size effects has a long history since Leonardo da Vinci, and interest in this topic has risen over recent decades due to the development of advanced simulation capability, particularly finite element analysis. Both deterministic and statistical aspects of scaling can influence structural and material failure theories (Bažant, 1997, 2000). The present study focuses on developing a deterministic methodology to predict mesh size effects for ductile fracture.

When simulating ductile fracture using the finite element method, mesh size effects are encountered. It is common that finer mesh sizes are needed for better results when spacial gradients of deformation are high. However, this is not necessarily true when one encounters simulation processes in which material failure is significant as in, for example, impact, explosion, implosion, ship grounding, and sheet metal forming studies (Kuroiwa, Kawamoto and Yuhara, 1992, Kitamura, 2001, Servis, Samuelides, Louka and Voudouris, 2001). For such large scale simulations, a common approach for analyzing the response of hull structures due to grounding and impact, for example, is to eliminate elements (Li 2002) or to allow elements to split (Simonsen and Tornqvist., 2004) when a critical strain to failure is achieved. However, an important complication arises because of the observed mesh size sensitivity whereby strain to failure generally increases with finer finite element meshes.

For decades, researchers found the value of strain to failure is mesh-dependent and attempts were made to find their relation, although the results are for the most part based on empirical relationships. For example, the International Ship and Offshore Structures Congress reviewed the state-of-the-art of rupture strain in research on ships' collision and grounding (Wang et al. 2006), and organized a series of benchmark studies to compare some formulae (Paik et al. 2003). Lehmann and Yu (1998) presented an empirical power law model to handle the tri-axial rupture criteria, and it was improved by Broekhuijsen (2003). The range of critical values of rupture strain was studied by Okazawa et al (2004), Yamada et al (2005), and Alsos and Amdahl (2005). Other efforts, with particular emphasis on failure of aluminum, are reported by Lee and Wierzbicki (2005). In this investigation, it is argued that mesh-size dependence can be determined by the constitutive relations and the microscale imperfections of the material, either geometric or material. Although theoretical studies of size effects are presented, notably Bažant and Guo (2002), and Engelen et al. (2006) using strain-gradient theory (Fleck and Hutchinson,1993, 2001), there still are gaps between the theory and industrial application. The purpose of this study is to explain size effects physically and present a methodology to predict size effects for marine structures involving ductile fracture of metals including aluminum, magnesium, and steel alloys.

Damage and fracture models of various complexities consider the nucleation, growth and coalescence of voids in a homogenous matrix such as the classical references by McClintock (1968, 1971), Rice and

Tracey (1969), Gurson (1977), and Needleman and Tvergaard (1984). Implementation of plasticity and damage models in finite element codes often involves the use of a material characteristic length or involves explicitly modeling the micro structural features. In the present study, this kind of constitutive model is also used together with the simplified power law plasticity model. Initiating from the one dimensional analysis, extensions to two and three dimensional stress states are also discussed.

Problem Formulation

An intuitive idea about size effect is shown in Fig. 1 qualitatively. It is obvious that the average strain in mesh 2 is larger than that in mesh 1, at the time when fracture is occurring. In fact, within subsets of mesh 2, facture is in fact complete; a continuum description of the strain in such zones leads to infinite strains. To study size effects quantitatively, a simplified three-piece-cell, shown in Fig. 2, is used (Li and Karr 2007(a)) representing a typical unit cell or single finite element. Different from typical finite element descriptions with homogeneous stress and strain, it has an imperfect part and allows strain localization. The total strain and nominal stress of this cell is then considered in a manner similar to uniform averaged stresses and strains of conventional finite elements.

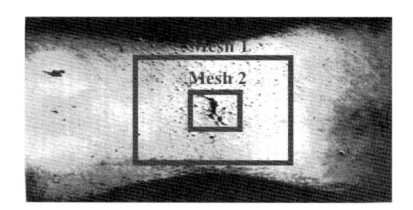

Fig. 1: Necking of a copper tensile specimen with profusion voids and central crack (from Garrison and Moody, 1987)

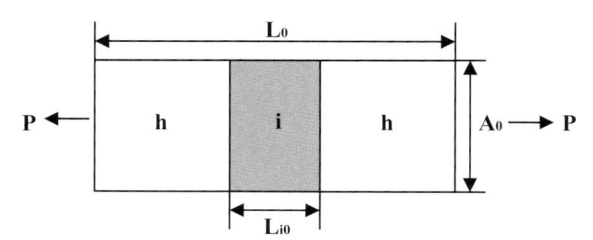

Fig. 2: Three-piece-cell

The fracture strain will be mesh-independent if the material is ideally incompressible and perfectly homogeneous. However, there are always imperfections within the material and strain localization is often concentrated at sites such as micro voids, inclusions and cracks etc. The parameter we use to describe the size of the imperfect part is defined as:

$$\lambda = \frac{L_{i0}}{L_0} \qquad (1)$$

where, L_{i0} is the characteristic size of microscale material imperfection, considered here a material property. L_0 is the initial length of the whole cell, (it thus directly describes mesh size). Equation (2) is derived (Li, 2006, Li and Karr 2007b) by using compatibility conditions, which is satisfied until fracture occurs.

$$e^{\varepsilon_{total}} = (1-\lambda)e^{\varepsilon_h} + \lambda e^{\varepsilon_i} \qquad (2)$$

where, ε_{total} is the total true strain of the cell, ε_h and ε_i are the true strains in the homogeneous piece and imperfect piece, respectively.

For the multi-piece-cell, which is more realistic than the three-piece-cell, the total fracture strain of the whole cell will be

$$\varepsilon_{total} = \ln(\sum_1^m \lambda_i e^{\varepsilon_i}) \qquad (3)$$

where, λ_i and ε_i is the geometric parameter and true strain in each part.

Rearranging equations (1) and (2), the quantitative relation between the strains within the homogeneous and imperfect part at fracture is

$$\varepsilon_f(f, \lambda, n) = \ln(\frac{a}{L_0} + b) \qquad (4)$$

where:

$$\begin{cases} a(f,n) = (e^{\varepsilon_i^*} - e^{\varepsilon_h^*})L_{i0} \\ b(f,n) = e^{\varepsilon_h^*} \end{cases} \qquad (5)$$

and where $\varepsilon_h^*, \varepsilon_i^*$ are true strains at fracture in the homogeneous part and imperfect part respectively and can be determined by constitutive bifurcation criteria, either one-dimensional or multiple-dimensional. For one-dimensional stress control loading conditions, it corresponds to the maximum load with strains concentrated in the imperfection zone. Also, f represents the size of imperfection and n is the material property index for the power law plasticity equation $\sigma = K\varepsilon^n$.

Size effects for power law plastic material

For incompressible power law plasticity, where n is the index, the quantitative relation between the strains within the homogeneous and imperfect parts is:

$$\varepsilon_h^n e^{-\varepsilon_h} = (1-f)\varepsilon_i^n e^{-\varepsilon_i} \qquad (6)$$

Here, the parameter f is the size of the geometric imperfection of the three-piece cell, representing the cross section area reduction. It can be shown, with $f = 0$, that the maximum nominal stress is $\sigma/K = n^n$ obtained at $\varepsilon_i = n$. This is the Considère criterion (see also Malvern, 1969). Returning to equation (6), the relationship between ε_i and ε_h can be established for various values of f. For nonzero values of f, the curves contain turning points where the strain in the imperfect zone increases and the strain in the homogeneous portions decreases, hence indicating the localization of strain and the onset of fracture. This is shown in Fig.3 where the bifurcation strains or fracture points are obtained as:

$$\begin{cases} \varepsilon_i^* = n \\ \varepsilon_h^* = \varepsilon_h^*(f,n) = -n LambertW[-(1-f)^{\frac{1}{n}}] \end{cases} \quad (7)$$

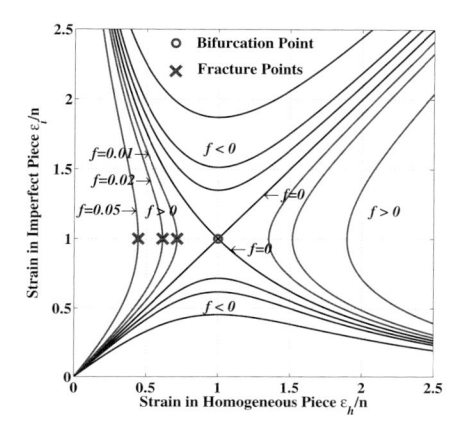

Fig. 3: Fracture points determined by Strain Bifurcation Diagram for different geometric imperfections

The 'LambertW' in equation (7) represents the Lambert W function, which has the form $W(z)e^{W(z)} = z$ (see for example Corless, et al., 1996). Substituting equation (7) into equation (5) and equation (4), the influence of the geometric imperfection f and the material hardening index n on the size effects can be obtained. Shown in Fig. 4 are the effects of varying f.

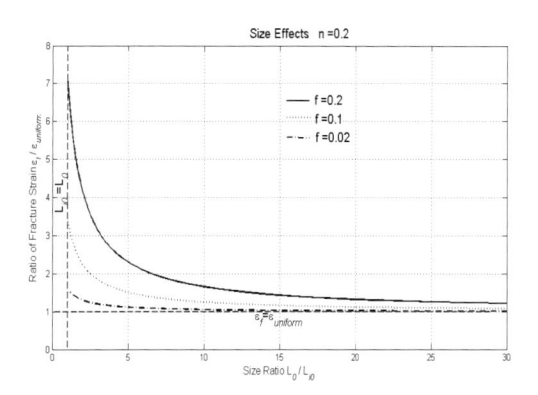

Fig. 4: Effects of imperfection size on the ratio of fracture strains for various values of the area ratio.

The size effects predicted by equation (4), (5) are compared with the FEM analysis performed by Li et al. (2002). Since the micro parameters of the material are not known, we use the least square method with two parameters (a and b) optimization to fit the curve from the FEM analysis, see Fig. 5. The trend is captured by these formulae. If the micro scale parameters are known, equations (4) and (5) provide a quantitative relation to predict the fracture strain input in FEM analysis for given mesh size of the FE model.

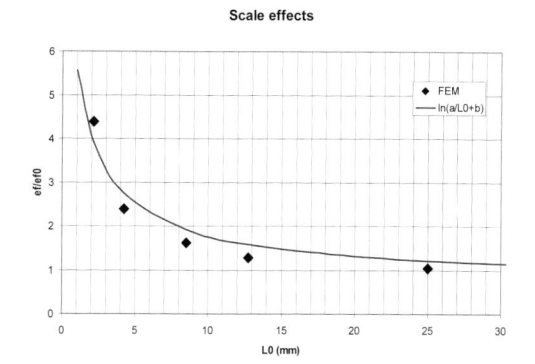

Fig. 5: Comparison between FEM results and analytical relation

Size effects prediction

With the development of tomography technology, the imperfection of the specimen can be measured (Weiler, et al 2005). Thus quantitative prediction of size effects is possible. Die-cast magnesium alloy AM60B samples were examined by Weiler and colleagues with the use of X-ray tomography (Fig. 6). The size and locations of pores in five tensile samples were obtained from the X-ray tomography data. In this section the size effects of AM60B is predicted by using data provided in Weiler's experiments, which is an application of the methodology described above.

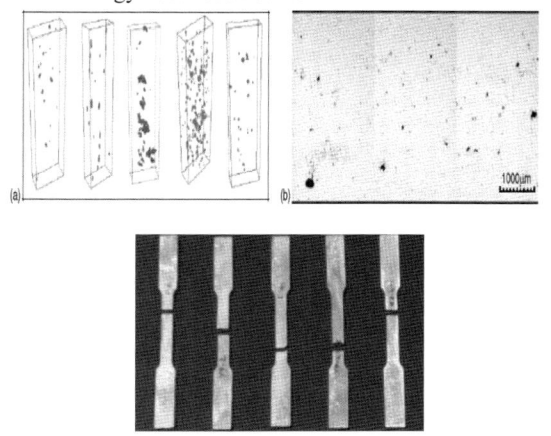

Fig. 6: 3D X-ray image for specimens in Weiler's experiment and image of final fracture (from Weiler et al., 2005)

The yield function of the randomly voided material developed by Gurson (1977) was modified by

Tvergaard and Needleman (1984). This function is referred to as the GTN model, which is shown in equation (8).

$$\phi = \frac{\sigma_e^2}{Y_m^2} + 2q_1 f_g \cosh(q_2 \frac{\sigma_1+\sigma_2+\sigma_3}{2Y_m}) - q_3 f_g^2 - 1 = 0 \quad (8)$$

Here, Y_m is the flow stress of the matrix material, σ_i are the principal values of the Cauchy stress, and f_g is the current volume fraction of voids. For spherical voids, $q_2 = 1$, and for cylindrical voids $q_2 = \sqrt{3}$. The incremental constitutive relation is developed by Needleman and Triantafyllidis (1978) as follow:

$$\dot{\sigma}_i = C_{ij}(E_{ij}, Y_m, \dot{Y}_m, f_g, \dot{f}_g, \sigma_i)\dot{\varepsilon}_j \quad (9)$$

where:

$$C_{ij} = E_{ij} - \frac{E_{ik}\phi_{,\sigma_k}E_{lj}\phi_{,\sigma_l}}{\phi_{,\sigma_i}(\phi_{,Y_m}\dot{Y}_m/\dot{\varepsilon}_i^p + \phi_{,f}\dot{f}/\dot{\varepsilon}_i^p) + \phi_{,\sigma_i}E_{ij}\phi_{,\sigma_j}} \quad (10)$$

For plastic loading

$$\phi_{,\sigma_i}\dot{\sigma}_i > 0 \quad (11)$$

The stress strain curves and fracture stresses and strains were obtained from Weiler, et al's test of simple tension. In this section, the fracture strains and stresses predicted by GTN model are compared with those obtained from the experiments.

We use the cross section with the largest pores to serve as the imperfection portion in the model. Since the samples were thin, the area porosity is set equal to the volume porosity and the GTN model is used. For samples 1, 2, 3 and 4 the porosities in the imperfection regime are 0.0075, 0.0165, 0.04, and 0.062, respectively; and the porosities in homogeneous regime are 0.001, 0.002, 0.007 and 0.013, respectively. The stress strain relation from the experimental data approximately follows the power law with hardening exponent n=0.14, this value is used for the matrix of all samples. Fig. 7 shows that, with the parameter $q_1 = 1.9$, the modified Gurson model can predict the fracture strain and fracture stress accurately.

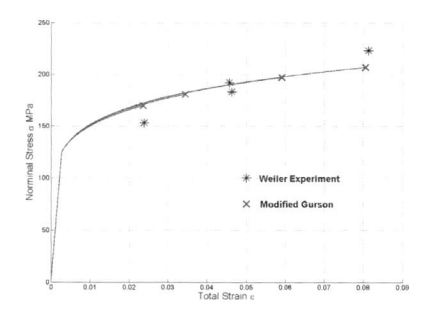

Fig. 7: Comparison of fracture stress and strain predictions and test results

Since the specimens used in Weiler's experiment were of constant length, the size effects are not obvious.

However, if one was to simulate the results of the experiments using the finite element method, size effects do arise. To simulate the experiments, we model the cross section with largest pore to extend to a homogeneous zone with length 1mm encompassing the entire width and thickness of the sample and located at the center. The volume porosity of this zone remains unchanged at 0.062. All the material properties outside this zone are the same as before. Also, 1/8 of the specimen is used in a finite element model with mesh size 0.5mm, shown in Fig. 8. Shear free end and axial symmetric boundary conditions are used to simulate simple tension.

Four 'elements' of different sizes with the same size of imperfection are studied. The size of the 'elements' are 3mm, 6mm, 12mm and 25mm separately. The total strain of these models when fracture occurs is considered the "strain to failure" of the 'elements'. A porous plastic constitutive model is used in the simulation using the computer program ABAQUS (2004).

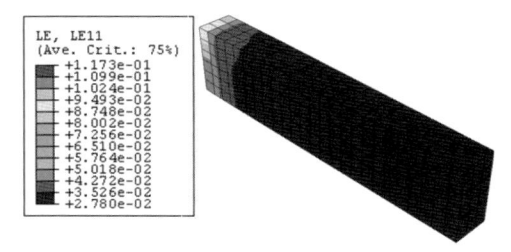

Fig. 8: ABAQUS for strain localization

The constitutive bifurcation in the imperfect zone is used as our fracture criterion. It is predicted by the three-dimensional constitutive bifurcation criteria and the results are shown in Fig. 9, which indicates that $\varepsilon_i^* = 0.115$.

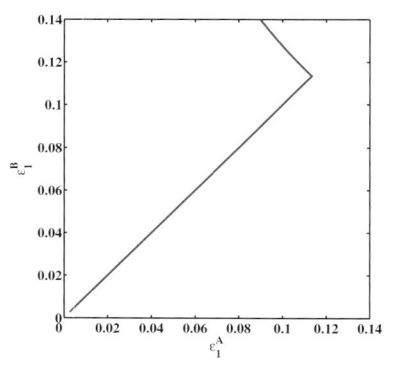

Fig. 9: Constitutive bifurcation in the imperfect zone predicted by the GTN model

Fig. 10 shows that when the displacement of the end of the total FE model reaches 0.395mm, the elements outside the imperfection part begin to unload. This state can be treated as the initiation of fracture in simulation, because normally in a material coupon test, fracture takes place shortly after this point. In the simulation, it is assumed that fracture occurs when the strain in the imperfect part reaches 0.115. For a sample length of 25 mm, the overall average fracture strain is 0.0238 and the data predicted by the GTN model is 0.0236; this corresponds to a strain in the homogeneous portion of 0.0276, which is close to the experimental data of sample 4. The total or overall true strains for different 'element' sizes are shown in Fig. 11 with the evolution of strain in the imperfect part. The corresponding fracture strain can be read from Fig. 11 and is plotted in Fig. 12.

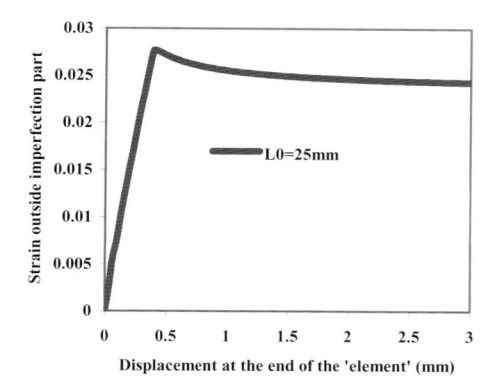

Fig. 10: Relation of displacement and strain

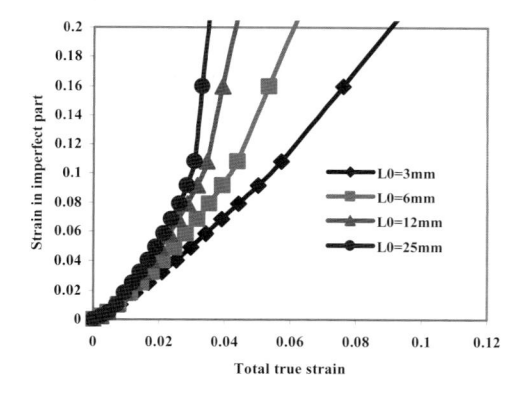

Fig. 11: Total strain and strain in imperfect zone outside the imperfect zone

Using equations (4) and (5), with $L_{i0} = 1mm$, $\varepsilon_i^* = 0.115$, $\varepsilon_h^* = 0.0276$, The size effect is predicted by the solid line in Fig. 12. Very nice agreement with the results from the finite element analysis is shown in Fig. 12.

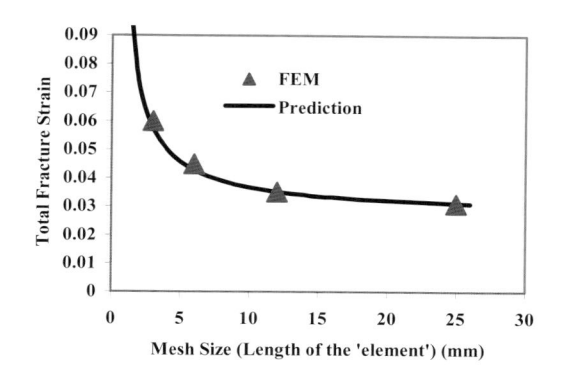

Fig. 12: Comparison of size effects obtained from FE simulation and Prediction by equation (4) and (5)

Recent studies of the fracture of structural steels also emphasize the importance of characteristic length parameters. Material tests and analyses of mild, low-carbon steels were presented by Kanvinde and Deierlein (2006). They used both void growth and stress modified critical strain models for several steels. When incorporated in finite element models to simulate fracture of steel structures, a critical average value of strain is to be achieved over a volume of material to form a crack. The question again arises as to the size of the critical volume. Note that in some applications, the finite elements may generally be smaller than the critical volume, also expressed by the characteristic length l^*.

This issue is addressed also by Chi, Kanvinde and Deierlein (2006). Material specific parameters for A572 Grade 50 steel were found using notched tensile tests. Results of the tests were analyzed using the finite element method and fracture predictions based on various levels of characteristic lengths of .09mm, .20mm and .38 mm, with the upper and lower limits being estimates based on the material substructure. Their approach was to simulate fracture based on a given stress modified critical strain. The predicted end displacement at fracture increased as the characteristic length increased. Using the data provided in Table 1 presented by Chi et al., we reduced the critical strain to failure as the characteristic length increased in accordance with equation (4). Excellent agreement is found by applying this approach to the results of the three point bending tests and compact tension tests of Table 1 of Chi et al., as presented in Figure 13. In the figure, we have normalized the failure strains with respect to the value for the smallest characteristic length and we have used the smallest characteristic length for our L_{i0}.

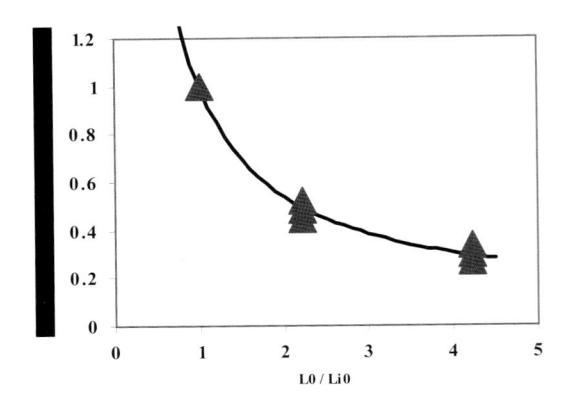

Fig.13: Prediction of Size effects for mild A572 Grade 50 steel

Three-Dimensional Constitutive Bifurcation Criteria for Material Failure

For ideally homogenous material, either compressive or incompressive, there is a critical three dimensional stress-strain state $\sigma_i^*(\underline{\sigma},\underline{\dot{\varepsilon}},\underline{\varepsilon})$ and $\varepsilon_i^*(\underline{\sigma},\underline{\dot{\sigma}},\underline{\dot{\varepsilon}})$, in principal directions, when constitutive bifurcation occurs, in the theory of material instability. Li (2006) proposed three-dimensional constitutive bifurcation criteria for two bifurcation modes: splitting and shear band.

First, we assume fracture is caused by splitting in the direction perpendicular to the principal direction. Consider one cubic cell shown in Fig. 14(a), whose edges are parallel to the local principal directions. Thus the differential equilibrium equations in the local principal coordinates for this cell are first determined. For force equilibrium, we get

$$\Delta(\sigma_i L_j L_k) = 0 \quad i,j,k = 1,2,3 \quad i \neq j \neq k \quad (12)$$

where σ_i is one of the principal stresses, L_j, L_k are the

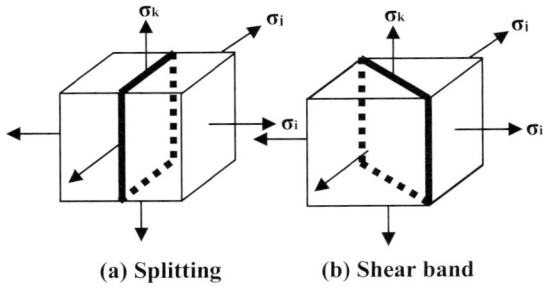

(a) Splitting **(b) Shear band**
Fig. 14: Sketch of bifurcation modes

dimensions of the cubic cell in other two principal directions. Also, Δ represents the difference between the force inside the necking band and that outside it. It

functions like a total derivative. Introducing the definition of natural strain:

$$\dot{\varepsilon}_i = \frac{\dot{L}_i}{L_i} \quad i = 1,2,3 \quad (13)$$

We find from equation (12),

$$\sigma_i L_j L_k \left[\dot{\sigma}_i + \sigma_i (\dot{\varepsilon}_j + \dot{\varepsilon}_k) \right] = 0 \quad (14)$$

For the trivial solution $\sigma_i = 0$, equilibrium equation is satisfied automatically. The non trivial solution is to let the bracket equal to zero, yielding a characteristic equation. Therefore, the characteristic equation for bifurcation is shown in equation (14) which is a general criterion for 3D fracture criteria based on the splitting mode:

$$\dot{\sigma}_i + \sigma_i (\dot{\varepsilon}_j + \dot{\varepsilon}_k) = 0 \quad i \neq j \neq k \quad (15)$$

It should be noticed that for the strain control loading process, the stress state and state of stress rate depend on the strain state and the state of strain rate, which influence each other by, for example, a particular plastic flow rule. This criterion should be checked in all of the three principal directions to determine which one is satisfied first, then the bifurcation will occur in that direction. This criterion is not constrained by associative flow rule as Drucker's postulate does. Any kind of plastic flow rule can be used. In fact, it can be applied to not only plastic material, but also all kinds of material models in continuum mechanics, either brittle or ductile, elastic or nonelastic. In addition, no assumption of small deformation is made.

The bifurcation point and direction is determined by the current stress state and the state of stress and strain rate. To this point of view, it can also be applied to history dependent constitutive bifurcation. For the one dimensional case, if the incompressibility assumption is used, it is straightforward to show that it coincides with Considére's criterion $d\sigma_1 / d\varepsilon_1 = \sigma_1$, by rearranging equation (14).

Similarly, the 3D general criterion with periodic shear band bifurcation is proposed. In Fig. 14 (b), a unit cubic of material was cut along the principal directions. Assume the bifurcation mode will be a periodical shear band in the i-j plane; k is the direction orthogonal to the i-j plane, where i, j, k are the principal directions. It is assumed that the principal directions inside the shear band are the same as those outside it. Also, t is defined as the thickness in the k direction. Note the following:

$$\Delta(\sigma_i t) = 0 \quad i = 1,2,3 \quad (16)$$

$$\dot{\sigma}_i + \sigma_i \dot{\varepsilon}_k = 0 \quad i \neq k \quad (17)$$

This is the three-dimensional characteristic equations for bifurcation within the periodic shear band mode.

The well known bifurcation criteria for simple tension and plane stress biaxial tension for incompressible power law plastic material with isotropic work hardening in sheet metal forming can be derived from the general three-dimensional criteria, too. The final analytical results are shown in Fig. 15, and the numerical results are exactly consistent with the analytical ones. It can be seen for the shear band mode, the triaxiality is always positive, while for necking mode, negative triaxiality can be obtained.

The results from sixteen experiments in Bao's thesis (2003) are also included. As is described in his thesis, all these specimens are made of Al 2024-T351, whose behavior is close to the power law with n = 0.21. Since the experiments are either one-dimensional or two-dimensional, it is expected that the analytical criteria can predict the fracture. The results are also shown in Fig. 15. The analytical criteria derived in this section provide a lower limit to the experimental results.

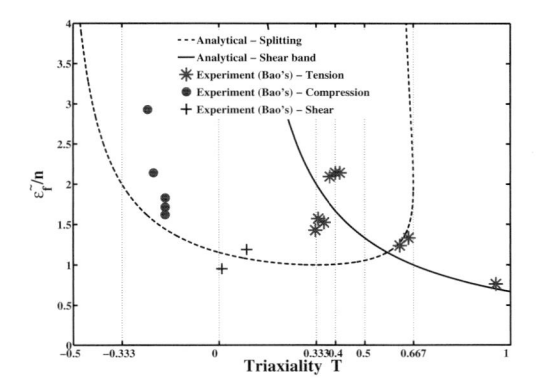

Figure 15: Comparison of analytical results and experimental results for aluminum alloy

For the special case of biaxial tension (plane stress), the shear band criterion simplifies considerably for a power law plastic material with exponent n. As shown in Li (2006) the effective strain to failure is

$$\frac{\widetilde{\varepsilon}^*}{n} = \frac{2}{3T} \qquad (18)$$

where the triaxiality, T, is defined in terms of the mean and effective stresses by:

$$T = \frac{\sigma_m}{\widetilde{\sigma}} \qquad (19)$$

This is qualitatively similar in form to the empirical relationships proposed by Kitamura (2001) and Broekhuijsen, 2003 and those shown by Lehmann & Yu 1998.

Conclusions

The relations found for size effect descriptions are derived based on localization models for fracture initiation. We note that these formulae show qualitatively similar relationships to the empirical curves provided by other authors. Our relations are derived for power law plastic materials and are shown to be in approximate agreement with more sophisticated void growth models. For uniaxial analyses, a single formula is presented in terms of the power law exponent, and the ratio of the microscale flaw length to the element length.

A quantitative relation of size effects is proposed, equations (4) and (5), based on a three-piece-cell model. This logarithmic relation catches the trend of mesh size effects observed in finite elements simulation. Different materials have different mesh size effects. With the development of X ray tomography technology, the important microscale material properties are measurable. The imperfection-induced nonuniform strain distribution is the physical reason of mesh size effects. Based on the methodology discussed in this paper, "strains to failure" along the principal directions according to different mesh sizes can be predicted accurately. In addition, it is shown the triaxiality effects can also be included in such analyses when three-dimensional localization models are adopted.

Acknowledgement

Support from the Office of Naval Research through Grant N00014-03-0983 to the University of Michigan is gratefully acknowledged.

References

ABAQUS 2004.User's Manual version 6.5.

Alsos, H. S., Amdahl, J., 2005. Intentional grounding of disabled ships, Marine 2005- Computational Methods in Marine Engineering, Oslo, Norway, 27-29.

Bao, Y. July 2003. Prediction of Ductile Crack Formation in Uncracked Bodies. Ph. D thesis in the Department of Ocean Engineering in MIT.

Bažant, P. Z., 1997. Scaling of Structural Failure. Appl. Mech. Rec. Vol. 50, No.10, 593-620.

Bažant, Z.P., 2000. Size effect, International Journal of Solids and Structures 37, 69-80.

Bažant, Z.P., Guo, Z., 2002. Size effect and asymptotic matching approximations in strain-gradient theories of micro-scale plasticity, International Journal of Solids and Structures 39, 5633-5657.

Broekhuijsen, J., 2003. Ductile failure criteria and energy absorption capacity of the Y-shape test section, Master degree thesis, Technical University of Delft.

Chi, W.-M., Kanvinde, A.M. and Deierlein, G.G., 2006. Prediction of Ductile Fracture in Structural Steel Connections Using SMCS Criterion, J. of Structural Engineering , Feb. 171-181.

Considère, A.G., 1885. Memoire sur l'Emploi du Fer et de l' Acier dans les Constructions. Annales des Ponts et Chausses, ser. 6 (9), 574-775.

Corless, R.M., Gonnet, G.H., Hare, D.E.G., Jeffrey, D.J., Knuth, D.E., 1996. On the Lambert W Function. Adv. Comput. Math. 5, 329-359.

Engelen, R.A.B., Fleck, N.A., Peerlings, R.H.J., Geers, M.G.D., 2006. An evaluation of higher-order plasticity theories for predicting size effects and localization, International Journal of Solids and Structures 43, 1857-1877.

Flech, N.A., Hutchinson, J.W., 1993. A phenomenological theory for strain gradient effects in plasticity, J. Mech. Phys. Solids 41, No.12, 1825-1857.

Flech, N.A., Hutchinson, J.W., 2001. A reformulation of strain gradient plasticity, Journal of Mechanics and Physics of Solids 49, 2245-2271.

Garrison, W. M. and Moody, N. R. 1987. Ductile fracture. J. Phys. Chem. Solids 48, 1035-1074.

Giovanola, J. H., Kirkpatrick, S. W., 1998. Using the Local Approach to Evaluate Scaling Effects, International Journal of Fracture 92, 101-116.

Gurson, A. L. 1977. Continuum theory of ductile rupture by void nucleation and growth: part I- yield criteria and flow rules for porous ductile media. Transactions of the ASME. J. of Engineering materials and Technology, Jan. 2-15.

Kanvinde, A.M. and Deierlein, G.G., 2006. Void Growth Model and Stress Modified Critical Strain Model to Predict Ductile Fracture in Structural Steels, J. of Structural Engineering , Dec. 1907-1918.

Kitamura, O., 2001. FEM approach to the simulation of collision and grounding damage. Proceeding of 2nd International Conference on Collision and Grounding of Ships, Copenhagen, Dammark,2001.

Lee, Y. W., Wierzbicki T. , 2005. Fracture prediction of thin plates under localized impulsive loading. Part I: dishing, International Journal of Impact Engineering, 31(10): 1253-1276.

Lehmann, E., Yu, X., 1998. On ductile rupture criteria for structural tear in the case of ship collision and grounding, International Symposium on Practical Designs of Ships and Floating Structures (PRADS), The Hague, The Netherlands.

Li, Y.N. 2006. Ductile Fracture due to Localization and Void Growth for 3D Randomly Voided Materials, Ph.D thesis

Li, Y.N., Karr, D. G. (2007a) Study of Uniaxial Tension from a New Point of View (Submitted to International Journal of Nonlinear Mechanics)

Li, Y.N., Karr, D. G. (2007b) Prediction of Ductile Fracture in Tension by Bifurcation, Localization, and Imperfection Analysis, (Submitted to International Journal of Plasticity)

Li, Y.N., 2003. Study on Nonlinear Finite Element Simulation of Ship-bridge Collision, Master Degree thesis (in Chinese).

Li, Y.N., Gao, Z. and Gu, Y., 2002. The Benchmark Study of the Tensile Coupon Test and Model Test of Ship Grounding. Journal of Ship Engineering 6, 13-17. (in Chinese)

Malvern, L. E. 1969. Introduction to the Mechanics of a Continuous Medium. by Prentice-Hall, Inc. Englewood Cliffs, N. J.

McClintock, F. A. 1968. A criterion for ductile fracture by the growth of holes, J. Appl. Mech. Jun., 363-371.

McClintock, F. A. 1971. Plasticity aspects of fracture. In "Fracture" (Liebowitz, H. Ed.), Academic Press, New York.

Needleman, A. and Triantafyllidis, N. 1978. Void Growth and Local Necking in Biaxially Stretched Sheets, Transactions of the ASME 100, 164-169.

Needleman, A., Tvergaard, V., 1984. An Analysis of ductile rupture in notched bars. J. Mech. Phys. Solids32 (6), 461-490.

Okazawa, S., Fujikubo, M. and Hiroi, S., 2004. Static and dynamic necking analysis of steel plates in tension, Third International Conference on Collision and Grounding of Ships (ICCGS), Izu, Japan, 25-27.

Paik, J. K. 2003. ISSC V.3 Committee Collision and Grounding, ISSC, San Diego, CA.

Kuroiwa, T., Kawamoto, Y. and Yuhara., T., 1992. Study on damage of ship bottom structure due to grounding. The Conference on Prediction Methodology of Tanker Structural Failure.

Rice, J. R. and Tracey, D. M. 1969. On the Ductile Enlargement of Voids in Triaxial Stress Fields. J. Mech. Phys. Solids, Vol. 17, 201-217.

Servis, D., Samuelides, M., Louka, T. and Voudouris, Giorgos, 2001. The implementation of finite element codes for the simulation of ship-ship collisions. Proceeding of 2nd International Conference on Collision and Grounding of Ships, Copenhagen,Danmark.

Simonsen, B. C., Tornqvist, R., 2004. Experimental and numerical modeling of ductile crack propagation in large-scale shell structures, Marine Structures 17, 1-27.

Wang, G. 2006. ISSC V.1 Committee Collision and Grounding, ISSC, Southampton, UK.

Weiler, J.P., Wood, J.T., Klassen, R.J., Maire, E., Berkmortel, R. and Wang, G., 2005. Relationship between internal porosity and fracture strength of die-cast magnesium AM60B alloy. Material Science and Engineering A 395, 315-322.

Yamada, Y., Endo, H., Pedersen, P. T., 2005. Numerical study on the effect of buffer bow structure in ship-to-ship collisions, International Offshore and Polar Engineering Conference (ISOPE), Seoul, Korea, 19-24.

Simulation of Response of Steel Plates under Pressure Pulses

M.S. Samuelides [1], D. Daliakopoulos [1], and J.K. Paik [2]

[1] School of Naval Architecture and Marine Engineering, National Technical University of Athens
Athens, Greece
[2] Department of Naval Architecture and Ocean Engineering, Pusan National University,
Busan, Korea

Abstract

The paper investigates the dynamic response characteristics of steel plates under impact pressure loads (or pressure pulses). In particular, the work reported herein is focused on the applicability of analytical methods for the prediction of the permanent deflections of steel plates under dynamic pressure loads and the simulation of the dynamic response using finite element codes. These methods are applied to predict the deformations of steel plates under blast loads that are reported in the literature. The effects of strain-rate and temperature on material properties are investigated and discussed. The range of applicability analytical formulae based on plastic analysis is discussed. Appropriate elements for the simulation of the structural response using finite element packages are identified in terms of element size and material modeling. Furthermore, the effects of the shape of the pressure pulse and the spatial distribution of pressures are examined.

Keywords

Impact pressure loads; Pressure pulse; Elasto-plastic structural response; Dynamic material properties; Finite element simulation of structural response.

Introduction

Plate panels in ship structures are subjected to both static and dynamic transverse loading, as a result of the operating conditions or accidents. Operating loads are usually hydrodynamic low-frequency pressures arising from wave actions, or relatively higher frequency pressures that arise from sloshing and slamming. Whenever these loads are considered by the rules in the design phase, they are usually treated as quasi-static loads, i.e., both inertia effects and strain-rate effects on the material properties are ignored. Accidental transverse loads on ship plating include those arising from contacts, i.e., collisions, grounding, dropped objects, as well as impact pressures resulting from blast or gas explosions. These types of loads are usually not taken into account when designing trading ship structures according to classification rules.

An extensive study was made by Jones (1989) on the response of beams and plates under impact loading employing the theorems of plastic analysis. In order to determine the impact response, Jones derived the equations of motion of the structural component, presuming a set of plastic hinge pattern and velocity field of the rigid areas of the hinged components. Then the equations of dynamic equilibrium are integrated in order to obtain the displacement field versus time.

If the displacements and the internal forces thus obtained do not violate the yield criterion anywhere in the structure, then the response is supposed to be the exact response of the component, provided that it obeys the yield criterion that has been postulated. If the yield criterion is violated the analysis may be repeated assuming another set of different pattern of plastic hinges and velocity field. Observations from tests could help select the appropriate plastic hinge modes of response.

If the duration of the load application is relatively long, with respect to the natural frequency of the structure, the response of the structure may be determined in the "quasi-static" domain. This approach assumes a response mode of the structural component, but contrary to the dynamic analysis described in the previous paragraphs, it ignores the inertia effects. The displacement of the structure is obtained by equating the work done by the external forces – or the initial kinetic energy of the striking mass in case that the problem under examination is an impact between two bodies – with the energy absorbed by the structural component as it is deformed. Oliveira (1981) developed expressions for the prediction of the permanent deflections of beams and plates under localized impact that may occur by falling objects.

The analytical formulae may be modified to include strain-rate effects. This aspect has been reviewed by Jones (2006) and Langdon et al (2004). From tests and observations it is concluded that strain-rate effects do not concern solely the yield stress, but also the ultimate stress, and the failure strain of the material and the associated Cowper-Symonds equation that is widely used, is in some cases too simple for an accurate modelling of the effect. However it seems that when the structural component is made of mild steel a correction made on the basis of the Cowper–Symonds rule gives results that are in good agreement with experimental measurements. A recent approach for the definition of design curves against impact loading taking into account the strain-rate effect has been reported by Paik and Thayamballi (2003, 2007), and Paik et al (2006). A further model for modelling the effect of strain-rate and temperature on the constitutive equation of materials is proposed by Johnson et al (1985). However it was not possible to find in the literature the values of the parameters that are needed in order to implement the model of Johnson for mild steel.

The increase of the speed of computers and the capacity and speed of storage devices, made it possible to use extensively, finite element codes for the simulation of the structural response under impact loading conditions. Both explicit and implicit codes may be used for dynamic analysis and the standard packages offer a wide variety of elements, material models and contact algorithms in order to suit the needs of the problems to be solved. Strain-rate and temperature effects on yield stress may be included in the analysis using material models that have been derived on the basis of tests under rather simple loading conditions. Failure criteria may be also incorporated in the analysis, but the accuracy of the results is still an open question.

Recent experiments on stiffened and unstiffened steel plates under impact loads have been reported by Yuan et al (2005), Langdon et al (2005), Pan and Louca (1999) and Schleyer et al (2003). These tests include uniform and localized blasts on small scale, i.e., 126×126 mm², panels, and uniform impacts on plate panels 2660×2630 mm² and 1000×1000 mm². The pressures were generated by explosions and varied from a couple of bars in the case of large plates to some hundred bars in the case of the small scale panels. The duration of the impact varied from a few μs to some ms.

The paper presents an investigation of the dynamic response of plates under pressure pulses. In particular the work reported herein is focused on the applicability of analytical methods for the prediction of the deformations of plates under dynamic loading and the simulation of the dynamic response using finite element codes. These methods are applied to predict the deformations of plates under blast loads that are reported in the literature. The effect of strain-rate and temperature on material properties as well as the effect of the shape of the pressure pulse and the spatial distribution of pressures are investigated and discussed.

Analytical Methods

Dynamic Response under Uniform Pressure Pulse

According to Jones (1989) the maximum displacement w(t) versus time, of a rectangular plate having a length 2L, breadth 2B and thickness H, which is fully restrained along its edges and loaded with a uniform pressure pulse of magnitude p for time τ is given as a function of time t by the formulae ($\beta = B/L$):

$$w(t) = \frac{(1-\eta) \cdot \{\cos(a_3 \cdot t) - 1\}}{a_2/2} \quad \text{if } t \leq \tau \tag{1a}$$

and

$$w(t) = \frac{\{1 - \eta + \eta \cdot \cos(a_3 \cdot \tau)\} \cdot \cos(a_3 \cdot t)}{a_2/2} +$$

$$+ \frac{\eta \cdot \sin(a_3 \cdot \tau) \cdot \sin(a_3 \cdot t) - 1}{a_2/2}$$

if $t \leq \tau$ \hfill (1b)

where

$$a_1 = \frac{\mu \cdot B^2}{6 \cdot M_p} \cdot \frac{2 - \beta \cdot \tan\phi}{1 + \beta \cdot \cot\phi}, \quad a_2 = \frac{2}{H} \cdot \left(1 + \frac{1 - \beta \cdot \tan\phi}{1 + \beta \cdot \cot\phi}\right)$$

$$a_3^2 = \frac{a_2}{a_1}$$

and η is the ratio of the applied uniform pressure p_0, over the collapse static collapse pressure p_p, and M_p is the maximum plastic bending moment per unit length that the cross section of the plate may carry, i.e.

$$p_p = \frac{12 \cdot M_p}{B^2} \cdot \frac{1}{\sqrt{3 + \beta^2} - \beta}, \quad M_p = \frac{\sigma_Y \cdot H^2}{4}, \quad \eta = \frac{p_0}{p_p},$$

where σ_Y is the yield stress of the material.

The maximum displacement is reached when the motion of the plate ceases - at time T_m - and in case this occurs after the removal of the pressure pulse, the following equation holds:

$$\tan(a_3 \cdot T_m) = \frac{\eta \cdot \sin(a_3 \cdot \tau)}{1 - \eta + \eta \cdot \cos(a_3 \cdot \tau)}$$

Thus the maximum displacement w_a may be determined from (1b), by substituting t with T_m.

Strain-rate effect

The above formulae do not take into account the effect of strain-rate on the yield stress of the material. In order to include this aspect in the analysis it is possible to select the yield stress in such a way, so that it satisfies the relation between the dynamic yield stress and the strain-rate, as the latter is obtained from the analysis. In the case of the rectangular plate under investigation, the rate of strain at any time t may be approximated by dividing an average strain ε_{av} by time t. The average strain rate $\dot{\varepsilon}_{av}$ could be estimated from

$$\dot{\varepsilon}_{av} = \frac{\sqrt{1 + (w(t)/B)^2} - 1}{t}$$

Thus it is possible to estimate at any time t, during the motion of the plate the strain-rate and the corresponding dynamic yield stress $\sigma_{Y,dyn}$ applying the Cowper-Symonds equation, which for mild steel is:

$$\sigma_{Y,dyn} = \sigma_Y \cdot \left[1 + \left(\frac{\dot{\varepsilon}_{av}}{40.4}\right)^{1/5}\right]$$

where σ_Y is the yield stress at zero rate of strain. By applying the formulae above and performing a few iterations it is possible to determine the dynamic maximum strain-rate during the motion of the plate and consecutively the corresponding dynamic yield stress and the maximum displacement that satisfy equations (1a, 1b).

Effect of temperature on material properties

In the case of gas explosion or in general when there is heat emission during the response of the structural component, the rise in temperature may affect the properties of the material, i.e., the Young's modulus, yield stress and rupture strain. In case of blast loading, where the heat is emitted by the conversion of the plastic work, and assuming that under adiabatic process the total of the dissipated work is converted to heat that raises uniformly the temperature of the material, it is possible to estimate the rise in temperature $\Delta\Theta$ by equating the energy needed to raise the temperature of the mass m of the beam or plate to the dissipated plastic work. An upper bound of the latter equals the work E_p done by the applied pressure as the plate deforms, i.e.,

$$E_p = p_0 \cdot \frac{L^2 \cdot w(\tau)}{3} = p_0 \cdot \frac{L^2}{3} \cdot \frac{(1-\eta) \cdot \{\cos(a_3 \cdot \tau) - 1\}}{a_2/2}$$

and the subsequent rise of temperature $\Delta\Theta$ is given by

$$E_p = p_0 \cdot \frac{L^2}{3} \cdot \frac{(1-\eta) \cdot (\cos a_3 \cdot \tau - 1)}{a_2/2} = a_T \cdot m \cdot \Delta\Theta$$

where a_T is the specific heat capacity of the material, which for mild steel is taken equal to 660 J/(Kg·C°).

Having estimated the rise in temperature the yield stress may be calculated by the relations proposed by Masui (1989), whereby the yield stress at temperature T, $\sigma_{Y,T}$ is given by

$$\sigma_{Y,T} = \sigma_Y \cdot [1 - 0.00178 \cdot (T - 200)]$$

if the temperature is between 200°C and 700°C, and

$$\sigma_{Y,T} = \sigma_Y \cdot [0.133 - 3.884 \cdot 10^{-4} \cdot (T - 700)]$$

for temperatures between 700°C and 1000°C.

However it should be stated that this approach is based on the assumption that the temperature of the plate is uniform. In actual cases plastic work is dissipated at the hinges and the temperature of hinge lines may rise faster than the part of the plates that remain elastic. Nevertheless for small plates this approach gives a first-cut estimation of the temperature effect on the yield properties and subsequently the response in the plastic region.

Simulation of blast tests

Yuen et al (2005)

The above methodology has been applied to simulate the blast test conducted by Yuen et al (2005), who performed numerous blast tests on small scale stiffened and unstiffened plates. The method described has been applied to predict the response of two unstiffened square plates, having an edge length of 126 mm and thickness of 1.6 and 1.63 mm, under blast loads. The plates were manufactured from steel having yield stress of 242 MPa and the impulse was applied uniformly on their surface. The magnitude of the impulses and the maximum displacements that were measured after the application of the blast load were 31 N·s and 25.6 mm for the test designated as S56 and 43.4 N·s and 35.5 mm for the test designated as S01 respectively. Figure 1, full lines, shows the displacement of the mid point of the plates versus time as obtained from equations (1a) and (1b). The yield stress was selected after 4 iterations to be 663 MPa for test S56 and 716 MPa for test S01. With these values of yield stress the average maximum strain-rate as calculated from equations are 663 s^{-1} and 1162 s^{-1} respectively, and the corresponding dynamic yield stresses according to equation coincide with the assumed values.

The rise of temperature according to the equations is in both cases less than 200°C, and therefore the Masui equations do not result in any significant effect of the temperature on the yield stress. The comparison of the measurements and the results obtained by the application of method of Jones, with the modification to take into account the strain-rate effects and the consideration of temperature rise, is considered to be excellent. The strain-rate and the temperature effects have been considered uniformly on the plate. Under this assumption the effect of the strain-rate is significant, i.e., the values of the dynamic yield stress reached approximately 3 times the static value, whereas the temperature appears not to influence the results. If the strain-rate effect is not taken into account the displacements would have been 56 mm for test S56 and 61 for test S01.

The above predictions were based on the assumption that the pressure pulse lasted for 14.5 μs, as suggested by Yuen et al (2005). In order to examine the sensitivity of the pulse duration on the results we repeated the calculations assuming that the pressure pulse was four or eight times longer. The respective displacement-time curves are shown in dotted lines in Figure 1. No significant changes are observed.

Langdon et at (2004) and Pan et al (1999).

The very good correlation that we have observed between the analytical and experimental results motivated the authors to simulate further blast tests with the same method. However the analytical predictions were not good in the case of the tests performed by Langdon and Schleyer (2004) and Pan and Louca (1999). It is believed that the main reason for the discrepancy between the analytical and measured values of the displacement at the centre is the presence of significant elastic strain energy that has been involved in the response. Another reason may be due to the boundary conditions, which were thoroughly investigated by Pan and Louca (1996).

Finite element modeling

Recent literature contains numerous investigations of impact response of structures using finite element packages. However there is still a lack of widely accepted procedure to perform the simulations in the large strain, elasto-plastic range and the results do depend on the selection of parameters, for some of which there is still an uncertainty. Mesh size and selection of elements, material characterization and failure criterion, if the latter is included in the analysis, are aspects that are still under investigation and their treatment are dependent on the experience of the investigator as well as the existing knowledge of the failure mechanisms and material behaviour in multi-axial stress patterns. It should be always kept in mind that finite element simulations are directly dependent on the description of the material and boundary conditions and if those are not incorporated in an appropriate manner, there will be no confidence on the results that are obtained.

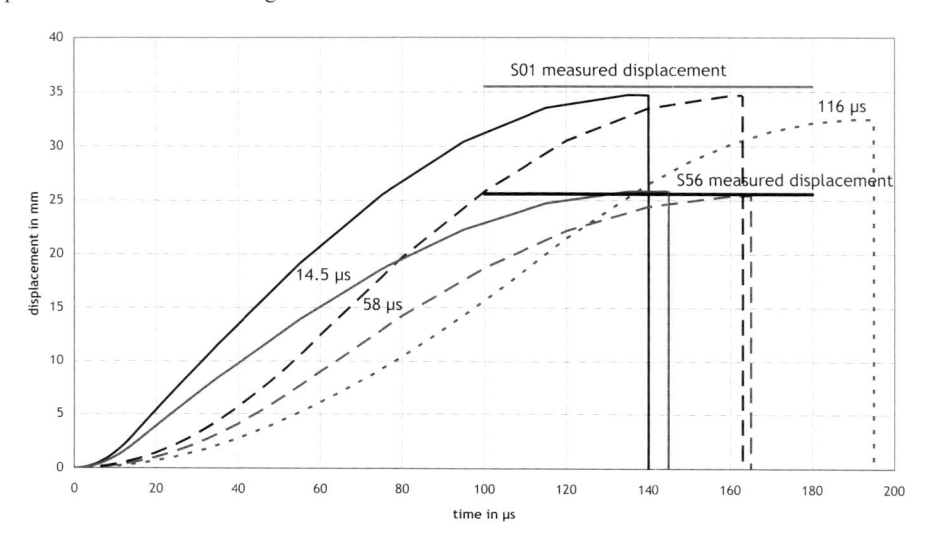

Figure 1: Comparison of measurements from Yuan et al (2005) with analytical predictions

FE code and selection of elements and mesh

ANSYS, version 10, was selected to perform the simulations. The package offers the possibility of a variety of elements. Two types of elements have been tested:

✓ SOLID186, which is a 20 node, 60 degree of freedom solid cubic element, and
✓ SHELL181, which is a 4 node, 24 degree of freedom shell rectangular element.

For the convergence studies a quarter of the plate was modeled. Three types of meshes were tested for each element, namely a coarse mesh, a relative fine mesh and a mesh between these two.

For the solid elements the meshes were 5×5×2, 10×10×2 and 15×15×2 and for the shell elements there were 5×5, 10×10 and 15×15. From the results it was concluded that the shell elements were appropriate for the modeling of the plate and that a 20×20 discretization of the whole plate could give numerically accurate results. For a square plate having an edge of 126 mm and thickness of 1.6 mm this selection implies that the length over thickness ratio of the shell elements is approximately 4.

Material model

The material was selected to be elastic-rigid plastic whereby the yield stress depends on the rate of strain by neglecting the effect of strain-hardening.

Applied load

In each case the pressure has been applied in four different ways. Yuen et al (2004) suggested that the duration of the pressure pulse was 14.5 μs. In order to investigate the effect of the pulse shape on the displacements four different pressure pulses were applied to test S56 and S01. The patterns are presented on Figure 2, with the pressure p_{max} given by

$$p_{max} = \frac{I}{A \cdot \tau}$$

whereby τ equals to 14.5 μs, I is the impulse and A is the area of application of the pulse that equals to 159 cm².

Results

The results obtained from the simulations of the two tests illustrate that the effect of the shape of the pressure pulse is negligible. All four pressure pulses produced the same response in each one of the tests S56 and S01. Figure 3 shows the maximum displacement at the mid-point (y axis in m·10⁻²) of the plate vs. time, for the test S56 and it can be seen that irrespective of the shape of the pressure pulse, the maximum displacement was approximately 28 mm, which compares well with the displacement 25.6 mm, which was measured during the test. It is also observed that the response is practically plastic and the elastic vibration about the maximum displacement is negligible.

Figure 3 also shows the plastic von Mises strain field. These figures confirm the previous finding, i.e., that the four pressure pulses produce the same plate response. The same conclusions may be drawn from the results of the simulation of tests S01. In this case the maximum displacement at mid-point was found to be 37.5 mm, whereby the maximum displacement, which was measured during the test was 35.5 mm.

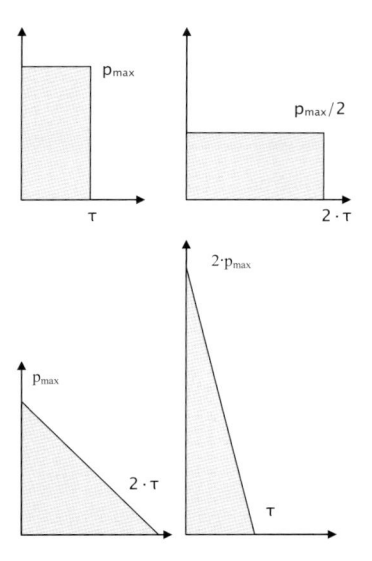

Figure 2: Applied pressure pulses

Effect of spatial distribution of pressures

In all simulations that have been reported up to this point the pressure pulses have been applied uniformly on the surface of the plate. In order to investigate the effect of the spatial variation of the applied pressures, we have simulated the response of the plate under an impulse I equal to 31 N·s, that corresponds to the test S56, but the pressure was applied non–uniformly over the surface of the plate.

For the definition of the pressures, the plate was divided in 16 same square segments. A peak pressure p_p was applied to one of these square segments, whereby the squares adjacent to the segment, where the peak pressure was applied, were loaded with a pressure that equals half the peak pressure.

As we move away from the area, where the peak pressure was applied the pressure levels were half the levels of the segments that are closer to the area of maximum pressures. The value of the peak pressure was calculated, so that the applied impulse equals 31 N·s. Two load cases, which are schematically shown in Figure 4, were investigated. In the time domain the pressures followed a rectangular pressure pulse, i.e., there were kept constant for $0 \leq t \leq \tau$, and then dropped to zero. The duration of the pressure pulses was taken equal to 14.5 μs, as in the cases described in the previous sections.

(a) Case S56a

(b) Case S56b

Figure 4: Spatial distribution of pressures

The results of the sensitivity study, in terms of maximum displacement versus time and displacement patterns are presented in Figure 5.

It is observed from Figure 5 that the spatial variation of the pressure has a moderate effect on the maximum displacements: the pressure distribution corresponding to case S56a, produces a displacement that is practically the same as the case of uniform pressure distribution and case S56b, a displacement that is slightly higher. It is also found that the displacement patterns show a shift of the location, where maximum displacement is observed towards the area of application of maximum pressures.

(a) Triangular pulse – duration of pulse τ-2·14.5 μs

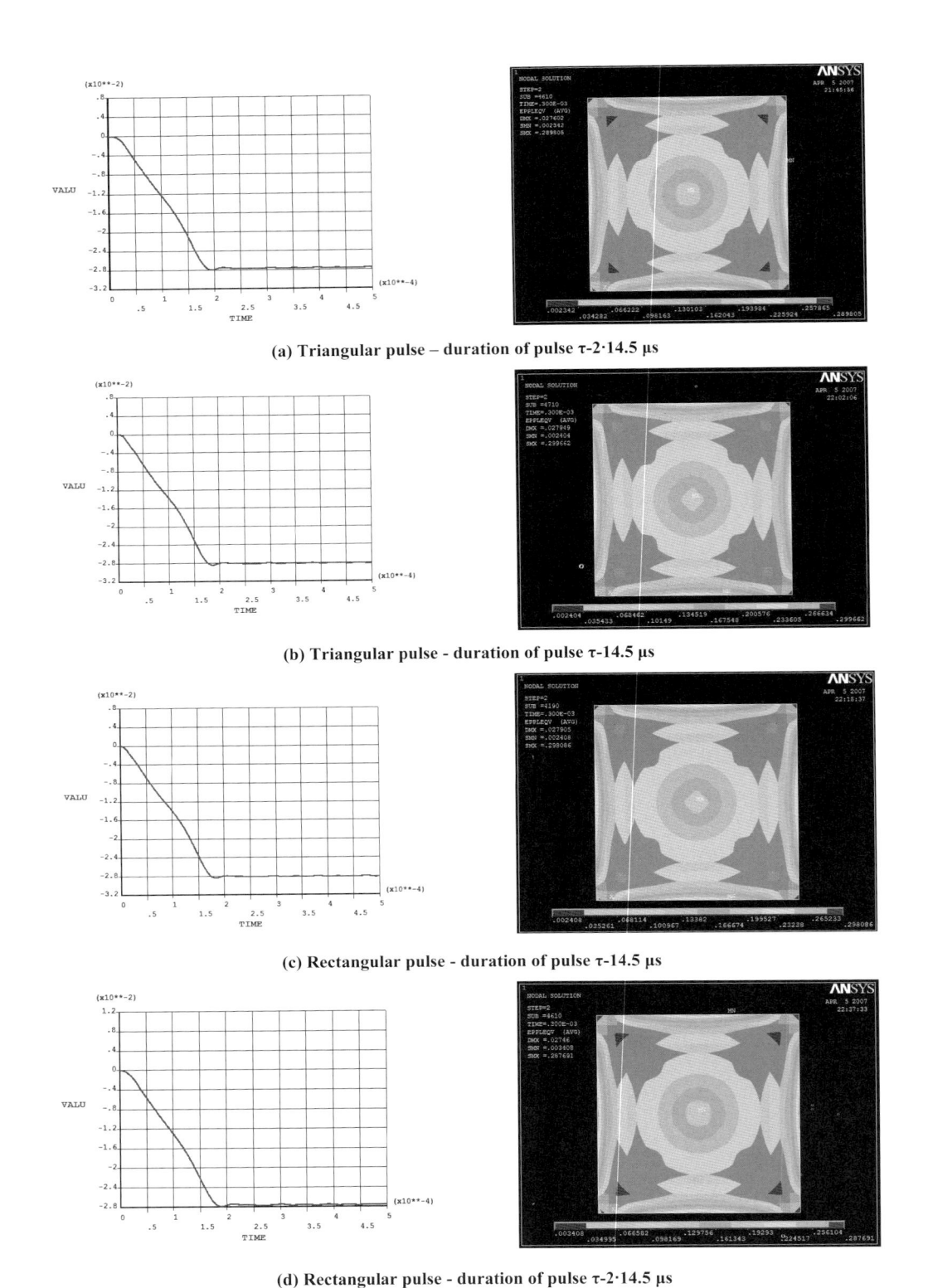

(b) Triangular pulse - duration of pulse τ-14.5 μs

(c) Rectangular pulse - duration of pulse τ-14.5 μs

(d) Rectangular pulse - duration of pulse τ-2·14.5 μs

Figure 3: Displacement at mid-point (left) and von Mises strain distribution (right) obtained by FE simulations for test S56

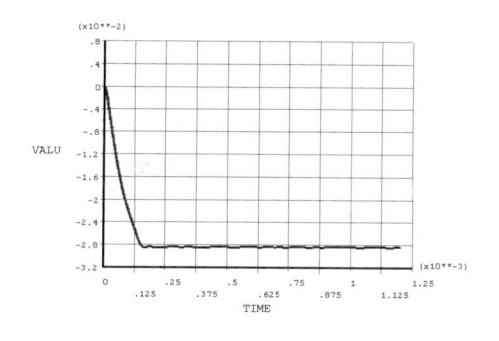

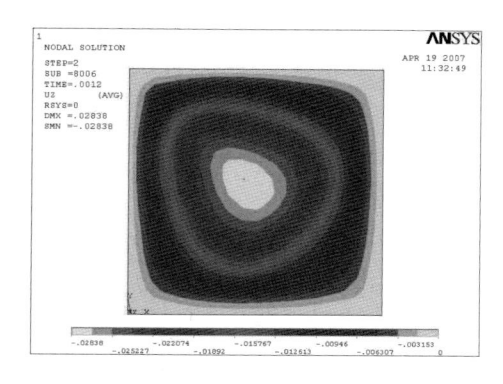

(a) Case S56a

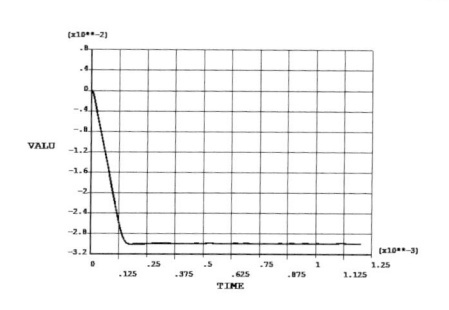

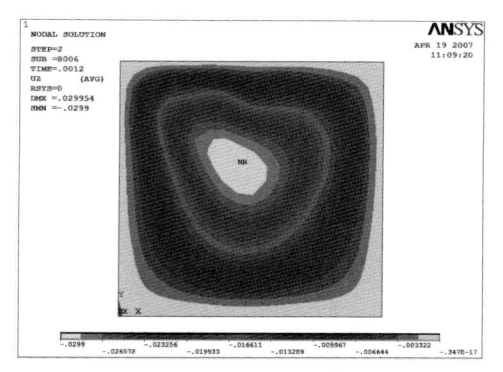

(b) Case S56b

Figure 5: Displacement at mid-point (left) and von Mises strain distribution (right) obtained by FE simulations for test S56

Conclusions

The analytical formulae of Jones (1989), which are derived using the dynamic equilibrium have been employed to predict the displacements of small scale square plates under blast loading. Strain-rate effects on yield stress were incorporated in the analysis and the effect of the temperature was investigated. The tests were also simulated using the ANSYS package. The following conclusions were drawn:

The analytical and numerical predictions were in very good agreement with the measurements.

The analytical predictions were poor in the case of tests, whereby the elastic response was significant. This was expected since the approach of Jones assumes a rigid-plastic material.

Strain-rate effects could be easily incorporated in the analytical method, using a simple iterative procedure. Similarly the effect of temperature could be also incorporated. However in the cases that have been examined the plastic work was not enough to heat the plate uniformly at temperatures, which will affect significantly the yield stress.

The duration of the pulse and the shape of the pulse do not have any effect on the response, as long as the duration remains short with the respect to the time needed to reach the maximum displacement. Variations on the spatial pressure distribution show no significant effect on the magnitude of maximum displacements.

Transverse response resulting in large deflections could be accurately predicted by ANSYS ver. 10, using shell elements with 4 nodes and 24 degrees of freedom. A 20×20 mesh was appropriate and the ratio of element length to thickness was approximately 4.

Acknowledgements

Part of the work has been performed during a visit of the first author to the Department of Naval Architecture and Ocean Engineering of Pusan National University, which was supported by the Korea Research Foundation and The Korean Federation of Science and Technology Societies. The third author is pleased to acknowledge the support of the Korea Science and Engineering Foundation via the National Research Laboratory project (Grant No. ROA-2006-000-10239-0). The authors acknowledge the contribution of Mr. Dimitris Dimou regarding the numerical simulations.

References

Johnson, GR and Cook, WH (1985). "Fracture characteristics of three metals subjected to various strains, strain-rates, temperatures and pressures," Engineering Fracture Mechanics, Vol.21, No.1, pp.31-48.

Jones, N (1989). "Structural impact", Cambridge University Press.

Jones, N (2006). "Some recent developments in the dynamic inelastic behaviour of structures", Ships and Offshore Structures, Vol. 1, No.1, pp. 37-42.

Langdon, GK and Schleyer GK, (2004). "Unusual strain rate sensitive behaviour of AISI 316L austhenitic stainless steel," Journal of Strain Analysis, Vol. 39, pp. 71-86.

Langdon, GS, Yuen, CKS and Nurick, GN (2005) "Experimental and numerical studies on the response of quadrangular stiffened plates. Part II: localized blast loading", International Journal of Impact Engineering, Vol. 31, pp. 85-111.

Masui T, Nunokawa T, and Hiramatsu T, (1987). "Shape correction of hot rolled steel using an on line leveler," Journal of Japanese Society of Technology in Plasticity, Vol. 28, pp. 81–87.

Oliveira, JG (1981), "Design of steel offshore structures against impact loads due to dropped objects," Proceedings of 3rd Onternational Symposium on Offshore Engineering Structures, Edited by FLLB Carneiro, Rio de Janeiro, Brazil..

Paik, JK and Shin, YS (2006). "Structural damage and strength criteria for ship stiffened panels under impact pressure actions arising from sloshing, slamming and green water loading," Ships and Offshore Structures, Vol. 1, No.3, pp. 249-256.

Paik, JK and Thayamballi, AK (2003). "Ultimate limit state design of steel-plated structures", John Wiley & Sons, Chichester, UK.

Paik, JK and Thayamballi, AK (2007). "Ship-shaped offshore installations: design, building, and operation", Cambridge University Press, Cambridge, UK.

Pan, Y and Louca, LA (1999). "Experimental and numerical studies on the response of stiffened plates subjected to gas explosions", Journal of Constructional Steel Research, Vol. 52, pp. 171–193.

Schleyer, GK, Hsu, SS, White, MD and Birch, RS (2003). "Pulse pressure loading of clamped mild steel plates", International Journal of Impact Engineering, Vol. 28, pp. 223-247.

Schleyer, GK, Kewaisy, TH, Wesevich, JW and Langdon, GS (2006). "Validated finite element analysis model of blast wall panels under shock pressure loading", Ships and Offshore Structures, Vol. 1, No.3, pp. 257-272.

Yuen, CKS and Nurick, GN (2005) "Experimental and numerical studies on the response of quadrangular stiffened plates. Part I: subjected to uniform blast load", International Journal of Impact Engineering, Vol. 31, pp. 55-83.

10th International Symposium on Practical Design of Ships and Other Floating Structures
Houston, Texas, United States of America
© 2007 American Bureau of Shipping

Finite Element Analysis of a 1.2 Tonnes WIG Craft under Water Impact Loads

Bok Won Lee[1], Chun-Gon Kim[1], Mi Young Park[2], Han Koo Jeong[3]* and Kuk Jin Kang[3]

[1] Division of Aerospace Engineering, Korea Advanced Institute of Science and Technology, 373-1 Guseong-dong, Yuseong-gu, Daejeon 305-701, Korea
[2] Transit Division, Hankuk Fiber Glass Co., Ltd., Miryang-si, Kyungnam 627-852, Korea
[3] Maritime and Ocean Engineering Research Institute, KORDI, 171 Jang-dong, Yuseong-gu, Daejeon 305-343, Korea

Abstract

Demand for high-speed sea transportation modes has increased dramatically in the last few decades. Various transportation modes were introduced and are being used today; Hydrofoil ship, Air cushion vehicle, Wave-piercing Catamaran vessel and WIG (Wing-In-Ground effect) craft are all a case in point. Among these transportations, the WIG is considered as the next generation maritime transportation system through the employment of advanced modern technologies such as lightweight structural materials, digital flight controls and advanced propulsion system. Noted advantages of the WIG craft compared to equivalent aircraft and marine vessels would be better economy and faster speed. In this paper, the Arbitrary Lagrangian-Eulerian (ALE) finite element method is used to simulate the water impact of a 1.2 tonnes WIG craft during a landing phase. A full 3D shell element is used to model the WIG craft in carbon composites, and a developed FE model is used to investigate the effect of the water impact loads on the structural responses of the WIG craft. In the analysis, two different landing scenarios are considered, and their effects on the structural responses are investigated.

Keywords

Finite element analysis; WIG craft; Composite structure; Water impact loads; Structural responses.

1. Introduction

In the structural design of high-speed marine vessels, an estimation of water impact loads is essential. The dynamic structural responses of those high-speed vessels excited by the water impact loads may bring an important contribution to their damage process. The work presented in this paper is focused on the numerical simulation of the water impact on a 1.2 tonnes WIG craft when it lands. The aim of this work is to study the structural responses of the WIG craft subjected to the water impact loads. Eulerian fluids/Lagrangian solid coupling capabilities from LS-DYNA, finite element analysis software, is used to simulate the water impact. With regards to fluid-structure interaction problems, the main problem in numerical calculation is that the fluid element of nearby structure is largely distorted and the time step becomes very small for explicit calculations. The arbitrary Lagrangian-Eulerian (ALE) finite element (FE) method is able to create a new, undistorted mesh for fluid domain and allows us to continue the calculation. The ALE FE method solves the transient equations of motion of the fluid and structure using the explicit time integration method. This method is suitable for analyzing highly dynamic, non-linear phenomena lasting for a short time such as water impact on the bottom hull of the WIG craft during a landing phase.

The first study of the water impact problem was probably by Karman (1929) in relation to seaplane landing. He considered the body to be a circular cylinder, representing its immersion as an expanding flat plate with the water surface remaining flat. Wagner (1932) extended this approach for the wedge-entry problem by incorporating some local jet analyses. Recently, Steinus et al(2006), Fasanella et al(2003), and Zhang et al(2006) studied the fluid-structure interaction problems using the ALE FE method. Whereas, the fluid subjected to large deformation at the free surface was modeled as multi-material Eulerian, the structure was modeled as Lagrangian. The different model parts were connected using fluid-structure coupling algorithm. The moving flexible Lagrangian structure imposed displacement and velocity boundary conditions on the Eulerian fluid, which, in turn, imposed traction boundary conditions on the structure. The advantage with this technique was that it enabled the modeling of the complete fluid-structure interaction problem.

In this paper, the ALE FE method is used in the LS-DYNA to analyze the fluid-structure interaction

---

* Corresponding author: hkjeong@moeri.re.kr

between the water surface and the bottom hull of the WIG craft. A nonlinear finite element model is developed to simulate the water impact of the WIG craft during a landing phase. From the developed FE model, the structural responses of the WIG craft due to complex water reaction loads are investigated, and, as a result, the structural integrity of the WIG craft is investigated as well.

2. Validation of the ALE FE model

To validate the ALE FE model in the fluid-structure interaction, two-dimensional and three-dimensional analyses of hydrodynamic impact of a wedge are carried out using the ALE FE method in conjunction with the LS-DYNA. Results are compared with the published test data performed by E. Yettou et al (2006).

2.1 Description of the ALE FE method

The fluid is solved by use of the Eulerian formulation on a Cartesian grid that overlaps the structure, while the structure is discretised by the Lagrangian approach. For simplicity, the numerical simulations in this paper are restricted to the Eulerian formulation for the fluid, although the formulation can be extended to an ALE formulation. The ALE equations can be derived by the use of the relationship between material time derivative and reference configuration time derivative,

$$\frac{\partial f(X_i,t)}{\partial t} = \frac{\partial f(x_i,t)}{\partial t} + (v_i - u_i)\frac{\partial f(X_i,t)}{\partial x_i}$$
$$= \frac{\partial f(X_i,t)}{\partial t} + w_i \frac{\partial f(X_i,t)}{\partial x_i} \quad (1)$$

Where X_i is the Lagrangian coordinate, i is the referential coordinate, x_i is the Eulerian coordinate, and v_i and u_i are the material and the mesh velocities, respectively.

In order to simplify the equations, the convective velocity of $w_i = v_i - u_i$ is introduced. Thus, the governing equations for the ALE formulation are given by

(i) The conservation of mass equation

$$\frac{\partial \rho}{\partial t} = -\rho \frac{\partial v}{\partial x_i} - w_i \frac{\partial \rho}{\partial x_i} \quad (2)$$

(ii) The conservation of momentum equation

$$\rho \frac{\partial v_i}{\partial t} + \rho w_i \frac{\partial v_i}{\partial x_j} = \sigma_{ij,j} + \rho b_i \quad (3)$$

(iii) The conservation of total energy equation

$$\rho \frac{\partial E}{\partial t} + \rho w_j \frac{\partial E}{\partial x_j} = \sigma_{ij} v_{i,j} + b_j v_j \quad (4)$$

where ρ is density, b_i is body force and E is energy

At the Euler-Lagrange interface, the Lagrange mesh acts as a moving boundary to the fluid, while fluid pressure is applied to the Lagrange mesh. Use of a penalty coupling allows the treatment of impact problems in the presence of fluid because the penalty coupling manages the interactions between a Lagrangian formulation modeling for the structure and the Eulerian formulation modeling for the fluid: the fluid flows around the structure, not through the structure. Prevention of the "flow of fluids through the structure" is achieved by applying penalty forces on the fluid and the structure. As soon as the Eulerian node penetrates into a Lagrangian structure, a force of recall is exerted on the contravening node and puts it back on the surface of the structure. More accurately, for each Lagrangian node, a search of the Eulerian element containing this node is done. Then, the penetration depth of each fluid node into the structure surface is evaluated. Finally, penalty forces are determined proportionally to the penetration depth. The coupling method behaves like a spring system.

2.2 Experimental background

E. Yettou (2006) carried out water impact tests as illustrated in Fig. 1. Items tested were the hydrodynamics of the water entry process of a V-shaped wedge. Five different wedges were made with a thick plywood wall for the test. The wedges had a square top section of 1.2m×1.2m that could support additional pieces with masses. The wedges were launched vertically from a resting position. In the test, they considered five wedges, four different masses and two different drop heights. Thus, a total of 40 test configurations were used. They provided the test results with 5% standard deviation. In the validation step of the ALE FE model, the single configuration is chosen for a comparison purpose as follows: an impact wedge having a deadrise of 25°, a drop height of 1.3m and a mass of 94kg.

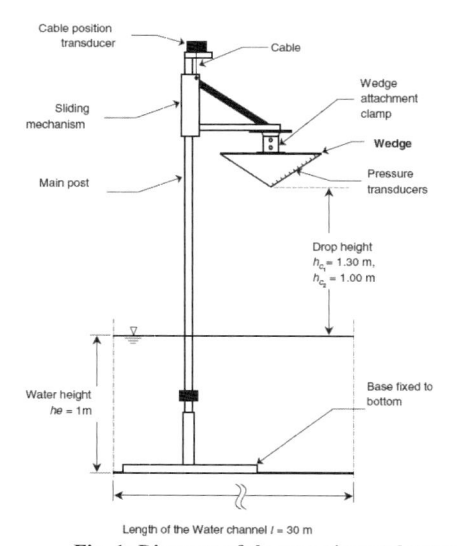

Fig. 1: Diagram of the experimental setup

2.3 ALE FE analysis

A double precision version of the LS-DYNA is used to simulate water impact of the wedge. Gravity and viscous effects are neglected because these effects are quite small compared to impact force. The fluid, water and air are modeled with solid-3 point ALE (Arbitrary-Lagrange-Euler, multi-material element formulation No. 12). In the water domain, the Gruneisen equation of state formulation is used with a water density of 1000kg/m^3, while the air domain is modeled as void allowing the water to redistribute. The fluid density of the 2D and 3D ALE analysis after a water impact load are shown in Fig. 2 and Fig. 3.

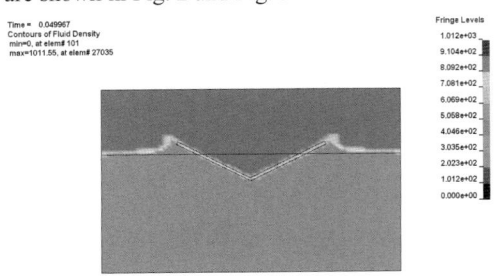

Fig. 2: 2D fluid density plot of a 25 degree wedge impact

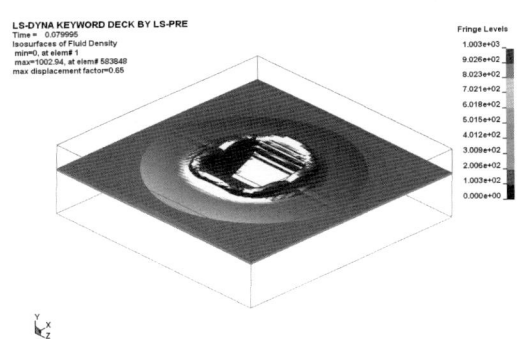

Fig. 3: 3D fluid density plot of a 25 degree wedge impact

The time variations of the peak pressure on the wedge surface and the wedge quadratic velocities obtained from the experiment and the numerical analysis are plotted in Fig. 4 and Fig. 5. In measuring the time-varying pressure distribution on one side of the wedge, equally spaced twelve pressure transducers are used. The peak pressure for each transducer appears during a penetration process of the wedge. Experimental curve in Fig. 4 is constructed by extracting peak pressure distribution at specific times of the transducers. The peak pressure curves of the FE analysis are also constructed in the same manner. In order to achieve reasonable correlation between the experimental and numerical results, appropriate approaches for the determination of fluid discretization, simulation time steps and contact parameters are required. In the FEA models, parameters like mesh density, time step, contact damping and number of impact points are empirically adjusted to correlate with test data and they are used in this FE analysis. 2D numerical results show over-estimated values compared to the experimental findings.

It is judged that this overestimation occurred due to the allowed fluid-flow at the extremities of the test section of the experiment. Since 3D effects help in the explanation and illustration of this overestimation, a 3D numerical modeling of the test section is performed to obtain a better comparison between the experimental and numerical results.

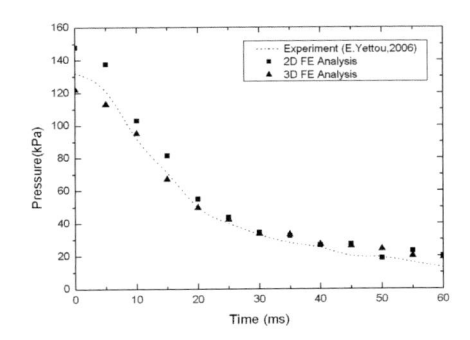

Fig. 4: Comparison between the time variations of peak pressure from the experimental and 2D, 3D numerical results (deadrise angle=25°; mass of the wedge=94kg; drop height =1.30m)

In order to reduce the cost of the simulation, the convergence of the results regarding the element size is investigated in 2D numerical analysis.

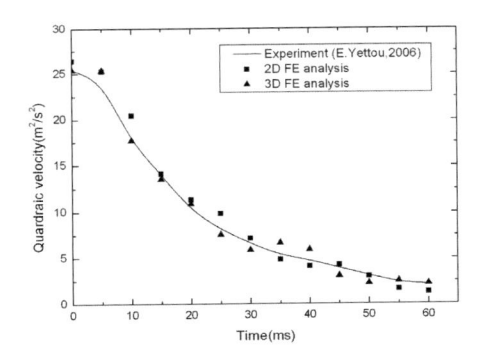

Fig. 5: Comparison between the time variations of the quadratic velocity from the experimental and 2D, 3D numerical results (deadrise angle=25°; mass of the wedge=94kg; drop height =1.30m)

From Fig. 4 and Fig. 5, the results from 3D numerical analysis are shown in better agreement with the experimental results while 2D numerical results overestimate the experimental results by about 20% at the maximum. The same difference in percentage was reported by Zhao (1993). These results confirm that the modeling method used in this paper is suitable for the simulation of the water impact on the WIG craft structure.

3. The WIG craft

The WIG craft considered in this research work is a 1.2-ton 1/2-scale manned test one for the development of full scale WIG craft having a capacity of carrying 20 passengers. Materials used for this WIG are pre-preg carbon/epoxy composites to achieve excellent strength to weight ratio. Additionally, a closed cell PVC foam core and a honeycomb core are used for the bottom hull and the longitudinal stiffeners of the WIG craft, respectively. Principal dimensions of the WIG are presented in Table 1.

Fig. 6: Artist's impression of a 1.2 tonnes WIG craft

Table 1: Principal dimensions of the WIG craft

Parameter	Dimension/details
Length	12.5m
Breadth	10.5m
Height	4.0m
Wing Span/Area	6.376m/29m^2
Take-off weight	1,200 kg
Cruising speed	120km/h
Engines	100 hp×2

3.1 Landing scenarios

In this analysis, two cases of landing scenarios are considered. The first landing scenario is that of the WIG craft landing at a horizontal speed of 16m/s and a descending speed of 4.5m/s with 5° angle of attack. The water surface is considered as free surface condition. In this landing scenario, the primary contact area would be the main bottom hull of the WIG craft. Afterward, the two side hulls attached to the main wings would contact free surface. This landing scenario can achieve directional stability. The second landing scenario is that of one of the side hulls touching the water surface before the main bottom hull does due to an unwanted roll angle of the WIG craft that is induced from gust of wind or other unexpected factors. This landing manner could affect the structural integrity of the WIG craft significantly, especially on the wing-fuselage attachment areas. The two landing scenarios are illustrated in Fig. 7.

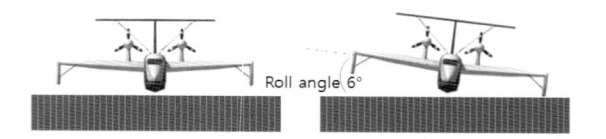

Fig. 7: Two landing cases

4. FE analysis of the WIG craft under water impact loads

In the design phase, numerical modeling is the most logical, least expensive approach to study the effect of the water impact to the WIG craft during a landing phase. With the advent of higher performance workstation computers, the numerical modeling of the WIG craft subjected to the water impact loads can be modeled using explicit nonlinear dynamic codes. In this paper, the ALE method is used to estimate the water impact pressure acting on the bottom hull of the WIG craft using the LS-DYNA. The size, shape, and discretization of the water and air volumes are chosen from the previous experiment and analysis comparison study. (See section 2.) The FE model of the WIG craft's structure is developed to accurately predict its structural response under the computed water impact loads from the LS-DYNA. The developed FE model of the WIG craft is shown in Fig. 8. The geometry, element mesh, material properties and groups are defined using ABAQUS preprocessor. All FE nonlinear analyses are performed by ABAQUS/Standards. The FE model contains meshes for structural components such as longerons, bulkheads, skin panels and other remaining structures. Predominantly, quadrilateral and triangular layered shell elements are used along with rod, beam and 3D solid elements. The shell element used in the FE modeling is 3D element and is of Mindlin type element allowing transverse shear strains and stresses. Hence, it has 3 integration points through-thickness direction and 6 global degrees of freedom per node (3 translations and 3 rotations).

(a) Side view

(b) Top view

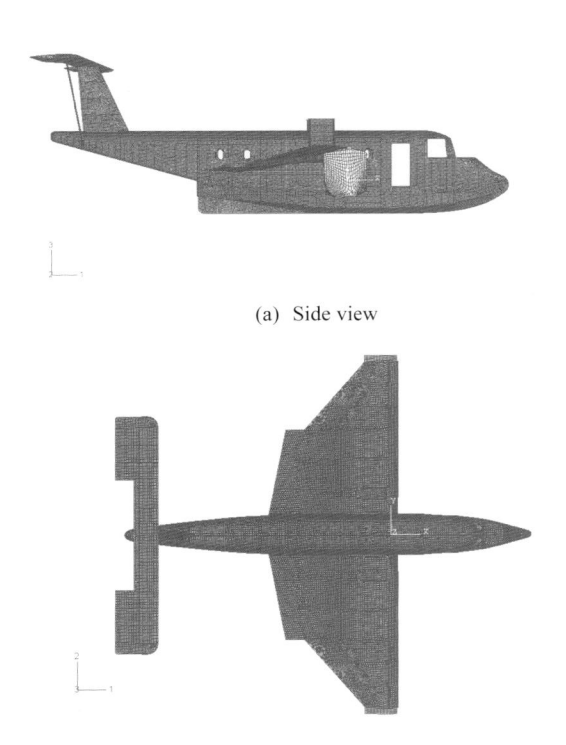

Fig. 8: Developed FE model of the WIG craft

In general, the FEM representation of the WIG craft joints is made with overlapping elements and common grid points. The FE model consists of approximately 202,900 nodes and 210,700 elements, resulting in approximately 1,217,800 degrees of freedom.

4.1 Water impact load calculations

In order to estimate the water impact loads, the FE model of the WIG craft is exported to the LS-DYNA. The WIG craft's structure is modeled with the lagrangian mesh composed of rigid elements with associated nodes that move with the elements. The fluid is modeled using a stationary Eulerian mesh in which the fluid material flows, while conserving mass, momentum, and energy. The water impact loads are modeled using 33cm cubic Eulerian elements to fill a water domain of 20m × 20m × 6.6m deep with 5,000 elements. The air is modeled as empty volume or void. The two landing scenario cases are analyzed with the fluid densities of those landing cases shown in Fig. 9. The first case is for the landing by the bottom hull of the WIG craft. The second case is for the landing by one of the side hulls with a 6° roll angle followed by the bottom hull landing. In Fig. 9, the color red represents the high density of water and the color blue represents the low density of air. In this simulation, an entry object, the WIG craft, is completely rigid and therefore structural deformations are not considered in this analysis.

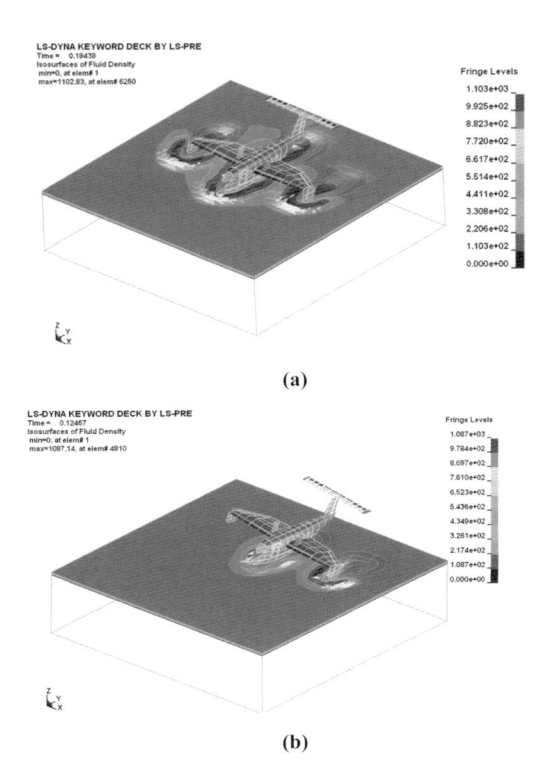

(a)

(b)

Fig. 9: Fluid density plots of the two landing cases (a) the main bottom hull landing (b) the side hull landing

The water impact pressure of 4 points for the main hull and 1 point for the side hull are selected, Fig. 10, for the purpose of comparing pressure distribution differences between the two landing cases.

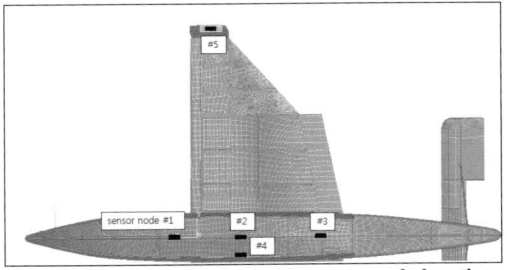

Fig. 10: Selected water impact pressure node locations

Fig. 11 shows the pressure distributions with respect to the time variation at the selected 5 sensor nodes. In the bottom hull landing case, a maximum peak pressure of 19.8MPa occurs at 0.061sec at the sensor node #2. This sensor node location corresponds to the primary landing area scenario in the bottom hull landing. Pressure value obtained from the sensor node #5 located at the side hull shows 70% of that of the sensor node #2 at 0.10sec. In the side hull landing case, a maximum peak pressure of 29.3MPa occurs at 0.068sec at the sensor node #5. This sensor node location is the first touching area due to 6° roll angle. This maximum peak pressure value is 30% greater than that of the bottom hull landing case.

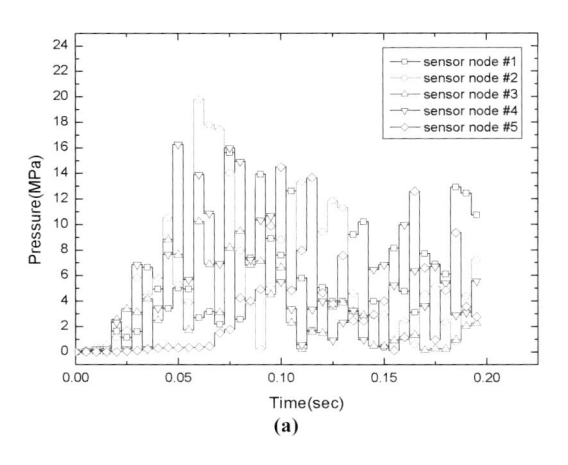

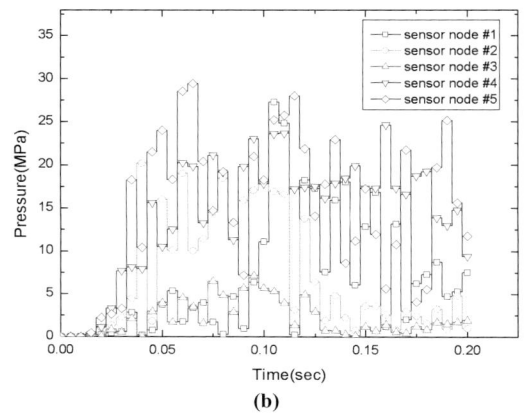

Fig. 11: Pressure time variation for the two landing cases (a) the bottom hull landing case (b) the side hull landing case

Different time history characteristics and spatial distributions are observed in the impact process of a solid object having low and high angles. (See Fig. 12.)

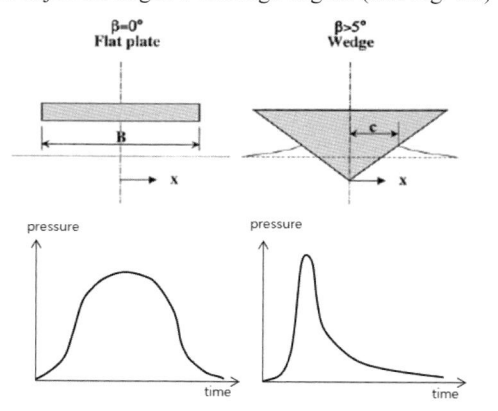

Fig. 12: Time-dependent pressure history

Considering the roll angle, the deadrise angles of the bottom hull and the side hull touching the water surface are reduced. This reduction in the deadrise angles contributes to the pressure distribution differences between the two landing cases. The overall pressure distributions for the two landing cases show the similar patterns seen in Fig. 12: a sudden localized pressure increase followed by sudden disappearing pressure for the wedge, and a relatively uniform pressure rise followed by gradual decreasing pressure for the flat plate.

4.2 Structural responses under the water impact loads

In order to calculate the structural responses of the WIG craft subjected to the water impact loads obtained from the LS-DYNA, the quasi-static equivalent pressure is introduced in this analysis. This term is defined as the quasi-static pressure that gives rise to the same maximum pressure at the impact. The quasi-static equivalent pressure is applied to the FE model of the WIG craft. It should be mentioned that current FE analysis programs cannot provide accurate results when the dynamic impact behavior of composite structures is concerned due to their complicated damage mechanism. This is why design guidance like DNV and FAR standards use global static impact loads in their rules. In this analysis, the effect of the maximum impact loads on the structural behavior is only considered to provide valuable information for the static strength design of the WIG craft. The equivalent static loads are extracted from maximum impact pressure history.

Global constraining of the loaded model is avoided by adopting a free body support arranged by providing the necessary reference point for the Inertia Relief facilities of the ABAQUS/standard. The inertia forces experienced by the WIG structure are included in the static solution through inertia relief loading that balances the water impact loading. Applying inertia relief loading establishes exact balances to unbalanced external impact loads and places the structure in static equilibrium. This allows the WIG craft to translate freely in the longitudinal and the height directions and rotate freely about the transverse direction. The constraints on a CG (center of gravity) reference point, which is connected to bulkheads of the fuselage by a rigid bar, prevent the WIG craft's translation from the transverse direction and rotation from the longitudinal and the transverse directions.

The vertical deflection plots of the FE model for the two landing cases are presented in Fig. 13. When the bottom hull landing case is considered, the maximum vertical deflection of about 27mm is obtained at the forward end of the WIG structure. On the other hand, when the side hull landing case is considered, the maximum vertical deflection of 38mm is obtained at the wing tip.

(a)

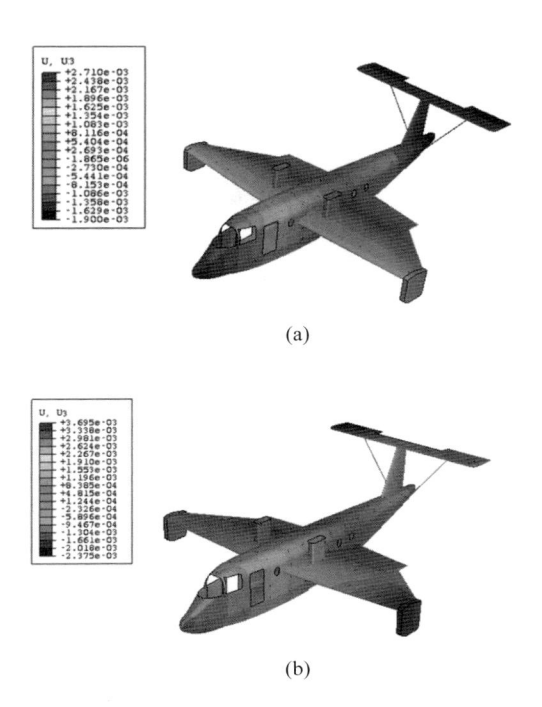

(b)

Fig. 13: Vertical deflection plots of the WIG craft (a) the bottom hull landing case (b) the side hull landing case

Fig. 14 shows the principal stress distribution of the WIG structure in the bottom hull landing case. Principal stress concentration is found at the bulkheads located in the bottom hull area as seen in Fig. 14-B. Additionally, the wing-fuselage joint area shows the principal stress concentration due to the inertia force of the wing and engine weight. Principal stresses of the WIG craft's structural components in both the bottom hull and the side hull landing cases are compared in Fig. 15. The comparison reveals that the maximum principal stress is obtained from the upper wing-fuselage joint area for the side hull landing case, and the minimum principal stress is obtained from lower keel beam, again, for the side hull landing case. In general, calculated principal stresses are higher for the side hull landing case than those of the bottom hull landing case. When the bottom hull landing case is considered, the maximum principal stress occurred in the order of bulkhead #7, lower side longeron, upper wing-fuselage joint area, bottom hull skin, lower keel beam, bulkhead #6, lower wing-fuselage joint area and finally bulkhead #5. However this order of the maximum principal stresses is not true in the landing scenario change to the side hull landing case. In this case, the order of the maximum principal stress becomes upper wing-fuselage joint area, bulkhead #7, lower side longeron, lower wing-fuselage joint area, bulkhead #6, bottom hull skin, bulkhead #5 followed by lower keel beam. These results indicate that the landing scenarios affect the WIG craft's structural integrity, and it should be understood in the design processes.

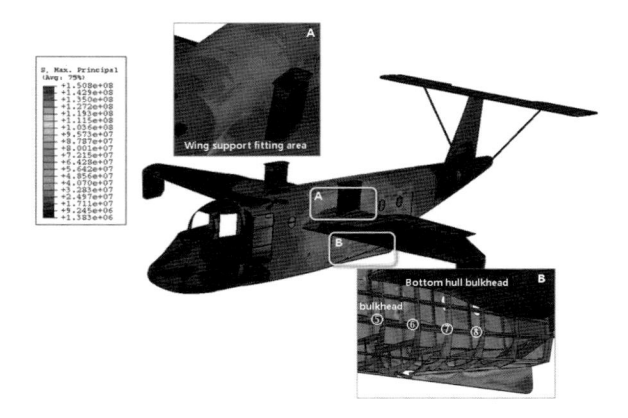

Fig. 14: Principal stress distribution plot of the WIG craft for the bottom hull landing case

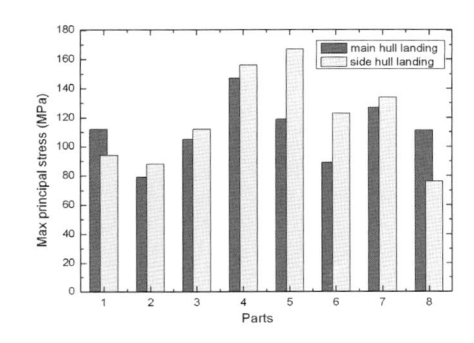

1: bottom hull skin, 2: bulkhead #5
3: bulkhead #6, 4: bulkhead #7
5: upper wing-fuselage joint area
6: lower wing-fuselage joint area
7: lower side longeron, 8: lower keel beam

Fig. 15: Maximum principal stress comparisons for the WIG craft's structural components

5. Concluding remarks

The ALE FE model is developed to simulate the water impact loads for the structural analysis of the 1.2 tonnes WIG craft during a landing phase. In the structural analysis, a full 3D shell element is used to model the WIG craft. The simulated dynamic water impact loads are converted to the quasi-static equivalent loads using the load spectrum conversion. The calculated quasi-static equivalent loads are applied to the developed FE model for the WIG craft assumed to have two different landing scenarios, the main bottom hull and the side hull landing cases. The structural responses of the WIG craft are studied in deflections and principal stresses. Between the two landing cases, the side hull landing case produces larger deflections at the side hull touching the water surface and its adjacent area in the main wing and higher principal stresses at the bulkhead located in the bottom hull and wing-fuselage joint area than those of the bottom hull landing case. It is noticed that the state of the structural responses of the structural components is varied as the landing scenario is changed. From those results, it is learned that the possible various landing scenarios of the WIG craft need to be realized and considered during the design process as they directly affect the structural integrity of the WIG craft.

6. Acknowledgement

This research work was supported through Dual Use Technology Program, Development of 20 passengers Wing-In-Ground Effect Ship Project. The project is funded by Korea Ministry of Commerce, Industry and Energy (MOCIE). The authors wish to thank MOCIE for funding the project.

7. References

Steinus, I, Rosen, A, and Kuttenkeuler, J(2006). "Explicit FE-modelling of fluid-structure interaction in hull-water impacts", International Shipbuilding Progress, Vol 53, pp 103-121.

Zhao, R, and Faltinsen, OM(1993). "Water entry of two dimensional bodies", Journal of Fluid Mechanics, Vol 246, pp 593-612.

Fasanella, FL, and Jackson, KE(2003), "Water Impact Test and Simulation of a Composite Energy Absorbing Fuselage Section", Proceeding of American Helicopter Society 59th Annual Forum, Phoenix, AZ.

Yettou, EM, Desrochers, A, and Champoux, Y(2006), "Experimental study on the water impact of a symmetrical wedge", Fluid dynamics research, Vol 38, pp 47-66.

Aquelet, N, Souli, M, and Olovsson, L(2005),"Euler-Lagrangian coupling with damping effects: Application to slamming problems", Comput. Methods Appl. Mech. Engrg. Xxx

Olovossion, L, and Souli, M(1999), "Multi-material capabilities in LS-DYNA", Proceedings of the 2nd European LS-DYNA Users Conference, Gothernburg, Sweden.

Okada, S, and Sumi, Y(2000), "On the water impact and elastic response of a flat plate at small impact angles", Journal of Mar. Sci., Vol 5, pp 31-39.

Ojeda, R, Prusty, BG, and Salas, M(2004), "Finite element investigation on the static response of a composite catamaran under slamming loads", Ocean Engineering, Vol 31, pp 901-929

Zhang, A, and Suzuki, K(2006) "Numerical simulation of fluid-structure interaction of liquid cargo filled tank during ship collision using the ALE finite element method", International Journal of Crash, Vol 11, pp 291-298.

Design Optimization of Steel Sandwich Hoistable Car-Decks Applying Homogenized Plate Theory

Jani Romanoff, Alan Klanac

Ship Laboratory, Helsinki University of Technology
Espoo, Finland

Abstract

This paper describes an approach for concept design of laser-welded web-core steel sandwich panels. The method utilizes a newly developed theory for the bending response of laser-welded web-core sandwich plates. Structural optimization is carried out using enumeration and newly developed vectorization-based Genetic Algorithm. To demonstrate these concepts, a case study in design of a hoistable car-deck is considered. Finally, the optimization is conducted considering the objectives of deck weight.

Keywords

Web-core; Laser-weld; Structural analysis; Vectorization; Genetic algorithm.

Nomenclature

A	In-plane stiffness
E	Young's modulus
B	Plate breadth or coupling stiffness
D	Bending stiffness
D_Q	Shear stiffness
d	Distance between mid-planes of the face plates
f	Objective function
g	Constraint function
h_c	Core height
h	Plate total height
k	Stiffness parameter
k_θ	T-joint rotation stiffness
L	Plate length
M	Bending moment
N	Normal force
Q	Shear force
q	External loading
s	Stiffener spacing
t_t	Thickness of the top face plate
t_b	Thickness of the bottom face plate
t_w	Thickness of the web plate
ε	Strain
φ	Fitness
κ	Curvature
υ	Poisson's ratio
θ	Slope
Ω	Feasible domain
σ	Normal stress

Introduction

Demand for lighter, safer and space-saving structures has stimulated the need of industry to study new structural configurations as ship structures. Laser-welded all-metal sandwich panels offer an option to fulfill these requirements. These panels are composed of face plates separated by a core material, which can be composed of various types of stiffeners, e.g. flats (Roland, 2000), corrugations (LASCOR, Marsico et al., 1993), C-profiles (Fung et al., 1996) and Z-profiles (Fung et al., 1994). The simplest core geometry of all-metal sandwich structures is built from flat web-plates perpendicular to the face plates; see Fig. 1.

Detailed 3D FE-modeling of the laser-welded web-core sandwich plates is very time-consuming, becoming impractical to use in conceptual design of ship structures. Therefore, the simplified models based on application of plate theory become attractive. Romanoff and Varsta (2007) presented a method to calculate the bending response of laser-welded web-core sandwich plate accurately using homogenized sandwich plate theory and its FE implementation to solve the internal forces and displacement of the sandwich structure. The periodicity of the actual structure was included into the equivalent stiffness properties of the homogenized plate, but also to the stress calculations. Further, it was concluded that this periodicity is very important when the maximum normal stress in the plate is evaluated.

Klanac and Jelovica (2007) presented a novel optimization method based on a genetic algorithm where the constraints are treated as objectives and the single-objective optimization problem is treated as a special multi-objective optimization problem.

This paper then combines the approaches of structural assessment and optimization. The outcome of this synergy is demonstrated through a case study on hoistable car deck.

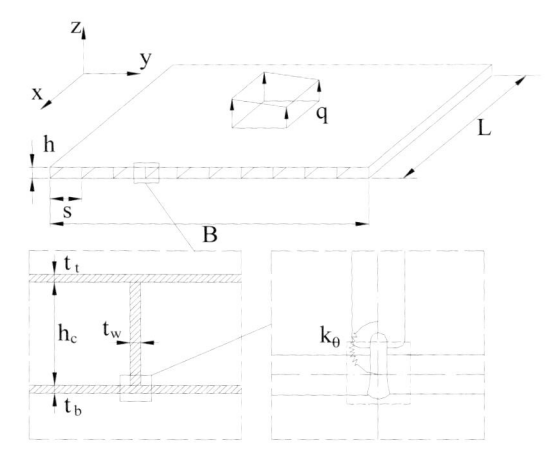

Fig. 1: Laser-Welded Web-core Sandwich Plate with Notations Used.

Definitions

The web-core sandwich plate consists of web and face plates, which are connected using laser-welding. The web plates are parallel to the xz-plane and have a thickness t_w and a height h_c, see Fig. 1. The web plate spacing is marked with s. The top and bottom face plates are parallel to xy-plane and have a thickness t_t and t_b respectively. The plate has length L, breadth B, total height $h=h_c+t_t+t_b$, and the mid-planes positioned $d=h_c+(t_t+t_b)/2$ apart. The T-joint between a faceplate and web consists of the laser-weld and parts of the face and web plates connected to it, see Fig.1. The welded connection has rotation stiffness k_θ. A unit cell is a representative cut of the sandwich plate in the yz-plane, which borders neighboring web plates and the parts of the face plates between these; length is infinitesimal dx and breadth is s. The sandwich plate has two coordinate systems, namely the global xyz and the local xy_lz_l. The origin of the global coordinate system xyz is located at the geometrical mid-plane of the plate. The origin of the local coordinate xy_lz_l is located on the mid-plane of the face or the web plate under consideration. Notation q is used for the external distributed loads. The Young's modulus and Poisson's ratio are denoted with E and υ, respectively. Subscripts t, b and w are used for the top face, the bottom face and the web plates, respectively.

Design Principle

The design is carried out using homogenized plate theory, enumeration and genetic algorithm. Firstly, FE-mesh is created for the plate under investigation. The mesh size is selected to describe the sandwich plate bending and shear response with sufficient accuracy, thus obtaining the gradients of internal forces accurately. The boundary conditions and loading are modeled as they are in the actual structure.

Optimization is used to sequentially create a population of design alternatives **x** with the size N, see Fig. 2. Each alternative is defined with the cross-sectional properties, which are then used to determine the equivalent shell element stiffness properties, see Fig. 2.

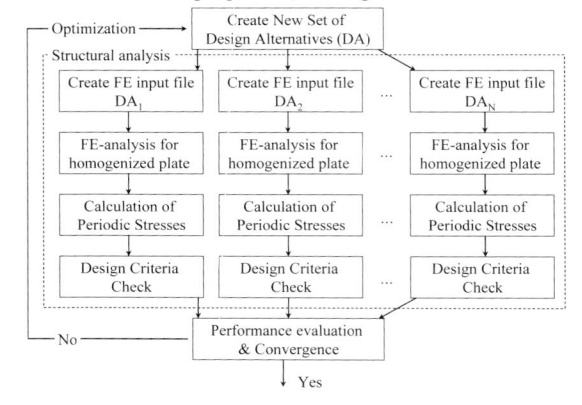

Fig. 2: Structural Design Process.

The FE-analysis is carried out for each design alternative. The internal forces are used to calculate the stress response of the plate induced by bending and shear. The local bending of the patch-loaded face plate is solved using the design formulae presented by DNV (2003). Then, different design criteria are evaluated for each alternative, marking their feasibility. This information is then taken to the optimization algorithm to produce the new population of alternatives.

Structural Analysis

Bending of Homogenized Plate

The bending response of the homogenized plate can be obtained through the solution of the differential equations given in Romanoff and Varsta (2007). The external load q applied on the sandwich plate and the stress resultants N, M, and Q are presented in Fig. 3A. Resulting deformations u, v and w in x-, y- and z-directions are presented in Fig. 3B. The differential equations read (Romanoff and Varsta (2007):

$$A_{11}\frac{\partial^2 u_0}{\partial x^2} + A_{33}\frac{\partial^2 u_0}{\partial y^2} + (A_{12}+A_{33})\frac{\partial^2 v_0}{\partial x \partial y} - B_{11}\frac{\partial^2 \theta_x}{\partial x^2} \quad (1)$$
$$- B_{33}\frac{\partial^2 \theta_x}{\partial y^2} - (B_{12}+B_{33})\frac{\partial^2 \theta_y}{\partial x \partial y} = 0$$

$$A_{22}\frac{\partial^2 v_0}{\partial y^2} + A_{33}\frac{\partial^2 v_0}{\partial x^2} + (A_{12}+A_{33})\frac{\partial^2 u_0}{\partial x \partial y} - B_{22}\frac{\partial^2 \theta_y}{\partial y^2} \quad (2)$$
$$- B_{33}\frac{\partial^2 \theta_y}{\partial x^2} - (B_{12}+B_{33})\frac{\partial^2 \theta_x}{\partial x \partial y} = 0$$

$$D_{Qx}\left(\frac{\partial^2 w}{\partial x^2} - \frac{\partial \theta_x}{\partial x}\right) + D_{Qy}\left(\frac{\partial^2 w_{RM}}{\partial y^2} - \frac{\partial \theta_y}{\partial y}\right) + q_{RM} = 0 \quad (3)$$

$$B_{11}\frac{\partial^2 u_0}{\partial x^2} + B_{33}\frac{\partial^2 u_0}{\partial y^2} + (B_{12}+B_{33})\frac{\partial^2 v_0}{\partial x \partial y} - D_{11}\frac{\partial^2 \theta_x}{\partial x^2}$$
$$- D_{33}\frac{\partial^2 \theta_x}{\partial y^2} - (D_{12}+D_{33})\frac{\partial^2 \theta_y}{\partial x \partial y} - D_{Qx}\left(\frac{\partial w_{RM}}{\partial x} - \theta_x\right) = 0 \quad (4)$$

$$B_{22}\frac{\partial^2 v_0}{\partial y^2} + B_{33}\frac{\partial^2 v_0}{\partial x^2} + (B_{12}+B_{33})\frac{\partial^2 u_0}{\partial x \partial y} - D_{22}\frac{\partial^2 \theta_y}{\partial y^2}$$
$$- D_{33}\frac{\partial^2 \theta_y}{\partial x^2} - (D_{12}+D_{33})\frac{\partial^2 \theta_x}{\partial x \partial y} - D_{Qy}\left(\frac{\partial w_{RM}}{\partial y} - \theta_y\right) = 0 \quad (5)$$

$$\frac{\partial^4 w_{tf}}{\partial x^4} + 2\frac{\partial^4 w_{tf}}{\partial x^2 \partial y^2} + \frac{\partial^4 w_{tf}}{\partial y^4} = \frac{q_{tf}}{D_f} \quad (6)$$

where the in-plane, coupling and bending stiffness are

$$[A] = \int_{-h/2}^{h/2} [E]_i dz \quad (7)$$

$$[B] = \int_{-h/2}^{h/2} [E]_i d_i dz \quad (8)$$

$$[D_0] = \int_{-h/2}^{h/2} [E]_i d_k z dz, \quad i = t,c,b \quad (9)$$

$$[D]_t = \frac{t_t^3}{12}[E]_t \quad (10)$$

$$[D]_b = \frac{t_b^3}{12}[E]_b \quad (11)$$

and the shear stiffness

$$D_{Qx} = k_{11}^2 \cdot \left(G_t t_t + G_b t_b + \frac{t_w}{s}G_w h_c\right) \quad (12)$$

$$D_{Qy} = \frac{12 D_w}{s^2 \left(k_Q\left(\frac{D_w}{D_b}+6\frac{d}{s}\right)+12\frac{D_w}{k_\theta^b s}-2\frac{d}{s}\right)} \quad (13)$$

where

$$k_{11} = \sqrt{\frac{1}{A\left(\sum_i \int \left(\frac{\tau_i}{Q_{Q,x}s}\right)^2 t_i ds_i\right)}}, \quad i=t,c,b. \quad (14)$$

$$k_\theta^i = Q_{Q,y} s / \theta_c^i$$

$$k_Q = \frac{1+12\frac{D_t}{s}\left(\frac{1}{k_\theta^t}-\frac{1}{k_\theta^b}\right)+6\frac{D_t}{D_w}\frac{d}{s}}{1+12\frac{D_t}{D_w}\frac{d}{s}+\frac{D_t}{D_b}} \quad (15)$$

$$k_1^t = 1-k_Q$$
$$k_1^b = k_Q$$
$$k_2^t = 2-3k_Q$$
$$k_2^b = 3k_Q - 1$$

and $D_f = D_t + D_b$ where

$$D_i = \frac{E_i t_i^3}{1-v_i^2}, \quad i=t,w,b. \quad (16)$$

Further *[E]* is the elasticity matrix for isotropic material in plane stress condition.

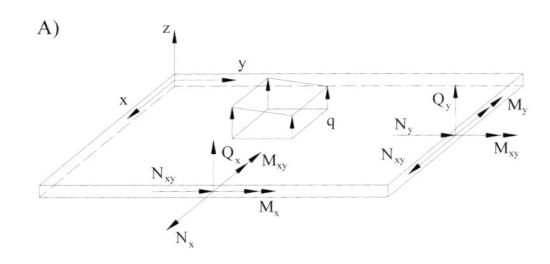

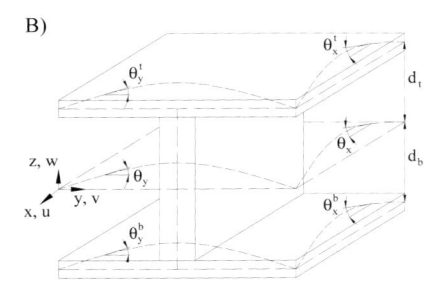

Fig. 3: A) External loading and stress resultants and B) deformations in web-core sandwich plate.

FE-Solution of the Homogenized Plate

The numerical solution is carried out by Finite Element Method (FEM). The solution is obtained using ABAQUS 6.5.1 FE-software, using eight-node shell elements with reduced integration (S8R). The solution produces the resultant deflections and normal forces *{N}*, bending moments *{M}* and shear forces *{Q}*.

Discrete Strain and Stress Response

Due to very low shear stiffness in *y*-direction transverse to the core web stiffeners, the secondary shear induced bending stresses in the face and web plates may become significant. The strain is determined from

$$\begin{Bmatrix}\varepsilon\\-\kappa\end{Bmatrix} = \begin{bmatrix}A & B\\B & D_0\end{bmatrix}^{-1}\left(\begin{Bmatrix}N\\M\end{Bmatrix}_{RM} - \begin{Bmatrix}0\\M_Q\end{Bmatrix}\right) + \begin{Bmatrix}0\\\kappa_l\end{Bmatrix} \quad (17)$$

where
$$M_{Q,x}^i = \nu M_{Q,y}^i$$
$$M_{Q,y}^i = \int Q_{Q,y}^i dy_l - \left[\iint \frac{Q_{Q,y}^i}{s} dy_l dy_l\right]_{y_l = s} \quad (18)$$
$$M_{Q,xy}^i = 0$$

Assuming constant shear force inside an element gives the shear induced moment as

$$M_{Q,x}^i = \nu_i \frac{Q_{Q,y}^i s}{2}\left(\frac{y}{s}-1\right)$$
$$M_{Q,y}^i = \frac{Q_{Q,y}^i s}{2}\left(\frac{y}{s}-1\right) \quad (19)$$
$$M_{Q,xy}^i = 0$$

where

$$Q_{Q,y}^{t} = (1-k_{Q})Q_{RM,y}$$
$$Q_{Q,y}^{b} = k_{Q}Q_{RM,y} \quad (20)$$

When the stress of unit cell is considered, the shear-induced moment $M_{Q,y}^{i}$ will induce stresses with opposite signs into the top and bottom surface of the face plates; for moment see Fig. 4. If the ends of the unit cell are considered, they will also have opposite signs and equal magnitude in stress. In order to determine the maximum stress knowledge on the sign of the membrane stress is needed; when it is negative, also the negative shear induced stress should be considered. The stress is obtained from standard relation between stress and strain in plane stress; von Mises stress is further derived for yield checks.

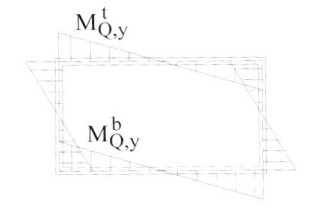

Fig. 4. Shear-induced bending moment in unit cell.

Local Stress Response Due to Patch-Load

The local strain in Eq. (17) is transferred to local stress, which is calculated with the wheel load approach used in DNV (2003) guidelines, i.e. the equation for minimum thickness of decks under wheel loads is used. Writing the minimum plate thickness equation for stress (von Mises) gives

$$\sigma = 5991 \frac{k_a^2 k_w csq}{m(t-t_k)^2} [MPa] \quad (21)$$

where q is given in $[kN/m^2]$ and t in $[mm]$. Other parameters are as given in DNV (2003), Pt.5, Ch.2, Sec.4, C300.

Optimization

Description of the Algorithm - VOP

Optimization is performed using a specific Genetic algorithm (GA). This GA considers vectorization and omni-optimization, hence the name *VOP*. Vectorization assumes converting all constraints into objectives, and their optimization alongside the original objective or a set of objectives. On the other hand omni-optimization assumes capability to perform any type of optimization, e.g. single and multi-objective, using a single optimization algorithm, or the omni-optimizer. See Klanac & Jelovica (2007a), for further details on these concepts.

To illustrate VOP let us consider a general relaxed multicriterion optimization problem over a vector of design variables **x**

$$\min_{x \in X}\{f_0(\mathbf{x}), f_1(\mathbf{x}),..., f_l(\mathbf{x})\} \quad (22)$$

where f(**x**) is a criterion to be minimized, and any **x**∈**X** describes a design alternative belonging to a set **X**. **X** then contains all possible design alternatives, both feasible and infeasible, between lower x_{min} and upper bounds x_{max} of variables. Set **X** is then evaluated fully through enumeration. Contrary to the most of standard structural optimization methods, which operate strictly on a feasible domain of design alternatives **Ω**

$$\Omega = \{\mathbf{x} \in \mathbf{X} \mid \mathbf{g}(\mathbf{x}) \geq 0\} \quad (23)$$

VOP in addition operates over infeasible domain. Let now all the criteria **f**(**x**), except **f**₀(**x**), in VOP be understood as l constraints **g**(**x**). Klanac & Jelovica (2007b) suggest the following absolute constraint transformation function for their association with criteria:

$$f_j(\mathbf{x}) = |g_j(\mathbf{x})|, j \in [1,l] \quad (24)$$

See Fig. 5 for the illustration of this concept.

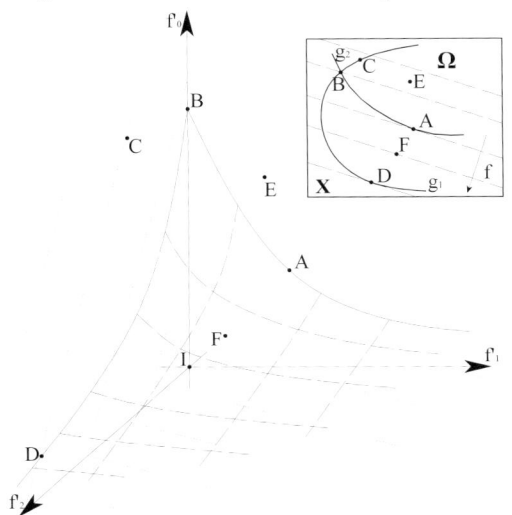

Fig. 5. A criteria and a design (in window) space for a vectorized single-objective constrained problem. Notice the correspondence between the objective f and criterion f'₀, and the constrains g₁ and g₂ and criteria f'₁ and f'₂. Pareto front is indicated by a dotted surface.

This concept of vectorization can be applied directly into GA through fitness φ calculations using the following expression

$$\varphi(\mathbf{x}^i) = \begin{cases} \max d(\mathbf{x}) + \dfrac{1}{d(\mathbf{x}^i)}, & if \ \mathbf{x}^i \in (\Omega \cap \hat{\mathbf{X}}) \\ \max d(\mathbf{x}) + d(\mathbf{x}^i), & otherwise \end{cases} \quad (25)$$

where $\hat{\mathbf{X}}$ marks all the non-dominated design alternatives in Equation (22). Non-dominated alternatives are defined through weak Pareto optimality

$$\hat{\mathbf{X}} = \{\mathbf{x} \in \mathbf{X} \mid \text{there does not exist } \mathbf{x}^k, \\ f(\mathbf{x}^k) < f(\mathbf{x}), \forall \mathbf{x}^k \in \mathbf{X} \text{ except } \mathbf{x}\} \quad (26)$$

Here **f** stands for a vector of criteria defined in Equation (22), and applied inequalities "<" and "≤" are vector inequalities.

The fitness expression in Equation (25) ranks designs on the basis of attained weak Pareto optimality within one population of alternatives, feasibility and the distance $d(\mathbf{x})$ of a design alternatives to the reference point **I** in a multicriterion space. **I** can be arbitrary, but in this case it is chosen as the set containing the minimum values of every criterion in Equation (22) within a population of design alternatives.

Treatment of Design Variables

Design variables in this case are binary coded to GA with a variable bit long strings, based on their integer representation. Details are given in Table 1. Thus, the faceplates are coded with a 3-bit long string, stiffener thickness with 1-bit, while the stiffener spacing and height possess 4-bit long strings.

Table 1: The lower and upper bound values of design variables used in optimization with step of variations

Variable	Lower [mm]	Upper [mm]	Step [mm]
Top face thick.	2.5	4.25	0.25
Web plate thick.	4	5	1
Bott. face thick..	1.5	3.25	0.25
Stiffener space.	80	230	10
Core height	120	270	10

A population of 30 design alternatives, or individuals, is created within each generation following a hand-picked generated initial population. Based on the computed fitness of an individual, the VOP uses the weighted roulette wheel to select designs for the mating pool. Individuals' chromosomes, or a binary string of variable values, are mated with a probability of 0.8 using the randomly selected single point cross-over between two consecutive individuals in the mating pool. Subsequently, the individuals' chromosomes are mutated bit-wise with a probability of 0.03. The optimization was performed for 20 generations.

Enumeration

In order to show the power of GA, enumeration with reduced number of possible variable values is also considered. The variables' values used in enumeration are given in Table 2. Altogether enumeration lead to 1800 design alternatives which took with Pentium M715 having 512 RAM about 10 hours to perform. The original GA problem, if enumerated, would have demanded 32768 different design alternatives, while now GA computed 600 alternatives. The total time to perform GA optimization was about a third of that needed for enumeration, as most of the time is anyway consumed for FE calculations of response.

Table 2: The values of design variables used in enumeration.

Variable	Values used [mm]
Top face thickness	1.5, 2.0, 2.5, 3.0, 4.0
Web plate thickness	4
Bottom face thickness	1.5, 2.0, 2.5, 3.0, 4.0
Stiffener spacing	80, 100, 120, 140, 160, 180, 200, 220, 240
Core height	120, 150, 180, 210, 240, 270, 300, 330

Design Criteria

General

Use of minimum rule thickness requirement would lead to inefficient structure. Therefore, it is assumed that the loads, deformation, fabrication aspects and other practical aspects are to be known well enough to carry out the selection of dimensions based on direct calculations.

The design criteria used in this study includes the plate maximum deflection $L/250$ being 40 mm, and buckling and yielding of structural members. Details on buckling, yielding and fatigue criteria are given below. The design criteria is violated if the ratio between the existing value and critical value is above one, i.e. $\eta > 1$.

Buckling

Local buckling of the face and web plates structure is taken into account using the DNV Guidelines for laser-welded sandwich panes (DNV, 2003). There linear elastic buckling stress for uni-axial or shear stress is calculated from

$$\sigma_e = 0.9 \cdot kE \left(\frac{t}{s}\right)^2 \qquad (27)$$

where the buckling coefficients used are given in Table 3 for different buckling modes and structural members. The Johnson-Ostenfield and interaction formulae are applied as presented in the mentioned DNV guidelines.

Table 3: Buckling coefficients for elastic buckling stress for different structural members and buckling modes (DNV 2003).

Buckling mode	Face plate	Web plate
Longitudinal	4.00	-
Transverse	1.00	-
Shear	$5.34 + (s/l)^2$	$5.34 + (s/l)^2$
In-plane bending	-	21.6

Yielding

Yielding of the faces and web plate is calculated according to the von Mises equivalent stress. When seagoing conditions are used, the maximum equivalent stress in the face and web plate is $\sigma = 320 f_1$ and $\sigma = 160 f_1$ respectively.

Case Study

Loads

A hoistable car deck of 10 m x 10 m is considered as a case study to illustrate the approach. It is loaded by eight vehicles weighing 2.57 tons with wheel print size of 200 mm x 200 mm; the weight is distributed equally to both axels. The ship hosting this deck has the main dimensions as presented in Klanac (2002), and given below in Table 4. Safety factor of 1.2 is introduced for loading.

Table 4: The main dimensions of the ship.

Dimension	Value
Length between perpendiculars	165 m
Breadth	31.1 m
Block coefficient	0.54
Speed	19.0 kn

Description of the Structure and Idealization

Fig. 6 presents the applied FE-mesh. The structure is idealized to a simply supported plate. Only one quarter of the plate is considered, loaded by two cars parallel to stiffener direction. Eight patch-loads of 235 kPa are used. The patch load is modeled to one element which has an area of 200 x 200 mm. The spacing between the patch loads is 2.8 m and 1.6 m (breadth of the car is 1.8 m) in x and y-directions respectively. The spacing between the cars is 0.7 m in y-direction. The material is steel with Young's modulus of 206 GPa and Poisson's ratio 0.3. The yield strength in top and web plates is chosen to be 355 MPa due to higher loads on these; the bottom face has the yield strength of 235 MPa. The laser-weld rotation stiffness is taken as 107 kN (Romanoff et al. 2007).

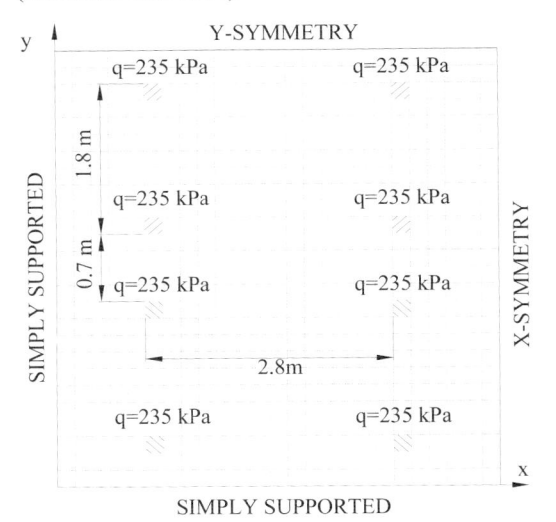

Fig. 6. FE-mesh used in optimisation.

Furthermore, an additional beam-model study is conducted, similar to that of Romanoff & Kujala (2001), using enumeration and assumption that a beam with breadth equal to one stiffener spacing carries the averaged vehicle load as a uniform pressure. See also Klanac & Kujala (2004) for additional explanation on this simplified load modeling. The purpose of this study is to connect this new approach with some of the earlier works and recommendations on design of steel sandwich panels for decking.

Results

Fig. 6 presents the convergence of the plate enumeration and the GA. Table 5 presents the comparison of the best design alternatives obtained with enumeration of the plate and beam models and with GA.

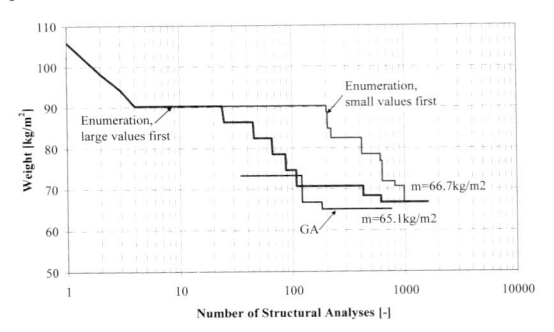

Fig. 7. Convergence of the enumeration and GA.

Table 5: The best design alternatives. The maximum allowed value for different design criteria is 1.

Parameter	Enum. Plate	Enum. Beam	GA
Top face [mm]	3	3	3
Web plate [mm]	4	4	4
Bottom face [mm]	1.5	1.5	1.5
Stiff. spacing [mm]	180	240	190
Height of core [mm]	180	330	180
Mass [kg/m^2]	66.7	77.2	65.1
Buckling, top [-]	0.29	0.81	0.32
Buckling, web [-]	0.04	-	0.04
Buckling, bottom [-]	0.36	-	0.50
Yield, top [-]	0.93	0.36	0.99
Yield, web [-]	0.52	0.36	0.53
Yield, bottom [-]	0.87	0.73	0.85
Deflection [-]	0.98	0.995	0.998

As Fig. 7 shows, the convergence of the GA is very good even though the design space is smaller than with enumeration. Carrying out enumeration so that the small values are used first leads to many calculations of infeasible alternatives. While with enumeration 1800 calculations are needed, with GA only about 200 analyses are required to get better structural configuration. Fig. 6 also shows how with GA the weight becomes smaller than with enumeration mainly due to consideration of the design space with finer set up of design alternatives. This difference of 1.6 kg/m^2 corresponds 2.4% of the total weight.

As given in Table 5, the best design alternative has relatively thick top face plate. This follows from the top face yield criterion which is actively bounding the optimum. In that sense additional active constraint is the plate maximum deflection. Also the bottom face plate yielding is close to being active. However, it should be noted that the allowed stress in top face and bottom face were taken as $\sigma=320f_1$ and $\sigma=160f_1$ respectively.

Comparison of the beam analysis with the plate analyses reveals that the use of simple beam approach can lead to 19% heavier structure than using the homogenized plate approach. Also, further plate investigation on the obtained beam optimum reveals that the structure is not feasible since it violates the yield criteria of the face plate. This is caused by the fact that the beam approach cannot predict periodic shear induced normal stresses in y-direction, and therefore it underestimates the stresses in the structure. On the other hand, this solution is limited by the deflection constraint, which the plate analysis shows, is not valid in reality.

Figs. 8 and 9 present the difference on the feasible designs in the top and bottom face plates. While in top face yield criterion dominates with low plate thicknesses, in larger plate thickness the maximum deflection criterion is active. In optimum both of these are active. In bottom face plate both yield and maximum deflection criterion constraint the design all the time. In both cases buckling criterion is found to be not active at all.

Fig. 10 to 13 show the mapped design space. The depicted points are feasible design alternatives attained through enumeration. It can be noticed that the space is slightly non-convex within the chosen lower and upper limits of the design variables.

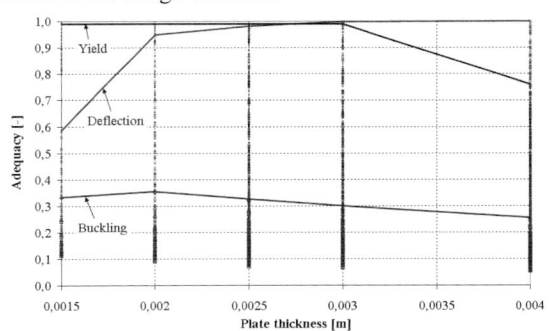

Fig. 8. Active constraints for top face plate.

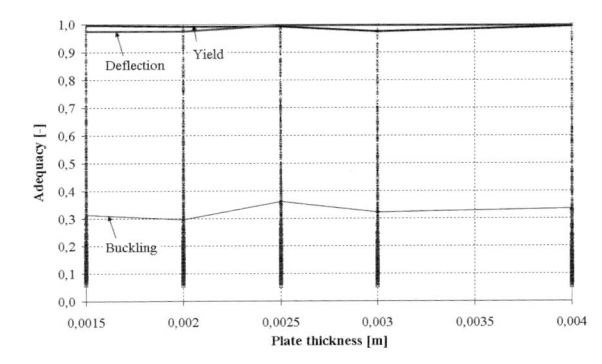

Fig. 9. Active constraints for bottom face plate.

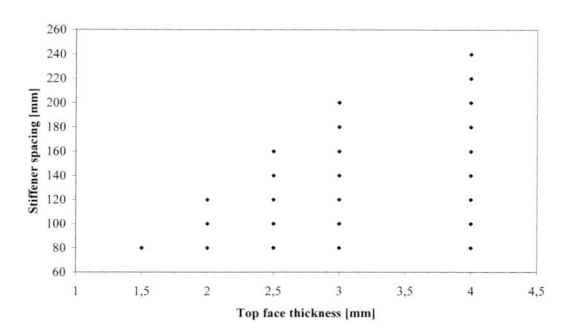

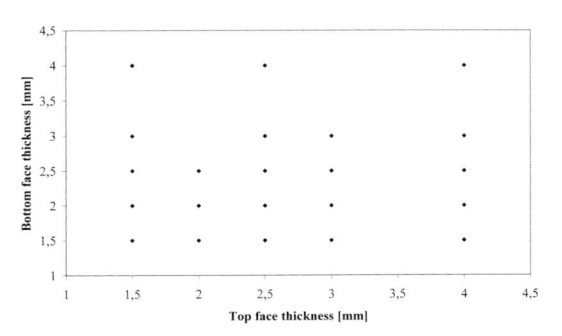

Fig. 10. Design space, top face plate thickness and stiffener spacing.

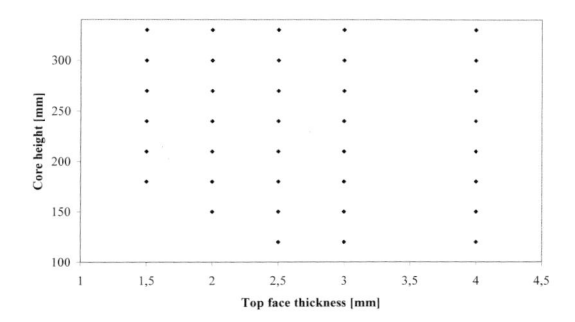

Fig. 11. Design space, top face plate thickness and core height.

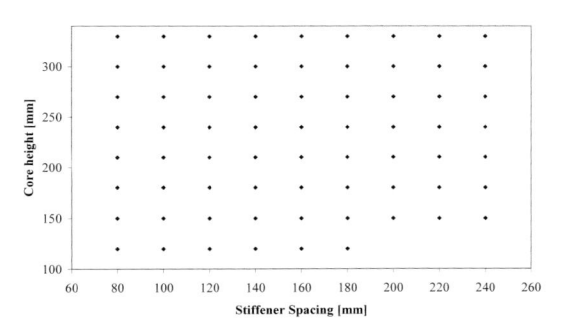

Fig. 12. Design space, stiffener spacing and core height.

Fig. 13. Design space, top face plate thickness and stiffener spacing.

Conclusions

The paper presents a structural design method for steel sandwich panels that utilizes newly developed structural analysis and optimization methods with the existing design criteria given by DNV guidelines for all steel sandwich panels. The method is applied to a case study of hoistable car deck. The comparison is done against two enumeration analyses, one based on the use of simple beam theory, and another on the use of homogenized plate theory as presented in the paper.

The case studies show that with proposed approach the structural design of steel sandwich panels can be carried out within few hours, which makes the approach very interesting within the conceptual stage of ship design. The case study shows also that using GA reduces the required amount of analyses when compared to enumeration. Therefore the design space can be mapped more accurately and lighter structures can be attained. It is also seen that a simple beam analysis leads to 19% heavier structure than a plate analysis, revealing more strongly the lightweigthing benefits for decking of the steel sandwich panels. In addition further study of so-obtained structure reveals that the beam analysis leads to structure that is infeasible. This mainly due to the fact that simple beam analysis cannot consider the shear-induced periodic normal stresses at all.

The paper considered only design based on yield, deflection and buckling checks. Fatigue of these structures poses an interesting design issue as well. However, this has been left for future work.

Acknowledgements

This work has been supported by EU-funded research project "DE-Light Transport – Developing lightweight modules for transport systems featuring efficient production and lifecycle benefits at structural and functional integrity using risk based design". This financial support is gratefully appreciated.

References

Det Norske Veritas, "Technical Report: Project Guidelines for Metal-Composite Laser-Welded Sandwich Panels – Public Version", Report No. 2003-0751, 2003.

Fung, T.C., Tan, K.H. and Lok, T.S. Elastic Constants for Z-core Sandwich Plates. Journal of Structural Engineering, Vol. 120, No. 10, October, 1994: 3046-3055.

Fung, T.C., Tan, K.H. and Lok, T.S. Elastic Constants for C-core Sandwich Plates. Journal of Structural Engineering, Vol. 122, No. 8, August, 1996: 958-966.

Klanac, A. "Optimal design of cardeck applying sandwich panels", Master Thesis, Tehnički fakultet, Rijeka, 2002. (In Croatian)

Klanac, A., Kujala, P.: *Optimal Design of Steel Sandwich Panel Applications in Ships*, 9th International Symposium on Practical Design of Ships and Other Floating Structures - *PRADS*, Travemuende – Luebeck, Sept. 2004.

Klanac, A. Jelovica, J.: *A concept of omni-optimization for ship structural design*, Advancements in Marine Structures, Guedes Soares & Das (eds), Proceedings of MARSTRUCT 2007, The 1st International Conference on Marine Structures, 12-14 March 2007a, Glasgow, UK. p. 473-481 (Taylor & Francis: London).

Klanac, A., Jelovica, J., "Vectorization in the structural optimization of a fast ferry", Brodogradnja-Shipbuilding, Vol. 58, No. 1, 2007b,: 11-17.

Marsico, T.A., Denney, P.E. and Furio, A. Laser Welding of Lightweight Structural Steel Panels. Proceedings of the Laser Materials Processing Conference – ICALEO'93, Orlando, LIA Vol. 77: 444-451.

Roland, F. and Reinert, T. Laser Welded Sandwich Panels for the Ship Building Industry. In Lighweight Construction – Latest Developments. 24 & 25 February, 2000, London, SW1: 1-12.

Romanoff, J, and Kujala, P (2001). "The Optimum Design for Steel Sandwich Panels Filled with Polymeric Foams", 6th FAST, Vol. 3, Southampton.

Romanoff, J. and Varsta, P. "Bending Response of Web-Core Sandwich Plates", Composite Structures, 2007.

Romanoff, J., Remes, H., Socha, G., Jutila, M. and Varsta, P., "The Stiffness of Laser Stake Welded T-joints in Web-core Sandwich Structures", Thin-Walled Structures. Accepted for publication.

The Problem of Fatigue on Large High Speed Craft and the Comparison between the Behavior of High Tensile Steel Structures and Aluminum Alloy Ones: The View of an International Shipbuilder

S. Ferraris [1], V. Farinetti [2]

[1] Ship Basic design, Fincantieri C.N.I. Naval Vessel Business Unit
Genoa, Italy
[2] Sales & Marketing, Fincantieri C.N.I. Systems and Components Unit
Genoa, Italy

Abstract

Fatigue is a leading factor in the design of ships and particularly of high speed vessels, where designers focus their efforts on how to define optimized structural solutions, which often imply higher design stress levels and higher flexibility. Fatigue problems may arise as a consequence of ship response to environmental loads and, locally, to the vibrations induced by the propulsion systems.

The paper aims at supplying some information about the experience matured in this field by a big European shipbuilding company, also pointing out the differences between steel structures and aluminum alloy ones. The precautions in design, production and through–life maintenance, needed to prevent fatigue cracks arising after a short service period are also taken into consideration, showing that fatigue problems can be limited, if not avoided, only if every party involved is fully aware of its role and of the possible troubles induced by any deviation from the correct way to act.

Keywords

High speed craft; Fatigue; Steel; Aluminum; Design; Production; Maintenance.

Introduction

Fatigue is indeed a driving parameter in the design of vessels. Its importance is even more emphasized in the HSC field, for a remarkable amount of reasons:

- the increase in size of such vessels (see for instance Fig. 1, referred to the last decade of XX century), which has led to a rise in the importance of global loads and of the dynamic phenomena related to the flexibility of hull girders;

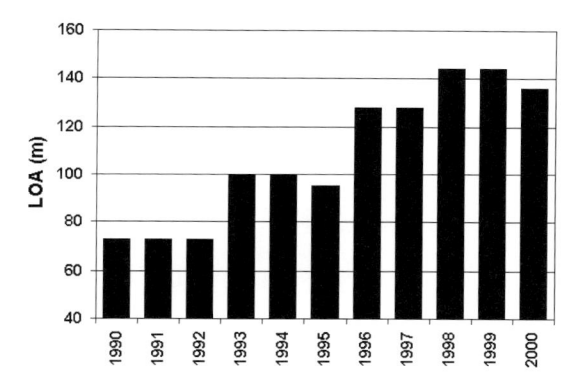

Fig. 1: The increase in HSC L_{OA} in the last decade of XX century

- the increase in installed power, which means vibrations with significant energy contents;
- the higher wave encounter frequency due to the higher operative speeds;
- the use of light and/or high strength materials, trying to exploit their mechanical properties as much as possible;
- the fact that such ships are quite often operating close to their design limits (ISSC 2000, Specialist Committee V.2);
- the still limited experience of designers, builders, classification societies and owners.

The subject, which is indeed complex and hard to study, face and solve, has a strong impact on all the activities related to shipbuilding and ship-operating. It is therefore possible to logically separate the different phases (design, production, running) and highlight the matters pertinent to each of them.

A few practical examples will help to better understand the view of the matter of a big shipbuilding company. Some ideas will also be given about the recent developments in the approach to the topic and about the differences between the behaviors of the most common metallic materials for HSC construction, high tensile steel and aluminum alloys.

Dealing with fatigue phenomenon

Design

In terms of design, the fatigue phenomenon has to be faced by using both a qualitative and a quantitative approach. The former implies the need to study more refined structural details so as to keep stress concentration factors as low as possible. The latter is now feasible thanks to both the availability of design procedures for the estimation of structure durability and the skyrocketing development in computational capabilities.

Fig. 2: An example of "bad" structural detail

The effects of global loads on flexible hulls are not easy to study due to the nonlinearity in hydrodynamic loads and the dynamic structural response, which both result in a nonlinear relationship between wave amplitudes and stresses. Spectral fatigue analysis, based on linearity assumptions, can not be widely applied to HSC (ISSC 2000, Specialist Committee V.2). Anyway the load cycles remain within the "classical" limits and the matter can be faced by means of a careful use of conventional methods, taking account that mentioned nonlinearity may significantly increase the cumulative damage.

On the contrary, it is hardly possible to predict the long-term behavior of structures subjected to a very high number of load cycles. This is for instance the case of water jet compartments, where the vibration regimes can subject the structures to more than 10^8 cycles in rather short periods. There are very few experimental results beyond 10^7 cycles and it is proven that in some cases the asymptote is not actually horizontal, which means that the fatigue strength at 10^6 cycles is higher than at 10^8 cycles (ISSC 2006, Technical Committee III.2).

The matter is critical for both steel and aluminum alloys, but the latter tends to be more susceptible to fatigue due to the loss of strength in Heat Affected Zone, the higher notch sensitivity and the consequent lower capability of withstanding cyclic loads (Ferraris and Volpone, 2005). There is further concern about the use of new alloys with enhanced yield strength, without adequately documented corresponding increases in fatigue strength (ISSC 2000, Specialist Committee V.2).

Aluminum alloys are much less forgiving than steel as they do not allow mistakes: this implies the need for a substantial change in the design approach, as the use of a "conventional steel design" would easily mean severe failures. On the contrary, especially in the HSC field, many concepts and ideas developed for aluminum constructions can be, and often are, adopted to make steel structures more reliable and less prone to fatigue.

Production

High speed vessel construction requires special care: difficult building sequences or incorrect production processes may cause distortions, misalignments, heat-induced buckling, notches or even crack initiations, which could easily give rise to fatigue failures in highly stressed thin structures (Farinetti, 1998). Fig. 3 gives a clear example of how secondary details, if wrongly executed, may cause fatigue damages even after only a few load cycles. This is true for both steel and aluminum alloys, but in the latter case the impact can become even dramatic due to the notch sensitivity of the material.

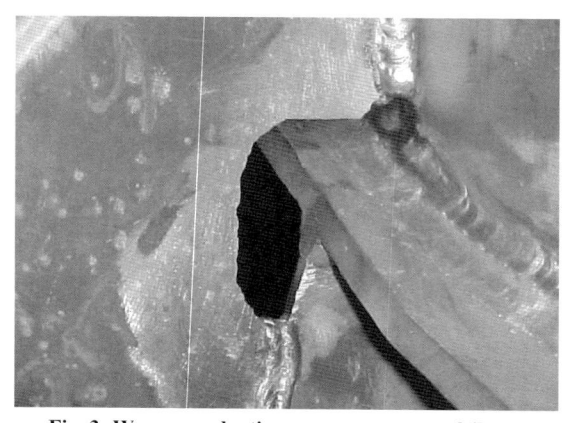

Fig. 3: Wrong production may cause severe failures

Another critical aspect of production is the possible lack of care in the integration between outfitting and structure. If hangers and other supports are put without thinking that a wrong location may cause hard points and notches, then significant failures are likely to occur, despite a good structural design and construction. Once again, incorrect solutions, often stood by steel structures, are hardly bearable by aluminum ones, which may suffer from the troubles generated both by the presence of hard points or abrupt discontinuities and by the decreased mechanical properties in heat affected areas not foreseen at the design stage.

Fig. 4: An example of "dangerous" integration between structure and outfitting

Feedback from operations

Classification societies now have feedback from several high speed vessels in service and are aware of where problems are most likely to occur. Many files are for internal use only, but some useful information can be also found in open literature (Wilhelmsen, 2000; Fach and Krüger, 2006).

The record of various structural failures has shown the lack of design experience, but has also allowed a better understanding of physical phenomena. Hull monitoring systems have provided another important contribution to the validation of design assumptions. This is particularly important in areas subjected to remarkable vibration regimes, where FEM analyses can give good indications, but the availability of measurements onboard is deemed fundamental and also allows tuning the design methodology (Ferraris et al., 2006).

A one year structural monitoring campaign was carried out on MDV 3000 at the end of the Nineties, allowing a better understanding of the structural response of those, which are still the largest fast ferries ever built (Fig. 5).

Fig. 5: One of MDV 3000 at sea

Owners, who are fully aware of the peculiarities of HSC with respect to conventional ships, perfectly know that good management also implies continuous monitoring and periodical structural surveys, together with a photographic record to allow present and subsequent operators to be aware of the structural history of the craft (Ferraris and Simpson, 2000).

Some practical examples

Design solutions

As already said, a correct design approach is essential to minimize the risk of fatigue failures and increase the expected life of structures. This means a different way of thinking both the overall geometry and the specific details. A good example of such a qualitative approach is the structural layout of transom main vertical girders, between the two lateral steering water jets, as adopted on the aluminum alloy SuperSeaCat fast ferries about ten years ago. To avoid critical welds in an area subjected to significant fatigue loading (as confirmed by Wilhelmsen, 2000), the web was locally cut to leave only transom plating between the jets and let it act in bending with not too stiff and hard points (Figs. 6 and 7). After about ten years of continuous service, no failures have been reported on any of the four vessels of the class, thus confirming the reliability of the design choice.

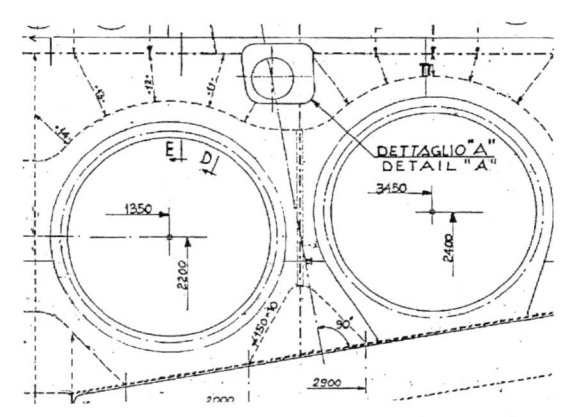

Fig. 6: The cut transom vertical girder between the steering water jet units – view from aft

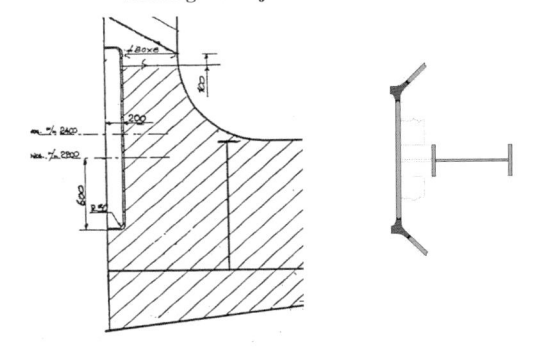

Fig. 7: The cut transom vertical girder between the steering WJ units – long. and hor. sections

Direct calculations

The progress of computational capabilities gives now the chance to carry out sophisticated verifications. This allows predicting the fatigue life of structures as never before, even though the actual problem is the uncertainty in the appropriateness of the environmental data used as a basis for design and so in the long-term distribution of loads. Another problem is the lack of established and well documented and tested methods of defining fatigue loadings for explicit calculations, particularly when nonlinear effects are present (ISSC 2000, Specialist Committee V.2).

Despite these uncertainties, most Classification Societies have issued rules or guidelines for the evaluation of the fatigue life of structural details, which can be used for design and verification purposes. Nowadays, such calculations are performed for whole structures and details subjected to both global loads and local vibrations.

One typical example of the former case is the FEM fatigue prediction of expansion joint lower end. Leading stress flow outside superstructures, expansion joints allow the designer to calculate superstructure scantling disregarding the longitudinal stresses due to the global behavior of the hull girder. This permits sparing weight and improves the stability of the vessel. On the other hand, in case of wrong design, the expansion joint might be subjected to serious damages, as shown by Fig. 8. The problem is not easy to solve since superstructures are generally made by using aluminum alloys and the hulls are often so flexible, to contain structural weight, that global deflections are very significant.

Fig. 8: Typical fatigue crack in way of expansion joint lower end

Fig. 9 shows one single snapshot of a complex fatigue analysis carried out by Fincantieri in 2005 on their last large HSC, the MDV 2000 Destination Gotland.

The circular shape of joint end and its diameter had been chosen on the basis of previous optimization studies carried out on naval ships, where use of such details is quite usual (Ferraris et al, 2002).

Another field, where current calculation capabilities give real chances to achieve results, which were hardly conceivable only some years ago, is the prediction of long-term behavior of those structures, which are constantly subjected to severe vibration regimes. This is the case of water jet compartments, where pressure pulses induce high frequency loads. All structures are to be thought taking account of the main vibration sources and considering that water jet impellers cause cyclic loads with high energy contents at rather high frequencies, often very close to the resonant ones of typical structural configurations.

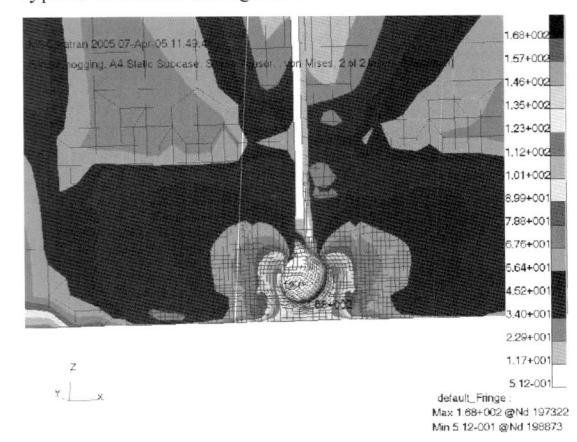

Fig. 9: One step of the fatigue life estimation of an expansion joint lower end

The problem is general, due to the high number of cycles, but obviously aluminum alloy structures need an even more careful design, as the stress range they can withstand is much lower than for steel ones. In both cases, a suitable direct calculation approach can help to avoid severe failures, but onboard monitoring at sea trials and during the operating life of the ship is indeed advisable to become more confident in the reliability of theoretical results as well as to help crews to better understand the loading conditions acting on vessels and to operate them accordingly (ISSC 2003, Specialist Committee V.4).

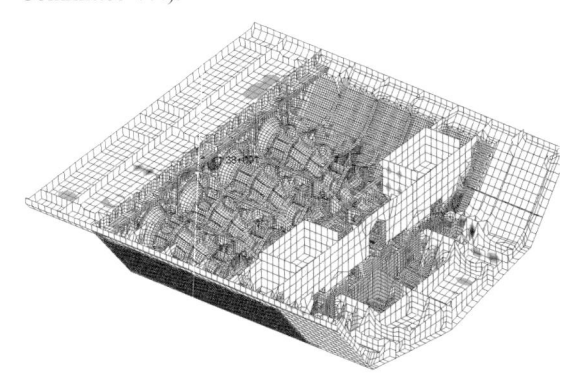

Fig. 10: WJ compartment: a snapshot of some dynamic calculation results

Sea trials

As mentioned above, structural tests during sea trials are very important to validate the design assumptions. Till some years ago, apart from few ashore tests to find the resonant frequencies of structures located in critical areas, measurements in operating conditions were the only actual way to identify possible glaring mistakes and then verify the reliability of the solutions to same.

Such a practice was adopted in the second half of nineties and allowed to prevent potentially serious failures. As an example, the study on a floor panel of the water jet compartment of SuperSeaCat (aluminum alloy fast ferries) is presented hereafter.

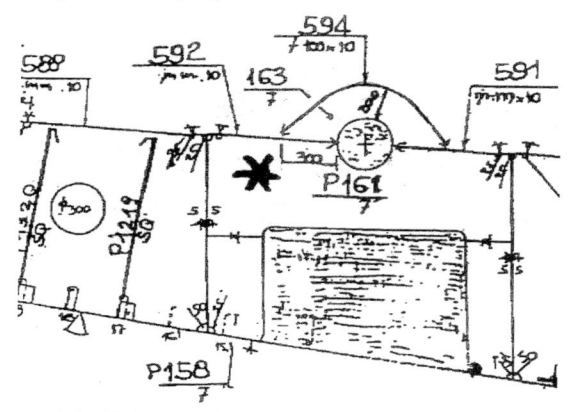

Fig. 11: Extract from floor configuration showing the critical panel and accelerometer location

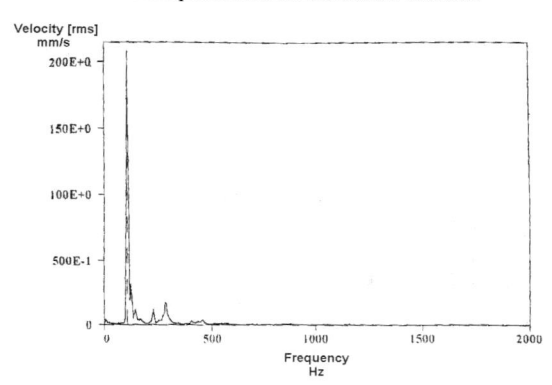

Fig. 12: Original vibration levels: peak is 208 mm/s at 115 Hz

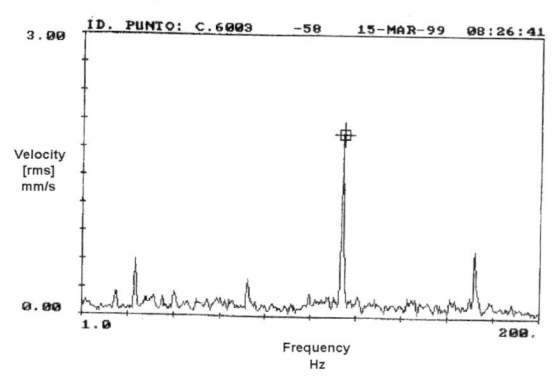

Fig. 13: Vibration levels after the modification: peak is reduced to 2.15 mm/s at 114.8 Hz

Figs. 11 through 13 show the location of the panel, above an external water jet, and the comparison between the measures before and after structural adjustments, consisting of the implementation of suitable intercostal stiffening elements to tie floors and water jet ducts together (Fig. 14).

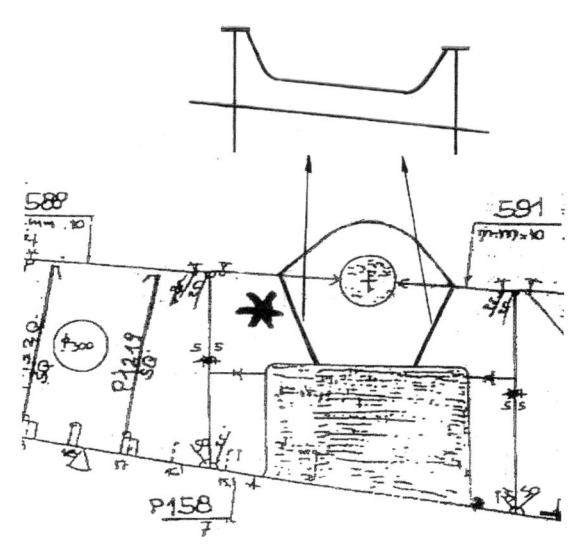

Fig. 14: The structural modification

Ship management

Owners, who want to acquire and operate high speed craft, must be fully aware that these can hardly be compared with conventional ships. The extreme and sometimes novel design solutions; the uncertainties about the applied loadings and the structural response; the uncertainties about the influence of initial deformations and residual stresses, especially when considering the fatigue strength of welded aluminum structures; the limited feedback from the operating field; the restricted service and the operational limits, basis for the HSC concept; the uncertainty about the crew ability to ensure that the craft always stays within its specified operating envelope: these are some of the reasons, which make the management of high speed vessels so delicate. Such ships can be compared with sports cars, which need due care and accurate running.

Frequent inspections, periodical surveys, ordinary and extraordinary maintenance are a must to prevent serious failures and take immediate care of minor ones.

Fig. 15: A bad executed cut out below a foundation

Usually, limited troubles can be easily solved: this is for instance the case of small cracks due to incorrect integration between structure and outfitting or inaccurate production (Fig. 15 - in this latter case, grinding, re-welding and an overlapped collar solved the matter).

Major problems, generally deriving from erroneous design assumptions or from unforeseen excessive loadings (irrespectively of their quasi-static or fully dynamic nature), must be faced trying to analyze and understand all the possible causes and then studying different design approaches to limit the risk of relapses.

Fig. 16 shows fatigue cracks in a vertical girder inside a void space: the successful repairs included the complete deletion of the notches and the stagger of welds.

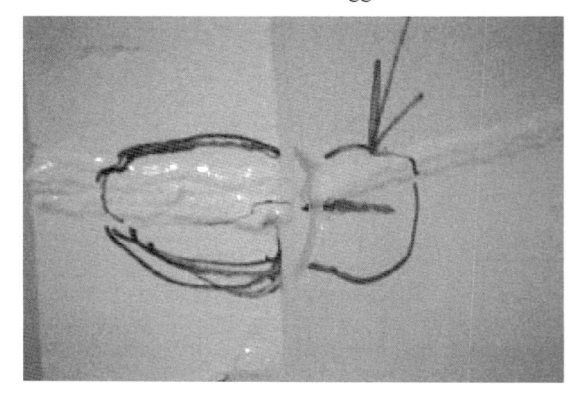

Fig. 16: Notch-induced cracks

Another failure, quite common in fore void spaces, is shown by Fig. 17: here the cyclic loads due to high frequency wave impacts caused cracks in deck beams in way of bracket weld toe. The main cause proved to be poor scantling rather than inefficient detail design: a suitable insert in the beam (Fig. 18) allowed a better distribution of stresses and the prevention of rising of buckling phenomena. Such a crucial modification prevented any failure to occur again in the same position.

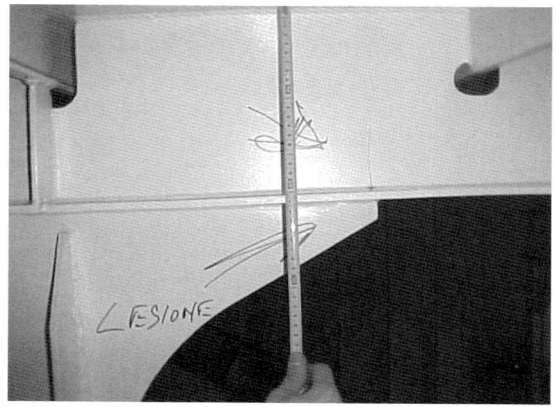

Fig. 17: Cracks in deck beam in fore void spaces

Other failures typically occurred on large HSC, especially when the increase in length and displacement led to a shift of emphasis in load types and combinations, with global loads playing a more significant role than previously, are those related to windows.

Fig. 18: The insert that solved the problem

Irrespective of the kind of superstructure implemented, either taking part into global hull girder strength or provided with expansion joints to avoid this, cracks tended to appear at few stressed window corners, sometimes due to sailing in unexpected extreme environmental condition, close to the design limits or even beyond them, otherwise due to the cumulative damage deriving from wave encounters. In latter case, the higher speed and the more flexible structure could give rise to springing, as the wave encounter frequency may coincide with the lowest hull girder natural one.

While metallic hulls can be made of either high tensile steel or aluminum alloys, superstructures are generally made of the second. This fact increases the risk of failures, even though the experience matured through several designs and constructions in the last decade has clearly shown the critical aspects of both design and production, giving the chance to build safer structures.

Figs. 19 and 20 show a few severe cracks occurred in way of some windows of the first tier of superstructures of SuperSeaCat aluminum alloy fast ferries.

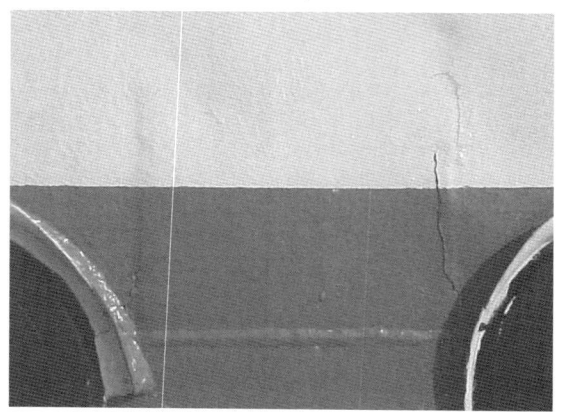

Fig. 19: Typical cracks in way of window corners

The vessels were provided with expansion joints, which prevented the superstructure from directly sustaining global bending moments, but induced serious secondary effects. A refined FEM analysis proved the cracks had been caused by pulsing shear forces acting in way of mullions. Mullion design was reviewed and bone-shaped doublers (Fig. 21), attached to the existing structure by gluing and riveting, were successfully used (Ferraris and Simpson, 2000).

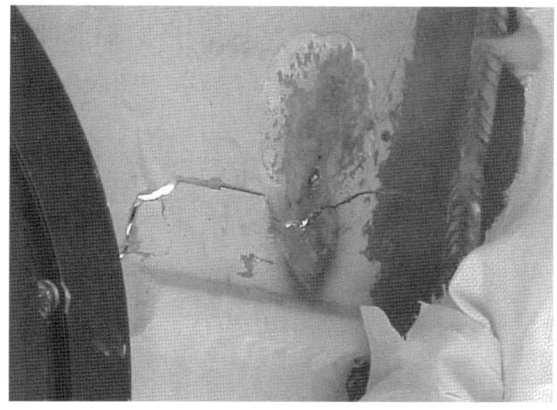

Fig. 20: A serious crack seen from inside

Fig. 21: A successful repair by using riveted and glued doublers

Such structures are constantly monitored and no other failures have been reported since then.

Nowadays the design approach to this kind of structures is considerably different. Few main aspects can be mentioned hereafter:

- when in presence of expansion joints, no openings should be foreseen in the closest web frame spacings;
- use of large extruded profiles should be avoided in way of windows, as the preparation for the integration of window frames often leads to notches and crack initiations. In that area, one single machine holed plate and a traditional "plate plus stiffeners" structure should be preferred;
- among structural details, mullions are quite critical: the secondary shear effects induce remarkable torsion on such girders, so that in areas, where high stress peaks or significant stress ranges may occur, a box solution is normally preferable;
- in general, a smooth transition of structural stiffness from highly stressed areas to rather quiet ones can ensure that stresses and strains are correctly taken up.

In any case, an accurate FEM analysis is highly advisable, if not mandatory, to carefully evaluate the long-term behavior of superstructures, including as much secondary effects as possible. The uncertainties deriving from nonlinear phenomena still remain, but the overall figure can be identified as well as the areas more likely to become structurally critical.

Conclusions

The daily progress in knowledge, which turns dedicated studies into reference design rules, the development of computational methods, the increasing amount of information about the results of practical tests as well as the feedback from operational scenarios: these are some of the reasons, which make dealing with fatigue of HSC structures more feasible than a few years ago.

Nevertheless, despite the tremendous progress in this field, direct calculation approaches can hardly solve the whole problem, due to the persisting uncertainties about the physical nature of some loadings and their combinations, especially when nonlinear effects may occur (as in statically indeterminate cases, where the direct integration of external loads to obtain sectional forces may be misleading and may cause underestimated loads and responses).

Direct analyses are very important as they can help to find out the most critical areas, can give a pretty good idea of the problems and give the great chance to compare different structural solutions and choose the most reliable of them.

Further R&D work is expected and indeed necessary to reduce uncertainties, which still have a strong influence on structural design, and to address certain design aspects, like fatigue assessment of structures subjected to a number of cycles exceeding the traditional limits (10^7-10^8), as also suggested by ISSC 2003, Specialist Committee V.4.

In the last decade, several research activities have been devoted to the durability of aluminum alloy structures. Such studies included fatigue life assessment of typical details and the development of new computational techniques for the evaluation of the fatigue life of aluminum alloy welded joints. However, there is still a remarkable gap between the knowledge about the long-term behavior of steel structures and the long-term behavior of aluminum alloy ones. As emphasized by ISSC 2006, Technical Committee III.2, there is not only need for more design data about arc welded aluminum alloy structures, but also corresponding data for other welding processes, like friction stir welding; considering the existing codes and standards, there are often significant differences between the proposed design S–N curves and the fatigue test database available for large-scale structural specimens. Last but not least, there is little information in the literature on remaining life assessment procedures.

In terms of production, Q.A. and stringent Q.C. are essential, because low thickness and uncommon materials, especially aluminum alloys, imply higher quality of workmanship. Here a conceptual leap is mandatory, since high quality in structural details and in the integration between structure and outfitting is crucial to achieve a substantial reduction of fatigue failures.

Owners can play an active role, giving designers and shipbuilders a constant feedback about any possible damage through a careful monitoring of their vessels and a precise recording of the environmental conditions, in which they are operated.

References

Fach, K, and Krüger, D (2006). "Damages on Lightweight Structures", Proc 1st European Conference on Production Technologies in Shipbuilding, Rostock-Warnemünde, Germany, Schiffbauforschung 45, pp 89-96.

Farinetti, V (1998). "General considerations on high tensile steel versus aluminum alloy and technical aspects related to the aluminum construction", Proc 3rd International Forum on Aluminum Ships, Haugesund, Norway.

Ferraris, S, Grillo, R, Mueller, S, and Volpone, LM (2006). "Lightweight Metallic Structures in Large High Speed Vessels: established technologies and future trends", Proc 1st European Conference on Production Technologies in Shipbuilding, Rostock-Warnemünde, Germany, Schiffbauforschung 45, pp 71-88.

Ferraris, S, Grillo, R, Volpone, L, Ivaldi, A, Gambaro, C, and Nicchia, D (2002). "Fatigue assessment and optimisation of a naval ship expansion joint", Proc 10th International Congress of the International Maritime Association of the Mediterranean, Rethymnon, Crete, Hellas.

Ferraris, S, and Simpson, M (2000). "Structural Design, Production and Operational Experience of SuperSeaCat Fast Ferries", Proc 4th International Forum on Aluminum Ships, New Orleans, USA.

Ferraris, S, and Volpone, LM (2005). "Aluminum Alloys in Third Millennium Shipbuilding: materials, technologies, perspectives", Proc 5th International Forum on Aluminum Ships, Tokyo, Japan.

ISSC (2000). "Structural Design of High Speed Vessels", Report of Specialist Committee V.2, Proc 14th International Ship and Offshore Structures Congress, Elsevier, Nagasaki, Japan, Vol. 2, pp 43-99.

ISSC (2003). "Structural Design of High Speed Vessels", Report of Specialist Committee V.4, Proc 15th International Ship and Offshore Structures Congress, Elsevier, San Diego, USA, Vol. 2, pp 109-147.

ISSC (2006). "Fatigue and Fracture", Report of Technical Committee III.2, Proc 16th International Ship and Offshore Structures Congress, Southampton, UK, Vol. 1, pp 439-520.

Wilhelmsen, Ø (2000). "Hull Structural Damage and Repairs", Proc 4th International Forum on Aluminum Ships, New Orleans, USA.

Application of Sandwich Panels in Design and Building of Dredging Ships

Jeroen (J) Kortenoeven[1], Bart (B) Boon[2], Arnold (A) de Bruijn[3]

[1] M.Sc, IHC HOLLAND Dredgers BV, Kinderdijk, The Netherlands
[2] M.Sc, Bart Boon Research and Consultancy, Aerdenhout, The Netherlands
[3] M.Sc, IHC HOLLAND Dredgers BV, Kinderdijk, The Netherlands

Abstract

Main objective of this paper is to assist shipyards and ship owners to actually decide to examine and implement sandwich panels in ship structures. The awareness that the application of sandwich panels may lead to substantial lower production costs, relatively shorter product delivery times, improved ship performance due to a lower structural weight and improved fatigue and corrosion characteristics is increasing. As a world market leader in building and supply of dredging ships and dredging equipment IHC Holland Dredgers (Member of the IHC Holland Merwede Group) is continuously seeking ways to improve the performance of its complex and special ship designs, to further reduce production costs and shorten delivery times. Sandwich panels have already been applied in commercial vessels, but on a rather modest scale. After some exploratory studies, IHC is convinced of the potential benefits for the ship yard and its customers, mainly dredging companies. However several factors affect the potential use of sandwich panels in the design and building processes including acceptance by clients, class societies and the shipyard's own personnel.

Keywords

Sandwich panel; Dredging ship structure; Weight; Production cost.

Introduction

Thorough feasibility studies have been performed at IHC for the application of sandwich panels in the ship structure of dredging ships and in detail for a complete, sandwich superstructure. Furthermore, IHC joined national and international co-operative projects with other ship yards, ship owners, sandwich suppliers, research institutes and universities. Research studies have been carried out in close cooperation with classification societies. The in-house studies included practical application tests in the yard fabrication facilities leading to a better understanding of avoiding the pitfalls that are inherent when introducing novel concepts in a well-established production environment.

Based upon the significant technical advantages and substantial cost and fabrication time saving IHC decided to start applying steel sandwiches at a modest scale expecting, that the applications will rapidly grow. Design of the first sandwich application has been done in close cooperation with the supplier of the sandwich panels.

This paper will present the main issues of an extensive research project including results regarding the application of sandwich panels. The results of the design process at IHC, the classification of the structure and the actual building, outfitting and handling of the steel sandwich switch board room at IHC will be discussed in detail. The pro's and con's for the ship owner are presented. The paper will finish with an outlook to next steps regarding the design and building of sandwich applications at IHC in the ship structure of dredging ships. Feasible new sandwich applications at IHC will be pointed out.

Advantages and disadvantages of the application of sandwich panels

Advantages

Sandwich panels in the present context consist of two steel or aluminum skins at a certain distance with a relative light-weight core either of the same material or of a plastic. Due to the distance between the skins the ratio of the sectional modulus and the sectional area of sandwich panels is high in comparison with plates only. The strength of the ship structure of (dredging) ships is determined for a great deal by local bending moments due load or water pressures. Generally, the application of sandwich panels can reduce the structural weight of a specific part (e.g. decks) in a dredging ship with 39% (see paragraph "Research at IHC Holland Dredgers). As a result the ship owner can buy a lighter ship with a large deadweight-displacement ratio and reduced operational costs and the shipyard is able to reduce production time and material costs.

Steel cored sandwich panels are produced with laser welding machines because only in this way through-plate welding is possible (e.g. I-core®, Figure 1).This means that production involves large semi-products thus reducing the amount of traditional yard work. Large sandwich panel areas are produced by suppliers as semi-finished products, thus decreasing the production time in the yard itself dramatically. The number of panel stiffeners still to be installed by the yard is reduced when applying sandwich panels because of the high sectional modulus compared to a single plate panels. Production costs at a shipyard can be reduced by applying sandwich panels instead of conventional stiffened panels due to the reduction of panel stiffeners and therefore the reduction of brackets, cut-outs, collar plates and buckling stiffeners.

Figure 1: I-core® sandwich panel (Jos L. Meyer GmbH)[1]

By applying sandwich panels instead of conventional stiffened panels production costs will shift from the shipyard to the supplier of sandwich panels. Most of the welding work at the shipyard during section assembly is done manually, but the assembly of the sandwich panels is done semi-automatically, which is relative cheap. Therefore in most cases total production costs (production of panels and assembly of the section) will be reduced when applying sandwich panels in (ship) structures. Generally the application of sandwich panels will reduce the total production costs (material, panel and section assembly) with 25% (Van der Zwaal, 2005).

Due to the reduction in parts not only the assembly costs for the specific sandwich application will reduce, but also the throughput time of the assembly. Transport, handling, welding, surface treating and inspection work will be reduced by applying sandwich panels. In case of the Switch Board Room (Chapter "First Results") the throughput time of the section assembly is reduced with 70%!

Additional benefits of the application of sandwich panels are improved fatigue and corrosion characteristics. It is difficult to judge these benefits in a quantitative way. But the number of parts will reduce the risk of fatigue cracks and the number of corrosion sensitive details. Finally the use of sandwich panels can result in more available space for non-structural parts, which is particularly interesting in accommodation areas.

Disadvantages

Disadvantages for the application of sandwich panels compared to conventional stiffened panels are: the low resistance of the shell plates in case of impact loads and local (point) loads, the low shear strength of the core (metal or polymer) of the sandwich panel and the panel joints as well as the low freedom in structural design.

One of the main objections when proposing steel cored sandwich panels at a shipyard or for ship owners is the possible, lower impact resistance of the sandwich panels. Of course when applying 2.5 mm shell plates or less for a sandwich panel the local impact strength of the shell plates for metal core panels will be lower. In case of polymer cores the local, impact strength will be significantly better compared to conventional stiffened panels. The influence of impact loads on all-metal sandwich panels during grounding on rocks of a cutter suction dredger has been investigated authored by IHC Dredgers (Figure 2).

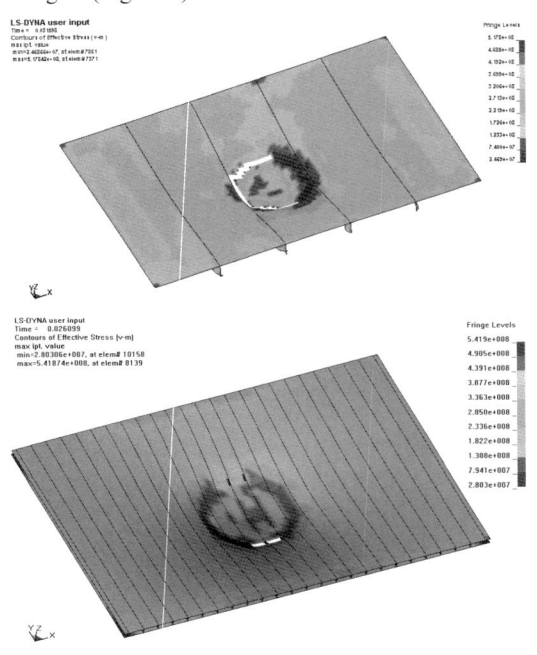

Figure 2: finite element results for conventional and I-core® sandwich panel under impact loads (large indenter)

As a result of this analysis it was concluded that the behavior of a standard I-core panel was significantly better than that of conventional panel with comparable strength characteristics; once damaged, it possessed a higher capacity to resist in-plane loads before collapse. This is a major improvement if considering prevention of a total ship loss. Sandwich panels behaved better

---

[1] Pictures are being presented with approval of the Meyerwerft.

when impacted by the sharp rock of a small size (assessed with 120 mm indenter), only for the impact of larger rocks (600 mm indenter) the performance was below the level of the conventional panel. Assessing the overall results one can conclude that is it sensible to use steel sandwich panels as bottom shell, and that the grounding problem does not represent a significant problem. Also, additional safety could be achieved for most of the cases of grounding (crash worthiness) without damaging the performance of the ship due to an additional shell plate once the other plate is damaged. The sandwich panel thus acts as a small dimension double hull and may prevent or delay flooding of holds and other large compartments. One cannot conclude that the impact resistance of all-metal sandwich panels is lower compared to conventional stiffened panels based on the information above, this should be considered on a case by case basis.

Due the thin shell plates compared to the plates in conventional stiffened panels and the low tensile strength out-of-plane point loads have to be spread out over a greater area or internal sandwich transitions have to be designed and fabricated to transfer out-of-plane point loads through the sandwich panel to supporting structures at the other side of the panel. This is the case, when applying foundations of gantries, winches on deck structures. This could lead to the non-application of sandwich panels due to the lack of technical sandwich solutions or due to higher fabrication costs.

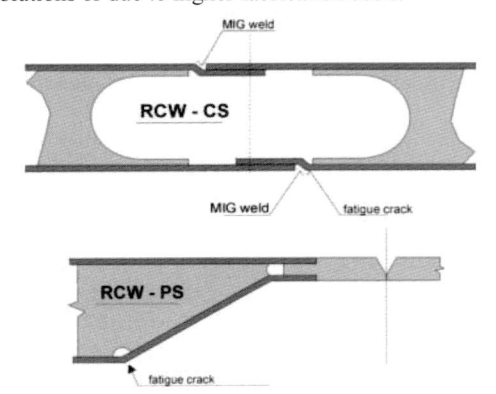

Figure 3: possible sandwich panel joints for I-Core with relative high fatigue strength, but quite expensive to fabricate (www.SAND.CORe.net, 2006)

One of the main disadvantages of the application of sandwich panels in parts involving large in-plane stresses is the relative low strength of the joints of the individual welded I-core® panels. At these joints it is only possible with relative high fabrication costs and time consuming techniques to connect the cores of the sandwich panels. In plane and shear strength of the joints will be reduced due to the missing of core strength and additional plates or profiles have to be provided to compensate for the lack of static and fatigue strength. For this reason panel joints cannot be applied highly loaded areas or can be applied with high production costs compared to joints within conventional stiffened structures. For instance the fatigue performance of joints can be improved by applying detailed designs as presented in Figure 3; however production costs of these joints will be rather high. Because of this IHC as yet mainly considers applications with out-of-plane loads only.

Concept design shall, wherever possible, take measures to prevent the transfer of global loads to the sandwich structure. This can be easily done in cases like sun decks or moveable ramps and will make joints easier and less costly in assembly. Joints shall be put as close as possible to supporting girders, which makes fitting work easier.

Due to objections and disadvantages mentioned before the freedom in structural design compared to conventional stiffened structures is low. This can be stated as an objection and not as a disadvantage, because technical solutions can always be found for locations with possible impact loads or panel joints at highly loaded areas However technical solutions always have to be "balanced" with the comparison between total production costs of conventional and sandwich panel applications.

Research at IHC Holland Dredgers

Thorough feasibility studies have been performed at IHC for the application of sandwich panels in the ship structure of dredging ships and in detail for a complete, sandwich superstructure. Research started with a feasibility study of sandwich applications in trailing suction hopper dredgers. A complete ship structure of a 7400 m^3 trailing suction hopper dredger (TSHD) has been analyzed for the application of sandwich panels taking into account the possibility of joints between sandwich panels and between conventional stiffened and sandwich panels, strength, weight and stiffness of the panels, overall production costs, classification rules, fire resistance, corrosion and wear. Results of this study show that cost savings for the specific (steel) sandwich application can be up to 57% and average 25% (Van der Zwaal, 2005) for the investigated locations. Weight savings can be more than 70% for FRP sandwiches and average 39% for steel sandwich applications. Steel-polymer-steel sandwich panel applications have been investigated too, but the results of the study show no cost or weight benefits for internal decks and bulkheads (mainly because of the small plate thickness needed in the conventional structure). Steel-concrete-steel sandwich panel applications haven't been investigated because of the lack information about these sandwich types. Specific areas where sandwich panel applications are feasible based on cost savings are given in **Figure 4**.

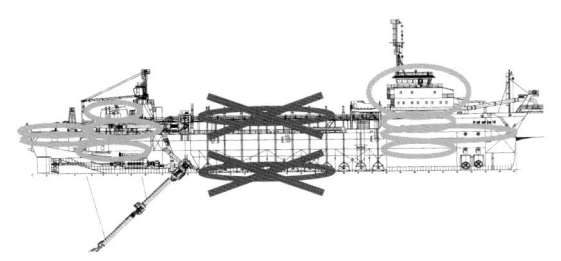

Figure 4: feasible areas for the application of sandwich panels for a 7400 m3 TSHD based on cost savings (IHC Holland Dredgers BV, 2005)

Based on positive cost and weight results and taking into account technical complexity, number of foundations and holes the superstructure has been further investigated (Van der Zwaal, 2005).

Engineering, all production stages and the final usage of a superstructure have been evaluated. The results of this sub study show a 12% saving of the structural weight of a superstructure by applying steel sandwich panels and a 20% reduction in overall production cost. The occurring deflections of the sandwich panels are large compared to the deflection of conventional panels, while the stresses are low. It also appeared that the conventional structural design was not optimal for the application of sandwich panels. With a modified sandwich structural design using the full strength potential of the sandwich panels the reductions in price and weight can be even larger.

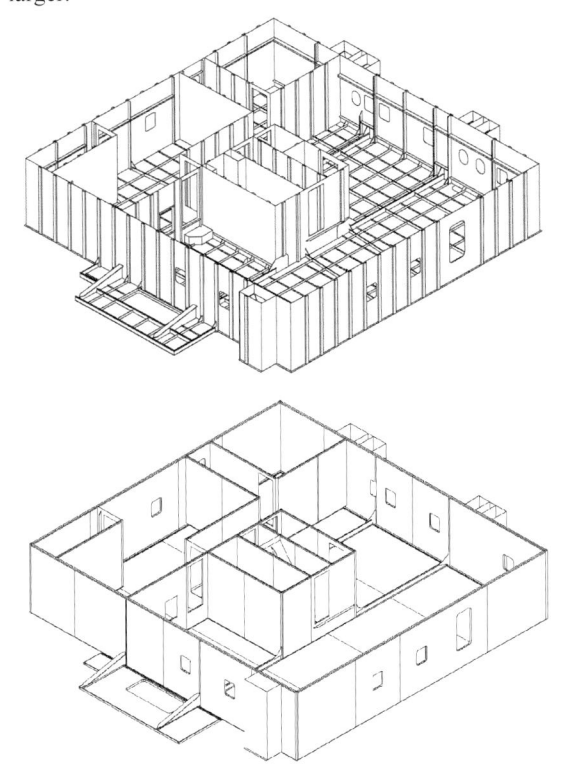

Figure 5: conventional stiffened tier of a superstructure (3D-view upside down) and an all-steel sandwich tier (IHC Holland Dredgers BV, 2005)

A second study of the application of steel sandwich panels in a smaller superstructure of a 3500 m3 TSHD has been performed later on as a basis for the actual application of steel sandwich panels in the superstructure for a new build dredger. The results of this study showed smaller reductions in structural weight and overall production costs, but with a 50% reduction in steel building hours and throughput time. The difference in structural design is shown in Figure 5.

It should be clear, that also costs of insulation work are reduced (22%) due to the flat sandwich panel areas (Van der Zwaal, 2005). Just like in the previous study results showed low stresses in the steel sandwich panels compared to the conventional stiffened structure. The results of the superstructure studies indicate, that in that case cost and weight savings are possible but for relative large superstructures (relative large hopper dredgers) and a modified structural design compared to a conventional stiffened structure is necessary to gain maximum cost and weight reductions.

After performing feasibility studies concerning the application of sandwich panels in the total ship structure and the superstructure (2x) of a TSHD IHC Dredgers decided not to actually build an all-sandwich superstructure yet. Management of IHC Dredgers was concerned about the risk of the new method of building the all-sandwich superstructure. Feasible alternative sandwich applications have been inventoried and a cooperative project with engineering bureaus (Bart Boon Research and Consultancy, Spaarnwater), a classification bureau (Bureau Veritas) and research institute (TNO) was done in which the application of steel sandwich panels in the pontoon structure of a cutter suction dredger was investigated, but cost and weight results were insufficient. The reason, the extent of the sandwich application in the pontoon structure turned out to be small due to several practical problems during production and after delivery. Finally during design of a 6000 m^3 the application of steel sandwich panels in a switch board room was decided. Results of the research, engineering and production of the sandwich SBR will be discussed in "First results".

Practical application tests at the ship yard were performed to gain experience with welding on and flame cutting, sawing and drilling in steel sandwich panels (I-core®). Square profiles have been connected to the panel, holes were drilled and edge reinforced, stiffeners welded onto the panel and the panel was outfitted with insulation pins and pipe clamps. Types of welds and welding speed were investigated. And finally the sandwich panel including outfitting was used as a presentation model for colleagues at design, engineering and production departments, clients of IHC Dredgers and project partners (Figure 9).

Focus during design

Prior to the engineering of a sandwich application preliminary strength calculations, cost and weight estimates are made, to investigate if the specific sandwich application will lead to benefits for the ship yard as well as the ship owner. Cost and weight reductions should be significant (10 to 15 %) to compensate for unforeseen technical, practical and financial problems during the engineering, production and exploitation of sandwich applications and to convince ship owners, classification societies and management of the ship yard to actually decide to apply sandwich panels.

Type of sandwich panel

The choice for the type of sandwich panel, all-metal, metal polymer or plastic, is made based on available technical, practical and cost information. Because the ship construction of merchant vessels is mainly done by welding plates and profiles to each other, the application of plastic sandwich panels is a step too far, but could be possible in the future. Steel sandwich panels however can be connected to the conventional stiffened ship structure by welding and normal steel production handlings like flame cutting, sawing, drilling are (limited) possible. Steel-polymer sandwich types like the Sandwich Plate System (SPS) could be useful when A60 fire protection regulations have to be fulfilled, when the structure must dampen vibrations, in case of local impact loads or when two types of metals have to be connected with the polymer core for example normal steel and wear resistant steel (difficult to weld). However the weldability of the sandwich skin with polymer underneath is restricted by a certain amount of heat input to prevent delamination. All-steel sandwiches do not have this problem and are lighter too. For the engineering of the superstructures and final production of the switch board room steel I-core® sandwich panels have been chosen based on practical (weldability), cost, but mainly weight advantages compared to other sandwich types.

Scantlings and joints

At the moment scantlings of conventional stiffened structures are still determined prior to the scantlings of the sandwich design to investigate if the application of sandwich panels will lead to lower costs and structural weight. The thickness of shell and core plates and the distances in between if necessary in combination with stiffeners are determined at first based on equal strength (allowable (buckling) normal and shear stresses) compared to the conventional stiffened structure and second based on allowable stiffness. In general equal strength will lead to a relative lower stiffness for the sandwich application, which could lead to unacceptable deformations. Also the thickness of the shell plating of the panels is tied to minimum thickness requirement of classification societies. According to Lloyd's Register for the present SBR application (see later) the combined skin thickness may be taken equal to the minimum required thickness in the conventional structure. A lot of attention should be paid to joints of the sandwich panels, which are relatively weak elements in the sandwich application. Panel joints are already discussed in the previous paragraph. Summarizing the required stiffness, minimum thickness and strength of panel joints can determine the geometry of the sandwich panels such as described later for the SBR.

Application area

The extent of the sandwich application in the ship structure is not only determined by cost and weight but also by the possibility of the modification of the structure after design and production, fitting of foundations, water or gas tightness, type of loads and the number and dimensions of penetrations and other holes. For example the cutter suction dredgers are build in series. The dredgers remain in port until purchased by a client. The client could ask for lengthening of the pontoon structure or the installation of winches on the deck structure, which makes it more complex and costly to apply sandwich panels in the pontoon structure compared to conventional stiffening because of the complex sandwich panel joints and complex foundations.

Design loads

Finally the evaluation is done of the response of the sandwich panels (e.g. (cyclic) stresses, deformations and vibration behavior) and panel connections under design loads, extreme loads (impact for example) and loads during transport and production of the sandwich application. Cyclic stresses and fatigue life of joints between sandwich panels or between sandwich and conventional panels should be acknowledged or even calculated if desired by the ship yard or classification society. Based on finite element analysis and test results of sandwich panel (2x) joints, sandwich-conventional panel joints and weld joints between two conventional panels stress calculations are done for the analysis of the static strength and fatigue life of the specific details.

Classification

Classification societies will pay special attention during classification to the connection of the sandwich panels and sandwich-conventional panels regarding static and fatigue strength especially in case of possible misalignments. The approval of these joint will be done after delivery of finite element analysis and test results provided by the supplier of the sandwich panels.

Focus during production

The application of sandwich panels will affect the organization during all stages of production of ship structures. The production of ship structures is being done in several stages; metal preparation, panel fabrication, section building and hull assembly. The application of sandwich panels will lower the amount of girders, stiffeners and brackets significantly, therefore reducing the amount of parts, handling and welding work. The panel production in the panel hall will be reduced; sandwich panels produced by the sandwich supplier will be transported to the yard and integrated in conventional panels in the panel hall or directly connected to panels in ship sections (all-metal sandwich panels like I-Core®), the overall building time will be reduced. In the case of metal-polymer sandwich panels (SPS) can be made in the panel section hall or elsewhere (at supplier) depending on the location and size of the sandwich application.

Metal preparation

The metal preparation is still being done for panels and sections with sandwich panels integrated but on a smaller scale. The number of girders, stiffeners and brackets is reduced significantly, therefore the package of parts is reduced. For the integration of sandwich panels internally or into the conventional ship structure extra (metal) joints are needed, that can be delivered by the metal preparation department or sandwich supplier. Some examples of steel sandwich panel connection elements are given in Figure 6.

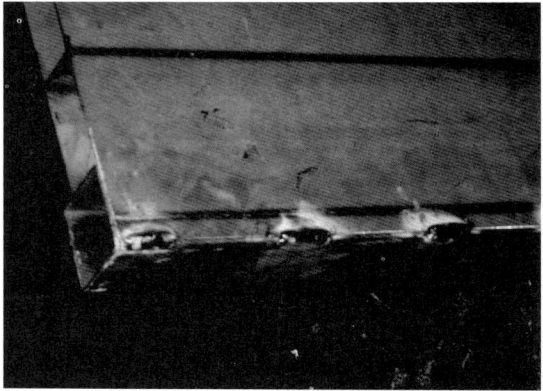

Figure 6: S-profile and square tube profile for the connection of steel sandwich panels to the conventional ship structure (IHC Holland Dredgers BV, 2005)

Panel fabrication

The sandwich panels are fabricated outside the yard by the supplier of the panels (I-core® panels for example) or fabricated at the yard, as is often the case for SPS. The dimensions of the supplied sandwich panels depend on the maximum allowable weight and dimensions for transport by truck, rail of boat of the sandwich panels.

If a deck or bulkhead structure only consists of a set of coupled sandwich panels, the sandwich panels will be directly integrated in the ship section in the section hall after delivery. Optional coupling of a set of sandwich panels (in case of large sandwich panel area's) or connecting sandwich panels to conventional stiffened structures can be done in the panel hall. Before sandwich panels will enter the section hall all edges will be provided with the joint components. The arrangement of such elements is necessary for the integration of sandwich panels into the conventional ship sections and to increase the strength of the edges in case of collisions during handling and transport at the shipyard. The joint edges are preferably integrated by the supplier of the sandwich panels to reduce total production costs and to increase also the strength of edges in case of collisions during transport from supplier to the shipyard. Joints can be welded at the ship yard using traditional welding methods, like submerged arc or gas metal arc welding in case of the application of metal sandwich panels.

The connection of the few girders and stiffeners to the sandwich panels will be done in the panel hall (Figure 7). To decrease the welding work the weld connection between sandwich panel and girder can be intermittent depending on the location in the ship structure.

Figure 7: Installation of girders onto steel sandwich (I-core®) panels (Jos L. Meyer GmbH)

Preferably the arrangement of openings, holes, the strengthening of holes or openings or providing pipe sockets in bulkheads will be done in the panel hall (Figure 7). Strengthening of the holes and openings is necessary when these holes or openings will weaken the strength of the panel. For example when the internal bulkheads of an I-core® sandwich panel will be cut through, a pipe ring has to be provided and welded into the hole (Figure 8).

Figure 8: plasma cut hole in a steel sandwich panel reinforced with a pipe ring (IHC Holland Dredgers BV, 2005)

In the case of all-metal sandwich panels an owner or classification society can require pressure test to check the water or gas tightness or the panels. Pressure tests should preferably be done during panel building.

Section building

The reduction in worked hours for the application of sandwich panels in ship sections decreases time that the floor area is required. When there is a shortage of free section hall floor this will be an advantage because the floor will be available earlier for other sections.

Vacuum clamps instead of hoisting clamps for transport of the panels can be used for handling and transport of the panels to minimize the risk of damage to the thin skin plates of the panels due to local hoisting loads. The use of vacuum clamps is possible because of the relative flat surface of sandwich panels. For hoisting complete sandwich panel it is possible to use normal hoisting brackets. Like with the conventional sections the panels have to be connected to those parts of the structure that can withstand the hoisting forces. Possible locations are reinforced edges of sandwich panels (Figure 6) or the connection of decks and bulkheads.

Hull assembly

To take into account misalignments (of conventional stiffened panels due to weld shrinkage) some adjustment in three directions should be possible to integrate sandwich panels. Every steel structure will deform when large thermal differences occur within the structure. This means that production methods like welding and flame cutting will deform the structure. Although this is a well known phenomenon it is very difficult to perform these activities without any unpredicted deformations.

Sandwich panels require far less welding then conventional panels which will decrease the shrinkage due to welding. On top of that the connection method using the square tubes will allow some size adjustment making the panels fit even better. When it is necessary to make extra cut-outs it is possible to cut the panels with a saw which will eliminate heat deformations.

On-site outfitting

Rework is always mentioned as being a big problem for the application of sandwich panels. It is generally agreed upon at a shipyard, that it is not possible to work on sandwich panels after installation, which is a misunderstanding. It is almost always possible to make extra penetrations in a sandwich panel and always possible to weld extra parts on a sandwich panel. But making big penetrations will be more expensive if they will have to be added during section building (or even later). For penetrations there are solutions:

Pipe clamps have to be welded onto the stiffeners of a conventional panel. On steel sandwich panels it is allowed to weld the pipe clamps directly on skin plates of the panel (at the position of internal bulkheads, Figure 9). It is therefore possible to route the pipe without aligning it to weld the clamps on specific locations. The penetrations on the other hand have to be made as described in the previous paragraph. The freedom in placing pipe clamps will increase the possible routings which will be compromised by the choice of locations of holes. Making extra penetrations afterwards can be more work than with conventional panels. Preferably pipes pass through a panel at the given locations which will therefore limit the routing options. Sometimes depending on the specific location in the ship structure the (hollow) sandwich panels have to be pressure tested. Pipe routing is easier because of fewer obstructions due the decrease in amount of stiffeners for the application of sandwich panels.

During outfitting pipe clamps (previous paragraph), cable trays, insulation pins and handrails have to be attached to the sandwich panels. At Meyer Werft a special contract is made which has to be signed by all personnel and subcontractors that have to work on the I-core panels. It is stated that people should be aware of the thin plates and use the prescribed welding procedures, which will have to be built up. The subcontractors will have to supply their employees with the necessary welding equipment according to the contract.

Figure 9: handrail and pipe clamps attached to an I-core® sandwich panel (IHC Holland Dredgers BV)

The application of sandwich panels will not alter the kind of insulation but because of the flat panels and the significant reduction of stiffeners the amount of insulation work and material will decrease.

Focus during exploitation

By applying sandwich panels in the ship structure the ship owner should not be limited in the use of his ship. For dredging ships it is common to alter the location of dredging pipe lines and components, to install new types of dredging equipment, to increase the strength of specific foundations, to increase the hold volume by increasing the height of the coaming or even lengthening of the ship. Such modifications will affect the initial design of the sandwich application concerning the application area and possible outfitting (see previous paragraphs).

No general conclusion can be made about the complexity of modifications and repairs when comparing sandwich and conventional panel applications. The modification and repair of panel and panel joints is more difficult to design, but due to the smaller number of stiffeners compared to the conventional equivalent structural design the implementation of the modification or repair may be relatively easy.

Corrosion and wear of steel plates are particular important for the structural design of dredging ship, because dredging activities imply corrosion and wear of not only dredging pipes and components but also of plates and profiles in and directly outside the hopper (hold) of the ship. By applying sandwich panels with thin plates thicknesses corrosion and wear will have a greater impact on the residual strength when compared to conventional structures with bigger plate thicknesses. Thickness measurements should be done in an earlier stage during ship exploitation at locations with a lot of wear. The use of sandwich panels in wear and corrosive environments should be considered on a case by case basis.

First sandwich application

At the moment of writing this paper IHC Holland Dredgers B.V. has built its first sandwich application. I-core sandwich panels have been applied for the structure of a Switch Board Room (SBR) in the engine room of a 6000 m^3 TSHD (Figure 10).

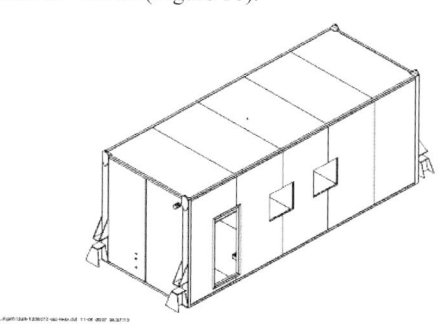

Figure 10: Structural design of a sandwich Switch Board Room

Preliminary calculations showed a reduction of total costs (material plus production) of 34%, a weight reduction of 20% and a reduction of the production throughput time equal to 63% (!). A risk estimate was made taking into account possible problems during design and production (for example drilling extra holes and pressure testing afterwards if required by the classification society). IHC decided to actual design and build the all-sandwich SBR, based on an estimation of the risk being smaller than the cost benefit.

Design

Design of the SBR was done in close cooperation with the Meyerwerft, as a supplier of I-core® sandwich panels. Static and dynamic calculations have been performed at IHC Dredgers, Meyerwerft has supplied results of a finite element analysis of the bottom panel of the SBR. Standard I-core panels have been applied with a shell and core thickness of respective 2.5 and 4.0 mm and a distance between shell and core plates of respective 40 and 120 mm. The sandwich panel geometry has been compared with a conventional panel structure with 6 mm shell plate and HP120x7 bulb profiles at a distance of 614 mm, being the minimum scantling design for this particular application.

From a comparison between standard I-core panel design and conventional design the following conclusions could be drawn:

The results of direct calculations showed a modulus of inertia and section modulus of the conventional stiffened panels (6 mm plate with (11x) HP120x7) being 3 respective 4 times as high as the sandwich panel, the shear area and weight per metre are also higher (15%). For example a 4 mm plate with bulb profiles HP80x6 (9x) would have the same strength and a 5 mm plate stiffened with HP80x6 (14x) would have a comparable stiffness. The weight benefit of the sandwich panel is thus being caused by a difference in strength between conventional and sandwich panel. Comparing the sandwich and conventional structure based on equal sectional modulus would lead to a sandwich design being cheaper (15%) but heavier (29%). However a conventional structural design with 4 mm plate thickness and frame distance of 820 mm (9 stiffeners) is not workable during production and would lead to additional weight due to extra stiffeners to prevent large welding distortions of the thin plates. A plot of the stresses in the bottom panel of the SBR is presented in Figure 11.

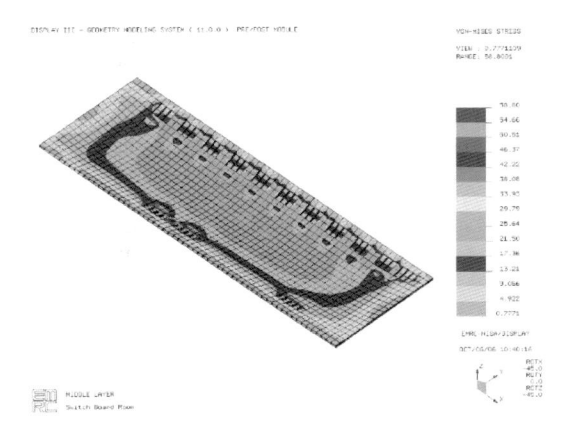

Figure 11: a plot of the maximum Von Mises stresses in the sandwich panel (Jos L. Meyer GmbH, 2006) for a distributed load

The vibration behavior of the SBR has been analyzed based on direct and finite element calculations. The results show a relative low natural frequency of the total sandwich panel, which fortunately falls in between operational frequencies of the engines, dredge pump and propeller for this specific sandwich application and design of the TSHD. The natural frequencies of the conventional panel (6 mm stiffened with HP120x7 profiles) are relative high and because of the high values, the possibility of resonance is lower compared to the sandwich panel (Figure 12). However the number of natural frequencies of the sandwich panel with risk of resonance (10 from 0-100 Hz) is low in comparison with the number of vibration modes (panel and local plate vibration modes) of the conventional panel (59 from 0-100 Hz), which makes it easier to prevent resonance by shifting the operational frequencies (rates) or by changing the stiffness of the structure (natural frequency).

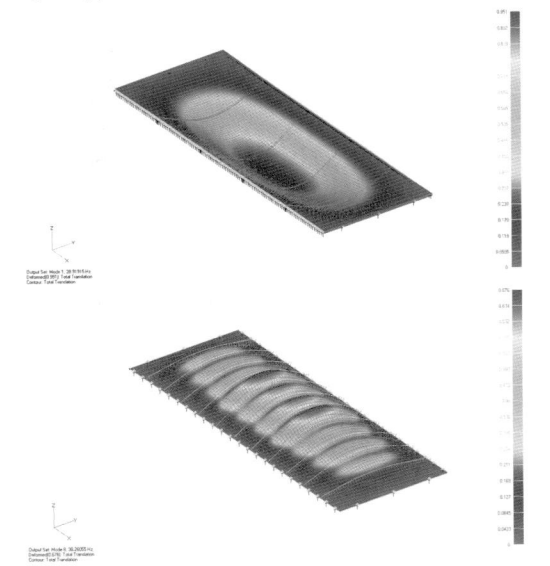

Figure 12: Normalized deformation plots of the lowest natural frequencies of sandwich (upper figure) and conventional panel (IHC Holland Dredgers BV, 2007)

Production

The fatigue strength of specific details of the sandwich structure is determined by the detailed geometrical and weld design, the stiffness and strength of both structural designs (sandwich and conventional). Fatigue calculations haven't been made for the structure of the SBR. However the fatigue life of the sandwich structure has been improved compared to the conventional design based on the number of (fatigue sensitive) parts like cut-outs and brackets (roughly 50% parts reduction).

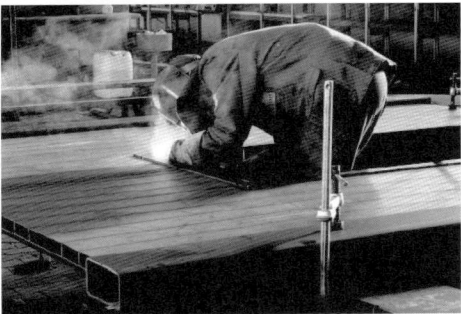

Figure 13: Grinding and conventional welding of connections / outfitting parts (Jos L. Meyer GmbH, 2006) of the sandwich walls of the SBR

All openings and holes were investigated during the detailed design of the SBR, indicated in the section drawing and sent to the Meyerwerft. Large opening for doors were strengthened with square tubes and holes for the penetration of electrical cables were strengthened with curved flat profiles both during production already of the sandwich panels (Figure 13). This was done because of the wide experience at the Meyerwerft with making and strengthening of cut-outs in steel sandwich panels.

The sandwich panels were transported by lorry to IHC Dredgers and hoisted from the trailer making use of vacuum clamps. First impression was the flat panel area compared to conventional welded steel structures. The box structure of the SBR was build up quite fast, in a couple of days, one of the short sides of the SBR was left open to install switch board and several other equipment including foundations, piping and electrical cabling before closing and final welding of the SBR structure (Figure 14). Insulation and coating of panel areas was relatively easy because of the flat panel areas. Overall response of the production people was very positive and questions were put up "why not use sandwich panels for our accommodation and engine room superstructures?"

Figure 14: SBR including insulation but without switch boards (IHC Holland Dredgers BV, 2007)

The hour report showed slightly more hours to place and weld the panels (15% more) compared to the preliminary cost calculations, but hours to produce the conventional structure were estimated to be far more compared to the preliminary estimations (50%) resulting in a total cost reduction by applying sandwich panels equal to 34% (equal to estimated value) and a reduction in throughput time of 71% (!).

Classification was done by Lloyds's Register and did not differ from normal classification procedures. At the moment of writing vibration and sound tests in the SBR are prepared for the nautical and dredging tests of the TSHD.

Future applications

The results of research at IHC Dredgers and the actual design and production of the sandwich switch board room has shown, that the application of steel sandwich panels in the ship structure of dredging ships can lead to significant overall cost reductions, weight reductions and a large reduction of the throughput time. IHC is ready for the production of a larger sandwich application, which would probably be a deckhouse or funnel structure. A sandwich deckhouse has already been engineered and a sandwich funnel structure has been produced at the Flensburger Schiffbau Gesellschaft with SPS sandwich panels as well as I-core® panels. The production of such sandwich applications could lead to a larger extent in application of sandwich panels in ship structures, because experience and confidence are build up.

Conclusions

Sandwich panels can be applied to a large extent in the ship structure of trailing suction hopper dredgers. Significant production cost and weight reductions as well a large reduction in the production throughput time are possible. Disadvantages of the application of sandwich panels are the relative weak panel joints and a limitation in freedom of structural design. The building of an all-sandwich Switch Board Room has shown significant cost and weight savings and has lead to enthusiasm at the engineering and production departments. IHC Holland Dredgers is convinced about the advantages of sandwich panels and has laid the foundation for future sandwich applications like a sandwich superstructure or funnel structure.

References

J.R. van der Zwaal (2005) "Feasibility study of an all-sandwich superstructure for hopper dredgers" (M.Sc. thesis Naval Architecture, Delft University Delft of Technology).

Mechanical Collapse Testing on Aluminum Stiffened Plate Structures for Marine Applications

Jeom Kee Paik[1], Celine Andrieu[2], and H. Paul Cojeen[3]

[1] Pusan National University, Korea, [2] Alcan Marine, France, [3] U.S. Coast Guard, USA

Abstract

The present paper is a summary of the R&D results obtained through SSC SR-1446 project sponsored by Ship Structure Committee together with Alcan Marine, France. It is recognized that the use of ultimate limit state (ULS) design method in addition to more conventional structural design standards will help make possible to move high speed vessels to open ocean transiting of very large high speed vessels, which is what the US Navy is certainly trying to do.

The aim of the project is to investigate the collapse characteristics of aluminum stiffened plate structures used for marine applications by mechanical testing, together with nonlinear FEA. Fabrication related initial imperfections significantly affect the ULS behavior, and thus it is of vital importance to identify the features of initial imperfections prior to ULS computations. In the present study, statistical database of fabrication related initial imperfections on welded aluminum stiffened plate structures is also developed. The database and insights developed will be very useful for design and building of welded aluminum high-speed ocean-going vessel structures.

Keywords

Aluminum stiffened plate structures; High-speed ocean-going vessels; Ultimate limit state design; Mechanical collapse testing; Fabrication related initial imperfections; Nonlinear finite element analysis.

Introduction

The use of high strength aluminum alloys in shipbuilding provides many benefits but also presents many challenges. The benefits of using aluminum versus steel include lighter weight, which helps increase cargo capacity and/or reduce power requirements, excellent corrosion resistance and low maintenance. Challenges include reduced stiffness causing greater sensitivity to deformation, buckling, and plastic collapse and different welding practices.

The benefits noted above are now well recognized, particularly for the design and construction of war ships, littoral surface crafts, and littoral combat ships as well as fast passenger ships. The size of such ships is increasing, causing various related design challenges compared to vessels with shorter length. In addition to aluminum alloys being less stiff than mild steel, no refined ultimate limit state (ULS) design methods involving local and overall ULS assessment exist unlike steel structures where the necessary information is plentiful. The use of ULS design method in addition to more conventional structural design standards will be able to help design and build very large ocean-going aluminum high speed vessel structures.

The present paper is a summary of the R&D results obtained through SSC SR-1446 project sponsored by Ship Structure Committee together with Alcan Marine, France. Buckling collapse characteristics of welded aluminum stiffened plate structures were investigated by mechanical testing on a total of 78 single- and multi-bay prototype structures, which are full scale equivalent to subs-structures of an 80m long aluminum high speed vessel structure. Welding induced initial imperfections significantly affect the ULS behavior, and it is thus of vital importance to identify the features of initial imperfections prior to the ULS computations and design. In this regard, the statistics of welding induced initial imperfections on the prototype structures are measured and analyzed. The buckling collapse testing is undertaken until and after the ULS is reached. Nonlinear FEA solutions are also obtained for the prototype structures. Based on the experimental and numerical results, closed-form ULS formulae are developed.

In the past, useful studies on mechanical collapse testing of welded aluminum structures have of course been undertaken. In the early 1980s, a series of 76 aluminum un-stiffened plate collapse tests were carried out by Mofflin (1983) and Mofflin & Dwight (1984) at the University of Cambridge, UK; and these are regarded as perhaps one of the largest and most relevant test programs for the collapse strength of aluminum plating (un-stiffened plates) until now. After TIG (tungsten inert gas) welding in the longitudinal direction and MIG (metal inert gas) welding in the transverse direction, weld induced initial distortions and residual stresses were measured and their influences on the plate collapse behavior were studied on two of the most common aluminum alloys used for the construction of high speed vessels, i.e., 5083 and 6082 alloys.

In the late 1980s, Clarke & Swan (1985) and Clarke (1987) at the Admiralty Research Establishment (ARE), UK carried out the buckling collapse testing on a total of five aluminum stiffened plate structures. This was one of the earliest collapse test programs to use ship-shaped aluminum stiffened plate structures using full-scale prototype models of all-welded construction with multiple frame bays. All material of the test structures was equivalent to 5083 aluminum alloy.

Over a decade after the ARE tests, several collapse test programs on aluminum stiffened plate structures constructed by welding were carried out together with various surveys of weld induced initial imperfections. These include Hopperstad et al. (1998, 1999), Tanaka & Matsuoka (1997), Matsuoka et al. (1999), Zha et al. (2000), Zha & Moan (2001, 2003) and Aalberg et al. (2001). The material of most test structures was 5083 aluminum alloy for plating and 6082 aluminum alloy for stiffeners.

Except perhaps for those by Tanaka & Matsuoka (1997) and Matsuoka et al. (1999) which were full-scale prototype models with multiple frame bays, most of these test structures were small scale models composed of a single stiffener with attached plating or a thin-walled cruciform structure. Although the nature and extent of test structures were somewhat limited, these test results were still very useful in studying the statistics of weld induced initial imperfections as well as the compressive collapse strength characteristics themselves.

Even in light of the existing excellent research results on the weld induced initial imperfections and ultimate strength of aluminum structures noted above, more studies are certainly required, because a systematic survey of the initial imperfection and buckling collapse characteristics is very lacking for a variety of aluminum alloy types and structural dimensions typical of ship-shaped full-scale prototype structures considering the recent trends in the application of aluminum marine structures.

A significant motive for initiating the present research project was to contribute to resolving the issue noted above to a good degree, by developing relevant design database on fabrication related initial imperfections and ultimate strength of welded aluminum stiffened plate structures for marine applications.

Design and fabrication of test structures

Table 1 indicates the overall dimensions of prototype structures. A total of 78 prototype aluminum structures that are full-scale equivalent to sub-structures of an 80m long all aluminum high-speed vessel are considered. They are designed in terms of single and multi-bay stiffened plate structures as those shown in Fig.1.

While various methods for fabricating aluminum ship structures are today relevant, the present test program adopts the MIG welding technique, which is now one of the most popular methods of welding in aluminum ship construction.

Fig.1(a): One-bay prototype structure

Fig.1(b): Three-bay prototype structure

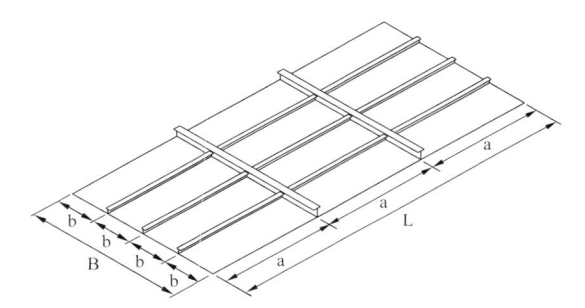

Fig.2: Nomenclature: A stiffened plate structure

To cover the possible diverse range of in-service aluminum marine structures representative of various collapse failure modes, a variety of structural dimensions, material types, plate thicknesses, stiffener types and stiffener web heights are considered as follows (see Fig.2 for the nomenclature):

- Panel width: B = 1000 mm;
- Stiffener spacing: b = 300 mm;
- Panel length: 1000 mm (one-bay structure), 1200 mm (one-bay structure), 3000 mm (three-bay structure of 1000 mm length);
- Material types: plate – 5083-H116 (rolled), 5383-H116 (rolled), stiffeners – 5083-H116 (rolled), 5383-H112 (extruded), 5383-H116 (rolled), 6082-T6 (extruded);

- Thickness: plate – 5 mm, 6 mm, 8 mm, stiffeners – 4 mm, 5 mm, 6 mm, 8 mm;
- Stiffener types: flat bar, built-up T-bar, extruded T-bar;
- Stiffener web height: 60 mm, 70 mm, 80 mm, 90 mm, 100 mm, 120 mm, 140 mm.

Table 2 indicates the minimum values of mechanical properties of aluminum alloys used for building the prototype structures.

Statistics of weld induced initial imperfections

When aluminum alloys are locally heated, the heated part will expand but because of adjacent cold part it will be subjected to compressive stress and distortion. When the heated part is cooled down, it will tend to locally shrink and thus now be subjected to a tensile stress. While the same happens in steel structures as well, it is the case that in aluminum structures the aluminum material in the HAZ is typically softened and subsequently the strength (yield stress) of the HAZ is generally reduced, which is termed a material softening phenomenon.

Figure 3 represents a profile of the weld induced initial distortions in a stiffened plate structure, where stiffeners distort in the direction of web and also sideways and plating deflects in the lateral direction. Due to welding, tensile residual stresses remain in the HAZ, and compressive residual stresses develop in the other areas to be in equilibrium of internal forces as shown in Fig.4. The distribution of residual stresses in plating which is welded along multiple stiffener lines or edges may differ from that in stiffener web itself as shown in Fig.5.

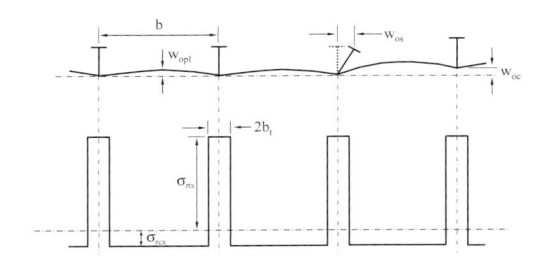

Fig.4: Weld induced initial distortions and residual stresses in a stiffened plate structure

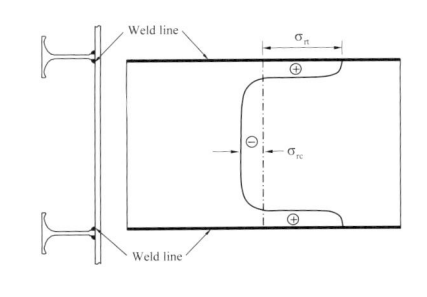

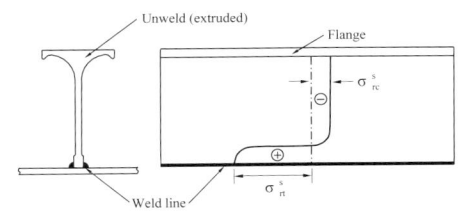

Fig.5: Schematics of the distribution of weld induced residual stresses in a plate welded at two edges, and in the stiffener web welded at one edge (left: plating, right: extruded stiffener web; +: tension, -: compression)

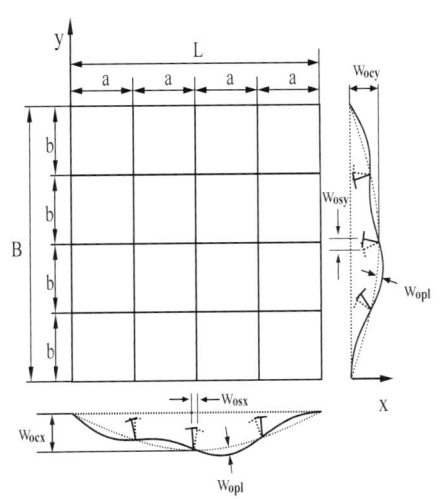

Fig.3: A profile of weld induced initial distortions in a stiffened plate structure

Figure 6 shows idealized schematics of softened regions in the HAZ. In the plating, since stiffeners are assumed to be welded in this case along all four edges, the softening zones develop along all edges as indicated. Its counterpart in the stiffener attached by welding is also shown. In terms of structural behavior in association with softening in the HAZ, the breadth of the softening zones together with the reduction of yield strength plays a primary role in strength characterization.

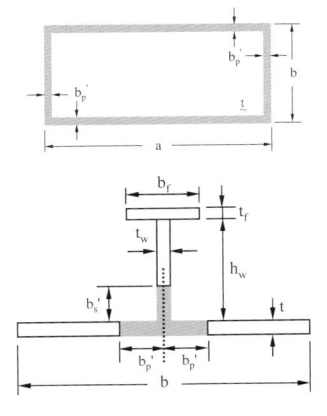

Fig.6: Idealized profiles of softening zones inside an aluminum plate welded at four edges, and its counterpart in the stiffener attachment to plating

While weld induced initial imperfections described above should be minimized by application of proper welding procedures and fabrication methods, it is nevertheless important to realize that their levels in specific cases can have a remarkable influence on the strength and stiffness of the structures. Hence their levels must be dealt with as parameters of influence in the analysis of load-carrying capacity. This means that such initial imperfection parameters must be properly determined in advance and accounted for in the design process including reliability analyses and code calibrations.

For aluminum stiffened plate structures constructed by welding, the following six types of initial imperfections will generally be pertinent, namely

- Initial distortion of plating between stiffeners;
- Column type initial distortion of stiffener;
- Sideways initial distortion of stiffener;
- Residual stresses of plating between stiffeners;
- Residual stresses of stiffener web;
- Softening in the HAZ in terms of reduction of the HAZ material yield stress and breadth of softened zone.

In the present study, the six types of initial imperfections noted above were measured for all the prototype structures (Paik et al. 2006, Paik 2007a). Figure 7 shows 3-dimensional configurations of selected test structures after welding, indicating initial distortions in terms of plate initial deflection, column type initial deflection of stiffeners, and sideways initial deflections of stiffeners. Figure 8 shows measurements of welding induced residual stresses in plating and stiffener web.

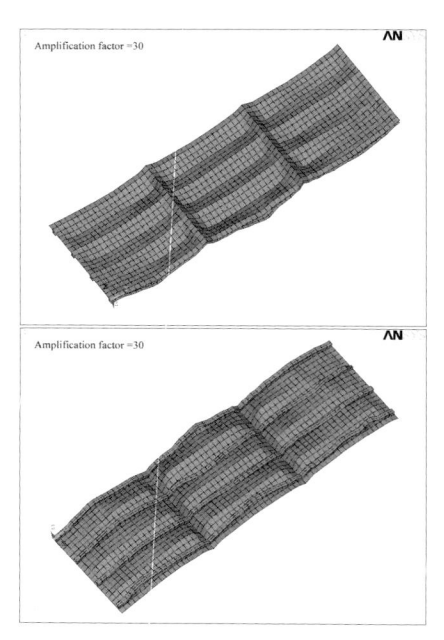

Fig.7(b): 3-dimensional displays of a selected prototype structure distorted after welding, for ID77 with amplification factor of 30

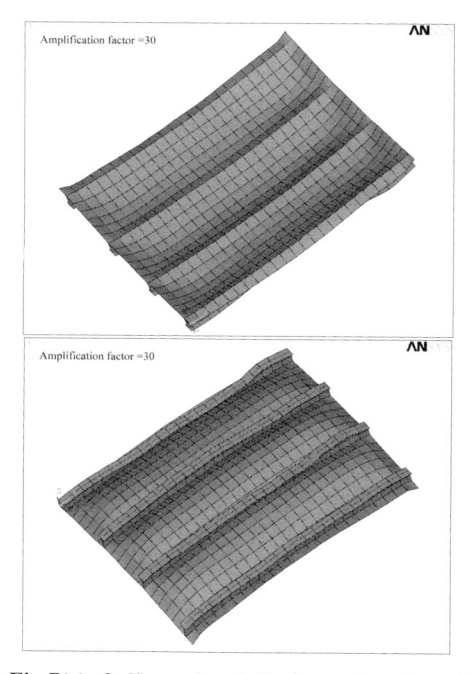

Fig.7(a): 3-dimensional displays of a selected prototype structure distorted after welding, for ID7 with amplification factor of 30

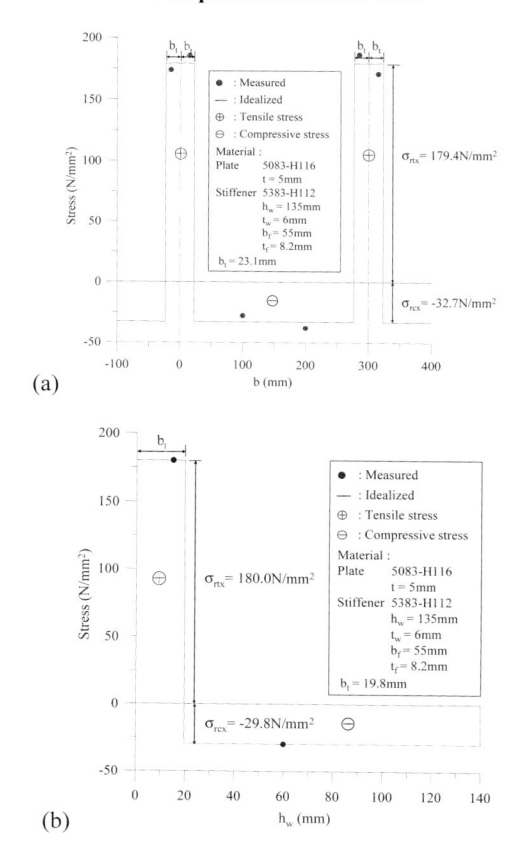

Fig.8: Residual stress distributions at (a) plating, (b) stiffener web for ID4 (5083-H116)

Based on the statistical analyses of the extensive initial imperfection measurements undertaken in the present study, the levels of initial imperfection parameters useful for design as well as reliability analyses and code calibrations can be suggested when 5% and below band data is applied for the slight level analysis and 95% and above band data is applied for the severe level analysis, as follows

Maximum initial distortion of plating:

$$w_{opl} = \begin{cases} 0.018\beta^2 t & \text{for slight level} \\ 0.096\beta^2 t & \text{for average level} \\ 0.252\beta^2 t & \text{for severe level} \end{cases} \quad (1)$$

where $\beta = \dfrac{b}{t}\sqrt{\dfrac{\sigma_Y}{E}}$ = plate slenderness ratio.

One half-wave initial distortion amplitude of plating:

$$w_{ol} = \begin{cases} 0.0059\beta^2 t & \text{for slight level} \\ 0.093\beta^2 t & \text{for average level} \\ 0.252\beta^2 t & \text{for severe level} \end{cases} \quad (2)$$

Localized initial distortion of plating:

$$w_{ob} = \begin{cases} 0.00033\beta^2 t \approx 0.0 & \text{for slight level} \\ 0.0101\beta^2 t & \text{for average level} \\ 0.0365\beta^2 t & \text{for severe level} \end{cases} \quad (3)$$

Buckling mode initial distortion of plating:

$$w_{om} = \begin{cases} 0.0 & \text{for slight level} \\ 0.00552\beta^2 t & \text{for average level} \\ 0.0468\beta^2 t & \text{for severe level} \end{cases} \quad (4)$$

Maximum column type initial distortion of stiffener:

$$w_{oc} = \begin{cases} 0.00016a & \text{for slight level} \\ 0.0018a & \text{for average level} \\ 0.0056a & \text{for severe level} \end{cases} \quad (5)$$

One half-wave column type initial distortion of stiffener:

$$w_{ol}^c = \begin{cases} 0.0 & \text{for slight level} \\ 0.00155a & \text{for average level} \\ 0.00525a & \text{for severe level} \end{cases} \quad (6)$$

Maximum sideways initial distortion of stiffener:

$$w_{os} = \begin{cases} 0.00019a & \text{for slight level} \\ 0.001a & \text{for average level} \\ 0.0024a & \text{for severe level} \end{cases} \quad (7)$$

One half-wave sideways initial distortion of stiffener:

$$w_{ol}^s = \begin{cases} 0.0 & \text{for slight level} \\ 0.000574a & \text{for average level} \\ 0.0018a & \text{for severe level} \end{cases} \quad (8)$$

Yield stress of the HAZ material for 5083-H116:

$$\dfrac{\sigma_{YHAZ}}{\sigma_Y} = \begin{cases} 0.906 & \text{for slight level} \\ 0.777 & \text{for average level} \\ 0.437 & \text{for severe level} \end{cases} \quad (9)$$

where $\sigma_Y = 215 \text{ N/mm}^2$.

Yield stress of the HAZ material for 5383-H116:

$$\dfrac{\sigma_{YHAZ}}{\sigma_Y} = \begin{cases} 0.820 & \text{for slight level} \\ 0.774 & \text{for average level} \\ 0.640 & \text{for severe level} \end{cases} \quad (10)$$

where $\sigma_Y = 220 \text{ N/mm}^2$.

Yield stress of the HAZ material for 5383-H112:

$$\dfrac{\sigma_{YHAZ}}{\sigma_Y} = 0.891 \text{ for average level} \quad (11)$$

where $\sigma_Y = 190 \text{ N/mm}^2$.

Yield stress of the HAZ material for 6082-T6:

$$\dfrac{\sigma_{YHAZ}}{\sigma_Y} = 0.703 \text{ for average level} \quad (12)$$

where $\sigma_Y = 240 \text{ N/mm}^2$.

Compressive residual stress at plating:

$$\sigma_{rcx} = \begin{cases} -0.110\sigma_{Yp} & \text{for slight level} \\ -0.161\sigma_{Yp} & \text{for average level} \\ -0.216\sigma_{Yp} & \text{for severe level} \end{cases} \quad (13)$$

Compressive residual stress at stiffener web:

$$\sigma_{rcx} = \begin{cases} -0.078\sigma_{Ys} & \text{for slight level} \\ -0.137\sigma_{Ys} & \text{for average level} \\ -0.195\sigma_{Ys} & \text{for severe level} \end{cases} \quad (14)$$

Width of the HAZ:

$$b_p' = b_s' = \begin{cases} 11.3\,\text{mm} & \text{for slight level} \\ 23.1\,\text{mm} & \text{for average level} \\ 29.9\,\text{mm} & \text{for severe level} \end{cases} \quad (15)$$

Collapse testing

Figure 9 shows the set-up of the physical collapse testing on the stiffened plate structures. The loaded edges are simply supported and the axial compressive loading is applied at the neutral axis of the panel cross section. A rigid circular bar at each side of loaded edges was inserted as shown in Fig.10 to reflect simply supported edge conditions along the loaded edges, i.e., by minimizing the rotational restraints.

Two types of unloaded edge condition are considered, namely free and simply support conditions, as shown in Figs.9(a) and 9(b) or 9(c), respectively. For the latter condition shown in Fig.9(b) or 9(c), a set of supporting jigs was attached to keep the unloaded edges straight. This condition was considered to reflect the behavior of stiffened panels in a continuous stiffened plate structure.

A total of 10 test structures with flat bar type stiffeners, namely ID40, 41, 42, 44, 45, 58, 59, 60, 62 and 63 were tested without the supporting jigs at unloaded edges, indicating a free edge condition. Figure 11 shows axial compressive loads versus shortening curves of selected test structures. It is seen from Fig.11 that the structures exhibit nonlinear behavior until and after the ultimate strength is reached. This is partly due to initial imperfections.

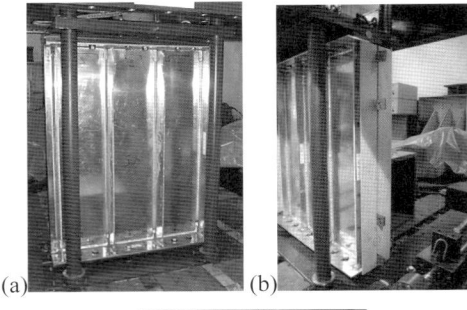

Fig.9: Test set-up for collapse testing on stiffened plate structures, (a) without supporting jigs at unloaded edges, (b), (c) with supporting jigs at unloaded edges to keep straight

Fig.10: Simply supported condition at loaded edges and axial compressive loading at the neutral axis of the panel cross section

Nonlinear finite element analysis

Nonlinear finite element analysis (FEA) using ANSYS (2006) was carried out on the test structures by a comparison with FEA and test results. Since some arguments in terms of selecting relevant FEA modeling techniques still remain, 8 types of FEA modeling are in the present study considered with varying the extent of analysis and the direction of column type initial deflection of stiffeners (with the abbreviations of CIP = compression in plate side, CIS = compression in stiffener side, SPM = stiffened panel model, PSC = plate-stiffener combination model), namely

- 1 bay SPM with initial deflection in CIP
- 1 bay SPM with initial deflection in CIS
- 2 bay SPM with initial deflection in CIP
- 2 bay SPM with initial deflection in CIS
- 1 bay PSC with initial deflection in CIP
- 1 bay PSC with initial deflection in CIS
- 2 bay PSC with initial deflection in CIP
- 2 bay PSC with initial deflection in CIS

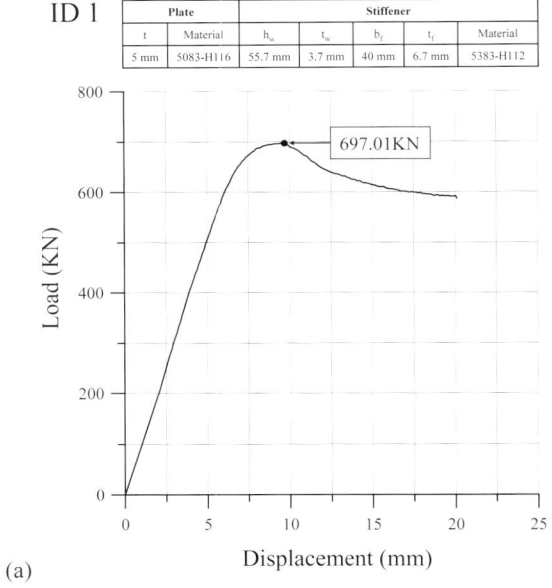

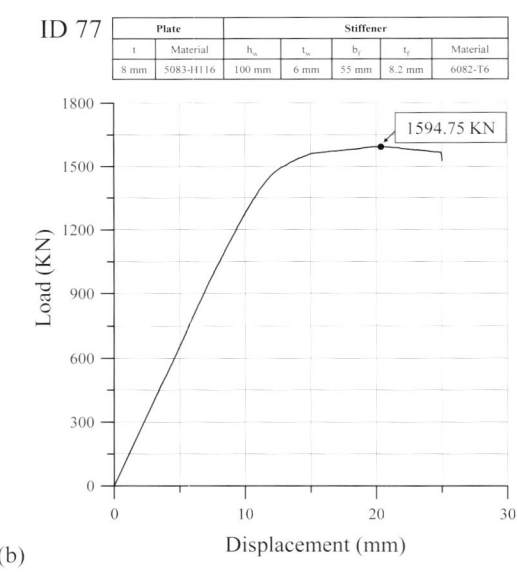

Fig.11: Axial compressive loads versus shortening curves for (a) ID1 and ID77, obtained by the experiment

In addition to the 8 types of modeling noted above, another 2 bay FE model was considered by reflecting the unloaded edges as being simply supported keeping them straight, namely

- 2 bay SPM with all (four) edges simply supported

While the test structures are primarily 1 bay system, i.e., considering the longitudinally stiffened panels between two transverse frames, 2 bay system including transverse frames as shown in Fig.12 are also considered in the present FEA to reflect the continuity support condition along the transverse frames in a continuous plate structure.

All of the 1 bay models are analyzed by a load control, while the 2 bay models are loaded by a displacement control, because of easier handling for the load application with regard to the neutral axis at the panel cross section.

After some convergence studies, the FE mesh size adopted has one plate-shell element representing the HAZ at plating and at the stiffener web. Ten plate-shell elements represent the plating between stiffeners and six elements model stiffener web, including the elements in the HAZ.

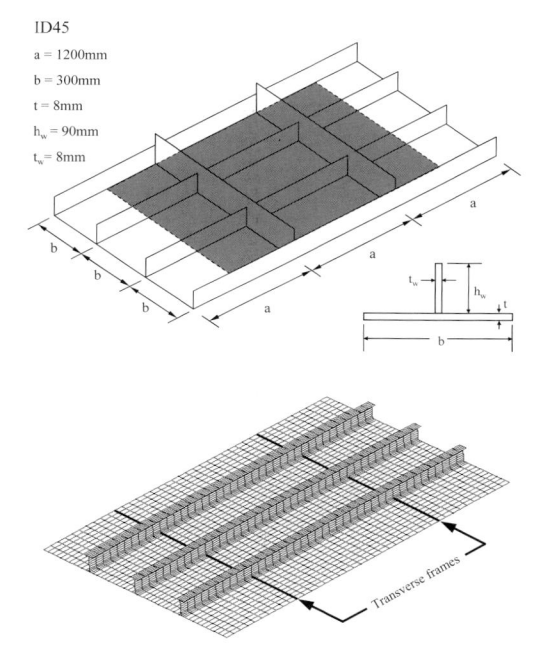

ID45
a = 1200mm
b = 300mm
t = 8mm
h_w = 90mm
t_w = 8mm

Fig.12(a): The extent and structural modeling for the 2 bay stiffened panel model (SPM) FEA

Figure 13 compares FEA solutions obtained by the 9 types of FE modeling noted above together with test data for two selected test panels until and after the ULS is reached. It is to be noted in Fig.13 that all FEA except for No. 10 were undertaken considering that the unloaded edges are free as in the actual testing, while No.10 was considered that the unloaded edges (as well as the loaded edges) are simply supported keeping them straight.

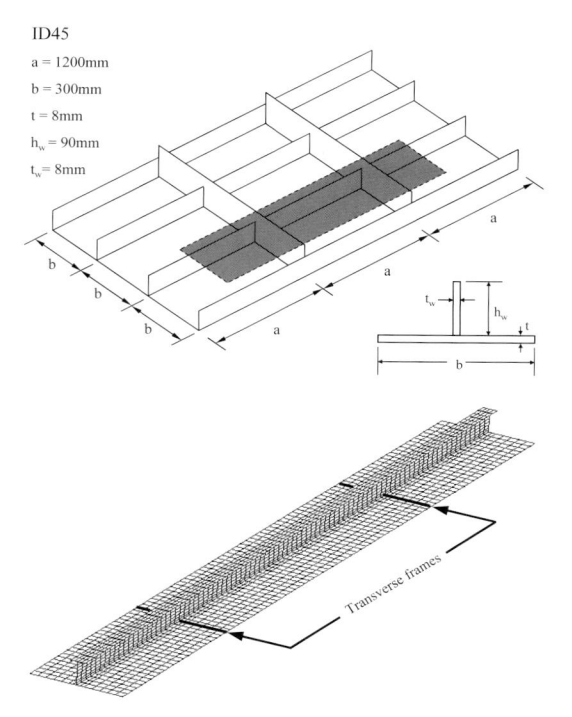

ID45
a = 1200mm
b = 300mm
t = 8mm
h_w = 90mm
t_w = 8mm

Fig.12(b): The extent and structural modeling for the 2 bay plate-stiffener combination (PSC) FEA

In the actual test, the panel ID 40 collapsed by column type collapse (Mode III) and ID 63 collapsed by stiffener tripping (Mode V). As would be expected, it is evident that the direction of column type initial deflection of stiffener significantly affects the FE solutions.

It is also seen that the 2 bay FEA always gives a larger ULS than 1 bay FEA. This is because the 2 bay FEA involves the rotational restraint effects along the transverse frames in the continuous plate structures.

It is to be noted that the different FE modeling approaches give quite different solutions. It is of vital importance to correctly reflect all of the influential parameters in the FE modeling in this regard. It is important to realize that the direction of column type initial deflections of stiffeners, among other factors may significantly affect the ultimate strength behavior when the magnitude of initial deflections is substantially large.

Also, it is evident that the model type or extent taken for the FE analysis must be determined carefully, while the real material stress-strain relationship rather than the elastic-perfectly plastic material approximation must always be employed unlike the ULS assessment of steel structures. Since softening in the HAZ plays a significant role on the welded aluminum plate structures, it must be carefully dealt with as well.

(a) 5083 panel

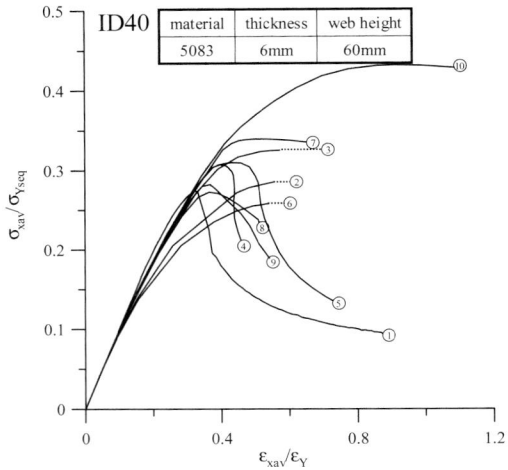

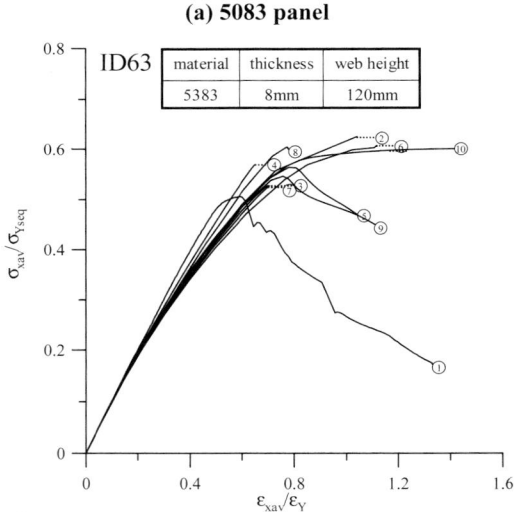

① Experiment, collapse mode III (CIP)
② 1 bay FEA(SPM), collapse mode III (CIP), column type initial deflection with CIP
③ 1 bay FEA(SPM), collapse mode III (CIP), column type initial deflection with CIS
④ 2 bay FEA(SPM), collapse mode III (CIP), column type initial deflection with CIP
⑤ 2 bay FEA(SPM), collapse mode V (CIS), column type initial deflection with CIS
⑥ 1 bay FEA(PSC), collapse mode III (CIP), column type initial deflection with CIP
⑦ 1 bay FEA(PSC), collapse mode III (CIP), column type initial deflection with CIS
⑧ 2 bay FEA(PSC), collapse mode III (CIP), column type initial deflection with CIP
⑨ 2 bay FEA(PSC), collapse mode V (CIS), column type initial deflection with CIS
⑩ 2 bay FEA(SPM), collapse mode III (CIP), column type initial deflection with CIP
(All edges simply supported keeping them straight)
Note: CIP = compression in plate side, CIS = compression in stiffener side

(b) 5383 panel

① Experiment, collapse mode V (CIS)
② 1 bay FEA(SPM), collapse mode III (CIP), column type initial deflection with CIP
③ 1 bay FEA(SPM), collapse mode V (CIS), column type initial deflection with CIS
④ 2 bay FEA(SPM), collapse mode III (CIP), column type initial deflection with CIP
⑤ 2 bay FEA(SPM), collapse mode V (CIS), column type initial deflection with CIS
⑥ 1 bay FEA(PSC), collapse mode III (CIP), column type initial deflection with CIP
⑦ 1 bay FEA(PSC), collapse mode V (CIS), column type initial deflection with CIS
⑧ 2 bay FEA(PSC), collapse mode III (CIP), column type initial deflection with CIP
⑨ 2 bay FEA(PSC), collapse mode V (CIS), column type initial deflection with CIS
⑩ 2 bay FEA(SPM), collapse mode V (CIS), column type initial deflection with CIS
(All edges simply supported keeping them straight)
Note: CIP = compression in plate side, CIS = compression in stiffener side

Fig.13: Comparison of FEA solutions as those obtained by 9 types of FE modeling together with test data for (a) a 5083 panel, (b) a 5383 panel

These aspects definitely make the aluminum panel ULS evaluation works cumbersome. In this regard, the present study adopts the following four types of FEA models for the test structures, namely

- 1 bay PSC model in CIP
- 1 bay PSC model in CIS
- 2 bay PSC model in CIP
- 2 bay PSC model in CIS

It is assumed that the material follows the elastic-perfectly plastic behavior neglecting strain-hardening effect. An 'average level' of initial imperfections including initial distortions, welding residual stresses and HAZ softening as measured for the test structures is applied for the FEA.

The mechanical properties (e.g., elastic modulus, yield stress) of aluminum alloys used for the present FEA were defined from the minimum values of classification society rules rather than actual values obtained from the tensile coupon tests.

Summary of experimental and numerical results

Table 3 summarizes the ultimate strengths of test structures together with collapse modes obtained by the experiment and nonlinear FEA. Theoretically, six primary modes of stiffened panel collapse under predominantly axial compressive loads are considered, namely (Paik & Thayamballi 2003)

- Mode I: Overall collapse of plating and stiffeners as a unit;
- Mode II: Collapse under predominantly biaxial compression;
- Mode III: Beam-column type collapse;
- Mode IV: Local buckling of stiffener web;
- Mode V: Tripping of stiffener;
- Mode VI: Gross yielding.

It was observed that the panel collapse patterns were clearly different depending on the panel geometries. For the ratio of stiffener web height to web thickness is relatively large, the stiffened panel mostly collapsed by lateral torsional buckling or tripping (Mode V), while the beam-column type collapse (Mode III) took place for panels with a smaller web height. For some panels with high T-bars, local web buckling (Mode IV) tends to occur.

Also, from the numerical computations, it is observed that the 2-bay FEA models give greater ultimate strength values than the 1-bay FEA models because the effect of rotational restraints along the transverse frames is taken into account in the 2-bay FEA models.

Closed-form ULS formulae

In ship design, the hull girder strength of ships is often governed by the buckling collapse behavior of deck or bottom panels. Hence the calculation of the buckling collapse strength of stiffened panels in deck and bottom structures under axial compressive loads, which are a primary load component due to ship's hull girder actions, is an essential task.

Closed-form empirical ULS formulae for aluminum stiffened plate structures under axial compressive loads are derived by the regression analysis of experimental and numerical database obtained from the present study (Paik 2007b).

To cover a wider range of plate slenderness ratio and column slenderness ratio in the developed ULS formulae, some additional FEA were undertaken for stiffened plate structures with different plate slenderness ratio and column slenderness ratio from those of prototype structures tested in the present study.

When the continuous stiffened plate structure is modeled as an assembly of plate-stiffener combinations, it is recognized that the ultimate compressive strength of the representative plate-stiffener combination is expressible as follows (Paik & Thayamballi 1997, 2003)

$$\frac{\sigma_u}{\sigma_{Yeq}} = \left[C_1 + C_2\lambda^2 + C_3\beta^2 + C_4\lambda^2\beta^2 + C_5\lambda^4\right]^{-0.5} \le \frac{1}{\lambda^2} \quad (16)$$

where $C_1 \sim C_5$ = coefficients to be determined from database.

For steel stiffened plate structures with an average level of weld induced initial imperfections, Paik and Thayamballi (1997, 2003) determined the coefficients of Eq.(16) by the least square method based on the experimental database as follows

$$\frac{\sigma_u}{\sigma_{Yeq}} = \left[0.995 + 0.936\lambda^2 + 0.170\beta^2 + 0.188\lambda^2\beta^2 - 0.067\lambda^4\right]^{-0.5} \le \frac{1}{\lambda^2} \quad (17)$$

It is to be noted that σ_{Yeq}/λ^2 is the elastic buckling stress of a column member simply supported at both ends, and the ultimate strength of a column member should not be greater than the elastic buckling stress. Eq.(17) is useful for predicting the ultimate compressive strength of steel stiffened panels with Tee, angle or flat bars, the last type of stiffeners having relatively large column slenderness ratio, when an average level of initial imperfections is applied.

For aluminum stiffened plate structures, the use of a similar approach to steel stiffened plate structures was attempted but with different formulae for different types of stiffeners. We then suggest the following constants for aluminum stiffened plate structures with extruded or built-up T-bars when an average level of weld induced initial imperfections are applied, namely

$$\frac{\sigma_u}{\sigma_{Yeq}} = \left[1.318 + 2.759\lambda^2 + 0.185\beta^2 - 0.177\lambda^2\beta^2 + 1.003\lambda^4\right]^{-0.5} \le \frac{1}{\lambda^2} \quad (18)$$

Figure 14 checks the accuracy of Eq.(18) together with Eq.(17) for steel stiffened plate structures. The bias and COV of Eq.(18) are 1.032 and 0.101, respectively. On the other hand, the ultimate strength of aluminum stiffened plate structures with flat bars can be given as a smaller value of the following two formula solutions, when an average level of initial imperfections is applied, namely

$$\frac{\sigma_u}{\sigma_{Yeq}} = \text{Min.} \begin{cases} \left[2.500 - 0.588\lambda^2 + 0.084\beta^2 + 0.069\lambda^2\beta^2 + 1.217\lambda^4\right]^{-0.5} \le \frac{1}{\lambda^2} \\ \left[-16.297 + 18.776\lambda + 17.716\beta - 22.507\lambda\beta\right]^{-0.5} \end{cases} \quad (19)$$

Figure 15 checks the accuracy of Eq.(19) by a comparison with experimental and numerical results. Considering the uncertainty associated with initial imperfections and structural modeling techniques, among other factors, it is interesting to see the upper and lower limits of the panel ultimate strength with relevant deviations. Except for very thick panels with T-bars, i.e., with $\beta = 2.08$ and 2.10, all experimental and numerical data of the panel ultimate strength are located in the range of $\pm 20\%$ deviations.

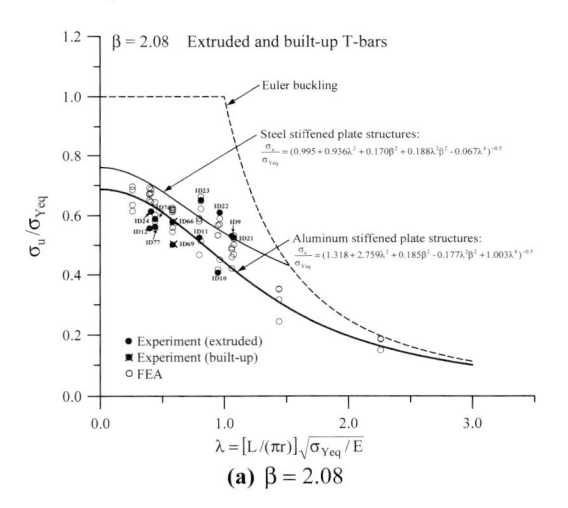

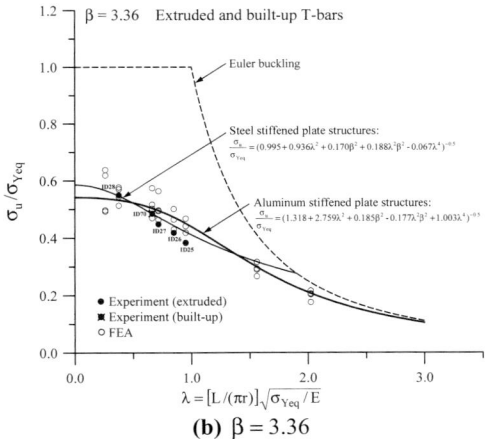

(a) $\beta = 2.08$

(b) $\beta = 3.36$

Fig.14: The accuracy of the closed-form empirical ULS formula, Eq.(18), for aluminum stiffened plate structures with T-bars, (a) $\beta = 2.08$, (b) $\beta = 3.36$

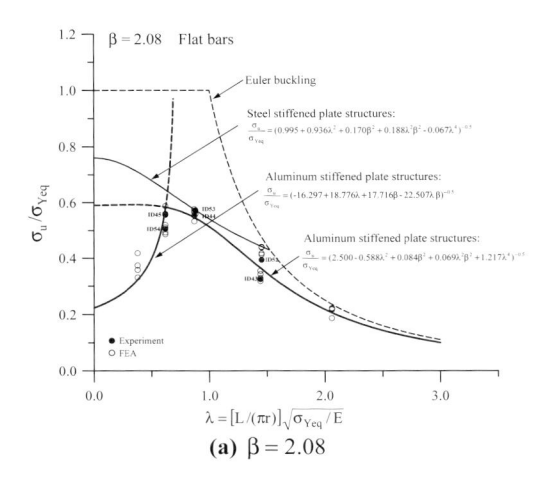

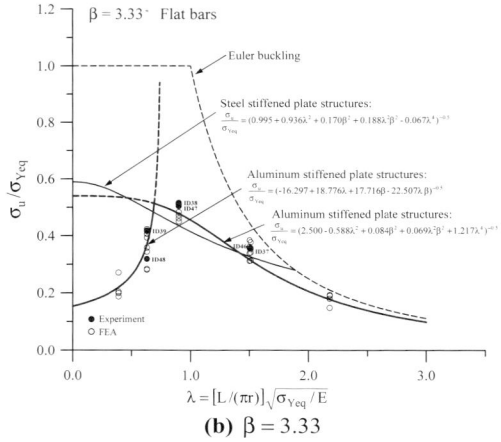

Fig.15 The accuracy of the closed-form empirical ULS formula, Eq.(19), for aluminum stiffened plate structures with flat bars, (a) $\beta = 2.08$**, (b)** $\beta = 3.33$

Concluding remarks

During the last decade, the application of aluminum alloys to marine structures such as high-speed vessels and littoral surface crafts has been rapidly increasing. To operate in increasingly harsher environments, the size of high-speed vessels has also grown. Subsequently, the structural design and building process to ensure the structural safety has become more complex in terms of limit state strength assessment and fabrication quality control among others.

In addition to more conventional structural design standards, the use of ULS design method will make possible to design and build very large aluminum high speed vessel structures that can operate in open ocean.

The aims of the present study have been to develop statistical database of fabrication related initial imperfections, and database of experimental and numerical results on the ultimate strength for aluminum stiffened plate structures, and also to derive closed-form empirical ULS formulae.

A total of 78 full-scale prototype aluminum structures, which are equivalent to sub-structures of an 80m long aluminum high speed vessel, were constructed by MIG welding and a total of 6 types of fabrication related initial imperfections, which govern the load-carrying capacity were measured.

By statistical analyses of initial imperfection measurements, three different levels (i.e., slight, average and severe levels) of each of the six type initial imperfection parameters were determined which can be used as reference levels of initial imperfections in ultimate limit strength assessment in association with reliability analyses and code calibrations for welded aluminum marine structures.

Buckling collapse testing on the prototype structures was undertaken. The load-axial displacement curves were obtained until and after the ultimate strength is reached. Nonlinear elastic-plastic large deflection finite element analyses were performed for the prototype structures. The ultimate strength characteristics of the structures together with collapse modes were investigated in terms of plate slenderness ratio and column slenderness ratio as well as initial imperfections.

Closed-form empirical ULS formulas for aluminum stiffened plate structures were developed by the regression analysis of experimental and numerical ultimate strength database obtained from the present study.

It is believed and hoped that the database and insights developed from the present study will be very useful for ultimate limit state design and strength assessment of aluminum stiffened plate structures which are used for building very large high speed ships such as passenger ships, war ships, littoral surface or combat ships.

Acknowledgements

The present study was undertaken at the Ship and Offshore Structural Mechanics Laboratory (SSML), Pusan National University, Korea, which is a National Research Laboratory funded by the Korea Science and Engineering Foundation (Grant No. ROA-2006-000-10239-0). The authors are pleased to acknowledge the support of Ship Structure Committee, USA, Alcan Marine, France, and Hanjin Heavy Industries & Construction Company, Korea.

References

Aalberg, A., Langseth, M. and Larsen, P.K. (2001). Stiffened aluminum panels subjected to axial compression. Thin-Walled Structures, Vol.39, pp.861-885.

Antoniou, A.C. (1980). On the maximum deflection of plating in newly built ships. Journal of Ship Research, Vol.24, No.1, pp.31-39

Antoniou, A.C., Lavidas, M. and Karvounis, G. (1984). On the shape of post-welding deformations of plate panels in newly built ships. Journal of Ship Research, Vol.28, No.1, pp.1-10

Bradfield, C.D. (1974). Analysis of measured distortions in steel box-girder bridges. Cambridge University Engineering Department, Report CUED/C-Struct/TR42.

Carlsen, C.A. and Czujko, J. (1978). The specification of postwelding distortion tolerances for stiffened plates in compression. The Structural Engineer, Vol.56A, No.5, pp.133-141

Czujko, J. and Kmiecik, M. (1975). Post welding distortions of ship shell plating. Ship Research Institute Report No.4-5, Technical University of Szczecin, Poland.

Czujko, J. (1980). Probabilistic estimation of load carrying capacity of axially compressed plates with random post-welding distortions. The Norwegian Institute of Technology, The University of Trondheim, Norway.

DNV (2003). Rules for ships / high speed, light craft and naval surface craft. Det Norske Veritas, Oslo, Norway

Ellis, L.G. (1977). A statistical appraisal of the measured deformations in several steel box girder bridge. Journal of Strain Analysis, Vol.12, No.2, pp.97-106.

EN 13195-1 (2002). Aluminum and aluminum alloys: wrought and cast products for marine applications (shipbuilding, marine and offshore). European Standard: French Standard, Association Francaise de Normalisation (AFNOR), Pasris.

Faulkner, D. (1975). A review of effective plating for use in the analysis of stiffened plating in bending and compression. Journal of Ship Research, Vol.19, No.1, pp.1-17

Hopperstad, O.S., Langseth, M. and Hanssen, L. (1998). Ultimate compressive strength of plate elements in aluminum: Correlation of finite element analyses and tests. Thin-Walled Structures, Vol. 29, pp.31-46.

Hopperstad, O.S., Langseth, M. and Tryland, T. (1999). Ultimate strength of aluminum alloy outstands in compression: experiments and simplified analyses. Thin-Walled Structures, Vol. 34, pp. 279-294.

Kmiecik, M (1970). The load carrying capacity of axially loaded longitudinally stiffened plates having initial deformation. Ship Research Institute Report No.R80, Technical University of Szczecin, Poland.

Kmiecik, M. (1971). Behavior of axially loaded simply supported long rectangular plates having initial deformations. SFI, Trondheim, Norway.

Kmiecik, M. (1981). Factors affecting the load-carrying capacity of plates. Ship Research Institute Report No.115, Technical University of Szczecin, Poland.

Kmiecik, M. (1986-1987). A review of fabrication distortion tolerances for ship plating in the light of the compressive strength of plates. Paper No.6, Lloyd's Register Technical Association, London.

Kmiecik, M., Jastrzebski, T. and Kuzniar, J. (1995). Statistics of ship plating distortions. Marine Structures, Vol.8, pp.119-132.

Kontoleon, M.J., Preftitsi, F.G. and Baniotopoulos, C.C. (2000). Butt-welded aluminum joints: a numerical study of the HAZ effect on the ultimate tension strength. The paramount role of joints into the reliable response of structures, Edited by C.C. Baniotopoulos and F. Wald, pp. 337-346.

Masubuchi, K. (1980). Analysis of welded structures – Residual stresses, distortion and their consequences. Pergamon Press, Oxford.

Matsuoka, K., Tanaka, Y. and Fujita, Y. (1998). Buckling strength of lightened aluminum hull structures. Proceedings of INALCO'98, International Conference on Aluminum Structural Design, Cambridge, UK, April 15-17.

Mazzolani, F.M. (1985). Aluminum alloy structures. Pitman Advanced Publishing Program, Boston.

Mofflin, D.S. (1983). Plate buckling in steel and aluminum. Ph.D. Thesis, University of Cambridge, UK.

Mofflin, D.S. and Dwight, J.B. (1984). Buckling of aluminum plates in compression. In: Behavior of Thin-Walled Structures, Elsevier, pp.399-427.

Paik, J.K., et al. (2006). The statistics of weld induced initial imperfections in aluminum stiffened plate structures for marine application. International Journal of Maritime Engineering, Vol.148, Part A4, pp.1-50.

Paik, J.K. (2007a). Characteristics of welding induced initial deflections in welded aluminum plates. Thin-Walled Structures, Vol.45, pp.493-501.

Paik, J.K. (2007b). Empirical formulations for predicting the ultimate compressive strength of welded aluminum stiffened panels. Thin-Walled Structures, Vol.45, pp.171-184.

Paik, J.K. and Thayamballi, A.K. (1997). An empirical formulation for predicting the ultimate compressive strength if stiffened panels. Proceedings of International Offshore and Polar Engineering Conference, Honolulu, Vol.IV, pp.328-338.

Paik, J.K. and Thayamballi, A.K. (2003). Ultimate limit state design of steel-plated structures. John Wiley & Sons, Chichester, UK.

Paik, J.K. and Thayamballi, A.K. (2007). Ship-shaped offshore installations: Design, building, and operation. Cambridge University Press, Cambridge, UK.

Paik, J.K., Thayamballi, A.K. and Lee, J.M. (2004). Effect of initial deflection shape on the ultimate strength behavior of welded steel plates under biaxial compressive loads. Journal of Ship Research, Vol.48, No.1, pp.45-60.

Paik, J.K. and Duran, A. (2004). Ultimate strength of aluminum plates and stiffened panels for marine applications. Marine Technology, Vol. 41, No 3, pp. 108-121.

Paik, J.K., Hughes, O.F., Hess, P.E. and Renaud, C. (2005). Ultimate limit state design technology for aluminum multi-hull ship structures. SNAME Transactions, Vol. 113, pp.270-305.

Raynaud, G.M. (1995). New aluminum products for high speed light crafts. Building High-speed Aluminum Marine Vessels in Victoria – A Feasibility Study, Business Victoria, Melbourne, Australia.

Smith, C.S. and Dow, R.S. (1984). Effects of localized imperfections on compressive strength of long rectangular plates. Journal of Constructional Steel Research, Vol.4, pp.51-76

Smith, C.S., Davidson, P.C., Chapman, J.C. and Dowling, P.J. (1988). Strength and stiffness of ships' plating under in-plane compression and tension, RINA Transactions, Vol. 130, pp. 277-296.

Somerville, W.L., Swan, J.W. and Clarke, J.D. (1977). Measurement of residual stresses and distortions in stiffened panels. Journal of Strain Analysis, Vol.12, No.2, pp.107-116.

Timoshenko, S.P. and Gere, J.M. (1961). Theory of elastic stability. McGraw-Hill, New York. Timoshenko, S.P. and Woinowsky-Krieger, S. (1981). Theory of plates and shells. McGraw-Hill, New York.

Tanaka, Y. and Matsuoka, K. (1997). Buckling strength of lightened aluminum hull structures. Proceedings of the 7th International Offshore and Polar Engineering Conference, Vol.4, Honolulu, pp.790-797.

Ueda, Y. and Yao, T. (1985). The influence of complex initial deflection modes on the behavior and ultimate strength of rectangular plates in compression. Journal of Constructional Steel Research, Vol.5, pp.265-302

Zha, Y., Moan, T. and Hanken, E. (2000). Experimental and numerical studies of torsional buckling of stiffener in aluminum panels. Proceedings of the 8th International Offshore and Polar Engineering Conference, Seattle, pp.249-255.

Zha, Y. and Moan, T. (2001). Ultimate strength of stiffened aluminum panels with predominantly torsional failure modes. Thin-Walled Structures, Vol.39, No.8, pp.631-648.

Zha, Y. and Moan, T. (2003). Experimental and numerical collapse prediction of flat bar stiffeners in aluminum panels. Journal of Structural Engineering, Vol.129, No.2, pp.160-168.

Table 1: Overall characteristics of the 78 prototype structures

One bay test plate structures (1200 mm × 1000 mm) with no replications:

ID	Plate t(mm)	Plate Alloy and temper	Stiffener Type	h_w(mm)	t_w(mm)	b_f(mm)	t_f(mm)	Alloy and temper
1	5	5083-H116	Extruded Tee	55.7	3.7	40	(6.7)	5383-H112
2	5	5083-H116	Extruded Tee	66.1	4	40	(5.7)	5383-H112
3	5	5083-H116	Extruded Tee	76.8	4	45	(5.6)	5383-H112
4	5	5083-H116	Extruded Tee	135	6	55	(8.2)	5383-H112
5	6	5083-H116	Extruded Tee	55.7	3.7	40	(6.7)	5383-H112
6	6	5083-H116	Extruded Tee	66.1	4	40	(5.7)	5383-H112
7	6	5083-H116	Extruded Tee	76.8	4	45	(5.6)	5383-H112
8	6	5083-H116	Extruded Tee	135	6	55	(8.2)	5383-H112
9	8	5083-H116	Extruded Tee	55.7	3.7	40	(6.7)	5383-H112
10	8	5083-H116	Extruded Tee	66.1	4	40	(5.7)	5383-H112
11	8	5083-H116	Extruded Tee	76.8	4	45	(5.6)	5383-H112
12	8	5083-H116	Extruded Tee	135	6	55	(8.2)	5383-H112
13	5	5083-H116	Extruded Tee	55.7	3.7	40	(6.7)	6082-T6
14	5	5083-H116	Extruded Tee	66.1	4	40	(5.7)	6082-T6
15	5	5083-H116	Extruded Tee	76.8	4	45	(5.6)	6082-T6
16	5	5083-H116	Extruded Tee	135	6	55	(8.2)	6082-T6
17	6	5083-H116	Extruded Tee	55.7	3.7	40	(6.7)	6082-T6
18	6	5083-H116	Extruded Tee	66.1	4	40	(5.7)	6082-T6
19	6	5083-H116	Extruded Tee	76.8	4	45	(5.6)	6082-T6
20	6	5083-H116	Extruded Tee	135	6	55	(8.2)	6082-T6
21	8	5083-H116	Extruded Tee	55.7	3.7	40	(6.7)	6082-T6
22	8	5083-H116	Extruded Tee	66.1	4	40	(5.7)	6082-T6
23	8	5083-H116	Extruded Tee	76.8	4	45	(5.6)	6082-T6
24	8	5083-H116	Extruded Tee	135	6	55	(8.2)	6082-T6
25	5	5383-H116	Extruded Tee	55.7	3.7	40	(6.7)	5383-H112

Table 1: Overall characteristics of the 78 prototype structures (continued)

ID	Plate t(mm)	Plate Alloy and temper	Stiffener Type	h_w(mm)	t_w(mm)	b_f(mm)	t_f(mm)	Alloy and temper
26	5	5383-H116	Extruded Tee	66.1	4	40	(5.7)	5383-H112
27	5	5383-H116	Extruded Tee	76.8	4	45	(5.6)	5383-H112
28	5	5383-H116	Extruded Tee	135	6	55	(8.2)	5383-H112
29	6	5383-H116	Extruded Tee	55.7	3.7	40	(6.7)	5383-H112
30	6	5383-H116	Extruded Tee	66.1	4	40	(5.7)	5383-H112
31	6	5383-H116	Extruded Tee	76.8	4	45	(5.6)	5383-H112
32	6	5383-H116	Extruded Tee	135	6	55	(8.2)	5383-H112
33	8	5383-H116	Extruded Tee	55.7	3.7	40	(6.7)	5383-H112
34	8	5383-H116	Extruded Tee	66.1	4	40	(5.7)	5383-H112
35	8	5383-H116	Extruded Tee	76.8	4	45	(5.6)	5383-H112
36	8	5383-H116	Extruded Tee	135	6	55	(8.2)	5383-H112
37	5	5083-H116	Flat	60	5	-	-	5083-H116
38	5	5083-H116	Flat	90	5	-	-	5083-H116
39	5	5083-H116	Flat	120	5	-	-	5083-H116
40	6	5083-H116	Flat	60	6	-	-	5083-H116
41	6	5083-H116	Flat	90	6	-	-	5083-H116
42	6	5083-H116	Flat	120	6	-	-	5083-H116
43	8	5083-H116	Flat	60	8	-	-	5083-H116
44	8	5083-H116	Flat	90	8	-	-	5083-H116
45	8	5083-H116	Flat	120	8	-	-	5083-H116
46	5	5083-H116	Flat	60	5	-	-	5383-H116
47	5	5083-H116	Flat	90	5	-	-	5383-H116
48	5	5083-H116	Flat	120	5	-	-	5383-H116
49	6	5083-H116	Flat	60	6	-	-	5383-H116
50	6	5083-H116	Flat	90	6	-	-	5383-H116
51	6	5083-H116	Flat	120	6	-	-	5383-H116
52	8	5083-H116	Flat	60	8	-	-	5383-H116
53	8	5083-H116	Flat	90	8	-	-	5383-H116
54	8	5083-H116	Flat	120	8	-	-	5383-H116
55	5	5383-H116	Flat	60	5	-	-	5383-H116
56	5	5383-H116	Flat	90	5	-	-	5383-H116
57	5	5383-H116	Flat	120	5	-	-	5383-H116
58	6	5383-H116	Flat	60	6	-	-	5383-H116
59	6	5383-H116	Flat	90	6	-	-	5383-H116
60	6	5383-H116	Flat	120	6	-	-	5383-H116
61	8	5383-H116	Flat	60	8	-	-	5383-H116
62	8	5383-H116	Flat	90	8	-	-	5383-H116
63	8	5383-H116	Flat	120	8	-	-	5383-H116

Table 1: Overall characteristics of the 78 prototype structures (continued)

ID	Plate		Stiffener					
	t(mm)	Alloy and temper	Type	h_w(mm)	t_w(mm)	b_f(mm)	t_f(mm)	Alloy and temper
64	5	5083-H116	Built-up Tee	80	5	60	5	5083-H116
65	6	5083-H116	Built-up Tee	60	5	60	5	5083-H116
66	8	5083-H116	Built-up Tee	100	5	60	5	5083-H116
67	5	5083-H116	Built-up Tee	80	5	60	5	5383-H116
68	6	5083-H116	Built-up Tee	60	5	60	5	5383-H116
69	8	5083-H116	Built-up Tee	100	5	60	5	5383-H116
70	5	5383-H116	Built-up Tee	80	5	60	5	5383-H116
71	6	5383-H116	Built-up Tee	60	5	60	5	5383-H116
72	8	5383-H116	Built-up Tee	100	5	60	5	5383-H116

One bay test plate structures (1000 mm × 1000 mm):

ID	Plate		Stiffener					
	t(mm)	Alloy and temper	Type	h_w(mm)	t_w(mm)	b_f(mm)	t_f(mm)	Alloy and temper
73	6	5083-H116	Extruded Tee	76.8	4	45	(5.6)	6082-T6
74	8	5083-H116	Extruded Tee	100	6	55	(8.2)	6082-T6
75	8	5383-H116	Extruded Tee	100	6	55	(8.2)	5383-H112

Three bay test plate structures (3000 mm × 1000 mm):

ID	Plate		Stiffener					
	t(mm)	Alloy and temper	Type	h_w(mm)	t_w(mm)	b_f(mm)	t_f(mm)	Alloy and temper
76	6	5083-H116	Extruded Tee	76.8	4	45	(5.6)	6082-T6
77	8	5083-H116	Extruded Tee	100	6	55	(8.2)	6082-T6
78	8	5383-H116	Extruded Tee	100	6	55	(8.2)	5383-H112

Notes: t = plate thickness, h_w = web height (excluding flange thickness), t_w = web thickness, b_f = flange width, t_f = flange thickness, t_f where given in brackets indicates the effective value of for an idealized plate-stiffener combination with the same moment of inertia as the actual case.

Table 2: Minimum values of mechanical properties of aluminum alloys used for the construction of prototype structures (DNV 2003)

Alloy and temper	Yield strength of base metal (N/mm^2)	Tensile strength of base metal (N/mm^2)	Elongation of base metal (%)	Type of production	Yield strength of welded material (N/mm^2)
5083-H116	215	305	10	Rolled	125
5383-H116	220	305	10	Rolled	145
5383-H112	190	310	13	Extruded	145
6082-T6	240	290	5	Extruded	100

Note: Elastic modulus E = 70,000 N/mm^2, Poisson's ratio ν = 0.33.

Table 3: Summary of the ultimate strengths of test structures together with collapse modes obtained by FEA and experiment

ID	Exp. σ_u/σ_{Yeq}	Exp. Mode	1 bay-CIP σ_u/σ_{Yeq}	1 bay-CIP Mode	1 bay-CIS σ_u/σ_{Yeq}	1 bay-CIS Mode	2 bay-CIS σ_u/σ_{Yeq}	2 bay-CIS Mode	2 bay-CIS σ_u/σ_{Yeq}	2 bay-CIS Mode
ID1	0.462	III	0.380	III	0.413	III	0.474	III	0.449	V
ID2	0.487	V	0.426	III	0.459	III	0.508	III	0.471	V
ID3	0.517	III,IV	0.460	III	0.490	III	0.517	III	0.492	V
ID4	0.546	IV,V	0.452	III	0.456	III	0.550	V	0.562	V
ID5	0.448	III	0.434	III	0.482	III	0.478	III	0.471	V
ID6	0.530	III	0.490	III	0.536	III	0.516	III	0.495	V
ID7	0.516	III	0.521	III	0.559	III	0.554	III	0.526	V
ID8	0.615	V	0.554	III	0.560	III	0.604	V	0.590	V
ID9	0.531	V	0.459	III	0.421	V	0.485	III	0.491	V
ID10	0.407	V	0.568	V	0.417	V	0.533	III	0.534	V
ID11	0.526	V	0.589	V	0.467	V	0.590	III	0.581	V
ID12	0.557	V	0.673	III	0.692	III	0.670	V	0.650	V
ID13	0.435	III	0.354	III	0.390	III	0.491	III	0.474	V
ID14	0.477	III	0.399	III	0.434	III	0.531	III	0.479	V
ID15	0.492	III,IV	0.433	III	0.464	III	0.602	III	0.543	V
ID16	0.596	III,IV	0.505	III	0.511	III	0.582	V	0.593	V
ID17	0.431	III	0.402	III	0.452	III	0.506	III	0.491	V
ID18	0.460	III	0.458	III	0.528	III	0.532	III	0.500	V
ID19	0.513	III,IV	0.487	III	0.529	III	0.602	III	0.556	V
ID20	0.627	III,IV	0.503	III	0.514	III	0.575	V	0.582	V
ID21	0.525	III	0.501	III	0.468	V	0.521	III	0.533	V
ID22	0.610	V	0.590	III	0.451	V	0.570	III	0.570	V
ID23	0.651	IV,V	0.622	III	0.514	V	0.662	III	0.647	V
ID24	0.613	III,IV	0.614	III	0.645	III	0.674	V	0.687	V
ID25	0.384	III	0.383	III	0.419	III	0.468	III	0.442	V
ID26	0.418	III	0.430	III	0.464	III	0.501	III	0.464	V
ID27	0.448	III,IV	0.464	III	0.494	III	0.564	III	0.497	V
ID28	0.549	III,IV	0.513	III	0.544	III	0.577	V	0.570	V
ID29	0.447	V	0.433	III	0.485	III	0.486	III	0.475	V
ID30	0.515	V	0.488	III	0.537	III	0.532	III	0.508	V
ID31	0.494	III,IV	0.525	III	0.564	III	0.564	III	0.543	V
ID32	0.548	III,IV	0.552	III	0.590	III	0.608	V	0.594	V
ID33	0.544	V	0.518	III	0.407	V	0.551	III	0.538	V
ID34	0.538	V	0.536	III	0.401	V	0.575	III	0.564	V
ID35	0.491	V	0.564	V	0.448	V	0.612	III	0.600	V
ID36	0.516	V	0.602	III	0.628	III	0.664	V	0.645	V
ID37	0.356	III	0.312	III	0.339	III	0.361	III	0.384	V
ID38	0.512	III	0.471	III	0.460	V	0.513	III	0.510	V
ID39	0.416	V	0.406	III	0.393	V	0.423	III	0.418	V
ID40	0.301	III	0.290	III	0.304	III	0.312	III	0.326	V
ID41	0.463	III	0.457	III	0.465	III	0.523	III	0.482	V
ID42	0.430	V	0.427	III	0.413	V	0.465	III	0.440	V

Table 3: Summary of the ultimate strengths of test structures together with collapse modes obtained by FEA and experiment (continued)

ID	Exp.	FEA 1 bay-CIP	1 bay-CIS	2 bay-CIS	2 bay-CIS

			FEA							
	σ_u/σ_{Yeq}	Mode	σ_u/σ_{Yeq}	Mode	σ_u/σ_{Yeq}	Mode	σ_u/σ_{Yeq}	Mode	σ_u/σ_{Yeq}	Mode
ID43	0.325	V	0.318	III	0.329	V	0.343	III	0.355	V
ID44	0.553	V	0.543	III	0.570	III	0.577	III	0.566	V
ID45	0.556	V	0.520	III	0.560	V	0.588	III	0.558	V
ID46	0.357	III	0.313	III	0.341	III	0.353	III	0.377	V
ID47	0.504	V	0.472	III	0.483	V	0.514	III	0.516	V
ID48	0.319	V	0.284	III	0.281	V	0.344	III	0.358	V
ID49	0.271	III	0.264	III	0.288	III	0.314	III	0.327	V
ID50	0.559	V	0.522	III	0.545	V	0.567	III	0.569	V
ID51	0.513	V	0.507	III	0.484	V	0.530	III	0.495	V
ID52	0.394	III	0.413	III	0.418	V	0.451	III	0.449	V
ID53	0.572	III	0.572	III	0.559	III	0.581	III	0.583	V
ID54	0.506	V	0.493	III	0.486	V	0.560	III	0.511	V
ID55	0.323	III	0.295	III	0.315	III	0.332	III	0.343	V
ID56	0.467	V	0.440	III	0.411	V	0.476	III	0.450	V
ID57	0.386	V	0.369	III	0.349	V	0.425	III	0.410	V
ID58	0.312	III	0.292	III	0.306	III	0.312	III	0.324	V
ID59	0.432	III	0.436	III	0.446	III	0.472	III	0.447	V
ID60	0.419	V	0.435	III	0.389	V	0.402	III	0.422	V
ID61	0.405	III	0.385	III	0.380	V	0.397	III	0.405	V
ID62	0.687	V	0.575	III	0.635	III	0.616	III	0.621	V
ID63	0.561	V	0.570	III	0.556	V	0.579	III	0.558	V
ID64	0.518	III,IV	0.465	III	0.500	III	0.567	III	0.522	V
ID65	0.508	III	0.468	III	0.500	III	0.510	III	0.486	V
ID66	0.579	V	0.612	III	0.545	V	0.612	III	0.619	V
ID67	0.526	III,IV	0.464	III	0.520	III	0.579	III	0.523	V
ID68	0.466	III,IV	0.467	III	0.523	III	0.510	III	0.487	V
ID69	0.501	V	0.617	III	0.560	V	0.625	III	0.621	V
ID70	0.485	III,IV	0.469	III	0.502	III	0.574	III	0.517	V
ID71	0.460	III	0.472	III	0.531	III	0.505	III	0.480	V
ID72	0.619	V	0.633	III	0.547	V	0.619	III	0.614	V
ID73	0.526	III	0.520	III	0.554	III	-	-	-	-
ID74	0.589	III,IV	0.603	III	0.644	III	-	-	-	-
ID75	0.592	III,IV	0.612	III	0.651	III	-	-	-	-
ID76	0.529	III	-	-	-	-	0.564	III	0.541	V
ID77	0.563	III,IV	-	-	-	-	0.581	III	0.557	V
ID78	0.607	III	-	-	-	-	0.643	III	0.620	V

Improving Fatigue Life for Aluminum Cruciform Joints by Weld Toe Grinding

Naiquan Ye, Torgeir Moan

Department of Marine Technology, Norwegian University of Science and Technology (NTNU)
Trondheim, Norway

Abstract

Fatigue improvement by weld toe grinding for aluminum welded joints has been investigated in this paper. Fatigue tests were performed for a number of as-welded and toe-ground non-load carrying cruciform joints. Finite element analyses were carried out to further study the influence of the variation of the main weld parameters such as the weld toe angle, weld toe radius and weld leg length on the stress concentration factors (SCF). Fatigue test results were presented by both a nominal stress based approach and a more refined structural stress based approach for the as-welded joints. Test results show that the weld toe grinding doubles the fatigue life compared to the as-welded joints. It is found that an optimal grinding depth is required to obtain a reasonable fatigue improvement factor.

Keywords

Fatigue; Aluminum; Weld; Toe grinding; Stress concentration.

Introduction

The fatigue life of components is reduced when parts are welded due the presence of weld defects and stress concentrations. Sometimes, often late in the design process or during operation, it is necessary to utilize an increased fatigue life of a particular joint detail by an improvement method. Significant increase in the fatigue life of welded joints has been reported by various kinds of local treatment methods in the steel industry.

Aluminum has been widely used in many areas such as high-speed light crafts (HSLC) in recent years. As the size of vessels becomes larger, fatigue has become a critical design criterion. The possibility of improving the fatigue life of welded joints in fatigue-prone regions is therefore desirable. Weld toe grinding is one of the successful methods in practice for aluminum welded joints (Haagensen et al. 1998; Haagensen and Maddox 2004).

Weld toe grinding technique is a widely accepted fatigue life improvement method due to the reliability and ease by which it can be performed. The main purpose of weld toe grinding is to reintroduce a fatigue initiation period by removing possible defects at the weld toe. The general view today is that a crack initiation period in as-welded steel joints is insignificant due to the existing weld defects (i.e., slag intrusions at the fusion line), which allow the crack growth to initiate very early in the fatigue life. However, the same is not absolutely agreed on for aluminum welded structures, where studies have indicated that the fatigue initiation period may account for a larger portion of the total fatigue life. For this reason, it is argued that the crack initiation period becomes more dominant for aluminum welds than for steel welds. This implies that the weld toe grinding method for aluminum weldments could have a lesser effect on the improvement of fatigue life compared to that of steel joints. In addition, weld toe grinding changes the local weld toe geometry, which alters the local stress concentration. It is therefore an open question whether the weld profile of aluminum and steel welds is comparable so that the modification of the weld notch by the grinding process has a comparable effect on the fatigue life. For example, Tveiten (1999) reported that little improvement was achieved by grinding the weld toe of an aluminum flat bar with a welded bracket while Haagensen and Maddox (2004) pointed out in a summary report that significant improvement could be achieved by using one or a combination of several improvement methods.

A test program was therefore established to investigate the effect of the toe grinding on the fatigue improvement of a non-load carrying cruciform welded joints. Finite element analyses were conducted to calculate different SCFs as well as study the influence of variation of weld parameters on the fatigue behavior of the joints.

Joints Specifications

Specimens and welds

A total umber of thirty-one (31) non-load carrying cruciform welded joints were fabricated, among which the weld toes of thirteen (13) specimens were post-treated by burr grinding while the rest were left in the as-welded condition. The specimens were made from a parent plate 206 mm wide and 12 mm thick. Fig. 1 shows a picture of the tested specimen as fabricated. Fig. 2(a) schematically illustrates the geometrical properties of the specimens. Possible fatigue cracking sites are marked by $C_1 - C_4$. Fig. 2(b) and Fig.2(c) show typical weld toe profiles of the as-welded and toe-ground joints. Some key weld parameters such as the weld toe angle θ, weld leg length λ and weld toe radius ρ are also shown in the same figure. These parameters have been reported to have great influence on the fatigue behavior of welded joints (Engesvik and Moan, 1983; Ye and Moan, 2001)

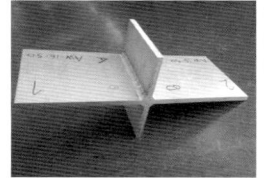

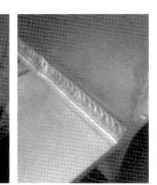

Specimen full view   As-welded   Toe-ground

Fig. 1: Picture of the test specimen

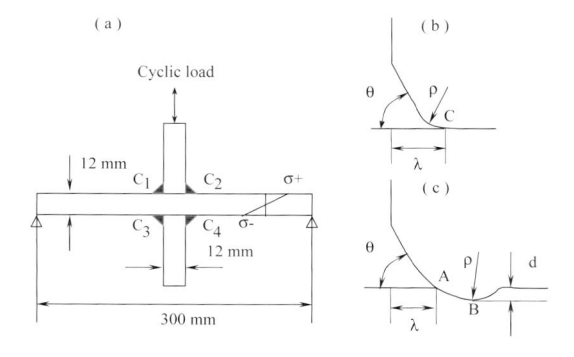

Fig. 2: (a) Geometrical properties; (b) As-welded toe profile; (c) Weld toe profile after grinding

These weld parameters were measured and summarized in Table 1. It is shown in the table that the mean weld toe radius of the toe-ground joints (3.2 mm) is nearly two and half times than that of as-welded (1.3 mm). The weld toe angle is increased by grinding; however, the weld leg length is reduced by the material removal at the weld toe. The mean grinding depth is about 0.8 mm into the thickness and this depth is the least requirement in the IIW documentation to assure satisfactory fatigue life improvement (Haagensen and Maddox, 2004).

Table 1: Measured main weld parameters, unit: ρ (mm), θ (deg.), λ (mm), d (mm), STDV=standard deviation

Parameters		Min.	Max.	Mean	STDV
ρ	As-welded	0.1	4.2	1.3	0.90
	Toe-ground	2.5	4.8	3.2	0.38
θ	As-welded	17.0	90.0	52.1	14.40
	Toe-ground	28.0	100.0	72.9	12.92
λ	As-welded	7.2	11.8	9.0	1.05
	Toe-ground	5.9	9.5	7.5	0.81
d	Toe-ground	0.2	1.6	0.8	0.28

Stress analysis

Stress at the weld toe is usually raised by the structural geometry as well as by the weld itself. The structural and notch stresses are correspondingly defined to capture stress raising factors relating to the structural and weld geometry. As a consequence, different fatigue assessment methods have been developed depending on the stress range used in designing SN curves. Fig. 3 schematically illustrates how these stresses are defined for a general joint detail.

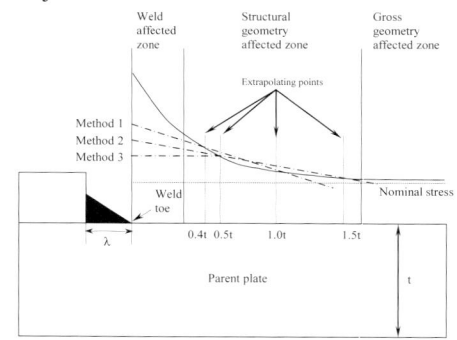

Fig. 3: Stress components near the weld toe

Nominal stress

The failure of the non-load carrying fillet welded cruciform joints occurred at the weld toe. The nominal stress range at the weld toe can be obtained either by simply using elastic beam theory or coarse finite element analysis. For complex joint details, difficulty may arise in calculating the nominal stress and care should be taken to use the calculated nominal stress in the fatigue analysis (Niemi et al., 2006).

For the three point bending load case as shown in Fig. 2(a) in this study, the nominal stress was simply obtained by a beam solution under bending, i.e., $\sigma = My/I$, where M, I, and y represent the bending moment, inertia moment, and the distance of the interested point to the neutral axis of the section, respectively. The difference between the analytical solution and the measured value by strain gauge was less than 2% for both the as-welded and toe-ground joints. The nominal stress applied to the test specimen was 37.7 MPa. It should be noted that the thickness reduction effect of the toe-ground joint was not taken into account while calculating the nominal stress, rather it was reflected in the SCFs.

Structural stress

The nominal stress only reflects the response of the joint to global forces. A traditional fatigue assessment uses this stress as a design stress by including all the other factors, such as the effect of the structural geometry and the weld geometry implicitly in the design of the SN curves. Some more refined fatigue assessment methods have been developed recently based on a deeper understanding of the influence of the structural geometry and weld on the stress at the fatigue cracking area, such as the weld toe. The structural stress range approach has recently been one of the most interesting methods by which structural stress is used to capture the stress raising factor due to structural geometry. However, the contribution of the weld to stress concentration is excluded by performing an extrapolation to the weld toe within the structural geometry affected zone, as shown in Fig. 3. Various methods have been proposed, however, a universal method that can be applied to all kinds of joint types is still needed. The structural SCF can be obtained either by strain gauge measurements or finite element analysis; the latter method was used in this study to calculate the stress concentration. A full model was built in the analysis. However, only a quarter portion of the full finite element models, as well as the sub-models, are shown in Fig. 4 for the sake of symmetry.

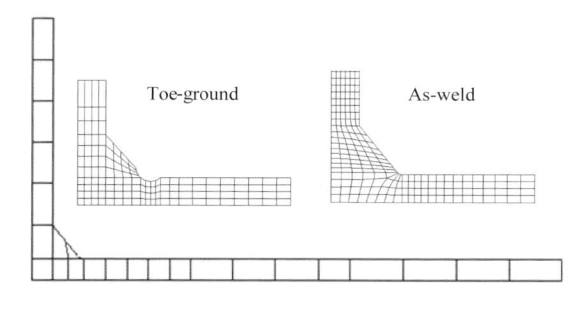

Fig. 4: Finite element model

The structural stress range approach is designed so that the stress raising effects due to the weld can be excluded from the structural SCF. It has been agreed based on experience that the influence of the weld on the stress concentration at the weld toe is confined to a short distance of 0.3-0.5t, i.e., 3.6-6 mm for the specimens studied herein. Three representative structural SCF calculation methods were investigated in this study for the as-welded specimens. Method 1 is a linear extrapolation method in which the stresses at 0.4t and 1.0t were used to perform the extrapolation. Niemi (1995) reported this method after investigating a gusset attachment joint and this is used as a standard method by IIW(2003 ,Hobbacher) . Method 2 is another linear extrapolation method used by DNV (1995, 2000) in which the points 0.5t and 1.5t were used. No extrapolation was required for Method 3, rather the stress value at 0.5t was taken as the structural stress. This method is used by Lloyd's Register. It is seen that in the aforementioned methods, the distance of the leading point is either 0.4t or 0.5t. However, this distance is dependent on the joint type, as reported by Tveiten and Moan (2000).

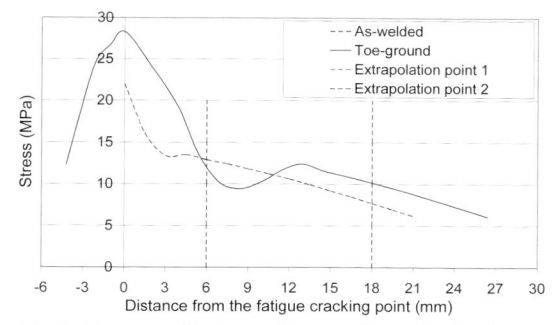

Fig. 5: Stress gradient near the cracking point for the as-welded and toe-ground joints

Fig. 5 shows typical stress distributions near a normal weld toe for the as-welded joint and a "new" toe after grinding based on mean weld parameters in Table 1. It should be noted that different origins were used for the illustration in order to compare the SCFs at the fatigue cracking point. For the as-welded joints, the origin point refers to C in Fig. 2(b), however, the origin refers to B for the toe ground joints, that is, the deepest point B as shown in Fig. 2(c).

The structural stress range approach is based on an assumption and observation that there exists a consistent stress gradient near the weld toe, as shown in Fig. 3. The stress gradient for the as-welded joint, as shown in Fig. 4, reveals the same pattern, therefore it was reasonable to apply the structural stress range approach. However, as shown in Fig. 5, the toe grinding caused redistribution of the stress adjacent to the cracking point B in Fig. 2(c). A consistently increasing stress gradient no longer appeared. This made the application of the structural stress range approach to the toe-ground joint more difficult or even impossible. For instance, a structural SCF of 1.02 was obtained if the stresses at 0.5t and 1.5t were used as the basis for a linear extrapolation. This value was unreasonably small compared to the as-welded cases, which is also in contrast to experience. For instance, a recent IIW documentation pointed out that grinding may introduce further stress concentration at the weld toeHaagensen) (2004 ,and Maddox. Therefore, the structural SCF appears unable to capture the real stress concentration at the fatigue cracking point.

Very little information regarding the influence of weld parameters on structural SCFs is available in the open literature. Moreover, no public literature exists related to the effect of weld parameters for a toe-ground joint when the structural stress range approach is used to present the fatigue test results.

The weld toe radius, weld leg length, and weld toe angle were modeled in the FEM. In each case, the minimum, mean, and maximum values of each of the parameters were chosen to investigate the influence of that parameter, while the mean values of the other parameters were utilized in the model. The results are shown in Tables 2, 3, and 4, respectively.

Table 2: Influence of toe radius on structural SCF

Extrapolation Method	As-welded ($\lambda=9.0$, $\theta=52.1$)		
	$\rho=0.1$	$\rho=1.3$	$\rho=4.2$
0.4t/1.0t	1.09	1.09	1.09
0.5t/1.5t	1.08	1.08	1.08
0.5t	1.07	1.07	1.07

Table 3: Influence of leg length radius on structural SCF

Extrapolation Method	As-welded ($\rho=1.3$, $\theta=52.1$)		
	$\lambda=7.2$	$\lambda=9.0$	$\lambda=11.8$
0.4t/1.0t	1.09	1.09	1.09
0.5t/1.5t	1.07	1.08	1.08
0.5t	1.06	1.07	1.06

Table 4: Influence of toe angle on structural SCF

Extrapolation Method	As-welded ($\rho=1.3$, $\lambda=9.0$)		
	$\theta=17.0$	$\theta=52.1$	$\theta=90.0$
0.4t/1.0t	1.09	1.09	1.09
0.5t/1.5t	1.08	1.08	1.08
0.5t	1.06	1.07	1.06

It is shown in Tables 2, 3, and 4 that, in general, the closer the distance of the leading point in the extrapolation methods to the weld toe, the higher the structural SCF. It can be easily understood that extrapolation points at a short distance from the weld toe may bring the notch effect into the extrapolation procedure and result in a higher stress value at the leading point. The distance necessary to avoid this from occurring has been further clarified by Tveiten and Moan (2000). Extrapolation points must fall within the structural geometry affected zone (Fig. 3) to obtain a reasonable structural SCF. A procedure to calibrate this structural geometry affected zone and the notch affected zone has also been proposed.

The change of weld parameters had little influence on the structural SCFs by all the methods used for the as-welded joint, and the use of different methods did not cause a significant change in the structural SCFs. Therefore, the effect of the weld parameters has been reasonably excluded in the calculation of the structural SCFs.

Notch stress concentration

The notch stress concentration factor included not only the structural geometry related stress raising factors, but also the stress raising factors due to the weld. This factor was assessed by direct finite element calculation by means of the sub-modeling technique (Fig. 4). The notch refers to the weld toe for the as-welded joints (point C in Fig. 2(b)) and the deepest point in the ground profile (point B in Fig. 2(c)). It should be pointed out that no reduction of thickness for the ground joints was applied in the calculation of the nominal stress because it had already been captured in the stresses obtained by the finite element analysis. The results are summarized in Tables 5, 6, and 7. 20-nodes solid elements were used with an element size of 1/16t for weld toe radius larger than 3 mm. However, smaller elements were used for small weld toe radius. The figure below shows the mesh detail for the weld toe radius $\rho=0.1$ mm. The element size at the weld toe is approximately 0.02 mm.

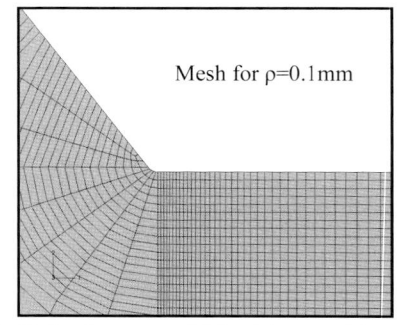

Fig. 6: Finite element model for 0.1 mm weld toe radius

Table 5: Influence of weld toe radius on the notch SCF

As-welded ($\lambda=9.0$, $\theta=52.1$)			Toe-ground ($\lambda=9.0$, $\theta=72.9$, $d=0.8$)		
$\rho=0.1$	$\rho=1.3$	$\rho=4.2$	$\rho=2.5$	$\rho=3.2$	$\rho=4.8$
3.78	1.83	1.32	2.01	1.91	1.82

Table 6: Influence of weld leg length on the notch SCF

As-welded ($\rho=1.3$, $\theta=52.1$)			Toe-ground ($\rho=3.2$, $\theta=72.9$, $d=0.8$)		
$\lambda=7.2$	$\lambda=9$	$\lambda=11.8$	$\lambda=5.9$	$\lambda=7.5$	$\lambda=9.5$
1.88	1.83	1.80	1.91	1.91	1.91

Table 7: Influence of weld toe angle on the notch SCF

As-welded ($\rho=1.3$, $\lambda=9.0$)			Toe-ground ($\rho=3.2$, $\lambda=7.5$, $d=0.8$)		
$\theta=17$	$\theta=52.1$	$\theta=90$	$\theta=28$	$\theta=72.9$	$\theta=100$
1.62	1.83	1.79	1.93	1.91	1.93

It was found, in principle, that notch SCF for the toe-ground joint was greater than those of the as-welded joint when the weld toe radius is larger than 1 mm.

The notch SCF can also be roughly estimated according to the equation $K = 1 + 0.21(\tan\theta)^{1/6}(t/\rho)^{1/2}$ for cruciform joints under bending, in which t represents the parent plate thickness while θ and ρ have the same meaning as indicated in Fig. 2(b, c), as suggested by Yung and Lawrence (1985). For instance, the notch SCF will be 3.38, 1.67 and 1.37 for weld toe radius $\rho=0.1$, 1.3 and 4.2 mm, respectively ($\lambda=9.0$ mm, $\theta=52.1$ degree). The FE results are close to the values obtained by the empirical equation.

Figs. 2 and 4 showed that a "notch" was introduced by grinding that caused more severe stress concentration compared to the as-welded joint. This is revealed in Fig. 5 as well. Moreover, it was also found that the change of weld parameters did not have as significant an influence on the notch SCFs as for the as-welded joint.

Table 5 shows that the increase of the weld toe radius for the toe-ground joint caused a reduction of the notch SCFs for the same reason as the influence of the weld toe radius on the structural SCFs. This also confirms the IIW requirements that the new weld toe radius should not be too small; otherwise a sharp discontinuity may appear accompanied by a high SCF (Haagensen and Maddox, 2004).

The change of the other two parameters, i.e. the weld leg length and weld toe angle had little influence on the notch SCFs for the toe-ground joint, as shown in Tables 6 and 7.

The effect of grinding depth on the notch SCF is further studied by keeping the weld leg length λ=9.0 mm, weld toe angle θ=72.9 degrees and weld toe radius ρ=3.2 mm. Fig. 6 accordingly shows that the notch SCF increases linearly proportional to the increase of the grinding depth.

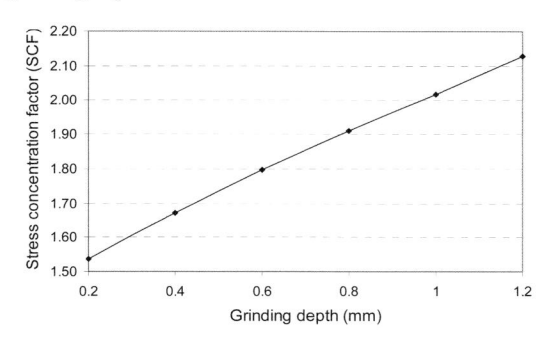

Fig. 7: Influence of grinding depth on notch SCF

Some material including the parent material and weld will be removed by performing the toe grinding. The purpose of the grinding is to take away the small defects introduced by the welding procedure so that the fatigue performance can be improved. However, the removal of the parent material cause a reduction of the thickness of the parent material so as to raise the stress level as it is shown in Fig. 6. Therefore, there exists an optimal grinding depth by which the defects are removed while the stress level is not raised unreasonably high.

Fatigue tests

Test program

Fig. 2(a) is an illustration of the test set-up. The specimens were mounted in a three-point bending test rig under a frequency of 12 Hz. In order to eliminate the compressive residual stress introduced by the welding procedure, a stress ratio of 0.44 was applied to ensure that only tensile stress may occur at C_1 and C_2. All tested joints were cracked from either of these two locations. The fatigue life as number of cycles was recorded when the specimen was fully cracked through the thickness of the plate.

Fatigue behavior of a structural component can be expressed by the equation, $\log N = \log A - m \log S$, in which N represents the fatigue life corresponding to a given stress range S, A is a constant depending on the joint features and load parameters, and m is a statistically obtained parameter. The fatigue strength is usually expressed in terms of the number of cycles at a given level of stress range and the fatigue life is referred to as the number of cycles at a specified stress range. A detail class number assigned to a particular joint type in a design code represents the stress range at the characteristic fatigue life of two million cycles.

Test data

The fatigue life in terms of the number of cycles was recorded when a full thickness crack developed. Eighteen (18) as-welded and thirteen (13) toe-ground specimens were tested and the test data are summarized in Table 8.

Table 8: Recorded fatigue life

No.	Number of cycles to failure	
	As-welded	Toe-Ground
1	930806	2423027
2	1042485	2830036
3	916920	1846428
4	1057019	1421794
5	1774631	2694688
6	1050289	3268021
7	923797	3609481
8	1348637	2765445
9	1051069	3108286
10	1150013	2520398
11	866263	1963157
12	1099022	2262469
13	1041857	2827378
14	1252033	-
15	1063280	-
16	789209	-
17	1202075	-
18	1582690	-
Mean	1119005	2580047
Stdv of logN	0.09	0.11

Fatigue analysis based on nominal stress

The detail classes for the investigated cruciform joints from different codes based on nominal stress are differed in different classifications or standards. The lowest detail class for a non-load carrying cruciform joint was 28, given by Eurocode 9 (1998) and the IIW (Hobbacher, 2003), however, a clear indication of as-welded condition is only specified by the IIW. The highest class, 36, is given by both the IIW and

Aluminum Association(1994) and toe-grinding is clearly indicated by the IIW. It should noted that the IIW is the only code in which the as-welded and toe-ground joints are clearly classified into two detail classes, 28 for as-welded joints, and 36 for ground joints; as a consequence, there is an improvement of approximately 29% in terms of stress range at a given number of cycles. In other words, by applying the above SN curve equation, the fatigue life in terms of cycles at a given stress range level for a toe-ground joint is about twice that of the as-welded joint. Therefore, the IIW SN curves, 28 and 36, were chosen in this study to compare the test data for the as-welded and toe-ground joints in Figs. 6 and 7. The nominal stress applied to the test specimen was 37.7 MPa as can be seen in those two figures.

It seems that that the tested data agreed quite well with the IIW SN curves. The fatigue strength of the as-welded and toe-ground joints was approximately 2.4% and 1.3% below the SN curves, 28 and 36, respectively. The grinding improved the fatigue strength by about 30% in terms of stress range, which was nearly equivalent to a doubling in fatigue life improvement in terms of the number of cycles. This occurred despite the fact that the notch SCF of the toe-ground joint was about 30% greater than the as-welded joint. The contribution of grinding in improving fatigue life is therefore primarily due to the removal of the defects. The grinding depth is therefore the decisive parameter in determining the effect of grinding. This is also reflected by the test data in Figs. 8 and 9 where a rather low fatigue life was recorded and the corresponding grinding depth was found to be the smallest one, i.e. 0.2 mm.

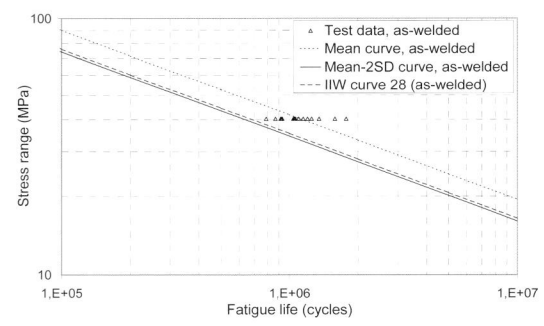

Fig. 8: Test data of as-welded specimens compared with IIW SN curve 28 based on nominal stress

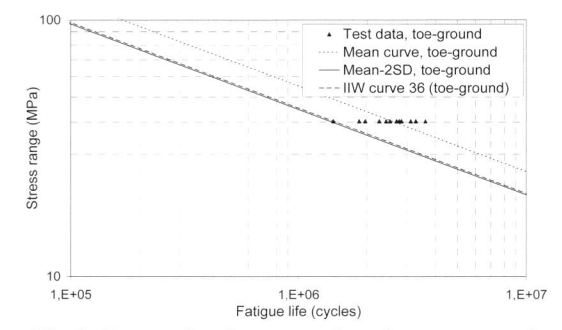

Fig. 9: Test results of toe-ground specimens compared with IIW SN curve 36 based on nominal stress

It should be mentioned that, as indicated in Fig. 2(c), the original weld toe disappeared after grinding and the fatigue cracking was found to be located at point B, which is the deepest point in the ground profile. The effect of the thickness reduction on the determination of the nominal stress was not taken into account when presenting the data against the nominal SN curves. This effect should have been embedded in the specified SN curves for the toe-ground joints. The grinding effect will tend to be more significantly conservative if the nominal stress is corrected by the thickness reduction, i.e., a higher nominal stress was used in the presentation of the test data.

It should also be noted that the standard deviations of logN for the as-welded and toe-ground joints were 0.09 and 0.11, which indicates that the grinding did not reduce the scatter of the test data. Instead, the scatter was slightly expanded. This was probably due to the scatter of the grinding depth, which was from 0.2-1.6 mm, as shown in Table 1. An insufficient grinding depth may cancel off the fatigue life improvement effect compared to those sufficiently ground specimens. As can be seen in Table 8, the lowest fatigue life (cycles to failure 1421794) of toe-ground specimen did not improve significantly compared to the mean fatigue life of the as-welded specimens (cycles to failure=1119005).

Fatigue analysis based on structural stress

Fatigue assessment based on structural stress range has been used in the design of steel tubular joints since the 1970s (HSE, 1996). The structural stress, $\sigma_{structural}=K_g \times \sigma_{nominal}$, is taken as the design stress, where K_g represents the structural SCF. However, the derivation of a universal structural SCF calculation method and consistent design SN curves are still needed for both steel and aluminum plate structures. Moreover, rather limited data for aluminum structures are available up to now.

Eurocode 9 (1998) issued six structural stress design SN curves. The choice of SN curve is dependent on the thickness of the stressed member of the structure, for instance, detail class 35 is proposed for structures with the thickness of a stressed member between 10 and 15 mm. However, no corresponding structural stress calculation process is specified in the code. A detail class of 40 has been accepted, to some extent, as a suitable design SN curve for butt and fillet welded aluminum joints of relatively thin plates (up to 6 mm) failing from the weld toe location ,Partanen and Niemi) (2001 ,Maddox ;1999. A thickness penalty factor was suggested by Niemi(1995) to further apply the detail class 40 to the structures with a thickness exceeding 6 mm. In the case of a 12 mm thickness, a modified detail class will be approximately 35. Tveiten et al. (2002) commented that the use of the penalty factor should be further investigated since the reduction in design fatigue strength would be unacceptably large once the large thickness appears. More description on the choice of a suitable structural stress design SN curve was summarized recently by Tveiten et al. (2002).

The test data of the as-welded specimens are presented against the Eurocode 9 SN curve 35 in Fig. 9. The structural SCFs correspond to the mean weld parameters. The as-welded joint falls quite below the SN curve 35 because the structural SCFs of the as-welded joint is low as shown in Table 2. It should be remembered that the application of the structural stress range approach to the toe-ground joint can bring uncertainties because there is no consistent stress gradient towards the fatigue cracking point.

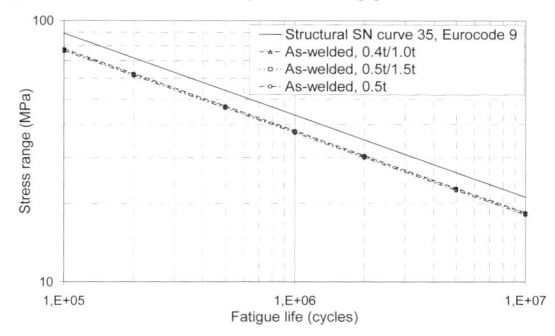

Fig. 10: Test results compared with Eurocode 9 SN curve 35 based on structural stress

Conclusions

The following conclusions can be drawn based on the stress analysis and fatigue tests, which corresponds very well to the IIW recommendation (Haagensen and Maddox, 2004): 1) the weld toe grinding significantly improved the fatigue life of the cruciform joint based on a nominal stress range approach and 2) a near doubling of the fatigue life was observed in terms of the number of cycles for the toe-ground joint.

The test data agreed quite well with the IIW nominal SN curve 28 for the as-welded joints and 36 for the toe ground joints.

The weld parameters had little influence on the structural SCFs for the as-welded joint.

The Eurocode structural SN curve, 35, was found to be non-conservative for the as-welded joints. The structural stress approach appears to be not applicable to toe-ground joints due to the stress redistribution caused by the new weld profile after grinding.

The notch SCFs based on FE analysis of the as-welded joints were generally below those of the toe-ground joints when the weld toe radius is larger than 1 mm, while the latter one had better fatigue performance than the former one. Therefore, the defects introduced by the welding procedure played a decisive role in determining the fatigue behavior of the welded joints. The removal of those defects by grinding significantly improved the fatigue life of the joints.

Larger weld toe radius caused a reduction in the notch SCFs for the toe-ground joints, while other parameters did not affect the value appreciably. It is also important to point out that the grinding depth should exceed a limit, for instance 0.8 mm, for most joints so that the defects can be removed with certainty and to achieve a reasonable fatigue life improvement. On the other hand, excessive grinding reduced the effective plate thickness and, hence, represents a stress raiser.

Acknowledgement

The authors appreciate the financial support of the DASS project that made the experimental study possible. Thanks are also extended to the engineers in the structural laboratory at the Marine Technology Center of NTNU, who contributed to the fatigue testing.

References

Cledwyn-Davies, DN (1954). "The Effect of Grinding on the Fatigue Strength of Steels." Institution of Mechanical Engineers, London.

DNV-Det Norske Veritas (2000). "Fatigue Strength Analysis of Offshore Steel Structures." Høvik, Norway.

DNV-Det Norske Veritas (1993). "Fatigue Assessment in Ship Structures." No 93-0432, Høvik, Norway.

DNV-Det Norske Veritas (1997). "Fatigue Analysis of High Speed and Light Craft." Classification Notes, CN30.9, Høvik, Norway.

ECCS (1992). "European Recommendations for Aluminium Alloy Structures Fatigue Design." First edition.

Engesvik, KM, Moan, T (1983). "Probabilistic Analysis of the Uncertainties in the Fatigue Capacity of Welded Joints." Eng. Frac. Mech., Vol 18, No 4, pp743-762.

Eurocode 9 (1998). "Design of Aluminium Structures-Part 2: Structures Susceptible to Fatigue." EC-ENV 1999-2, CEN, Brussels.

Fisher, JW, and Dexter, RJ (1993). "Weld Improvement and Repair for Fatigue Life Extension." OMAE-Vol. III, Material Engineering, pp 875-881.

Haagensen, P J (1994). "Effectiveness of Grinding and Peening Techniques for Fatigue Life Extension of Welded Joints." OMAE-Vol. III, Material Engineering, pp 121-127.

Haagensen, PJ, Statnikov, ES, and Lopez-Martinerz L (1998). "Introductory Fatigue Tests on Welded Joints in High Strength Steel and Aluminium Improved by Various Methods including Ultrasonic Impact Treatment (UIT)." Doc.IIW-XIII-1748-98.

Haagensen, PJ, and Maddox, SJ (2004). "Recommendations on Post Weld Improvement for Steel and Aluminium Structures." Doc.IIW-XIII-1815-00, Rev. 5.

Hobbacher, A (2003). "Recommendations for Fatigue Design of Welded Joints and Components." Doc. XIII-1965-03/XV1127-03, Paris

HSE (1995). "Offshore Installations: Guidance on Design, Construction and Certification." London.

Maddox, SJ (2001). "Hot-spot Fatigue Data for Welded Steel and Aluminium as a Basis for Design." Doc. IIW-XIII-1900-01, IIW.

Niemi, E, Fricke, W, and Maddox, SJ (2006). "Fatigue Analysis of Welded Components – Designer's Guide to the Hot-Spot Approach," Woodhead Publ., Cambridge.

Niemi, E, (1995). "Recommendations Concerning Stress Determination for Fatigue Analysis of Welded Components." Abington Publ., Abington, Cambridge.

Partanen, T, and Niemi, E (1999). "Hot spot S-N Curves Based on Fatigue Tests of Small MIG-welded Aluminium Specimens." Welding in the World, Vol 43, No 1, pp 16-22.

Smith, IFC, and Smith, RA (1982). "Defects and Crack Shape Development in Fillet Welded Joints." Fatigue Eng. Mater. Struct., Vol 5, No 2, pp 151-165.

The Aluminium Association (1994). "Aluminium Design Manual." Washington, D.C., U.S.A.

Tveiten, BW (1999). "Fatigue Assessment of Welded Aluminium Ship Details." Doctoral thesis, Department of Marine Structures, Norwegian University of Science and Technology, Trondheim, Norway.

Tveiten, BW, and Moan, T (2000). "Determination of Structural Stress for Fatigue Assessment of Welded Aluminium Ship Details." J. of Marine Struct., Vol 13, No 3, pp 189-212.

Tveiten, BW et al. (2002). "Recommendations on the Selection of Structural Stress Design S-N Curves for the Fatigue Assessment of Welded Aluminium Structures." The 8th Int. Fatigue Cong., Stockholm, Sweden.

Ye, N, Moan, T and Tveiten, BW (2001). "Fatigue Analysis of Aluminium Box-stiffener Lap Joints by Nominal, Structural, and Notch Stress Range Approaches." Proc. of the 8th Int. Symp. on Practical Design of Ships and Other Floating Struct. Shanghai, China.

Ye, N, Moan, T (2002). "Fatigue and Static Behaviour of Aluminium Box-stiffener Lap Joints." Int. J. Fatigue, Vol 39, pp 581-589.

Yung, JY and Lawrence, FV (1985). "Analytical and graphical aids for the fatigue design of weldments" Fatigue Fract. Eng. Mater. Struct, Vol 8(3), pp 223-241.

Valaire, B (1993). "Optimisation of Weld Toe Burr Grinding to Improve Fatigue Life." OMAE-Vol. III_B, Material Engineering, pp 869-873.

Watkinson, F et al. (1970). "The fatigue strength of Welded Joints in High Strength Steels and Methods for Its Improvement." Proc. Conf. On Fatigue of Welded Structures, pp 97-113, Brighton.

Welding Distortion Analysis of Hull Blocks Using Equivalent Load Method Based on Inherent Strain

Chang Doo Jang [1], Yong Tae Kim [2], Young Chun Jo [2], Hyun Su Ryu [2]

[1] Research Institute of Marine Systems Engineering, Seoul National University, Seoul, Korea
[2] Dept. of Naval Architecture & Ocean Engineering, Seoul National University, Seoul, Korea

Abstract

Welding deformation reduces the dimensional accuracy of ship hull blocks and decreases productivity due to the correction work. Prediction and minimizing of welding distortion at the design stage will lead to higher quality as well as higher productivity. Therefore, it is strongly required to develop an effective method to accurately predict the weld distortion of hull blocks considering the fabrication sequences.

In the case of hull block welding work in shipyard, the welding process of curved stiffened plate has large amounts of workload. This paper suggests an efficient method for predicting the welding deformation of stiffened curved plates based on the inherent strain theory combined with the finite element method. The equivalent load was determined by integrating inherent strain components which are calculated in the vicinity of heat affected zone using the highest temperature and the degree of restraint. The welding distortion of curved stiffened panels under equivalent load are calculated by elastic analysis and compared with that by intensive elasto-plastic finite element analysis. It is verified that the proposed method has a high efficiency and accuracy.

Keywords:

Welding deformation; Curved stiffened plate; Inherent strain; Highest temperature; Degree of restraint; Finite element method.

Introduction

Nowadays, most commercial and naval ships are constructed by the block building method in shipyards. The blocks which constitute the ship hull are built in a series of production process and transferred to the pre-erection area for the preparation works including the correction of distortion. The distortion of a block is inevitably induced by welding and is accumulated during the sequential fabrication process.

As the block erection step accounts for about one-third of the whole shipbuilding process, the accuracy of a block's shape and size has a close relation with the overall efficiency of production in the shipyard. To increase the precision of fabrication, the welding distortion and the exact distortion margin at every fabrication stage should be estimated to meet the allowable tolerances of ship hull blocks.

The inherent strain method has been used as one of the most efficient analysis method to predict the welding deformation (Jang and Lee, 1999). Inherent strain method is an approach to calculate the deformation by elastic equivalent forces which are obtained by integration of inherent (irrecoverable) strain in the HAZ region. Due to its accuracy and efficiency, the inherent strain method will be able to substitute thermal elasto-plastic 3-D FEM analysis which requires much more computing time.

The object of the present work is to develop an analysis method that can predict the welding distortion of stiffened flat plates considering the fabrication sequences, phase transformation and free convection (Jang and Lee, 2004; Jang, Ha, and Ko, 2003). Considering that the shape of a block is complex, the analysis method should predict the distortion in not only stiffened flat plate but also a stiffened curved plate.

The main purpose of this study is to develop the welding distortion analysis method for the stiffened curved plate by using the improved equivalent load method based on the inherent strain method, considering the fabrication sequences. For testing and evaluation of this method, various stiffened and curved plates, which have different curvature, will be analyzed with different fabrication sequences. The developed welding distortion analysis method can be applied to predict the plate forming by line heating (Jang, Ko and Seo, 1997) and line heating with weaving motions (Jang, Ha, and Kim, 2006) of a curved plate.

Inherent strain due to welding

The plastic strain that causes the welding deformation can be defined as the inherent strain. In the case that inherent stress is distributed in continuum, the stress can be removed by separating element from the continuum. The residual strain in the separated element is called the inherent strain(Fujimoto, 1967).

$$\varepsilon^* = \frac{dS_2 - dS_0}{dS_0}$$

(a) Initial state (stress free)

(b) Stressed state

(c) Stress-released state by cutting

Fig. 1 Definition of inherent strain

General inherent strain by welding has six components ε_x^*, ε_y^*, ε_z^*, γ_{xy}^*, γ_{yz}^*, γ_{zx}^*. However, in the case that a plate has a large length/thickness ratio such as a ship hull plate, only two components ε_x^* and ε_y^* are dominant.

Calculation of the inherent strain

The inherent strain distribution can be formulated by using the simplified thermal elastic-plastic analysis model as shown in Figure 2(Jang 1996). The welding region, where the inherent strain occurs, can be modeled as a bar and a spring.

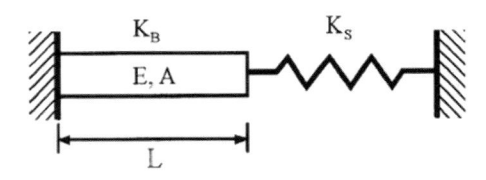

where E : Young's modulus
       A : Section area of a beam
       L : Length of a beam
       KB : Stiffness of a beam
       KS : Stiffness of a spring

Fig. 2 One-dimensional bar-spring model

In the case of the curved plate, the bar-spring model can be applied. Although the plate has a curvature, the HAZ region is small enough to apply for the bar-spring model.

Distribution of the highest temperature

The plastic strain is dependent on the highest temperature as shown Fig.3, and the highest temperature is needed to calculate the inherent strain.

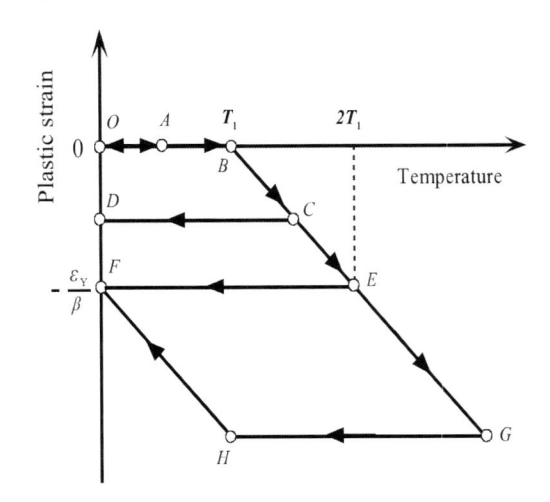

Fig. 3 Thermal history of plastic strain according to T_{max}

The highest temperature of each region is calculated by the FE heat transfer analysis as shown Figure 4.

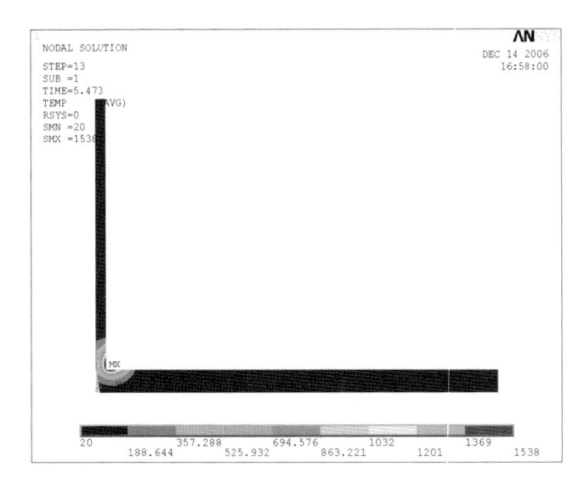

Fig. 4 Heat transfer analysis

Calculation of degree of restraint

The degree of restraint represents the level of resistance against the thermal deformation of the welding region. In order to calculate the degree of restraint, it is necessary to know the rigidity of the welding area and surround area. The unit load method is used to calculate the rigidity. The deformation from the elastic analysis of a stiffened plate under the unit load along the weld line is used to calculate the rigidity.

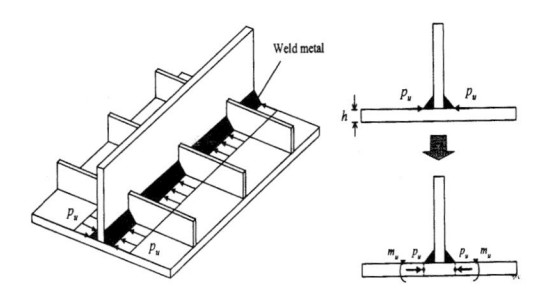

Fig. 5 Application of unit load along weld line

The distributed load p_u shown in Fig 4 is applied at the end of leg length of the weld on the plate surface, so the distributed load p_u and bending moment m_u are applied in the middle plane of the plate.

$$m_u = \frac{h}{2} \times p_u$$

$$\delta_S = \delta + \frac{h}{2} \cdot \theta$$

$$R_S = \frac{p_u}{\delta_S} = \frac{p_u}{\delta + \frac{h}{2} \cdot \theta} = k_S + K_B$$

where m_u : moment distributed along weld line
p_u : force distributed along weld line
δ_S : surface shrinkage
θ : rotation angle
R_S : stiffness of structure
k_S : stiffness of spring
K_B : stiffness of bar

Equivalent nodal loads

The equivalent forces and moments are obtained by the inherent strain which is calculated by the highest temperature and the degree of restraint. There are four types of equivalent loads; transverse shrinkage force, transverse bending moment, longitudinal shrinkage force, and longitudinal bending moment as shown Figure 5.

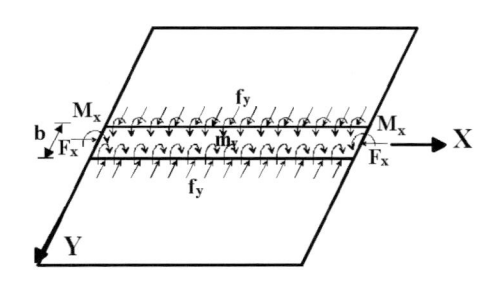

Fig. 6 Distribution of equivalent loads along weld line

Transverse shirinkage force $\quad f_y = \int_A E\varepsilon_y^* dA$

Transverse bending moment $\quad m_y = \int_A E\varepsilon_y^*(\frac{h}{2}+z)dA$

Longitudinal shirinkage force $\quad F_x = \int_A E\varepsilon_x^* dA$

Longitudinal bending moment $\quad M_x = \int_A E\varepsilon_x^*(\frac{h}{2}+z)dA$

where ε_x^* : plastic strain in x – direction
ε_y^* : plastic strain in y – direction
h : plate thickness

The longitudinal shrinkage force of a stiffened flat plate and a curved plate should be applied in different ways. As shown in Fig 6, the shrinkage force of the flat plate is applied at the both ends of the plate. In the curved plate case, however, the shrinkage force should be applied to each node toward the tangential direction of the welding line. Also, the application of equivalent load to a stiffened curved plate is shown in Fig 7.

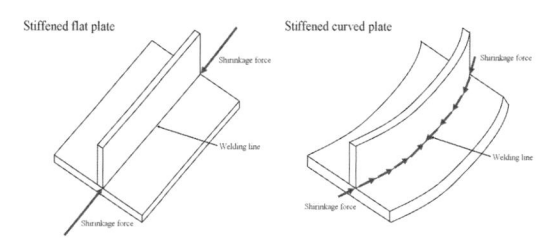

Fig. 7 Application of equivalent loads

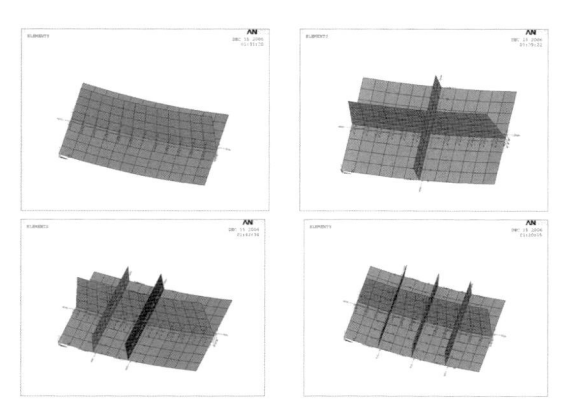

Fig. 8 Application of equivalent loads in FE model

Simulation of welding deformation

The welding deformation of stiffened curved plates was simulated by using both the inherent strain method and the FE analysis. The simulation procedures can be summarized into three steps. The first step analyzes the heat transfer; it calculates the highest temperature of each location with the welding information, considering convection on the plate surface. The second step calculates the degree of restraint by the unit load method using the FE analysis. The third step calculates the inherent strain components and their equivalent loads. Therefore, the welding deformation of the structure was solved by FE analysis.

Welding deformation experiment

The welding distortion experiment was performed for 4 kinds of stiffened curved plate models. As shown in Fig. 9, the experimental models have three kinds of curvatures (ρ = 1000, 2000, 5000mm ,respectively). The curvatures were selected by investigating actual fabrication data in the shipyards.

The girth length ($\rho\theta$), breadth, and thickness of base plate are 1200(mm), 800(mm), and 16(mm), respectively.

In order to study the effect of welding sequence on the welding distortion, the 2nd and 3rd experimental models were made to have the same curvature (ρ = 2000mm) but different welding sequences of case 1 and case 2 respectively. In case 1 (2nd model), the girder was welded after 3 longitudinal stiffeners are welded in order. In case 2 (3rd model), the girder was welded at first and then 3 longitudinal stiffeners are welded in order.

As shown in Fig.10, the arc welding process was adopted. The welding condition was 30(V) of voltage, 300(A) of current, and 5(mm/s) of welding velocity, and each welding was conducted after the air cooling.

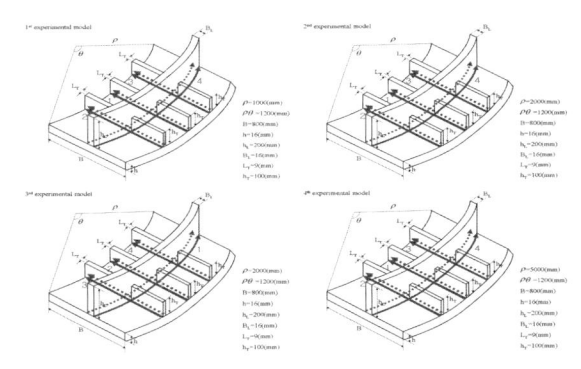

Fig. 9 Experimental models with the welding sequences

Fig. 10 Picture of welding distortion experiment

Comparison of analysis and experiment

1st experimental model

2nd experimental model

3rd experimental model

4th experimental model

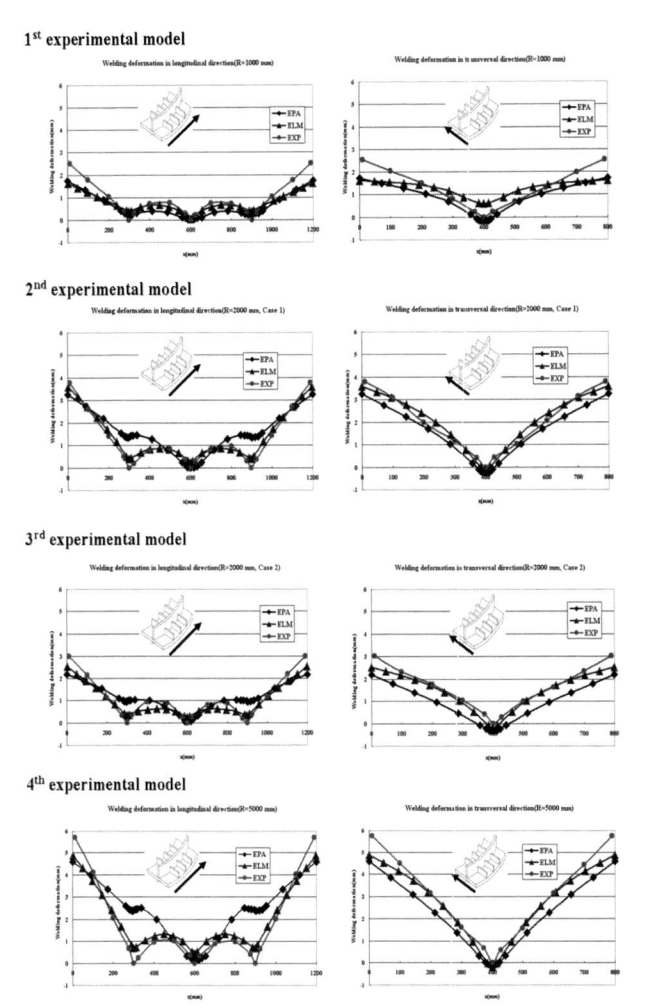

Fig. 11 Comparison of analysis and experiment

Table. 1 Analysis time

	ELM	EPA
Analysis time (Experimental model)	3~4(min)	1.5~2(day)
Pentium 4 CPU 3.20GHz, 2.00GB RAM		

As shown in Fig. 11, the welding deformation by the experiment show fairly good agreements with those by the ELM (Equivalent Load Method) suggested in this paper, but the welding deformation by the EPA (Thermal Elasto-Plastic Analysis) has a different tendency compared with the cases of ELM and EXP(Experiment). The discrepancy between EPA and EXP is remarkable especially at the location of 1st and 3rd longitudinal stiffeners.

In Fig. 11, the welding deformation increases with increasing radius of curvature, and the welding deformation with different welding sequence has a different value.

The welding deformation of case 1 (2nd model) is larger than that of case 2 (3rd model). From this result, it is recommended that the curved girder should be welded first before the smaller longitudinal stiffeners are welded from the view point of welding distortion control.

As shown above, the proposed method can estimate the welding distortions of stiffened curved plates considering welding sequence according to the fabrication stages.

Due to its efficiency from elastic analysis and accuracy, the present method can provide a powerful solution to predict the welding distortion of actual ship hull blocks with high complexity in structural shape. Some welding distortion control of actual ship hull block to reduce the welding deformation can be devised.

Conclusions

The main conclusions of this study are summarized as follows:

(1) This paper suggests an efficient method (Equivalent Load Method) for predicting the welding deformation of stiffened curved plates based on the inherent strain theory combined with the finite element method.

(2) The proposed method can consider the various modes of welding distortions such as angular distortion, in-plane shrinkage, longitudinal and transverse bending deformations.

(3) The proposed method can estimate the welding distortions of stiffened curved plates considering welding sequence according to the fabrication stages.

(4) It is recommended that the curved girder should be welded first before the smaller longitudinal stiffeners are welded from the view point of welding distortion control.

(5) The welding distortion analysis by the proposed method showed fairly good agreements with those by experiment.

(6) Due to its efficiency and accuracy, the present method can provide a powerful solution to predict the welding distortion of actual ship hull blocks with high complexity in structural shape.

Acknowledgement

Part of this work was supported by the Ship Structures Committee (SSC). The authors wish to acknowledge for its support.

References

Jang, C.D. and Seo, S.I. (1996) "A study on the automatic fabrication of welded built-up beams." Trans. of the Society of Naval Architects of Korea, 33(1), pp. 206-213

Jang, C.D. and Lee, C.H.(1999) "Prediction of Welding Deformation of Stiffened Plates using inherent Strain Method" Proceedings of the Thirteenth Asian Technical Exchange and Advisory Meeting on Marine Structures, pp. 485-492

Jang, C.D., Lee, C.H. and Ko, D.E. (2002) "Prediction of welding deformations of stiffened panels" Journal of Engineering for the Maritime Environment, Vol. 216, No. M2, pp. 133-143

Kim, S.I., Han, J.M., Cho, Y.K., Kang, J.K. and Lee, J.Y. (1997) "A study on the accuracy control of block assembly in shipbuilding." ICCAS '97, pp. 367-381

Masubuchi, K. (1980) "Analysis of welded structures."Pergamon Press, pp.239-243

Murakawa, H., Luo, Y. and Ueda, Y. (1997) "Prediction of welding deformation and residual stress by elastic FEM based on inherent strain" J. of the society of naval architects of Japan, 180, pp. 739-751

Seo, S.I. and Jang, C.D. (1999) "A study on the prediction of deformations of welded ship structures." Journal of Ship Production, 15(2), pp. 73-81

Tekriwal, P.(1989) Three-dimensional transient thermo-elasto-plastic modeling of gas metal arc welding using the finite element method." U. of Illinois at Urbana-Champaign, Urbana, Ill., USA

Ueda, Y. and Ma, N.X. (1995) "Measuring Methods of Three-Dimensional Residual Stresses with Aid of Distribution Function of Inherent Strains(Report3)." Trans. of Japanese Welding Research Institute, 24(2), pp.123-130

Watanabe, M. and Satoh, K. (1965) "Welding mechanics and its applications. Asakura Publication, pp.367-411

A CIP-based Cartesian Grid Method for Nonlinear Wave-body Interactions

Masashi Kashiwagi[1], Changhong Hu[1], Ryuji Miyake[2], Tingyao Zhu[2]

1) RIAM, Kyushu University, Fukuoka, Japan
2) Nippon Kaiji Kyokai (ClassNK), Chiba, Japan

Abstract

At Research Institute for Applied Mechanics (RIAM) of Kyushu University, extremely nonlinear wave-body interactions have been studied by means of CFD techniques and the computer code developed in partial cooperation with ClassNK, named RIAM-CMEN (computational method for extremely nonlinear hydrodynamics), is validated in several ways. In this paper, the frequency response characteristics of the wave-induced motions and added resistance on a ship running at constant forward speed in waves are compared to various results measured in a newly conducted experiment and computed by NSM (new strip method), EUT (enhanced unified theory), RSM (Rankine source method), and RIAM-CMEN. It is shown that the overall agreement of computed results by RIAM-CMEN is relatively good as compared to other linear-theory results.

Keywords

CFD; CIP; RIAM-CMEN; Interface capturing method; Extremely nonlinear; Ship motions; Added resistance.

Introduction

Numerical computations of nonlinear seakeeping problems, such as ship motions in large-amplitude waves and resultant green-water impact on deck, are presently our main concern. To make it possible to treat 'local' nonlinear hydrodynamic phenomena such as generation of splash, fragmentation and coalescence of a fluid, a CFD method using a Cartesian grid has been developed at RIAM (Research Institute for Applied Mechanics) of Kyushu University on the basis of the CIP (constrained interpolation profile) scheme initiated by Yabe *et al.* (2001). The computer code developed is named RIAM-CMEN (computational method for extremely nonlinear hydrodynamics) and its validation has been made through comparisons with experiments.

So far main interest has been placed on the prediction of the water on deck and its effect on the motions of a floating body or a ship running at forward speed in waves (Hu and Kashiwagi, 2006). However, we need to realize how accurately the RIAM-CMEN can predict 'global' quantities such as the wave-induced motions and the added resistance in waves for a wide spectrum of frequencies, even for the case of no prominent nonlinear phenomena.

In fact, using a modified Wigley model with wider breadth, the pressures by green water on the horizontal deck and vertical wall of an upstructure have been measured at a few selected wavelengths. However, the frequency response characteristics (response amplitude operators) of this ship model are not known for the wave-induced motions and the added resistance. Therefore, the present study started with the measurement of the 'global' ship motions and the added resistance for a wide range of wave frequencies.

On the other hand, through comparisons of the time histories of impulsive pressure by green water, it was revealed that the free-surface capturing scheme adopted in RIAM-CMEN must be improved in reducing the numerical diffusion and hence in keeping compact thickness of an interface even when the interface is largely distorted. To achieve this improvement, the THINC (tangent of hyperbola for interface capturing) scheme proposed by Xiao *et al.* (2005) is incorporated, which uses the hyperbolic tangent function to represent a step-like change of the density function across the interface (between water and air). Performance of this new scheme will be checked through a comparison between experiments and computations in this paper.

Because the time-domain calculation methods are usually time-consuming regardless of whether the fluid is assumed to be inviscid, the frequency-domain calculation methods in terms of the velocity potential have been used for routine use to compute global seakeeping characteristics. Typical examples of these methods are NSM (new strip method), EUT (enhanced unified theory) developed by Kashiwagi (1995, 1997), and RSM (Rankine source method); these are based on the linear formulation in the frequency domain but relatively reliable in the computational stability and accuracy. Therefore, in this paper, numerical computations corresponding to the experiments are performed by these linear frequency-domain calculation methods, and computed results are compared with the results by RIAM-CMEN and the experiments. Through this comparison, we expect to be able to realize what are the problems needing improvement in the present version of RIAM-CMEN.

Outline of RIAM-CMEN

Numerical computations by RIAM-CMEN are based on the finite difference method, and the present version of RIAM-CMEN is featured in (1) the use of a rectangular Eulerian grid, (2) the C-CUP (CIP-combined unified procedure) method as a flow solver for both water and air, (3) the THINC (tangent of hyperbola for interface capturing) scheme for the free-surface capturing, and (4) the use of virtual particles to impose the boundary condition and to compute the pressure forces on a moving rigid-body surface. These features except for the THINC scheme are described in Hu et al. (2006) and Hu and Kashiwagi (2006). Therefore, just the THINC scheme for the free-surface capturing and the associated flow solver are briefly described below.

Flow Solver

The wave-body interaction problem is treated in this paper as a multi-phase flow with liquid phase (water), gas phase (air), and solid phase (ship), and the C-CUP method developed by Yabe et al. (2001) is basically employed as the flow solver.

Both water and air are assumed to be incompressible, and thus the governing equations for the fluid velocity u_i in the i th direction ($i=1,2,3$ for x,y, and z respectively) and the pressure p are expressed as follows:

$$\frac{\partial u_i}{\partial x_i} = 0 \quad (1)$$

$$\frac{\partial u_i}{\partial t} + u_j \frac{\partial u_i}{\partial x_j} = -\frac{1}{\rho}\frac{\partial p}{\partial x_i} + \frac{1}{\rho}\frac{\partial}{\partial x_j}(\mu S_{ij}) + f_i \quad (2)$$

where $S_{ij} = \partial u_i/\partial x_j + \partial u_j/\partial x_i$, ρ is the fluid density, μ is the viscosity coefficient, and f_i denotes a body force. The surface tension is neglected and no turbulence models are introduced.

Eq.(2) is solved by a fractional step method, with the equation divided into three temporal steps: 1) advection phase ($q^n \rightarrow q^*$), 2) first non-advection phase ($q^* \rightarrow q^{**}$), and 3) second non-advection phase ($q^{**} \rightarrow q^{n+1}$), where q represents u_i or p, and $\Delta t = t^{n+1} - t^n$ is one time-step size.

In the advection phase, only the advection equation is solved using the CIP method. In the first non-advection phase, all terms on the right-hand side of Eq.(2), except for the pressure-related term are evaluated using an Euler explicit scheme with a central finite difference. In the second non-advection phase, the coupling between the velocity and pressure is treated by an implicit scheme, and thus the following Poisson-type equation

$$\frac{\partial}{\partial x_i}\left(\frac{1}{\rho}\frac{\partial p^{n+1}}{\partial x_i}\right) = \frac{1}{\Delta t}\frac{\partial u_i^{**}}{\partial x_i} \quad (3)$$

is solved for the pressure.

Free-Surface Capturing Method

The interface between water and air is called the free-surface to be determined by an interface capturing method, for which a number of CIP-based methods have been used so far (Hu et al., 2006), such as the original CIP method combined with function transformation for sharpness enhancement and the CIP-CSL3 (conservative semi-Lagrangian scheme with 3rd-order polynomial function) method.

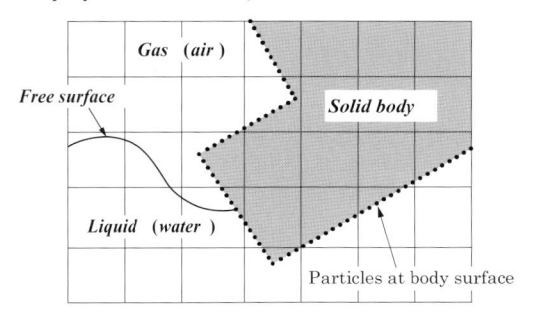

Fig. 1: Concept of multi-phase computation using a Cartesian grid and particles

To recognize different phases in a multi-phase flow, we define density functions ϕ_m for liquid ($m=1$), gas ($m=2$), and solid ($m=3$) phases (see Fig. 1). Whichever methods are adopted for free-surface capturing, the density function for a solid body ϕ_3 will be computed first by integrating in time the equations of body motions, thus determining the exact position of the rigid-body surface. Next the density function for liquid ϕ_1 will be computed, and then the remaining density function for gas ϕ_2 can be determined from a simple identity $\phi_1 + \phi_2 + \phi_3 = 1$.

In this paper, the THINC scheme proposed by Xiao et al. (2005) is employed as the free-surface capturing scheme. The value of the density function near the free surface changes abruptly from 1 to 0. The scheme to be used must reproduce this step-like change and keep compact thickness of largely distorted interface without numerical diffusion and oscillation. The THINC scheme uses the cell-averaged density function, with temporal integration carried out by the finite volume method, and thus the conservation of mass flux may be guaranteed. Since the hyperbolic tangent function is used to represent a step-like behavior, no spurious oscillation appears. Furthermore, a semi-Lagrangian method is employed to evaluate the flux across the cell boundary, which is effective in eliminating the numerical diffusion.

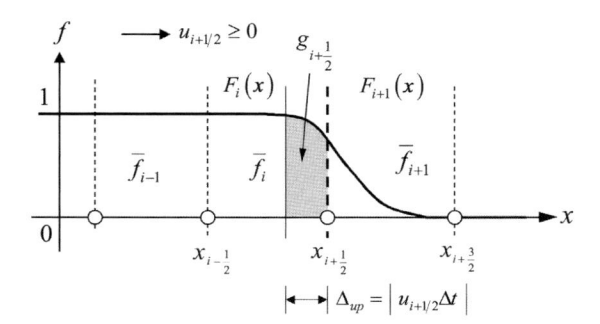

Fig. 2: Concept of THINC scheme for $u_{i+1/2} \geq 0$

In order to explain the calculation procedure of the THINC scheme, the basic 1-D advection equation for the density function $f(x,t)$ is considered in the following form:

$$\frac{\partial f}{\partial t} + \frac{\partial (uf)}{\partial x} = 0 \qquad (4)$$

Extension to multi-dimensional problems may be achieved with the directional splitting method, which uses the 1-D calculation procedure explained below.

Let $\overline{f}_i^n$ denote the cell-averaged density function, defined over $[x_{i-1/2}, x_{i+1/2}]$ at the n th time step ($t = t^n$). Then, with a finite-volume integration of Eq.(4), the density function f may be updated as

$$\overline{f}_i^{n+1} = \overline{f}_i^n + (g_{i-1/2} - g_{i+1/2})/\Delta x_i \qquad (5)$$

where

$$g_{i+1/2} = \int_{t^n}^{t^{n+1}} (uf)_{i+1/2} dt \qquad (6)$$

is the flux and $\Delta x_i = x_{i+1/2} - x_{i-1/2}$ (see Fig. 2).

A step-like distribution of the density function within cell i is approximated using a modified hyperbolic tangent function of the form

$$F_i(x) = \frac{\alpha}{2}\left[1 + \gamma \tanh\left\{\beta\left(\frac{x - x_{i-1/2}}{\Delta x_i} - \delta\right)\right\}\right] \qquad (7)$$

where α, β, γ and δ are the parameters to be determined as follows.

First α and γ can be explicitly determined as

$$\alpha = \begin{cases} \overline{f}_{i+1} & \text{if } \overline{f}_{i+1} \geq \overline{f}_{i-1} \\ \overline{f}_{i-1} & \text{otherwise} \end{cases} \qquad (8)$$

$$\gamma = \begin{cases} 1 & \text{if } \overline{f}_{i+1} \geq \overline{f}_{i-1} \\ -1 & \text{otherwise} \end{cases} \qquad (9)$$

Parameter β is associated with the steepness of the jump in the interpolation function. Following a result after several numerical experiments by Xiao et al. (2005), $\beta = 3.5$ is used in the present paper as well.

Parameter δ is associated with the middle point of the transition jump and can be determined by the relation below:

$$\frac{1}{\Delta x_i}\int_{x_{i-1/2}}^{x_{i+1/2}} F_i(x) dx = \overline{f}_i \qquad (10)$$

and thus

$$\delta = \frac{1}{2\beta}\ln\left|\frac{e^A - e^\beta}{e^A - e^{-\beta}}\right|, \quad A = \frac{2\beta}{\alpha\gamma}\left(\overline{f}_i - \frac{\alpha}{2}\right) \qquad (11)$$

Having determined a step-like profile, the flux $g_{i+1/2}$ across the cell boundary at $x_{i+1/2}$ can be evaluated in a semi-Lagrangian way as follows:

$$g_{i+1/2} = \int_{x_{i+1/2}-\Delta_{up}}^{x_{i+1/2}} F_i(x) dx$$

$$= \frac{\alpha}{2}\Delta_{up} + \frac{\alpha\gamma}{2\beta}\Delta x_i \ln\frac{\cosh\beta(1-\delta)}{\cosh\beta(1-\delta-\Delta_{up}/\Delta x_i)} \qquad (12)$$

where, as shown in Fig. 2, $\Delta_{up} = |u_{i+1/2}\Delta t|$. Eq. (12) is valid for $u_{i+1/2} \geq 0$, and a similar result may be obtained for $u_{i+1/2} \leq 0$ in the same manner.

Outline of EUT

The CFD calculation methods for the prediction of seakeeping performance of a ship, like RIAM-CMEN, are usually time-consuming and not yet well validated. For the purpose of routine use, EUT (enhanced unified theory) was developed by Kashiwagi (1995, 1997), which is an extension from the unified slender-ship theory initiated by Newman (1978) and Sclavounos (1984), and includes various important terms especially for the prediction of the added resistance in waves.

The formulation of EUT is based on the assumption of linearized potential flow, and the velocity potential is introduced and expressed as

$$\Phi = U\phi_S(\boldsymbol{x}) + \mathrm{Re}\left[\phi(\boldsymbol{x})e^{i\omega t}\right] \qquad (13)$$

$$\phi = \frac{ig\zeta_a}{\omega_0}(\phi_0 + \phi_7) + \sum_{j=1}^{6} X_j \phi_j \qquad (14)$$

$$\phi_0 = \exp\{k_0 z - ik_0(x\cos\chi + y\sin\chi)\} \equiv \psi_0(y,z)e^{i\ell x} \qquad (15)$$

$$\omega = \omega_0 - k_0 U\cos\chi, \quad k_0 = \omega_0^2/g, \quad \ell = -k_0\cos\chi \qquad (16)$$

where $\boldsymbol{x} = (x, y, z)$ in a Cartesian coordinate system, shown in Fig. 3; ϕ_0 denotes the incident-wave potential; $\zeta_a, \omega_0, k_0, \chi$ are the amplitude, circular frequency, wave-number, and incident angle of a regular incident wave, respectively; g is the gravitational acceleration. ϕ_7 denotes the scattering potential, and ϕ_j the radiation potential of j th mode with complex amplitude X_j ($j = 1$ for surge, $j = 3$ for heave, and $j = 5$ for pitch). ϕ_S in Eq. (13) denotes the steady disturbance potential by a ship moving at constant forward speed U.

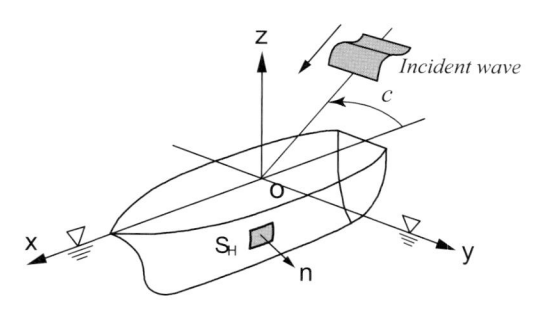

Fig. 3: Coordinate system for calculation of ship motions and added resistance

Radiation Problem

In the inner region close to the ship hull, ϕ_j may be sought to satisfy

$$\nabla_{2D}^2 \phi_j = 0 \quad \text{for } z \leq 0 \quad (17)$$

$$\frac{\partial \phi_j}{\partial z} - K\phi_j = 0 \quad \text{on } z = 0 \quad (18)$$

$$\frac{\partial \phi_j}{\partial n} = i\omega n_j + U m_j \quad \text{on } S_H(x) \quad (19)$$

where $K = \omega^2/g$. n_j and m_j denote the j th components of the unit normal and so-called m term representing an interaction with the steady flow, respectively.

The inner solution of the EUT satisfying Eqs. (17)-(19) takes the form

$$\phi_j = \phi_j^P(y,z) + C_j(x)\phi^H(y,z) \quad (20)$$

Here ϕ_j^P denotes the particular solution that is identical to the solution in strip methods, e.g. NSM (new strip method), and ϕ^H denotes a homogeneous solution with $C_j(x)$ the unknown coefficient. This coefficient can be determined after solving an integral equation that may be obtained through matching between the inner and outer solutions in an overlap region. Therefore, through this coefficient, 3-D and forward-speed effects (ignored in the strip methods) are accounted for.

Unlike the strip methods and the original unified theory, the solution for the surge mode ($j = 1$) is also given in the form of Eq.(20). The calculation procedure for surge can be the same as those for heave and pitch, only if the x-component of the normal vector is given; which is obtained by differentiating a shape function used for representing the ship hull.

Diffraction Problem

Since the incident-wave potential is given as Eq. (15), the scattering potential is assumed to be of the form $\phi_7 = \psi_7(x;y,z)e^{i\ell x}$. Then the slowly-varying part ψ_7 may be sought to satisfy the following:

$$\left(\nabla_{2D}^2 - \ell^2\right)\psi_7 = 0 \quad \text{for } z \leq 0 \quad (21)$$

$$\frac{\partial \psi_7}{\partial z} - k_0 \psi_7 = 0 \quad \text{on } z = 0 \quad (22)$$

$$\frac{\partial \psi_7}{\partial n} = \left(n_3 + in_1 \cos\chi + in_2 \sin\chi\right)$$
$$\times k_0 e^{k_0 z - ik_0 y \sin\chi} \quad \text{on } S_H(x) \quad (23)$$

It should be noted that the wave diffraction ahead of the ship's bow is taken into account, in an approximate manner, by retaining the n_1 term in the body boundary condition. The solution method for Eqs. (21)-(23) is very similar to that in the original unified theory by Sclavounos (1984), and the only difference is the use of $n_3 + in_1 \cos\chi$ in place of n_3. However, this minor difference provides a big difference in the pressure prediction near the bow and the resulting exciting force in surge and the added resistance in waves.

In the same manner as in the radiation problem, the coefficient of a homogeneous solution can be determined, which plays an important role in accounting for the 3-D and forward-speed effects as well as the effect of bow wave diffraction.

Once the inner solutions of the radiation and diffraction problems are determined, hydrodynamic forces can be readily computed, and then the equations of coupled motions among surge, heave, and pitch may be solved. Furthermore, the added resistance in waves can be computed from Maruo's formula (1960) in terms of ship-generated progressive waves (i.e. Kochin functions) to be determined with the outer solution in EUT. More details are described in Kashiwagi (1997).

Outline of RSM

In the framework of linear potential theory, RSM (Rankine source method) may account for genuine 3-D and forward-speed effects connected with the derivatives of the velocity potential with respect to x which are neglected as higher-order terms in the Laplace equation and the free-surface condition in the EUT.

In the formulation of RSM, the free-surface condition for the unsteady velocity potential generally includes various contributions from the steady flow, and thus a simple Rankine source rather than a complicated free-surface Green function is used as a kernel function in an expression of the velocity potential:

$$\phi(\boldsymbol{x}) = \iint_{S_F} \sigma_F(\boldsymbol{x}') G(\boldsymbol{x},\boldsymbol{x}') dS(\boldsymbol{x}')$$
$$+ \iint_{S_H} \sigma_H(\boldsymbol{x}') G(\boldsymbol{x},\boldsymbol{x}') dS(\boldsymbol{x}') \quad (24)$$

where

$$\left.\begin{array}{l}G(\boldsymbol{x},\boldsymbol{x}') = \dfrac{1}{r} + \dfrac{1}{r_1} \\[6pt] \left.\begin{array}{l}r \\ r_1\end{array}\right\} = \sqrt{(x-x')^2 + (y-y')^2 + (z \mp z')^2}\end{array}\right\} \quad (25)$$

and $z' = 0$ in the integral on the free surface S_F.

The strengths of the source distribution on the free surface (σ_F) and on the wetted surface of a ship (σ_H) must be determined so as to satisfy the free-surface and body boundary conditions. In addition, the so-called radiation condition must be satisfied as well. The computer program of RSM used in the present study was the same as that developed by Miyake et al. (1999, 2001). Thus, following Yasukawa (1990), the radiation condition is incorporated in the free-surface condition by approximating the terms of Kelvin-type waves with the upstream 4-point finite difference and by introducing Rayleigh's artificial viscosity for the terms associated with ring-type waves.

Once the velocity potentials for the radiation and diffraction problems are determined, as in the EUT, hydrodynamic forces can be computed and then the equations of coupled motions of surge, heave, and pitch can be solved.

Regarding the computation of the added resistance in waves, the so-called near-field method is employed, which is based on the time average of the direct pressure integration on the ship hull, but only the second-order quantities with respect to unsteady terms are consistently retained.

Overview of Experiment

In order to validate the performance of RIAM-CMEN, 3-D experiments have been carried out (Hu and Kashiwagi, 2006), measuring the impulsive pressure due to green water impinging upon a modified Wigley model; which is of mathematical form represented by

$$\eta = (1-\zeta^2)(1-\xi^2)(1+a_2\xi^2+a_4\xi^4) \\ + \zeta^2(1-\zeta^8)(1-\xi^2)^4 \quad (26)$$

where $\xi = 2x/L$, $\eta = 2y/B$ and $\zeta = -z/d$, with L, B, and d the length, breadth, and draft, respectively. The bluntness parameters, a_2 and a_4, are chosen as $a_2 = 0.6$ and $a_4 = 1.0$.

Main concern in the previous experiments was placed on the time variation of the local nonlinear phenomena, and thus measurements were carried out only at a few wavelengths. However, the response characteristics of wave-induced motions of the present ship model should be clarified for a wide range of frequencies, and a comparison of measured results with computed ones by various kinds of existing calculation methods should be made as a part of validation of RIAM-CMEN. For this purpose, measurements of the motions of surge, heave, pitch and the added resistance in head waves were newly conducted in the towing tank (65 m long, 5 m wide, and 7 m deep) at RIAM, Kyushu University. The principal particulars of the ship model tested are shown in Table 1.

Table 1: Principal particulars of the ship model

Length: L (m)	2.500
Breadth: B (m)	0.500
Draft: d (m)	0.175
Freeboard: f (m)	0.075
Displacement volume: ∇ (m^3)	0.1388
Gyrational radius in pitch: κ_{yy}/L	0.258
Height of gravitational center: $\overline{KG}/d$	0.851

In the experiments, the ship motions were free in surge, heave, and pitch, while towing the model with constant torque exerted by a print motor so as to keep the model at a time-averagely constant location. In this way, the forward velocity (i.e. Froude number) was kept constant at $Fn = U/\sqrt{Lg} = 0.15$. The wavelength was varied in the range of $\lambda/L = 0.3 \sim 3.0$. The force acting upon the model was measured with the use of a load cell installed in the lowest part of the heaving rod, and the measured data was Fourier-analyzed.

The added resistance in waves (R_{aw}) is the difference between the steady component of the unsteady force in the Fourier-series expansion used in the Fourier analysis (F_0) and the resistance in still water (R_S). Namely

$$R_{aw} = F_0 - R_S \quad (27)$$

Computational Conditions

Numerical computations by RIAM-CMEN were performed in a numerical wave tank, whose size was taken as $-4.9L \sim 2.6L$ in the x-axis, $-2.1L \sim 2.1L$ in the y-axis, and $-1.3L \sim 1.3L$ in the z-axis, with L being the ship's length and the origin of the coordinate system taken at amidships and undisturbed free-surface. The coordinate system (grid) moves with the mean forward speed U of a ship.

A non-uniform grid of $180\times80\times80$ points along the x-, y-, and z-axes respectively was used, where the minimum grid spacing was $\Delta x = 0.006L$ near the bow and stern (taken symmetrically) and $\Delta y = \Delta z = 0.005L$ near the ship hull and free surface. The time step size was taken equal to $\Delta t / T_w = 2000$, where T_w is the period of the incident wave.

The surge motion was fixed in the computations of RIAM-CMEN to shorten the computation time, because of the difficulty in attaining a steady harmonic oscillation with surge free or restrained using a weak spring.

For numerical computations of RSM, the number of grid points on the whole area of free surface ($z = 0$) and ship hull ($z \leq 0$) was 4,000 and 1,200, respectively. The computational domain is varied depending on the wavelength (λ) of an incident wave. Specifically, we took $-(2.0\lambda + 0.5L) \leq x \leq 1.5\lambda + 0.5L$ along the x-axis and $-(\lambda + 0.5B) \leq y \leq \lambda + 0.5B$ along the y-axis.

The steady flow, which is needed in evaluating the free-surface and ship-hull boundary conditions for the unsteady flow, is approximated by the so-called double-body flow. The source strengths on the free surface and ship hull are assumed constant, and the resultant influence coefficients in a linear system of simultaneous equations for the source strengths are evaluated using the Hess and Smith method.

Numerical computations by EUT are very fast compared to RSM, even if we take 50 terms in the Chebyshev polynomials, which are employed in solving the unified-theory integral equation for the source strength distributed along the x-axis.

Numerical computations of NSM can be done as a part of the computations of EUT, for which the number of segments along the ship's length was taken as 60 and the number of segments along the contour at each transverse section was taken as 80.

Comparison and Discussion

First, examples of the time histories of computed results by RIAM-CMEN are shown in Figs. 4 and 5 for the cases of $\lambda/L = 0.5$ and 1.5 respectively; these are the forces in surge (F_1) and heave (F_3) and the moment in pitch (M_2), and also the motions of heave (ξ_3) and pitch (ξ_5). (Note that the surge motion is fixed.)

It can be seen that it takes at least $6T_w$ for $\lambda/L = 0.5$ to attain to a steady harmonic oscillation and at least $3T_w$

for $\lambda/L = 1.5$ (with T_w the period of incident wave). In addition, the motion amplitudes at $\lambda/L = 0.5$ are very small compared to those at $\lambda/L = 1.5$. The amplitude and phase lead are obtained from the first harmonic components in each mode of motion by the use of the Fourier analysis using these time histories of the motions. The phase reference is taken as the time instant when the crest of the incident is at the center of a ship.

The results for heave are shown in Fig. 6. A somewhat large peak in amplitude around $\lambda/L = 1.2$ is predicted by RIAM-CMEN, and the existence of a peak around $\lambda/L = 1.2$ is also predicted by EUT and RSM. On the other hand, no prominent peak can be seen in the result of NSM, which conforms to the result measured in the experiment. However, a close look at the phase reveals that the result of NSM is discrepant around $\lambda/L = 0.8$, which may be attributed to 3-D effects, because the results by EUT and RSM taking account of 3-D effects are in good agreement with the measured ones.

Computed results of the phase by RIAM-CMEN are somewhat scattered and different from the variation tendency of the results by other linear-theory calculation methods. The phase calculation in RIAM-CMEN was performed in the same way as that in the experiment; that is, the wave elevation at amidships but enough apart from the centerline were also Fourier-analyzed and the difference in phase between the motion of a ship and the wave elevation was taken as a computed value. Therefore the wave at the reference point might be disturbed by the ship-generated waves or might be slightly changed by some numerical errors, which may be a reason of scattered values in the phase computed by RIAM-CMEN.

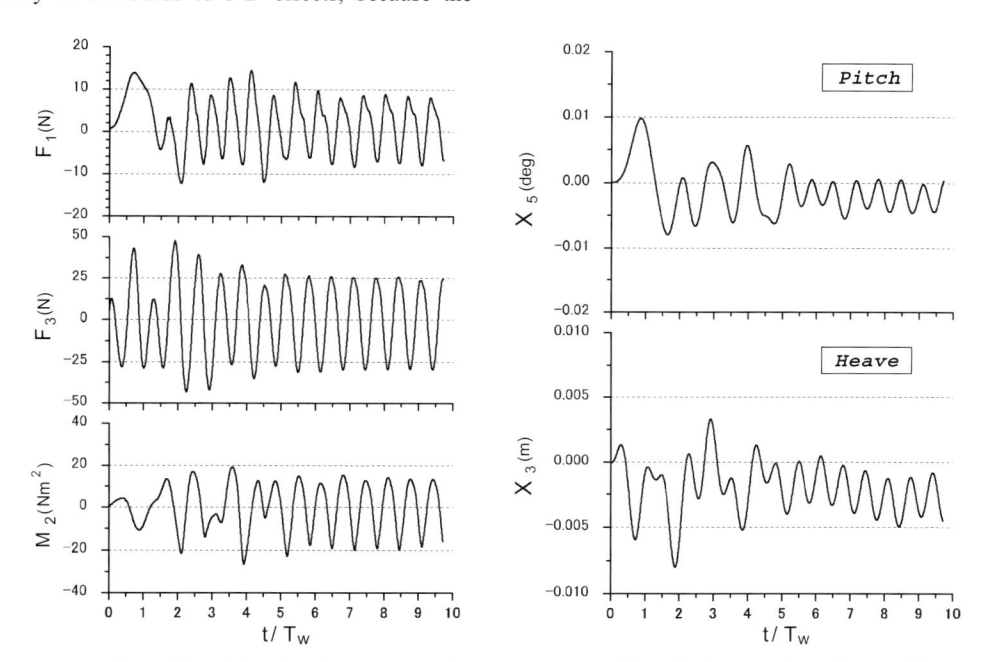

Fig. 4: Time histories of forces on and motions of a modified Wigley model at $Fn = 0.15$ in regular head wave of $\lambda/L = 0.5$, computed by RIAM-CMEN

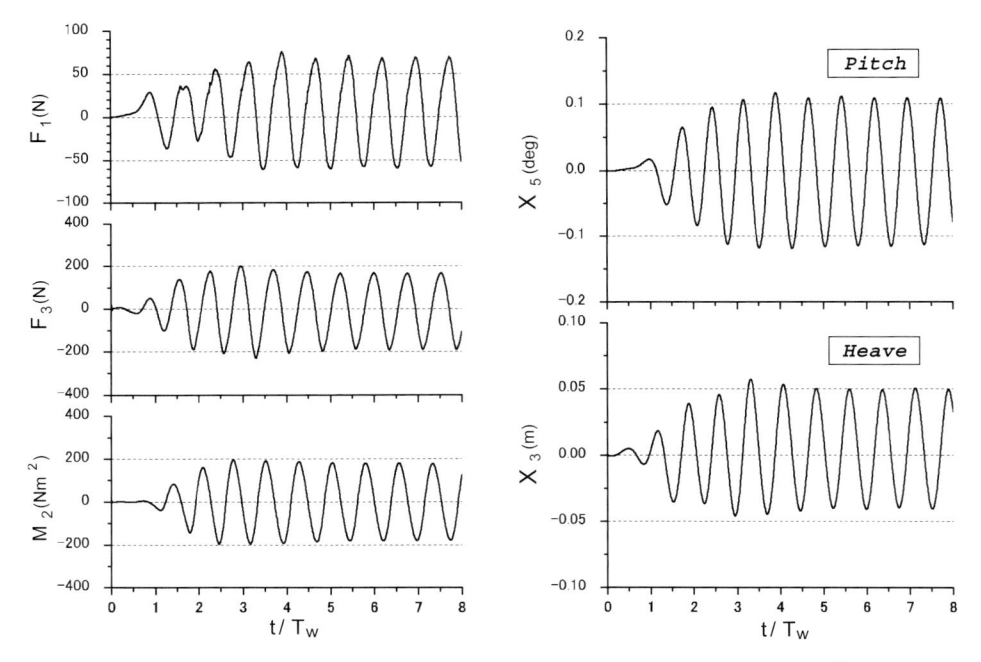

Fig. 5: Time histories of forces on and motions of a modified Wigley model at $Fn = 0.15$ in regular head wave of $\lambda/L = 1.5$, computed by RIAM-CMEN

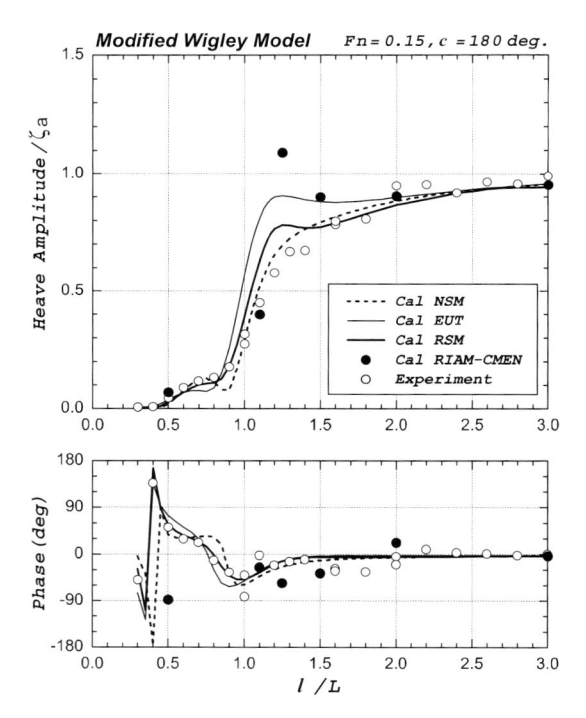

Fig. 6: RAO of heave of a modified Wigley model at $Fn = 0.15$ in head waves

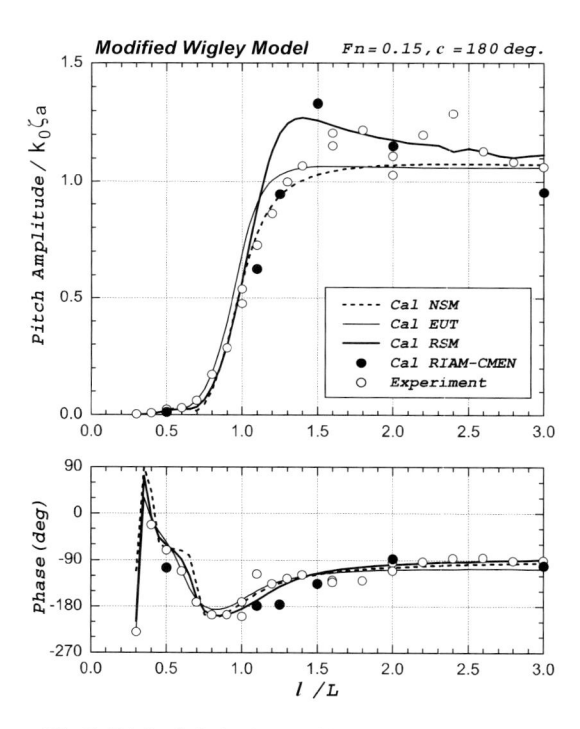

Fig. 7: RAO of pitch of a modified Wigley model at $Fn = 0.15$ in head waves

The results of the pitch motion are shown in Fig. 7. Measured values are scattered a little in the range of $1.5 < \lambda/L < 2.5$, but yet the amplitudes computed by RIAM-CMEN agree well with the measured ones, except for a larger value at $\lambda/L = 1.5$. This larger value around $\lambda/L = 1.5$ is also predicted by RSM and thus corresponds to a peak near the resonant frequency in pitch. Computed results by RSM look fluctuated in amplitude at longer wavelengths, but the agreement with measured results is favorable. In particular the phase is well predicted by RSM. Theoretically, EUT must be superior to NSM, but computed amplitudes by EUT look worse than those by NSM.

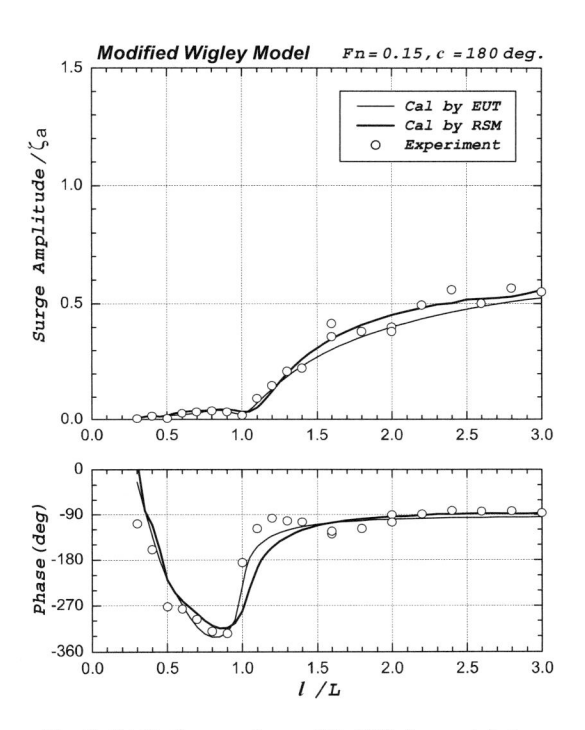

Fig. 8: RAO of surge of a modified Wigley model at $Fn = 0.15$ in head waves

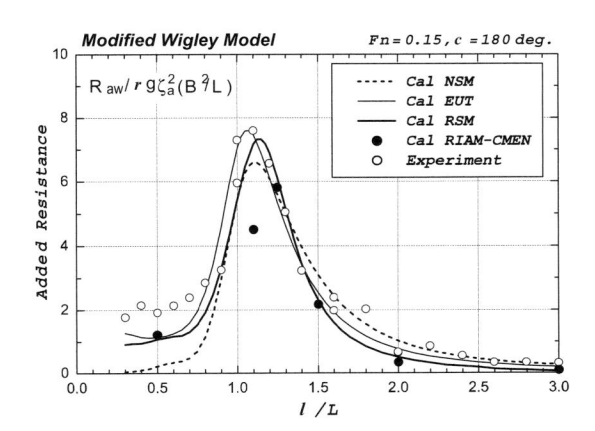

Fig. 9: Added resistance of a modified Wigley model at $Fn = 0.15$ in head waves

The surge motion can be predicted by EUT and RSM, whereas the surge is fixed in the computation of RIAM-CMEN. A comparison with measured results is shown in Fig. 8. Computed results by RSM are in good agreement with measured ones. The results by EUT are also in favorable agreement, although EUT tends to under predict the amplitude.

Figure 9 shows the results of the added resistance in waves in a nondimensional form of $R_{aw}/\rho g \zeta_a^2 (B^2/L)$. Since the computational burden in RIAM-CMEN is large, numerical computations by RIAM-CMEN were performed only at a few wavelengths. Nevertheless, it is obvious that the predicted peak value around $\lambda/L = 1.1$ is smaller than the measured one.

In the range of shorter wavelengths of $\lambda/L < 0.7$, the measured values are larger than the computed ones by any calculation method considered in this paper. It is natural that the values by EUT and RSM are much larger than those by NSM, because the wave diffraction near the ship bow is taken into account in EUT and RSM at least in the framework of linear theory. The difference between the measured and computed results by EUT and RSM may be attributed to nonlinear effects such as wave breaking (energy dissipation) near the bow. In this regard, we expected better agreement between the experiment and the prediction by RIAM-CMEN. However, the results by RIAM-CMEN are still smaller than the measured results.

Of course there is room for improvement in RIAM-CMEN; for example, the number of grids must be increased for higher resolution, since it is true that the accuracy of computed results does depend on the number of grids. In order to increase the number of grids, the computation must be much accelerated, which may be accomplished by making the computer code parallel. Furthermore, the effect of surge motion on the added resistance must be studied, and the dependency of the wave amplitude on the added resistance must also be checked in the computations of RIAM-CMEN.

Conclusions

Performance of a CIP-based Cartesian grid method, RIAM-CMEN, for computing the wave-induced motions and the added resistance on a ship with forward velocity has been validated through comparisons with newly conducted experiments and computed results by various linear-theory methods in the frequency domain such as RSM (Rankine source method), EUT (enhanced unified theory), and NSM (new strip method). It was confirmed that the overall agreement of computed results by RIAM-CMEN with measured ones is relatively good. However, the calculation of the phase of ship motions with reference to the incident wave must be improved, and the surge motion must be included in numerical simulations.

As an improvement in RIAM-CMEN, a new free-surface capturing scheme, THINC, using the hyperbolic tangent function is incorporated in the present version of RIAM-CMEN, which is believed to contribute to the enhancement of the resolution. However, to increase the numerical resolution, the calculation efficiency must be greatly improved so that we can increase the number of grids.

Acknowledgments

The experiments presented in this paper were carried out with help of Prof. H. Iwashita and his students as a part of collaboration, for which we greatly appreciate. We also acknowledge Mr. M. Inada for his constant help in the experiments.

References

Hu, C, and Kashiwagi, M (2006). "Validation of CIP-based Method for Strongly Nonlinear Wave-Body Interactions", Proc 26th Symp on Naval Hydrodyn, Rome, Vol 4, pp 247-258.

Hu, C, Kishev, Z, Kashiwagi, M, Sueyoshi, M, and Faltinsen, OM (2006). "Application of CIP Method for Strongly Nonlinear Marine Hydrodynamics", Ship Tech Res, Vol 53, No 2, pp 74-87.

Kashiwagi, M (1995). "Prediction of Surge and Its Effect on Added Resistance by Means of the Enhanced Unified Theory", Trans West-Japan Soc Nav Arch, No 89, pp 77-89.

Kashiwagi, M (1997). "Numerical Seakeeping Calculations Based on the Slender Ship Theory", Ship Tech Res, Vol 4, No 4, pp 167-192.

Maruo, M (1960). "Wave Resistance of a Ship in Regular Head Seas", Bulletin of Faculty of Eng, Yokohama National Univ, Vol 9, pp 73-91.

Miyake, R, Kagemoto, H, and Fujino, M (1999). "Calculation of Hydrodynamic Forces Acting on a Ship in Waves by Rankine Source Method (in Japanese)", J Soc Nav Arch Japan, Vol 185, pp 49-60.

Miyake, R, Zhu, T, and Kagemoto, H (2001). " On the Estimation of Wave-Induced Loads Acting on Practical Merchant Ships by a Rankine Source Method (in Japanese)", J Soc Nav Arch Japan, Vol 190, pp 107-119.

Newman, JN (1978). "The Theory of Ship Motions", Advances in Applied Mechanics, Vol 18, pp 221-283.

Sclavounos, PD (1985). "The Diffraction of Free-Surface Waves by a Slender Ship", J Ship Res, Vol 28, No 1, pp 29-47.

Xiao, F, Honma, Y, and Kono, T (2005). "A Simple Algebraic Interface Capturing Scheme Using Hyperbolic Tangent Function", Int J Numer Methods Fluids, Vol 48, pp 1023-1040.

Yabe, Y, Xiao, F, and Utsumi, T (2001). "The Constrained Interpolation Profile Method for Multiphase Analysis", J Comp Physics, Vol 169, pp 556-569.

Yasukawa, H (1990). "A Rankine Panel Method to Calculate Unsteady Ship Hydrodynamic Forces (in Japanese)", J Soc Nav Arch Japan, Vol 168, pp 131-140.

CFD Hull Form Optimization of a 12,000 cu. yd. (9175 m³) Dredge

Bruce L. Hutchison [1], Karsten Hochkirch [2]

[1] Sr. Principal, Ocean Engineering & Analysis, The Glosten Associates, Inc.
Seattle, Washington, U.S.A.
[2] Managing Director, FRIENDSHIP SYSTEMS GmbH
Potsdam, Germany

Fig. 1:   M/V *Glenn Edwards* at sea trials

Abstract

Manson Construction Company's 12,000 cu.yd. (9175 m³) trailing suction hopper dredge *M/V Glenn Edwards* is the newest and largest hopper dredge in the U.S. fleet. Unusual among large hopper dredges, the *Glenn Edwards* is propelled by three 1,920 kW azimuthing Z-drive units fitted with nozzles. This paper describes the formal CFD hull form optimization process for the *Glenn Edwards*. An unusual feature of this formal hull form optimization process was the CFD evaluation of performance both in deep and shallow water operations, as both regimes are important to the operation of a hopper dredge. The paper describes the development of the constraint set, CFD modeling considerations, the optimization process and the results obtained. Comparison is made between CFD results and results obtained from model tests of the selected optimum hull at MARINTEK in Trondheim, Norway. Mention will also be made of observations and results from sea trials and early service.

Keywords

Hull form; Optimization; CFD; Parametric geometry; Wavemaking resistance

Nomenclature

$(1+k)$	form factor as given by Holltrop (1984)
C_{TS}	thrust loading coefficient of propeller
F_N	Froude number
GM_T	transverse metacentric height
L_{OA}	length overall
L_{WL}	length at waterline
R_{PT}	pressure resistance
R_{PRP}	pressure induced additional resistance of the acting propeller on the hull
R_{PRV}	change of viscous resistance due to propeller action
R_{PRW}	change of wave making resistance due to propeller action
R_T	total resistance
R_V	viscous resistance
T	draft
$\tilde{T}$	first approximation to the thrust
t	thrust deduction fraction

Introduction

Manson Construction Company's 12,000 cu.yd. (9175 m^3) trailing suction hopper dredge *M/V Glenn Edwards* (Fig. 1) is the newest and largest hopper dredge in the U.S. fleet. The *Glenn Edwards* is 112.2 m LBP, with a beam of 23.17 m and a design draft of 7.47 m. The *Glenn Edwards* is propelled by three 1,920 kW azimuthing Z-drive units fitted with nozzles, an unusual arrangement for its class.

This paper describes the formal CFD hull form optimization process used to develop the hull form for the *Glenn Edwards*. As depicted in Fig. 2, that process begins with the formulation of a constraints set, followed by development of a parametrically defined hull geometry (or perhaps one should say family of geometries) that expresses the different attributes thought to be candidates for a successful hull. The optimization process then proceeds by stages. First, a coarse survey of parameter space is accomplished; this is followed by a directed search for near optimum hulls, beginning from the region of parameter space determined to be most promising from the survey.

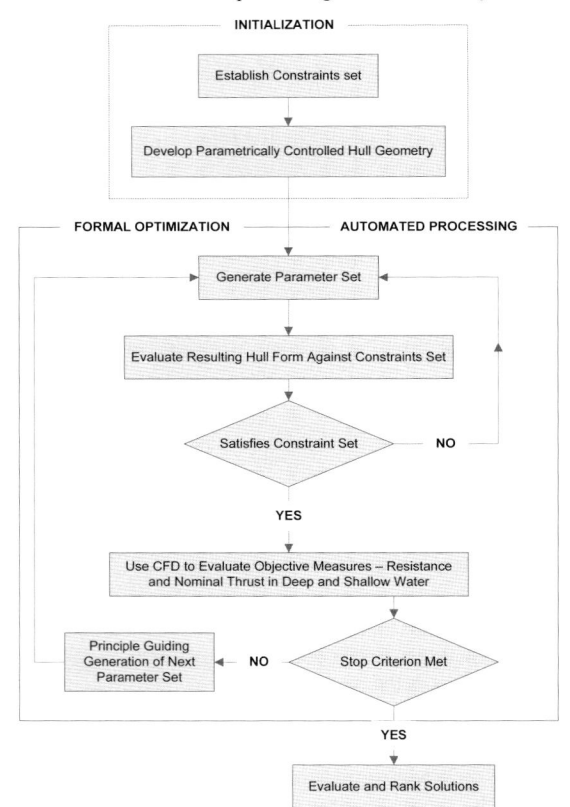

Fig. 2: Hull form optimization process

Each parametrically generated candidate hull is first checked for compliance with the constraints set. In general, not all candidates comply, and if the problem is over-constrained few will comply. Non-compliant hull forms are discarded without further analysis. Objective functions are evaluated for each compliant hull form using nonlinear free surface potential flow CFD, empirical values for the form factor and ITTC friction.

Typically, the objective measure of merit might be the scalar value of resistance or nominal thrust at a design service speed. However, given the nature of the service for a suction hopper dredge, the objective measure of merit for the *Glenn Edwards* was the two component vector comprising the nominal thrust in both deep and shallow water. In the nonlinear free surface potential flow computation, the influence of the propulsors was modeled using a source distribution on the propeller disc, representing a specified thrust of the propeller.

The first, exploratory phase examined about 150 different hull designs, of which 47 conformed to all of the given constraints. The second phase commenced from the best design identified during the exploratory phase, and proceeded to seek an optimum hull form using a Tangent Search Method. The rate of improvement essentially vanished after 136 successive designs were evaluated.

The hull form recommended by this process was then subjected to a detailed RANS evaluation. During the RANS computation, actuator discs were introduced and the thrust was adjusted to balance the resistance force – thus simulating a free running propulsion test.

Compared to other CFD hull form optimization methods, this approach based on parameterized hull geometry is thought to be both practical and superior for the following reasons:

1. The parameterized hull geometry can be devised such that it is only capable of generating realistic (and '*fair*') hull forms that one would genuinely consider building.

2. The procedure is automated so that it is practical to evaluate hundreds (upwards to thousands) of geometries for compliance with constraints, and the objective functions can be evaluated for hundreds of compliant hull forms using nonlinear free surface potential flow CFD.

The parameterization of the hull geometry minimizes the degrees-of-freedom (DOF) to a practical and manageable level. Twenty (20) free parameters were used in the optimization of the *Glenn Edwards*, of which thirteen (13) were handled implicitly in the geometric modeling, and the remaining seven (7) were explicitly explored during the optimization process. Compared, for example, to automated hull form optimization procedures that make each vertex on the hull form mesh a free (vector) variable (see for instance Hendrix *et al* 2001), the present approach based on parameterized geometry represents a reduction in DOF by many orders of magnitude.

The present approach is advantageous, too, when compared to man-in-the-loop hull form optimization procedures guided by experience and judgment. Man-in-the-loop procedures can evaluate only a very few hull forms (typically two to six), and therefore are unable to offer any convincing evidence that a near optimum has been achieved. Usually, at best, they can only claim improvement over the initial hull form, but cannot provide any genuine confidence that the potential for further gains has been (nearly) exhausted.

Constraints Set

Hull forms were validated against a set of constraints established by the naval architect in consultation with the owner at the beginning of the hull form optimization effort. The constraints set and parametric geometry model embodied hull constructability, as well as other concerns.

In the service of brevity, the full rationale behind each constraint will not be described here. Care should be taken in establishing the constraints set to determine those constraints that are truly necessary and to avoid otherwise overly constraining the problem, as over-constraint will needlessly reduce the number of constraint compliant hull forms, and may prevent finding a desirable optimum.

Constraints are presented under class subheadings, such as: symmetry, length, volume, etc. More generally, there are conceivable useful constraints that may fall under headings not used for the *Glenn Edwards,* and some of these possibilities will be briefly discussed at the conclusion of this section.

Symmetry

It may appear obvious and even trivial, but the number of planes of symmetry is an appropriate constraint. The parametric exploration for the *Glenn Edwards* was constrained to one plane of symmetry. On a concurrent double-ended ferry project, however, there were two planes of symmetry.

Length

For the *Glenn Edwards*, constraints were set on several lengths: L_{OA}, wetted length, L_{WL}, waterline beam, draft, still water trim and midship bilge radius. Most of these were constrained by exact equalities, an unusual choice. More typically, these might be constrained to fall within some acceptable range.

Following the initial exploration of parametric design space, it was realized that a constraint (acceptable range) on the position of the longitudinal center-of-buoyancy was also required.

Area

There were no constraints measured as areas for the *Glenn Edwards,* but more generally there could be constraints in this classification. Examples might be minimum (and/or maximum) waterplane area.

Volume

A minimum displaced volume of 17,047 m^3 was set for the *Glenn Edwards,* corresponding to a minimum displacement of 17,200 long tons in salt water. While displacement is the most obvious volume constraint, on some projects there have been other volume constraints, such as the tank volume between specified transverse boundaries.

Other Geometric Constraints

Other geometric constraints for the *Glenn Edwards* included the following:

- Clearances for the azimuthing Z-drive propulsors imposed with a 2.713 m clearance circle in a plane 3.901 m above base and centered on the rotation axis for Z-drive azimuth.
- Minimum extent (and location) of parallel mid-body.
- Aft hopper door clearance enforced by requiring the bottom tangent for the flat of bottom to fall outside (aft of) a specified control point.
- A requirement that the main deck (30 foot (9.1 m) elevation) be maintained at full breadth to within 72 feet (22.0 m) forward of the transom.
- A requirement that the poop deck (42 foot (12.8 m) elevation) continue at full breadth all the way aft to the transom.

Gaussian Curvature

Except in the forebody and bilge radius, it was desired/required that the hull be a developable surface with zero Gaussian curvature. To the maximum extent possible, it was desired that the forebody also be comprised of developable surfaces. This constraint was handled implicitly within the parametric modeling.

Other Possible Constraints

As mentioned at the beginning of this section, only necessary constraints should be established, and the optimization problem should not needlessly be over-constrained. With these caveats in mind it is useful briefly to note constraints that have been found both necessary and practical in other projects. These include measures of transverse stability (e.g., GM_T) and non-submergence of a margin line following damage between specified transverse stations. Also useful have been specific control points necessary for clearance around machinery or outfit (e.g., reduction gears).

Parametric Geometry Model

Parametric approach

In order to generate and vary functional surfaces of complex shape such as ship hull forms with a degree of freedom suitable for optimization, a parametric approach is preferred. A context-dependent and solution-oriented description is established, allowing production of those shapes that are beneficial in performance and acceptable with regard to the many constraints from as small a data set as possible. Fig. 3 depicts a selection of different parameterizations provided for different design tasks ranging from fully appended round bilge sailing yachts, hard chined hulls, container carriers and multi hull arrangements such as SWATH.

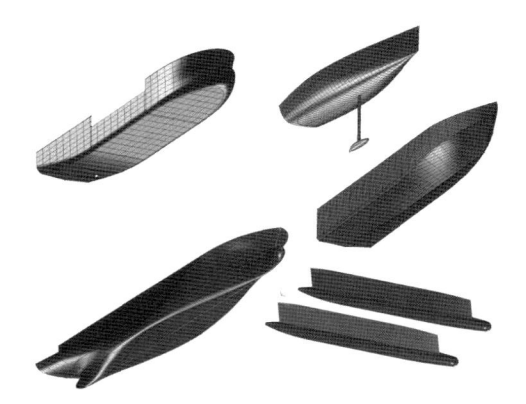

Fig. 3: The FRIENDSHIP-Modeler provides specific parametric models for various design tasks

The *FRIENDSHIP-Modeler* grants a high-level definition of hull shapes via form parameters such as beam, deadrise, draft, entrance angles, sectional areas, etc., and was therefore selected for the modeling of the dredge hull. For details see (Harries and Abt, 1999), (Harries *et al.*, 2001) and (Harries and Heimann, 2003). Also, see http://www.FRIENDSHIP-SYSTEMS.com for more information.

Form parameters

Fig. 4 depicts the hull geometry of the dredge generated with the *FRIENDSHIP-Modeler*. The shape of the dredge called for a specific parameterization which was developed by FRIENDSHIP SYSTEMS on the basis of a baseline design by Hockema and Assoc. The form features were closely examined via curvature plots and other measures, and suitable form parameters were identified.

Fig. 5 through Fig. 12 illustrate eight of the parametrically controlled geometric 'modes'.

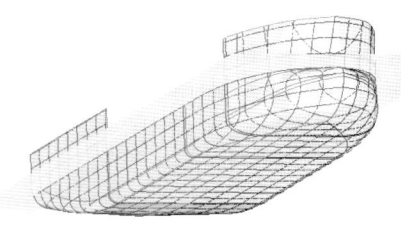

Fig. 4: Perspective view of the parametrically modeled dredge hull

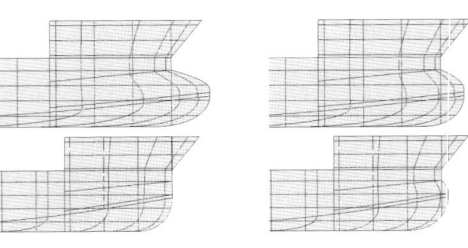

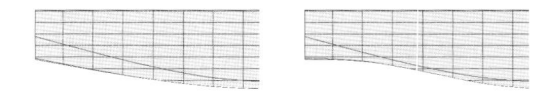

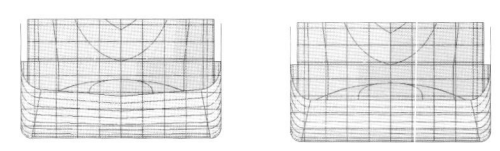

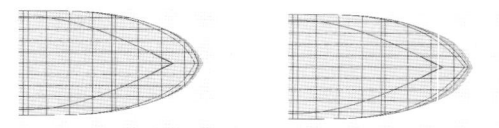

Fig. 5: Parametric dredge model: Variation of bulb length

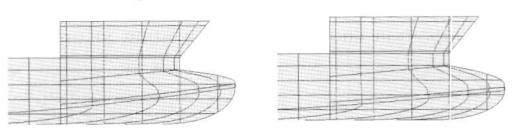

Fig. 6: Parametric dredge model: Modification of vertical position of straight part of bulb

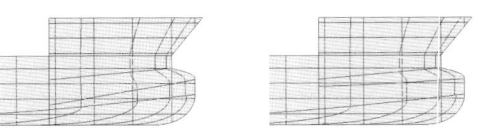

Fig. 7: Parametric dredge model: Variation of straight length at intersection to hull

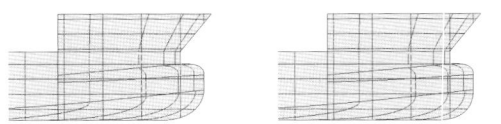

Fig. 8: Parametric dredge model: Variation of fullness of bulb's top and bottom

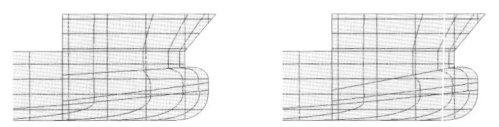

Fig. 9: Parametric dredge model: Variation of bulb height at FP and intersection to hull

Fig. 10: Parametric dredge model: Variation of run configuration

Fig. 11: Parametric dredge model: Variation of transom deadrise

Fig. 12: Parametric dredge model: Variation of bow plan view

Overview of Optimization Process

The complete process of generating a new hull form geometry, checking the constraints and eventually evaluating the measure of merit was setup by means of the FRIENDSHIP-Optimizer. This generic optimization toolkit facilitates building a process chain from a selection of arbitrary programs to generate a new design based on a number of controlling parameters. It then triggers the tools necessary to evaluate the design features and applies a variety of methods for design space exploration and formal optimization in order to find a superior design.

Constraints can be included and monitored during the optimization. The program has an advanced graphical interface, and can also be run in batch mode for time consuming numerical computations on mainframe computers.

In addition to a wide selection of well known formal algorithms, advanced users may also incorporate their own algorithms to control the optimization, while still taking advantage of the file and directory handling provided by the FRIENDSHIP-Optimizer.

Fig. 13 depicts the principal setup of such an optimization chain. For the problem at hand, the FRIENDSHIP-Modeler was used to generate the new hull geometry, and the well known Rankine source panel code SHIPFLOW (Larsson, 1997) was used to evaluate the wave making resistance in deep and shallow water.

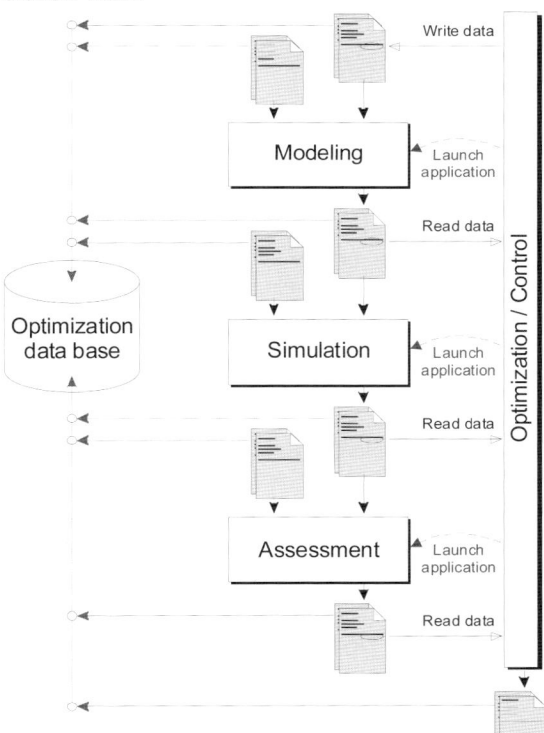

Fig. 13: Automated formal optimization process

Objective Functions in Deep and Shallow Water

As the main objective, the nominal thrust in deep water for a speed of 6.69 m/s (13.0 kts) was considered, corresponding to a Froude number of F_N=0.199.

$$T = R_T + R_{PRP} + R_{PRW} + R_{PRV} = \frac{R_T}{1-t} \qquad (1)$$

Additionally, the nominal thrust in shallow water (depth 45 ft or 13.7 m) and a speed of 6.43 m/s (12.5 kts) was monitored during the optimization procedures.

The nominal thrust, used as an objective function, was computed from the results of the free surface flow solution with the activated propeller source model by pressure integration over the hull panels. The viscous components were approximated using the ITTC'57 base line and a form factor estimate.

As the form factor might change with changes in the geometry, an approximation for the form factor in relation to geometric characteristics as introduced by Holtrop (1984) was employed.

The thrust must be input into the panel code. Before the parameterization, the value is unknown, and would require a time consuming iterative calculation. In order to speed up the optimization, a constant value for the thrust loading coefficient, C_{TS}=0.850, – giving a first approximation to the thrust of $\widetilde{T}$ – was used. An algebraic correction was developed to approximate the total pressure resistance at the correct thrust, $R_{PT}(T = R_T)$:

$$R_{PT}(T) = R_{PT}(\widetilde{T}) - t[\widetilde{T} - R_{PT}(\widetilde{T}) - R_V] \qquad (2)$$

$R_{PT}(\widetilde{T})$ denotes the calculated pressure resistance when using the thrust $\widetilde{T}$ in the calculation, t is the thrust deduction factor as calculated by comparing calculations with and without acting propeller. t = 0.22 and 0.23 for the deep water and the shallow water conditions, respectively.

Using the approximation above, the objective for the total nominal thrust becomes:

$$T = R_{PT}(T) + R_V \qquad (3)$$

Computational Fluid Dynamics Tool

For the performance assessment, the well-known code SHIPFLOW was employed. The wavemaking resistance was calculated by the potential-flow module xpan with nonlinear free-surface boundary conditions. In addition, viscous calculations were performed using SHIPFLOW's boundary layer module xbound and RANS module xvisc.

The potential module of the code SHIPFLOW employs a Rankine source panel representation of the hull, appendages and free surface geometry, and adjusts the source strength on each panel to fulfill the boundary conditions on the surface of the body and on the elevated free surface, respectively. Dynamic sinkage and trim are considered.

The Froude number of the dredge being $F_N=0.199$ for the deep water case, and the transom being submerged substantially, no flow clearance was expected; instead, a recirculating flow region just aft of the ship was anticipated. The flow past the large submerged transom cannot be adequately described as long as viscous effects are neglected. After discussing the issue with representatives of Flowtech A/B, it was decided not to impose any boundary conditions in that region. The transom and a triangular region of the free surface right behind the transom were left unpanelized, see Fig. 4. Within SHIPFLOW, the pressure integration is carried out over the panelized surface of the hull; the hydrostatic and hydrodynamic pressures on the transom are not accounted for in the code. It was therefore decided to add the hydrostatic component, and to neglect the hydrodynamic effect on the transom. This would certainly bias the resulting value for the wavemaking resistance; however, as the optimization was focused on the forebody, it was felt that the ranking would not be influenced severely, as the aft part of the hull remained largely unchanged.

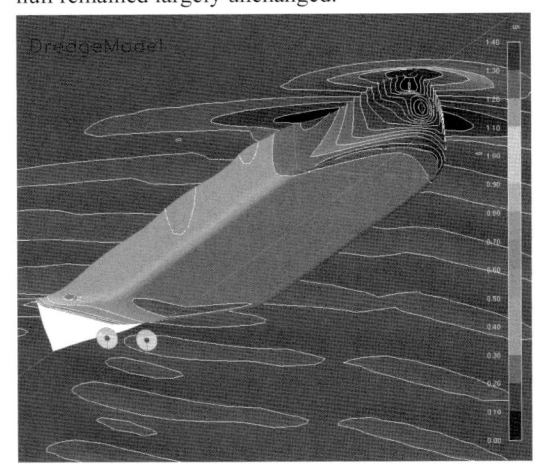

Fig. 14: Free surface flow computation with propeller disks and open transom

Since the SHIPFLOW code is limited to modeling only twin propellers, the effect of the triple screw configuration was approximated by using twin screws with accordingly changed loadings.

As the dredge is to operate regularly in shallow water, the wavemaking resistance was also calculated by adding environment panels at a depth of 45 feet (13.7 m) below the waterline.

For the RANS calculations, the aft half of the hull was covered with a grid of 120x40x40 nodes in the longitudinal, circumferential and radial directions, respectively. Thus a grid with 180999 nodes was used.

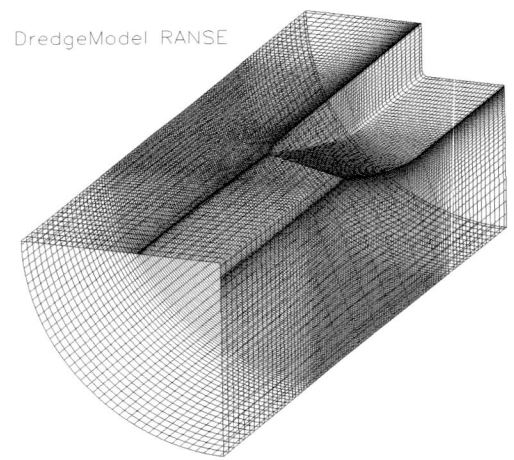

Fig. 15: Discretization of fluid domain about hull

The grid structure was improved by Poisson smoothing with respect to orthogonality of the cells, and a cell height at the boundary adequate for the actual Reynolds number. The grid cells were clustered in the vicinity of the transom to improve the resolution in that region. The grid extended beyond the hull 40% of the waterline length downstream. The radius of the grid was 25% of the waterline length. Fig. 15 shows the computational domain.

The inflow condition was calculated from a double body potential flow simulation and a boundary layer calculation, using a Reynolds number of 6.1 million and conforming to a model scale of 1:25.

Hierarchy of Search Strategies

As the dependence of the objective function on the generating parameters is considered rather complex, a multimodal problem with many local minima is very likely. Therefore, as first step of the optimization; a design space exploration was conducted to investigate the full range of the design space for possible areas with promising design properties. In order to provide a uniform distribution of hulls within the design space, a Sobol sequence (Press *et al*, 1988) was used. As a quasi-random strategy, the Sobol sequence ensures a statistically well represented design space, with increasingly finer resolution as more samples are produced, while avoiding clustering the design parameters. Within this phase, about 150 different hull designs were examined, of which 47 conformed to all of the given constraints. The best parametric design was identified as a suitable starting point for the subsequent directed search.

The focus of the second phase of the optimization is to converge to the optimum design in the vicinity of the starting point. Therefore, the direction of advancement for the free variables was triggered by the achieved values on the objective function (nominal thrust) while subject to the considered constraints. The Tangent Search Method, as described by Hilleary (1966), was considered an adequate strategy, as this method implicitly handles the optimization of an objective function within a constrained domain. The rate of improvement essentially vanished after 136 successive designs were evaluated, and the optimization was considered converged.

Results of Optimization

The optimization achieved a significant improvement in the nominal thrust. As shown in Fig. 16, the most advantageous design with respect to deep water was candidate DES_0106. However, DES_0047 exhibited significant advantages in shallow water, with only a modest degradation in deep water performance relative to DES_0106. Since the client indicated that performance in shallow water should be emphasized, DES_0047 was selected as the basis for the new suction hopper dredge *Glenn Edwards*.

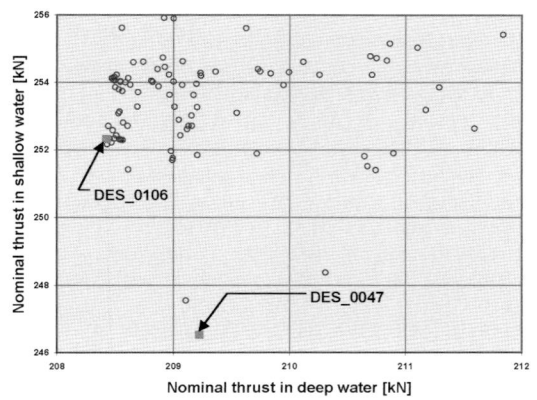

Fig. 16: Nominal thrust of solutions in deep and shallow water

Fig. 17 shows a color-coded plot of the axial velocity with acting propulsors as computed by the RANS code for DES_0047. There were no indications of premature flow separation on the bilge radii, a result similarly indicated in the model tests.

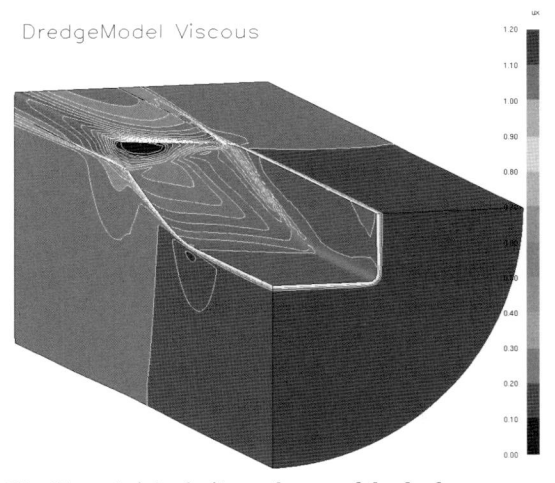

Fig. 17: Axial velocity on the run of the dredge

Model Tests

Model tests at 1:17.333 scale were performed at MARINTEK in Trondheim, Norway. The test program commenced with self-propelled course stability tests in deep water with various skeg configurations. A single centerline skeg was found to be acceptable, and was selected for the remainder of the program in shallow water (45 foot (13.7 m) depth full-scale equivalent).

The shallow water test program was carried out at two drafts, one corresponding to full-load (7.47 m draft) and the other corresponding to a no-load operating condition with trim aft. The shallow water test program included flow visualization, resistance, self-propulsion, detailed wake surveys in the propeller plane, and longitudinal wave cuts of wake-wash, see Fig. 18.

At the full-load draft in shallow water, the thrust deduction fraction averaged 0.261, which is slightly higher than the value of 0.23 estimated for that same condition using SHIPFLOW. The form factor determined from a Prohaska plot was $(1+k) = 1.2881$ from the model tests, while a form factor of $(1+k) = 1.34$ was predicted from SHIPFLOW RANS calculations.

Thrust at 12.5 knots from the model tests in shallow water was 2,312 kN which may be compared to 2,001 kN estimated as the nominal thrust in the optimization process, which included an estimated correction for the submerged transom. The thrust estimated from a direct pressure integration without such correction was higher than that determined from the model tests. It should be noted, however, that the CFD model did not account for additional resistance due to the double bow thruster opening, skeg and thruster supports which were present in the model test.

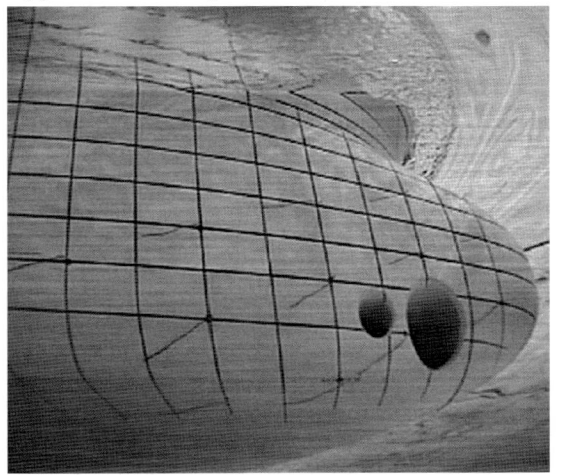

Fig. 18 Model test at MARINTEK with tuff flow visualization on the bow of the dredge

Full Scale Experience

Manson Construction Company has reported that they are very pleased with the hydrodynamic performance of the *Glenn Edwards*. They have reported that expectations regarding speed and power have been met or exceeded, and they have particularly noted the low wake wash when operating in shallow and/or restricted channels.

Conclusions

The approach to formal hull form optimization used for the dredge *Glenn Edwards* is practical and produced measurable improvement to performance both in deep and shallow water operations. Optimization is subject to a constraint set defined by the naval architect. Proper definition of that constraint set both engages the practicing naval architect and imposes a discipline to identify only the truly essential constraints. The parameterized geometry makes possible the limitation of optimization DOF to practical values, while simultaneously (and implicitly) enforcing selected constraints. The parameters of the geometry are physical (not abstract), and hence, intuitive for practicing naval architects.

This approach gives the ability to investigate compliance of thousands of potential hull forms with the constraints, and to evaluate the relative hydrodynamic performance of hundreds (or potentially thousands) of constraint compliant hull forms. This breadth of investigation, together with the application of directed search strategies, ensures that the final selected hull form is a credible near optimum, while the parametric geometry ensures that the selected hull adheres to conventional notions of fairness. All of these contribute to acceptance of the optimized hull by owners. Finally, the favorable results obtained in actual service are recognized and appreciated by owners.

Acknowledgement

The authors gratefully acknowledge the support of owners of the *Glenn Edwards*, Manson Construction Company, and of Hal Hockema, the lead and managing naval architect for the project.

References

Harries, S. and Abt, C. (1999). "Formal Hydrodynamic Optimization of a Fast Monohull on the Basis of Parametric Hull Design," 5th International Conference on Fast Sea Transportation, Seattle, WA, USA, August 1999.

Harries, S. and Heimann, J. (2003). "Optimization of the Wave-making Characteristics of Fast Ferries," 7th International Conference on Fast Sea Transportation, Ischia (Gulf of Naples), Italy, October 2003.

Harries, S.; Valdenazzi, F.; Abt, C.; and Viviani, U. (2001). "Investigation on Optimization Strategies for the Hydrodynamic Design of Fast Ferries," 6th International Conference on Fast Sea Transportation, Southampton, UK September 2001.

Hendrix, Dane, Percival, Scott and Noblesse, Francis (2001). "Practical Hydrodynamic Optimization of a Monohull," SNAME Transactions, Vol. 109, pp 173-183.

Hilleary, Roger R. (1966). "The tangent search method of constrained minimization," Technical Report/Res. Paper No. 59, Naval Postgraduate School, Monterey, CA, USA.

Holtrop, J. (1984). "A statistical re-analysis of resistance and propulsion data," International Shipbuilding Progress, 31(363), pp 272–276.

Larsson, L. (1997). "SHIPFLOW User's manual and theoretical manual," FLOWTECH Int. AB, Gothenburg.

Press, William H., Teukolsky, Saul A., Vetterling, William T., and Flannery, Brian P. (1988). Numerical Recipes in C, 2nd ed., Cambridge University Press, New York, NY, USA.

Hydrodynamic Performance and Structural Design of a SWATH Ship

You-Sheng Wu [1], Qi-Jun Ni [1], Wei Xie [2], Sa-Ya Zhou [2], Guo-Hong You [1], Chao Tian [3], Yan Zhang [4] and Qiang Wu [5]

[1] China Ship Scientific Research Center, CSIC,
Wuxi, Jiangsu, China
[2] China Ship Design and Development Center, CSIC,
Wuhan, Hubei, China
[3] School of Naval Archi & Ocean Eng, Shanghai Jiao Tong University,
Shanghai, China
[4] Dalian Scientific Test and Control Technology Institute, CSIC
Dalian, Liaoning, China
[5] China Shipbuilding Industry Corporation (CSIC)
Beijing, China

Abstract

The present paper describes the practical design technique of SWATH ships developed by China Shipbuilding Industry Corporation. This includes the systematic approaches of conceptual design, optimization of shipform and principal dimensions, predictions of powering performance, seakeeping behavior and motion stability, assessment of structural loads, static and dynamic strengths of a SWATH ship traveling in random waves. The design and evaluation of an Ocean-Survey SWATH Ship with the displacement of 1500t is illustrated as an example. In the design process, the linear and non-linear three-dimensional hydroelasticity theories (Bishop, Price and Wu, 1986; Wu, Maeda, and Kinoshita, 1997) were applied to predict the loads and to assess the structural safety of the vessel traveling in rough seas (Li and Wu, 2005; Tian and Wu, 2006a, b, 2007). The resistance, seakeeping and maneuvering behaviors and the wave loads of the designed vessel were verified by a set of restricted and free-running model tests carried out in towing tank and wave basin at CSSRC. These are briefly described in the paper.

Keywords

SWATH Ship; Design optimization; Structural design; Hydrodynamic performance; Hydroelastic analysis; Non-linear responses.

Introduction

Relying on the excellent performance in waves resulting from the small waterplane area concept, more than 60 SWATH (Small Waterplane Area Twin Hull) ships have been built since 1973 in the world. Generally speaking, the seakeeping behavior of a well-designed SWATH ship may be as good as a larger mono-hull ship with 3 to 10 times of displacement. However the specific twin hull form implies much more design parameters than a mono-hull ship in the optimization of its hydrodynamic performances and structural strengths. Based on years of research work and accumulated experiences, China Shipbuilding Industry Corporation has developed a comprehensive package of practical design tools for SWATH ships traveling in waves, including the systematic approaches of conceptual design, optimization of principal dimensions and shipform, predictions of powering performance, seakeeping behavior and motion stability, assessment of structural loads and dynamic strengths etc. This is briefly described in the present paper. As an example, the design and evaluation of an Ocean-Survey SWATH Ship with the displacement of 1500t is illustrated.

Conceptual Design Method

Optimization of Principal Dimensions

Following the functions and technical specifications of the ship particularly defined, and the displacement preliminary required by the ship owner, the designers out of several options are able to initiate the overall layout and configuration of the ship based on their experiences. Different from design of conventional mono-hull ships, in the following design procedures the most important work that comes at first in SWATH ship design is to carefully tackle the hydrodynamic qualities of the ship. The first stage in this direction is the optimization of principal dimensions to the target of low resistance and the selection of the main engine to approximately reach the initial displacement and satisfy the overall design requirements of the ship. A simple mathematical model consisting of 10 independent optimization parameters was introduced to describe the outlines and principal dimensions of the SWATH ship

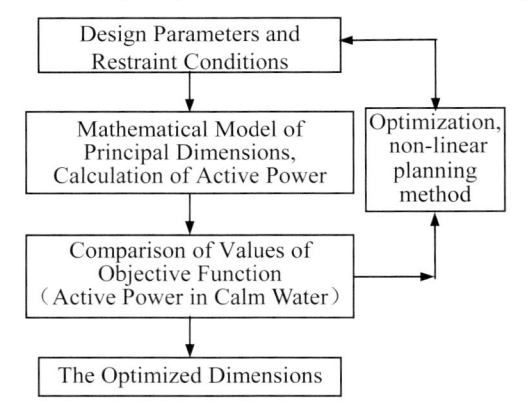

Fig.1: Optimization of the Principal Dimensions

(Ge, 1992). These parameters include the lengths of strut and main hull, the beam of strut at waterline, the maximum cross section area of main hull, the submerged depth of strut, the horizontal distance between strut nose and main hull nose, and the relative lengths of nose to midsection and tail to midsection of strut and main hull respectively. Applying these parameters the corresponding prediction method of active power in calm water was established (Ge, 1985) based on the slender body linear wave resistance theory. With the total displacement of the ship and the upper and lower limits of the parameters being the prescribed restraints, and the active power of the ship as the objective function, the Flexible Tolerance Method of non-linear planning approaches (Chen, 1981) was used to achieve the optimization of the principal dimensions. The procedure is shown in Fig. 1.

Conceptual Design and Shipform Optimization

The preliminarily defined principal dimensions should be further modified to satisfy or balance other requirements, especially seakeeping behavior, stability, endurance, transportation efficiency etc. Hence the second stage of SWATH ship design is the optimization of the shipform. To this purpose, a computer added conceptual design package was developed (Yi, 2004; Ni and Ye, 2005), where except the above mentioned 10 parameters, the ship displacement and the transverse metacentric height were added as variables. The SWATH ship was therefore described by 12 independent design parameters. For a set of initial values of the parameters, each running of the program produced 8 sets of their variations, and the simplified methods for predictions of the powering performance, seakeeping (Yi, 2004), stability (Ge and Guo, 2000) behaviors, and wave loads (Lin, Qian, and You, 2006) were further used to provide the results of 9 different designs. Each set of results include the geometries of the hull, metacentric heights, resistance, active power in calm water, added power in waves, design shaft power, sea endurance, resonant frequencies, seakeeping behaviors in typical sea conditions, characteristics of motion stability, roughly estimated weights of structure, machineries and effective loads individually etc. These were created in the form of a database and the corresponding figures to show the variation trends of different designs, allowing the designers to compare the results, modify the parameters and by iteration, achieve the optimized design. The procedure of the conceptual design and the shipform optimization is shown in Fig.2.

Based on the shipform produced by iterative applications of the optimization software of principal dimensions and the conceptual design package, the detailed ship-lines were further optimized to reach the geometric smoothness and minimum resistance (Ge, 1986).

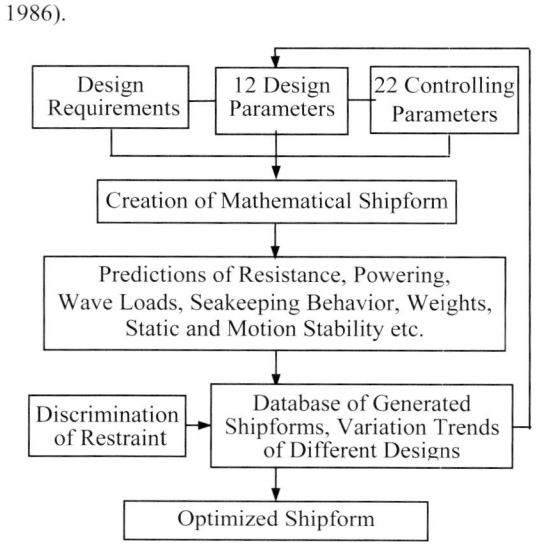

Fig.2: Procedure of the Conceptual Design

Assessment Methods of Structural Loads

In addition to the regular structural design and safety assessment using design guides issued by classification societies, China Ship Industry Corporation established a first-principle-based direct calculation method of wave loads. This is based on the three-dimensional hydroelasticity theories. The linear three-dimensional hydroelasticity theory (Bishop, Price and Wu, 1986; Du, Wu and Price, 1998) and the corresponding numerical method (Li, 2005; Tian and Wu, 2007) have been used to predict the wave loads and the structural dynamic strengths of a ship traveling in design sea conditions. While a non-linear three dimensional hydroelasticity theory (Wu, Maeda, and Kinoshita, 1997) and the corresponding numerical method (Tian and Wu, 2006a,b, 2007) has been used to modify the linear predictions and to provide a reference of confidence to the model test results of design wave loads, as well as to check the structural strengths of a ship traveling with a moderate or high speed in rough seas.

The importance and attractiveness of three-dimensional hydroelastic analyses to a SWATH ship comes from the fact that it is especially suitable to a complicated multi-hull floating structure, and more over it predicts simultaneously both the seakeeping behaviors and the structural responses (deformations, strains, stresses, internal forces and moments).

According to the three-dimensional hydroelasticity theory, under the assumption of the linear structure, the displacement at any position of the structure may be expressed as the aggregation of the principal modes of the dry structure u_r^o (r = 1,2,..., m):

$$u = \sum_{r=1}^{m} u_r^o p_r(t) \quad (1)$$

where the principal modes u_r^o are defined in the body-fixed coordinate system with the first six (r =1, 2,..., 6) being the rigid body modes, and $p_r(t)$ (r =1, 2,..., m) are the principal coordinates. In general when the ship travels with a constant forward speed in irregular waves, the generalized equations of motion may be written to the second order in the matrix form (Tian and Wu, 2006):

$$(a+A)\ddot{p}(t)+(b+B)\dot{p}(t)+(c+C+\Delta C)p(t)$$
$$= \Xi^{(1)}(t) + \widetilde{F}^{(2)}(t) + \widetilde{D}^{(2)}(t) + \widetilde{S}^{(2)}(t) \quad (2)$$

where a, b and c are matrices of generalized modal inertial, modal damping and modal stiffness of the dry structure; p is the vector $\{p_1(t), p_2(t),..., p_m(t)\}$; A, B and C are respectively the matrices of generalized hydrodynamic inertial, damping and restoring coefficients; $\Xi^{(1)}$ is the generalized first-order wave exciting forces; $\widetilde{F}^{(2)}$, $\widetilde{D}^{(2)}$ and $\widetilde{S}^{(2)}$ are respectively the wave frequency components, difference- and sum-frequency components of the generalized second-order hydrodynamic forces (Wu, Maeda and Kinoshita, 1997; Tian and Wu, 2006b).

A program package LTHAFTS was developed to solve the linear problem of Eq.2. The boundary integral method together with the Kelvin translating source Green function for the non-uniform steady flow around the body surface and the translating and pulsating source Green function for the radiation flow are used to solve the generalized hydrodynamic coefficients A, B and C and the generalized exciting forces $\Xi^{(1)}$ to allow for the effect of forward speed being more rigorously considered in the analyses. A program NTHAFTS was developed to further solve the second order non-linear problem of Eq.2, where the non-linear hydrodynamic forces resulting from the large motions and the instantaneous wetted surface effect are calculated (Tian and Wu, 2006a, b, 2007).

For a given sea state described by a wave energy spectrum, the first and second order principal coordinates could be solved by adopting LTHAFTS and NTHAFTS respectively. The structural responses of the ship can be evaluated by the modal superposition:

$$\sigma(x) = \sum_{r=7}^{m} \sigma_r(x) p_r(t), \quad F_y(t) = \sum_{r=7}^{m} F_{yr} p_r(t),$$
$$M_x(t) = \sum_{r=7}^{m} M_{xr} p_r(t), \quad M_z(t) = \sum_{r=7}^{m} M_{zr} p_r(t) \quad (3)$$

where σ denotes the von Mises stress at any position $x = \{x, y, z\}$ of the structure, F_y, M_y and M_z represent respectively the global horizontal prying force, prying moment and yaw splitting moment acting along the longitudinal cross section of the bridge structure. The quantities with a subscript r denote the corresponding r-th mode of the dry structure *in vacuum*.

The 1500t Ocean Survey SWATH Ship

The design methods briefly described above have been applied to design more than 7 SWATH ships in CSIC, among which was an ocean survey ship of the displacement 1500t as shown in Fig.3. This ship was designed for multi-purposes of research and survey of oceanography, marine biogeography, geomorphology and resources in the territorial sea of China.

The principal particulars of the ship produced based on the mission of the ship and the applications of the optimization method of principal dimensions and the conceptual design package is partly listed in Table 1. The optimized ship-lines are shown in Fig. 4.

Fig.3: The 1500t Ocean Survey SWATH Ship

Table 1: Principal particulars of the SWATH ship

Items	Data
Length Overall (m)	65.8
Length of Strut (m)	52.0
Maximum Beam (m)	23.0
Depth to the Main Deck (m)	7.8
Draught (m)	5.0
Full Load Displacement Mass (t)	1500
Distance between the Centerlines of the Struts (m)	18.0
Maximum Speed (kn)	12.0 (6.17 m/s)
Economic Cruising Speed (kn)	11.0 (5.67 m/s)
Power of Driving Motor (kw)	2x800
Range at Cruising Speed (n mile)	1500 (2780 km)
Endurance (days)	15
Crew and Researchers (persons)	32+20

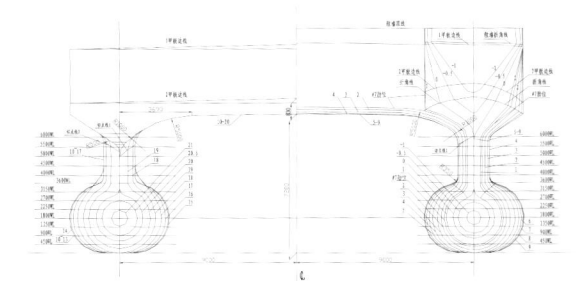

Fig. 4: The Ship-lines of the 1500t SWATH Ship

Prediction of Behaviors and Model Tests

Powering Performance

The resistance and powering performance of the ship in design condition of draught 5m and displacement 1500t was predicted at different speeds from 5 to 14kn. The resistance and self-running model tests were carried out at the towing tank of CSSRC with the model scale of 1:17. The comparisons between the predictions and the test results of active power are shown in Fig.5. Apparently good agreement was achieved, and the cruising speed possesses the plateau position of the active power curve, providing attractive powering efficiency.

The propeller was designed with the assistance of the lifting surface method. The powering performance exhibited in Fig.6 shows that with two 800kw driving motors rotating at 250rpm, the maximum speed of the ship could reach 12.25kn.

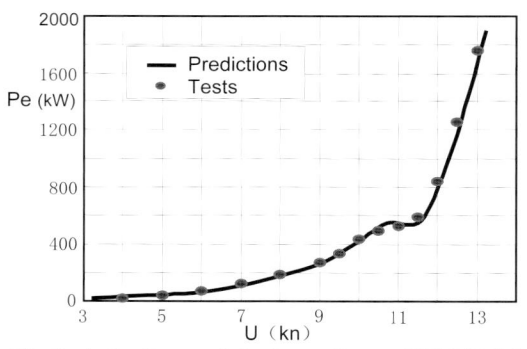

Fig. 5: Active Power of the Ocean-Survey SWATH Ship

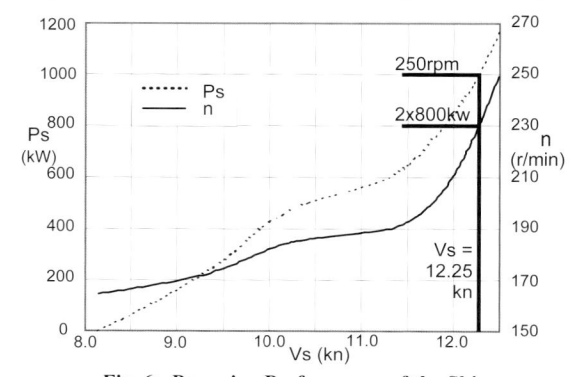

Fig. 6: Powering Performance of the Ship

Seakeeping Behavior of the Ship

The seakeeping model tests were carried out in the wave basin of CSSRC to verify the design optimization and the numerical predictions. The model scale was also 1:17. The ISSC wave spectrum with two-parameters of $H_{1/3}$ and T_{01} was used to simulate the irregular waves. Part of the test results of the ship under design condition of displacement 1500t and draught 5m are presented in Table 2. The numerical predictions by the three-dimensional hydroelasticity theory are close to the model test results as compared in Table 3. The predicted heave motions are apparently higher than the test results,

Table 2: Test results of Seakeeping behavior of the SWATH ship

Headings (°)	Forward Speed (kn)	Waves $H_{1/3}$(m) T_{01}(s)	Pitch (°)	Roll (°)	Heave (m)	Accel. at Bow (g)
180	0	2.5m 6.95s	1.36	/	0.99	0.058
90			0.36	3.08	1.99	0.057
180	3	2.5m 6.95s	1.20	/	0.95	0.060
	8		1.10	/	0.53	0.053
	11		1.03	/	0.42	0.053
180	8	3.25m 7.53s	1.90	/	1.17	0.083
	11		1.79	/	1.02	0.138
180	0	3.25m 7.53s	2.20	/	1.41	0.084
135			1.80	2.61	1.50	0.071
90			0.57	5.07	1.56	0.073
45			1.98	2.89	1.47	0.069
0			2.51	/	1.36	0.072
Oscillating Period			11.7s	17.4s	8.9s	/

Table 3: Comparison between predictions and test results of significant values of motions

	Waves	Motion	(a) Prediction	(b) Tests	(a-b)/a
Beam Sea 0 kn	$H_{1/3}$=2.5m T_{01}=6.95s	Heave (m)	1.24	1.19	4.03 %
		Pitch (°)	0.35	0.36	-2.86 %
	$H_{1/3}$=3.25m T_{01}=7.53s	Heave (m)	1.76	1.56	11.4 %
		Pitch (°)	0.52	0.57	-9.61 %
Head Sea 11 kn	$H_{1/3}$=2.5m T_{01}=6.95s	Heave (m)	0.596	0.42	29.5 %
		Pitch (°)	1.012	1.03	-1.78 %
	$H_{1/3}$=3.25m T_{01}=7.53s	Heave (m)	1.127	1.02	9.49 %
		Pitch (°)	1.835	1.79	2.45 %

Table 4: Comparison of significant values of motions between a mono-hull ship and the SWATH ship (0 kn, $H_{1/3}$ =3.25m, T_{01}=7.53s)

Particulars	A Mono-hull Ship	The SWATH
Length Overall (m)	158.6	65.8
Length of Waterline	156.4	52.0
Maximum Beam (m)	23.0	23.0
Draught (m)	8.81	5.00
Full load displacement (t)	17590	1500

Headings	Motions		
180°	Pitch (°)	2.27	2.20
90°	Heave (m)	2.51	1.56
90°	Roll (°)	9.31	5.07
90°	Amidships Acceleration (g)	0.15	0.074

partly due to the neglect of the viscous damping in the numerical calculations.

The attractive seakeeping behaviors of the ship in waves can be more clearly observed by comparison with a mono-hull ship with 10 more times of displacement as shown in Table 4.

Predictions of Maneuverability

Self-propulsion maneuvering model tests were performed and the results are listed in Table 5. The stable rotating diameter of the ship at speed 12kn is about 5 times of the ship length L with maximum heel angle of 3.28°. The results shown in Table 5 indicate that the maneuvering behavior of the ship is satisfactory.

Table 5: Test results of maneuvering behaviors

Test Items	Maneuvering Parameters		Rudder Angle δ_r(°)	Test Results
Turning Test (12kn)	Steady turning diameter	D_S	±35°	5.18 L
	Transfer	S_l	±35°	2.68 L
	Advance	I_m	±35°	4.20 L
	Tactical diameter	D_T	±35°	5.23 L
Zig-Zag Test	Non-dimensional initial turning time	t_a'	±10°/±10°	2.60
			±20°/±20°	2.86
	First overshoot angle ψ_{OV1}		±10°/±10°	2.86
			±20°/±20°	6.92
	Second overshoot angle ψ_{OV2}		±10°/±10°	3.46
			±20°/±20°	7.51
Pulling Out Maneuvering Test	Remnant yaw velocity	r_o	±20°	0.0
Full Astern Stopping Tests	Track reach	R_T	0	2.34 L

Wave Loads Assessment

Wave loads of the ship were carefully assessed by both model tests and numerical predictions. Since the ship was designed to operate in the territorial sea of China, the survival wave condition was defined as $H_{1/3}$= 4.0m.

Wave Load Model Tests

Self-running model tests with the model scale of 1:22 were performed at wave basin of CSSRC to measure the wave loads. For a SWATH ship, the most important global loads are evidently the prying force F_y, prying moment M_X, yaw splitting moment M_Z and torque moment M_y. Here x, y and z are the axes of the body fixed frame with x-axis horizontally pointing from stern to bow and z-axis vertically pointing upwards. Hence the model was cut to port and starboard potions along the longitudinal centerline of the bridge structure. Two sets of load sensors were mounted fore and aft midsection of the model to connect the two portions and to measure the above-mentioned components of global loads. The tests were carried out at three wave conditions corresponding to the full-scale significant wave heights of $H_{1/3}$=2.5m (operational wave condition, T_{01}=5.61s), 4.0m (survival wave condition, T_{01}=7.1s) and 7.7m (extreme wave condition, T_{01}=10.71s) at different forward speeds and wave headings.

The tests results revealed the following aspects:

(1). In all wave conditions, forward speeds and wave headings, the maximum prying forces F_y and moments M_X occurred in the zero speed and beam sea case.

(2). The resultant prying forces F_y in those cases were acting at the positions a little bit above the half of the draught.

(3). Due to the fact that in the irregular waves of $H_{1/3}$=7.7m and T_{01}=10.71s the amount of long wave length components became relatively more along with the increase of wave height, although motions of the ship appeared larger than other wave conditions, the prying force F_y and moment M_X exhibited smaller maximum values than the case when the ship was in survival wave condition of $H_{1/3}$=4.0m and T_{01}=7.1s.

(4). The maximum value of yaw splitting moment M_Z appeared in the zero speed and oblique sea (45°) case.

(5). In any cases the torque moment M_y was small. Its maximum value occurred when the ship was traveling with 12kn in oblique (45°) sea of the survival wave condition.

Some typical test results of the significant wave loads of the ship in survival wave condition are shown in Table 6.

Table 6: Comparison between predictions and test results of significant wave loads ($H_{1/3}$=4.0m, T_{01}=7.01s)

Headings / Speed	Global Wave Loads	(a) Prediction	(b) Test Results	(a-b)/a
Beam Sea 0 kn	F_Y (kN)	3127	3716	-18.8 %
	M_X (kN·m)	24166	20685	14.4 %
	M_Z (kN·m)	6900	5974	13.4 %
Head Sea 12 kn	F_Y (kN)	207	267	17.6%
	M_X (kN·m)	1502	1506	1.4%
	M_Z (kN·m)	3343	3982	22.1%

Design Wave Loads

Classification Society Guides were used to provide the design loads. Apparently the results obtained by applying the guides issued by different classification societies were quite different. The differences between each other could be greater than 140%. The results based on one of the design guides are shown in Table 7.

The test results proved that the required design wave loads for prying force and moment that the ship structure has to withstand could be reasonably decided relying on the maximum wave loads that the ship would encountered at zero speed in beam seas of the survival wave condition. Though need to be multiplied by a safety factor.

For the present ship the safety factor was taken as 2, and the maximum wave loads were converted from the test results of significant wave loads F_Y and M_X listed in Table 6. While the maximum yaw splitting moment was obtained from the test result in oblique wave condition. Thus obtained values of design loads are given in Table 7. They are smaller than the results calculated following the design guide by a factor from 0.65 to 0.80.

Table 7: Design wave loads based on the classification society guide and the test results

Design Wave Loads	(a) Design Guide	(b) Test Results	(b)/(a)
Prying Force (kN)	19322	13824	0.72
Prying Moment (kN·m)	117864	76947	0.65
Yaw Splitting Moment (kN·m)	125593	101009	0.80

Preliminary Design of the Structure

The preliminary design of the mainframe structure was based on the design wave loads obtained from the model tests. The local structures were designed to satisfy the guidelines of classification societies. A preliminarily designed hull structure of the ship allowed the hydroelasticity method being used to directly calculate and check the wave loads.

Calculation of the Wave Loads

The Finite Element Analysis of the ship structure *in vacuum* was performed at first to obtain the principal modes of the ocean survey SWATH ship. A symmetric modal shape corresponding to the 14th mode is shown in Fig. 7.

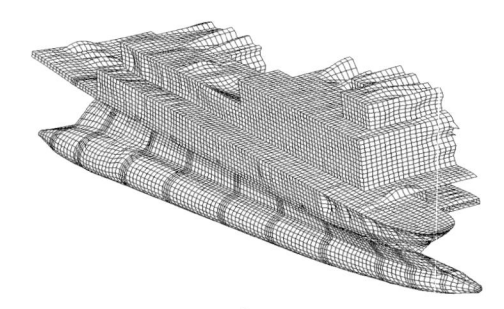

Fig. 7: The symmetric 14th modal shape of the SWATH ship (showing half body, Natural frequency 7.8676Hz)

The program LTHAFTS based on the linear three-dimensional hydroelasticity theory and the program NTHAFTS based on the non-linear three-dimensional hydroelasticity theory were further employed to calculate the structural deflections, stresses, global forces and moments etc. of the ship encountering either beam sea with 0 speed, or head sea with forward speed of 11 and 12kn in different wave conditions of significant wave heights 2.5m, 3.25m and 4.0m. In the calculation the mean wetted surface of the ship was represented by 1206 panels, and two incident wave spectra were used, which were the same as the target and the measured incident wave spectra of the model tests.

The predictions exhibited the same phenomena as revealed by the test results. In the survival wave conditions described by the target incident wave spectrum of the model tests, the global wave loads of the ship predicted by the non-linear program NTHAFTS are compared with the test results in Table 6. The differences between the predictions and the test results are less than 22%. The differences may partly be caused by the fact that the calculation was for the preliminary designed ship, which was slightly different from the test model produced from the conceptual design.

The comparison confirmed that the design loads based on the test results or the direct calculations were reasonable to be applied in the detailed design of the SWATH ship concerned.

Assessment of Local Strengths

The typical structural configuration and the weight critical nature of SWATH ship require more attention in the assessment of structural design and safety than a mono-hull ship. During the detailed design stage of the structure, the Finite Element Analysis and the program NTHAFTS were used to check the local strengths.

Fig. 8 exhibits a simplified example of the NTHAFTS predicted maximum von Mises stresses within a portion of the port hull, including a transverse bulkhead (amidships, 25m from the bow). The ship is traveling with forward speed of 12kn in irregular head waves of the significant wave height $H_{1/3}$=3.25m. The color contour plot of Fig. 8 illustrates the stress variations within the entire bulkhead. Among the hot spots A~E in the outer plate, the node D sustains the largest stresses.

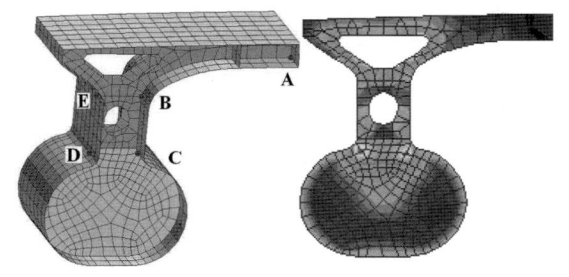

Fig. 8: A typical portion of the structure including a transverse bulkhead and the distribution of the maximum von Mises stress over the bulkhead (12kn, Head sea, $H_{1/3}$=3.25, T_{01}=7.53s)

Fig. 9 shows the linear and non-linear predictions of the time variations of the von Mises stress at the node D. "Non-linear (1)" denotes the non-linear prediction including the second order effect of the rigid body rotations of the ship in rough seas. Since the SWATH ship has very good seakeeping behavior, the rigid body rotation effect provides little influence on the stresses, hence is close to the linear solution. "Non-linear (2)" represents the non-linear prediction taking into account both the instantaneous wetted surface and the rigid body rotation effects. Obviously the variation of instantaneous wetted surface over the SWATH ship in rough seas provides noticeable influence on the stress level at the hot spot D. Thus produced maximum von Mises stress at D is greater than the linear solution up to about 30%. However this phenomenon and the increased quantity need to be further verified.

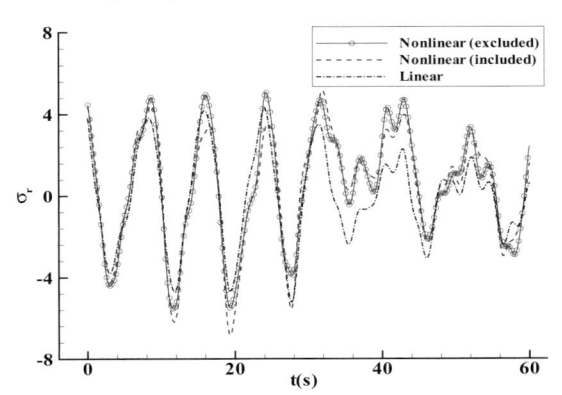

Fig. 9: Time variations of linear and nonlinear predictions of von Mises stress at node D (12kn, Head sea, $H_{1/3}$=3.25, T_{01}=7.53s)

Even though the non-linear solutions predicted greater stresses than the linear solutions, it is obvious that the value of the maximum stresses at the hot spots are still far below the allowable stress, when the SWATH ship is traveling with 12kn in head seas within a wide range of significant wave height from 2.5m to 4.0m. Only when the SWATH ship is encountering beam seas with zero forward speed in survival wave conditions, the predicted stresses at several hot spots along the joint lines between the strut-bridge structure and the strut-pontoon structure appear to be large. According to the calculation results, certain modifications of the local structural design were made, and the materials were carefully chosen to ensure the structural safety.

Conclusions

Three SWATH ships are now in operation and two more will be in service in the near future in China. Systematic approaches have been developed in CSIC to provide a comprehensive package of practical design tools for SWATH ships. These include: (1) The optimization program of principal dimensions for low resistance; (2) Predictions of powering performance, seakeeping behavior and motion stability; (3) A computer aided conceptual design package with 12 independent parameters for optimization of shipform and overall behaviors; (4) The techniques of model tests for hydrodynamic behaviors and wave loads; (5) The direct calculation methods of structural loads and safety assessment based on linear and non-linear hydroelastic analyses etc.

It is shown in this paper that these methods were successfully applied in the design of an ocean survey SWATH ship of 1500t displacement. However the developed techniques are not restricted to SWATH ships only, but may be applied to other multi-hull ships and high performance mono-hull ships.

Acknowledgement

The authors would like to thank Prof. Ge, WZ, Prof. Shi, LG, Prof. Yi, QL, Prof. Lin, JR, Prof. Guo, ZX and Prof. Zhu, BQ for their contributions to the development of the design techniques briefly described in this paper, and their effort in the conceptual and preliminary design of the SWATH ship concerned, also acknowledge Mr. Suo, HX and Mr. Yao, QR for their hard work in structural design.

References

American Bureau of Shipping (1999). "Guide for Building and Classing Small Waterplane Area Twin Hull (SWATH) Vessels," Provisional.

Bishop, RED, Price, WG, and Wu, YS (1986). "A General Linear Hydroelasticity theory of Floating Structures Moving in a Seaway", Phil. Trans. Royal Soc. London, A316, pp 375 – 426.

Chen, JT (1981). "The Mathematical Methods of Design Optimization", National Defense Industry Press, December, 1981.

China Classification Society (2004). "Guidelines of Small Waterplane Area Twin Hull Craft".

Du, SX, Wu YS and Price, WG (1998). "Forward Speed Effect on the Structure Responses of a Ship Traveling in Waves". Hydroelasticity in Marine Technology, Kashiwagi et al. (eds), Yomei Printing Cooperative Society, pp 401-410.

Ge, WZ (1985). "Prediction Method of SWATH Ship Resistance", J. Ship Behavior Research, No. 2.

Ge, WZ (1986). "Optimization Method of Low Resistance Shipform of SWATH Ships", Proc 1st Symp of Ship Resistance, Chinese Society of Naval Architects and Marine Engineers, Wenzhou, China.

Ge, WZ (1992). "Optimization Method of Principal Dimension of SWATH Ships", J. Naval Ship Science & Technology, Vol 14, No.2.

Ge, WZ, and Guo, ZX (2000). "Motion Stability of SWATH Ship", J. of Shipbuilding of China, Vol 41, No 3.

Guo, ZX, Shun, QW et al (2005). "Wave Basin Test of Self-running SWATH Ship Model", Proc 10th China Int Boat Show and High Performance Marine Vehicles (HPMV) Conference, Shanghai, China.

Li, ZW (2005). "Hydroelastic Analysis of Wave Loads of SWATH Ships", MSc Dissertation, Shanghai Jiao Tong University.

Lin, JR, Qian, JY, and You, GH (2006). "Design Wave Loads of SWATH Ships", Proc Ship Mechanics & Ship Design Conf, Nanjing, China.

Ni, QJ and Ye, YL (2005). "Optimal Design for the Complex Navigation Performance of A SWATH-type Comprehensive Scientific Research Vessel", FAST'2005, Saint-Petersburg, Russia.

Shun, QW, Guo, ZX et. al. (2004). "Prediction Method of Heave and Pitch Motions of SWATH ships", Proc 9th China Int Boat Show and High Performance Marine Vehicles (HPMV) Conference, Shanghai, China.

Tian, C, and Wu, YS (2006a). "The Non-Linear Hydroelastic Responses of a Ship Traveling in Waves", Hydroelasticity in Marine Technology, Wu and Cui (eds), National Defense Industry Press, pp 14-24.

Tian, C, and Wu, YS (2006b). "The Second-order Hydroelastic Analysis of a SWATH Ship Moving in Large-amplitude Waves", J. Hydrodynamics, Ser.B, Vol 18, No 6, pp 631-639.

Tian, C, and Wu, YS (2007). "Three-dimensional Non-linear Hydroelasticity Analysis of Ships with Forward Speed", J. Ship Mechanics, Vol 11, No 1, pp 68-78.

Wu, YS, Maeda, H, and Kinoshita, T (1997). "The Second Order Hydrodynamic Actions on a Flexible Body", J. of SEISAN-KENKYU, Institute of Industrial Science of Univ. of Tokyo, Vol 49, No 4, pp 8 – 19.

Yi, QL (2004). "Conceptual Design Package of SWATH Ship", Proc High Performance Ship Symp, Chinese Society of Naval Architects and Marine Engineers, Suzhou.

Development of New Applied Models for Steel Corrosion in Marine Applications Including Shipping

Robert E Melchers
Centre for Infrastructure Performance and Reliability, The University of Newcastle
Newcastle, NSW, Australia 2308

Abstract

Models for the prediction of corrosion mostly give the misleading impression that corrosion of steel in seawater environments is a linear function of time (the 'corrosion rate'). Non-linear functions have been proposed also, These have been calibrated to aggregated data from a wide variety of sources. This produces predictions with wide uncertainty and it is difficult to make assessments of the effect of steel composition and environmental influences. Recent research has produced a model based on the fundamental characteristics of steel corrosion, including the effect of biological influences. Detailed investigations show that the process controlling the (instantaneous) rate of corrosion changes as corrosion progresses. This is represented as a sequence of phases for which fundamental theoretical justifications and mathematical relationships have been derived. To ensure the model has practical validity it has been calibrated to actual field observations rather than laboratory data. Research findings for the effect of water temperature, dissolved oxygen levels, nutrient pollution, depth, water velocity, water salinity and steel composition are reviewed briefly. Some observations about applications and research directions are given.

Keywords

Corrosion; Steel; Seawater; Mathematical models; Environment; Composition.

Introduction

Despite protective coatings and cathodic protection, ships do corrode. One question is how long it takes before corrosion commences, a matter about which there is much anecdotal information, mostly in the private domain, but little recorded quantitative data (Melchers & Jiang 2006). In practice good housekeeping ought to be able to prevent corrosion becoming a serious problem but in fact many structures show (apparently) advanced corrosion. In such situations the questions that arise are (i) how serious is the visible corrosion, (ii) is immediate action required, and (iii) if not, how much longer can action be deferred? These are not wholly engineering questions and involve economics, risk assessment and related criteria. But they do need an understanding of the corrosion processes and a model (or quantitative understanding) of how the corrosion process operates and what amount of corrosion is likely in future under defined operational conditions. This paper is concerned with the latter problem.

Fig. 1 shows that the prediction of the future corrosion (thickness loss or pitting) can be very much in error if only a simplistic approach based on a 'corrosion rate' is used.

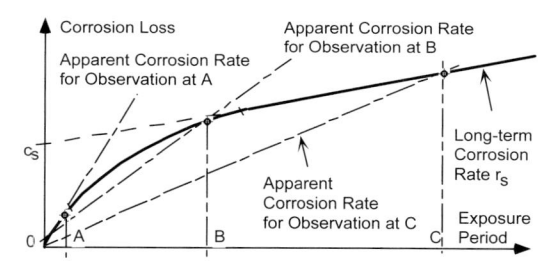

Fig. 1: Effect of non-linear corrosion loss function on measured corrosion rates

Typically thickness measurements on ship plates, etc. are made ultrasonically and are available at one or more points in time, say at A. Assuming the time when corrosion first commenced can be identified (0), the estimated projection for corrosion loss is as shown. Clearly it is different from what might be predicted from measurements at some other time (B or C) and from what a realistic corrosion loss model would predict, such as the long-term rate r_s (coupled with the intercept c_s). The challenge, then, is how to interpret measurements such as made at A, B or C, to obtain the best estimate of the future amount of corrosion. Moreover, there is little point in knowing that 'on average' a ship bulkhead plate, for example, experiences, say, 2mm of corrosion loss in 5 years when the statistics produce a standard deviation of, say, 3 mm or more.

Models based on oxidation

Corrosion loss models may be categorized as those based on some level of theoretical input and those that are essentially empirical. In the first category belong those proposed by Tammann (1923), Booth (1948), Evans (1960), Tomashev (1966), Chernov (1990), Benarie & Lipfert (1986), Feliu et al. (1993). They all consider metal oxidation as the controlling mechanism and that this reduces with time as the layers of corrosion products build-up. After some serious simplifications in boundary conditions, material properties and mathematics (cf. Melchers 2003a) the corrosion loss $y(t)$ as a function of exposure period t is given by

$$y = At^B \qquad (1)$$

where A and B are empirical constants. Although B should be 0.5 for pure Fickian diffusion, calibration to field data invariably shows that B varies between about 0.3 and 0.8 and that both A and B are highly sensitive to small changes in data or to additional data. Data that deviates too much from Eqn (1) often has been dismissed in the corrosion literature as caused by 'experimental error'.

There are also a number of (semi-) empirical models (Reinhart & Jenkins 1972, Mikhailovskii, et al. 1980, Chernov & Ponomarenko 1991) starting from different assumptions. Some of these attempted to allow for water temperature, dissolved oxygen and water velocity. Overall, these have not proved any better in fitting to longer-term data.

Corrosion wastage models

'Corrosion wastage' models have been proposed in the shipping literature. Typically they start from the assumption that understanding of the corrosion process and the many factors that influence it is difficult and that therefore only data collected from ships (such as in the periodic classification society condition surveys) has validity for model development. Moreover, typically observations from ships of widely differing size and operational conditions are lumped together. The shipping data also does not come with information about the environmental conditions (e.g. temperature, humidity, seastates) that almost certainly is relevant to interpreting it in more detail (Melchers 2001). The result is a population that is far from homogeneous and, almost in every case, shows very wide scatter. The problems were seen already in the work of Yamamoto & Ikegami (1996) and have been pointed out repeatedly (e.g. Melchers 2001, Gardiner & Melchers 2003).

The large scatter in the data for corrosion losses is not confined to ship plates. Even for corrosion coupons exposed at natural open-sea or coastal seawater test sites the scatter can be large if data from different sources is combined without discrimination. Fig. 2 shows an example of immersion corrosion loss data for all such sites as at 1994 (Melchers & Ahammed 1994)). Note that in many cases these data were obtained at coastal seawater test sites used for commercial purposes for predicting future corrosion losses, so they cannot easily be discredited. The data from exposures at any one of these sites typically show remarkably little scatter. This highlights the problem with aggregation of data - the resulting population is highly inhomogeneous.

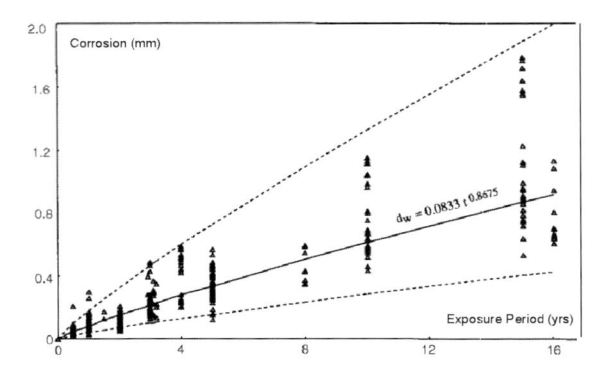

Fig. 2: Marine immersion corrosion loss data for steel coupons from various sources to 1994

Following the very high corrosion losses experienced by military equipment deployed in the tropics during WW2, a major long-term corrosion project was commenced in the Panama Canal Zone. Coupons 225 x 225 x 6 mm were exposed to natural seawater (and in the atmosphere) and sampled periodically over a period of 16years. This was considered to provide realistic corrosion data for design purposes. Examining the data led Southwell et al. (1979) to conclude that long-term corrosion was controlled by sulphate reducing bacteria (SRB). They recognized also that short-term corrosion loss is not representative of long-term corrosion behavior. They proposed a simple linear relationship for corrosion after one year (see Fig. 3).

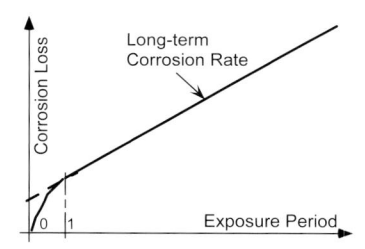

Fig. 3: Schematic model of Southwell et al. (1979)

Despite the extensive nature of the PCZ tests, the conclusions reached by Southwell et al. (1979) appear to have gone largely unnoticed. Subsequent researchers attempting to deal with corrosion losses under field exposure conditions, Yamamoto & Ikegami (1998), were unaware of these findings. They assumed that general corrosion results from pitting corrosion through the coalescence of many independent hemispherical pits, a process that was taken to go on indefinitely. This produced a complex non-linear model with corrosion loss levelling-off with exposure time. Attempts to fit the model to data were not particularly successful. For a further discussion see Melchers (2001).

A model with somewhat similar overall characteristics was proposed by Guedes Soares & Garbatov (1998). It has three phases (Fig. 4), representing (i) a period of no corrosion (such as due to protective coatings), (ii) damage of the corrosion protection system and the start of the corrosion process and (iii) a gradual decrease in the rate of the corrosion such that it eventually becomes zero. This is considered the result of the buildup of protective rusts. It is unclear how the second phase differs from the third phase.

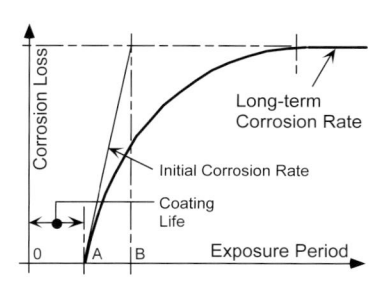

Fig. 4: Model proposed by Guedes Soares & Garbatov (1998)

Qin & Cui (2002) assumed that the coating protection system deteriorates gradually. Also, they assumed that coating breakdown led to early corrosion by pitting. The later corrosion loss is defined relative to the volume of pitting corrosion with pitting depth represented by Eqn (1). It was assumed that the long-term instantaneous corrosion rate asymptotes to zero (Fig. 5).

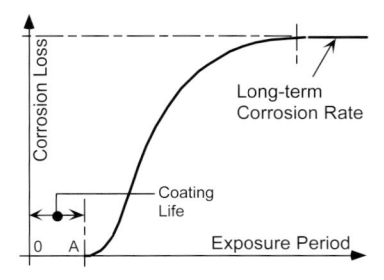

Fig. 5: Model proposed by Qin & Cui (2002)

Paik et al. (1998, 2003) also proposed three phases. The first is coating life, assumed to follow a lognormal distribution. The second, assumed to be exponentially distributed, is the transition when the coating breaks down and corrosion commences. The third is a corrosion loss curve that may be concave, convex or linear (Fig. 6). The choice between the corrosion loss curves is entirely empirical, i.e. by fitting to data. Importantly, there is no insistence that the long-term corrosion rate becomes zero.

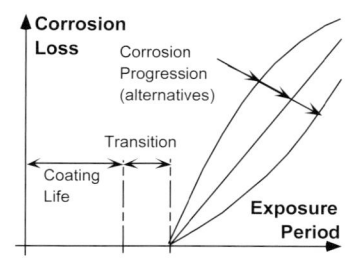

Fig. 6: Model proposed by Paik et al. (1998)

The models by Paik et al. (1998), Guedes Soares & Garbatov (1998) and Qin & Cui (2002) attempt to model both the loss of protective coatings and the progression of corrosion with time. This is a brave effort given the complexities of each of the two processes involved (coating deterioration and corrosion) (Melchers 2001). Realistically, however, the modeling of coating deterioration belongs to a completely different domain of investigation and should be treated as such, despite their obvious interaction as the coating begins to fail (TSCF 2002). Until there is sufficient fundamental understanding of the breakdown of organic coatings under realistic operational conditions any modeling attempt will remain entirely empirical. Laboratory studies of coating breakdown for research and for life expectancy studies tend to use accelerated testing including UV exposures. There is very little long-term data obtained under controlled conditions and objective field data is extremely scarce (Melchers & Jiang 2006). For this reason coating deterioration will not be considered herein.

A number of papers mainly in the conference literature have applied the model proposed by Guedes Soares & Garbatov (1998) to ship corrosion wastage data. However, no corrosion science theoretical justification for the model appears yet to have been published. To allow for the influence of environmental influences, various adjustments, based on text-book information, have been proposed (Guedes-Soares et al. 2005) Unfortunately, reference back to the original sources shows that mostly these adjustments are based on simplistic models derived from studies using short-term exposures (days, weeks) under laboratory conditions without the use of natural seawater (Guedes-Soares et al. 2006). This is a serious deficiency.

It is now well-established that artificial exposure conditions almost always produce misleading results compared to exposures under natural seawater conditions (Little & Ray 2002), even for short-term exposures. The reason is that natural seawater is a complex 'soup' of chemical and biological components, both of which have important influences on corrosion, not necessarily concurrently or in combination. Moreover, corrosion data and trends obtained from short-term exposures, even to study the effect of environmental variables, do not predict longer term behavior. These fundamental issues were pointed out already in 2001 (Melchers 2001) although, as noted above, much earlier Southwell et al. (1979) had provided a clear pointer to the importance of biological influences in longer-term corrosion. Importantly, the realistic corrosion tests in the warm waters of the PCZ showed clearly that there is no evidence of a leveling-out of corrosion loss with time, as proposed in Figs 4 and 5. Such a proposition also does not accord with experience with real structures.

If the corrosion process does eventually stop, the long-term deterioration and disintegration of ship wrecks and other steel objects in shallow seawaters simply would not occur. Moreover, it would suggest that merely by increasing the plate thickness beyond the level of ultimate corrosion loss would permit the design of 'corrosion-proof' structures.

There is no doubt that the instantaneous rate of corrosion declines with time, in general, owing to the build-up of corrosion products. This will inhibit the diffusion of oxygen to the corroding surface, as is the basis for Eqn (1). But, as will be explained below, the corrosion process is rather more complex than indicated by the simple models so far considered. This applies both to short-term and to long-term corrosion. For the latter, only Southwell et al. (1979) were close to capturing the essentials involved.

A model based on fundamentals

Background (1) - The role of rusts

When a steel surface is first exposed to natural seawater there is a build-up localized biofilm and bacteria resulting in a short-term effect on corrosion (Beech & Sunner 2004). In most cases this lasts for only days-weeks and may be ignored for structural engineering modeling purposes. Soon the oxidation of the (ferrous) iron in the steel is established. For seawater this produces the commonly observed red-brown ferrous oxi-hydroxide rusts at seawater pH of around 8:

$$4Fe + 2H_2O + 3O_2 \rightarrow 4FeOOH \quad (2)$$

This shows immediately that both oxygen and water are essential for corrosion to occur by oxidation. It follows readily that the rate of immersion corrosion depends on the rate of supply of oxygen.

At first the rate-controlling step is the rate at which oxygen can diffuse out of the bulk seawater to the metal surface. However as the rust layers build up the diffusion of oxygen becomes increasingly more difficult and eventually the diffusion of oxygen through the rust layers becomes the rate-controlling step. The result is a gradual slowing of the oxidation corrosion process. With some assumptions it may be modeled as a 'moving-boundary' diffusion problem described by Fick's second law. Eqn (1) is an approximate solution.

Note that there is no specific mention of salt (NaCl) in Eqn (2). Its precise role is still not completely clear, although the aggressiveness of the chloride ion resulting from the dissolution of NaCl in water is well-known. In principle it would react to form ferric chloride (FeCl$_3$) and as this is still highly aggressive further reaction will convert it to ferrous chloride (FeCl$_2$). However, these iron chlorides are only seldom detected in rust layers (e.g. Gilberg & Seeley 1981).

The rusts FeOOH are a complex mix of different 'phases', the most common and most stable being the red-brown, brittle and flaky Goethite (α–FeOOH). Typically, it overlies a thin layer of hard black Magnetite (Fe$_3$OH$_4$). These products are readily identified by Scanning Electron Microscope (SEM) and X-Ray Diffraction (XRD) analysis. However, other corrosion products are sometimes identified by these techniques, including iron sulphides FeS. Typically they appear as black, soft and slimy and may emit H$_2$S gas. They are known to be associated with corrosion of iron under highly anaerobic conditions. Evidently, the oxidation of iron as in Eqn (2) is not the only process involved in the marine corrosion of steel.

Background (2) - Bacteria in corrosion

The presence of FeS in rusts has long been associated with the activity of the sulphate reducing bacteria (SRB). They are ubiquitous in nature and are obligatory anaerobes. It is recognized that the biofilms that form on first exposure in seawater can provide an appropriate anaerobic environment for SRB activity (Hamilton 1985). However, as will be seen, this is not the only environment in which SRB can flourish.

The SRB metabolize the (calcium and magnesium) sulphates abundantly present in seawater to hydrogen sulphide, which is highly corrosive with respect to iron. The bacteria themselves do not directly attack the steel. The (partial) chemical reactions involved are

$$SO_4^- + \rightarrow H_2S + \quad \text{and} \quad H_2S + Fe \rightarrow FeS + ... \quad (3)$$
SRB metabolism $\quad\quad\quad$ electrochemical reaction

The SRB need sufficient food including nutrients for metabolism. Nutrients are available in seawater in various quantities. In general, the availability of one or more of Fe, organic carbon and nitrogen (nitrates, nitrites, ammonium) limits the rate of metabolism. However, for the corrosion of steel typically the availability of nitrogen is limiting in seawater (Postgate 1984).

Multi-phase immersion corrosion model

The above preliminaries provide the necessary background for the model first proposed in 1997 (Melchers 1997) and since refined to that shown in Figure 7. A key feature is the recognition that the corrosion process changes with the development of corrosion products with time. This has a profound effect on conditions at the corroding surface. It is represented in a number of consecutive 'phases' (Melchers 2003b) summarized very succinctly in Fig. 7.

The model recognizes that (i) oxygen diffusion through the rust layers can not be the rate-controlling mechanism at the very start of immersion when there is no rust, (ii) corrosion controlled by oxygen diffusion through the rust layers as expressed by Eqn (1) is only represented in Phase 2 and (iii) long-term corrosion involves the activity of sulphate reducing bacteria (SRB) in Phases 3 and 4. Following the idea of Southwell et al. (1979), phase 4 can be modeled as a (near-) linear function of time (Melchers & Wells 2006).

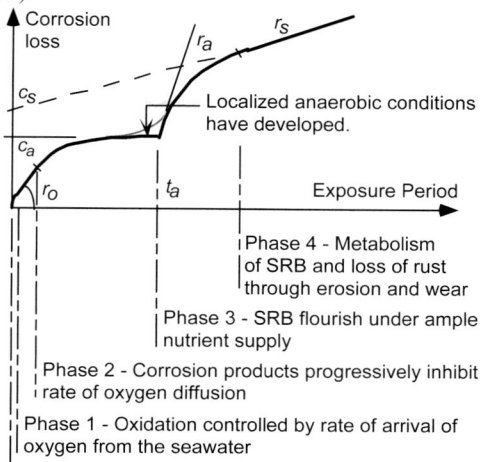

Fig. 7: Corrosion loss – exposure time model for immersion corrosion of steel in natural seawater showing the parameters for each of the phases

The model is clearly an idealization. Actual corrosion loss and pitting will vary from point to point on a corroding surface and the transitions from one phase to another will occur at slightly different points in time. Nevertheless, the model has been successfully calibrated to a wide range of field data drawn from many parts of the world (Melchers 2003b,c). Moreover, direct evidence of the influence of SRB in the corrosion products corresponding to phases 3 and 4 of the model has been obtained from in-situ field studies using scanning electron microscope (SEM), X-ray diffraction (XRD) and bacterial culturing techniques (Jeffrey & Melchers 2003).

Although there are many potential influences that can affect corrosion loss, the basic calibration was done for unpolluted, low velocity, coastal seawaters that typically are near fully oxygenated. In this case the predominant remaining influencing factor is average seawater temperature T. Table 1 shows the calibration functions describing the model parameters (Fig. 7) for both general and pitting corrosion (Melchers 2003b, Melchers and Wells 2006, Melchers 2004a).

Table 1: Calibrated model parameters for general and for pitting corrosion as functions of average seawater temperature T.

	General corrosion	Pitting corrosion
r_0	$r_0 = 0.076 \exp(0.054T)$	-
c_a	$c_a = 0.32 \exp(-0.038T)$	$c_{ap} = 0.99 \exp(-0.052T)$
t_a	$t_a = 6.61 \exp(-0.088T)$	$t_a = 6.61 \exp(-0.088T)$
r_a	$r_a = 0.066 \exp(0.061T)$	$r_{ap} = 0.596 \exp(0.0526T)$
c_s	$c_s = 0.141 - 0.00133T$	$c_{sp} = 0.641 \exp(0.0613T)$
r_s	$r_s = 0.039 \exp(0.0254T)$	$r_{sp} = 0.353 \exp(-0.0436T)$

r_0, r_a, r_s (mm/yr), c_a, c_s (mm)

Fig. 8 shows that seawater temperature T has a significant effect on corrosion loss at all stages. The parameter t_a that marks the idealized changeover from oxidation to anaerobic bacterial action is seen to be strongly dependent on T. This means that in tropical waters anaerobic conditions will be reached much sooner (within one year) of first exposure than for colder waters and it may take many years to reach this state in arctic waters. This immediately provides one explanation for the wide scatter seen in Fig. 2. It also provides a strong reason why it is not valid to use aggregated data for ships.

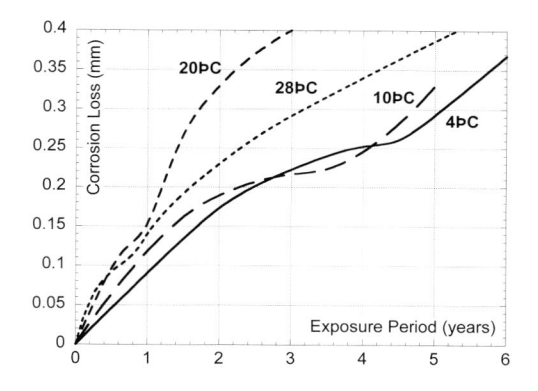

Fig. 8: Corrosion loss curves for different mean seawater temperatures

Effect of other influences

The effect of various influences can be summarized as in Fig. 9. As noted, water temperature is part of the original model. A summary of other influences follows.

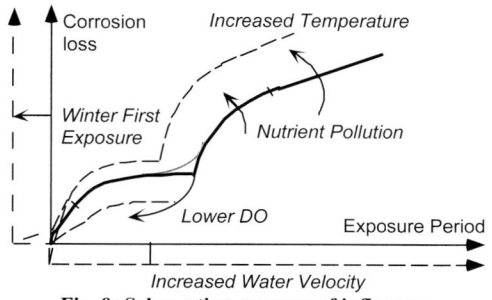

Fig. 9: Schematic summary of influences

Water pollution

Chemical pollutants, unless in extremely large and environmentally completely unacceptable amounts, do not have a significant effect on corrosion in phases 1 and 2 since aerobic corrosion is governed by oxygen diffusion and thus not influenced by the precise chemical composition of seawater (Mercer and Lumbard 1995). One important exception is nutrient pollution. Elevated levels of nitrogenous pollutants in particular tend to increase r_0 (Melchers 2007a) and to increase the corrosion loss in phase 3 and the long-term rate r_s (Melchers 2005a). These phenomena occur because SRB and other bacteria in the consortia are very sensitive to the rate of nutrient supply (Postgate 1984).

Dissolved oxygen (DO)

Depression of the dissolved oxygen (DO) content in seawater affects phases 1 and 2, causing a direct reduction of parameters t_a, r_0 and c_a. This has the effect of establishing anaerobic conditions (i.e. phase 3) earlier in time (Melchers & Jeffrey 2005). Since most open waters are subject to wind and wave action they tend to be close to fully aerated near the surface and for this reason there has been little evidence of a DO effect in coastal seawater corrosion trials.

Water velocity

Water velocity such as resulting from wave action typically has an effect only early in the process when the rust layers are insufficient to protect the corroding surface underneath. Melchers & Jeffrey (2004) showed that the net effect is to move the corrosion loss curve (Fig. 7) upward. This result is considerably different to the widely-quoted classical result (LaQue 1975) based on 36 days of laboratory testing in a closed loop.

Timing of first immersion

The available evidence (LaQue 1975, Melchers 2001) indicates that steel first exposed in autumn or winter has an initially slower rate of corrosion loss. This can be accounted for by a horizontal shift of the corrosion loss curve and a slight early adjustment.

Depth of immersion exposure

There is no evidence that increased water pressure has any noticeable effect on the corrosion of relatively small objects and that any effects on corrosion of immersion depth can be associated closely with the temperature, DO and nutrient levels present at the exposure location (Melchers 2005b).

Salinity

An extensive review of literature data and careful analysis of the effects of carbonate solubility and pH has shown that these rather than salinity account for differences in longer-term corrosion loss for fresh, brackish and seawaters (Melchers 2006). This is quite different to observations from short-term laboratory studies. Salinity has only a short-term effect (Mercer & Lumbard 1995).

Changes in steel composition

Very small changes in steel composition have no significant effect on corrosion loss or pitting particularly when oxidation controls the rate of corrosion. However, there is an effect for larger changes. Importantly, the model has been able to clarify the seemingly conflicting data in the literature for the effect of alloying both for corrosion loss and for pitting corrosion (Melchers 2003d, 2004b). Fig. 10 summarizes the findings. In addition, increased carbon content tends to increase corrosion in phases 3 and 4 (Melchers 2003d).

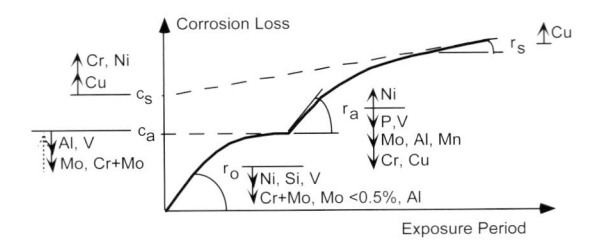

Fig. 10: Schematic effect on corrosion of small increases in alloying for low alloy steels

Some applications

The above model has been applied together with models for atmospheric corrosion loss to predict the internal corrosion in naval vessel ballast tanks, accounting for changes in temperature, RH, etc. and operational factors (e.g. number of ballast changes). These have been compared with detailed monitored in-situ corrosion loss observations on an operational naval vessel (Gudze et al. 2004, 2006). Earlier, slightly less developed models were used to model the corrosion losses in the holds of bulk carrier ships used for coal and iron ore (Gardiner & Melchers 2001, 2002, 2003).

Recently it has been shown that the model of Fig. 7 also applies to marine tidal and coastal atmospheric corrosion (Fig. 11) (Melchers 2007b). Efforts are currently underway to calibrate the model for these exposure conditions using both literature data and new data being obtained at several locations along the Eastern Australian seaboard.

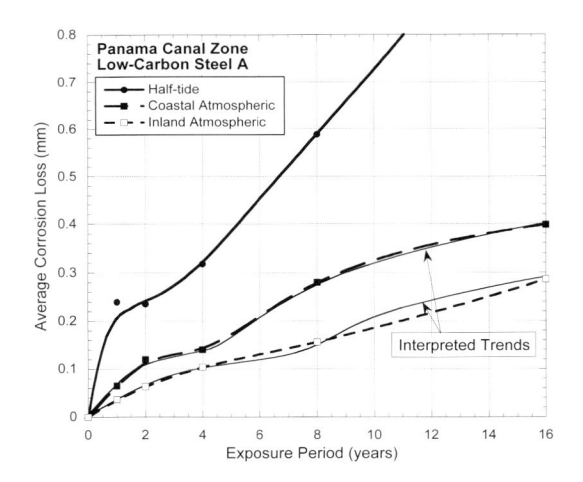

Fig. 11: Typical data trends for long-term atmospheric corrosion loss (Melchers 2007b)

Discussion

Criticisms leveled at the above approach include (i) that the model has been calibrated to coupon data rather than data for full-scale structures, (ii) that there are a myriad of details and variations in practice that coupons cannot measure (iii) that it is laboratory-based and (iv) that it assumes the environmental conditions can be measured whereas in practice this is not the case (e.g. Guedes-Soares et al. 2005, 2006). Apart from the fact that (iii) is wrong, as examination of the original papers will show, the others simply illustrate that the starting point for this research is completely different from the purely empirical approach represented by the 'wastage models'.

No progress in understanding of corrosion losses under in-situ conditions can be made if the fundamentals are not understood and the variables involved not isolated. This may require a lot of detailed data and measurement, but it is clearly not something the present ship data can provide. Broadly, there are two ways forward.

One is to use the type of point-wise ultrasonic corrosion loss data already being obtained as part of certification studies but coupled closely with observations of the environmental conditions and the voyages undertaken (cf. Gudze & Melchers 2006). This will require a considerable change in the way data is currently collected.

The other and complementary way forward is to perform more in-situ testing using coupons, including on ships, to elucidate the relationships involved. There is ample evidence in the corrosion literature that coupons can provide accurate corrosion estimates and that size is not a significant variable within the one exposure environment (Evans 1960). On the other hand, metal surface orientation is very important where tidal and atmospheric corrosion is concerned. This is clearly a matter for detailed investigation, and as yet has received insufficient attention. The important point is that most effort so far has been spent in attempting to understand the essential corrosion processes, using coupons for simplicity. By comparison, the effect of orientation is relatively straight-forward and can be determined by appropriate testing programs.

The model outlined herein clearly relies on input of environmental variables. Ii is important to understand also that the corrosion process is an integration process. It smoothes out variations in the environmental conditions and (apart from very early, short-term corrosion) tends to be sensitive only to long-term trends. This implies that only relatively short-term sampling of the environmental conditions is required. It means also that representative estimates may be sufficient. Both are much easier to obtain in practical applications. Moreover, better understanding of the relative importance of environmental variables will enable the optimal structuring of monitoring programs for practical applications. It also may permit improved approaches to the management of ships and other structures to minimize corrosion losses.

Conclusion

A review of existing models for corrosion loss showed that mostly these are based on insufficient understanding of the corrosion process, including that due to bacterial activity. The development of a model that considers these matters was outlined. It is based on corrosion fundamentals and has provided considerable insight to explain matters such as the effect of water temperature, water velocity, dissolved oxygen levels, water pollution including nutrient pollution, depth of immersion and water salinity. Some applications were outlined. It was noted that ship based corrosion loss data would be much more valuable if it were not aggregated before attempting to develop empirical corrosion 'wastage' models.

Acknowledgement

The financial support of the Australian Research Council is acknowledged.

References

Beech IB & Sunner J (2004) Biocorrosion: towards understanding interactions between biofilms and metals, Current Opinion in Biotech. 15: 181-186.

Benarie M & Lipfert FL (1986) A general corrosion function in terms of atmospheric pollutant concentrations and rain pH, Atmospheric Environment, 20(10) 1947-1958.

Booth F 1948. A note on the theory of surface diffusion reactions, Trans. Faraday Soc. 44: 796-801.

Chernov BB (1990) Predicting the corrosion of steels in seawater from its physiochemical characteristics, Protection of Metals 26(2) 238-241.

Chernov BB & Ponomarenko SA (1991) Physiochemical modelling of metal corrosion in seawater, Protection of Metals 27(5) 612-615.

Evans UR (1960) The corrosion and oxidation of metals: Scientific principles and practical applications, Edward Arnold (Publishers) Ltd. London.

Feliu S, Morcillo A & Feliu Jr S (1993) The prediction of atmospheric corrosion from meteorological and pollution parameters - 1. Annual corrosion, Corrosion Science, 34(3) 403-422.

Gardiner CP and Melchers RE (2001) Enclosed atmospheric corrosion within ship structures, British Corrosion Journal, 36 (4) 272-276.

Gardiner CP and Melchers RE (2002) Corrosion of mild steel by coal and iron ore, Corrosion Sci., 44(12) 2665-2673.

Gardiner, CP & Melchers RE (2003) Corrosion analysis of bulk carriers, Part 1: Operational parameters influencing corrosion rates, Marine Structures, 16(8) 547-566.

Gilberg MR & Seeley NJ (1981) The identity of compounds containing chloride ions in marine iron corrosion products: A critical review, Studies in Conservation, 26: 50-56.

Gudze MT, Melchers RE (2006) Prediction of naval ship ballast tank corrosion using operational profiles, Transactions of the Royal Institution of Naval Architects Part A: International Journal of Maritime Engineering, 148; 77-86.

Gudze MT, Cannon S and Melchers RE (2004) Ballast tank corrosion using naval ship operational profiles, Proc. Pacific 2004 Intl Maritime Conf, Sydney, 3-5 Feb., Vol. 1, Engineers Australia, 280-289.

Guedes Soares C & Garbatov Y (1998) Non-linear time dependent model of corrosion for the reliability assessment of maintained structural component, (in) Safety and Reliability, (Ed) S Lydersen, GK Hansen and H Sandtorv, Balkema, 929-036.

Guedes Soares C & Garbatov Y (1999) Reliability of maintained, corrosion protected plate subjected to non-linear corrosion and compressive loads, Marine Structures 12: 425-445.

Guedes-Soares C, Garbatov Y, Zayed A and Wang G (2005) Non-linear corrosion model for immersed steel plates accounting for environmental factors, Trans. SNAME, 111: 194-211.

Guedes-Soares C, Garbatov Y, Zayed A, Wang G, Melchers RE, Paik JK and Cui W (2006) Non-linear corrosion model for immersed steel plates accounting for environmental factors, Transactions 2005 SNAME, 113: 306-329.

Hamilton WA (1985) Sulphate-reducing bacteria and anaerobic corrosion, Ann. Rev. Microbiol. 39: 195-217.

Jeffrey R and Melchers RE (2003) Bacteriological influence in the development of iron sulphide species in marine immersion environments, Corrosion Science, 45(4) 693-714.

LaQue F (1975) Marine Corrosion, Wiley, New York.

Little B & Ray R (2002) A perspective on corrosion inhibition by biofilms, Corrosion, 58(5) 424-428.

Melchers RE (1997) Modeling of marine corrosion of steel specimens, (in) Corrosion Testing in Natural Waters, (Ed) RM Kain and WT Young, ASTM STP 1300, Philadelphia, 20 - 33.

Melchers RE (2001) Probabilistic models of corrosion for reliability assessment and maintenance planning, Proc. Offshore Mechanics and Arctic Engineering Conference, Rio de Janeiro, 3-8 June, 2001: Paper OMAE2001/S&R-2108, CDRom

Melchers RE (2003a) Mathematical modeling of the diffusion controlled phase in marine immersion corrosion of mild steel, Corrosion Sci. 45(5) 923-940.

Melchers RE (2003b) Modeling of marine immersion corrosion for mild and low alloy steels - Part 1: Phenomenological model, Corrosion, 59(4) 319-334.

Melchers RE (2003c) Modeling of marine immersion corrosion for mild and low alloy steels - Part 2: Uncertainty estimation, Corrosion, 59(4) 335-344.

Melchers RE (2003d) Effect on marine immersion corrosion of carbon content of low alloy steels, Corrosion Science 45(11) 2609-2625.

Melchers RE (2004a) Pitting corrosion of mild steel in marine immersion environment - 1: maximum pit depth, Corrosion, 60(9) 824-836.

Melchers RE (2004b) Effect of small compositional changes on marine immersion corrosion of low alloy steel, Corrosion Science, 46(7) 1669-1691.

Melchers RE (2005a) Effect of nutrient-based water pollution on the corrosion of mild steel in marine immersion conditions, Corrosion, 61(3) 237-245.

Melchers RE (2005b) Effect of immersion depth on marine corrosion of mild steel, Corrosion, 61(9) 895-906.

Melchers RE (2006) Modelling immersion corrosion of structural steels in natural fresh and brackish waters, Corrosion Science 48(12) 4174-4201.

Melchers RE (2007a) The influence of seawater nutrient content on the early immersion corrosion of mild steel – 1 Empirical observations, Corrosion, 64(1) 318-329.

Melchers RE (2007b) The transition from marine immersion to coastal atmospheric corrosion for structural steels, Corrosion, 63(6) 500-514.

Melchers RE & Ahammed M (1994) Non-linear modelling of corrosion of steel in marine environments, Res. Rept 106.09.1994, Dept of Civil Engineering and Surveying, The University of Newcastle.

Melchers RE & Jeffrey R (2004) Influence of water velocity on marine corrosion of mild steel, Corrosion, 60(1) 84-94.

Melchers RE & Jeffrey R (2005) Early corrosion of mild steel in seawater, Cor. Sci. 47(7) 1678-1693.

Melchers RE & Jiang X (2006) Estimation of models for durability of epoxy coatings in water ballast tanks, J. Ships and Offshore Structures 1(1) 61-70.

Melchers RE & Wells PA (2006) Models for the anaerobic phases of marine immersion corrosion, Corrosion Science 48(7) 1791-1811.

Mercer AD and Lumbard EA (1995) Corrosion of mild steel in water, British Corrosion J, 30(1) 43-55.

Mikhailovskii YN, Strekalov PV & Agafonov VV (1980) A model of atmospheric corrosion of metals allowing for meteorological and aerochemical characteristics, Prot. of Metals 16(4) 396-323.

Paik JK, Kim SK, Lee S and Park YE (1998) A probabilistic corrosion rate estimation model for longitudinal strength members of bulk carriers, Journal of Ship and Ocean Technology, 2: 58-70.

Paik J, Lee J, Hwang J and Park Y (2003) A time-dependent corrosion wastage model for the structures of single and double hull tankers and FSOs and FPSOs, Marine Technology, 40: 201-217.

Postgate JR (1984) The sulphate-reducing bacteria, Second edition, Cambridge University Press.

Qin S & Cui W (2002) Effect of corrosion models on the time-dependent reliability of steel plated elements, Marine Structures 15: 15-34.

Reinhart FM & Jenkins JF (1972) Corrosion of materials in surface seawater after 12 and 18 months of exposure, Technical Note N-1213, Naval Civil Engineering Laboratory, Port Hueneme, CA.

Southwell, CR, Bultman, JD and Hummer, CW (1979) Estimating service life of steel in seawater (in) Seawater Corrosion Handbook, (Ed) M. Schumacher, Park Ridge, NJ; Noyes Data Corp, 374-387.

Tammann G (1923) Lehrbuch der Metallographie, 2nd Edn, Leipzig, 1923.

Tomashev ND (1966) Theory of Corrosion and Protection of Metals, The MacMillan Co., New York.

TSCF (2002) Guidelines for ballast tank coatings systems and surface preparation, Tanker Structure Cooperative Forum, London.

Yamamoto N & Ikegami K (1996) A study on the degradation of coating and corrosion of ships hull based on the probabilistic approach, Proc. of the 15th International Conference on Offshore Mechanics and Arctic Engineering, Vol. II, ASME, 159-166.

Strength and Deformability of Corroded Steel Plates Estimated by Replicated Specimens

Yoichi Sumi

Department of Systems Design for Ocean-Space, Faculty of Engineering, Yokohama National University
Yokohama, Kanagawa-ken, Japan

Abstract

Strength and deformability of corroded steel plates are investigated by using artificially pitted and replicated specimens processed by a CAD-CAM system which numerically controls a desktop milling machine in order to produce or replicate the surface geometry of a corroded surface. Periodical array of surface pits are made for self-similar specimens. Also, corroded surfaces are measured by scanning a plate by a laser displacement sensor, so that the surface data are stored to generate the input for the CAM system. As a typical example of plates with general corrosion, surface geometries of a sample specimen taken from the bottom plate of an aged tanker are reproduced, and the corresponding tensile test are carried out. The reduction of the tensile strength is slight, while that of the elongation is significant. In order to examine the extent of the corroded surface, test specimens having different sample area but with the same thickness are tested, where the surface undulation is machined in the same scale. The test results show slight dependence on the extent of the surface area.

Keywords

Corroded plate; Replica specimen; Tensile strength; Deformability; Similarity; Size effect.

Introduction

In order to assess the structural performance of aged ships, it is of essential importance to predict the strength and absorbing energy during collapse and/or fracture of corroded plates. Since it is well-known that the effect of corrosion is basically the geometrical effect and chemistry does not come into play (Oka et al., 1990), tests are carried out for plates with their surfaces processed to geometrically simulate corroded surfaces. Although the strength reduction due to periodical array of pits as studied by Nakai et al. (2004a, b) is known, the size effects in experiments and random undulation due to general corrosion are still open to question because of difficulties in preparing appropriate test specimens.

In the present paper the reduction of strength and deformability of a corroded plate is investigated by using pitted specimens or geometrically reproduced replica specimens of a corroded plate sampled from an actual aged ship. The geometries of corroded surfaces are generated by a CAD system, and mechanically processed by NC milling machine by a CAM system, so that one can directly investigate the mechanical properties of corroded plates in details. In order to investigate the size effect of specimens with surface pits, we first examine the yielding strength, ultimate strength, and elongation of self-similar but using different size specimens.

In order to reproduce a replica specimen of an actual corroded surface, surface geometry is scanned by the use of a laser displacement sensor. As a typical example of plates with general corrosion, surface geometries of a sample taken from the bottom plate of an aged tanker are reproduced, and the corresponding tensile tests are carried out. In order to examine the effects of the extent of the corroded surface, test specimens having different sample areas with the same thickness are tested, where the surface undulation is in the same scale. As will be seen later, the test results show a slight dependence on the extent of the surface area.

Replica Production of Corroded Surface

In order to process a specimen surface, we first generate the data of surface coordinates by using a CAD system (MasterCam Design), which is transmitted to a CAM system (MasterCam Mill 9.1). Then, the CAM system generates the necessary tool path for the milling machine (SG01). Arbitrary surface geometries can be generated including periodical array of pits, numerically simulated random array of pits (Yamamoto and Ikegami, 1998), and reproduction of actual corroded surfaces. In the present study, we first investigate the various periodical arrays of circular conical pits, which are observed in side frames of bulk carriers.

With regard to the replica specimens of a corroded plate in an actual ship, we first precisely measure the surface geometry by scanning the surface height by a laser displacement sensor. The results are translated to the 3D geometrical data of the CAD system, and the same procedure follows in the CAM system and milling machine to process the surface geometry. Having measured the machined surface, it has been confirmed that the accuracy of the surface geometry is within 10μm, so that the accuracy is quite satisfactory for the simulation of corroded plates with surface undulation of the order of several millimeters.

Size Effect of Strength and Deformability of Pitted Steel Plates

Test Specimen and Test Method

Test specimens are shown in Fig.1, where the M-size and S-size specimens are reduced to half and quarter from the L-size specimens, respectively. The material is SM490 steel, and the tests are carried out for its roll direction. In order to simulate the pitting corrosion observed in side frames of bulk-carriers, three types of pitting pattern are processed on the both sides of the parallel part of the specimen (see Fig.2). The pit has a circular conical shape with its diameter/depth ratio, 8, and the pitting patterns on the both sides are made asymmetric with respect to the middle plane. The pit diameters are 20mm, 10mm, and 5 mm, for L, M, S specimens, respectively, and the degree of pitting intensities are 0.314, 0.471, and 0.628 for the pitting patterns, 1, 2, and 3, respectively. Tensile tests were carried out for specimens with these pitting patterns and for flat plates without pits under quasi-static loading conditions, where the crosshead speed is 3 mm/min. for S-size specimens, and 5 mm/min. for the rest of the specimens. The list of test specimens and test results are shown in Table 1, where the notation, P-L1, for example, indicates the artificially pitted L-size specimen with the pitting pattern-1. Specimens L0, M0, and S0 are flat specimens, so that the conventional yielding stress and the ultimate tensile strength of the material should be read from the results of these specimens.

It should be noted that the specimens of these three sizes are self-similar, so that the same quantity of the geometrical information of a surface is contained in these specimens with the scaling factors of 1.0, 0.5 and 0.25.

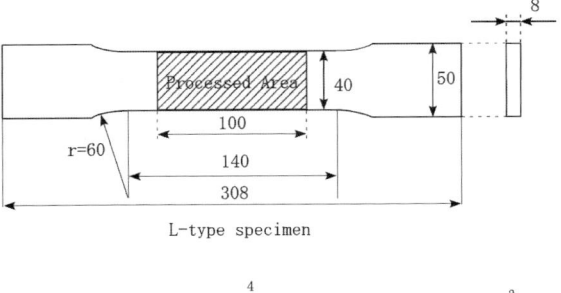

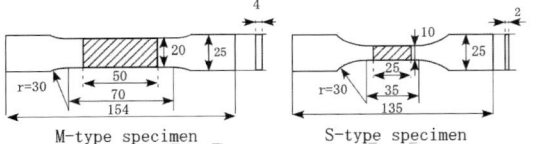

Fig.1: Similar specimens having different test volume

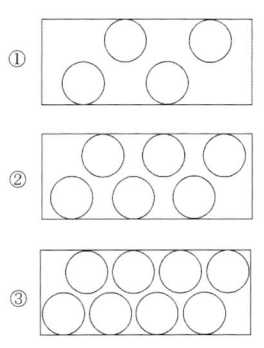

Fig.2: Three pitting patterns 1, 2, and 3

Results of Tensile Tests

The deformed shape of the L-size specimens after fracture are compared in Fig.3, in which we can see the fracture occurring in the pitted section and considerable reduction of elongation in comparison with that of the flat specimen. In the flat specimen, ductile fracture occurs perpendicular to the tensile direction, while in the pitted specimens, plastic strain localization is first observed in the cusp of the pits, followed by the initiation of a ductile crack there. Sometimes the initiated ductile crack propagates perpendicular to the tensile direction, while in certain cases it has an inclined angle to the width direction so as to propagate along the adjacent pits.

Table 1: Test results of nominal upper yielding stress, σ_{YU}, lower yielding stress, σ_{YL}, ultimate strength, σ_U, and elongation

Specimen	σ_{YU} [MPa]	σ_{YL} [MPa]	σ_U [MPa]	Elongation [%]
L0-1	387.5	369.9	517.19	32.46
L0-2	388.3	370.3	515.25	33.88
P- L1	324.2	319.5	466.41	20.76
P- L2	288.7	287.1	439.47	24.66
P- L3-1	286.3	280.5	429.69	25.90
P- L3-2	288.7	284.3	432.03	28.16
M0	394.1	377.5	525.31	32.18
P- M1	322.3	321.3	464.06	16.28
P- M2	307.5	305.4	455.94	23.62
P- M3	301.6	297.6	444.54	25.94
S0	374.5	366.0	510.50	31.52
P- S1	300.5	300.0	447.82	20.18
P- S2	269.5	-	451.57	22.84
P- S3	274.5	274.0	421.57	27.60

We shall next compare the fracture behavior of self-similar specimens. In the pitting patterns-1 and 2, a ductile crack initiates in at the cusp of a pit, and it propagates perpendicular to the tensile direction for all sizes of specimens as shown from the second and third specimens from the top in Fig.3. On the contrary, in the case of the pattern-3, an initiated ductile crack propagates so as to join the adjacent pits, but the fracture pattern is not unique. The reason for various possible crack paths may be explained by the existence of closely located zones of high strain localization caused by the high density of pitting.

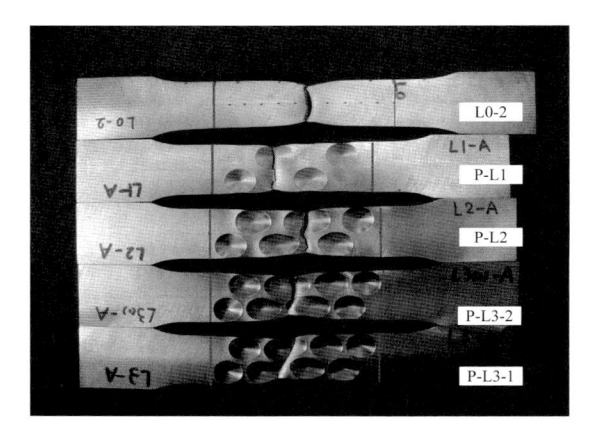

Fig. 3: L-type specimens after fracture

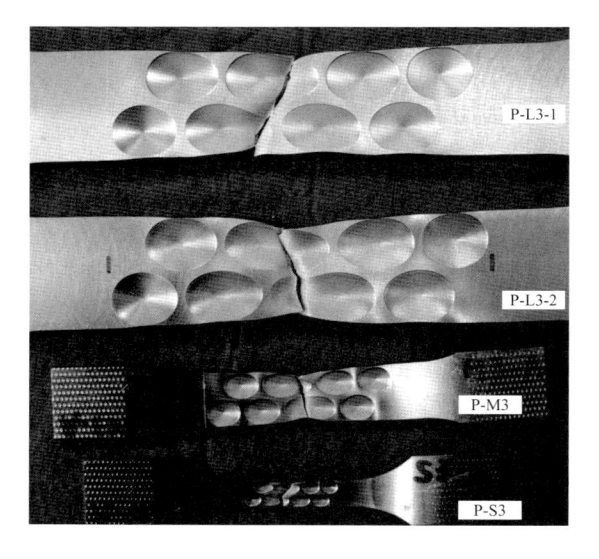

Fig.4: Fracture behavior of pitting pattern 3

If the material degradation due to corrosion can be disregarded, strength and deformability of corroded plates are governed purely by the surface geometry. This assumption may lead to the results that the size effect does not appear in experiments, if the material of specimens is homogeneous and isotropic. Since the strength of material with geometrical defects often shows certain size effect, it should be examined based on the experimental results. As is illustrated in Fig.4, the fracture morphology is the same for different size specimens. In Figs. 5 and 6, the relations between the nominal stress and nominal strain of flat specimens and pitting pattern-2 are compared for different size specimens, respectively. These results as well as those of the other pitting patterns show fairly good agreement with each other. With regard to the size effect, it may be noted that the initial yielding behavior is less significant for the smallest S-size specimens.

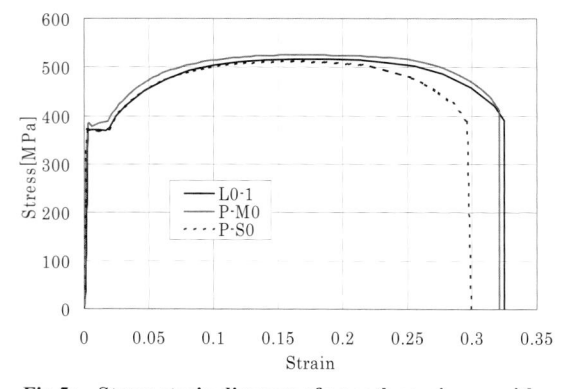

Fig.5: Stress-strain diagram of smooth specimens with different size

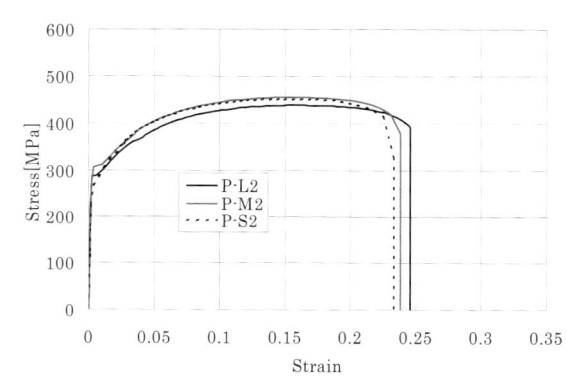

Fig.6: Stress-strain diagram of different size specimens with pitting pattern 2

Figure 7 shows the ultimate strength of M-size and S-size specimens normalized with respect to those of L-size specimens, in which we can see the same results for these specimens, so that there is no size effect in this range of size changes. With regard to the elongation, Fig.8 shows the results of M-size and S-size specimens normalized with respect to those of L-size specimens, where the correlation is fairly good except for the result of M1-specimen. The slightly larger scatter of elongation data may be due to the different initiation sites of ductile cracks and their different propagation paths.

Figure 9 illustrates the strength and deformability of the L-size specimens with different pitting patterns. In the following discussion, the nominal strength of a specimen is defined by

$$\sigma_U = P_{max}/A_0 \qquad (1)$$

where P_{max} is the maximum load, and A_0 is the sectional area without pits. Obviously, the ultimate strength and elongation are reduced for pitted specimens, where the upper and lower yielding points do not clearly appear in the pitted specimens. In pitted specimens, plastic flow behavior is observed in the range of 3-5% of the nominal strain. This behavior may correspond to the not localized but global formation of the slip bands.

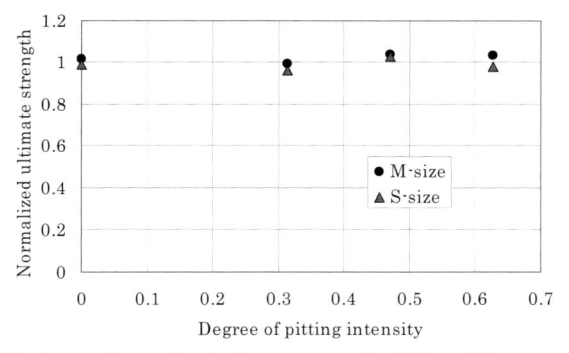

Fig.7: Normalized ultimate strength of M- and S-type specimens for the three pitting patterns

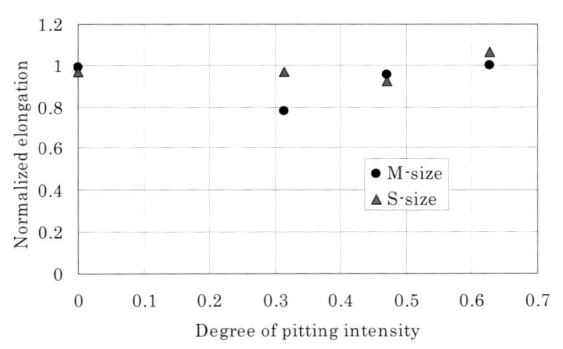

Fig.8: Normalized elongation of M- and S-type specimens for the three pitting patterns

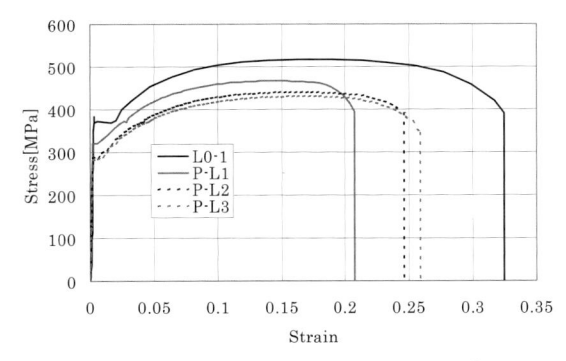

Fig.9: Stress-strain diagrams of L-type specimens

Discussions

The relation between the nominal ultimate strength of pitted specimens and the degree of pitting intensity is illustrated in Fig.10, where the ultimate strength is normalized with respect to that of the flat specimen. The reduction of the ultimate strength is 10-13% for pitting pattern-1, 13-15% for pitting pattern-2, and 15-18% for pitting pattern-3, respectively, and these results coincide with those predicted by the formula proposed by Nakai et al. (2004a) based on the minimum sectional area of the pitted specimens.

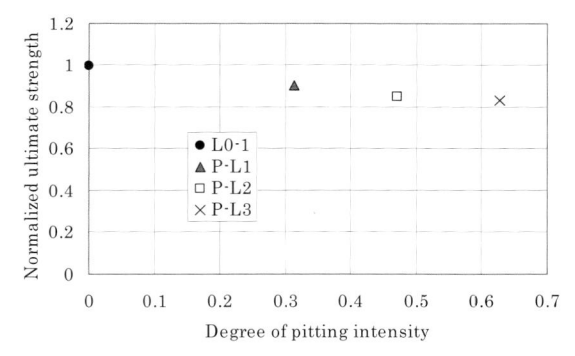

Fig.10: Relation between ultimate strength and pitting intensity

Figure 11 shows the relation between the elongation and the degree of pitting intensity, in which the elongation is normalized with respect to that of flat specimen. The maximum reduction of elongation is observed for the pitting pattern-1, whose pitting intensity is smallest among the three pitting patterns. The elongation recovers with increasing the pitting intensity because of the less strain concentration at the cusps of pits. In actual ship structural members, corrosion pits may locate randomly, and since the elongation reduction due to pits is very sensitive to the arrangement of pits, the deformability of corroded members should be considered based on the random array of pits (Nakai, Sumi, Saiki, and Yamamoto, 2006).

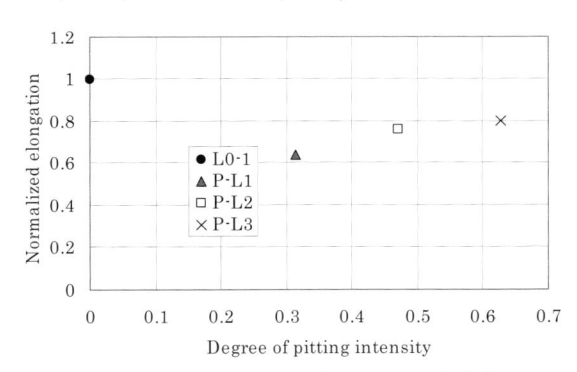

Fig.11: Relation between elongation and pitting intensity

Tests of Steel Plate with General Corrosion by Using Replica Specimens

Test Specimen and Test Method

In order to investigate the mechanical behavior of plate subjected to general corrosion, a steel plate (250mm×100mm) was sampled from the bottom plate of an aged heavy oil carrier, whose two surfaces had been in contact with heavy oil and sea water, respectively. Based on the results of the previous section, the replica specimens are reduced to 40% of the original size of the sample (100mm×40mm), and the plate thickness before surface processing is 8mm. These are C-L-1 and C-L-2 specimens. In order to investigate the extent of the replica specimens, the whole sample area is bi-sectioned in the length and width directions, so that four specimens having the half size (C-M-1, 2, 3, and 4 specimens) are also prepared. These areas are further bi-sectioned in the length and width directions, in which the two sub-domains with the least mean thicknesses and the two sub-domains with largest thickness variations are selected as the test specimens (C-S-2, 3, 7, and 14 specimens). Table 2 shows the specimen list.

Table 2: List of Replica Specimens

Specimen	G.L. [mm]	w [mm]	Δa [mm]	Δb [mm]	Δt [mm]
L0-1	100	40	No surface diminution		
L0-2					
C-L1-1			0.323	0.345	0.668
C-L1-2					
C-M1	50	20	0.328	0.379	0.707
C-M2			0.316	0.368	0.684
C-M3			0.317	0.281	0.598
C-M4			0.331	0.350	0.681
C-S2	25	10	0.337	0.386	0.723
C-S3			0.366	0.500	0.866
C-S7			0.386	0.457	0.843
C-S14			0.379	0.442	0.821

N.B. G.L.: gauge length; w: specimen width; Δa: surface diminution on surface A; Δb: surface diminution on surface B; Δt: total diminution

Test specimens are produced based on the following procedures;
1. The surface geometry of the sample plate from an aged ship is scanned by 0.5mm interval by a laser displacement sensor, and the results are stored as the data for the CAD system. The surface data in the CAD system is displayed in Fig.12.
2. The specimen surfaces are processed by the use of numerically controlled milling machine with the use of CAD-CAM system.
3. The accuracy of the surface geometry is confirmed by scanning the specimen surface after milling process, and the results are satisfactory as illustrated in Fig. 13.

All test specimens having different extents of sample areas are shown in Fig.14.

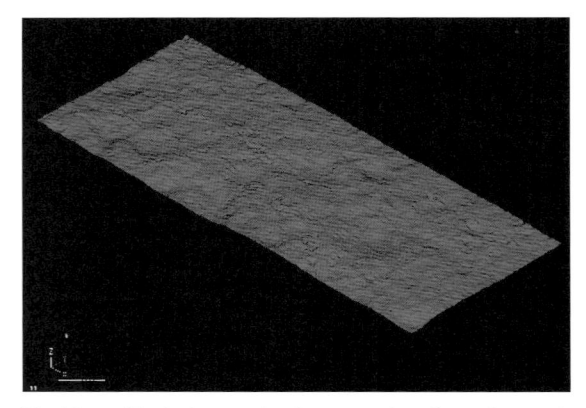

Fig.12: Typical example of measured surface of general corrosion

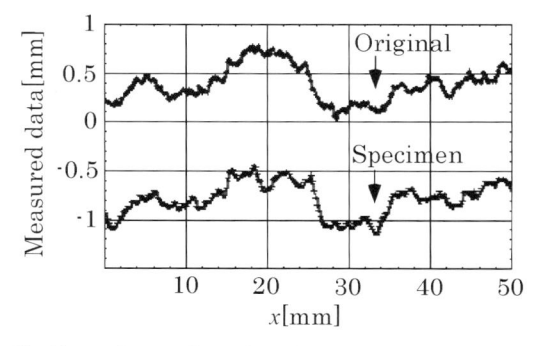

Fig.13: Comparison of original and machined surfaces

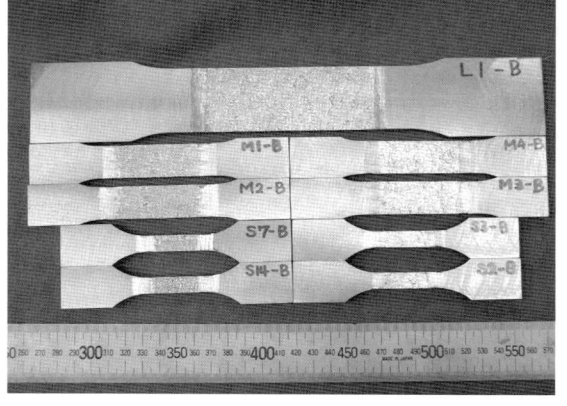

Fig.14: Test specimens

Results and Discussions

The test results are listed in Table 3 and the relation between the width/thickness ratio and the nominal tensile strengths are illustrated in Fig.15. In the present study, the width/thickness ratios are 5.0, 2.5, and 1.25, for C-L, C-M, and C-S specimens, respectively. In the case of C-L specimens, tensile ultimate strength is reduced by 7%, while the strength reduction is not clearly observed in C-S specimens. One of the reasons of this observation may be attributed to the fact that a larger specimen may contain larger pits in the sample area. In order to estimate the mechanical properties of corroded members of aged ships, it may be desirable to have experimental data corresponding to the higher range of the width/thickness ratio to confirm this tendency.

With regard to the elongation, it should be noted that the specimens show considerably larger elongation with decreasing the width/thickness ratio as illustrated in Fig.16. This is due to the relatively weak constraint in the width direction of the specimen, so that this may also cause some influence to relatively narrow specimens such as C-S specimens. The effects of the specimen width were investigated by Miklowitz (1948) for flat plates, where he concluded that the width effects could be disregarded if the width/thickness ratio is greater than 7. In the present study, since this ratio is less than 5, the width effect may appear in the results for especially narrow specimens.

In Fig.17 the elongation is normalized by those of the flat plates, in which we can see the reduction by 30% with some scatters in comparison with the flat plate. As far as the reduction of elongation is concerned, no clear dependence was observed with respect to the width/thickness ratio.

Table 3: Test results

Specimen	σ_{YU} [MPa]	σ_{YL} [MPa]	σ_U [MPa]	Elongation [%]
L0	387.50	367.95	517.19	32.46
C-L1	342.27	332.90	478.21	23.92
C-L1-2	337.99	335.86	479.51	23.26
C-M1	359.08	357.37	497.91	28.44
C-M2	357.95	355.94	500.19	30.84
C-M3	354.22	347.46	484.67	26.48
C-M4	360.36	357.38	494.86	25.20
C-S2	379.96	373.09	507.08	32.00
C-S3	376.37	369.36	510.93	32.32
C-S7	380.05	371.66	519.77	36.84
C-S14	371.22	366.35	521.66	37.24

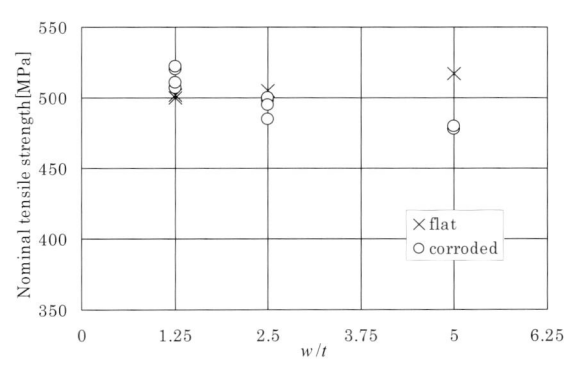

Fig. 15 Nominal tensile strength for various sizes of specimens

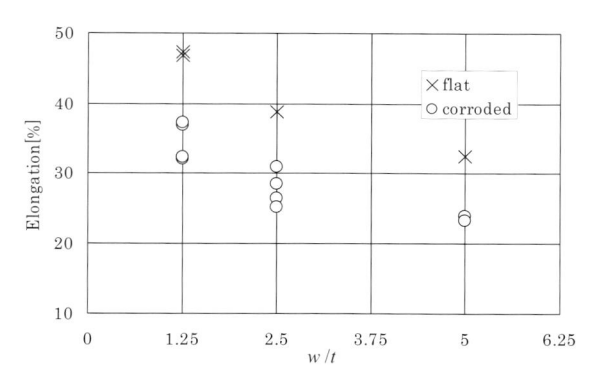

Fig. 16: Elongation for various sizes of specimens

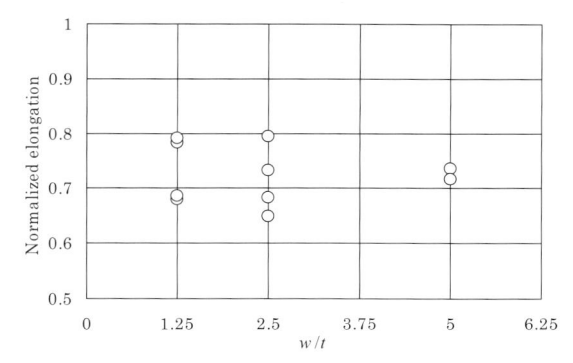

Fig. 17: Normalized elongation for various sizes of specimens

Conclusions

In order to investigate strength and deformability of corroded steel plates by using artificially pitted and replicated specimens, a CAD-CAM system, which numerically controls a desktop milling machine, has been successfully developed. Periodical array of surface pits are made for self-similar specimens, and the results do not show any significant size dependency, so that it becomes possible to carry out experiments by using self-similar small specimens. In order to examine the mechanical properties of plates with general corrosion, surface geometries of a sample specimen taken from the bottom plate of an aged tanker are reproduced, and the corresponding tensile tests are carried out. Slight reduction of the tensile strength is observed, while the reduction of elongation is considerable. In order to investigate the extent of the sample area of a corroded surface, specimens having different sample areas but with the same thickness and with the surface undulation in the same scale are tested. The ultimate tensile strength shows slight dependence on the extent of the surface area, which may suggest a further research using wider specimens.

Acknowledgement

The author expresses his gratitude to Mr. N. Yamamura and Mr. Y. Yamamuro, former students, for their supports of the present work. This work has been in parts supported by Grant-in-Aid for Scientific Research (No. B(2)14350519, and No. A(2)1720608600) from the Ministry of Education, Science and Culture to Yokohama National University. The author is grateful for their support.

References

Miklowitz, J (1948). "The Influence of the DimensionFactors on the Mode of Yielding and Fracture in Medium-Carbon Steel-I, The Geometry and Size of the Flat Tensile Bar," J. Applied Mechanics, ASME Vol 70, pp 274-287.

Nakai, T, Matsushita, H, Yamamoto, N, and Arai, H (2004a). "Effect of Pitting Corrosion on Local Strength of Hold Frames of Bulk Carriers (1st Report)," Marine Structures, Vol 17, pp 403-432.

Nakai, T, Matsushita, H, and Yamamoto, N (2004b). "Effect of Pitting Corrosion on Local Strength of Hold Frames of Bulk Carriers (2nd Report) - Lateral-Distortional Buckling and Local Face Buckling," Marine Structures, Vol 17, pp 612-641.

Nakai, T, Sumi, Y, Saeki, K, and Yamamoto, N (2006). "Stochastic Modeling of Pitting Corrosion and Tensile Tests with Artificially Pitted Members," J. Japan Society of Naval Architects and Ocean Eng., Vol 4, pp 247-255 (in Japanese).

Oka, M, Kitada, H, and Watanabe, T (1990). "Experimental Study on Statistical Strength of Corrosive Mild Steel," J. Society of Naval Architects of Japan, Vol 167, pp 229-235 (in Japanese).

Yamamoto, N and Ikegami, K (1998). "A Study on the Degradation of Coating and Corrosion of Ship's Hull Based on the Probabilistic Approach," J. Offshore Mechanics and Arctic Eng, ASME Vol 120, pp 121-128.

Simulation of Inspections on Ship Plates with Random Corrosion Patterns

A.P. Teixeira & C. Guedes Soares

Unit of Marine Technology and Engineering,
Technical University of Lisbon, Instituto Superior Técnico,
Av. Rovisco Pais, 1049-001 Lisboa, Portugal
E-mail: teixeira@mar.ist.utl.pt, guedess@mar.ist.utl.pt

Abstract

This paper investigates how the number of thickness measurements and the location of each measurement influence, both the correct representation of the level of corrosion, and indirectly the correct assessment of the collapse strength of the corroded plates. For this propose, the corrosion patterns are represented by random fields, as recently suggested by Teixeira and Guedes Soares, (2006), which are then discretized using the Expansion Optimal Linear Estimation method proposed by Li and Der Kiureghian, (1993). This approach is used to simulate the present practice on thickness measurement patterns and to identify what would be the effect of other strategies of measurement patterns for representing the corrosion in terms of prediction of the average reduction of plate thickness. Finally, the collapse strength of the plates with nonuniform corrosion is calculated by nonlinear finite element analysis and its correlation with the average reduction of plate thickness obtained from the different measurement patterns is assessed.

Keywords

Nonuniform corrosion; Random fields; Thickness measurement patterns; Collapse strength of plates.

Introduction

Corrosion is one of the major issues for the structural condition assessment of aged ships. The condition of the steel structure of ships is subject to requirements of classification societies, as stipulated in the rules for classification, and to international requirements being controlled by statutory regulations specified in several IMO resolutions. In particular, the Enhanced Survey Programme (ESP) Guidelines (IMO, (2005) resolution A.744 (18), as amended) defines the requirements for planning, execution and reporting for hull surveys of oil/chemical tankers, obo and bulk carriers. The ESP program survey schedules and extent of surveys are based on the understanding that the real condition can only be revealed with detailed close-up inspections and extensive thickness measurements, and that the deterioration process happens slowly over time. It is therefore considered more effective to have fewer thorough surveys rather than more frequent superficial ones.

Another instrument is the MARPOL's Condition Assessment Scheme (CAS) (IMO, (2001)) that is a mandatory statutory survey scheme that single hull oil tankers must satisfactorily complete by 15 years of age or by the first intermediate or renewal survey due after 5 April 2005 (which ever occurs later) in order to trade to their respective phase out date as per MARPOL 13G, which was accelerated by resolution MEPC.111(50) (IMO, (2003)).

CAS is required to be conducted in conjunction with the mandatory Enhanced Survey Program (ESP) and builds upon ESP by requiring additional thickness measurements and close-up surveys. The main differences between CAS and ESP are related to survey planning, survey reporting, flag state involvement and the strict timeline needs to be followed. Moreover, the minimum requirement to thickness measurements under CAS increases, as the measurements are to be taken in areas subject to close-up inspection.

The purpose of thickness measurement is to establish, in conjunction with a visual examination that the condition of the existing structure is, or will be after the required repairs, fit for continued service during the subsequent survey interval. The gauging requirements include measurements which are used to verify remaining longitudinal strength, transverse sections, as well as measurements of areas known to be potential problem areas, main deck plates and wind and water strakes.

According to the current practice, in the execution of the thickness measurements on board the surveyor will direct the gauging operation by selecting locations such that readings taken represent, on average, the condition of the structure for that area. When a single reading is not representative of the corrosion in a particular area of platting, additional readings are taken and assessed together with close visual examination by the Surveyor for determination of the extent of corrosion pattern. In this case, the Surveyor assesses the average condition based on observations of the structure from visual examination and the gauged readings.

A key question concerns which parameters are appropriate for evaluating corrosion; average thickness, minimum thickness, pit intensity, etc. Class societies generally require average thickness, pit maximum depth and pit intensity (as a percentage of the plate surface).

There is a trend towards a more quantitative definition of corrosion intensity, as the current practice of gauging, even if carried out according to the rule requirements, may not represent the reality (ABS, (2001)).

Moreover Teixeira and Guedes Soares, (2006) showed recently that the strength of plates with spatial distribution of corroded thickness is usually lower than the one obtained for uniform corrosion and, therefore, taking the average of the measurements to represent the corroded plate thickness in alternative to a more correct representation of the corrosion patterns, can lead to optimistic assessment of strength of the structural elements.

The present paper investigates how the number of thickness measurements and their location influence the correct representation of the corrosion patterns and the correct assessment the collapse strength of the corroded plates. For this propose the nonuniform corrosion patterns are represented by random fields, as suggested by Teixeira and Guedes Soares, (2006), which are then discretized using the Expansion Optimal Linear Estimation method proposed by Li and Der Kiureghian, (1993). A non-linear corrosion model proposed by Guedes Soares and Garbatov, (1999) is used to define the probabilistic characteristics of the random fields based on corrosion data measured in plate elements at different locations of several bulk carriers reported by Paik et al., (1998).

This approach is used to simulate different thickness measurement patterns on plates with simulated nonuniform corrosion in order to assess the effect of the various options on the prediction of average reduction of plate thickness and its correlation with the collapse strength of the plates calculated by nonlinear finite element analysis.

Discretization of random fields

In many structural problems, the basic structural parameters were often assumed to be discrete, allowing them to be represented as single-valued random variables. This assumption is valid for quantities that are concentrated at discrete points or uniformly distributed in space. However, most parameters in a structure are distributed in space. Examples of such parameters are distributed loads, material and geometric properties and the reduction of thickness due to corrosion that vary over the length of a beam or the area of a plate. Such quantities cannot be expressed as single random variables, but only as a collection of many random variables or more appropriately, as random processes or fields.

In probabilistic analyses, it is however convenient to represent the random fields in terms of a discrete set of random variables. This is known as discretization of random fields. Since these random variables are obtained from the same random field, there is statistical correlation among them and the mathematical understanding of the correlation relationships in a random field is therefore essential in order to correctly discretize the field.

Several methods have been proposed for discretization of random fields in particular for use in finite reliability analysis of structures as reviewed by Li and Der Kiureghian, (1993), Ditlevsen, (1996) and Schuëller, (1997). In this study the random field of corrosion is discretized using the Expansion Optimal Linear Estimation method (EOLE) proposed by Li and Der Kiureghian, (1993).

The EOLE discretization method assumes that the random field $H(x)$ can be defined as a linear function of a vector $h = \{H(x_1),....,H(x_N),\}$ of N nodal values $H(x_i)$ of the original random field given by:

$$\hat{H}(x) = a(x) + \sum_{i=1}^{N} b_i(x) H(x_i) = a(x) + b^T(x) h \quad (1)$$

where $a(x)$ is a scalar function of x, $b(x)$ is a vector function of x and N in the number of nodal points in the domain.

Assuming that the vector h of random variables can be expressed in terms of its spectral decomposition it is possible to determine the functions $a(x)$ and $b(x)$ that minimize the variance of the error $(H(x) - \hat{H}(x))$, subjected to $\hat{H}(x)$ being an unbiased estimator of the $H(x)$ in the mean, i.e., $(H(x) - \hat{H}(x)) = 0$. Hence, according the called Expansion Optimal Linear Estimation method (EOLE), the random field is given by (Li and Der Kiureghian, 1993):

$$\hat{H}(x) = \mu(x) + \sum_{i=1}^{r} \frac{\zeta_i}{\sqrt{\theta_i}} \phi_i^T C_{Hh} \quad (2)$$

where $\mu(x)$ is the mean function of the random field, C_{Hh} is a $r \times 1$ vector containing the covariances of $H(x)$ with the elements of h, θ_i, ϕ_i are the eigenvalues and eigenvectors of the covariance matrix of h and ζ_i is a set of r independent standard normal distributions (zero mean, unit variance and zero correlation).

Therefore, this method requires first the definition of the grid size, i.e. the dimension $N \times N$ of the matrix C_{hh} for the eigenvalue problem and then the number of terms r with the largest eigenvalues that correspond to the number of random variables that are used to represent the random field.

The variance of the Expansion Optimal Linear Estimation method is given by:

$$VAR[\hat{H}(x)] = \sum_{i=1}^{r} \frac{1}{\theta_i} (\phi_i^T C_{Hh})^2 \quad (3)$$

Thus, the variance error in the EOLE method can be estimated by comparing the variance of random field the variance of the represented field i.e.,

$$VAR[H(x)-\hat{H}(x)] = \sigma^2(x) - \sum_{i=1}^{r} \frac{1}{\theta_i}(\phi_i^T C_{Hh})^2 \qquad (4)$$

The high level efficiency of this approach in the sense that it requires a small number of random variables to represent the random field, within a given level of accuracy, makes this model particular useful for stochastic analysis, and therefore it will be used on further calculations.

The probabilistic characteristics of the random field, namely its mean value and standard deviation, are defined based on available statistical data of the corrosion damage in plates of existing bulk carriers (Paik et al., (1998). For the numerical analysis presented in this paper the following autocorrelation function of multidimensional homogeneous random fields has been considered:

$$\rho(x,x') = e^{-\frac{|x-x'|^2}{l_c^2}} \qquad (5)$$

in which the parameter l_c is a measure of the rate of fluctuation of the random filed, commonly known as the correlation length. A correlation length of 0.3m was chosen in the present study, which allows the study of the effect of the spatial representation of the corrosion patterns on the collapse strength of the plates.

Fig. 1 shows three realizations of the random field of reduction of plate thickness due to the corrosion process.

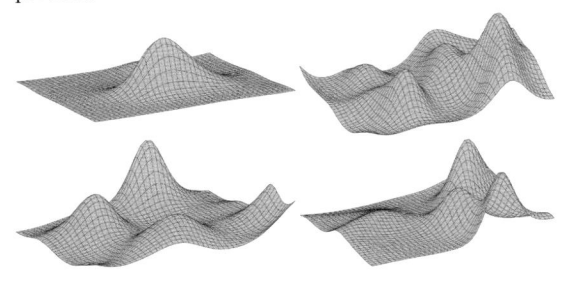

Fig. 1: Realizations of the lognormal random field of thickness reduction due to corrosion.

Thickness measurements for corrosion monitoring

Corrosion monitoring of ship structures is typically performed through ultrasonic thickness measurements (UTM) carried out by qualified operators using specialized measurement equipment. Procedures for UTM are well established and mostly governed in general terms by IACS requirements (IACS, (2006b), IACS, (2006a), IACS, (2004)) and by the individual Classification Societies at a more detailed level (e.g. DNV, (2004)) .

The IACS's Procedural Requirement PR 19 IACS, (2004), is mandatory and stipulates that the thickness measurements required in the context of hull structural classification surveys are to be witnessed by a surveyor, which requires the attendance of a surveyor during gauging.

The associated Recommendation No 77 "Guidelines for the Surveyor on how to control the thickness measurement process" (IACS, (2006a)), contain items that should be addressed at the survey meeting prior to the survey to ensure a safe and efficient execution of the surveys and thickness measurements. The guidelines also contain items related to monitoring the thickness measurement process on board, such as: selection of locations; special consideration of structures where protective coating is found to be in good condition; additional measurements of areas with substantial corrosion or excessive diminution.

Thickness measurement processes

During the execution of the thickness measurements on board the surveyor directs the gauging operation by selecting locations such that readings taken represent, on average, the condition of the structure for that area.

According to the current practice (DNV 2004) the measurements shall be taken at the forward, middle and aft area of all plates, minimum 3 measurements per plate. This applies for e.g. deck, bottom and wind- and water strakes. However, the requirements at CAP surveys may be stricter, e.g. one measurement in the middle of each plate and one in each corner, five in all.

If a single reading is not considered to be representative for an area, additional readings shall be carried out, with a comment in the report stating that these are additional readings. Alternatively, the average value of several readings in a small area may be included in the report together with a comment stating that this is an average value. In such cases all the readings to be averaged are to be taken within the affected area. The size of such a "small area", shall typically be the spacing of the stiffeners (longitudinals in tankers or side frames in bulk carriers), with the same length used both in the ship's transverse and longitudinal direction. The average thickness of that area shall then be entered in the report, and used to compare with minimum thickness and substantial thickness values, even if single readings within that area are less.

Where thickness measurements indicate substantial corrosion or excessive diminution the surveyor should direct locations for additional thickness measurements in order to delineate areas of substantial corrosion and to identify structural members for repairs / renewals.

Substantial Corrosion is defined as, "an extent of corrosion such that assessment of corrosion pattern indicates wastage in excess of 75% of the allowable margins, but within the acceptable limits". In this case, the number of readings needed to obtain a representative average will depend on the ship type and structural element, but typically a 5 point pattern over 1 m^2 of plating or for each panel between longitudinals are usually required (IACS, (2006b)). This higher density of readings will provide a higher degree of accuracy in determining the corrosion pattern and will provide sufficient data to establish appropriate recommendations for extent of repair, if required.

Thickness measurement patterns and averaging

The present study investigates the effect of several thickness measurement patterns on the assessment of the level of corrosion of plate elements. The approach is based on the statistical analysis of the corrosion wastages calculated from different measurement criteria of corrosion patterns on square plates ($a=b=1m$) obtained by stochastic simulation of random fields of corrosion.

Table 1 summarizes the characteristics of the plate element and of the random field of thickness reduction due to corrosion of inner bottom plates of a 10 years old bulk carrier (Teixeira and Guedes Soares, (2006)).

Table 1: Probabilistic characteristics of the random field of corrosion.

Plate model	a (mm)	b (mm)	t (mm)	b/t
	1000	1000	20	50

Random field	Distrib.	Mean, μ_c	St. dev., σ_c	Corr. length, $l_{c,x}=l_{c,y}$
	Lognormal	1.021mm	0.883 mm	300 mm

Fig. 2 illustrates the measurement patterns adopted in this study that differ on the number of readings per plate and by their locations. The figure shows a 1, 3, 5 and 8-point patterns along the centerline of each plate, represented by "1P", "C$_1$-3L", "C$_2$-5L" and "C$_3$-8L", respectively. The effect of the thickness measurement locations is accounted for by two 5-point measurement patterns "C$_4$-5A" and "C$_5$-5CM", and a 9-point pattern (C$_6$-9P), as illustrated in Fig. 2.

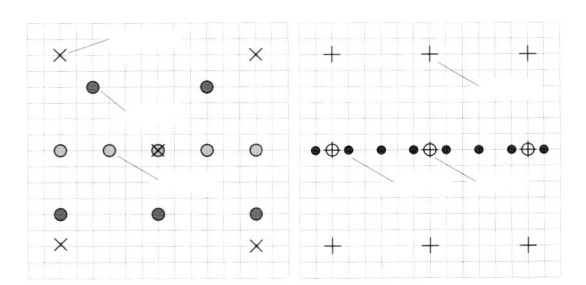

Fig. 2: Location of the readings of each measurement pattern.

Table 2 shows the results of the statistical analysis of the average reduction of plate thickness due to corrosion (t_r) obtained by the different thickness measurement patterns, based on over 5000 simulations of the lognormal random field of corrosion. The results are compared with the thickness reduction, $t_r(\text{all})$, derived from averaging 289 readings corresponding to measurement locations defined by the mesh illustrated in Fig. 2. It can be seen that the squared correlation coefficients (R^2) between the predictions of the various measurement patterns and the best estimate "$t_r(\text{all})$" are considerably different. The best correlation is obtained by the 9-point pattern "C$_6$-9L" followed by the two 5-point measurement patterns, "C$_4$-5A" and "C$_5$-5CM", as illustrated in Figs. 3-6. It is also interesting to see that all measurement patterns of readings along the centerline of the plate element ("C$_1$-3L", "C$_2$-5L" and "C$_3$-8L") give identical results leading to the conclusion that, in statistical terms, the increase of line readings does not increase the accuracy of the predictions of the average reduction of plate thickness. Therefore, it is much more efficient to distribute the readings over the plate under examination, as can be seen by the higher correlation coefficients obtained from the 9-point pattern (C$_6$-9L) and the 5-point alternated measurement pattern (C$_4$-5A).

Table 2: Statistics of average reduction of plate thickness, t_r.

$n = 5000$	Mean	St. Dev.	COV	R^2	% Δ (Mean)	% Δ (COV)
$t_r(\text{all})$	1.027	0.367	0.357	-	-	-
$t_r(\text{C}_6\text{-9P})$	1.027	0.376	0.366	0.960	0.0	2.5
$t_r(\text{C}_4\text{-5A})$	1.025	0.457	0.445	0.800	-0.2	24.4
$t_r(\text{C}_5\text{-5CM})$	1.024	0.421	0.411	0.701	-0.2	14.8
$t_r(\text{C}_3\text{-8L})$	1.044	0.613	0.588	0.561	1.6	67.1
$t_r(\text{C}_2\text{-5L})$	1.045	0.632	0.605	0.556	1.7	72.3
$t_r(\text{C}_1\text{-3L})$	1.043	0.611	0.586	0.551	1.5	66.4
$t_r(1P)$	1.027	0.885	0.862	0.169	0.0	141.1

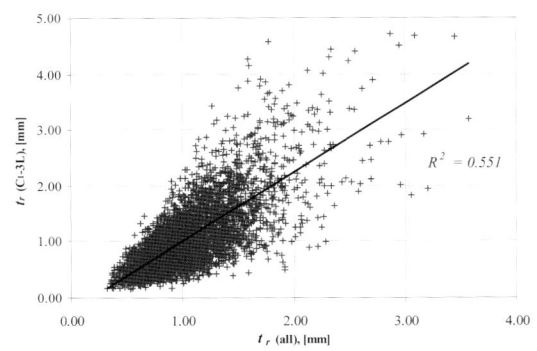

Fig. 3: Correlation between the average reduction of plate thickness "$t_r(\text{C}_6\text{-3L})$" and "$t_r(\text{all})$".

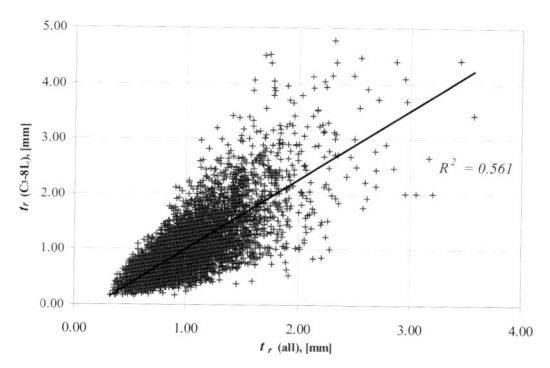

Fig. 4: Correlation between the average reduction of plate thickness "$t_r(C_6\text{-}8L)$" and "$t_r(\text{all})$".

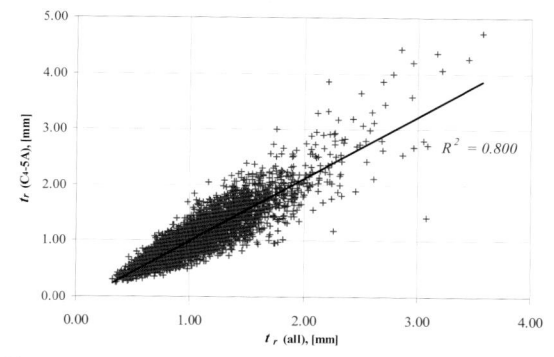

Fig. 5: Correlation between the average reduction of plate thickness "$t_r(C_6\text{-}5A)$" and "$t_r(\text{all})$".

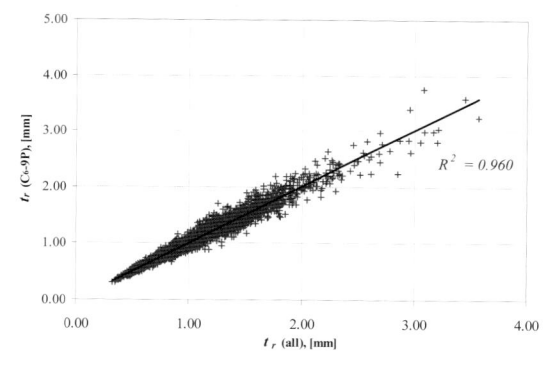

Fig. 6: Correlation between the average reduction of plate thickness "$t_r(C_6\text{-}9P)$" and "$t_r(\text{all})$".

It is clear from Figs. 3-6 that the accuracy of each individual method in predicting the real average reduction of plate thickness is significantly different, as indicated by the differences in the level of dispersion around the regression lines. The level of dispersion is often characterized by a constant conditional variance $Var(Y|x)$ within the range of x. In this case an unbiased estimate of this variance, $\left(s_{Y|x}^2\right)$, can be obtained from the correlation coefficient (R) by:

$$R^2 = 1 - \frac{s_{Y|x}^2}{s_Y^2}, \qquad (6)$$

which reflects the effect of linear regression on the reduction of the original variance of Y from s_Y^2 to $s_{Y|x}^2$ resulting from taking into account the general trend with x. Moreover, the sample of the differences to the regression line follows a normal distribution with mean $\mu = 0$ and variance $s_{Y|x}^2$. According to the central limit theorem, the mean of this sample ($\mu = 0$) also follows a normal distribution $N\left(\mu = 0, s_{Y|x}/\sqrt{n}\right)$, from which it is possible to determine the confidence intervals (CI) or alternatively the sample size (n) of measured plates necessary to obtain a level of accuracy (ε) in terms of the assessment of average thickness reduction, i.e.:

$$\varepsilon = CI = \left| \mu + \frac{s_{Y|x}}{\sqrt{n}} k_{CL} \right| \qquad (7)$$

where k_{CL} is a value of a standard normal variate with cumulative probability level related with a particular confidence level (CL) given by:

$$k_{CL} = \Phi^{-1}\left(\frac{1+CL}{2}\right) \qquad (8)$$

These calculations are presented in Table 3 for the different measurement patterns considered in this study. The table shows that only 54 plates are need to be inspected according to measurement pattern "$C_6\text{-}9P$" to obtain a 2% error on the average reduction of plate thickness, at a 95% confidence level. This value increases to around 1600 for the line measurement patterns ("$C_1\text{-}3L$", "$C_2\text{-}5L$" and "$C_3\text{-}8L$"), almost independent of the number of readings.

Table 3: Sample size (n) for a given level of accuracy on the on the average reduction of plate thickness t_r (margin of error $\varepsilon = 2\%$ at a 95% confidence level).

$\varepsilon = 2\%$ on t_r, $CL=0.95$, $k_{CL}=1.96$							
Method	C_6-9P	C_4-5A	C_5-5CM	C_3-8L	C_2-5L	C_1-3L	1P
Sample size	54	401	509	1586	1706	1607	6250

Effect of the correlation length of the random field

The level of fluctuation of the corrosion over the plate surface influences the form of the realizations of the random field and consequently the performance of each measurement criteria in obtaining the average reduction of plate thickness. This effect can be investigated by varying the correlation length (l_c) of the random field of reduction of plate thickness due to corrosion. Fig. 7 illustrates the effect of increasing the correlation length (l_c) from 0.2m to 0.5m in one realization of the random field of corrosion.

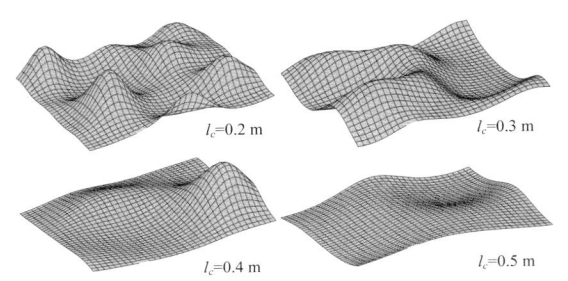

Fig. 7: Effect of the correlation length (l_c) on the realizations of a lognormal random field of thickness reduction due to corrosion.

Fig. 8 shows the effect of the correlation length of the random field on the correlation (R^2) between the average reduction of plate thickness obtained from the different measurement patterns and t_r(all). As one would expect, the increase of the correlation structure of the random field increases the accuracy of all measurement criteria. It can also be seen that the correlations of the most accurate measurement pattern (C$_6$-9L) tend to stabilize after $l_c = 0.3 m$. For the less accurate methods of measurement, the increase of the correlation is almost linear with the increase of the correlation length of the random field.

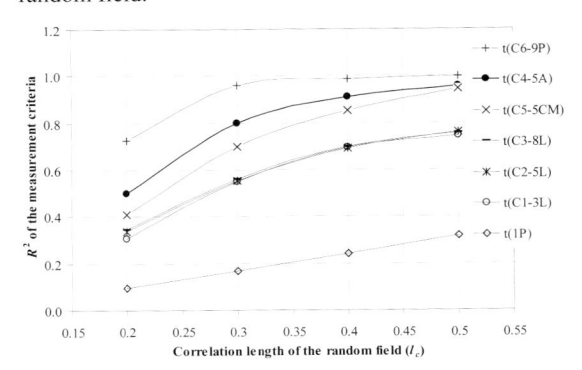

Fig. 8: Effect of l_c on the correlation between the average reduction of plate thickness "t_r(C$_\cdot$-..)" and "t_r(all)".

Fig. 9 shows the effect of the correlation length of the random field on the sample sized required to obtain a level of accuracy (ε) of 2% on the assessment of average thickness reduction. It is clear that for the most accurate measurement patterns (C$_6$-9L, C$_4$-5A and C$_5$-5CM), the increase of the correlation structure of the random field results in a decrease on the number of plates that need to be measured. It is also interesting to see that all line measurement patterns require considerably larger samples to obtain the specified level of accuracy on the assessment of average thickness reduction. Moreover, the general trend of decreasing the sample size (n) as the correlation length (l_c) increases, obtained for the measurement patterns C$_6$-9L, C$_4$-5A and C$_5$-5CM, is not identified for the line measurement patterns. This indicates that line measurement patterns are not able to capture the correlation structure of the corrosion field in the transverse direction, and increasing either the line readings or the 2D correlative structure of the random field of corrosion does not increase their performance in assessing the average reduction of plate thickness.

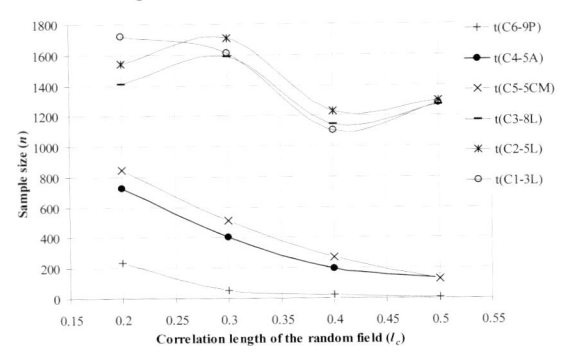

Fig. 9: Effect of l_c on the sample size for a given level of accuracy on the on the average reduction of plate thickness t_r.

Ultimate strength of plates with random fields of corrosion

The calculations were carried out for simply supported square plates with $a=b=1.0$m of slenderness $b/t=50$ with longitudinal edges restrained against transverse displacement. The load is a uniform prescribed longitudinal displacement (δ) applied along the transverse edge of the plate as illustrated in Fig. 10. An initial geometric imperfection shape (w_z) represented by with only one component of a Fourier series was considered in this study:

$$w_z = w_o \sin\frac{\pi x}{a} \sin\frac{\pi y}{b} \qquad (9)$$

where the mean value of the amplitude of the shape of the initial imperfection (w_o) is given as function of the plate slenderness (β) by:

$$w_o = 0.1\beta^2 t \quad \text{with} \quad \beta = (b/t)\sqrt{\sigma_o / E} \qquad (10)$$

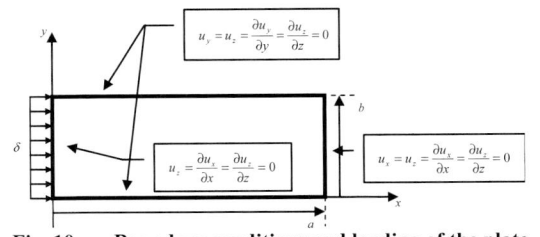

Fig. 10: Boundary conditions and loading of the plate model.

Table 4 presents the statistics of the normalized collapse strength (ϕ_u) of the plates with nonuniform corrosion represented by random fields, obtained by Monte Carlo simulation and nonlinear finite element analysis. Fig. 11 illustrates the average normalized longitudinal stress-displacement curve of the plate with corrosion represented by random fields (R.F.) and the one corresponding to the plate without corrosion.

940

Table 4: Statistics of the collapse strength (ϕ_u) of corroded plates with $b/t=50$ ($n=5000$ simulations).

Average	St. Deviation	Skewness	COV
0.739	0.026	-1.666	0.035

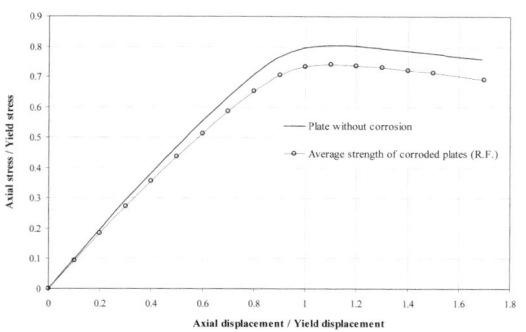

Fig. 11: Longitudinal normalized stress-displacement curves of square plates of ($b/t=50$).

Table 5 presents the sample squared correlation coefficient between the average reduction of plate thickness, obtained from the different measurement patterns, with the collapse strength of the plates with nonuniform corrosion patterns represented by the random field. These results are also illustrated in Figs. 12-15, respectively for the average reduction of plate thickness "t_r(all)" and for each one derived from measurement patterns "C_6-9P", "C_4-5A", "C_1-3L" and "1P". It can be seen that the squared coefficient of correlation of ϕ_u with the best prediction of the average reduction of plate thickness t_r(all) is 0.943. This result reflects mainly the correlation between the collapse strength of the plate with nonuniform corrosion represented by random fields and the one obtained assuming the uniform reduction of plate thickness t_r(all), as illustrated in Fig. 16. It can be seen from Fig. 16 that on average the differences between the collapse strengths are small, but increase for larger levels of corrosion and are more evident for slender plates for which a higher dispersion of the results is observed, as shown by Teixeira and Guedes Soares, (2007). This situation illustrates that the assumption of uniform reduction of plate thickness can in many situations underestimate the real collapse strength of the corroded plate.

Table 5: Correlation between the average reduction of plate thickness "t_r(C_-..)" and the collapse strength of the plate (ϕ_u).

Method	t_r(all)	C_6-9P	C_4-5A	C_5-5CM	C_3-8L	C_2-5L	C_1-3L
R^2	0.943	0.907	0.693	0.654	0.627	0.621	0.622

Table 5 also shows that the 9-point measurement pattern is the one that has the best correlation with the collapse strength of the plate, as it provides the most accurate assessment of the average reduction of plate thickness. Finally, it is possible to see that the thickness measurement pattern "C4-5A", although being substantially more accurate than the line measurement patterns in assessing the average reduction of plate thickness, as shown in Table 2, its correlation with the collapse strength decreases considerably. Therefore, it can be concluded that this measurement pattern is not able to capture the highly localized shapes of corrosion that contribute more to the reduction of the collapse strength of the plates.

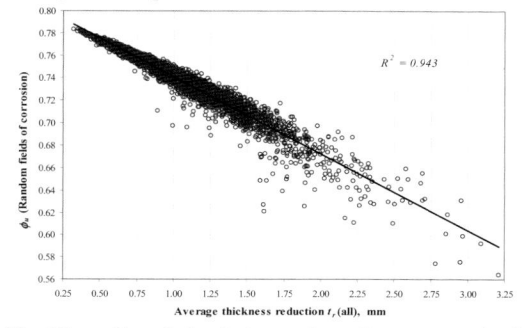

Fig. 12: Correlation between the collapse strength of plate and the average reduction of plate thickness "t_r(all)".

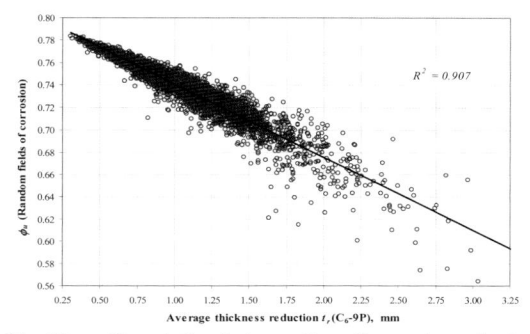

Fig. 13: Correlation between the collapse strength of plate and the average reduction of plate thickness "t_r(C_6-9P)".

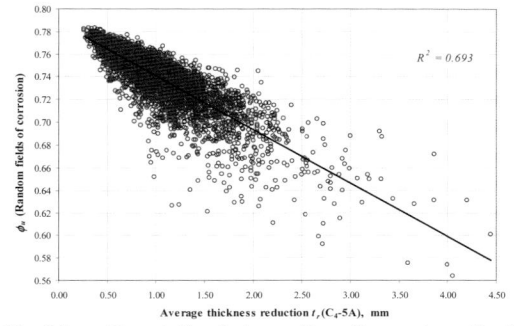

Fig. 14: Correlation between the collapse strength of plate and the average reduction of plate thickness "t_r(C_4-5A)".

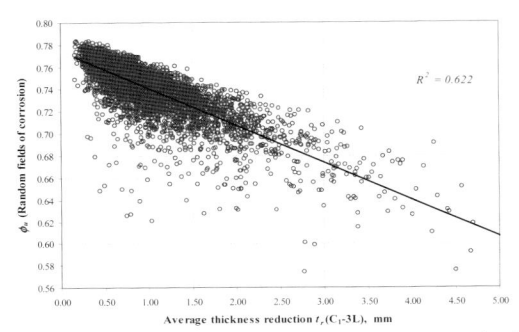

Fig. 15: Correlation between the collapse strength of plate and the average reduction of plate thickness "$t_r(C_1\text{-}3L)$".

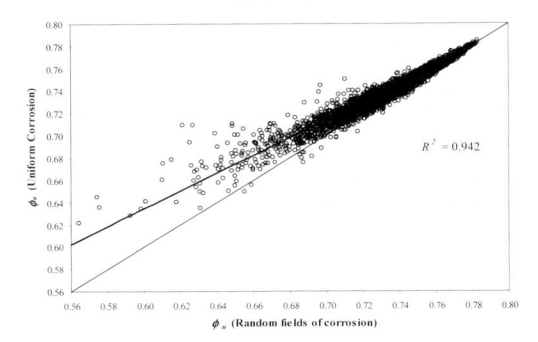

Fig. 16: Collapse strength of plates with corrosion represented by random fields and uniform reduction of thickness "$t_r(\text{all})$".

Conclusions

This paper has presented a study on the effect of different measurement patterns on the prediction of the average reduction of thickness of plates with nonuniform corrosion obtained by stochastic simulation of random fields. It has been shown that the accuracy of each individual measurement pattern in assessing the average reduction of plate thickness is considerably different. In particular it was demonstrated that, in statistical terms, the increase of line readings does not increase the accuracy of the predictions leading to the conclusion that is much more efficient to distribute the readings over the plate under examination. It was also shown that the line measurement patterns are not able to capture the correlation structure of the corrosion field in the transverse direction, and increasing either the line readings or the 2D correlative structure of the random field of corrosion does not increase their performance in assessing the average reduction of plate thickness.

The correlation between the average reduction of plate thickness, obtained from the different measurement patterns, with the collapse strength of the plates with nonuniform corrosion patterns has also been investigated. The results showed that the 9-point measurement pattern is the one that has the best correlation with the collapse strength of the plate, as it provides the most accurate assessment of the average reduction of plate thickness. Moreover, it was possible to see that the thickness measurement pattern "C4-5A", although being substantially more accurate than the line measurement patterns in assessing the average reduction of plate thickness, its correlation with the collapse strength decreases considerably. Therefore, it can be concluded that this measurement pattern is not able to capture the highly localized shapes of corrosion that contribute more to the reduction of the collapse strength of the plates. This suggests that these particular patterns of localized corrosion should be carefully characterized during inspections or even mapped separately, as carried out for pitting corrosion.

The examples presented demonstrate the potential of this method but the conclusions are related to the example studied. There is still the need to conduct field experiments that will allow realistic models of spatial distribution of corrosion to be modeled by this theoretical model and it is expected that the spatial distribution may be different in various areas of the ships.

Acknowledgement

The present paper has been prepared within the project "MARSTRUCT - Network of Excellence on Marine Structures", which has been funded by the European Union through the Growth program under contract TNE3-CT-2003-506141.

References

ABS, (2001), Final report of Investigation into the damage sustained by the M.V. Castor on 30 December 2000, American Bureau of Shipping, http://www.eagle.org/news/press/castorreport.pdf.

Ditlevsen, O., (1996), Dimension reduction and discretization in stochastic problems by regression method, Mathematical models for structural reliability analysis, CRC Mathematical Modelling Series, F. Casciati and B. Roberts (Editors), 2, pp. 51-138.

DNV, (2004), Guideline for Ultrasonic Thickness Measurements of ships classed with Det Norske Veritas, MTPNO864, September 2004, http://www.dnv.com/binaries/UTM_tcm4-77272.pdf.

Guedes Soares, C. and Garbatov, Y., (1999), Reliability of Maintained Corrosion Protected Plate Subjected to Non-Linear Corrosion and Compressive Loads, Marine Structures, N. 6, Vol. 12, pp. 425-446.

IACS, (2004), PR 19 -Procedural Requirement for Thickness Measurements, Revision 3, June 2004, http://www.iacs.org.uk/document/public/Publications/Procedural_requirements/PDF/PR_19_pdf104.pdf.

IACS, (2006a), Guideline 77 -Guidelines for the Surveyor on how to Control the Thickness Measurement Process, Revision 2, April 2006, http://www.iacs.org.uk/document/public/Publications/Guidelines_and_recommendations/PDF/REC_77_pdf217.pdf.

IACS, (2006b), UR Z - Requirements concerning Survey and Certification, Revision 12, 2006, http://www.iacs.org.uk/document/public/Publications/Unified_requirements/PDF/UR_Z_pdf160.pdf.

IMO, (2001), Condition Assessment Scheme, Resolution MEPC.94(46).

IMO, (2003), Amendments to regulation 13G, addition of new regulation 13H, Resolution MEPC.111(50).

IMO, (2005), Guidelines on the enhanced programme of inspections during surveys of bulk carriers and oil tankers, Resolution A.744(18), as amended.

Li, C.-C. and Der Kiureghian, A., (1993), Optimal discretization of random fields, Journal of Eng. Mechanics, N. 6, Vol.119, pp. 1136-1154.

Paik, J. K., Kim, S. K., and Lee, S. K., (1998), Probabilistic corrosion rate estimation model for longitudinal strength members of bulk carriers, Ocean Engineering, 10, Vol. 25, pp. 837-860.

Schuëller, G. I. et al., (1997), A state-of-the-art report on computational stochastic mechanics, Probabilistic Engineering Mechanics, No. 4, Vol. 12, pp. 285-308.

Teixeira, A. P. and Guedes Soares, C., (2006), Ultimate strength of plates with random fields of corrosion, Advances in Reliability and Optimization of Structural Systems, Sorensen & Frangopol (eds), Taylor & Francis Group, London, pp. 179-186.

Teixeira, A. P. and Guedes Soares, C., (2007), Probabilistic modelling of the ultimate strength of plates with random fields of corrosion, Proc. of the 5th International Conference on Computational Stochastic Mechanics, G. Deodatis & P.D. Spanos (eds), Millpress, Rotterdam, pp. 653-661.

The Impact of Fusion Welds on the Ultimate Strength of Aluminum Structures

Matthew D. Collette [1)]

[1)] Science Applications International Corporation
Bowie, Maryland, U.S.A.

Abstract

In the quest to minimize lightship weight, structural researchers and engineers are turning to limit-state design techniques for aluminum high-speed vessels (HSVs). In adapting techniques used for other materials for use on aluminum, one of the central problems faced is how to account for the reduced strength region in and around fusion welds in aluminum structures. The common marine aluminum alloys in both the 5000 and 6000 series alloys lose a significant portion of their strength when fusion welded. The properties of fusion welds in common marine alloys are reviewed in this paper, and previous work in this field is summarized along with new investigations into the tensile strength of such welds. Examples of loss of strength in tensile loading are given along with the implications for limit-state formulation and structural strength.

Keywords

Aluminum; Welds; Ultimate strength; Heat-affected zone (HAZ); Strain concentration.

Introduction

Aluminum high-speed vessels are being employed on increasingly demanding routes and missions by civilian and military operators around the world. As the roles of these vessels expand, there is growing interest in applying limit-state design techniques in the vessels' structural design and optimization in place of current allowable-stress techniques. Limit-state design has been extensively investigated for steel vessels, with many notable publications in this area. Paik and Thayamballi (2003) give an excellent overview of steel-based limit-state design. For steel structures, research to date has been dominated by limit states involving collapse following large deformations, fracture, and corrosion. Steel structures can usually be successfully idealized as having homogenous material properties within each member of the structure and usually only two or three grades of material are used within a single structure.

While the three failures modes – collapse, fracture, and corrosion – must be addressed with aluminum as well as steel, welded marine aluminum structures cannot normally be idealized as having homogenous material properties. Fusion welds in marine-grade aluminum are under-matched, or weaker, than the surrounding structure. Careful use of extrusions and friction-stir welding can significantly reduce the number of fusion welds in an aluminum vessel; however, at the present time it is not practical to remove all fusion welds from the structure. Transverse welds at frames and construction block boundaries are likely to remain for some time, along with longitudinal welds in places where extruded integral panels have not proven popular, such as bottom structure. In current allowable-stress design techniques, these under-matched welds can be accounted for by adjusting the allowable stress level in the structure, or treating the structure as if the entire structure was made of the weakest material, both of which impose a significant weight penalty on the structure. However, for limit state design where the non-linear collapse of the structure must be evaluated, this material inhomogeneity must be accounted for in the limit state formulations.

Fusion welds in marine alloys, such as the 5000 or 6000 series alloys, lead to a region of reduced strength near the weld, which is often referred to as the heat-affected zone (HAZ). For common marine alloys, the reduction in proof strength in this region is often on the order of 30%-50%, and the HAZ normally extends between 10mm and 30mm from the centerline of the weld. Thus, fusion welds are marked by pronounced material inhomogeneity in material strength, and this inhomogeneity occurs at a much smaller length scale than what characterizes the other dimensions of the structure, such as the panel length, which is normally on the order of 1 meter, and the vessel breadth and depth, which are on the order of 10 meters. This difference in length scales requires limit state models that are able to integrate both the local material failure near fusion welds and the overall structural failure modes that are similar to existing steel limit states. A similar situation can occur when high-strength steels are joined by under-matched welds, but the under-match in these joints is often closer to 10% than 50%.

One feature of the response of a structure with under-matched welds is that the plastic flow of the structure in the post-elastic regime is concentrated in the under-matched region. As this region is small compared to the overall dimensions of the structure, it is often possible to see ductile rupture in these regions when the average global strains of the overall structure are still quite low. This leads to an overall structural response and failure that can appear similar to a brittle failure, although it is important to note that the failure is still fundamentally a ductile failure on the local level. This limitation of ductility indicates that failure modes – such as rupture in tension – that are often not investigated for steel vessels may be important for aluminum vessels.

In the following sections, the implications of welds on the ultimate limit state of aluminum structures will be further explored. First a review of previous works in this field will be presented, followed by a detailed review of fusion welds in 5000 and 6000 series aluminum alloys. Simple models of a welded aluminum joint are reviewed, followed by a summary of existing data on the effect of welding in compressive collapse. The results of several new models and studies for the influence of welding on tension limit states are presented, and conclusions are drawn.

Review of Previous Work

As aluminum limit-state analysis is a relatively new area of research in the marine field, much of the existing work on aluminum welds originates from the civil engineering, offshore, and aerospace fields. However, similar issues have been tackled in the marine industry when examining under-matched welds used in conjunction with high-tensile strength steel, where using under-matched welds can reduce fabrication costs. Ship Structure Committee report SSC-384 (Dexter and Ferrell, 1995) presents a good overview of this work and several experimental investigations into shipbuilding steels. Additional significant aluminum studies are briefly reviewed below, presenting first studies on local weld behavior, followed by studies on in-plane compressive collapse of ship-like shell structures, in-plane tension and bending collapse, and lateral collapse.

Weld Properties

Several studies have experimentally investigated local material properties near aluminum fusion welds. Hill, Clark, and Brungraber (1966) present one of the first studies of the influence of welding on structural response. Scott and Gittos (1983) present tensile and toughness measurements for a range of 5083 and 6082 butt welds. Malin (1991) presents a detailed study of welds in 6061-T6 extrusions used for panels as part of temporary bridging. Övreas, Thaulow, and Hval (1992) present material properties and FEM analysis of 6000-series butt welds. Matusiak and Larsen (1998) present material properties near a 6082-T6 butt weld as well as deformation and strength studies on butt and fillet welds in 6082-T6. Hval et al. (1998) present similar data for numeric modeling of fracture in 6005 and 6082 alloys, while Missori and Sili (2000) present similar data.

Compressive Collapse

Several authors have investigated the impact of welds on the compressive collapse of shell structures, where the primary mode of failure is structural instability. Mofflin (1983) investigated a wide range of 5083 and 6082 alloy plates with welds on both the plate boundaries parallel to the applied load and in the mid-region of the plate perpendicular to the applied load. Additionally, three panel tests have incorporated either longitudinal or partial transverse welds (Clarke and Swan 1985, Zha and Moan 2001, and Aalberg et al. 2001). Kristensen (2001), Paik and Duran (2004), and Rigo et al. (2003) performed numerical modeling of plates and stiffened panels including welds in compression. These studies have indicated that both longitudinal and transverse welds will impact the structure's strength in compression. In general, it is easier to formulate methods that include the effects of longitudinal welds on the ultimate strength, but transverse welds in the panel's mid-region can have a large impact on the predicted strength, especially for structures with low slenderness.

Tensile Collapse

There have also been several investigations into tensile collapse of welded aluminum structures, investigations that tend to focus on the reduction of ductility in a structure with under-matched weld regions and the related influence either on impact or crash resistance or on plastic capacity. The majority of the work to date has focused on plastic capacity under quasi-static loading. In an aerospace application, Verderaime (1989, 1991) studied the response of a butt weld in 2219-T87 aluminum, including formulating a simple model to predict the response of the weld under tension and bending loading. A similar weld was investigated by Vaughan and Schonberg (1995). Hval, Johnsen, and Thaulow (1995) investigated the impact of welds on 6082-T6 frameworks for offshore applications, and estimated the reduction in ductility from such welds. Roberts and Newark (1997) investigated welds in 7000-series aluminum tapered plate girders, finding that the girders' shear capacity was limited by sudden fracture of the HAZ where the web meets the flange and panel breakers on the girder. Moen, Hopperstad, and Langseth (1999) investigated the rotational capacity of welded and unwelded 6082-T6 beams, noting that the failure mode of the welded beams was rupture in the tensile HAZ near the weld. More recently, Chan and Porter Goff (2000) examined welded finger connections in 7000-series alloys, and formulated a weld failure model considering the material properties in the HAZ. Wang, Hopperstad, Larsen, and Lademo (2006) formulated and tested a finite-element approach for modeling the fillet weld connection in aluminum alloys.

While the studies above focus primarily on quasi-static loading, the weak region near welds also causes concern for impact and crash loading. An extensive European

Union project, ALJOIN (2007), has investigated "unzipping" of fusion welds in 6000-series aluminum rail cars during accidents, where the welds fail with little deformation of the surrounding structure. Such failure modes may be relevant for ship structures under collision, grounding, or blast loading.

Collectively, these studies represent a large body of work examining the tensile response of aluminum welds. These studies indicate that the weaker region near the welds can significantly impact the overall strength and ductility of the structure, and that an understanding of the properties of the local region around the weld is important when moving towards a limit-state design approach.

Lateral Collapse

The impact of welds on the strength of aluminum panels loaded laterally, or out-of-plane, has not been investigated as extensively as in-plane loadings. Abildgaard, Hansen, and Simonsen (2001) investigated the lateral plane response of welded plates through both experimental means and the use of a yield-line theory approach. Again, the potential for fracture or premature failure in the HAZ was noted.

Properties of Welds in 5000 and 6000 Series Alloys

The response of welded aluminum depends strongly on the underlying metallurgy of the particular aluminum alloy. 5000 and 6000-series alloys are the two most commonly used alloys in marine construction, and the metallurgy and resulting material properties of each will be reviewed below. In this work, the Ramberg-Osgood stress-strain relation will be used to model the response of the aluminum alloy. While this relation may not always capture the profile of the entire stress-strain curve, it has the advantage of being simple and useful for both analysis and design activities, where the type of data required for more advanced models may not always be available. The Ramberg-Osgood relation relates applied stress, σ, to strain, ε, via the material's elastic modulus, E, a proof stress $\sigma_{0.2}$, and an exponent, n.

$$\varepsilon = \frac{\sigma}{E} + 0.002\left(\frac{\sigma}{\sigma_{0.2}}\right)^n \qquad (1)$$

Sample parameter values for common alloys are show in Table 1.

Table 1: Typical material properties for thin 5000 and 6000 series marine alloys (Strengths are minimums per ABS 2006, Ramberg-Osgood exponents are typical)

Property	5083-H116	6061-T6
Un-welded proof stress	214 MPa	241 MPa
Un-welded ultimate stress	303 MPa	262 MPa
Un-welded RO exponent, n	12	29
Welded proof stress	165 MPa	138 MPa
Welded ultimate stress	276 MPa	165 MPa
Welded RO exponent, n	8	16
Approximate failure strain	8%	10%

5000-Series Alloys

The 5000-series alloy is one of the most common aluminum alloys used in marine construction; it is typically used for shell plating, although it is possible to extrude it. In the 5000-series, the primary alloying elements is Magnesium, and the resulting microstructure can be made stronger by cold-working or strain hardening the alloy. The marine tempers of – H116 or –H321 have had a significant amount of strain hardening. When fusion welded, the high heat of the welding process anneals the alloy and causes the metal to loose its strain hardening in the region around the weld. The resulting weld will show smooth decline in material properties, with a minimum strength typically located near the center of the weld. A typical hardness profile of a 5000-series weld is shown in Fig. 1. While the weld region has a noticeably lower proof stress than the surrounding metal, it retains the ability to strain-harden, and as such the reduction in ultimate stress of the weld region is typically much smaller than the reduction in proof stress. Sample material properties are given in Table 1 and the corresponding stress-strain curve is presented in Fig. 2

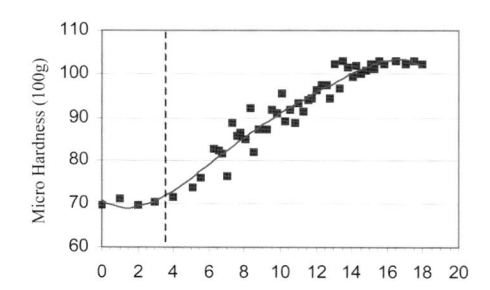

Fig. 1: 5000-Series Weld Hardness Profile (Paik and Duran, 2004)

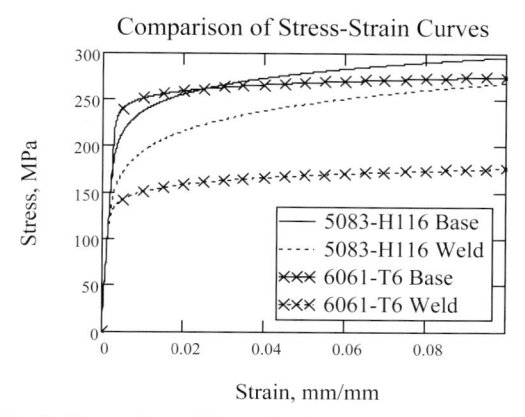

Fig. 2: Comparison of Stress-Strain Curves for Alloys

6000-Series Alloys

The 6000-series alloys commonly encountered in marine construction are in the form of extruded profiles or custom shapes. In this series, the primary alloying elements are Magnesium and Silicon, which are added so that Magnesium Silicide precipitates are formed by heat treating. Controlling the size and distribution of these precipitates allows tempers with high-strength to be developed. In a 6000-series fusion weld, the weld heat input will cause the weld metal and base metal immediately adjacent to the weld to reach a high enough temperature that the Magnesium Silicide will go back into solution and then re-precipitate over time, a process known as natural aging. Near the weld centerline, the weld may recover a significant portion of its pre-welded strength; however, at some distance off the centerline, the temperature will not be high enough to place the Magnesium Silicide back in solution and the precipitates will grow in size, a process known as over-ageing. This over-aged zone will be weaker than either the base material or the weld material, resulting in a "W" shape distribution of strength through the weld, as shown in Fig. 3 Depending on the choice of filler metal and weld process parameters, the central hump in the "W" may be more or less pronounced. Additionally, the 6000 series does not strain harden as readily as the 5000 series, so both the proof stress and ultimate stress of the material will be significantly impacted by welding; this impact can be seen in Table 1 and in the stress-strain curve plotted in Fig. 2.

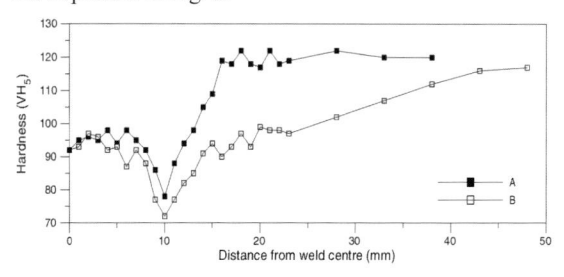

Fig. 3: 6000-Series Weld Showing "W" Hardness Profile at two locations, A, B, and over-aged zone 0.3-0.6" away from weld (Wang, Hopperstad, Larsen, and Lademo 2006)

Tension Weld Models

The previous work on aluminum structures has indicated that the tensile plastic capacity of welded aluminum structures may be less noticeable than the unwelded material properties, and the concentration of plastic strains in the weak regions around the weld may make the structure susceptible to failure at very low global strains. Thus, a logical place to begin a limit state analysis of welded structures is to investigate the tensile response of welds. There are several locations in typical aluminum vessel structures where welds will be subject to stress perpendicular to the direction of welding, including:

- module and building block joints
- fillet welds at the intersection of web frames and plating
- fillet welds joining sandwich-type deck extrusions to bulkheads.

Such connections in the strength deck or bottom structure may be subject to high levels of in-plane loading, and thus it is important to check for rupture potential in these welds when investigating global limit states of the hull girder. Additionally, it is important to determine the effective stress-strain response of the welded connection in tension in order to determine the total resistance force and moment for compressive collapse limit states elsewhere in the hull girder.

Series Model

The most basic model of a welded connection is a simple series model where the total strain across a series of i different "zones" in the weld is combined under the assumption that each zone acts independently of each other and that the total force, F, on each zone is equal according to

$$\varepsilon_{TOTAL} = \frac{\sum_i \varepsilon_i L_i}{L_{TOTAL}} \qquad (2)$$

where ε is the strain, L is the length of each zone and the total length. While very simple, this model can provide useful insight for interpreting tensile test specimen results and understanding the relative importance of the different material parameters on the weld's capacity. Fig. 4 shows the results of applying such a model to a simple weld specimen with a 50mm HAZ. The HAZ was assumed uniform, and the material properties were as per Table 1, where a 10" gauge length is implied for proof stress measurements. Fig. 4 shows that, as the gauge length increases, the apparent proof stress of the specimen increases while the overall specimen strain at failure decreases, to less than 1% for the 6061 specimen. This is a result of inelastic strains building up in the HAZ once the applied stress exceeds the proof stress in the HAZ. The ductility of the specimen is then governed by the HAZ, and larger gauge lengths do not significantly increase the overall deformations because the added gauge material only undergoes comparatively low elastic strains. The ability of the 5000-series welds to strain harden in the HAZ means that the strain concentration is significantly less in 5000-series than it is in 6000-series alloys. This graph also clearly demonstrates that proof stress and gauge length are interrelated for inhomogeneous specimens.

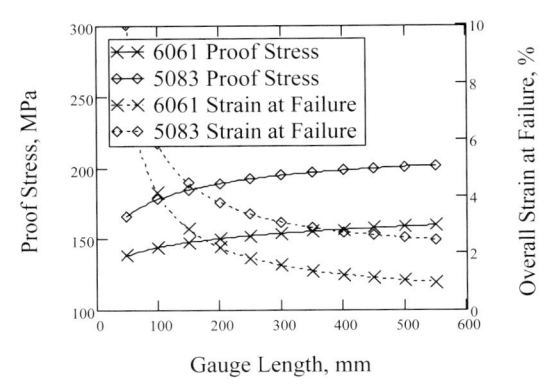

Fig. 4: Comparison of Proof Stress (Solid Lines) and Overall Strain at Failure (Dotted Lines) for Two-Zone Series model with 50mm HAZ

Three-Dimensional Model

There are several objections to applying the simple series model presented above to structures that are more complex than simple weld tensile specimens. In large welded structures such as aluminum HSVs, there are significant structural constraints working on most of the welds of interest: consider a transverse block join butt weld or the HAZ in front of a web frame fillet weld subjected to longitudinal stress. The neighboring base material that does not undergo large plastic strain with the HAZ will attempt to restrain HAZ contractions parallel to the weld and through the thickness of the material at the HAZ/base material interface; at the same time, volume conversation requires the HAZ material to shrink parallel to the weld and through the thickness of the plate as it elongates perpendicular to the weld. Several authors have proposed approaches that consider these effects. A model proposed by Satoh and Toyoda (1970) for a transverse weld in an infinitely wide plate is presented here. This model assumes that the weld can be modeled as a two-material combination, that the base metal can be assumed to be totally rigid compared to the weld metal, and that the weld will deform as a necked specimen as loading increased, as show in Fig. 5.

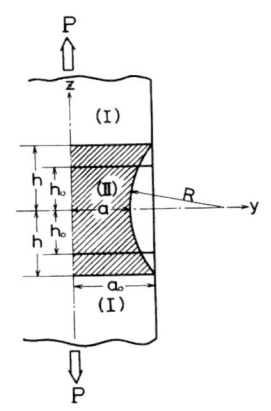

Fig. 5: Assumed weld deformation pattern by Satoh and Toyoda (1970)

In the model of Satoh and Toyoda, the stress-strain curve is represented by a simple power law, relating equivalent stress σ to strain ε by two coefficients K and n:

$$\overline{\sigma} = K\overline{\varepsilon}^n \quad (3)$$

It is assumed in the infinite weld that the true strain in the x-direction (along the length of the weld) is zero, and thus true stress, s, in the x-direction is equal to the average stress in the y and z directions. Thus the von Mises yield condition simplifies to:

$$s_Z - s_Y = \frac{2}{\sqrt{3}}\overline{\sigma} \quad (4)$$

By making some assumptions about how the stresses are distributed in the necking region of the weld, the equivalent stress can be related to the true strain perpendicular to the weld, e_z, through the relation

$$\overline{\sigma} = \left(\frac{2}{\sqrt{3}}\right)^n K e_z^n \quad (5)$$

and the engineering axial stress perpendicular to the weld, σ_z, can be related to the engineering strain perpendicular to the weld, ε_z, by the equation

$$\sigma_Z = \left(\frac{2}{\sqrt{3}}\right)^{n+1} \frac{K\{\ln(1+\varepsilon_Z)\}^n}{1+\varepsilon_Z}(1+Y_T) \quad (6)$$

where Y_t is found by solving the following equation with h_0 and a_0 defined in Fig. 5:

$$X_t = \frac{h_0}{y_0}, \varepsilon = \frac{1}{1+\varepsilon_z}$$
$$X_t = \frac{1}{\sqrt{3}}\sqrt{(1-\varepsilon)\left\{\frac{2\varepsilon}{Y_t}-3(1-\varepsilon)\right\}}\left(\frac{2\varepsilon+1}{3}-\frac{(1-\varepsilon)^2 Y_t}{2\varepsilon}\right) \quad (7)$$

Comparison of the Models

The simple series model and the three-dimensional model of Satoh and Toyoda were compared to a series of butt weld tension tests published by Scott and Gittos (1983). These were axial tension tests on 5083 and 6083 13mm thick plates, joined by fusion welds. The 5083 plates were welded with 5556A filler metal, while the 6082 plates were welded with both 5556A and 4043A filler metal. The welded tension test specimens consisted of a reduced-width tension coupon, where the width at the weld was 25mm. Thus, this experimental program falls between assumptions of the series model and the infinite-width approach from Satoh and Toyoda. Average material properties for the base and weld metal specimens are listed below in Table 2. These values were determined from 6.4mm round tensile specimens consisting of either all-base or all weld-metal. While this gives material that is data compatible with the presented models, it is insufficient to determine any variation in material property across the weld in the HAZ zone, which may be significant for welds such as the 6082 weld, where a combination of naturally-aged and over-aged metal may be present.

Table 2: Average proof stress, $\sigma_{0.2}$ ultimate stress, σ_{ULT}, and elongation at failure, ε_f for Scott and Gittos samples

Material	$\sigma_{0.2}$ MPa	σ_{ULT} MPa	ε_f %
5083 Base	189.8	333.0	20.8
5083 Weld w/5556A	155.0	318.0	28.5
6082 Base	273.8	300.2	19.0
6082 Weld w/5556A	139.5	284.0	20.5
6082 Weld w/4043A	127.5	233.7	11.7

The results from the two weld models are summarized in Tables 3 and 4 below. In applying both models, a HAZ extent of 25mm was assumed on each side of the weld centerline. Additionally, Scott and Gittos present elongation over two gauge lengths of 50mm and 75mm.

Table 3: Comparison of Predicted Ultimate Strains, %, for Weld Specimens at different gauge lengths (GL) for the Series and 3-D (Satoh and Toyoda Models)

Base Material Weld Filler	5083 5556A	6082 5556A	6082 4043A
Exp. – 50mm GL	15.5	9.0	6.5
Series – 50mm GL	28.5	20.5	11.7
3-D – 50mm GL	28.0	19.4	10.6
Exp. – 75mm GL	13.5	7.0	5.0
Series – 75mm GL	23.8	14.4	7.9
3-D – 75mm GL	21.1	13.4	7.2

Table 4: Comparison of Predicted Ultimate Stress, MPa, for Weld Specimens

Material Weld Filler	5083 5556A	6082 5556A	6082 4043A
Experiment	308.5	232.5	222.0
Series Model	318.0	286.0	233.7
3-D Model	292.5	281.6	248.9

Tables 3 and 4 show that neither of the prediction methods is entirely successful, and both appear to have trouble for the 6082 weld with the 5556A filler metal. Both approaches also overestimate the ductility of the 6082 welds. This could be a result of the actual failure taking place in a narrow over-aged zone in the weld, thus making the HAZ width effectively smaller than what was assumed here.

Influence of Welds in Tension on Global Limit States

While the impact of welds on the local ultimate limit state of beams and panels has been clearly demonstrated in a number of experimental studies, the influence of welds on global limit states has received less attention. An initial investigation was made into how the response of aluminum welds may impact one of the principal global limit states, such as hull girder collapse under bending moments. A box girder was used to represent a large stiffened-panel structure, as shown in Fig 6, with the properties as listed in Tables 5 and 6, including reduced 5083-H116 properties for compressive loading. The box girder features 5000-series bottom and sides, and a 6000-series top flange. This material use is broadly representative of the use of aluminum on high-speed vessels, where shell plating in contact with seawater tends to be 5000-series alloys, while large decks are often assembled from 6000-series extrusions. The box girder was tested under hogging moments to create a tension load on the 6000-series material in the top flange. The girder's response was determined by applying an incremental curvature Smith-type approach (Smith 1977). An approximate response of the plate-stiffener combinations in compression was obtained using the simplified approach discussed in Collette (2005).

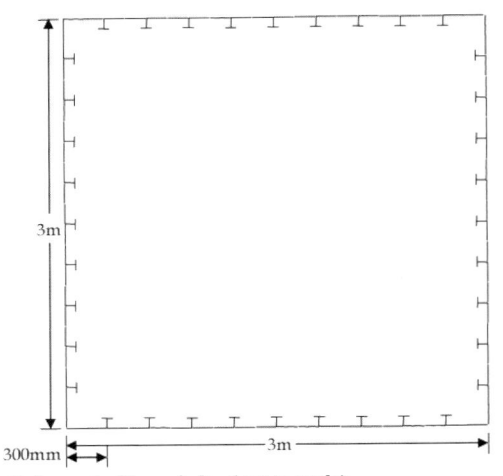

Fig. 6: Layout of box girder (not to scale)

Table 5: Box Girder Properties

Section	Plate mm	Stiffener Dimensions, mm	Matl.
Bottom	12	120x55x5.5x7.7 T	5083
Sides	8	80x45x4.5x6.2 T	5083
Top	6	70x40x4.0x6.1 T	6082

Table 6: Box Girder Material Properties

Property	5083-H116	6082-T6
Un-welded proof stress	180 MPa	260 MPa
Un-welded ultimate stress	305 MPa	290 MPa
Un-welded RO exponent, n	12	30
Welded proof stress	144 MPa	138 MPa
Welded ultimate stress	240 MPa	173 MPa
Welded RO exponent, n	8	16
Approximate failure strain	`12%	8%

The tension response of the top flange was modeled under three different assumptions:

- The tensile response of the material is represented by the base properties of the 6082-T6 alloy.
- The tensile response of the material is represented by all-weld properties of the 6082-T6 alloy.
- The tensile response of the material is represented by the application of the series-model presented in this paper. This model was adjusted to include the effects of longitudinal welds as well as transverse welds.

The three different responses of the top flange are shown in Fig. 7, and the corresponding response of the overall box girder in hogging is shown in Fig. 8. In Fig. 8, the response of a perfectly linearly elastic girder of the same cross section is also shown in heavy line for comparison. The results clearly indicate that the type of model assumed for the tensile response will have a noticeable impact on the computed ultimate strength of the girder. Notably, using the base material properties give unconservative predictions. Note that changing the effective resisting force from the tension flange also moves the neutral axis location, causing the peak in the moment-resisting curve to occur at different overall curvatures. The all-base material response has a sharper ultimate load, which occurs at an early curvature value than the cases where the impact of the HAZ is included. Such changes affect the strain levels that each component of the girder is subjected to during the loading. Another area of concern is the potential for fracture in the HAZ of the welds on the girder's tension flange, before the complete collapse of the compression flange, although results on two similar girders (Collette, 2005) indicated that the bottom structure must be quite stocky, and the fracture strain must be quite low in the HAZ for this to occur. For all of these reasons, it is important to have a solid local model for the response of welds when considering global failure modes for aluminum structures.

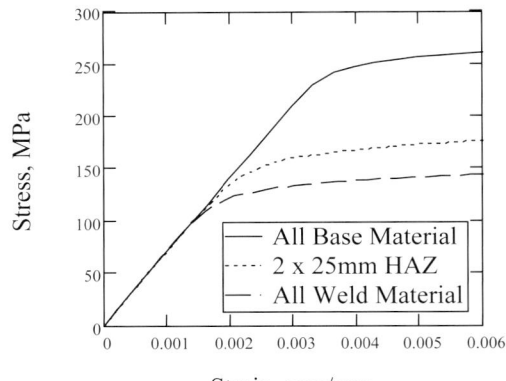

Fig. 7: Tensile Response of Deck Panels

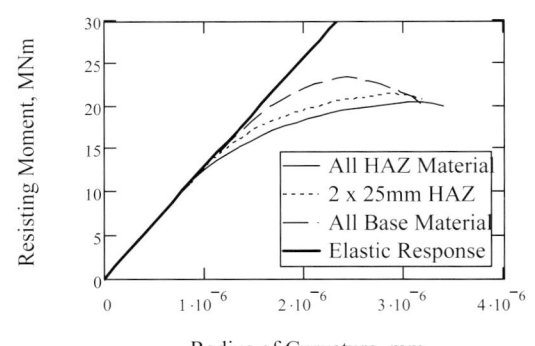

Fig. 8: Overall Resisting Moment Vs. Curvature, Hogging Loading

Conclusions

The impact of fusion welds on aluminum limit states was examined during the effort described in this paper. It is clear that the under-matched HAZ near welds in aluminum structures may accumulate plastic strains much faster than the rest of the structure, and have a significant impact on limit state calculations. Existing work on the role of welds in aluminum limit states has focused mainly on the compressive and tensile failure of welds and HAZ in local structures. The metallurgy of the 5000 and 6000 series alloys was reviewed, showing that the metallurgy of 6000-series fusion welds makes them more susceptible to plastic strain concentration. Simple weld models were compared to experimental test data for 5000 and 6000 series butt welds. Fair agreement with the simple models was shown; however, the restraint on the test welds fell between the idealized restraint in the two theories which could impact the comparison. A comparison of a global hogging collapse limit state was made by applying a Smith-type approach to a box girder, with three different tension weld models. The resisting moment plots are different in both magnitude and shape, indicating that the local tensile weld model may have a noticeable impact on global limit states. As the marine structural community moves towards limit state design for aluminum structures, it is clear that there is a need for practical limit-state models for aluminum welds.

Acknowledgements

The author wishes to thank Dr. Paul Hess of the Office of Naval Research (ONR) who has provided support for this work.

References

Aalberg, A., M. Langseth, and P.K. Larsen, (2001) "Stiffened Aluminium Panels Subjected to Axial Compression", Thin-Walled Structures, 2001. 39(10): 861-885.

Abildgaard, PM, Hansen, PW, Simonsen, BC, (2001), "Ultimate Strength of Welded Aluminium Strucutures", Proceeding of HIPER 2001, pp. 4-18.

ABS (2006), "Rules for Materials and Welding 2006: Part 2 Aluminum and Fiber Reinforced Plastics", Houston, TX: American Bureau of Shipping, 2006 including January 2007 update.

ALJOIN (2007), Project Website, http://www.aljoin.net/ accessed on April 30th, 2007.

Chan, TK, Porter Goff, RFD (2000), "Welded Aluminum Alloy Connections: Test Results and BS8118", Thin-Walled Structures, Vol. 36, pp 265-287.

Clarke, JD and Swan JW, "Interframe Buckling of Aluminium Alloy Stiffened Plating", Admiralty Research Establishment Dunfermline, 1985, AMTE(S) R85104. October, 1985.

Collette, M, (2005), "Strength and Reliability of Aluminium Stiffened Panels", PhD Thesis, School of Marine Science and Technology, University of Newcastle upon Tyne.

Dexter, R, and Ferrell, M (1995), "Optimum Weld-Metal Strength for High-Strength Steel Structures", Ship Structure Committee Report SSC-383, Washington DC, July 1995.

Hill, HN, Clark, JW, and Brungraber, RJ (1966). "Design of Welded Aluminum Structures", Journal of the Structural Division, Proceedings ASCE, Vol 86, No ST6, pp 101-124.

Hval, M, Johnsen, RH, Thaulow, C (1995), "Strength and Deformation Properties of Welded Aluminum Structures with Reference to Local Design and Material Properties", Proceedings of INALCO 1995 pp 167-182.

Hval, M, Thaulow, C., Lange, JH, Høydal, SH, and Zhang, ZL (1998), "Numerical Modeling of Ductile Fracture Behavior in Aluminum Weldments", Welding Journal Research Supplement, May, 1998, 208s-217s.

Kristensen, OHH., "Ultimate Capacity of Aluminium Plates Under Multiple Loads, Considering HAZ Properties", Department of Marine Structures, Norwegian University of Science and Technology, 2001.

Malin, V (1991). "Efficient Welding Fabrication of Extruded Aluminum Mat Panels", ElectroCOM GARD Report A1-161, September 1991. Available online via http://stinet.dtic.mil/ , Accession number ADA279638.

Matusiak, M, and Larsen, LK, (1998). "Strength and Ductility of Welded Connections in Aluminium Alloys", INALCO 1998, Cambridge, UK, April 1998, pp 299-310.

Missori, S, and Sili, A, (2000). "Mechanical Behaviour of 6082-T6 Aluminum Alloy Welds", Metallurgical Science and Technology, Vol 18, No 1, pp 12-18.

Moen, LA, Hopperstad, OS, Langseth, M (1999), "Rotational Capacity of Aluminum Beams Under Moment Gradient I: Experiments", Journal of Structural Engineering, Vol 125. No. 8 910-920.

Mofflin, DS, "Plate Buckling in Steel and Aluminium", Phd Thesis, University of Cambridge, 1983.

Övreas, L, Thaulow, C, and Hval, M (1992). "Effect of Geometry and Size on the Mechanical Properties of AlMiSi1 Weldments" INALCO 1992, Munich, Germany, Paper 10.1.

Paik, JK and Duran, A (2004),"Ultimate Strength of Aluminum Plates and Stiffened Panels for Marine Applications", Marine Technology, 2004, 41(3): 108-121.

Paik, JK and Thayamballi, AK (2003), "Ultimate Limit State Design of Steel-Plated Structures", Chichester, England: John Wiley and Sons, 2003.

Rigo, P, et al., "Sensitivity Analysis on Ultimate Strength of Aluminium Stiffened Panels", Marine Structures, 2003. 16(6): 437-468.

Roberts, TM, and Newark, ACB (1997). "Shear Strength of Tapered Aluminum Plate Girders", Thin-Walled Structures, Vol 29, No 1-4, pp 47-58.

Satoh, K and Toyoda, M (1970), "Static Strength of Welded Plates Including Soft Interlayer under Tension across a Weld Line", Transactions of the Japan Welding Society, Vol. 1 No. 2 pp 10-17.

Scott, MH, and Gittos, MF, (1983). "Tensile and Toughness Properties of Arc-Welded 5083 and 6082 Aluminum Alloys", Welding Journal Research Supplement, Vol. 62, Sept 1983, pp 243s-252s.

Smith, CS (1977), "Influence of Local Compressive Failure on Ultimate Longitudinal Strength of a Ship's Hull", Proceeding of PRADS 77, Tokyo, Japan, pp 73-79.

Vaughan, R, and Schonberg, WP, (1995), "An Inelastic Analysis of Welded Aluminum Joint", Metallurgical and Materials Transactions B, Vol. 26B, pp 1253-1261.

Verderaime, V (1989), "Weld Stresses Beyond the Elastic Limit", NASA Technical Paper 2935, available at http://ntrs.nasa.gov/search.jsp

Verderaime, V (1991), "Plate and Butt-Weld Stresses Beyond the Elastic Limit, Material and Structural Modeling", NASA Technical Report 3075, available at http://ntrs.nasa.gov/search.jsp.

Wang, T, Hopperstad, OS, Larsen, PK, and Lademo OG, (2006), "Evaluation of A Finite Element Modeling Approach for Welded Aluminum Structures", Computers and Structures, Vol. 84 pp 2016-2032.

Zha, Y and Moan, T, "Ultimate Strength of Stiffened Aluminum Panels with Predominantly Torsional Failure Modes", Thin-Walled Structures, 2001. 39(8): 631-648.

Ultimate Strength of Frames and Grillages Subject to Lateral Loads – an Experimental Study

Claude Daley[1], Greg Hermanski[2], Mihailo Pavic[3], Amghad Hussein[1]

[1] Faculty of Engineering, Memorial University,
St. John's, Newfoundland, Canada
[2] Institute for Ocean Technology, NRC,
St. John's, Newfoundland, Canada
[3] BMT Fleet Technology Limited,
St. John's, Newfoundland, Canada

Abstract

This paper describes experimental research conducted in part for the Ship Structures Committee project # 1442 - Investigation of Plastic Limit States for Design of Ship Hull Structures. The research program consisted of a series of increasingly large experiments to investigate the plastic behavior of ship framing and grillages subject to lateral loads. The initial tests were conducted as single frames, fixed on the ends and loaded with a small patch load at either the center or near the ends, so that two forms of plastic collapse, bending and shear, could be investigated. After eight single frames were tested, the experiments proceeded to test two small grillages (3 frames attached to one plate panel) and then two large grillages (9 frames plus two stringers, attached to 3 plate panels, in a 6.8m x 2.46m panel). The experimental procedures, data sensors and the full range of results are described. Extensive ANSYS finite element analysis of frames has been conducted, and some comparisons are presented. The study found a number of interesting relationships between various buckling mechanisms (shear buckling, web compression buckling and tripping) and the overall plastic collapse. Implications for design, especially goal-based design, are discussed.

Keywords

Ship structures; Plastic limit states; Experiments; Finite element analysis; Nonlinear; Ship design.

Introduction

The design of ship structures is undergoing considerable change. The reasons for the change are many. New and larger ships are continuing to address new commercial opportunities. Continuing improvements in materials and ship construction technology are encouraging change. The constant improvement of computational power is letting researchers and designers contemplate and execute ever more sophisticated simulations of ship structural behavior (loads and failure mechanisms). An increasingly sensitive public has lead to demands on the governments, shipping companies and classification societies to find way to make ships safer. The International Maritime Organization (IMO) is the focal point for much of the discussion and debate.

As part of this trend, new ship structural rules are going beyond the traditional approach of just checking structures against a yielding criterion. The ice class rules developed during the 1980s and 90s (Transport Canada 1995, IACS 2006) have all been formulated using plastic limit states for the sizing of plating and framing. The new IACS Common Structural Rules (IACS 2005) have included certain assessment of plastic limit states in their formulations.

The research described here is being conducted as part of a comprehensive study of the ultimate strength of ships frames (Daley, Pavic and Hermanski, 2004; Daley and Hermanski, 2005). The current focus is on frames subject to intense local lateral loads, such as ice loads. The work was begun with support from Transport Canada to study single frames. Eight single frames were tested. The US Coast Guard then joined in the project and enabled an expansion of the experimental and numerical analysis to include the testing of two three-frame grillages. The experimental program was then further expanded with the support of the Ship Structures Committee, which funded the experimental investigation of two large grillages.

This paper represents a summary and overview of the work. The complete set of results will be reported to the Ship Structures committee in a comprehensive report.

Experimental Program

The experimental program has provided empirical evidence to support the numerical and analytical investigations. The experiments explored the influence of frame geometry (for single frames), load position (central and end) and frame boundary conditions. In ships, any single frame is joined laterally to neighboring frames through the shell plating. At their ends, frames typically continue to the next bay, through a supporting stringer (or similar). The experiments examined a range of frame support conditions. In the single frame tests, the frame ends are held rigidly (as rigidly as possible), while the sides were free. In the small grillage the ends were held rigidly, while to the side (of the central frame) there was plating and a similar frame. Also attached to the plate beside the side frames, there is a heavy bar that is designed to approximate additional frames. This construction created realistic boundary conditions to the side of the test frame. In the large grillage the frames continued through a stringer and on to a remote fixed support. Thus in the large grillage, both the side and end conditions (for the central frame) are realistic. Fig. 1 shows the cross sections of the frames tested. The grillages were all made with the T75 frame section.

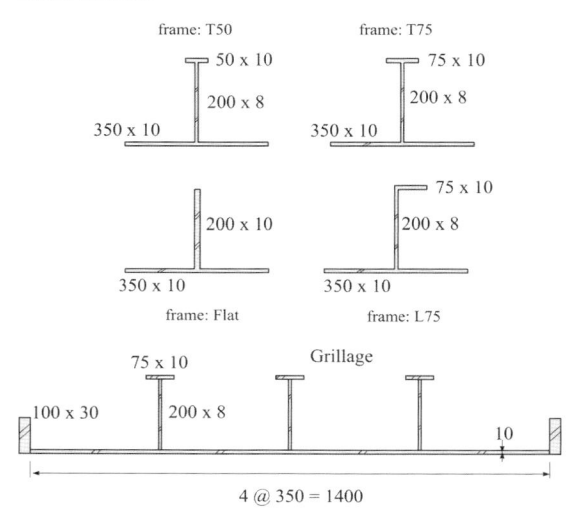

Fig. 1: Frame Sections

Single Frame Tests

The first six single frame tests were conducted using the support frame illustrated in Fig. 2. Photos of two tests are shown in Figures 3 and 4. At first, a 350x350mm (14"x14") silicon filled loading pillow was used to apply the load (see Fig 3). This proved to be problematic, so that after two tests, the load was applied through a 102x102mm (4"x4") square steel block (Fig. 4).

After the first six single frame tests were complete, the new grillage test apparatus was ready for use. This large support structure was then used to test that last two of the single frames (Figures 5 and 6). Table 1 summarizes the eight single frame tests that have been conducted.

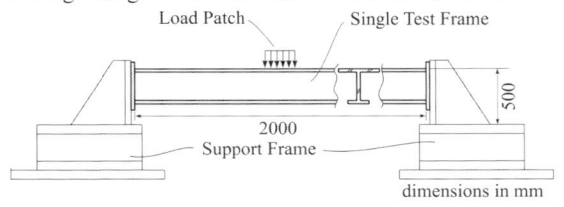

Fig. 2: Single Frame Tests (first six)

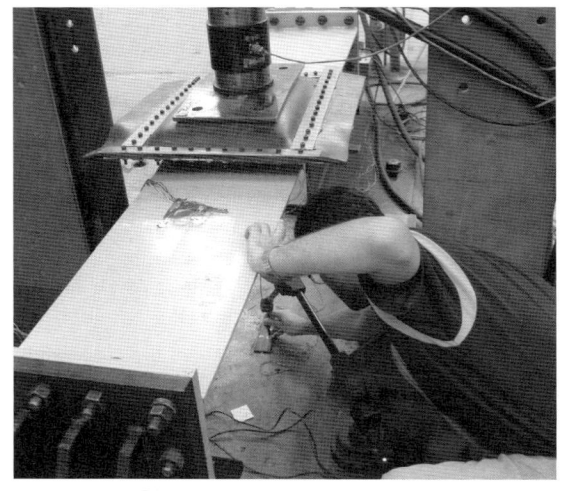

Fig. 3: Single Frame Test L75c

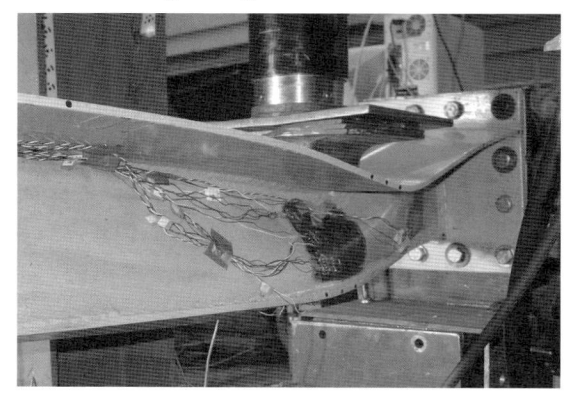

Fig. 4: Single Frame L75e

Table 1: Single Frame Tests Conducted

Test Name	Load Position	Test Date	Frame Description*
L75e	End	8/18/2004	200x8,75x10 L
L75c	Center	10/7/2004	200x8,75x10 L
T75e	End	5/19/2004	200x8,75x10 T
T75c	Center	8/12/2004	200x8,75x10 T
T50e	End	7/16/2004	200x8,50x10 T
T50c	Center	6/16/2005	200x8,50x10 T
Fe	End	7/28/2004	200x10 Fl
Fc	Center	6/6/2005	200x10 Fl

*dimensions in mm.

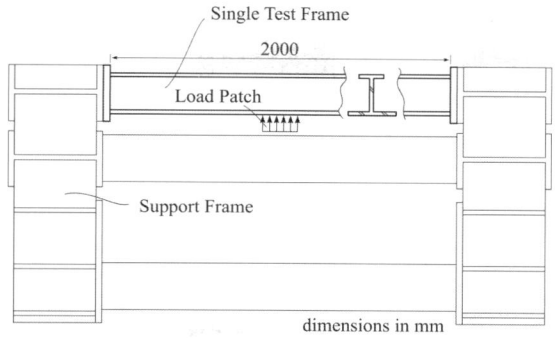

Fig. 5: Single Frame Tests (for T50c and Fc)

Fig. 6: Single Frame Test (Fc)

Data Collection

The components of the data collection system are shown in Fig. 7. The data collection system was very similar for all tests conducted. In the first six single frame tests, the load was measured with a load cell, in line with the actuator. In the later tests, the load was determined by measuring the hydraulic pressure in the load jack. The system was calibrated in a press, to ensure that the calculated and measured loads were in agreement. Strain was measured with a set of resistance strain gauges. The strain gauges were long-elongation gauges, chosen to give values well up into the plastic strain region. Deflections were measured with a set of wire-reel extensometers ('yo-yo' pots.). The strain, deflection and loads were all gathered Local deformations were also recorded automatically throughout the test using hardware and software (LabView™) from National Instruments. In addition, a 3D coordinate measurement device (microscribe from Immersion Corporation) was used to determine the distortion of the frame under load. The microscribe was connected to a computer running Rhinoceros (from McNeel and Associates), where the 3D deformation data was recorded. At each load step, the microscribe was used to manually measure the x,y,z coordinates of about 15 points on the cross section above the load.

In addition to the numerical data, digital still and video images of the tests have been recorded. One 6mp still camera was used to gather time-lapse images of the later tests. These images can be viewed individually or as a motion video. The digital video used DV format tapes.

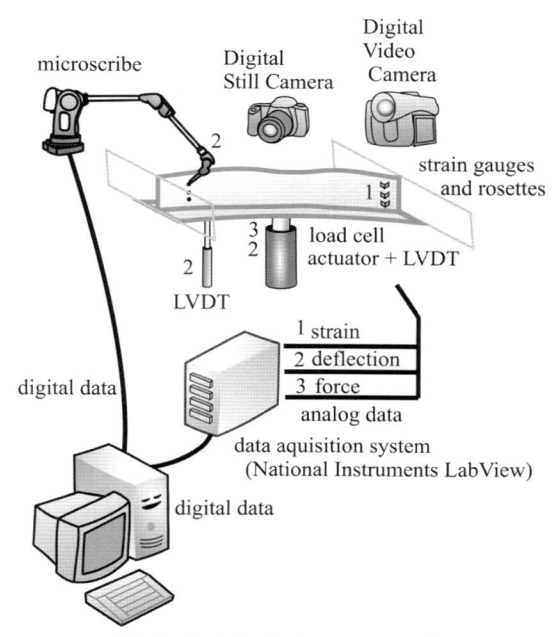

Fig. 7: Data Collection components

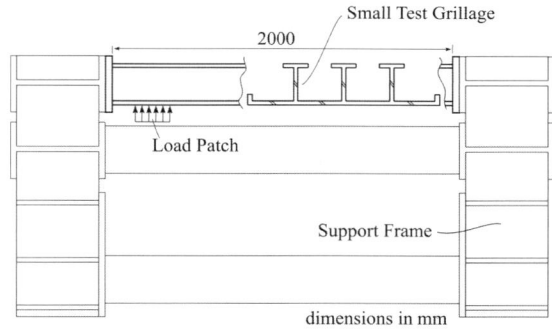

Small Grillage Tests

With the single frame tests complete, the next stage was the testing two small grillages. Fig. 8 illustrates the test setup. The ends of the small grillages were bolted into a large support frame. The load was applied from below using a hydraulic jack. One test involved a central load on the central frame, while the other involved an end load on the central frame. Fig. 9 shows the end-loaded small grillage after removal from the test frame. The local distortion of the central frame at the end is clearly visible.

Fig. 8 : Small Grillage Tests

Fig. 9 : Small Grillage Panel after End-Load Test

Large Grillage Tests

The final stage in the current program has been the testing of two large grillages. The grillages are supported in a support frame as illustrated in Fig. 10. Each test grillage is 6.8m (22.8ft) long and 2.46m (7.9ft) wide (Fig. 11). The ends of the 2m frames are supported by a cross stringer with the frames extending through the stringer to a clamped (bolted) support at the extreme ends. The stringers are held by brackets bolted into the main support frame. The load is applied from below as described earlier.

The large grillages were tested with three applications of load, rather than one. After the first load was applied and removed, the hydraulic ram was moved and the structure was tested again. This has given an indication of the capacity of the frames after there is damage at nearby locations. This has proven to be very interesting. It is important to note that all testing should be considered as the testing of one frame. Even in the grillage cases, the load is applied to a single frame. The grillage is there to give the correct boundary conditions for the test frame. It is very interesting to see how much more capacity a frame has when part of a grillage. This increased capacity and increased forces applied, resulted in the large grillages failing finally by punching shear in the 10mm shell plate. The load reached 1470kN, applied through a 102x102mm load patch.

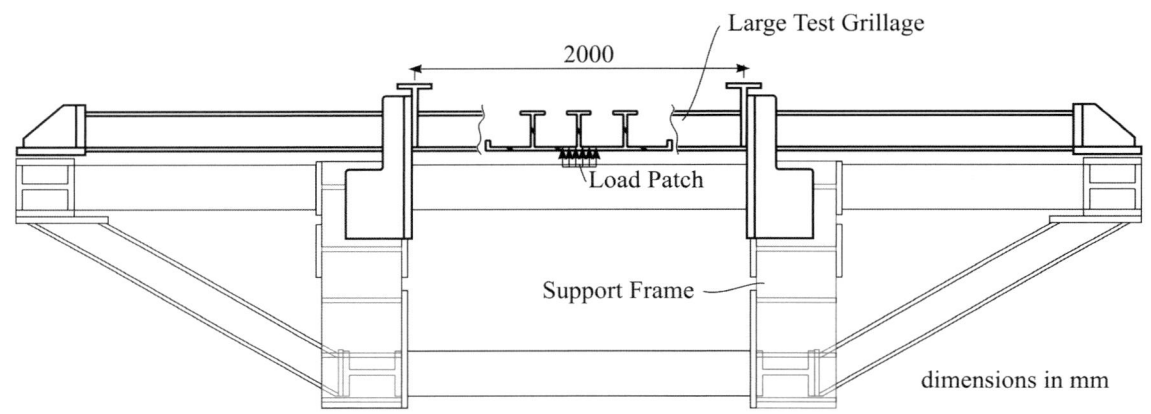

Fig. 10 : Large Grillage Test Setup

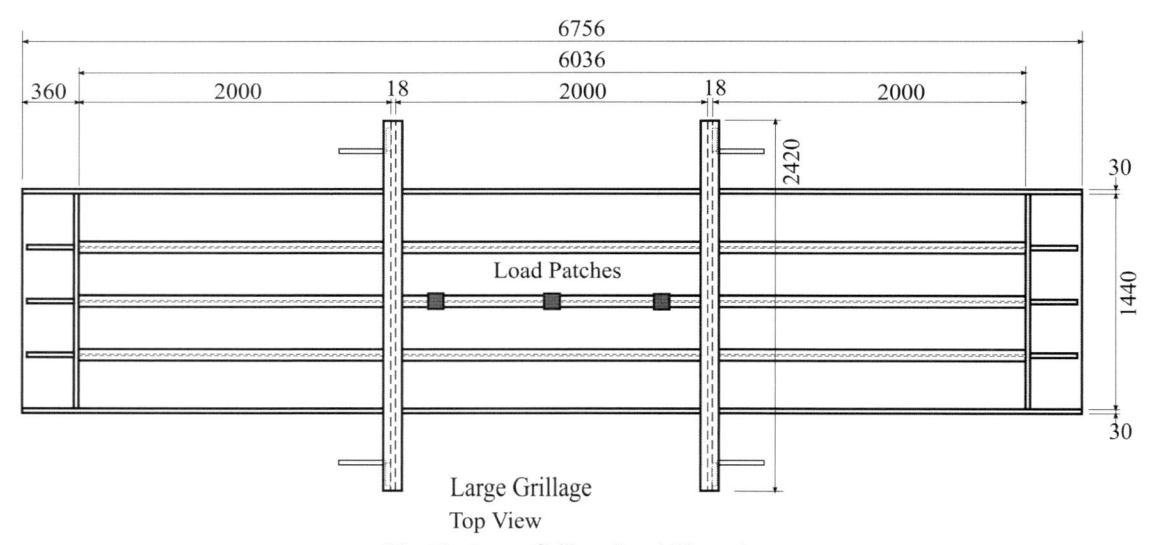

Fig. 11 : Large Grillage Panel Dimensions

Fig. 12 : Large Grillage Test Arrangement

Samples of Test Results

Fig. 13 shows one of the stress-strain curves taken from a sample of the steel in the webs of the single frames. The steel grade was 300W, a weldable construction steel commonly available in Canada. The measured yield strengths were in the range of 340MPa to 425MPa. Some of the shell plating was made from 250W, and had measured strength as low as 280MPa. Typically the steel exhibited the usual yield plateau, with a subsequent strain hardening region. The (linear-equivalent) post-yield modulus was taking to be about 1.2 GPa.

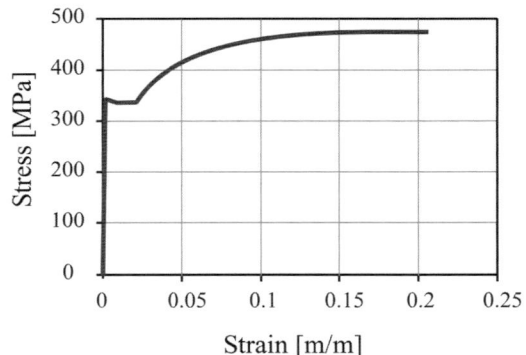

Fig. 13 : Load vs. deflection for three of the single frame tests.

Fig. 14 shows three forces vs. deflection curves for three of the single frame tests. Fig. 15 shows force vs. deflection for one of the large grillage tests. It is clear that the presence of the surrounding frames in a grillage has a significant influence on the capacity of a loaded frame. This would not matter when all frames are loaded similarly and have the same capacity. However, in the case of local loads from ice or small collisions, the surrounding structure plays a significant role in supporting the loaded frame. The initial (linear) region is larger, and the post-yield reserve region is much larger.

Fig. 16 shows how the microscribe data can be viewed after the tests. In this case the measured microscribe point data (x,y,z coordinates) has been used to construct before and after (deformed) sections of the test frame.

This data can be subsequently used to compare with finite element simulations of the tests.

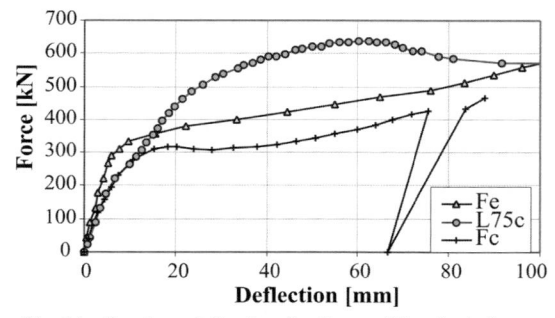

Fig. 14 : Load vs. deflection for three of the single frame tests.

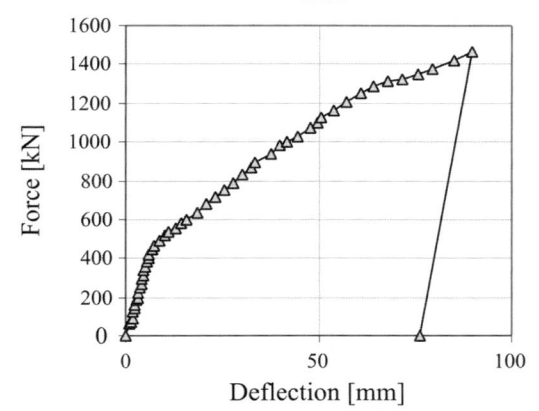

Fig. 15 : Load vs. deflection for the 2nd Large Grillage Test (end load)

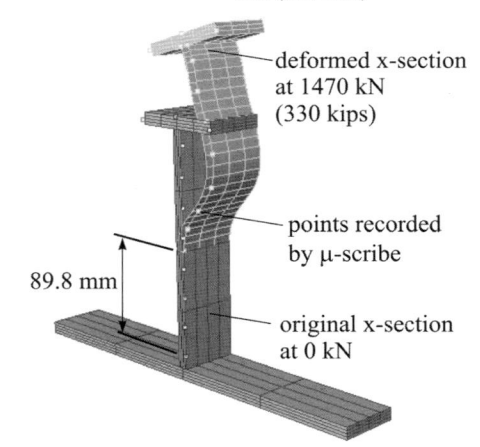

Fig. 16 : Microscribe data for first and last load step on Large Grillage Test LG2

Fig. 17 shows one of the many photos taken during the tests. This one illustrates the web buckling which occurred during the large grillage end-load test. The photo also shows one of the intriguing plastic phenomena which was seen in various forms in many tests. The paint is showing a pattern of failure which is believed to reflect plastic shear slip planes in the underlying steel. While not initially intended as such, the paint acted as a strain visualization coating. While this only occurred at very large deformations (well above yield), it showed that the steel tended to form 'fingers' when highly stressed in shear. This may be peculiar to the particular steel used in the tests, or this may be a more general result. This kind of strain localization is very difficult to create in a finite element model, and would normally not be seen in finite element models. These 'fingers' imply very high local strains, and may well have a significance for later fatigue strength. Note that there are both horizontal and vertical finger patterns showing in Fig.17. Such fingers would also tend to cause coating breakdown, and so would have an impact on the corrosion process. The fingers did not appear to affect the overall frame capacity.

Fig. 17: Web of Large Grillage test LG2.

Discussion

The experiments described above provide insight into the plastic behavior and reserve capacity of ship frames. Fig. 15, for example, shows that there is a very large plastic capacity reserve, and that even with loads of say twice yield, the frame deflections would remain less than 1% of the frame span. Ship structural design can benefit greatly if this kind of behavior is considered at the design stage. Traditionally, ship structures have been designed using 'working stress' methods. This approach considers the elastic stresses in a structure and sets limits on stresses. Consequently, the elastic properties of structures (e.g. moment of inertia, elastic section modulus) are controlled and optimized. Unfortunately, this approach does not assure that structures behave adequately in overload situations. Consider the two frames sketched in Fig. 18. The two frames have the same elastic section modulus, though all other geometric measures (area, inertia) are different. The two frames would be considered equally satisfactory in any 'working stress' design. However, they have quite different plastic capacities. Fig. 18 illustrates the different plastic behaviors of the two frames. The flat bar frames has greater initial capacity, followed by a greater reserve and more stable behavior. The flat bar stays upright while the tee section folds over under high loads. Not all flatbar frames will out-perform flanged frames. The comparisons will be quite dependent on the specific geometry.

120 x 15 flange
325 x 12 web   374 x 24 web
400 x 15 plate
A = 117 cm^2 A = 150 cm^2
Ze = 907 cm^3 Ze = 907 cm^3 (same elastic modulus)
Zp = 1275 cm^3 Zp = 1650 cm^3

4.31
yield strength (same for both)

Frame span = 3000 mm
Load patch = 500 x 400 (centered)
E = 200,000 MPa, E_t = 500 MPa
σ_y = 360 MPa
dimensions in mm

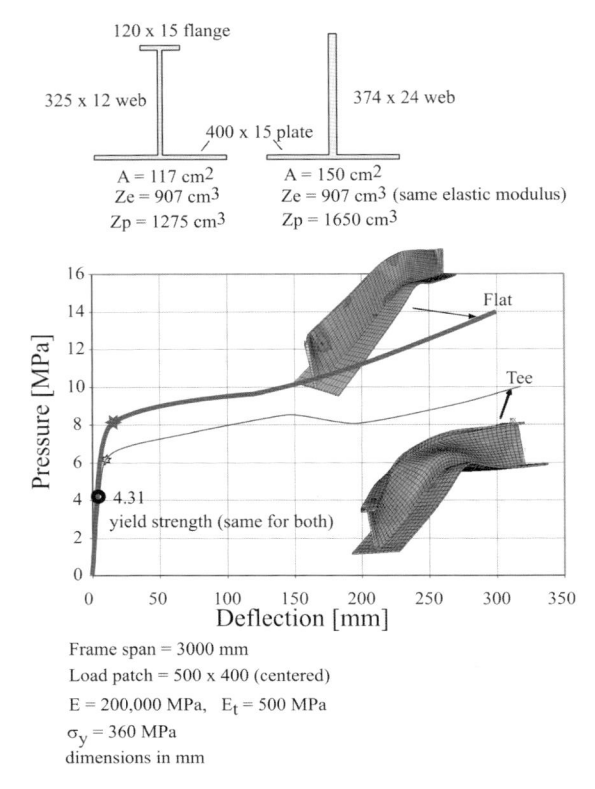

Fig. 18 Comparison of load-deflection behavior of two equal modulus frames.

The frames in Fig. 18 have identical modulus, but not the same weight. From one perspective the figure shows the value of considering plastic capacity, but at the cost of steel weight. In this way, conventional rules result in the flatbar being doubly penalized, once by not recognizing its superior linear and reserve performance, and secondly by adding steel weight. The next comparison shows an example where the frame weights are identical. Fig. 19 shows two frames with the same weight. The tee section has a very thin web, at the limit of allowable thickness (for buckling). The flatbar actually exceeds the usual aspect ratio, but still behaves acceptably. Fig. 19 compares the load-deflection curves for the two frames. Also shown are the nominal yield capacities (load which would case yield stress in simple bending). Note that the flatbar has a lower elastic modulus, but is both initially and ultimately stronger than the slender tee. This demonstrates a number of important points. The first is that elastic properties may have little relation to structural behavior. Second is that even the plastic section modulus may be a poor indicator of capacity, especially if plastic bending is not the dominant plastic structural mechanism. The design rules should reflect actual capacity, rather than using a single simple measure like modulus.

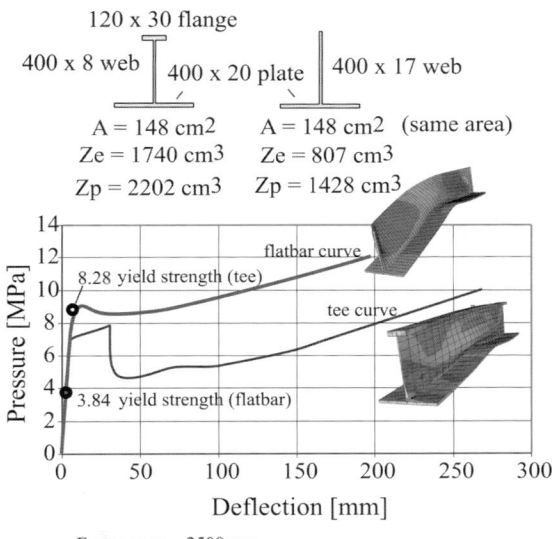

120 x 30 flange
400 x 8 web 400 x 20 plate 400 x 17 web
A = 148 cm2   A = 148 cm2 (same area)
Ze = 1740 cm3 Ze = 807 cm3
Zp = 2202 cm3 Zp = 1428 cm3

Frame span = 2500 mm
Load patch = 500 x 400 (centered)
E = 200,000 MPa, E_t = 750 MPa
σ_y = 360 MPa
dimensions in mm

Fig. 19 Comparison of load-deflection behavior of two equal weight frames.

Fig 20 sketches the typical load deflection pattern that we tend to have in laterally loaded frames. The deflection is the maximum deflection of the web under at the plate-web connection. After yield, but prior to the full formation of mechanism 1, the load-deflection curve is essentially linear and follows the slope of the original elastic trend. Yielding occurs well before mechanism 1, and initially produces a tiny volume of yielded material. This is followed by the expansion of the yield zone, during which stress redistribution takes place. Once the plastic zone fills one or more critical cross sections, a plastic mechanism forms that allows large and permanent deformations to occur. Mechanism 1 might be called 'collapse', though this term is not exactly correct. Subsequent to mechanism 1, while the frame is 'collapsing' in bending, internal forces tend to rise and support the growing load. Further along this curve, additional mechanisms can occur, including buckling and fracture. There is no standard way to evaluate frames that takes into account this multiplicity of behaviors.

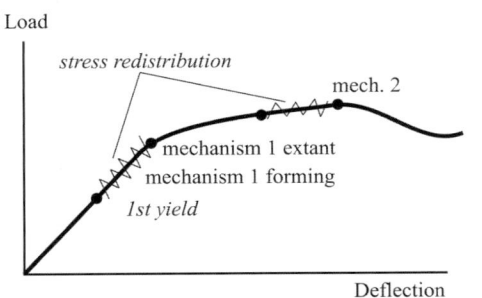

Fig 20. Idealized load-deflection curve for a frame.

Conclusions

The results and descriptions presented have been an overview of a large series of structural experiments conducted at Memorial University. The results will be fully described in a Ship Structures Committee (SSC) report. The experiments have shown a number of interesting and in some cases surprising results. It is clear that a simple measure such as elastic section modulus is not representative of the capacity of a ship frame, especially as regards the full behavior and post-yield reserve. It may well not even be a good indicator of the linear range capacity. Another surprising result is the post-damage capacity of frames. Small damages appear to strengthen, not weaken, the surrounding structure. This has implications for inspection and timing of repairs. And finally, the presence of shear strain localization (fingering) deserves further attention, especially as it may affect fatigue and corrosion of dented structures.

Acknowledgement

The work presented has had the support of many people and organizations. The key sponsors have been Transport Canada, DRDC (Atlantic), US Coast Guard and the Ship Structures Committee. As well, important contributions of needed equipment have been provided by the Canada Foundation for Innovation (CFI), the Atlantic Canada Opportunities Agency (ACOA), The Province of Newfoundland and Labrador, Memorial University, the National Research Council (NRC) and the National Science and Engineering Research Council (NSERC). All this support is gratefully acknowledged. There is one person whose support and contribution was particularly important. Mr. Victor Santos Pedro of Transport Canada was the initial instigator and a continuing supporter throughout the work.

References

Daley, C, Pavic, M, Hermanski, G, Hussein, A, (2004) "Ship Frame Research Program- A Numerical Study of the Capacity of Single Frames Subject to Ice Load", Memorial University OERC Report 2004-02 and NRC/IOT Report TR-2004-04

Daley, C, and Hermanski, G (2005) "Ship Frame/Grillage Research Program- Investigation of Finite Element Analysis Boundary Conditions", Memorial University OERC Report 2005-02 and NRC/IOT Report TR-2005-05

IACS (2005) - IACS Common Structural Rules for Bulk Carriers, and Common Structural Rules for Tankers.

IACS (2006) Unified Requirement URI -" Structural Requirements for Polar Class Ships"

Transport Canada (1995), Equivalent Standards for the Construction of Arctic Class Ships, TP12260.

Research Needs in Aluminum Structure

Robert A. Sielski

Naval Architect—Structures
Indio, California, USA

Abstract

The technology required for the design, fabrication, operation and maintenance of aluminum structures for ships and craft are reviewed to assess the needs for improvements in that technology. The areas reviewed are: material property and behavior, structural design, structural details, welding and fabrication, joining aluminum to steel, residual stresses and distortion, fatigue design and analysis, fire protection, vibration, maintenance and repair, mitigating slam loads and emerging technologies.

Keywords

Aluminum ship structures; Aluminum high-speed vessels.

Introduction

Aluminum has been used for the construction of ships and craft for more than a century. In many cases, the vessels have served well for several decades of use without any serious structural problems. However, there have been some difficulties. From the very beginning, and continuing up to very recently, there have been instances where the selection of the wrong aluminum alloy has led to corrosion problems so severe that the vessels had to be scrapped within a few years of construction. Aluminum has been used for the deckhouse structure of US Navy combatant and amphibious ships for more than 70 years. Those ships served well, but the aluminum structure was the source of significant maintenance problems, mostly from fatigue damage. Serious concerns for survival in shipboard fire and for maintenance reduction led to the discontinuation of the use of aluminum for major US Navy combatant ships in the 1980s.

Towards the close of World War II, some merchant ships built in the U.S. had aluminum in their deckhouses, and this practice continued after the war, primarily in the superstructures of passenger ships. Aluminum began to be adopted worldwide for fabrication of the superstructure of passenger ships, a practice that continues today. Aluminum began to be used in the 1940s for pleasure craft and for workboats, the size of which has increase greatly over the years. The use of aluminum for the hulls of high-speed merchant vessels began in the 1990s with increased construction of high-speed ferries. These vessels have become so technologically advanced that they have surpassed the capabilities of many naval vessels; many navies today are adapting derivatives of these high-speed vessels to combatant craft.

The interest in aluminum structure has increased greatly over the past decade. Evidence of international interest in aluminum ship structure is the International Forum on Aluminum Ships, the fifth of which took place in Tokyo in 2005. The Ship Structure Committee (SSC) has recently completed a number of projects concerning aluminum ship structures:

- SSC-410, Fatigue of Aluminum Structural Weldments
- SSC-438, Structural Optimization for Conversion of Aluminum Car Ferry to Support Military Vehicle Payload
- SSC-439, Comparative Structural Requirements for High Speed Craft
- SSC-442, Labor-Saving Passive Fire Protection Systems for Aluminum and Composite Construction
- SR-1434, In-Service Performance of Aluminum Structural Details
- SR-1446, Mechanical Collapse Testing on Aluminum Stiffened Panels for Marine Applications
- SR-1447, Fracture Mechanics Characterization of Aluminum Alloys for Marine Structural Applications
- SR-1448, Aluminum Marine Structure Design and Fabrication Guide
- SR-1454, Buckling Collapse Testing on Friction Stir Welded Aluminum Stiffened Plate Structures

Additionally, the US Navy's Office of Naval Research has begun a multi-year research program, Aluminum Structure Reliability Program, aimed at improving the technology for design construction, operation, and maintenance of high-speed aluminum naval vessels.

This paper is based on the aluminum guide and on the ONR program. Research needs will be discussed in the following areas:

- Material property and behavior
- Structural design
- Structural details
- Welding and fabrication
- Joining aluminum to steel
- Residual stresses and distortion
- Fatigue design and analysis
- Fire protection
- Vibration
- Performance metrics, reliability and risk assessment
- Maintenance and repair
- Structural health monitoring
- Emerging technologies

Material Property and Behavior

There is vast experience with aluminum alloys in both the 5xxx and 6xxx-series; the most commonly used marine alloys. However, there are still fairly large knowledge gaps in basic knowledge on these alloys. The most common gap is in fatigue properties and fracture toughness, particularly dynamic fracture toughness, with much of the existing fracture data coming from non-standard tests with invalid data.

An important discrepancy in basic material properties is the variation among different sources on the strength of welded aluminum. Table 1 illustrates this discrepancy for several alloys. The differences come in part from different standards for determining the yield strength from a "dog bone" sample cut across the weld in a plate. Some use a 50-mm gage length that measures only weld metal and heat-affected zone (HAZ), but others use a 250-mm gage length sample that includes base metal.

Perhaps even more important than the difference in yield strength is the manner in which this property is used in design. The welded strength is typically 30 to 50 percent of the strength of the base metal, and this reduced strength is used for most design calculations. There are indications that the approach is overly conservative. In studies on the compressive strength of welded panels, Paik et al (2006) used a weighted average based on the relative volumes of base metal, weld metal, and HAZ. In a simplified analysis of a welded panel in tension, Collette (2005) found that the yield strength of a 5xxx-series welded plate was close to the yield strength of the base metal, although for a 6xxx-series alloy, the strength was closer to that of the HAZ. Research in this basic material property could result in significantly increased allowable stresses and reduced weight.

Table 1: Yield Strength of Some Alloys as Specified by Different Authorities (MPa)

Alloy	Authority				
	ABS	DnV	Aluminum Association	AWS Hull Welding	US Navy
5086-H116	131	92	95	131	152
5083-H116	165	116	115	165	
5383-H116	145	140			
5456-H116	179		125	179	179
6061-T6	138	105	105	138	

Aluminum alloys, particularly those of the 5xxx-series have shown excellent corrosion resistance in service, with some bare hulls operating for more than 30 years without discernable corrosion. However, there is a general reluctance to place 6xxx-series alloys in similar service. Indeed, classification societies and the U.S. Navy prohibit most uses of 6xxx-series alloys in contact with seawater. A review of available corrosion data fails to provide any experimental basis for this prejudice against 6xxx-series alloys.

The 6xxx-series alloys generally have excellent resistance to general corrosion over the surface, but compared to 5xxx-series exhibit more localized pitting. Most of the corrosion testing of aluminum in seawater occurred in the 1950 through the 1960s. Goddard et al. (1967) report that the maximum pit depth in three 5xxx-series alloys (5052, 5056, and 5083) was 0.18 and 0.86 mm after five and ten years of immersion in seawater, respectively. In the same tests, 6061-T6 had 1.30 and 1.65 mm of pit depth when samples were removed after 5 and 10 years of immersion. Although the 6061 had twice the depth of pitting in this test, the rate is not necessarily unacceptable. Other 6xxx-series, such as 6082 have less copper that 6061 and should have better corrosion resistance, although data is lacking

The 6xxx-series are beginning to be used more extensively in integrally stiffened deck panels, and there is a desire to use these light panels for general hull structure. A systematic comparative test of different alloys in corrosive environments will demonstrate if more extensive use of the 6xxx-series alloys is possible and if this can be safely done will result in significant weight and cost savings.

While the 5xxx-series alloys have generally shown to have excellent resistance to corrosion, there is concern that material is becoming sensitized over time to intergranular corrosion and stress-corrosion cracking, particularly when subjected to higher service temperatures on exposed decks. An accelerated test that would be based on the thermal profile of the decks of operational ships must be developed to screen the material.

There are also indications that there are reductions in corrosion resistance in the heat-affected zones of welds in the 5xxx-series alloys such as shown in Fig 1. The standard ASTM G 67 NAMALT test is designed to measure weight loss in a relatively large surface area, not in the narrow band of the HAZ of a weld. A standard for weight loss in the HAZ should be developed to allow comparison and optimization of welding methods.

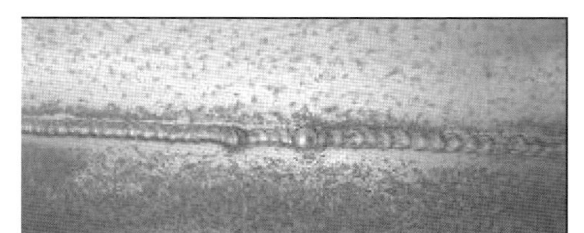

Fig. 1: Corrosion at a weld in 5xxx-series plate.

Testing in accordance with ASTM G 67 as well as the ASTM G 66 G66 (ASSET) test to determine susceptibility to exfoliation are required for marine-grade 5xxx-series aluminum alloys ordered in accordance with ASTM specification B 928, which was developed following extensive stress corrosion cracking that was experienced in 5083-H321 material ordered in the late 1990s (Bushfield et al, 2003). However, recent experience (Kieth and Blair, 2007) showed some 5083 H321 that had been ordered to ASTM B 928 to have considerable excess magnesium precipitating as a secondary phase, Mg_2Al_3 or β-phase, in the grain boundaries of the metal. The β-phase is an electrochemically active phase. When the β-phase forms as a continuous and complete network on the grain boundaries, the material becomes "sensitized" or susceptible to intergranular forms of corrosion. The 5083-H321 may have had more than 15 mg/cm^2 mass loss in ASTM G 67. This experience indicates that further research into sensitization of higher-magnesium 5xxx-series alloys may be needed.

Structural Design

Methodologies for computing the compressive strength of plates and welded panels are well established and validated for steel structure. For welded aluminum structure, that is not the case. The work of Paik and by a few others such as Rigo et al. (2003, 2004) represents a good start on this validation, but many questions remain such as the effect of transverse welds and the effect of localized heat-affected zones resulting from welded attachments. There is limited guidance on how to incorporate such welds into finite element models. A conservative approach is to treat such a panel as all-HAZ material; however this may incur a large weight penalty and does not shed any light on strain concentration and other effects from the differences in material properties over the panel.

Other design issues include:

- Ultimate strength of plates and panels undergoing combined loading such as biaxial compression in multi-hull cross decks, or a combination of in-plane compression and lateral pressure in the slamming zone of high-speed vessels.
- The effect of initial imperfections and residual stresses on the strength of common aluminum structures needs further validation, including guidance on how to incorporate these values into finite-element models for ultimate strength along with simplified methods able to incorporate a range of imperfection magnitudes in ultimate strength prediction.
- Guidance on how to incorporate HAZ effects on ultimate strength calculations needs to be defined, including techniques for incorporating HAZ into finite element models, including estimates of the effect of strain concentration on tensile ultimate strength, and estimates of the effect of various types of HAZ (GMAW, Laser, FSW) on in-plane and lateral loads of panels.
- Simplified methods for predicting the load-shortening curves of plate and panels under combined loading for use in overall hull-girder ultimate strength calculations.
- Ultimate strength methods for advanced extrusions, where the plate thickness may not remain constant.

Structural Details

Although many structural details that have been used over the year with steel ships are acceptable in aluminum construction, many are not, particularly because of concern for fatigue strength. Likewise, many details that boatbuilders have used for years on smaller craft are not acceptable on larger craft because of longitudinal strength and fatigue concerns. The Ship Structure Committee has sponsored many projects over the years on the suitability of different steel structural details and their fatigue strength, but has not yet produced significant guidance for aluminum details. Fig. 2 shows one of the new types of details being used in aluminum structures today—a detail of questionable strength.

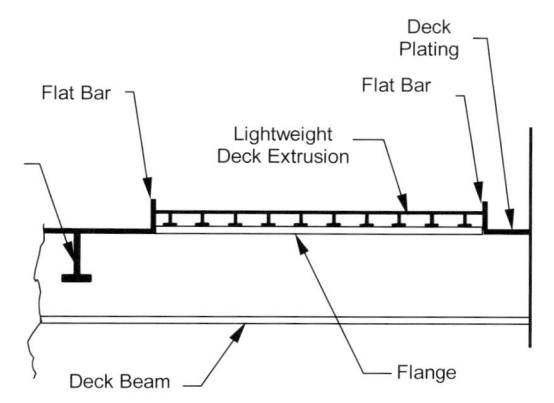

Fig. 2: Detail with lightweight deck extrusions.

Joining Aluminum to Steel

Many ships combine an aluminum superstructure with a steel hull. The standard for performing the joint between the metal is the roll-bonded or explosively bonded bimetallic (actually trimetallic strip), which has to be at least four times wider than the thickness of the plate that it joins. If 10-mm aluminum plate is to be joined to similar thickness steel plate, the bimetallic strip has to be about 40 mm wide, which is unsightly and somewhat difficult to paint, and it must be painted to avoid galvanic corrosion. Kimapong and Watanabe (2004) explored a simpler method to use friction stir welding to join 2-mm 5083 plate to mild steel of the same thickness. This work should be continued to produce a less expensive and cleaner joint between the two dissimilar metals.

Residual Stresses and Distortion

The residual stresses and distortions associated with welding aluminum structures have advantages and disadvantages compared to steel. The elastic modulus of aluminum is one-third that of steel, but the coefficient of thermal expansion is about twice as much. This means that the strains that occur from the cooling of the welds and surrounding areas will produce lower residual stress in aluminum. However, the reduced elastic modulus means that when residual stresses do occur, they will tend to produce greater distortion than in steel structure. Because aluminum conducts heat anywhere from 2.5 to 9 times faster than steel, the area heated during welding processes is greater but not as intense. In general, welded aluminum structure tends to exhibit greater overall distortion than steel structure, and tolerances for ship construction reflect this, with greater allowance for distortion being permitted in aluminum structure than in comparable steel structure. Although there has been much research done on the residual stresses and distortion of steel ship structure, particularly by the National Ship Research Program, much comparable work is needed for aluminum.

Fatigue Design and Analysis

Design of aluminum structure to resist fatigue damage is severely limited by a lack of information on the fatigue strength of typical structural details used in aluminum high-speed vessels. Several organizations have compiled databases relating to the fatigue strength of aluminum structural details and have published design codes. The most recent of these codes is Eurocode 9, which was developed by merging data from most of the other sources and developing new data from testing of medium-scale specimens typical of the details used in civil engineering structures. These codes all assume that the fatigue strength of welded details is the same for all aluminum alloys, and that mean stress effects are not significant.

The data from which these design codes were developed does not reflect many of the structural details currently used or proposed for use in construction of high performance aluminum marine vehicles. Rather, they are for the structural details used for civil engineering structures such as buildings and bridges, for which aluminum is sometimes used. Comparison of the limited data that is available for the structural details used for ship structure with the Eurocode 9 standard shows that the international standard is far more conservative than the data for ship details indicate. A testing program is needed to address these deficiencies. Some of the details used today for which no data is available include joints in extruded aluminum sandwich panels and other complex details commonly used with other lightweight extruded panels.

A deficiency in Eurocode 9 is illustrated by Fig.3, which has experimental data for a common ship-type aluminum structural detail compared to the more conservative fatigue strength of Eurocode9. In the figure, the dotted line represents the lower 5 percent limit of the data, and the solid line represents a Eurocode 23, 3.4 fatigue classification, which would apply to a detail of this sort. The Eurocode 9 standard is considerably more conservative than the data would suggest. This illustrates the need for more fatigue data on specific ship structural details.

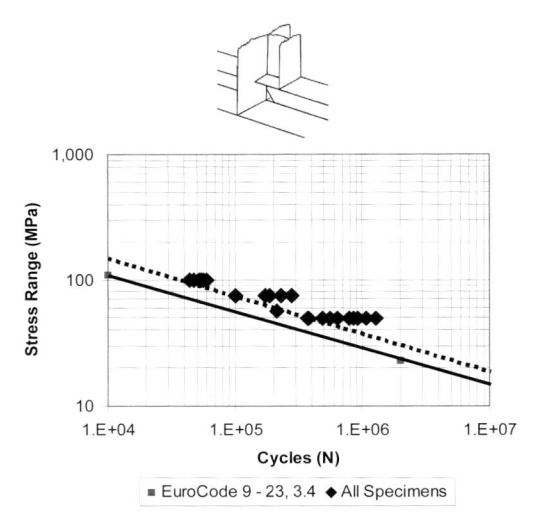

Fig. 3: Fatigue data for stiffener intersection compared to Eurocode 9.

To perform fatigue analysis during structural design, an accurate fatigue-loading spectrum is needed, which is typically developed in the latter stages of design through the use of hydrodynamic analysis or model testing. However, fatigue considerations frequently control many of the scantlings of aluminum vessels, including hull girder strength and methods of performing fatigue analysis in the early design stages are needed. Although the format of fatigue allowable stress levels developed by classification societies for initial guidance in the design of steel ships for fatigue has some merit, the method is too restrictive for the design of most aluminum vessels because of their high speeds and sometimes unusual hull forms. Rather, a simplified way to develop a fatigue-loading spectrum is needed, perhaps tied to the various methods of estimating hull girder loads during early design stages.

The different multi-axial loadings occur at different phases during a loading cycle, and a means of combining all of the different loads to assess the fatigue strength of structural details is needed. There is currently no universal parameter for correlating cyclic multiaxial stress/strain with fatigue life for marine structures. Very few methods have been investigated for welded joints as a group, particularly in aluminum, and additional validation efforts are required before they can be recommended for application to marine structures. Potentially useful tools for extrapolating the responses of aluminum structural details from one stress state to another and for life correlation in high cycle multiaxial regimes include the use of maximum shear stress for crack initiation and maximum principal stress for crack growth.

Aluminum has a crack propagation rate under fatigue loading that can be as much as 30 times greater than that of steel under the same applied stress intensity factor range. Fig. 4 illustrate a fatigue crack growth calculation for a steel hull and an aluminum hull that were designed to the ABS HSC guide, with the section modulus of the aluminum hull increased significantly over minimum rule requirements because of a fatigue crack initiation analysis. An initial 24-mm crack in the aluminum propagated to 50 mm in 24 months of service, but the same size initial crack in the steel propagated to only 30 mm. When a crack reaches appreciable size in an aluminum hull, it can grow quickly and lead to catastrophic hull failure.

In steel hulls, placing significantly tougher grades of steel in critical areas to serve as crack arrestors reduces the chance of catastrophic hull failure from fast fracture. Recognizing that that fatigue crack growth resistance and fracture toughness are entirely different metallurgical phenomena, an effective means must found to arrest a crack in an aluminum hull before catastrophic failures occur.

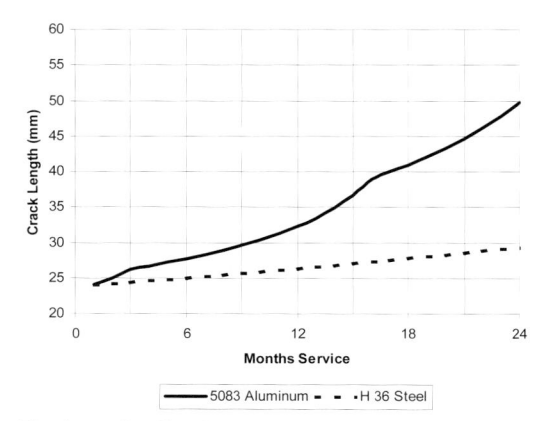

Fig. 4: Predicted crack growth for a 4.39-m 32-knot craft.

Riveted seams may be an answer to crack arrest, but they represent a significant maintenance problem in aluminum structure because they can lead to crevice corrosion and are prone to leakage. Solutions such as welding thicker bars of aluminum that will temporarily reduce the stress intensity may be effective, but the concepts need to be analyzed and experimentally verified prior to use.

Fire Protection

The structural insulation requirements for aluminum are more extensive than for steel because the aluminum structure itself must be protected from the heat of the fire by using fire protection insulation to prevent the aluminum from softening or melting during the fire. The goal of aluminum fire protection insulation is to prevent the aluminum being heated to more than 230 °C.

Table 2 shows the results of two comparative studies that were made of the weight of aluminum structure. The first is a 42.7-m, 32-kt crew boat and the second is the deckhouse of a naval combatant. In the first study the aluminum structure alone weighed 56 percent of the weight of the steel structure, but the total weight of aluminum structure and fire protection insulation was 62 percent of the weight of the steel structure. In the second study the aluminum structure alone weighed 49 percent of the steel, but 84 percent of the weight of the steel when the insulation was added, negating much of the weight advantage of aluminum.

Table 2: Comparative Weights of Aluminum and Steel Structures with Fire Protection Insulation (tonnes)

Ship	Items	Steel Weight	Aluminum Weight	% of Steel
42.7-meter 32-kt Crew Boat	Structure	84.4	47.5	56%
	Insulation		4.5	
	Total	84.4	52.0	62%
Naval Combatant Deckhouse	Structure	134.9	66.2	49%
	Insulation		46.6	
	Total	134.9	112.8	84%

The weight increase for the crew boat is probably acceptable, especially as a conservative assumption was made in the study to insulate all transverse bulkheads and the bottom of the entire main deck, which is not always required for a vessel of this size. Insulation provided IMO A-60 protection and weighed 8.64-kg/m^2 to cover both sides of a transverse bulkhead. For the combatant's deckhouse, the U.S. Navy N-30 protection was provided, with the insulation weighing 18.94-kg/m^2 with both sides of a bulkhead covered.

The U.S. Navy N-30 protection is designed to withstand the heat of a hydrocarbon fire as well as the fire from the residual fuel of an unexpended missile, a more significant threat than the wood fire that is the basis of A-60 protection. However, hydrocarbon fires are a threat for commercial vessels, particularly above vehicle decks on ferries, where some builders use a steel framework to support the deck above rather than using IMO H-60 insulation, which weighs only slightly less than N-30 insulation. There is a clear need for the development of better fire protection methods for aluminum structure.

The National Shipbuilding Research Program has conducted a study of improved fire protection insulation for aluminum structure aimed particularly at the vehicle deck of ferries (NSRP, 2001). The product studied under project was estimated to weigh about 0.2 to 0.4 pounds per square foot (1.0 to 2.0 kg/m2), and have an installed cost ranging from $0.07 to $1.00 per square foot. Because the product was tested in hydrocarbon fires, it seems promising to meet the IMO H-30 and the U.S. Navy N-30 requirements. However, regulatory bodies have not yet approved the product.

Reductions can be made in the placement and configuration of structural fire protection insulation through modeling potential fire scenarios, and examining how the structure responds with different types of insulation. This is in line with established IMO procedures for alternate design and arrangements for fire safety that are used for Class A fires. However, the experimental basis for such evaluation with hydrocarbon fires is not as well established, especially for structure surrounded by fire, such as stanchions and deep girders. SNAME Technical and Research Bulletin 2-21, Aluminum Fire Protection Guidelines, was issued in 1974 and should be updated through a program that included analysis and testing.

Vibration

Vibration problems can be more acute in aluminum structure than in steel because aluminum has greater potential for fatigue damage. Structural details located in areas not normally subjected to significant stresses can develop fatigue cracks if the structure vibrates significantly.

Although aluminum has one-third the elastic modulus of steel, it also has one-third the density. The natural frequency of a system is proportional to the square root of the stiffness divided by the mass, so similar aluminum and steel structures will have similar modes of vibration. Because the scantlings for aluminum structure are generally greater than for steel structure designed to the same criteria, aluminum structures will have higher natural frequencies than steel structures unless a significant amount of mass is associated with the mode of vibration, such as machinery foundations.

The methodology for analyzing structure for vibration is well developed and equations reflect both density and elastic modulus, so that calculations for aluminum structure are as valid as for steel structure. One area of concern is for structural damping when making forced response calculations, for which information is scarce for aluminum ships.

For ship structures, there is greater uncertainty into the magnitude of the forcing function for such sources as waterjet propulsors, and research is needed in order to properly design structure subjected to such loading.

Performance Metrics, Reliability and Risk Assessment

A need to apply quantifiable performance metrics to evaluate the capability of a structural design has influenced research into applying formal reliability analysis and risk assessment to marine structural design. These methods offer an advantage for aluminum marine structures because there is little experience with design and long-term operation of many of these ships. Traditional design methods may lead to over-designed structures or a higher level of risk than desired. Development of the methodology for applying performance metrics to ship design requires research in several areas:

- Development of specific aluminum limit states, and the uncertainty associated with the variables in these limit states.
- Development of an automated process to calculate and document the probabilities associated with individual failure modes.

- Application of the methodology to existing ship designs to establish baseline values of these metrics.
- System level aggregation of each reliability-based performance evaluation.

Research in several key areas is needed for further application of reliability assessment to aluminum vessels:

- Development of ultimate strength and fatigue analysis methodologies as mentioned above.
- Obtaining better information on the mean values and stochastic properties of the variables used in ultimate strength and fatigue analysis, including basic material properties.

Application of risk assessment to design of ship structures is less advanced than its application to other ship systems, but it offers a systematic method of assuring equivalence between aluminum and steel structures. There are several ongoing efforts in this area, including the POP&C, MARSTRUCT, and ASRANet projects that should be monitored to see how they could be applied to aluminum ships and craft.

Maintenance and Repair

Properly designed and maintained, aluminum marine structures can see many years of service with minimal problems. Aluminum can be very prone to fatigue crack propagation if cracking of structure does occur. Corrosion of aluminum, once initiated, tends to be rapid and concentrated, generally requiring immediate action to restore structural integrity. Although the 5xxx-series aluminum alloys do not generally require painting to avoid corrosion, improper painting procedures can lead to corrosion problems. Contact with most other metals, which are anodic to aluminum, can lead to rapid wastage of aluminum. Use of improper alloys, especially those containing copper, will also lead to rapid corrosion, against which coating systems offer little protection if the aluminum is constantly exposed to seawater.

The research needs for fatigue analysis methods in design were mentioned above, and are equally important for repair, where little time or money is generally available for the repair of fatigue cracks. The Ship Structure Committee has sponsored work in the past on improving the fatigue life of common structural details on steel ships, and that work should be extended to include aluminum. Knowledge of the corrosion resistance of marine aluminum alloys is needed to determine if a structural problem is material related.

Structural Health Monitoring

Structural health monitoring systems have seen application to some aluminum vessels, including the simple installation of accelerometers that warn ship operators when to reduce speed or take a more favorable heading when design levels of loads are being exceeded. These systems are sometimes misunderstood or are perceived as being too sensitive, and components such as audible alarms are frequently turned off.

The lack of confidence of the operators in such monitoring systems demonstrates the need for improvements in those systems. There are other needs that are more specific to aluminum vessels, particularly for the early detection of fatigue cracks. Because aluminum structures may have more insulation than ships built with steel, early detection of cracks by visual inspection is more difficult, although it is more important because of the rapid fatigue crack propagation rates in aluminum. Methods for early crack detection such as installation of trip gages should be explored for use on aluminum vessels.

Monitoring of the structural health of an aluminum vessel over its lifetime would be enhanced by the development of methods of analyses of the fatigue of the structure over the operational lifetime of the vessel. Such a model would be updated during the life of the ship from information gathered on actual fatigue cracking events, indicating if the forecasted behavior is optimistic or pessimistic.

Emerging Technologies

Friction stir welding of aluminum ship structures has gained rapid usage over the last few years, with new applications and methods under exploration. The research issues are similar for other welded properties. Paik is investigating the effect of the different properties on the compressive strength of panels, but the effect on other failure modes needs to be determined too. The basic material properties for all alloys being joined need determination, including their statistical properties. The effect of friction stir welds on corrosion strength is being investigated by NSWCCD, but this needs to be done in the context of standardized testing of aluminum alloys for marine service.

Conclusions

Aluminum has become the material of choice for many types of vessels, particularly high-speed vessels where lightweight structure is important for meeting design goals. The methods of design and fabrication of aluminum contain many areas of conservatism that if overcome by aggressive research will lead to even greater performance at reduced cost.

Acknowledgement

This work was sponsored by the interagency Ship Structure Committee as well as by the Office of Naval Research. I would like to thank the members of the SSC Project Technical Committee, which had technical oversight for this project, especially committee chair Derek S. Novak of the American Bureau of Shipping, Sergei Petinov of St. Petersburg Polytechnic University, Matthew Collette of SAIC, Jeom Kee Paik of Pusan National University, and Paul Hess of the Office of

Naval Research, all of whom made many helpful suggestions and provided much reference material.

Grateful assistance was received from members of the Office of Naval Research Aluminum Structure Reliability Program, especially program manager Paul Hess and planning committee members Catherine Wong of NSWCCD who provided much useful advice and information on corrosion, Edward Devine, Liming Salvino, Daniel Stiles, and Chandra Ullagaddi of NSWCCD, Matthew Collette of SAIC, and Pradeep Sensharma of Fulcrum corporation. The material on fire protection was reviewed by Usman Sorathia of NSWCCD.

I received help from many shipyard personnel, especially Grant Pecoraro of Gulfcraft, Al Dodson of Swiftships, Jim Towers of Kvichak Marine Industries, Michael Duquesnoy of Austal USA, Paul Kotzebue of Swath Ocean Systems, W. Philip Nuss of Trinity Yachts, and George Lundgren of Workskiff.

Many producers and suppliers of aluminum were helpful, including Michael Skillingberg of The Aluminum Association, Stan Guess of Tower Extrusions, Larry Moffett of Taber Extrusions, Joseph B. Wolf and Rob Menard of Aluminum and Stainless, Inc., Douglas J. Waldron of Advanced Joining Technologies, Harold Bushfield of Alcoa, and Mike Farrell of G. James Australia Pty. Ltd. I was kindly received at the Alcoa Technical Center, and received helpful information from Nathaniel Beavers, Francine Bovard, Israel Stol, Michael Brandt, James Burg, Roger Kaufold, James Marinelli, Jean Ann Skiles, and Rebecca Wyss.

References

Bushfield, Harold Sr., Marc Cruder, Rendall Farley, and Jim Towers, Marine Aluminum Plate - ASTM Standard Specification B 928 And The Events Leading To Its Adoption. Presented at the October 2003 Meeting of the Society of Naval Architects and Marine Engineers, San Francisco, California.

Hay, Robert A. and Chester H. Holtyn (1980). "The Effect of Thermal Fabrication Practices on Aluminum," Naval Engineers Journal, pp. 37–43, 1980.

Keith, Donald, J. and Amy Blair. Fracture Mechanics Characterization of Aluminum Alloys for Marine Structural Applications, Ship Structure Committee report SSC-448, 2007.

Kimapong, K. and T. Watanabe (2004). "Friction Stir Welding of Aluminum Alloy to Steel," Welding Journal, October 2004, pp. 277-S–282-s.

NSRP, 2001. Results of Enhanced Fire Protective Material Systems, National Shipbuilding Research Program report ASE_932006, 2001.

Paik, Jeom Kee, Jae Myung Lee, Jung Yong Ryu, Jun Ho Jang, Celine Renaud, and Paul E. Hess III (2006). "Mechanical Buckling Collapse Testing on Aluminum Stiffened Plate Structures for Marine Applications", Presented at the World Maritime Technology Conference, March 6–10, 2006, London.

Rigo, P. et al. (2004) "Ultimate Strength of Aluminum Stiffened Panels: Sensitivity Analysis" 9th Symposium on Practical Design of Ships and Other Floating Structures (PRADS), Lubeck, Germany 2004. 156-162.

Rigo, P., R. Sarghiuta, S. Estefen, E. Lehmann, S.C. Otelea, I. Pasqualino, Bo C. Simonsen, Z. Wan, and T. Yao, (2003) "Sensitivity Analysis on Ultimate Strength of Aluminium Stiffened Panels", Marine Structures Vol. 16, No. 6 pp. 437-468.

Significance of the EFFORT Project for the Design of Complicated Sterns

A. de Jager [1], M. Visonneau & P. Queutey [2], J. Windt [3], A. Thoresson [4]

[1] IHC HOLLAND Dredgers BV, Kinderdijk, The Netherlands
[2] Fluid Mechanics Laboratory UMR CNRS, ECN, Nantes, France
[3] MARIN, Wageningen, The Netherlands
[4] BERG PROPULSION, Öckerö Gothenburg, Sweden

Abstract

July 2002 the research project EFFORT (European Full-scale FlOw Research and Technology) started. This project, initiated by the Maritime Research Institute Netherlands (MARIN), focused on the validation of the existing CFD-codes of six reputable institutes and universities in Europe. The intention was to realize reliable prediction tools and as a consequence a European hull design standard of a high quality. Industriële Handels Combinatie (IHC) was involved in this project as an industrial partner. Because its designs are not only characterized by a high degree of complexity, but also meant for extreme circumstances, the use of CFD is very attractive and consequently its reliability even more significant. Directly after the finish of this research project, the improved CFD has been used for new designs.

Keywords

Hull design; Scale effects; CFD; Propeller design.

Introduction

The traditional way of hull design was setting up the lines by experience and checking the performance by model tests. When the performance was found not acceptable, the lines and the model were changed and the tests redone. This (common) procedure is time consuming, expensive and on top of that not very flexible. CFD gives the opportunity to check several alternatives in the design stage and only the very best are then used for model tests. Another important advantage of CFD is that scale effects can be avoided by calculating with the right Reynolds Number [6], [7].

It must be said that further development of CFD was (and still is) necessary to comply with all wishes of the industry, however, the codes of some well known institutes are very useful nowadays. The above-mentioned development is mainly necessary to enable proper treatment of appendages and to cope with extreme circumstances as shallow water. These details are essential from the flow point of view, that is.

The CFD development of the last decade has raised the need for validation, especially on full scale [8], [9]. For that reason the EFFORT project was initiated. Bringing in a vessel with a complicated stern to be subjected to full scale measurements resulted in an attempt to test as well the capability of CFD to deal with appendages.

The necessity for a certain ship type having a complicated stern with appendages for deviating circumstances will be described hereunder. Then a description will be given of the EFFORT project. Furthermore an investigation of a recently designed complicated hull with help of CFD will be presented. In the end the use of the results of this investigation, the propeller blade design, will be shown.

A complicated hull and its origin

For building ease (thus cost reduction) there will always be a striving for a simple hull. However, there are limits which are enforced by hydrodynamics. The vessel type which was subjected to full scale research was, amongst others, a hopper dredger. Its main characteristics briefly are:

- A full block ship with C_B = 0.87 and a low L/B ratio of 4.5
- A twin screw vessel with nozzles and a high demand on thrust for dredging purposes
- The vessel is sailing empty as much as loaded
- Extreme shallow water is the vessel's normal work area, with a Depth / Draught ratio of 1.5

It needs no evidence that the full stern, the confined flow in shallow water, the high thrust and the two conditions of similar importance were (and still are) making the design a challenge. Extensive model tests in a shallow water basin were carried out in the past and gradually the knowledge so obtained led to a more or less satisfying stern design. Sea trial experience with many dredgers confirmed that good feeling.

In fact, the stern of European inland vessels served as an example. This type of vessel is always sailing in shallow water and has a full stern with a large B/T ratio, identical to a hopper dredger. An additional joint problem of these ship types is the restricted diameter of propeller due to that full stern. Consequently the power density of their propellers is high. As said before the demand for thrust is high for dredgers, resulting in a typical high thrust loading during dredging. So, to avoid a random flow towards the propellers, a kind of covering proved essential. The relatively low draught in empty condition (due to ship's fullness) enhanced the need for this covering as it avoids air suction of the propellers. This covering is normally named "tunnel" or "head box". Old designs without such a covering suffered of serious vibration problems and a significant drop of propeller efficiency. At several dredgers retro fit of these appendages have taken place short after sea trials. Another problem that had to be solved was the arisen flow separation at the center skeg. A usual simple flat skeg was not sufficient, but a rounded transition to the main hull proved necessary.

These apparently necessary appendages are making the stern complicated (Fig. 1), all the more because the nozzles and rudders must be integrated to fit (Fig. 2).

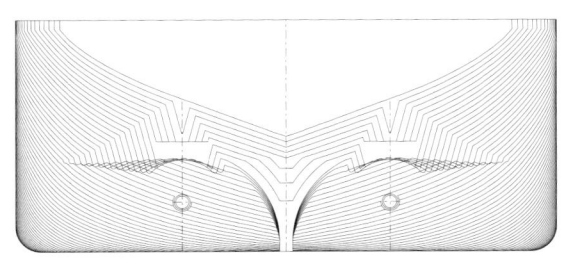

Fig. 1: Stern complexity

Fig. 2: Integration of nozzle and rudder

A "good feeling", however, is not the right scientific attitude. To be honest, the results of the model test were not always satisfying, but deliberations about scale effects brushed our objections aside.

Two disappointing phenomena at model scale in shallow water were encountered regularly:

- Flow separation
- Chaotic wake field structure (Fig. 3)

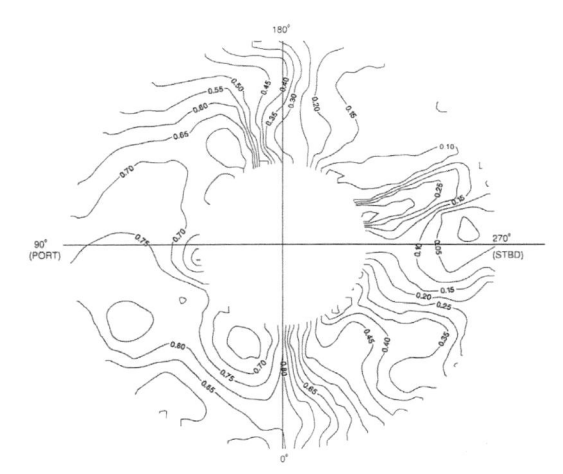

Fig. 3: Model axial wake in shallow water

The location and extent of the flow separation proved to be strongly depending on the action respectively loading of the propeller. Without propeller action, separation occurred just in front of the propeller (to be qualified as unacceptable), but with propeller action it disappeared at that spot (Fig. 4) and arose somewhere behind the nozzles.

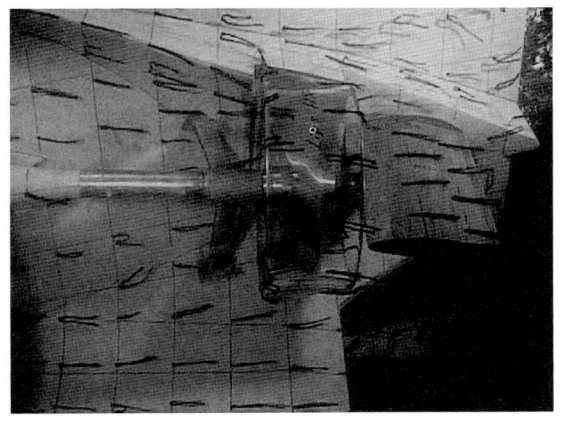

Fig. 4: Flow towards propeller in shallow water

This last fact set our mind at rest, but the problem of the chaotic wake field (measured without propeller) remained. The propeller manufacturer was not able to translate this nominal wake into an effective wake for a full scale situation, to be used for the blade design. Sad to say, nothing could be done by the industry with this information. Meanwhile it was experienced frequently on board the dredgers that the mechanical pitch range of the CPP was hardly sufficient in free sailing mode whereas a reasonable margin on the pitch range was provided during the design, one thought……

Both phenomena are, amongst others, depending on viscosity and can therefore be categorized under "scale effects". Nevertheless, at the moment it is not clear to what extent viscosity is responsible for the observed phenomena. Possibly a not well shaped hull or not properly oriented appendages are affecting the flow negatively. Because the flow in shallow water is completely different from that in deep water, this last assumption sounds plausible. Some improvements have been achieved with the help of model tests, but we were not successful in fully sorting out viscous effects from misalignments in the past. Furthermore, it was insupportable to accept that the wake information of the ship's actual operational condition could not be used.

January 2001 IHC ordered MARIN for the first time to make viscous CFD calculations for a dredger stern with aforementioned appendages. From that very beginning up to now a certain development in the use of this technique has taken place. The first calculations concerned the hull at laden draught without propeller action in deep water at model scale. The possibility of comparing calculation results with model test results without too many complicating factors was the main reason for this careful start. Next steps were the empty draught with trim by stern, full scale situation, propeller action, shallow water, complete hull and finally transom immersion. Although the first calculations were of an experimental nature, soon after the validity (at model scale) was established the results have been directly used for shipbuilding purposes.

The main advantages of this application for the dredger with its characteristic complicated stern were:

- Several alternatives of the appendages could be investigated in short time. Ultimately this process led to an appendage orientation which differs from that of the past.

- The full scale calculation results showed that the flow in shallow water is not that unfavourable as indicated by model tests. Hence, shallow water model test results must be interpreted with caution.

- The wake field at full scale in shallow water proved to be not chaotic as indicated by model test, but on the contrary rather smooth and usable for the design of the propeller blade.

- Additionally, the effective wake could be obtained from the calculation results. This made the usual but a bit uncertain translation of the nominal wake unnecessary.

- Now, an even more complicated stern (as a twin gondola stern is) which suffers even more of scale effects in shallow water on model scale, can be investigated with more confidence. Just this alternative stern is very attractive for this ship type and nowadays applied as a standard.

Needless to say this development has been welcomed very much by the shipyard in question. However, one important question still remained: are the calculation results similar in reality? For the model scale situation a lot of validation material is available, but to be convinced of the reliability of full scale viscous CFD calculation results, full scale validation material is necessary. Being aware of the importance of this last statement and taking into consideration of dredger's sensitivity for viscous effects, a passion arose to subject a dredger to full scale research. So, the participation of IHC in the EFFORT project became self-evident.

The EFFORT project

Viscous effects in the flow around a stern are qualifying for the wake field. To enable validation of full scale wake field computations, the main objective, full scale measurements are indispensable. Because such measurements are as well difficult as expensive, full scale data are scarce. To deal with the difficulty experts, high tech equipment and cooperation with a willing ship owner is essential. To deal with the costs a group of participants is necessary, but even then subsidy is very welcome. After the usual preparatory work the project could start in July 2002. The name of the project "EFFORT" is an acronym of **E**uropean **F**ull-scale **Fl**O**w R**esearch and **T**echnology. The European character of this project is expressed by its European participants and the subsidy from the European Commission.

Organization of the project

Initiator and general coordinator of the whole project was MARIN. The project consisted of six work packages which will be described here below briefly.

WP 1: Full scale measurements, coordinated by MARIN. For this task two vessels were selected, research vessel "NAWIGATOR XXI" and hopper dredger "UILENSPIEGEL" (Fig 5).

Fig. 5: hopper dredger "UILENSPIEGEL"

The first vessel is a single screw vessel with its characteristic boundary layer effects in the propeller plane and the second vessel has a complicated stern with viscous effects as described in the former section. The stern of these vessels must be provided with plane windows (Fig. 6) for the purpose of measuring the wake fields by means of Laser Doppler Velocimetry (LDV). For this kind of measurements very clear water is necessary and for that reason the research vessel has been subjected to measurements in the Sogne Fjord, Norway, and the dredger in the Mediterranean

Sea. Besides the wake fields also the wave pattern of the vessel has been measured by means of laser technique.

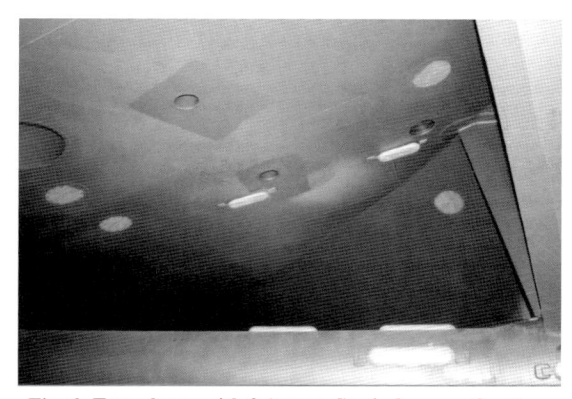

Fig. 6: Two planes with 2 (covered) windows on the stern of the "UILENSPIEGEL"

WP 2: Model Tests, coordinated by Centrum Techniki Okretowej S.A. (CTO), Gdansk, Poland. Model tests were found essential to enable the investigation of scale effects. These tests, which must be conducted in similar conditions as those of the vessels, could not be started until the full scale trials were finished. Furthermore, because the full scale wake plane of the vessels could only be measured with propeller action, the application of the Particle Image Velocimetry (PIV) technique on model scale was necessary.

WP 3: CFD Development, coordinated by Centre National de la Recherche Scientifique (CNRS), Nantes, France. This task was added for checking the robustness and the accuracy of the simulation tools in full scale flow conditions. Specifically, research has been done on free-surface computation at full scale; turbulence modelling and hull-propeller interaction. Recommendations to prepare the simulation tools (to be used for validation purpose) have thus been issued.

WP 4: Validation, coordinated by Helsinki University of Technology (HUT), Finland. This was the key task with objectives to perform an evaluation of the accuracy, applicability and efficiency of the different approaches used. The grids and the convergence must be verified and the wake, the wave profile, the pressure distribution and resistance must be validated. Not only the information obtained from WP1 of the two vessels which were subjected to measurements, but also that of six data base vessels, a valuable contribution of Hamburgische Schiffbau-Versuchsanstaltt GmbH in Germany (HSVA), must be taken into account. Because the outcome of this work package is the crux of the project, a more comprehensive description will follow in the next subsection.

WP 5: Application & Demonstration, coordinated by IHC. This work package was added to enhance the involvement of the industry. Several yards, propeller manufacturers and a classification society participated in this project. With the help of case studies, proposed by themselves, they must be convinced of the value, reliability and effectiveness of CFD.

WP 6: Exploitation & Dissemination, coordinated by Lloyd's Register, London, United Kingdom.

Work package 4: Validation

Work Package 4 of the EFFORT project consists of verification and validation of model and full-scale predictions of the flow around hull and wake field. Verification as well as validation are considered to be essential to obtain reliable flow predictions and both are not easy to achieve. At the start of the project full scale predictions often suffered from numerical difficulties because of the required resolution and high aspect ratio of cells close to the wall. In addition, the complex geometry of the dredger results in a complex flow which means that it is more difficult to achieve sufficiently accurate numerical results. Moreover, the performance of turbulence models for ship flows at model scale is well known now, but how do they perform at full scale, and how accurate is a full-scale wake field prediction? Very limited full-scale experimental data were available, and EFFORT has provided, brought together and exploited most of these. Here we present a short summary of calculations performed by Ecole Central de Nantes (ECN) and MARIN.

ECN's computations are performed with the ISIS-CFD flow solver developed by the CFD Department of the Fluid Mechanics Laboratory [8]. Turbulent flow is simulated by solving the incompressible unsteady Reynolds-averaged Navier-Stokes equations (RANSE). The solver is based on a finite volume method with non-overlapping unstructured grids. Free surface flow is simulated by a surface capturing method. Several turbulence models ranging from one equation models to Reynolds stress transport model are implemented in ISIS-CFD [9]. Here a standard k-ω SST turbulence model is used. MARIN's computations are performed with their in-house computer code PARNASSOS, [3] and [5], which solves the incompressible steady RANS equations. It is based on a finite difference method with multi-block structured body fitted grids and allows non-conforming coupling between blocks. Free surface flow is simulated with the 'composite approach', i.e. the viscous flow is computed in a fixed domain bounded by the wave surface found form a potential flow solution, or by surface fitting. Various isotropic eddy viscosity turbulence models are available. Here the one-equation model by Menter ("UILENSPIEGEL") and the two-equation k-ω SSTmodel both with a correction for longitudinal vorticity according to Dacles-Mariani et al., are applied. No wall functions are used, not even at full-scale.

As mentioned, the validation work addressed eight vessels altogether, six data base vessels and one of the two EFFORT vessels were single-screw vessels without appendages. For such ships, the wake field is affected by longitudinal vorticity that can be a difficult feature to predict; and the question was how this would be at full scale. A similar flow feature is present for twin-gondola shape hulls. A conclusion of this part of the work was that turbulence models that perform well at model scale, also were found to be generally adequate at full scale. The two codes ISIS and PARNASSOS performed best in these validations, and provided almost identical predictions when the same turbulence model was used. Additional information about these calculations performed by ECN and MARIN can be found in [1],[2].

The "UILENSPIEGEL" case

The "UILENSPIEGEL" has the additional interest of the appendages, complicated geometry and ducted propeller. First we present a verification study by MARIN. After that, computations by ECN and MARIN for model- and full-scale conditions are presented.

Verification
Many aspects influence the accuracy of the flow field predictions: the number of grid nodes, the quality of the grid e.g. orthogonality and smoothness, the type of grids, structured or unstructured, all play a role. Secondly, flow solver details, discretisation of derivatives, highly influence the overall accuracy of the calculations for a given grid density. All these details are strongly related to the complexity of the flow. At MARIN accuracy is continuously guarded by background research and comparison with tank tests. Important for a dredger is a study on flow around open shaft (rotating or not) configurations and on the flow around tunnel/headbox configurations. For open shafts, a systematic study was done of the flow around a cylinder protruding from a flat plate at an inclination angle of 8 degrees. Different grid structures and grid densities have been used and insight was obtained on the effect on the accuracy of the flow predictions. More details can be found in [4]. Next we profoundly studied the flow around a stern with headbox and a triangular shaped body fitted to a flat plate. We found that flow reversal regions may appear and grow with increased number of grid nodes and may vanish again after refining even more [1]. These verification studies were done prior to the EFFORT project. A first step in EFFORT was a grid study for the "UILENSPIEGEL" itself. Calculations are performed for full-scale but *without* propeller action. The tunnel, headbox and propeller shaft were included in the geometry but the support struts, duct and rudder were omitted. The total number of grid nodes was varied from 0.4 to 6 million. Grid refinement in streamwise direction, and on the other hand in wall-normal and girthwise directions, was applied separately. The study showed that the flow upstream of the appendages can be considered as sufficiently grid independent. Further downstream the level of grid-dependence increases. The axial flow field around the shaft that determines the inflow to the propeller is presented (Fig. 7). It shows the effect of streamwise grid refinement on the wake field around the propeller shaft (compare top left to bottom left figure). The predicted wake of the propeller shaft moves outwards, and the depth of the wake is found to reduce slightly. An almost opposite effect is found for the refinement in the wall-normal and the girthwise direction (compare top right to bottom left figure). There a significant increase of the depth of the wake of

the propeller shaft can be seen, while the location of the wake remains practically unaltered. The flow separation region between the tunnels (not plotted) is also highly grid dependent. Refinement in streamwise direction leads to an increased velocity between the tunnels. A refinement in wall-normal and girthwise direction leads on the other hand to a lower velocity between the tunnels.

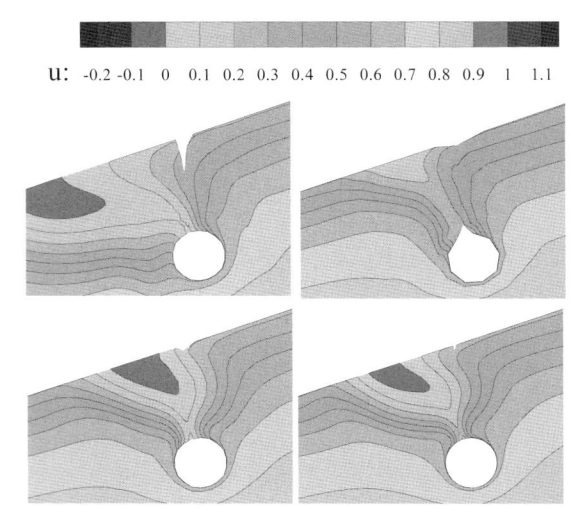

Fig. 7: The effect of mesh refinement on the axial velocity field behind the bossing of the "UILENSPIEGEL". Top left: 91x141x121 nodes, top right: 361x71x61 nodes, bottom left: 361x141x121 nodes, bottom right: final grid, 9 million nodes using non-conforming connection between blocks.

The grid study showed that the structured mesh, with over 6 million cells might not be sufficiently dense to ensure a grid-independent solution of the flow field around the appendages even while some geometric features (shaft support struts, duct and rudder) had been omitted. It shows how complex details and sharp knuckles in the hull form can increase the resolution demands far beyond those for e.g. smooth tanker or container ships. After EFFORT, the PARNASSOS code had been extended by allowing a non-conforming coupling in main stream direction between blocks. Much denser grids can thus be used locally in blocks around the appendages. Around the shaft and headbox, we again doubled the number of nodes in streamwise and girthwise direction and used about 30% more nodes in wall normal direction. About 9 million grid nodes were used in 6 blocks. We found (compare bottom left part and bottom right part of Fig. 7) that the predicted wake of the propeller shaft moves slightly inwards and the depth of the wake is reduced a little bit more. So the grid with 6 million nodes gave a nearly grid independent solution after all.

Scale effects and validation of wake fields
ECN used unstructured meshes generated by HEXPRESS while MARIN used structured meshes, generated by in-house elliptic grid generation methods

(Fig. 8). MARIN did not model the duct, shaft and rudder while ECN modelled the fully appended hull. The unstructured grid contains about 6 million nodes, among them about 340000 are located on the hull. The structured grid contains 9 million nodes with 33000 nodes on the hull. The unstructured grid is very dense on the hull and local grid refinements are applied, but is substantially coarser away from the hull.

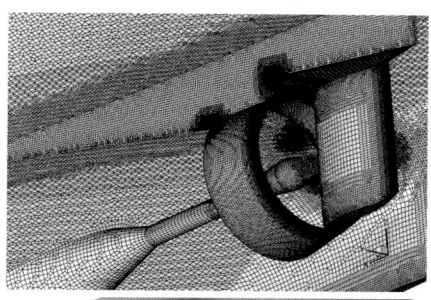

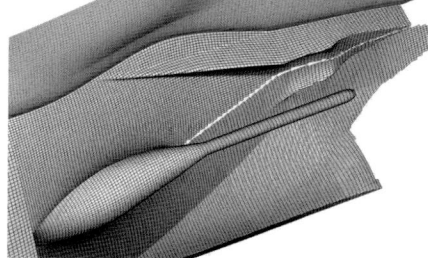

Fig 8: "UILENSPIEGEL": Grid on aftpart of ISIS (top) and PARNASSOS (bottom).

Calculations are performed for model scale (Re = 10^7) and full-scale (Re=10^9) with and without propeller. ECN computed the free surface flow with a surface-capturing strategy and the propeller action is modelled by a classical actuator disk approach. The propeller thrust is obtained by updating at each time step the balance between the thrust of the propeller and the total drag of the ship. This leads to an increase of computation time of 20%. MARIN computed the free surface flow with the composite approach. The propeller action is modelled by an actuator disk while the thrust is estimated by an in-house model. This gives a slightly lower propeller thrust.

Scale effects

The limiting wall streamlines, at model scale for free-surface flows, with and without propeller, are computed. Due to computational resources limitations and for time saving, the air/water volume fraction for the simulation with propeller (WIP) is frozen to the field obtained without propeller (WOP), and, consequently, the influence of the propeller on the free surface elevation near the stern cannot be analyzed here. One can observe the strong upstream influence of the ducted propeller on the near-wall flow and the drastic reduction of separated flow regions when the propeller is working (Fig. 9). It is to be noted, however, that the propeller effect is exaggerated by including the nozzle in the computation without propeller; as it then acts as an obstruction to the flow. At model scale and without propeller, one can see the print of a very complex structure made of three longitudinal vortices visible from their focal prints near the intersection between the hull and the propeller shaft. At full scale with free-surface, with and without propeller (Fig. 10), one can observe again the strong upstream influence of the ducted propeller on the near-wall flow and the drastic reduction of separated flow regions when the propeller is operating. Compared to the computations performed at model scale, the Reynolds number influence appears to be very significant since, even without propeller, the three focal points related with the strong longitudinal vortices emanating close to the intersection between the propeller shaft and the hull, have totally disappeared. This noticeable influence of Reynolds number on the flow topology will have a strong impact on the isowake distribution in sections located in front of the ducted propeller, as it will be shown later.

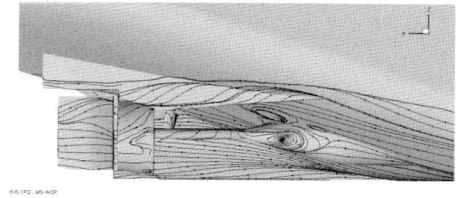

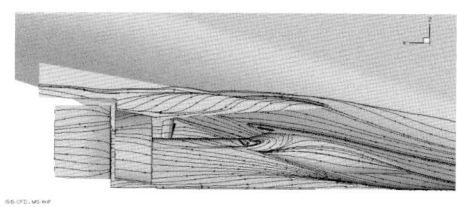

Fig. 9: "UILENSPIEGEL" (ISIS), Limiting streamlines MS, WOP (top), WIP (bottom).

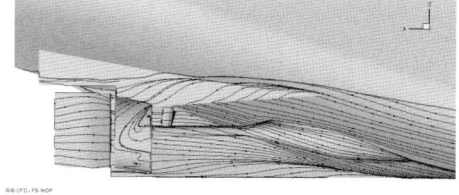

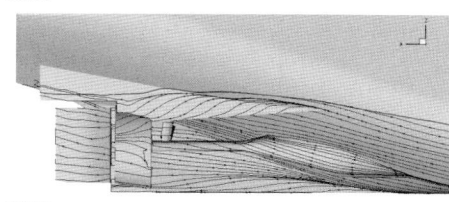

Fig. 10: "UILENSPIEGEL" (ISIS), Limiting streamlines FS, WOP (top), WIP (bottom).

The limiting streamlines at model- and full-scale are also predicted by PARNASSOS (Fig. 11). At model scale, the patterns are generally quite similar, but there is a difference close to the intersection between propeller shaft and the hull. PARNASSOS predicts a strong flow separation region behind this intersection at the inner side. There is no drastic reduction of this when the propeller is operating; but here the nozzle was absent from both computations, only the nozzle thrust was modelled. Another aspect is that the Reynolds number effect is less significant; the flow separation region at the inner side remains.

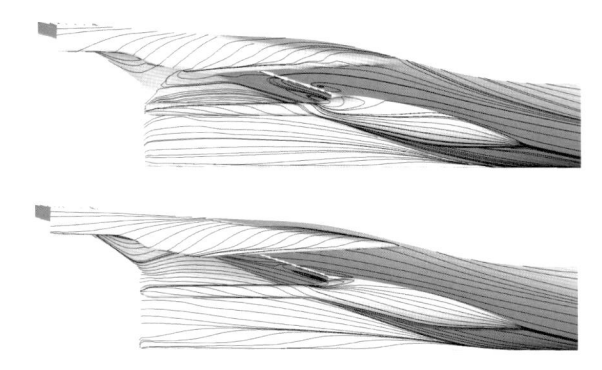

Fig. 11: "UILENSPIEGEL" (PARNASSOS), Limiting streamlines MS, WIP (top), FS WIP (bottom).

Comparisons to model scale experiments

PIV model-scale experiments with operating propellers were carried out by the Polish Ship Design and Research Center within the EFFORT consortium at a section called WinDE which is not located precisely for confidentiality reasons but corresponds to the same location used for the full scale measurements. Global views of the computed isowakes and secondary velocities are provided by ISIS (Fig. 12). At this measurement section and the rectangular zone indicates precisely the PIV window for which measurements are provided (Fig. 13 top).

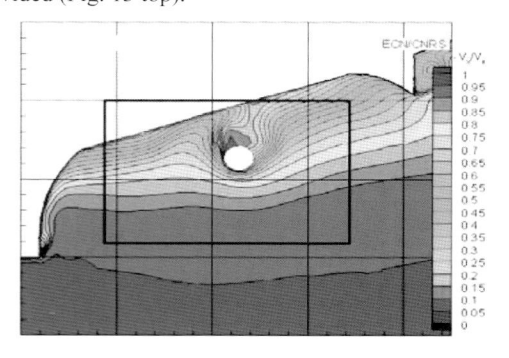

Fig. 12: "UILENSPIEGEL": MS:WIP : WinDE - Global views of isowake at modelscale with propeller. The rectangular zone indicates the PIV measurement window

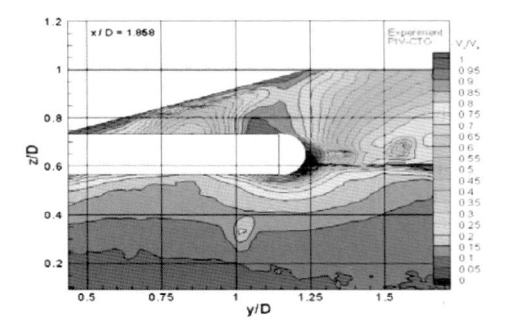

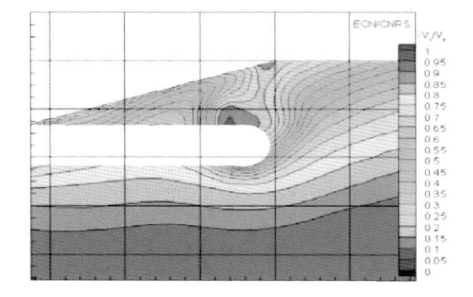

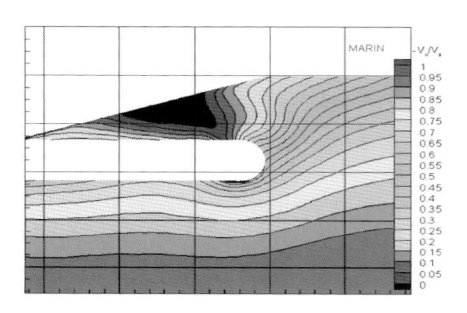

Fig. 13: "UILENSPIEGEL": MS, WIP, WinDE - Comparison of isowake distribution at model scale, PIV experiments with ISIS & PARNASSOS computations at section WinDE

One can observe a region of low longitudinal velocity between the hull and the propeller shaft (Fig. 13). The strong distortion of the isowakes between the shaft and the hull is associated with the presence of a clockwise longitudinal vortex.

Then, a comparison between PIV measurements and computations of both ISIS and PARNASSOS is made and shown in the same rectangular region as indicated above (Fig. 13). The white rectangle located in the prolongation of the propeller shaft corresponds to a region where no measurements are available since the PIV setup is located in the right part of this figure. The global agreement between experiments and computations is very satisfactory for the predictions by ISIS since the distortion of the isowakes and the shape of the low speed region between the shaft and the hull is well reproduced by this blind simulation. The computational result by PARNASSOS is less satisfying. The predictions show a large region with reversed flow between the shaft and the hull which is not present in the measurements. The solution is proven to be grid independent and neither an increased thrust nor a more forward position of the actuator disc to enhance the nozzle presence improved the results significantly, so most probably the influence of turbulence modeling is important here. Because investigations are still going on, a clear conclusion cannot be drawn at this moment. Another interesting item is the secondary velocity distribution in the same rectangular region as predicted by ISIS (Fig. 14). The existence of a clockwise longitudinal vortex is confirmed by the experiments and one can observe that the location and the intensity of this vortical structure is well predicted by the computations.

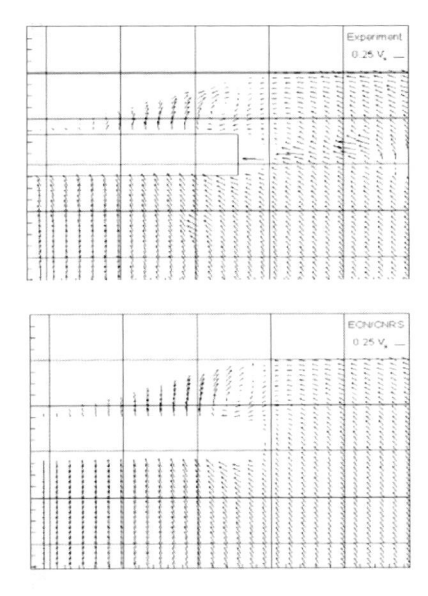

Fig. 14: "UILENSPIEGEL", MS, WIP, WinDE - Comparison of the secondary velocity distribution between model scale PIV experiments and ISIS-CFD computations at section WinDE

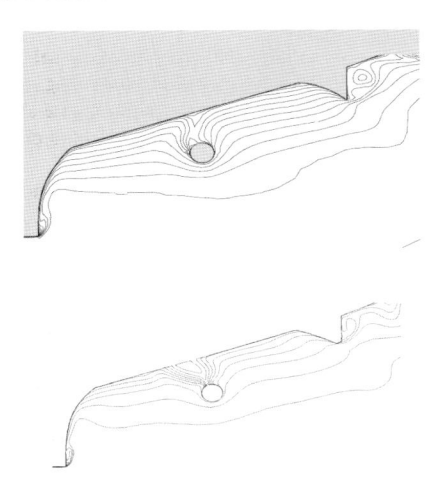

Fig. 15: "UILENSPIEGEL": FS, WIP, WinDE - Global view of full scale isowakes. Top figure: ISIS. Bottom figure: PARNASSOS.

Comparisons to full scale experiments

This part is devoted to a comparison of ISIS-CFD and PARNASSOS computations with the experimental isowake distribution at two different sections for Windows D & E and Windows C & A which will not be explicitly located for confidentiality reasons. The computed flow fields are shown at section WinDE (Fig. 15). This last section is the same as the one shown at model scale. Although not coarse, the used unstructured mesh already comprised of about 6 million nodes should be refined in the vicinity of the appendices. A grid dependency study would be welcome but unfortunately impossible to carry out on the available computational facilities.

Then, a comparison of experimental and computed isowakes at windows D and E, located between the hull and the propeller shaft, is shown (Fig. 16).

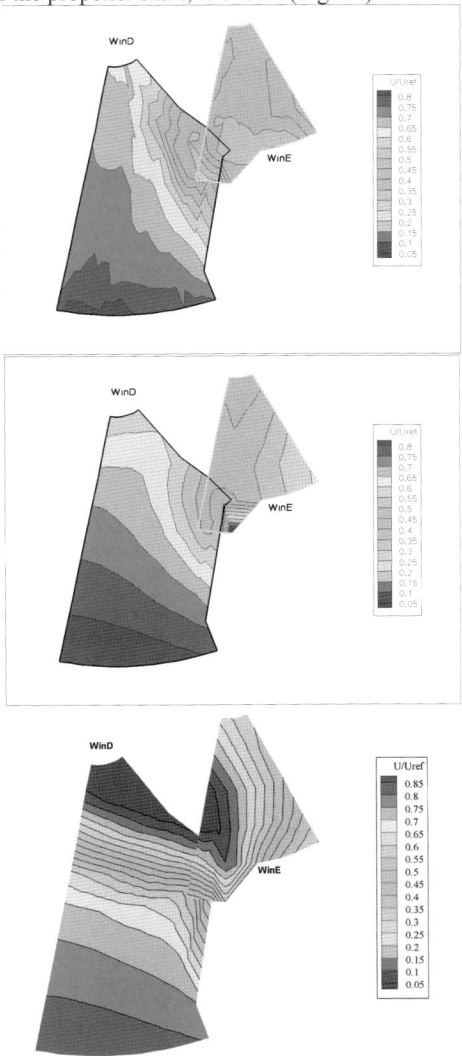

Fig. 16: "UILENSPIEGEL": FS, WIP, WinDE - Comparison on the isowake distribution between full scale experiments (top) and computations: ISIS (middle), PARNASSOS.(bottom)

Compared to the similar results shown in the previous section at model scale, one can observe that the isowake distortion is less pronounced at full scale, indicating a less intense longitudinal vorticity in that region. Moreover, the mean value of the longitudinal component of the velocity between the hull and the propeller shaft is around 0.45Uref at full scale when it is about 0.10Uref at model scale. This observation confirms the huge difference between model and full scale flows already observed on the topology of the near-wall flow discussed before. This scale effect is accurately predicted by ISIS-CFD, which provides computational isowakes in very good agreement with the sea measurements although computed with a standard k–w SST turbulence model. Examining the full-scale PARNASSOS prediction shows that the boundary layer thickness is predicted well but a clear over-estimation of the depth of the wake of the shaft is found in the computation.

Furthermore the flow behaviour at another section called WinAC located closer to the propeller nozzle are shown, but in front of the struts supporting the shaft hose and the nozzle (Fig. 17). In the ISIS results one can see the upwind influence of the struts illustrated by the distortion of the isowakes which is more pronounced than in the previous examined section. The PARNASSOS results, in which the struts are not present, show the acceleration of the flow in the wake of the shaft.

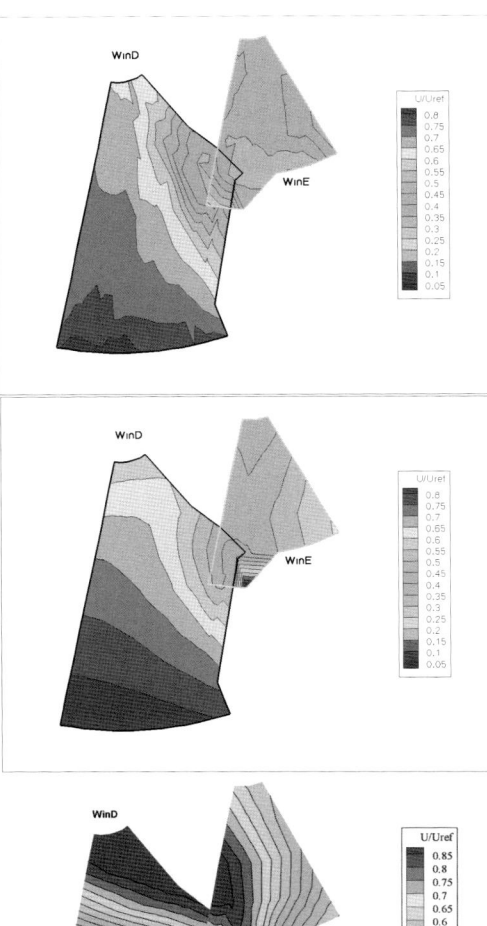

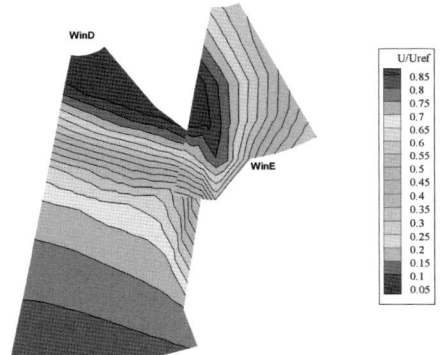

Fig. 16: "UILENSPIEGEL": FS, WIP, WinDE - Comparison on the isowake distribution between full scale experiments (top) and computations: ISIS (middle), PARNASSOS.(bottom)

As previously, a comparison between the full scale experiments and the computations at windows A and C is made (Fig. 18). Window C, located on the right hand side of the figure shows the thick boundary layer developing outside of the propeller shaft. The agreement between both computations and experiments is very good. Window A shows a more complex flow located between the hull and the shaft. Both experiments and ISIS computations reveal a distorted region of decelerated longitudinal flow with a mean value of 0.60Uref for the experiments and a slightly more pronounced deceleration in the computations with a mean value around 0.55Uref. The PARNASSOS computations show a slightly different shape of the wake.

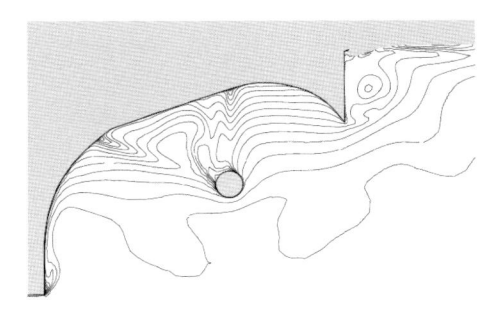

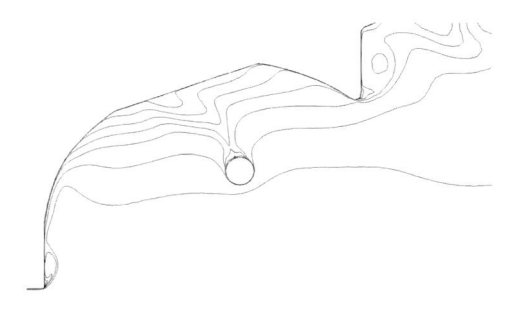

Fig. 17: "UILENSPIEGEL": FS,WIP, WinAC - Global view of the full scale isowakes Top figures: ISIS, bottom figure: PARNASSOS.

It may be concluded now that these CFD tools are suitable for a reliable prediction of the full scale flow. This means for the propeller manufacturers, amongst others, that they enter a new era of full scale based design without the need of translation from model scale to full scale wake data and its intrinsic doubts. The next paragraphs will show an actual design approach with the availability of full scale data.

A new design with the help of ISIS-CFD

Description

This case concerns a new dredger built by IHC HOLLAND Dredgers BV and referenced here as "IHC co 1246". For this hull, full scale flow is considered with working propeller and free surface under two conditions: loaded (CD1) configuration with shallow water and an empty (CD2) condition in deep water. For both cases, the hull has a prescribed constant speed and draught which will not specified for the sake of brevity.

Numerical details

Geometries have been meshed using the HEXPRESS grid generator. The computational domain is made of a rectangular box of size [-500m,500m]x[0,500m]x[-13.5mx8m] for (CD1) and [-500m,350m]x[0,500m]x[-200mx8m] for (CD2). For all configurations, the highest vertical resolution for free surface capturing is dZ=5cm leading to grids comprised of about 5 million nodes with 150 000 located on the hull.

Results

Wave profile along the hull and the symmetry plane are

Fig. 19 : IHC_Co_1246 : Loaded condition (CD1)

plottedfor the two conditions (Fig. 19 resp. 20).

Fig. 20: IHC_Co_1246 : Empty condition(CD2)

Although not illustrated, it is observed that the propeller influence is stronger with empty case (CD2) than with the loaded one (CD1). Flow field results are simply presented from limiting streamlines on the walls and plotted in stern region from a symmetry plane point of view for the loaded (Fig. 21) and for the empty conditions (Fig. 22), both with propeller in operation. For loaded conditions in finite depth (CD1), the separation near the symmetry plane and before the transom appears amplified when propeller is running. From the point of view of dredger builder, due to propeller suction and lack of water in front (in relation to that suction demand), the propeller obtains its needs from behind and trying to avoid this phenomenon in shallow water should be a progress.

For empty condition in deep water (CD2), the propeller suction cancels the small separation zone observed on the hull, just behind the headbox and no separation is detected from streamlines near the transom with/without propeller.

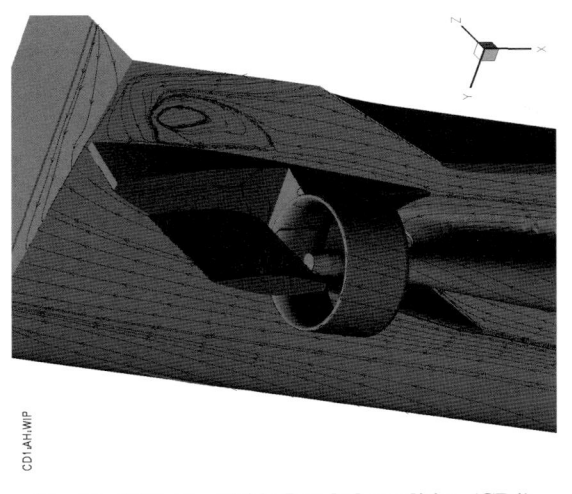

Fig. 21: IHC_Co_1246 : Loaded condition (CD1) with propeller- Wall streamlines

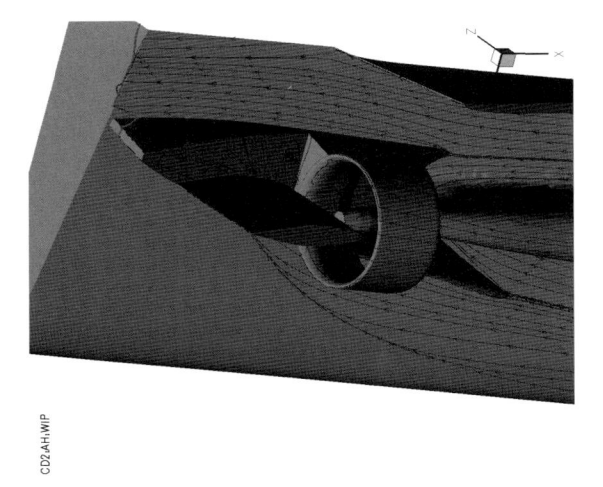

Fig. 22: IHC_Co_1246: Empty condition (CD2) with propeller- Wall streamlines

Propeller blade design on basis of a full scale wake field

It is really a challenge to make a propeller blade design for a dredger. The propeller is often extreme with respect to:

- Propeller load: high due to restricted draft.
- The mission profile: this covers conditions from idling at full shaft speed to full power in free running at ballast.

- Ducted propeller: the nozzle should work well also at free running at full power.

The highly loaded propeller requires a wake field with low density peaks else it will be difficult to avoid vibration and noise problems from the propeller. CFD, valid for full scale, is a fantastic tool for prediction of the real wake field. The results where the nozzle is included are beneficial to use, especially when a high skew design is necessary.

During the design of the propeller blade all the running conditions have to be taken into consideration. It is not possible to decide one design condition and make the best blade design and only do a small check for other conditions. The design process must be an iteration process which includes traditional model propeller data, lifting surface design tools as well as analysis tools. Input in the analysis is the propeller geometry and water velocities, what means wake field data.

Propeller nozzles are normal to use for towing ships such as tugs and trawlers. Then, the propeller is optimized to give the best thrust at low ship speed. The free running condition is not interesting in that case. For a dredger too the purpose of the nozzle is to have a high thrust at low speed: when dredging the resistance is high due to the draghead force when down to the sea bottom. Nevertheless, when free sailing at maximum speed, the nozzles must still give an addition to the propeller thrust. In that condition the nozzles proved to reduce noise and vibrations caused by the propeller. To optimize the propeller with respect to noise and vibrations, the wake field is very important. Normally, available data of the wake field is obtained from measurements on model scale with no nozzle mounted. One reason for this is the tradition of treating the nozzle and the propeller as one propulsion unit. For this unit it has been possible to get data from model series. Another reason is as earlier mentioned the flow separation and a chaotic wake field (Fig 3). Due to scale effect and to an operating propeller the situation will be so different from that was shown by the model test. Nevertheless, also a good model wake has to be scaled to full scale. Normally this is done by using the mean value from the wake field measurement and the effective wake at full scale. In this scaling also assumptions on effects of the nozzle and the running propeller are taken into consideration.

For a blade design that is made for IHC dredger Co. 1246, results from CFD calculations at full scale were available. The results covered wake field from the hull without appendages (Fig. 23), the hull with appendages and nozzle (Fig. 24) and finally the hull with appendages, nozzle and operating propeller (Fig. 25).

In all given wake fields as well as on different drafts and water depths there cannot be seen any tendency of flow separation or chaotic structure. Both wake fields (Fig. 23, Fig. 24) have been used in the design to determine a radial wake distribution which is used as input for lifting surface calculations. It is interesting to see the difference between these two. The speed is higher with the nozzle. The difference in speed over the disc is more or less the same but the wake peak is more pronounced for the case without nozzle. The nozzle has smoothed out the difference and the speed gradient has been smaller. This is what can be expected.

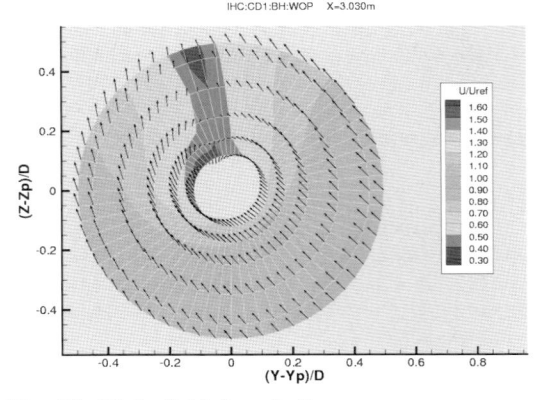

Fig. 23: Wake field, bare hull

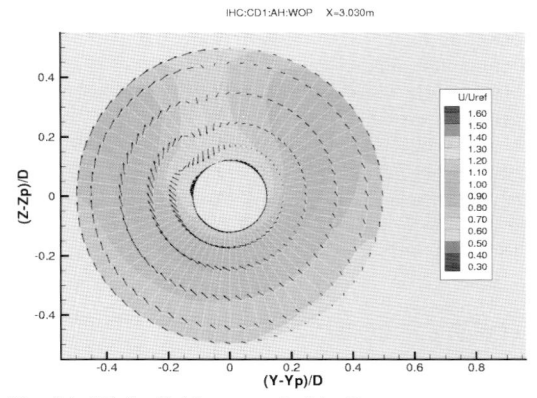

Fig. 24: Wake field, appended hull

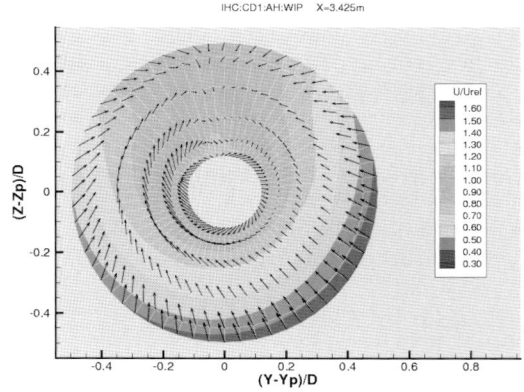

Fig. 25: Wake field, appended hull with working propeller

For the evaluation of the propeller design a lifting surface program for unsteady analysis has been used. The input is: shaft speed, propeller geometry and three dimensional wake data (Fig. 25). The propeller pitch and speed were adjusted to fit the propeller thrust and the torque. The sheet cavitation and tip vortex at free running at full power in ballast condition (Fig. 26) was believed to be critical.

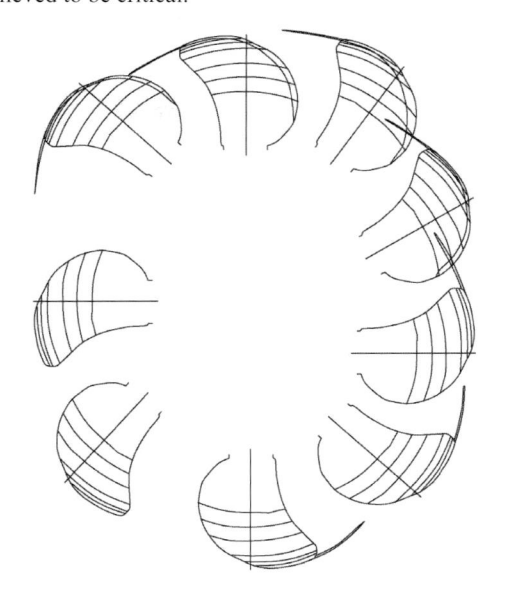

Fig. 26: Cavitation in free running condition

Also the criteria to avoid pressure side cavitation at dredging conditions at low drafts were investigated and finally fulfilled by adjusting pitch and camber of the propeller blade, combined with acceptable sheet cavitation at the same time.

The final blade design (Fig. 27) shows a moderate skewed propeller with a normal loaded blade tip. Both skew and tip load is favorable with respect to propeller efficiency. This was possible due to a moderate loaded propeller but also on confirmation from the analysis. The analysis is reliable because of the good wake field data from the CFD calculations.

For both design and analysis a lifting surface program still has been used. However, we believe that in a near future the power of CFD also will cover evaluation of cavitation phenomena for a rotating propeller in a unsteady wake field.

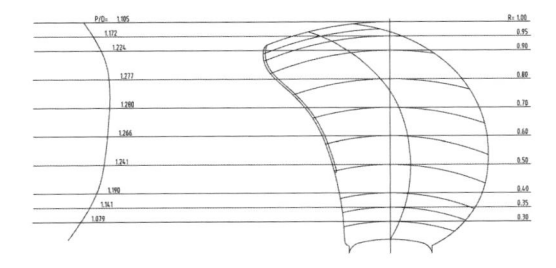

Fig. 27: Final blade design for IHC_Co_1246

Conclusions

The following conclusions can be drawn after the realization of the EFFORT project, some experience with improved CFD tools and the use of CFD results:

- Validation of CFD tools is indispensable.
- Full-scale flows are not dramatically more complicated to compute than model-scale flows.
- The turbulence modelling has influence on the wake prediction at full-scale for some hulls, but it proved to be less crucial at full scale than at model scale for some others. This shows that there is still a need for improved anisotropic turbulence models.
- Complex details as appendages require a high dense grid. However, extremely dense grids do not result in significant further improvements.
- There are only some CFD tools available which are suitable for a reliable prediction of the full scale flow and to deal with complicated ship hulls.
- The availability of accurate full scale wake data proved to be profitable for propeller blade design.

Acknowledgement

The EFFORT project was supported by the EC 5th Framework GROWTH program under grant G3RD-CT-2002-00810. This support is gratefully acknowledged.

References

[1] Starke, A.R., Windt, J., Raven, H.C., 'Validation of viscous flow and wake field predictions for ships at full scale', 26th Symp. Navel Hydrodyn., Rome, Italy, 2006

[2] Visonneau, M., Deng, G.B., Queuty, P., 'Computations of model and full scale flows around fully-appended ships with an unstructured RANSE solver', 26th Symp. Naval Hydrodynamics, Rome, Italy, 2006

[3] Eça, L., Hoekstra, M., 'An evalution of verification procedures for CFD applications', 24th Symp. Naval Hydrodynamics, Fukuoka, Japan, 2002

[4] Windt, J., 'Towards accurate wake predictions of twin-screw ships with an open-shaft stern configuration', 6th Num. Towing Tank Symp., Rome, Italy, 2003.

[5] Hoekstra, M., 'Numerical simulation of ship stern flows with a space-marching Navier Stokes method', Thesis, Technical University of Delft, October 1999.

[6] Hoekstra, M., Jager, A. de, Valkhof, H.H., 'Viscous flow calculations used for dredger design', PRADS2001, Shanghai, P.R. of China, September 2001.

[7] Starke, A., Windt, J., 'Two Examples of Hull-Form Optimization Using Viscous-Flow Computations', CFD Technology in Ship Hydrodynamics conference, London, United Kingdom, 2003.

[8] Hay, A. & Visonneau, 'Adaptive finite-volume solution of complex turbulent flows', Computers & Fluids, Vol. 36, Issue 8, pp. 1347-1363, September 2007.

[9] Duvigneau, R., Visonneau, M., Deng, G.B., 'On the role played by turbulence closures for hull shape optimization at model and full scale', Marine Science and Technology, Vol. 153, No 8(1), pp. 1-25, 2003.

Stern Flow Analysis and Design Practice for the Improvement of Self-propulsion Performance of Twin-skeg Ships

D. W. Park [1], M. G. Kim [1], S. H. Chung [1] and Y. K. Chung [2]

[1] Maritime Research Institute, Hyundai Heavy Industries Co., Ulsan, Korea
[2] Ship Development Team, Hyundai Heavy Industries Co., Ulsan, Korea

Abstract

Hydrodynamic standards have been derived for the improvement of propulsive performance of twin-skeg hull forms. Three important physical observations were used in the optimization of design practice for the stern hull form of twin-skeg ships: flow line patterns on the skeg surface, flow balance on both sides of skeg surface and nominal wake distribution in the propeller plane. Numerical calculations and model tests have been compared to validate a CFD code used in the current work. Based on the stern flow analysis for the evaluation of self-propulsion performance, effects of stern skeg arrangement on the propulsion efficiency, i.e. the distance between skegs and the angle of the skeg with respect to shaft centerline, were intensively investigated. An optimized hull form design for a twin-skeg ship was developed using the design practice derived in this work.

Keywords

Twin-skeg ship; Hydrodynamic standards; Stern flow; Optimized hull form; CFD; Model test at towing tank

Introduction

As the ship size becomes larger, twin-skeg ships whose engine power is transmitted to the propellers through twin shafts have recently emerged as a design alternative. For example, for large LNG carriers of the cargo capacity over 200,000 m^3, the propulsion system consisted of two diesel engines, two shafts and two propellers. Shipyards are currently taking orders for the 267,000 m^3 ultra-large LNG carrier, which requires studies on hull form design for the improvement of speed performance. CFD is now widely used in the study of hull form design and ship flow analysis using CFD showing good agreements, at least qualitatively, with the model tests at towing tank.

Besides the analysis of resistance and propulsion, CFD is also applied to the assessment of the maneuvering performances of ships. Kim et al. (2004, 2005) treated propeller-induced hydrodynamic force as body force and performed viscous flow analysis to assess self-propulsion performance of ships. Kim et al. (2006) carried out viscous flow analysis for the bare hull, bare hull-rudder and bare hull-rudder-propeller. Kim et al. (2006) predicted self-propulsion performance of ships by solving the unsteady hull-propeller interaction problem using body force distribution and RANS equations.

In this work, hull form design of an ultra-large LNG carrier and flow analysis for the ship using a commercial CFD code (FLUENT) is presented. Emphasis was laid on the derivation of the most critical and practical skeg parameters to achieve the improvement in ship speed. The initiative of the present work was to establish design practice to improve self-propulsion performance of the twin-skeg ships when the shape of the stern skeg was changed.

Numerical flow simulations and as well as model tests were carried out for the two ships whose design of stern skeg was largely different. Interrogations were made on the pattern of the limiting streamlines on the skeg surface, flow balance between the inner and outer side of the skeg, and nominal wake distribution in the skeg tunnel. Through the interrogations for stern flow of the ships, an effective standard to assess the self-propulsive performance of the twin-skeg ship was established.

Based on the standard established in the present work, self-propulsion performance was investigated when geometrical variation in the inclined angle of the skeg and the distance between the two skegs was imposed on the ship stern. Through the investigation, an optimized stern hull form was derived. Model tests were carried out for the optimized hull and the existing hull design and the speed performance was compared. Model tests also provided validation data for the hydrodynamic standards derived in this work.

Work flow of the present study

The primary objective of the current work is to establish efficient standards using numerical calculations to improve the propulsive performance of twin-skeg ships. Extensive numerical simulations were carried out to investigate stern flow to evaluate the self-propulsion performance. Using the design practice based on the numerical calculations, optimized stern hull form of a twin-skeg ship was developed. Model tests in the towing tank were conducted to interrogate the validity of the design practice and performance evaluation based on the numerical calculations. Finally the speed performance of the optimized hull form was evaluated in the model tests. The design procedure used in the present work is summarized in Fig. 1.

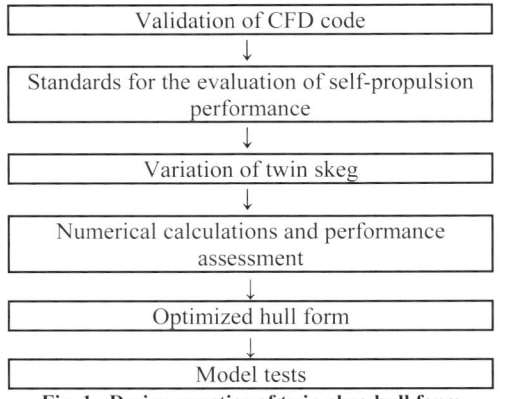

Fig. 1 Design practice of twin-skeg hull form

Numerical method

Coordinate system and governing equations

The coordinate system(x,y,z) is defined as positive x in the flow direction, positive y starboard and positive z upward where the origin locates at the intersection of centerplane, amidships and undisturbed free surface as shown in Fig. 2. All the physical quantities in the present study are nondimensionalized by the ship length (Lpp), ship speed (Vs) and fluid density (ρ). The continuity equation and momentum equation for the flow field is shown in Equations (1) and (2) respectively:

$$\frac{\partial U_i}{\partial x_i} = 0 \tag{1}$$

$$\frac{\partial U_i}{\partial t} + U_l \frac{\partial U_i}{\partial x_l} = -\frac{\partial p}{\partial x_i} + \frac{\partial}{\partial x_l}\left(\frac{1}{R_N}\frac{\partial U_i}{\partial x_l} - \overline{u_i u_l}\right) \tag{2}$$

where $U_i = (U,V,W)$ are velocity components in $x_i = (x,y,z)$ directions while p, R_N and $-\overline{u_i u_l}$ are pressure, Reynolds number and Reynolds stress, respectively.

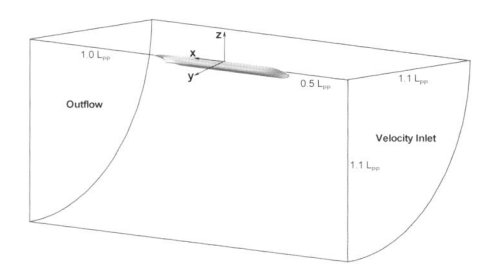

Fig. 2 Computational domain and coordinate system

Numerical grid and calculation conditions

A commercial code, Gridgen V15, was used to generate the ship hull surface and spatial grid system. The number of grids for the object ship was about 530,000. The distance of the first grid point off the ship surface maintained y+ $\approx$ 100 that is within a log-law region.

Since the main concern of this work was to investigate self-propulsion performance when the distance between skegs and the angle of the skeg of aft-body are varied, the grid of fore-body remained to be the same but the grid of aft-body was changed according to the variation of stern hull shape. An example of grid system of the aft-body of a twin-skeg ship used in the present work is shown in Fig. 3. The flow computation was conducted for double-body model of the bare hull using a commercial CFD code (FLUENT). The computational condition of flow field applied in this work is shown in Table 1.

Using the commercial CFD code flow fields around the stern skeg were computed: limiting streamlines along the aft-body, velocity vectors, pressures on the hull surface and nominal wake distribution in the propeller plane were calculated. These hydrodynamic characteristics were visualized to provide engineering data for use in the assessment of the hydrodynamic performance of the ships.

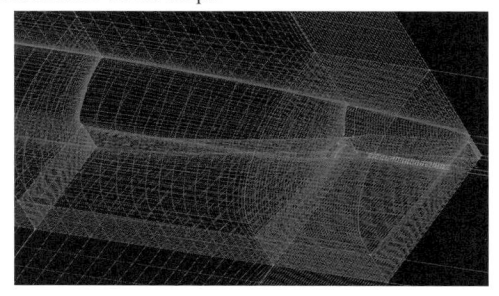

Fig. 3 Numerical grid for the aft-body of a twin-skeg ship

Stern flow analysis

Numerical flow analysis in model scale was performed for the two existing ship designs (hereafter referred to as ship A and B) whose experimental data was already acquired in the model tests at a towing tank. The geometric features for the stern part of the ships A and B are illustrated in Fig. 4. A photo of a ship model used in the model tests is presented in Fig. 5. The direction of propeller rotation is inward for both of the ships.

For the validation of the CFD code used in the present work, numerical flow characteristics in the stern region of the model ships were intensively compared with those in the experiments. Fig. 6 and Fig. 7 demonstrate experimental and computational wake distribution in the starboard propeller plane of the ships A and B, respectively.

The experimental wake distributions shown in Fig. 6 exhibit important flow characteristics between the two stern shapes: Shown in zone I, left-hand half side of the propeller plane, higher axial flow velocities are achieved in ship B when compared to ship A. On the contrary, in the upper right-hand side of the plane, zone II, axial flow velocities in ship B are lower than ship A.

Table 1 Computational conditions

	Specified condition	Remark
Computational domain	$-L_{PP} \leq x \leq 1.5\ L_{PP}$, $0 \leq y \leq 1.1\ L_{PP}$, $0 \leq z \leq -1.1\ L_{PP}$	Model ship length (L_{PP}): 7.79 m Domain for ship model: $-0.5\ L_{PP} \leq x \leq 0.5\ L_{PP}$
F_N	0.176	Design speed
R_N (Model)	11.708×10^6	Design speed
Boundary conditions	Inlet region: velocity Inlet Outlet region: outflow Hull surface: wall Remaining region: symmetry	
Turbulence model	Reynolds stress	Near wall, standard wall function is used
Velocity-pressure coupling	SIMPLE	

The velocity contour of ship B is skewed to the direction of propeller rotation when com-pared to ship A. Low flow velocity distribution is clearly observed in ship B in zone III. As can be observed in zone IV where transverse velocity vectors are presented, stronger rotational flow is induced in ship B in the upper left-hand inner region of the propeller plane.

The numerical flow simulations for the two ships indicated the validity of the CFD code. Axial and transverse flow velocities illustrated in Fig. 7 demonstrate that the code simulates the stern flow with satisfactory accuracy at least in the qualitative sense. It is likely that the quality and the number of grids used in the present simulations are adequate for the comparative assessment of the stern flow field between the design alternatives.

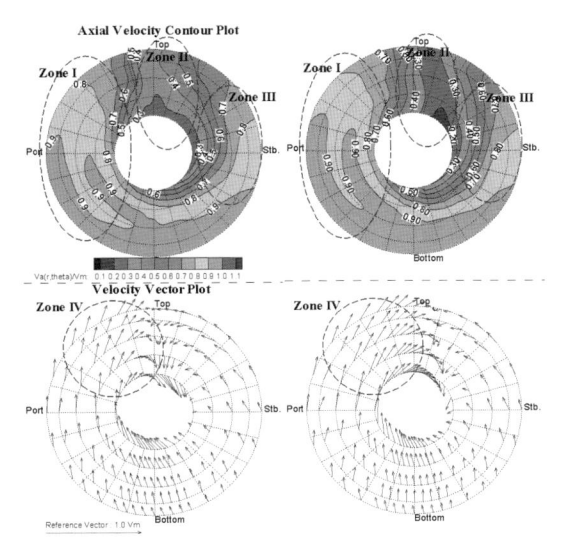

Fig. 6 Distribution of experimental velocity components in the propeller plane (left: Ship A, Right: Ship B)

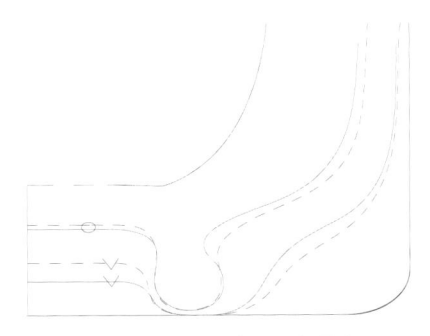

Fig. 4 Comparison of stern hull forms (solid line: Ship A, dashed line: Ship B)

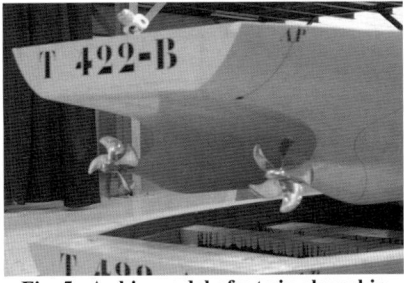

Fig. 5 A ship model of a twin-skeg ship

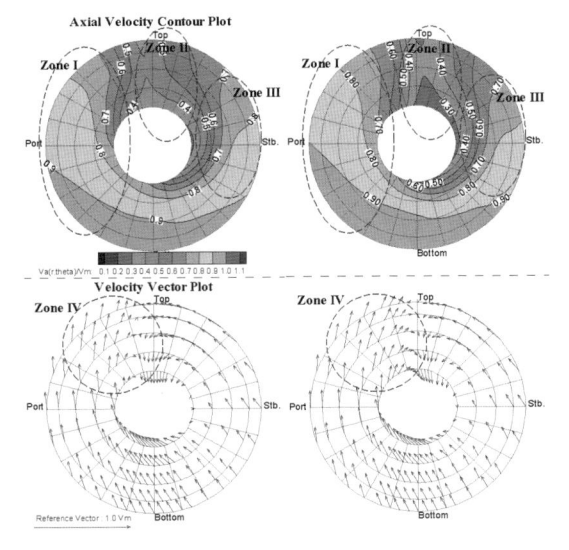

Fig. 7 Distribution of computational velocity components in the propeller plane (left: Ship A, right: Ship B)

Standards for the evaluation of self-propulsion performance of the twin-skeg ships

Standards to be used in the assessment of the self-propulsion performance of twin-skeg design alternatives were established in this work. The standards are based on the analysis of stern flows in the twin-skeg ship. Self-propulsion characteristics for ships A and B were used to provide solid background in the establishment of the standards. Table 2 shows experimental comparison of propulsive coefficients and effective power of ships A and B. Although ship A exhibits superior efficiency in effective horsepower by 2.7%, ship B has superior performance in quasi-propulsive efficiency by 1.8%. The standards for the superior propulsive efficiency have been established based on the experiments and numerical simulations:

Table 2 Comparison of model tests between Ship A and Ship B

Ship	EHP (%)	w_{TS}	t	η_H	η_O	η_D (%)	BHP (%)
Ship A	100.0	0.300	0.246	1.078	0.677	100.0	100.0
Ship B	102.7	0.291	0.216	1.105	0.682	101.8	101.0

Standard 1

Experimental and numerical circumferential mean axial velocities in the propeller plane are presented in Fig. 8 and 9 respectively where r denotes radial distance from shaft center, R is radius of propeller, V_A denotes axial flow velocity, and V_M denotes incoming flow velocity. In the figures, marked solid line represents mean velocity over the entire propeller plane but marked dashed line represents mean velocity over the left-hand half plane only. Numerical simulations show quite good agreement with the experimental mean velocities.

Observed in the mean velocities over the entire propeller plane, axial flow velocities in the stern region of ship A are slightly higher than ship B. In the left-hand half plane, flow velocity for ship B is much higher than ship A. From this investigation on the mean flow velocities in the propeller plane in the stern region, together with the propulsive coefficient estimated from the model tests, it can be deduced that acceleration of inflow on to the propeller plane, i.e. high velocity in the inner region of the skeg will improve propulsive efficiency when the propeller is rotating inward or counterclockwise.

Standard 2

Numerical pressure distribution and limiting streamlines on the inner and outer skeg stern are presented in Fig. 10 and Fig. 11 respectively. As seen in Fig. 10, in the inner side of the skeg, flow lines on ship B are straightened out in the upper part of the stern bulb without the twisting of streamlines. On the contrary, in the outer side of the skeg, streamlines of ship A exhibit relatively smooth distribution resulting in smaller dead water area. Accordingly, in viewpoint of self-propulsion, streamline distribution over both sides of the stern skeg is to be straightforward since it implies less flow separation in the stern area.

Standard 3

Numerical pressure and streamline distribution on the bottom of the stern area including stern hangover are shown in Fig. 12. Flow line patterns from the end of the stern bulb to the transom stern are clearly observed. The flow of ship B in the area over stern bulb to transom stern shows straightforward flow lines when compared to that of ship A. The pronounced smooth flow line in ship B implies that a balance between the flow intensity over the inner and outer side of the stern skeg can be an important parameter for the self-propulsion efficiency.

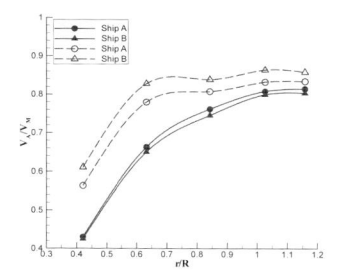

Fig. 8 Experimental circumferential mean value for the r/R
(solid line: mean velocity over the entire propeller plane
dashed line: mean velocity over the left-hand half plane)

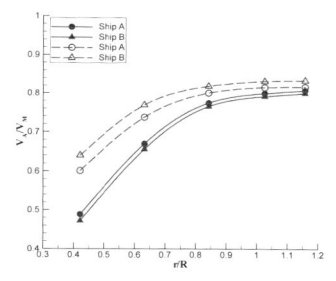

Fig. 9 Computational circumferential mean value for the r/R
(solid line: mean velocity over the entire propeller plane
dashed line: mean velocity over the left-hand half plane)

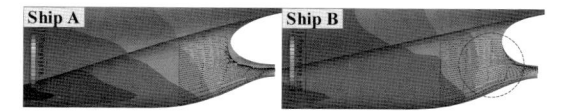

Fig. 10 Limiting streamlines on the inner skeg stern (computation)

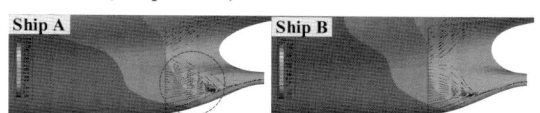

Fig. 11 Limiting streamlines on the outer skeg stern (computation)

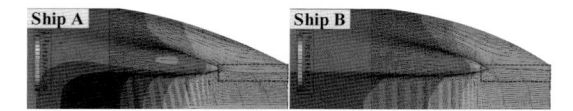

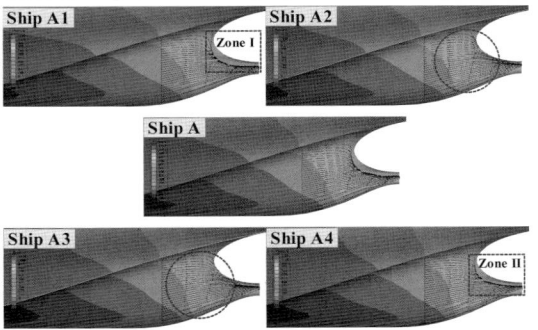

Fig. 12 Limiting streamlines on the bottom skeg stern (computation)

Variations of stern-skeg arrangement and stern flow analysis

To validate the standards for use in the improvement of the self-propulsion performance of twin-skeg ships, ship A was selected as a mother ship to which geometric variations in stern skeg would be applied. Although ship B exhibited superior quasi-propulsive efficiency to that of ship A as shown in Table 2, ship B could not be selected as a design practice since she did not satisfy propeller cavitation requirement due to the low flow velocities shown in Fig. 6 and Fig. 7.

Two design parameters in stern skeg arrangement were selected for variation: distance between two skegs and the inclination angle of a skeg. Figure 13 shows a schematic view of the variations in stern skeg arrangement applied in the present work. For ship A the ratio of the distance between the skeg and the half-breadth of the ship is 40% and its skeg inclination angle is 7 degrees.

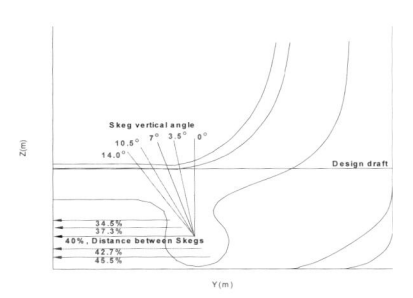

Fig. 13 Variations in stern skeg arrangement

Effects of the distance between skegs on the stern flow

The distance between the skegs of ship A was varied in two ways: narrower ships (ship A1 and ship A2) and wider ships (ship A3 and ship A4). Table 3 shows the skeg distance of the ships of whose stern flow characteristics were investigated.

Table 3 Skeg distance of the ship

Ship	Percentage of Skeg distance/Ship half-breadth	Remark
Ship A1	34.5%	
Ship A2	37.3%	
Ship A	40.0%	Mother ship
Ship A3	42.7%	
Ship A4	45.5%	

Numerical flow simulations for the ships were carried out to investigate flow patterns in the skeg stern area that may impact the self-propulsion performance of the ships. Figures 14 to 16 present the pressure distribution and limiting streamlines of the ships listed in Table 3 in the stern area at the inner side of skeg, the stern area at the outer side of skeg, and the bottom area including stern overhang respectively.

In zone I, the inner side of stern skeg, the streamlines along the upper part of the stern bulb of ship A1 (the ship with the smallest skeg distance) shows a twisting pattern which indicates large flow separation in the zone. The flow separation and the resulting distorted flow over the stern bulb will have a negative impact on the propeller efficiency. Similarly in zone II of ship A4 (the ship with the largest skeg distance), a twisting flow pattern is observed in the upper part of the stern bulb. On the contrary, as observed in the circled area on the upper part of the stern bulb, flow lines of ships A2 and A3 are straightened out without twisting. The investigation in flow pattern at the inner side of the stern skeg indicates that there are critical skeg distances as demonstrated in ship A2 and A3 to accelerate the flow into the propeller plane which in turn will improve the propulsion efficiency. As shown in Fig. 15, when investigating the streamlines at the outer side of the skeg, it is likely that ship A1 has the best flow characteristic and the other ships have almost identical flow patterns.

Figure 16 shows the streamlines on the bottom of the skeg area including stern overhang. Special attention is necessary on the streamlines emitting from the end of the stern bulb to the stern overhang. The streamlines in this area exhibit the flow balance between flow velocities in the inner and outer side of the stern sekg. As can be seen in the squared region of ship A1, no flow balance is retained due to the interaction between the slow flow in the inner side of the skeg demonstrated in Fig. 14 and the relatively fast flow in the outer side of the skeg in Fig. 15. The flow balance for ship A2 is also disturbed due to the interaction between the fast flow in the inner side of the skeg and the slow flow in the outer side of the skeg. The most prominent flow balance is achieved in ship A3. Streamlines from the end of stern bulb in ship A4 are bending toward the stern skeg overhang.

In addition to the interrogations onto the flow characteristics in the stern skeg area according to the Standard 2 and 3, wake distribution on the propeller plane was also investigated in accordance with Standard 1. Accordingly ship A3 was selected a candidate design that will improve the self-propulsion efficiency.

Fig. 14 Limiting streamlines on the inner skeg stern (computation)

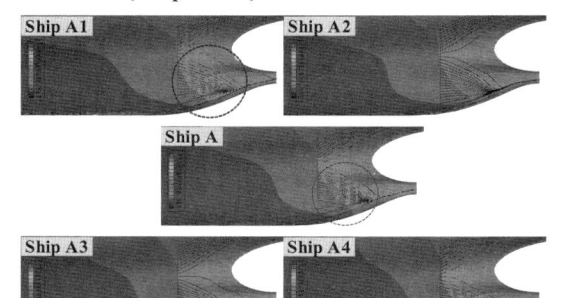

Fig. 15 Limiting streamlines on the outer skeg stern (computation)

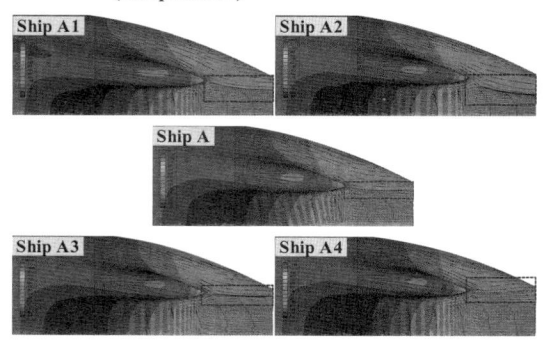

Fig. 16 Limiting streamlines on the bottom skeg stern (computation)

Effect of the skeg angle on the stern flow

Skeg angles of ± 3.5 degrees and ± 7 degrees were systematically added to the candidate ship A3 whose original skeg angle was 7 degrees. The resulting skeg arrangements are shown in Fig. 13 and Table 4.

Stern flow analysis was performed for the five design alternatives listed in Table 4 in accordance with the standards derived in the present work, resulting in the final selection of ship A3 as a candidate design to improve the self-propulsion efficiency of the twin skeg ship. In the variation of skeg angles, no prominent discrepancies in the stern flow characteristics were investigated. The investigation implies that the variation in skeg angle had little influence on the stern flow around the skeg area but the distance between the skegs are critical design parameter to improve the stern flow.

Table 4 Skeg angle of the ship

Variation in skeg angle	Absolute inclination angle	Remark
Ship A3 -7.0°	0.0°	
Ship A3 -3.5°	3.5°	
Ship A3	7.0°	Selected to be final candidate
Ship A3 +3.5°	10.5°	
Ship A3 +7.0°	14.0°	

Optimized stern hull form and validation of the standards

An optimized stern hull form of ship A3 (hereafter referred to as the optimized ship) showing favorable flow characteristics was selected out of nine candidates design practices. The design parameters and body plan of stern hull forms for the mother ship and the optimized ship are presented in Table 5 and Fig. 17.

Table 5 Design parameters of the mother ship and optimized ship

Ship design	Skeg distance/Ship half-breadth	Skeg angle
Mother ship	40.0%	7.0°
Optimized ship	42.7%	7.0°

Fig. 17 Comparison of stern hull forms (Mother ship vs. Optimized ship)

Numerical stern flow analysis

Fig. 18 shows comparison of wake distribution at the propeller plane for the mother ship and the optimized ship. Investigating the zones I to IV in the wake distribution, the flow quality of the optimized ship was much improved: more pronounced and faster axial flow distribution in the top part of the propeller plane, extension of higher velocity flow in the left-hand and right-hand side of the propeller plane, and higher transverse flow distribution in the upper left-hand side of the plane implying less propeller pitch. Figure 19 shows circumferential mean axial velocity in the radial direction averaged over the entire and left-hand half of the plane. It is easily observed that the overall flow velocity of the optimized ship is much improved in the entire propeller plane and left-hand half plane as well.

Model tests at the towing tank

Resistance, self-propulsion tests and wake measurement to evaluate the speed performance and to validate the design standards derived in the present work were carried out for the mother ship and the optimized ship in the towing tank. The final predictions of the resistance and self-propulsion performance are summarized in Table 6.

Resistance performance for the bare hull of the optimized ship shows 0.5% improvement in effective horsepower when compared to the mother ship. Wake measurements for the optimized ship and the mother ship are presented in Fig. 20 and Fig. 21. As can be observed in Fig. 20, wake in the propeller plane of the optimized ship was evenly distributed and the velocity distribution showed improvement in the left-hand side of the propeller plane for the propeller rotating counterclockwise. Figure 21 shows circumferential mean axial velocities over the entire propeller plane and left-hand half plane. It can be concluded from the measurements that the numerical stern flow simulations demonstrated excellent qualitative agreement with the experiments.

Hull efficiency of the optimized ship exhibits improvement because of the simultaneous decreases in the effective wake fraction and the thrust deduction fraction, clearly indicating that the modified stern skeg arrangement was effective in the self-propulsion performance of the ship. In addition, due to the improvement in wake distribution in the propeller plane of the optimized ship, advance ratio of the propeller was increased. This increase in the advance ratio subsequently resulted in the improvement of propeller efficiency as was expected in the numerical stern flow analysis. In total, the quasi-propulsive efficiency of the optimized ship achieved 2% increase when compared to the mother ship. Finally 2.5% improvements in brake horsepower and a speed gain of 0.15 knots were achieved in the optimized ship when compared to the mother ship.

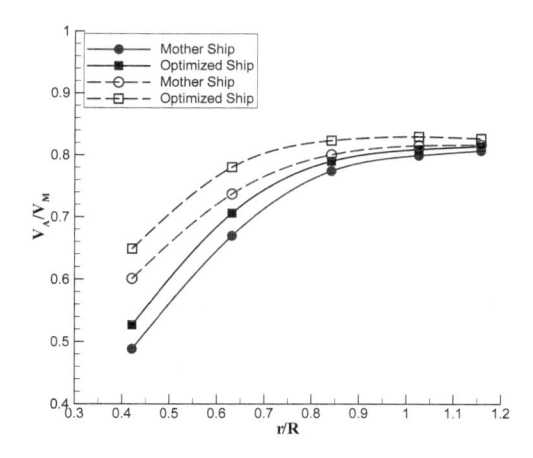

Fig. 19 Computational circumferential mean value for the r/R
(solid line: mean velocity over the entire propeller plane
dashed line: mean velocity over the left-hand half plane)

Table 6 Comparison of model tests between the mothership and the optimized ship

Ship	EHP (%)	w_{TS}	t	η_H	η_O	η_D (%)	BHP (%)
Mother Ship	100.0	0.300	0.246	1.078	0.677	100.0	100.0
Optimized Ship	99.5	0.282	0.218	1.090	0.687	102.0	97.6

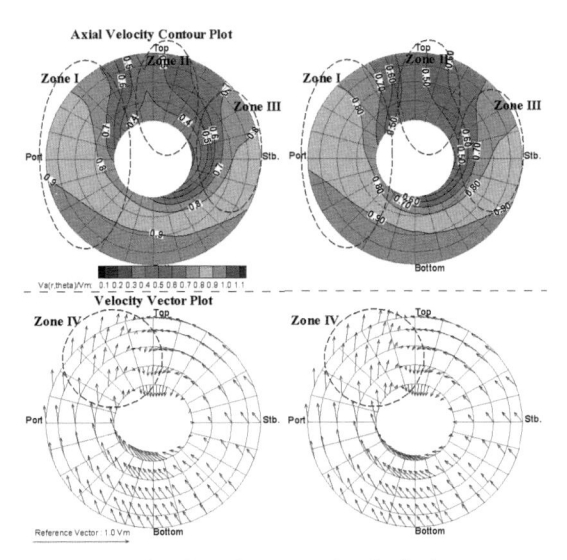

Fig. 18 Distribution of computational velocity components in the propeller plane
(left: mother ship, right: optimized ship)

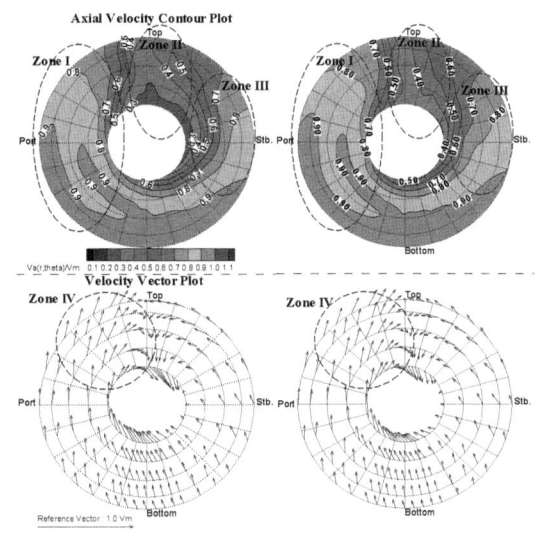

Fig. 20 Distribution of experimental velocity components in the propeller plane
(left: mother ship, right: optimized ship)

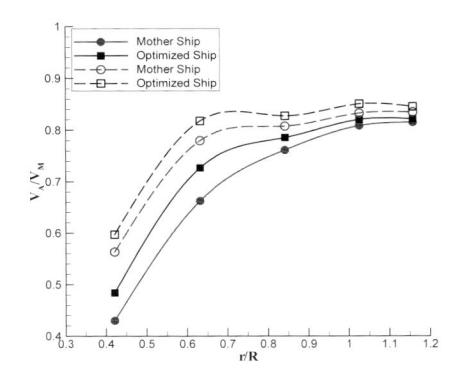

Fig. 21 Experimental circumferential mean value for the r/R
(solid line: mean velocity over the entire propeller plane
dashed line: mean velocity over the left-hand half plane)

Conclusions

Three important hydrodynamic standards that can be effectively used in the hull form design practice of twin-skeg ships have been derived in the present work. The three hydrodynamic standards for use in the improvement of propulsive efficiencies of the twin-skeg ships involve high axial velocities in the skeg tunnel, straightforward flow lines along the stern bulb, and flow balance between the inner and outer side of the stern skeg to ensure straightforward streamlines along the stern overhang. The establishment of the standards was based on the numerical stern flow simulations and model experiments. Numerical analysis has been extensively used in the assessment of the complicated ship stern flows that impacts the propulsive efficiencies of the twin-skeg ships. The validity of a CFD code for use in the numerical stern flow analysis was investigated through the comparison with the experimental flow behaviors.

Effects of the variation of design parameters in the stern skeg arrangement on the behavior of stern flow have been interrogated to optimize the stern hull form of twin-skeg ships in viewpoint of self-propulsion performance. Starting with a mother ship that was adopted in the design practice for a large LNG carrier in shipyard, an optimized hull form was derived out of nine design alternatives through the numerical stern flow analysis and the three hydrodynamic standards.

Finally hydrodynamic performance of the mother ship and the optimized ship were compared through the model experiments at a towing tank. The optimized hull form showed a speed gain of 0.15 knots when compared to the speed of the mother ship. This experimental comparison exhibited the validity of the three hydrodynamic standards established in the present work. It was shown that a minor change in stern hull form of the twin-skeg ship, although it is a small fraction of total hull geometry, might result in critical change in stern flow and subsequently in speed performance of the twin-skeg ship.

References

Boo, K. T. and Hong, C. B. (2006), "Self-Propulsion Performance using CFD", SNAK Annual Autumn Meeting

Hino, T. (2005),"Proceeding of CFD Workshop". Tokyo, Japan

Kim, K. H., Kim, J. J. and Choi, S. H. (2005), "Computation of Viscous Flow around Hull-Propeller-Rudder with Body Force Method", SNAK Annual Autumn Meeting

Kim, H. T., Kim, H. T. and Van, S. H. (2006), "Numerical Analysis of Turbulent Flows around a Ship with Twin-skegs by skeg distance", SNAK Spring Autumn Meeting

Kim, J. J., Paik, K. J., Lee, Y. C. and Kim, H. T. (2006),"A Numerical Study of Tubulent Viscous Flow around a Self Propelled Ship", SNAK Spring Autumn Meeting

Kodama, Y. (1994), "Proceedings of CFD Workshop Tokto 1994", Janpan

Larsson, L. (1980), "SSPA-ITTC Workshop on Ship Boundary Layers", SSPA Publication No. 90.

Larsson, L., Patel, V. C. and Dyne, G. (1991), "Ship Viscous Flow : Proceedings of 1990 SSPA-CTH-IIHR Workshop", Flowtech International AB, Gothenburg, Sweden

Larsson, L. F., Stern, F. and Bertram, V. (2000),"A Workshop on Numerical Ship Hydrodynamics, Gothenberg, Sweden.

Park, I. R., Kim, W. J. and Van, S. H. (2004), "Grid Generation and Flow Analysis around a Twin-Skeg Container Ship", Journal of the Society of Naval Architects of Korea, 15-22.

Ship Hull Simulations with a Coupled Solution Algorithm

Philip J. Zwart [1], Philippe G. Godin [1], Justin Penrose [2], Shin Hyung Rhee [3]

[1] ANSYS Canada
Waterloo, Ontario, Canada
[2] ANSYS Europe
Milton Park, U.K.
[3] Seoul National University
Kwanak-gu Seoul, Korea

Abstract

An accurate, efficient algorithm for solving free surface flows around ship hulls is described. Accuracy is achieved using a compressive advection discretization which maintains a sharp free surface interface representation without relying on a small timestep. Efficiency is obtained using a solution algorithm which implicitly couples velocity, pressure, and volume fractions. The algorithm has been implemented in the ANSYS CFX software package, and is validated by comparing with experimental data on a number of ship hull benchmark cases in both steady and transient conditions.

Keywords

VOF; Marine; Free-surface; Ship hull; CFD.

Introduction

Simulating fluid flow around ship hulls is useful for a number of reasons, including exploring the effect of hull shape on drag and understanding ship dynamics in seakeeping exercises. For CFD to be fully accepted in the marine industry for these applications, CFD solvers need to deliver accurate, efficient simulations in both steady-state and transient situations.

Accuracy requires careful attention to both physical modeling (particularly the effects of turbulence) and numerical discretization. There have been a variety of numerical approaches to free surface flows, including surface-adaptive methods, interface-capturing methods, and interface-tracking methods. Surface-adaptive methods such as (Raithby, G. D., Xu, W.-X., and Stubley, G. D. (1995)), are useful for certain classes of flows, but become very cumbersome for complex geometries and complex interface topologies.

Interface-capturing and interface-tracking methods overcome these limitations by having a fixed mesh which spans the interface location. They solve an additional equation for the volume fraction of one of the phases; they are therefore often called Volume-of-Fluid (VOF) methods. Interface-tracking methods obtain a high fidelity by having an explicit representation of the interface geometry at all times (Kothe, D.B., Rider, W.J., Mosso, S.J., and Brock, J.S. (1996)). Interface-capturing methods, on the other hand, use a continuum advection discretization leading to a smeared representation of the interface. The smearing can be minimized by using a compressive advection scheme, such as the donor-acceptor (Hirt, C.W. and Nichols, B.D., (1981)) or CICSAM (Ubbink, O. and Issa, R. I. (1999)) methods. These methods use controlled downwinding, and therefore small timesteps, to obtain compressiveness, even for steady-state simulations. The method described here uses a compressive advection scheme whose compressive properties are independent of the timestep (Zwart, P. J. (2005)).

The other requirement for practical free surface calculations is an efficient solution algorithm. Usual solution algorithms require small timesteps or heavy underrelaxation factors and long solution times. The convergence difficulties may be traced to the use of a segregated solution algorithm, which treat the strong inter-equation couplings between pressure, velocity, and volume fraction explicitly. Small timesteps are therefore required for numerical stability. In a recent paper (Zwart, P. J., Burns, A. D. B, and Galpin, P. F. (2007)), a new implicitly-coupled approach developed by ANSYS CFX has been described; it removes the need for small timesteps and leads to efficient solutions. This method will be described in this paper, together with its application to some ship hull calculations.

Mathematical Model

Free surface flows are a special class of multiphase flow in which it is often appropriate to assume a single velocity field u^i at each point in space. We refer to the resulting model as *homogeneous multiphase flow*. Let ρ_α and r_α represent the density and volume fraction of phase α. There is one continuity equation for each phase:

$$\frac{\partial(r_\alpha \rho_\alpha)}{\partial t} + \frac{\partial(r_\alpha \rho_\alpha u^i)}{\partial x^i} = 0. \quad (1)$$

Momentum conservation requires that

$$\frac{\partial(\rho_m u^i)}{\partial t} + \frac{\partial(\rho_m u^j u^i)}{\partial x^j}$$
$$= -\frac{\partial P}{\partial x^i} + \rho_m g^i + \frac{\partial \tau_m^{ji}}{\partial x^j}. \quad (2)$$

where P is the pressure; ρ_m is the mixture density

$$\rho_m = \sum_{\alpha=1}^{N} r_\alpha \rho_\alpha; \quad (3)$$

and τ_m^{ji} is the mixture stress tensor

$$\tau_m^{ji} = \mu_m \left(\frac{\partial u^i}{\partial x^j} + \frac{\partial u^j}{\partial x^i} \right) \quad (4)$$

$$\mu_m = \sum_{\alpha=1}^{N} r_\alpha \mu_\alpha. \quad (5)$$

This mathematical model is general for N phases, although in practice it is usually two (air and water).

We also have the volume continuity constraint that the volume fractions must sum to unity:

$$\sum_{\alpha=1}^{N} r_\alpha = 1. \quad (6)$$

These equations are augmented by a model for turbulence stress. Various eddy viscosity, Reynolds Stress, and boundary layer transition models are available in the solver.

NUMERICAL MODEL

Domain Discretization

The conservation equations described above are discretized using an element-based finite volume method (Schneider, G. E. and Raw, M. J. (1987)). The mesh may consist of tetrahedral, prismatic, pyramid, and hexahedral elements. A polyhedral control volume is constructed around each mesh vertex, as illustrated in Figure 1. Fluxes are discretized at the subfaces, or integration points, between adjacent control volumes within a particular element. Integration point quantities such as pressure and velocity gradients are obtained from vertex values using finite element shape functions, with the exception of advected variables which are obtained using an upwind-biased discretization.

Equation Discretization

We now consider the discretization of the conservation equations (1) and (2) at each control volume. The discretization is fully conservative and implicit. The conservation equations are integrated over each control volume, volume integrals are converted to surface integrals using Gauss' divergence theorem. In the following discussion V represents the volume of a control volume, A_{ip}^i the area vector of a subface corresponding to an integration point, δt the time step, and the superscripts $n+1$ and n mean that the quantity is evaluated at the new and old time step, respectively.

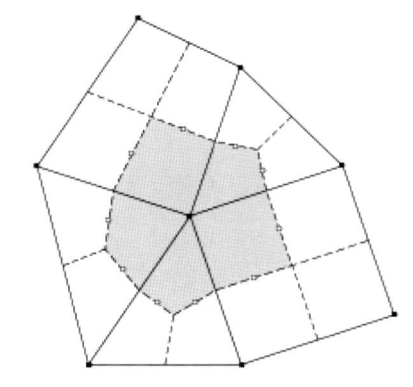

Figure 1: Element-based finite volume discretization of the spatial domain. Solid lines define element boundaries and dashed lines divide elements into sectors. Solution unknowns are colocated at the vertices (●), and surface fluxes are evaluated at integration points (○). A polyhedral control volume is constructed around each vertex as the union of all element sectors which touch it (shaded region).

Continuity Equation

The discrete representation of Eq. (1) is:

$$\frac{V}{\delta t} \left((\rho_\alpha r_\alpha)^{n+1} - (\rho_\alpha r_\alpha)^n \right)$$
$$+ \sum_{ip} (\rho_\alpha u^i A^i)_{ip}^{n+1} (r_{\alpha,ip})^{n+1} = 0. \quad (7)$$

Note that the transient term is discretized using a first-order scheme. This term is retained even for steady-state problems as a means of underrelaxing the solution updates in a physical manner. For time-accurate simulations, a second order scheme is used instead for better accuracy.

The advection scheme used to evaluate $r_{\alpha,ip}$ in terms of neighboring vertex values must give solutions which are both bounded and accurate. We write it in the form

$$r_{\alpha,ip} = r_{\alpha,up} + \beta \nabla r_\alpha \cdot \vec{R}, \quad (8)$$

where $r_{\alpha,up}$ is the upwind vertex value and $\vec{R}$ is the vector from the upwind vertex to the integration point. A bounded high-resolution scheme can be obtained by making β as close to 1 as possible, but reducing where necessary to prevent overshoots and undershoots. The calculation procedure is similar to that described by Barth, T.J. and Jesperson, D.C. (1989).

This high resolution scheme gives good advection accuracy when modeling most flows. However, for free surface applications, it is still overly diffusive when applied to $r_{\alpha,ip}$ in Eq. 7. In this situation, we introduce a compressive scheme as described in Zwart et al (2007). Of particular note is the fact that this compressive scheme does not rely on small timesteps to obtain its compressiveness, and is therefore equally applicable to steady state and transient problems.

The mass flows must be discretized in a careful manner to avoid pressure-velocity decoupling. This is performed by generalizing the interpolation scheme proposed by Rhie, C. M. and Chow, W. L. (1983).

Note that Eq. (7) is fully implicit, and therefore involves the product of implicit variables u^i and r_α at time level $n+1$. This implicit product is linearized as follows:

$$(u^i r_\alpha)^{n+1} \approx (u^i)^{n+1} r_\alpha^n \\ + (u^i)^n r_\alpha^{n+1} \\ - (u^i)^n r_\alpha^n \qquad (9)$$

Momentum Equations

The discrete representation of Eq. (2) is:

$$\frac{\rho_m V}{\delta t}\left((u^i)^{n+1} - (u^i)^n\right) \\ + \sum_{ip}(\rho_m u^j A^j)^{n+1}(u^i)^{n+1} \\ = -\sum_{ip} P_{ip}^{n+1} A^i + \rho_m^{n+1} g^i V \\ + \sum_{ip}(\tau^{ji})^{n+1} A^j)_{ip}. \qquad (10)$$

As with the volume fraction equation, a first-order transient scheme is used as a means of underrelaxing the solution in a physical manner; for time-accurate simulations a second order scheme is used instead. For the advected velocity, a standard second-order or high-resolution scheme is used. Note also that the buoyancy term is fully implicit, and therefore introduces coefficients on volume fraction in the coupled matrix system.

Constraint

The discrete representation of Eq. (6) is

$$\sum_{\alpha=1}^{N} r_\alpha^{n+1} = 1. \qquad (11)$$

Numerical Beach Condition

In order to avoid reflections from the waves hitting the outlet, a momentum loss term Eq. ((12) is added in the z-direction on a region next to the outlet but far enough away from the stern of the ship to absorb the waves traveling in this region. This term is linearly ramped in the x-direction from the start of the damping region to the outlet. This is a modified version of the formulation in Park, J.-C., Kim M.-H., and Miyata H. (1999).

$$loss = \frac{|z|}{A^2}\rho w |w| \qquad (12)$$

where:

$$A = \text{wave amplitude at inlet} \\ \rho = \text{density} \\ w = \text{vertical velocity component} \\ z = \text{vertical distance from calm water line} \\ x = \text{streamwise direction} \qquad (13)$$

Solution Strategy

The set of algebraic equations (7), (10) and (11), represent equations for the volume fraction, velocity, and pressure fields. With two phases, these equations form a 6×6 coupled system of equations at each control volume.

These equations are solved simultaneously, leading to a fully coupled algorithm. Retaining the variable coupling is a key component of a scalable solution algorithm. By scalable we mean that the solution cost increases linearly with mesh size. Note also that additional transport equations (such as turbulence) are not implicitly coupled with the mass and momentum system because they involve weaker interequation couplings.

The solution strategy proceeds as follows:
1. Assemble equations (7), (10), (11) in a coupled manner. Solve using an algebraic multigrid method. Update the velocity, pressure, and volume fractions fields accordingly.
2. Assemble and solve other relevant equations (eg, turbulence model equations).
3. Return to step 1 until convergence has been achieved. This occurs when the normalized residuals are reduced to an acceptable level.

All steps of this algorithm have been fully parallelized using a domain-decomposition technique.

WIGLEY HULL

The Wigley hull is an academic hull shape which is frequently used as a benchmark for free surface flow. This problem has also been described in Zwart et al (2007) but a summary is included here for completeness. CFD calculations are compared with the experimental data of Sarda, O. P. (1986). The hull length is 3.014 m, the half-width is 0.301 m, and the draught is 0.188 m.

Two hexahedral meshes are considered: a coarse mesh of 100 000 vertices and a fine mesh of 500 000 vertices. The geometry (together with a visualization of the free surface interface) is illustrated in Figure 2.

The inlet fluid velocity is $1.452 m/s$ which gives a Froude number (based on ship length) of 0.267 and a Reynolds number of 4.9×10^6. A hydrostatic pressure profile is specified for the outlet. The mid-plane is modeled as a symmetry plane, and the hull surface as a no-slip wall. The far-field side and bottom boundaries are modeled as free slip walls, and the top surface as an entrainment opening.

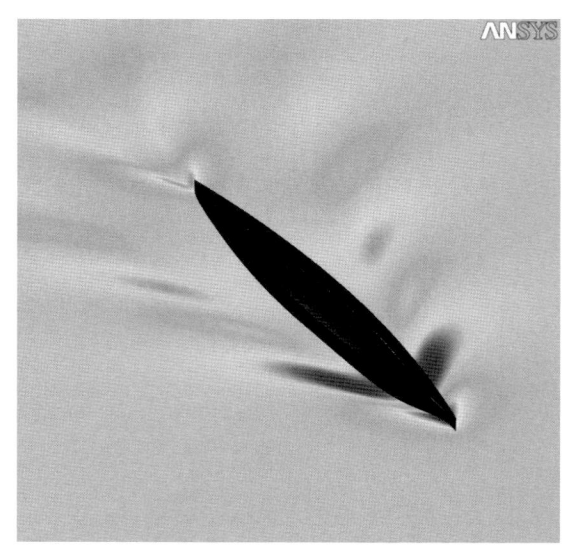

Figure 2: Wigley hull geometry and free surface visualization

Turbulence is modeled using the $k-\varepsilon$ model. Although this is a steady-flow simulation, a physical timestep is still used as a means of providing underrelaxation as the solution approaches steady-state. The time step is chosen to be 0.2 s, which represents about 10% of the advection timescale based on the inlet velocity and hull length.

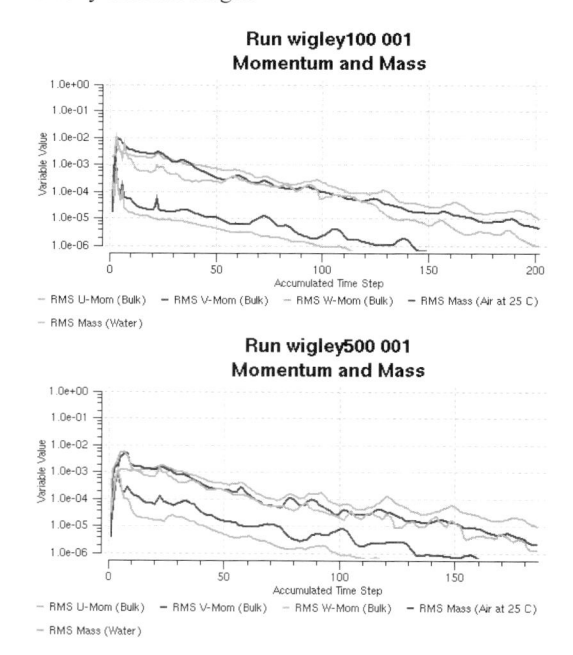

Figure 3: Residual convergence plot for Wigley hull case. Top: coarse mesh; bottom: fine mesh.

Convergence is declared when the RMS average of normalized residuals drops below 10^{-5}. Residual convergence plots are illustrated in Figure 3, and drag convergence plots in Figure 4. Residuals are converged in about 200 iterations, while drag stabilizes after about 100-150 iterations. These plots illustrate that the solution algorithm is *scalable*; ie, the number of iterations is independent of the mesh size and the CPU effort is a linear function of mesh size.

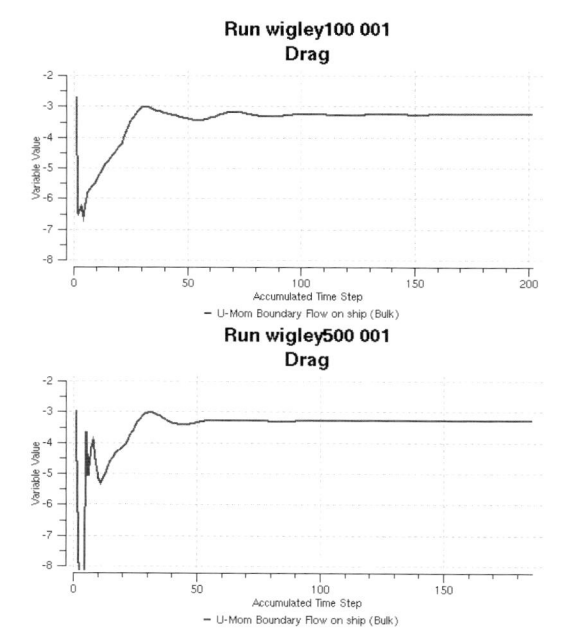

Figure 4: Drag convergence plot for Wigley hull case. Top: coarse mesh; bottom: fine mesh.

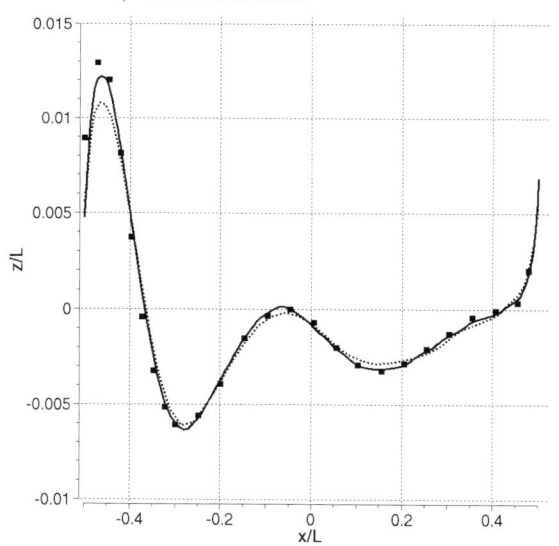

Figure 5: Water level on hull surface: experimental - points, coarse grid - dotted line, fine grid - solid line.

The water level on the hull surface for the coarse and fine meshes is compared with experimental data in Figure 5. It indicates excellent agreement with data.

DTMB 5415

The DTMB 5415 model was conceived as a preliminary design for a Navy surface combatant. The hull geometry (Figure 6) includes both a sonar dome and transom stern. There is a large experimental fluid dynamics (EFD) database for Model 5415 due to a current international collaborative study on EFD/CFD and uncertainty assessment between Iowa Institute of Hydraulic Research (IIHR), Istituto Nazionale per Studi ed Esperienze di Architectura Navale (INSEAN) amd the Naval Surface Warfare Center, Carderock Division (NSWC). In 2005 a CFD Workshop was held in Tokyo (Hino, T., (2005)).

In this section, we compare computed results with experimental results presented at this Workshop by Olivieri, A., Pistani, F., and Penna R. (2001), Gui, L., Longo, J., and Stern, F. (2001), Longo, J., Shao, J., Irvine M. and Stern, F. (2002) for the two cases. The first involves steady flow around the destroyer, while the second involves the transient diffraction of a wave train around the hull. These cases have been studied by other researchers, including (Rhee, S.H. and Skinner, C. (2006)). Dynamic sinkage and trim calculations are also underway. Validation data is difficult to obtain, however, and these results will not be described in this paper.

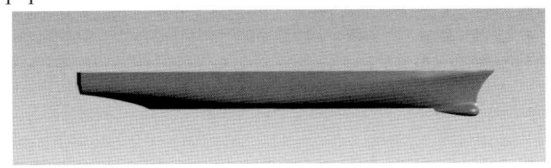

Figure 6: DTMB 5415 hull geometry

Steady Resistance Case

In this setup the ship (Length=5.72m) is traveling at a constant speed of $2.1m/s$ and fixed attitude in calm water. Hence the Froude number for this case is 0.28 and the Reynolds number is 1.27×10^7. Most calculations use the SST turbulence model, although some $k - \epsilon$ results are also presented.

The physical timestep (used as a means of underrelaxing the solution) is set initially to 0.05 s and then ramped up to 4 s. With this approach, the drag converges to within 1% of its final value in 85 iterations, which took less than 2 hours of wall-clock time using 8 CPUs on a 1.8 million node grid. The normalized RMS residuals dropped below 10^{-4} in 175 iterations.

A grid refinement study was performed using three grid sizes (see Table 1). The total drag and skin friction component for these calculations, together with the difference with experimental results, are reported in Table 2. It is interesting to note that these results seem to suggest that the error increases with mesh refinement. However, mesh refinement reduces only discretization error; the remaining discrepancy is due to a combination of model error and experimental error. Note also that the $y+$ on the finest grid is still somewhat large.

Figure 7 and Figure 8 illustrate the computed wave profile along the ship hull and along a plane which is $0.984m$ away from the symmetry plane. The comparison with data is very good and the results also indicate that mesh dependence is small.

This case was solved using both the $k - \epsilon$ and SST turbulence models. The computed drag for these cases is compared in Table 3, and the wave profiles are compared in Figure 9 and Figure 10. These results indicate somewhat better accuracy with the SST model.

Table 1: Grid Resolution and y+ values

	Coarse	Medium	Fine
Nodes	630 000	1 844 000	5 085 000
Average y+	80	43	27

Table 2: Calculated drag for different mesh sizes (T=Total Drag, S=Skin Friction Drag)

	Expt. [N]	Coarse [N]	% diff.	Medium [N]	% diff.	Fine [N]	% diff.
T	45.08	44.07	2.2	43.99	2.4	43.83	2.8
S	30.69	30.38	1	31.60	3.0	32.30	5.2

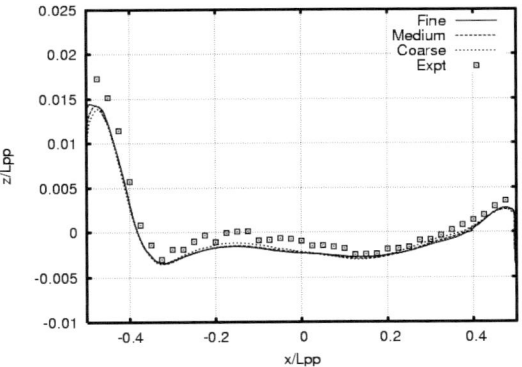

Figure 7: Wave profile along hull for different grids

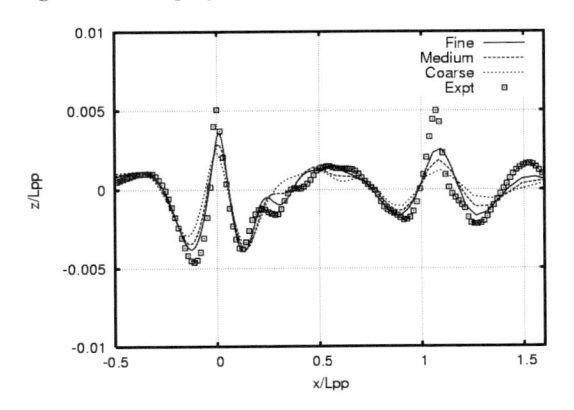

Figure 8: Wave profile along $y/L_{pp} = 0.172$ plane for different grids

Table 3: Drag vs turbulence models on fine grid (T=Total Drag, S=Skin Friction Drag)

	Expt. [N]	SST [N]	SST % diff.	$k-\epsilon$ [N]	$k-\epsilon$ % diff.
T	45.08	43.83	2.8	50.32	11.6
S	30.69	32.30	5.2	33.72	9.9

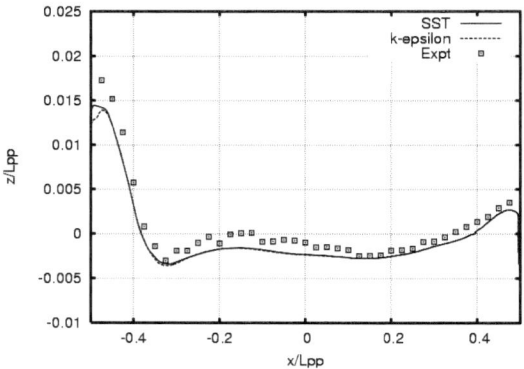

Figure 9: Wave profile along hull for $k-\epsilon$ and SST turbulence models

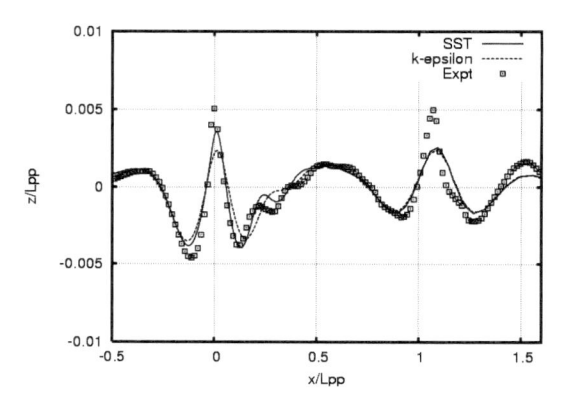

Figure 10: Wave profile along $y/L_{pp} = 0.172$ plane for $k-\epsilon$ and SST turbulence models

Diffraction Case

For the transient diffraction case, the ship (Length=3.048m) travels at constant speed of $1.53m/s$ (or Fr=0.28) and fixed attitude into incoming head waves of height $0.018m$ and wave length of $4.572m$. The waves are generated at the inlet using linear wave theory. The resulting encounter period (T_e) is $1.088s$ and encounter velocity (V_e) is $4.2m/s$. Since the domain of the grid is $39m$ in the streamwise direction it takes $9.3s$ for a wave to the travel the length of the domain, from inlet to outlet. The $k-\epsilon$ turbulence model with scalable wall function was used for these results.

A grid of 3 million nodes was used in this analysis. A timestep and grid resolution study was performed on a similar 2D geometry, not shown here. The purpose was to find the largest allowable timestep and streamwise grid resolution so that the waves remain relatively undamped when reaching the bow of the ship. This resulted in a timestep of $\Delta t = T_e/80$ and streamwise grid resolution of $\Delta x = \lambda/40$.

Figure 11 shows the wave profile along the symmetry plane of the ship at $t = 20s$ simulation time and shows that the waves propagate relatively undamped upstream of the ship but are absorbed by the numerical beach condition which extends from $x = 15m$ to the outlet.

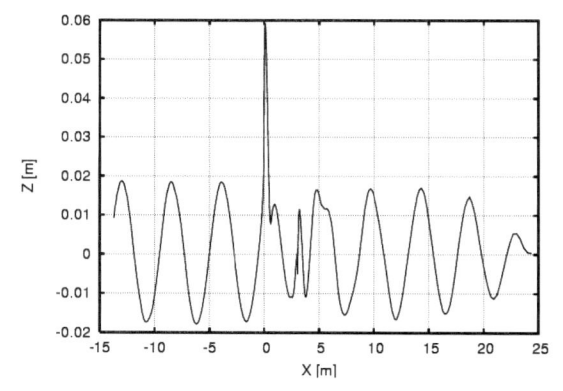

Figure 11: Wave profile along symmetry plane at t=20s

Predicted and measured time histories of resistance and heave force and pitching moment are shown in Figure 12, Figure 13 and Figure 14. The amplitudes of these three quantities are slightly over-predicted. A phase lead is apparent for all three quantities. Although it is hard to come up with a suitable explanation for this phase lead, similar phase disagreements have been reported by (Wilson R, Stern F. (2000)) amongst others. Also of note, the total drag force becomes negative during part of the cycle, implying that a brief portion of each cycle, the ship is propelled forward.

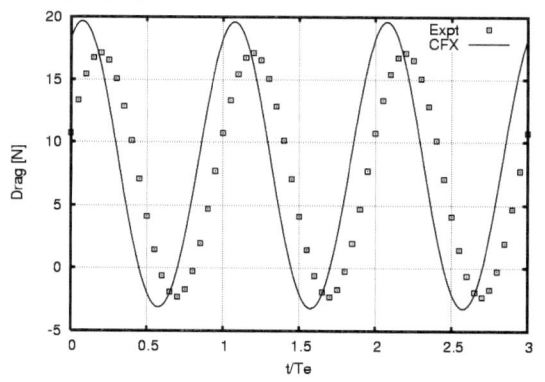

Figure 12: Drag vs t/Te

The heave force as reported in Figure 13 is corrected by subtracting the running average from the time dependent quantity. This eliminates the long period oscillations present in the solution which are approximately 6s in period and 4% of the heave total amplitude.

Figure 13: Heave force vs t/Te

Figure 14: Pitching moment vs t/Te

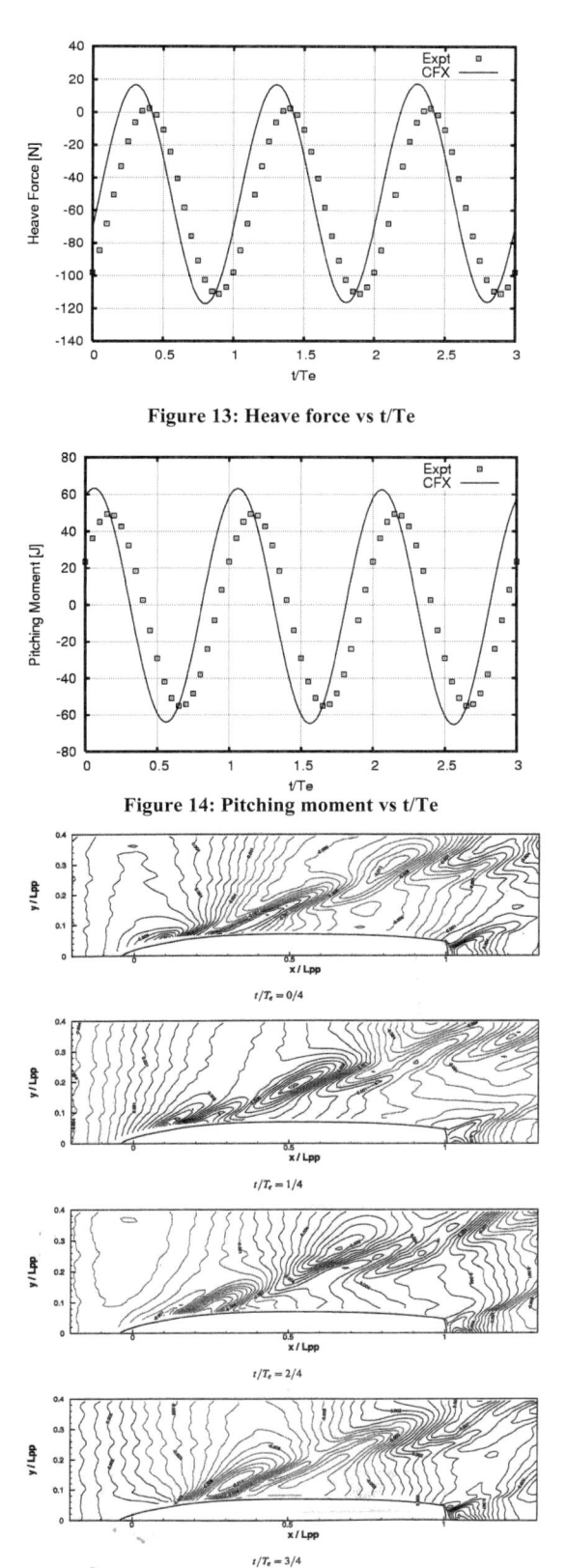

Figure 15: Experimental wave elevation contours

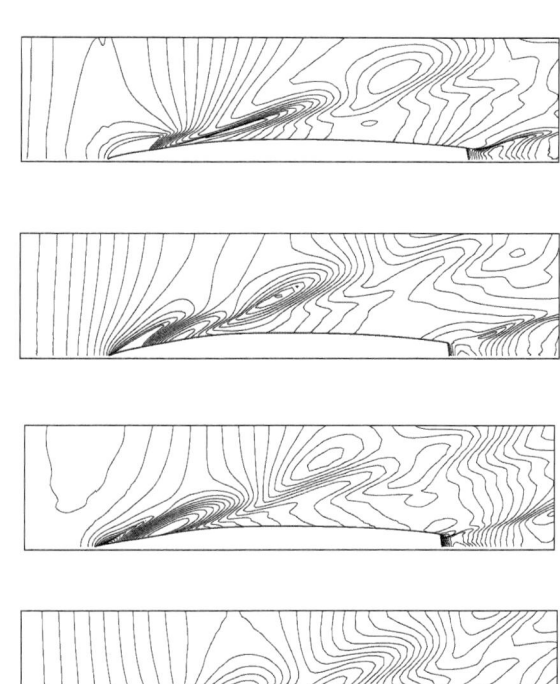

Figure 16: Predicted wave elevation contours. From top to bottom t/Te=0,1/4,1/2,3/4.

Figure 15 and Figure 16 display good agreement between experimental and predicted wave elevation contours at 4 equally spaced time intervals along the encounter period (T_e).

Each timestep was converged until the RMS residuals dropped below 10^{-4}. This typically took about 6 inner loops per timestep. The resulting calculation time was about 14 wall-clock hours on 10 Intel 32-bit 3.4MHz CPUs with 2Gb of RAM for each period (T_e) of simulation. Subsequent testing indicated that fewer inner loops could be used for each timestep, but those results are not given here. By initializing from the steady resistance solution, a periodic-in-time solution was achieved after about 8 seconds of simulation time.

Conclusions

A robust, accurate CFD model for predicting free surface flow around ship hulls has been developed. It combines an accurate discretization scheme with a coupled solution algorithm having excellent convergence properties. The algorithm has been validated on the Wigley hull and DTMB 5415 ship hulls under steady and transient flow conditions.

Acknowledgement

This work was partially sponsored by the United States Department of the Navy, Office of Naval Research, as a subaward under Grant No. N00014-05-1-0875.

References

Barth, T.J. and Jesperson, D.C. (1989) "The design and application of upwind schemes on unstructured meshes" *AIAA Paper 89-0366*.

Gui, L., Longo, J., and Stern, F. (2001) "Towing Tank PIV Measurement Systems, Data and Uncertainty Assessment for DTMB 5512. Exp. In Fluids, 31:336-346.

Hino, T., (2005) *"CFDWS05 Tokyo"*, Tokyo, Japan, National Maritime Research Institute.

Hirt, C.W. and Nichols, B.D., (1981) "Volume of fluid (VOF) method for the dynamics of free boundaries" *Journal of Computational Physics*, 39:201-225.

Longo, J., Shao, J., Irvine M. and Stern, F. (2002) "Phase-averaged PIV for surface combatant in regular head waves" In: 24th ONR symp. on naval hydrodynamics, Fukuoka, Japan.

Olivieri, A., Pistani, F., and Penna R. (2001) "Towing Tank Experiments of Boundary Layer and Wake, and Free Surface Flow Around a Naval Combatant". In Proc. of 26th American Towing Tank Conference, Glenn Cove, New York.

Park, J.-C., Kim M.-H., and Miyata H. (1999) "Fully non-linear free-surface simulations by a 3D viscous numerical wave tank" Int. J. Numer. Meth. Fluids 29: 685-703.

Kothe, D.B., Rider, W.J., Mosso, S.J., and Brock, J.S. (1996) "Volume tracking of interfaces having surface tension in two and three dimensions" *AIAA Paper 96-0859*.

Patankar, S.V. (1980) *"Numerical Heat Transfer and Fluid Flow"* Hemisphere Publishing Corporation.

Raithby, G. D., Xu, W.-X., and Stubley, G. D. (1995) "Prediction of incompressible free surface flows with an element-based finite volume method" *Computational Fluid Dynamics Journal*, 4:353-371.

Rhee, S.H. and Skinner, C. (2006) "Computational Validation of Flow Around Surface Ships Using an Unstructured Grid Based RANS Method", Trans. RINA, Int. J. Maritime Eng., Vol.148, Part A

Rhie, C. M. and Chow, W. L. (1983) "Numerical study of the turbulent flow past an airfoil with trailing edge separation" *AIAA Journal*, 21:1525-1532.

Sarda, O. P. (1986) "Turbulent Flows Past Ship Hulls -- An Experimental and Computational Study", PhD thesis, University of Iowa.

Schneider, G. E. and Raw, M. J. (1987) "Control volume finite-element method for heat transfer and fluid flow using colocated variables -- 1. Computational procedure", *Numerical Heat Transfer*, 11:363-390.

Ubbink, O. and Issa, R. I. (1999) "A method for capturing sharp fluid interfaces on arbitrary meshes", *Journal of Computational Physics*, 153:26-50.

Wilson R, Stern F. (2000) "Unsteady viscous ship hydrodynamics, In: ONR workshop on free surface turbulence and bubbly flows, California Institute of Technology, Pasadena, California.

Zwart, P. J., Burns, A. D. B, and Galpin, P. F. (2007) "Coupled Algebraic Multigrid for Free Surface Flow Simulations", *Proceedings of OMAE2007*, Paper OMAE2007-29080.

Zwart, P. J. (2005) "Numerical modelling of free surface and cavitating flows", In *VKI Lecture Series: Industrial Two-Phase Flow CFD*.

Experimental Investigation on Fatigue Behavior of Side Longitudinals of Tanker under Periodic Storm Loading

Kukbin Kim [1], Jinsoo Park [1], Pan Young Kim [1], and Wha Soo Kim [2]

Structure Research Department [1] and Hull Initial Design Department [2]
Hyundai Heavy Industries Co., Ltd., 1, Cheonha-Dong, Dong-Ku, Ulsan, KOREA

Abstract

Results of an experimental study on fatigue behavior of typical side longitudinals of tanker under periodic storm loading are presented. Four full-scale models of side longitudinals are tested under the storm loading simulated by the Weibull distribution as a programmed block loading. Tested fatigue lives are compared with those calculated from the linear damage accumulation rule based on the IACS S-N curve. Measured data of crack growth and crack shape on the fracture plane are presented. Crack growth lives obtained from the test are compared with those predicted from the LEFM based crack growth analysis, resulting in a good agreement.

Keywords

Storm loading; Variable-amplitude fatigue test; Miner's rule; Hot-spot stress; Crack growth analysis.

Introduction

Since the pioneering work of Palmgren and Miner, the linear damage accumulation rule has widely been adopted in most fatigue design guidances such as BS5400 (1980), ECCS (1985) and IACS (2006). Despite the practical aspects of the Miner's rule, many experimental investigations (Head and Hook, 1956; Kowalewski, 1961; Gassner, 1956; Schijve, 1961) suggested two major shortcomings of the Miner's rule for variable-amplitude (VA) loading. First, the Miner's rule is unable to take into account the effects of overload or underload on fatigue damage. Some fatigue tests showed that after the application of underload fatigue failure can occur by low stresses even if they are below the fatigue limit (Gurney, 1979; Frost, 1974). Second, the Miner's rule takes no account of the load sequence effect. Ship structures often undergo periodic storm loading, which is a typical kind of VA loading. Some storm loading models were proposed by Terai et al (2001), which showed that fatigue crack growth life largely depends on the order and the size of storm load. In the meantime Bayley et al. (2000) investigated the discrepancy among fatigue lives calculated using the Miner's rule, crack growth approach and strain life approach from the storm loading fatigue tests of butt welded joints and suggested that the Miner's rule and fatigue propagation approaches are conservative while the strain life predictions are unconservative. This paper presents the results of an experimental investigation on the effects of the periodic storm loading on fatigue for conventional side longitudinals in tankers. Fatigue lives measured from the variable-amplitude storm loading fatigue test are discussed and compared with prediction based on the Miner's rule.

Fatigue Tests

Fatigue tests were carried out using full-scale single hull side shell longitudinal models under periodic storm loading. Structural behavior and strength evaluation of the subject models under constant-amplitude loading are given in detail in authors' previous study (Park and Kim, 2001). Fig. 1 shows the test setup, where the both ends of the model are clamped by bolts to the test floor and a hydraulic actuator (± 500kN) is installed onto the top of the web frame. The test frequency ranges 1Hz~7Hz considering the load variation in the storm block loading. Tests were conducted in the as-welded condition in the air at room temperature. Surface crack length at the weld toe of the hot-spot areas was measured in a regular interval using the penetrant testing.

Fig. 1: Fatigue test setup

Test Models

Four full-scale test models (4,400×1,600×1,200mm) were prepared using the structural mild steel by the yard practice, including two Angle-type side longitudinal models and two T-type ones. Detailed geometry of the test models is shown in Fig. 2. Comparison of structural responses of the two types of longitudinals is well described in Park and Kim (2001).

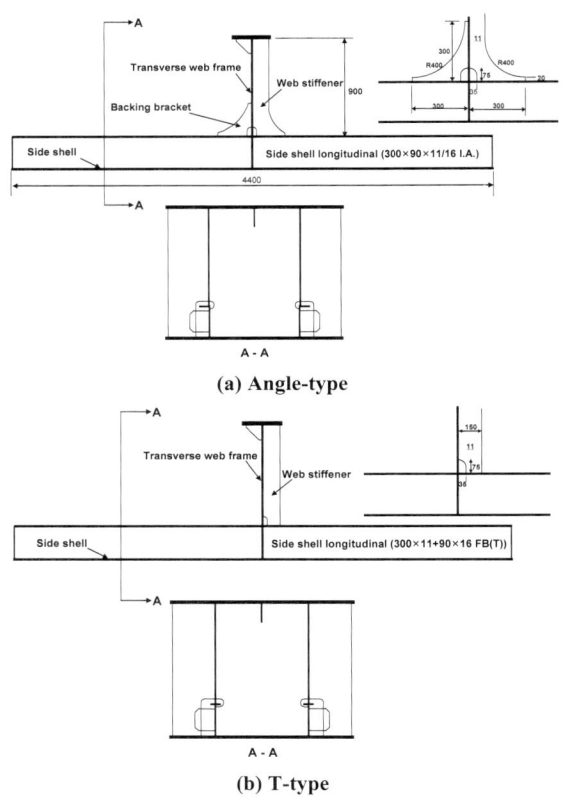

Fig. 2: Geometry of test models
(a) Angle-type
(b) T-type

Loading

The shape of storm loading was simulated by a Weibull function and the related parameters were chosen from the direct load calculation for a tanker under the North Atlantic Ocean sea-state condition. From the direct load calculation results, Weibull shape parameter (h) was determined to be 0.921, average zero crossing rate (f) 0.1098, and dynamic pressure on the side shell near the water line at a probability of exceedance 10^{-5} 114.4kPa. Considering the half area of the side shell of the test models (800mm×4400mm) and the external dynamic pressure, equivalent point load was determined to be 215kN. The maximum forces in the storm loading are 300kN for Angle-type and 340kN for T-type. The test sequence was arranged in a low-high-low order with the highest load spectrum in the center as shown in Fig. 3.

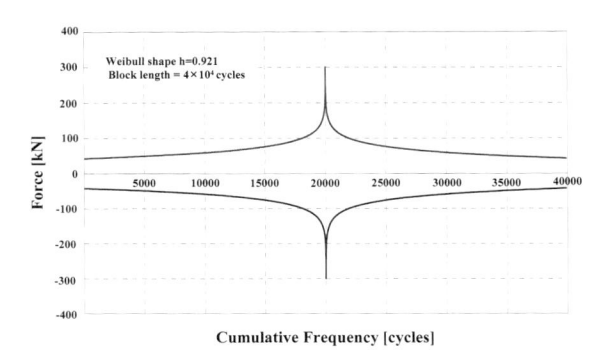

Fig. 3: Simulated storm loading (Angle-type)

The duration of the storm loading was assumed as 15 days. Therefore, the number of load cycles per block is 1.4×10^5 cycles. However, the sequence was shortened to be 4×10^4 cycles by omission of small loads below 15% of the maximum load because the stress ranges induced by these small loads was regarded as negligible in their contribution to the total fatigue damage. The storm loading spectrum was simplified as a stepwise pattern for the test. The simplified block loading for T-type model was composed of 23 sub-block loads as shown in Fig. 4.

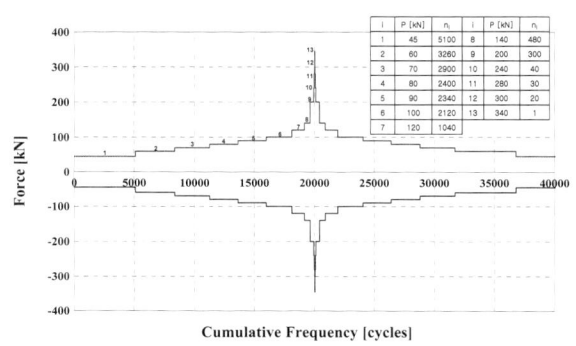

i	P [kN]	n_i	i	P [kN]	n_i
1	45	5100	8	140	480
2	60	3260	9	200	300
3	70	2900	10	240	40
4	80	2400	11	280	30
5	90	2340	12	300	20
6	100	2120	13	340	1
7	120	1040			

Fig. 4: Test block loading (T-type)

Hot-spot Stress

Generally the critical points, i.e., hot spot areas of the side longitudinals are the connections of the flange and web frame stiffeners, where fatigue cracks usually often occur (Fig. 5).

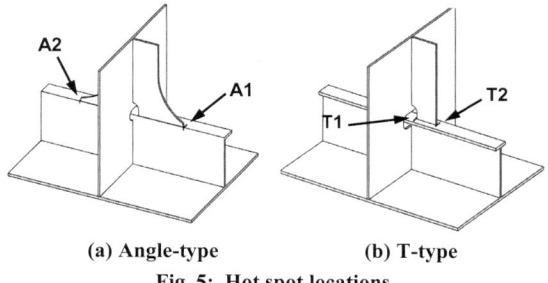

Fig. 5: Hot spot locations
(a) Angle-type
(b) T-type

In order to calculate the hot-spot stresses of the two types of longitudinals, strain measurement and finite element analysis were conducted. Finite element models were made using 20-node solid elements (Fig. 6). Stress concentration areas were finely meshed to the half of the plate thickness to calculate hot-spot stresses.

For comparison, hot-spot stresses for a reference force of 100kN were calculated by the linear extrapolation method using the measured principal stresses at 0.5t and 1.5t distance away from the hot-spot point as shown in Fig. 7 and the results from the strain measurement and finite element analysis are listed in Table 1 for the hot spot locations of each type model. Hot-spot stresses at A-1 and T-1 are 82.9MPa and 79.0MPa on the average, respectively, about 5% larger in the Angle-type model for the same reference load of 100kN.

Table 1: Hot-spot stresses from measurement and analysis

Model	Hot spot location	Hot-spot stress (MPa) Measured	FEA
Angle-type 1	L-A1	83.7	88.4
	R-A1	82.9	
Angle-type 2	L-A1	83.5	
	R-A1	81.5	
T-type 1	L-T1	79.7	80.8
	R-T1	78.1	
T-type 2	L-T1	79.9	
	R-T1	78.1	

(R: Right longitudinal, L: Left longitudinal)

Test Results

The fatigue life of the test models was defined as the number of loading blocks (N) until the surface cracks propagate 50mm long. The fatigue lives obtained from the VA (variable amplitude) storm loading fatigue test (N_{test}) were compared with the predicted lives by the Miner's rule (N_{pred}). The cumulative fatigue damage (D) by the Miner's rule is generally given as

$$D = \frac{n_1}{N_1} + \frac{n_2}{N_2} + \cdots = \sum \frac{n_i}{N_i} \quad (1)$$

where n_i is the number of cycles of the stress range $\Delta\sigma_i$, N_i is the fatigue life for the stress range $\Delta\sigma_i$. Based on the Miner's rule, an equivalent stress range $\Delta\sigma_e$ (IIW, 1982) was adopted to represent the VA stress block used in the test.

$$\Delta\sigma_e = \sqrt[m]{\frac{\sum n_i \Delta\sigma_i^m}{\sum n_i}} \quad (2)$$

Table 2 shows the measured and predicted lives of the test models for the hot-spot areas, where the life ratio (N_{test}/N_{pred}) ranges 2.3 to 3.0 for Angle-type and 6.8 to 7.5 for T-type. It may indicate that the linear damage accumulation results in more conservative life prediction in the T-type longitudinals. Measured fatigue lives in cycles are compared in Fig. 8 with those obtained from the previous study for CA (constant amplitude) loading (Park and Kim, 2001), where it can be seen that the fatigue behavior for this periodic storm loading goes well with that for CA loading in the overall. All the test data show conservative results in view of the IACS D-type mean curve (IACS, 2006), especially in the T-type.

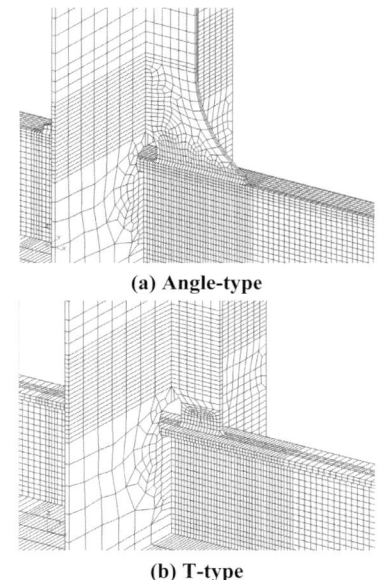

(a) Angle-type

(b) T-type

Fig. 6: Finite element model

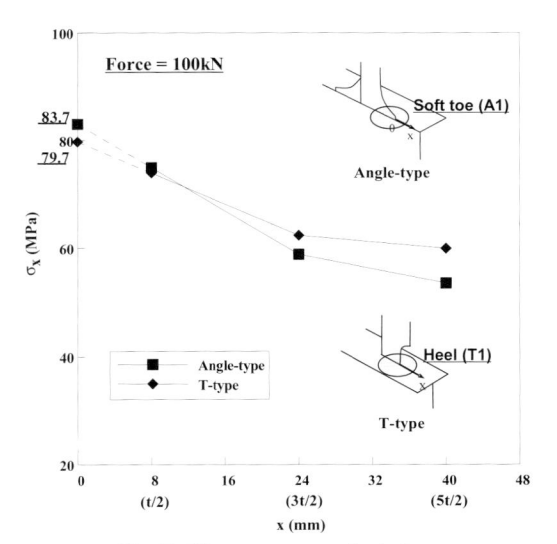

Fig. 7: Hot-spot stress calculation

Table 2: Comparison between fatigue lives obtained from the VA fatigue tests and the Miner's rule

Model	Hot-spot location	N_{test} (blocks)	$\Delta\sigma_e$ (MPa)	N_{pred} (blocks)	N_{test}/N_{pred}
Angle-type 1	L-A1	42	129	18	2.3
	R-A1	52	128	18	2.8
Angle-type 2	L-A1	41	129	18	2.3
	R-A1	57	126	19	3.0
T-type 1	L-T1	97	143	13	7.5
	R-T1	96	139	14	6.9
T-type 2	L-T1	96	143	13	7.4
	R-T1	95	139	14	6.8

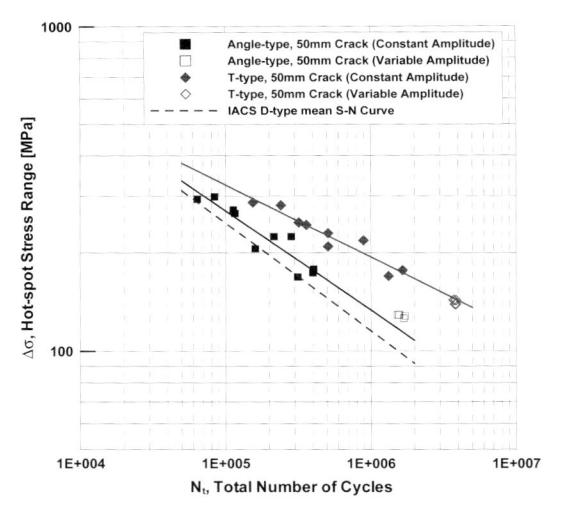

Fig. 8: Comparison of fatigue lives

Crack Growth Analysis

Crack growth data of surface crack length versus number of blocks are plotted in Fig. 9, where it can be noted that the growth rate in the Angle-type is more or less higher than that in the T-type, resulting in the similar behavior as the CA loading test.

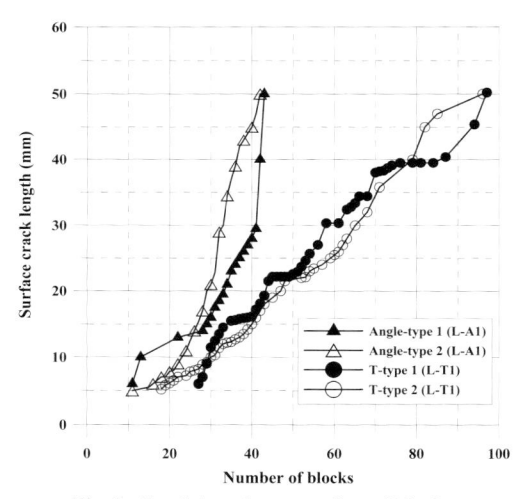

Fig. 9: Crack length vs. number of blocks

From the tested models, the part of the cracked area was taken and the fracture surface was pictured as in Fig. 10, where it can be seen that beach marks were well made and grew semi-elliptically. Figs. 10(a) and 10(b) show the fracture surface in Angle-type 1 (L-A1) and T-type 1 (L-T1), respectively. In the Angle-type test, quarter-elliptical shapes were developed in the later stage.

Crack growth analysis was carried out in order to predict crack growth lives and compare those with measured growth lives. For the analysis, the Paris-Elber's model (Elber, 1971) was used:

$$\frac{da}{dN} = C(\Delta K_{eff})^m \qquad (3)$$

$$\Delta K_{eff} = K_{max} - K_{op} \qquad (4)$$

$$K_{op} = \begin{cases} 0.333 \times K_{max} & (K_{max} \leq 50) \\ -0.75 \times K_{max} + 54.15 & (K_{max} > 50) \end{cases} \qquad (5)$$

where da/dN is the crack growth rate, ΔK_{eff} is the effective stress intensity factor range, K_{max} and K_{op} are the maximum and opening stress intensity factors, and C and m are material constants. K_{op} was used as given from the storm model fatigue test results of Kawata (1996). Weight function method was used to determine the stress intensity factors at the crack tips. In this study the crack growth analyses for semi-elliptical surface crack were performed using the weight function of Shen and Glinka (1991). The material constants, C and m given in the reference (SR219, 1996) were used.

$$C = 1.45 \times 10^{-11}, \ m = 2.75 \qquad (6)$$

The fatigue crack shape definitions for the crack growth analysis are shown in Fig. 11 for the Angle-type and T-type models.

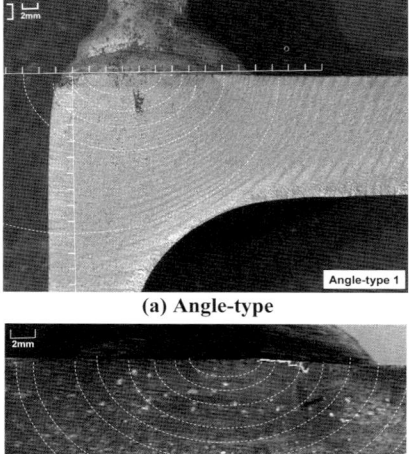

(a) Angle-type

(b) T-type

Fig. 10: Crack growth shapes on fracture plane

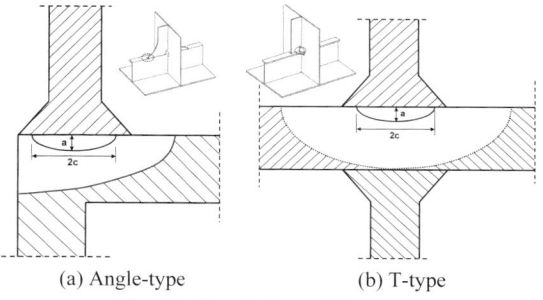

(a) Angle-type (b) T-type

Fig. 11: Crack shape definitions

As input data for the crack growth analyses, the initial depth and the final depth of surface crack were chosen to be 1mm and 20mm, respectively. The aspect ratio of the initial crack was assumed to be 0.2 based on the measured beach mark shape. The stress distribution in the thickness direction on the fracture plane was obtained from the finite element analysis.

Fig. 12 and Fig. 13 show the comparison between the predicted and measured aspect ratio of the crack at it grows from the initial crack in the range of $0.06 < a/2c < 0.43$ for the two types of longitudinals. The value of $a/2c$ increases linearly in the early stage and it becomes seemingly constant to be about 0.43.

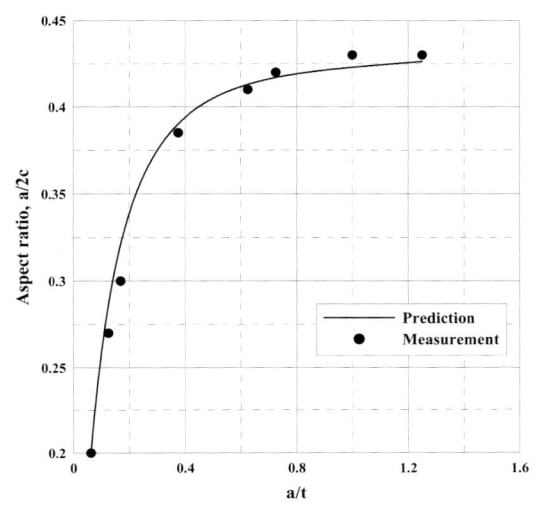

Fig. 12: Crack aspect ratio development (Angle-type 1)

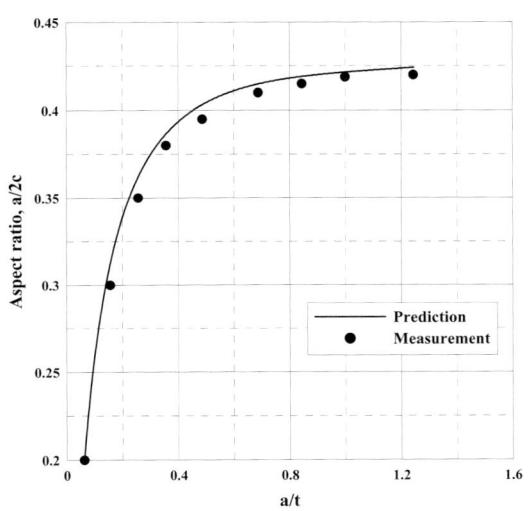

Fig. 13: Crack aspect ratio development (T-type 1)

Results of crack depth versus number of blocks calculated from the analysis are compared with the measured data in Figs. 14 and 15, which show a good agreement in the overall. For the Angle-type as shown in Fig. 14, it is seen that after the crack grew about 12mm deep, the difference started to be noticed. This difference may be explained by the fact that the corner crack developed around this depth and grew fast along the web. Table 3 summarizes predicted and measured crack growth lives from 1mm to 16mm depth in number of blocks for all the cracks occurred in the hot spot areas.

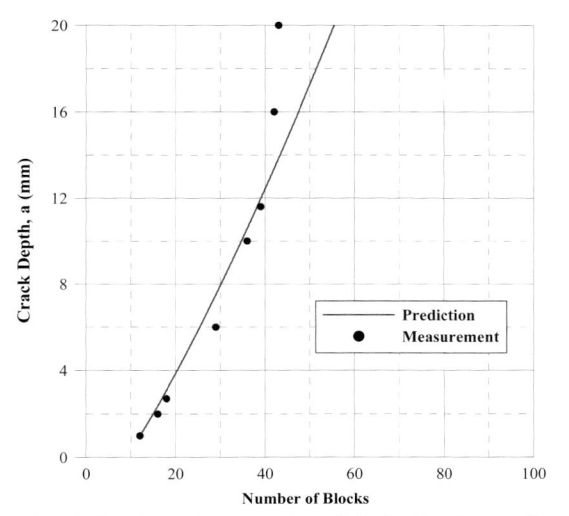

Fig. 14: Crack depth vs. number of blocks (Angle-type 1)

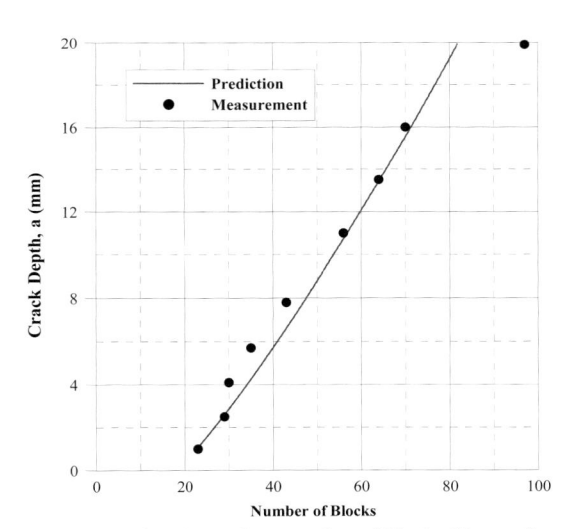

Fig. 15: Crack depth vs number of blocks (T-type 1)

Table 3: Comparison of crack growth lives (blocks)

Model	Hot spot location	N_{test}	N_{pred}	N_{test}/N_{pred}
Angle-type 1	L-A1	31	35	0.89
	R-A1	29		0.83
Angle-type 2	L-A1	32	35	0.91
	R-A1	28		0.80
T-type 1	L-T1	48	49	0.98
	R-T1	45		0.92
T-type 2	L-T1	51	49	1.04
	R-T1	44		0.90

During the fatigue tests, it was observed that one crack on a longitudinal was growing while the other crack initiated on the other longitudinal tend to stay in recess. Fig. 16 shows the switching behavior of crack growth between the two longitudinals of a model.

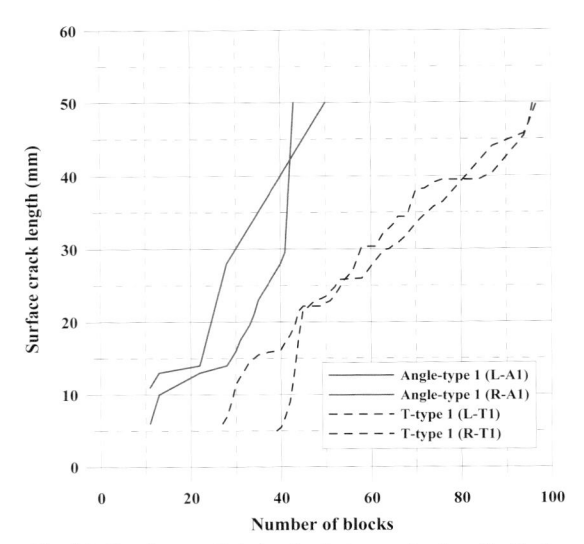

Fig. 16: Crack growth behavior between the longitudinals

Conclusions

Predictions and experimental investigations for fatigue life of full-scale side longitudinals under periodic storm loading were performed and followings are concluded.

1. The life ratio (N_{test}/N_{pred}) using the IACS D-type mean S-N curve ranges 2.3 to 3.0 for Angle-type and 6.8 to 7.5 for T-type. It may indicate that the linear damage accumulation rule results in more conservative life prediction in the T-type longitudinals.
2. The load sequence effects of the periodic storm loading on fatigue damage are not significant. It may be explained that because the storm loading spectrum in this study is stepwise and periodic the load sequence give insignificant effect on the fatigue damage.
3. The fatigue crack growth prediction by the Paris-Elber's model and weight function method agrees well with the experimental result. The aspect ratios of the cracks measured from the fractured plane are also well predicted by the crack growth analysis.

References

Bayley, C, Glinka, G, and Porter, J (2000). "Fatigue Crack Initiation and Growth in A517 Submerged Arc Welds under Variable Amplitude Loading," Int J Fatigue, Vol 22, pp799-808.

BS5400 (1980). Specification for Steel, Concrete and Compositive Bridges, Part 10: Code of Practice for Fatigue, British Standard Institution.

ECCS (1985). Recommendation for the Fatigue Design of Steel Structures, Technical Committee 6-Fatigue.

Elber, W (1971). "The Significance of Fatigue Crack Closure," Damage Tolerance in Aircraft Structures, ASTM STP 486, American Society for Testing and Materials, pp230-42.

Frost, NE (1974). "Metal Fatigue," Oxford, Clarendon Press.

Gassner, E (1956). "Effect of Variable Load and Cumulative Damage on Fatigue in Vehecle and Airplane Structures," Proc Int Conf Fatigue Metals, Inst Mech Eng, pp304.

Gurney, TR (1979). "Fatigue of Welded Structures (2nd Edition)," Cambridge, University Press.

Head, AK and Hook, FH (1956). "Random Noise Fatigue Testing," Proc Int Conf Fatigue Metals, Inst Mech Eng, pp301-3.

IACS (2006). Common Structural Rules for Double Hull Oil Tankers.

IIW (1982). Design Recommendations for Cyclic Loaded Welded Steel Structures, Welding in the World, Vol 20, pp153-65.

Katawa, N (1996). "Experimental Study on Fatigue Crack Growth Behavior under Storm Model," Graduation Thesis, Department of Naval Architecture and Ocean Engineering, Faculty of Osaka University.

Kowalewski, J (1961). "On the Relation between Fatigue Lives under Random Loading and under Corresponding Program Loading," Full-scale Fatigue Testing of Aircraft Structures, Oxford: Pergamon Press, pp60-75.

Park, J, Kim, K, Kim, WS and Kim, DH (2001). "An Experimental Investigation on Fatigue Behavior of Inverted Angle- and T-type Side Longitudinals in Tankers," Proc of 9th PRADS, Shanghai, Vol 2, pp189-95.

Schijve, J (1961). "The Endurance under Fatigue-Program Test," Full-scale Fatigue Testing of Aircraft Structures, Oxford: Pergamon Press, pp41-59.

Shen, G and Glinka, G (1991). "Weight Functions for a Surface Semi-elliptical Crack in a finite thickness plate," Theoretical and Applied Fracture Mechanics, Vol 15, pp247-55.

Ship Research Panel 228 (1996). "Study on Practical Use for Fatigue Crack Growth Analysis," Shipping Research Association of Japan.

Terai, K, Tomita, Y, and Osawa, N (2001). "Fatigue Design Method of Ship Structural Members Based on Fatigue Crack Growth Analysis," Proc 11th ISOPE, Stawanger, Vol 4, pp589-94.

Tomita, Y, Hashimoto, K, Osawa, N, Terai, K, and Wang, YH (2002). "Experimental Study of Mean Stress Effect on Fatigue Crack Growth under Variable Amplitude," Symposium on Fatigue Testing and Analysis under Variable Amplitude Loading, ASTM.

Wang, YH, Tomita, Y, Hashimoto, K, Osawa, N, and Terai, K (2002). "A New Approach to Fatigue Strength Evaluation of Ship Hull," Proc 12th ISOPE, Kitakyushu, Vol 2, pp198-204.

Fatigue Design of Web Stiffened Cruciform Connections

Inge Lotsberg, Trond A. Rundhaug, Harald Thorkildsen, Åge Bøe and Torbjørn Lindemark

Det Norske Veritas
Norway

Abstract

Fatigue design of dynamic loaded ship structures is normally based on finite element analysis using shell elements where the welds are not included in the analysis models. FE analyses of a fatigue tested hopper knuckle type specimen were performed for calibration of analysis methodology in a joint industry project. The test specimen was analyzed using 20-node solid elements, 4-node and 8-noded shell elements. Only the solid element models included the weld geometry. In the present work the FE analyses were extended to that of other geometries at web stiffened cruciform joints such as typical found at hopper connections, at stringer heels and at joints connecting deck structures to vertical members in ship structures. Based on the result from these analyses a methodology for derivation of hot spot stress at welded connections using shell finite element models was developed. The weld size is accounted for in the analysis procedure even if the weld is not included in the shell finite element model. The basis for this procedure is presented in this paper.

Keywords

Fatigue; Finite element analysis; Shell elements; Web stiffened cruciform connections; Hot spot stress; Weld size; S-N curves.

Introduction

Fatigue design of dynamic loaded ship structures is normally based on finite element analysis using shell elements where the welds are not included in the analysis models; reference is e. g. made to DNV Classification Note 30.7 (2005). A joint industry project on fatigue capacity of floating production vessels, the FPSO Fatigue Capacity JIP, was carried out in two phases from 1998 to 2003, (Lotsberg, 2001 and Bergan and Lotsberg, 2006). This project provided a number of fatigue test data and analysis results of typical welded connections in ship structures. Fatigue analysis of fatigue tested side longitudinals using FE models with shell elements showed in general good agreement with measured stress where the hot spot is a result of global force flow through the structural details. It was found to be less good for details where the hot spot stress is a result of local behavior such as at bracket connections between transverse frames and bulb longitudinals (Storsul et al. 2004). In this project also a number of fatigue tests of hopper knuckle connections were performed; Kim and Lotsberg (2005). FE analyses were performed for calibration of the analysis methodology; Fricke (2001) and Lotsberg (2004, 2006). The test specimen was analyzed using 20-node solid elements, 4-node and 8-noded shell elements. The solid element model included the weld.

The current method for hot spot stress derivation at web stiffened cruciform joints given in DNV Classification Note 30.7 "Fatigue Assessment of Ship Structures" is considered to be conservative. Results from the FPSO Fatigue Capacity project showed that an effective stress can be obtained by reducing the plate bending stress as explained in the next section. In the present work the FE analyses were extended to that of other connections at stiffened cruciform joints such as typical found at hopper connections, at stringer heels and at joints connecting deck structures to vertical supports in ship structures, ref. Figure 1. The present project is performed in order to develop a procedure for derivation of hot spot stress at such joints using shell elements, also taking into account the actual weld size.

Procedure for Derivation of Effective Hot Spot Stress

At hot spots with significant plate bending one may derive an effective hot spot stress for fatigue assessment based on the following equation:

$$\Delta\sigma_{e,spot} = \Delta\sigma_{a,spot} + 0.60\,\Delta\sigma_{b,spot} \qquad (1)$$

where

$\Delta\sigma_{a,spot}$ = membrane stress

$\Delta\sigma_{b,spot}$ = bending stress

The reduction factor on the bending stress can be explained by redistribution of loads to other areas during crack growth while the crack tip is growing into a region with reduced stress. The effect is limited to areas with a localized stress concentration, which occurs for example at a hopper knuckle. However, in a case where the stress variation along the weld is small, the difference in fatigue life between axial loading and pure bending is much smaller. Therefore it should be noted that it is not correct to generally reduce the bending part of the stress to 60 percent. This has to be restricted to areas with a pronounced stress concentration. The procedure is also supported by fatigue tests subjected to bending; Kang et al. (2002). The procedure can also be explained based on crack growth analysis using fracture mechanics as shown in Figure 2 and Figure 3, Lotsberg and Sigurdsson (2004). Figure 3 shows crack growth curves through the thickness of the flange for different stress gradients having the same hot spot stress. Semi-elliptic crack growth is assumed as indicated in Figure 2. The S-N curve for specimens subjected to pure membrane stress is at a level of 60 % of that of specimens subjected to bending load. Thus equation (1) represents physical behavior and applies to members where the stress can be divided into membrane and bending based on finite element analyses using either three-dimensional elements or shell elements.

Finite Element Analysis

Analysis Models

The present study has covered hot spot stress related to a 135 degrees, 120 degrees and 90 degrees stiffened cruciform connection. The FE analyses included models with 20-node solid elements and 8-nodes shell elements. Finally the procedure has also been verified using models with 4-node shell elements. The solid model included a weld created by 15-nodes solid elements. The analyses cover variation of weld size expressed by weld leg length (full penetration weld without additional weld leg, with additional weld leg length equal to half plate thickness, t/2, and with additional weld leg length equal to plate thickness, t), and extrapolation of calculated stresses to the weld toe from t/2 and 3t/2. The shell element models were made without any weld.

A hopper knuckle model that was tested by HHI in Korea and in the laboratories of DNV was selected for structural analysis. The critical weld toe is located at the transition from the beam consisting of 10 mm thick flange (simulating the tankers inner bottom plate) and plates simulating the sloped hopper plate, Figure 2. The specimen was subjected to a vertical point load at the end of the cantilever resulting in a bending moment at the hot spot area. The DNV Sesam programs were used for the analyses. The test specimen from the FPSO Fatigue Capacity project contained eccentricity and the target hot spot stress values used for calibration are derived for this geometry. Therefore also one of the finite element models included the same eccentricity. Thus the finite element models for the 135 degree connection were created with and without eccentricity. The main emphasis of a finite element analysis is to make a model giving stresses with sufficient accuracy at the hot spot region, ref. Figure 4. (Analysis using a flat weld profile gave analysis results not significantly different from that of the shown concave profile). The finite element models consist of two types of three-dimensional solid elements, isoparametric triangular prisms, used for modeling of welds, and isoparametric hexagons for the remaining structure. The fillet welds below the upper flange (below inner bottom/tank top) has been included in the model. The welded connection is typically modeled by use of two separate superelements in order to connect the plates through the fillet weld only.

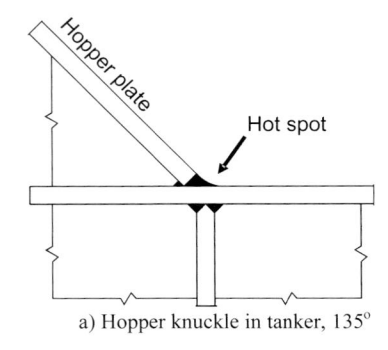

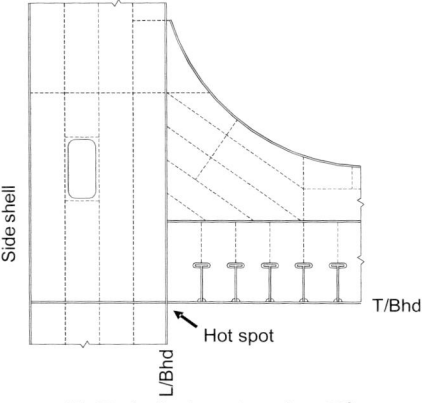

a) Hopper knuckle in tanker, 135°

b) Heel of stringer in tanker, 90°

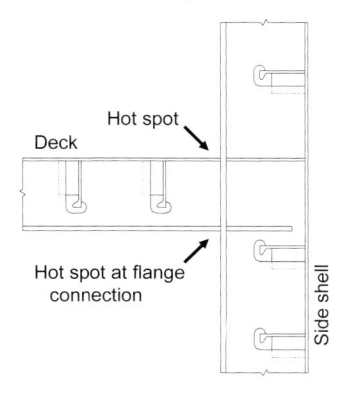

c) Connection between deck web frame in car carrier, 90°

Fig. 1 Examples of web stiffened cruciform connections

Derivation of Hot Spot Stress

Element stresses in the solid FE models are derived at the Gaussian integration points (stress result points). The Gaussian stresses are manually extrapolated to the surface and further interpolated within the element for derivation of stress at the read out points. The 8 node shell element has 4 surface stress result points in the upper (top) surface (at the Gaussian points). These stresses are extrapolated to nodes in the upper top surface from the result points. The element stresses in the top surface point for the two closest elements to the system line corresponding to a distance t/2 and 3t/2 from the intersection line are used directly as extrapolation points to calculate the hot spot stress.

Results for 135 degrees hopper knuckle based on 20-node solid model without weld leg and with weld leg = t/2 and t, is compared with results based on 8-nodes shell elements. The stresses at positions 10 mm and 20 mm away from weld toes/intersection line is derived by fitting a second order function through the values derived at 5, 15 and 25 mm.

The hot spot stresses from the solid models were derived from linear extrapolation of stresses at t/2 and 3t/2 from the weld toe. These hot spot stresses are used as basis for derivation of target hot spot stress that is used for calibration of analysis methodology.

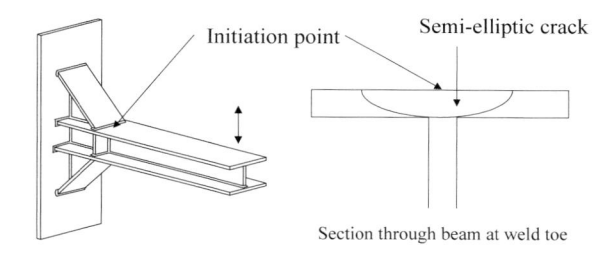

Fig. 2 Crack growth analysis of hopper knuckle

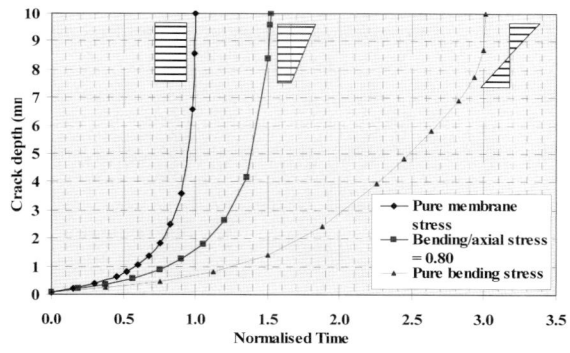

Fig. 3 Crack growth curves for same hot spot stress with different stress gradients through flange

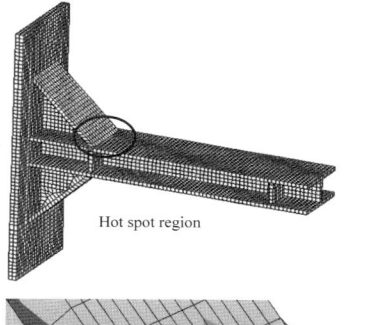

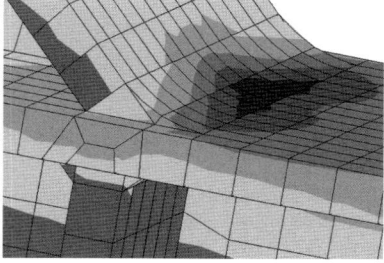

Fig. 4 Solid element model of tested specimen

Analysis Results

Cruciform connection 135 deg. with eccentricity

Calculated results for cruciform connection 135 deg. with eccentricity are shown in Figure 5. From this figure it is seen that approximately the same stresses at the hot spot region is derived using solid element model (20 node elements) as from the shell element model (8-node elements). From this figure it is also seen that addition of weld material increases slightly the stress distribution in front of the weld as compared to calculated stress using a FE model where the weld is not included. Thus, if some additional weld is added, and if the stresses are read out at the relevant weld toe position, they should be increased by a factor corresponding to this stress increase. The target hot spot surface stress value from fatigue tests is 1.64 when linked to a design hot spot stress fatigue S-N curve that corresponds to 90 MPa at 2 mill cycles (Denoted FAT 90 by IIW (1996) and curve D in DNV-RP-C203 (2005)), Lotsberg and Sigurdsson (2004). From FE analyses the target hot spot surface stress is somewhat larger, in the range 1.84-1.96. The calculated stress from the present three-dimensional analysis is 2.08. Then the stress is reduced by the factor 1.96/2.08 = 0.942 to get a target factor equal 1.96. The same factor is used for all the three-dimensional analyses for derivation of target values. Based on the performed analyses the target values in Table 1 are derived. It is assumed that there is a relative difference in the target values as derived from the three-dimensional models where the actual weld geometry is included.

Cruciform connection 135 deg. without eccentricity

Calculated stresses for cruciform connection 135 deg. without eccentricity are shown in Figure 6. From this figure it is seen that approximately the same stresses at the hot spot region is derived using solid element model (20 node elements) as from shell element model (8-node elements). From this figure it is also seen that addition of weld material increases slightly the stress distribution in front of the weld as compared to calculated stress using a FE model where the weld is not included. The stress distribution at the hot spot area for the geometry without additional weld is shown in Figure 7. The stress distribution at the hot spot area for the geometry with additional weld equal t is shown in Figure 8. From these figures it is seen that it is the local bending that is the main contribution to the stress increase at the hot spot. This bending stress is located within an area of 1.5 t from the weld toe (t = 10 mm). By adding weld, it is seen that the bending stress is moved to the right in Figure 8 as compared with that of bending stress in Figure 7. However, the absolute value of the bending stress is also slightly reduced by addition of a fillet weld at the hot spot.

Table 1 Target hot spot stresses

Geometry	Weld leg length x_{wt}		
	0	t/2	t
135° (with eccentricity)	1.96	1.62	1.42
135° (without eccentricity)	2.15	1.66	1.47
120 (without eccentricity)	2.37	1.85	1.72
90° (with eccentricity)	2.42	2.05	1.87
90° (without eccentricity)	2.56	2.07	1.88

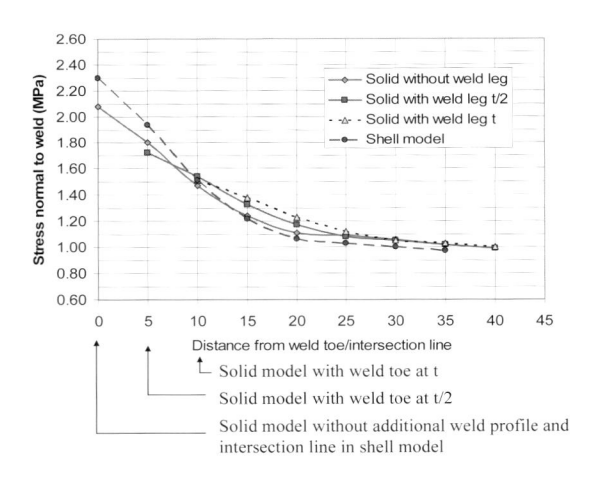

Fig. 5 Surface stress at hot spot region of 135° model with eccentricity

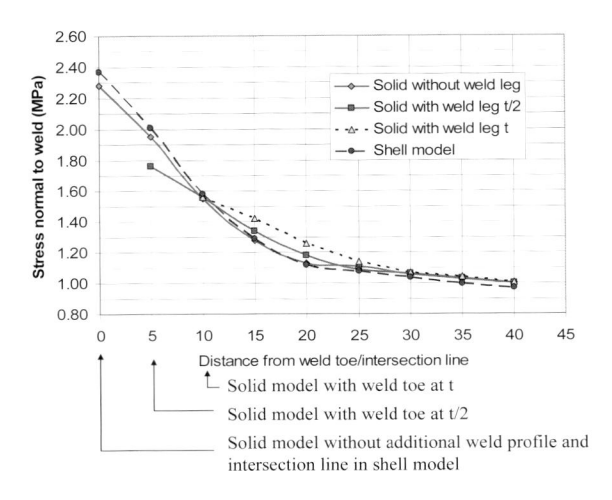

Fig. 6 Surface stress at hot spot region of 135° model without eccentricity

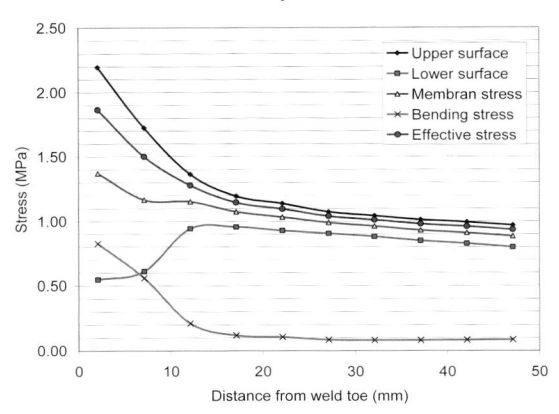

Fig. 7 Stress at hot spot region of 135° solid element model without eccentricity and no additional weld

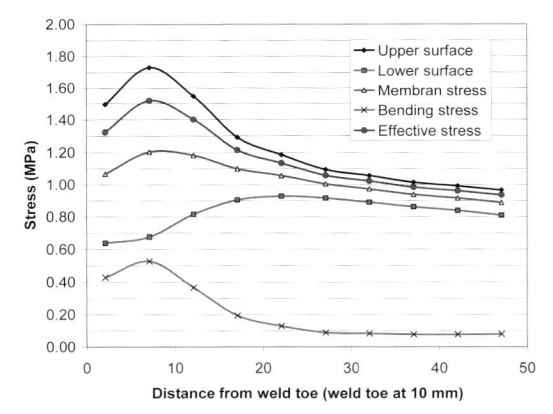

Fig. 8 Stress at hot spot region of 135° solid element model without eccentricity and with weld leg length t

Cruciform connection 120 deg. without eccentricity

Calculated results for cruciform connection 120 deg. without eccentricity are shown in Figure 9. It is seen that approximately the same stresses at the hot spot region is derived using solid element model (20 node elements) as from shell element model (8-node elements). The result for the solid model with weld leg t, shows slightly higher stress than for the other.

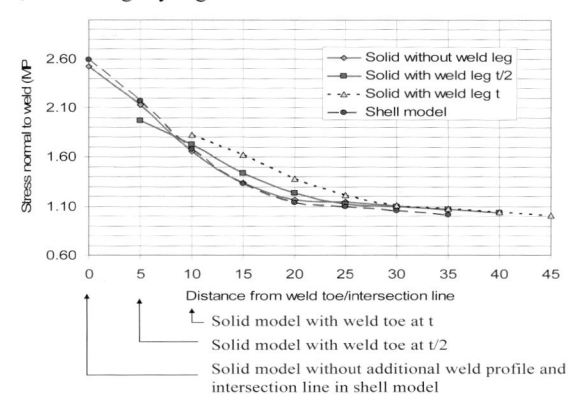

Fig. 9 Surface stress at hot spot region of 120° model without eccentricity

Cruciform connection 90 deg. without eccentricity

Finite element model for 90 degree web stiffened cruciform connection with weld leg length equal the plate thickness is shown in Figure 10. The calculated stresses for this model are shown in Figure 11. From this figure it is seen that approximately the same stresses at the hot spot region is derived using solid element model (20 node elements) as from shell element model (8-node elements). The stress distribution at the hot spot area for the geometry without additional weld leg is shown in Figure 12. The stress distribution at the hot spot area for the geometry with additional weld leg equal t is shown in Figure 13. From these figures it is seen that the local bending is the main contributor to the stress increase at the hot spot. This bending stress is large within an area of one times the plate thickness from the weld toe. By adding weld it is seen that the area with high bending stress is moved to the right when comparing Figure 13 with Figure 12. In addition, the absolute value of the bending stress is slightly reduced by addition of a fillet weld at the hot spot. Target values for different weld size are assessed as shown in Table 1. For the 90 deg. geometry we do not have target values from fatigue tests or other FE analysis. However, it is assumed that the same conservatism is inherent the finite element analysis for this detail without any weld as for the 135° hopper connection, as the finite element modeling is similar. Thus the same procedure is used to derive target values. This gives target values for weld size t/2 and t as shown in Table 1.

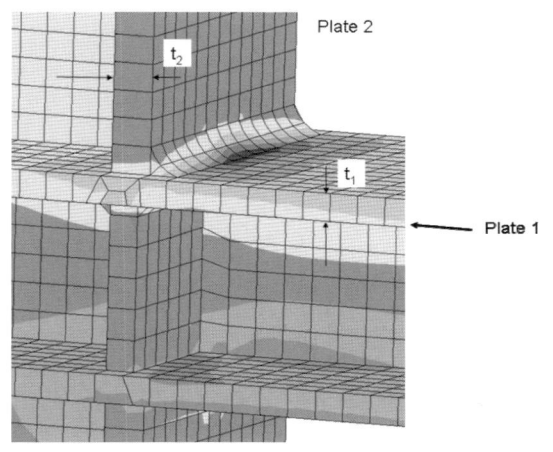

Fig. 10 Finite element model of 90° connection with weld leg length equal t

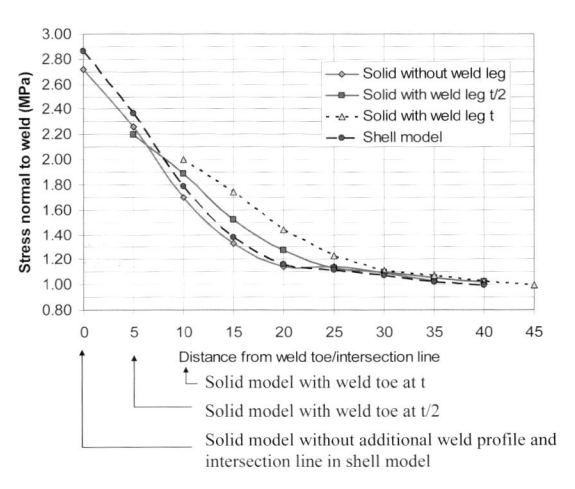

Fig. 11 Surface stress at hot spot region of 90° model without eccentricity

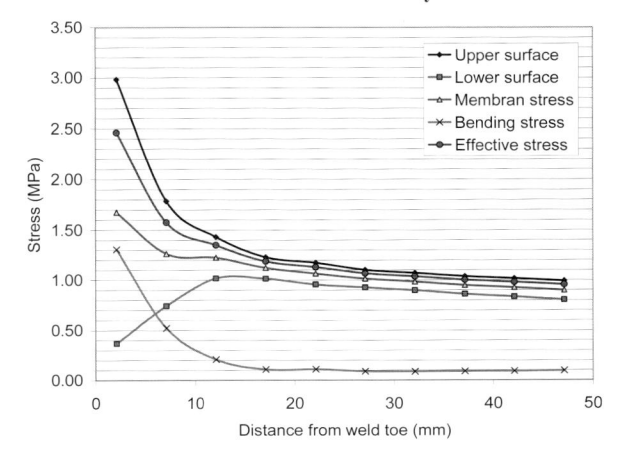

Fig. 12 Stress at hot spot region of 90° solid model without eccentricity and additional weld leg length

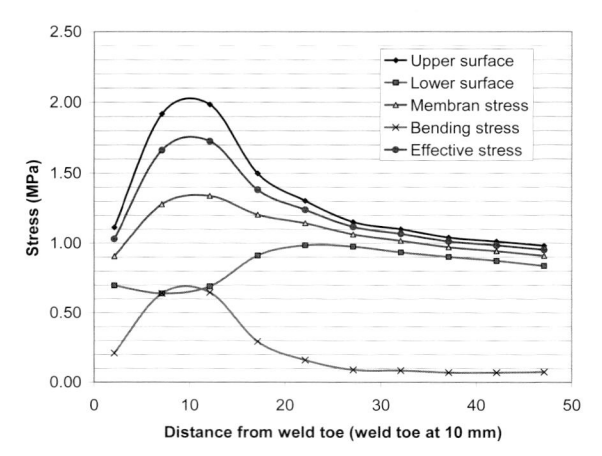

Fig. 13 Stress at hot spot region of 90° solid model without eccentricity and with weld leg length equal t

Discussion of numerical results

The methodology and target hot spot stress values in this investigation were derived from FE analysis and fatigue testing of a hopper knuckle connection (in this study denoted cruciform joint, 135°, with full penetration weld with no additional weld leg length, but with eccentricity. There is a weld, but no significant fillet weld from the hopper plate into the bottom plate). Then target values were derived for geometries without eccentricities as listed in Table 1. FE analyses without fillet weld and with additional fillet weld leg lengths equal t/2 and t were performed (t = thickness of bottom plate). Based on this an assessment of stress read out points from shell FE models, where the weld is not included, was made. It is suggested to read out stresses from a shell finite element model at read out points shifted away from the intersection line for derivation of surface hot spot stress by the following value

$$x_{shift} = \frac{t_1}{2} + x_{wt} \quad (2)$$

where t_1 = plate thickness of plate number 1 in Figure 10 and x_{wt} = additional fillet weld leg length as shown in Figure 15. ($t_1 = t_2 = 10$ mm is used for the calibration). The stress at the shift position is denoted $\sigma (x_{shift})$. Then the surface hot spot stress is increased by a factor β to account for the local bending due to presence of an additional weld leg length by the following equation

$$\sigma_{hot\,spot} = \sigma(x_{shift}) * \beta \quad (3)$$

where

$$\beta = \gamma + \alpha_1 \frac{x_{wt}}{t_1} + \alpha_2 \left(\frac{x_{wt}}{t_1}\right)^2 \quad (4)$$

where t_1 is plate thickness at the considered hot spot region.

The factor β is shown in Figure 14. This figure is derived for the different cruciform connections without eccentricity.

The ratio of bending stress to the total stress in the shell finite element model relative to that of the three-dimensional model, where the weld toe is included at different positions, is assessed. It is found that this ratio is similar in the shell finite element model as in the three-dimensional model. Thus, it is also considered acceptable to reduce the local bending stress derived from a FE analysis using shell elements at hot spots of this type by a factor 0.6 before an effective hot spot stress is entered into the S-N curve for fatigue assessment as explained earlier. It is observed that some negative eccentricity is beneficial for the fatigue life as calculated hot spot stress is less with eccentricity included as compared without eccentricity for the 135 degree joint. The difference was found to be less for the 90 degree joint.

Based on an assessment of the derived numerical results it is found acceptable to use results from shell finite element analysis, where the weld is not included, also for read out of hot spot stress at a position of the actual weld toe when a fillet weld is added. From the analyses with three-dimensional solid elements it is seen that addition of a fillet weld increase the local bending stress at the weld toe area. It is observed that the local bending stress is moved to be in front of the new weld toe. However, its absolute value is reduced by addition of a fillet. The net result is a slight increase of stress in front of the new weld toe. This increase in stress should be accounted for by a correction factor as expressed by equation (4).

Based on the performed work it is suggested to read out stress from a shell finite element model at read out points shifted away from the intersection line for derivation of surface hot spot stress as expressed by equation (2). This stress is derived directly from the analysis (without any extrapolation of stresses). The surface stress (including membrane and bending stress) is denoted $\sigma_{surface}(x_{shift})$. The membrane stress is denoted $\sigma_{membrane}(x_{shift})$ and $\sigma_{bending}(x_{shift})$. Then the hot spot stress is derived as

$$\sigma_{hot\,spot} = (\sigma_{membrane}(x_{shift}) + \sigma_{bending}(x_{shift}) * 0.60) * \beta \quad (5)$$

where

$$\sigma_{bending}(x_{shift}) = \sigma_{surface}(x_{shift}) - \sigma_{membrane}(x_{shift}) \quad (6)$$

For 135° connections the correction factor β is derived as

$$\beta = 1.07 - 0.15 \frac{x_{wt}}{t_1} + 0.22 \left(\frac{x_{wt}}{t_1}\right)^2 \quad (7)$$

For 120° connections the correction factor β is derived as

$$\beta = 1.09 - 0.16 \frac{x_{wt}}{t_1} + 0.36 \left(\frac{x_{wt}}{t_1}\right)^2 \quad (8)$$

For 90° connections the correction factor β is derived as

$$\beta = 1.20 + 0.04 \frac{x_{wt}}{t_1} + 0.30 \left(\frac{x_{wt}}{t_1}\right)^2 \quad (9)$$

The β-factors are shown in Figure 14. The procedure is calibrated for $0 \leq x_{wt}/t_1 \leq 1.0$. The derived hot spot stress should be entered the D-curve (DNV-RP-C203) or FAT90 curve (IIW (1996)). The analysis procedure is illustrated in Figure 15. It is recommended to use the same element size at hot spots of models of actual structural details as used in the presented calibration work, i.e. mesh size t x t where t = plate thickness.

Additional analyses

The calibration analyses reported above were related to a test specimen with a rather small thickness (10 mm) and a limited flange width. Therefore, a number of additional analyses were performed to investigate

- Increased plate widths
- Increased plate thickness and weld size
- Other loading conditions: One load case with pure membrane stress in the flange plate and one load case with normal pressure on the flange plate.

In general the results for different types of loading and with larger plate widths did not deviate much from that of the original calibration. The analyses showed that plate thickness was not a significant parameter beyond that already included in equations (7-9).

The methodology has been tested on a hopper knuckle section investigated by ISSC (2003). The model was a hopper knuckle section for a double hull VLCC in approximately 1/3 scale, Ship Research Panel 245 (2001).

The model was fixed to a rigid wall at the double hull side, with the ship's bottom being upside and the inner bottom being downside. The load was applied by three synchronized hydraulic jacks on the centerline of the double bottom, see Figure 16. The proposed procedure was found to be in agreement with the test results using both 4-node and 8-node shell elements.

The proposed procedure has also been used in full scale fatigue analysis by DNV. The procedure has been assessed using the sub modeling technique in a stochastic analysis, Figure 17. Results using models with three-dimensional elements including the welds have been compared with results from simple shell models using 4-node and 8-noded shell elements without welds in the model. After this it was suggested to increase the β correction factor for the 90° connection slightly as compared with the original calibration presented in Figure 14. The resulting correction factor is expressed by equation (9).

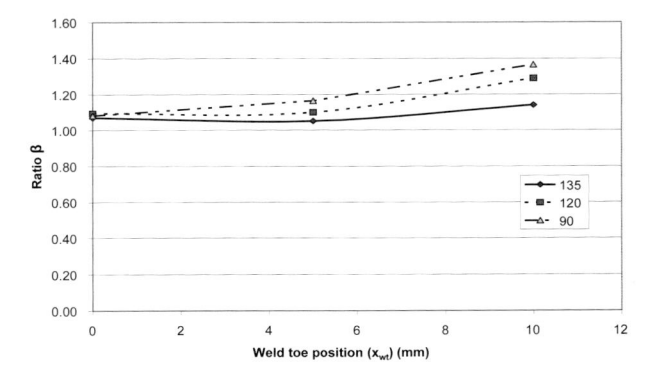

Fig. 14 Ratio β as function of weld toe position

$$\sigma_{hot\ spot} = (\sigma_{membrane}(x_{shift}) + \sigma_{bending}(x_{shift}) * 0.60) * \beta$$

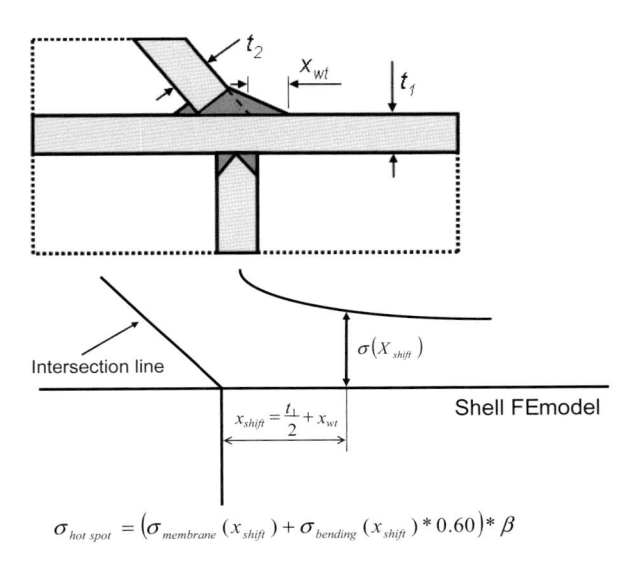

Fig. 15 Illustration of procedure for derivation of hot spot stress using shell finite element model

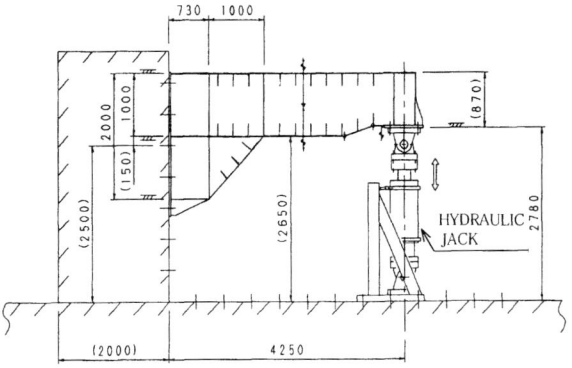

Fig. 16 Hopper knuckle model

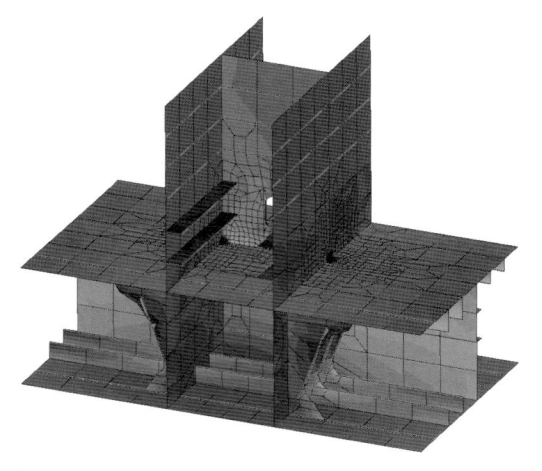

Fig. 17 Detail in full ship model analyzed by sub modeling

Hot spot areas on back sides at welds between plate to web

It is observed from the present analyses that also the welded connections on the back side (below inner bottom plate to double bottom web) may be critical with respect to fatigue, especially if one accepts use of improvement methods for the weld toes such that the total stress range in the considered area is increased.

This implies that if weld improvement of the front side weld toe is required to achieve sufficient fatigue life, one should also consider describing weld improvement of the weld toes on the back side. Then a full/partial penetration weld is recommended over some length in the most severe stressed area. To avoid fatigue cracking from the weld root it is recommended to use full/partial penetration welds over a length of min. 150 – 200 mm from the corner of crossing plates. In case of NDT with ultrasonic examination a full penetration weld is necessary.

The size of fillet welds and depth of penetration for partial penetration welds should be checked for sufficient fatigue strength. In assessing this region it should be noted that this detail is a cruciform connection and that a stricter S-N curve should be used in the fatigue assessment as compared with the standard hot spot S-N curve, see e. g. DNV-RP-C203 (2005) for more details.

The calculated hot spot stress in the corner region is significantly higher in a shell element model than in a model with solid elements where the welds are included. Based on the present analysis with use of t x t element mesh size it is observed that the stresses in the element in the corner may be neglected when analysis results in a shell element model is considered based on comparison with results from the three-dimensional model, Figure 18.

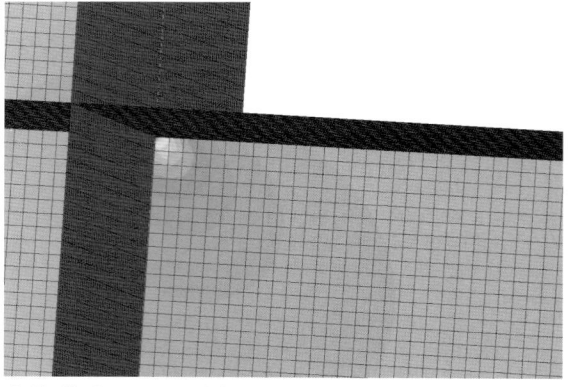

a) Shell element model (8-node elements)

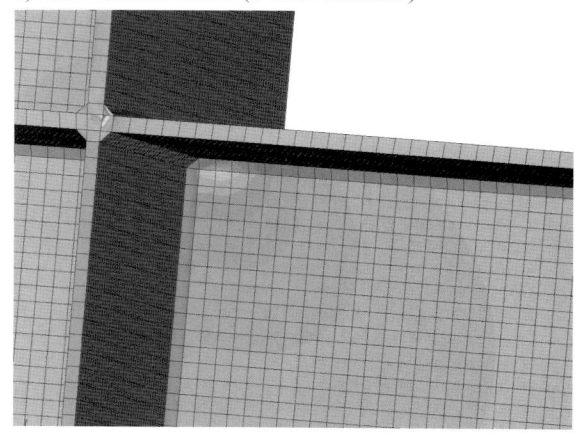

b) Three-dimensional element model
Fig. 18 Calculated principal stresses at back side plate

Conclusions

Fatigue design of dynamic loaded ship structures is normally based on finite element analysis using shell elements where the welds are not included in the analysis models. These analyses do not account for the weld geometry which is considered to be a significant parameter for details with large stress concentrations. Typical details are web stiffened cruciform connections such as hopper knuckles, stringer heels and joints connecting deck structures to vertical primary members in ships. In the present work a number of calibration analyses have been performed using three-dimensional solid elements that included the weld geometry and shell elements with 4-nodes and 8-nodes. Based on the results from these analyses a methodology for derivation of hot spot stress at welded connections using shell finite element models has been developed. The weld size is accounted for in the analysis procedure even if the weld is not included in the shell finite element model. This procedure will be included in the revision of the DNV Classification Note 30.7 "Fatigue Assessment of Ship Structures" scheduled for release in January 2008.

References

Bergan, P. G. and Lotsberg, I. (2006). "Fatigue Capacity of FPSO Structures". Journal of Offshore and Arctic Engineering. Vol. 128, May, pp. 156 -161.

Berge, S., Kihl, D., Lotsberg, I., Maherault, S., Mikkola, T. P. J., Nielsen, L. P., Paetzold, H., Shin, C. –H., Sun, H. –H and Tomita, Y. (2003). "Special Task Committee VI.2 Fatigue Strength Assessment". ISSC, San Diego, 2003. In Proceedings of the 15th International Ship and Offshore Structures Congress. Vol. 2. Edited by A. E. Mansour and R. C. Ertekin, Elsevier. ISBN: 0-08-044076-2.

CN 30.7 (2005) "Fatigue Assessment of Ship Structures". DNV, Oslo.

DNV- RP- C203 (2005) "Fatigue Analysis of Offshore Steel Structures".

Fricke, W. (2001). Recommended Hot Spot Analysis Procedure for Structural Details of FPSO's and Ships Based on Round-Robin FE Analyses. Proc. 11th ISOPE, Stavanger. Also International Journal of Offshore and Polar Engineering. Vol. 12, No. 1, March 2002.

Lotsberg, I. (2001). "Overview of the FPSO Fatigue Capacity JIP". OMAE, Rio deJaneiro, June.

Lotsberg, I. (2004). "Recommended Methodology for Analysis of Structural Stress for Fatigue Assessment of Plated Structures". OMAE-FPSO'04-0013, Int. Conf. Houston.

Lotsberg, I. (2006). "Fatigue Design of Plated Structures using Finite Element Analysis". Journal of Ships and Offshore Structures. Vol. 1, No 1, pp. 45-54.

Lotsberg, I. and Sigurdsson, G.(2004). "Hot Spot S-N Curve for Fatigue Analysis of Plated Structures". OMAE-FPSO'04-0014, Int. Conf. Houston. Also in Journal of Offshore and Arctic Engineering November 2006, pp. 330-336.

Kang, S. W., Kim, W. S. and Paik, Y. M. (2002). "Fatigue Strength of Fillet Welded Steel Structure under Out-of-Plane Bending", International Welding / Joining Conference – Korea.

Kim, W. S. and Lotsberg, I.(2004). "Fatigue Test Data for Welded Connections in Ship Shaped Structures". OMAE-FPSO'04-0018, Int. Conf. Houston. Also in Journal of Offshore and Arctic Engineering, Vol. 127, Issue 4. November 2005, pp 359-365.

Ship Research Panel 245. (2001). "Study on Ship Structural Life of the Double Hull Tanker". Shipping Research Association of Japan. (in Japanese).

Sesam User Manuals, DNV, Oslo. 2004.

Storsul, R., Landet, E. and Lotsberg, I.(2004). "Calculated and Measured Stress at Welded Connections between Side Longitudinals and Transverse Frames in Ship Shaped Structures". OMAE-FPSO'04-0017, Int. Conf. Houston.

On Corrosion Fatigue Crack Propagation of TMCP Steel in Seawater Ballast Tanks

Won Beom Kim and Jeom Kee Paik

Department of Naval Architecture and Ocean Engineering, Pusan National University
Busan, Korea

Abstract

Corrosion fatigue crack propagation is a challenging issue in seawater ballast tank structures under corrosion environment. The aim of the present study is to investigate the corrosion fatigue crack propagation characteristics of TMCP steel in synthetic seawater.

Corrosion fatigue testing on TMCP steel specimen with tensile strength of 490MPa is carried out in synthetic seawater with and without the application of cathodic protection.

In the present study, the loading speed of fatigue test was set at 0.17Hz that is supposed to be equivalent to typical sea wave period. Stress ratio in the fatigue test loading was set to be 0.1.

It is found that the fatigue crack propagation rate of TMCP steel in synthetic seawater condition is faster than that in air condition by almost two times. Also, it is observed that the fatigue crack propagation rate of TMCP steel in seawater condition with cathodic protection is in between air condition and seawater condition without cathodic protection. The results and insights developed from the present study will be useful for corrosion fatigue crack propagation management of seawater ballast tank structures.

Keywords

Corrosion fatigue crack propagation; Cathodic protection; TMCP steel; Seawater ballast tank; Synthetic seawater.

Introduction

Recently, in order to enhance the efficiency of the transportation by the ship, ships have become bigger and progressed with an exclusive use of the ship. At the same time, fast and light-weight ships are being used expeditiously. For this purpose, TMCP steel has contributed greatly. Additional reasons for the wide use of TMCP steel include the enhancement of the weldability and a good quality of high heat-input weldment that makes thick plate weld possible.

Recent unpublished investigation made in Korea, shows that generally more than 30% of the weights in large merchant ships are credited to the use of TMCP steel. Accordingly, the investigation of the characteristics of TMCP steel is an important task that should be promptly undertaken.

The IMO performance standard for protective coatings has recently been updated. By the application of this updated standard, a longer coating life should be expected. However with regard to the corrosion environment of the ballast tank, the reverse side of the upper deck (which is the upper side of the ballast tank) is exposed to severe variations of temperature in a day's time. In addition, the wet atmosphere of the ballast tank makes it vulnerable to corrosion.

Another example that leads to further corrosion involves the heated fuel oil tank, adjacent to the ballast tank, which is harmful to the environment of the ballast tank. The continuous degradation of the coating of the ballast tank is to be presumed when taking these causes into account.

If the coating is complete, corrosion will not occur. However, if the degradation of the coating continues, corrosion will start. In this case, cathodic protection is an effective method. In this paper focusing on the ballast tank concerns as mentioned above, the fatigue crack propagation behavior of TMCP steel under the circumstances of "in air, in seawater condition (Kim and Paik, 2007) and under the cathodic protection" are investigated.

Test of TMCP steel for corrosion fatigue crack propagation

Configuration of test specimen

Two kinds of specimen were used for the corrosion fatigue crack propagation test: the CCT (Center-Cracked-Tension) specimen that has a large-sized centrally penetrated slit in the middle of the specimen and the CT (Compact Tension) specimen by ASTM E647, respectively. The configuration and size of the specimens are shown in Figures 1 and 2 respectively. The chemical composition and mechanical properties of the TMCP steel used are shown in Tables 1 and 2 respectively.

Table 1: Mechanical properties of TMCP steel plate used

Yield Stress	Tensile Stress	Elongation
390MPa	496MPa	29%

Table 2: Chemical composition TMCP steel plate used

C	Si	Mn	P	S
0.14	0.20	1.14	0.016	0.004

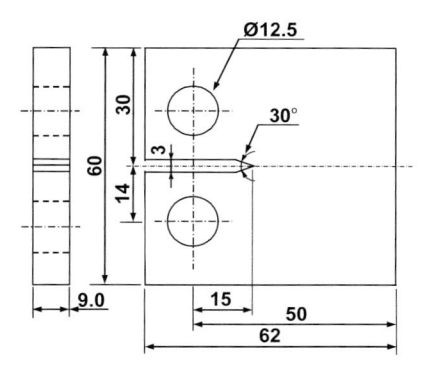

Fig. 1: Shape and dimensions of CT specimen

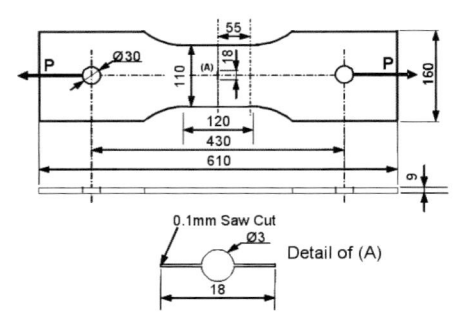

Fig. 2: Shape and dimensions of CCT specimen

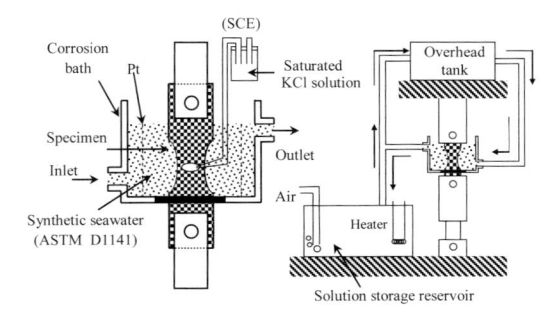

Fig. 3: Circulation system of synthetic seawater for corrosion fatigue crack propagation tests

With these specimens, corrosion fatigue crack propagation tests were carried out.

Experimental circumstances

Fatigue tests were performed using hydraulic fatigue test machines with capacities of 98kN and 490kN respectively in air, in synthetic seawater and under the cathodic protection condition. For seawater condition, ASTM (ASTM D1141) standard synthetic seawater was used at 25°C in fully air saturated condition with pH adjusted to 8.2 with NaOH solution.

The synthetic seawater solutions were circulated from a reservoir. In addition, for cathodic protection condition, corrosion potentials were adjusted to be -800mV vs. Saturated Calomel Electrode (SCE).

It is known that corrosion fatigue is affected by the conditions of the temperature, loading speed, flow rate of solution and stress etc. Accordingly, in this research, loading speed of fatigue test was set to be 10cpm because it is known that the sea wave period is 6~10cpm (Ebara, 1988). The stress ratio of the fatigue loading was set at 0.1. Figure 3 shows the schematic circulation system of synthetic seawater for the corrosion fatigue crack propagation test.

The test specimen was immersed into a corrosion bath made of acryl resin, and the synthetic seawater was circulated at a uniform speed of 0.004m/s. It is known that the corrosion current density of the steel in a seawater environment condition is stabilized 8 hours later (Nagai et al., 1977), loading was exerted 12 hours later since the specimen was immersed in the synthetic seawater.

Measurement of corrosion fatigue crack

From the tip of a slit, at interval of 1mm, a rule was inserted in the direction of crack propagation for CCT and CT specimen for the convenience of the observation. Also, for the specimen that was used at seawater environment, transparent anti-corrosion tape was attached on the surface of the specimen for the clear view of the crack observation. The measurement of the fatigue crack was carried out by the use of a traveling microscope with the accuracy of 1/100mm.

Crack propagation characteristics of TMCP steel plates

Evaluation of stress intensity factor K for CT specimen

Manufacturing of the specimen and calculation of the stress intensity factor K for the CT specimen were carried out according to the ASTM E647,

$$\Delta K = \frac{\Delta P}{B\sqrt{W}} \frac{(2+a/W)}{(1-a/W)^{3/2}} \times$$
$$[0.886 + 4.64(a/W) - 13.32(a/W)^2$$
$$+ 14.72(a/W)^3 - 5.6(a/W)^4] \quad (1)$$

where P is applied load, B is specimen thickness and W is specimen width, respectively.

Evaluation of boundary correlation factor of CCT specimen

With regard to CCT specimen, as the loading was exerted through the pin, it was thought that the stress is not uniform at parallel part of the specimen. If the stress is exerted uniformly, Isida's solution (Stress Intensity Handbook, 1987) is applicable. However, in the strict sense, Isida's solution is not applicable for this case.

Accordingly, in this research, to get the boundary correlation factor $F(\alpha,\beta)$ for the CCT specimen, the calculation of J as a path-independent line integral was carried out. With the solutions of J integral similar values were shown in spite of the different path. From this J integral value, the stress intensity factor of the present CCT specimen by pin loading was obtained. The J integral can be obtained from the following equation (Anderson, 1997):

$$J = \int_\Gamma (Wdy - T_i \frac{\partial u_i}{\partial x})ds \quad (2)$$

where W is strain energy density, T_i is components of the traction vector, u_i is displacement vector components and ds is length increment along the contour, with

$$W = \int_0^{\varepsilon_{ij}} \sigma_{ij} d\varepsilon_{ij}$$

$$T_i = \sigma_{ij} n_j \quad n_j : \text{unit vector}$$

When it is plane stress condition, the stress intensity factor K can be obtained from the following equation by using previously obtained J, where E is Young's modulus.

$$J = \frac{K^2}{E} \quad (3)$$

For the verification of the accuracy of the calculated K by FEM, boundary correlation factor $F(\alpha,\beta)$ as shown in Figure 4 was derived from the calculated K by changing the crack length 2a for the plate which width is 110mm and 2H is 110mm for the uniform stress condition. The calculation result of $F(\alpha,\beta)$ was compared with Isida's graph (Stress Intensity Factors Handbook, 1987) and shown in Figure 4 as the symbol ●.

Based on this fact, the accuracy of the present calculation was verified. In addition, $F(\alpha,\beta)$ for CCT specimen, which is in pin loading condition, was calculated by changing the crack length 2a and shown in Figure 4 as the symbol ■. Figure 5 shows FEM mesh generation of CCT specimen for J integral calculation. Figure 6 shows the result of curve fitting for the symbol ■ which represents the $F(\alpha,\beta)$ of the present pin loaded CCT specimen. The range of the stress intensity factor ΔK of the CCT specimen was calculated by the following equation.

$$\Delta K = \Delta\sigma\sqrt{\pi a} \cdot F(\alpha,\beta) \quad (4)$$

Figure 7 shows the relationship between da/dN-ΔK using

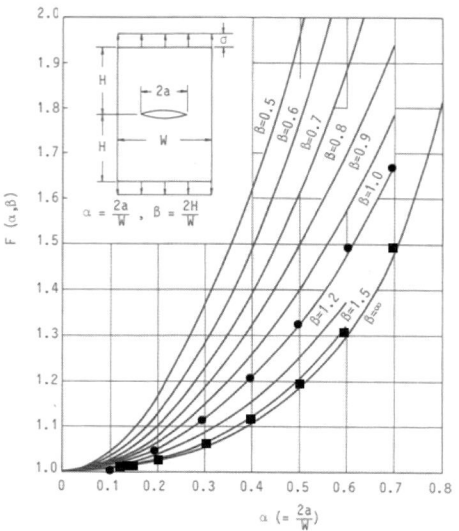

Fig.4: Boundary correlation factor F(α,β) of CCT specimen

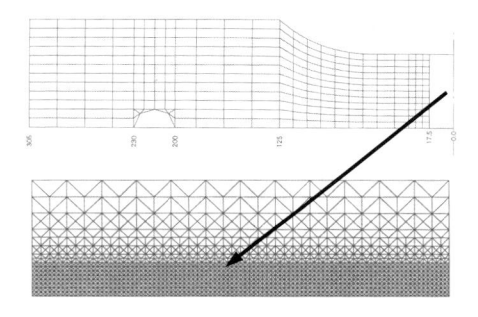

Fig. 5: FEM model for J integral calculation

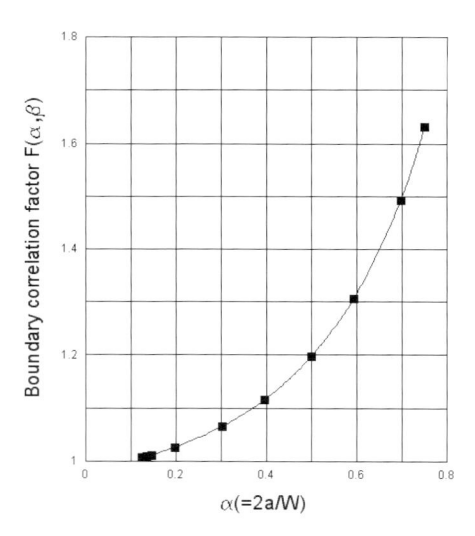

Fig. 6: Calculated boundary correlation factor F(α,β) for the used CCT specimen

In air condition (without cathodic protection)

Comparing the crack propagation speed in air and in seawater condition with the same ΔK in Figure 7, although it is different according to the ΔK, it can be generally said that the crack propagation speed in seawater condition is twice as fast or more than in air condition. The da/dN-ΔK data in air condition was plotted almost on one line (Kim and Paik, 2007). This shows that the crack propagation in air condition is governed by the stress intensity factor alone.

In seawater condition without cathodic protection

From da/dN-ΔK data in seawater condition, it was observed that the data of the synthetic seawater condition is much more scattered than that of air condition (Kim and Paik, 2007). In addition, it was observed that the crack propagation occurred intermittently. That means that other factors, for example, the formation of the rust, electrocoating, stress concentration of the pit at the tip of the crack, corrosive dissolution etc. are thought to be related to the crack propagation behavior in seawater condition. Further research with regard to these matters is to be needed.

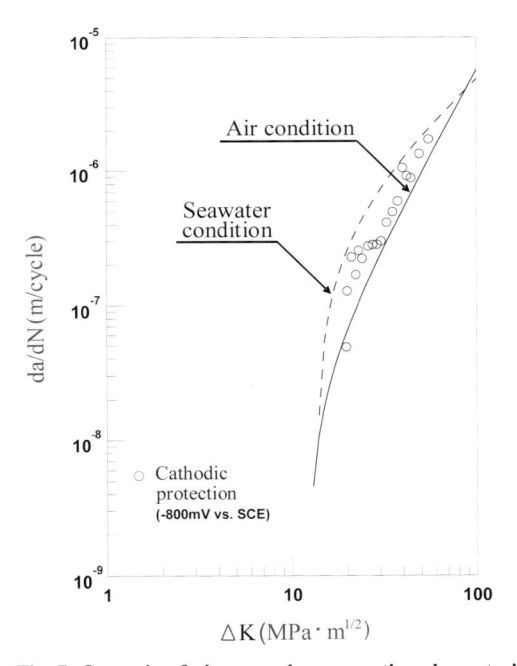

Fig. 7: Corrosion fatigue crack propagation characteristics

In seawater condition with cathodic protection

Corrosion fatigue crack propagation characteristics under the cathodic protection were compared with those of in air and in seawater condition. For this purpose, the least square method was used to get the fitting line of in air and in seawater condition seen in Figure 7. In Figure 7, it is obvious that the fatigue crack propagation rate of steel with cathodic protection is in between those of seawater condition without cathodic protection and air condition.

Concluding remarks

It is found that the fatigue crack propagation rate of TMCP steel in synthetic seawater condition is almost two times faster than that in air condition. Also, it is observed that the fatigue crack propagation rate of steel with cathodic protection is in between those of seawater condition without cathodic protection and air condition. The test results and insights developed from the present study will be useful for practical design of seawater ballast tank structures in association with corrosion fatigue crack performance.

Acknowledgements

This study was undertaken at the Ship and Offshore Structural Mechanics Laboratory (SSML), Pusan National University, which is a National Research Laboratory funded by the Korea Science and Engineering Foundation (Grant No. ROA-2006-000-10239-0). The authors thank Emeritus Professor M. Iwata, Hiroshima University, Japan, for his valuable guidance and comments.

References

Kim, WB and Paik, JK (2007). "Corrosion Fatigue Crack Propagation Characteristics of TMCP Steel in Synthetic Seawater Condition under Wave Period," Proc. 10th Int. Conf. on the Mechanical Behavior of Materials, ICM10, Busan.

Ebara, R (1988). "Corrosion Fatigue Test Method for the Material," Bulletin of the Society of Naval Architects of Japan, Vol.703, pp.34-43 (in Japanese).

Nagai, K, Mori, M, Yajima, H, Yamamoto, Y, and Fujimoto, Y (1977). "Studies on the Evaluation of Corrosion Fatigue Crack Initiation," Journal of The Society of Naval Architects of Japan, Vol.142, pp.239-250 (in Japanese).

ASTM E647 (1999). "Standard Test Method for Measurement of Fatigue Crack Growth Rates," Annual Book of ASTM Standards, American Society for Testing and Materials, Philadelphia, pp.591-630.

Stress Intensity Factors Handbook (1987). Vol.1., Pergamon Press, New York, USA.

Anderson, TL (1995). "Fracture Mechanics," CRC Press, Florida, USA.

10th International Symposium on Practical Design of Ships and Other Floating Structures
Houston, Texas, United States of America
© 2007 American Bureau of Shipping

New Directions in Ship Structural Regulations

Claude Daley [1], Andrew Kendrick [2], Mihailo Pavic [2]

[1] Faculty of Engineering, Memorial University
St. John's, Newfoundland and Labrador, Canada
[2] BMT Fleet Technology Limited
Kanata, Ontario, Canada

Abstract

A recent review of ship structural regulations (Ship Structures Committee Project 1444) was aimed at clarifying best practice in regulations. The review focused on the hull girder and bottom structure. The majority of rules reviewed are formulated in terms of elastic stresses. It was expected that the review would be able to identify implicit as well as explicit factors of safety in either the load or strength formulations or both. However, no such factors of safety against yielding were found. While this was initially surprising, it leads to an interesting and useful insight into the question of why ships are able to operate safely. The best explanation is that ships, especially new ships, rely on small levels of plastic deformation to create a significant strength reserve, easily capable of withstanding not only the design loads, but overload conditions as well. Ductility is thus a crucially important material property for keeping ships safe. The complexity of plastic response raises the question of how best to reflect this issue in rules. This is especially important when considering the safety of aging ships. The issues of coating design, corrosion and fatigue deserve to be reexamined with a view to the effects of the plastic behavior during ageing.

Keywords

Ship design; Ship structures; Regulations; Plastic response; Classification.

Nomenclature

B : beam [m]
Cb : block coefficient [-]
f_1 : material factor [-]
H : height [m]
kw : function of frame geometry [-]
Lbp : length between perpendiculars [m]
p : pressure [kPa]
p_C : pressure causing 3 hinge plate collapse [MPa]
p_{dp} : dynamic pressure [kPa]
p_{EH} : pressure to cause edge hinges in plate [MPa]
p_Y : pressure to cause plate yield [MPa]
s : frame spacing [m, mm]
T : draft [m]
t : thickness [mm]
t_k : corrosion addition [mm]
Zpns: normalized plastic modulus [-]
σ : stress (design) [MPa]
$σ_x$: longitudinal stress
$σ_y$: lateral stress
$σ_{VM}$: von-Mises equivalent stress

Introduction

A review of various ship structural regulations has been conducted as part of a Ship Structures Committee project (Kendrick, Daley and Pavic 2006). The review has shown that while ship structural rules can appear to be complex, they are based on quite simple structural mechanics. It was not a surprise to find that the rules are formulated with simple combined elastic stresses. On the other hand, it was surprising to find that the combined stresses appear to exceed the yield stress. This led to the realization that ship rules, being based on real world experience (strong empirical evidence), reflect an intrinsic plastic capacity that ships have. At deformations that are too small to observe, ship structures can exceed yield and be perfectly safe. The ductility of modern steel ships is implicitly providing a substantial 'factor of safety'. The rational next step is to have the rules explicitly recognize this capability and reflect this behavior in the rules we use to design the structure. This will result in better ship designs, with improved safety and economy, a win-win outcome for everyone.

Background

The desire to develop more rational approaches to ship structural design is not new. The foreword to 'A Guide for the Analysis of Ship Structures' published in 1960, starts:

> "It has been the dream of every ship designer to rise above the conventional empirical methods of

structural design and create a ship structural design based on rational methods."

In order to understand the need for a unified and rational approach to ship structure design, it is necessary to review the history and nature of current methods, and of alternatives to these.

"Traditional" Ship Structural Design Standards

The origins of most current commercial and naval ship structural design approaches can be found in the work of a number of mid-19th century pioneers, including Rankine, Smith and Reed. They developed methods of estimating hull girder bending loads due to waves, and also developed response criteria for bending and shear. Early iron-framed ships tended to have wooden decks and hulls, meaning that buckling did not become an issue. Formal approaches to buckling date from the 1940s to 1960s. Material property issues (notch toughness, weldability) started to be addressed systematically within the same timeframe, partly through the early work of the SSC on fatigue and fracture. One hundred and fifty years of research and development, cross-fertilized by efforts in other engineering disciplines have been incorporated in commercial and naval ship design standards in somewhat different ways.

Most commercial ships are constructed under the Rules of a Classification Society, such as the American Bureau of Shipping (ABS), Det Norske Veritas (DNV), Lloyds Register (LR), Bureau Veritas (BV), Germanischer Lloyd (GL), etc. These and other classification societies developed, starting in the 19th Century, in order to meet the growing needs of both governments and commercial interests to ensure that ships were adequately reliable and safe. Initially, they largely focused on national interests and fleets (or imperial, in the case of LR and BV); and most were wholly or partly government controlled. More recently, the market for ship classification services has become international in nature (in most cases) and so the classification societies have become more independent of national ties. However, most classification societies retain strong links with maritime administrations in their home countries.

In keeping with their origins, classification society rules developed in some level of isolation from each other for many years, meaning that (for example) ABS, DNV and LR requirements for different areas of design were presented in very different ways and could lead to significantly different outcomes in terms of scantlings. As technologies developed (new ship types, faster operating speeds, replacement of rivets by welding), rules governing their use were introduced into the various Rules, extending their scope.

Advances in analytical methodologies have also been incorporated as they have been developed. For example, prior to the work of Rankine and others noted above, LR's rule scantlings were proportional only to displacement, which led to decreasing factors of safety for larger ships. Subsequently, the rules were modified to incorporate a more systematic treatment of wave bending. Similarly, local strength and stability rule requirements were initially based on successful past practice and "rules of thumb"; and modified as the state-of-the-art expanded. However, some of the historical features were retained, making the rule systems a mixed bag of analytical and prescriptive requirements.

The differences in Rules systems, and organizational issues that influenced their application, led to differences in outcomes in terms of safety and reliability. Accordingly, a group of the leading Classification Societies formed the International Association of Classification Societies (IACS) in 1968.

Recent Structural Standards Development

As noted previously, some recent convergence in classification society rule systems has been generated by IACS. IACS can trace its origins back to the International Load Line Convention of 1930 and its recommendations. The Convention recommended collaboration between classification societies to secure "as much uniformity as possible in the application of the standards of strength upon which freeboard is based...". Milestones towards achieving this included the formation in 1948 of the International Maritime Consultative Organization (now IMO), by the United Nations, and major conferences of the leading classification societies in 1939, 1955, and 1968. The last of these led to the formation of IACS, which has since developed more than 200 Unified Requirements (URs) and many Unified Interpretations and Recommendations of rule requirements. The first UR dealing with structural strength unified the classification societies' approaches to maximum wave bending moment, almost 100 years after Rankine's first theoretical model.

IACS was given consultative status with IMO, and works closely with IMO (though with frequent tensions) to address structural and other safety issues through the development of new URs and by other mechanisms. Two notable models can be cited. Under the High-Speed Craft Code, IMO has left structural requirements at a very broad and performance-based level. The responsibility for the development of appropriate rules was left to the classification societies, each of which has developed its own approach. Conversely, in the new Guidelines for Ships Operating in Arctic Waters (Polar Code) IMO has specifically referenced new IACS URs for structural and mechanical design. Representatives of the national administrations and of the classification societies have been involved in the development of both the Guidelines and the URs.

Other important developments within the last decade have included the move towards the use of numerical analysis (FEA) to optimize scantlings, and the development of automated systems (ABS Safehull, DnV Nauticus, etc.) to generate and check most structural components. To some extent, these have led to less standardization amongst class, although in principle all structures should still comply with the intent of the relevant URs. The classification societies' various software packages (e.g SafeHull from ABS) simplify the work of the average ship structural designer. However, by capturing many important issues into software that tends to be used as a 'black-box', these developments do not encourage insight into the structural issues involved. The use of FEA also carries risk for the unwary and for the occasional user, and classification society guidance notes are an imperfect substitute for training and experience.

In parallel with these 'organizational' changes to standards and to their implementation, the ship rule systems have continued to incorporate some of the developments in the technical state-of-the-art.

Another recent development is the increased involvement of national and international standards organizations (ASTM, CSA, ISO) in the development of structural standards for ships and offshore structures. To date, these have gained only limited acceptance in the shipping community, but they represent increased competition for traditional rule systems.

The two key technical aspects that are to be found in recent developments are the treatment of the mechanics of structures (load and strength models) and the treatment of uncertainty (probability models, risk reduction strategies). Both developments are aimed at inserting more rational understanding into the process of specifying structural requirements.

Load and Resistance Factor Design (LRFD)

LRFD (Load and Resistance Factor Design) is a relatively recent development, although it has been employed in some standards for a few decades. In certain areas, notably related to buildings, bridges and offshore structures, it is common to use LRFD. The approach attempts to achieve a consistent risk level for all comparable structures by employing calibrated partial safety factors. Various parameters affecting the design, both load and strength related measures, are individually factored to reflect both the level of uncertainty and the consequences of failure, which may range from loss of serviceability to catastrophic collapse. The approach relies on several assumptions about the nature of risk and failure, many of which are reasonable when thinking of the types of hazards (wind, seismic) that a static building will face. The approach implicitly assumes that failure is a consequence of an uncertain load exceeding an uncertain strength, which is a very simplistic model of an accident. The approach does not attempt to model complex (nonlinear) paths to failure, including feedback and interdependence, gross errors or any but the simplest of human errors. LRFD has not been implemented in ship structural design, at least partly due to concerns about its suitability.

LRFD is often implemented along with concepts from Limit States (LS) design. LS design attempts to look beyond the intact behavior, and establish the limits, both from a safety and operational perspective, so that the design point(s) reflect the boundary of unacceptable behavior. Traditional elastic design, on the other hand, tended to focus on a design point far below a level where actual negative consequences arose. When combined, LRFD and LS design purport to both properly balance risk and reflect, to all concerned, the actual capability limits of the structure. Together, this is intended to clarify and communicate the realistic structural risks. There are ship structural rules that have employed LS design, without LRFD. Two notable examples include the new IACS Unified Requirements for Polar Ships, and the Russian Registry Rules for Ice Class Vessels. In both cases the rules contain checks for post-yield limit states, but do not include load or resistance factors, as are typically included in LRFD codes.

Formal Safety Assessment (FSA)

Formal Safety Assessment (FSA) is a recent development in the area of structural standards. FSA is actually more of a standards development approach than a design standard. The International Maritime Organization (IMO) has led the development of this concept. They describe it as "a rational and systematic process for assessing the risks associated with shipping activity and for evaluating the costs and benefits of IMO's options for reducing these risks."

The IMO, and others, are evaluating FSA as a method to comparatively evaluate the components in proposed new regulations or to compare standards. FSA allows for a cost-risk-benefit comparison to be made between the various technical and other issues, including human factors. The FSA approach is based on the recognition that many risks arise from multiple causes (i.e. from system behavior) and can be mitigated in a variety of ways. This view leads to the approach of allowing safety to be based on the most cost effective risk control option (RCO) rather than on some standard, prescribed, one-size-fits-all approach. This is especially beneficial for innovative designs, where the standard approach to reducing risk may not be optimal.

FSA is largely a development out of the UK, developed partly in response to the Piper Alpha offshore platform disaster of 1988, where 167 people lost their lives. FSA is being applied to the IMO rule-making process.

FSA offers much promise. The complexity of risk assessment technology itself is probably the major obstacle standing in the way of wider use of the FSA approach.

Performance Based Standards

In recent years, there has been a strong trend towards what is generally referred to as performance-based standards (PBS). These standards describe a context and safety targets that they expect the design to meet, and then leave it to the proponent to achieve the targets in any manner they wish. CSA S471 is one example of this approach. In PBS, there are no specific loads or strength levels prescribed. The designers are expected to demonstrate the achievement of a target level of safety by an analysis of the loads and strength. In effect, the proponent is asked to both develop a design standard for their own structure and evaluate it against a risk criterion.

This approach is very popular in certain industries, especially the offshore oil and gas industry, as it enables them to examine a variety of structural and system concepts (gravity based platforms, semi-submersibles, tension-leg platforms, ship shape FPSOs, and others) on a more consistent basis.

The obvious drawback with this approach is the divergence of designs and the possibility for divergence in safety attainment when each project group develops an essential custom design standard. In reality, for most aspects of a design, the proponents will have neither the resources nor the time to develop a complete standard from scratch, and will instead apply existing standards as demonstration that requirements have been met.

Discussion of Structural Standards Development

Taken as a whole, there has been a piecemeal approach to structural design standards. As technical developments occur (models of various structural behaviors, risk methodologies), they have been incorporated into structural standards. Individuals and rule committees have framed their own rules with an emphasis on certain load/strength/failure models, coupled with some risk avoidance strategy (explicit or implicit). It is hardly surprising that various standards are different, even quite different. More, rather than fewer, concepts are available to those who develop structural standards. In the absence of a binding philosophy of structural behavior, there will continue to be divergence along the way to improved standards.

It must be appreciated that all current standards "work". Any of the current commercial ship design approaches can be used to produce structural designs that function with adequate reliability over a 20+ year life expectancy, unless subjected to poor maintenance, human operational error, or deliberate damage. Changes to standards are, therefore, resisted by all those who have invested time and effort in them as developers and users. The rationale for change must be presented well, and its benefits have to outweigh its costs.

Experienced designers recognize that structural behavior can be very complex. Despite this, it is necessary to use simple, practical approaches in design standards, to avoid adding to the problem through overly-complex rules that are difficult to apply and more so to check and audit. Stress is the primary load-effect that standards focus on, partly because it is so readily calculated. The main concerns are material yielding, buckling and fatigue. All of these are local behaviors, and all are used as surrogates for actual structural failure. A structure is a system, comprised of elements, which in turn are built from materials.

As an example, yielding can be considered. Yielding is a material level 'failure', very common, usually very localized, and usually producing no observable effect. It can be quite irrelevant. The important issue is the behavior and failure of the structural system, even at the level of the structural components. Ship structures are especially redundant structures, quite unlike most civil structures and buildings. Ship structures are exposed to some of the harshest loading regimes, yet are usually capable of tolerating extensive material and component failure, prior to actual structural collapse. An essential deficiency of all traditional structural standards has been the failure to consider the structural redundancy (path to failure) and identify weaknesses in the system. Areas of weakness are normally defined as those parts that will first yield or fail. However, far more important is the ability of the structure to withstand these and subsequent local/material failures and redistribute the load. The real weaknesses are a lack of secondary load paths. It is often assumed, wrongly, that initial strength is a valid indicator for ultimate strength, but it is certainly far simpler to assess. There is a need to focus on ways of creating robust structures, much as we use subdivision to create adequate damage stability.

As another example, consider frames under lateral loads. When designed properly, frames can exhibit not only sufficient initial strength, but substantial reserve strength, due to the secondary load path created by axial stresses in the plate and frame. In effect, it is possible to create a ductile structure analogous to a ductile material. If we instead use current design standards that emphasize elastic section modulus, we risk creating a 'brittle' structure, even when built from ductile materials

In the case of fatigue and buckling, it is again necessary to stand back from consideration of the initial effects, and examine whether there is sufficient reserve (secondary load paths). When there is no such reserve, there is the structural equivalent of a subdivision plan that cannot tolerate even one compartment flooding.

The above discussion talks only about structural response, and indicated some gaps. Similar gaps exist in our knowledge of loads. The complexity of ship structures, the complexity of the loads that arise in a marine environment, and the dominating influence of human factors in any risk assessment for vessels, all present daunting challenges.

Classification Society Rules

The DNV Rules for Ships (DNV, 1998) are typical of individual society rules. They will be used for illustration of several points that are common to may classification societies' rules. The discussion presented below is summarized from Daley, Kendrick and Pavic (2007). The analysis examines the combined design stresses on the bottom structure. The aim is to dissect the design requirements to see how they work, and if and where the rules contain a factor of safety. The factor of safety is seldom explicit, so each term is examined to see if there are implicit reserves, equivalent to a factor of safety. The plating requirements are first examined. Then the combined stresses are presented.

Plating Requirements

The DNV plate formula for shell thickness is given by;

$$t = \frac{15.8 \cdot s \cdot \sqrt{p}}{\sqrt{\sigma}} + t_k \quad (1)$$

The equation is essentially a plate response equation, inverted to become a thickness design equation. When converted to an equation with consistent units (t and s in mm, and p and σ, in MPa), it becomes;

$$t = .5 \cdot s \sqrt{\frac{p}{\sigma}} + t_k \quad (2)$$

Converted to a capacity equation (ignoring the corrosion addition);

$$p = 4 \cdot \sigma \cdot \left(\frac{t}{s}\right)^2 \quad (3)$$

The standard plate capacity equation, giving the pressure to cause yielding, (see Table 1) has a constant of 2.25, rather than 4. Clearly the DNV equation assumes a response beyond yield. The standard load and deflection equations for a long plate with a uniform load, and fixed at the edges are given in Table 1. As well, Fig. 1 shows a sketch of the three conditions. If the plate design equation were to have been based on yield, the constant, in the units used by DNV, would have been 21.1 instead of 15.8.

Eq. 2 underestimates the stress that will occur when the pressure p is applied. This must be considered when combined elastic stresses are examined. Is it reasonable to think of the plate being partially plastic, and then to combine stresses in an elastic manner?

Table 1. Plate response equations.

Behavior	Load	Deflection
Yield	$p_Y = 2.25 \cdot \sigma \left(\frac{t}{s}\right)^2$	$\delta_Y = \frac{1}{384}\frac{p_Y s^4}{D}$
Edge hinge	$p_{EH} = 3.375 \cdot \sigma \left(\frac{t}{s}\right)^2$	$\delta_{EH} = \frac{1}{384}\frac{p_{EH} s^4}{D}$
Collapse	$p_C = 4.5 \cdot \sigma \left(\frac{t}{s}\right)^2$	$\delta_C = \frac{2}{384}\frac{p_C s^4}{D}$

Based on the above, it can be concluded that the plate design equation implies some yielding, close to nominal 3 hinge collapse. This appears at first to be non-conservative, but when added to other factors, is a reasonable statement of plate capability. These other factors that will tend to raise the plate capacity are;

- real plates will have finite aspect ratio (i.e. length to breadth of less than 6), and will tend to be stronger than long plates (this aspect may add 5-10% to the strength)
- actual yield strength tends to be above specified values (this aspect adds an uncertain amount, though often significant)
- stress redistribution and strain hardening while hinges begin to form will tend to add capability in the post yield region. (this adds approximately 50% to the plate strength)
- membrane effects will tend to help, though only at very large deflections.

As well, there are factors that tend to reduce plate capacity. These include;
- aging effects (fatigue, corrosion)
- poor workmanship and random flaws
- non-uniform load patterns

As a result of the above factors, it is most likely that a plate designed with Eq. 1 would yield, but would not have started to show visible permanent deformation.

From the above, it is concluded that the 15.8 constant in Eq. 1 may well be quite adequate, but does certainly not include a factor of safety against yielding. On the contrary, it represents a condition in which the plate has yielded, though with very small permanent deflection.

Continuing to the other terms in Eq. 1, the design pressure (for bottom plating near midships) is given by

$$p = 10 \cdot T + p_{dp} \quad (4)$$

The constant 10 is the weight density of seawater (in kN/m^3). In other words the design pressure is just the static head at the design draft, plus some dynamic increase. The equation for p_{dp} is somewhat complex, but typically adds only about 20% to the static head. As such, the design pressure does not appear to include any factor of safety. It is perfectly plausible that a typical plate panel will experience the design pressure on a regular basis, even when the ship is in the undamaged condition. Damage may well lead to deeper drafts. There does not appear to be any allowance for other types of loads, or uncertainties, contained in the pressure term.

Next, the allowable plate bending stress σ is examined. Mild steel is assumed (yield strength of 235 MPa), so that the material factor f_1 is 1.0. The allowable plate bending stress (see Kendrick, Daley and Pavic 2006, or Daley Kendrick and Pavic, 2007) for a transverse plate is 55 MPa and for a longitudinal plate is 120 MPa. To see whether the allowable stress contains a factor of safety, it will be necessary to check the combined plate/frame/hull girder stresses.

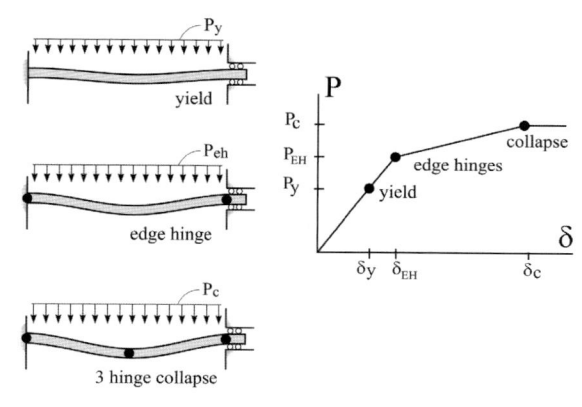

Fig 1. Plate behavior diagram

Combined Stress Results

In the DNV plating formula, the allowable stress formula depends on the type of framing, longitudinal or transverse. The reason for this has to do with combined stresses and is illustrated in Fig. 2. For location 1, the maximum plate bending stresses are aligned with the hull girder stresses and at right angles with the frame bending stresses. For location 2 the maximum frame bending stresses are aligned with the hull girder stresses and at right angles with the main plate bending stresses. At both locations 1 and 2, the frame bending stress is assumed to be 1/8 of the design value This is because the moment at the center of the frame is half of the end values, and the modulus on the shell plate side is assumed to be 1/4 of the flange side value. In the case of the plate, there is always a Poisson's ratio effect producing a biaxial stress state. The Poisson's effect gives a 30% stress of the same sign in the other direction (i.e., in the along frame direction).

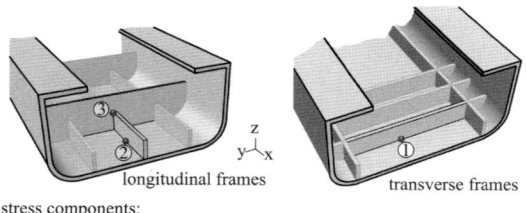

stress components:
① hull(x) + frame(y) + plate(x+y)
② hull(x) + frame(x) + plate(y + x)
③ hull(x) + frame(x)

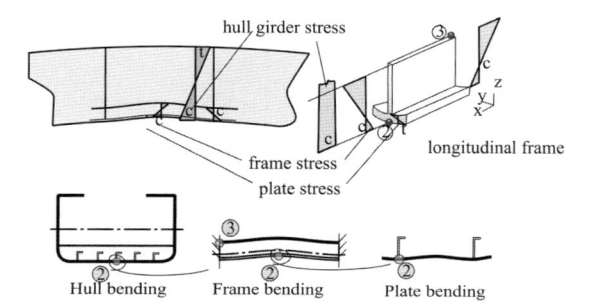

Fig 2: Stress Locations (Transverse and Longitudinal)
The combination of stresses for locations 1, 2 and 3 (in Fig 2) are shown in Table 2. Comparable values from the DNV rules, the Joint Bulker (JBR), Joint Tanker (JTR) rules and the Bureau Veritas (BV) rules are given. The details of these calculations are shown in Kendrick, Daley and Pavic (2006), and Daley Kendrick and Pavic, (2007). From the sum of the local and hull girder stresses x and y direction stresses, the von-Mises equivalent stress is also calculated;

$$\sigma_{VM} = \sqrt{\sigma_x^2 - \sigma_x\sigma_y + \sigma_y^2} \qquad (5)$$

The combined stresses are all close to yield, with the average being slightly above yield (at 246 MPa or 5% above yield). Note that the numerical constant in the plate equations (the 15.8 value) does not actually represent the proper relationship between loads and elastic stresses. The actual plate bending stresses are higher by 1.78x (=$(21.1/15.8)^2$). Table 2 includes this adjustment in the von-Mises stresses.

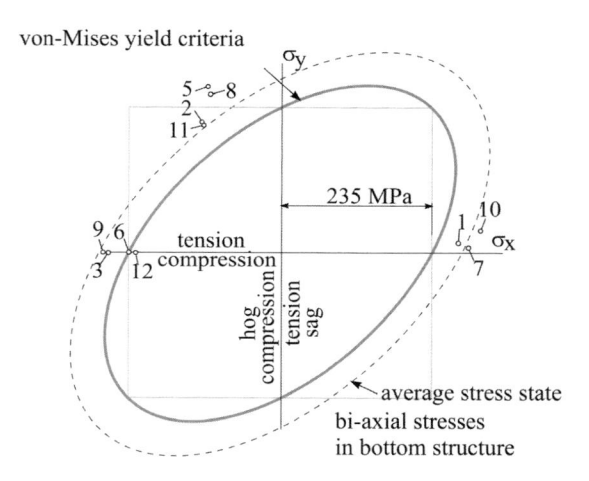

von-Mises yield criteria

Figure 3: Von-Mises Stresses (12 cases in Table 2).

The basic plate equation (the constants) is non-conservative against yield. The plate pressures are not very high, meaning that one might be able to actually measure these pressures in a field trial in rough weather. The allowable stresses, while individually well below yield, are such that the combined stresses (plate+ frame + hull) are generally at or above the yield stress. One can only conclude that if the design loads were to occur, the structure would certainly begin to yield. Kendrick, Daley and Pavic (2006) discuss the hull girder design bending moment, and conclude that it does not contain a sufficient factor of safety to change this conclusion.

Table 2: Combined Stresses at the Locations Shown in Figures 2 and 3 for DNV, JBR, JTR and BV

Rule Set	Case	Location	Hull Girder Stress [MPa] (note 1, 2)	Plate Stress [MPa]	Ordinary Frame Stresses [MPa]	Combined Stresses [MPa]	VM Total Stress [MPa]
DNV	1	1	175 (x-t)	97 (x-t), 29 (y-t)	~ 16 (y-c)	273 (x-t), 13 (y-t)	266
	2	2	175 (x-c)	64 (x-t), 213 (y-t)	~ 12 (x-c)	123 (x-c), 213 (y-t)	295
	3	3	175 (x-c)		95 (x-c)	270 (x-c)	270
JTR	4	1	Not Permitted				
	5	2	190 (x-c)	81 (x-t), 270 (y-t)	~ 6 (x-c)	114 (x-c), 270 (y-t)	343
	6	3	190 (x-c)		45 (x-c)	235 (x-c)	235
JBP	7	1	175 (x-t)	117 (x-t), 35 (y-t)	~ 26.5 (y-c)	292 (x-t), 9 (y-t)	288
	8	2	175 (x-c)	77 (x-t), 258 (y-t)	~ 13 (x-c)	110 (x-c), 258 (y-t)	328
	9	3	175 (x-c)		103 (x-c)	279 (x-c)	279
BV	10	1	175 (x-t)	135 (x-t), 41 (y-t)	~ 7 (y-c)	310 (x-t), 34 (y-t)	295
	11	2	175 (x-c)	62 (x-t), 208 (y-t)	~ 7 (x-c)	120 (x-c), 208 (y-t)	287
	12	3	175 (x-c)		53 (x-c)	228 (x-c)	228

Note 1: It is assumed that section modulus at the locations considered (Z_B for the bottom) are the design values.
Note 2: The stress direction (x for longitudinal dir'n, y for transverse dir'n) and the sense (c-compression, t- tension) are indicated. The worst combinations are assumed.

Plastic Behavior

The above analysis of various rules suggests that the combined stresses on a bottom panel tend to exceed yield. The design loads and the strength formulations do not contain any significant factor of safety that would prevent yielding. Many people know that ships contain residual stress from construction, and so will likely experience local plasticity during 'shakedown' as the self-equilibrating residual stresses are redistributed. However, few people in the field would expect that yielding would occur due to normal sea loads. This somewhat surprising result is not, in fact, in conflict with the experience that ships are safe when built to the various above mentioned rules. The reason is that the local plating and framing has considerable plastic capacity and reserve to resist the local hydrostatic pressures. This will be examined in the following section.

Elasto-Plastic Response of a Bottom Grillage

To examine the design of a simple bottom grillage, a 3-frame (3x4 bay) stiffened panel has been designed. The basic design satisfies Germanischer Lloyd's rules. (GL 2006). This was taken to represent another typical example of classification society rules. A 50,000 tonne deadweight bulk carrier was chosen as the vessel. The vessel properties are:

- Length - Lbp: 218.5m
- Breadth - B: 32.24 m
- Height - H: 20m
- Draft - T: 14.5m
- Block - Cb: .75

With these properties, the design bottom panel is as shown in Fig. 4. The hull hog bending stress at the design condition is 126 MPa. The design lateral pressure on the outer shell is 210 kPa. The finite element analysis examined the ability of the grillage to resist lateral load. Fig. 5 shows the deflection at the center of the frame plotted for each load level. The two curves show the influence of the hull bending stress. Up to the design pressure, the hull stress has almost no influence on the response. For higher lateral pressures the presence of the hull stress increases the deflection of the grillage. Nevertheless, the grillage can withstand twice the design pressure with only 2mm of permanent deflection. This level of deflection is very minor.

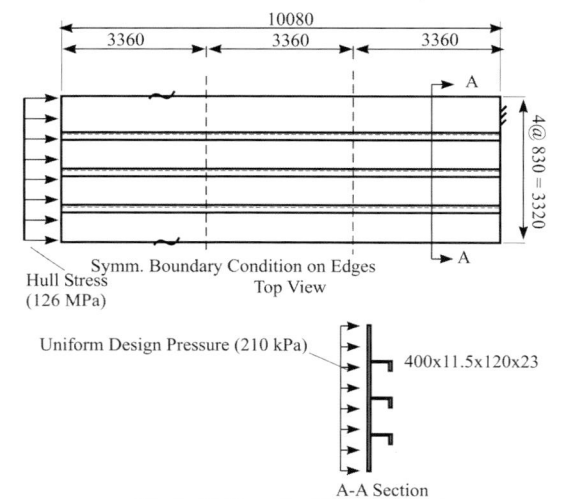

Fig 4: Grillage for Stress Analysis

The analysis showed that at the design pressure, while the peak stress exceeds yield, there is only a very small zone of plastic strain, and the deflections are too small to be seen. Further, the structure can withstand two or even three times the local design pressure without any visibly significant deformation.

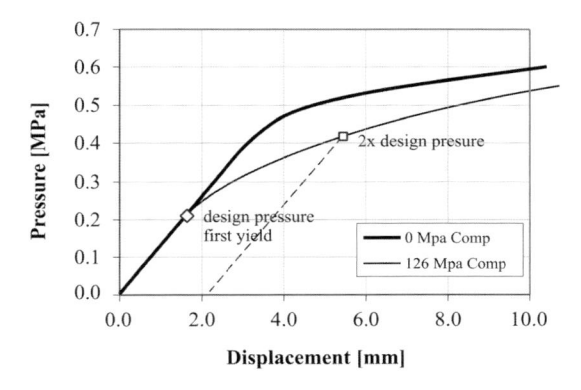

Fig 5: Load vs. Lateral Deflection of the Grillage

Elasto-Plastic Response of Transverse Frames

While the above analysis has shown that plastic capacity can provide a significant contribution to strength, it is important to recognize that there are still no simple design equations that can predict the full plastic behavior of ship frames. In the IACS Polar Rules (IACS 2006), the frame design equations are formulated using energy methods and the assumption of rigid plastic behavior. Eq. (6) expresses 3-hinge strength of the frame and should be the onset of large deformations. A full explanation is given by Daley (2002).

$$P_{3h} = \frac{(2-kw)+kw\cdot\sqrt{1-48\cdot Zpns\cdot(1-kw)}}{12\cdot Zpns\cdot kw^2+1} \cdot \frac{Zp\cdot\sigma_y\cdot 4}{\left[S\cdot b\cdot L\cdot\left(1-\frac{b}{2\cdot L}\right)\right]} \quad (6)$$

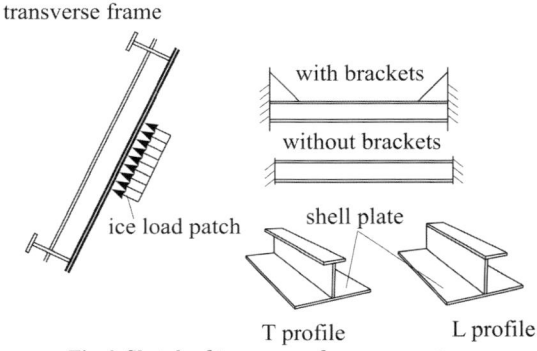

Fig 6. Sketch of transverse frame geometry.

In order to compare a variety of frames, a set of transverse frame finite element models have been created and analyzed. Fig. 6 shows the type of frame and load. Fig. 7 shows the load vs. deflection plots for nine example frames. The frame dimensions and geometry are given in the figure index. For example, the designation L2400nb_W8/309_P20_F16/95 means an 'L' frame, with 2400mm span, a web of 309x8mm and a flange of 95x16mm. All frames were spaced at 400mm and had a yield strength of 315MPa, and a post-yield modulus of 500 MPa. The loads have been normalized by the nominal plastic capacity as given by Eq. (6). It is clear from Fig. 7 that while Eq.6 may well predict the 'collapse' strength (i.e. the load causing the onset of large deformations) to within 10%, the various frames behave quite differently. Some frames exhibit a substantial reserve capacity, while others 'collapse' completely at relatively small deflections. These differing behaviors are not accounted for in any design standards, and yet these differing behaviors would have an important influence on the consequences of overloads. Thus these differing behaviors have an influence on safety that is not captured in design standards.

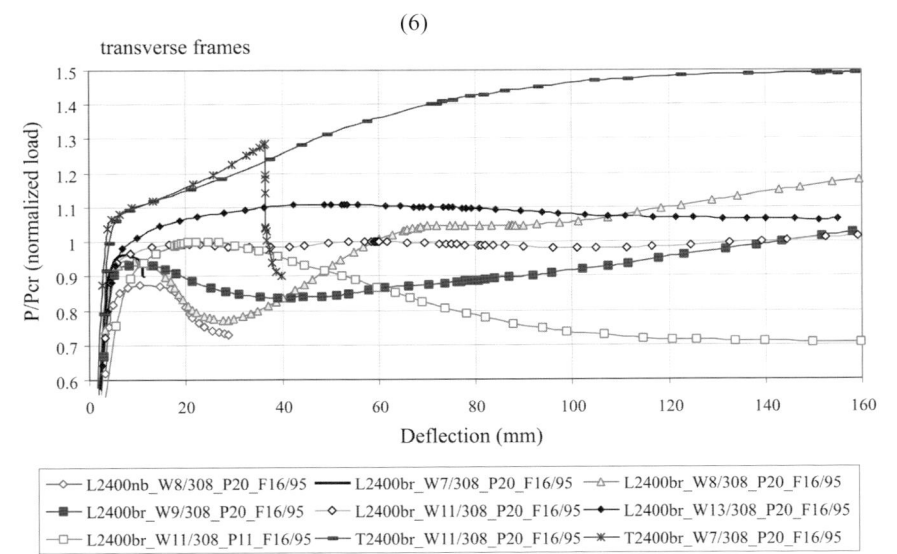

Fig 7: Response analysis of various frames.

Discussion

These results show that both the plating and framing can have significant post-yield capacity without significant deflections. This reserve provides a significant factor of safety, in contrast with the lack of nominal safety factors. However, this result raises a number of questions. Class rules are based on a linear-elastic idealization of structural response, but appear to rely on plastic behavior to ensure safety and serviceability. It is also shown that there is variability in the ultimate capacity and plastic reserve for different configurations, something not accounted for in current rule approaches. Local structure is designed to meet requirements for elastic section modulus. Unfortunately, elastic section modulus (the 2nd moment of area) does not reflect plastic capacity. Even the concept of the plastic section modulus is too simple to reflect the capacity accurately. In effect, the wrong measures are being optimized. There is a significant opportunity for improvement in both safety and cost of ship structures.

Conclusions

The paper has presented several findings. One is that classification society rules do not appear to have any significant factor of safety against yield at the design point. A second key point is that there is a significant strength reserve, and thus a factor of safety to be found in the plastic capacity of the shell structure. Consequently, it becomes clear that while classification society rules generally result in quite safe structures, different notionally equivalent structures can have quite different capacities, and thus different true factors of safety. The latest developments (e.g. Common Structural Rules) have added considerable complexity to the formulations, but do not appear to have addressed the points being raised here. The new requirements are still based on the traditional elastic section properties, and so are still encouraging the optimization of the wrong measures.

The plastic reserve is, at least for new construction with proper steel, quite significant and comes with little cost. How to optimize this is still not clear. Unlike elastic response, there is no one measure (such as section modulus) that predicts behavior. This is because plastic behavior is nonlinear and so superposition does not hold. Each structure requires a full nonlinear analysis. A method of assessing and comparing behaviors is needed. A measure, based on the full plastic capacity, would encourage better proportions and more effective steel. This is a direction that could give structures that are both safer and less expensive, and would serve everyone's interests.

Acknowledgements

The funding for this SSC project was provided by the Maritime Administration of the US Department of Transportation, and is gratefully acknowledged. The input and guidance from the project technical committee is appreciated.

References

BV (2005), Rules for the Classification of Steel Ships

Daley, C, (2002), "Derivation of Plastic Framing Requirements for Polar Ships", Journal of Marine Structures, Elsevier, 15(6) pp 543-559

Daley, C, Kendrick, A, Pavic, M, (2007) "Comparative Study of Ship Structural Regulations", Proceedings of RINA Conference: Developments In Classification & International Regulations, 24-25 Jan., London, UK

DNV (1998) Rules for Ships

Dorton, RA (1982), "Implementing the New Ontario Bridge Code" Intl. Conf. on Short and Medium Span Bridges, Toronto

GL (2006), Rules and Guidelines

IACS (2001), Unified Requirement URS - "Requirements Concerning Strength of Ships", Section S11 – Longitudinal Strength Standard, rev.2001

IACS (2005) - IACS Common Structural Rules for Bulk Carriers, and Common Structural Rules for Tankers

IACS (2006) Unified Requirement URI -"Structural Requirements for Polar Class Ships"

Kendrick, A, Daley, C, Pavic, M, (2006) "Comparative Study of Ship Structure Design Standards", Ship Structures Committee Report SR-1444, submitted to US Maritime Administration, by BMT Fleet Technology, May 2006

Nitta, A, Hironori,A, Atsushi, M,(1992) "Basis of IACS Unified Longitudinal Strength Standard",Marine Structures 5-1

Parunov, J, Senjanovic, I, and Pavicevic, M,(2004) "Use of Vertical Wave Bending Moments from Hydrodynamic Analysis in Design of Oil Tankers". International Journal of Maritime Engineering, Royal Institution of Naval Architects

A Method for the Quantitative Assessment of Performance of Alternative Designs in the Accidental Condition

Jonathan Downes [1], Colin Moore [2], Atilla Incecik [1], Estelle Stumpf [3], Jon McGregor [3]

[1] School of Marine Science and Technology, Newcastle University,
Newcastle upon Tyne, NE1 7RU, UK
[2] Herbert Engineering Corporation, 2417 Mariner Square Loop
#125 Alameda, CA 94501, USA
[3] Bureau Veritas - Marine Division, 17 bis, place des Reflets,
La Defense 2, 92400 Courbevoie, France

Abstract

Following various high profile incidents, the role of residual strength in accident scenarios is becoming more important in the design process, in particular when considering the effects on the structural integrity of competing designs. Accidental damage of ships can occur in any number of ways including damage due to Collision and Contact, Grounding, Non- accidental structural failure, Fire and Explosion.

Risk based design of ships is becoming an accepted design process for most ship types providing a rational basis for making decisions in the design, operation and regulation of these ships. One area that has become of much greater concern to the design and operation of ships is that of accidental damage. This paper addresses the question of how to combine probabilities of failure and probabilities of occurrence into a useful process for the quantitative assessment of performance of alternative designs in the accidental condition

Keywords

Residual strength of a ship's hull; Accidental damage; Structural reliability; Probability of failure.

Introduction

Risk based design of ships is becoming an accepted design process for most ship types, providing a rational basis for making decisions in the design, operation and regulation of these ships. One area that has become of much greater concern to the design and operation of ships is that of accidental damage. Accidental damage to ships can occur in any number of ways but generally damage due to collision and grounding are of the most concern. Following high profile incidents, such as the *Herald of Free Enterprise*, the *Estonia*, *Exxon Valdez*, and more recently, the *Sea Empress*, the *Prestige* and the *Sea Diamond*, comparison of the response of alternative designs to accident scenarios is becoming more commonplace in the design process, in particular when considering the effects on the structural integrity of the competing designs.

The damaged case represents a considerably different challenge to the general design condition. Different hull girder loadings and the loss of structural integrity need to be accounted for. Structural reliability methods can be used to develop the probability of failure for each design and each individual accident case. Each individual accident scenario can also have an individual probability of occurrence associated with it. However to provide the design team with useful data, a range of accident scenarios need to be considered, leading to the question of how to combine this range of probabilities of failure with probabilities of occurrence, into a useful process.

Probabilities of failure and probabilities of occurrence are combined, within this study, into a potentially useful process for the quantitative assessment of performance of alternative designs in the accidental condition. A methodology has been developed and case studies for two ships, an Aframax tanker, and a VLCC tanker, are presented for a series of developed accidental damage scenarios. Damage statistics are based upon those developed for use by the IMO and other data developed by the European Union funded project Pollution Prevention and Control (POP&C).

Probability of Occurrence of Accidental Damage

Damage Statistics

Accident scenarios typically include Collision and Contacts (or Allisions), Grounding, Non-accidental structural failure, Fire and Explosion. The scenarios define the situations that will affect the risk to the ship and/or the environment e.g. a major pollution incident. The scenarios should represent as closely as possible actual situations that could be encountered by ships. Some incidents have major implications to the ship and or the environment but only have a very small likelihood of occurring whereas others have smaller impacts but potentially occur much more frequently. Therefore the probability of occurrence should be taken into account.

The accident scenarios, and their associated probability of occurrence, are typically derived using the following approaches:

- Statistics from historical data
- Expert opinion
- First principle tools

Much work into the identification of scenarios and the probability of occurrence of incidents has been undertaken for Aframax Tankers by Papanikolaou et al (2005) within the POP&C project, by developing a database of historical incident data from which incident statistics could be developed. In combination with relevant "fleet at risk" data, the incident rates per ship year could be calculated. While analysis of historical data sources can be a useful tool, sufficient data is not always available for the analysis and expert judgement is often used in risk analysis, as discussed by Delautre et al (2005). The extent of damage and the location of the damage will also have a probability associated with each as discussed later in this paper.

Probability of Occurrence

From the POP&C work the following incident rates are taken. These rates are specific to Aframax tankers but similar information could be developed for other vessel sizes and types. For evaluation of new Aframax vessels the most recent rates, 1999-2003, shown in Table 1, are most relevant.

Table 1: Incident Rates

Incident type	Average Incident Rates Per Shipyears
Structural Failure	1.82E-03
Collision	4.41E-03
Contact	1.48E-03
Grounding	3.64E-03
Fire	1.83E-03
Explosion	1.84E-03

The structural failure analyses considered within this work, assume rupture of hull structure and thus the incident rates need to be adjusted for the probability of loss of watertight integrity (LOWI), and associated extents of flooding, given the basic event. The POP&C project provides the rate of LOWI (for Aframax tankers) for the various accident types as shown in Table 2.

Table 2: Probability of LOWI

Incident type	% of Incidents where L.O.W.I. occurred
Structural Failure	29.8
Collision	16.7
Contact	23.8
Grounding	18.6
Fire	1.00
Explosion	12.8

Probability of Failure

Structural Reliability Analysis

The construction of a typical risk model requires that the probability estimates for the various events in the model are determined. Traditional approaches, using historical data or expert judgement, whilst applicable as previously discussed in this paper, are not particularly applicable to developing the probability of failure of a hull structure and would not be able to respond to small but significant changes in variables such as plate thickness or hull component loadings.

Structural reliability theory attempts to estimate the probability that a structure will fail at some time when in service and includes the uncertainties associated with the estimates of the strength and loadings appropriately calculated. It therefore accounts for the natural variations in the load and strength components arising from the stochastic nature of the ocean and variability in geometric and material properties of the structure, and the inherent uncertainty with the actual engineering calculation processes themselves. As discussed by Collette et al (2005), reliability methods express the problem being investigated in the form of a limit state equation which relates the loading and strength variables in such a manner that structural failure occurs when the result of the limit state equation is less than zero.

Fully determining the probability that an equation of stochastic variables will be less then zero is an extremely complex problem and one that results in structural reliability theory being implemented in a simplified manner. Melchers (2002) discusses that the result of this simplification of the otherwise complex mathematics in determining the probability of failure, combined with limited knowledge of the variation of material, strength and loading properties related to the structure, and the conclusion is that the determined probability of failure is a "nominal" value.

Methods for considering the probabilities of failure of the hull girder due to overall collapse in bending are discussed by Downes and Pu (2005), and Das and Dow (2000) among others.

Longitudinal Hull Girder Strength

Overall bending of a ship's hull girder is a very important failure mode, which is normally catastrophic and has severe consequences. It is thus of great importance to accurately predict the ultimate strength of hull girders so that an adequate but not excessive safety margin for this failure condition can be ensured at the ship design stage. The methods for estimating the ultimate strength of hull girders could be classified as empirical methods (Paik *et al* 1996), progressive collapse analysis (Smith 1977), and numerical methods, such as finite element methods. Amongst these methods, progressive collapse analysis is preferred in practice because it is reasonably accurate and computationally efficient (Jensen *et al* 1994).

Empirical methods are typically based upon the conventional section modulus of the midship section with various procedures suggested for the strength calculation. They develop only the predicted ultimate strength value and cannot give any further information about the collapse mechanism of the hull girder. One method is the single step approach given in the Common rules for Double Hull Oil Tankers (IACS, 2006), January 2006 edition which has been adopted by IACS and came into force on the 1st April 2006.

Finite Element methods have been applied to various hull girder analyses. Both geometric and material nonlinearities can be considered, however the effects of residual stress are often neglected. The evaluation of the ultimate longitudinal strength of a hull girder is still an extremely daunting task due to the amount of data preparation and computational time required. The length of the model and the application of boundary conditions are of particular importance. This approach is more suited to the final design validation stage.

Progressive collapse Moment-Curvature methods idealise the transverse section of the hull girder into specific elements as developed by Smith (1977). Bending occurs about the instantaneous conventional neutral axis, which is initially calculated using elastic analysis assumptions. The section is also assumed to remain plane. Curvature, C, is then applied about this axis. At each increase of curvature the strain in each individual element, ε_i, can be calculated.

$$\varepsilon_i = Cy_i \tag{1}$$

where y_i is the vertical distance of ith element from the neutral axis.

The corresponding axial stresses (σ_i) are then found from the relevant stress-strain curves. Hard spots, e.g. joint regions, between plating in a structure can be considered to have sufficient stiffness to resist premature buckling and will follow an elastic-perfectly plastic path in both tension and compression. The corresponding overall current vertical bending moment capability is then calculated using a summation process.

$$M = \sum_{i=1}^{n} (\sigma_i, A_i, y_i) \tag{2}$$

where M is the vertical bending moment, σ_i is the stress in the ith element and A_i is the cross-sectional area of ith element

As the applied curvature is incrementally increased, the corresponding position of the neutral axis must be altered in order to maintain overall equilibrium of the structure. This can be calculated by checking the longitudinal force equilibrium over the whole transverse section and hence adjusting the currently assumed neutral axis until the change in position is less than 0.0001m

$$F_i = \sum_{i=1}^{n} A_i \sigma_i \tag{3}$$

Where F_i is the total force on the section.

In a damaged ship, the hull may become unsymmetrical due to this damage, which will therefore result in unsymmetrical bending occurring. In addition, it can be typically assumed that flooding has occurred to some extent and that this is likely to induce an angle of heel and hence also induce horizontal bending. These considerations should be accounted for in the analysis of the ultimate longitudinal strength. Wang *et al* (2002) considered the longitudinal hull girder strength of a range of ships in the damaged condition.

The ultimate longitudinal strength of a hull girder is typically analysed at the point in which maximum bending, and hence zero shear force, occurs. Therefore the effects of shear and torsion are typically neglected from the analysis procedure. In the damaged case, shear forces in the area of the damage can be significant and influence the position of collapse. Yao *et al* (2004) suggested a methodology for considering the effects of warping on the ultimate strength when using 2-D approach. The influences of shear stress were considered in two ways; the influence on buckling and yield strength of the structural components and secondly, the influence of warping on the stress distribution in the cross-section.

Loadings

The loads acting on the hull girder are primarily due to the ship's own weight, cargo, buoyancy, and operations at sea. As discussed by Ayyub *et al* (2002), the loads can be grouped into three main categories.

- Stillwater loads
- Wave loads
- Dynamic Loads

Stillwater loads can be evaluated from proper consideration of the mass distribution over the ship length, the variability in the cargo loading and the buoyancy of the ship.

Previous studies on the wave loading on damaged ships have been fairly limited, and the two of most notable studies have been concentrated on passenger vessels. As part of the EU 4th-Framework project DEXTREMEL, which investigated the structural safety of a typical Ro-Ro ferry under extreme conditions including damage, an extensive study was carried out on the response of the ship (Chan et al, 2003). This included the formulation of a new time-domain nonlinear strip theory for predicting the wave induced loading at zero forward speed, and a comparison of the predicted loads with those from model tests. The numerical theory agreed well with the test results in most cases, and the wave loads were higher in the damaged condition than those in the intact condition.

Similar studies were carried out for a cruise ship in a joint U.S. Coast Guard and Ship Structures Committee project (Tagg & Akbar, 2004, Iversen, Moore & Tagg, 2006). In the first study, several damage scenarios were investigated for a large cruise ship. Again, a midship damage case led to reduced still water hogging bending moments that were judged to be the most critical for survival given the weak compressive strength of the upper decks. In the second study the possibility that midship flooding would lead to sagging moments was investigated. Sea loading was estimated by the linear strip theory program SMP originally developed by the US Navy. Based on the results of the EU 5th Framework HARDER project, a 3.5m significant wave height was selected for the survival condition, which should be equal to or greater than the actual wave height for 98% of the damage cases.

Large amplitude motions and resulting structural responses, which cannot be accurately predicted by linear theory, are key issues for determining maximum demand and subsequent assessments of ultimate hull girder strength of intact ship and residual strength of damaged ship in extreme wave conditions. In particular nonlinear effects associated with large amplitude motions and loads are much pronounced for RoRo hull having fine form with large bow flare, as the water plane area of the damaged RoRo hull varies significantly as the vessel oscillates. Moreover, the wetted body sections become asymmetrical during roll motion and flood water dynamics are present inside a damaged compartment. As a result there is a need to use techniques being capable to take into account these nonlinear effects. Although the nonlinear boundary element technique is applicable to solving full nonlinear ship motion problem, its computational cost is prohibitively expensive in practical design office applications.

The added mass approach is one method that can be used for modelling one effect of the damage. In this approach, the seawater which floods into the vessel is assumed to become part of the vessel's mass, and to move with the vessel. For calculating the hydrodynamic forces, the damage opening is assumed to have negligible impact on the overall hydrodynamic properties of the hull. This approach should be accurate for damage extents which are small compared to the size of the tanks which are breached. For larger breaches, an alternative approach would be to remove the damaged tank and all of its mass from the vessel, and remove its surface area from the hydrodynamic model. However the hydrodynamic interaction between the waves and the structure of the opening remains after removing the tank from the ship hull, which needs to be modelled.

Method for Integration of Probabilities

The approaches described in the previous sections develop detailed information about the damage extent, damage location, loading, and ultimate longitudinal hull girder strength, which is necessary for structural reliability analysis to be undertaken for each actual or assumed damage scenario.

In the design evaluation case, information on damage extent probabilities is used to modify the initial probability of failure by also taking into account the probability of occurrence of damage, and details of its probability of extent and location.

In the POP&C work, damage extent statistics are used to develop damage cases for evaluating the potential oil outflow performance of alternative designs. These assessments potentially involve thousands of feasible damage cases which would be impractical to evaluate using the structural reliability methods described here. Instead it is proposed that a representative set of damage cases be developed that explore major examples of damage and to assign relative probabilities to each case based upon the damage extent statistics that are available. Stumpf and DeLautre (2006) established a set of damage cases that test the structural capability of tankers. These were largely based upon damage extents consistent with MARPOL criteria. This set has been expanded by the authors to account for additional basic events including Grounding, Non-Accidental Structural Failure (NASF), Fire and Explosions. Table 3 provides the damage cases selected with a short description of their extent. For the purpose of this work, damage was assumed to have occurred at the midships. Further details of these cases can be found in Downes et al (2006).

These damage cases have been assigned to the basic events as shown in Table 6 in the Results section. Within each basic event grouping, e.g. collision, grounding, etc. the damage extent statistics have been combined with engineering judgment to develop relative weighting for each case. For NASF and Explosion the weighting is assumed to be uniform. Collisions and Contacts have been combined into a single category as the damage extent statistics do not distinguish between them. Fires have been discarded due to the low probability of LOWI.

Table 3: Damage Cases for Aframax Tanker.

Case	Location	Vertical Extent (m)	Horizontal Extent (m)
1	Side Shell	9.345	-
2	Side Shell + Inner Side Shell	9.345	2.50
3	Bilge	6.98	1.60
4	Bottom Shell	-	4.25
5	Bottom Shell + Inner Bottom	2.50	4.25
6	Bottom Shell + Bilge	2.00	4.675
7	Inner Bottom	-	4.25
8	Inner Side Shell	9.345	-
9	Hopper Joint	0.2	0.6
10	Deck - small	-	5.94
11	Deck - large	-	19.44
12	Side Shell above Bilge	14.445	2.50
13	Side Shell including Bilge	21.00	2.50
14	Full Side of Ship	21.00	8.00
15	Bottom Shell	-	19.44
16	Bottom Shell + Inner Bottom	2.5	19.44
17	Keel	-	2.127
18	Keel + Inner Bottom	2.5	2.127

The suggested methodology is given in Equation 4.

$$P_{f_{MOD}} = P_b \times P_{LOWI} \times P_D \times P_f \quad (4)$$

Where

P_{fMOD} = Modified Probability of Failure.
P_b = Probability of Basic Event
P_{LOWI} = Probability of LOWI
P_D = Probability of Damage Extent.
P_f = Probability of Structural Failure.

This equation could be further modified to account for the severity of the incident. This would allow for scenarios other than loss of ship to be considered in more detail.

Case Studies

Case studies on two ships have been undertaken; an Aframax tanker and a VLCC tanker. Both ships are double hull construction and their particulars are given in Table 4.

Table 4: Ship Particulars

	Aframax	VLCC
Length BP (m)	239.00	320.00
Breadth (m)	44.00	60.00
Depth (m)	21.00	30.50
DWT (MT)	112,700	320,000
Arrangement	6x2	5x3

Analysis of the ultimate longitudinal hull girder strength of the ships has been undertaken for both the intact condition and for 18 damage cases. The damage cases are described in Table 3 using the Aframax Tanker as an example and were appropriately scaled for the VLCC tanker.

The Stillwater loading was calculated using the Herbert Software Solutions Inc HECSALV™ software. The effects of flooding of both cargo spaces and void spaces, and the corresponding oil outflow were incorporated into the analysis. Stillwater bending moments can be significantly increased due to flooding. Damage cases developed from the damage extents for Aframax tankers in POP&C were evaluated to determine the stillwater bending moment in the damaged condition. The change in bending moment compared to the class allowable is shown in Fig. 1. For example, in the full load condition 10% of the cases lead to an increase in sagging moment of 25% or more of the allowable stillwater bending moment.

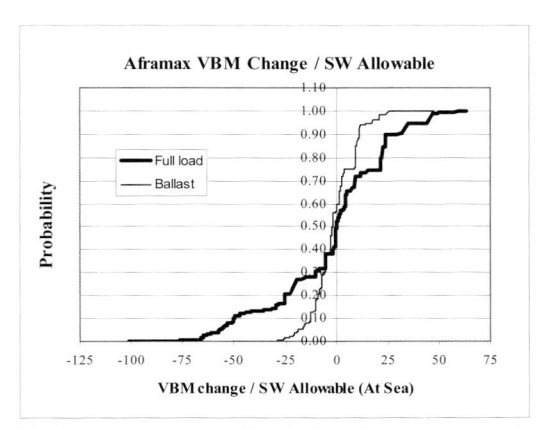

Fig. 1: Change in Stillwater bending moment due to flooding after side damage

The analysis of wave induced bending moments was initially limited to the vertical bending moment, which is typically the dominant loading in head seas, using linear response theory and the added mass model for flooding water (Collette et al 2005). A range of damage cases were considered as shown in Table 5. These cases cover a wide range of side damage, raking damage and bottom damage.

Table 5: Damage Loading Cases

Damage Case	Tanks Damaged
1	FP
2	FP, 1C-S, 1B-S
3	All Tanks 1&2 - S
4	All Tanks 3&4 - S
5	All Tanks 5&6 – S, Pump room, Slop, CO Sludge, Void
6	SG, ER
7	1-3B-S
8	1-6B-S
9	1-2 B tanks, FP

The comparison of the intact condition and the different damage cases RAOs for vertical bending moment are shown in Fig.2 Comparison of RAOs for Aframax Damage Cases

where it can be seen that the RAO peak value increases, with increasing damage and heel. It can also be seen however, that there is no significant difference between the RAOs due to the effects of damage.

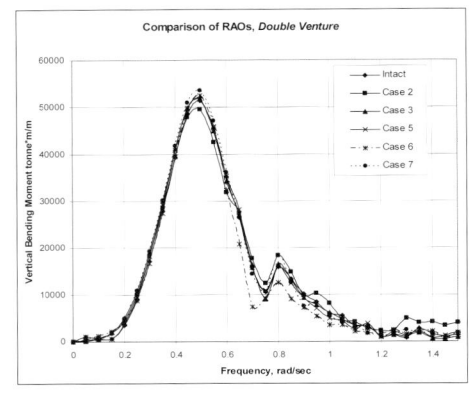

Fig.2 Comparison of RAOs for Aframax Damage Cases

This study indicated that the change in global hull loading may be much smaller for tankers than for Ro-Ro ferries and cruise ships. Furthermore, the deck of a tanker, while still usually weaker in compression than the bottom, is not as lightly built as the upper decks of a passenger vessel.

Table 6 Combined Probability of failure for Aframax and VLCC tankers

	Case	Prob of Damage Extents	Prob of Event per Ship Year	Prob of LOWI	Aframax Probability of Failure (Structural)	VLCC Probability of Failure (Structural)	Aframax $P_{f\,MOD}$	VLCC $P_{f\,MOD}$
1	Collision*	0.23	5.89E-03	0.203	1.53E-03	2.01E-05	4.20E-07	5.52E-09
2	Collision*	0.22	5.89E-03	0.203	2.86E-03	1.52E-05	7.50E-07	3.99E-09
12	Collision*	0.53	5.89E-03	0.203	2.90E-03	4.54E-05	1.83E-06	2.87E-08
13	Collision*	0.01	5.89E-03	0.203	3.68E-03	6.57E-05	4.39E-08	7.84E-10
14	Collision*	0.01	5.89E-03	0.203	2.31E-03	3.41E-04	2.76E-08	4.07E-09
3	Grounding	0.23	3.64E-03	0.186	1.09E-03	9.88E-06	1.67E-07	1.51E-09
4	Grounding	0.22	3.64E-03	0.186	1.23E-03	1.22E-05	1.80E-07	1.79E-09
5	Grounding	0.05	3.64E-03	0.186	1.69E-03	2.01E-06	6.16E-08	7.33E-11
6	Grounding	0.15	3.64E-03	0.186	1.20E-03	1.14E-05	1.20E-07	1.14E-09
15	Grounding	0.15	3.64E-03	0.186	4.75E-03	2.24E-05	4.83E-07	2.28E-09
16	Grounding	0.04	3.64E-03	0.186	8.95E-03	3.31E-06	2.26E-07	8.38E-11
17	Grounding	0.03	3.64E-03	0.186	3.54E-03	8.20E-05	6.95E-08	1.61E-09
18	Grounding	0.14	3.64E-03	0.186	1.47E-03	2.57E-05	1.38E-07	2.42E-09
7	NASF**	0.33	1.82E-03	0.298	2.13E-03	1.65E-06	3.85E-07	2.98E-10
8	NASF**	0.33	1.82E-03	0.298	2.79E-03	2.53E-06	5.04E-07	4.57E-10
9	NASF**	0.33	1.82E-03	0.298	2.11E-03	1.56E-06	3.81E-07	2.83E-10
10	Explosion	0.50	1.84E-03	0.128	3.49E-03	7.03E-06	4.11E-07	8.28E-10
11	Explosion	0.50	1.84E-03	0.128	1.88E-03	1.67E-04	2.21E-07	1.96E-08
						Totals	6.42E-06	7.55E-08

*Including Contacts. **Non-Accidental Structural Failure

Results

The probability of failure was calculated using a FORM methodology in conjunction with the singular progressive collapse limit state function. Combining the probabilities of failure with the basic event probability, the probability of LOWI, and the relative weighting within each of the basic events leads to an overall probability (P_{fMOD}). This could then be converted to a reliability index to be used for comparison between designs. Table 6 shows the analysis of the two case study vessels.

The POP&C Project considered 5 different sea areas for the location of potential incidents around the European Coastline. The assessment in this paper has been made, for both vessels, for the full load condition only, using sea conditions representing the Bay of Biscay which was the most severe of the areas considered by the POP&C project.

Preliminary calculations have indicated that the probability of failure is sensitive to the wave loading, however further investigations are needed to confirm this.

It can be seen that there is a difference between the results for the Aframax and the VLCC. This may be due to larger vessels being less sensitive to larger wave loading than smaller vessels.

Conclusions

The question of how to combine probabilities of failure and probabilities of occurrence into a useful process has been addressed by developing a methodology for the quantitative assessment of the relative performance of alternative designs in the accidental damaged condition.

This methodology has been used in the analysis of an Aframax tanker and of a VLCC tanker. The combined probability of failure (P_{fMOD}) was developed from the probability of failure using a FORM based analysis, the probability of damage extent, the probability of LOWI and the probability of the event per ship year for each of the postulated damage scenarios.

It should be noted that the developed probability of damage extent, the probability of LOWI and the probability of the event per ship year for each of the damage scenarios are specific to the Aframax fleet. It has been used for the VLCC to show the application of the methodology and such data could be further developed for the VLCC fleet.

Whilst this study considered tankers, there is no reason that similar data couldn't be developed for the analysis of other ship types such as Ro-Ro's or passenger ships.

The resulting combined probabilities (P_{fMOD}) were developed and it is shown how alternative designs can then be quantitatively compared for design development purposes.

This analysis considered hull girder bending only, however the procedure could be applied when considering other design tradeoffs such as comparison of scantlings, spacings or framing schemes etc. This would require modification of the limit state used when developing the probability of structural failure (P_f)

Acknowledgements

The authors wish to acknowledge the valuable contribution of Severine Delautre, formerly of Bureau Veritas Marine Division and of Dr Matthew Collette, formerly of Newcastle University.

Part of this work herein was financially supported by the European Commission under the FP6 Sustainable Surface Transport Programme. The support is given under the scheme of STREP, Contract No. TST3-CT-2004-506193. The European Commission and the Authors shall not in any way be liable or responsible for any use that might be made of any knowledge, information or data contained in this paper, or the consequences thereof.

This paper has also been partially prepared within the project "MARSTRUCT – Network of Excellence on Marine Structures", (www.mar.ist.utl.pt/marstruct/), which is being funded by the European Union through the Growth program under contract TNE3-CT-2003-506141.

References

Ayyub, B., Assakkaf, I., Kihl, D. and Siev, M. (2002) Reliability-Based Design Guidelines for Fatigue of Ship Structures Naval Engineers Journal, 114, 2 113-138.

Chan, H. S., Atlar, M. and Incecik, A. (2003) Global Wave Loads on Intact and Damaged Ro-Ro Ships in Regular Oblique Waves Marine Structures, 16, 4 323-344.

Collette, M., Cooper, M., Mesbahi, A. and Incecik, A. (2005) "An Integrated Reliability, Risk Analysis, and Cost model for Preliminary Structural Design: A module of the Safety@Speed Design Methodology." Proceedings of the International Conference on Fast Sea Transportation FAST '2005, June, St. Petersburg, Russia.

Collette, M. (2005) "Deliverable D4.2 – Loading Procedures and Loading Data Sets for Finite Element Models" POP&C: "Pollution Prevention and Control", EU project, 6th Framework Programme Contract No. FP6-PLT-506193.

Delautre, S., Aksu, S., Tuzcu, C., Mikelis, N. and Papanikolaou, A. (2005) Hazard Identification & Risk Ranking of Aframax Tankers by Expert Judgement: Proceedings of the 12th International Congress of the International Maritime Association of the Mediterranean, IMAM 2005. Lisboa, Portugal, 26-30th September 2005. Taylor & Francis/Balkema. pp. 1511-1519.

Das, P.K., and Dow R.S., (2000) "Reliability Analysis of a Naval Hull Girder under Extreme Load." Ship Technology Research / Schiffstechnik, 47:186-196

Downes, J., and Pu, Y., (2005) "Reliability-based Sensitivity Analysis of Ships." Proceeding of the IMechE Part M: Journal of Engineering in the Maritime Environment, 219, pp.13.

Downes, J., Incecik, A., and Dow, R.S., (2006) "Deliverable D4.4 – Report on Probabilities of Failure for WP2 Damage Scenarios" POP&C: "Pollution Prevention and Control", EU project, 6th Framework Programme Contract No. FP6-PLT-506193.

International Association of Classification Societies (IACS). (2006) Common Rules for Double Hull Oil Tankers.

Iversen, R,, Moore, C. and Tagg, R., (2006) "Structural Survivability of a Modern Passenger Ship," Marine Technology, Vol.43, No. 2, pp63-73.

Jensen JJ, Amdahl J, Caridis P, Chen TY, Cho S-R, Damonte R, Kozliakov VV, Reissmann C, Rutherford SE, Yao, T. and Estefen, SF. "Report of ISSC Technical Committee III.1 - Ductile Collapse". In: Jeffrey NE and Kendrick AM, editors. 12th International Ship and Offshore Structures Congress; 1994 1994; St John's, Canada: Elsevier Science Ltd; 1994. p. 299-387.

Melchers, R.E., (2002) "Probabilistic Risk Assessment for Structures" Proceedings of the Institution of Civil Engineers: Structures and Buildings, 152:4: 351-359

Paik JK, Thayamballi A and Che JS. "Ultimate Strength of Ship Hulls Under Combined Vertical Bending, Horizontal Bending and Shearing Forces". Transactions of SNAME 1996;104:31-59.

Papanikolaou, A., Eliopoulou, E., Alissafaki, A., Aksu, S., Delautre, S. and Mikelis, N. (2005) Systematic Analysis and Review of Aframax Tankers Incidents: Proceedings of the 12th International Congress of the International Maritime Association of the Mediterranean, IMAM 2005. Lisboa, Portugal, 26-30th September 2005. Taylor & Francis/Balkema. pp. 1573-1581.

Stumpf, E. and Delautre, S. (2006) "Deliverable D4.1 – Identified Damage Scenarios" POP&C: "Pollution Prevention and Control", EU project, 6th Framework Programme Contract No. FP6-PLT-506193.

Smith, C. S. (1977) Influence of Local Compressive Failure on Ultimate Longitudinal Strength of a Ship's Hull: Proceedings of the PRADS: International Symposium on Practical Design in Shipbuilding. Tokyo, Japan, 18-20 October 1977. Society of Naval Architects of Japan. pp. 73-79.

Tagg, R. and Akbar, R. (2004) "Structural Survivability of a Modern Passenger Ship," Marine Technology, Vol. 41, No. 1, pp22-30.

Wang, G., Chen, Y., Zhang, H. and Peng, H. (2002) "Longitudinal Strength of Ships with Accidental Damages". Marine Structures, Vol. 15, pp119-138.

Yao, T., Imayasu, E., Maeno, Y. and Fujii, Y. (2004) Influence of Warping due Vertical Shear Force on Ultimate Hull Girder Strength: 9th Symposium on Practical Design of Ships and Other Floating Structures. Luebeck-Travemuende, Germany, Schiffbautechnische Gesellschaft e.V., pp. 322-328.

Extreme Waves and Ship Design

Craig B. Smith

Dockside Consultants, Inc.
Balboa, California, USA

Abstract

Recent research has demonstrated that extreme waves, waves with crest to trough heights of 20 to 30 meters, occur more frequently than previously thought. Also, over the past several decades, a surprising number of large commercial vessels have been lost in incidents involving extreme waves. Many of the victims were bulk carriers. Current design criteria generally consider significant wave heights less than 11 meters (36 feet). Based on what is known today, this criterion is inadequate and consideration should be given to designing for significant wave heights of 20 meters (65 feet), meanwhile recognizing that waves 30 meters (98 feet) high are not out of the question. The *dynamic* force of wave impacts should also be included in the structural analysis of the vessel, hatch covers and other vulnerable areas (as opposed to relying on static or quasi-dynamic analyses).

Keywords

Extreme waves; Rogue waves; Ship design; Ship losses; Sinking; Risk.

Nomenclature

CSR, Common structural rules
ft, foot, feet (0.305 m)
grt, Gross register ton
H_{ext}, Extreme wave height, m
H_S, Significant wave height, m
HTS, high strength steel
HY, high yield strength steel
IACS, International Association of Classification Societies
m, meter
N, Newton
Pa, Pascal (N/m^2)
psf, pounds force per square foot
psi, pounds force per square inch
SSC, Ship Structure committee

Introduction

Recent research by the European Community has demonstrated that extreme waves—waves with crest to trough heights of 20 to 30 meters—occur more frequently than previously thought (MaxWave Project, 2003). In addition, over the past several decades, a surprising number of large commercial vessels have been lost in incidents involving extreme waves. Many of the victims were bulk carriers that broke up so quickly that they sank before a distress message could be sent or the crew could be rescued.

There also have been a number of widely publicized events where passenger liners encountered large waves (20 meters or higher) that caused damage, injured passengers and crew members, but did not lead to loss of the vessel. This is not a new phenomenon; there are well-documented events dating back to at least the early 1940s.

These two facts, vessel losses combined with knowledge that waves larger than previously considered likely may be encountered, suggest that reviewing vessel design criteria may be necessary. (Smith, 2006).

Ocean Wave Environment

Marine weather forecasts report the significant wave height (H_S), which is defined as the average of the highest one-third of the wave heights. A working definition for an extreme wave is one with a height greater than 2.3 times the significant wave height. In mathematical terms, this is:

$$H_{ext} = 2.3 \times H_S \qquad (1)$$

Such waves are often referred to as rogue waves or freak waves, as their height lies at the extreme of what would be expected for a Rayleigh distribution of wave heights. Based on observations made by ship's crews and on limited data from offshore platform measurements and satellite observations, these waves are asymmetrical and have unusually steep faces. They may be preceded or followed by a deep trough.

Ship Design

Ship design is based on a set of prescriptive rules or standards. While this standardization ensures that designs meet operating requirements, it is important that these standardized requirements reflect the actual operating conditions that a ship will see during its service life. As a first approximation for structural design purposes, a seagoing vessel is considered to be a structural beam or girder. A fundamental difference is the fact that it is not connected to rigid supports, but rather is supported by fluid pressure. In addition, because a vessel is in constant motion, it is also subjected to dynamic forces.

Reduced to basic terms, the design of the vessel can be considered in two parts: first is the design of the hull as a girder capable of resisting the bending moments, shear forces, and torsion resulting from the cargo weight distribution and the forces of wind and wave. The second part is the detailed design of local structural elements such as hatch openings, hatch covers, engine and crane supports, bridge windows, and so on. The latter case is an important aspect of structural design whether for aircraft, civil structures, or ships. Failure often occurs at connections, local details, and other areas where stress concentrations can occur.

The reader is assumed to be familiar with ship design, so for conciseness I will not discuss it here. Readers interested in a general overview can consult my book (Smith, 2007), or for an excellent detailed discussion and comparison of ship design standards, see Kendrick and Daley (2007). Central to any design methodology is estimating the prevailing sea state and selecting a design wave height.

As larger and larger ships have been built, alternate methods of determining the design wave height have been used. Current design criteria generally consider significant wave heights less than 11 meters (36 feet). For example, the International Association of Classification Societies (IACS) has issued standard wave data—called IACS Recommendation 34—for use in the design of cargo-carrying vessels in the North Atlantic. (IACS, 2001). Table 1 in the IACS document indicates that most waves (88%) will have periods of 7 to 14 seconds and significant heights of 1m to 10.9 m (3.3 to 35.7 ft) or less. Only 0.2% of these significant wave heights will fall in the range of 11m to 17 m (36 to 55.7 ft).

Ship design necessarily must consider many service conditions, wave height being but one. Military vessels, for example, are designed to withstand shock and overpressure loads not experienced by commercial vessels. Basic ship design considers the moments and shear forces imposed by hogging and sagging loads with the vessel supported on or between waves having the maximum expected height.

The United States Navy uses a design wave height based on the length of the vessel (Fee, 2005), as noted in (Eq. 2).

$$H = 1.1\,(L_s)^{0.5} \qquad (2)$$

Here L_s is the length of the ship in feet. Thus, for a vessel 900 feet long, the design wave height would be $(1.1)(30) = 33$ feet high. Note: Converting the formula to metric units it becomes $H = 0.61\,(L_s)^{0.5}$, where now H and L_s are in meters. Historically, the U.S. Navy has taken the position that the largest wave likely to be encountered was 21.4 m (70 ft.) Based on more recent experiences the navy now believes that larger waves can occur, but that they are unstable and only last for a brief period. The possibility of extreme waves that are steeper and possibly do not have longer wavelengths is now recognized.

Once the loads are established, finite element methods are used to calculate the primary stresses in the ship's ribs, longitudinals, and other main structural elements, to ensure that the sizing of steel members is adequate for the expected loads. The navy's general criterion is built around a Sea State 8 condition. In Sea State 8, the significant wave height is about 14 m (45 ft). This is typical for most hurricanes. Hurricane Camille is one of the best recorded hurricanes, and the navy uses a wave scenario based on this hurricane in their ship models to check for dynamic stability and survivability. On the basis of other analyses, the navy has not had to make any fundamental changes in ship design as a result of the prospect of a wave greater than 21.4 m (70 ft). Naval vessels appear to already have sufficient strength built into them to survive an encounter with a larger wave using the existing criteria.

The energy carried by a wave is proportional to the square of its height. For this reason, a 30.5 meter (100 foot) high wave will hit a vessel with four times the force of a 15 meter (50 foot) high wave. If a high wave is traveling at 35 knots and a vessel traveling at 20 knots runs into it bow first, the combined velocity of the impact is 55 knots. The resulting slamming force has the potential to seriously damage the bow structure.

Consequently, other parts of the ship structure that may be subject to wave forces are also examined to ensure that they are sufficiently strong to resist the forces that will occur. The next step is the design of the deck plate for "deck wetness." Those areas subject to extreme deck wetness are the bow area and parts of the superstructure that encounter extreme wave loading due to wave slap and the dynamic load of large amounts of water pouring onto the deck in an extreme wave encounter. The basic design criterion is to assume a pressure of 24 kPa (500 psf) for any area that is prone to "green water" (wave slap). Most navy vessels are designed for at least 71.9 kPa (1500 psf), and some unique parts of a structure, such as the sponsons on an aircraft carrier, are designed for as high as 359 kPa (7,500 psf). In addition, a static head equivalent to a column of green water 2.4 to 3.1

meters (8 to 10 feet) high is designed in the forward part of the vessel that is likely to encounter waves. This is reduced linearly as you move aft from the bow of the vessel where a value of 30.6 kPa (640 psf) is used to a minimum value of 1.2 meters (4 feet) of head, equivalent to about 12.3 kPa (256 psf). Military vessels include additional design conservatism to account for the need to resist blast over pressure during combat operations.

Both military and commercial vessels are designed to stay afloat with one or more hull compartments flooded. In the case of commercial vessels, one or two flooded compartments is the norm, while for the navy it is three.

The military has progressed from using steel with a yield strength of 207 to 276 MPa (207 to 276 N/mm^2 or 30,000 to 40,000 psi) called HTS or high strength steel to using high yield strength steels (called HY steels) that have a yield strength of 551 MPa (80,000 psi). Submarines use 714 MPa (100,000 psi) HY steel. The norm for commercial ships is HTS at 276 MPa (40,000 psi). Further verification of ship designs is accomplished by carrying out model tests in wave tanks. Once the vessel is commissioned, it will undergo sea trials to verify performance and operational characteristics.

IACS Common Structural Rules

One of the vagaries of ship design is that there are no uniform codes or international standards as in the case of building design. Instead, ship design has evolved from centuries-old traditions where ship insurers inspected and classified vessels in accordance with the risks they perceived and the premiums they would impose. Over time this system evolved from vessel inspection to a classification system that stipulated design rules for a vessel to be eligible for rating in a specified class. Today there are more than 50 classification societies worldwide, each with different rules. The rules vary depending on the type of vessel as well.

In 1968 a group of classification societies formed the International Association of Classification Societies (IACS). Today the IACS membership consists of 10 classification societies representing China, France, Germany, Italy, Japan, Korea, Norway, Russia, United Kingdom, and United States. The IACS claims that its members collectively class more than 90 percent of all commercial tonnage involved in international trade. Historically IACS resolutions have not been mandatory for implementation by member organizations, which have been free to develop their own rules for ship design.

In response to growing discontent by ship owners concerned about the fact that ships being built today are less robust, three classification societies announced in 2001 that they would work together to establish common design criteria for standard ship types, beginning with tankers. Subsequently, a task force was formed to develop common structural rules for bulk carriers (IACS, 2006). As part of this effort, vessel inspection reports were reviewed to assess problem areas. The IACS reported that the majority of bulk carriers lost were more than 15 years old, were carrying iron ore at the time, and failed as the result of corrosion and cracking of the structure within cargo spaces, and as a result overstressing by incorrect cargo loading and cargo discharging operations. (IACS 1997). Curiously, there was no mention of extreme waves or rough seas as a cause of failure. The *Derbyshire*, only 4 years old, likely sank when 20+m (70 ft) high waves collapsed hatch covers (Tarman and Heitman, no date). Incidentally, bulk carriers continue to sink, the most recent example being May 2006 when 190,000 gt *M/V Alexandros T* broke up off the coast of South Africa in an area noted for extreme waves.

In 2004, the chairman of the IACS council, Ugo Salerno, issued a letter reporting on the status of common rules for oil tankers and bulk carriers. (IACS, 2004). Salerno stated that IACS's objective is that the new rules will be adopted and applied uniformly by all IACS members. The new ship design criteria—called *Common Structural Rules*—were released in April 2006, and will apply to tankers and bulk carriers designed and constructed after that date. The design wave loads in the new rules will be based on IACS Recommendation 34, described previously.

Should Design Loads be Increased?

Although the IACS Common Structural Rules (CSR) for bulk carriers state that they are based on IACS Recommendation No. 34, "Standard Wave Data," the relationship is not obvious. (IACS 2001). The CSR (see Chapter 1 page 17) defines a "wave parameter" C that is a function of vessel length and has a maximum value (dimensionless) of 10.75. The CSR rules specify material properties and design calculations that are required for vessel classification. The rules also contain a number of "check values" that stipulate certain minimum parameters, such as minimum hull plate thickness, that must be met by the design. In other words, the designer can use his or her own methods to size structural members but must ensure that results meet or exceed the checking criteria.

To get a feel for applying the CSR, I made a series of calculations for a hypothetical bulk carrier based on these parameters:

    Rule length L = equal to 275 m (900 feet)
    Breadth B = 45 m (147.5 feet)
    Depth D = 23.8 m (78 feet) depth.
    Draught T = 17.5 m (57.4 feet) displacement.
    Displacement Δ = 161,000 metric tons

Here the nomenclature is as given in the CSR chapter 1 page 16.

Applying the CSR formula in this example gives a wave parameter of C = 10.625. (The maximum value of C = 10.75 is to be used for vessels 300 to 350 meters in length.) The wave parameter is used in various formulas in the CSR to calculate the bending moment and shear forces at various positions along the length and height of the hull and also in determining the hydrodynamic pressure at various locations. The procedures consider hogging and sagging as well as various sea states, such as bow-on, following seas, beam seas, et cetera.

In the CSR formulation the wave parameter is dimensionless but has a numerical value very close to the design wave height determined by the US Navy criteria (Eq. 2), i.e., $C = 0.61 (L)^{0.5} = 10.56$ meters when L = 300 meters.

Table 1 summarizes the results of my sample calculations. The notation "min or max" in the table means that this is a check value and the actual value calculated by the ship designer must be greater than or less than this value.

Table 1: CSR Sample Calculations

Material = AH steel with minimum yield stress 315 N/mm^2 and k= 0.78
Vertical wave bending moment, midship, deck level
- Hogging 4.98×10^6 kNm
- Sagging 5.68×10^6 kNm

Vertical wave shear force = 56,200 kN
Hydrostatic pressure, 8.75 m below waterline = 88 kN/m^2
Hydrodynamic pressure = 122 kN/m^2
Pressure on exposed decks and hatch covers = 35.8 kN/m^2
Normal stress due to vertical bending = 315 N/mm^2 (max value)
Shear stress = 154 N/mm^2 (max value)
Material thicknesses:
- Cargo area hull plate thickness, 22.6 mm
- Bow area, intact condition, 27.8 mm
- Bottom, inner bottom, 13.75 mm (min value)
- Weather strength deck, 10.0 mm (min value)
- Side shell, bilge, 14.1 mm (min value)
- Hatch cover plate thickness, 10 mm (calculated)
- Hatch cover plate thickness, 5-6 mm (min value)
- Note: thicknesses are "net" and must have a corrosion allowance of 2 to 4 mm added.

Lateral pressure, side of superstructure 29.9 kN/m^2
Pressure on exposed deck at superstructure level, 22.4 kN/m^2. Toughened window glass, 8 mm (min value).

The effort to develop the CSR is laudable, and hopefully will lead to greater consistency in the design of new vessels. One question is whether or not a maximum wave parameter of 10.75 is adequate.

Ship Failure Modes

There are several ways in which a large vessel could conceivably founder under the impact of wind and wave. Typically it is a chain of occurrences rather than a single event. For example, due to wave damage, a vessel could lose power or sustain rudder failure, which might then cause it to wallow in beam seas, in turn causing the cargo to shift and the vessel to list, take on water, and capsize. Or, wave damage to hatch covers, hatch coamings, deck equipment, or the hull itself could lead to flooding of holds or compartments, loss of freeboard, and eventual sinking.

Failure of structural integrity is common to several loss scenarios so it is of interest to estimate the order of magnitude of stresses imposed by large waves. Such stresses can be considered in three categories: hydrostatic loads, hydrodynamic loads, and impulse loads.

In Table 2 I compiled the hydrostatic force of a column of sea water of various heights. This could be considered the deck or hatch cover static load caused by green water flowing over the vessel (keep in mind that the actual load would be greater due to hydrodynamic forces acting in addition to the static load). The table also includes the original design criteria for the Derbyshire hatch covers, the Derbyshire hatch load at failure (as determined by SSC), typical deck and hatch loads using the CSR methodology (Chap. 4 pg. 23, Chap. 5, p.29) and some of the United States Navy guidelines mentioned above.

Table 2: Hydrostatic Load Points

Static Head (m)	Static pressure psi	kN/m^2	Notes
1.0	1.46	10.1	
1.7	2.48	17.1	(1)
2.0	2.92	20.1	
2.38	3.47	23.9	(2)
3.0	4.37	30.2	
3.56	5.19	35.8	(3)
5.0	5.29	50.3	
5.32	7.76	53.49	(4)
6.0	8.75	60.3	
7.15	14.4	71.9	(5)
10	14.6	100	
15	21.9	151	
20	29.2	201	(6)
25	36.5	251	

Notes:
1. *Derbyshire* DnV design load.
2. USN 500 psf criteria.
3. CSR design load, decks, hatches.
4. *Derbyshire* hatch load at ultimate Stress (3.125 x design), (Tarman and Heitman).
5. USN 1,500 psf criteria.
6. *Derbyshire* hatch load likely during

Typhoon Orchid, (Tarman and Heitman).

Hydrodynamic loads ("wave slap") can impose greater stresses on marine structures than the hydrostatic load of green water. In heavy seas, an envelope of operating conditions bounded by predominant wave periods of 7 to 18 seconds, wave lengths of 50 to 250 meters, wave heights of 10 to 30 meters, and wave crest velocities of 10 to 35 meters/seconds would encompass dangerous conditions. Using Bernoulli's equation, the hydrodynamic loads for typical conditions can be found as noted in Table 3 using Eq. 3.

$$P_d = \tfrac{1}{2}\, C_p\, \rho v^2 \qquad (3)$$

Where P_d is the hydrodynamic pressure in N/m^2, C_p is a factor to account for concentrated loads, ρ is sea water density, 1,025 kg/m^3, and v is velocity, m/sec. C_p is given the value of 3 for global loadings and 9 for local, concentrated loads. (Faulkner, 2001).

Table 3: Hydrodynamic Loads

Velocity m/sec	Pressures, kN/m²		
	$C_p=1$	Global $C_p=3$	Local $C_p=9$
10	51.3	154	461
15	115	346	1,040
20	205	615	1,850
25	320	961	2,880
30	461	1,380	4,150
35	628	1,880	5,650

In addition to the dynamic loads estimated above, plunging or breaking waves can cause short-lived impulse pressure spikes called Gifle peaks. These can reach pressures of 200 kN/m^2 or more for milliseconds, leading to brittle fracture of mild steel. Evidence for this type of failure was found when *Derbyshire's* wreckage was surveyed. (Faulkner, 2001).

As noted above in Table 2, the CSR design load for hatches is a static head of 3.6 m corresponding to a pressure of 35.8 kN/m^2. This value would be exceeded by waves 4 m high or by waves with an incident velocity of 10 m/sec. But would the hatch fail?

Are the CSR design criteria adequate?

The IACS CSR design criteria are intended to insure that stresses remain less than the yield stress of the selected material. This being the case, the expectation is that there is a safety factor of around 3 before the ultimate stress is exceeded and failure occurs. In the case of exposed decks and hatch covers this value corresponds to a wave 10.7 meters high or a pressure of 107 kN/m^2. Considering that the hatch covers, deck, and hull are structures fabricated of plates supported by beams and stiffeners, failure could occur by bending or shear.

In bending, the plate deforms elastically until some point reaches the yield point. In the case of a plate rigidly supported at the edges and uniformly loaded, yielding occurs at the center and edges. Plastic failure occurs when yielding and resulting plastic flow propagates throughout the section. This is known as a three-hinge plastic collapse because the three yield points at the center and edges act as hinges and allow the plate to collapse under the applied load.

To fail in shear, the applied load has to be considerably greater, sufficient to exceed the ultimate shear strength at the edge supports.

To check hatch failure for the hypothetical vessel described above, I made two further assumptions: hatch plate material thickness 12 mm (10 mm + corrosion allowance of 2 mm) and unsupported span distance b of 600 mm. Material is still AH steel with a minimum yield stress σ of 315 N/mm^2. Shear yield stress is taken as $\tau = \sigma/(3)^{1/2}$. Two potential failure modes to consider are the three-hinge plastic collapse and the edge shear yield.

The three-hinge plastic collapse pressure P_c in kN/m^2 can be found from equation 4 and the edge shear yield pressure P_e from equation 5. (Faulkner, 2001).

$$P_c = 4.5\, \sigma\, (t/b)^2 = 423 \text{ kN/m}^2 \qquad (4)$$

$$P_e = 2\, \tau\, (t/b) = 5,430 \text{ kN/m}^2 \qquad (5)$$

These results indicate that a large, fast moving wave (v ≥ 35 m/sec) could possibly cause edge shear failure for a hatch designed in accordance with the CSR. However, and more importantly, plastic collapse would most likely occur first, either from the impact of a wave crest traveling at 20 to 30 m/sec or from the combined load of a slower moving wave with a head of 10 meters or so.

No doubt it can be argued that more sophisticated analyses can be made. Nonlinear finite element models of hatch covers can be developed and subjected to time-dependent wave loadings that more realistically simulate actual sea conditions. For example, in heavy seas, a vessel would be pitching up and down and the freeboard would not be constant. Also, if the vessel is underway, the impact velocity is the sum of the vessel velocity and the incident wave velocity. For a vessel underway at 16 knots and struck by a single rogue wave (as opposed to a vessel hove to in a storm) this velocity difference can be significant.

However, for the purposes of this study these refinements are not important.

The wave loads developed above suggest that vessels designed in accordance with CSR minimum values may in fact be vulnerable to high waves that can reasonably be expected in a 25 year service life. My conclusion is that the current design criteria spelled out in the CSR are inadequate and need to be increased. Specifically, hatch covers, coamings, wheel house windows and deck and bow structures and equipment subject to direct wave impacts should be designed to withstand the impact of fast moving waves 20 meters (66 feet) high.

Evidence for Higher Waves

Today there is considerable evidence for the existence of higher waves. In addition to observations by mariners at sea, there are measurements based on buoys, subsurface pressure transducers, wave height measuring instruments on offshore platforms, and satellite-based radar altimeters. Researchers are looking at installation of ship board wave height measuring instruments to gather more comprehensive data under actual conditions at sea. See Table 4 for examples ranging from 24 to 40 meters (80 to 140 feet).

Table 4: Some Evidence for Extreme Waves

Description and Location (Year)	Wave heights (m) Significant/Extreme
Sydney-Hobart Race (1998)	12-18 43 (M)
Weather ship data ca. 1980:	
Atlantic	13-23 40 (C)
Pacific	11-20 36 (C)
Offshore platforms	
North Sea	-- 34 (C)
USS *Ramapo* N. Pacific 1933	-- 34 (M)
East Dellwood N. Pacific 1993	12 31 (M)
Ocean Ranger N. Atlantic 1982	-- 31 (E)
SS *Bremen* S. Atlantic 2001	-- 30 (E)
Submarine *Grouper*, Atlantic	Calm seas 30 (M)
Caledonian Star S. Atlantic 2001	-- 30 (E)
Athene Indian Ocean 1977	-- 30 (E)
Queen Elizabeth 2 N. Atlantic 1995	-- 29 (E)
Hurricane *Ivan* Atlantic 2004	-- 28 (M)
Queen Elizabeth N. Atlantic 1943	-- 27 (E)
Draupner platform N. Sea 1995	12 26 (M)
Esso Nederland Agulhas	-- 25 (E)
MaxWave satellite study 2001	-- 24+(M)

Notes: M= Measured, C=Calculated, E=Estimated
Source: Smith (2006) p. 215

Historic Ship Losses

A few decades ago, commercial vessels were lost at the rate of one per day somewhere in the world. Not all of these losses were attributed to heavy seas or extreme waves; the statistics indicated that 41% were wrecked, 28.5 % were lost to collisions, fire or explosion, 28 % foundered, and 2.5% simply disappeared and were never found, "missing and presumed lost." (Bascom, 1980). Today the size of the global merchant fleet is only about half the number of vessels that existed in 1980, but the cargo carrying capacity is actually increased through the use of larger vessels.

While many improvements have been made in vessel safety through improved operations, better weather forecasts, improved radar, and satellite navigation techniques, a surprisingly large number of vessels are still lost each year. For example, in 2006, a total of 261 vessels sank. Of this total, 75 were over 500 gross tons. These numbers are based on data that I have been able to gather; the actual losses are probably greater. Of the 75 vessels that sank, 25% were lost due to the effects of wind and wave. There were at least 10 rogue wave incidents reported in 2006, along with 15 other "large wave" incidents. I cite the following examples to show that the risks are real.

In May, 2006, bulk carrier *Alexandros T*, carrying iron ore from Brazil to China, broke up off the coast of Port Alfred, South Africa, a notorious location for rogue waves. Of the crew of 33, only 5 persons made it to life rafts before the vessel sank. A fishing vessel called *Super Suds II* capsized off shore from South Carolina after taking a big wave on the starboard bow, but the five crew members were rescued. Also in May, a large ferry, the *M/V Pont-Aven*, with 1,100 passengers on board, was hit by a rogue wave, breaking windows, flooding berths, and injuring 5 passengers. It was on its way from Plymouth, England to Santander, Spain, traversing the Bay of Biscay, another rogue wave hot spot. In August, the fishing vessel *Challenger* was swamped by a sudden, unexpected large wave and driven onto the rocks at the west end of Hoy, Orkney Islands, Northern Scotland. The two crewmen were saved. In November 2006, an offshore utility vessel called *M/V Hawk* disappeared off the east coast of South Africa, with no sign of the 4 crewmen. An empty life raft was later discovered. Its condition suggested that it was torn from the boat before any of the crew could get in, and they are lost and presumed drowned. November saw a large tanker, *M/T FR8 Venture*, with a load of crude oil from Scapa Flow, Orkney Islands, and headed for Houston, take a huge wave over the bow off the east coast of Scotland. Two seamen were killed and a third injured. Also in November, the German fishing vessel *Hohe Weg* was capsized by a huge wave in the North Sea, north of Bremerhaven. There was no time for the two crew members to escape; a month later their bodies washed ashore. A fishing vessel named *Joe Green* was hit by a rogue wave in the Atlantic Ocean off the coast of South Carolina, smashing bridge windows and damaging electronic gear, but the boat and crew survived. In November, a cargo ship 440 feet long, the *Westwood Pomona*, was hit by a wave 70 feet high that smashed in the windows on the bridge, damaged essential electronics, and forced the vessel to seek shelter in Coos Bay, Oregon for repairs. In December, a large wave came out of nowhere and smashed the tug *M/V Kathleen* in the Gulf of Mexico while it was offshore from Padre Island, Texas. It lost power and suffered one injured crewman, but was able to recover. Finally, in December the tall ship *Picton Castle* sailing from Nova Scotia to the Caribbean was hit by a rogue wave that washed a female crew member over board to her death in the Atlantic.

Risk-Benefit Considerations

Let's assume that the design lifetime of a new vessel is 25 years or 1300 weeks. During this period of time, we can anticipate at least five haul outs, each lasting four weeks. Assume that an average ocean crossing trip (Atlantic or Pacific) has a duration of three weeks with a one-week layover at each end. This corresponds to 75% sea time and 25% port time. The equivalent lifetime sea time for the vessel is 960 weeks or 581 million seconds.

Then assume that the vessel experiences waves with periods in the range of 7 to 14 seconds. On average during its lifetime, it would experience approximately 55 million waves. According to IACS Bulletin 34, Table 1, 99.8% of these waves would have a significant height less than 11 m (36 feet), and only 0.2% of these waves would fall in the category of 11 to 17 m in height. This suggests that 110,000 waves over 11 m in height could be encountered during the life of a vessel plying North Atlantic waters. The probability of waves over 17 m in height is not given.

The trend today is to make commercial vessels bigger and bigger. The *Maersk Emma*, reportedly the world's largest container ship at 397 m (1300 ft) long and 170,000 grt, is an example. Orders are in place to build more than ten additional container ships this size. Passenger ships keep getting bigger and bigger, with the new Royal Caribbean Line's *Freedom of the Seas* (339 m, 1,112 ft) and a 4,000 passenger capacity outpacing the *Queen Mary 2* (3,000 passengers). The largest double-hull tanker is the *Hellespont Fairfax*, at 380 m (1,246 ft); the largest bulker is the *Berge Stahl*, at 343 m (1,125 ft).

It would be of interest to see a comparative study demonstrating how these longer vessels fare in large, long wavelength waves, compared to vessels 200 to 250 meters long.

In the last several decades emphasis has been placed on increasing the cost effectiveness of vessels. More sophisticated computer design tools and the use of high strength steel alloys has enabled ship designers to reduce the quantity of structural steel per ton of cargo capacity. Using more advanced design techniques designers have also reduced areas of design uncertainty with the consequence that safety margins have also been reduced. The use of thinner plates and structural elements is advantageous, because it not only reduces shipbuilding costs but improves fuel economy. Improved corrosion protection methods and coatings have been developed that in theory reduce the likelihood of wastage of structural metal due to corrosion. However, with thinner sections, rigorous inspection and maintenance takes on an even greater importance, since there is less margin for error.

New vessel construction costs range from approximately $1,000/grt for container ships to $5,000/grt for cruise ships like the *Freedom of the Seas*.

Designing for higher waves will mandate the use of more steel in critical structural components, increasing the cost of construction. The benefit of increased vessel reliability and a reduced risk of damage to the vessel and cargo, or of the loss of the vessel and its crew, must be weighed against this added cost. At first glance the incremental cost appears to be small, the benefit, huge.

Consider the cost of losing a *Maersk Emma* or a *Freedom of the Seas*. For the container ship, the value of vessel and cargo could easily exceed one billion dollars. For a giant cruise ship such as *Freedom of the Seas*, the vessel alone reportedly costs $800 million; the loss of thousands of passengers has an incalculable cost. In either case the damage to the marine insurance industry and the loss of public confidence in marine transport would lead to bankruptcies and increased government regulation.

Ship Losses and Vulnerability

Review of ship accident reports and US Coast Guard casualty reports indicates a number of areas where ships have been vulnerable to rogue wave damage. These areas should have priority for improved design. For bulk carriers, as discussed above, hatch covers and deck penetrations are extremely important, since they represent a potential path for seas to enter the vessel. In addition to the static load of green water on hatch covers, they should be designed to withstand the dynamic load of the impact of the design wave breaking on the vessel.

Consideration should also be given to installing seawater intrusion detection systems in forward sections of the vessel, as well as pumps that can be activated remotely from the bridge in the event leaks are detected.

In many of the reported rogue wave incidents, the wave smashed bridge windows and flooded instrument panels, disabling critical instruments and in a number of cases caused a complete loss of power. The obvious solution is to strengthen bridge windows. Less obvious is to weather-proof critical instrumentation systems within the bridge. Waves have also ripped lifeboats from their davits, suggesting that safety systems must be especially rugged.

Findings

I believe there is sufficient evidence to conclude that significant wave heights of 20 meters (66 feet) can be experienced in the 25-year lifetime of oceangoing vessels, and that 30 meter (98 foot) high waves are less likely, but not out of the question. Therefore, a design criterion based on an 11 meter (36 feet) high significant wave seems inadequate when risk of losing crew and cargo is considered. This is particularly true for large vessels that are intended for service in areas where extreme waves are likely to be encountered. IACS Recommendation 34 should be modified so the *minimum* significant wave height for design is at least

20 meters. The *dynamic* force of wave impacts should also be included in a dynamic structural analysis of the vessel, hatch covers and other vulnerable areas (as opposed to relying on static or quasi-dynamic analyses).

After selecting design loads, further steps are necessary to complete a ship design. An overall structural arrangement has to be selected; methods have to chosen to calculate the response of the structure (prescriptive rules, computer simulations, linear vs. non-linear analyses, et cetera); and finally the designer has to decide what are stress or deformations are acceptable, including determination of how much yielding or plastic response is allowable. Different classification societies take different approaches, with wide variation in results and safety factors. (Kendrick and Daley, 2007). This lack of consistency should be alarming to ship owners, insurers, passengers, and ship's crews.

Dedication

This paper is dedicated to the more than 2,700 merchant seaman, sailors, and passengers who lost their lives in marine disasters during 2006.

References

Bascom, Willard (1980). *Waves and Beaches*, Anchor/Doubleday, New York, p. 158.

Faulkner, Douglas (2001). "An Analytical Assessment of the Sinking of the M.V. Derbyshire," *Transactions,* Royal Institution of Naval Architects.

Fee, Captain Jerry, USN Ret (2005). Personal communication with Craig B. Smith.

The International Association of Classification Societies (2006). *Common Structural Rules forBulk Carriers,* January.

The International Association of Classification Societies (2004). Letter to shipping and shipbuilding associations, et cetera, from Ugo Salerno. Subject: *IACS common rules for oil tankers and bulk carriers.* Genoa: May 17.

The International Association of Classification Societies (1997). Recommendation No.46, *Bulk Carriers— Guidance on Bulk Cargo Loading and Discharging to Reduce the Likelihood of Over-Stressing the Hull Structure,* p. 1.

The International Association of Classification Societies (2001). Recommendation No. 34, *Standard Wave Data,* p. 2. (See IACS website at www.iacs.org.uk.)

Kendrick, A. and Daley, C. (2007). *Comparative Study of Naval and Commercial Ship Structure Design Standards,* Report No. SSC-446, Ship Structure Committee: Washington, D.C.

MaxWave Project (2003). Research project no. EVK: 3-2000-00544. Bergen: Commission of the European Communities. Available at: http://w3gkss.de/projects/maxwave.

Smith, Craig B. (2006). *Extreme Waves*, Joseph Henry Press: Washington D.C., pp 238-239.

Tarman, Daniel, and Heitmann, Edgar. (No date.) "Case Study II. *Derbyshire*—Loss of a Bulk Carrier." *Ship Structure Committee.*, pp 1-18. http:www.shipstructure.org/derby.shtml.

An Integrated Approach for Hydrodynamic Optimization of SWATH Hull Forms

Claus Abt [1], Gregor Schellenberger [2]

[1] FRIENDSHIP SYSTEMS GmbH
Potsdam, Germany
[2] Nordseewerke GmbH, ThyssenKrupp Marine Systems
Emden, Germany

Abstract

This paper presents objectives and results of a challenging R&D project for SWATH design at a very advanced level. In 2005 the model basin Hamburgische Schiffbau-Versuchsanstalt (HSVA), the consultancies MTG Marinetechnik GmbH and FRIENDSHIP SYSTEMS GmbH joined forces under the leadership of the German shipyard Nordseewerke GmbH in order to develop an integrated computer aided design environment for SWATH ships – called OptiSWATH. The idea behind OptiSWATH was to bring together design and analysis tools for the preliminary design of SWATH vessels in one program suite, so as to be able to perform design studies and formal optimization in a very efficient way and therewith increase competitiveness of each partner involved. The paper will provide an overview on the strategy of tool design and challenges during the software implementation. Some of the remarkable results that have been achieved during a real life design project will be presented. Nordseewerke's latest design, a fast offshore patrol SWATH, is shown as a practical example for the hydrodynamic optimization of a high speed hull form utilizing the newly developed tool OptiSWATH.

Keywords

Hydrodynamic design; multi-criteria optimization; parametric design; CFD; seakeeping; SWATH; offshore patrol vessel.

Introduction

"The Whole is more than the Sum of Its Parts" states an old Greek saying. The word *Whole* in this sentence captures *synergy* which means *working together*. Ship design is a very complex task, and ship designers make use of many different tools in the course of the design. State-of-the-art ship design software aims on integration of increased functionality to support the designer in his or her design work. In other words, it is a common standard for hull design programs to provide hydrostatic calculations. Several programs already provide power prediction modules on the basis of empirical methods additionally. Integrating several analysis tools in one suite, or, alternatively providing streamlined interfaces between the different pieces of software are common approaches to achieve the synergy which is required to make the *Whole* from the *Parts* already available. Once a system is established that supplies the designer with the information needed to judge the quality of a design, many design alternatives can be taken into account and a trade off between different, often contradictory objectives and constraints can be considered.

A prerequisite for selecting from a set of alternatives is the availability of design alternatives. The Potsdam based company FRIENDSHIP SYSTEMS has specialized on developing parametric computer aided design (CAD) models for functional surfaces – with emphasis on marine applications. FRIENDSHIP SYSTEMS was responsible for the development of the parametric SWATH models within OptiSWATH. These parametric models allow directed changes and represent an excellent starting point for formal optimization, see (Harries, 2004). FRIENDSHIP SYSTEMS also provided their new engineering framework as an integration platform for OptiSWATH.

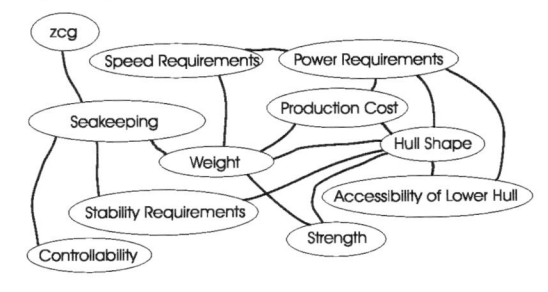

Fig.1: Simplified mind map for SWATH design

The hydrodynamic performance of a vessel in terms of resistance and local flow phenomena can be evaluated to an increasing extent by the use of computational fluid dynamics (CFD). Beside HSVA's expertise in model testing, their CFD department provided the latest developments for non-linear potential flow calculations adapted to SWATH vessels on the basis of their code v-Shallo. Further viscous computations have been made for selected designs in order to gather knowledge about correlations between design variables and the resulting wake field.

The Hamburg based engineering consultant MTG Marinetechnik has a strong background in the design work of naval vessels of various types. MTG provided their seakeeping code SEDOS to the consortium, which was developed for twin hull vessels of any kind. SEDOS is based on the linear strip theory and takes the interaction of the demi-hulls into account. Most modern SWATH designs make use of stabilizer fins which therefore are also considered in the seakeeping analysis and CFD software.

The shipyard Nordseewerke took the leadership in this research and development project. Nordseewerke's product portfolio ranges from the latest submarine and surface vessels for the German Navy to very efficient medium size container carriers and special ships including SWATH. The company is part of ThyssenKrupp Marine Systems (TKMS), one of the leading companies in the naval and merchant shipbuilding sector in Europe. Nordseewerke's initiative to develop OptiSWATH and the immediate use of it in their design work has pushed the project to a real powerful design tool in record time.

This paper will cast light on the various *parts* of OptiSWATH and their integration as a *whole* in one software suite. Results from the application of the framework in exercises and for a real design case, the development of a fast offshore patrol SWATH, will be shown.

OptiSWATH

In the early design phase of a project so-called "Mind maps" can be of help to perform a first analysis of the problem to be solved. Mind maps help to identify properties and parameters of a design task and their relations. Fig. 1 shows an extremely simplified mind map for a SWATH design problem. In contrast to many other engineering disciplines, where relations often can be expressed by physical laws or correlation formulas, this mind map already displays at least three items which can only be evaluated by numerical methods – seakeeping, power and stability requirements. In most marine design processes the problems clarified in the mind map are decomposed, and solutions for each part are developed sequentially. This procedure is done iteratively after changing parameters or requirements and ends up in the well-known design spiral.

A more holistic view can be taken, if the effect of changed design variables can be seen immediately for all items of interest. In other words, what happens to resistance, seakeeping and stability if a specific property of the lower hull is changed? The favor of such holistic approaches to design is addressed in several European research projects – for hydrodynamic design a current research activity is VIRTUE (Duffy, 2006).

The mind map in Fig. 1 also provides valuable information for the design of the envisaged software implementation. Some of the items can only be predicted fuzzy at the preliminary design stage. Production costs e.g. can not be estimated with sufficient accuracy at that stage and relating these estimates to changes in the shape of the hull will not support the decision making of the designer. Other calculations may require huge computational resources and the response time for such computations may also exceed the acceptable. Possibly, these computations can not even be conducted by their own design team, e.g. complicated viscous CFD computations. Consequently those elements were chosen to be integrated in OptiSWATH that can be evaluated with

- sufficient relative accuracy between variants
- an acceptable response time.

Early 2005 the project plans were settled and agreements were signed between the parties involved in OptiSWATH. At that time FRIENDSHIP SYSTEMS was in the middle of their development of a new engineering framework which was designed for integrating parametric modeling techniques for ship hull design, CFD applications for hydrodynamic assessment and optimization algorithms for automated hull form optimization. The advantages of formal hull form optimization have been promoted by Harries (1998) over the past decade and have become a well received consultancy work for FRIENDSHIP SYSTEMS by today. However, a key requirement for running formal optimization constitutes the availability of parametric modeling approaches for SWATH vessels.

Parametric SWATH design

The nature of parametric models can be characterized as follows: Every change of an input value within reasonable limits will create a valid design of the same topology but different shape. The freedom of a parametric model for a sphere is defined by its radius – the sphere will stay a sphere in any case. If the aim is to find an optimal solution of different shape, e.g. a cuboid, a different model has to be developed.

Taking this nature of parametric models into account, it was decided to develop a set of different SWATH types to accommodate the variety of practical hull forms. A thorough investigation of existing SWATH vessels lead to a specification of several different topologies for lower hull and strut, see Fig. 2.

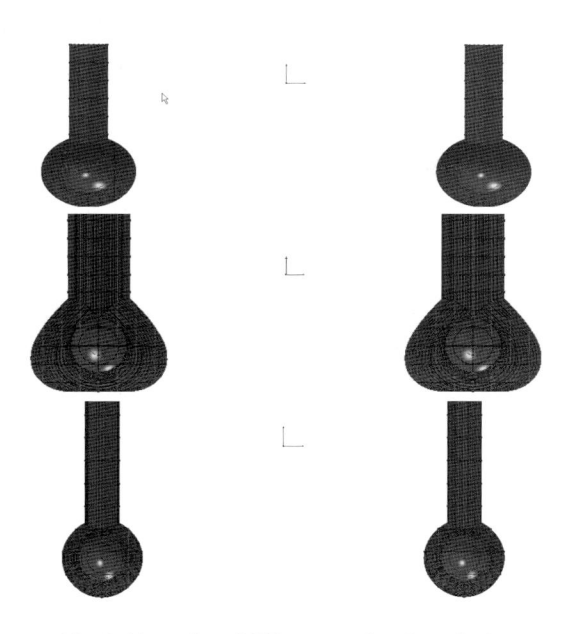

Fig. 2: Examples of different sectional topologies

Over the past years different concepts for strut design have been utilized. While some designs favor a single strut concept, an alternative is the twin strut approach, which has also been made available for the different parametric models, see Fig. 3.

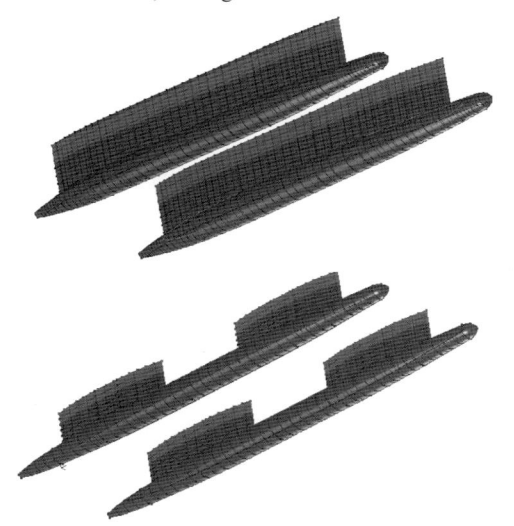

Fig. 3: Single and twin strut arrangements

Parametric design approaches have been used in ship design for a long time. Interpolation from systematic series and the Lackenby transformation are the most prominent examples for parametric design methods. However, they have very little in common with modern parametric design approaches, where either local or global properties of the hull can be addressed very efficiently. Fig. 4 shows the change of the bow shape of a SWATH vessel by changing the values of only two parameters, namely the diameter and the relative position of the forward frame. Fig. 5 depicts two different stern configurations: the upper is implemented as an attachment to the strut while the lower one connects both strut and lower hull. More insight in the parametric description of SWATH hulls is given by Richardt and Wetterling (2006).

Fig. 4: Parametric variation of a SWATH's bow shape

Synergy is only achieved if the parts of the whole work together well. Introducing subtle changes to a shape, these changes have to be propagated correctly to the analysis tool. Whenever different shapes are compared by numerical methods it is essential to maintain the format and topology of the panel meshes or offset data to get reliable and comparable results. The absolute value of the computational results from the flow simulation is not crucial, but the ranking of different designs usually points into the right direction, if the parameterization of the panel data is done with care and the changes of the shape are not too extreme. Fig. 6 shows the panel output as passed from CAD to the CFD-solver for two different single strut SWATH designs. The upper design features an offset of the forward tip of the strut from the centerline while the lower design has a centered strut over the entire length.

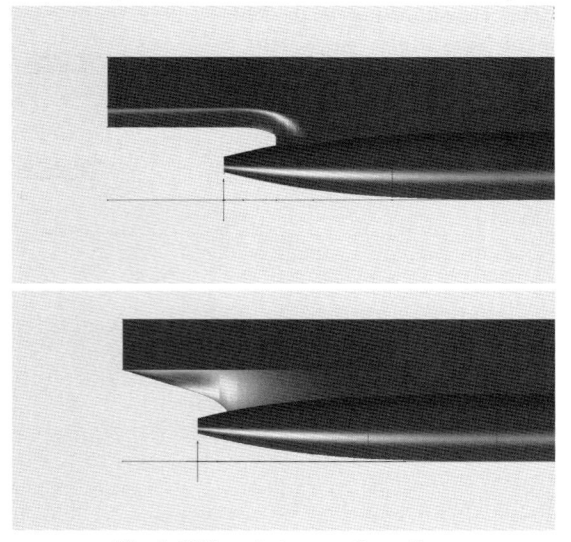

Fig. 5: Different stern configurations

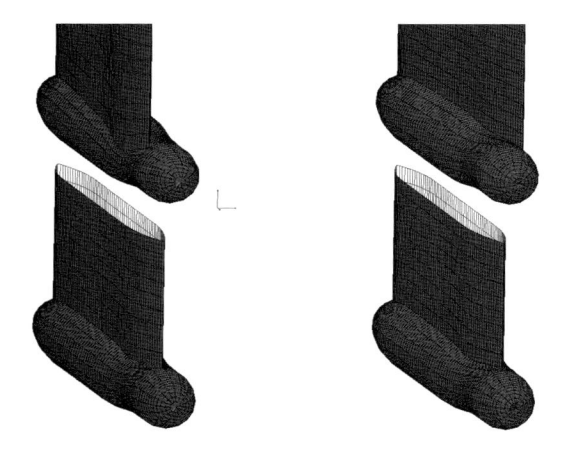

Fig. 6: Propagation of geometry changes to CFD-input

Resistance calculation

For wave resistance analysis the potential flow code, v-Shallo-SWATH, an extension to the standard v-Shallo wave resistance code by HSVA was used. The potential flow code solves the fully nonlinear free surface wave resistance problem using Rankine panels. Although potential flow methods cannot be expected to attain the same accuracy level as model tests, past exercises have shown that they are well suited to compare hull design variants (Marzi, 2004, Harries 2006). Due to their computational efficiency potential flow codes are very well suited for automated optimization procedures. The wave patterns of two different designs are compared in Fig. 7.

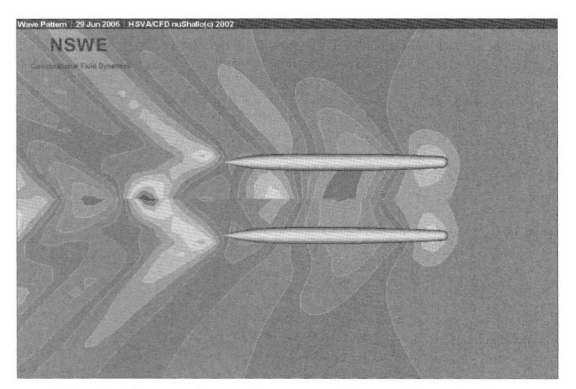

Fig. 7: Comparison of wave pattern of two designs

SWATH vessels suffer from additional dynamic trimming moments. The so-called Munk Moment (induced by the asymmetric flow past the demi-hulls) and the low restoring moment of the small waterplane area may lead to strong trim variations. The use of stabilizer fins on the bow and the aft end of the submerged floating bodies is common practice in SWATH design. To consider these fins and their forces, an additional module based on lifting line theory was implemented into v-Shallo-SWATH. In addition to wave field data and integrated quantities such as wave resistance and dynamic sinkage, fin forces and angles of attack are results of the CFD simulation.

Seakeeping analysis

The prime reason for an owner to choose a SWATH vessel is its favorable behavior in moderate to heavy sea states. In order to analyze the seaworthiness of a ship, significant amplitudes and frequencies of the ship's response at various sea states have to be evaluated. MTG shared their expertise of seakeeping analysis within OptiSWATH by providing their program system SEDOS. This code is based on linear strip theory and accounts for the interaction between the demi-hulls by interfering the waves radiated from one demi-hull with the incident sea waves on the other demi-hull and vice versa.

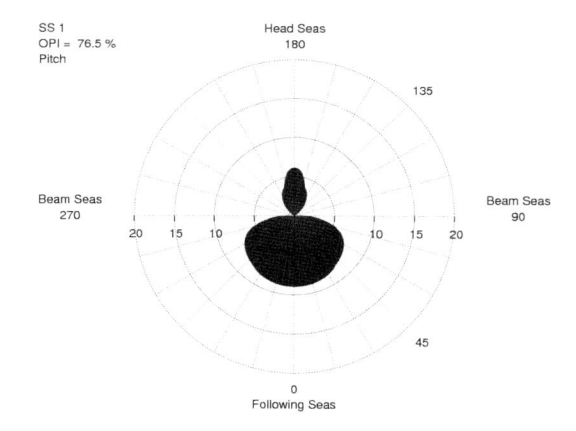

Fig. 8: Polar plot for pitch motion and associated OPI

SEDOS is utilized to investigate the motion of SWATH ships in various sea states, defined by e.g. JONSWAP or

Pierson-Moskowitz spectra. In addition to the rigid body motions, significant acceleration amplitudes at specified motion prediction points as well as the probability of wet-deck slamming, deck-wetness, and propeller emergence can be calculated.

A post-processor is employed to determine the Operability Performance Index (OPI) and the Seakeeping Performance Index (SPI). The OPI describes the percentage a ship operates in a specified sea state without exceeding given limits of motion amplitudes, while the SPI defines the percentage of downtime of a ship in a sea territory characterized by a specific distribution of sea states. As an example, Fig. 8 displays the OPI for the pitch motion in a selected sea state. The red area indicates the angles of encounter and the speeds at which roll motions are expected to exceed a specified limit. Fig. 9 depicts the resulting transfer functions of the heave motion for different speeds and headings as they are provided by the SEDOS computation.

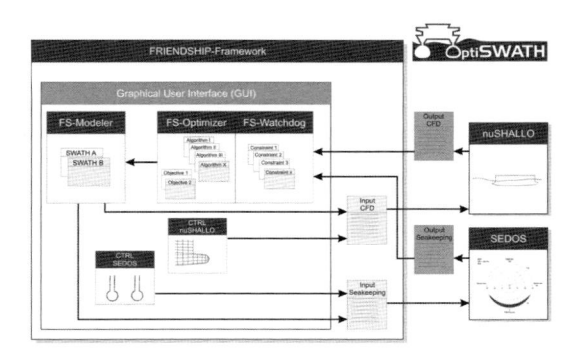

Fig. 10: Integration schema of OptiSWATH

The object oriented approach of the FS-Framework allows for distinguishing between data items that are input to modeling and simulation and those that are pure output data. Input data is kept in the data structure as part of the model, i.e. they are displayed in the object tree of the framework and can be edited through an object editor. Output data in contrast, can be regarded as 'read only' data, and the way they are displayed can be configured by the user. In this way result data, like the wave field of the CFD calculation, can be directed to one window, while the current geometry or a seakeeping plot can be directed to a different window. The graphical user interface of the FS-Framework allows configuring many windows which enables the user to get the full picture of the current design with regard to simulation results. Fig. 11 shows the user interface of the FS-Framework displaying seakeeping results in the central window. The upper left window contains the tree view of the model.

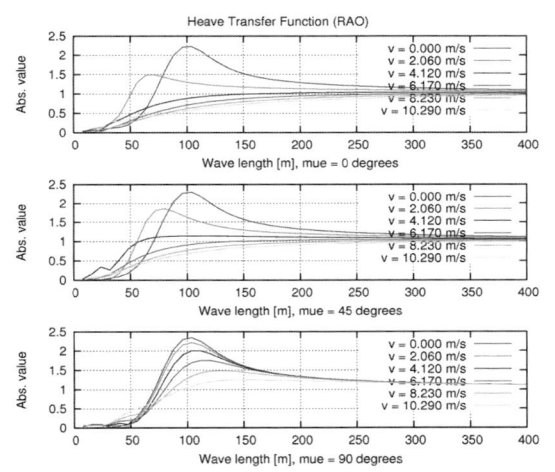

Fig. 9: Example of heave transfer functions for different speeds and headings

Integration

The intention of bringing the software tools together has already been stated in the motivation of OptiSWATH. The further development of the FRIENDSHIP-Framework aimed for the integration of FRIENDSHIP SYSTEMS' parametric modeling approaches, the generic optimization environment FS-Optimizer and a newly developed constraint management system called FS-WatchDog. In addition to these software components, which are all based on a set of common source code, two external programs – namely v-Shallo-SWATH and SEDOS had to be integrated. The integration schema can be seen in Fig. 10.

Taking into account the wide range of input data for modeling and simulation on one side and the variety of results on the other side, a general approach had to be developed to handle these data – not only for a single design, but for hundreds of variants.

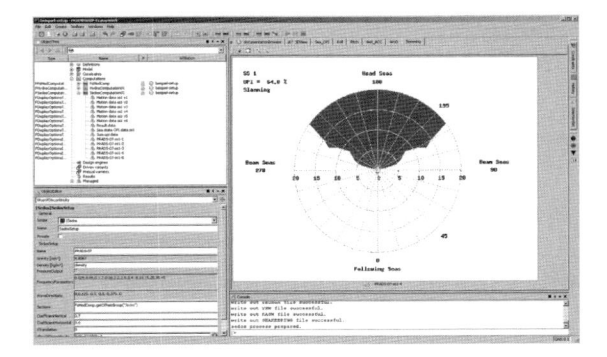

Fig. 11: Visualization of seakeeping analysis results

Design variants can be created either manually by the user or automatically through so-called design engines. These design engines provide algorithms for systematic variation of the model as well as for single and multi-objective optimization, as applied in the design example for the offshore patrol SWATH. The user defines design variables and allows the selected design engine to act on the variable in order to improve the model with regard to one or several specified objective functions. Design variables are most often used in geometric modeling, but can also be introduced in configurations for external computations or ensemble investigations.

The variants can be accessed in the tree view, see Fig. 12. Once selected, all windows that are addressed will display the result objects of the selected design variant. Fig. 13 shows the wave pattern and pressure distribution of a selected variant in the central window, while the lower left window displays the associated geometry from the parametric model. This technique enables the user to breeze through all the variants in very short time. The naval architect does not only see an excerpt of the design he or she is working on, but the complete set of simulation results which shall be taken into account – not only for one design but for a comprehensive exploration of the design space.

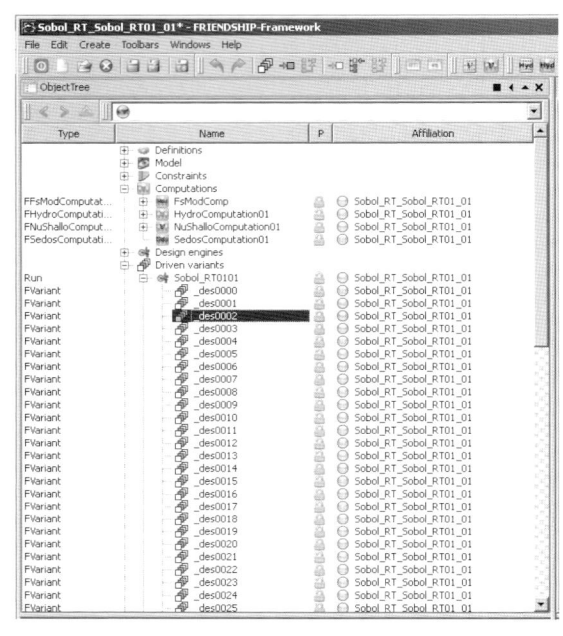

Fig. 12: Representation of variants

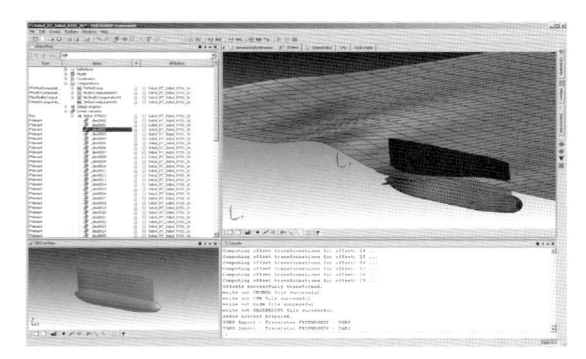

Fig. 13: Visualization of CFD results (wave pattern and pressure distribution) within the framework

Fast Offshore Patrol SWATH

The German shipyard Nordseewerke GmbH gained experience on SWATH development during design and construction of the 3.500 t research vessel 'Planet' for the German Navy. With a length over all of about 73 m and a speed of 15 knots, this vessel is a typical low speed application for SWATH vessels (HANSA 2004). The yard's latest design, a fast offshore patrol SWATH, represents Nordseewerke's entrance to the high-speed segment of the SWATH market.

Fig. 14: Nordseewerke's Fast Offshore Patrol SWATH

Design

At the end of 2006 the Emden-based shipyard Nordseewerke won the contract for the design and construction of two offshore patrol vessels (OPV) in SWATH technology for the German Federal Customs Authority. These ships, measuring approximately. 50 m length and 19 m beam will serve within the German Coast Guard on weekly turns in the German Bight/southern North Sea (Fig. 14 and 15, Table 1).

Length o. a	appr. 49.70 m
Length b. p.	45.00 m
Beam	19.00 m
Depth to maindeck	9.00 m
Draught (design)	4.55 m
Crew	13+8
Displacement	appr. 900 t
Max. speed	20 knots
Range (at 15 knots)	2300 nm

Table 1: Main dimensions

The reason for the German Federal Customs Authority to apply the costlier SWATH technology for their next generation of ships was the change in responsibilities within the German Coast Guard resulting in the requirement for extended service time at sea. The SWATH concept was chosen to reduce downtime of the patrol vessels due to bad weather conditions and to decrease the danger of crew fatigue. Therefore, the customer set stringent requirements for the seakeeping behavior of the SWATH vessels.

The challenge in designing these SWATH vessels with approximately 900 t displacement was the demanding speed requirement with a maximum of 20 knots. Up to now only smaller SWATH vessels with a displacement less than about 450 t are known for high speed applications while SWATH designs with a displacement of 1.500 t and above are generally operating at lower speeds.

For the fast patrol SWATH the expected speed profile requires maximum speed of 20 knots for only about 10% of the operation time. Commonly, the ships will operate at more economic speeds between 10 and 15 knots.

Nordseewerke's fast offshore patrol SWATH vessels are fully diesel-electric driven. Power is generated by four MTU 16V4000 GenSets arranged in two separate power plants on main deck. Each engine can be dismounted and removed off the ship easily through service hatches. The ships are equipped with five bladed fixed pitch propellers driven over a reduction gear by asynchronous electric motors positioned in the lower hulls.

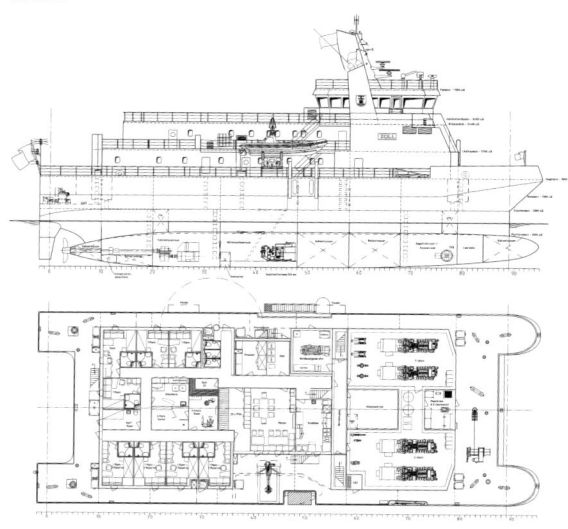

Fig. 15: General arrangement plan

To fulfil their assigned surveillance and protection duties the vessels are each equipped with a 30 kn RIB boat launched by a C-frame davit with wave motion compensation. For boarding, rescue, and miscellaneous operations the ships are each equipped with a hoistable platform on starboard side which can be lowered to sea level. A winch area at the after end of the bridge deck allows co-operation with helicopters. For planning, execution, and controlling of patrol operations the SWATH vessels are equipped with a mission control center integrated on the bridge.

Good maneuverability is achieved by a pair of balanced rudders behind the propellers and a 300 kW bow thruster positioned in the starboard lower hull.

A general challenge in SWATH design is the weight issue. For this reason the hull below main deck is designed as a high-tensile steel lightweight structure while the deckhouse is made of aluminum alloy. All implemented components are selected with reference to their weight.

Hull Form Optimization

The available propulsive power at the propellers was limited by a maximum of 4 MTU 16V4000 high-speed engines with a mechanical power of 2080 kW each and by the efficiency losses due to the diesel-electric propulsion concept. Furthermore, the challenging speed requirement of 20 knots resulting in a Froude number of about 0.5 with a highly unfavorable flow regime made it necessary to use state-of-the-art analysis techniques to minimize resistance. Therefore, from the very beginning of the design process OptiSWATH was used to analyze and optimize the hull form for the fast patrol SWATH vessels.

Resistance Characteristics

The main focus was set on minimizing wave making resistance for maximum speed. After conducting design exploration using a SOBOL search algorithm a set of relevant design parameters was analyzed with a tangent search method to find an optimal hull form within the given geometrical and hydrostatic constraints. The result from the optimization runs is a typical high speed hull form showing the characteristic prismatic hump (Kenell, 1992) in the residuary resistance at Froude numbers of about 0.3 with almost similar height to the primary hump at Froude numbers of about 0.45 to 0.5. The residuary resistance coefficient for the fast patrol SWATH as determined by model tests is presented in Fig. 16.

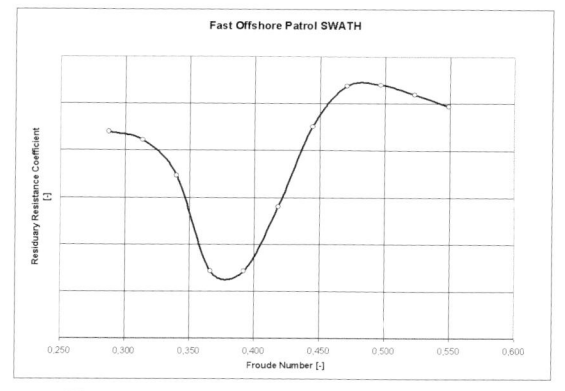

Fig. 16: Residuary resistance coefficient C_{Res}

Resistance and propulsion model tests were performed at the Maritime Research Institute Netherlands (MARIN) showing a significant reduction in propulsive power at maximum speed of more than 7% compared to a statistical power prognosis for the hull form under investigation based on a multitude of MARIN tested SWATH vessels (Fig.17). This is assessed to be a result of the optimization efforts undertaken using OptiSWATH.

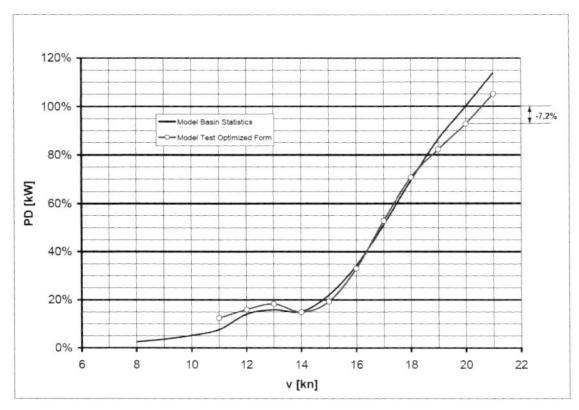

Fig. 17: Speed power diagram: statistics vs. model test

Fig. 18: Seakeeping tests, $H_{1/3}$=3.5 m, Tp=10 s, v=20 kn, bow quartering seas

Seakeeping Performance

The main reason for a customer to spend money on a SWATH vessel is its advantageous seakeeping behavior. Therefore, it is of importance to analyze the seakeeping behavior from the early design stage with adequate analysis tools. Nordseewerke used OptiSWATH to support the design process and to regularly check for compliance with the customer set seakeeping criteria.

The fast patrol SWATH vessels will operate in the southern North Sea corresponding to Gridpoint 10 of the NATO wave climate. For a significant wave height of $H_{1/3}$=3.5 m and a peak period T_p=6.5 to 10 s the following seakeeping criteria are to be observed for all ship speeds:

- significant amplitude of roll	< 6°
- significant amplitude of pitch	< 6°
- max. vertical acceleration	< 1.5m/s²
- slamming events (wet deck)	< 20/hour

To further enhance the good seakeeping behaviour due to the hull characteristics of SWATH ships, the fast patrol SWATH vessels will be equipped with four controllable fins reacting on pitch, pitch velocity, roll, roll velocity and heave velocity.

Calculations as well as initial model tests in the most unfavorable sea conditions show good seakeeping behavior for the fast patrol SWATH design. The required seakeeping criteria are met for all speeds and headings in the described sea states. Especially the pitch motions are of a significant lower level than specified by the owner. Fig. 18 shows the model during testing.

Further Applications

The fast patrol SWATH is a new generation of SWATH vessels with a maximum speed of up to 20 knots featuring a convenient diesel-electric propulsion system. Apart from being applied for Coast Guard operations, the stable SWATH platform can as well be used for military applications. Furthermore, with its spacious decks and excellent seakeeping behavior a variant of the fast patrol SWATH could be of interest for yacht owners.

Conclusions

OptiSWATH - a newly developed SWATH design and optimization program suite utilizing a holistic approach for hull form modeling, resistance performance assessment and seakeeping analysis was presented. The *parts* of the program suite, the parametric modeling module, the CFD and seakeeping analysis tools and the optimization procedures were introduced and the implementation into the *whole* within FRIENDSHIP SYSTEMS' engineering framework was shown. A progressive SWATH design, Nordseewerke's fast offshore patrol SWATH, was presented as an example for the successful application of OptiSWATH in real life design projects.

References

Abt, C, Harries, H (2007) "A new Approach to Integration of CAD and CFD for Naval Architects", COMPIT'07, Ischia

Duffy, A, Harries, S, Marzi, J, Petz, Ch, Wu, Z (2006) "VIRTUE: integrating CFD ship design", 7th International Conference on Hydrodynamics, Ischia

Harries, S (1998) "Parametric design and hydrodynamic optimization of ship hull forms", Dissertation, Mensch & Buch Verlag, ISBN 3-933346-24-X

Harries, S, Abt, C and Hochkirch, K (2004). "Modeling meets Simulation – Process Integration to improve Design", Honorary colloquium for Prof. Hagen, Prof. Schlüter and Prof. Thiel.

Harries, S; Abt, C; Heimann, J; Hochkirch, K, (2006), "Adanced Hydrodynamic Design of Container Carriers for Improved Transport Efficiency", Royal Institution of Naval Architects, Design & Operation of Container Ships, London

Kennell, Colen (1992). "SWATH Ships", Technical and Research Bulletin No 7-5, The Society of Naval Architects and Marine Engineers

Marzi, J, Grashorn, H (2004) „Hullform Analysis and Optimisation - A Model Basin's Approach", International Symposium on Practical Design of Ships and Other Floating Structures (PRADS), Lübeck-Travemünde.

NN (2004). "Forschungs- und Erprobungsschiff 'Planet', HANSA International Maritime Journal, Vol 09/2004.

Richardt, T, Wetterling, P (2006) "OptiSWATH – a new way towards optimum SWATH design", HANSA International Maritime Journal, Vol 09/2006.

Study on Reduction of Wave-making Resistance in Multiple Load Conditions using Real-coded Genetic Algorithm

Akihito Hirayama [1], Jun Ando [2]

[1] Numerical Analysis Department, Akishima Laboratories (Mitsui Zosen) INC.
Akishima, Tokyo, Japan
[2] Department of Marine Systems Engineering, Faculty of Engineering, Kyushu University
Fukuoka, Fukuoka, Japan

Abstract

Practical ships have different operating speeds, draft and trim in multiple load conditions. Therefore, in the hull form improvement, it is necessary to develop a different hull form in substance for every condition, from a viewpoint of hydrodynamics. The present paper proposes a hull form optimization method for reducing wave-making resistance using the real-coded genetic algorithms in multiple load conditions. The real-coded genetic algorithm (GA) of the optimization method, employs the UNDX (Unimodal Normal Distribution Crossover) as a crossover operator, and employs the POSS (Pareto Optimal Selection Strategy) as a generation-alternation model. The hull form optimization for Series60 (CB=0.6) is carried out using the program that is based on the present method. In the optimization, many Pareto solutions are obtained. These hull forms have lower wave-making resistance with the panel-shift type Rankine source method on both the full load condition and the ballast condition, in comparison with the original hull form.

Keywords

Hull form optimization; Real-coded genetic algorithm; Multiobjective optimization; Wave-making resistance; Pareto optimal solution; UNDX; POSS; Multiple load conditions.

Introduction

The hull form improvement of practical ships is basically one of multiobjective optimization problems. There are many requirements on practical ships. It is difficult to satisfy multiple requirements simultaneously. The requirement to reduce resistance in multiple load conditions is known as a difficult problem on merchant ship design. Many kind of merchant ships have different operating speeds, draft and trim in multiple load conditions. The fact means that there is necessity to develop a different hull form in substance for each load condition, from a viewpoint of hydrodynamics.

In conventional design for a hull form of a practical ship, these requirements are satisfied by human efforts using their own experience. However, it becomes difficult to achieve the requirement because the speed-power performances of ships have been enhancing rapidly.

Many numerical optimization methods have been proposed for hull form design. In the primary stage of this research field, almost all of the methods treated single design objective. As examples, Tahara (1996a, 1996b) proposed the improvement method of stern form to minimize viscous resistance using CFD, Hirayama (1996, 1998) applied numerical wave analysis to hull optimization for reduction of wave-making resistance.

In recent years, to satisfy multiple requirements in ship design, some multiobjective hull optimization methods were proposed. Peri (2003) proposed the method to minimize the resistance and the motion in wave for naval combatant. Chen (2003) proposed the method to minimize the wave-making resistance for two speeds.

On the other hand, not only targets of optimization but also techniques to solve optimization problem are important. For use of the practical ship design, optimiztion technique should be able to find solutions quickly. In addition, the optimization technique should be able to handle a lot of design parameters whose degrees of influence on the objective function are different.

Gradient methods, such as the SQP (Successive Quadratic Programming) methods, have been used for hull form optimization problems so far. For the effective use of gradient methods, we have to know the behavior of objective functions. The GA is widely known as a global optimization technique, because the GA can surely find the optimum solution even if the objective function is multimodal or discontinuous. Some attempts of hull optimization using the GA have been made (e.g. Yasukawa, 1999; Chen, 2003; Ando, 2004).

In this paper, a hull form optimization method is proposed, and the optimization example is shown. The present hull form optimization method aims to reduce wave-making resistance in multiple load conditions using the real-coded GA. The example of hull form optimization are for Series60 (CB=0.6).

Optimization method

Pareto solutions

Let us consider the hull form optimization to minimize a summation of the required horsepower of the full load condition and the ballast condition. This technique to deal with multiple evaluation items has been widely used. In this case, the obtained optimum hull form is only optimum for the ship that has the same ratio of operation time for the full load and the ballast condition.

In other words, the technique is able to provide a limited solution on a certain tradeoff condition only. This point is the biggest weak point of the method.

In recent years, a concept to find Pareto solutions for dealing with an optimization problem has been proposed to avoid the weak point.

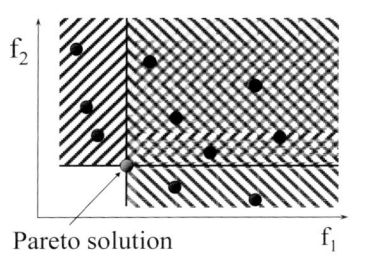

Fig. 1: Pareto solution

A Pareto solution is defined as a solution having a superior fitness value by at least one or more objective function in comparison with all other solutions of an objective function field. Figure 1 shows a Pareto solution example in case to minimize two objective functions. In the multiobjective optimization that deals with Pareto solutions, the results are the set of many solutions that have advantages in a tradeoff of the multiple objective functions.

A case of hull form optimization, which uses the two performances for two loading conditions, is picked up. In this case, a set of Pareto solutions which consists of many hull forms is obtained as the results of the optimization. Each hull form has a superior performance by at least one or more loading condition. These hull forms are individual feasible solutions on a certain tradeoff condition. A ship designer can choose a hull form from the Pareto solutions considering requirements in ship design.

For the above reason, the multiobjective optimization obtaining a set of Pareto solutions is more flexible than a method that replaces a multiobjective optimization problem with a mono-objective problem. Therefore the multiobjective optimization can be adopted for various kinds of optimization problems.

Real-coded GA for multiobjective optimization

The GA is known as a method with the outstanding feature for multiobjective optimization method.

A lot of optimization methods using the GA have been produced in many studies. Ordinary GA uses binary coding to keep genetic information. This kind of GA is called the binary coding GA (e.g. Yasukawa, 1999), and this method has so far been widely used.

The binary coding GA expresses genetic information with 0 and 1. In the case of using binary coding, even if a solution is located near the optimum solution in genotype space, the solution is not always located near the optimum solution in phenotype space. Here, phenotype space means the space consists of actual hull forms. In other words, there is a possibility that the hulls having similar genes look like different form each other. According to the experiential knowledge in which similar hull forms show the similar hydrodynamic performance, this is very inconvenient in hull form optimization.

The real-coded GA was proposed to overcome the problem. In the real-coded GA, solutions which resemble each other in genotype space also resemble in phenotype space because the solution genes are expressed by real number.

Ono (2000) proposed a multiobjective GA method to satisfy the requirement. The method is using the UNDX (Unimodal Normal Distribution Crossover) as a crossover operator, the POSS (Pareto Optimal Selection Strategy) as a generation-alternation model, and non-satisfied solution removing as a satisfaction method for constraint.

The UNDX selects three solutions as parent solutions to generate solutions for the next generation. This crossover operator makes offspring around two solutions of the previous generation using the distance between two solutions and another solution. Figure 2 shows locations of three parent solutions and new offspring in the case of two parameters. a_1, a_2 are the parameters which represent shapes of solutions.

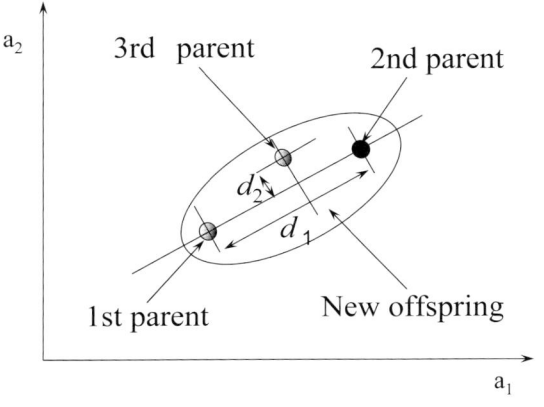

Fig. 2: Concept of UNDX

The mathematical operation of the UNDX is described in Eq.1:

$$\vec{C}_1 = (\vec{P}_1 + \vec{P}_2)/2 + z_1 \vec{e}_1 + \sum_{k=2}^{n} z_k \vec{e}_k$$

$$\vec{C}_2 = (\vec{P}_1 + \vec{P}_2)/2 - z_1 \vec{e}_1 - \sum_{k=2}^{n} z_k \vec{e}_k$$

$$z_1 \sim N(0,\sigma_1^2)$$

$$z_k \sim N(0,\sigma_2^2) \quad (k=2,\cdots n)$$ (1)

$$\vec{e}_1 = (\vec{P}_1 - \vec{P}_2)/|\vec{P}_1 - \vec{P}_2|$$

$$\vec{e}_i \perp \vec{e}_j \quad (i,j=1,2,\cdots n)(i \neq j)$$

$$\sigma_1 = \alpha d_1$$

$$\sigma_2 = \beta d_2/\sqrt{n}$$

where

$\vec{C}_1, \vec{C}_2$: vector of offspring
$\vec{P}_1, \vec{P}_2, \vec{P}_3$: vectors of parent
d_1 : distance between $\vec{P}_1$ and $\vec{P}_2$
d_2 : distance between $\vec{P}_3$ and the line $\overrightarrow{P_1 P_2}$
n : number of parameters
$z_1 \sim N(0,\sigma_1^2), z_k \sim N(0,\sigma_2^2)$: normal random number
$\vec{e}_i \ (i=1,\cdots n)$: orthogonal basis vectors
σ_1, σ_2 : standard deviation
α, β : constants defined by parameter study

The POSS selects Pareto optimum solutions for the next generation group. This alternation of generations is suitable for the GA. In case of optimization methods except the GA, such as the gradient method, to obtain Pareto solution causes the increase of a calculation cost. On the other hand, the GA does not need to increase the cost for a calculation because the GA is keeping a group while proceeding with optimization.

Objective function

The objective functions are wave-making resistance coefficient of full load condition and ballast condition.

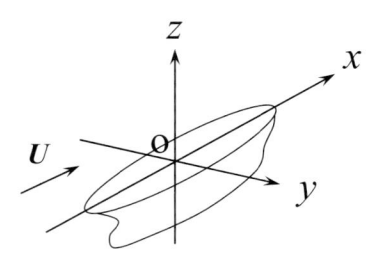

Fig. 3: Definition of the coordinate system

The panel shift type Rankine source method (Ando, 1988, 1990) was chosen for the evaluation method of the objective functions. The panel shift type Rankine source method is widely known with comparatively providing a high accuracy result in a short time. The values of wave-making resistance coefficients are determined to use wave analysis that Eggers proposed (1967). The coordinate system in the present method is shown in Figure 3.

Panels of singular points distribution for the hull surface are 40 panels in the x direction, and are 10 panels along girth direction. Free surface, the range from -75% Ship Length (L) to 250%L, is divided with a panel of a square of 2.5%L. Wave data at 200%L are used for wave analysis. Fig.4 shows the comparison of wave-making resistance coefficients between experiment (ITTC, 1987) and Rankine source method for Series60 (CB=0.6). Wave-making resistance coefficient C_w is defined as Eq.2:

$$C_w = R_w /(1/2\rho U^2 L^2)$$ (2)

where

R_w : wave - making resistance
ρ : density of water
U : ship speed
L : ship length

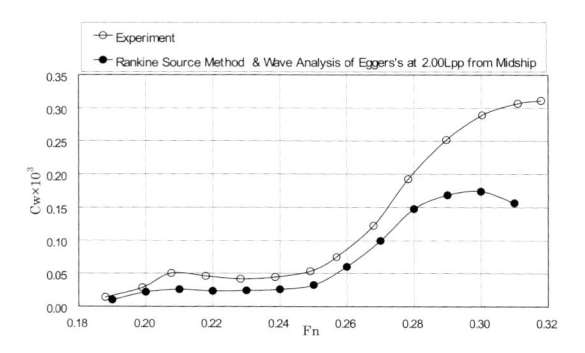

Fig. 4: Comparison of wave-making resistance coefficient

Expression of hull form

A function to express offsets of a hull form under an optimization process is defined as Eq.3 (Suzuki, 1999):

$$f(x,z) = f_0(x,z) \times w_{a,f}(x,z)$$

$$w_a(x,z) = 1 - \sum_{m=1}^{3}\sum_{n=1}^{3} A_{mn} \sin\left\{\pi\left(\frac{x}{L/2}\right)^{m+2}\right\} \sin\left\{\pi\left(\frac{z_{0a}-z}{z_{0a}+d}\right)^{n+2}\right\}$$ (3)

$$w_f(x,z) = 1 - \sum_{m=1}^{3}\sum_{n=1}^{3} B_{mn} \sin\left\{\pi\left(\frac{-x}{L/2}\right)^{m+2}\right\} \sin\left\{\pi\left(\frac{z_{0f}-z}{z_{0f}+d}\right)^{n+2}\right\}$$

$$m = 1,2,3, \quad n = 1,2,3$$

where $f(x,z)$ is offsets of a modified hull, $f_0(x,z)$ is offsets of the original hull, d is draft, z_{0a}, z_{0f} are upper end of modified parts in the z direction, A_{mn}, B_{mn} are parameters to define amplitude. Total number of optimization parameters is 20 in the present method. The modified part under the optimization process is shown in Figure 5.

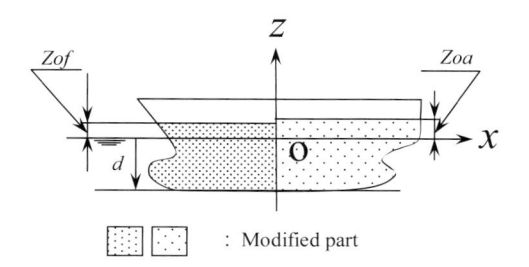

Fig. 5:   Part of the modification

Constraint

The following constraints are imposed as the minimum requirements:

$$f(x,z) \geq 0.0$$
$$1.00 \leq \nabla/\nabla_0 \leq 1.05 \quad (4)$$

Where ∇ is the displacement volume of modified hulls, ∇_0 is the displacement volume of the original hull. Although constraints concerning a center of buoyancy or the stability should be imposed for practical design, we dared to limit the number of constraints in order to examine whether this optimization method can provide the reasonable solution or not, in terms of hydrodynamics.

If the generated hull does not satisfy the above constraints, the hull is generated again by the UNDX.

Procedure of Optimization method

Before showing the example of hull form optimization, the procedure of the present method is described as follow:

Step 1: Generation of Initial Population

  Hull forms, as the initial population, are generated at random using Eq.3.

Step 2: Generation of Offspring using UNDX

  New hull forms, as offspring solutions, are generated using the UNDX.

Step 3: Check for Satisfaction of Constraints

  It is confirmed whether new hull forms are satisfied the constraints of Eq.4. If the constraints are satisfied, the procedure is preceded to Step 4. In case that the constraints are not satisfied, the procedure is returned to Step 2.

Step 4: Evaluation of Wave-making resistance

  The wave-making resistances of all forms are evaluation about full-load condition and ballast condition, using Rankine source method.

Step 5: Selection of Solutions using POSS

  Pareto optimum solutions, from the view point of low wave-making resistance, are selected for the next generation using the POSS.

Step 6: Judgment to Finish the Procedure

  Judgment to finish this procedure is made, in consideration of the wave-making resistance and the shapes of the obtained hull forms. When optimization is continued, the procedure is returned to Step 2.

Example of Hull Form Optimization

A hull form optimization is carried out by the present method described in a foregoing chapter. Series60 (CB=0.6) is used as the original hull form. Draft, initial trim and design-speed of each condition are shown in Table 1. Population size is defined 50.

Table 1:   Condition of calculation

	Full load	Ballast
Draft at midship (% Ship length)	5.33	3.20
Initial trim (deg.)	0.0	1.0
Design speed Froude number	0.24	0.27

Pareto solutions

The obtained Pareto solutions of each generation are shown in Figure 6. The horizontal axis and vertical axis indicate the wave-making resistance coefficient of full load condition and ballast condition respectively.

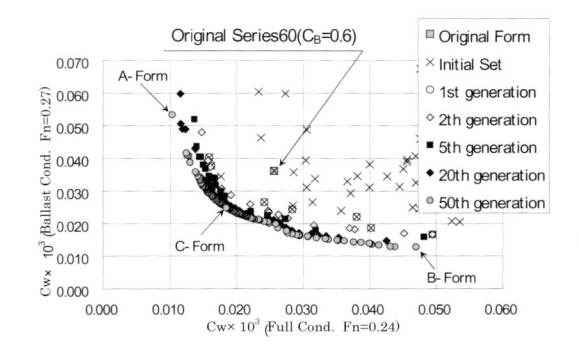

Fig. 6:   Pareto solutions in objective function field

In the initial stage of optimization, solutions are scattered in objective function space. As the generation proceeds, the Pareto front clearly forms, and the wave-making resistance coefficient decreases. In addition, in an early generation, significant wave-making resistance reduction is achieved.

At 50th generation, 31 hull forms that have smaller wave-making resistance compared with Series60 (CB=0.6) are obtained, and the Pareto front consists of 112 hull forms.

Obtained hull form

"A-Form" in Figure 6 is the hull form with the lowest wave-making resistance in full load condition and "B-Form" is the hull form with the lowest wave-making resistance in ballast condition. Here we choose one Pareto solution located in the middle of the Pareto front of the 50th generation as a typical hull form (see Figure 6). We call this hull form "C-Form". At the design of hull form, we can choose the appropriate hull form from the Pareto front considering various requirements.

The body plans of A-From, B-Form and C-Form are shown in Figure 7.

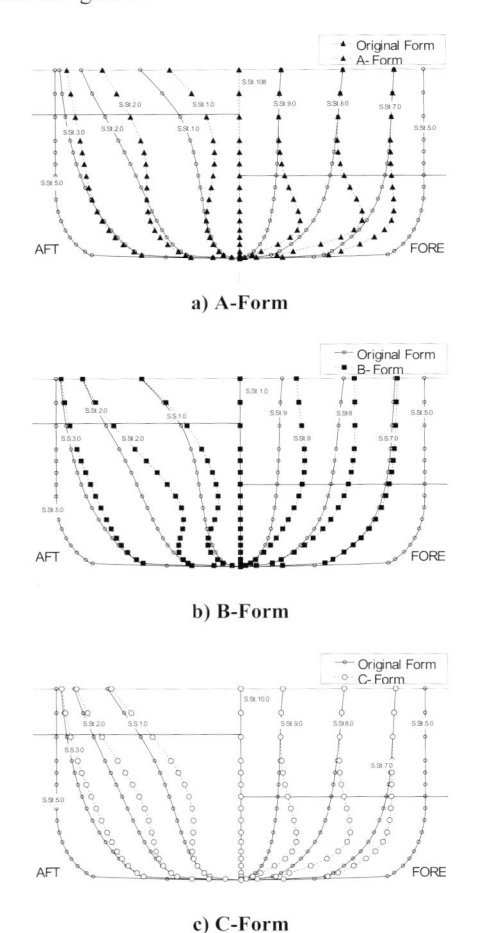

Fig. 7: Comparison of body plan

It seems that the displacement volume moves towards the bottom of ships. These features are similar to the hull form of the SSC (Semi-Submerged Catamaran) or the SWATH (Small Water-plane Area Twin Hull). The changes of hull forms agree with the way in practical ship design. The sectional area curves of these forms are compared in Figure 8. The center of buoyancy of all improved hull forms move forward when compared with Series60 (CB=0.6).

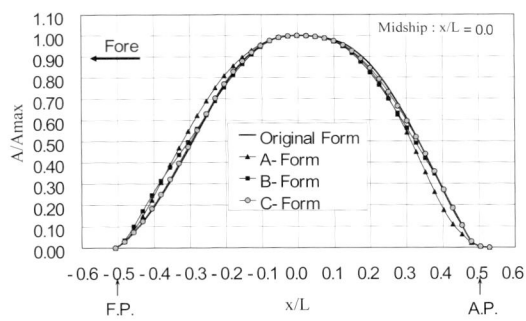

Fig. 8: Comparison of sectional area curves

Wave Profile

The wave profiles of the original hull form and the three improved forms obtained by the present method are shown in Figure 9. The full-load's wave profile of A-From, which has the smallest wave-making resistance, becomes bigger than other profiles in the aft part from the point x/L=0.4. This characteristic means that the pressure recovery appears, and it causes the reduction of wave-making resistance.

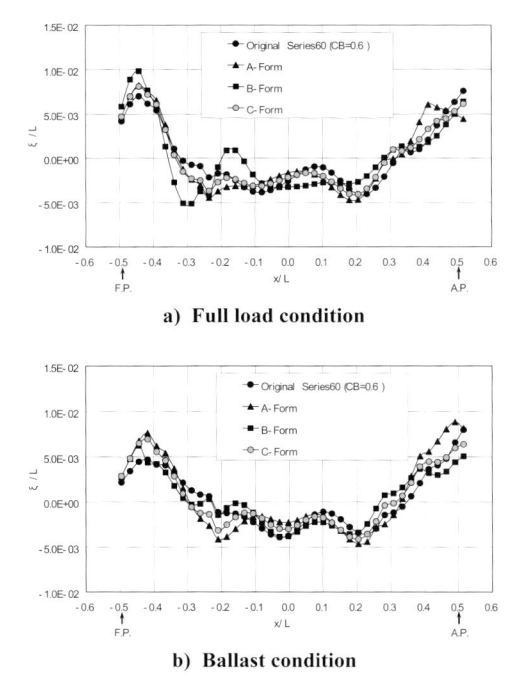

Fig. 9: Comparison of wave profiles

Concerning the wave profiles of ballast condition, the profile of B-Form shows the same tendency in full load condition of A-Form.

Wave amplitude function

The wave amplitude functions of the original hull form and the three improved hull forms by the present optimization are shown in Figure 10, where θ indicates the direction of the elementary waves, $\overline{A}$ indicates the amplitude of elementary waves.

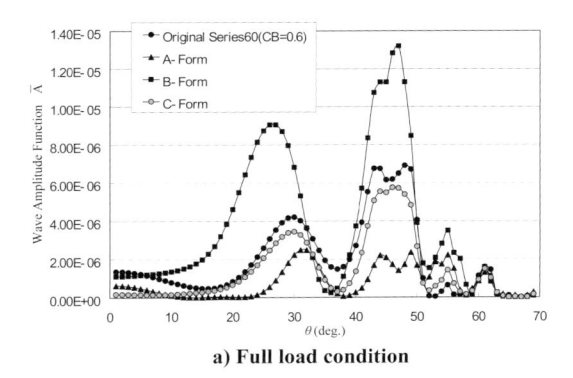

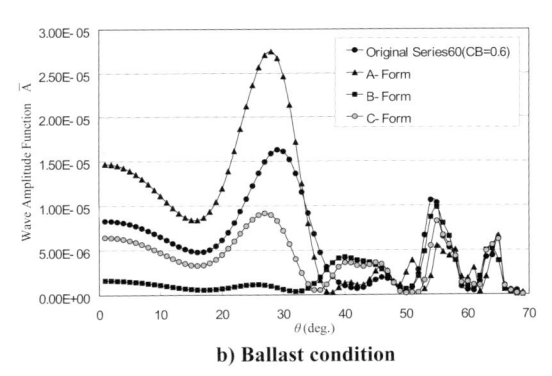

Fig. 10: Comparison of wave amplitude functions with Rankine source method

Concerning the wave amplitude function of full load condition, wave amplitude function of A-Form becomes smaller than that of the original hull form in the range of all angles. The wave amplitude function of B-Form and C-Form become smaller in θ > 35degree. In case of the wave amplitude function of ballast condition, amplitude function of B-Form becomes smaller than amplitude functions of other forms in θ < 35 degree. C-Form shows smaller amplitude functions in both conditions, compared with the original hull form.

The wave-making resistance coefficients of the original hull form and the three improved hull forms obtained by the present method are shown in Figure 11.

The A-Form shows the smallest wave-making resistance at design speed Fn=0.24 in full load condition, and also B-Form's resistance shows the smallest value at design speed Fn=0.27 in the ballast condition.

On the other hand, the wave-making resistance of C-Form becomes smaller than that of the original hull form in the wide speed range.

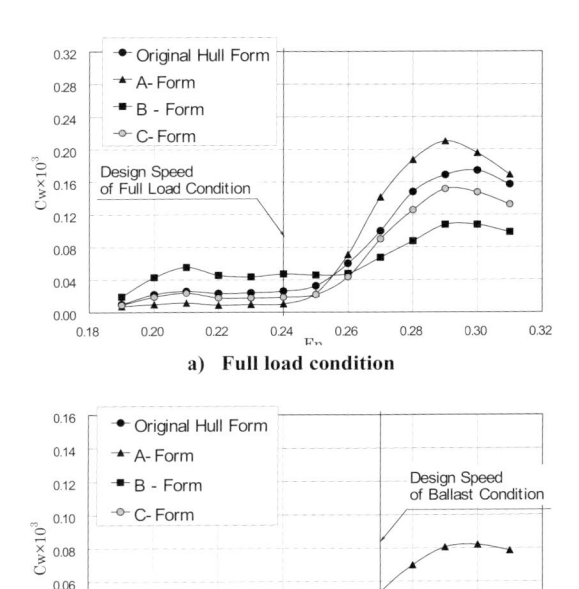

Fig. 11: Comparison of wave-making resistance coefficient curves with Rankine source methods

Conclusions

This paper proposes the multiobjective hull form optimization method using Real-coded Genetic Algorithm to reduce wave-making resistance in multiple load condition. The real-coded GA employs the UNDX (Unimodal Normal Distribution Crossover) as a crossover operator, and employs the POSS (Pareto Optimal Selection Strategy) as a generation-alternation model.

The application examples of the present optimization method for Series60 (CB=0.6) are shown. The hull forms that have small wave-making resistance at different speed and on different load condition were obtained. These improved hull forms have reasonable shapes in terms of wave-making resistance. These hull forms are individual feasible solutions and a ship designer can choose a hull form from the Pareto solutions considering requirements in ship design. The results show the present optimization method is effective for ship design for reduction of wave-making resistance in multiple load condition.

References

Tahara, Y et al. (1996a). "Hull Form Optimization by Nonlinear Programming (Part 3) -Improvement of Stern Form for Minimizing Viscous Resistance, " Journal of Kansai Society of Naval Architects, No.225, pp.1-6.

Tahara, Y et al. (1996b). "Hull Form Optimization by Nonlinear Programming (Part 4) -Improvement of Stern Form for Wake and Viscous Resistance, " Journal of Kansai Society of Naval Architects, No.226, pp.15-21.

Hirayama, A et al. (1996). "An Application of Wave Pattern Analysis Employing Rankine Source Method for Ship Form Optimum, " Transactions of the West-Japan Society of Naval Architects, No.92, pp.19-28.

Hirayama, A et al. (1998). "Optimum Hull Form Design using Numerical Wave Pattern Analysis, " 7th International Symposium on Practical Design of Ships and Mobile Units Proceedings, pp. 421-428.

Chen, S et al. (2003). "Multi-Objective Optimization of Ship Hull Form for Wavemaking Resistance, " Transactions of the West-Japan Society of Naval Architects, No.106, pp. 191-200.

Peri, D et al. (2003). "Multidisciplinary Design Optimization of Naval Surface Combatant," Journal of Ship Research, Volume 47, Number 1, pp.1-12.

Yasukawa, H et al. (1999). "Improvement of Fore Ship Form by a Genetic Algorithm, " Journal of the Society of Naval Architects of Japan, No.186, pp.1-6

Ando, J et al. (2004). "A Trial to Reduce Wavemaking Resistance of Catamaran - Hull Form Improvement Using Real-Coded Genetic Algorithms-, " Transactions of the West-Japan Society of Naval Architects, No.107, pp.1-13

Ono, I et al. (2000). "Optimal Lens Design by Real-Coded Genetic Algorithms Using UNDX," Computer methods in applied mechanics and engineering, No. 186, pp. 483-497.

Ono, I et al. (1999). "A Real-Coded Genetic Algorithm for Function Optimization Using the Unimodal Normal Distribution Crossover," Journal of Japanese Society for Artificial Intelligence, Vol.14 No.6, pp. 1146-1156.

Kobayashi, S et al. (1996). "Generating a Set of Pareto Optimal Decision Trees by Genetic Algorithms," Journal of Japanese Society for Artificial Intelligence, Vol.11 No.5, pp. 102-109.

Ando, J et al. (1988). "A Method to calculate Wave Flow by Rankine Source, " Transactions of the West-Japan Society of Naval Architects, No.75, pp.1-12

Ando, J et al. (1990). "Free Surface Effect on the Propulsive Performance of a Ship (3rd Report) , " Transactions of the West-Japan Society of Naval Architects, No.79, pp. 13-20

Eggers, K.W.H. et al. (1967). "An Assessment of Some Experimental Methods for Determining the Wave-making Characteristics of a Ship Form," Trans. of SNAME, Vol. 75, pp. 112-157.

ITTC (1987). "18th International Towing Tank Conference," Proceedings Vol.1, pp. 50-92.

Suzuki, K et al. (1999). "Studies on Minimization of Wavemaking Resistance Based on Rankine Source Method," Journal of the Society of Naval Architects of Japan, No. 185, pp. 9-19.

Investigations into the Effect of Bulb Shape on Wave Resistance of Ro Ro Vessel

Rahul Subramanian, G.Dhinesh, K.Murali

Department of Ocean Engineering, Indian Institute of Technology
Madras, India

Abstract

This paper presents the results of numerical and experimental investigations with a view to bringing out the kinematics in terms of the wave pattern as well as drag reduction of a RO-RO ship tested with and without the bulbous bow. The numerical estimation uses a 3D fluid dynamics RANSE solver with a volume of fluid (VOF) method with geo-reconstruct surface capturing scheme.

The flow effects at the bulbous bow are quite complex in nature and the effect of the bulbous bow in reducing the gradient of the bow waves is known to be Froude number dependent. Earlier works have considered the use of analytical methods like Michell's method of obtaining wave resistance for the purpose of optimizing the bulb geometry. Studies have also been done using commercial optimization packages and potential flow solvers. In the present work, the ship model has been investigated both with and without bulb by re-modeling the forward region keeping both buoyancy and center of buoyancy unchanged in the two cases. The numerical and experimental wave patterns are presented. The consistent simulation of the wave pattern at the design Froude number of 0.27 and good match with the experimental wave pattern is brought out in the study. The results establish that integration of CFD tools in the analysis/optimization process can reliably and effectively cut down the lead time and associated costs in the design process.

Key words

Bulbous bow; CFD; VOF; Turbulence; Free surface elevation; Resistance.

Introduction

Today the bulbous bow is an elementary device in practical shipbuilding. It changes the hydrodynamic characteristics at the bow. The most important effect is its influence on different resistance components and consequentially on power consumption. The two main effects for bulb design are interference and wave-breaking effect .The interference effect deals with wave resistance change due to interfering free wave systems of main hull and bulb. This is crucial for slender fast ships. The effect depends on the volume of bulb and longitudinal position of the center. The wave breaking effect deals with the prevention of energy loss due to breaking of the very steep bow waves. This effect depends on the volume of bulb. A bigger bulb will deflect the flow better in the vicinity of the bow region. Optimal volume distribution in the longitudinal direction reduces the gradients of hull surface in the region of rising bow waves. This fact is predominant in full, slow ships. Both effects are Froude number dependent. It has indirect effects on propulsive characteristics like wake and thrust deduction fraction. Other beneficial effects of the bulb include mitigating pitching motion by means of higher damping. The bulb also provides aperture for bow thruster and acoustic sounding devices. On the negative side, the additional bulb surface increases frictional resistance, but this effect is small compared to the beneficial effect of reduced wave resistance.

Methodology

A RO-RO ship model with details as shown in Table 1 has been considered in this study. The particulars of the bulb are shown in Table 2. The shaping of the forebody with and without bulb is shown in Fig.1. It may be noted that the bulb conforms to the Nabla shape characteristic of higher speed vessels (Kracht, 1978). The design Froude number is 0.27.

The scope of the investigation consists of numerical modeling of the fluid in the control volume defined around the ship model to obtain the pressure effects and drag, and experimental simulation at corresponding speeds on the basis of Froude number identity. Therefore, a validation has been attempted to obtain the kinematic aspects as well as the dynamic aspects in terms of quantifying drag as well as drag reduction due to the presence of the bulb.

Table 1 Main particulars of the vessel for simulation studies

Particulars	Prototype	Model (scale1:60)
LBP(m)	180.0	3.0
Beam(m)	28.0	0.466
Depth(m)	18.0	0.3
Draft(m)	7.5	0.125
Displacement(t)	22012	0.1019
CB	0.62	0.62
Designed speed (knots)	22	1.46
Fn.	0.27	0.27

Table 2 Particulars of the bulb

Particulars	Value
Length from FP (m)	8.2
Area at FP (m^2)	15.6
Volume (m^3)	95

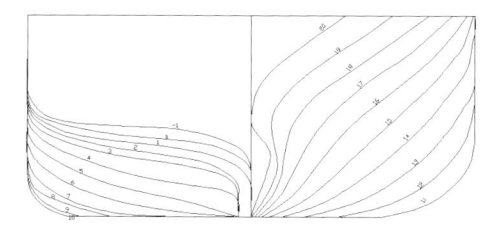

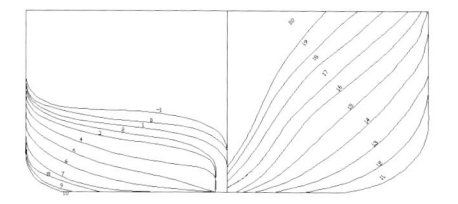

Fig.1 Body plan of the RO-RO model with and without bulb

Numerical simulation

Simulations of the flow field around the model hull were performed using a general purpose RANSE solver FLUENT v6.2.

Governing equations

Once the Reynolds averaging approach for turbulence modeling is applied, the Navier-stokes equations can be written in Cartesian tensor form as:

$$\frac{\partial \rho}{\partial t} + \frac{\partial}{\partial x_i}(\rho u_i) = 0$$

$$\frac{\partial}{\partial t}(\rho u_i) + \frac{\partial}{\partial x_j}(\rho u_i u_j) =$$

$$-\frac{\partial p}{\partial x_i} + \frac{\partial}{\partial x_j}\left[\mu\left(\frac{\partial u_i}{\partial x_j} + \frac{\partial u_j}{\partial x_i} - \frac{2}{3}\delta_{ij}\frac{\partial u_i}{\partial x_i}\right)\right] + \frac{\partial}{\partial x_j}\left(-\overline{\rho u_i' u_j'}\right)$$

where μ is the molecular viscosity, δ_{ij} the Kronecker delta, and the $\overline{\rho u_i' u_j'}$ the Reynolds stresses.

To close the above set of equations, among the various turbulence models, the present study used Shear-Stress Transport (SST) k-omega turbulence model. The SST $k - \omega$ model was developed by Menter to effectively blend the robust and accurate formulation of the $k - \omega$ model in the near-wall region with the free-stream independence of the $k - \varepsilon$ model in the far field.

VOF Method

The volume of fluid (VOF) method with geo-reconstruct surface capturing scheme has been used to capture the free surface (Hirt and Nicholas (1981)). The location of the two fluids is specified using a volume fraction function, α_q, with $\alpha_q = 1$ inside one fluid and $\alpha_q = 0$ in the other. The cell identifying α_q lies between 1 and 0 contains the interface between q[th] fluid and one or more other fluids.

$\Sigma \alpha_q = 1$ and for two phases, $\rho = \alpha_1 \rho_1 + (1 - \alpha_1)\rho_2$

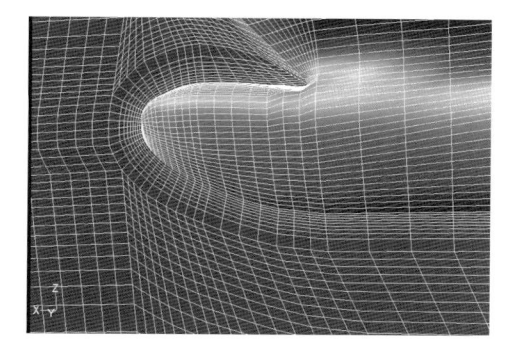

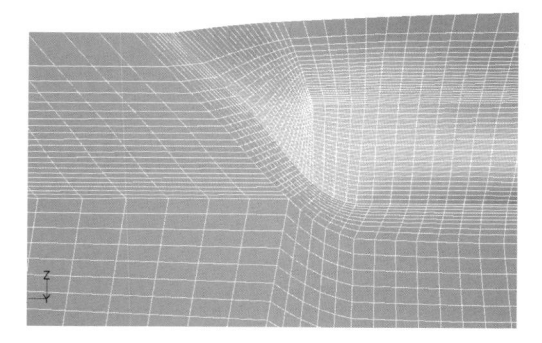

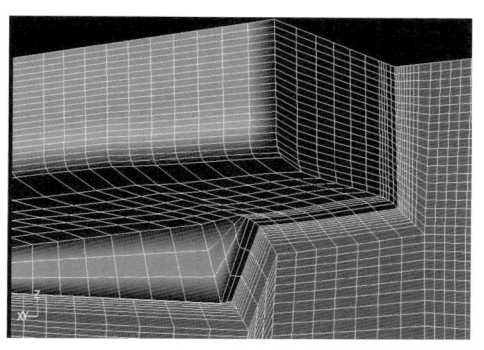

Fig. 2 Surface mesh over the hull

Fig. 2 shows the surface mesh over the bow with bulb, without bulb and aft of the model respectively. The domain extends from -3.67m≤x≤4.83m, 0≤y ≤1.67, 0.21m≤z≤-0.81m with around 0.35 million hexahedral cells in the domain. The wall with zero shear is used for the top, bottom, and side wall boundaries. One half of the ship is modeled and a symmetry boundary condition is imposed at the middle plane. No slip wall boundary condition is imposed on the hull surface. Velocity inlet and velocity outlet boundary condition are imposed at the inlet and outlet of the computational domain as shown in Fig. 3.

Grid independence and convergence studies were carried out to obtain the optimal mesh sizing as part of the standardization (Manoj and Subramanian 2007). The results for dynamic pressure distribution in the forebody for the cases of (i) with bulb and (ii) without bulb are shown in Fig.4. It may be noted that the bulbous bow wave system destructively interferes with the primary ship bow wave system and in effect produces a subdued wave pattern at the bow. The effect is visibly pronounced when compared with the much larger and spread out wave breaking seen at the bow in the case without bulb. The surface elevations in the two cases are shown in Fig.5 a and 5 b. The subdued wave pattern in the case with bulb is evident.

Fig. 6 gives an additional perspective view where the breaking wave at the bow is very much evident for the case without bulb. In comparison the wave system is very much subdued in Fig. 6 (b).

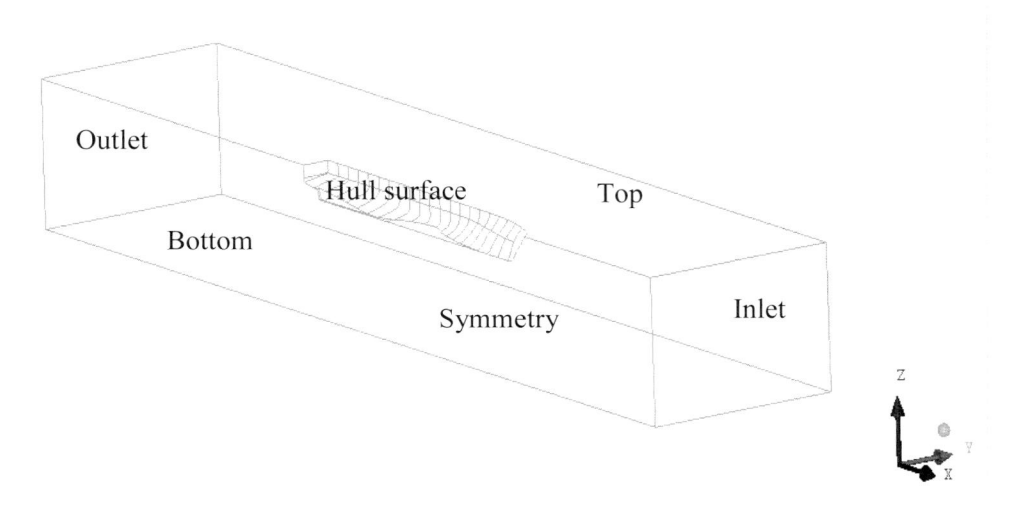

Fig. 3 Boundary conditions

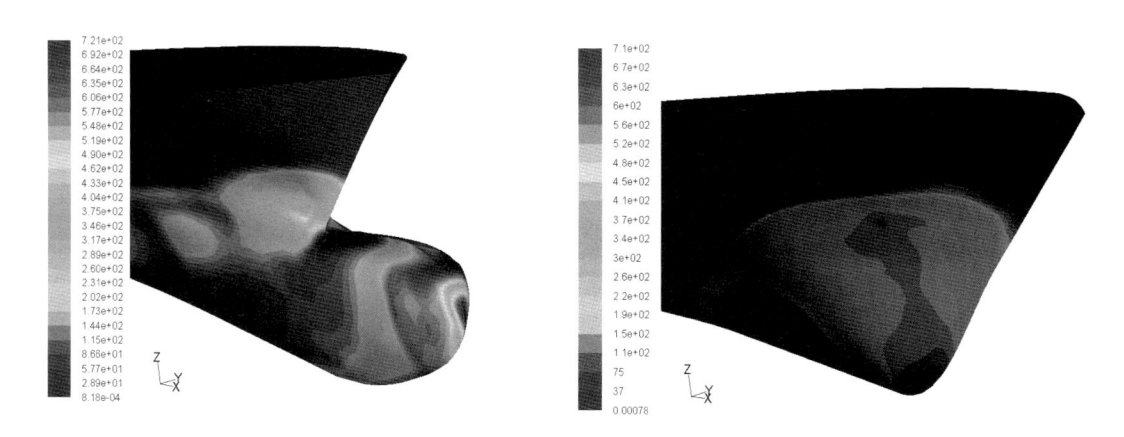

Fig. 4 Dynamic pressure contours from numerical simulation for Fn=0.27

(a) (b)

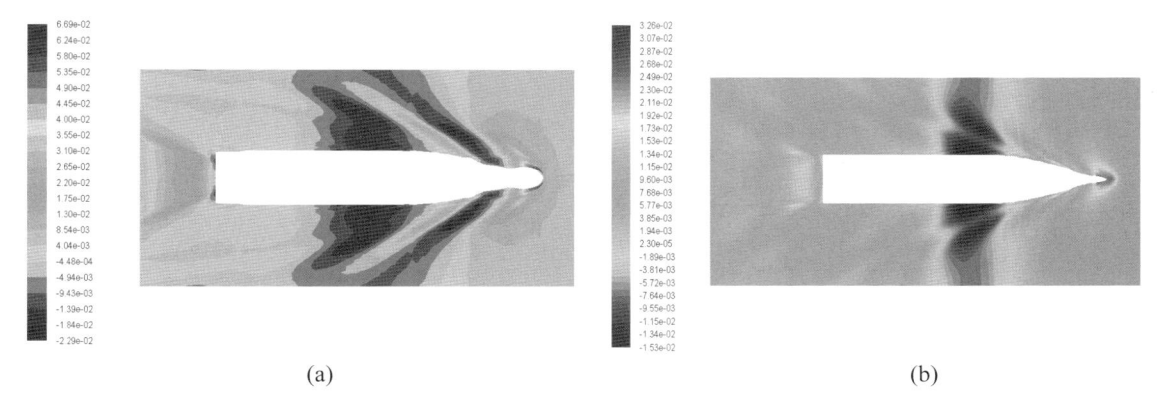

Fig. 5 Free surface elevation plots around the hull for Fn=0.27

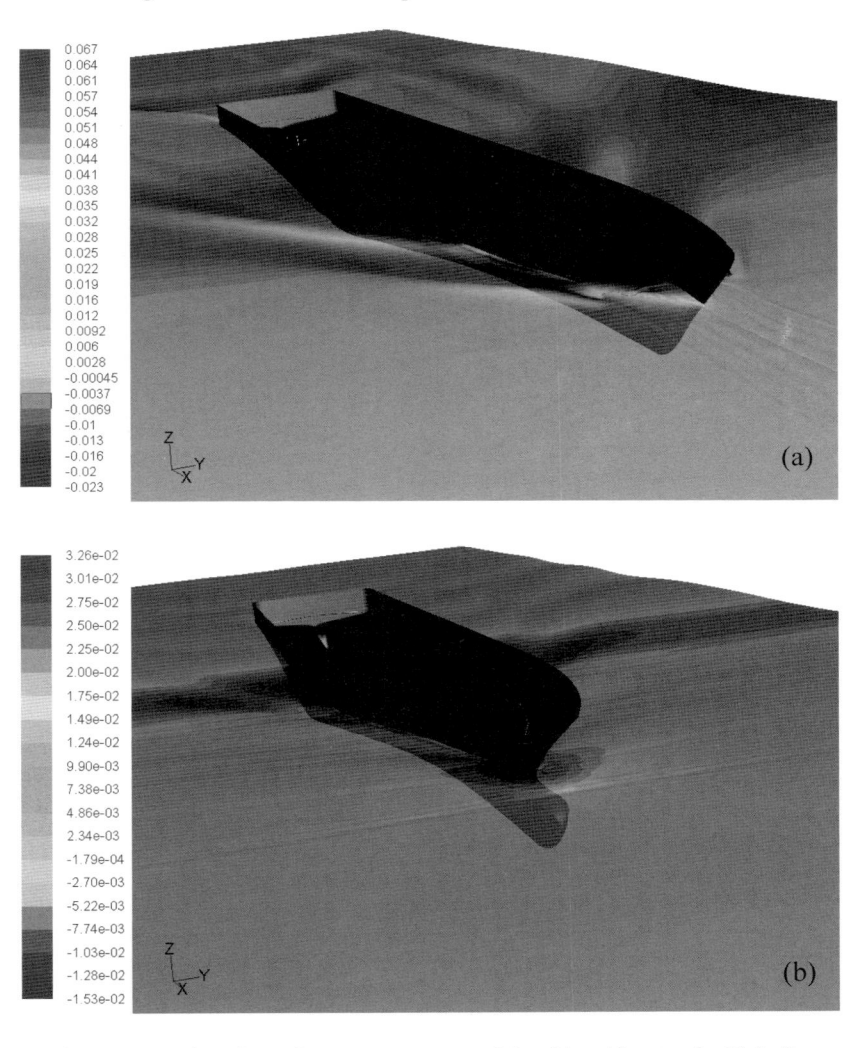

(a)

(b)

Fig. 6 Perspective view of wave pattern around the ship without and with bulb

Experimental study

The bow region of the same RO-RO model was modified to conform to the two body plan shapes shown in Fig.1. The body plan at the bow was re-faired keeping draught, volume of displacement as well as longitudinal center of buoyancy constant in both the cases. Iterative checks were made on both the volume of displacement as well as the longitudinal center of buoyancy within a pre-fixed tolerance limit (within 0.1%). All experiments were carried out in the towing tank at IIT Madras. The tank dimensions are 82m x 3.2m x 2.8m depth. The comparative resistance measurements are shown in Fig.6. The presence of the bulb shows a benefit of resistance to the order of 5% reduction at the designed speed. The values of resistances have been compared with numerical simulation based results, see Table 3.

The breaking waves from the physical model tests are captured and shown for comparison in Fig.7. The wave pattern on the sides of the bow is shown in Fig. 8.

Table 3 Comparison of resistance for different Froude numbers

Fn	Total resistance from experiment (N)	Total resistance from CFD (N)	% Error
0.15	2.3	2.47	6.9
0.27	9.3	9.88	6.2

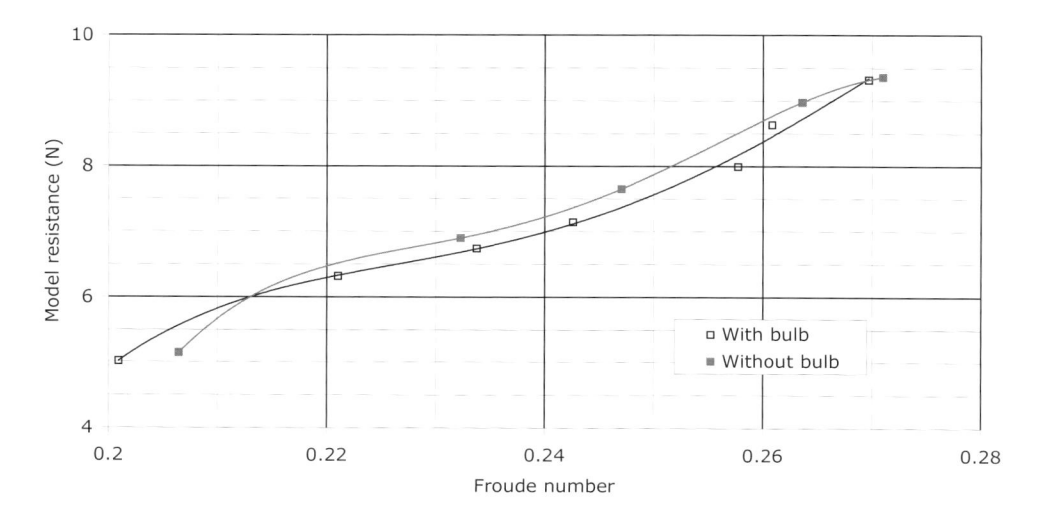

Fig.7 Comparative resistance plots from experimental study

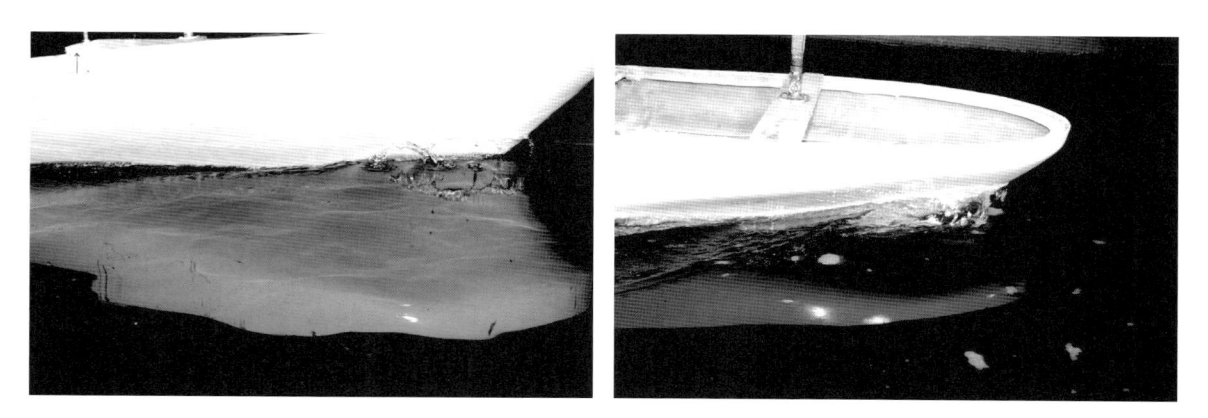

Fig. 8 Bow waves in comparison for the cases of with bulb and without bulb

Fig. 9 Wave pattern around the ship hull with bulb and without bulb

Conclusion

The combined numerical/ experimental study has been undertaken with care and the obtained results show that the numerical model captures the physical event of the wave pattern around the ship hull as well as the breaking waves at the bow of the ship. The results show good comparison when compared with photographs from the experiments. The study establishes the validity of application of the numerical tool for design optimization.

References

Hirt, C.W. and Nichols, B.D., (1981) "Volume of Fluid (VOF) Method for the Dynamics of Free Boundaries," Journal of Computational Physics Vol 39, pp 201-221.

Kumar, M., Subramanian. A., (2007) "A numerical and experimental study on tank wall influences in drag estimation," Ocean Engineering, Vol 34, pp192-250.

Kracht, M. A.,(1978) "Design of bulbous bows'' SNAME transactions Vol 86 pp 186-213.

Application of the Two-parameter Unified Approach for Fatigue Life Prediction of Marine Structures

Weicheng Cui[1], Rugang Bian[1], Xiangchun Liu[2]

1 China Ship Scientific Research Center, Wuxi, Jiangsu, China
2 College of Shipbuilding Engineering, Harbin Engineering University, Heilongjiang, China

Abstract

Marine structures are subjected to complex loading histories and one of the most significant failure modes is fatigue. Accurate prediction of the fatigue life of marine structures under service loading is very important for both safe and economic design and operation. However, due to the complex loading and geometries of marine structures, the current technology for the prediction of fatigue life of marine structures is far from satisfactory. This situation might change due to one of the latest developments of FCP theory, the two-parameter unified approach proposed by Vasudevan, Sadananda and their co-workers. The purpose of this paper is to carry out a feasibility study for the application of the unified approach for fatigue life prediction of marine structures. First an overview on the two-parameter Unified Approach for fatigue life prediction is given. Then potential problems encountered in the application of the unified approach are discussed. Finally, the feasibility of the application procedure and the capabilities of the unified approach for fatigue life prediction are demonstrated using a simple example of a finite width plate with a center crack subjected to remote uniform fatigue loading.

Keywords

Marine structures; fatigue; fatigue crack propagation theory; two-parameter unified approach.

Introduction

Marine structures such as ships and offshore platforms are subjected to complex loading histories and one of the most significant failure modes is fatigue. Accurate prediction of the fatigue life (or more completely the whole process of fatigue crack propagation (FCP)) of marine structures under service loading is very important for both safe and economic design and operation [1]. However, due to the complex loading and geometries of marine structures, the current technology for the prediction of fatigue life of marine structures is far from satisfactory. One of the significant reasons is that current fatigue strength assessment methods for marine structures are largely based on the cumulative fatigue damage (CFD) theory using S-N curves [2]. The CFD theory does not capture all the important factors affecting the fatigue life. The effects of initial defects and the load sequence have not been accounted for. The extent of final fatigue failure in real structures is also not specified [3]. Furthermore, the linear accumulation of fatigue damage itself is an assumption and it is well proved now that this assumption has wide scatter [4]. These factors will result in a large difference between the actual fatigue life and the predicted one [5]. In fatigue community, more and more researchers have realised that fatigue crack propagation (FCP) theory could overcome these deficiencies and has the potential to provide more accurate predictions to fatigue lives [6-9].

FCP theory is not new and Paris equation is well-known. Various improvements based on the crack closure concept [10] have achieved some successes [e.g. 7, 11] but now this concept is subjected to some challenges [12, 13]. Because of the much complexity involved in the application and limited improvement in the accuracy of the predicted fatigue lives, the adoption of FCP theory in marine community received great resistance [2]. However, this situation might change due to one of the latest developments of FCP theory, the two-parameter unified approach proposed by Vasudevan, Sadananda and their co-workers [14-21]. According to the unified approach it is both K_{max} (σ_{max}) and ΔK ($\Delta \sigma$) which are responsible for the fatigue crack propagation. The implication of this statement is that past practice based on both S-N curves or Paris equations is incomplete and that might explain the incapability of predicting good fatigue lives. Through their efforts the unified approach has been demonstrated that many recognized special phenomena can be explained, e.g. compression-tension [15], compression-compression [18], load sequence effects [16], environmental interactions [17], superimposed monotonic fracture modes [19], non-propagating incipient cracks [20], vacuum behavior [21]. Now more and more people in fatigue community tend to believe that this unified approach might be a correct way forward [22-27]. However, little work has been seen to apply this unified approach to marine structures.

The purpose of this paper is to carry out a feasibility study for the application of the unified approach for fatigue life prediction of marine structures. After an overview on the two-parameter Unified Approach, the potential problems encountered in the application of the unified approach are discussed. Finally, the feasibility of the application procedure and the capabilities of the unified approach for fatigue life prediction are preliminarily demonstrated using a simple example of a finite width plate with a center crack subjected to remote uniform fatigue loading.

Brief Overview of the two-parameter Unified Approach

A Historical Overview to FCP theory before the Two-parameter Unified Approach

As pointed out in the introduction, fatigue life prediction methods based on CFD theory suffers from many deficiencies because of neglecting many important factors such as the effects of initial defects and the load sequence and the extent of final fatigue failure in real structures. In theory, fatigue crack propagation (FCP) theory based on the crack growth rate curves has the capability to account for the neglected factors in CFD theory [1]. A historical overview on FCP theory before 2002 was given in Cui [9]. The earliest crack driving force was ΔK and then ΔK_{eff} using the concept of crack closure [10]. This concept has been highly appraised in 1980s and 1990s but now it is subjected to some challenges [e.g. 12]. Particularly many people have agreed that the physical effects of crack closure have been greatly over-estimated in the past [e.g 13]. Partial crack closure model [28,29] was proposed to overcome the difficulty the crack closure model met. Comparison with some experimental data showed that the constitutive relationship proposed by McEvily and Ishihara [29] is able to explain the six special phenomena they concerned. McEvily's partial crack closure model was further extended by Cui and Huang [30] by introducing the concept of "virtual strength" (σ_V). The virtual strength of the material may represent the material strength at limit of "perfect" condition ($r_e=0$) while the actual ultimate strength of the material (σ_u) represents the strength under the condition that the defect size is equal to the inherent flaw length ($r_e>0$), a minimum crack size for engineering metals. What it says here is that the virtual strength is only an ideal value when all the inherent flaws have been removed. However, for any existing engineering metal, the inherent flaws exist and its maximum strength is the ultimate strength which will be lower than its virtual strength. When a body contains a crack its ultimate strength (σ_{ua}) will be lower than the ultimate strength of the material (σ_u). As crack length increases, the ultimate strength will decrease.

The extended constitutive relation [30] can be applied from the low cycle fatigue (LCF) down to the static failure to the high cycle fatigue (HCF) up to the fatigue limit and from "crack-free" plain specimens to cracked bodies. For a body containing an existing initial crack length a_0, the maximum fatigue stress has to be in the range between fatigue limit ($\sigma_{\infty a}$) and ultimate strength (σ_{ua}). If the stress is lower than the fatigue limit, then fatigue crack will not propagate. If the stress approaches to the ultimate strength, static failure will occur. Therefore, a sigmoidal shape of the general crack growth rate curve also reflects a sigmoidal shape of an S-N curve.

Vasudevan and Sadananda [13] criticized the FCP methods based on the crack closure concept. They pointed out that the drawbacks in the current fatigue life prediction methods stem from several sources: (1) the assumption of plasticity induced crack closure, (2) the lack of terms in the model that relates to the environmental effects and slip deformation behavior, and (3) several adjustable parameters needed to fit the observed data. In order to overcome these drawbacks and develop a more reliable fatigue life prediction model, Vasudevan, Sadananda and co-workers have proposed a two-parameter unified approach [14-21].

The two-parameter Unified Approach

The fundamental assumptions made in the Unified Approach [13-21] are: (1) the true material behavior is represented by the long crack growth properties, (2) fatigue damage must be described by two driving force parameters ΔK and K_{max} instead of one, and (3) the deviations from the long crack growth behavior arise from the *internal stresses* present ahead of the crack tip which *contribute to* K_{max}. These *internal stresses* are responsible for the accelerated growth in short crack, underload region and decelerated growth during overloads.

Since there are two driving forces required to obtain fatigue crack growth, K_{max} and ΔK, there are two fatigue thresholds, $K_{max,th}$ and ΔK_{th} corresponding to two driving forces. These are asymptotic values in the $\Delta K - K_{max}$ plot. Both must be satisfied simultaneously for fatigue crack growth to occur. Existence of dependence of ΔK_{th} on R is a trivial consequence of the existence of two thresholds. Extrinsic mechanisms (such as crack closure) therefore are not necessary to account for R dependence of ΔK_{th}. Crack growth is driven by total crack tip stresses, i.e., the superimposition of the externally applied stress and any internal stress that exist. Internal stresses exist due to, for example, defects, scratches, inclusions, or other stress concentrators; residual stresses such as from welding or heat treatments, cold work, transformation induced stresses, and plasticity, including overload plasticity. The basic effect of internal stress is to offset the total stress intensity at the crack tip relative to the externally applied stress, so that both K_{min} and K_{max} would generally be affected similarly. Consequently, the primary effects of internal stress manifest through K_{max} and not the ΔK parameter. Environmental effects manifest primarily in the K_{max} term. This is because the K_{max} driving force is what opens and increments the crack, therefore it is more sensitive to environmental modification of the material at the crack tip.

Role of K_{max} in fatigue crack growth has been considered in the past [e.g 28,29], but mostly in a phenomenological sense to correct for the superimposition of monotonic modes of crack growth at high ΔK. In the Unified Approach, the role of K_{max} is different. In this approach, K_{max} is the primary driving force for fatigue crack growth. In fact, it is considered as a fundamental fracture mechanics parameter needed to quantify all fracture processes, including monotonic fracture, stress corrosion crack growth and sustained load crack growth. Cyclic loads introduce an additional perturbation bringing amplitude, ΔK, as the second parameter. The Unified Approach further considers that there are two thresholds, one in terms of K_{max} and the other in terms of ΔK, which must be met simultaneously for fatigue crack to grow. Existence of threshold in terms of K_{max} is a definite indication that it is a crack tip driving force.

Physically, although both driving forces are essential, only one will be the controlling parameter for a given range of R. For example, at low R, K_{max} is the controlling force, and at high R, ΔK is the controlling force. Crack arrest occurs if either of the two forces falls below their respective thresholds. The experimental validity for the existence of K_{max} threshold, in addition to threshold ΔK, has been demonstrated for a variety of materials. A broad classification of material behavior has been presented [19,21]. The physical significance of K_{max} has also been explained recently [25] on the basis of shielding effect of dislocations in the plasticity ahead of the crack tip.

Problems to be solved for the application of the Unified Approach

The crack growth rate expression

The two-parameter Unified Approach was proposed by Vasudevan and Sadananda and described in many papers [14-21]. According to these works, the growth of the crack depends on two load parameters: ΔK and K_{max}, and in order for a crack to grow, two thresholds values (ΔK_{th}^*, K_{maxth}^*) must be met. Although many papers have been published to use the two-parameter unified approach to explain various special phenomena, there is no unified expressions for the two-parameter crack growth rate law.

In Vasudevan, Sadananda and Louat of 1994 [13], the following general expression was given:

$$\frac{da}{dN} = f\left[\left(\Delta K - \Delta K_{th}^*\right), \left(K_{max} - K_{maxth}^*\right)\right] \quad (1)$$

In Sadananda and Vasudevan of 1997 [14], the following specific expression was given:

$$\frac{da}{dN} = A\left(\Delta K - \Delta K_{th}^*\right)^n \left(K_{max} - K_{maxth}^*\right)^m \quad (2)$$

Note that K_{maxth}^* and ΔK_{th}^* depends on da/dN, and the general expressions are:

$$K_{maxth}^* = K_{maxth0} f_1\left(\tfrac{da}{dN}\right), \quad \Delta K_{th}^* = \Delta K_{th0} f_2\left(\tfrac{da}{dN}\right) \quad (3)$$

This expression can only describe the behaviour near the threshold region. Maymon [27] used that expression to study an aluminum 2024-T351 and the detailed values for the model parameters are given. In order to describe the sigmoidal shape of the crack growth rate curve, Bukkapatnam and Sadananda [31] proposed an expression based on the mathematical properties of sigmoidal functions.

Although their expression can capture the sigmoidal shape, the physical meanings of the parameters are unclear. We recommend to write the general expression of the two-parameter unified approach following the same idea as Eq.(2) as follows:

$$\frac{da}{dN} = \frac{A\left(\Delta K - \Delta K_{th}^*\right)^n \left(K_{max} - K_{maxth}^*\right)^m}{\left(1 - \left(K_{max}/K_{cf}\right)^{\gamma_1}\right)} \quad (4)$$

Where A, n, m, γ, K_{cf}, ΔK_{th}^*, K_{maxth}^* are the model parameters. ΔK_{th}^*, K_{maxth}^* can be functions of da/dN similar as Eq.(3) [31] or can be functions of R [30]. In this paper, we assume

$$\begin{cases} \Delta K_{th}^* = \Delta K_{th0}(1-R)^{\gamma_2} \\ K_{maxth}^* = K_{maxth0}(1-R)^{\gamma_2} \end{cases} \quad (5)$$

K_{max} can be defined either within linear elastic fracture mechanics or modified by elastic-plastic fracture mechanics. In this paper, K_{max} is defined by the following equation according to Ref. [30]:

$$K_{max} = \sqrt{\pi r_e \left(Sec\frac{\pi}{2}\frac{\sigma_{max}}{\sigma_V} + 1\right)}\left(1 + Y(a)\sqrt{\frac{a}{2r_e}}\right)\sigma_{max} \quad (6)$$

where the "virtual strength" (σ_V) can be determined from the following equation:

$$\frac{\sigma_V}{\sigma_u} = \frac{\pi}{2} \cdot \frac{1}{\cos^{-1}(\frac{1}{\alpha^2-1})},$$
$$\alpha = \frac{K_c}{\sigma_u \sqrt{\pi r_e}\left(1 + \frac{Y(r_e)}{\sqrt{2}}\right)} > \sqrt{2} \quad (7)$$

In the following, the performances of this two-parameter crack growth rate curve, Eq.(4), will be studied through a simple example of a center crack in a finite width plate. The total number of model parameters are 11 which are: A, n, m, γ_1, γ_2, r_e, K_c, K_{cf}, σ_u, ΔK_{th0}, K_{maxth0}.

Determination of K_{cf}

Based on the crack growth rate law, for a given fatigue problem (known fatigue load and crack size), one can plot out a~N curve. From the curve one can determine a value of a_c, crack length at which unstable crack propagation occurs. Using this value of a_c, one can calculate K_{cf}, fracture toughness value in fatigue failure. By comparing K_{cf} with K_c, one can find that these two values are different. This may be the consequence of fatigue loading history. Schijve [8] has emphasized this point that fracture toughness in fatigue is different from the static fracture toughness.

Determination of other model parameters

Since there are so many model parameters, many tests have to be carried out in order to determine these parameters. This could be a great obstacle to the practical application. Further difficulty is how to measure some of the parameters such as K_{maxth}. Standard measurement methods need to be agreed. One way to overcome these difficulties is to estimate these model parameters from quasi-static material properties such as hardness, elastic modulus and ultimate strength.

Performances of the two-parameter crack growth rate curve

The problem and the realistic values for model parameters

Let us consider the problem of a center crack in a plate of finite width subjected to remote fatigue loading, see Fig.1. For this problem, the geometrical factor Y can be calculated by the following formula:

$$Y(a/w) = \left(\sec \frac{\pi a}{w} \right)^{1/2} \quad (8)$$

The width of the plate w=100mm = 0.1 m. The material is assumed to be a 0.45 wt% carbon steel as-heat-treated. The yield stress σ_Y=750 MPa, the ultimate tensile strength σ_u=833 MPa, the inherent flaw length $r_e = 10^{-6}$ m and A=1.5×10^{-10} (MPa)$^{-2}$[10]. The two threshold values are assumed to be K_{maxth0}=4.1MPam$^{1/2}$; ΔK_{th0}=3.0MPam$^{1/2}$ in this paper. This material is chosen as a reference material and the values of these parameters are regarded to be realistic for a representative high strength carbon steel. The other model parameters will be assumed in each individual case accordingly.

Effects of load and crack length on fatigue crack growth rate

If 9 model parameters are known, then the crack growth rate will vary with the maximum stress and the crack length. Fig.2 shows the crack growth rate increases with the maximum stress for a/r_e=100. It can be seen that the crack growth rate curve is of a sigmoidal shape and the stress ratio has significant influence on the threshold but no influence on the unstable condition as expected. Fig.2 shows the variation of the crack growth rate with the crack length for a constant stress intensity factor range

$$\Delta K = 60 \, \text{MPa}\sqrt{\text{m}}.$$

The model parameters used in the calculation are:

$r_e = 10^{-6}$ m, A=1.5×10^{-10} (MPa)$^{-2}$, $\gamma = 20$, n=0.75,

m=1.15, σ_u=825MPa, K_c=150 MPa$\sqrt{\text{m}}$,

K_{cf}=120 MPa$\sqrt{\text{m}}$, $\Delta K_{th0} = 3.0$MPa$\sqrt{\text{m}}$,

$K_{maxth0} = 4.1$MPa$\sqrt{\text{m}}$.

Fig.2 is very similar to Fig.3 of McEvily et al [8] and the slowing down of a crack growth rate with crack advance at constant ΔK is known as anomalous fatigue crack growth behavior.

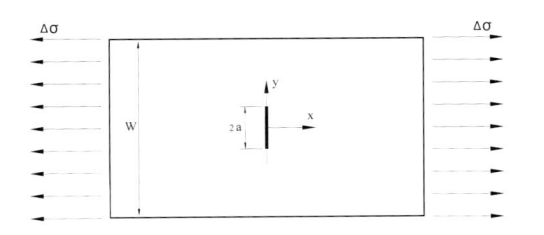

Fig.1 A center crack in a plate of finite width subjected to remote fatigue loading

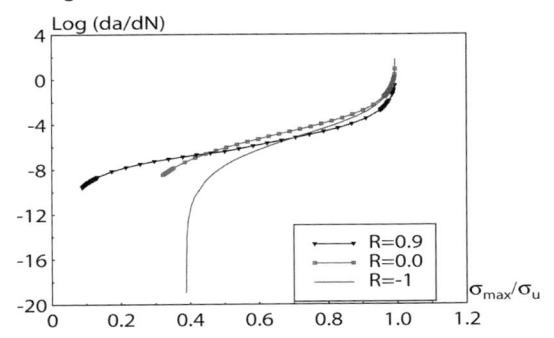

Fig.2 Crack growth rate increases with the maximum stress for a/r_e=100

Various Factors on Fatigue Strength

a ~ N curve for constant amplitude loading

If the constitutive relation for fatigue crack propagation is known, then through the use of Eq.(4), we can study the crack propagation behavior under constant amplitude loading from initial a_0 to final fracture. Fig.3 shows the predicted a~N curves for three different stress levels. The model parameters used in the calculation are:

$r_e = 10^{-6}$ m, A=1.5×10^{-10} (MPa)$^{-2}$, $\gamma = 20$, n=0.75,

m=1.15, σ_u=825MPa, K_c=150 $MPa\sqrt{m}$,

$\Delta K_{th0} = 3.0 MPa\sqrt{m}$, $K_{maxth0} = 4.1 MPa\sqrt{m}$.

The initial crack length is a_0=10r_e, the stress ratio is R=0.1. It can be seen that initially the crack propagation is stable then it will be unstable and final fracture occurs. The maximum crack length allowed depends on the applied stress level. The higher the stress, the lower the maximum crack length. This maximum crack length is generally smaller than the physically allowed length such as half of the plate width in this case.

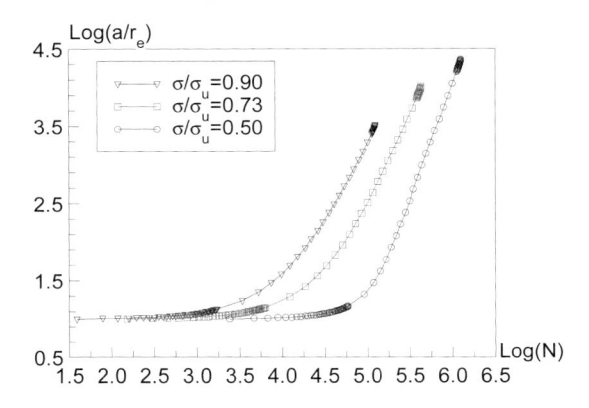

Fig.3 Predicted a~N curves for three different stress levels

S-N curves

If the stress cycles remain to be constant amplitude ($\sigma_{min}, \sigma_{max}$), then S-N curves can be derived by repeatedly using Eq.(4). Generally speaking, they are functions of (a_0, R). The parameter γ which reflects the threshold property will also has some effect on the predicted S-N curves, especially in the fatigue limit region. Fig.4 shows several example calculations for different R levels and two different γ values. The other parameters are:

$r_e = 10^{-6}$ m, A=1.5×10^{-10} (MPa)$^{-2}$, $\gamma = 20$,

n=0.75, m=1.15, σ_u=825MPa, K_c=150 $MPa\sqrt{m}$,

$\Delta K_{th0} = 3.0 MPa\sqrt{m}$, $K_{maxth0} = 4.1 MPa\sqrt{m}$.

The initial crack length is a_0=10r_e. From this figure, the three regions of upper limit (controlled mainly by fracture toughness), the middle linear part and the lower fatigue limit (controlled mainly by fatigue threshold) can be seen clearly. According to the current crack growth rate model, the fatigue limit will depend on several parameters as discussed in previous section. The indifference of R variation in the negative region to the crack growth rate value needs further study.

$\gamma = 0.75$

$\gamma = 1.0$

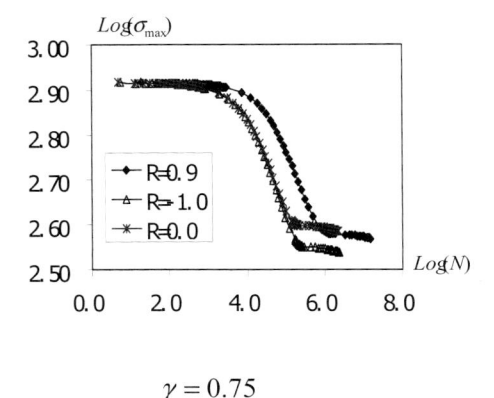

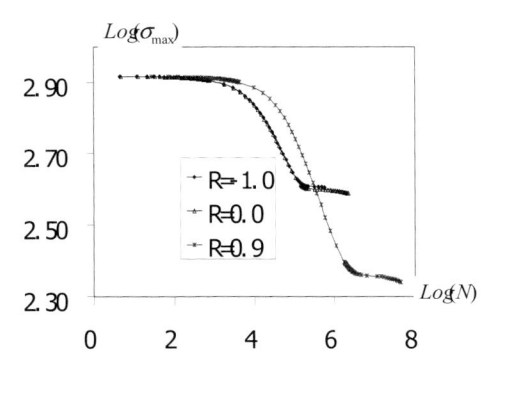

Fig.4 Predicted typical S-N curves by the general constitutive relation

Effect of initial crack size on fatigue strength

If the constant stress reversals ($\sigma_{min}, \sigma_{max}$) are fixed as R=0.2, σmax=551MPa, then the effect of initial crack size a0 on fatigue life can be studied. Fig.5 shows an example calculation where

$r_e = 10^{-6}$ m, A=1.5×10^{-10} (MPa)$^{-2}$, $\gamma = 20$, n=0.75,

m=1.15, σ_u=825MPa.

K_c=150 MPa$\sqrt{m}$, $\Delta K_{th0} = 3.0$MPa$\sqrt{m}$,

$K_{maxth0} = 4.1$MPa$\sqrt{m}$.

From Fig.5, it can be seen that when initial crack size a_0 varies from 0.01 mm to 1 mm, the fatigue life could have 4.5 times difference. This certainly provides some explanations to the scatter observed in an S-N test. A through-thickness crack may be a bit severe than the actual situation. Other models such as a surface elliptical crack model may also be used for the similar investigation.

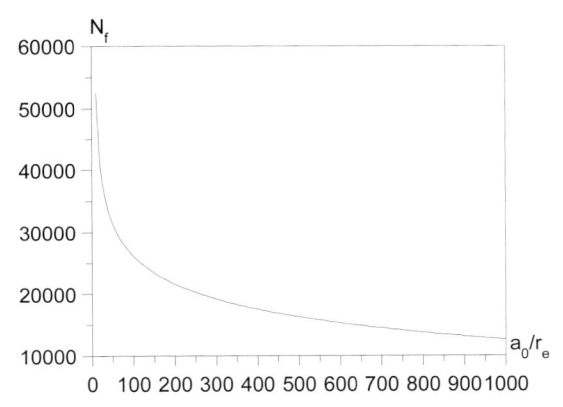

Fig.5 Effect of initial crack size a₀ on fatigue life

Effect of load sequence

Sadananda et al [16] have analyzed the overload effects using the two-parameter unified approach and they concluded that residual stresses due to the overlaod plastic zone are the major factor contributing to retardation. However, up to now there is no method suggested how to calculate these residual stresses. Therefore, this problem needs further study.

Summary and Conclusions

Accurate prediction of the fatigue life of marine structures under service loading is very important for both safe and economic design and operation. A feasibility study for the application of the two-parameter unified approach for fatigue life prediction of marine structures has been done. Following conclusions can be drawn.

1. Theoretically speaking, the two-parameter Unified Approach is more reasonable than the modified single parameter approach and it has the ability to explain many of the phenomena encountered in fatigue. However, there are lots of works to be done in the future to determine the model parameters.
2. Many special fatigue phenomena such as the load sequence effect and the compression-compression fatigue are explained by using the concept of the *internal stresses*. How to determine the internal stresses are a big challenge.
3. In order for applying the two-parameter Unified Approach to predict the fatigue life of marine structure, we have to establish some of the empirical methods to estimate model parameters in order to reduce the test requirements.

References

[1] Cui, W.C. (2003). A feasible study of fatigue life prediction for marine structures based on crack propagation analysis. Journal of Engineering for the Maritime Environment, Vol.217, No.5, pp. 11-23.

[2] Wästberg, S. et al. (2006). Fatigue and Fracture, TC III.2 Report, Proceedings of 16th International Ship and Offshore Structures Congress, edited by P.A. Frieze and R.A. Shenoi, 20-25 August, Southampton, UK, Vol.1, pp. 459-541.

[3] Cui, W.C. and Wu, Y.S. (2002). Towards a more rational first-principle-based strength assessment system for ship structures. Presented at ASRANET conference in Glasgow, July 8-10 2002.

[4] Schutz, W. (1996). A history of fatigue, Engineering Fracture Mechanics, Vol.54, No.2, pp.263-300.

[5] Fricke, W., Cui,W.C., Kierkegaard,H., Kihl,D., Koval,M., Lee,H.L., Mikkola, T., Parmentier, G., Toyosada, M., Yoon,J.H. (2002). Comparative Fatigue Strength Assessment of a Structural Detail in a Containership using various Approaches of Classification Societies, Marine Structures, Vol.15, No.1, pp.1-13.

[6] Fatemi, A. and Yang, L. (1998). Cumulative fatigue damage and life prediction theories: a survey of the state of the art for homogenus materials, International Journal of Fatigue, 20(1): 9–34.

[7] Newman Jr, J.C. (1998). The merging of fatigue and fracture mechanics concepts: a historical perspective, Progress in Aerospace Sciences, 34: 347-390.

[8] Schijve, J. (2003). Fatigue of structures and materials in the 20th century and the state of the art, International Journal of Fatigue, 25: 679–702.

[9] Cui, W.C. (2002). A state-of-the-art review on fatigue life prediction methods for metal structures, Journal of Marine Science and Technology, Vol.7, No.1, pp.43-56.

[10] Elber, W. (1970). Fatigue crack closure under cyclic tension, Engineering Fracture Mechanics, Vol.2, pp.37-45.

[11] Lee, SY and Song, J.H. (2000). Crack closure and growth behavior of physically short fatigue cracks under random loading. Engng Fract Mech, 66(3):321-346.

[12] Hertzberg,R.W., Newton,C.H., Jaccard,R. (1988). Crack closure: correlation and confusion. In: Mechanics of Fatigue Crack Closure, ASTM STP 982. Philadelphia,PA: American Society for Testing and Materials, pp.139-148.

[13] Vasudevan, A.K., Sadananda, K. and Louat, N. (1994), A review of crack closure, fatigue crack threshold and related phenomena. Materials Science and Engineering, A188, pp.1-22.

[14] Sadananda, K. and Vasudevan, A.K. (1997). Short crack growth and internal stresses, Int. J. Fatigue, 19(93): S99–S108.

[15] Vasudevan, A.K. and Sadananda, K. (1999). Application of unified fatigue damage approach to compression–tension region, International Journal of Fatigue, 21(s1): S263–S273.

[16] Sadananda, K., Vasudevan, A.K., Holtz, R.L. and Lee, E.U. (1999). Analysis of overload effects and related phenomena, International Journal of Fatigue, 21(s1): S233–S246.

[17] Sadananda, K., Vasudevan, A.K. and Holtz, R.L. (2001). Extension of the Unified Approach to fatigue crack growth to environmental interactions, International Journal of Fatigue, 23: S277–S286.

[18] Vasudevan, A.K. and Sadananda, K. (2001). Analysis of fatigue crack growth under compression–compression loading, International Journal of Fatigue, 23: S365–S374.

[19] Sadananda, K., Vasudevan, A.K. and Kang, I.W. (2003). Effect of superimposed monotonic fracture modes on the ΔK and Kmax parameters of fatigue crack propagation, Acta Materialia, 51: 3399–3414.

[20] Sadananda, K. and Vasudevan, A.K. (2004). Non-propagating incipient cracks from sharp notches under fatigue, Acta Materialia, 52: 4239–4249.

[21] Vasudevan, A.K., Sadananda, K., and Holtz, R.L. (2005). Analysis of vacuum fatigue crack growth results and its implications. International Journal of Fatigue, 27:1519–1529.

[22] Noroozi, A.H., Glinka, G. and Lambert, S. (2005). A two parameter driving force for fatigue crack growth analysis. International Journal of Fatigue, 27:1277–1296.

[23] Stoychev, S. and Kujawski, D. (2005). Analysis of crack propagation using ΔK and Kmax, International Journal of Fatigue, 27:1425–1431.

[24] Kujawski,D. (2005). On assumptions associated with ΔK_{eff} and their implications on FCG predictions, International Journal of Fatigue, 27:1267–1276.

[25] Zhang,J.Z, He, X.D. and Du, S.Y. (2005). Analyses of the fatigue crack propagation process and stress ratio effects using the two parameter method. International Journal of Fatigue, 27:1314–1318.

[26] Maymon,G. (2005a). A 'unified' and a $(\Delta K^+ \cdot K_{max})^{1/2}$ crack growth models for aluminum 2024-T351. Internal Journal of Fatigue, 27:629-638.

[27] Maymon, G. (2005b). Probabilistic crack growth behavior of aluminum 2024-T351 alloy using the 'unified' approach. International Journal of Fatigue, 27:828–834.

[28] Kujawski, D. (2001b). Enhanced model of partial crack closure for correlation of R-ratio effects in aluminum alloys. International Journal of Fatigue, Vol.23, pp.95-102.

[29] McEvily,A.J. and Ishihara,S. (2001), On the dependence of the rate of fatigue crack growth on the $\sigma_a^n (2a)$ parameter, International Journal of Fatigue, Vol.23, pp.115-120.

[30] Cui, W.C. and Huang, X.P. (2003). A general constitutive relation for fatigue crack growth analysis of metal structures. Acta Metallurgica Sinica (English Letters), Vol.16, No.5, pp.342-354.

[31] Bukkapatnama,S.T.S. and Sadananda, K. (2005). A genetic algorithm for unified approach-based predictive modeling of fatigue crack growth. International Journal of Fatigue, 27:1354–1359.

Local Stress Analysis of Welded Ship Structural Details under Consideration of the Real Weld Profile

Wolfgang Fricke [1], Adrian Kahl [2]

[1] Ship Structural Design and Analysis, Hamburg University of Technology
Hamburg, Germany
[2] Germanischer Lloyd,
Hamburg, Germany

Abstract

The fatigue strength of welded ship structural details can be assessed by local stress approaches. In contrast to the widely applied nominal and structural hot-spot stress approaches, the notch stress approach can explicitly consider the shape of the weld. Usually a quite simplified weld profile is assumed, but it is also possible to reproduce the real weld profile, if data is available. In the paper, the notch stress approach is described and techniques are introduced for measuring the weld profile, focusing especially on the laser-based sheet-of-light measurement system. Taking different bracket connections as an example, which have been analyzed in a recent research project, the derivation of a realistic weld profile from the laser measurement is described, introducing a fictitious notch radius to account for micro-support effects of the material. The so-called effective notch stress is then analyzed using finite-element submodels of the coarse bracket models. The fatigue test results are compared with design S-N curves based on the computed effective notch stresses as well as with the structural hot-spot stresses derived from the coarse models. Finally, conclusions are drawn with regard to the practical application in ship structural design.

Keywords

Fatigue; Welded joint; Structural hot-spot stress; Local stress; Weld profile; Ship structural detail; Bracket.

Introduction

Ships are today mainly welded steel structures. The fabrication-related notches at the welded joints reduce the fatigue strength considerably. The high stress utilization due to weight optimization and application of higher-tensile steel contribute to the susceptibility to fatigue calling for appropriate fatigue assessments. At present, mainly the nominal stress approach and occasionally the structural hot-spot stress approach are applied. The so-called notch stress approach offers a refined procedure.

The approaches mentioned, which are described by Hobbacher (2005) and Radaj et al. (2006) among others, allow different types of stress to be evaluated which are illustrated in Fig. 1 for a bracket toe on a plate surface. The nominal stress approach uses the nominal stress σ_n being calculated from internal forces and moments as well as sectional properties. The structural hot-spot stress approach considers the structural stress σ_s, which includes the stress increase due to the overall structure, i. e. the bracket, but excludes the effect of the local notch at the weld toe. The notch stress approach evaluates the fatigue-effective, linear-elastic notch stress σ_k, which contains the stress increase due to the weld toe.

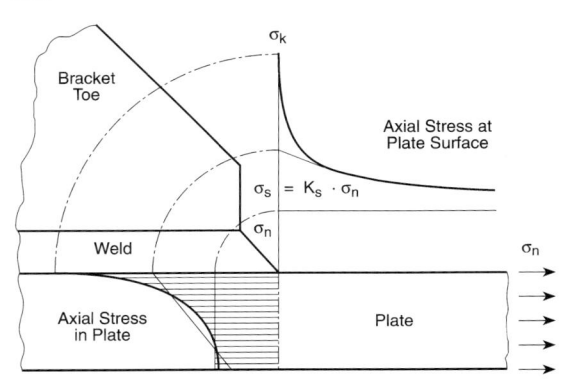

Fig. 1: Different stress types at a bracket toe

The fatigue assessment is usually performed with the S-N approach, i. e. using a design S-N curve for constant amplitude loading and a damage accumulation law. In the nominal stress approach, a specific S-N curve is required for the structural detail in question which contains the effects of the structural and local stress increases. Problems may arise if no suitable S-N curve is available for the actual case. Also, it might be difficult to define an appropriate nominal stress. The other two 'local' approaches avoid these difficulties by using a stress which includes the effects of the structure so that principally one S-N curve is sufficient to describe the fatigue strength. However, refined stress analyses are required particularly in the case of complex structures.

The further development of computer hard- and software allow the local approaches to be applied efficiently to complex structures. In the following, the notch stress approach is considered more closely. When the notch stress is computed, the weld profile has to be taken into account explicitly. Normally, an idealized shape is assumed. Alternatively, the real weld profile can be modeled if it is known. In this paper, possibilities for recording the real weld profile are discussed and the laser-based sheet-of-light measurement technique is described in more detail. By the example of different bracket connections, which have been investigated in a recent research project, the derivation of a weld contour close to reality from laser measurements and the subsequent computation of the notch stress the plane and 3D finite element models are presented.

The Notch Stress Approach

In the notch stress approach, the fatigue-effective stress in the notch root is considered as single fatigue parameter. The approach has been developed for non-welded as well as welded structures, for the latter with different variants (Radaj et al., 2006). In the following, the notch stress approach according to Radaj (1990) is described, which has been implemented in the fatigue design recommendations of the International Institute of Welding (IIW) as effective notch stress approach (Hobbacher, 1996), using specimen fracture as failure criterion.

The approach has originally been derived for the fatigue assessment of welded joints at the endurance limit. The fatigue-effective stress is the theoretical elastic notch stress, which is computed taking into account the micro-structural support effect of the surrounding material according to a hypothesis by Neuber (1968). The effect can be considered by fictitious rounding of the rather sharp weld toe using the following formula

$$\rho_f = \rho + s \cdot \rho^* \quad (1)$$

where ρ is the actual notch radius, ρ^* is a material constant and s is a multiaxial coefficient. For mild steel and the assumption that the crack initiation occurs in the cast weld material at the weld toe, ρ^* may be taken as 0.4 mm. The multiaxial coefficient is suggested to be 2.5 for plane strain condition and the applicability of the distortion energy hypothesis. In case of lacking information about the actual radius or consideration of the worst case, $\rho = 0$ mm should be assumed, so that eq. (1) yields a fictitious radius of 1 mm.

Fig. 2 shows the arrangement of the fictitious notch radii ρ_f at the weld toes and roots of a cruciform and a butt joint as proposed in the IIW fatigue design recommendations for the effective notch stress approach (Hobbacher, 2005).

The fillet welds in Fig. 2 have a strongly idealized profile being characterized by the nominal throat thickness and a weld flank angle of 45 degrees. If the real weld profile deviates from this shape and can be ensured by quality control measures, larger notch radii may occur allowing a more favourable fatigue assessment.

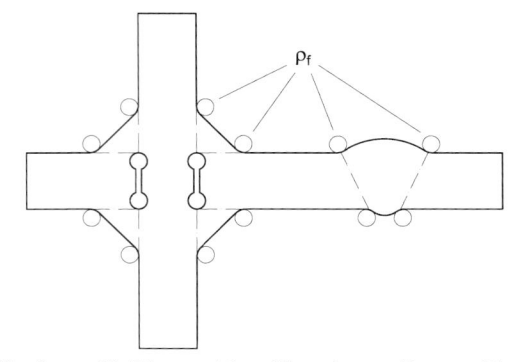

Fig. 2: Fictitious notch radii ρ_f at a cruciform and butt joint

The notch stress can be computed by fatigue notch factors together with the nominal or structural hot-spot stress or by the finite element or boundary element method. The latter requires the explicit consideration of the notch at the weld toe or root in the model, which demands a sufficiently fine discretization of the weld and particularly the fictitiously rounded weld toe or root. Here, the element size should be $\rho/4$ or less in case of higher-order elements (Fricke, 2006). The global model is usually refined in the notch area. Alternatively, the submodel technique is applied, either with 3D submodels or 2D submodels in plane strain condition, if the principal stress is acting perpendicular to the weld line. The approach has disadvantages particularly with relatively thin plates where the fictitious rounding can lead to substantial weakening of the plate section considered. An alternative approach has been proposed using a fictitious radius of 0.05 mm (Eibl et al., 2003).

The fatigue strength reference value FAT, defining the design S-N curve at $2 \cdot 10^6$ load cycles for 97.7% survival probability, has been proposed in the IIW fatigue design recommendations to be 225 N/mm^2 (FAT 225). In this connection, the effective notch stress has to be computed for the fictitious radius $\rho_f = 1$ mm corresponding to the worst case approach proposed by Radaj.

Measurement of the Actual Weld Contour

In the following, two techniques are outlined which allow the actual weld profile to be measured. The first is the traditional manual measurement technique and the second the laser-based sheet-of-light technique which has found application due to the development of computer-based optical measurement systems in various industrial sectors.

Manual Measurement Technique

The manual measurement of the weld profile is the technique mostly applied up to now, which requires no extraordinary measurement tools. A negative replica of the weld is produced in the investigated area using e. g.

silicon rubber. The replica is cut at locations of further evaluation for subsequent measurement of the weld contour. Fig. 3 shows a cut replica of a weld around a bracket toe on a bulb plate profile.

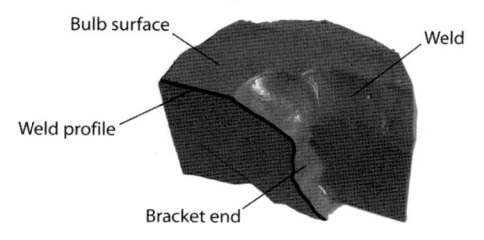

Fig. 3: Replica of a weld around a bracket end

In order to measure parameters of the weld contour in detail, e. g. the weld toe radius, enlarged images have to be produced by taking pictures or scanning the cut surface. Disadvantages of the technique are the extensive preparation and probably the reliability of the pure manual measurement.

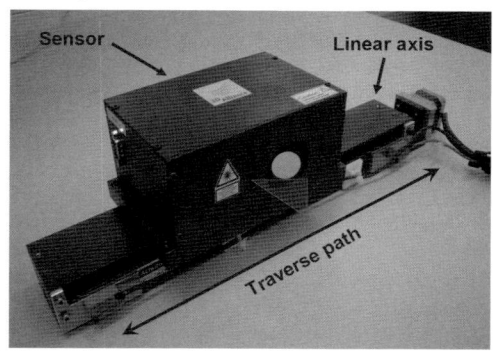

Laser-Based Sheet-of-Light Measurement Technique

During the past years, the evolution of digital photography and image processing has led to the development of contact-less optical measurement techniques. A wide-spread technique, which is continuously further developed, is the sheet-of-light measurement. The measurement principle is schematically shown in Fig. 4. A sheet of light, which is created by widening a laser beam, is projected on the measurement object. The laser beam can be widened by an oscillating mirror in the projector. The object is observed by a CCD camera which is placed in a defined distance and angle away from the projector. The sheet of light is reflected by the object, from which the contour can be converted into the real profile by triangularization using the known distance and angle between projector and camera. If the projector and camera are moved along the measurement object, sheets of light are continuously recorded so that a 3D image of the object surface is generated. Actually, the pixels of the CCD chip create a digital 3D cloud of points.

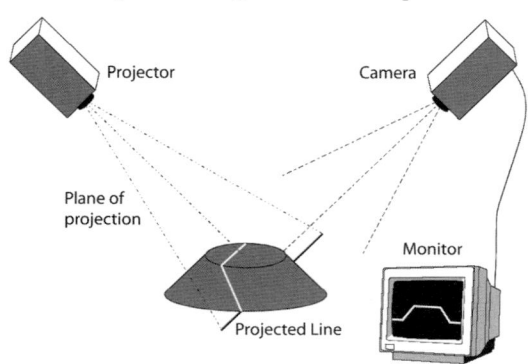

Fig. 4: Principle of the sheet-of-light measurement (Wolf, 1998)

The laser-based sheet-of-light measurement technique is today used by the industry for the quality control during fabrication. An example is the online measurement of mechanically produced welds to control the process and to check for defects. The technique has been applied by Lieurade et al. (2003) for the automatic measurement of fillet welds with the aim to investigate effects of the weld geometry on fatigue strength.

Within the research project mentioned, the measurement system shown in Fig. 5 has been acquired. Projector and camera are combined in a casing which can be traversed over a distance of 300 mm. The emergence of the sheet of light is indicated in the figure by a triangle. The resolution of the measurement system along a 25 mm wide sheet of light on the object is about 45 µm, which means that 22 points per mm and 520 points in the whole section can be measured. Various sections are measured in distances of 100 µm. Fig. 6 shows the surface of a fillet weld around a bracket toe generated from the measured point cloud. With special software the point cloud can be further evaluated with respect to geometric parameters such as the weld toe radius.

Fig. 5: Laser-based sheet-of-light measurement system

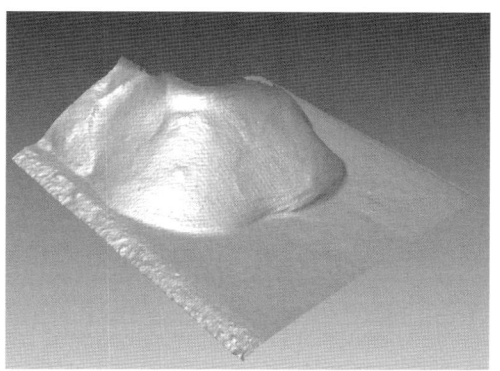

Fig. 6: Measured surface of a fillet weld around a bracket toe

The measurement accuracy on rough surfaces is physically limited due to the optical technique. The resolution of the measurement system allows the toe radius of a typical fillet weld of 0.2 mm and more to be reliably measured. A disadvantage is that shiny surfaces disturb the result which can be overcome by treatment of the object surface with chalk spray.

Notch Stress Analysis for Different Bracket Types

The notch stress approach has already been applied in research and in the industry using mainly idealized weld profiles, but sometimes also parameters of the actual weld geometry such as toe radius, flank angle and weld reinforcement. Radaj et al. (2006) give some examples. Related to ship and offshore structures, the approach was applied by Gimperlein (1990) to knuckled frame corners and by Petershagen (1992) to hyperbaric dry butt welded specimens using the actual weld profiles.

As an example for notch stress analyses of the idealized and actual weld profile, the results of the aforementioned research project are described in the following. The objective was the comparison between the fatigue strength of inserted and overlapped brackets connecting stiffeners made either of bulb plate stiffeners or flat bars. The different connections are shown in Figs. 7 and 8. The abbreviations 'HP-O', 'HP-I', 'FB-O' and 'FB-I' are used in the following to distinguish between the four variants. 'HP' stands for bulb plate profile (Holland profile), 'FB' for flat bar, 'O' for overlapped and 'I' for inserted.

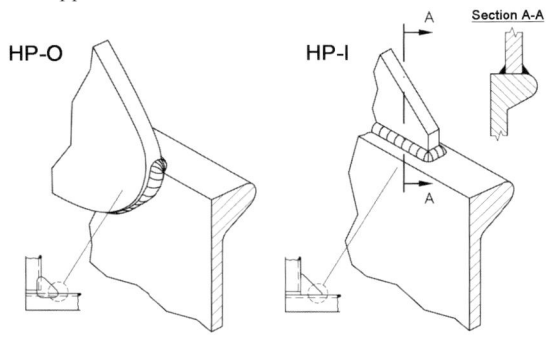

Fig. 7: Overlapped and inserted bracket at a bulb plate stiffener (Holland profile)

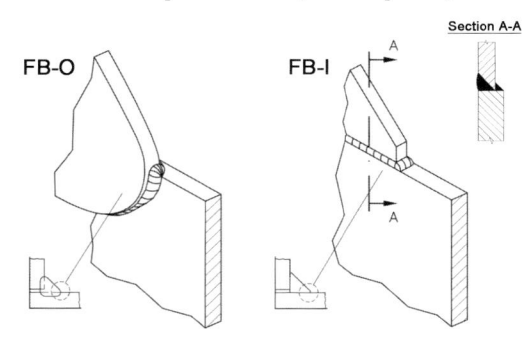

Fig. 8: Overlapped and inserted bracket at a flat bar stiffener

In the research project, the fatigue strength behavior of all four variants was investigated. In parallel, the notch stresses as well as the structural hot-spot stresses were computed.

Fatigue Tests

Each of the four variants was fatigue tested with four large-scale test models, which contained two bracket connections. The test set-up is shown in Fig. 9 for the variant with overlapped brackets on bulb plate profiles HP 160x9 (HP-O). The symmetrical test models were loaded by diagonal acting hydraulic cylinders such that tensile stresses are acting at the bracket toes. The test models with bulb plate stiffeners were subjected to a cyclic force range of $\Delta F = 30$ kN. The load ratio was $R \approx 0$. The test models with flat bar stiffeners FB 160x15 were subjected to a slightly smaller load in order to achieve the same nominal stress at the bracket toes. Fatigue cracks appeared generally at the weld toes on the stiffeners in front of the bracket ends.

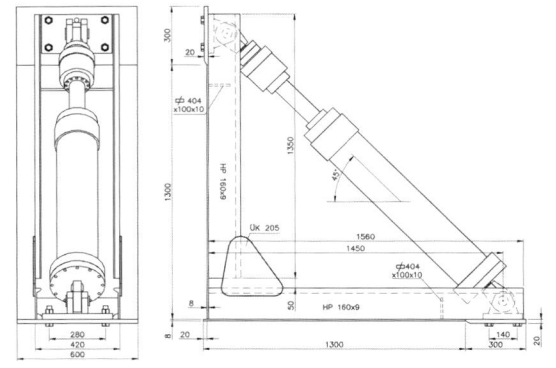

Fig. 9: Test set-up for variant HP-O

Fig. 10 shows a comparison of the endured stress cycles for all cracked stiffeners in the four variants up to a length of the fatigue crack of 10 mm on the stiffener surface. The survival probabilities $P_s = 10\%$, 50% and 90% resulting from a statistical evaluation are indicated in the figure. The direct comparison of endured stress cycles is reasonable because the nominal stresses in the stiffeners are equivalent. It can be seen that the variants with overlapped brackets are superior to those with inserted brackets, which might be surprising as adverse opinions exist in the shipbuilding community.

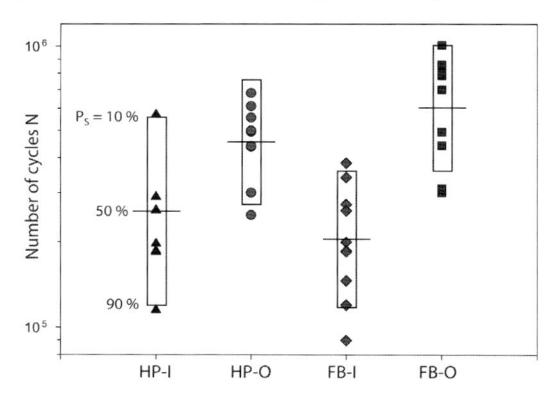

Fig. 10: Endured stress cycles of the different variants for $\Delta F = 30$ kN up to a crack length of 10 mm

Derivation of realistic weld profiles for the notch stress analysis

The weld profiles in the different test models were measured before the tests with the laser-based sheet-of-light system as described in the previous chapter.

To implement the weld profiles in finite element models, characteristic geometry parameters were derived from the measured point clouds at all locations where cracks were observed. Fig. 11 displays the derived parameters for a fillet weld, i. e. the weld leg length l_w and h_w, the weld toe radii r_{top} and r_{bottom}, and the weld toe angle θ at the crack location. The characteristic geometry parameters were evaluated from the point cloud by arranging several sections in way of the crack initiation point having a distance of 0.5 mm from each other. Fig. 12 shows this by the example of a weld around the bracket end of the variant HP-I.

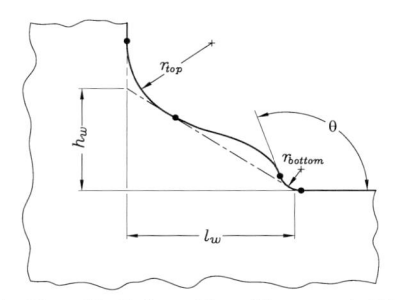

Fig. 11: Realistic weld profile generated from characteristic parameters

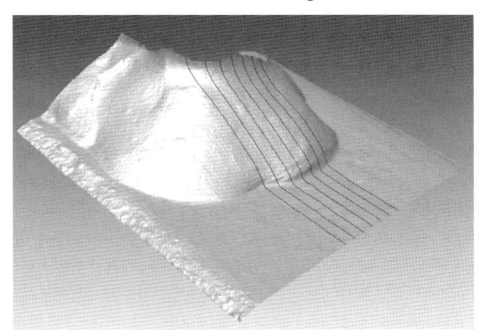

Fig. 12: Measured weld surface of variant HP-I with section lines

The individual section lines were subdivided into parts from which the individual parameters were manually evaluated. Fig. 14 exemplifies this for the lower weld toe radius and angle for the section line plotted in Fig. 13.

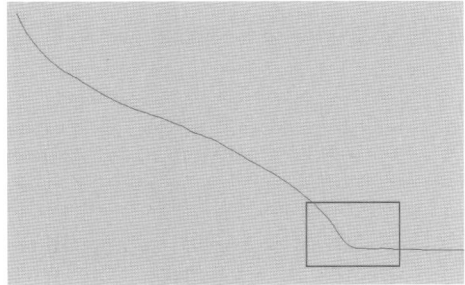

Fig. 13: Individual section line

The evaluation of the characteristic parameters can principally be automatized, as shown by Lieurade et al. (2003) for the investigation of the effect of weld quality on fatigue strength. A special software was developed which identifies the weld toe and derives the characteristic geometry parameters with special algorithms. Problems arise if the weld contour differs considerably from usual ones. In the investigation presented here, this approach was not followed because the profiles of welds performed in the upwards position or around the bracket end are very irregular where similar problems occur.

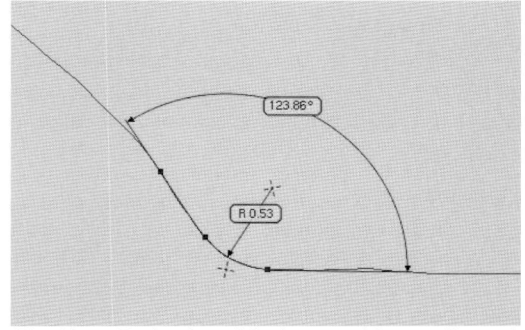

Fig. 14: Evaluation of the lower weld toe radius and angle for the example in Fig. 13

For the notch stress analyses of the welds at the bracket connections, the realistic weld profile as illustrated in Fig. 11 was applied. The parameters were derived from the individual section lines (Figs. 12-14). The curve between the lower and upper weld toe radii in Fig. 11 was approximated by a spline function which runs tangentially into the circles. The critical weld toe radius was fictitiously increased by 1 mm according to eq. (1). Some further modifications were necessary in cases with undercuts or unusual weld profiles.

In addition, the effective notch stress was computed also for an idealized weld profile according to Fig. 2 using a fictitious radius $\rho_f = 1$ mm, a flank angle θ = 45 deg. and the nominal throat thickness. Only for variant FB-I, a larger flank angle was assumed because the full-penetration weld results in steeper flank angles at the bracket toe than for a usual fillet weld (see Section A-A in Fig. 8). The additional computation of notch stresses for these idealized weld profiles corresponds to the common situation of designers who have no information about the weld profiles occurring actually.

Performance and Results of the Notch Stress Analyses

The notch stress analyses were performed using coarse global finite element models and 3D and 2D submodels. Fig. 15 shows the procedure using a 2D submodel and the realistic weld profile for the variant HP-I.

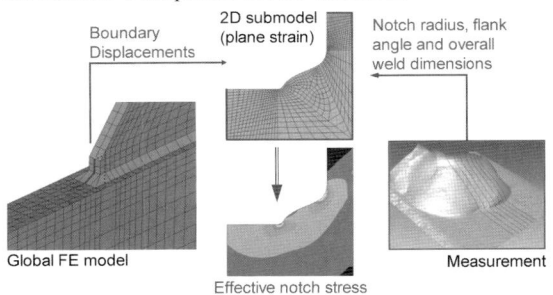

Fig. 15: Procedure of the notch stress analysis using a 2D submodel and realistic weld profile

Basis is a global finite element model which represents the structural behavior of the whole test model. In addition, local submodels are generated for the fatigue-critical welded joints which contain either the realistic weld profile derived from the measurements or alternatively the idealized one. The submodel is loaded at the boundaries with the displacements obtained from the global model. Assuming plane strain conditions for the 2D submodels, the effective notch stress is computed given by the highest surface stress in the weld toe radius.

For each crack location, several section lines and corresponding weld profiles have been derived. For each of them, a separate submodel was created and analyzed, i. e. seven submodels for the weld shown in Figs 12 and 15. From the results, the highest notch stress was assumed as relevant for the fatigue failure.

In all test models with inserted brackets (HP-I and FB-I), the fatigue cracks appeared generally at the toe of the weld around the bracket end. In these cases, 2D submodels were sufficient as their orientation is almost parallel to the direction of the largest principal stress. However, in the test models with overlapped brackets (HP-O and FB-O), almost all cracks appeared at the toe of the weld on the flat side of the stiffener, i. e. 5 - 30 mm below the upper edge of the stiffener. Here, the arrangement of a 2D submodel was impracticable because the direction of the largest principal stress differed notably from the longitudinal stiffener direction due to shear. Therefore, 3D submodels were created. Fig. 16 shows such a submodel together with the corresponding global model. The submodel was generated by extrusion of the weld profile at the crack initiation along the weld line. The crack initiation point is marked in Fig. 16.

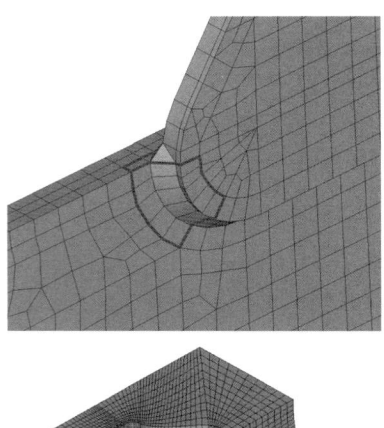

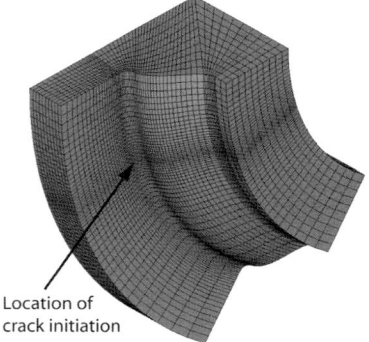

Fig. 16: Global and submodel for the variant FB-O

As the modeling of the weld of the overlapped bracket is rather complicated in a 3D submodel and several individual submodels have to be generated, the computation was performed only for all cracks appearing on the flat side of the stiffener. The stress calculation for each crack was individually performed for the location of the actual crack initiation. Fig. 17 shows the resulting notch stresses for the realistic weld profiles together with the endured load cycles in an S-N diagram. The failure criterion is again a surface crack length of 10 mm. The results of a statistical analysis yielding survival probabilities P_s = 10%, 50%, 90% and 97.7% are included in the diagram, assuming the common slope exponent m = 3 for S-N curves of welded joints. Also the standard deviation s of log(N) is given. In addition, the design S-N curve FAT 225 according to the IIW fatigue design recommendations is included.

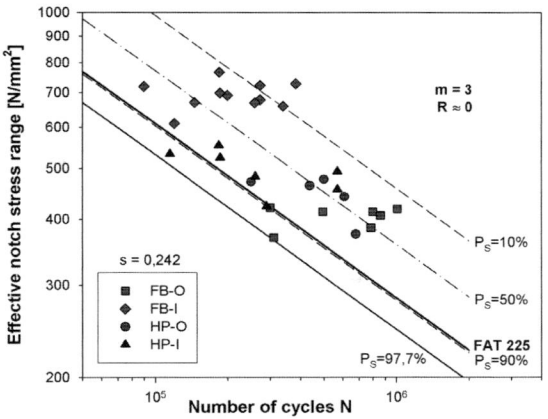

Fig. 17: S-N diagram for 10 mm crack length using the notch stresses computed for realistic weld profile (notch radius increased by 1 mm)

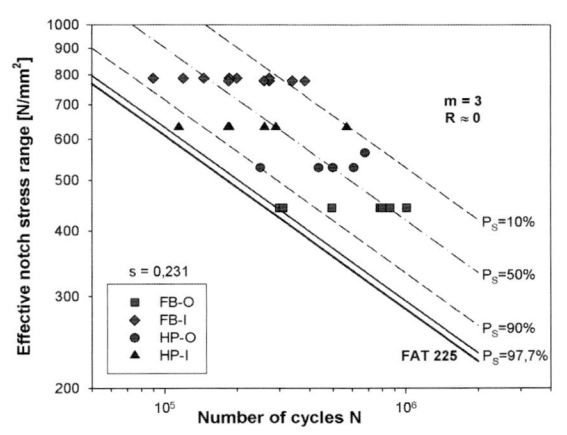

Fig. 18: S-N diagram for 10 mm crack length using the notch stresses computed for idealized weld profile (notch radius $\rho_f = 1$ mm)

As mentioned before, additional notch stress calculations were performed for idealized weld profiles as principally shown in Fig. 2. Again 2D and 3D submodels were generated to compute the effective notch stress in the weld toe which was fictitiously rounded by $\rho_f = 1$ mm. For the overlapped brackets, the notch stress was generally computed for a location 5 mm below the upper edge of the stiffener so that the same stress occurs in each variant. The stress results are again shown together with the endured load cycles in an S-N diagram, Fig. 18.

If the stress results for the realistic and idealized weld profiles are compared with each other, the effect of the actual weld geometry can be recognized which is partly larger and partly smaller. Surprising is that the standard deviation is almost the same. Obviously, the consideration of the realistic weld geometry does not reduce the scatter. However, the scatter for individual variants, e. g. HP-I and HP-O is reduced. A possible reason for the remaining large scatter might be that the chosen kind of modeling does not consider geometry changes along the weld. These are relatively large, especially at the welds around the bracket ends and in upwards position. Furthermore, residual stress effects are not considered which may be different in structural details with different geometry.

The notch stresses for the idealized weld profiles are - due to the smaller toe radius (1 mm) and steeper flank angles - generally larger than those for the realistic weld profiles. These results are conservative with regard to the design S-N curve FAT 225, see Fig. 18, which confirms the procedure proposed by the IIW fatigue design recommendations (Hobbacher, 2005). This is not the case for the realistic weld profiles with the actual toe radii enlarged by 1 mm. This means that a lower design S-N curve than FAT 225 has to be used if fictitiously enlarged weld toe radii are assumed.

It is interesting to note that both variants with inserted brackets (HP-I and FB-I) show higher notch stresses than the others with overlapped brackets. This is in line with the fatigue test results in Fig. 10 showing the superiority of the overlapped brackets. The notch stress approach is able to predict this behavior.

Comparison with Structural Hot-Spot Stress Results

As mentioned in the beginning, the structural hot-spot stresses were computed in addition to the notch stresses. Different approaches exist for the determination of structural stresses (Radaj et al., 2006). The numerical analysis was performed in accordance with the IIW fatigue design recommendations (Hobbacher, 2005), using the global finite element models of the bracket connections. The structural hot-spot stress is typically determined by extrapolation of the normal or principal stress at definite locations on the surface to the weld toe. Fig. 19 shows the recommended extrapolation types. It is distinguished between relatively fine and coarse meshes. Furthermore, a distinction is made between hot spots on a plate surface and at a plate edge, which affects the distances of the extrapolation points from the weld toe. In the first case, these depend on the plate thickness, while in the second, which represents an in-plane notch, fixed distances are chosen.

The structural stress analyses were performed with relatively fine and coarse models of the bracket connection. The stress extrapolation points were chosen for almost all variants according to the situation at a plate edge. This is quite obvious for the inserted brackets forming together with the stiffener an in-plane notch. For the overlapped variants, where the cracks mostly appeared on the side of the stiffener, the sketches in Fig. 19 represent the structure seen from above. Hence, the overlapped bracket on a bulb plate stiffener (HP-O) is again considered to form an in-plane notch because the bulb cannot be regarded as a plate with a reasonable thickness. Only the overlapped bracket on the flat bar stiffener (FB-O), where cracks have appeared on the flat side, allows the plate thickness of the flat bar to reasonably define the location of the extrapolation points.

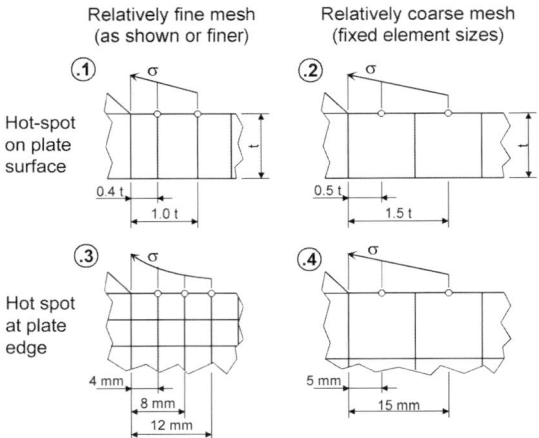

Fig. 19: Structural hot-spot stress determined by surface stress extrapolation (Hobbacher, 2005)

The welds modeled correspond to those with idealized weld profile in the notch stress analysis. Generally the largest principal stress at the crack initiation point was evaluated.

Fig. 20 shows the structural hot-spot stresses computed with the coarse meshes together with the endured load cycles up to a crack length of 10 mm. The S-N diagram contains again the results of a statistical analysis. Fig. 21 shows the corresponding results with the stresses from the finer meshes.

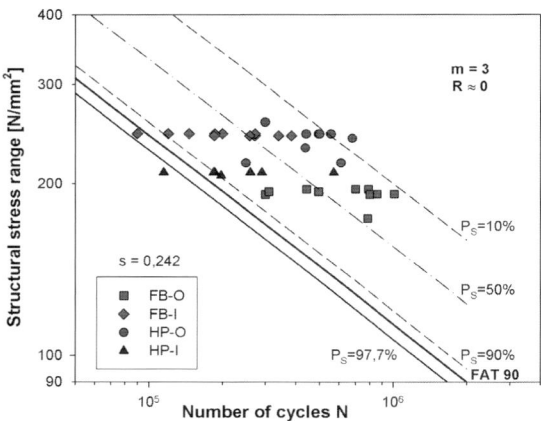

Fig. 20: S-N diagram for 10 mm crack length using structural hot-spot stresses computed with coarse meshes

The different structural stresses within one variant result from the stress evaluation stress at the crack initiation point and partly from the differences at the two ends of one bracket.

The scatter of the results in both diagrams is comparable, but slightly higher than in the notch stress analysis. For load-carrying fillet welds, a design S-N curve FAT 90 has to be assumed according to the IIW fatigue design recommendations (Hobbacher, 2005). This is reasonable also for the variant FB-I, which has a full penetration weld, but a rather steep flank angle. The results obtained from the fine meshes are conservative in relation to the FAT 90 curve. This is not fully the case for the results from the coarse meshes.

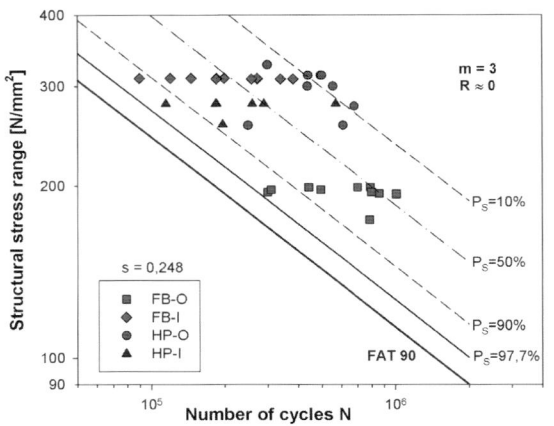

Fig. 21: S-N diagram for 10 mm crack length using structural hot-spot stresses computed with finer meshes

The comparison of the individual results with those of the notch stress analysis shows that the structural stresses of the variants HP-O seem to be too high. The assumption of a plate edge for stress extrapolation seems to be over-conservative here. On the other hand, a plate thickness cannot reasonably be defined here. For this reason, the different behavior of the bracket connections is not well predicted by this method.

Conclusions

The notch stress approach is a suitable approach for the fatigue assessment of welded ship structural details. Compared to the nominal and the structural hot-spot stress approaches it offers the possibility to explicitly take into account the local weld geometry.

In order to consider the microstructural support effects of the material in the relatively sharp notches of the weld toe or root, fictitious notch rounding is performed leading to a radius enlarged by 1 mm or - in the worst case - to a minimum radius of 1 mm at steel joints.

With modern optical techniques, the weld profile can be measured and afterwards evaluated with respect to geometry parameters relevant to fatigue behavior. Such an evaluation has been performed for test models of different bracket connections before fatigue testing.

The finite element analysis included the determination of the notch stress for realistic weld profiles including the enlarged weld toe radius as well as for an idealized weld profile using the nominal weld geometry together with the fictitious radius of 1 mm (worst case approach). In addition, the structural hot-spot stress was determined using the IIW fatigue design recommendations. Following conclusions can be drawn from the results:

- The realistic weld profile with enlarged weld toe radius resulted naturally in smaller notch stresses than the idealized weld profile with 1 mm radius. The latter were conservative in relation to the design S-N curve recommended by IIW (FAT 225).

- Realistic weld profiles with fictitiously enlarged weld toe radius have to be assessed with a lower S-N curve, which, however, allows improved weld shapes to be assessed on a rational basis.
- The scatter of the endured load cycles was not reduced when using realistic weld profiles.
- The structural hot-spot stress approach yields a slightly larger scatter.
- Compared to the structural hot-spot stress approach, the notch stress approach predicts better the different fatigue behavior of structural variants.

Acknowledgement

The work described was performed within the research project 'Comparative investigation of the fatigue strength of bracket connections' funded by the Forschungsvereinigung der Arbeitsgemeinschaft der Eisen und Metall verarbeitenden Industrie e. V. (AVIF) through the Center of Maritime Technologies (CMT).

References

Eibl, M.; Sonsino, C.M.; Kaufmann, H. und Zhang, G. (2003): Fatigue assessment of laser welded thin sheet aluminium. Int. J. of Fatigue 25, pp 719-731.

Fricke, W. (2006): Round-Robin Study on Stress Analysis for the Effective Notch Stress Approach. Doc. XIII-2129-06 / XV-1223-06, Int. Inst. of Welding.

Gimperlein, D. (1990): Tragverhalten von Rahmenecken mit geknickten Gurten. Schweißen und Schneiden, 52:5, pp 234 - 240.

Hobbacher, A., Ed. (1996): Fatigue Design of Welded Joints and Components. Abington Publ., Cambridge.

Hobbacher, A., Ed. (2005): Recommendations for Fatigue Design of Welded Joints and Components, Final Draft. IIW-Doc. XIII-1965-03 / XV-1127-03, International Institute of Welding.

Lieurade, H.-P.; Huther, I. und Lebaillif, D. (2003): Weld quality assessment as regard to Fatigue. Proc. of the IIW Fatigue Seminar 2003, Rep. 14, Lappeenranta University of Technology, Finland.

Neuber, H. (1968): Über die Berücksichtigung der Spannungskonzentration bei Festigkeitsberechnungen. Konstruktion 20:7, pp. 245 - 251.

Petershagen, H. (1992): Fatigue tests with hyperbaric dry butt welded specimens, Rep. 522 Inst. Schiffbau Univ. Hamburg and IIW-Doc. XIII-1445-92.

Radaj, D. (1990): Design and analysis of fatigue-resistant welded structures. Abington Publ., Cambridge.

Radaj, D.; Sonsino, C.M. und Fricke, W. (2006): Fatigue assessment of welded joints by local approaches. 2nd ed., Woodhead Publishing, Cambridge.

Wolf, H. (1998): Absolute Moirémeßtechnik zur Formerfasssung nicht notwendigerweise stetiger Oberflächen. 5. ABW-Workshop, Jan. 1998, Esslingen.

Estimate Method of Hotspot Stress for Ship Structural Members Based on FE Analysis

Norio Yamamoto [1], Naoki Osawa [2], Koji Terai [1],

[1] Nippon Kaiji Kyokai, Research Institute, 1-8-3 Ohnodai, Chiba 267-0056, Japan
Tel: 81-43-294-5894, Fax: 81-43-294-5896, E-mail: ri@classnk.or.jp
[2] Osaka University, 2-1 Yamadaoka, Suita 565-0871, Japan
Tel: 81-6-6879-7576, Fax: 81-6-6879-7594, E-mail: osawa@naoe.eng.osaka-u.ac.jp

Abstract

Generally, hotspot stress (HSS) is calculated by the simplified method or estimated by FE analysis. Therefore, the accurate estimate method of HSS from the FE analysis results is needed.

In this paper the following applies:

(1) The FE analysis was performed and earned stress distributions using ship structure models that were modeled by shell elements (shell element model) and by solid elements (solid element model) respectively.

(2) The procedure that earns the stress distribution from the analysis results of the shell element model equivalent to that of the solid element model was considered in the large-scale structure model.

(3) The estimate method of HSS from these stress distributions was examined.

(4) The efficiency of current methods that estimates HSS was confirmed at the ship structural members.

Keywords

Fatigue; Hotspot stress; FE analysis.

Introduction

Ship structural members where fatigue strength must be considered are generally complex structures. Stress concentration around the hotspot depends on the structural details and loading conditions. It is necessary to accurately understand and know the stress distribution around the hotspot and at the structural members where fatigue damages might occur in order to perform the fatigue strength analysis. In addition, accurate HSS at the subject structures are needed in order to perform the fatigue strength analysis for the structural members where the HSS or fatigue performance are not directly monitored by the strain gage or the fatigue damage sensor (Muragishi, O, et al, 2004). It is desirable that accurately measuring stresses through experiments for the structural members where fatigue strength analysis is performed in order to know the stress distribution around the hotspot. However, it is not realistic that experiments performed for various structural members and stresses are measured. Furthermore, measuring the HSS at experiments is difficult. Therefore, the FE analysis is performed instead of experiments, and the HSS is estimated from the FE analysis results.

The FE analysis is performed using FE models that are modeled in detail with solid elements in order to accurately estimate stress distributions at actual structural members. However, there are some limits, such as computer performance, spending time for modeling and so on. For these reasons, the FE analysis is usually performed using the shell element model that is not as precisely modeled with structural details as when large-scale structures are chosen as the subjects of analysis. However, the shell element models are usually modeled at the centerline of plate thickness without local structural details like weld beads. Therefore, stress distributions in the vicinity of the hotspot of the shell element models sometimes differ largely from those of the solid element models or actual structural members. Consequently, the evaluated HSS of both models are sometimes largely different. Some procedures that modify HSS have been proposed (e.g. Niemi, E, 1995).

The procedure that has been proposed by one of the authors (Osawa, N, et al, 2007a) is mainly applied to simple welded joints and loads. However, actual ship structural members and actual loads due to wave and cargo are complex. Therefore, verification is needed as to whether or not the procedure can be applied to any ship structural members. Then, the procedure is applied to the ship structural members subjected to the loads likely acting on the actual ship structures. Stress distributions of the shell element model and the solid element model were compared. Then, the procedure that estimated the HSS from the stress distribution was considered.

Evaluation method of HSS

Difference of analysis model

The HSS and stress distributions in the FE analysis are affected whether or subject structures are truly modeled. Therefore, it is desirable that the structural details of subject structures are modeled with solid elements as truly as possible. But, analysis models are usually modeled by shell elements (see Fig. 1). Figure 1 schematically shows the difference of models of the structural details around the hotspot by the shell and solid elements and the difference of position of the hotspot. Needless to say, the stress distribution and the HSS do not correspond with each model.

Modification of stress distributions

There are many studies that consider the differences of stress distribution and HSS due to the difference of modeling (e.g. JIP FPSO Fatigue Capacity, 2000). In this paper, the stress distribution of the shell element model was modified according to the procedure proposed by one of authors. In the case in which the stress distributions of the solid element model and the shell element model are compared, the origin of coordinate system is usually the hotspot position of each model. However, stress distributions are not correlated in this way. Then, one of authors showed that the stress distribution of the solid element model (whose origin of the coordinate system is the hotspot) is correlated with that of the shell element model (whose origin of the coordinate system) is the intersection of plate surfaces (see Fig. 2, Osawa, N, et al, 2007a).

Loads due to wave, dry bulk and liquid work at the inner and outer hull of ships. In the case when the FE analysis is performed in these conditions, deformation behaviors of the shell and solid elements near the primary supporting members (girder, floor, etc.) are different. This reason is one of the factors why stress distributions are not correlated between the shell element model and the solid element model. Osawa (2007b) has considered the use of this factor, and the procedure that modified the stress distribution has been proposed. In this paper, this procedure was also applied in order to modify the stress distribution of shell element model.

FE analysis for ship structural members

The FE analysis was performed to the ship structural members where fatigue damages might occur. Then, the modified procedure described in the above section was applied to the stress distributions that were earned from the analysis results of the shell element model and the solid element model, and modified stress distributions were compared.

Analysis model and analysis procedure

A cape-size bulk carrier that has single side skin was chosen as the subject ship (see Fig. 3). Principal dimensions are shown in Table 1. Subject cargo hold for analysis is No.5 cargo hold. Structural members for the FE analysis were the intersection between bilge hopper sloped plate and inner bottom plate (at the port side of the mid of the cargo hold, see Fig.4) and the intersections between lower stool sloped plate and inner bottom plate (at aft. and fore. ends of the mid cargo hold on the centerline of ship, see Figs.5 and 6). MSC.Nastran and MSC.Marc were used as the analysis code. Yong's modulus was 206000 MPa. Poisson' ration was 0.3. Plate thickness was net thickness that was subtracted corrosion addition from gross thickness according to Common Structural Rules for Bulk Carriers (CSR-B; IACS, 2006a). The net thickness of the subject structures is shown in Table 2. The analysis procedure is as follow:

1. The cargo hold model with 3 holds length was modeled by shell elements. Mesh size of the members within about 400mm around the hotspot, which were chosen as the subjects for analysis, was about net plate thickness.

2. The FE analysis was performed according to the combinations of 4 loading conditions (full load condition, alternate load condition, normal ballast condition and heavy ballast condition) and 8 design waves (H1, H2, F1, F2, R1, R2, P1 and P2) that were defined in CSR-B (IACS, 2006a). Totally 32 loading cases of FE analyses were made.

3. Around the hotspots of the subject structures were modeled by solid element. The solid model was divided into 8 in the direction of the plate thickness. Shell elements and solid elements were coupled with the perpendicular shell element method (Osawa, N, et al, 2007a). Then, zooming analysis was performed. Referring to the analysis results of the shell element models, relatively sever 4 loading cases (alternate condition: H1, heavy ballast condition: F2, R1, P1) were applied to the solid element models.

Analysis results

Examples of the analysis results are shown in Figs. 7 to 12. The analysis results that were analyzed in alternate loading condition and design wave H1 (head sea) are shown in Figs. 7 to 9 and in heavy ballast condition and design wave P1 (beam sea) are shown in Figs. 10 to 12. Hull girder stress was not contained in these results because the purpose of this study was to compare the stress distributions between analysis results of the shell element model and the solid element model due to external and internal pressure. In Figs. 7 to 12, "Solid (vs d)" and "Shell (vs x)" show the stress distributions according to the each coordinate system whose origin is the hotspot. On the other hand, "Shell (Modified: vs ξ)" shows the stress distribution that was modified according to the procedure described in the above section, and to the coordinate system whose origin is the intersection of plate surfaces.

Figures 7 to 12 show that the absolute values of the stresses of "Shell (vs x)" are higher than those of "Solid (vs d)" in the vicinity of hotspot regardless of loading conditions, design waves and angles of sloped plates.

On the other hand, the absolute values of the stresses of "Shell (Modified: vs ξ)" are almost the same as that of "Solid (vs d)". The same tendency is shown in other loading conditions and design waves.

These results show that the procedure described in the above section can estimate the stress distribution of the solid element model from that of the shell element model in the ship structural members subjected to the pressure load.

Hotspot stress

The HSS estimated from the stress distribution that was modified by the procedure described above was compared with the HSS estimated from the shell element model, the solid element model and CSR's procedure.

Hotspot stress

The HSS based on the analysis results of the shell element model was estimated by the liner extrapolation using stresses at the points where 0.5 times (0.5t) and 1.5 times (1.5t) of net thickness of the inner bottom plate from the origin of the coordinate system x (Panel, SR202, 1991). The HSS based on the analysis results of the solid element model and modified stress distributions of the shell element model were estimated by the extrapolation using stresses at 0.5t and 1.5t from the origin of coordinate system d and ξ. The HSS of CSR-B and CSR-T (Common Structural Rules for Double Hull Oil Tankers; IACS, 2006b) were also estimated according to their procedures.

The estimate results of the HSS at the intersection between bilge hopper sloped plate and inner bottom plate in alternate loading condition and design wave H1 were shown in Fig. 13 and in heavy ballast condition and design wave P1 were shown in Fig. 14 respectively. Figures 13 and 14 show that the HSS estimated by the stress distribution of the shell element model based on axial x (the hotspot is at the intersection of centerline of plate thickness) is in excess of the HSS of the solid element model. This finding means that some procedures that modify HSS of the shell element model to match the HSS of the actual or the solid element model are needed. On the other hand, the HSS based on the modified stress distribution of the shell element model, CSR-B and CSR-T are relatively the same as the HSS of the solid element model. From Figs. 13 and 14, the mean value of the HSS and the stress at 0.5t in modified stress distribution of the shell element model is almost the same as the HSS of the solid element model. Therefore, the mean of these stresses can be considered as the provisional HSS. The HSS and the ratio to the HSS of the solid element model in alternate loading condition and design wave H1 are shown in Table 3. Adding analysis results of other three loading cases, the HSS ratio to the solid element model is as follow:

- about 1.1 in CSR-B
- about 0.9 to 1.1 in CSR-T
- about 0.95 to 1.05 in the provisional HSS

However, in order to obtain generalized results, it is necessary to increase the number of analysis cases and reconsider this trend.

Conclusions

The evaluation method of the HSS was considered in this paper. For the large-scale structure like ship structure, the FE analysis using the shell element model is a practical procedure in order to estimate the HSS. In this case, there are some difficulties in trying to accurately estimate the stress distributions around the hotspot based on the FE analysis results of the shell element model and to express the stress concentration due to actual structural details. One of the reasons is that locations of the hotspot at FE models are different from the actual positions at the actual structures.

The solid element model is needed in the FE analysis because the actual hotspot position can be considered. But, it is usually difficult to use the solid element model due to extensive time and labor required in making the solid element model. One of the authors developed (Osawa, N, et al, 2007a and 2007b) the procedure that estimates the stress distribution around the hotspot by the shell element model that is equivalent to the stress distribution by the solid element model. However, this procedure is mainly applied to simple welded joints and loads. On the other hand, actual ship structural members and actual loads due to wave and cargo are complex. Therefore, verification is needed as to whether or not the procedure can be applied to any ship structural members. In this paper, this procedure was applied to the actual ship structural members where fatigue strength analysis was performed thereby confirming its effectiveness. According to this procedure, an accurate fatigue strength analysis for structures that have complex structural details in variable loading conditions becomes possible without using the solid element model. Furthermore, it is considered that the examinations for other structures and loading cases are performed efficiently.

Now, procedures that estimate the HSS from the FE analysis results of the shell element model are defined in CSR-B and CSR-T. In this paper, HSS of CSR-B and CSR-T were compared with that of the solid element model. Then, it was shown that both procedures were given the HSS that were almost same as the HSS of the solid element model.

References

IACS (2006a) "Common Structural Rules for Bulk Carriers," the International Association of Classification Societies

IACS (2006b) "Common Structural Rules for Double Hull Oil Tankers," the International Association of Classification Societies

JIP FPSO fatigue Capacity (2000). "Hot Spot Stress Analysis of Five Structural Details and Recommendations for Modeling, Stress Evaluation and Design S-N Curve," Germanischer Lloyd.

Muragishi, O, Nihei, K, and Kobayashi, T (2004). "Remaining Life Evaluation by Fatigue Detecting Sensor," International Institute of Welding, Work in Progress on Fatigue Strength of Welded Joints in Japan, IIW Document No. XIII-2018-04, 2004

Niemi, E (1995). "Recommendations Concerning Stress Determination for Fatigue Analysis of Welded Components," IIW-Doc. XIII-1458-92/XV-797-92, Abington Pub., Cambridge, UK.

Osawa, N, Hashimoto, K, Sawamura, J, Nakai, T, and Suzuki, S (2007a). "Study on the Relationship between Shell Stress and Solid Stress in the Vicinities of Ship's Welded Joints," the 17th International Offshore (Ocean) and Polar Engineering Conference & Exhibition, ISOPE, Lisbon.

Osawa, N, Hashimoto, K, Sawamura, J, Nakai, T, and Suzuki, S (2007b). "Study on the Relationship between Shell Stress and Solid Stress in Fatigue Assessment of Ship Structure," the 10th International Symposium on Practical Design of Ships and Other Floating Structures, PRADS, Houston.(contributing)

Panel, SR202 (1991). "Annual Report of Panel SR202," The Shipbuilding Research Association of Japan, (in Japanease)

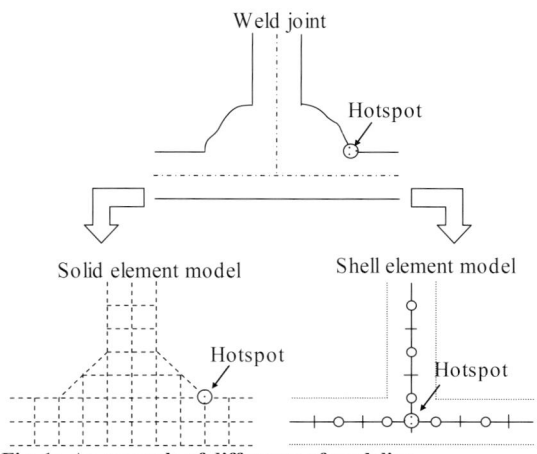

Fig. 1: An example of difference of modeling

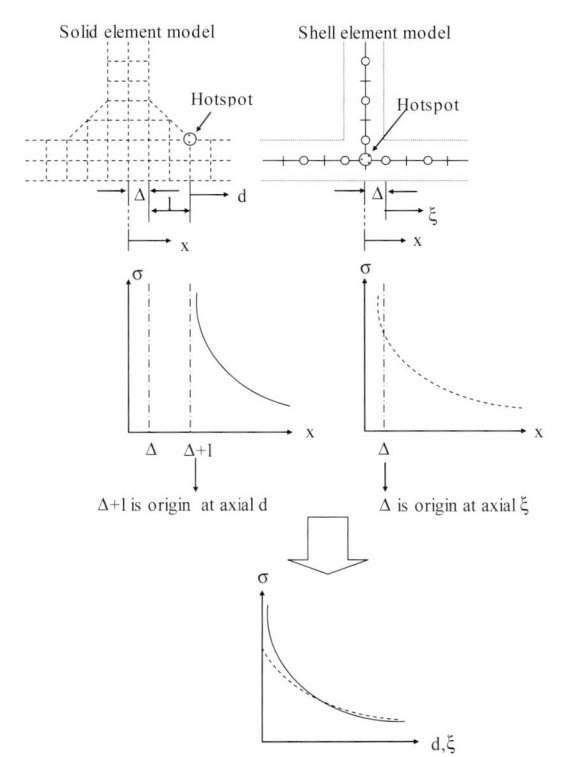

Fig. 2: Comparison way of stress distributions

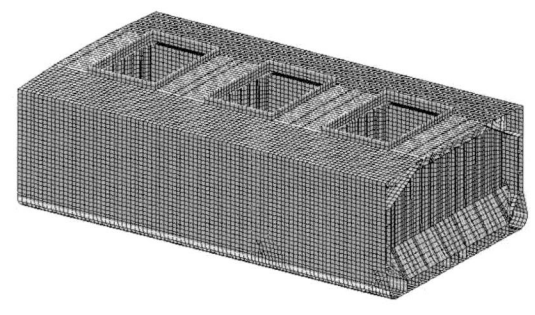

Fig. 3: Cargo hold model for analysis

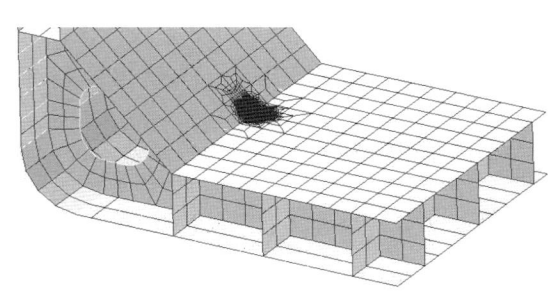

Fig. 4: Intersection of bilge hopper sloped plate and inner bottom plate (angle between plates is 45 deg)

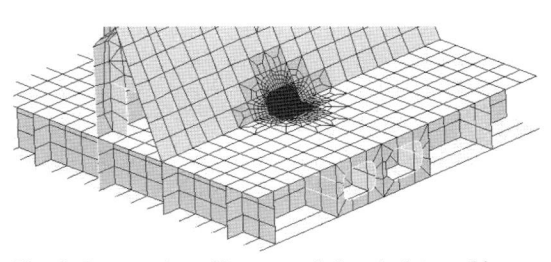

Fig. 5: Intersection of lower stool sloped plate and inner bottom plate (angle between plates is 65 deg)

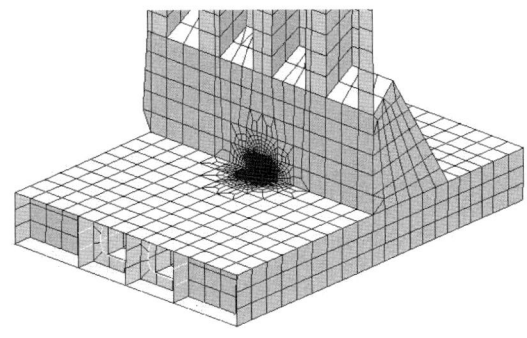

Fig. 6: Intersection of lower stool sloped plate and inner bottom plate (angle between plates is 90 deg)

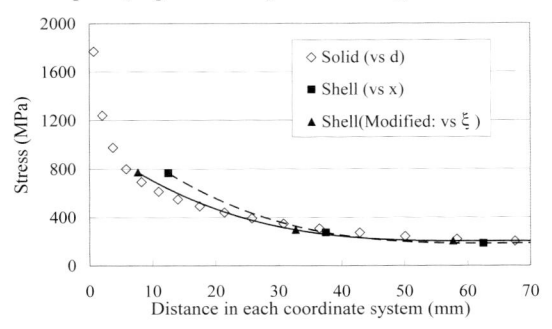

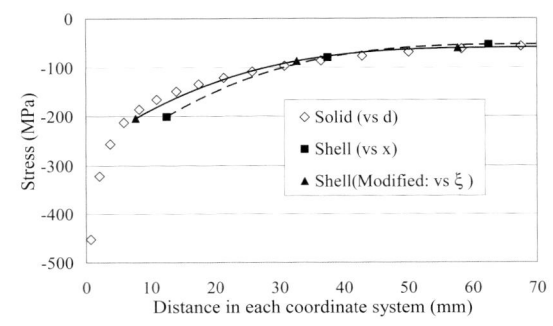

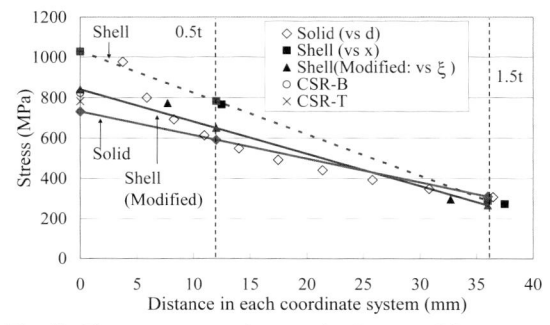

Fig. 7: Stress distributions at intersection between bilge hopper sloped plate and inner bottom plate (alternate loading condition, design wave H1: angle between plates is 45 deg.)

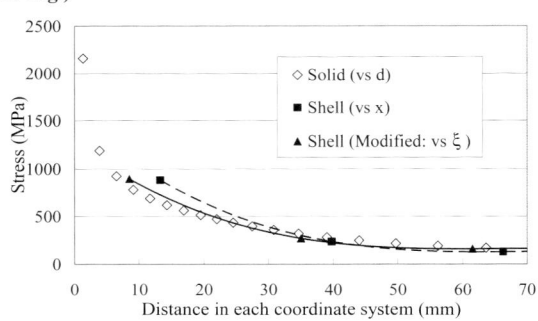

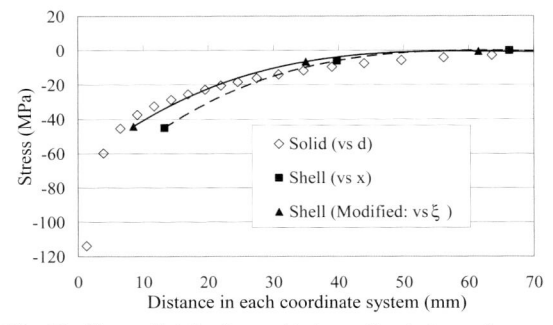

Fig. 8: Stress distributions at intersection between lower stool sloped plate and inner bottom plate (alternate loading condition, design wave H1: angle between plates is 65 deg.)

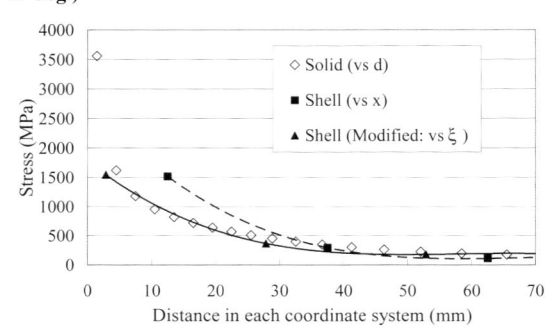

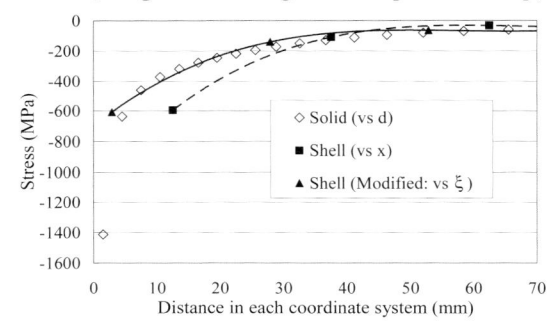

Fig. 9: Stress distributions at intersection between lower stool sloped plate and inner bottom plate (alternate loading condition, design wave H1: angle between plates is 90 deg.)

Fig. 10: Stress distributions at intersection between bilge hopper sloped plate and inner bottom plate (heavy ballast condition, design wave P1: angle between plates is 45 deg.)

Fig. 11: Stress distributions at intersection between lower stool sloped plate and inner bottom plate (heavy ballast condition, design wave P1: angle between plates is 65 deg.)

Fig. 12: Stress distributions at intersection between lower stool sloped plate and inner bottom plate (heavy ballast condition, design wave P1: angle between plates is 90 deg.)

Fig. 13: Hotspot stress at intersection between bilge hopper sloped plate and inner bottom plate (alternate loading condition, design wave H1: angle between plates is 45 deg.)

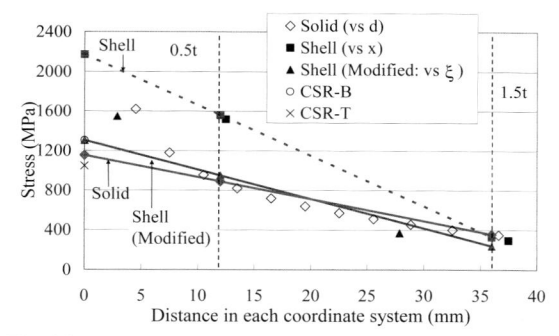

Fig. 14: Hotspot stress at intersection between bilge hopper sloped plate and inner bottom plate (heavy ballast condition, design wave P1: angle between plates is 45 deg.)

Table 2: Plate thickness of subject structures

	Thickness (mm)	
	Gross	Net
Inn BTM	26.50	24.00
Bilge knockle slant	26.50	23.75
L.Stool slant (65deg.)	22.00	18.75
L.Stool slant (90deg.)	22.50	19.25

Table 1: Principal dimensions of subject ship

L (m)	275.5
B (m)	45.0
D (m)	24.3
T_S (m)	17.8
C_B	0.85
V (knot)	14.0

Table 3: Hotspot stress and ratio in alternate loading condition and design wave H1

Alternate, H1	Bilge-InnBTM (45deg.)		L.Stool-InnBTM (65deg.)		L.Stool-InnBTM (90deg.)	
	HSS (MPa)	Ratio	HSS (MPa)	Ratio	HSS (MPa)	Ratio
Solid	731.5	1.00	865.8	1.00	1152.2	1.00
Shell	1028.6	1.41	1259.6	1.45	2169.7	1.88
Provisional HSS	745.0	1.02	896.3	1.04	1125.7	0.98
CSR-B	822.9	1.12	1007.7	1.16	1301.8	1.13
CSR-T	782.1	1.07	799.0	0.92	1046.2	0.91

Design of X-joints in Sandwich Structures for Naval Vessels

Brian Hayman[1], Christian Berggreen[2], Christian Lundsgaard-Larsen[2], Kasper Karlsen[2], Claus Jenstrup[2]

[1] Section for Structural Integrity and Laboratories, Det Norske Veritas
Høvik, Norway
and Department of Mathematics, University of Oslo
Oslo, Norway
[2] Department of Mechanical Engineering, Technical University of Denmark
Kongens Lyngby, Denmark

Abstract

In many naval ships of fiber composite sandwich construction, an X-joint exists where the end bulkhead of the superstructure is attached to the deck, with an internal bulkhead placed in the same vertical plane below the deck. This joint is subjected to alternating tensile and compressive loading in the vertical direction for respectively hogging and sagging bending deformation of the hull girder. When the core material is polymer foam, such joints are often strengthened by the insertion of a higher density core material in the deck panel in the immediate region of the joint. The paper aims to improve the basis for the design of such X-joints, focusing on the prevention of crushing of the core under compressive load while ensuring adequate damage tolerance for the case of tensile load. Extensive material tests are reported, strain distributions are investigated by both laboratory tests and numerical modeling, and design guidance for core inserts is presented.

Keywords

Sandwich; X-joint; Debond; Fiber bridging; Core inserts.

Introduction

Sandwich construction with polymer foam core and face laminates of fiber reinforced plastics has been used in the hulls and superstructures of a number of naval ships where low weight has been an important factor. In several cases the superstructure does not cover the full length of the hull, and in some cases it also does not cover the full width. In such an arrangement, the end bulkhead of the superstructure is usually attached to the deck in a position lined up with a transverse bulkhead placed underneath the deck. This situation results in an X-joint configuration with the deck running continuously through the joint and the bulkheads connected to its face laminates (Fig. 1).

Fig. 1: Naval vessel in sandwich construction, illustrating typical location of X-joint

As the hull girder flexes due to motion of the ship in waves, compressive and tensile vertical loadings are exerted alternately on such an X-joint for respectively sagging and hogging bending deformation. The compressive loading may lead to crushing of the sandwich core within the deck as it passes through the joint, while the tensile loading tends to pull the upper face laminate off the deck. If this happens, the in-plane compressive strength of the deck panel may be significantly reduced, because the detached face laminate has little buckling capacity. Thus it is important to prevent these modes of failure through good detailing of the joint. An important aspect is to ensure that the core inside the deck panel has sufficient strength, and for this purpose it is common to use a higher density piece of core in the region of the joint than is used in the remainder of the deck panel. Damage at such joints has been observed in service, suggesting that current practice for joint design is inadequate.

A literature search has revealed an appreciable amount of research into the behavior and optimization of sandwich T-joints (e.g. Kildegaard, 1992; Efstathios and Moan, 1996; Toftegaard and Lystrup, 2005), but very little information about X-joints. On this basis it is tempting to conclude that X-joint design has up to now been largely based on experience of testing and analysis of T-joints. As the X-joint is a "harder" detail than the T-joint, in the sense that the stresses are likely to be more concentrated and that possibilities for redistribution may be more limited, it is suggested that such a procedure may be unconservative and thereby an important cause of the observed joint failures.

Typical polymer foam core materials, such as the Divinycell "H" series of cross-linked PVC foams, have lower strength in compression than in tension. This is because, under compressive loading, the cells of such foams undergo crushing deformation with local buckling of the cell walls, while the tensile strength is governed more by the tensile strength of the cell walls. Thus, if the tensile and compressive loads are roughly equal, initial selection of material and extent for the core insert should be based on the compressive loading case. For tensile loading, however, it is important to ensure that a local stress concentration or an initial production defect or local damage will not reduce the strength unacceptably. The most relevant type of defect or damage to consider is a lack of bond between the sandwich face and core, commonly referred to as a debond.

The objective of the work reported in the present paper is to provide an improved basis for the design of such X-joints. The following aspects are addressed:

- Determination of stress distributions in X-joints under compressive loading, using both laboratory tests and numerical modeling, validation of the FE (finite element) modeling approach, and establishment of design criteria for core inserts (regarding both dimensions and material properties) to avoid core crushing.

- Determination of pull-off resistance for a range of face laminate / core combinations with debond defects, also using both laboratory tests and numerical modeling, to determine optimal material combinations and selection criteria to ensure that tensile loading will not lead to uncontrolled growth of the debond.

- Determination of relevant fracture mechanics parameters by advanced laboratory testing to support the pull-off resistance studies, taking account of the mode-mixity that arises in this scenario.

The studies on pull-off behavior are an extension of the previous work by Berggreen (2004) and Berggreen et al. (2007a), and include an investigation of the effect of including chopped strand and woven mats in the face-core interface when the laminates are made with non-crimp fabrics.

X-joint Configurations and Material Lay-ups

Two alternative designs of X-joint with GFRP face laminates and overlaminates and PVC foam core have been studied, with different fillet radii and overlamination details at the joint, see Fig. 2. The fillet radius (and thus the radius of the overlamination at the joint) is an important design parameter (Kildegaard, 1992), and influences the shape and extent of the compressive and tensile stress distributions in the core. Fig. 3 shows the geometry of the specimens used for testing of the X-joints under compression loading. Note that the overlaminations are shown in a schematic representation in Fig. 2 and Fig. 3. Wooden inserts have been used to reinforce the core at all loaded and free ends of the specimens. Five specimens of each type have been manufactured and tested.

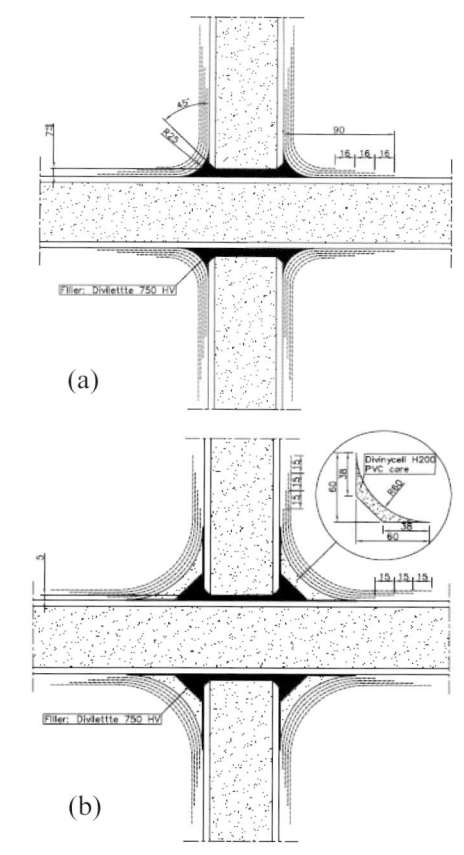

Fig. 2: Schematic representation of fillet and overlamination details. (a) Type X1. (b) Type X2

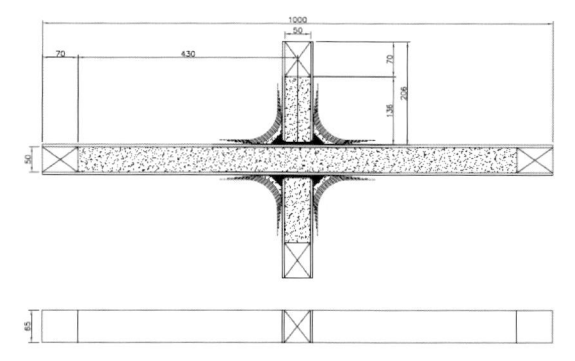

Fig. 3: Test specimen geometry. Shown for type X2, but type X1 has similar dimensions

In both X-joint specimen types, the face laminates each consist of four quadri-axial, E-glass mats (Devold AMT DBLT-850, 850 g/m^2) in a $(0/45/90/-45)_{2s}$ configuration, together with polyester resin (Polylite 720-691), manufactured using vacuum assisted resin injection. The resulting face thickness is approximately 3 mm.

The core is a 50 mm thick cross-linked PVC foam of the relatively heavy Divinycell H200 type, with a density of approximately 200 kg/m^3. The filler Norpol FI 177-10 has been applied in all joints.

For the X1-type specimens the fillet radius is 25 mm and the overlaminations are made using E-glass fibre mats corresponding to the lay-up in the face laminates. The overlamination mats have a length of 150 mm and are placed staggered 16 mm in each layer relative to one another, as indicated in Fig. 2.

Apart from filler and overlaminations, the X2-type specimens also have a specially designed Divinycell H250 foam insert embedded in the filler material, thus increasing the fillet radius to 60 mm and reducing the weight. The fibre mats (same as for the X1 type) used for the overlaminations are of different length, increasing with 30 mm between each layer, i.e. four layers in all, in order to resemble the face laminate lay-up of the faces. The mats are placed symmetrically around the angle bisector of the fillet radius.

Determination of Material Properties

Face Laminate Properties

In the modeling studies, the face laminates and overlaminations were represented by a linear-elastic, orthotropic material model. In-plane material parameters (E-moduli and Poisson's ratio) were measured in tensile tests. The remaining in-plane and out-of-plane properties were estimated based on resin properties and an assumption of quasi-isotropic material behavior for the quadri-axial laminates. The applied material properties can be seen in Table 1.

Table 1: Mechanical properties for face laminates and overlaminations.

E_1	E_2	E_3	ν_{12}	ν_{13}	ν_{23}
14.50 GPa	14.50 GPa	3.65 GPa	0.33	0.33	0.33

G_{12}	G_{13}	G_{23}
5.45 GPa	1.37 GPa	1.37 GPa

Core Properties

To model the inelastic crushing and densification regimes of the H200 PVC foam core material, it was decided to use the crushable foam material model in ABAQUS. Extensive material tests were carried out to establish the material input parameters. The applicability of the foam material model was then checked by performing FE analyses of material specimens and comparing the results with those of the corresponding experimental tests. The resulting stress-strain relation assumed for the material model is shown in Fig. 4. This displays an initial, linear-elastic regime with Young's modulus and Poisson's ratio 250 MPa and 0.32, respectively. A crushing regime follows, during which the stress increases more slowly with increasing strain. The strain at crushing initiation was found to be in the region of 2% for all the specimens tested. Finally, for strains above about 44% densification of the foam occurs.

These properties were obtained on the basis of samples taken from a single sheet of H200 core material. The density was found to vary significantly between these sheets and those used for the X-joint specimens. To allow for this the mechanical properties for the X-joint cores were scaled linearly with the density (DIAB, 2007). The elastic properties for the H250 foam fillets were based on datasheet values (DIAB, 2007) and the inelastic properties were scaled from the H200 material test results.

Details of the foam core material tests and modeling are given by Karlsen and Jenstrup (2007) and will be the subject of a later publication.

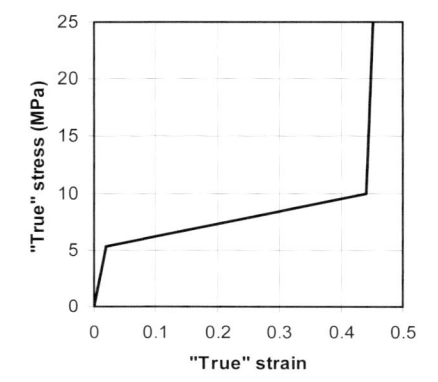

Fig. 4: Assumed stress-strain curve for H200 core material of density 240 kg/m^3, based on test data.

Adhesive Filler Properties

The Reichhold NORPOL FI-177 adhesive filler was modeled as an isotropic, linear-elastic material. It was found that the compressive stresses in the adhesive filler do not reach the plastic yield limit during the analysis. The values assumed for Young's modulus and Poisson's ratio were 289 MPa and 0.30 respectively, in accordance with the manufacturer's data sheet.

X-joints under Compressive Loading

Load-deflection Curves and Strain Distributions

The deformations of the two X-joint designs illustrated in Fig. 2 have been investigated both numerically using a commercial FE-code (ABAQUS) and experimentally using advanced digital deformation measurements (Berggreen et al., 2007b).

The analyses were performed using a two-dimensional plane strain model as shown for the X1-type joint in Fig. 5.

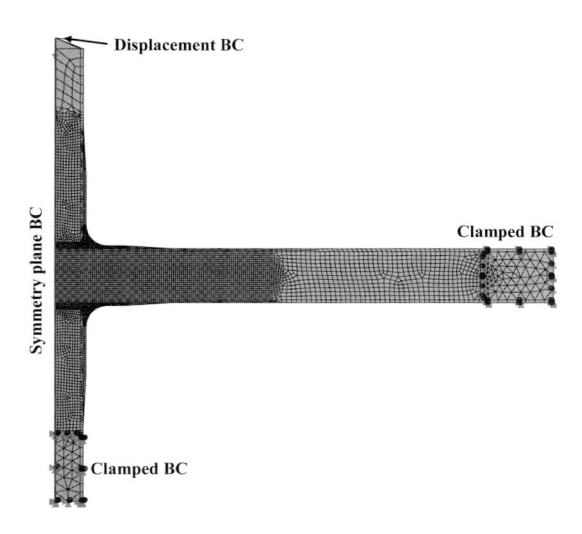

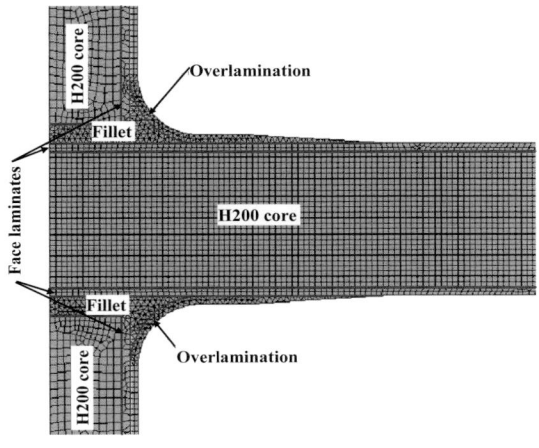

Fig. 5: FE mesh for X1 joint analysis, with enlarged view of central region.

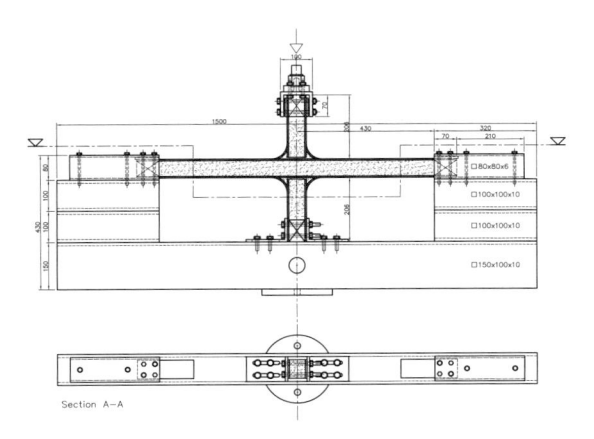

Fig. 6: Test specimen and arrangement for X-joint compressive loading tests.

Fig. 7: Test rig with X1 specimen and digital cameras.

The test arrangement is shown in Fig. 6 and Fig. 7. The test rig was mounted in an Instron 8502 servo-hydraulic test machine. The ends of the horizontal and vertical sandwich elements were reinforced with hardwood inserts and rigidly clamped to the test rig fittings. Compression loads were introduced into the specimens at a displacement-controlled loading rate of 1.5 mm/min, and measured by a 100 kN load cell. (While the loading rates experienced by such an X-joint in practice may be somewhat higher than applied in these tests, strain rate effects are assumed not to have a major influence on the behavior.) Full-field displacements and surface strains were measured at one side of the specimen using an advanced digital optical system (ARAMIS 4M) operating at a frequency of 0.25 Hz.

Fig. 8 shows the load-displacement behavior for each of the joints as obtained from measurements and analyses. Good agreement was obtained between laboratory tests and FE calculations for strain distributions in the core of the horizontal deck panel and for the load-displacement response in the elastic range. Agreement was less good for the load-displacement response in the core crushing regime, though the initiation of core crushing was well predicted. As discussed by Berggreen et al (2007b), this may well be due to the necessity to assume plane strain deformation in the core crushing model, while the tested X-joints were in a condition closer to plane stress and developed significant out-of-plane distortion of the cross-sections (Fig. 9).

From the test results it is seen that the X1 joints first experience significantly non-linear behavior at a load of about 650 kN/m, when significant core crushing is developing. The load increases to about 750 kN/m before final failure occurs by separation of the overlaminates (Fig. 9). In the X2 joints the development of core crushing is more gradual, with non-linearity becoming evident at a load of about 800 kN/m and failure of the overlaminations at loads in the region of 1000 kN/m.

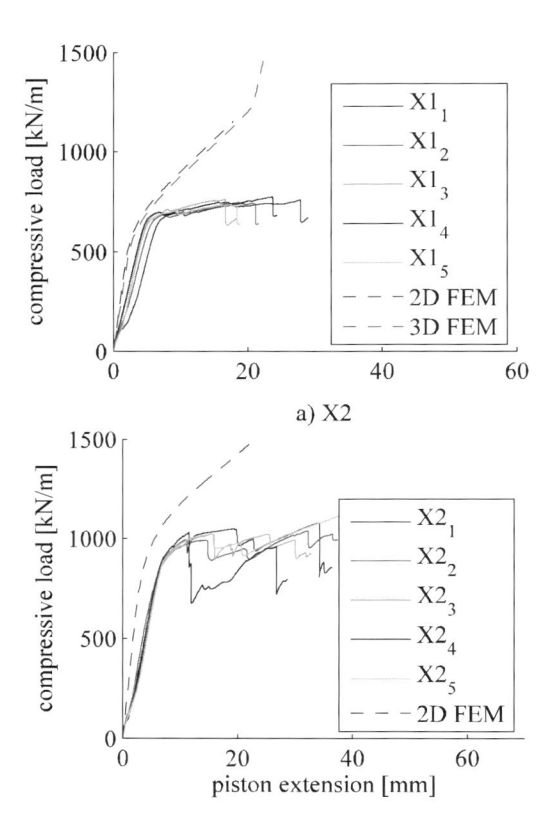

Fig. 8: Compressive load per unit width as a function of the applied vertical displacement for specimen types X1 and X2.

Fig. 9: Final failure of specimen $X1_1$ and large deformations in the core and failure of upper overlaminations in the $X2_1$ specimen

Conclusions for Selection of Core Material and Design of Core Inserts

Fig. 10 shows the von Mises strain as measured by the ARAMIS system on specimen $X1_3$ at a load of approximately 461 kN/m. Fig. 11 shows the maximum compressive principal strains, plotted against position along a series of horizontal section lines through the core of the deck panel, for each of the X1 joints at similar load levels within the elastic regime. The corresponding results from the FE analyses are also shown.

The section lines are defined in Fig. 10. With the exception of specimen $X1_5$, the test results show a reasonable degree of symmetry about the vertical symmetry axis of the specimens. A similar plot to those of Fig 11 is shown for section line 0 for the X2 joints in Fig. 12.

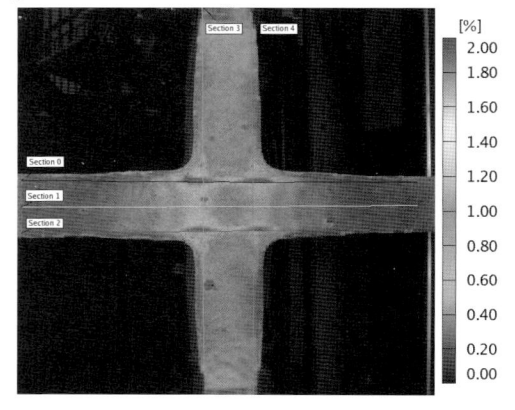

Fig. 10: Von Mises strains obtained by ARAMIS system for joint X13 at 461 kN/M, showing section lines used for data extraction.

Figs. 11 and 12 allow some conclusions to be drawn regarding the selection of core material for the joints. Firstly it is possible, by scaling these results or by studying the responses at successive load steps in the analysis, to deduce the loads at which crushing of the H200 core begins. This represents a limiting load beyond which some permanent damage may be expected in an X-joint having H200 core throughout the joint. Assuming that crushing of H200 foam core begins at a compressive strain of 2%, and basing the estimates on the FE analysis, gives the resulting limits for the X1 and X2 joints as approximately 550 kN/m and 715 kN/m respectively. For each type of joint the greatest compressive strain in the core occurs close to the upper face laminate of the deck panel just below the end of the face laminate of the vertical panel. The strain at the corresponding position above the lower face laminate is slightly smaller as a result of the asymmetry introduced by the clamping of the ends of the deck panel.

It is also possible to draw some tentative conclusions regarding designs with an insert of higher-strength core material in the most highly loaded part of the horizontal deck panel, as illustrated in Fig. 13. Two alternative cases may be considered: (a) when a higher strength foam insert is to be used in a panel that is made otherwise with H200 foam core, and (b) when an H200 foam insert is used in a panel that is made otherwise with a lower strength foam.

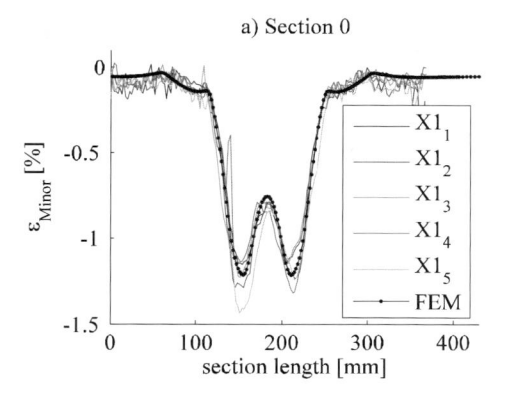

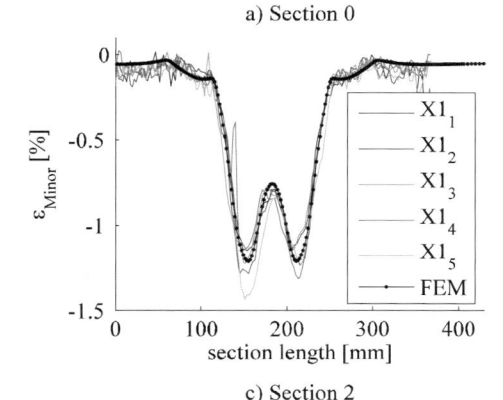

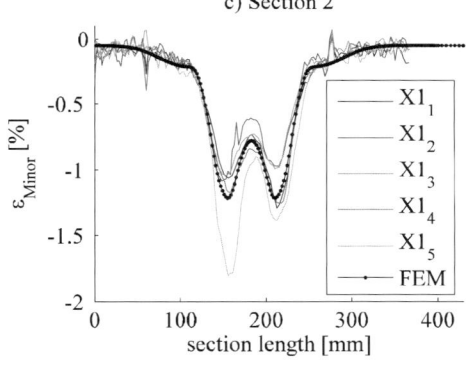

Fig. 11: Maximum compressive principal strains plotted along section lines for the X1 joints. Applied loads: $X1_1 = 310$ kN/m, $X1_2 = 308$ kN/m, $X1_3 = 318$ kN/m, $X1_4 = 315$ kN/m, $X1_5 = 315$ kN/m, FEM = 333 kN/m.

(a) H200 Core with Higher Strength Insert

It is readily seen from Fig. 11 that the compressive strains, and hence the compressive stresses, in the core drop very rapidly at distances greater than about 50 mm to each side of the vertical centerline of the X1 joint, and become quite small at distances over about 70 mm. Thus, if a stronger material were substituted for the H200 foam over a total length of 100 mm or more, the joint would be able to carry a greater load without suffering permanent damage to the core. With an insert length of 140 mm or more the increased capacity could be quite considerable. The strain level, and hence the stress level, in the core region outside the insert is then very much lower than in the central part of the insert, so the parameters determining the limiting load for the joint will be primarily the strength of the inserted core material and the strength of the other components in the joint, such as the overlaminations. Based on the observations in the tests, it is reasonable to suppose that the overlaminations etc. will be able to withstand a load of at least 700 kN/m, though this would need to be confirmed in the presence of an insert. An insert to support this loading without crushing would need to have the strength about 30% higher than H200.

The picture is similar for the X2 joint, though the rate, at which the compressive strains and stresses decline for increasing distance from the joint, is lower (Fig. 12). The length of insert needed to reinforce the entire region experiencing local stresses is now increased to about 190-200 mm, though some appreciable benefit would be gained with any insert length greater than about 100 mm.

For either type of joint, an accurate estimate of the limiting load can only be found by analyzing or testing the joint with the actual combination of core materials.

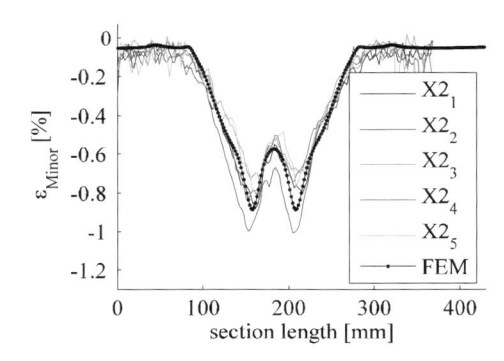

Fig. 12: Maximum compressive principal strains plotted along section line 0 for the X2 joints. Applied loads: $X2_1 = 317$ kN/m, $X2_2 = 367$ kN/m, $X2_3 = 311$ kN/m, $X2_4 = 329$ kN/m, $X2_5 = 314$ kN/m, FEM = 320 kN/m

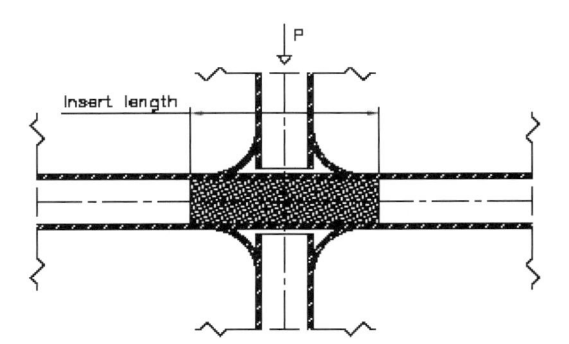

Fig. 13: Schematic layout of core insert in X-joint, with insert length definition.

(b) Lower Strength Core with H200 Insert

Similar conclusions may be drawn for the case when the core insert is of H200 material and the core outside the insert is a lower grade material. For the X1 joint a core insert of length 140 mm or more would ensure that the lower grade core material outside the joint was only lightly stressed, so it could be of appreciably lower strength without significantly influencing the limiting load for the joint. Furthermore, since the foam outside the insert is so lightly stressed, the substitution of a lower grade and lower-modulus material will not be expected to cause significant redistribution of stresses in the joint as compared to the case that has been analyzed and tested. The required strength of the lower grade core in the deck will now be determined by other loadings on the deck panel, while the joint capacity will be maintained at about 550 kN/m.

For the X2 joint, the same arguments may be used provided the insert length is 190 mm or more. Shorter inserts will give a benefit but this can only be quantified by testing or analysis of the configuration in question.

Further Consideration of the Insert Length

It is interesting to compare the required insert lengths described above with the geometry of the respective joints. For the X1 joint the thickness of the vertical panel extended by the radii of the two fillets and the widths of overlaminations before they start to taper down (about 17 mm each side) is 140 mm. For the X2 joint the corresponding dimension is approximately 192 mm. These dimensions agree extremely well with the length of the core region in the deck panel experiencing increased stresses, and thus the required insert length. However, this will not necessarily be the case for other joint designs.

Other Considerations

In addition to considering the modes of failure seen in the reported tests, it is necessary when selecting core inserts to consider the local stresses that are induced in the face laminates in the region of a joint between core blocks with differing stiffnesses, as shown by Bozhevolnaya et al. (2005) and Lyckegaard et al. (2006). Such stresses could be checked by means of FE analysis carried out on a joint with core insert.

X-joints under Tensile Loading

An X-joint located at the connection between a deck and a superstructure end bulkhead is subjected to similar tensile and compressive load levels if the hull girder hogging and sagging moments are roughly equal. As the tensile strength of the foam core material is higher than its compressive strength, the critical regions of the deck panel for tensile loading on the X-joint are then the core-laminate interfaces and the laminates themselves. (The strength of the connections between the vertical bulkheads and the deck face laminates will not be addressed here.) As the pull-off strength of the core-laminate interface and through-thickness tensile strength of the face laminate are sensitive to initial defects in the form of debonds or delaminations it is of interest to study ways of ensuring an acceptable level of defect/damage tolerance in this region. The study by Lundsgaard-Larsen et al. (2007), which uses cohesive zone modeling in a FE analysis, combined with laboratory test results obtained by Karlsen and Jenstrup (2007), allows some conclusions to be drawn regarding the selection of materials and design of the joint.

Materials Considered in Damage Tolerance Studies

Four different laminate lay-ups were considered in the damage tolerance studies:

I: 4 x DBLT850 as in the compression load studies

II: As I but with a 450 g/m^2 layer of chopped strand mat (CSM) at the interface

III: As II but with an additional layer of woven mat (tex68) between the DBLT850 and the CSM

IV: As III but without the CSM

Fracture Toughness and Cohesive Laws

A detailed description of the FE modeling carried out by Lundsgaard-Larsen et al. (2007) using cohesive zone modeling at the sandwich core/face interface is beyond the scope of the present paper. Extensive fracture mechanics testing under mixed-mode conditions was performed by Karlsen and Jenstrup (2007) to obtain parameters for the cohesive model and to compare the performance of different face laminate lay-ups when combined with Divinycell H200 foam core. The test method was based on a Double Cantilever Beam specimen loaded by Uneven Bending Moments (DCB-UBM), see Sørensen et al. (2006). The FE modeling focused on lay-up II only. The other lay-ups showed behavior that indicated that the J-integral method used for developing the cohesive zone model would be invalid.

Pull-off Tests on Debonded Sandwich Beams

To simulate the tensile loading case on an X-joint without the complication of possible failure in the overlaminations, a series of pull-off tests was carried out on sandwich beams representing the horizontal deck panel with a debond between the upper laminate and the core (Lundsgaard-Larsen et al, 2007; Karlsen and Jenstrup, 2007). The sandwich specimen was mounted in the same test-rig as used for the compression testing, and loaded by an Instron 8502 servo-hydraulic test machine, see Fig.14. The replacement of the lower bulkhead portion by a rigid attachment is believed to have a minor effect on the behavior.

The middle of the bottom face is fixed to the test rig, and the middle of the top face is clamped to the cross-head as shown. The sandwich specimen has wooden inserts at the ends which are clamped to the test rig. A Teflon film is inserted between the upper face and core along half the specimen length, so that the crack will only propagate to one side and hence only one fracture incidence will occur in the measurements. The half of the beam with the Teflon film incorporated maintains some symmetry, and prevents excessive horizontal forces from being exerted on the piston of the test machine. The displacement field of the specimen surface was recorded using the ARAMIS optical system as in the compression tests.

The specimen was loaded by moving the cross-head upwards with a rate of 2 mm/min. The face laminate had to be lifted 30-40 mm before the crack had fully propagated to the end support. During this time the crack propagated slowly, with an increasing amount of fiber bridging. A specimen with a fully propagated crack is seen in Fig. 15.

During each test the lift as measured by the test machine piston displacement, the lift force as measured by the load cell and the crack length found by tracking the opening between the core and face at different locations along the interface were all recorded. Five specimens of each of the types I – IV were tested. Each specimen had a width of 60-67 mm.

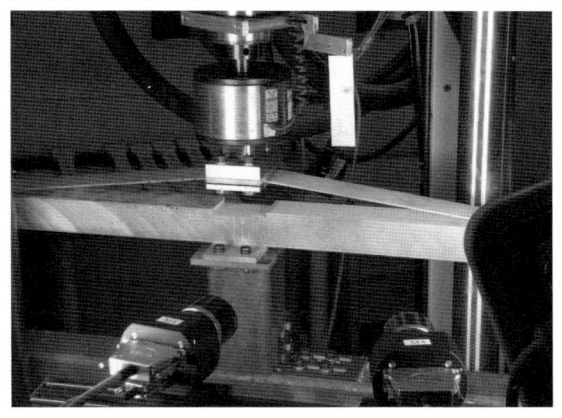

Fig. 14: Loaded beam specimen in tensile test machine.

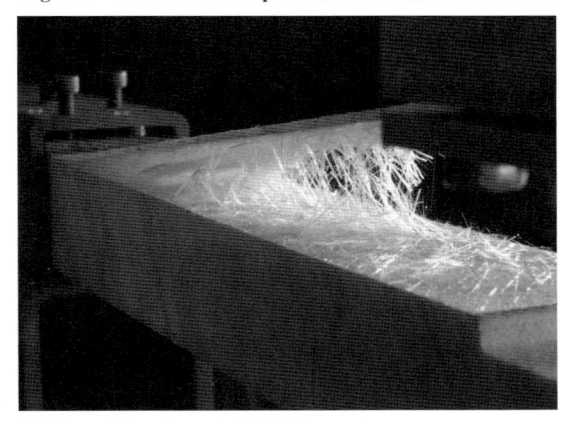

Fig. 15: Tested beam specimen with fibre bridging between the crack faces.

FE Modelling

A 2D finite element model was created using ABAQUS version 6.6 and the explicit solver was used. Due to symmetry only half the specimen was modeled. A schematic illustration of the model, with dimensions, is given in Fig. 16.

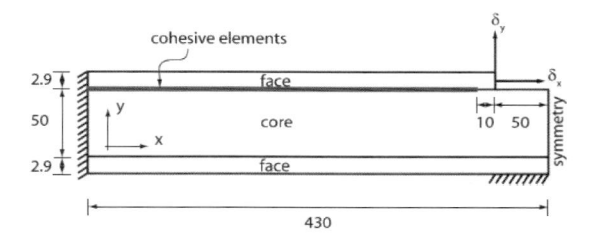

Fig. 16: Schematic drawing of the finite element model indicating boundary conditions, cohesive section and loading points.

The model consists of two faces and a core, where the top face and the core are connected through zero-thickness cohesive elements which represent the traction-separation behavior in the interface. The left edge of the sandwich beam is fixed, and the right edge is exposed to symmetry conditions. A length of 50 mm of the bottom right edge is fixed, since this part is clamped to the test rig in the experiments.

The finite element model is meshed uniformly with 4-noded bilinear rectangular elements each with 8 degrees of freedom. The element size is approximately 0.5 mm, which corresponds to 6 elements through the thickness direction of the face. The sandwich specimen is loaded in displacement control so that the edge of the face is displaced as shown in Fig. 16.

Analysis and Test Results for Pull-off Tests

For the purposes of assessing damage tolerance, and for considering the design of a core insert block, it is relevant to evaluate the results in terms of a plot of lift force against crack length. Fig. 17 shows such a plot as obtained by testing and FE analysis for the type II beams. The lift force reaches a local maximum just before the crack starts propagating, which is in good agreement with the results obtained in Berggreen et al. (2007a). It is seen that the FE analysis over-predicts this initial peak load, but that agreement improves as the crack propagates. Fig. 18 shows the averaged results for each specimen type. Here the forces have been divided by the specimen width.

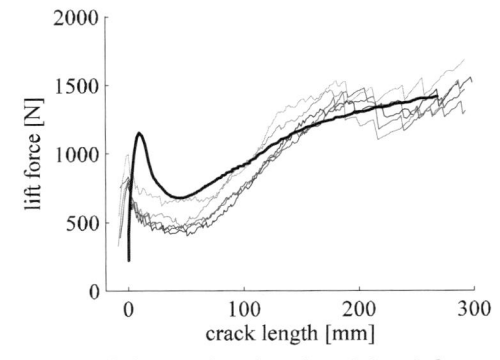

Fig. 17: Lift force as function of crack length for type II lay-up. The FE results are shown by the thick curve.

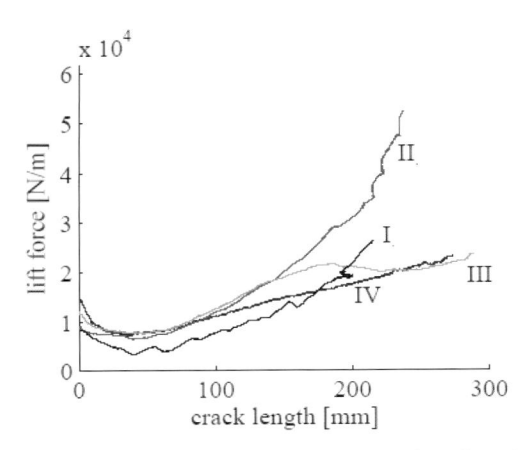

Fig. 18: Lift force per unit width as function of crack length: Average values for each specimen type

Conclusions from Pull-off Tests

Both the pull-off tests and the FE analyses show that, with H200 core, crack lengths of 100-200 mm are needed before the beneficial effects of fiber bridging raise the load capacity to the initial value it had before crack propagation began. The exact extent depends on the laminate lay-up.

The differences between the lay-ups can be at least partly explained as follows. The two interfaces without CSM, types I and IV are relatively brittle and show little or no fiber bridging. Lay-ups II and III, with CSM, give a tougher interface with fiber bridging. However, in case II the crack is seen to kink into the laminate so that further crack propagation results in even more effective fiber bridging but at the same time weakening the main load-carrying laminates. This contrasts with type III, for which the crack remains in the CSM. The type II lay-up also has the disadvantage that propagation begins at a relatively low load level.

The use of a CSM layer clearly has only a modest effect on the performance, as it only initiates scattered fiber bridging and the load carried by bridged fibers is limited by the length of each of the chopped fibers in the mat. It is possible that the use of continuous strand mat, with a layer of randomly arranged continuous fibers in place of the CSM, may increase the magnitude of the load that can be carried by the bridged fiber. This will be investigated in the next stage of the studies.

Implications for Core Insert Design

Attention is focused on the case when a block of H200 material is to be inserted in a core of lower grade material. The first item to note is that the load levels reached in the pull-off tests are of the order 10- 50 kN/m, which are very much lower than in the compression tests. The tension load that could be applied to a complete X-joint, however, would be greater because in the beam tests the face laminate on one half of the beam was already separated from the core. This part of the beam provides no resistance to lifting at small crack lengths, but as the lift increases there is an increasing contribution from the membrane tension in the laminate itself. Thus the load applied to a complete X-joint would be approximately twice that measured in the beam tests initially, but the ratio reduces somewhat for larger crack lengths.

The second observation is that the required insert length to gain any benefit from the fiber bridging at large crack lengths are 200-400 mm depending on the lay-up. (Note that the required insert lengths are twice the single crack lengths at which the benefits are seen.) These lengths are similar to or greater than the lengths that typically emerged from the compression case.

The main conclusions from the damage tolerance studies are thus that the lay-ups with CSM at the interface provide the best damage tolerance in combination with an H200 core, and that fiber bridging will ensure that this damage tolerance is activated provided the H200 core extends over a width of at least 200 mm, which is similar to the minimum width required for the compression case. However, the tensile capacity of the joint with a debond defect is considerably lower than the compressive strength.

Conclusions

The laboratory tests and FE analyses have provided useful information for assessing the load-carrying performance of foam core materials and laminate-core interfaces in sandwich X-joints, and in particular for determining the required lengths of higher-strength blocks to be inserted in the through-going panel to avoid compressive core failure. The FE analyses reproduce the essential features of the behavior for both compression and tension loading cases, though quantitative agreement is best for the compression case.

The tensile load-carrying capacity of X-joints with face-core debond defects is limited but can be influenced by the choice of reinforcement adjacent to the interface. Further studies are planned in this area.

The studies reported here are limited to in-plane compressive and tensile loading on the bulkhead panels that are perpendicular to the through-going deck panel. These are considered to be the primary loads experienced by an X-joint connecting a superstructure end bulkhead, deck panel and internal bulkhead below the deck. The effects of shear and bending loadings may also need to be considered in some cases. A further phenomenon that is not considered here is the possibility of growth of a face-core debond under repeated loading; this type of damage growth is the subject of ongoing research.

Acknowledgements

This work has been performed within the context of the Network of Excellence on Marine Structures (MARSTRUCT), partially funded by the European Union through the Growth Programme under contract TNE3-CT-2003-506141. The provision of test specimens and materials by Kockums AB (Karlskronavarvet) and DIAB AB is highly appreciated.

References

Berggreen, C (2004). "Damage Tolerance of Debonded Sandwich Structures", PhD Thesis, Technical University of Denmark, Department of Mechanical Engineering.

Berggreen, C, Simonsen, BC and Borum, KK (2007a). "Experimental and numerical study of interface crack propagation in foam-cored sandwich beams. Journal of Composite Materials", Journal of Composite Materials, 41(4):493-520

Berggreen, C, Lundsgaard-Larsen, C, Karlsen, K, Jenstrup, C and Hayman, B (2007b). "Improving performance of polymer fibre reinforced sandwich X-joints in naval vessels – Part I: Design aspects", 16th Int. Conf. on Composite Materials, Kyoto, Japan.

Bozhevolnaya, E, Lyckegaard, A and Thomsen, OT (2005). "Localized Effects Across Core Junctions in Sandwich Beams Subjected to In-Plane and Out-of-Plane Loading", Applied Composite Materials, Vol.12, pp. 135-147.

DIAB (2007). "Technical Manual – Divinycell H", http://www.diabgroup.com/europe.

Efstathios, E and Moan, T (1996). "Experimental and numerical study of composite T-joints", Journal of Composite Materials, Vol. 30, No. 2, 190-209.

Karlsen, K and Jensrup, C (2007). "Design of core inserts in sandwich X-joints – Experimental and numerical analysis", MSc Thesis, Department of Mechanical Engineering, Technical University of Denmark.

Kildegaard, C (1992). "Experimental and numerical fracture mechanical studies of FRP-sandwich T-joints in maritime constructions", 2nd Int. Conference on Sandwich Constructions, Gainesville, USA.

Lundsgaard-Larsen, C, Berggreen, C, Karlsen, K, Jenstrup, C and Hayman, B (2007). "Improving performance of polymer fibre reinforced sandwich X-joints in naval vessels – Part II: Damage Tolerance", 16th Int. Conf. on Composite Materials, Kyoto, Japan.

Lyckegaard, A, Bozhevolnaya, E and Thomsen, OT (2006). "Parametric Study of Structurally Graded Core Junctions", Journal of Sandwich Structures and Materials, Vol. 8, No.5.

Sørensen, BF, Jørgensen, K, Jacobsen, TK and Østergaard, RC (2006). "DCB-specimen loaded with uneven bending moments", International Journal of Fracture, Vol. 141, No. 1-2, pp 163-176.

Toftegaard, H and Lystrup, A (2005). "Design and test of lightweight sandwich T-joint for naval ships". Composites: Part A, Vol. 36, No. 8,1055-1065.

Hydrodynamic Pressure and Structural Loading of High-Speed Catamaran and SES

William S. Vorus[1], Robert D. Sedat[2]

[1] School of NAME, University of New Orleans, New Orleans, LA
[2] US Coast Guard R&D Center, Groton, CT

Abstract

A theory and engineering model for seaway dynamic response of high-speed catamaran and SES hull forms was developed and applied to configurations of interest. Zero gravity semi-planing theory was used initially for both calm-water analysis and seaway dynamics. From this initial work it was concluded that while the typical operating Froude number of the larger vessels of interest is high (slightly above unity), it is probably not high enough to justify discarding the effects of gravity in the hydrodynamics. A main effort was then to incorporate gravity into the hydrodynamics, for both calm water operations and in waves. The Mauro "flat ship" theory was found to be useful as the basis for this extension. The development is demonstrated by comparing calculations from the extended code to the model experiments conducted on the Bell-Halter110 SES at the old Lockheed tank in San Diego, CA back in the 1970's.

Keywords

Catamaran; Hydrodynamics; Resistance; Seakeeping; SES.

Introduction

The criteria most widely available to the design community for determining hydrodynamic forces and hull surface pressure for use in vessel design are embodied in Guidelines and Rules promulgated by the various Classification Societies. When applied to fast multi-hull designs, with service speeds of 50 to 60 knots or higher, formulas published by ABS, DnV, and Lloyd's Register (for example) may produce significantly different values of design and impact pressure loads. This produces a corresponding variation in scantling requirements, particularly for hulls with sandwich-skin composite construction.

It was recognized as a worthwhile service to the ship design community to develop a comprehensive tool for evaluation of high-speed catamaran and catamaran/SES design pressure and wave impact loading. Ideally, this tool should be based on an analytical/numerical model, developed from first principles, and validated by comparison with test data for the hull types of interest. Such an analysis tool has been developed and has been applied to the Bell-Halter 110 ft SES built in the late 1970's. Both calm water and seaway model test data was available here for making definitive comparisons with the calculations.

Approach

The base computer codes employed, that implement the general hydrodynamics outlined above, existed originally in the VAI EDITH system. EDITH (Engineering Development in Theoretical Hydrodynamics) is a computer system dedicated to the application of sound theoretical hydrodynamics to relevant engineering challenges in marine hydrodynamics. With regard to the work described here, the relevant EDITH code was the pre-existing EDITH 2, or CatSea, for analysis of high speed planning catamarans.

The new code series assembled for the SES analysis is EDITH 2-AG, or CatSeaAir.

All of the EDITH-series algorithms prior to EDITH 2-AG had implemented the zero gravity high-speed theory of Vorus(1996). The new CatSeaAir code was adapted for approximate inclusion of vessel generated gravity waves, and now that algorithm has been back-fit into the other programs of the series.

Non-zero Gravity Theory

The base theory used here for gravity wave effects is the linearized planning monohull theory of Maruo (1967), adapted for bi-hulls, including SES. The Maruo formulation is based on ideal flow theory and represents a solution to the Laplace equation for a velocity potential subject to the linearized free-surface boundary condition, with gravity included, and a radiation condition of no waves upstream. It is a steady flow theory, and therein lies the major approximation of this application. The unsteady seaway dynamics of EDITH 2-AG assumes that the wave-making is quasi-steady.

That is, with changing vessel attitudes in the seaway, this application assumes that at any instant the temporal effects in the wave-making, as regards loading changes, are small. The unsteady effects in the wave making are generated by the Maruo solution at any instant for the craft geometry varying generally with time.

Referring to Figure 1, x is downstream with the coordinate system located at the bow, and y is up. The planing surface is considered to occupy the region of the y = 0 plane corresponding to $-Z(x) \leq z \leq -Z_k$ and $Z_k \leq z \leq Z(x)$ with $0 \leq x \leq L$, L being the instantaneous waterline length. Z(x) is the waterline offset and Zk is the demi-hull keel offset, taken as constant in x. The kinematic boundary condition is satisfied on this plane surface, which requires that the craft bottom have a flat characterization. Planing craft are consistent with the assumption of flatness in satisfying boundary conditions on the y = 0 plane, and this has been a universal assumption for conventional analysis of planing craft at zero gravity, as built upon the original work of vonKarman(1929) and Wagner (1932). The current CatSeaAir code uses the non-linear slender-body formulation of Vorus (1996), with the addition of the specially adapted Mauro gravity routines.

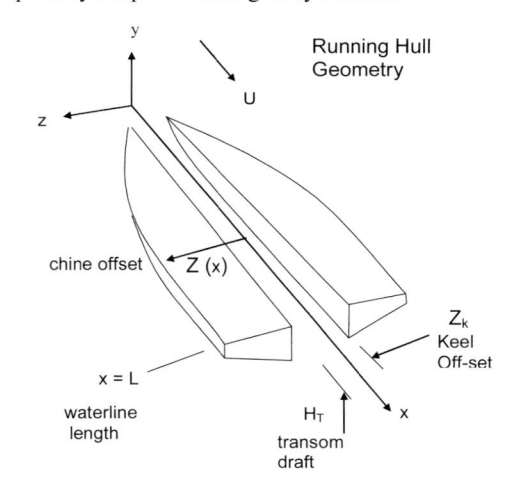

Fig 1: Catamaran/SES Geometry

The Maruo velocity potential, adapted for the catamaran geometry, is:

$$\Phi(x,y,z) = -\frac{1}{\pi} \int_{\zeta=-Z(x)}^{-Z_k} +$$

$$\int_{Z_k}^{Z(x)} \int_{\xi=0}^{x} \gamma_z(\xi,\zeta) \int_{\lambda=0}^{\infty} \cos[\sqrt{\kappa\lambda}(x-\xi)]\cos[\lambda(z-\zeta)]e^{\lambda y} d\lambda d\xi d\zeta \quad (1)$$

Referring back to Figure 1, Φ is the velocity potential in the fluid region, $y \leq 0$. γ_z is the unknown transverse (z-directed) vortex density component on the surface projection. (The companion axial vortex density component, γ_x, is the usual subject of the conventional zero gravity slender body formulation of planing, but the two components are related by the condition of zero divergence of the two dimensional surface vector.) κ in (1) is the wave number:

$$\kappa = g/U^2 \quad (2)$$

κ entered the derivation of (1) in satisfying the linearized free surface boundary condition in allowing for gravity wave generation.

Note from (1) that only the sections at $\xi < x$ upstream convect into the current x – solution section; γ_z for $\xi < x$ will always be known from upstream computation steps. This x-marching characteristic of the elliptic solutions in the z-coordinate is common to the parabolic reduction in x associated with all slender body theories.

The linearized kinematic boundary condition to be satisfied on the craft surface projection is:

$$\frac{\partial \Phi}{\partial y} = U \frac{\partial y_0}{\partial x} \quad \text{on y} =$$

$0, -Z(x) \leq z \leq -Z_k$ and $Z_k \leq z \leq Z(x)$, $0 \leq x \leq L$ (3)

$y_0(x,z)$ is the definition of the planing surface $y - y_0(x,z) = 0$, which is presumed to be known for purposes of the theoretical development.

Substitution of (1) into (3) produces an integral equation that is solved numerically for the vortex density $\gamma_z(x,z)$. This solution is difficult in that it exhibits a higher order singularity that must be carefully treated, Tuck (1975). But it is made easier by the downstream marching, for which each successive x-station is solved in terms of the already available solutions from the stations upstream.

The axial perturbation velocity on the surface is given in terms of $\gamma_z(x,z)$ as:

$$u(x,z) = -\gamma_z(x,z) \quad (4)$$

The coefficient of pressure on the surface is then:

$$C_p(x,z) = -2\left(\frac{u}{U}\right) \quad (5)$$

This pressure distribution, (5), is integrated over the surface to produce the force components needed in Newton's Law for stepping the vessel motion to the next time.

Note that $\kappa \to 0$ corresponds to vanishing gravity by (2). $\kappa = 0$ in (1) therefore gives the zero gravity solution $\gamma_{zi}(x,z)$. The vortex density due only to waves is therefore:

$$\gamma_{zw} = \gamma_z - \gamma_{zi} \quad (6)$$

(5) and (6) give the pressure due to wave-making as:

$$C_{pw}(x,z) = 2\left(\frac{\gamma_{zw}(x,z)}{U}\right) \quad (7)$$

A subroutine has been added in CatSeaAir to solve (1) and (3) and to compute (7) at each time step as the hull wetted geometry changes. $C_{pw}(x,z)$ is added to the g = 0 surface pressure currently calculated in CatSeaAir to obtain the total pressure field including the gravity wave effects.

Hydrostatic pressure relative to the undisturbed water surface is also included in the pressure sum in CatSeaAir, as well as is air pressure associated with SES operations.

The new version of CatSeaAir with the gravity routines included (as an option under user control) is designated as EDITH 2-AG.

EDITH 2-AG is simple to execute and interpret. However, with the gravity option exercised, the code is time consuming. It executes about 200 time steps per hour. With 10,000 to 20,000 time steps desirable for achieving statistically stationary conditions in a random seaway analysis, approximately 50 to 100 hours of running time is required. This is on a 3.2 Ghz workstation. Most of the calculation is serial in x and then serial in time, so it is not clear that parallel processing (or cluster computing) would help much. With the gravity option off, CatSeaAir runs about 20 time steps per minute.

The extended code is robust, however, and never crashes and it has a restart capability. Effort will be made, by programming refinements, to reduce the time consumption requirement as time permits.

Comparison of Code Predictions with Model Tests

The EDITH 2-AG CatSeaAir code was applied to the Bell-Halter 110 ft SES. This design was extensively model tested in the 1970's at the old Lockheed, San Diego facility (LOLTB), as reported in LMSC/D682700, December 1979. Fig. 2 is the arrangement of the 1/15-scale (7 ft) model that was tested. Figs. 3a and 3b are the body plan from which the geometry input for CatSeaAir was extracted. Note from Figs. 2 and 3 that the BH110 is a "rockered" hull with 2.6 degree of keel rocker aft.

Analysis versus Experiments - Calm-Water

The model experiments in calm water reported the following data needed for comparison with the analysis:

Steady speed, U

Weight, W

Longitudinal center of gravity, xcg

Air cushion pressure, p_{ac}

Transom draft, Ht/Zk

Trim

Drag coefficient, Cd

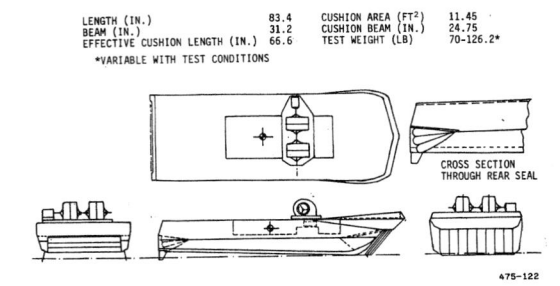

Fig 2: BH 110 Test Model

From the above list the % air support, WA, was obtained from the cushion pressure by multiplying p_{ac} by the cushion ceiling area and dividing by the model weight, W. The transom draft was extrapolated from the measured mid-cushion draft using the measured trim angle.

The theoretical model has three degrees of freedom: heave, pitch, and surge. But the physical model tested was restrained in surge, so that drag represents the surge equation. This requires that of the seven variables listed above only three can be predicted by CatSeaAir and the others must be considered as input to the analysis. The normal choice for input would be U, W, xcg, and WA, with the trim, transom draft and drag considered as output to be compared with the test measurements. This is the context of the experimental data presentation.

However, with trim, draft, and drag as the output, the calculations were very poorly behaved in some cases and failed to converge to reasonable values, if at all, in others. After a great deal of calculation it was decided that xcg and WA given for the tests were not uniformly consistent. WA had to be estimated from the cushion pressure measurement by assuming the cushion pressure uniform and constant over the wet deck. There was also some seeming confusion over the experimental xcg determination. Two xcg's were reported; one in air and a CG in "hover" on the air cushion at zero forward speed. They were different and it was not always clear which was being reported. These tests were conducted 30 years ago, and while one or two of the TEXTRON people involved were still available and helpful, the xcg issue, particularly, remained confusing.

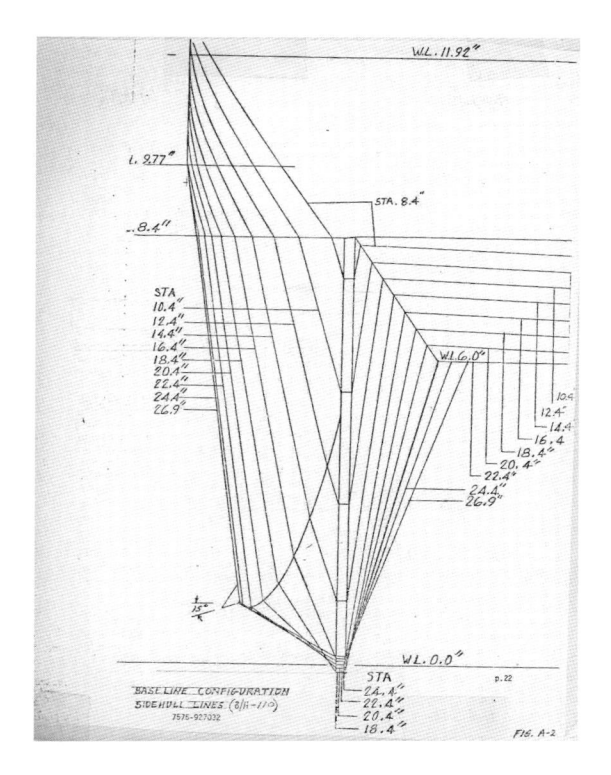

Figure 3a: BH110 (Model B-34C) Body Plan Forward

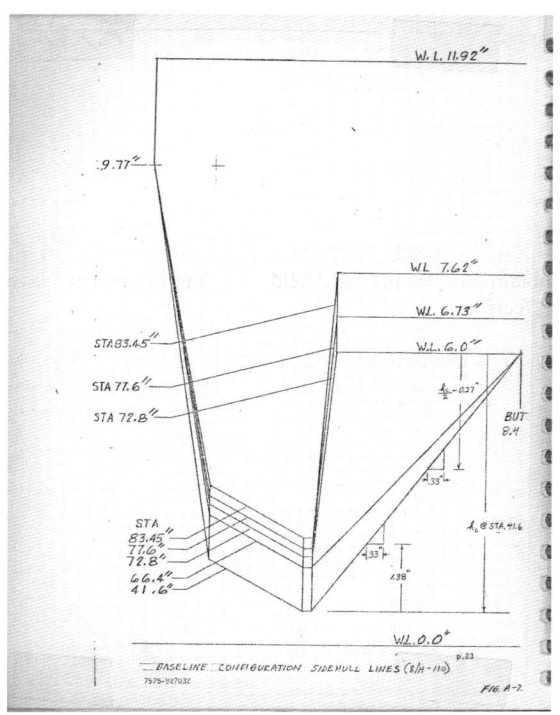

Figure 3b: BH110 (Model B-34C) Body Plan Aft

It was therefore finally decided to take the trim and draft as the two input variables, along with U and W, for the calm water analysis, and to calculate WA, xg and Cd for comparison to the test data. This result is reported below in Table 1 for the three model weights of Condition 1: W = 70, 81.5, and 93 lbs.

Table 1: BH 110 Calm Water Runs, Model B34C, Configuration 1 LMSC/D682700, 12/79, Book 5 VAI Analysis of 9-06

No.	U(fps)	Vfs(k)	W(#)	%xge	Trim	Ht	Cl	%WAe	%WAc	xcge	xcgc	%xcgc	Cde	Cdc
362	12.91	29.60	70.0	0.0	1.28	0.1229	0.3935	87.5	81.0	2.623	2.485	-2.61	0.0233	0.0169
363	17.26	39.58	70.0	0.0	0.57	0.0785	0.2202	85.5	78.8	2.623	2.713	1.70	0.0126	0.0194
364	13.10	30.04	70.0	-0.7	1.59	0.1273	0.3822	78.7	81.9	2.586	2.465	-2.99	0.0221	0.0158
365	17.48	40.08	70.0	-0.7	0.97	0.0874	0.2147	83.7	82.9	2.586	2.499	-2.52	0.0103	0.0118
366	24.28	55.68	70.0	-1.5	0.75	0.0738	0.1113	81.7	86.3	2.544	2.536	-1.65	0.0069	0.0095
367	13.12	30.08	70.0	-1.5	1.81	0.1407	0.3811	85.0	81.9	2.544	2.466	-2.97	0.0215	0.0161
368	17.48	40.08	70.0	-1.5	1.17	0.1012	0.2147	82.9	82.7	2.544	2.498	-2.37	0.0108	0.0118
370	24.08	55.22	70.0	-2.0	0.88	0.0823	0.1131	78.4	85.4	2.517	2.526	-1.84	0.0068	0.0094
371	30.90	70.86	70.0	-2.0	0.63	0.0634	0.0687	75.4	86.8	2.517	2.554	-1.31	0.0049	0.0083
372	9.20	21.10	70.0	-0.5	2.27	0.1233	0.7751	82.6	87.0	2.597	2.433	-3.60	0.0409	0.0216
378	17.32	39.72	70.0	-1.0	1.00	0.0941	0.2187	82.0	84.4	2.571	2.502	-2.29	0.0102	0.0120
393	17.40	39.90	70.0	-1.0	1.14	0.0980	0.2168	86.7	83.0	2.571	2.495	-2.42	0.0106	0.0117
397	9.15	20.98	81.5	0.0	2.48	0.2307	0.9125	86.5	75.0	2.623	2.459	-3.10	0.0549	0.0393
398	13.08	30.00	81.5	0.0	1.45	0.1315	0.4465	89.1	79.1	2.623	2.478	-2.74	0.0268	0.0183
399	9.15	20.98	81.5	-0.5	2.68	0.2374	0.9125	85.2	75.0	2.597	2.458	-3.12	0.0562	0.0397
400	13.08	30.00	81.5	-0.5	1.74	0.1344	0.4465	87.7	82.3	2.597	2.460	-3.08	0.0251	0.0173
401	17.41	39.92	81.5	-0.5	0.98	0.0984	0.2509	86.3	83.3	2.597	2.520	-1.95	0.0132	0.0134
402	24.00	55.03	81.5	-0.5	0.61	0.0777	0.1326	85.1	79.5	2.597	2.743	2.27	0.0088	0.0145
403	13.10	30.04	81.5	-1.0	1.96	0.1499	0.4451	87.4	81.9	2.571	2.462	-3.05	0.0252	0.0178
404	17.44	39.99	81.5	-1.0	1.22	0.1103	0.2509	84.7	81.5	2.571	2.504	-2.25	0.0117	0.0130
405	24.06	55.17	81.5	-1.0	0.85	0.0834	0.1320	84.0	85.4	2.571	2.537	-1.63	0.0080	0.0100
406	12.35	28.32	81.5	-1.5	2.37	0.1775	0.5008	85.4	81.3	2.544	2.458	-3.12	0.0302	0.0205
407	17.43	39.97	81.5	-1.5	1.38	0.1113	0.2514	83.6	83.4	2.544	2.488	-2.55	0.0122	0.0123
408	24.08	55.17	81.5	-1.5	0.94	0.0830	0.1317	81.1	84.4	2.544	2.523	-1.89	0.0074	0.0097
416	17.40	39.90	81.5	-1.0	1.24	0.1104	0.2524	84.3	81.8	2.571	2.501	-2.31	0.0114	0.0129
422	9.08	20.82	81.5	0.5	2.30	0.2215	0.9265	85.9	74.6	2.649	2.469	-2.91	0.0543	0.0398
423	23.89	54.78	81.5	-2.0	1.05	0.0953	0.1339	81.4	83.0	2.517	2.531	-1.74	0.0074	0.0102
425	9.16	21.00	93.0	0.0	2.75	0.2617	1.0380	85.4	73.8	2.623	2.469	-2.91	0.0657	0.0485
426	13.09	30.02	93.0	0.0	1.75	0.1500	0.5082	86.7	79.8	2.623	2.469	-2.91	0.0299	0.0203
434	13.09	30.02	93.0	-0.5	1.99	0.1517	0.5082	86.5	82.1	2.597	2.457	-3.14	0.0293	0.0195
435	17.29	39.65	93.0	-0.5	1.17	0.1125	0.2913	83.6	83.0	2.597	2.506	-2.21	0.0135	0.0142
436	17.42	39.95	93.0	-1.0	1.40	0.1160	0.2870	84.4	82.9	2.571	2.489	-2.54	0.0131	0.0133
437	17.44	39.99	93.0	-1.5	1.54	0.1271	0.2863	83.4	82.4	2.544	2.493	-2.46	0.0312	0.0135

Key:

No.: run number from test book 5

U: model speed in tank

Vfs: Froude scaled full scale speed in knots

W: weight of model, lbs

%xg: xcg shift as % of cushion length from cushion center from report

Trim: trim angle, deg, from report *(input)*

Ht: transom draft/Yk; Yk demi-hull keel offset from report *(input)*

Cl: hull lift coefficient, $W/1/2\rho U^2 Yk^2$ *(calc)*

%WA: percent of W supported by air *(experimental and calc)*

xcg: location of center of gravity forward of transom/Yk *(experimental and calc)*

Cd: hull drag coefficient, $D/1/2\rho U^2 Yk^2$ *(experimental and calc)*

sub – e: experimental

sub – c: CatSeaAir calculation

Description of the data is provided above below the table. The comparisons were made for all of the data for model Condition 1. The differences in the several Conditions are generally superficial non-systematic variations in the model. Condition 1 was considered adequate coverage.

Choosing not to invert the equations of motion for steady trim and transom draft avoided the time stepping and actually made the CatSeaAir calculations much simpler. CatSeaAir was first run with WA set to zero with the trim and draft set to the Table 1 measured values. This produced W_h and xcg_h, with W_h being the weight supported by hydrodynamics/hydrostatics with zero air cushion pressure at the given trim and draft, with xcg_h being the center of application of W_h. Weight and moment component summation gives:

$$1 = \frac{WA}{W} + \frac{W_h}{W} \qquad (8)$$

$$xcg = \frac{WA}{W} xcg_A + \frac{W_h}{W} xcg_h \qquad (9)$$

with xcg_A being the known center of the air cushion from the transom.

Equation (8) is first solved for WA/W, which is substituted into (9) to calculate the required xcg. These are the values listed in Table 1 as %WAc and %xcgc[1].

Fig 4a and 4b are plots of the trim and draft input values from Table 1 for each of the three model weights.

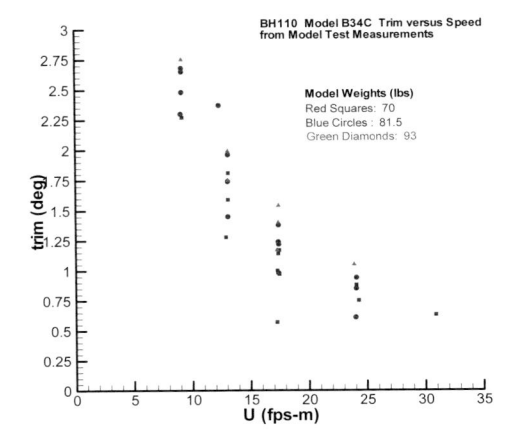

Fig 4a: Measured Trim versus Speed for the Three Model Test Weights of 70, 81.5 and 93 lbs.

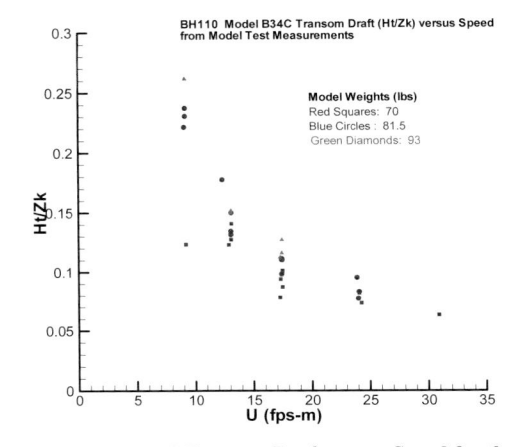

Fig 4b: Measured Transom Draft versus Speed for the Three Model Test Weights of 70, 81.5 and 93 lbs.

The Table 1 data displayed on Fig 4a and Fig 4b is difficult to plot as conventional curves versus speed because so much is varying. Some of the variation is systematic input variation and some seems to be random experimental variability. It seems to be best displayed

---

[1] %xcg = 100(xcg − xcg_A)/xcg_A

in terms of the unconnected data points as "scatter graphs," as on Fig 4. The interpretation of Fig 4, and of the additional scatter graphs to follow, is that the degree of cluster at any speed reflects the degree of data consistency, with high cluster reflecting high consistency. Spreading vertically does correctly occur due to the xcg variations.

It must be kept in mind that the trim and draft data of Fig 4 is considered the input data from the experiments.

So the calculated output from this input, via CatSeaAir, should reflect, at best, the same level of scatter.

Figs 5 to 10 are the calculated WA fraction and %xcg forward of mid-cushion from (8) and (9) via the Table 1 runs for each of the three weights.

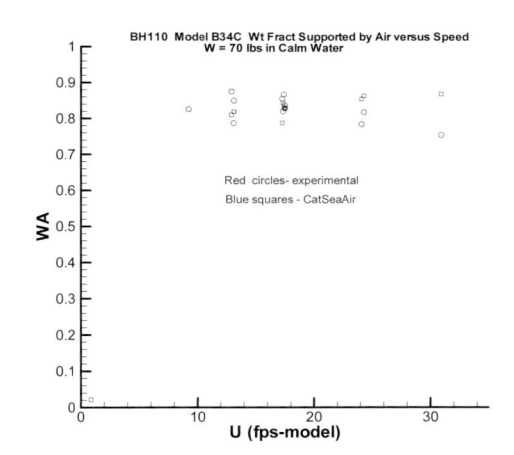

Fig 5: Calculated WA/W versus Model Speed for 70 lb Model

The calculated WA/W displayed on Figs 5, 6, and 7 are considered to be quite close to the experimental in consideration of the variability of the input trim and transom draft measurements displayed on Fig 4.

As for the xcg data on Figs 8, 9, and 10, the test values were considered to be part of the experimental set-up. Except for a few irregular points, the xcg implied by CatSeaAir are slightly lower (xcg further aft) and the variability, or sensitivity to speed differences, seems to be lower, in general. It should be kept in mind that a 1% CG shift is only about 3/8 inch relative to the length of the 7-foot model. It seems likely that movements of this magnitude would be hard to set by the simple balance and leveling methods used. And then there was uncertainty about "in air" or "in hover" cited in the preceding.

The xcg comparisons are considered to contribute to establishing the validity of CatSeaAir, and not to diminish it.

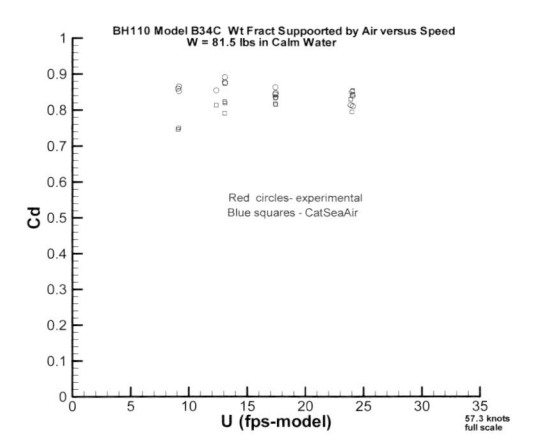

Fig 6: Calculated WA/W versus Model Speed for 81.5 lb Model

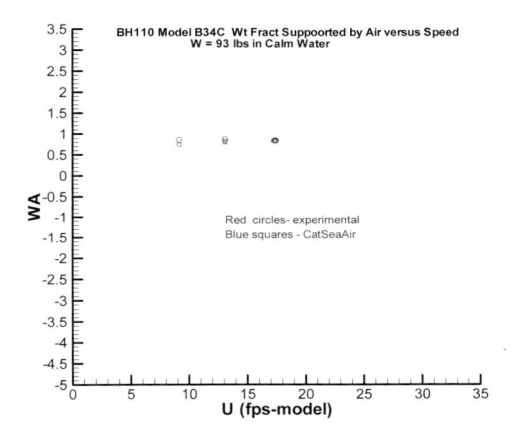

Fig 7: Calculated WA/W versus Model Speed for 93 lb Model

Another supportive CatSeaAir calculation is considered to be that of the calm-water drag. This is Figs 11, 12, and 13, in the same format as the preceding comparisons.

Drag, in representing craft resistance, is of primary importance in the calm-water performance prediction. It is also a second order variable and generally challenging to predict with accuracy.

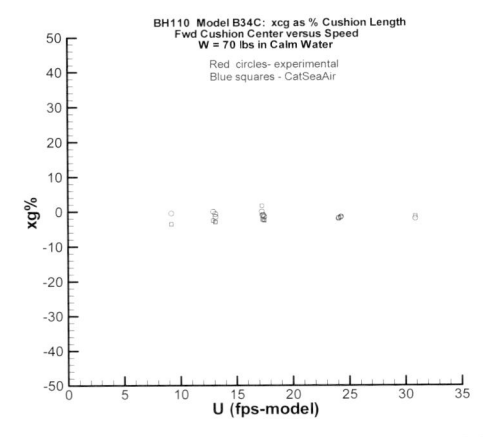

Fig 8: Calculated %xcg Versus Speed for 70lb Model

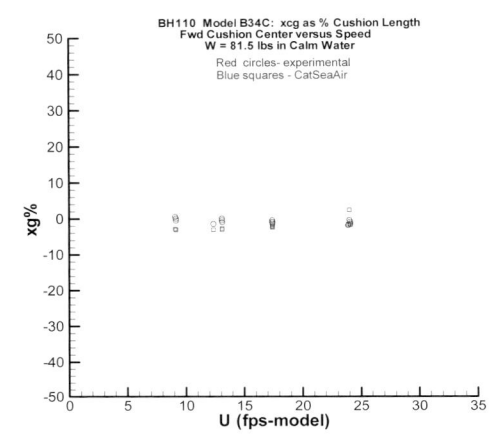

Fig 9: Calculated %xcg Versus Speed for 81.5lb Model

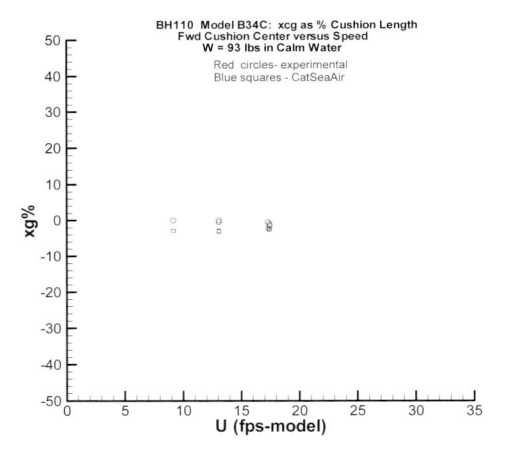

Figure 10: Calculated %xcg Versus Speed for 93lb Model

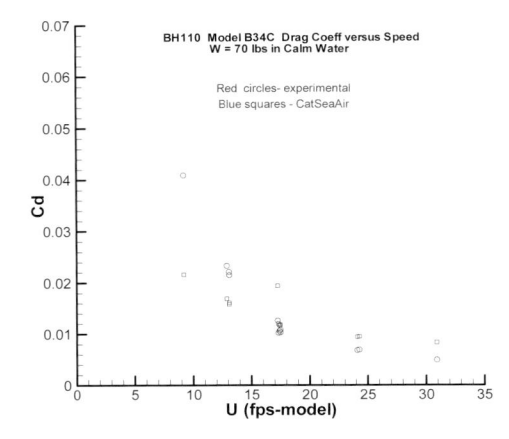

Figure 11: Calculated Cd Versus Speed for 70lb Model

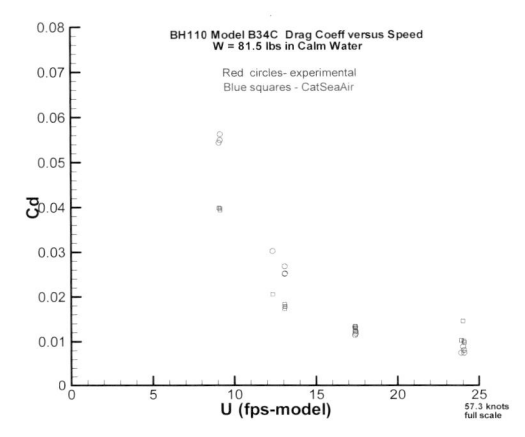

Figure 12: Calculated Cd Versus Speed for 81.5lb Model

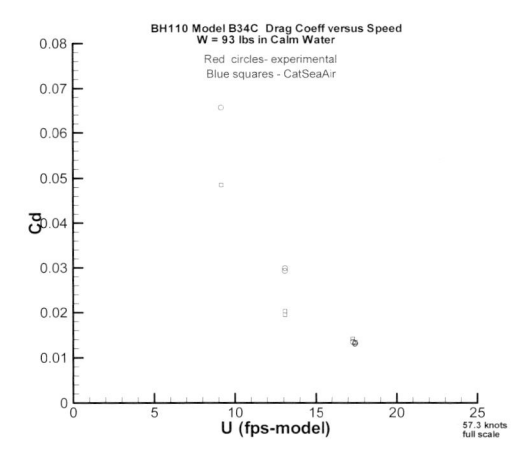

Figure 13: Calculated Cd versus Speed for 93lb Model

As a matter of record, the drag coefficient is by the previous definition:

$$C_d = \frac{drag}{\frac{1}{2}\rho U^2 Z_k} \qquad (10)$$

As these last three figures show, the calculated calm water drag is generally a little lower than the measured, but with the differences diminishing at the higher speeds. This is just as would be expected in consideration of the theory employed in CatSeaAir. The Maruo theory is a linearized theory and looses some effectiveness at lower Froude number corresponding to the lower speeds of the test series; 9 ft/sec was the lowest model speed tested. The length Froude number at U = 9 fps is .6, still high speed but associated with substantial wave-making and wave resistance. At the model speed of 30 fps, on the other-hand, Fn = 2, for which the wave making should be small and within the linearized theory. This is the observation in Figures 10 to 13.

Analysis versus Experiments - Seaway Dynamics

The principal test data reported from the seaway measurements were statistical accelerations at the bow, center of gravity, and transom.

The model test procedure was somewhat different than that of the calculation by CatSeaAir; the model was accelerated to speed in the fully-developed wave system and then measurements were made for a distance of 110 ft down the tank. The data was then statistically processed.

In the CatSeaAir calculations the model is started with the calm water equilibrium at the test speed and the wave system is ramped-up to the fully developed condition over a short time period. The statistical processing of the calculated data is delayed in the interest of achieving a statistically stationary response to the seaway.

The comparisons were limited to two of the seaway runs: #390 for Sea-State 2 and W = 70 lbs model weight and #438 for Sea-State 3 at W = 93 lbs model weight. The seaway runs were both fewer in number and time intensive to compute, as discussed. The speed for both runs is the design speed of nominally 17.45 fps (40 knots full scale). The starting calm-water runs are #393 at 70lbs and #437 at 93lbs. As shown on Table 1, the CG positions for these two cases are essentially identical; the calculated xcgc and WAc are used in all the seaway calculations. The results are summarized on Table 2 to follow.

There was a concern about achieving statistically stationary response from the numerical time-stepping solution in CatSeaAir, as well as in the model tests. The scaled Pierson-Moskowitz spectrum was inverted into the time domain for the time-stepping response solution by CatSeaAir. The wave input is thereby stationary random. The response output is meaningless as a statistical measure, e.g., RMS, unless it is likewise statistically stationary.

Figure 14 is a plot of calculated displacement response components of the Run #438 computation at SS3.

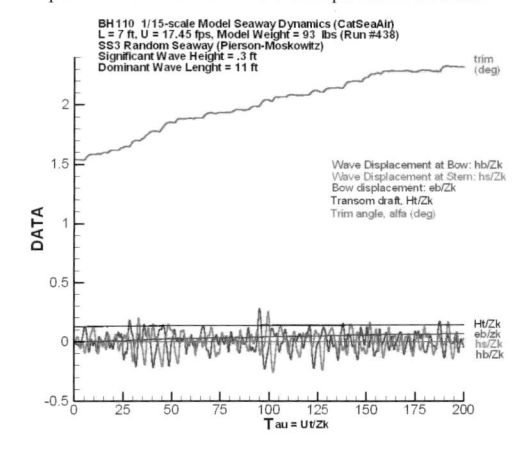

Fig 14: Displacement Distributions versus Time from Seaway Dynamic Analysis; Run 438, SS3, W = 93 lbs, U =17.43 fps, 10,000 time steps

The seawave dimensionless elevations at the bow and stern, as converted from the Pierson-Moskowitz spectrum with the .3 ft significant wave height (4.5 ft full scale), is plotted along the dimensionless time axis of Fig 14. The seaway is ramped-up as an inverse exponential from calm-water to its full stationary state at about $\tau = 10$, where the statistical data collection commences. Note that Ut is the distance the model has traveled down the tank. With the demi-hull keel offset Zk = 1.05 ft, $\tau = Ut/Zk = 10$ is slightly more than one model length of travel.

Figure 14 clearly shows that the model is predicted to have risen in the time mean, more in the bow than in the stern. This is because the wave pounding in slams is dominantly up, and dominantly in the bow, thus almost doubling the trim angle. The most relevant implication of Fig 14 is that the non-linear rise has essentially ceased at large time, which would imply that stationarity has been achieved. But it has taken 10,000 time steps at $\Delta\tau = .02$ to reach that state.

The companion SS2 time history (Table 2) although not shown, exhibits the same character, but converges to the apparent stationary random state slightly sooner.

Table 2: Seaway Dynamic Analysis – Calculations and Experiments

A. Run # 390 - SS2, U = 17.43 fps, W = 70 lbs

No.	N	Tau	D (ft)	Bow (RMS g's)	CG	Trans	Cl (Mean)	Cd	L/D
390	2500	50	52.5	0.485	0.103	0.254	0.229	0.0150	15.3
	5000	110	115.5	0.400	0.091	0.221	0.228	0.0135	16.8
	6000	120	126.0	0.420	0.095	0.246	0.228	0.0137	16.7
	8000	160	168.0	0.374	0.099	0.245	0.227	0.0130	17.4
	10000	200	210.0	0.351	0.101	0.240	0.227	0.0127	17.9

From experiement / Calm Water Calculation

| 390 | 4190 | 105 | 110.0 | 0.250 | 0.190 | 0.140 | 0.217 | 0.0117 | 18.4 |

B. Run # 438 - SS3, U = 17.43 fps, W = 93 lbs

No.	N	Tau	D (ft)	Bow (RMS g's)	CG	Trans	Cl (Mean)	Cd	L/D
438	3000	60	63.0	0.418	0.128	0.158	0.306	0.0297	10.3
	5000	110	115.5	0.390	0.129	0.160	0.305	0.0273	11.2
	6000	120	126.0	0.380	0.125	0.175	0.304	0.0258	11.8
	8000	160	168.0	0.381	0.123	0.175	0.304	0.0248	13.1
	10000	200	210.0	0.354	0.115	0.168	0.303	0.0231	21.2

From experiement / Calm Water Calculation

| 438 | 4190 | 105 | 110.0 | 0.520 | 0.330 | 0.210 | 0.286 | 0.0135 | 21.2 |

Turning to Table 2, the 10,000 time step analysis was done using the dump-restart capability of CatSeaAir for both of the calculations; the files are written on the dump and saved. The total of 10,000 time steps is accomplished in 5 segments for each of the runs A and B; the distance down the tank (D) corresponding to the advancing time is shown. It is being assumed that stationary response is achieved at 10,000 steps on the basis of Fig 14.

It is relevant to consider that the actual tank data collection was over 110 ft of tank length, with the measurements commencing from a transient start-up in the wave system.

But the 5th – 7th columns impact acceleration data of Table 2 would suggest that the stationary random state of the model response was hardly achieved in 110 ft.

The experimental statistics on RMS model acceleration is the last line in each of the Table 2 segments A and B. It is noteworthy that the Lockheed tank tests were done under Bell-Halter (now TEXTRON Marine and Land Systems) as an engineering design effort in the development of the BH110, and not as a research program. The model at 7 feet (1/15 scale) was really too small for the expectation of high absolute accuracy. Relative, rather than absolute, accuracy is needed for continuous improvement in design development. In view of both the experimental and numerical modeling uncertainties, the Table 2 comparisons are considered to exhibit supportive agreement.

One further Table 2 observation is worthy of attention. The right sides of the tables are calculated lift and drag coefficients. The upper-right sub-tables are the time means of the variations, with the last line being the calm-water calculated values of Table 1. There are no measurements available for the lift coefficients in the seaway. In this regard, the Cl might be expected to be close to the calm water value, even in waves. Cl is equivalent to the boat weight in calmwater. But continuing from Table 2B, for example, the predicted time mean Cl at $\tau = 200$ is 6% above the calm water Cl. It is this increased mean lift that produces the rise of the vessel above its calm water position, which is indicated and discussed on Figure 14.

The increase in mean drag over the calm water level indicated in Table 2 is believed to be consistent with expected levels of added resistance in waves. The drag increase is 71% over calm-water drag in the SS3 seaway at 40 knots full scale, by the predicted numbers of Table 2.

Hull Pressure and Structural Loading

It would seem inappropriate for a paper with "pressure and structural loading" featured in the title to not include material on pressure and structural loading. But pressure and structural loading was not part of the BH-110 experimental program, so there was nothing on this material to report from the focus of the work.

In the total development program, however, unsteady hull pressure distributions on a notional 10m bi-hull SES with B/L = .275 and Fn = 2.6 were evaluated. A sample of this is included here for the purpose of demonstrating the use of the extended CatSeaAir (EDITH 2-AG) code for dynamic load analysis in the seaway.

Fig 15 is the distribution of force coefficient, $C_f(x,\tau)$, corresponding to the predicted pressure sectionally integrated at the time $\tau = 50$ for the notional SES design at 75% cushion support.

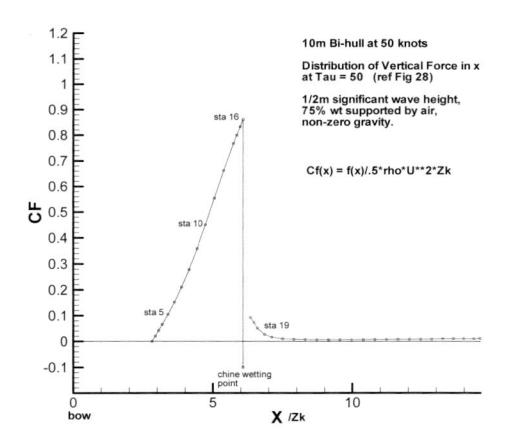

Fig 15: Vertical Force Distribution in x at time $\tau = 50$ for 75% Cushion Support, Non-zero Gravity

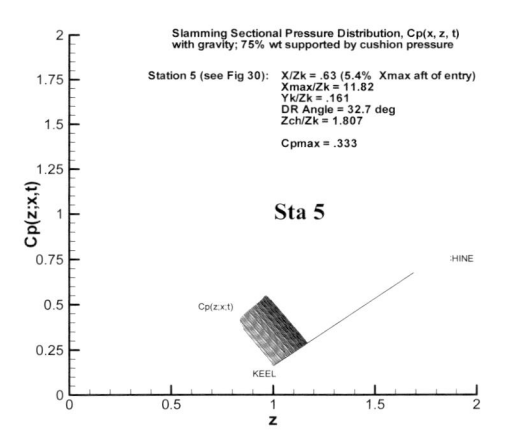

Fig 16: Half Demi-hull Section $C_p(x, z, t)$ at Station 5, 5.4% of Wetted Length Aft of Entry (refer to Figure 15); 75% Wt by Cushion Pressure

The near discontinuity on Fig 15 is the occurrence of 'chine-wetting.' Just as in calm-water planing, the hull pressure (and lift) drop by an order of magnitude when the jet-head reaches the chine, proceeding outward. This is for the case of approximately cylindrical wetted geometry in x at chine-wetting and aft, which is the common case and the case here. Vessel-generated gravity waves then boost the pressure and lift aft in calm water. In the case of Fig 15 at $\tau = 50$, the instantaneous motions and ambient waves, along with the cylindrical geometry, are responsible for almost nullifying the pressure loading aft.

The impact acceleration is largest at the bow around this time, implying high sectional and contour pressure loading there. Therefore, bow contour pressure distributions have been plotted at $\tau = 50$ at each of the four sections marked on Fig 15. The pressure plots are Figs 16 through 19. The plots are transverse in z from the demi-hull keel to the chine with the heights of the bars representing the pressure magnitudes (The colors on Figures 16 through 19 are intended only to indicate the distribution of points at which the pressures were computed.) The vertical component of the integral of the pressure across the section at each of numbered stations is the values of the corresponding vertical-axis force coefficients on Fig 15.

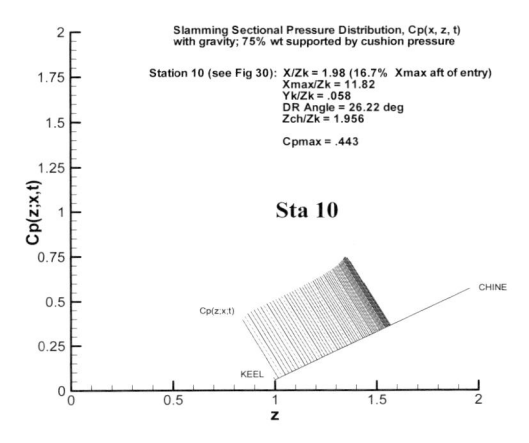

Figure 17: Half Demi-hull Section $C_p(x, z, t)$ at Station 10, 16.7% of Wetted Length Aft of Entry (refer to Fig 15); 75% Wt by Cushion Pressure

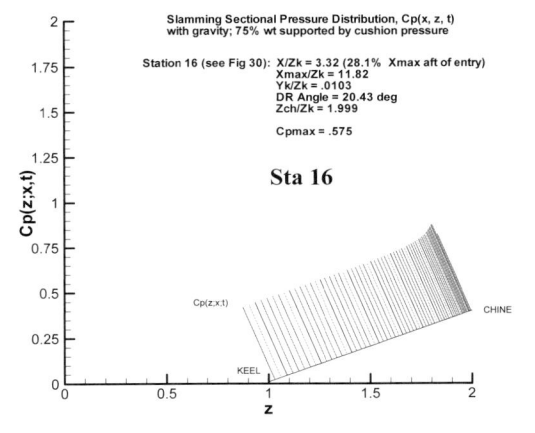

Figure 18: Half Demi-hull Section $C_p(x, z, t)$ at Station 16, 28.1% of Wetted Length Aft of Entry (refer to Fig 15); 75% Wt by Cushion Pressure

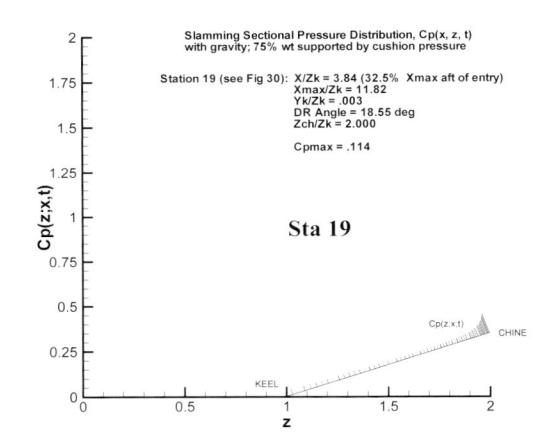

Figure 19: Half Demi-hull Section $C_p(x, z, t)$ at Station 19, 32.5% of Wetted Length Aft of Entry (refer to Fig 15); 75% Wt by Cushion Pressure

Recognize that Figs 16 through 19 are the pressures over the four section contours at a single time. The next time on the output record would show the pressures at the same sections slightly changed, and so forth. The time and spatially varying pressure field is available in this form for all times (10,000 steps) and for any of the 101 x-sections specified.

Conclusions

CatSeaAir is a computationally-intensive theoretical tool which has demonstrated useful agreement with the limited test data available. Pending further validation it could provide reliable prediction of structural loads on high-speed SES/Catamaran hull forms in a seaway.

It would be in order to further consider the quasi-steady approximation on wave effects employed for the time domain seaway dynamic analysis. It is not clear that this routine can be improved much for purposes of a design oriented computation tool for lifting hull forms. But its accuracy should be more thoroughly checked than time has yet permitted.

Probably of more importance is better treatment of the SES end seal leakage and drag. Seal drag has been included in CatSeaAir, but it is empirical, as deduced from past studies on operating SES craft. The air leakage rates largely determine the lift fan power. The drag equivalent to fan power was not included in the resistance estimates in the BH 110 model tests, and is therefore not an issue in the data comparisons of the last section. SES seal design reliability remains as a significant uncertainly in the technology of this very important craft type.

Acknowledgements

The authors have to thank primarily the Ship Structures Committee, who supported the work for two years; included, of course, is the US Coast Guard and the American Bureau of Shipping for their work in support of SSC.

The authors also thank Ms Leila Tahvildari at the University of New Orleans for her competence in producing the finished document.

This paper reflects the views of the authors and does not represent an official position, policy, or recommendation by the U.S. Coast Guard.

References

Von Karman, T. 1929 The impact of seaplane floats during landing. NACA TN 321 Washington, D.C., Oct.

Wagner, H. 1932 Uber stoss-und gleitvorgange an der oberflache von flussigkeiten. *Zeitschrift fur Angewandte Mathematik und Mechanik*, 12, 193, Aug.

Maruo, H. 1967 High and low-aspect ratio approximation of planing surfaces. *Schiffstechnik*, 72.

Tuck, E. 1975 Low-aspect ratio flat-ship theory. *Journal of Hydronautics*, 9, 1, January.

Stability and Seakeeping Tests with a 1/15 Scale Model of the Bell Aerospace Company Model B-34C, LMSC/D682700, December 1979.

Vorus, W. 1996 A flat cylinder theory for vessel impact and steady planing resistance. *Journal of Ship Research*, 40, 2, June.

Recent Hydrodynamic Tool Development and Validation for Motions and Slam Loads on Ocean-Going High-Speed Vessels

Woei-Min Lin [1], Matthew Collette [1], David Lavis [2], Stuart Jessup [3], John Kuhn [4]

[1] Science Applications International Corporation, Advanced Systems and Technology Division
Bowie, Maryland, USA
[2] CDI Marine, Systems Development Division
Severna Park, Maryland, USA
[3] Naval Surface Warfare Center, Carderock Division
Bethesda, Maryland, USA
[4] Science Applications International Corporation, Naval Hydrodynamics Division
San Diego, California, USA

Abstract

The marine community continues to push the boundaries of high-speed marine transportation, with both commercial and military operators seeking potential solutions for the safe and economic transportation of time-sensitive cargos on trans-oceanic routes. The design of such vessels becomes more complex when operational requirements dictate the use of shallow-draft ports with minimal supporting infrastructure. To provide the naval architect with a set of practical tools to design this type of vessel, the Office of Naval Research (ONR) commissioned, in 2005, several development and validation research projects as part of a high-speed sealift (HSSL) program. This paper presents the results of several key studies covering hullform development, prediction of unsteady motions and hull structural loads, model tests, and code validation undertaken by the SAIC-led HSSL research team.

Keywords

HSSL; High-speed; Sealift; Computation; Hydrodynamics; Simulation; Model test; Validation.

Introduction

There is continued interest in military circles for high-speed vessels that can combine trans-oceanic range with high sustained speed, yet still access austere ports. There are many challenges to designing such a vessel; one central challenge is obtaining reasonable estimates of the hydrodynamic performance of candidate hullforms. The primary objective of the SAIC-led HSSL effort was to assemble, evaluate, extend, and validate a set of software tools for the hydrodynamic design and performance assessment of HSSL ships. This set of software tools must reliably address ship performance issues such as unsteady motions and wave loads, impact loads, resistance, added resistance, maneuvering, viscous effects, and shallow-water effects. This set of tools must also handle innovative design features that may be used on such vessels, including multi-hull, SES (Surface Effect Ship), and waterjet propulsion.

To test the ability of this set of software tools, an innovative multi-hull vessel (HSSL hullform) design was developed that meets the ONR's design objectives. This HSSL hullform design combines aspects of catamaran, SES, and SWATH (Small Water plane Area Twin Hull) technology. It is capable of transporting 4,000 short tons of payload at high speed (43 knots) on trans-oceanic voyages, completing at-sea cargo transfers, and entering ports with less than 6.5m available water draft. Minimizing resistance, and hence deadweight consumed by fuel, was identified early on as a key design challenge in this effort. Building on the preliminary design developed by CDI Marine's Systems Development Division (CDIM-SDD), a process for resistance reduction through computational shape optimization was used. Subsequent integration of the resistance predictions with high-fidelity codes into the design optimization procedure was carried out by CDIM-SDD to develop the final HSSL hullform for model tests and code evaluations.

Model tests of the HSSL hullform were carried out at the Naval Surface Warfare Center Carderock Division (NSWCCD) to show the ship's performance characteristics and to generate validation data for the software tools. The tests were done at all three operation modes: catamaran, SES, and SWATH. In addition, a scale-model of the Sea Fighter hullform was also tested to generate a selected set of maneuvering force data and wetdeck slamming pressure using novel slam panels developed at NSWCCD.

The software tools selected and evaluated in this effort include ComPASS (Commercial Parametric Assessment of Ship Systems), Das Boot, VERES, LAMP (the Large Amplitude Motion Program), FANS (Finite-Analytic Navier-Stokes), and SHAPE. These software tools were validated to the extent possible and extended based on specified program needs.

More detailed description of these software tools, the HSSL hullform design, the hullform optimization process, model tests, validation results, lessons learned, and recommendations for future development are presented in this paper.

Software Tool Set for Design and Performance Predictions

The primary objective of the HSSL effort was to assemble, evaluate, extend, and validate a set of software tools for design and performance assessment of HSSL ships. The software tools were selected based on ONR's target performance prediction capabilities. The following criteria were used:

- Capabilities that are needed for HSSL ship design and performance analysis
- Physics-based rather than empirical approaches
- Maturity of capabilities and readiness to be used for its intended purposes
- Past performance experiences of the tools.

The major selected software tools and their intended functions are shown in Table 1 below.

Table 1: Selected Software Tools in the HSSL Program

Code Capabilities	ComPASS	Das Boot	VERES	LAMP	FANS
Unsteady motions and loads in waves			•	•	•
Wave resistance	•	•		•	•
Added resistance	•			•	•
Water-jet propulsion	•			•	
Maneuvering				•	•
Shallow water effects	•			•	•
Multi-hulls	•	•	•	•	•
Surface-effect ship	•			•	
Viscous effects					•

In addition to the software tools listed in the table, a shape optimization code, SHAPE, was also used. SHAPE can be used with all the codes described in the table for hullform optimization.

A brief description of each one of the software tools and their roles in the HSSL program is given below.

ComPASS

ComPASS is an acronym for "Commercial Parametric Assessment of Ship Systems". This software represents a unique design tool for navigating the ship design space. It has been widely validated and utilized in support of many government programs, building upon a long legacy (28+ years) of design synthesis module development at CDIM-SDD. The technical goals driving the software development were to provide early concept exploration and platform optimization, and to improve the process of evaluating the cost and potential technical benefits of newly emerging technologies to the overall ship system and the fleet as a whole.

During the development of ComPASS, the overall objective was to establish a design synthesis tool that recognizes current or projected future fleet requirements and operational priorities, and permits a realistic assessment of the cost benefits and "whole-ship" impacts of emerging technologies. Other common uses of the model include those in which the cost impact of changing operational requirements, such as vessel speed and range, are easily examined, and those in which "design-to-cost" trade-offs are conducted to determine the preferred selection of hullform, structural materials, and subsystem choices.

In the HSSL effort, ComPASS was the primary engine used for the HSSL hullform design. It was used first for the baseline HSSL hullform design and then with the embedded resistance surrogate model from Das Boot to produce the final HSSL hullform.

Das Boot

Das Boot is a de-singularized potential flow code with a nonlinear free surface boundary condition and iterative sinkage and trim. It is used for the analysis of steady speed performance in calm water for various types of surface vessels, including monohulls, catamarans, and trimarans. A version of the code with lift is available.

Wave resistance is calculated by both pressure integration and wave cut analysis. Skin friction drag is estimated with friction line methods, and form drag is estimated with a form factor. Das Boot has undergone extensive validation based on tank test data. More detail about Das Boot can be found in Wyatt (2000).

In the HSSL effort, Das Boot was the primary code for ship resistance prediction. It was used extensively with SHAPE for the HSSL hullform optimization.

VERES

VERES (Vessel Responses) is a strip theory program for predicting ship motions and loads with several extensions to increase accuracy for high-speed craft. VERES implements both conventional strip theory established by Salvesen, Tuck, and Faltinsen (1970), and the high-speed strip theory developed by Faltinsen and Zhao (1991), which extends the accuracy of conventional strip theory to higher speeds by considering the interaction effects between strips (this theory is also known as 2½D theory). Further extensions to the high-speed theory are available, which include hull interaction effects for catamarans. The basic version of the VERES is implemented as a linear, frequency-domain code that generates standard response amplitude operators (RAOs) for both motions and load responses. VERES is capable of calculating global resultant loads in both longitudinal and transverse directions, and can also account for torsional loading. Empirical add-on models are available for viscous roll damping, foils, and slamming pressure predictions. Both short and long-term post-processors are available for making statistical motion and load prediction in specific sea-states and for a given operational scatter diagram and operational profile. A time-domain solver is also implemented, which allows non-linearities from hydrostatic and Froude-Krylov forces to be estimated.

LAMP

The Large Amplitude Motions Program is a time-domain simulation model specifically developed for computing the motions and loads of a ship operating in extreme sea conditions. LAMP System development began with a 1988 DARPA project for advanced nonlinear ship motion simulation, and has continued under the sponsorship of the U.S. Navy, the U. S. Coast Guard, the American Bureau of Shipping (ABS), and SAIC's IR&D program. LAMP has been used extensively for performance assessment of ship motions and wave loads in the past 15 years (Shin *et. al.*, 2003).

LAMP uses a time-stepping approach in which all forces and moments acting on the ship, including those due to wave-body interaction, appendages, control systems, and green-water-on-deck, are computed at each time step and the 6-DOF equations of motions are integrated in the time-domain using a 4th-order Runge-Kutta algorithm. In addition to motions, LAMP also computes main hull-girder loads using a rigid or elastic beam model and includes an interface for developing Finite-Element load data sets from the 3D pressure distribution.

The core of the LAMP System is the 3D solution of the wave-body interaction problem in the time-domain (Lin and Yue, 1990, 1993). A 3D perturbation velocity potential is computed by solving an initial boundary value problem using a potential flow boundary element or "panel" method. A combined body boundary condition is imposed that incorporates the effects of forward speed, the ship motion (radiation), and the scattering of the incident wave (diffraction). The potential is computed using either a hybrid singularity model that uses both transient Green functions and Rankine sources (Lin *et al.*, 1999), or a Rankine singularity model with a damping beach condition. Once the velocity potential is computed, Bernoulli's equation is used to compute the hull pressure distribution, including the second-order velocity terms.

The perturbation velocity potential can be solved over either the mean wetted surface (the "body linear" solution) or over the instantaneously wetted portion of the hull surface beneath the incident wave (the "body nonlinear" approach). In either case, it is assumed that both the radiation and diffraction waves are small compared to the incident wave and the incident wave slope is small so that the free-surface boundary conditions can be linearized with respect to the incident-wave surface. Similarly, the incident wave forcing (Froude-Krylov) and hydrostatic restoring force can also be computed either on the mean wetted surface or on the wetted hull up to the incident wave.

The combinations of the body linear and body nonlinear solutions of the perturbation potential and the hydrostatic/Froude-Krylov forces provide multiple solution "levels" for the ship-wave interaction problem. These levels are:

- LAMP-1 (body linear solution): both perturbation potential and hydrostatic/Froude-Krylov forces are solved over the mean wetted hull surface
- LAMP-2 (approximate body nonlinear solution): the perturbation potential is solved over the mean wetted hull surface while the hydrostatic/Froude-Krylov forces are solved over the instantaneous wetted hull surface
- LAMP-3 (approximate body nonlinear solution with large lateral displacements): similar to LAMP-2, but the hydrodynamic formulation is revised so that large lateral displacements and yaw angles are accounted for; this allows accurate maneuvering simulations
- LAMP-4 (Body nonlinear solution): both the perturbation potential and the hydrostatic/Froude-Krylov forces are solved over the instantaneous wetted hull surface.

For most seakeeping problems, the most practical level is the "approximate body-nonlinear" (LAMP-2) solution, which combines the body-linear solution of the perturbation potential with body-nonlinear hydrostatic-restoring and Froude-Krylov wave forces. This latter approach captures a significant portion of nonlinear effects in most ship-wave problems at a fraction of the computational effort for the general body-nonlinear formulation. However, body-nonlinear hydrodynamics and nonlinear incident wave effects can be important, depending on ship geometry and operating conditions.

Other than the ship motions and wave loads calculations, LAMP also has extensive capabilities for solving many ship hydrodynamics and dynamics related problems such as impact loads, whipping responses, wetdeck slamming loads, green water effects (Liut *et al.*, 2002; Zhang *et al.*, 2005), parametric roll (Shin *et al.*, 2004) ship maneuvering in calm water and in waves (Lin *et. al.*, 2006), and ship-ship interactions (Zhang *et al.*, 2007). Even though LAMP is a potential-flow based program, it has the ability to incorporate external force models and has been used extensively as a dynamic simulation tools for marine vehicles.

LAMP was the primary code in the HSSL program for prediction of ship motions, wave loads, impact loads, added resistance in waves, and maneuvering. Under the program, LAMP was further developed to include the waterjet propulsion capability, to provide an initial SES modeling capability, and to use pre-corrected Fast Fourier Transfer (pFFT) method for an order of magnitude computation speedup of body nonlinear hydrodynamics calculations and problems involving large number of panels (>10,000).

FANS

The FANS code was developed by Dr. H.C. Chen at Texas A&M University (Chen and Yu, 2006; Pontaza *et al.*, 2005). It consists of the following main components: (1) finite-analytic method for the solution of compressible and incompressible Reynolds-Averaged Navier-Stokes (RANS) equations and energy equation in general curvilinear coordinates; (2) dynamic chimera domain decomposition technique for overlapped, embedded, or matched grids including relative motions; (3) near-wall Reynolds stress (second-moment) and two-layer k-ε turbulence models for turbulent boundary layer and wake flows; (4) large eddy simulation for unsteady chaotic eddy motions; (5) linear and nonlinear wave effects; (6) level-set method for interface-capturing between two different fluids; (7) detailed propeller flow simulations or interactive coupling with propeller performance programs; (8) coupling with six-degree-of-freedom motion program for ship, structure, wave, and current interactions; and (9) multi-processor parallelization for large-scale CFD applications. The combination of these methods provides a unique capability for modeling complex fluid flow and heat transfer, including viscous and violent free surface effects, around practical three-dimensional configurations. The FANS code has been used for a wide range of applications including the ship berthing operations, modular hybrid pier and multiple ship interactions, ship-ship interactions in navigation channel, unsteady propeller flow analyses under design and off-design operations, complete propeller-ship flow simulations, vortex-induced vibrations, green water effects, dam breaking, tank sloshing, bridge pier scour, abutment scour, channel migration, and internal cooling and film cooling of turbine blades.

SHAPE

The SHAPE code (Kuhn *et al.*, 2007) is a geometric hullform optimization tool that has been under periodic development by SAIC since the early 1990s. The optimization technique is based on sequential linear programming, and the geometric model is based on a series of basis functions that are added to a baseline design.

The coefficients of the basis functions are the unknowns of the optimization problem. The SHAPE code finds values for these unknowns that minimize a user-defined objective function subject to user-defined constraints. A generic architecture is available for the objective function and constraints. This allows the use of virtually any tool for their calculation. To facilitate this, each basis function is individually applied to the baseline design and the resulting series of hulls is evaluated by whatever tool is desired. The results of the evaluations are then used to derive the influence of each basis function on the metric that is calculated by the tool. The influence of each basis function is formulated as a derivative with respect to the coefficient of the basis function. For each metric of interest, these derivatives are used to define a Taylor Series Expansion about the point in design space that is defined by the baseline design. Having done this, each expansion is then input to the SHAPE code via the objective function or a constraint.

The SHAPE code also contains an assortment of relatively common objective functions and naval architectural constraints. In combination with the generic architecture described above, the code is capable of performing a broad range of optimization tasks.

It has been used for ship design and yacht design with objective functions based on isolated metrics (such as wave resistance), and also integrated metrics that involve comprehensive performance simulation. The SHAPE code, together with the Das Boot code, was used for HSSL hullform shape optimization in the HSSL program.

HSSL Hullform Design

The ability of the software tools was tested on an innovative multi-hull HSSL hullform. This HSSL hullform was designed to a demanding set of performance targets (speed $\geq$ 43 knots, un-refueled range $\geq$ 5000 nautical miles, payload $\approx$ 4000 tons, draft at port entry $\leq$ 6.5m, and full performance through at least sea state 4) necessitating a short overall length (~170m), high installed power, and the ability to function as a SWATH to reduce motions. Thus, the concept vessel features a hybrid catamaran-SWATH-SES hull shape as shown Fig. 1. The vessel is designed to transit at 43 knots, which gives a full-load condition Froude number of 0.542.

A baseline hullform design was developed at the beginning of the program by CDIM-SDD using ComPASS, and the hullform design evolved during the course of the HSSL program. Fig. 2 shows a photograph of the final hull surface from a scale model built to test the vessel's motions, and Table 2 lists the main particulars of the design.

The most notable step in the design process was hullform optimization to reduce drag using a high-fidelity resistance code, Das Boot, and the shape optimization code, SHAPE. To meet the demanding set of design objectives, it was necessary to reduce the total drag. SHAPE and Das Boot were used to optimize the hullform to minimize the total drag at 43 knots in calm water. Although SHAPE is capable of enforcing large numbers of design constraints, they were intentionally avoided for this particular application because the HSSL concept was at a very early stage in the evolution of its design. It is beneficial to allow the optimization process to freely explore design space without the limitations that are imposed by constraints; this allows the process to fully exploit various elements of physics, including concept-specific issues such as hull-hull interaction. Since some of these issues are relatively unusual, it is no surprise that the optimal hullform has a somewhat unusual geometry. In the shape optimization process, only three constraints are enforced based on SES operational goals:

- Draft is prevented from increasing
- Displaced volume beneath the 21.3 foot waterline is prevented from decreasing
- The inboard hull surface above the 21.3 foot waterline is not included in optimization.

The total drag of the final hullform is about 25% less than the original baseline design at the design speed. It is worthwhile to note that although the shape optimization was done to minimize total drag only at 43 knots, the total drag of the optimized hullform is lower than that of the original baseline design at all speed tested (20 – 43 knots).

A particular challenge of this hullform is the step-like transition between catamaran and SWATH hullforms that occurs just above the full-load still waterline. This rapid transition and the high forward speed of the vessel mean that a time-domain non-linear motion and load simulation is most suited for analysis of this concept.

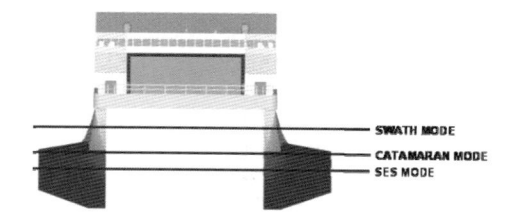

Fig. 1: Section View of the Conceptual HSSL Hullform

Fig. 2: View of the HSSL Hullform

Table 2: Key Parameters of the HSSL Design

Parameter	Value
LOA	179.0m
LWL	170.1m
Beam Overall	45.0m
Displacement	19,630mt
Transit Speed	43 Knots

Model Tests

One of the key objectives of the HSSL project is tool validation for HSSL ships. Model tests were carried out to validate key performance parameters of the HSSL hullform. In addition, model tests were carried out using the 1/15th scale *Sea Fighter* model to collect additional validation data. These two model test programs are described briefly below.

HSSL Hullform Model Test

The HSSL model test program represents a comprehensive data set for code validation with a numerically challenging hullform that can be used as an SES, catamaran, SWATH, or SWATH hull stabilized by SES cushion. A brief overview of the model test and data available is presented in this section.

A 1/55th scale model of the vessel was tested at the NSWCCD high-speed tank in December 2006. The model test program consisted of 282 runs, covering motions and resistance in all three operational modes. Fig. 3 shows snap shots of the model test in different modes. Both regular and irregular seas runs were made for the catamaran high-speed transit mode at 25 knots and 43 knots. Irregular seas runs were made for the SWATH mode at 0 knots, 5 knots, and 10 knots, both with and without the SES cushion deployed. Calm-water resistance runs were made for the catamaran mode and SES shallow-draft mode over the range of speeds that each mode operates in.

For each run, the following data was recorded at a 50Hz sampling speed: carriage speed, wave height at probe location, drag force, heave displacement, pitch displacement, vertical acceleration at the bow, vertical acceleration at the C.G., vertical acceleration at the stern, pitch rate, roll rate, and cushion pressures in the SES cushion and seals. In addition, all runs were videotaped at three angles, showing the profile of the vessel as well as bow and stern views. Digital photographs were taken of the model set-up, test configuration, and several of the runs.

After the completion of testing, the model was laser-scanned and the dimensions were compared to the specified dimensions. With the exception of some local swelling of the model where the unfinished interior got wet during testing, the dimensional scan revealed no significant discrepancies from the specified dimensions. Selected resistance runs were repeated during the experiment after the swelling was discovered, and no noticeable difference in the results was observed, suggesting that the swelling had a very minor impact on the responses of the model.

Fig. 3: Left: Catamaran Mode; Center: SWATH Mode; Right: Shallow Draft SES Mode

Sea Fighter Model Test

Additional model tests were carried out using a 1/15th scale *Sea Fighter* model. The *Sea Fighter*, FSF-1, is a high-speed experimental catamaran. The LOA is

79.9m, Beam is 22m, Draft is 3.5m, the maximum speed is ~ 50 knots, and the range is ~ 4000 nautical miles. Two sets of tests were performed using the 1/15 scale *Sea Fighter* model: (1) motion and slamming test for motion and slamming loads validation and (2) fix yaw towing test for hull lifting force prediction.

The motion and wetdeck slamming model tests were carried out at NSWCCD in October 2006. The *Sea Fighter* model was tested in regular head waves. Both fixed and 2-degree-of-freedom (DOF) tests were carried out. These tests provided the following data: kinematics for 2-DOF tests, pitch motion, heave motion, bow acceleration for 2-DOF tests, total body force for fixed tests, vertical force measured at the CG, pitch moment about the CG, and wetdeck slamming incidence and slamming pressures for both sets. A snap shot of the *Sea Fighter* encountering wetdeck slamming during the test is shown in Fig. 4.

Fig. 4: *Sea Fighter* Wetdeck Slamming

Results for four test conditions were analyzed carefully. Table 3 summarizes these four cases, referred to as "Spots". Note that two cases were free to heave and pitch, and two were fixed. As indicated in the table, wetdeck slamming was observed in Spots 149 and 206.

Table 3: Experimental Cases Provided by DSWCCD

Parameter	Spot 149	Spot 152	Spot 206	Spot 211
Model	Free	Free	Fixed	Fixed
Speed, kts	15.6	25.9	15.6	8.9
Froude No.	0.301	0.498	0.301	0.172
Dipl. LT	1377	1377	2079	2079
Draft, ft	11.96	11.96	16.31	16.31
Wave ht., ft	8.8	7.5	7.5	7.5
L_{wave}/L_{ship}	1.6	1	1	1
Slams	Yes	No	Yes	No

Sample time histories of measured wetdeck slamming pressure (equivalent full scale, psi) at pressure panels are shown in Fig. 5. The placement of the pressure panel under the wetdeck is shown in Fig. 6.

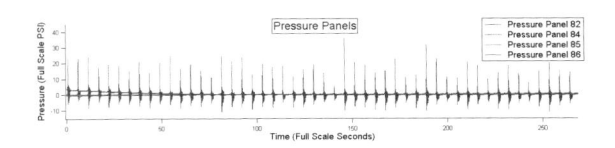

Fig. 5: Time History of Measured Wetdeck Slamming Pressure at Pressure Panels at Spot 149

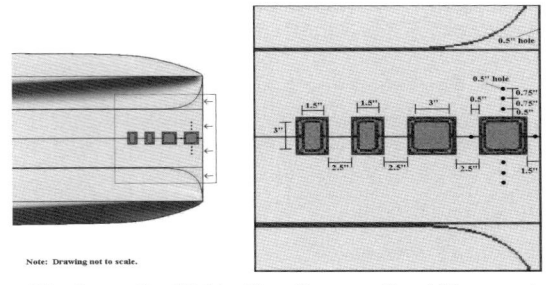

Fig. 6: *Sea Fighter* Slam Pressure Panel Placement

In addition to motions and wetdeck slamming, the model was also towed at fixed yaw angles to quantify the lifting forces and moments generated by the two hulls. These quantities are important to ship maneuvering predictions. More detail of this Sea Fighter model test is given in Lin *et al.* (2007).

Validation of Prediction Capabilities

Extensive validation of the prediction tools was done using the HSSL model test data and the Sea Fighter test data. A limited set of results are presented in this paper.

Ship Resistance

Das Boot resistance predictions have not yet been made for the model test hullform, which is somewhat heavier than the optimized design. However, existing Das Boot predictions for the optimized design have been scaled to estimate the model hullform resistance by applying a surrogate drag model that was specifically developed for the HSSL design. It is based on a series of predictions for scaled versions of the optimum that include displacement variation, so it is expected to be quite accurate for this purpose. A comparison of tank data with Das Boot results that have been scaled in this manner is shown in Fig. 7 for the high-speed catamaran mode of operation. The predicted and measured resistance is very well correlated. Overall, the Das Boot predictions and SHAPE optimization appear to have worked excellently for this design configuration.

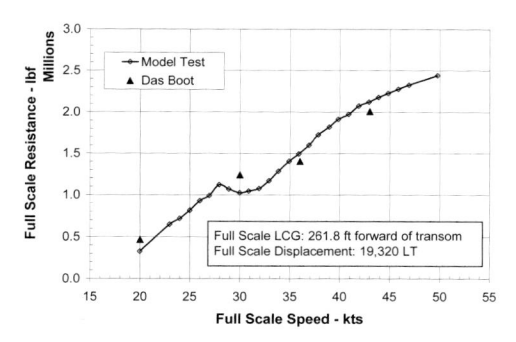

Fig. 7: Wave Resistance Comparison

Ship Motions and Slamming Loads

For both the *Sea Fighter* and HSSL hullform motion tests, the experimental wave time history was recorded by a wave probe. Fourier decomposition was used to reconstruct the experimental wave through a summation of sinusoidal wave components that could be input into the LAMP code, allowing LAMP to simulate the motion of the model for each tank pass on a wave-by-wave basis. For the *Sea Fighter* hullform, sample comparison of the heave and pitch motions at Spot 149 are plotted in Figs. 8 and 9, showing that LAMP captures the phasing and magnitude of the ship motion correctly.

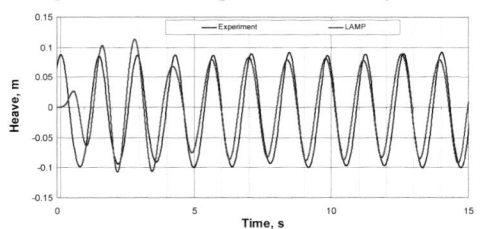

Fig. 8: Heave Motion Comparison for Spot 149

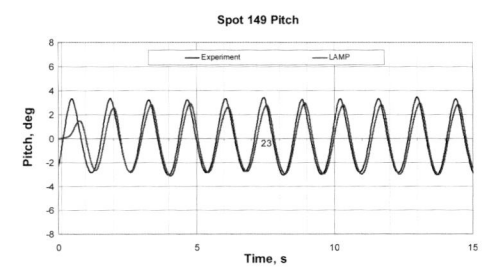

Fig. 9: Pitch Motion Comparison for Spot 149

Figs. 10 and 11 compare vertical acceleration near the bow and slamming pressure at Spot 149 for a run in which the *Sea Fighter* hullform was free to pitch and heave. Slamming pressures in the LAMP model are captured by coupling a semi-empirical wedge entry model to the motions and incident wave boundary conditions determined by the LAMP simulation. A slamming model based on the model proposed by Ge, Faltinsen, and Moan (2005) was used, and the forces resulting from such slamming pressures were then added to the motion of the vessel. As can be seen, LAMP captures the overall magnitude and phasing of both responses quite well. It should be noted that the pressure in the model test was obtained by converting a strain gauge measurement on the slam panel. As a result, the slamming pressure could appear to be negative after a slam event from structural vibration of the slam panel.

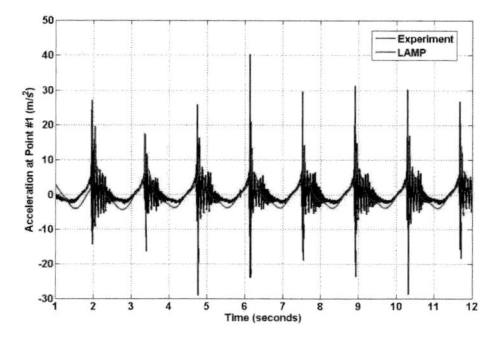

Fig. 10: Vertical Acceleration Comparison at Spot 149

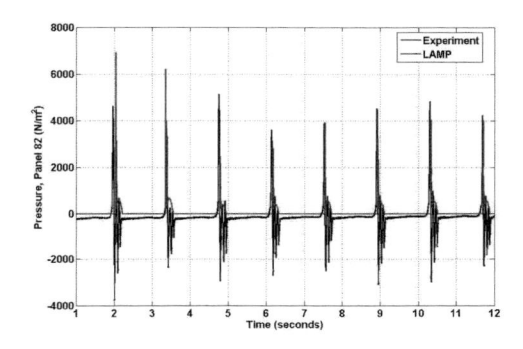

Fig. 11: Pressure Comparison at Spot 149

A similar series of comparison were carried out with the HSSL hullform in both regular and irregular waves. Again, generally good agreement was observed between the LAMP predictions and experimental results. It was clear from the experimental results that significant viscous damping and spray formation took place during high-speed runs when the step in the hull between catamaran and SWATH modes was placed near the still waterline. In these cases, LAMP tended to give higher motion predictions than the model test results. A sample comparison for pitch displacement in a simulated sea state 5 (significant wave height Hs=3.26m and modal period Tp=9.7sec) at 43 knots forward speed is shown in Fig. 12. More detailed results are summarized in Lin and Collette (2007).

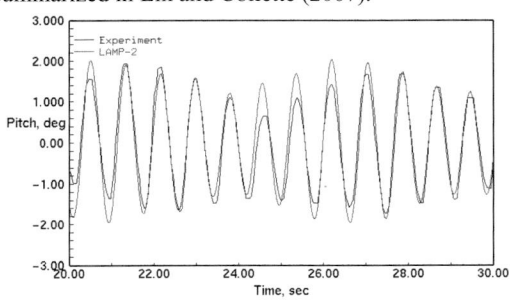

Fig. 12: Pitch Motions Comparison for HSSL Hullform

SES Motions in Head Seas

The initial LAMP SES model was also compared to the motions of the HSSL hullform tested in SWATH mode with the SES cushion deployed. The initial SES model in LAMP featured the effect of the cushion pressure on the free surface boundary condition and the hull. Leakage was modeled by constant-gap seal elements; an air supply was modeled with a linearized fan curve relating delivered air to cushion pressure. The pressure in the cushion was determined by an adiabatic ideal gas law, accounting for the changing cushion volume in waves, leakage of air from seals, and air supplied from the fans. In general, this simple SES model agreed quite well with experimental results at low speeds. Sample pitch motion results for zero speed in sea state 5 (Hs=3.26m and Tp=9.7sec), with the cushion supporting 24% of the vessel's weight, is shown in Fig. 13. At higher speeds, the constant-gap seal expression starts to break down, and the simple SES model will over-predict the SES motions.

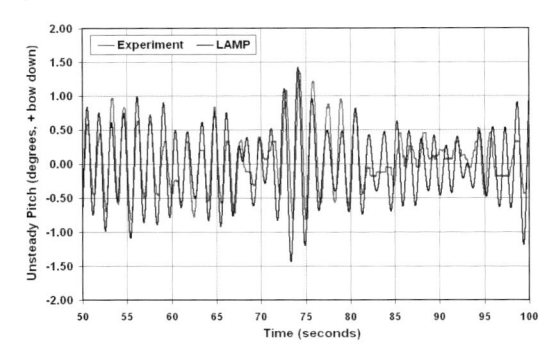

Fig. 13: SES Pitch Motions for HSSL Hullform

Ship Maneuvering in Calm Water

When dealing with unconventional hullforms, a numerical method for evaluating the maneuvering characteristics of the hullform is advantageous. The maneuvering characteristics predicted by the hybrid maneuvering model in LAMP (Lin et al., 2006) were compared to existing maneuvering model test results for the *Sea Fighter* hullform. A key test was to determine if the LAMP approach would correctly indicate that the bare hull was unstable, while the addition of a skeg made the hull stable. This was investigated by comparing the spiral maneuvers for the bare hull and hull with skeg. As can be seen from Figs. 14 and 15, the LAMP maneuvering approach was able to identify the unstable spiral tests that do not pass through the origin (Fig. 14) from the stable tests that do (Fig. 15).

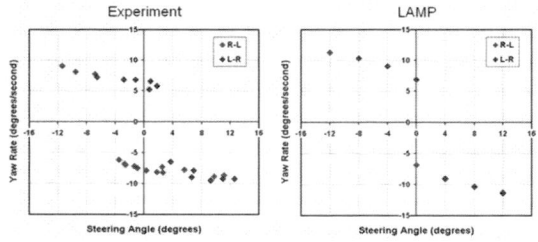

Fig. 14: Unstable Spiral Maneuver for Bare Hull

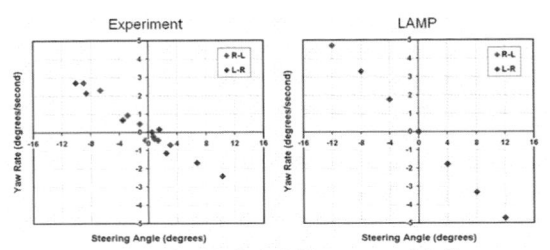

Fig. 15: Stable Spiral Maneuver with Skeg

A further comparison of turning circles at 20 knots full scale (Froude Number 0.385) was made between the LAMP results and the experimental data for the *Sea Fighter* hullform. As can be seen from the data in Table 4, the experimental results and LAMP results are in reasonable agreement.

Table 4: Comparison of Turning Circle Results

Fin Type	Experimental (ship lengths)	LAMP-3 (ship lengths)
Fin C	5.5	5.8
Fin D	3.7	4.3
Fin E	3.6	3.9

Yaw Test

In maneuvering simulations, lifting forces and moments generated by the body are required. However, potential flow codes such as LAMP cannot capture the lifting forces and moments properly; in the LAMP maneuvering approach, these forces must be determined by other means and included in the calculation as an additional force model (Lin et al., 2006). One approach to this problem is to use a viscous flow code to compute the hull lifting forces and moments. A surrogate model can be built based on the viscous flow computation results for use in the LAMP simulations. In the HSSL program, the viscous flow tool FANS was evaluated as a potential tool to build a surrogate maneuvering model. The Sea Fighter hullform was towed down the tank at several fixed yaw angles, and the total side force and moment on the hull was recorded. These experiments were simulated in the viscous flow code FANS, and the results were compared to the experimental values. Table 5 compares side forces, with excellent agreement between the codes and the experiments. Initial comparisons of the resulting moment were not as favorable; the experimental wave profile and FANS results are currently being compared in order to explain the difference.

Table 5: Side Force Comparison between FANS and Experimental Data, 20 Knots Full Scale (Fn=0.385)

Yaw Angle	Experimental Side Force (lbf)	FANS Side Force (lbf)
2°	43.38	41.98
4°	90.97	88.18
6°	127.08	128.11

Conclusions

The SAIC-led HSSL effort has extended and evaluated a set of software tools for the hydrodynamic design and performance assessment of innovative high-speed sealift hullforms. The current effort evaluated tools for resistance, motions, slamming loads, SES systems, and maneuvering. Using a series of model tests, these tools were assessed for their ability to provide useful guidance to designers. Non-linear potential flow codes such as Das Boot and LAMP have shown the ability to capture resistance and overall motions effects of innovative hullforms. Additionally, extending such potential flow codes with additional models has allowed a wide range of practical design problems to be tackled, including estimations of slamming pressures, modeling motions with active SES cushions, and investigating maneuvering. While viscous flow codes can be used for limited analysis of motions and loads on their own at this point, viscous flow predictions have proven useful in providing data for extensions models for potential flow code.

Acknowledgements

The authors would like to thank Dr. L. Patrick Purtell of ONR for his support of the HSSL program, and to thank the staff in the HPC office at ONR and at ARL who assisted with access and support for the JVN cluster. The authors would also like to thank the following team members of the SAIC-led HSSL team for their outstanding contribution to the overall HSSL program effort: Kenneth Weems, Sheguang Zhang, Daniel Liut, Michael Meinhold, Kristine Chevalier, Don Wyatt, and Tin-Guen Yen of SAIC; Greg Buley Volker Stammnitz and Chris Clayson of CDIM-SDD; Yuming Liu and Hongmei Yan of the Massachusetts Institute of Technology; Allen Engle, Ann Marie Powers, and Bryson Metcalf of NSWCCD; Gene Miller and Dave Helgerson of Computer Science Corporation; Ham-Chin Chen of Texas A&M University; Han Yu of the American Bureau of Shipping; and Gary Shimozono of Navatek.

References

Chen, HC, and Yu, K (2006). "Numerical Simulation of Wave Runup and Greenwater, on Offshore Structures by a Level-Set RANS Method," Proceedings of the 16th International Offshore and Polar Engineering Conference, San Francisco, California.

Faltinsen, OM, and Zhao, R (1991). "Numerical Predictions of Ship Motions at High Forward Speed," Phil. Trans. R. Society of London, A. Vol. 334, pp. 241-252.

Ge, C, Faltinsen, O., and Moan, T. (2005), "Global Hydroelastic Response of Catamarans Due to Wetdeck Slamming", Journal of Ship Research, Vol. 49, No. 1, pp 24-42.

Kuhn, JC, Chevalier, KL, Schlageter, EC, Scragg, CA, and Wyatt, DC (2007). "The Use of Linear Programming and Basis Functions for Hull Form Optimization," Proceedings of the 9th International Conference on Numerical Ship Hydrodynamics, Ann Arbor, Michigan.

Lin, WM, and Yue, DKP (1990). "Numerical Solutions for Large–Amplitude Ship Motions in the Time Domain," Proceedings of the Eighteenth Symposium on Naval Hydrodynamics, The University of Michigan, Ann Arbor, Michigan.

Lin, WM, and Yue, DKP (1993). "Time-Domain Analysis for Floating Bodies in Mild-Slope Waves of Large Amplitude," Proceedings of the Eighth International Workshop on Water Waves and Floating Bodies, St. John's, Newfoundland, Canada.

Lin, WM, Zhang, S, Weems, KM, and Yue, DKP (1999). "A Mixed Source Formulation for Nonlinear Ship-Motion and Wave-Load Simulations," Proceedings of the 7th International Conference on Numerical Ship Hydrodynamics, Nantes, France.

Lin, WM, Zhang, S, Weems, KM, and Liut, DA (2006). "Numerical Simulations of Ship Maneuvering in Waves," Proceedings of the 26th Symposium on Naval Hydrodynamics, Rome, Italy.

Lin, WM, and Collette, M (2007). "LAMP Validation and Modeling Recommendations – ONR HSSL Model Test Program," SAIC Report # ASTD 08-003.

Lin, WM, Zhang, S, Weems, KM, Jones, P, Meinhold, M, Bryson M, and Powers, A (2007). "Numerical Simulation and Validation Study of Wetdeck Slamming on High-Speed Catamaran," Proceedings of the 9th International Conference on Numerical Ship Hydrodynamics, Ann Arbor, Michigan.

Liut, DA, Weems, KM, and Lin, WM (2002). "Nonlinear Green Water Effects on Ship Motions and Structural Loads," Proceedings of the 24th Symposium on Naval Hydrodynamics, Fukuoka, Japan.

Pontaza, JP, Chen, HC, and Reddy, JN (2005). "A local-analytic-based discretization procedure for the numerical solution of incompressible flows." International Journal for Numerical Methods in Fluids, Vol. 49, No. 6, pp. 657-699.

Salvesen, N, Tuck, EO, and Faltinsen, O (1970). "Ship Motions and Sea Loads," Transactions of the Society of Naval Architects and Marine Engineers, Vol. 78, pp. 250-287.

Shin, YS, Belenky, V, Lin, WM, Weems, KM, and Engle, AH (2003). "Nonlinear Time Domain Simulation Technology for Seakeeping and Wave-Load Analysis for Modern Ship Design," Transactions of the Society of Naval Architects and Marine Engineers.

Shin, YS, Belenky, VL, Paulling, JR, Weems, KM, and Lin, WM (2004). "Criteria for Parametric Roll of Large Containerships in Longitudinal Seas," Transactions of the Society of Naval Architects and Marine Engineers.

Wyatt, DC (2000). "Development and Assessment of a Nonlinear Wave Prediction Methodology for Surface Vessels," Journal of Ship Research, Vol. 44, No. 2, pp. 96-107.

Zhang, S, Liut, DA, Weems, KM, and Lin, WM (2005). "A 3-D Finite Volume Method for Green Water Calculations," Proceedings of the 24th International Conference on Offshore Mechanics and Arctic Engineering (OMAE2005), Halkidiki, Greece.

Zhang, S Weems, KM, and Lin, WM (2007), "Numerical Simulations of Ship-Ship Interactions," Proceedings of the 9th International Conference on Numerical Ship Hydrodynamics, Ann Arbor, Michigan.

Speed Power Prediction Using Potential Flow Codes

Dr.-Ing. Uwe Hollenbach [1], Dipl.-Ing. Henning Grashorn [1]

[1] Hamburgische Schiffbau-Versuchsanstalt GmbH, HSVA
Hamburg, Germany

Abstract

The traditionally used comparative or statistical prediction methods for the calculation of resistance in the early design stage give only limited accuracy. Accuracy is expected to increase when potential flow codes are applied to the estimation of resistance, as the wave making resistance is no longer estimated, but directly calculated. calculated. HSVA compares the results of resistance tests being performed with the results of the numerical potential flow code v-Shallo. The aim of this ongoing investigation is to determine the conditions under which potential flow calculations can predict the resistance to a specified precision and what are the limits of potential flow theory today. This paper presents the results of the comparison of selected vessels. The resulting possibilities to increase the accuracy of the prognosis of resistance in the early design stage by using potential flow codes are discussed.

Keywords

Speed-power prediction; Resistance prediction; Model tests, Potential flow calculations; Comparison.

Introduction

Calculation of resistance and propulsion is one of the most important tasks during project development. Traditionally, comparative calculations or statistically based methods are used to predict the performance of a vessel in advance of model tests. These methods highly depend on the availability of a suitable database and, what is even more important, these methods can not take into account the actual hull form of a project vessel and therefore they must have only a limited accuracy.

The accuracy of statistical methods has been investigated by Hollenbach (1999). Maximum errors of a novel developed statistical method for estimating the resistance of single screw vessels with bulbous bow has been reported to be in the range of ±30%, with a standard deviation of about 10%.

Computational fluid dynamics play an increasingly important role in the investigation of hydrodynamic effects, and it is intended to use them for more accurate performance analysis in the future. While today potential flow codes are being used as a standard tool to optimize hull forms in the early design stage, there is little experience available addressing if these methods are suitable to predict the resistance in a more accurate way than using the traditional methods. Viscous flow calculations already give very promising results, though they still have the disadvantage of extensive preparatory work and long computation time, which makes them mostly unfeasible for the optimization process in the early ship design stage.

HSVA applies their in-house potential flow code v-Shallo to study free surface flows around ships. v-Shallo is a fully non-linear panel code based on state-of-the-art technology. Developed in 1998/99 the code continues HSVA's long tradition of free surface codes which dates back into the 1980's. v-Shallo is continuously updated to meet current and future requirements. This program has been successfully applied to a very large number of ship designs, analyzing the wave elevation and the pressure distribution for optimizing the hull form.

As a standard, HSVA compares the results of resistance tests being performed with the results of the numerical flow code v-Shallo. Not only the resistance at design draught at contract speed is compared, but the whole resistance curve on all drafts is investigated. In cases where variants have been investigated, where results of trim variation tests or results of shallow water tests are available, these results have been compared with numerical calculations as well. The aim of this ongoing investigation is to see under which conditions (e.g. ship type, hull form, draft, trim) the potential flow calculations can predict the resistance to a specified precision and what are the limits of potential flow codes today.

Previous Work

In a previous investigation Hollenbach and Christiansen (2005) presented a systematic comparison of model tank test results with results of two different potential flow codes. Ten different hull forms of small tankers and gas carriers have been investigated on different drafts using Kelvin of SVA-Potsdam and v-Shallo of HSVA. Both codes showed a similar performance, resulting in a mean error of −11% to −14% with a standard deviation of about 10% for Kelvin, and a mean error of –21% to –26% with a standard deviation of 5.4% to 7.4% for v-Shallo.

The mean error (aka mean error of estimate) is determined in such a way that for each speed predicted a deviation δC_T (in percent) to the model test result is calculated. The average deviation over the entire speed range gives the mean error. The standard deviation (aka standard error of estimate) is the root mean square deviation about the mean error and describes the scatter range of the deviations.

The following example may illustrate the meaning of "mean error" and "standard deviation". Assuming two different curves consisting of five points each, of which one curve represents the predicted values, and the second curve the measured values, further assuming a deviation of –20% between predicted and measured values for the first point, –10% for the second point, 0 for the third point, +10% for the fourth point and +20% for the fifth point, results in a mean error of ±0% and a standard deviation of 15.8% (Fig. 1). Assuming a second set of curves, with a deviation of +20% between predicted and measured values for all points, results in a mean error of +20% and a standard deviation of 0% (Fig. 2).

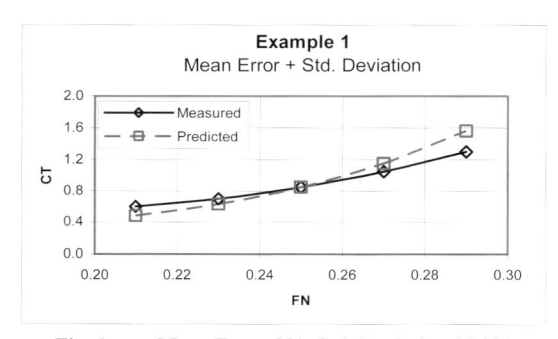

Fig. 1: Mean Error 0%, Std. Deviation 15.8%

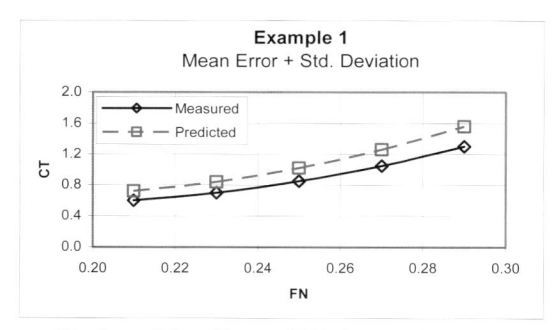

Fig. 2: Mean Error +20%, Std. Deviation 0%

Whereas the standard deviation is a measure for the deviation in the slope of both curves and can be interpreted as inaccuracy in the prediction of the wave resistance, the mean error is a measure for a parallel shift between both curves and can be interpreted as inaccuracy in the viscous resistance prediction.

Based on this, the predictions based on potential flow code results can be expected to have a larger mean error, but a lower standard deviation as statistically based methods, as the potential flow methods can not take into account any viscous effects, but should predict the wave making resistance in a more accurate way.

Vessels Investigated

A high percentage of models currently tested at HSVA are Container Vessels and Mega Yachts. For this paper the following projects have been selected for presentation. Some of the Container Vessels have been tested on different drafts (design, scantling and ballast). The High Speed Craft HSC 2 is a Catamaran.

Table 1: Container Vessels

Vessel	L/B [-]	B/T [-]	CB [-]
CV 1	8.79	2.68	0.650
CV 2	8.79	2.68	0.651
CV 3	8.77	2.68	0.669
CV 4	8.79	2.68	0.651
CV 5	6.09	2.88	0.649
CV 6	6.12	3.20	0.614
CV 7	6.18	3.11	0.765

Table 2: Mega Yachts

Vessel	L/B [-]	B/T [-]	CB [-]
MY 1	6.36	3.73	0.615
MY 2	5.09	3.58	0.571
MY 3	4.89	3.99	0.644

Table 3: High Speed Craft

Vessel	L/B [-]	B/T [-]	CB [-]
HSC 1	7.82	4.05	0.481
HSC 2	16.1	2.19	0.633
HSC 3	7.99	3.94	0.530

Table 4: Trim Effects (Container Vessel)

Vessel	L/B [-]	B/T [-]	CB [-]
CV 7	6.18	3.11	0.765

Table 5: Shallow Water Effects (RoRo Vessel)

Vessel	L/B [-]	B/T [-]	CB [-]
RR 1	7.45	3.54	0.737

Physical Model Tests

All model tests concerning resistance and ship powering are carried out at HSVA's large towing tank, which has a length of 300 m, a breadth of 18 m and a depth of 6 m. During the resistance tests, the model is towed by means of a thin, flexible rope. Thus, the resistance (being identical to the force in the tow rope) is measured. The guidance of the Model allows free sinkage and trimming. The tests and their analysis are carried out in accordance with Froude's method, i.e. the total resistance is split up into a frictional and a residual component. The frictional resistance coefficient is calculated according to the 1957 ITTC friction line.

CFD computations using v-Shallo

The HSVA developed non-linear free surface panel code v-Shallo dissolves the total resistance coefficient c_T as follows (Marzi and Hafermann, 2001):

$$c_T = c_R + c_F \qquad (1)$$

with c_F according to the 1957 ITTC friction line.

$$c_F = 0.075 / (\log R_n - 2)^2 \qquad (2)$$

The residual resistance coefficient c_R used is defined as following:

$$c_R = c_W + c_{Transom} + k_{Friction} * c_F + c_{VD} \qquad (3)$$

The predicted wave resistance c_W is the x-component of the pressure integral over the wetted surface of the hull:

$$c_W = \int_S p * n_x * ds / \frac{\rho}{2} * U_0^2 * S_0 \qquad (4)$$

Looking to the predicted pressure distribution of a hull, especially to the stern part, it is obvious that a potential flow assumption does not represent the physics of the local flow properly. The high pressure values indicate that there is too much positive x-force generated in this area. Thus the c_W coefficient is likely to be wrong and may even be negative (which is especially the case when there is a fine fore body that doesn't induce much resistance).

The $c_{Transom}$ contribution is introduced to take into account for the effect of the transom and the hydrostatic pressure in that area:

$$c_{Transom} = F_{x-static} \cdot g / (0.5 \cdot U_0^2 \cdot S_0) \qquad (5)$$

$k_{Friction}$ is an integral over the wetted surface, taking into account the effect of the local velocities at each panel – a quasi "form factor" for the hull similar to the k-factor used in model testing (influence of the hull form).

c_{VD} finally is an option to account for unlikely pressure rises in the stern part of the ship hull and an estimator for the viscous drag contribution.

Results for different Ship Types

For all vessels and all conditions presented here, the mean error and the standard deviation between Model Test Results and CFD calculations has been determined.

For model tests, where only data of self propulsion tests are available (e.g. the trim variation tests and the shallow water tests), the CFD results are compared with the measured relative thrust with the level trim condition respective the unrestricted water condition as reference.

Panmax Container Vessels

The Container Vessels CV 1 to CV 4 are all Container Vessels of Panmax size. Vessel CV 1 is the initial hull form of a project, while CV 2 is the optimized variant. Vessel CV 4 is an alternative hull form design with more forward longitudinal center of buoyancy for the same project as CV 1 and CV 2. Vessel CV 3 is another project with slightly higher block coefficient than the other Panmax vessels. The model test results and the CFD results of all four hull forms are shown in the following figures (Figs. 1~2).

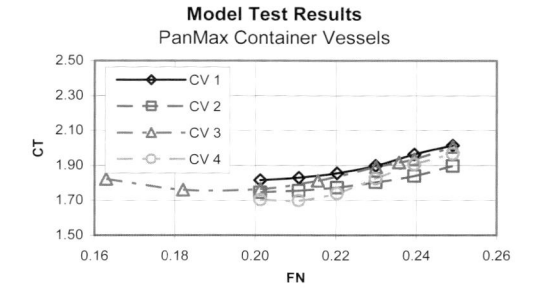

Fig. 1: Model Test Results Panmax Container Vessels

Fig. 2: CFD Results Panmax Container Vessels

The mean errors and the standard deviations for the Container Vessels are given in Table 6. A negative mean error indicates, that the resistance in model tests has been lower than has been predicted by CFD.

Table 6: Errors for the Panmax Container Vessels

Vessel	Mean Error	Standard Deviation
Container CV1	-6.1%	3.8%
Container CV2	+2.9%	3.3%
Container CV3	+6.0%	3.8%
Container CV4	-0.8%	1.8%

Comparing the model test results and potential flow results it is obvious, that the mean error and the standard deviation is smaller than is usually known from statistical methods. Furthermore, the standard deviation in the range between 1.8% and 3.8% is satisfyingly low for these four Panmax Container Vessels.

Based on the potential flow results, the variant CV 2 would have been selected as best variant of CV1, CV2 and CV4, which as well has been proven by the model tests. However, the improvement between CV 1 and CV 2 is not as large, as has been predicted by potential flow prediction. Based on this the Container Vessel CV 3 would have been expected to have a similar performance than the best variant CV 2, which could not be verified during the model tests.

Container Vessels on different Drafts

The Container Vessels CV 3, CV 5, CV 6 and CV 7 are tested on design, scantling and ballast draft. The model test results and CFD results are shown in the following figures (Figs. 3~10).

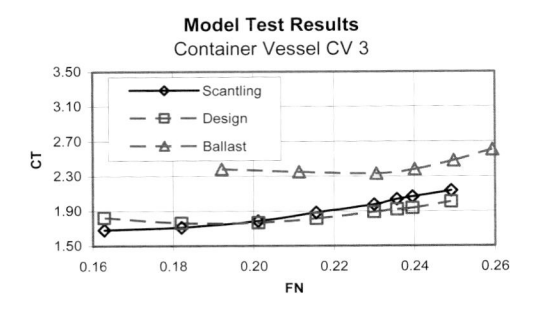

The results for Container Vessel CV 3 on design draft are quite good, the mean error is +6.0% with standard deviation of 3.8%.

The agreement both on scantling draft and on ballast draft is less accurate, the mean error rises up to +21.1% with standard deviation of 8.6% for scantling draft, and up to +15.2% with standard deviation of 7.7% for ballast draft.

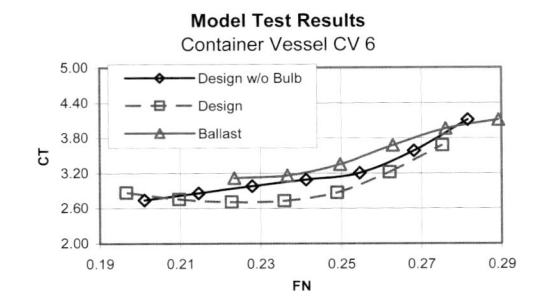

Fig. 3: Model Test Results of CV 3

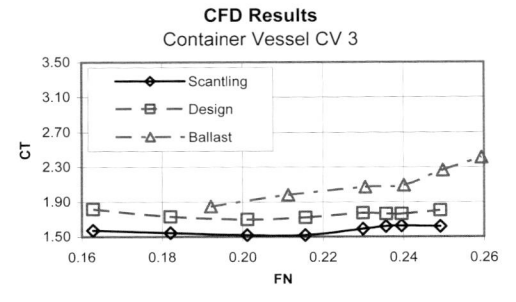

Fig. 4: CFD Results of CV 3

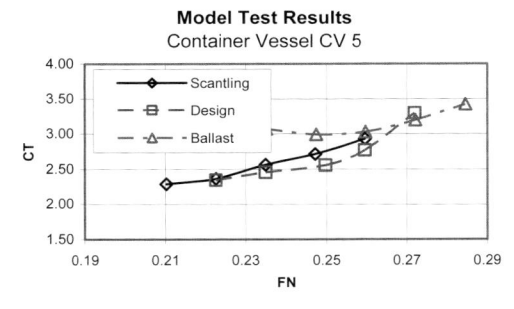

Fig. 5: Model Test Results of CV 5

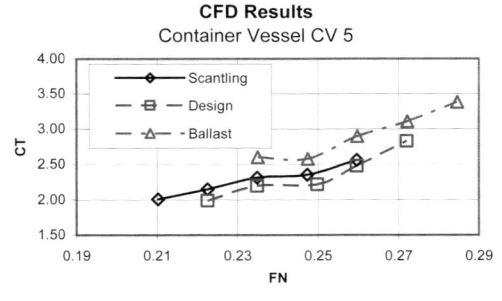

Fig. 6: CFD Results of CV 5

Fig. 7: Model Test Results of CV 6

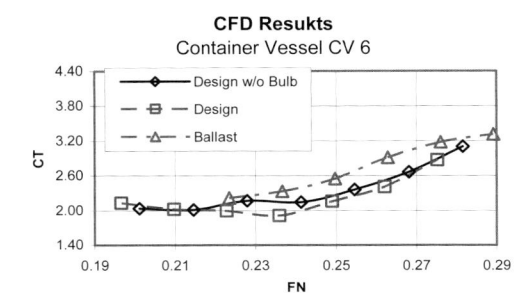

Fig. 8: CFD Results of CV 6

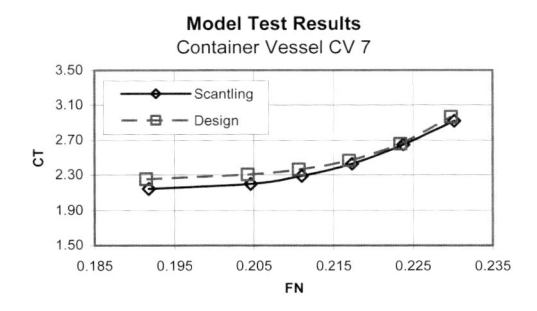

Fig. 9: Model Test Results of CV 7

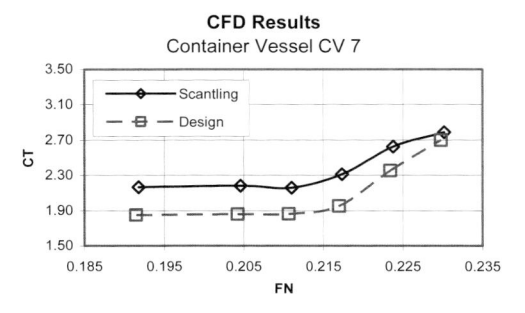

Fig. 10: CFD Results of CV 7

Although the mean error for the Container Vessel CV 5 with +12.9% on scantling draft and +14.6% on design draft are larger than for the Container Vessel CV 3, the standard deviation with 2.4% on scantling and 2.8% on design draft is as well fairly low. The agreement on ballast draft is a little less accurate with mean error of +8.6% and with standard deviation of 7.9%.

The Container Vessel CV 6 has been investigated on design draft with and without bulbous bow. Although the potential flow calculation predicts quite well the tendency between the variants with and without bulbous bow, the mean error in both cases with +37.3% (without bulb) and with +34.9% (with bulb) is too large. The standard deviation for these two variants with 4.3% respective 4.5% is fairly low. The agreement on ballast draft is a little less accurate with mean error of +30.4% and with standard deviation of 6.7%.

The Container Vessel CV 7 is a Multi-Purpose-Vessel also suitable for heavy lift cargo. The prediction for design draft with mean error +2.7% and standard deviation of 2.8% is satisfyingly low. The agreement on scantling draft is a less accurate with a mean error of +20.2% and a standard deviation of 7.1%.

Mega Yachts

Modern hull forms of Mega Yachts often face long overhangs, extremely long bulbous bows, wide transoms with large submerged transom areas, sometimes additionally with splash ducts arranged. The longitudinal center of buoyancy often is selected according to design constraints from the general arrangement, and not from hydrodynamic point of view.

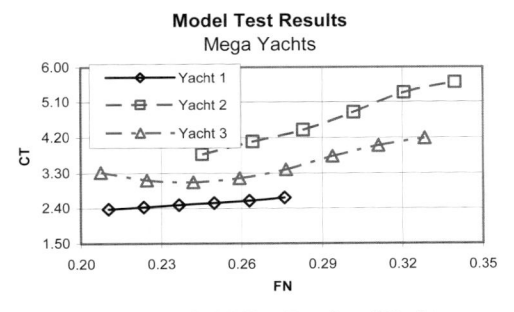

Fig. 11: Model Test Results of Yachts

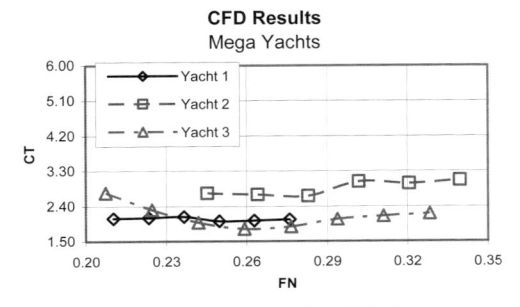

Fig. 12: CFD Results of Yachts

From hydrodynamic view some hull forms are the result of unfavorable design constraints and for accurate resistance predictions numerical tools with a proven reliability would be a great help during the design process and for discussions with shipyards, ship owners, consultants and designers. Although a large number of Mega Yachts has been tested during recent years at HSVA, only a few models have been tested in the bare hull condition, which allow a direct comparison with the potential flow calculations.

According to model test results the Yacht MY1 has the lowest total resistance coefficient of all three yachts. This could not be predicted by using CFD methods.

Table 7: Errors for the Mega Yachts

Vessel	Mean Error	Standard Deviation
Yacht MY1	+21.5%	6.9%
Yacht MY2	+62.9%	16.8%
Yacht MY3	+65.4%	25.6%

High Speed Craft

Actual hull forms of High Speed Craft usually face wide transom sterns with large submerged transom areas. Novel designs have to arrange a number of water jet drives. In some projects special bulbous bow designs are applied, in other projects monohull and catamaran variants have to be assessed.

Further to the maximum top speed, often a cruising speed in the range of 18 knots to 22 knots and a loitering speed in the range of 5 knots to 8 knots is a requirement within the specified speed profile. For the optimization of these hull forms, and to find the best possible compromise between concurrent design constraints, numerical tools are required for accurate resistance predictions at different speeds.

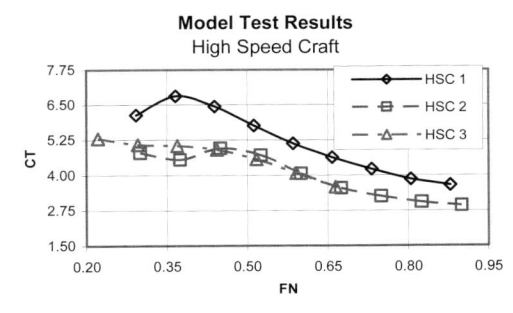

Fig. 13: Model Test Results of High Speed Craft

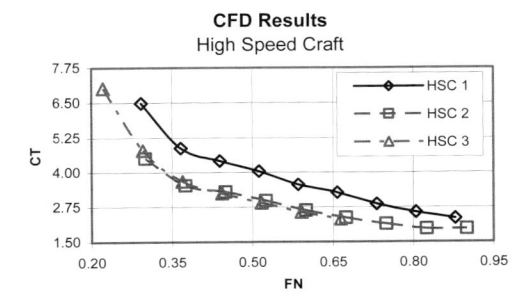

Fig. 14: CFD Results of High Speed Craft

The High Speed Craft HSC 1 is a conventional monohull design, HSC 2 is a wave piercing catamaran design and HSC 3 is a wave piercing monohull design. The model test results and potential flow results for three different hull forms of High Speed Craft are shown in the following figures (Figs. 13~14).

According to model test results, depending on the speed the High Speed Craft HSC 3 has the lowest total resistance coefficient of all three hull forms investigated. This has been predicted by the potential flow methods.

The mean error between model test results and potential flow results is +40.3% for High Speed Craft HSC 1, +44.8% for High Speed Craft HSC 2 and +34.5% for High Speed Craft HSC 3. The standard deviation in these cases is 17.8% for High Speed Craft HSC 1, 16.7% for High Speed Craft HSC 2 and 31.9% for High Speed Craft HSC 3.

Trim Variation Tests

Today more and more shipyards and ship owners require trim variation tests to find out, which is the optimum trim condition for certain drafts in respect to power consumption. As these trim variation tests usually are performed as self propulsion tests, no resistance data are available.

To compare model tests results with potential flow results the thrust measured in the self propulsion tests and the resistance predicted by the potential flow methods have been used, with the level trim condition as reference (100%).

For the Container Vessel CV 7 trim variation tests on three drafts have been performed: the Light Load Draft of T=8.1m, the Design Draft of T=8.7m and the Scantling Draft of T=9.5m.

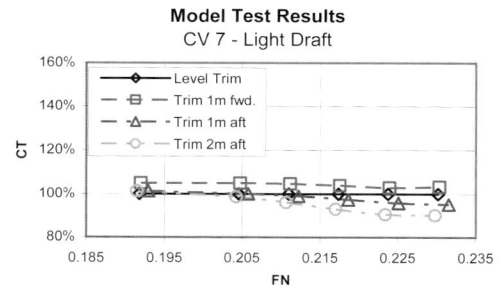

Fig. 15: Model Test Results on Light loaded Draft

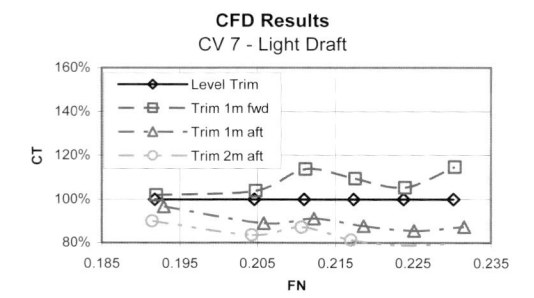

Fig. 16: CFD Results on Light loaded Draft

For all drafts the level trim condition, a trim of 1m to the head and a trim of 1m and 2m to the stern, with constant displacement for each draft condition, have been investigated.

The model test results and potential flow results of the trim variation tests of the three drafts investigated are shown in Figs. 15~20.

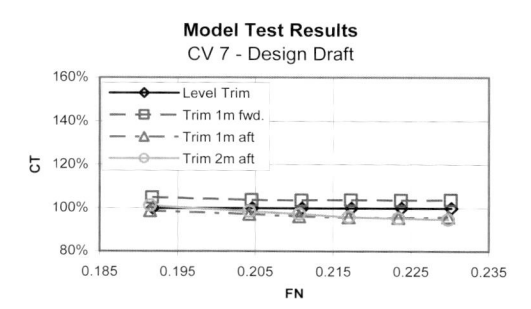

Fig. 17: Model Test Results on Design Draft

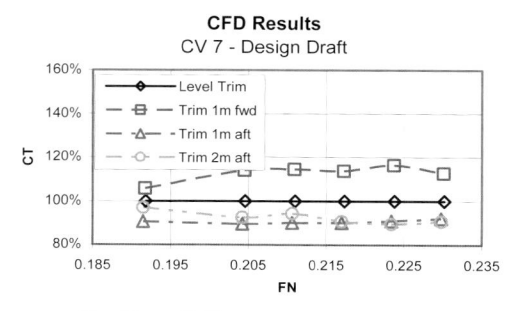

Fig. 18: CFD Results on Design Draft

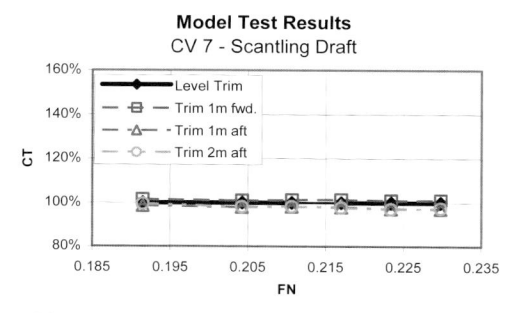

Fig. 19: Model Test Results on Scantling Draft

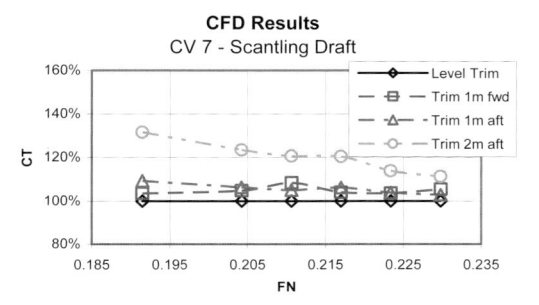

Fig. 20: CFD Results on Scantling Draft

In the Light loaded Draft Condition both model test results and potential flow results show the same trend. However, the influence of the trim is over estimated by the potential flow predictions.

In the forward trim condition the model test requires about 4% additional thrust, but the predicted additional resistance is about 8%. In the aft trim conditions the tests predict up to 4% less thrust, but the predicted decrease in resistance is between 10% and 17%.

In the Design Draft Condition both model test results and potential flow results show the same tendency. While in the forward trim condition the model test requires about 4.5% additional thrust, the predicted additional resistance is about 12.8%. In the aft trim conditions the model tests require between 1.9% and 3.3% less thrust, but the predicted decrease in resistance is between 7.5% and 9.4%.

In the Scantling Draft Condition the potential flow methods can not predict the trend of the model test results. While in the forward trim condition the model test requires about 1.4% additional thrust, the predicted additional resistance is about 5.0%. In the aft trim conditions the model tests require between 1.4% and 1.9% less thrust, but the CFD methods predict an increase in resistance between 5.6% and 20.2%!

Shallow Water Tests

Ship owners operating their vessels in coastal waters and in rivers require reliable predictions for shallow water conditions. As these shallow water tests usually are performed as self propulsion tests, no resistance data are available.

To compare model tests results with potential flow results the thrust measured in the self propulsion tests has been used deriving dimensionless coefficients. The trend can be compared with the coefficients derived from the potential flow results. However, as the model tests results base on the thrust measured, and the potential flow results base on the predicted resistance, the absolute figures can not be compared.

For the RoRo-Vessel RR 1 shallow water tests have been performed on water depth/draft ratios of H/T=2.0, H/T=1.6 and H/T=1.2.

The model test results and potential flow results of the shallow water tests on three different water depths are shown in the figures (Figs. 21~22).

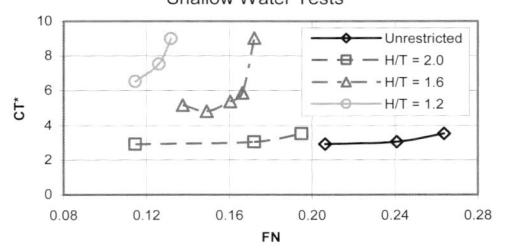

Fig. 21: Model Test Results in Shallow Water

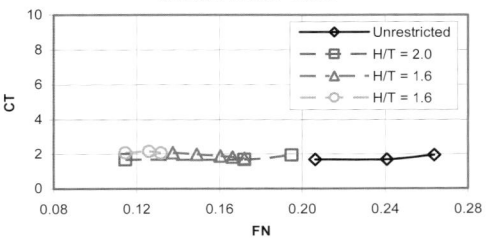

Fig. 22: CFD Results in Shallow Water

Unfortunately the potential flow calculations do not match the model tests results to a sufficient degree, except at the highest water depth/draft ratios. While model tests results indicate a higher thrust level at H/T=1.6 and H/T=1.2 compared to the unrestricted condition and predict a steep resistance increase with increasing Froude depth number, this effects is not predicted by the potential flow method at all.

Conclusions

Compared to resistance predictions based on comparative calculations or statistical methods the predictions based on potential flow calculations for Container Vessels on design draft are quite promising. Although the mean error of +11% (with minimum/maximum of -6% to +37%) is not satisfying, the standard deviation of 3.4% is satisfyingly low.

This standard deviation is much lower than that associated with typical statistical methods for predicting the resistance, where the standard deviation is about 10% and even higher.

However, taking into account not only the design draft, but also ballast and scantling drafts, the mean error rises from +11% to +14% and the standard deviation rises from 3.4% to 4.8%. This is still better than is achieved with typical statistical methods.

Further taking into account the Mega Yachts and High Speed Crafts investigated, the mean error rises from +11% to +23% and the standard deviation rises from 4.5% to 9.2%.

Having a closer look to the detailed results of the potential flow predictions for the Container Vessels it was noticed, that the discrepancies in accuracy e.g.

between design draft and scantling draft mainly arise from the transom correction $C_{Transom}$. As long as the transom is not immersed, this factor contributes with a positive value to the total resistance. With increasing immersion area of the transom (e.g. from design to scantling draft) and depending on the vessels speed this factor becomes negative, thus reducing the calculated residual resistance coefficient C_R.

Neglecting the transom correction at all did not led to an improvement. By taking into account the Container Vessels only, the mean error raised from +14% to +17% with the standard deviation rising from 4.8% to 7.0%.

Applying only the positive contribution and neglecting the negative contribution of the transom correction improves the mean error, reducing it from +14% down to +9%, while slightly increasing the standard deviation from 4.8% to 5.4%.

The potential flow predictions for the Mega Yachts as well could be improved by neglecting the negative contribution of the transom correction.

The potential flow predictions for the High Speed Craft however could not be improved in the same way, as in these cases the correction for the entire speed range contributes with a positive value to the total resistance.

The tendency in power demand during the trim variations tests is predicted correctly, but the effect is greatly overestimated. Applying only the positive contribution of the trim correction in these cases as well reduce the large discrepancies between model test result and potential flow prediction (Table 8).

Table 8: Effect of $C_{Transom}$ on the Prediction of Trim Variation Tests

Draft and Trim Condition	Model Test	CFD „as is"	CFD $C_{Tr.}>0$
Light Level	100%	100%	100%
Light 1m fwd	105%	108%	108%
Light 1m aft	98%	89%	92%
Light 2m aft	96%	83%	89%
Design Level	100%	100%	100%
Design 1m fwd	105%	112%	106%
Design 1m aft	97%	90%	94%
Design 2m aft	98%	93%	91%
Scantl. Level	100%	100%	100%
Scantl. 1m fwd	101%	105%	103%
Scantl. 1m aft	98%	105%	96%
Scantl. 2m aft	99%	120%	95%

The results of this investigation show the possibilities but also the limits of state of the art potential flow calculations. Although the potential flow predictions show a fairly good agreement with the model test results for Container Vessels on design draft, the accuracy in other cases is not as good. The lack of accuracy in these cases mainly arises from two effects, which can be improved in future potential flow code applications:

1. The potential flow code can not predict viscous effects. Further improvements of potential flow predictions can be expected using empirical correction factors derived from calculated pressure distribution and pressure gradients.
2. The flow situation at the stern and the related effect on the resistance is not predicted correctly. Further improvements can be achieved developing improved numerical models for transom stern predictions.

Current Developments / ABSS

To improve the quality of future numerical methods, HSVA has joined forces with Technical University Hamburg-Harburg (TUHH) to develop a better understanding and, in a second step improved numerical models for transom stern predictions, with a focus on potential flow methods.

The ABSS project, the acronym stands for the German title "Akkurate Berechnung der Strömung an einem Spiegelheck", is funded by the Federal Ministry of Economics and Technology under the umbrella of the National Maritime Research programme.

ABSS combines novel experimental techniques for optical wave pattern measurements in areas otherwise not accessible with standard wave probes and advanced numerical modelling approaches to improve the quality of transom flow predictions, particularly for potential flow models. These panel codes are still one of the work horses in everyday ship hull form analysis and optimisation. The quality of results obtained from such methods largely depends on an accurate capturing of the flow situation at a ship's transom.

To gain deeper insight in the different flow conditions which are encountered at a transom stern, e.g. a dry transom or a partially wetted one, special experiments were performed in the large towing tank. A novel test rig supporting a set of line lasers in combination of a water spray curtain behind the transom of a ship model was installed on the towing carriage. The stern wave at speed could be visualised and photographs taking during runs were analyzed with a dedicated image processing algorithm to determine the wave elevation behind the transom.

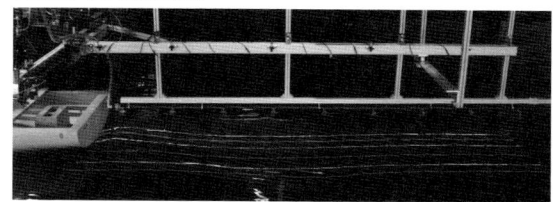

Fig. 23: Optical wave measurements behind the transom of a container ship model.

The image shown (Fig. 23) illustrates a set of six wave cuts measures behind a container ship model. This new measurement technique has been carefully validated; a comparison of the wave profile obtained from two methods, standard wave probes and the new optical technique, close to the side of the ship is shown in Fig. 24. This indicates excellent agreement.

The experimental data obtained for a number of different floating conditions provide a unique set of data which is presently used to develop advanced numerical models which are expected to improve the quality of future numerical predictions, particularly for operating conditions with a – partially – wetted transom. New dead water models are embedded in potential flow codes to allow also the prediction of cases where no dry transom is expected.

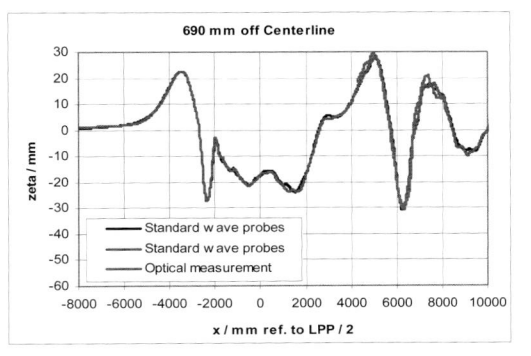

Fig. 24: Comparison of wave cuts obtained with standard wave probes (pink/blue) and optical measurements (green).

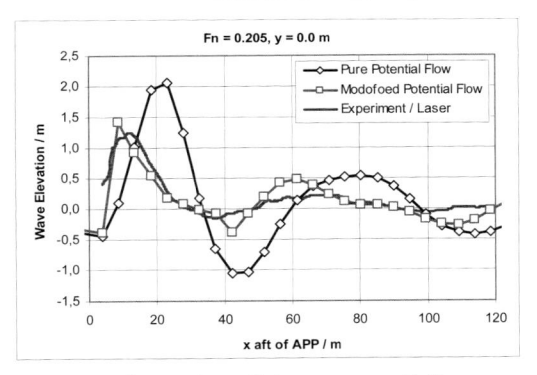

Fig. 25: Comparison of stern wave prediction – new model: pink, standard: blue – with experimental data (green).

First results obtained for test cases show promising results. Fig. 25 compares the predicted wave elevation behind the transom from the new model with experimental data, indicating a significant improvement over the previously used standard model.

The improved calculated wave elevation behind the transom will result in more accurate resistance predictions based on potential flow calculations in the near future.

Acknowledgements

Thanks from the authors to our colleagues Jochen Marzi and Hans-Uwe Schnoor and our students Adrian von Ramin and Fairuz Hazwan Zahari for their contribution to this paper.

References

Hollenbach, U. (1999). "Estimating Resistance and Propulsion for Single-Screw and Twin-Screw Ships in the Preliminary Design", Proceedings, 10th International Conference on Computer Applications in Shipbuilding ICCAS, 1999

Hollenbach, U., Christiansen, M. (2005). "Systematischer Vergleich von Modellversuchsergebnissen mit Ergebnissen von CFD-Berechnungen (Potential-Methoden)", Jahrbuch der STG, 99. Band, 2005

Jensen, G., Marzi, J., et. Al. (2000). "Wave Resistance Computations - A Comparison of different Approaches", 23rd Symposium Naval Hydrodynamics, Val de Reuil

Maisonneuve, J.J., Harries, S., Raven, H.C., Marzi, J., Viviani, U. (2003). "Towards Optimal Design of Ship Hull Shapes", IMDC 03, Athens 2003

Marzi, J., Hafermann, D. (2001). "The v-Shallo Users Guide", HSVA Report 1646, 2001

Marzi, J. (2003). "Use of CFD Methods for Hullform Optimization in a Model Basin", MARNET – CFD Workshop, Haslar 2003

Söding, H. (1993). "A Method for Accurate Force Calculation in Potential Flow", Ship Technology Research, Volume 40

Application of Artificial Neural Networks for the Prediction of Inland Water Units Resistance

Maged M Abdel Naby, Heba W Leheta, Adel A Banawan, Ahmed A Elhewy
Department of Marine Engineering and Naval Architecture, Alexandria University
Alexandria, Egypt.

Artificial Neural Networks (ANNs) have been successfully used in ship hydrodynamics field for pattern recognition and prediction of resistance coefficients. ANNs have been applied successfully also in the area of identifying, modeling, and controlling a wide range of marine systems and promising results were obtained in many fields. Accumulated experimental data of inland water units' resistance from the Versuchsanstalt fur Binnenschiffbau Duisburg (VBD) in Germany represent a very good record for formulating a general expression for the estimation of inland water units' resistance. In this paper ANNs' models have been created in order to be used in storing the data of methodical series for inland water units' resistance and predicting the resistance for new designs. The selected model can then be integrated into an optimization computer code for ship design. The ANN training data are based on numerous experiments done in the VBD, which allows a prediction of sufficient accuracy for single screw self propelled units. The predicted resistance results are compared to those computed by cubic spline interpolation method. The results show that ANNs have large capabilities in capturing the pattern from scatter data but the precision of the results obtained, particularly those for maximum error, should be treated with care.

Keywords

Artificial neural networks; Cubic spline interpolation; Inland water units; Ship design optimization; Residual resistance estimation

Nomenclature

B : Ship breadth
C_B : Block coefficient
C_m : Midship section area coefficient
F : Transfer function
Fn : Froude number
H : Water depth
L_{WL} : Length of water line
R_R : Residual resistance
T : Ship draft
V : Ship speed
∇ : Volume of displacement

Introduction

Ship design is a multidisciplinary and multi-objective design problem. Ship design traditionally was based on a sequential and iterative approach called the design spiral. This classical design procedure was more art than science as the designer should have an insight of the effect of his different decisions on the design under consideration.

With the availability of new optimization techniques, particularly Metaheuristic Algorithms, several attempts have been made to solve the ship design problem, which allow the development of new optimum designs while considering different aspects of the design problem. Ray, Gokarn, and Sha (1995) developed a full ship design model for a container ship in which simulated annealing was used to tackle the optimization problem. Wolf, Dickmann, and Boas (2005) used genetic algorithms for the design optimization of a US navy frigate. The FIRST project conducted by the department of Aerospace and Ocean Engineering at Virginia Tech developed a model for the optimization of container ships in which different optimization tools and ship design models were tested and verified. A review of optimization methods and their application in the ship design field can be found in Leheta (2002).

This optimization procedure requires that different design disciplines/modules are integrated together to formulate the whole design process. Estimation of ships' resistance represents a prime module for the design process. This has been based on extrapolation of resistance of models tested in towing tanks to that of full size ships. These results are commonly presented in the form of curves and equations with different non dimensional ship parameters used for representing the data. For inland water units one more parameter, which is the water depth, is presented in the design formula, which makes the prediction of the resistance of such units even more complicated.

Due to the complicated nature of the resistance estimation from model experiments and the large number of parameters involved in such estimation, a powerful means to store, generalize and predict the resistance from this database is of utmost importance.

ANNs represent a very powerful tool for pattern recognition and have been successfully used for the prediction of resistance from model experiments and in many other applications in the marine field in general.

In this study, the capabilities of ANNs versus those of cubic spline interpolation for the prediction of inland water units resistance based on available curves derived from model experiments are tested. The aim of this current work is to arrive at the most convenient method for utilizing these curves for the prediction of units' resistance and integrating this method in a computer code for inland water units design optimization.

Derivation of Inland Water Units Resistance

When a ship sails from deep to shallow water, a reduction in speed is noticed. This is due to the fact that the constraint in the vertical direction has two effects; a wave retardation effect which affects the ship wave pattern and an acceleration of the flow around the ship due to the constriction of the flow under her. These two effects augment the resistance of any ship in shallow water in comparison to that in deep water (Schlichting, 1934).

Calculation of resistance in shallow water has been of special interest for many scientists since a long time. Kempf (1923) derived a method for the correction of deep-water resistance at different h/T values and for different speeds, based on results of model and ship tests in shallow water. Schlichting (1934) made the first methodical procedure in this area. He developed a method for the determination of speed reduction in shallow water, from which shallow water resistance can be calculated based on ship's resistance in deep water. Landwerber (1939) extended the work of Schlichting to resistance estimation in confined waters using experimental results of a merchant ship model tested in various rectangular canal sections. Heuser (1980) analyzed the experimental results of the Versuchsanstalt fur Binnenschiffbau Duisburg (VBD) from 1954 to 1978, and made the first important systematic approach to determine directly the residual resistance of motor ships and push trains at different water depths. He developed a procedure for the determination of residual and total resistance, and the prediction of power demand of inland water units in deep and shallow water.

Between 1993 and 1996, Kamar (1993, 1996) developed equations for the calculation of shallow and deep-water form factors dependent on water depth and form parameters.

Theoretical and numerical methods have evolved during the 60's, and since the 80's a lot of computer codes have been developed for the determination of ship resistance in deep and shallow water. Most of the results coming out of these programs are time consuming and are still mainly used in a qualitative manner; for comparing hydrodynamic qualities of different hull forms in order to minimize the experimental work required. Jiang (2001) introduced a new trend for the prediction of the form factors and the resistance on different water depths by the measured resistance at one water depth. This was done through the determination of the so-called effective speed depending on the sinkage, as the sinkage can be calculated easily using numerical methods.

Heuser's method for the determination of shallow water resistance is based on the specific evaluation of systematic resistance and propulsion tests carried out during about 25 years in the VBD towing tank with self-propelled inland cargo ship models. For the systematic evaluation measurements, 10 self-propelled cargo ships were used to conduct the systematic experiments for the estimation of resistance and propulsive coefficients. Unfortunately, the prediction of power using Heuser's method is still limited for a very small range of application, therefore only the charts of specific residual resistance (R_R/∇) will be used in the calculations. Once the specific residual resistance is calculated, the frictional resistance can be derived and the total resistance can be estimated.

The data available for specific residual resistance calculations cover the range:

$$7 < L_{WL}/B < 12$$
$$2 < B/T < 7.5$$
$$0.75 < C_B < 0.94$$
$$5.2 < L_{WL}/\nabla^{1/3} < 8.4$$
$$\frac{h-T}{h} > 0.25$$

The deviation of results compared to full size ships are 1.0- 1.5% of the velocity and 10% of the total resistance.

For the presentation of the data, Heuser used $L_{WL}/\nabla^{1/3}$, as it is a good parameter for the description of the ship geometry. To account for the wave making resistance, he only considered the Froude number (Fn). In consideration of the change from unlimited to limited water depth, and its effect on the flow around the ship, Schlichting's assumption was adopted and $\sqrt{B.T.C_m}/h$ was used to account for the change in the potential flow around the ship, provided that there is no width restriction. A water width to L_{WL} ratio of 1.5 is a further condition to be fulfilled for the accuracy of obtained results. The data is presented in 11 charts, each chart for a constant value of specific residual resistance. One sample chart is presented in Appendix A.

As the method is applicable in a wide range of ship parameters and water depths for conventional inland ships forms, the above-mentioned procedure can be used for the early stage calculation of the total resistance for single screw ships, optimization of ship principal dimensions in a relatively wide range of applications, and the possibility to extend resistance calculations to deep water, if the ship working area is to include coastal service.

Data Analysis Methods
Artificial Neural Networks

Artificial Neural Networks (ANNs) are pure mathematical models based on the neural structure of the brain. This field does not utilize traditional programming but involves the creation of massively parallel networks and the training of those networks to solve specific problems. ANNs have the capability of establishing a functional relationship between two data spaces during a learning process and to generalize these data during a recall process.

Ray, Gokarn, and Sha (1996) predicted the number of containers a ship can carry based on main ship parameters using ANNs in conjunction with real ships data. Mesbahi and Atlar (1998) used ANNs for the design of bulbous bows based on curves developed by Kracht and in the design of marine propellers based on NSMB-B series. Mason et al (2005) used this ability in the prediction of the resistance of catamarans based on scatter experimental data from models tested in towing tanks. Alkan, Trincas, and Nabergoj (2005) predicted sea keeping properties of fast RO-RO ships and compared the results to those obtained by regression using Response Surface Methodology (RSM). Elhewy et al (2006) used ANNs for reliability analysis of composite structures.

ANNs, in one of their basic applications and after successful training, can provide the correlating mathematical relationship between multi-dimensional input/output data sets.

One and two layer feed-forward neural networks structures trained by back-propagation are used in this study. In general, an ANN structure consists of several layers and each layer consists of several neurons, which are also called processing elements (PEs). Fig. 1 shows a typical structure of a feed-forward ANN model, in which the left column is the input layer with the bias (+1), the right most column is the output layer. In between input layer and output layer is a hidden layer with the transfer function (F) and bias. Generally there could be more than one hidden layer.

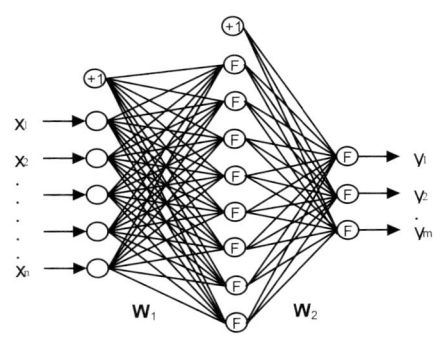

Fig. 1: General structure of an artificial neural network

The number of hidden layers and the number of processing elements in each hidden layer needs to be identified. In the current work, both the hidden layer and the output layer use hyperbolic tangent (tanh) activation functions. The number of PEs in the hidden layer is a very important parameter, which determines the accuracy of ANN models. Unfortunately there is no rule to determine this number. It is normally determined by a trial-and-error process, so this number will be optimized during the training process. Different numbers of PEs in the hidden layer will initially be used and the model with the best results will be saved.

To start the training process the initial weights are randomized. In this work, back-propagation training algorithm has been used to train all models. Successive runs are performed using different initialization weights to make sure that the model is not stuck at a local optimum.

The data is divided into three different sub-sets; Training, Cross validation and Testing. Cross validation set is used as a signal to stop the training and prevent over training. The model accuracy is measured using the correlation factor (r), mean relative error in percent, and maximum relative error in percent. Definitions of these parameters are mentioned in Appendix B.

More details of this procedure can be found in Principe et al (1999).

Cubic Spline (CS) Interpolation

The concept of spline came from the drafting technique, where a flexible strip is used to connect a set of points with flexible curves.

The objective of cubic splines is to connect each two points from n+1 points with a smooth curve of third order polynomial function. This involves n intervals and 4n unknowns, consequently 4n conditions are required.

The equality of function values, first, and second derivatives at interior knots provide 2n-2, n-1, and n-1 conditions respectively. The first and last functions must pass through the end points at which the second derivatives are equal to zero; this provides the last 4 conditions. The last two conditions implicate that the function is a straight line at the end points, and the spline is called a natural spline.

A complete explanation of cubic splines and the algorithm for programming them can be found in Chapra, S, and Canale, R (1998).

Prediction of Specific Residual Resistance Using ANNs and Cubic Spline Models

Since the aim of the present calculations is to provide a sub program for the residual resistance calculations to be integrated in a computer code for ship design optimization, the best procedure is to use $\sqrt{B.T.C_m}/h$, $L_{WL}/\nabla^{1/3}$ and V as inputs and the specific residual resistance at the required speed as an output.

This model can be achieved using ANNs by developing a three inputs – one output network. Data from all the charts were fed into the network. 594 random data points were divided into two sub-groups; one group for training and the other one for cross validation and another 396 random points were used for testing and evaluating the network performance.

Successive runs were performed while changing the architecture of the network; number of PEs and number of hidden layers. The networks different architectures for the most successful trials together with the results are presented in Table 1.

Since major errors were noticed in the prediction of specific residual resistance using one hidden layer, one more trial using two hidden layers was performed, and no noticeable progress was achieved.

Due to the major inconsistencies between real and predicted values by the previous ANNs model, particularly for the maximum error, further models to allow ANNs to better capture the pattern were performed.

In the new model, data points for each independent chart (54 points) were fed into the network after being divided into two sub-groups; one group for training and the other one for cross validation. The new inputs are $\sqrt{B.T.C_m}/h$, $L_{WL}/\nabla^{1/3}$ and the output is the speed at the given specific residual resistance specified on each chart. 36 random points from each chart were used for testing and evaluating the network performance. The ANNs' models for three sample charts were derived (1st, 6th, and 11th chart). Details of the networks architecture are presented in Table 2.

However, as the final output should be the specific residual resistance at the specified speed, this procedure has the disadvantage that V-R_R/∇ curve has to be calculated using all charts and one more interpolation step should be performed using this curve to calculate the specific residual resistance at the required speed.

The same data points used in the previous model are introduced for cubic spline interpolation. The data points are divided such that the points for each curve of constant $\sqrt{B.T.C_m}/h$ are used to derive a number of third degree polynomials to represent the curve. The inputs are still $\sqrt{B.T.C_m}/h$, $L_{WL}/\nabla^{1/3}$ and the output is the speed at the given specific residual resistance specified on each chart. The cubic spline interpolants for three sample charts were derived (1st, 6th, and 11th charts), which are the same charts used in the previous model.

The disadvantage mentioned for the previous model still holds for this one. In addition, this model has one more disadvantage, which is if the input $\sqrt{B.T.C_m}/h$ value does not coincide with one of the values mentioned on the curves in the charts, the speed should be calculated at the two values on the charts bounding the required value, and one more interpolation step is performed to calculate the speed at the required $\sqrt{B.T.C_m}/h$. The results for both of the previous models are presented in Table 3.

Since the results provided by the above mentioned three models still lack the required accuracy, the number of data points is increased to better capture the pattern. In these new models each curve in every chart was represented using 6 or 7 points depending on the curve geometry. These points contained the start point, endpoint, maximum point, points of inflection, and other 3 or 2 points to insure good description of the relevant curve. Finally, 78 points were used for representing each chart and a total of 858 points were tabulated to be used for training and cross validation. In addition, 132 random points (12 points from each chart) were picked to be used for testing and evaluating the performance of different models.

The three previous models are repeated using the new data set. Networks architecture and results are presented in Tables 4, 5, and 6.

For Further clarification, the results for using ANNs and cubic spline interpolation together with the original points from the 1st chart only are plotted in Fig. 2.

Table 1: ANNs' models architecture and results for processing all charts using 594 data points

Trial no.	No. of layers	Range of varying PEs	Final no. of PEs used	No. of runs/PEs variation	r	Max relative error in R_R/∇ (%)	Mean relative error in R_R/∇ (%)
1	1	12-18	16	10	0.992	35.245	5.99
2	1	18-30	29	5	0.995	24.17	4.41
3	1	-	50	3	0.995	49	4.988
4	2	-	16/8	1	0.992	41.19	4.23

Table 2: ANNS' model architecture for each of the three sample charts using 55 data points

Chart no.	No. of layers	Range of varying PEs	Optimum no. of PEs	No. of runs/PEs variation
1	1	4-12	10	5
6	1	4-12	9	5
11	1	4-12	11	5

Table 3: ANNS' and cubic spline interpolation results for each of the three sample charts using 55 data points

Chart no.	R		Max relative error in speed (%)		Mean relative error in speed (%)	
	ANNs	C.S.	ANNs	C.S.	ANNs	C.S.
1	0.991	0.952	5.812	9.919	1.297	2.462
6	0.999	0.998	3.241	3.397	0.44	0.606
11	0.999	0.998	4.08	4.423	0.619	0.611

Table 4: ANNs' models architecture and results for processing all charts using 858 data points

Trial no.	No. of layers	Range of varying PEs	Final no. of PEs used	No. of runs/PEs variation	r	Max relative error in R_R/∇ (%)	Mean relative error in R_R/∇ (%)
1	1	12-18	18	10	0.995	28	5.103
2	1	-	22	5	0.995	17.81	5.07
3	1	-	25	2	0.995	21.78	4.33
4	1	-	27	10	0.994	21.9	5.27
5	1	-	30	3	0.994	25	4.98
6	2	-	16/8	3	0.994	28	3.957

Table 5: ANNS' model architecture for each of the three sample charts using 78 data points

Chart no.	No. of layers	Range of varying PEs	Optimum no. of PEs	No. of runs/PEs variation
1	1	4-12	4	10
6	1	4-12	10	10
11	1	4-12	10	10

Table 6: ANNS' and cubic spline interpolation results for each of the three sample charts using 78 data points

Chart no.	R		Max relative error in speed (%)		Mean relative error in speed (%)	
	ANNs	C.S.	ANNs	C.S.	ANNs	C.S.
1	0.998	1	2.3	0.696	0.632	0.185
6	0.999	1	3.577	0.251	0.581	0.09
11	0.999	1	5.317	0.277	1	0.1

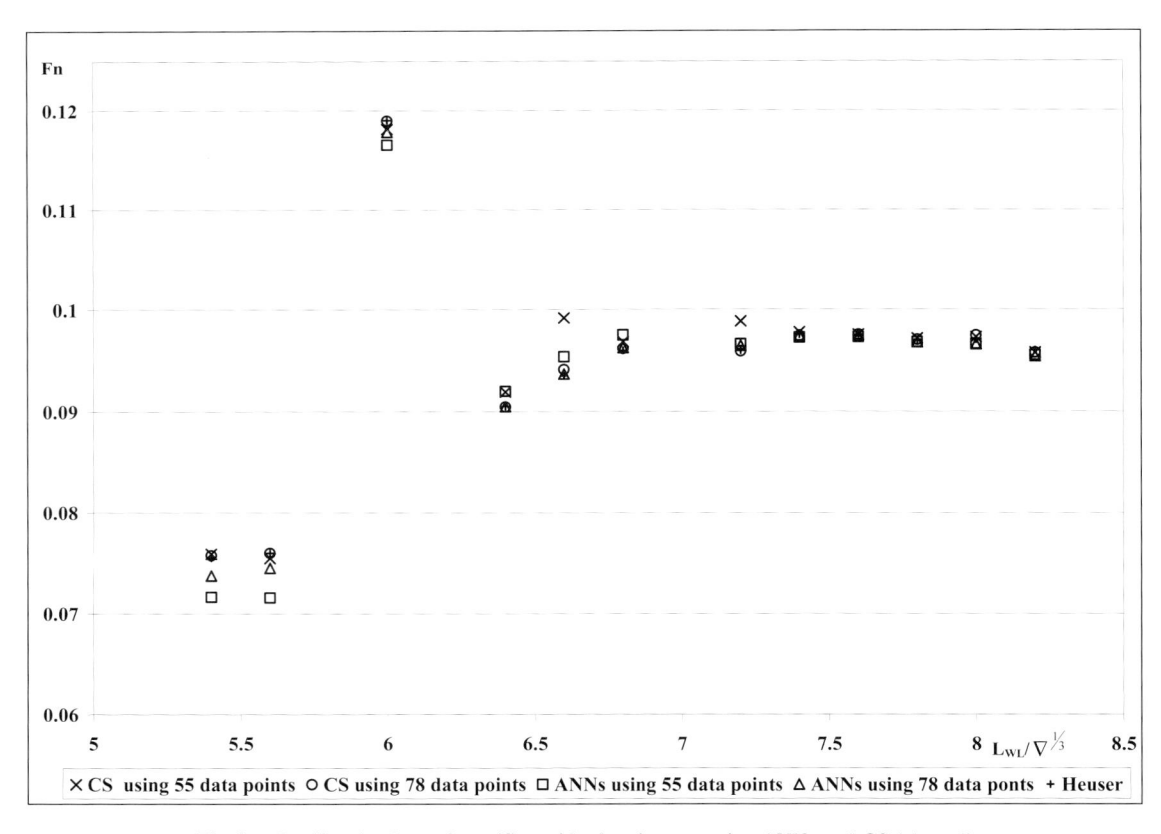

Fig. 2: Predicted values of specific residual resistance using ANNs and CS (chart 1)

5. Concluding Remarks

Based on the above mentioned models and the results obtained, no general rule can be derived on the best means for pattern recognition of specific residual resistance of ships, but this depends on the type of data and number of data points available. However the following remarks can be concluded.

The results outlined in Tables 1 and 4, show that although ANNs have large capabilities in capturing the pattern from scatter data, the accuracy of the results obtained should be treated with care, particularly those for maximum error.

Table 3 shows the superior capabilities of ANNs in comparison to cubic spline interpolation in predicting the specific residual resistance from a small number of random data points within a limited range of variation (the same chart), and within an acceptable error.

In the case where data are represented by curves of defined geometry and smooth nature, Table 6 shows that the ability of cubic spline interpolation for fitting polynomials to curves and recalculating the values at various points is by far more efficient than ANNs. The results obtained by cubic spline interpolation are the same as those measured from real charts, bearing in mind the error due to measurement precision from the charts. It should be mentioned that the capabilities of cubic splines are highly dependent on the selection of training points, as they should properly describe the geometry of the curves.

The error mentioned in Tables 3 and 6 due to the application of ANNs and cubic spline interpolation is not the final one. This is due to the fact that one more interpolation step is required for calculating the specific residual resistance at the required speed in case of ANNs. For cubic spline interpolation, two more interpolation steps are required, one for calculating the speed at intermediate values of $\sqrt{B.T.C_m}/h$ and the other for calculating the specific residual resistance at the required speed. Therefore, ANNs still have the advantage of one reduced interpolation step for the final required output (R_R/∇ at the required speed).

Integrating the results from one of the above mentioned methods for the estimation of residual resistance with other modules for different aspects of ship design and carrying out optimization using Genetic Algorithms (GA) is the intention of the authors in the future. This requires full evaluation of the design for each proposed unit and comparison of different alternatives and involves numerous evaluations for the residual resistance and consequently how fast it can be done is an important issue.

The added accuracy of CS can be counteracted by the requirement of two more interpolation steps within the optimization code which will augment the error and can be time consuming. Also, the requirement of this high accuracy in the conceptual design stage can be considered of no prime importance. The same result can be extended to the method of applying ANNs to each chart independently although it has one reduced interpolation step.

Although evaluating all the charts at once using ANNs has an increased error, this is the fastest way to evaluate the residuary resistance during optimization runs. CS can be applied to the best designs that will be chosen from the optimization process to have better prediction of their resistance.

However, it must be investigated if considering each chart independently using ANNs or CS will have a noticeable effect on the determination of the optimum design and on the speed of convergence of the optimization process.

Acknowledgement

The authors would like to thank Prof. A. S. Sabit for valuable comments and advice.

References

Alkan, AD, Trincas, G, and Nabergoj, R (2005). "Seakeeping Metamodel of Fast Ro-Ro Ships: RSM or ANN Technique?", IMAM 2005, Lisbon, Portugal, pp 789-806.

Chapra, SC, and Canale, RC (1998)." Numerical Methods for Engineering," third edition, WCB/McGraw-Hill.

Elhewy, AH, Mesbahi, E, and Pu, Y (2006). "Reliability Analysis of Structures Using Neural Network Method," Probabilistic Engineering Mechanics, Vol 21(1), pp 44-53.

Heuser, H (1980). " Widerstand und Leistungsbedarf von Binnenschiffen," VBD-Bericht 960.

Jiang, T (2001). "A New Method for Resistance and Propulsion Prediction of the Ship Performance in Shallow Water," 8th International Symposium on Practical Design of Ships and Other Floating Structures, Shanghai, China.

Kamar, L (1993). " Zur Ermittlung von Formfaktoren fuer Seeschiffe aus Modellversuchen auf Tiefem Wasser," Schiff & Hafen, Vol 45.

Kamar, L (1996). " Wassertiefe – Ihr Einfluss auf den Formfaktor von Seeschiffen," Schiff & Hafen, Vol 48.

Kempf, G (1923)." Wirtschaftliche Geschwindigkeit bei Fahrt auf Flachem Wasser," Werft, Reederei, Hafen, 4.Jahrgang, Heft 23.

Landweber, L (1939)." Test of a Model in Restricted Channels," USEMB Report No. 460.

Leheta, HW (2002)."Decision Making in the Marine Field," Internal Report, Department of Marine Engineering and Naval Architecture, Alexandria University, Egypt.

Mason, A, Couser, P, Mason, G, Smith, CR, and von Konsky, BR (2005). "Optimization of Vessel Resistance using Genetic Algorithms and Artificial Neural Networks," COMPIT 2005, Hamburg, Germany, pp 440-454.

Mesbahi, E, and Atlar M (1998)."Applications of Artificial Neural Networks in Marine Design and Modelling," AIOMA Workshop, Hamburg.

Principe, JC, Neil, RE, and Curt Lefebrre, W (1999). "Neural and adaptive system," John Wiley & Sons, Inc.

Ray, T, Gokarn, RP, and Sha, OP (1995). "A global Optimization Model for Ship Design," Computers in Industry, Vol 26, pp 175-192.

Ray, T, and Gokarn, RP, and Sha, OP (1996). "Neural Network Applications in Naval Architecture and Marine Engineering," Artificial Intelligence in Engineering, Vol 1, pp 213-226.

Schlichting, O (1934)." Schiffswiderstand auf Beschraenkter Wassertiefe," Widerstand von Schiffen auf Flachem Wasser, 34. Hauptversammlung, Schiffbautechnische Gessellschaft.

Wolf, R, Dickmann, J, and Boas, R (2005)."Ship Design Using Heuristic Optimization Methods," 46th AIAA/ASME/ASCE/AHS/ASC Structures, Structural Dynamics & Materials Conference, 18 - 21 April 2005, Austin, Texas.

APPENDIX A

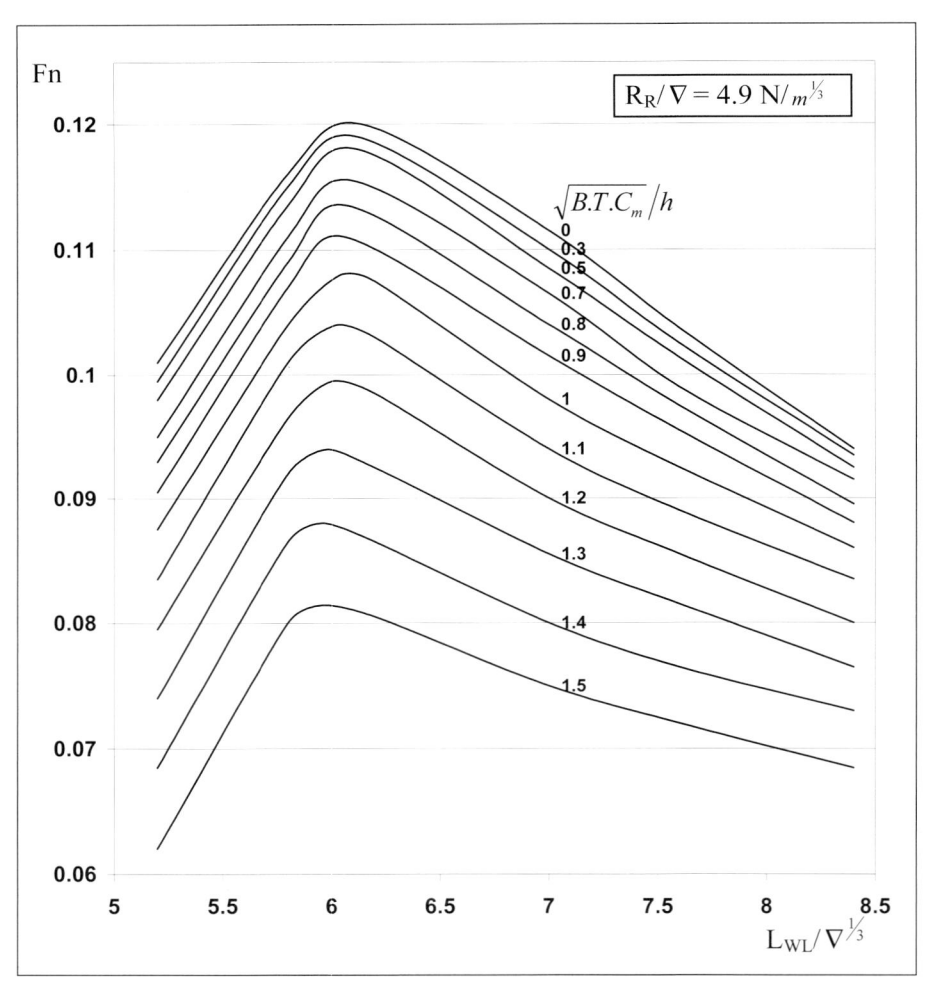

Chart 1 (Heuser, 1980)

APPENDIX B

Correlation Factor (r) = $\dfrac{\sum xy}{\sqrt{\sum x^2 \sum y^2}}$

Where:

x = $X - \bar{X}$

y = $Y - \bar{Y}$

X: observed values

$\bar{X}$: Mean of X

Y: Predicted values

$\bar{X}$: Mean of Y

Mean relative error = $(\sum abs(\dfrac{X-Y}{X}*100))/n$

Maximum relative error = $\max(\dfrac{X-Y}{X}*100)$

n: number of sampling points

A Comparative Study for the Fatigue Assessment of Typical Ship Structures using Hot Spot Stress and Structural Stress Approaches

Myung Hyun Kim[1], Sung Won Kang[1], Seong Min Kim[1], Jae Myung Lee[1],
Young Nam Kim[2], Sung Geun Kim[2], Kyoung Eon Lee[2], and Gyeong Rae Kim[2]

[1] Dept. of Naval Architecture and Ocean Engineering
Pusan National University, Busan, Korea
[2] Hull Design Team,
Hanjin Heavy Industries & Construction CO., LTD., Busan, Korea

Abstract

Recently, a mesh-size insensitive structural stress definition (structural stress method) is proposed that gives a stress state at weld toe with a relatively coarse mesh, such as up to 2t (t=plate thickness) or irregular mesh shapes while hot spot stress requires t mesh and regular shaped meshes. The structural stress definition is based on the elementary structural mechanics theory and provides an effective measure of a stress state in front of weld toe. In this study, a fatigue strength assessment for a side shell connection of a container vessel using both the hot spot stress and the Battelle structural stress method was carried out. A consistent approach to computing extrapolated hot spot stress for design purposes based on converged hot spot stresses is described and current fatigue guidance is evaluated. Fatigue strength predicted by the two methodologies, e.g. hot spot stress and structural stress approaches, at hot spot locations of a typical ship structure are compared and discussed.

Keywords

Fatigue design; Structural stress; Hot spot stress; Welded structures; Fatigue life; Fatigue strength evaluation.

Introduction

The welding procedure involves metallurgical discontinuity during heating and cooling processes. Defects such as inclusion, pores, cavities and undercuts are also inherent. In addition, residual stress and distortion are found to be inevitable. For these reasons, fatigue fracture of welded structure is even more complex to evaluate. As ship and offshore structures are also typical steel-plated structures involving welding procedure, they are directly exposed to fatigue damage.

The validity of fatigue design can be assessed by quantifying applied local stresses and by selecting proper S-N curve. Currently, there are three main approaches available in the definition of local stress, such as notch, nominal and hot spot stresses.

Notch stress is not normally applied to assess fatigue strength of welded structures due to difficulty in evaluating the exact non-linear peak stress at weld toe and due to uncertainty of weld toe shape. Thus, nominal stress has been extensively employed to assess fatigue strength of welded structures. A proper S-N curve classified with respect to weld joint type can be used considering geometric discontinuity. Difficulties are encountered occasionally in applying S-N curves available in the literature, particularly complex structures such as ships.

Hot spot stress method has been developed based on finite element method and its characteristics. The hot spot stress is defined as local stress obtained by extrapolating stresses at certain distances away from geometrically discontinuous area such as weld toe. The result of this approach, however, is known to be very sensitive to element type and mesh size in the vicinity of the weld toe due to stress concentration. The results also vary relying on commercial finite element codes due to the difference in the ways of interpolating or extrapolating stresses from Gaussian integration point. For these reasons, a proper guideline for the basis of calculating hot spot stress is required to remove the ongoing controversy.

Recently, the mesh-insensitive structural stress has been introduced as a mesh-size insensitive method. The structural stress is expressed in the form of membrane and bending stress components that satisfies equilibrium conditions based on finite element analysis. In this method, balanced nodal forces are used for estimating the local stresses in the vicinity of the considered weld toe. The results, therefore, have less deviation than the stress obtained from shape functions inside of elements.

Fatigue cracks in nearly all welded joints start at pre-existing flaws, the presence of which can be taken as the equivalent of an initial crack. In consequence the whole, or at least the major part, of the fatigue life is taken up by the propagation phase of crack growth (Gurney, 1979). Because fatigue lives of welded structures are more dependent on crack propagation than on crack initiation, the fatigue strength must be different corresponding size of the structures and type of loading modes even if shape of the structures is the same. In order to solve the problem of the size and loading mode effect, the structural stress approach can be considered by means of thickness correction and a function considering loading modes associated with the unified master S-N curve developed from crack propagation in the vicinity of weld toe from the fracture mechanics point of view (Battelle, 2004).

The aim of this study is to investigate fatigue assessment of typical ship structures employing structural stress approach and to compare with hot spot stress approach. FE analyses for side shell connections of a container vessel were performed to calculate structural stress and hot spot stress.

Structural Stress

Definition of structural stress

The stress gradient through plate thickness is formed as illustrated in Fig. 1 (a). The stress distribution can be divided into linear part and non-linear part due to the notch effect at weld bead. The former provides a clue to the definition of structural stress which is the summation of the membrane (σ_m) and the bending stress (σ_b) derived from mechanical equilibrium condition in front of the weld toes. The latter can be evaluated by crack propagation model with notch effect determined by plate thickness and type of loading mode to assess fatigue life.

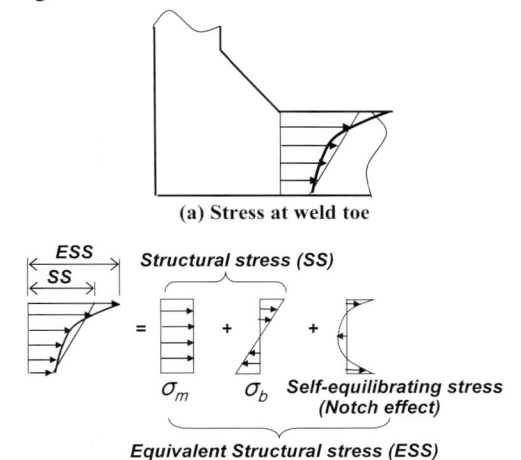

Fig. 1: Definition of structural stress

(a) Stress at weld toe

(b) Stress decomposition

In FE analysis using 2-D shell or plate element, balanced nodal forces can be derived from the element stiffness matrices and the nodal displacements as described Eq. (1). The same applies to the derivation of balanced nodal moments using nodal rotational displacement.

$$\{F\} = [K]\{d\} \qquad (1)$$

where $\{F\}$= vector of nodal forces, $[K]$= element stiffness matrix, $\{d\}$= nodal displacement

Once the nodal forces (F_{y1}, F_{y2}) in y direction and moments with respect to x axis are obtained as shown in Fig. 2 (a), the corresponding line forces (f_{y1}, f_{y2}) can be calculated with consideration of the mechanical equilibrium as derived to Eqs. (2), (3) and (4). The derivation of line moments (m_{x1}, m_{x2}) are the same as that of the line forces with respect to the nodal moments (M_{x1}, M_{x2}).

$$\sum F_{yi} + \int_0^l f_y(x)dx = 0 \qquad (2)$$

$$\sum F_{yi} x_i + \int_0^l f_y(x) \cdot x dx = 0 \qquad (3)$$

$$f_{y1} = \frac{2}{l}(2F_{y1} - F_{y2}), \quad f_{y2} = \frac{2}{l}(2F_{y2} - F_{y1}) \qquad (4)$$

$$m_{x1} = \frac{2}{l}(2M_{x1} - M_{x2}), \quad m_{x2} = \frac{2}{l}(2M_{x2} - M_{x1}) \qquad (5)$$

where l = element size along the weld line as described Fig. 2

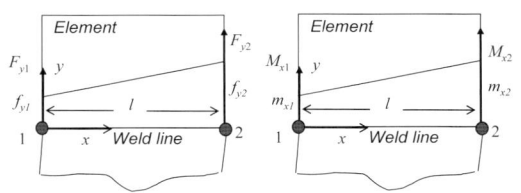

(a) Method in single element

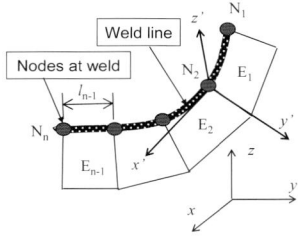

(b) Method in multi-elements

Fig. 2: Local line force and moment from nodal forces and moments for 4 node shell element

Once the line force and the line moment are available, the structural stress at each node can be given by Eq. (6).

$$\sigma_s = \sigma_m + \sigma_b = \frac{f_y}{t} + \frac{6m_x}{t^2} \qquad (6)$$

where, σ_s is stress concentration effects due to joint geometry and σ_m, σ_b are membrane and bending stress respectively.

Previous description is about how to calculate structural stress in single element. Structural stress in mutielements is available to calculate with similar manner. For more details, see the reference (Battelle structural stress JIP final report, 2004).

Equivalent structural stress with the master S-N curve

Equivalent structural stress parameter can be defined by normalizing the structural stress range ΔS_{eq} with two variables expressed in terms of t and r (bending ratio, $r = \sigma_b / \sigma_s$) on Eq. (7) (Dong, 2002).

$$\Delta S_{eq} = \frac{\Delta \sigma_s}{t^{\frac{2-m}{2m}} I(r)^{\frac{1}{m}}} = CN^{-\frac{1}{m'}} \quad (7)$$

where the thickness term $t^{(2-m)/2m}$ (m=3.6 according to Dong; the exponent of Paris crack propagation) becomes unity for t=1 (unit thickness) and therefore, the thickness t can be interpreted a ratio of actual thickness t to a unit thickness, rendering the term dimensionless. With this interpretation, the equivalent ΔS_{eq} retains a stress unit. $I(r)$ is the function of bending ratio (r) which indicates corrections depending on various loading modes, and it can be divided into load-controlled condition and displacement-controlled condition. For details to derive the $I(r)$ function, see the reference (Battelle, 2004). In this study, loading mode effects $I(r)^{1/m}$ is employed as Eq. (8) and Eq. (9) for edge crack and semi-elliptical crack, respectively.

$$I(r)^{\frac{1}{m}} = 2.4712r^6 - 5.5828r^5 + 5.0365r^4 \\ - 1.9617r^3 + 0.4463r^2 + 0.035r + 1.1392 \quad (8)$$

$$I(r)^{\frac{1}{m}} = 0.0011r^6 + 0.0767r^5 - 0.0988r^4 \\ + 0.0946r^3 + 0.0221r^2 - 0.014r + 1.2223 \quad (9)$$

Since the thickness correction, the loading mode effects and geometrical discontinuities have been already included in Eq. (7), any type of weld joints or loading modes can be evaluated consistently with the equivalent structural stress. Based on Eq. (7), over 2000 results of the existing fatigue tests for both various weld joints and loading modes are fitted in Fig. 3 and a master S-N curve is determined by Ha(2006). Based on Fig. 3, required parameters for S-N relationship can be obtained as Eq. (10) and Eq. (11). Here, the design master S-N curve is on the basis of two standard deviations with respect to mean S-N curve.

For the mean master S-N curve, C=21672.4, m'=3.08
$\log N_f$=13.33-3.08$\log \Delta S_{eq}$ (10)

For the design master S-N curve, C=15465.6, m'=3.08
$\log N_f$=12.88-3.08$\log \Delta S_{eq}$ (11)

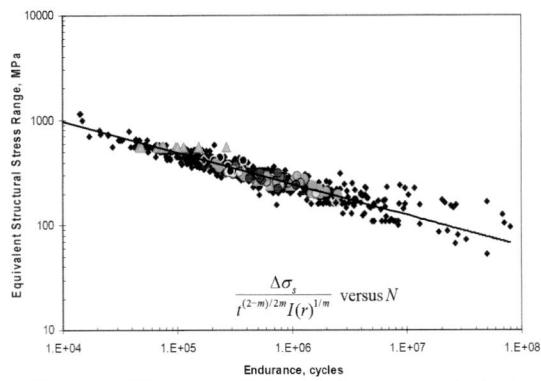

Fig. 3: The master S-N curve by using equivalent structural stress parameter

Hot spot stress

To evaluate stress for welded joints, hot spot stress has been adopted by major classification societies for obtaining local stresses at weld toe. Hot spot stress is defined as the stress obtained from extrapolation of surface stresses at certain distance from the weld toe. There are a few different stress extrapolation techniques as commonly recommended procedures for the calculation of hot spot stresses in welded. In this study, the hot spot stress was assumed as the linear extrapolation of stress over reference points at $0.5t$ and $1.5t$ away from the weld toe as illustrated in Fig. 4 if the mesh size is less than $1.0t$.

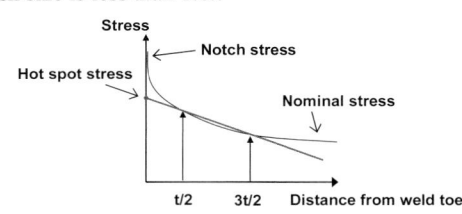

Fig. 4: Definition of hot spot stress in accordance with Classification societies

Fatigue life assessment of ship structures

Fatigue life assessment of welded joints in ship structures can be carried out using long term stress distribution and S-N curves.

In the case of simplified fatigue analysis, fatigue strength is analyzed using loadings defined from classification societies, not using ship motion analysis. The fatigue damage ratio is finally estimated using Palmgrens-Miner rule with long-term stress range distribution. The long-term stress range distribution is defined by the Weibull distribution. The fatigue life is calculated employing Weibull distribution factors (scale and shape parameter) and relevant S-N curves.

Flow diagram over fatigue analysis procedures are shown in Fig. 5 applying equivalent structural stress and notch stress using master S-N curve and DNV S-N curve. Load response in the diagram includes the loadings from internal or external pressure and hull girder wave bending moments. Using each equivalent structural stress and notch stress defined with respect to load cases, combined stress ranges can be obtained and fatigue damage ratio is calculated from long-term stress range distribution and the master S-N curve and DNV S-N curve.

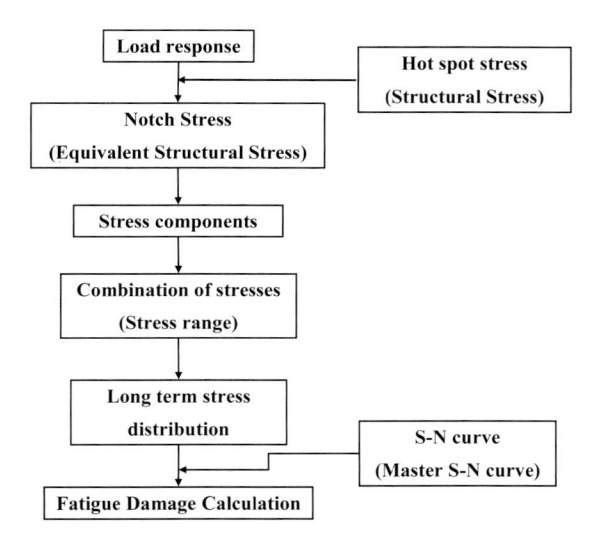

Fig. 5: Flow diagram over fatigue analysis procedures

Load responses

In the simplified method, dynamic loading may be divided into global wave bending moments and local load such as external pressure and internal pressure.

The following eight dynamic load cases have been applied to the FE model and the load cases applied are listed in Table 1. Boundary condition of the finite element model was applied as a simple support condition.

Table 1: Load cases considered for fatigue calculation

	Loading type	Loading condition
LC1	Vertical wave bending moment	Fully loaded / Ballast
LC2	Horizontal wave bending moment	Fully loaded
LC3	Horizontal wave bending moment	Ballast
LC4	Torsional moment	Fully loaded
LC5	Torsional moment	Ballast
LC6	External pressure	Fully loaded
LC7	External pressure	Ballast
LC8	Internal pressure	Ballast

Combined stress from load response

Since global wave bending moments are based on vertical wave bending moment and horizontal wave bending moment at 10^{-8} probability level of exceedance from IACS, they are modified to 10^{-4} probability level of exceedance to be compatible with pressure loading components defined at 10^{-4} probability level. Using correlation factor (ρ) which considers phase difference for combination of vertical and horizontal wave load, global combined stress range ($\Delta\sigma_g$) is finally defined by Eq. (12).

$$\Delta\sigma_g = \max \begin{cases} 2|\sigma_h + \sigma_{wt} + \sigma_{gt} + 0.45\sigma_v| \\ \sqrt{\Delta\sigma_v^2 + \Delta\sigma_h^2 + 2\rho_{vh}\Delta\sigma_v\Delta\sigma_h} \end{cases} \quad (12)$$

where $\Delta\sigma_g$ = combined grobal stress range

$\Delta\sigma_v$ = range of stress due to wave induced vertical hull girder bending moment ($\sigma_v = 1/2\ \Delta\sigma_v$)

$\Delta\sigma_h$ = range of stress due to wave induced horizontal hull girder bending moment ($\sigma_h = 1/2\ \Delta\sigma_h$)

σ_{wt} = warping stress due to torsion at position considered

σ_{gt} = bending stress of deck structure due to torsional deformation of hatch(=0)

ρ_{vh} = 0.10, average correlation between vertical and horizontal wave induced bending stress

External pressure is determined comparing dynamic pressures from ship rolling motion and ship pitching motion, whichever is higher. The internal pressure is determined from the acceleration of liquid cargo or ballast water among three directions and selected from whichever is the highest.

Local combined stress range ($\Delta\sigma_l$) is composed of external and internal pressures with a correlation factor expressed in Eq. (13). Local combined stress range is divided into full loaded condition and ballast condition.

$$\Delta\sigma_l = \sqrt{\sigma_e^2 + \sigma_i^2 + 2\rho_p\sigma_e\sigma_i} \quad (13)$$

where $\Delta\sigma_l$ = combined local stress range

σ_e = amplitude of stress due to the dynamic external sea pressure loads (tension=positive)

σ_i = amplitude of stress due to the dynamic internal pressure loads (tension=positive)

ρ_p = average correlation between sea pressure loads and internal pressure loads

$$= \frac{1}{2} - \frac{z}{10\cdot T_{act}} + \frac{|x|}{4\cdot L} + \frac{|y|}{4\cdot B} - \frac{|x|\cdot z}{5\cdot L\cdot T_{act}}$$

where L is rule length of ship in meter and T_{act} is actual draft. B is the greatest moulded of the ship and x, y, x are the longitudinal, transverse and vertical distance from the origin (at midship, centerline, baseline) to the load point of the considered structural detail.

If a combined long term stress response analysis is not carried out, the combined stress range response from the combined global stress and local stress range responses is the largest of (Hovem, L., 1993) :

$$\Delta\sigma_0 = f_e \cdot f_m \cdot \max\begin{cases} 0.6 \cdot \Delta\sigma_g + \Delta\sigma_l \\ \Delta\sigma_g + 0.6 \cdot \Delta\sigma_l \end{cases} \quad (14)$$

where f_e is the operation route reduction factor and f_m is the mean stress reduction factor (f_m=0.85 maybe applied on the long term stress distribution). A reduction in the effective estimated stress response is achieved for vessels that for longer periods operate in environments not as harsh as the North Atlantic. For world wide trade, the reduction factor may be taken as 0.8.

Cumulative damage

When the long-term stress range distribution is defined applying Weibull distributions for the different load conditions, and a one-slope S-N curve is used, the fatigue damage is given by (DNV, 2003),

$$D = \frac{v_0 T_d}{a} \sum_{n=1}^{N_{load}} p_n q_n^{m'} \Gamma(1+\frac{m}{h_n}) \leq \eta \quad (15)$$

where, D = accumulated fatigue damage

a, m = S-N fatigue parameters

N_{load} = total number load conditions considered

p_n = fraction of design life in load condition n

T_d = design life of ship in seconds

h_n = Weibull stress range shape distribution parameter for load condition n

q_n = Weibull stress range scale distribution parameter for load condition n

V_0 = long-term average response zero-crossing frequency

η = usage factor. Accepted usage factor is defined as η =1.0

$\Gamma(1+\frac{m'}{h_n})$ = gamma function

The Weibull scale parameter is defined from the stress range level, $\Delta\sigma_0$, as

$$q = \frac{\Delta\sigma_0}{(\ln n_0)^{1/h}} \quad (16)$$

where, n_0 is the number of cycles over the time period for which the stress level $\Delta\sigma_0$ is defined.

Fatigue strength assessment in side longitudinal web connections of a container vessel

Target structure

In this study, typical fatigue crack points are assumed in the vicinity of intersection of side longitudinals and transverse web frame for a 8,100 TEU class container carrier. Principal dimension of container vessel is listed in Table 2 and finite element model for full ship is shown in Fig. 6

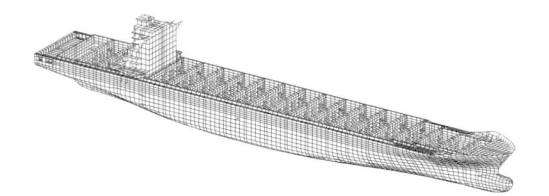

Fig. 6: Finite element model of container vessel

Table 2: Principal dimension of target vessel

Length of ship	305.356m
Breadth of ship	42.8m
Depth of ship	24.6m
Draft, Fully loaded	14.47m
Draft, Ballast loaded	7.42m
Max. Speed	26.4knot

Fatigue crack definition

FE analysis is carried out for full ship and structural stresses as well as hot spot stresses are calculated in critical details of side longitudinals located between design draft (T_F) and ballast draft (T_B). Fig. 7 shows the concerned section of web frame and local area in finite element model, and Table 3 lists the design details. In this study, two different types of stiffener were modeled to compare with fatigue life assessment with respect to stiffener type. One is L-type stiffener shown in Fig. 8 and the other is T-type stiffener shown in Fig. 9 with 1.0t mesh size. Three FC (Fatigue Crack) points for L-type slot detail and T-type slot detail are defined as shown in Fig. 8 and Fig. 9, respectively. For each HS (Hot Spot) point, semi-elliptical cracks are anticipated at HS 1 and HS 2 on the longitudinal face plate and collar plate, whereas edge cracks are expected at HS 3.

Table 3: Geometry of stiffener considered

Distance above keel	8.176m
Stiffener spacing	868mm
Height of stiffener	300mm
Thickness of web	11mm
Width of flange	90mm
Thickness of flange	16mm

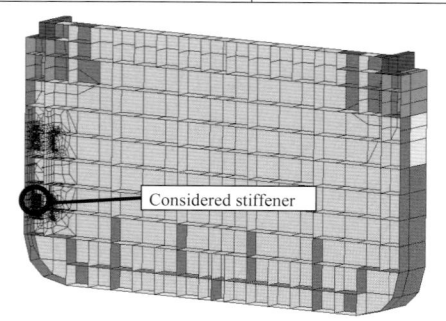

Fig. 7: Section of midship in finite element model

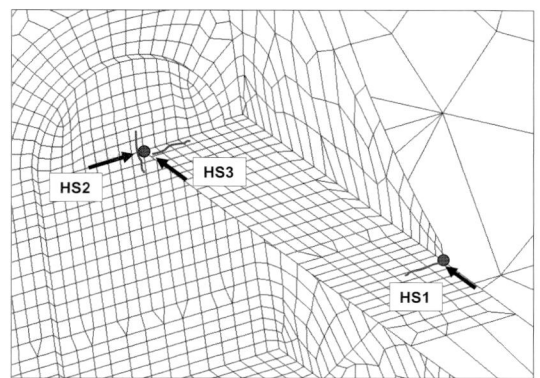

Fig. 8: Fatigue crack definition for L-type slot detail

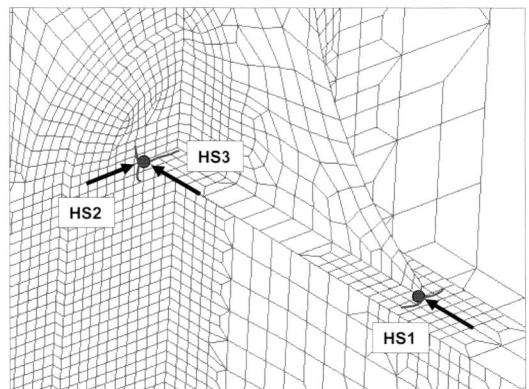

Fig. 9: Fatigue crack definition for T-type slot detail

Calculation of stresses at HS points using hot spot stress (HSS) and structural stress (SS)

The results of hot spot stress and structural stress are shown in Table 4, Table 5 and Table 6 for HS points, respectively. The result of stresses hot spot stress and structural stress is found to be similar as listed in tables. L-HS and T-HS mean hot spot point of L-type and T-type slot detail, respectively.

Table 4: Results of hot spot stress and structural stress with respect to load cases at HS 1

| | L-HS 1 || T-HS 1 ||
	HSS(MPa)	SS(MPa)	HSS(MPa)	SS(MPa)
LC1	46.74	44.93	39.98	38.92
LC2	43.34	41.68	36.78	35.93
LC3	32.14	30.92	27.3	26.65
LC4	41.05	39.40	34.34	33.28
LC5	33.15	31.23	27.72	26.88
LC6	-38.95	-36.23	-31.14	-21.99
LC7	-20.08	-18.78	-11.7	-8.50
LC8	18.79	17.01	12.13	10.89

Table 5: Results of hot spot stress and structural stress with respect to load cases at HS 2

| | L-HS 2 || T-HS 2 ||
	HSS(MPa)	SS(MPa)	HSS(MPa)	SS(MPa)
LC1	15.08	19.99	5.02	13.71
LC2	18.98	17.79	7.89	7.04
LC3	14.07	13.53	5.86	5.22
LC4	9.71	8.75	6.37	5.50
LC5	7.85	7.07	5.14	4.44
LC6	-59.78	-66.38	-76.53	-88.22
LC7	-71.71	-84.25	-89.56	-103.6
LC8	-11.19	-17.08	-9.65	-13.68

Table 6: Results of hot spot stress and structural stress with respect to load cases at HS 3

| | L-HS 3 || T-HS 3 ||
	HSS(MPa)	SS(MPa)	HSS(MPa)	SS(MPa)
LC1	39.87	39.33	33.39	32.90
LC2	32.25	32.29	29.97	29.63
LC3	23.93	23.95	22.23	21.98
LC4	28.53	28.95	18.70	18.10
LC5	23.04	23.38	15.10	14.62
LC6	-5.16	-6.89	-6.26	-5.70
LC7	8.845	6.37	-0.05	0.13
LC8	12.43	9.73	12.14	10.73

Fatigue life assessment using hot spot stress and structural stress

For the design life of 20 years, fatigue damage ratio has been calculated with the equivalent structural stress (ESS) and the design master S-N curve. In order to compare with the fatigue lives from the hot spot stress (HSS) approach, the S-N curve from DNV Classification Note No. 30.7 was employed. Parameters for the use of design master S-N curve and DNV curve are as given in Table 7. Palmgrens-Miner rule was used to calculate damage ratio.

Table 7: S-N parameters

$\log N = \log a - m \log \Delta\sigma$		
	$\log a$	m
Design master S-N curve	13.33	3.08
DNV curve	12.76	3.0

Calculation of Equivalent structural stress

With respect to the HS points, equivalent structural stresses are established as listed in Table 8 and Table 9. I(r) function for HS 1 and HS 2 is based on load controlled condition, while I(r) function for HS 3 is based on structural joint condition.

Table 8: Results of equivalent structural stress at L-type HS points (unit: MPa)

	HS 1	HS 2	HS 3
LC1	68.19	24.16	-63.71
LC2	62.99	23.05	52.39
LC3	46.92	17.6	38.86
LC4	59.80	11.93	-46.76
LC5	48.29	9.63	-37.76
LC6	-55.04	-90.76	-0.26
LC7	-28.55	-114.33	0.01
LC8	25.821	-19.28	15.11

Table 9: Results of equivalent structural stress at T-type HS points (unit: MPa)

	HS 1	HS 2	HS 3
LC1	59.05	17.82	53.45
LC2	54.33	9.29	48.04
LC3	40.43	6.89	35.64
LC4	50.50	7.55	25.19
LC5	40.78	6.09	20.34
LC6	-33.36	-122.89	-8.11
LC7	-12.91	-144.09	0.01
LC8	16.52	-14.35	13.27

Fatigue life at HS 1

Table 10 lists fatigue lives calculated based on the procedure above. The structural stress approach gives higher fatigue life but only a small difference in fatigue life is found between the two results of the hot spot stress approach. From fatigue life point of view with respect to slot detail, T-type slot detail gives much higher fatigue life at HS 1.

Table 10: Result of fatigue life at HS 1

		ESS	HSS
L-HS 1	Damage ratio	0.542	0.568
	Fatigue life (year)	37	35
T-HS-1	Damage ratio	0.267	0.322
	Fatigue life (year)	75	62

Fatigue life at HS 2

Calculated fatigue lives for HS 2 are listed in Table 11. According to these results, fatigue life from the structural stress is also higher than hot spot stress approach. Indeed, difference of about 20% in fatigue life is considered to be reasonable. In addition, the tendency of fatigue life with respect to slot detail is different to HS 1. It is considered that stress gradient under bending stress in unsymmetrical stiffener is lower than symmetrical stiffener at the end of the flange as illustrated in Fig. 10. At the same time, bending stress due to external pressure (LC6, LC7) is dominant at HS 2 as listed in Table 5.

Table 11: Result of fatigue life at HS 2

		ESS	HSS
L-HS 2	Damage ratio	0.388	0.349
	Fatigue life (year)	52	57
T-HS-2	Damage ratio	0.665	0.509
	Fatigue life (year)	30	39

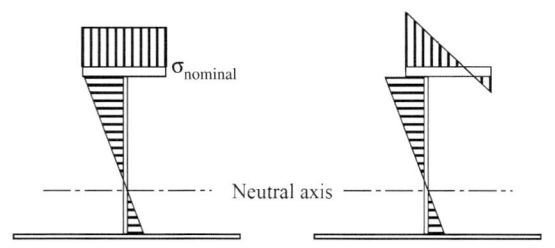

Fig. 10: Bending stress in symmetrical and unsymmetrical panel stiffener with same web and flange areas

Fatigue life at HS 3

Evaluation of fatigue lives at HS 3 is carried out in the same manner as HS 1 and HS 2. Result of fatigue life is similar structural stress approach and hot spot stress approach as listed in Table 12. Also fatigue life of T-type is higher than L-type slot detail as well known.

Table 12: Result of fatigue life at HS 3

		ESS	HSS
L-HS 3	Damage ratio	0.126	0.117
	Fatigue life (year)	158	171
T-HS-3	Damage ratio	0.057	0.061
	Fatigue life (year)	346	328

Conclusion

1. A consistent structural stress approach is employed for the fatigue strength assessment of side-longitudinal stiffeners of a 8100 TEU container vessel. The similar fatigue life results are compared with that of hot spot stress approach.

2. In general, T-type longitudinal stiffeners exhibit higher fatigue strength compared to that of L-type longitudinal stiffeners. At certain locations such as HS 2, however, L-type longitudinal stiffeners, which are unsymmetrical, exhibit higher fatigue strength under bending loads.

3. For fatigue strength assessment of ships, structural stress approach is found to be a viable alternative as employing the mesh size insensitive characteristics. Further study for the fatigue strength assessment of ship and offshore structures are required with different mesh size and shapes.

Acknowledgement

This study was performed under the ASERC research program. The authors are pleased to acknowledge the support of Hanjin Heavy Industries & Construction CO., LTD.

References

Center for welded structures research Battelle, "Mesh-Insensitive structural stress method for fatigue evaluation of welded structures", Battelle structural stress JIP final report No. N004431-01., 2004

C. I. Ha, "A study on the fatigue strength of welded joints using structural stress with consideration of stress singularity and its application to the fatigue life assessment of ship structures", M.S. Thesis, Pusan National University, Busan Korea 2006

C. G. Soares and Y. Garbatov, "Reliability based fatigue design of maintained welded joints in the side shell of tankers", The 3rd International Symposium on Fatigue Design, Editors: G. Marquis and J. Solin, European Structural Integrity Society (ESIS), pp. 13-28, 1998

C. H. Shin, "Simplified fatigue strength assessment of ship structures" Journal of the Korean Welding Society, Vol. 16 ,No. 5, pp.11-19, 1998 (Korean)

Det Norske Veritas, "Fatigue assessment of ship structure", Classification Notes No. 30.7, 2003

Det Norske Veritas, "Rules for classification of ships- Part 3 Chapter 1 Hull structural design ships with length 100 meters and above", 2003

Dong P, Hong JK, Cao Z., Structural stress based master S-N curve foe welded joints, IIW Doc XIII-1930-02/XV-1119-02, International Institute of Welding, 2002

H. Kyuba and P. Dong, "Equilibrium-equivalent structural stress approach to fatigue analysis of a rectangular hollow section joint", International journal of fatigue, pp. 85-94, 2004

Hovem, L., Loads and load combination for fatigue calculations – Background for the wave load section for the DNVC classification note : Fatigue assessment of ships, DNVC Report No. 93-0314, Høvik, 1993

T. R. Gurney, "Fatigue of welded structures", Cambridge university press, 1979

Study on the Relationship between Shell Stress and Solid Stress in Fatigue Assessment of Ship Structure

Naoki Osawa[1], Kiyoshi Hashimoto[1], Junji Sawamura[1], Tohei Nakai[1], Shota Suzuki[1]

[1] Department of Naval Architecture and Ocean Engineering, Osaka University
Suita, Osaka, Japan

Abstract

The relation between shell and solid stresses in T-shape cantilever beam models is examined. Based on the results, a technique to estimate true local stress only from shell stress components is proposed. The validity of the proposed technique is verified by examining the local stress in wide hopper corner joint models and BC lower stool joint. The following results were found:

(1) In T-shape beam, a linear relationship exists approximately between the shell / solid stress difference and the transversal shell surface bending stress. The transversal bending effective factor is closely proportional to the ratio of web thickness to flange thickness.

(2) It is possible to estimate solid surface stress with satisfactory accuracy from shell stress components alone using the relations described in the preceding paragraph.

(3) The relation between shell and solid stresses derived from T-shape beam results holds approximately true in wide hopper corner joint models and BC lower stool joint. This statement demonstrates the validity of the proposed true stress estimation technique in fatigue assessment of actual ship structures.

Keywords

Fatigue; Hot spot stress; Finite element analysis; Coupling analysis.

Introduction

The approaches to the fatigue strength assessment have been further developed during recent years (e.g. Fricke, 2003). In addition to the conventional nominal stress approach, local approaches such as the (structural) hot-spot stress (HSS) approach have reached the stage of practical application.

Regarding the HSS approach, experimental and analytical procedures have been derived for its determination by extrapolating the structural stress outside the localized notch-affected zone to the weld toe (e.g. Niemi, 1995). In most classification society rules where the weld geometry is neglected, the HSS is evaluated with shell FE models. In these cases, special care is needed to avoid misinterpreting the FE results.

The Common Structural Rules, CSR, went into effect in 2006. In the CSR, the fatigue design load has been raised drastically in comparison with the conventional rules. Over-conservative HSS evaluation could inadmissibly impair the economy of the ship design. It is necessary to establish a HSS determination technique based on shell FE analysis with a reasonable safety margin.

When a solid FE model is employed, modeling of welds is easily possible, and the stress field in the vicinity of the weld can be investigated with a high degree of precision. The safety margin of shell-based HSS determination techniques can be examined by comparing shell stress and solid stress. The HSS figures derived from shell and solid analyses are compared in some studies (e.g. Fricke, 2002). In these studies, relatively coarse solid meshes were used in order to exclude the notch effect. The calculated stress depends considerably on FE mesh. In this case the relation between shell and solid stresses cannot be clearly examined. This ambiguity can be eliminated by comparing shell stress with solid stress as calculated by the use of fine mesh that can reproduce the notch effect. The reference for the HSS can be determined by letting this solid stress be the measured stress.

The authors (Osawa et al., 2007b) examined the surface stress in the vicinity of the weld of small joint models. In their study, fine solid meshes that can reproduce the notch effect were used. They found that the solid stress at a distance of d from the weld toe agrees with the shell stress at a distance of d from the plate surface intersection apart from the shell element nearest to the structural intersection. This fact means that the true (solid) stress can be estimated by the use of a shell model when the point directory below the intersection of the plate surfaces is selected as the point to represent the weld toe in shell analysis.

The validity of the proposed technique was demonstrated only in the cases where cross-sectional deformation of the base plate is negligible. In actual ship structures, the cargo load induces the out-of-plane deformation of the inner walls, and cross-sectional deformation can be comparable to longitudinal bending deformation. The validity of the proposed technique has to be examined for these cases.

In this study, the local stresses of T-shape beam, wide hopper corner joint and BC lower stool subject to lateral pressure load are examined by shell and shell-solid coupling FE models. Based on the results, the relation between the shell and solid stresses in the cases where cross-sectional deformation of the base plate cannot be neglected is discussed.

Methodologies

Shell-solid coupling and shell FE analyses

Global shell FE models are usually employed in ship structural analysis for simplicity and low cost. Local solid FE models are used in the investigation of local stress field in the vicinity of the weld. It is needed to transfer the angular rotations or the moments of the global shell elements to the translational displacements or forces of the local solid elements. The rotation / moment can be easily converted by using shell-solid coupling FE models in the local analysis.

The shell-solid coupling can be achieved by use of a fictitious shell plane perpendicular to the original shell plane as shown in Fig. 1. Hereafter, this technique is called the 'perpendicular shell coupling method (PSCM)'. The authors (Osawa et al., 2007a) examined the local stresses of the stool-like welded joint models by using the PSCM-based shell-solid coupling FE models, and proposed the guidelines for PSCM technique for ship structural analysis as follows:

a) The thickness of the fictitious shell, t_S, is comparable to the plate thickness;

b) The 3-dimensional solid part extends to a minimum of five times of plate thickness from the hot spot.

In this study, solid surface stress on the solid part of a PSCM-based shell-solid coupling model created in accordance with the above guidelines is used as a reference for shell surface stress calculated by shell models. In solid modeling, the root gaps of the welds are not modeled.

Coupling analyses are performed by MSC. Marc 2005r2. Solid parts are comprised of three-dimensional arbitrarily distorted brick elements (Element 7). Shell parts are comprised of 4-node or 3-node bilinear thick-shell elements (Element 75). The number of the integration point in the direction of the thickness is 9 (default). The material properties of steel (E=200GPa, ν=0.3) are given to the models.

Shell analyses are performed by MSC. Marc 2005r2, and thick-shell (Element 75) elements are used.

The surface stresses are evaluated by linear extrapolation of solid element stresses (for solid parts of coupling models) or shell layer stresses (for shell models).

Definition of the hot spot

In a solid model, the notch is chosen as the hot spot. That is, the intersection of the plate surfaces is chosen for the model having no weld beads, and the weld toe for the model with weld beads.

In a shell model, three kinds of hot spot are considered:
- type-i: the intersection of the mid-planes of shell plates;
- type-ii: the point directory below the intersection of the plate surfaces (the hot spot of a solid model without weld bead);
- type-iii: the point directory below the weld toe.

Hereafter, let x, ξ and d denote the distances of the read-out-points (ROPs) from the hot spot type-i, type-ii and type-iii as shown in Fig. 2. They are related to each other through the following equations.

$$d = x - (\Delta + l), \ \xi = x - \Delta; \ \Delta = \frac{t_v}{2}\csc\phi - \frac{t_h}{2}\cot\phi, \quad (1)$$

where, t_h, t_v are the thicknesses of the base and cross plates, l the leg length, ϕ the angle at which the base and cross plates intersect.

The authors (Osawa et al., 2007b) showed that the solid stress at d=D and the shell stress at ξ=D are in fairly good agreement when d and ξ is larger than the plate thickness for the hopper corner model examined in JIP FPSO Fatigue Capacity (2000) and the perpendicular joint model examined in Sugimura et al. (2001) subject to longitudinal bending loads.

T-shape cantilever beams subject to pressure load

Finite element modeling

To examine the nature of the relation between shell and solid stresses, a T-shape cantilever beam shown in Fig. 3 subject to pressure load on the flange is examined. Thicknesses of the flange and web, t_f and t_w, are (t_f, t_w)= (10mm, 5mm), (10mm, 10mm), (10mm, 20mm), (20mm, 10mm), (20mm, 20mm). 'Downward pressure' and 'Upward pressure' loads shown in Fig. 4 are applied. In the later condition, downward point load is applied at the free end while upward pressure is applied on the faceplate. In this section, the model with (t_f, t_w)= (10mm, 10mm) is referred to as 'base' model. We consider the coordinates shown in Fig. 3, x in the longitudinal direction (directed from the fixed end to the free end), y in the transversal direction and z in the vertical direction.

The longitudinal (x-dir.) and transversal (y-dir.) components of surface stress, σ_{sx} and σ_{sy}, are calculated by the use of the shell and solid FE models. The element size of the shell model is $t_f \times t_f$. In the solid model, 8 layers of solid elements are arranged over the thickness. The minimum element size is $t_f/8 \times t_f/8 \times t_f/8$. These stress components are evaluated along the intersection between flange and web plates.

Deformation

The deformations calculated by solid models are in good agreement with the results of shell models without distinction of t_f and t_w. This means that solid models employed reproduce the bending rigidity of shell models.

Fig. 6 shows the calculated deformation of 'base' T-shape beam model. Both longitudinal and transversal bending deformations are produced. For 'downward pressure' condition, both bending deformations are convex upward. For 'upward pressure' condition, longitudinal bending deformation is convex upward, and transversal is convex downward. The degree of cross-sectional deformation is comparable to the longitudinal bending deformation in these cases.

Surface stress of 'base' model

Fig. 7 shows the comparisons of σ_{sx} calculated by shell and solid models of 'base' T-shape beam. Unlike the cases where cross-sectional deformation is negligible reported by the authors (Osawa et al., 2007b), large differences between shell and solid stresses are recognized. Fig. 6 and Fig. 7 show that shell stress overestimates true (solid) stress when the transversal bending is convex upward, while it underestimates when convex downward. It is also shown that the larger the transversal bending deformation is, the bigger the difference becomes between shell and solid stresses.

We define 'shell / solid stress difference' $\Delta\sigma_{sx}$ as

$$\Delta\sigma_{sx} = \sigma_{sx,SHELL} - \sigma_{sx,SOLID}, \quad (2)$$

where, $\sigma_{sx,SHELL}$ and $\sigma_{sx,SOLID}$ are the longitudinal surface stress components calculated by shell and solid models. Hereafter, the transversal shell surface bending stress is represented by $\sigma_{sy,B}$. The above results lead us to an assumption that a linear relationship exists approximately between $\Delta\sigma_{sx}$ and $\sigma_{sy,B}$. Fig. 8 shows the relation of $\Delta\sigma_{sx}$ and $\sigma_{sy,B}$. Fig. 9 shows the variation of the ratio of $\Delta\sigma_{sx}$ to $\sigma_{sy,B}$ with the distance from the fixed end, x. These figures show that the relation between them can be approximated as

$$\Delta\sigma_{sx} = k\,\sigma_{sy,B}, \quad (3)$$

with the exception of the vicinities of both ends. The coefficient k in Eq. (3) is almost the same as the ratio $\Delta\sigma_{sx}/\sigma_{sy,B}$ within the region of x>40mm, and it is about 0.1 for this 'base' model. Hereafter, this coefficient k is called the 'transversal bending effective factor'. Eq. (3) does not hold true near the fixed end (x≤30mm), but this does not significantly affect the accuracy of the estimated surface stress because $\Delta\sigma_{sx}$ is much smaller than true stress (=$\sigma_{sx,SOLID}$) in this region.

Effect of plate thickness

The relation between shell and solid stresses similar to that of 'base' model is observed for all other models. Fig. 10 shows the variation of the ratio of $\Delta\sigma_{sx}/\sigma_{sy,B}$ along the stress evaluation path for T-shape beams with various plate thicknesses. The transversal bending effective factor k for each model can be identified from $\Delta\sigma_{sx}/\sigma_{sy,B}$ within the region of x>40mm. This figure shows that k depends on web and flange thicknesses. Hereafter, the ratio of web thickness to flange thickness, $R=t_w/t_f$, is called 'thickness ratio'.

Fig. 11 shows the relation between k and R. It is shown that this relation can be approximated by a linear equation,

$$k = 0.09R = 0.09\,t_w/t_f. \quad (4)$$

Estimation of solid stress from shell stresses

The following equation is derived from Eqs. (2), (3) and (4):

$$\sigma_{sx,SOLID} = \sigma_{sx,SHELL} - 0.09(t_w/t_f)\sigma_{sy,B}. \quad (5)$$

Using this equation, we can estimate true surface stress (=solid stress) only from the shell calculation result.

Fig. 12 shows the comparisons of σ_{sx} calculated by shell and solid models of T-shape beams with various plate thicknesses. The estimated true stresses evaluated by Eq. (5) are also plotted in the figures. It is shown that the estimated true stress agrees well with the solid stress. This demonstrates the validity of the proposed true stress estimation technique for T-shape cantilever beams with various plate thicknesses.

Wide hopper corner models subject to pressure load

Finite element modeling

Wide hopper corner models subject to lateral pressure load are examined. Models with and without end girder are employed. The end plate of the model is fixed on the rigid wall, and downward pressure 0.2N/mm² is applied on tank top plate. We consider the (x,y,z) coordinates shown in Fig. 13, and the longitudinal (x-dir.) and transversal (y-dir.) components of surface stress, σ_{sx} and σ_{sy}, are calculated

Thicknesses of all plates, t, is 10mm. Weld bead is not modeled in solid modeling. The hot spot is located at the transition from the tank top plate to the sloped plate. The quantities in Eq. (1) are $l=0$, $t_v=t_h=t=10$mm, $\phi=\pi/4$ and $\Delta=\Delta+l=2.071$mm.

Shell FE meshes employed are shown in Fig. 13. The element size near the hot spot is t x t. Solid stress is evaluated by the use of the PSCM-based shell-solid coupling models. The fictitious shell thickness t_S is chosen so that t_S/t is 1.0. The solid parts extend to a minimum of seven times of plate thickness from the hot spot. In the solid part, 8 layers of elements are arranged over the thickness. The minimum element size is t/8 x t/8 x t/8.

Relation between shell and solid stresses

Fig. 15 shows the deformations of shell FE models. Both longitudinal and transversal bending deformations are produced. Transversal bending is smaller than the longitudinal one for the model with end girder while transversal bending is dominant for the model without end girder.

Fig. 16 shows the comparisons of σ_{sx} calculated by shell and coupling models. Distance ξ is plotted in abscissa. The estimated true stresses calculated by Eq. (5) are also plotted. As in the case of T-shape beam, there exists a difference between shell and solid stresses, and the larger the transversal bending deformation is, the bigger the shell / solid stress difference $\Delta\sigma_{sx}$. The estimated true stress agrees well with solid stress.

These results show that true stress (solid stress) cannot be evaluated accurately when we simply assume that $\sigma_{sx,SHELL}$ equals to $\sigma_{sx,SOLID}$ and choose the intersection of the plate surfaces as the point to represent the notch in shell analysis. The results also demonstrate the effectiveness of the proposed true stress estimation technique in local stress assessment of hopper corner-like structures subject to pressure load.

BC lower stool joint

Finite element modeling

In order to verify the effectiveness of the proposed true stress estimation technique in fatigue assessment of actual ship structures, the local stress in BC lower stool joint is examined. The local stress is examined by the submodeling technique. The nodal displacements near the joint is calculated by 1/2+1+1/2 hold FE model shown in Fig. 17, and they are transferred to local models as boundary conditions. Calculations are performed for two load cases; case 1 (alternate load condition) and case 2 (heavy ballast condition); the CSR-B's P2 wave is chosen as design wave.

The local stresses are calculated by shell model and shell-solid coupling model shown in Fig. 18. The hot spot is located at the intersection point of stool, girder and tank top. We consider the (x,y,z) coordinates shown in Fig. 18, and the longitudinal (x-dir.) and transversal (y-dir.) components of surface stress, σ_{sx} and σ_{sy}, are calculated. The evaluation path lies along the x-direction.

Plate thicknesses are 24.15mm for tank top (t_f) and 27mm for girder (t_w). The element size of the shell model near the hot spot is $t_f \times t_f$. Solid stress is evaluated by the use of the PSCM-based shell-solid coupling models. Both the solid part with weld beads and those without weld beads are used in coupling FE models. In the model with weld bead, beads of the weld between tank top's upper face and lower stool, and that between tank top's back face and girder, are modeled as shown in Fig. 19. The quantities in Eq. (1) are l=40mm, t_v=24.15mm, t_h=19.8mm, $\phi=\pi/2$ and Δ=12.08mm.

The fictitious shell thickness t_S is chosen so that t_S/t_f is 1.0. The solid parts extend to 200mm from the hot spot. In the solid part, 8 layers of solid elements are arranged over the thickness. The minimum element size is $t_f/8 \times t_f/8 \times t_f/8$.

Relation between shell and solid stresses

Fig. 20 shows the deformations of local shell FE models. Transversal bending is convex upward in case 1, and convex downward in case 2.

Fig. 21 shows the comparisons of σ_{sx} calculated by shell and coupling models. The distance ξ is plotted in abscissa for shell model and coupling model without beads, and d for coupling model with beads. Shell stress underestimates the true stress in case 1, and it overestimates in case 2. These results can be anticipated from the results in the previous sections. The estimated true stresses calculated by Eq. (5) are also plotted in Fig. 21. The estimated true stress agrees well with solid stress. This demonstrates that true local stress can be estimated with satisfactory accuracy from longitudinal and transversal shell surface stresses calculated by 'very fine' (t x t) shell mesh.

Conclusions

The relation between shell and solid stresses in T-shape cantilever beam models is examined. Based on the results, a technique to estimate true local stress from shell stress components alone is proposed. The validity of the proposed technique is verified by examining the local stress in wide hopper corner joint models and BC lower stool joint. The following results are found:

(1) In T-shape beam, a linear relationship exists approximately between the shell / solid stress difference and the transversal shell surface bending stress. The transversal bending effective factor is almost proportional to the ratio of web thickness to flange thickness.

(2) It is possible to estimate solid surface stress with satisfactory accuracy only from shell stress components using the relations described in the preceding paragraph.

(3) The relation between shell and solid stresses derived from T-shape beam results holds approximately true in wide hopper corner joint models and BC lower stool joint. This demonstrates the validity of the proposed true stress estimation technique in fatigue assessment of actual ship structures.

Acknowledgement

This research was carried out as a part of the joint research project between Osaka University and Nippon Kaiji Kyokai. The authors gratefully acknowledge Dr. Norio Yamamoto and Dr. Koji Terai for providing BC hold model and their guidance and comments.

References

Fricke, W. (2002) Recommended hot-spot analysis procedure for structural details of ships and FPSOs based on round-robin FE analysis. Int. J. Offshore and Polar Engineering; 12(1):40-47.

Fricke, W. (2003) Fatigue analysis of welded joints: state of development. J. Marine Structure; 16:185-200.

JIP FPSO Fatigue Capacity. (2000) "Hot Spot Stress Analysis of Five Structural Details and Recommendeations for Modeling, Stress Evaluation and Design S-N Curve", Germanischer Lloyd.

MSC. Software Inc. (2005), "MSC.Marc 2005 - Reference Manual", vol. B.

Niemi, E. (1995) Recommendations concerning stress determination for fatigue analysis of welded components. IIW-Doc. XIII-1458-92/XV-797-92, Abington Pub., Cambridge, UK.

Osawa, N., Hashimoto, K., Sawamura, J., Nakai, T. and Suzuki, S. (2007a) "Study on shell-solid coupling FE analysis for fatigue assessment of ship structure", J. Marine Structures, in Printing.

Osawa, N., Hashimoto, K., Sawamura, J., Nakai, T. and Suzuki, S. (2007b) "Study on the relationship between shell stress and solid stress in the vicinities of ship's welded joints", Proc. 17th International Offshore and Polar Engineering Conference, Lisbon, in Printing.

Sugimura, T., Inoue S., Shirakihara H. (2001) Study on fatigue assessment of perpendicular cross joint. In: Proc. 2001 Autumn Meeting of Kansai Soc. Naval Architects, Japan. p.63-66 (in Japanese)

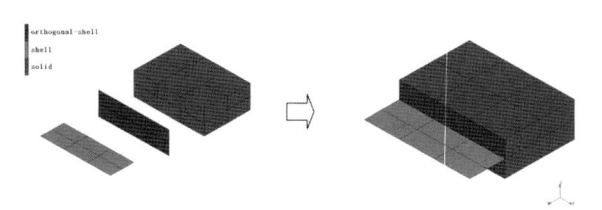

Fig. 1: The concepts of perpendicular shell coupling method (PSCM).

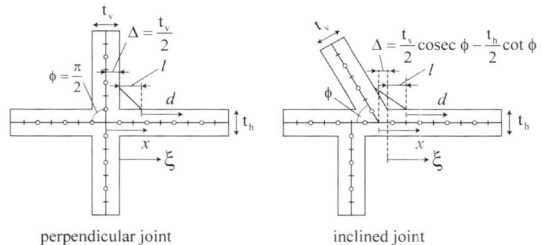

Fig. 2: Distance of the read-out-points (ROPs) from the hot spot.

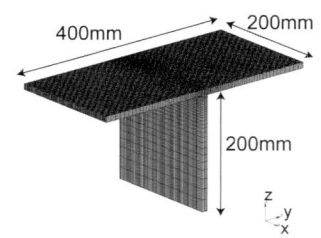

Fig. 3: A T-shape cantilever beam.

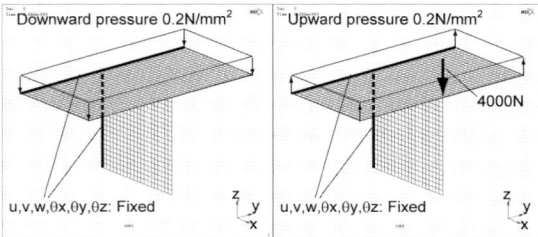

Fig. 4: Pressure load applied to the T-shape cantilever beam.

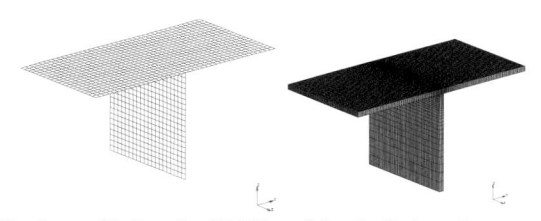

Fig. 5: Shell and solid FE models of a T-shape beam.

(a) Downward pressure load.

(b) Upward pressure load.

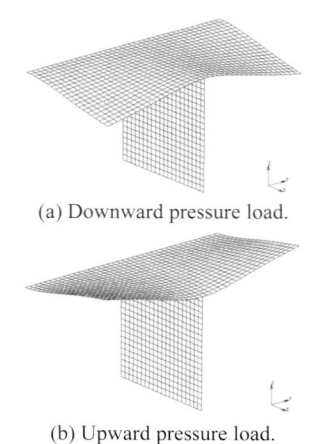

Fig. 6: Deformation of a 'base' T-shape beam subject to pressure loads.

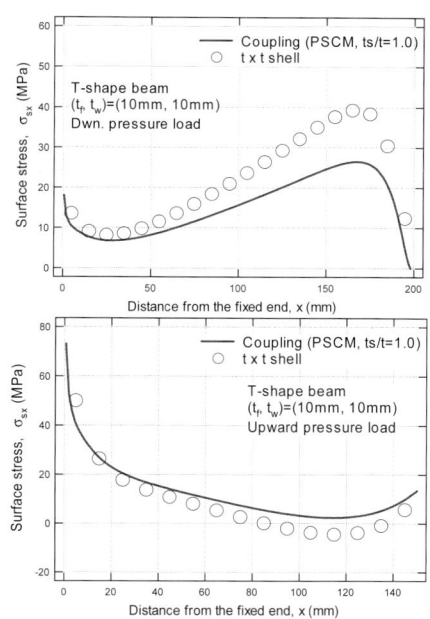

Fig. 7: The longitudinal surface stress components of a 'base' T-shape beam calculated by shell and solid models.

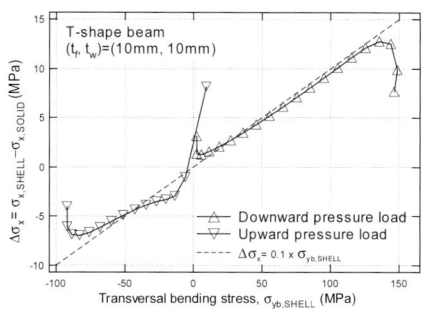

Fig. 8: Relation of the shell / solid stress difference and shell bending stress ('base' T-shape beam model).

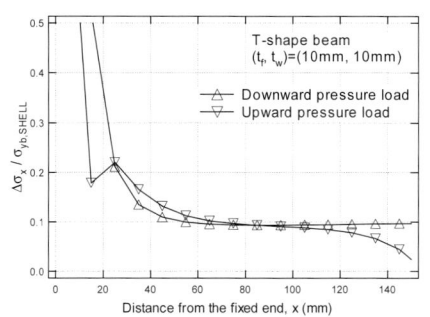

Fig. 9: Variation of the ratio of the shell / solid stress difference to the transversal bending stress along the stress evaluation path ('base' T-shape beam).

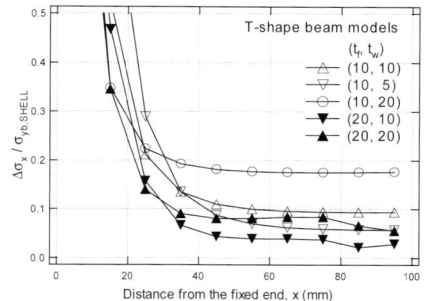

Fig. 10: Variation of the ratio of the shell / solid stress difference to the shell bending stress along the stress evaluation path (T-shape beams with various plate thicknesses).

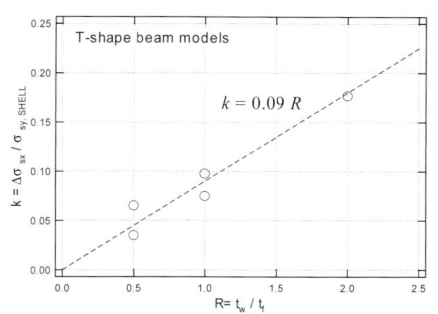

Fig. 11: Relation of the transversal bending effective factor and the thickness ratio.

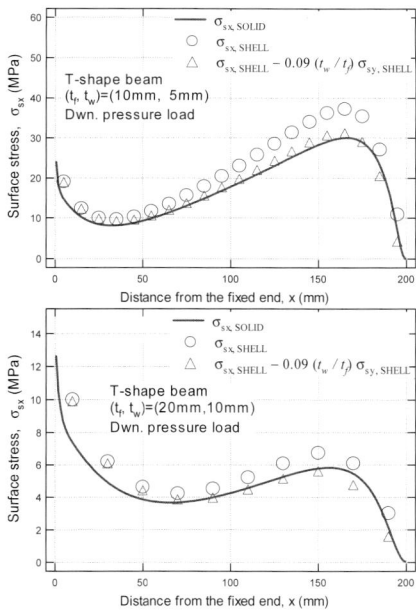

Fig. 12: The longitudinal surface stress components of T-shape beams with various plate thicknesses calculated by shell and solid models.

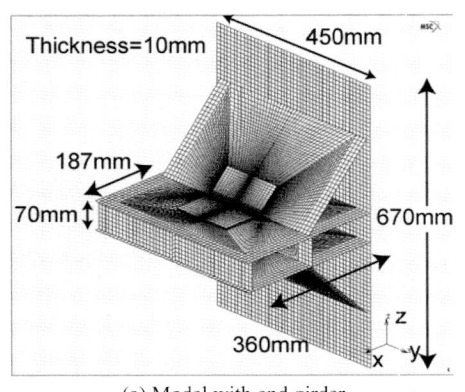

Fig. 13: Shell FE meshes of the wide hopper corner models.
(a) Model with end girder.
(b) Model without end girder.

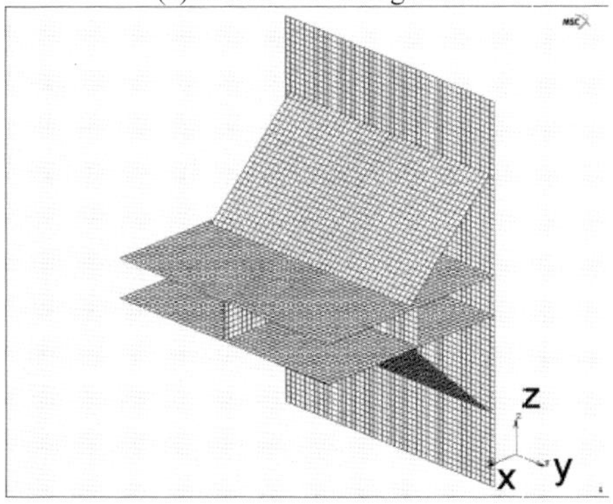

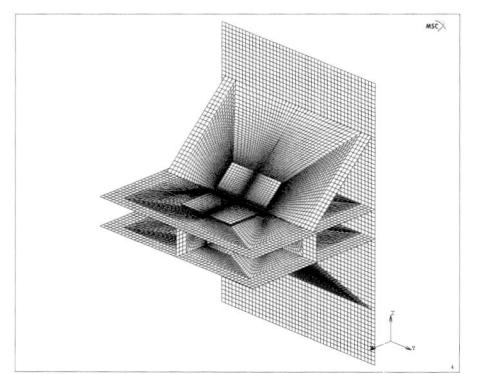

Fig. 14: Shell-solid coupling FE mesh of the wide hopper corner model without end girder.

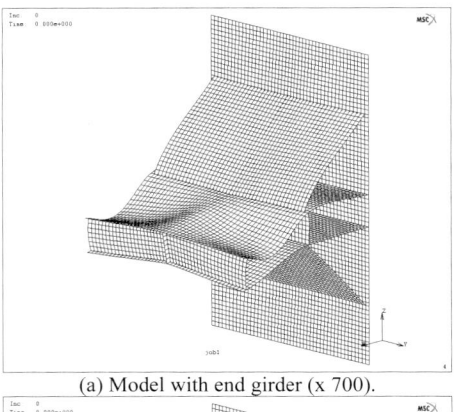

Fig. 15: Deformation of wide hopper corner models (shell FE models).
(a) Model with end girder (x 700).
(b) Model without end girder (x 50).

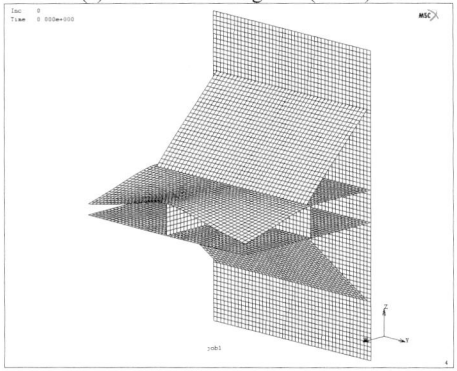

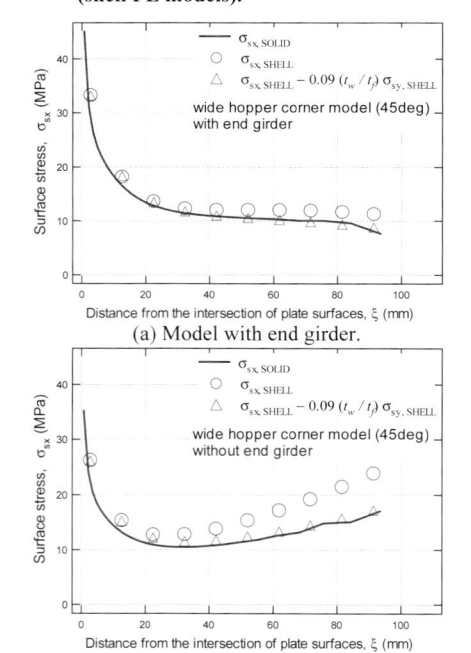

Fig. 16: The longitudinal surface stress components of wide hopper corner models.
(a) Model with end girder.
(b) Model without end girder.

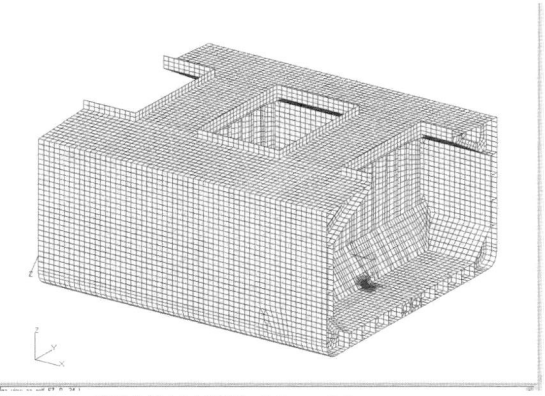

Fig. 17: BC 1/2+1+1/2 hold model.

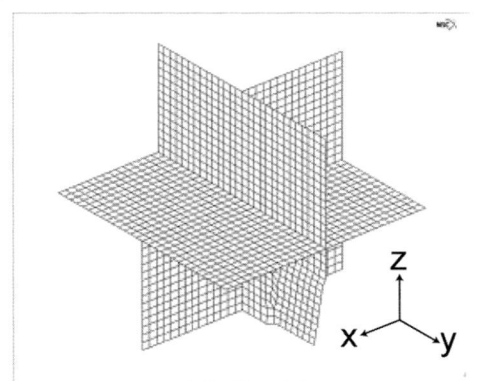

(a) Shell model.

(b) Shell-solid coupling model.

Fig. 18: Local FE models of BC lower stool joint.

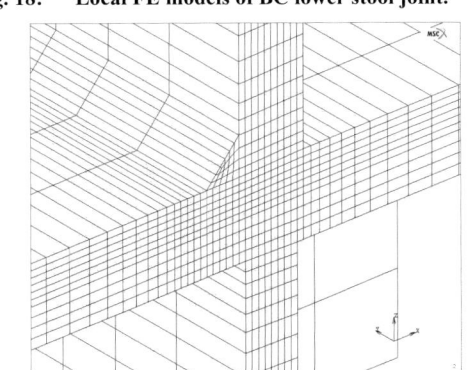

Fig. 19: Weld bead in the solid part of the coupling model with weld beads.

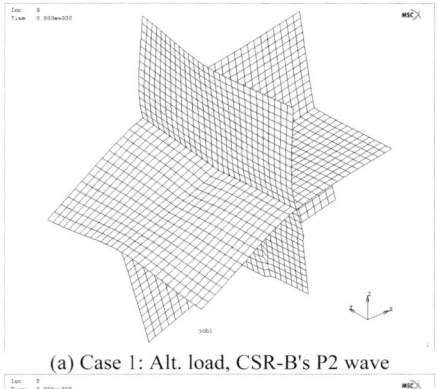

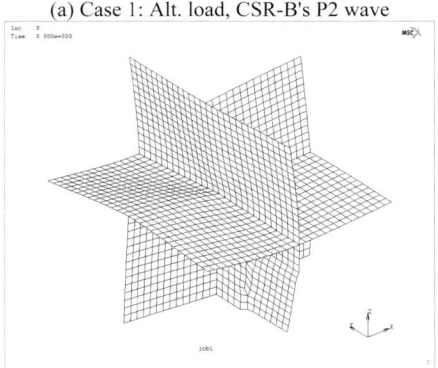

(a) Case 1: Alt. load, CSR-B's P2 wave

(b) Case 2: Heavy ballast, CSR-B's P2 wave

Fig. 20: Deformation of the local shell model of BC lower stool joint subject to actual loads.

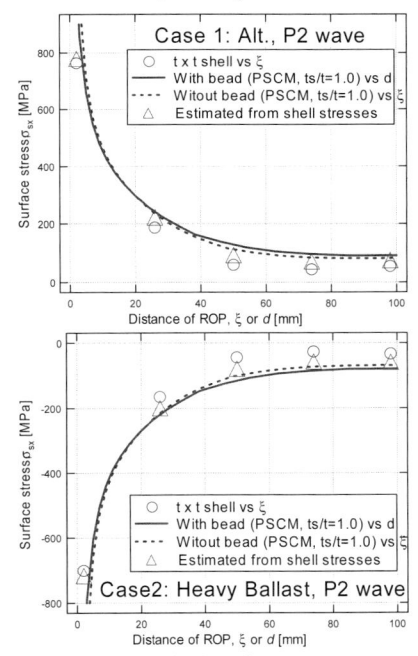

Fig. 21: The longitudinal surface stress components of BC lower stool joint.

A Study on the Fatigue under Combined Tensile and Compressive Mean Stresses in Ship Structure

Joo-Ho Heo[1], Joong-Kyoo Kang[1], Kyung-Su Kim[2], Hang-Sub Urm[3]

[1]Daewoo Shipbuilding & Marine Engineering Co.,Ltd.,
Keoje, Kyungnam, Korea
[2]Inha University
Incheon, Korea
[3]Det Norske Veritas Korea
Busan, Korea

Abstract Heading

A great deal of experimental validation work was performed in order to verify the combination method proposed by the DNV and the well-known linear combination of calculated damages due to low and high cycle loading. A number of fatigue tests using cruciform welded joints under the various loading cases that may consider the effect of various amplitude loadings were carried out. In order to evaluate a mean stress effect in high cycle loading, the various loading cases were also applied to fatigue tests. All of the fatigue test data with various loading cases were compared to the results from the low cycle fatigue test and the high cycle fatigue test, respectively. Fatigue damages due to combined fatigue test were calculated and compared based on pseudo hot spot stress and nominal stress. Based on the fatigue tests and damage calculation results using various methods, the most accurate damage calculation result from the combined damage test was obtained from the case of the linear combination method with peak-to-peak range based on pseudo hot spot stress considering mean stress effect.

Keywords

Low cycle fatigue; High cycle fatigue; Damage combination; Ship structure; Welded joint; Mean stress effect; Pseudo hot spot stress.

Introduction

Combined fatigue damage calculation is an established study for exact assessment of the fatigue life. This calculation will eliminate the uncertainty created by the combination of high cycle fatigue with low cycle fatigue as well as consider the mean stress effect with which high cycle fatigue loadings apply. The confidence of fatigue life superior to that typically assigned to conventional calculation method in combined fatigue loading history is expected. However, the current linear fatigue damage accumulations for combined fatigue loadings are not based on fatigue test data for high cycle loading with mean stress.

Also, most of the discussion about fatigue behavior has generally dealt with constant amplitude loading. In contrast, for many fatigue-critical parts of ships and offshore structures, most load history under service conditions basically involves random or variable-amplitude loading, rather than constant amplitude loading. Linear fatigue damage accumulation calculation for variable-amplitude load history combined low cycle loading with high cycle loading might make an unconservative result due to load interaction effect. Several methods have been developed to deal with variable-amplitude loading using the baseline data generated from constant amplitude tests. DNV proposed a fatigue damage formula combined with the low cycle fatigue damage and the high cycle fatigue damage in Technical Report for "Development of Low Cycle Fatigue Criteria for Ship Structures".

Therefore, this study has a plan to carry out the fatigue tests with combined-loading to examine load interaction effect and also confirm that the combination fatigue damage formula proposed by DNV is reasonable for predicting fatigue life.

Experimental process

Engineering material and test specimen

The type of all the specimens used in this study that are for combined fatigue damage test and for mean stress effect test is a welded cruciform joint whose detail is designed with a non-load carrying partial penetrated cruciform joint. The mechanical properties of those specimens are listed in Table 1. In Table 1, the steel grade of base metal is A. The geometry of the specimen is shown in Fig. 1. Welding was made on both side of the attachment with the number of pass 2 for each weld line. Weld leg length was approximately 8 mm and lack of penetration was 7 mm. The weld conditions for typical three specimens are shown in Table 2.

Table 1: Monotonic test results for engineering steels

Type	Young's Modulus (MPa)	Yield Strength (MPa) Upper YS	Yield Strength (MPa) Lower YS	Ultimate Strength (MPa)
Weld	208,161	564.734	547.604	603.229
Base Metal	200,033	264.281	264.282	440.793

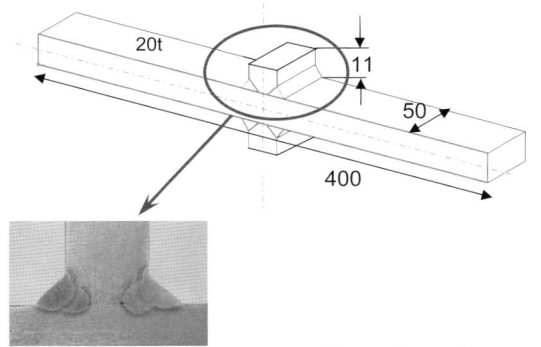

Fig.1: Geometry of welded cruciform joint (unit: mm)

Table 2: Weld conditions

No	Pass No.	Process	Current (A)	Voltage (V)	Speed (cm/min)
1	1	FCAW	260	27	105/1'42"
1	2	FCAW	260	31	105/2'30"
2	1	FCAW	260	27	105/2'03"
2	2	FCAW	260	30	105/2'32"
3	1	FCAW	260	27	105/2'04"
3	2	FCAW	260	30	105/2'32"

Load cases

Generally, fatigue damage calculation is based on completely reversed, constant amplitude loading. The mean stress effect is, for the most part, negligible on the fatigue life of a component. However, components in ships experience this type of loading, as variable-amplitude load history with some mean stress or mean strain is usually applied. Mean stresses may have a significant effect on the fatigue life. Mean stress effects are seen predominantly at longer lives. They can either increase the fatigue life with a nominally compressive load or decrease it with a nominally tensile value. Fatigue tests for three constant-amplitude loading cases and four combined-loading cases have been carried out in this study. As shown in Fig. 2, combined-loading cases are load histories combining LCF load cycles with HCF load cycles to examine the mean stress effect of HCF load cycle on combined fatigue damage. Three constant-amplitude loading cases are used to investigate the mean stress effect on fatigue damage.

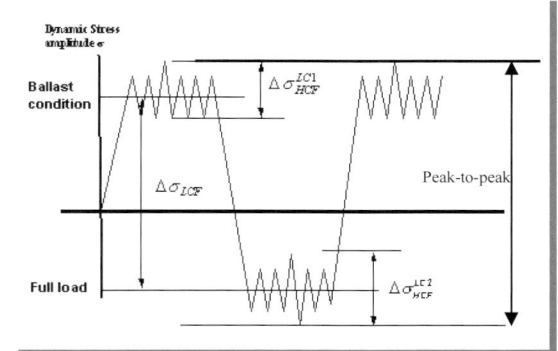

Fig.2: Variable-amplitude load history combining LCF load cycle with HCF load cycle

Therefore, combined-loading cases are designed as shown in Table 3 and Fig.3 (a) and (b). It is set to apply the LCF pseudo hot spot stress range above 1,000 MPa that significant yielding may occur from the cyclic stress-strain curve. For combined-loading cases, LC-1, 2, and 3, HCF cyclic loading amplitudes are controlled to examine the effect of HCF cyclic loading amplitude with mean stress in combined fatigue damage. LC-4 is the modified load case that eliminates the HCF cycle loading with compressive mean stress from LC-1. The constant-amplitude load cases are also designed for the investigation of the mean stress effect as shown in Table 4 and Fig. 3 (c). The combined-loading cases and constant amplitude load cases are listed in the following Tables 3 and 4:

Table 3: Combined-loading cases

Load Case	LCF Nominal Strain Range (%)	LCF Pseudo HSS Range (MPa)	HCF Nominal Strain Range (%)	HCF Pseudo HSS Range (MPa)	No. of HCF Cycles in Half of a LCF Cycle
LC-1	0.5 (0.600)	1,647 (1,989)	0.100	271	233
LC-2	0.5 (0.570)	1,647 (1,885)	0.070	192	814
LC-3	0.5 (0.532)	1,647 (1,755)	0.032	87	814
LC-4	0.5 (0.600)	1,647 (1,989)	0.100	271	233

Where ( ) is the value corresponding peak-to-peak

Table 4: Constant-amplitude load cases

Load Case	HCF Strain Range (%)	Mean Strain (%)
LC-5	0.1	0.00
LC-6	0.1	0.25
LC-7	0.1	-0.25

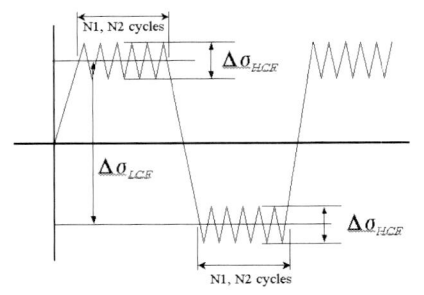

(a) Variable-amplitude load history for Load Case 1, 2, and 3

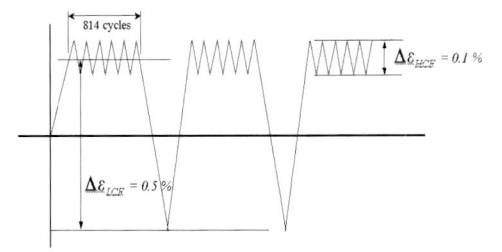

(b) Variable-amplitude load history for Load Case 4

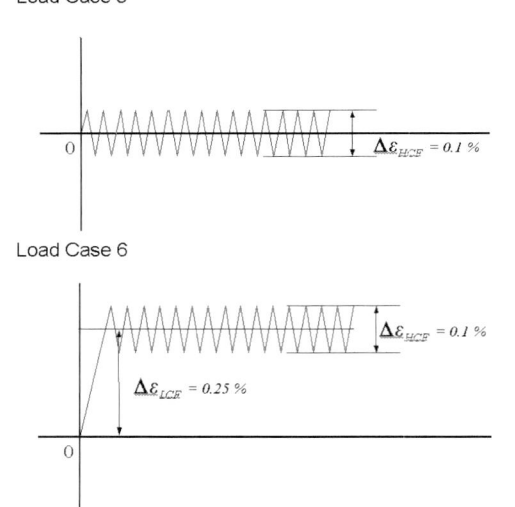

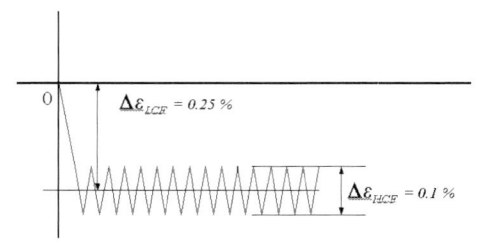

(C) Constant-amplitude loading histories for Load Case 5, 6, and 7

Fig.3: Load cases for combined fatigue damage test

Fatigue test method

The strain amplitude used in tests is in the LCF range. If fatigue tests are carried out using the load control mode, maximum strain around welding line will obtain increases with each cycle of load. So the strain control mode is used in all tests to perform the stable tests with at high strain amplitudes (0.25% above), where plastic strains are significant. Fatigue tests with combined load history are conducted with a load frequency, 0.5 Hz in a LCF load cycle and a load frequency, 3~5 Hz in a HCF load cycle.

All fatigue tests are conducted with the Universal Testing Machine (UTM) with 500kN load capacity, interfaced to a computer for machine control and data acquisition. Load-strain behavior is monitored for each of the tests using load cell and extensometer. With the use of the strain-control condition in fatigue test, expect to observe the slowdown of fatigue crack propagation after a significant amount of crack propagation. Hence, 50% load drop is selected to be the definition of fatigue life.

Combined fatigue damage test analysis

Test results

Fatigue test results are shown in Table 5 and 6. As shown in test results for LC-1, 2, and 3, a steady decrease of HCF strain amplitude results in an increase of fatigue life. Specifically, the test result for LC-4 shows considerable attention. The number of HCF cyclic loading for LC-4 is almost half of it for LC-1. This result indicates that HCF cyclic loading with large compressive mean stress of LC-1 does not contribute to fatigue damage.

Table 5: Fatigue test results for load cases with variable-amplitude loading

Load Case	Nominal Strain Range (%) LCF	Nominal Strain Range (%) HCF	Fatigue Life (cycles) LCF	Fatigue Life (cycles) HCF
LC-1	0.5	0.100 (233)	311	145,000
LC-2	0.5	0.070 (814)	316	515,000
LC-3	0.5	0.032 (814)	1,198	1,950,344
LC-4	0.5	0.100 (233)	327	76,000

Where ( ) is a number of cycle of HCF cyclic loading in a half of LCF cyclic loading.

As shown in test results for LC-5, 6, and 7(see Table 6), it is confirmed that mean stress has an effect on fatigue damage. Tensile mean stress induces an increase of fatigue damage, and compressive mean stress has a contrary position. It is assumed that an effect of mean stress in fatigue damage depends on the amplitude of mean stress. Additional fatigue tests with different mean stress are needed to consider the effect of mean stress in fatigue damage.

Table 6: Fatigue test results for load cases without LCF cyclic loading

Load Case	Mean Strain (%)	Nominal Strain Range (%)	Fatigue Life (cycles)
LC-5-1	0.00	0.1	180,000
LC-5-2	0.00	0.1	192,000
LC-6	0.25	0.1	134,000
LC-7	-0.25	0.1	Above 1,800,000

Welding residual stress

Although there is no information about welding residual stress on test specimens at this moment, test results for LC-5, 6, and 7 in Table 6 shows that relatively large mean stress, especially compressive one, affects the fatigue life of the specimens considerably. However, fatigue failure mechanisms of the specimens considering the residual stress are needed to be verified by the measurement or analysis of the residual stress of the specimens in relation with applied mean stress.

Combined fatigue damage calculation

On the application of nominal strain for LCF range, the base material response follows the cyclic stress-strain relationship of base material as shown in Fig. 4. The stabilized cyclic stress and strain approximate to a straight line. This line follows Ramberg-Osgood equation with material properties (K', n') determined by material tests (see Table 7). This relationship can be clarified with Appendix 1.

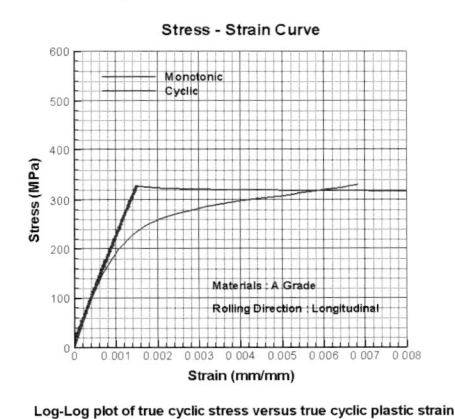

Fig.4: Cyclic and monotonic stress-strain relations

Table 7: Material properties

Material	K' Cyclic Strength Coefficient	n' Cyclic Strength Coefficient
Base material (A-Grade)	582	0.111

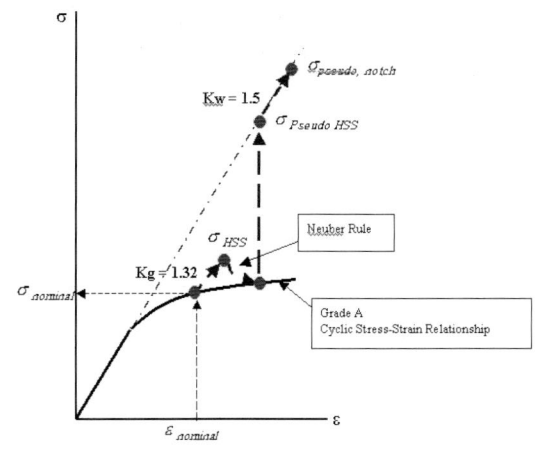

Fig.5: Definition of pseudo hot spot stress in LCF region

As shown in Fig. 5, theoretical hot spot stress is obtained by multiplying the nominal stress by K_g. In this analysis, geometric stress concentration factor, K_g, is approximated as 1.32. This value is obtained from the report of DNV's fatigue capacity in FPSO JIP in 2003. With theoretical HSS (Hot Spot Stress) known, actual Pseudo-HSS can be obtained using Neuber's rule. The elastic-plastic form of Neuber's rule is given as following Eq. (1).

$$\frac{(K_f \sigma_1)^2}{E} = \sigma_{actual\ HSS}\ \varepsilon_{actual\ HSS} \qquad (1)$$

where σ_1 = theoretical HSS

The actual HSS is determined by solving the simultaneous equation of cyclic stress-strain relationship of base material and Neuber's rule by iteration.

$$\sigma_{actual\ HSS}\left[\frac{\sigma_{actual\ HSS}}{E} + \left(\frac{\sigma_{actual\ HSS}}{K'}\right)^{1/n'}\right] - \frac{(K_f \sigma_1)^2}{E} = 0 \qquad (2)$$

where for A grade, $K' = 582$, $n' = 0.111$

Using cyclic stress-strain relationship of base material, the actual hot spot strain corresponding to the actual HSS is also determined. The pseudo-HSS is determined using the relationship defined as follows:

$$\sigma_{Pseudo\ HSS} = E\ \varepsilon_{actual\ HSS} \qquad (3)$$

Pseudo notch stress is determined by multiplying the pseudo-HSS by the stress concentration factor due to the weld, K_w of 1.5. Fatigue damage of LCF cyclic loading is calculated by using simplified fatigue damage assessment method based on not only the pseudo notch stress but also the pseudo hot spot stress. The fatigue life of pseudo notch stress range can be found from one-slope mean S-N curve for welded joint in DNV Classification Note No. 30.7. This is obtained using the relationship between stress range and fatigue life.

$$Log\ N = Log\ \bar{a} - m\ Log\ \Delta\sigma \qquad (4)$$

where

N = predicted number of cycles to failure for stress range $\Delta\sigma$

$\Delta\sigma$ = stress range

m = negative inverse slope of S-N curve

$Log\ \bar{a}$ = intercept of $Log\ N$ -axis by S-N curve

Table 8: One-slope mean S-N parameters from No.30.7 of DNV Classification Notes

S-N curve	Material	$Log\ \bar{a}$	m
Ib	Welded joint	13.16	3.0

On application of nominal strain for the HCF range, the nominal stress is in the significant elastic range. This makes the pseudo notch stress remain within elastic range despite the stress concentration due to weld. The fatigue life of pseudo-elastic notch stress range can be determined from the one-slope mean S-N curve for welded joint in DNV Classification Note No. 30.7. This fact is obtained by using the relationship between stress range and fatigue life as the same method in LCF range. HCF and LCF damage are calculated from the relationship between the calculated fatigue life and the fatigue test result.

$$D_{HCF\ or\ LCF} = \frac{n_{test}}{N_{cal.}} \qquad (5)$$

where

$D_{HCF\ or\ LCF}$ = damage due to low cycle fatigue or high cycle fatigue

n_{test} = number of cycle obtained from fatigue test

$N_{cal.}$ = number of cycle obtained from fatigue life calculation

With the fatigue damage of LCF and HCF known, the total fatigue damage can be calculated using the linear damage rule known as Miner's rule and combined fatigue damage rule proposed by DNV.

For Miner's rule

$$D_{total} = D_{LCF} + D_{HCF} \qquad (6)$$

For combined fatigue damage rule proposed by DNV

$$D_{total} = D_{HCF}\left(1 - \frac{v_{LCF}}{v_{HCF}}\right) + v_{LCF}\left\{\left(\frac{D_{LCF}}{v_{LCF}}\right)^{1/m} + \left(\frac{D_{HCF}}{v_{HCF}}\right)^{1/m}\right\}^m \le \eta \qquad (7)$$

where

D_{total} = total fatigue damage

D_{LCF} = damage due to low cycle fatigue

D_{HCF} = damage due to high cycle fatigue from full load and ballast conditions according to CN30.7

η = usage factor for fatigue, normally 1.0

v_{LCF} = mean zero up crossing frequency for the low frequency response

v_{HCF} = mean zero up crossing frequency for the high frequency response

m = inverse slope of the S-N curve
 = normally 3.0

Tables 9, 10 and 11 show the summary of resulting values for each Load Case. Table 9 is a fatigue damage calculation result based on nominal strain range using BS F mean curve. Table 10 is one based on pseudo-notch stress range using DNV one-slope mean S-N curve for welded joint. Table 11 is also one based on pseudo-hot spot stress range using BS D mean curve. It is confirmed that tensile mean stress in HCF cyclic loading results in an increase of fatigue damage, and compressive mean stress reverses it.

Table 9: Summary of fatigue damage calculation results based on nominal strain range

Load Case	Test Result, cycles	Miner's rule Nominal Strain	Miner's rule Peak-to-peak	DNV formula Nominal Strain	DNV formula Peak-to-peak
Case 1 L=0.5% H=0.10%, 233 cycles	311 145E3	D_{LCF} = 0.197 D_{HCF} = 0.367 D_{total} = 0.564	D_{LCF} = 0.340 D_{HCF} = 0.367 D_{total} = 0.707	D_{LCF} = 0.197 D_{HCF} = 0.367 D_{total} = 0.706	D_{LCF} = 0.340 D_{HCF} = 0.367 D_{total} = 0.906
Case 2 L=0.5% H=0.07%, 814 cycles	316 515E3	D_{LCF} = 0.200 D_{HCF} = 0.447 D_{total} = 0.647	D_{LCF} = 0.296 D_{HCF} = 0.447 D_{total} = 0.744	D_{LCF} = 0.200 D_{HCF} = 0.447 D_{total} = 0.743	D_{LCF} = 0.296 D_{HCF} = 0.447 D_{total} = 0.866
Case 4 L=0.5% H=0.10%, 233 cycles without comp. HCF	327 76E3	D_{LCF} = 0.207 D_{HCF} = 0.385 D_{total} = 0.592	D_{LCF} = 0.358 D_{HCF} = 0.385 D_{total} = 0.743	D_{LCF} = 0.207 D_{HCF} = 0.385 D_{total} = 0.741	D_{LCF} = 0.358 D_{HCF} = 0.385 D_{total} = 0.951

Table 10: Summary of fatigue damage calculation results based on pseudo notch strain range using DNV one-slope mean S-N curve for welded joint

Load Case	Test Result, cycles	Miner's rule Pseudo Notch	Miner's rule Peak-to-peak	DNV formula Pseudo Notch	DNV formula Peak-to-peak
Case 1 L=5% H=0.10%, 233 cycles	311 145E3	D_{LCF} = 0.325 D_{HCF} = 0.339 D_{total} = 0.663	D_{LCF} = 0.571 D_{HCF} = 0.339 D_{total} = 0.910	D_{LCF} = 0.325 D_{HCF} = 0.339 D_{total} = 0.850	D_{LCF} = 0.571 D_{HCF} = 0.339 D_{total} = 1.175
Case 2 L=5% H=0.07%, 814 cycles	316 515E3	D_{LCF} = 0.330 D_{HCF} = 0.428 D_{total} = 0.757	D_{LCF} = 0.495 D_{HCF} = 0.428 D_{total} = 0.922	D_{LCF} = 0.330 D_{HCF} = 0.428 D_{total} = 0.886	D_{LCF} = 0.495 D_{HCF} = 0.428 D_{total} = 1.089
Case 4 L=5% H=0.10%, 233 cycles without comp. HCF	327 76E3	D_{LCF} = 0.341 D_{HCF} = 0.355 D_{total} = 0.696	D_{LCF} = 0.600 D_{HCF} = 0.355 D_{total} = 0.955	D_{LCF} = 0.341 D_{HCF} = 0.355 D_{total} = 0.893	D_{LCF} = 0.600 D_{HCF} = 0.355 D_{total} = 1.235

Table 11: Summary of fatigue damage calculation results based on pseudo hot spot stress range using BS D mean curve

Load Case	Test Result, cycles	Miner's rule Pseudo HSS	Miner's rule Peak-to-peak	DNV formula Pseudo HSS	DNV formula Peak-to-peak
Case 1 L=0.5% H=0.10%, 233 cycles	311 145E3	D_{LCF} = 0.349 D_{HCF} = 0.364 D_{total} = 0.712	D_{LCF} = 0.613 D_{HCF} = 0.364 D_{total} = 0.977	D_{LCF} = 0.349 D_{HCF} = 0.364 D_{total} = 0.913	D_{LCF} = 0.613 D_{HCF} = 0.364 D_{total} = 1.262
Case 2 L=0.5% H=0.07%, 814 cycles	316 515E3	D_{LCF} = 0.354 D_{HCF} = 0.459 D_{total} = 0.813	D_{LCF} = 0.531 D_{HCF} = 0.459 D_{total} = 0.990	D_{LCF} = 0.354 D_{HCF} = 0.459 D_{total} = 0.952	D_{LCF} = 0.631 D_{HCF} = 0.459 D_{total} = 1.170
Case 4 L=0.5% H=0.10%, 233 cycles without comp. HCF	327 76E3	D_{LCF} = 0.366 D_{HCF} = 0.381 D_{total} = 0.748	D_{LCF} = 0.645 D_{HCF} = 0.381 D_{total} = 1.026	D_{LCF} = 0.366 D_{HCF} = 0.381 D_{total} = 0.959	D_{LCF} = 0.645 D_{HCF} = 0.381 D_{total} = 1.326

where

L = nominal strain range of LCF cyclic loading
H = nominal strain range of HCF cyclic loading
D_{LCF} = fatigue damage for LCF load
D_{HCF} = fatigue damage for HCF load
D_{total} = total fatigue damage added HCF damage to LCF damage

The term peak-to-peak is defined as the strain range of LCF cyclic loading that is determined in a peak value considering the amplitude of HCF cyclic loading.

Comparison of total fatigue damage according to calculation methods

As shown in Table 9, 10 and 11, total fatigue damage for each load case is calculated differently dependent on calculation methods. These results are compared to find a more reasonable method in combined fatigue damage calculation.

Total fatigue damage approximating to 1.0 indicates that combined fatigue damage calculation corresponds to fatigue test results, and the value above 1.0 means that the fatigue damage calculation is conservative. Bar graph (a) in Fig. 6 shows that all of the damage calculation methods are lower than value 1 although the calculation results from DNV formula is higher. In case of peak-to-peak base, bar graph (b) shows that much closer accuracy of damage results is obtained based on Miner's rule with peak-to-peak range, while DNV's formula gives relatively higher damage.

Bar graph (c) in Fig. 6 shows that the comparison results of damages among nominal strain, pseudo notch stress and pseudo hot spot stress base using peak-to-peak range with Miner's rule. Among them, the damage calculated based on pseudo hot spot stress with Miner's rule gives the most accurate calculation results.

All of calculation results in Fig.6 are obtained from considering the mean stress effect. If the damages due to high cycle fatigue are calculated without the mean stress effect, high cycle damage of case 4 should be lower than that of case 1 due to the fact that the test result from case 4 is almost half of case 1.

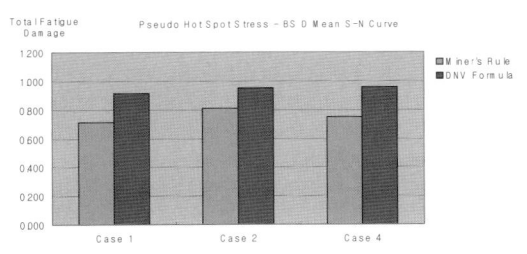

(a) Comparison Miner's rule with DNV formula on basis of Pseudo Hot Spot Stress

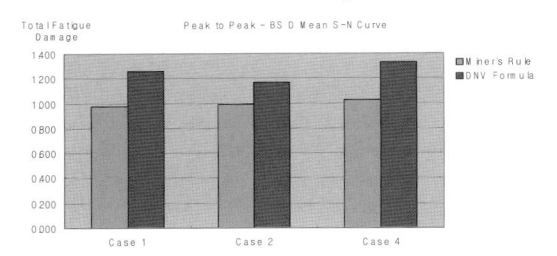

(b) Comparison Miner's rule with DNV formula on basis of pseudo hot spot stress using peak-to-peak

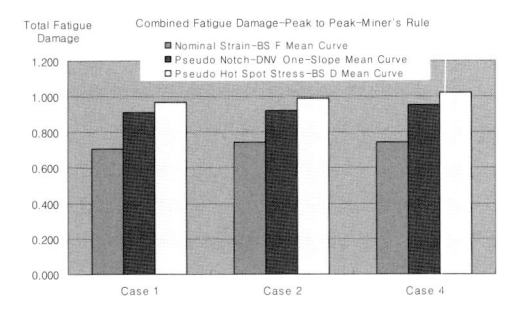

(c) Comparison nominal strain and pseudo notch stress with pseudo hot spot stress using peak-to-peak with Miner's rule

Fig.6: Comparison of combined fatigue damage calculation methods

Design Applications

Based on the combined fatigue test and damage calculation results, DNV applied the peak-to-peak stress range for LCF range and Miner's rule for damage calculation to their design guidance for low cycle fatigue strength assessment for ship structures. The combined stress range for low cycle fatigue strength assessment which represents a peak-to-peak stress range due to loading and unloading and wave action is given below,

$$\Delta \sigma_{comb}^{k} = \Delta \sigma_{LCF}^{k} + 0.5 \cdot \left(\Delta \sigma_{w}^{i} + \Delta \sigma_{w}^{j} \right) \quad (8)$$

where

$\Delta \sigma_{comb}^{k}$ = combined LCF stress range for the *k*-th load combination

$\Delta \sigma_{LCF}^{k}$ = static hot spot stress range for the *k*-th load combination between two load conditions *i* and *j*

$\Delta \sigma_{w}^{i}$ = dynamic stress range at 10^{-4} probability level for the *i*-th load condition

$\Delta \sigma_{w}^{j}$ = dynamic stress range at 10^{-4} probability level for the *j*-th load condition

With regard to mean stress effect, DNV suggested that no mean stress effect be considered for low cycle fatigue damage evaluation. However, when the dynamic stress range due to wave action is calculated, they proposed that the mean stress effect for the welded joints be taken into account as the same way in DNV Classification Note No. 30.7.

Conclusions

Based on the various combined fatigue test and damage calculation results carried out in this study, the following conclusions were derived.

- Based on strain controlled combined fatigue and constant amplitude fatigue test of welded cruciform joint, very stable fatigue test results were obtained. Through all of the fatigue test results, Miner'rule and DNV's formula's validities were checked.

- The peak-to-peak stress range for calculation of fatigue damage of LCF is more suitable than LCF range without HCF range. Therefore, HCF range due to wave load during fatigue damage calculation should add to the LCF range in design stage.

- The calculated damage using DNV's formula to consider load interaction effect between LCF and HCF showed somewhat conservative results compared to the results using Miner's rule.

- If it is possible, mean stress effect should be considered to calculate precisely the fatigue damage due to low and high cycle fatigue since there is no damage from compressive HCF.

- Damage calculation using pseudo hot spot stress is more accurate than those from nominal strain and pseudo notch stress.

- Finally, through lots of combined fatigue tests including constant amplitude loading tests, the most accurate fatigue damage calculation method is obtained as the damage calculation based on pseudo hot spot stress using peak-to-peak range with Miner rule considering mean stress effect.

Acknowledgement

This study has been performed from a task in the Joint Industry Project II between Daewoo Shipbuilding & Marine Engineering Co., LTD. (DSME) and Det Norske Veritas in 2005 - 2006. The authors would like to give thanks for DNV's support and valuable advices on the research.

All of the lab tests presented in this paper have been carried out in Inha University in 2005 - 2006. The Authors would like to thank the members of the impact and fatigue lab. department of naval architecture & ocean engineering in Inha University for their valuable contribution to combined fatigue damage tests.

References

Urm H.S.(2000), Low Cycle Fatigue Criteria for Ship Structures -Background of CN30.7 Addendum-, DNV Technical Report

Det Norske Veritas, Development of Low Cycle Fatigue Criteria for Ship Structures, Technical Report, Report No. 2004-0076, Revision No. 0

Heo, J. H., Kang, J. K., Kim, Y. I., Yoo, I. S., Kim, K. S., and Urm, H. S.(2004), "A Study on the Design Guidance for Low Cycle Fatigue in Ship Structures," PRADS2004, Hamburg, Germany

Det Norske Veritas, Fatigue Assessment of Ship Structures, Classification Notes, No. 30.7, January 2001

Urm, H. S., Yoo, I. S., Heo, J. H., Kim, S. C., and Lotsberg, I. (2004), "Low Cycle Fatigue Strength Assessment for Ship Structures," PRADS2004, Hamburg, Germany

Det Norske Veritas, Low Cycle Fatigue Strength Assessment for Ship Structures, Technical Report, Report No. 2006-9005, Revision No. 0

Appendix

Analogous to the monotonic stress curve as shown in Fig. 7, a log-log plot denoting the completely reversed stabilized cyclic true stress versus true plastic strain can be approximated by a straight line.

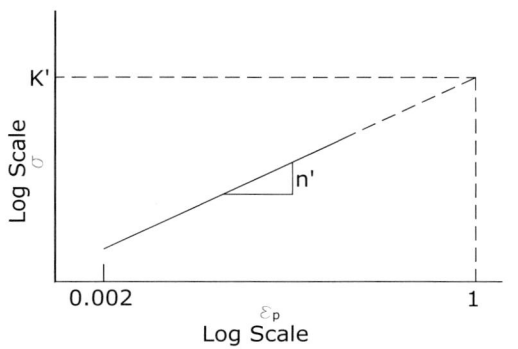

Fig. 7: Log-log plot of true cyclic stress versus true cyclic plastic strain

Similar to the monotonic relationship, we can develop power law function

$$\sigma = K'(\varepsilon_p)^{n'}$$

where
σ = cyclically stable stress amplitude
ε_p = cyclically stable plastic strain amplitude
K' = cyclic strength coefficient
n' = cyclic strain hardening exponent

Rearranging the above equation gives

$$\varepsilon_p = \left(\frac{\sigma}{K'}\right)^{1/n'}$$

The total strain is the sum of the elastic and plastic components. Using the above equation and Hooke's law, the total strain can be written

$$\varepsilon = \frac{\sigma}{E} + \left(\frac{\sigma}{K'}\right)^{1/n'}$$

Extreme Value Predictions for Wave- and Wind-induced Loads on Floating Offshore Wind Turbines using FORM

Sunvard Joensen[1], Jørgen J. Jensen[1], Alaa E. Mansour[2]

[1] Department of Mechanical Engineering, Technical University of Denmark
Kgs. Lyngby, Denmark
[2] Mechanical Engineering Department
University of California, Berkeley, USA

Abstract

The aim of the present paper is to advocate for a very effective stochastic procedure, based on the First Order Reliability Method (FORM), for extreme value predictions related to wave induced loads. Due to the efficient optimization procedures implemented in standard FORM codes and the short duration of the sequences of time domain simulations needed (typically 60-300s to cover the hydrodynamic memory effects in the response) the calculation of the mean out-crossing rates and hence also the extreme values of a given response are very fast. Thus complicated nonlinear effects can be included. The FORM analysis also identifies the most probable wave episodes that lead to given responses.

As an example, the motions of floating foundations for offshore wind turbines are analyzed taking into consideration both the wave and wind induced loads and considering different mooring systems. The possible large horizontal motions make it important to calculate the wave loads at the instantaneous position of the floater.

Keywords

Conditional stochastic processes; Critical wave episodes; FORM; TLP; Offshore wind turbines; Out-crossing rate.

Introduction

The First Order Reliability Method (FORM) has been widely used within structural reliability analyses. However, it is also an efficient method for extreme value predictions, as suggested by Der Kiureghian (2000). Due to the efficient optimization procedures implemented in standard FORM codes and the short duration of the time domain simulations needed (typically 60-300s to cover the hydrodynamic memory effects in the response) the calculation of the mean out-crossing rate of the response is very fast. Thus, complicated nonlinear effects can be included. When the mean out-crossing is known, extreme values are easily determined provided the out-crossing can be assumed statistically independent, i.e. considered as a Poisson process. The procedure then provides a fast, but accurate alternative to Monte Carlo simulation and to methods based on numerical fitting to asymptotic extreme value distributions.

The FORM analysis also identifies the most probable wave episodes that lead to given responses. These critical wave episodes can be applied in a model correction factor approach to account for even very complicated nonlinear effects (e.g. by applying the critical wave episodes in model tests).

Three different applications are summarized in Jensen (2007). The first dealt with a jack-up rig where the deck sway is considered taking into account second order stochastic waves. This procedure is usually not possible due to excessive computational time, but the efficiency of the FORM analysis makes it possible. The second order wave elevation is important as it increases the crest height, thereby the overturning moment, too.

The second application was the roll motion of ships. It was shown that both pure roll and parametric roll can be dealt with by FORM, even considering that parametric roll is a bifurcation type of response that cannot be solved by a gradient type of linearization.

Finally, the horizontal motion of a Tension Leg Platform (TLP) for an offshore wind turbine was analyzed taking into account large horizontal motions and the elastic deformation of the tower. The vertical and pitch motions were disregarded by taking the tendons to be inextensible.

The FORM is significantly faster than direct Monte Carlo simulations, but still very accurate as shown in the examples summarized in Jensen (2007). It is noted that the FORM approach is very similar to the spectral response surface method, developed by Tromans and colleagues, see e.g. Tromans and Vanderschuren (2004), where the effect of second order random waves on the crest statistics is discussed.

In the present paper a TLP is considered again but with focus on the interaction between the horizontal, vertical and pitch motions. Before, however, an outline of the FORM is given, emphasizing the application to extreme wave load predictions.

FORM applied to wave loads

Design Point and Reliability Index

The excitation or input process is considered to be a stationary stochastic process. The input process is the wave elevation and the associated wave kinematics. For moderate sea states the wave elevation can be considered as Gaussian distributed, whereas for more severe sea states nonlinearities in the wave model must be incorporated. For brevity, linear, long-crested waves are assumed in this Section, outlining the present application of FORM. Hence, the normally distributed wave elevation $H(x,t)$ as a function of space x and time t can be written,

$$H(x,t) = \sum_{i=1}^{n} \left(u_i c_i(x,t) + \overline{u}_i \overline{c}_i(x,t) \right) \quad (1.1)$$

where the variables $u_i, \overline{u}_i$ are uncorrelated, standard normal distributed variables to be determined by the stochastic procedure and with the deterministic coefficients given by

$$c_i(x,t) = \sigma_i \cos(\omega_i t - k_i x)$$
$$\overline{c}_i(x,t) = -\sigma_i \sin(\omega_i t - k_i x) \quad (1.2)$$
$$\sigma_i^2 = S(\omega_i) d\omega_i$$

where $\omega_i, k_i = \omega_i^2/g$ are the n discrete frequencies and wave numbers applied. g is the acceleration of gravity. Furthermore, $S(\omega)$ is the wave spectrum and $d\omega_i$ the increment between the discrete frequencies. It is easily seen that the expected value $E[H^2] = \int S(\omega) d\omega$ preserving the wave energy in the stationary sea.

As is seen in the wave elevation shown in Eqs. (1.1)-(1.2) and the associated wave kinematics, any nonlinear wave-induced response $\phi(t)$ of a marine structure can in principle be determined by a time domain analysis using a proper hydrodynamic model:

$$\phi = \phi(t | u_1, \overline{u}_1, u_2, \overline{u}_2, ..., u_n, \overline{u}_n) \quad (1.3)$$

Each of these realizations represents the response for a possible wave scenario. The realization which exceeds a given threshold ϕ_0 at time $t=t_0$ with the highest probability is sought. This problem can be formulated as a limit state problem, Der Kiureghian (2000):

$$G(u_1, \overline{u}_1, u_2, \overline{u}_2, ..., u_n, \overline{u}_n) \equiv$$
$$\phi_0 - \phi(t_0 | u_1, \overline{u}_1, u_2, \overline{u}_2, ..., u_n, \overline{u}_n) = 0 \quad (1.4)$$

An approximate solution can be obtained by use of first order reliability methods (FORM). The limit state surface g is given in terms of the uncorrelated standard normal distributed variables $\{u_i, \overline{u}_i\}$ and determination of the design point, $\{u_i^*, \overline{u}_i^*\}$, defined as the point on the failure surface, $G = 0$, with the shortest distance to the origin, is rather straightforward, Der Kiureghian (2000). A linearization around this point replaces Eq. (1.4) with a hyperplane in 2n space. The distance, β_{FORM}, from the hyperplane to the origin is denoted the (FORM) reliability index. The calculation of the design point $\{u_i^*, \overline{u}_i^*\}$ and the associated value of β_{FORM} can be performed by standard reliability codes, e.g. Det Norske Veritas (2002), or by standard optimization codes (ie. minimizing the distance β with the constraint Eq. (1.4)) in which $\phi(t_0)$ has to be calculated by numerical integration for a number of combinations of $\{u_i, \overline{u}_i\}$ until the design point is reached. The integration must cover a sufficient long time period $\{0, t_0\}$ to avoid any influence on $\phi(t_0)$ of the initial conditions at $t=0$, i.e. to be longer than the memory in the system. As no explicit expression for $\phi(t_0)$ is needed, any kind of nonlinearities can be incorporated. Note that the reliability procedure only gets $\phi(t_0)$ as input and no information about the time evolution leading to $\phi(t_0)$.

Proper values of t_0 would usually be 1-2 minutes, depending on the damping in the system. Hence, to avoid repetition in the wave system and for representation of typical wave spectra $n = 15$-50 would be needed.

Mean Out-crossing Rates and Peak Value Distribution

The time-invariant peak distribution follows from the mean out-crossing rates. Within a FORM approximation the mean out-crossing rate can be written, Jensen and Capul (2006), Koo et al. (2006)

$$\nu(\phi_0) = \frac{1}{2\pi \beta_{FORM}} e^{-\frac{1}{2}\beta_{FORM}^2} \sqrt{\sum_{i=1}^{n} \left(u_i^{*2} + \overline{u}_i^{*2} \right) \omega_i^2} \quad (1.5)$$

Thus, the mean out-crossing rate can be expressed analytically in terms of the design point and the reliability index. For linear processes it reduces to the standard Rayleigh distribution.

When the design point has been determined, the critical wave episode can be defined by the use of Eqs. (1.1)-(1.2) with $\{u_i, \overline{u}_i\} = \{u_i^*, \overline{u}_i^*\}$. This critical wave episode can be considered as a design wave and can be used as input in more elaborate time domain simulations to correct for assumptions taken in the hydrodynamic code, Eq. (1.3), applied in the FORM calculations. Such a model correction factor approach provides an effective tool to account for even very complicated nonlinear effects, Ditlevsen and Arnbjerg-Nielsen (1994).

Finally, extreme values are obtained assuming statistically independent out-crossings and hence, a Poisson distributed process. The number of exceedance of the level ϕ_0 in a given time T can then be calculated from the mean out-crossing rate $\nu(\phi_0)$:

$$P\{\max_T \phi > \phi_0\} = 1 - e^{-\nu(\phi_0)T} \quad (1.6)$$

Offshore wind turbines

Currently several studies have been performed in the US, Europe and Japan concerning the feasibility of installation of offshore wind turbines in water depths larger than 50 m. This might be the only possibility for offshore installation due to lack of availability of suitable areas close to the coast. It has also the advantage in that the wind speed is generally higher and more uniform due the absence of obstacles and, from an esthetical point of view, one avoids the visual and noise pollution, often the decisive factor for the installation of large wind turbine parks. However, the deepwater installations pose some severe problems. One is the electrical connection to shore or to an existing offshore installation. Another is maintenance that might require large crane vessels for servicing the nacelle. In addition, a fixed, bottom-supported base for the wind turbine becomes uneconomical and must be replaced by a floating base. Several possibilities have been suggested in the literature using different types of moorings: slack, taut or TLP, Musial et al. (2004), Henderson et al. (2002).

The present paper addresses the calculation of extreme sway, heave and pitch motions and tendon loads on a TLP type of floater. These responses are of importance for the operation of the wind turbine as they influence the blade loadings, and hence the downtime of the wind turbine energy production.

Table 1: Data used for the NREL TLP offshore wind turbine

Tower		Floater	
Height L_t	100 m	Height L_f	10 m
Bending rigidity EI_t	4.05 10^{11} Nm^2	Tank top submergence h_t	15 m
Mass of nacelle M_n	3.50 10^5 kg	Mass M_f	2 10^5 kg
Mass of tower M_t	3.47 10^5 kg	Diameter D_f	16 m
Structural damping ratio ξ	0.02	Inertia coeff. C_M, C_{mz}	2, 0.64
Diameter D_t	6 m	Drag coeff. C_d, C_{dz}	1, 2
Static wind force F_W	800 kN	Distance between tendons $2L_{ten}$	60 m

In the present study the tension leg platform, developed by National Renewable Energy Laboratory (NREL), Henderson et al. (2002), is considered. Only a static analysis has been published and the data available is somewhat limited. Those pertinent for the present study are given in Table 1 and a sketch of the geometry is shown in Figure 1. Most of the data is taken from the design study, Musial et al. (2004), Henderson et al. (2002), but some have been slightly modified for simplification purposes. In addition the bending rigidity has been estimated from the prescribed extreme tower base moment of 187,000 kNm and a corresponding allowable maximum bending stress of 175 MPa. Both the floater and the tower have been assumed to be prismatic cylinders. A previous study has dealt with the same TLP configuration, but with the assumption of inextensible tendons, Jensen and Mansour (2006).

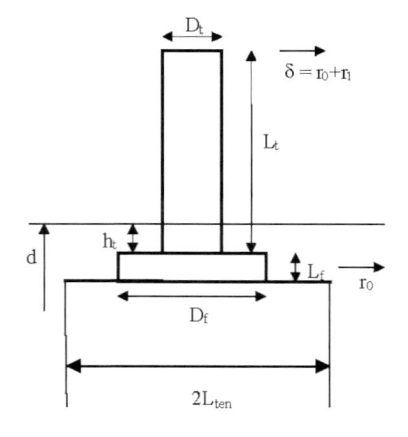

Fig. 1: Sketch (not to scale) of the TLP

The water depth d is taken to be 200m and the sea states are modeled by a standard JONSWAP wave spectrum together with long-crested waves. The spectrum is discretized into n =15 components with frequencies evenly distributed between $3/T_z$ and $8/T_z$. This discretization ensures that time periods up to 2 minutes can be simulated in Eq. (1.3) without repetition. The actual value of t_o is taken to 100s as the results do not change with larger lengths of the simulations. The memory in the model of the system is thus less than 100s.

Interactions between the aerodynamic and hydrodynamic loads and control system for the blade pitch can occur at resonant conditions, Nielsen et al (2006), and should be investigated in real applications. The present wind turbine is considered to be of a rated power equal to 5MW with a corresponding static maximum force $F_W = 800$ kN.

The fundamental frequency of the tower is

$$\omega_o = \sqrt{\frac{3EI_t}{M_t^* L_t^3}} \quad (2.1)$$

assuming half the tower mass concentrated in the position of the nacelle: $M_t^* = M_n + 0.5 M_t$. The equations of motions governing the horizontal motion r_o of the floater and the additional motion r_1 of the nacelle can be written

$$M_f^* \ddot{r}_o - M_t^* \left(\omega_o^2 r_1 + 2\xi \omega_o \dot{r}_1 \right) + F_{Tx} = F_H$$
$$\ddot{r}_0 + \ddot{r}_1 + \omega_o^2 r_1 + 2\xi \omega_o \dot{r}_1 = F_W \quad (2.2)$$

where a superscript dot implies differentiation with respect to time. The horizontal tendon restoring force F_{Tx} is given through the tendon forces F_{T1} and F_{T2} in the two tendons:

$$F_{Ti} = EA \left(\frac{\ell_i - \ell_0}{\ell_0} \right) + \frac{1}{2} F_{T0}; \quad i = 1, 2 \quad (2.3)$$

where EA is the axial stiffness of a tendon and ℓ_1, ℓ_2 the instantaneous lengths of each tendon. The length $\ell_0 = d - L_f - h_t$ is the tendon length when subjected solely to the total static pretension F_{T0} following from the difference between the buoyancy and the gravity of the structure:

$$F_{T0} = F_B - F_G = F_{Bf} + F_{Bt} - F_{Gf} - F_{Gt}$$
$$= \rho g \frac{\pi}{4} \left(D_f^2 L_f + D_t^2 h_t \right) - g \left(M_f + M_n + M_t \right) \quad (2.4)$$

Here indices t, f, n refer to the tower, floater and nacelle properties, respectively. The lengths ℓ_1, ℓ_2 of the two tendons are functions of the heave z_0, sway r_0 and pitch angle θ_0 of the floater:

$$\ell_i = \sqrt{\xi_i^2 + \eta_i^2}$$
$$\xi_i = r_0 \pm L_{ten} (1 - \cos \theta_0); \quad i = 1: +; i = 2: - \quad (2.5)$$
$$\eta_i = z_0 + \ell_0 \pm L_{ten} \sin \theta_0$$

where L_{ten} is the horizontal distance between a tendon and the center of the floater.

The horizontal F_{Tix} and the vertical F_{Tiz} components of F_{Ti} become

$$F_{Tix} = F_{Ti} \frac{\xi_i}{\ell_i}; \quad F_{Tiz} = F_{Ti} \frac{\eta_i}{\ell_i}; \quad i = 1, 2 \quad (2.6)$$

and,

$$F_{Tx} = F_{T1x} + F_{T2x}; \quad F_{Tz} = F_{T1z} + F_{T2z} \quad (2.7)$$

The hydrodynamic force (Morison's equation)

$$F_H = \int_{-h_t}^{H} \bar{q}_{Ht} dz + \int_{-h_t - L_f}^{-h_t} \bar{q}_{Hf} dz$$
$$\bar{q}_{Hi} = \rho \frac{\pi}{4} C_M D_i^2 \dot{v} + \quad (2.8)$$
$$\frac{1}{2} \rho C_d D_i (v - \dot{r}_0) |v - \dot{r}_0|; \quad i = t, f$$

The vertical z-coordinate is measured upwards from the still water surface and v is the horizontal wave particle velocity. Finally,

$$M_f^* = M_f + \frac{1}{2} M_t +$$
$$\rho (C_M - 1) \frac{\pi}{4} \left(D_t^2 (H + h_t) + D_f^2 L_f \right) \quad (2.9)$$

The heave z_0 is governed by the equilibrium equation:

$$\left(M_t^* + M_f^{**} \right) \ddot{z}_0 + \rho \frac{\pi}{4} D_t^2 z_0 = F_V - F_{Tz} + F_{T0} \quad (2.10)$$

where the vertical hydrodynamic force F_V is determined as the sum of the Froude-Krylov force, the drag force and the inertia force:

$$F_V = \frac{\pi}{4} \left[D_f^2 p_b - \left(D_f^2 - D_t^2 \right) p_t \right]$$
$$+ \frac{\pi}{8} D_f^2 \rho C_{Dz} (w_b - \dot{z}_0) |w_b - \dot{z}_0| \quad (2.11)$$
$$+ \frac{4}{3} \left(\frac{D_f}{2} \right)^3 \rho C_{mz} \dot{w}_b$$

Here w_b is the vertical wave particle velocity at the bottom of the floater. The pressure p_b and p_t are the incident wave pressures calculated at the bottom and the top of the floater, respectively. The pressures and the vertical velocity are assumed constant over the diameter D_f of the floater and calculated at the instantaneous horizontal position of the center of the bottom of the floater:

$$p_b = p(x, z = -h_t - L_f, t)$$
$$p_t = p(x, z = -h_t, t) \quad (2.12)$$
$$w_b = w(x, z = -h_t - L_f, t)$$

The change in vertical position due to heave is small and is ignored in calculation of the wave loads. The drag and inertia coefficients are denoted C_{Dz} and C_{mz}, respectively. The mass

$$M_f^{**} = M_f + \frac{1}{2}M_t + \frac{4}{3}\left(\frac{D_f}{2}\right)^3 \rho C_{mz}$$
$$+ \rho \frac{\pi}{4}\left(D_t^2(H+h_t) + D_f^2 L_f\right) \quad (2.13)$$

includes the added mass of water.

Finally, moment equilibrium with respect to the bottom of the floater yields

$$J\ddot{\theta} = F_W(L_f + L_t)\cos\theta_0 + F_G x_G - F_B x_B$$
$$+ M_H - (F_{T1x} - F_{T2x})L_{ten}\sin\theta_0 \quad (2.14)$$
$$- (F_{T1z} - F_{T2z})L_{ten}\cos\theta_0$$

The wave-induced moment is

$$M_H = \int_{-h_t}^{H} \bar{q}_{Ht}(z + L_f + h_t)dz$$
$$+ \int_{-h_t - L_f}^{-h_t} \bar{q}_{Hf}(z + L_f + h_t)dz \quad (2.15)$$

The mass moment of inertia J and the center of gravity x_G and center of buoyancy x_B follow directly from the assumed mass distribution and the geometry. The results are given in the Appendix.

The wave elevation $H(x,t)$ is given by Eq. (1.1). The associated incident pressure $p(x,z,t)$ and wave particle velocities $v(x,z,t)$ and $w(x,z,t)$ then follow from standard Airy theory. In the present calculation only linear stochastic waves are used, but it is straightforward to include second order stochastic waves, c.f. Jensen and Capul (2006) and Joensen (2007).

The four coupled equilibrium equations are solved within the FORM procedure by a standard 4th order Runge-Kutta method in terms of the horizontal motion components r_0, r_1, the heave motion z_0 and the pith angle θ_0. The FORM analysis is done by the commercial program PROBAN, DNV (2002).

Results

The following figures are based on prescribed nacelle sway $\delta = r_0 + r_1$ or pitch motion θ_0 of floater. The variations with time and space at the design point $\{u_i, \bar{u}_i\} = \{u_i^*, \bar{u}_i^*\}$, i.e. the scenario with the highest probability of occurrence, are shown. To avoid any notable influence of the arbitrary initial conditions, the prescribed values of nacelle sway and pitch motion of the floater are taken at a time t_0 sufficiently away from the start of the simulation. For the present examples, $t_0 = 100$ s was found to be appropriate. The results are presented for a nacelle sway of 30 m and a pitch motion of 0.6° for three different sea states. The shape of the responses does not change much with the prescribed values at $t = t_0$, only the magnitudes change.

The pertinent natural frequencies of the platform are: the natural frequency of the tower (4s), the natural frequency of the floater with tendon (38s) and the natural frequency of the pitch motion (3s).

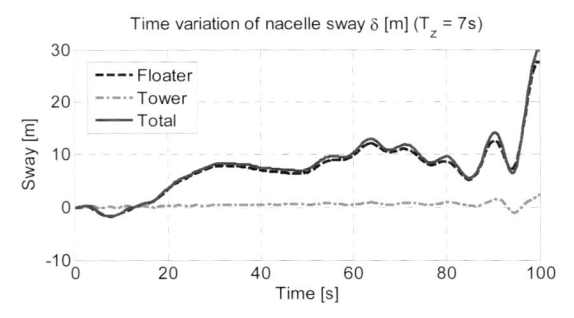

Fig. 2: Time variation of nacelle sway δ(t) at the design point, conditioned on δ(100s) = 30 m.

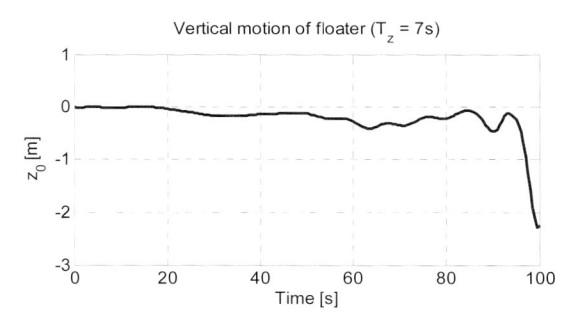

Fig. 3: Time variation of the vertical motion of floater z_0 at the design point, conditioned on δ(100s) = 30 m.

The results presented in Figure 2 are conditional of a nacelle sway equal to 30 m in a sea state with T_z=7s. It is possible to identify the natural frequency of the floater in the first half of Figure 2, and it is observed that the maximum sway builds up over around 2 periods. Over the whole time variation of nacelle sway, a force motion component with a period close to the exiting wave is also noticed.

The elastics vibration of the tower increases with decreasing wave period, but has a minor influence on the total motion in all cases considered. If either much larger or smaller wave periods were considered, resonance conditions could occur, but such periods will usually not be associated with the significant wave height of 7 m.

Figure 3 shows the vertical motion of the floater, and it appears that the vertical motion of the floater is naturally in opposite phase to the sway motion.

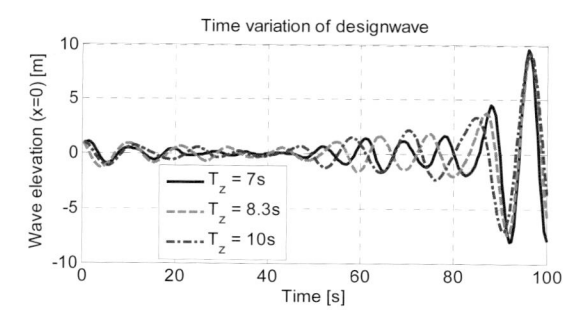

Fig. 4: Time variation of wave elevation at the design point, conditioned on $\delta(100s) = 30$ m.

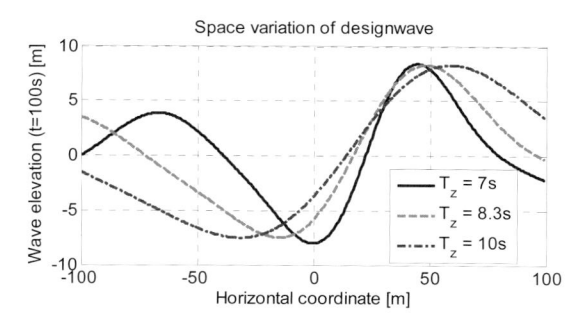

Fig. 5: Space variation of wave elevation at the design point, conditioned on $\delta(100s) = 30$ m.

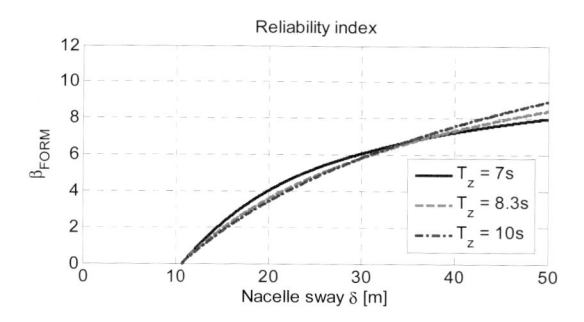

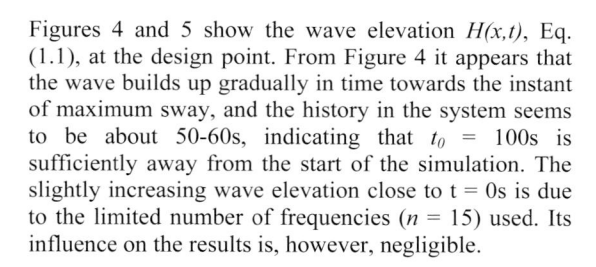

Fig. 6: Reliability index β_{FORM} as a function of maximum nacelle sway δ.

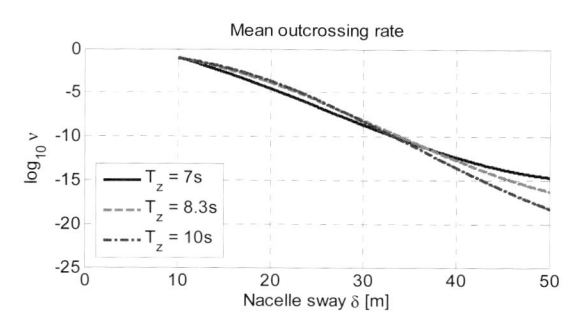

Fig. 7: Mean out-crossing rate ν as a function of maximum nacelle sway δ.

Figures 4 and 5 show the wave elevation $H(x,t)$, Eq. (1.1), at the design point. From Figure 4 it appears that the wave builds up gradually in time towards the instant of maximum sway, and the history in the system seems to be about 50-60s, indicating that $t_0 = 100$s is sufficiently away from the start of the simulation. The slightly increasing wave elevation close to t = 0s is due to the limited number of frequencies ($n = 15$) used. Its influence on the results is, however, negligible.

It is not straight forward to say whether the structure is inertia or a drag dominated because the system is oscillating, but Figure 5 shows that the wave elevation at maximum sway (30 m) for all three wave periods is about 4 m, corresponding to a more inertia dominated structure.

Figures 6 and 7 show the reliability index β_{FORM} and the mean out-crossing rate ν for all sea states and for a range of nacelle sway δ from 10 m to 50 m. The reliability index β_{FORM} is zero at 10 m, and this is due to the wind force F_w, yielding a static deflection of 10 m. The nonlinearity in the system is due to drag term in Morison's equation, Eq. (2.8). From the mean out-crossing rate the probability of exceedance follows from Eq. (1.6). The return period of a response level can be estimated as ν^{-1} and thus for instance $\nu = 10^{-5}$ s^{-1} corresponds to approximately one out-crossing every day. The corresponding nacelle sway is seen from Figure 7 to be about 20 m. The occurrence of a nacelle sway of 30 m in the three sea states is seen to be negligible.

The following figures are based on variation of the pitch motion θ_0 of the floater.

From Figure 8 it is seen that the natural frequency of the pitch motion is 3s. The average slope that can be seen in the figure from $t = 0$ to 50 s is due to the wind force F_w as it was made to build up linearly over the first 50 s to avoid numerical instabilities. The variation in the pitch angle θ_0 at $t = 75$-100 s can be characterized by mainly as a force motion with a period close to the exiting wave period. The same exiting wave period is noticed in Figure 9, from where it appears that the maximum sway does not occur at the instant of maximum pitch angle.

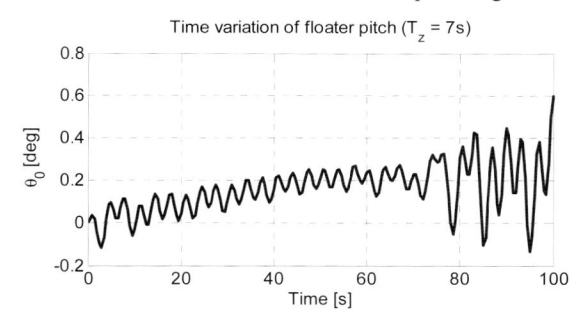

Fig. 8: Time variation of floater pitch $\theta_0(t)$ at the design point, conditioned on $\theta_0(100s) = 0.6°$.

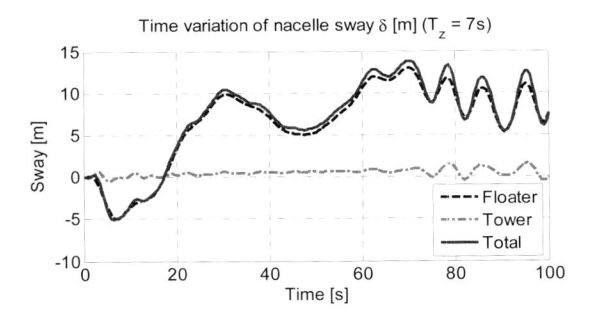

Fig. 9: Time variation of nacelle sway δ(t) at the design point, conditioned on $\theta_0(100s) = 0.6°$.

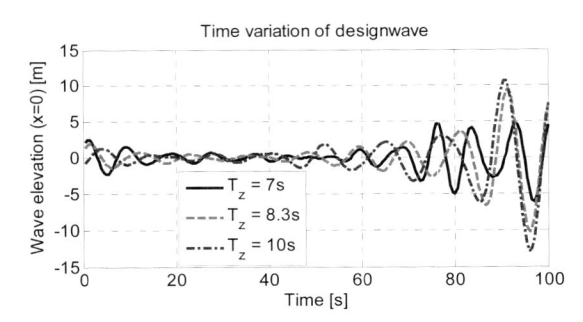

Fig. 10: Time variation of wave elevation at the design point, conditioned on $\theta_0(100s) = 0.6°$.

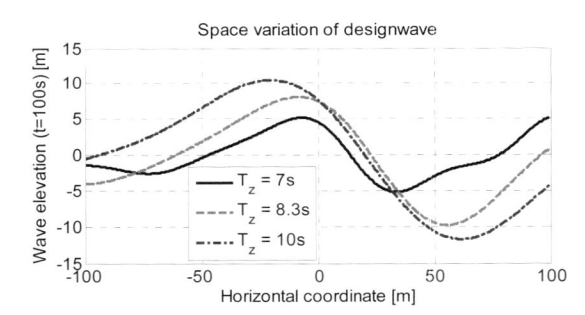

Fig. 11: Space variation of wave elevation at the design point, conditioned on $\theta_0(100s) = 0.6°$.

The results shown in Figure 10 and 11 are qualitatively similar to those in Figures 2-5, where the motion is conditioned on the sway. Note the time variation of the design wave with T_z =10s, where the wave is much higher than for the lower values of T_z.

The space variation of the wave elevation shows an increasing wave elevation at the position of the floater (x = 7 m at t = 100s) with increasing wave period.

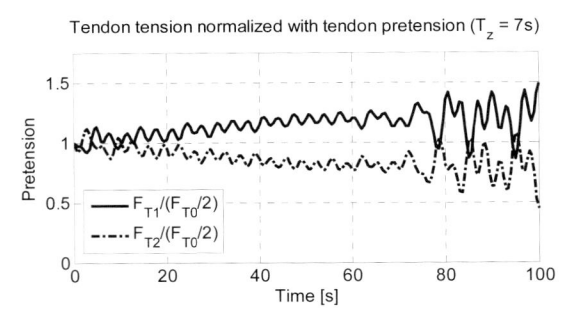

Fig. 12: Time variation of tendon tension normalized with tendon pretension at the design point, conditioned on $\theta_0(100s) = 0.6°$.

Figure 12 shows the time variation of the tendon tension normalized with tendon pretension. It is observed that tendon force variation follows the time variation of the floater pitch θ_0. At the design point, conditioned on $\theta_0(100s) = 0.6°$, the tension in the tendon F_{T1} and F_{T2} are respectively 1.5 and 0.5 times the pretension.

Figures 13 and 14 show the reliability index β_{FORM} and the mean out-crossing rate v for all three sea-states and for a range of pitch motion of the floater θ_0 from 0.2° to 1.2°. The reliability index β_{FORM} is zero at a pitch angle of 0.2°, which is the static response due to the wind force F_w. The variation of β_{FORM} with response level is more linear than when conditioned on the sway motion. The nonlinearity in the system is due to drag term in Morison's equation, Eq. (2.8) and some nonlinearity in the restoring moment from the gravity and buoyancy. The return period of a response $\theta_0 = 0.6°$ corresponds to approximately one out-crossing every third month. The pretension in the system will become zero if the pitch angle of the floater becomes approximately 1.2°, but the occurrence of this scenario is seen to be negligible.

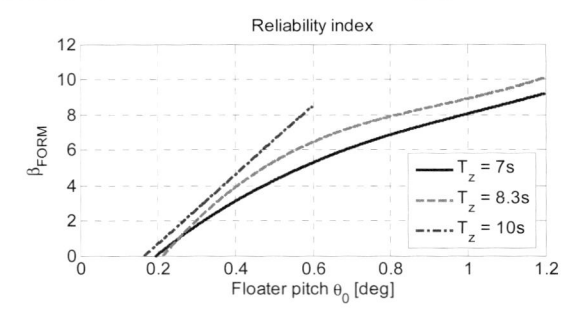

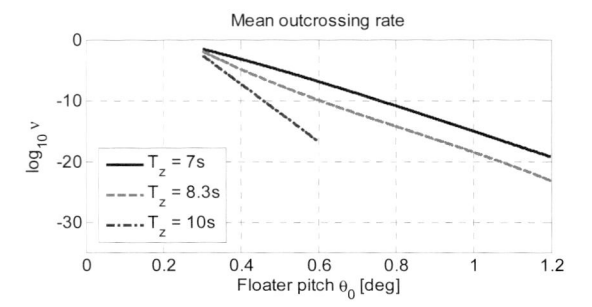

Fig. 13: Reliability index β_{FORM} as a function of maximum pitch motion θ_0.

Fig. 14: Mean out-crossing rate ν as a function of maximum pitch motion θ₀.

From a design point-of-view the calculation shows that an extreme sway of 30 m, which has a very low probability of occurrence, only gives rise to a vertical motion of 2.2 m, and a very small pitch motion. Therefore, the focus could be changed to the tendon forces, determining the probability distribution of the pretension to become zero or exceeding the yield stress. Such results can be found in Joensen (2007) together with further details of the present investigation.

Finally, the extreme value distributions for responses considered follow from Eq. (1.6) and should be applied if long-term predictions covering different sea states and operational parameters are requested.

Conclusion

The powerful tools of first order reliability method have been used to determine the most probable wave episode that produces a maximum response of a floating wind turbine. Based on this wave episode and a specified limiting (allowable) value of the response, the mean out-crossing rate and the safety index were determined using FORM. The method offers an efficient procedure for determining these safety indices for any response under consideration -- significantly faster than a typical time simulation procedure where the most critical wave episode is not identified beforehand. Because its efficiency the method allows for the inclusion of complicated nonlinear effects and the interaction of wind and wave as was done in this paper.

Appendix

The mass moment of inertia J with respect to the bottom of the floater:

$$J_{fk} = M_f^* \left(\frac{1}{16} D_f^2 + \frac{1}{3} L_f^2 \right)$$

Mass moment of inertia for nacelle with respect to the bottom of the floater:

$$J_{nk} = M_n^{**} \left(\frac{1}{16} D_n^2 + \frac{1}{12} L_n^2 + (L_f + L_t)^2 \right)$$

where

$$M_n^{**} = M_n^* - 3 M_b$$

is the mass of the nacelle excluding the blades (M_b = 17740 kg is the mass of one blade).

The blades are assumed to have an elliptic parabolic shape, where a = 2.31 m is half of the blade width and c = 61.5 m is the blade length.

The total mass moment of inertia for the three blades with respect to the bottom of the floater is then

$$J_{bk} = M_b \left(\frac{a^2}{2} + \frac{c^2}{3} + 3(L_f + L_t)^2 \right)$$

The mass moment of inertia J of the platform with respect to the bottom of the floater is finally:

$$J = J_{fk} + J_{nk} + J_{bk}$$

The horizontal center of gravity x_G for the platform in a heeled condition becomes

$$x_G = \frac{F_{Gt}(L_f + L_t) + 0.5 F_{Gf} L_f}{F_G} \sin \theta_0$$

where the gravity forces are given in Eq. (2.4). The horizontal center of buoyancy x_B is determined as, assuming that the floater do not penetrate the water surface

$$x_{Bt} = \left(L_f + \frac{h_t}{2} + \frac{D_t^2 (2 + \tan^2 \theta_0)}{32 h_t} \right) \sin \theta_0$$

$$x_{Bf} = \frac{1}{2} L_f \sin \theta_0$$

$$x_B = \frac{F_{Bt} x_{Bt} + F_{Bf} x_{Bf}}{F_B}$$

where the buoyancy forces are given in Eq. (2.4).

References

Der Kiureghian, A. 2000. The geometry of Random Vibrations and Solutions by FORM and SORM. *Probabilistic Engineering Mechanics*, 15: 81-90.

Det Norske Veritas. 2002. Proban Theory, General Purpose Probabilistic Analysis Program, Version 4.4.

Ditlevsen, O. and Arnbjerg-Nielsen, T. 1994. Model-Correction-Factor Method in Structural Reliability. *Journal of Engineering* 120: 1-10.

Henderson, A.R., Leutz, R. and Fulii, T. 2002. Potential for Floating Offshore Wind Energy in Japanese Waters. *Proc. of the Twelfth International Offshore and Polar Engineering Conference, Kitakyushu, Japan, May 26–31, 2002*, 505-512.

Jensen J.J. and Capul, J. 2006. Extreme Response Predictions for Jack-up Units in Second Order Stochastic Waves by FORM. *Probabilistic Engineering Mechanics* 21: 330-337.

Jensen, J.J., Mansour, A.E., 2006. Extreme Motion Predictions for Deepwater TLP Floaters for Offshore Wind Turbines. *Proc.Hydroelas'2006, Wuxi, China, September 2006*, 361-367.

Jensen, J.J. 2007. Extreme value predictions and critical wave episodes for marine structures by FORM. *Proc. Int. Conf. on the Advancements in Marine Structures, Glasgow, UK, March 12-14, 2007.*

Joensen, S. 2007. Stochastic Wave Loads on Floating Offshore Foundations for Wind Turbines (in Danish). *MSc Thesis, Depart. Mechanical Engineering, Technical university of Denmark.*

Koo, H., Der Kiureghian, A. and Fujimura, K. 2006. Design Point Excitation for Nonlinear Random Vibrations. *robabilistic Engineering Mechanics* 20:136-147.

Musial, W., Butterfield, S. and Boone, A., 2004. Feasibility of Floating Platform Systems for Wind Turbines. *Proc. 23rd ASME Wind Energy Symposium, Reno, Nevada, January 5-8, 2004.*

Nielsen, F.G., Hanson, T.D. and Skaare, B. 2006. Integrated Dynamic Analysis of Floating Offshore Wind Turbines. *Proc. EWEC 2006, Athens, Greece, 27 February - 2 March 2006.*

Tromans, P.S. and Vanderschuren, L. 2004. A Spectral Response Surface Method for Calculating Crest Elevation Statistics. *J. Offshore Mechanics and Arctic Engineering* 126: 51-53.

10th International Symposium on Practical Design of Ships and Other Floating Structures
Houston, Texas, United States of America
© 2007 American Bureau of Shipping

Hydrodynamic Design of a Monocolumn Platform Avoiding Excessive Heave and Pitch Motions

Fernando G. S. Torres[1], Sergio H. Sphaier[2], Isaias Q. Masetti[1] Ana Paula dos Santos Costa[1], Joel S. Sales Jr.[2]

[1] CENPES/PETROBRAS.
Rio de Janeiro, RJ, Brazil
[2] LabOceano/COPPE/UFRJ.
Rio de Janeiro, RJ, Brazil.

Abstract

Experimental tests have been carried out at the Ocean Basin of LabOceano to study the behavior of monocolumn structures provided with moonpool. The paper describes a study on the simultaneous use of moonpool, skirts and changes of the external diameter bellow the free surface to minimize the heave and the pitch motions of monocolumns. The results indicate that high resonant periods and low amplification can be obtained.

Keywords

Experimental tests; Moonpool; Monocolumn platform.

Introduction

The advance to deep waters in the oil exploitation changed the concepts of offshore platforms along the last decades. Fixed jackets have been viable solutions in shallow waters. Storage in shallow waters was not a problem once through pipe lines oil could be transferred to oceanic terminals or even to the continent. The advance to deeper waters put ships as a solution due to their storage capacity. Using ships as F(P)SO, Floating, (Production) Storage and Offloading units of production with capacity of storing the oil produced, the difficulties of transfer per pipelines are overcome. Nevertheless, ships also have some limitations once they may have excessive vertical motions that can damage the risers. The horizontal motion can be minimized by the choice of an anchorage system as SMS(Spread Mooring Systems) or in DICAS(Differentiated Compliance Anchoring System), but anchorage systems based on catenary lines cannot avoid the vertical motion. In order to minimize the vertical motions new concepts of hulls have appeared.

Further, the recent sequence of hurricane in Mexico Gulf caused strong damages to many installed platforms. The high intensity of the hurricanes seems to obey a 30 years cycle and these occurrences will imply in new platform concepts and new criteria for offshore platforms. New modern platforms will certainly decrease the risks even in adverse environmental conditions.

Within this context, coincidently, PETROBRAS, in cooperation with Universities and Research Institutes, is studying a potential hull based on vertical circular columns structures provided with a moonpool. The study is focused in the minimization of the heave and the pitch motion in waves. The behavior of the platform in the sea is based on the analysis of experimental results of reduced scale models excited by regular, transient and irregular waves, carried out at LabOceano (COPPE / UFRJ, Rio de Janeiro).

Different series of tests have been carried out concentrated in the study of the influence of some parameters in the heave and pitch motion in waves: the entrance of the moonpool, the volume relationship (volume of the moonpool to the volume of the structure), the use of skirts and the use of change of external diameter bellow the free surface.

A first set of tests has been carried out to study the influence of the opening of the moonpool at the base plan. Complementary experiments have been carried out decreasing the volume of the moonpool to increase the storage capacity of the structure. The decrease of the internal volume may imply a decrease on the effectiveness of the moonpool as a motion minimization device. Part of these results has been presented by Barreira, Sphaier, Masetti, Costa and Levi (2005).

A second set of tests has been carried out for a monocolumn with a moonpool, without skirts, with constant external diameter and lower volume relationship.

A third set of experiments has been carried out with a model which structure volume was increased (decreasing the volume of the moonpool) to create storage capacity to the structure.

Haslum and Faltinsen (1999) identified four different kinds of Mathieu instabilities that may occur in monocolumn structures, due to the change in the area of the waterline plan, due to the change in the position of the center of buoyancy (consequently changing the metacentric height), due to an amplification in the heave motion when the wave frequency is close to the heave frequency (the heave envelope instability) and due to the superposition of surge and pitch motion.

Basic Concepts

The basic idea to explore the effects of the moonpool can be first related with the Frahm absorber (see den Hartog, 1957). Let us consider a mass m1 and a spring with stiffness k1 oscillating at natural frequency w1. If a second mass m2 is connected to mass m2 through a spring with stiffness k12 and natural frequency w2, mass m1 will have an amplification factor equal to zero at frequency w2. Now the system has two natural frequencies different from w1 and w2. Den Hartog (1957) extended this concept introducing not only a spring but also a damper between the two masses. The damper causes a decrease on the amplification at both the natural frequencies. For large damping coefficient the system works like a single block. A second important point to highlight is that it is possible to get a low amplification for a large range of frequencies between the two natural frequencies.

If we consider the monocolumn as the first mass m1 and the moonpool (the water inside the moonpool) as the second mass m2 we may try to use the above ideas to design the moonpool to obtain a monocolumn structure with minimal vertical motion. Some additional questions arise for the analysis:

1 – the moonpool has its own dynamics. So, the water can have vertical motion even if the structure remains fixed. Thinking as a mechanical system the moonpool has restoring and damping forces.

2 – the motion of the moonpool implies in a hydrodynamic reaction force proportional to the acceleration of the moonpool. A coefficient like added mass should be introduced in the analysis.

3 – velocities and accelerations of the water particles in the moonpool are not constant.

3 – in waves, exciting forces act on the moonpool.

4 – when the moonpool moves, coupled hydrodynamic forces act on the structure.

5 – when the structures moves it induces hydrodynamic forces on the moonpool.

6 – viscous effects may play an important role depending on the entrance form of the moonpool at the structure baseline.

7 – the exciting forces depend on the frequency.

8 – the change in the damping of the moonpool is obtained by changing the entrance of the moonpool. A consequence is the change in the natural frequency and a change in the added mass.

It should be observed that for a mechanical system as above, we know the m1 and k1, and consequently the natural frequency w1. In principle we are able to choose a mass m2, a spring k12 and a damper c12 to interfere in the amplification curve.

In the case of a structure in waves we can not isolate the structure to test its behavior in a model basin. It is possible to estimate the behavior of the structure without the coupling effect of the moonpool using potential theory. The same can be done for the moonpool. But a final experimental study must be carried out with models to account for viscous effects.

Trying to incorporate some of these effects Sphaier, Torres, Masetti, Costa and Levi (2007) present an equivalent mechanical system consisting of two masses. They extend den Hartog model, by introducing additional spring k2 and damper c2 to the mass m2 to explain qualitatively the experimental results obtained for a monocolumn

Experimental Tests

The conceptual basic analysis indicates that the relation between the masses of the moonpool and the mass of the structure, the natural frequencies (consequently the added mass) and the damping factor play an important role in the design of a monocolumn with a moonpool.

The main dimensions of the Ocean Basin at LabOceano are: Length = 40 m, Width = 30 m and Depth = 15 m, with an additional pit 10 meters deep. The wavemaker consists of 75 rectangular panels (height: 1.2 m; width: 0.4 m); type wet-back. The model was moored by a simplified horizontal mooring system as show in fig. 1.

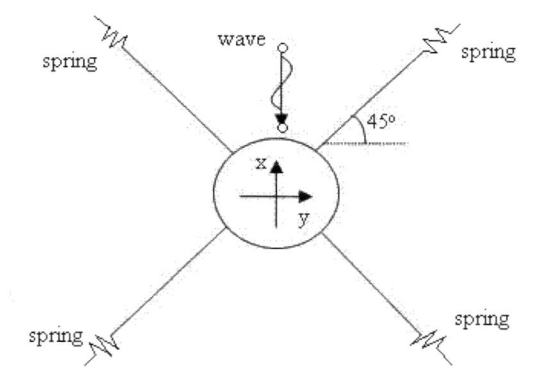

Fig. 1: Scheme of the horizontal mooring system at the Ocean Basin

For almost all experimental tests numerical calculations have been carried out using WAMIT (1995).

Model without storage capacity

A first design of a monocolumn structure was developed by Petrobras together with the University of São Paulo.

This initial concept did not have the capacity to store oil. Due to construction constraints the structure should have a maximal external diameter about 100 m. The diameter of the moonpool is about 70 m. The draft of the structure is equal to 38 meters. Both the structure and the moonpool have almost the same volume. A model in the scale 1:100 was tested at LabOceano at Federal University of Rio de Janeiro, to define the diameter of the moonpool, so that the vertical motion would be minimized. A plate with a circular hole was installed at the bottom line introducing a constraint to the water flowing from the moonpool to the external domain and vice-versa. The diameter of the circular opening of the moonpool has been varied to define an optimal solution from the point of view of minimal heave and pitch motion. Below the water line there is a change in the external diameter. The structure has an external skirt at the bottom line. Fig. 1 shows a scheme of the structure. In this figure the external diameter De, the moonpool diameter Dm, the diameter of the moonpool entrance Dr and the height of the entrance h are indicated. The height h can be varied in the internal part of the structure. The height of the skirt remains fixed.

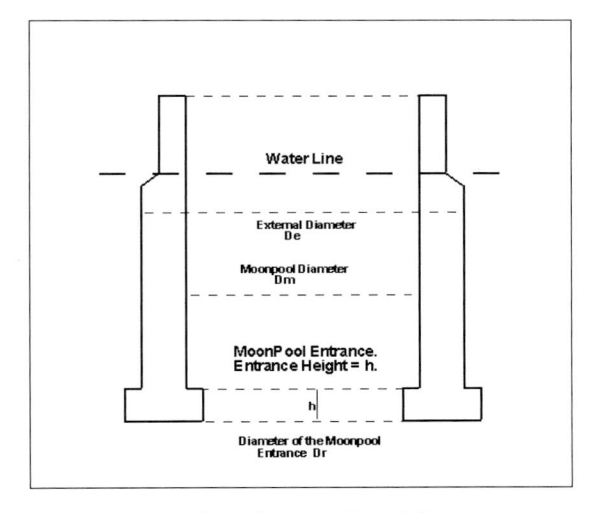

Fig. 2: Scheme of the first tested model

The volume of the moonpool is almost equal to the volume of the structure.

Transient wave tests have been carried out for the structure with different entrance diameters of the moonpool to determine the moonpool response when the structure remains fixed and the heave and pitch motions when the structure freely floats. The technique used to generate the transient wave was presented by Matos (2005). The response amplitude operator (RAO) for the vertical motion of the moonpool is presented in Fig. 3 for different entrance diameters with the use of a plate at the bottom with a circular hole. We can observe that the period of the damped oscillation increase with the increase of the constraint (smaller Dr). The amplification decreases with the increase of the constraint too. In the figure the different diameters Dr are indicated and also the relation between the internal area of the moonpool Am and the area of the entrance Ar.

Figs. 4~6 show the RAOs of heave motion for the different entrances. In these figures the heave RAOs for the different diameters of the entrance are presented. In each one figure the RAOs of the structure without moonpool and with no restriction is also presented. In order to observe the influence of an increase of the volume of the structure with reduction of the moonpool volume a ring was used at the bottom with h = 8 meters. From the results it is clear that this effect (change of the volume introducing a form like a tunnel in the entrance) introduces a decrease on the resonant period of heave and an amplification on the response for both the cases Dr = 33 and 47 meters.

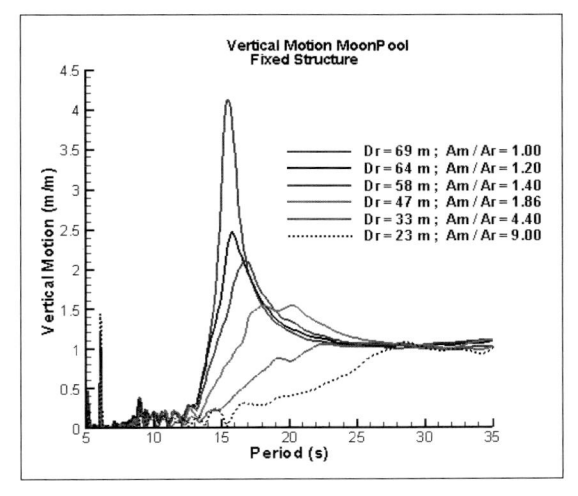

Fig. 3: RAO of vertical motion of the water inside the moonpool

From these figures we can observe that the best behavior was reached for Dr = 47 meters, in terms of minimization of the vertical motion.

The RAOs of the pitch motion of the structure in waves are presented in Fig. 7 for the case when a plate is used at the moonpool entrance. As we can observe the pitch response is very small. Even if we increase the volume of the structure, by increasing the height h, the pitch response is small, as we can observe from Fig. 8.

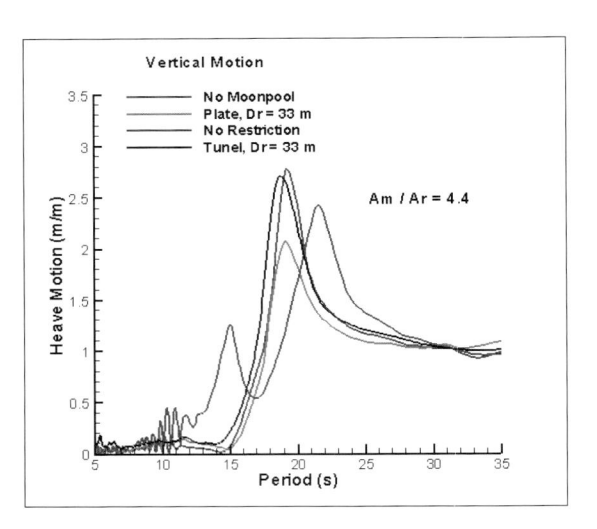

Fig. 4: RAO of heave when a restriction with diameter Dr = 33 m at the moonpool entrance.

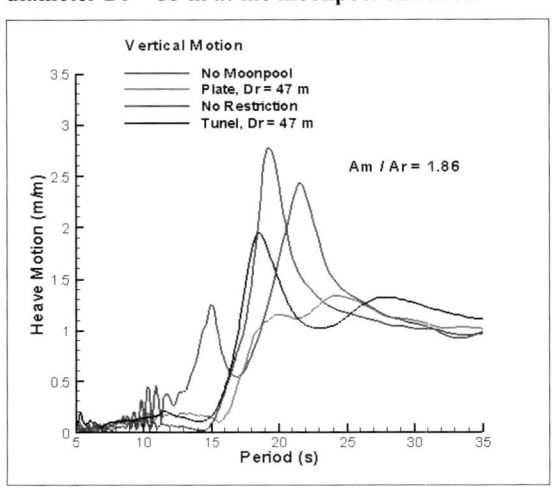

Fig. 5: RAO of heave when a restriction with diameter Dr = 47 m at the moonpool entrance.

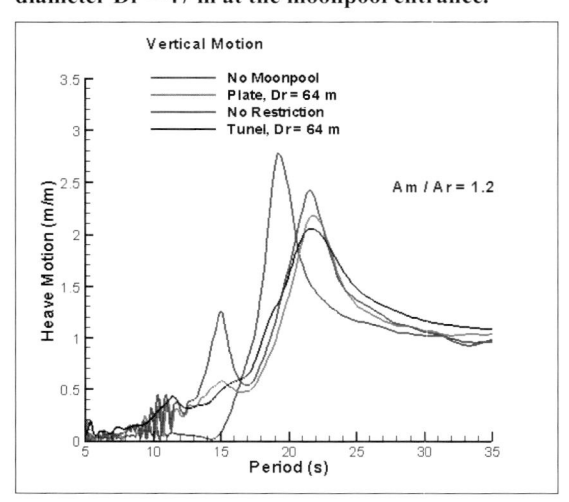

Fig. 6: RAO of heave when a restriction with diameter Dr = 64 m at the moonpool entrance.

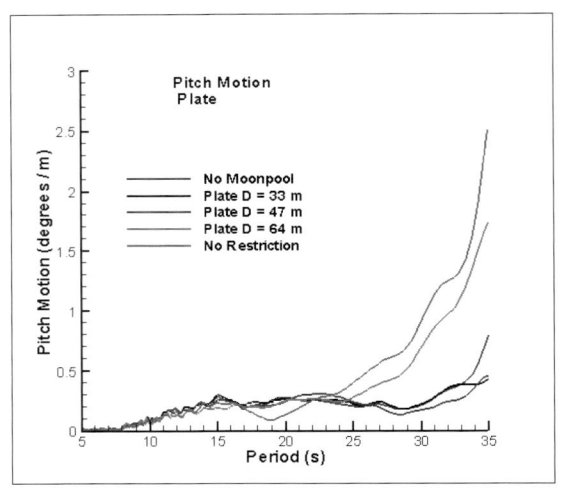

Fig. 7: RAO of pitch motion for the different entrances when a plate is used at the bottom.

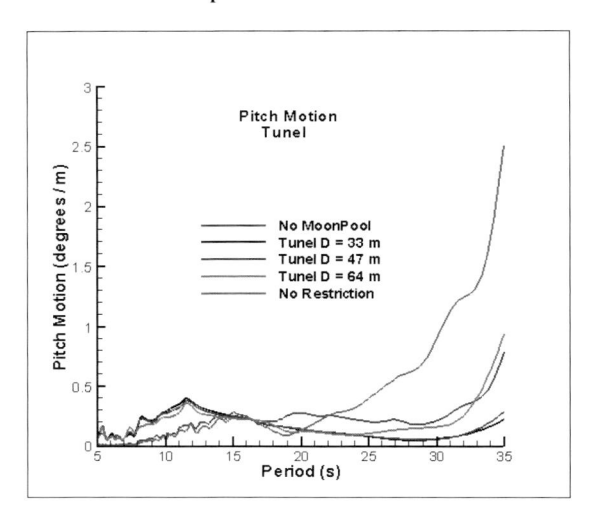

Fig. 8: RAO of pitch motion for the different entrances with h = 8 meters.

Monocolumn without skirt

A second set of tests were carried out with a monocolumn without change of the external diameter and without skirt. The external diameter of the monocolumn De = 110 meters. The internal diameter of the moonpool Dm = 50 meters. The structure was tested for a draft equal to 30 meters. Two entrances at the bottom of the moonpool were tested: Am / Ar = 1.0 and 2.0. In this case a plate at the bottom was used. The vertical motion inside the moonpool for the structure fixed was tested in transient waves. Similar tests have been realized for the structure in free floating condition. The motion of the water column inside the moonpool for the structure fixed, the heave and the pitch motion of the structure free floating in waves are shown in Figs. 9~11. From these results we can say that the moonpool does not act effectively as a device to minimize the heave and the pitch motion. Nevertheless, the vertical motion of the water column inside the moonpool is affected by the change of the entrance area. We should emphasize that the structure does not have with any skirt or change in the external diameter. In this case the volume of the moonpool is about 26 % the volume of the structure.

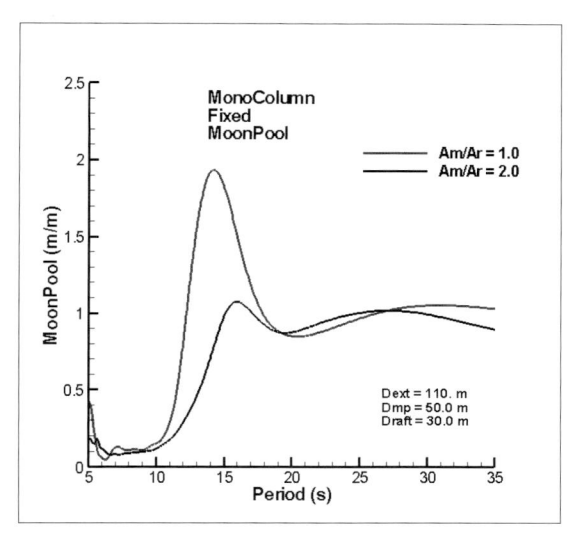

Fig. 9: Vertical Motion of the water column inside the moonpool for the monocolumn fixed in waves.

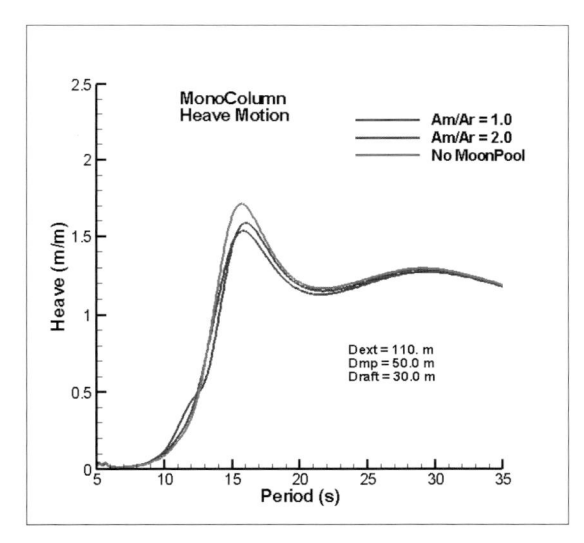

Fig. 10: Heave motion of the monocolumn free-floating in waves.

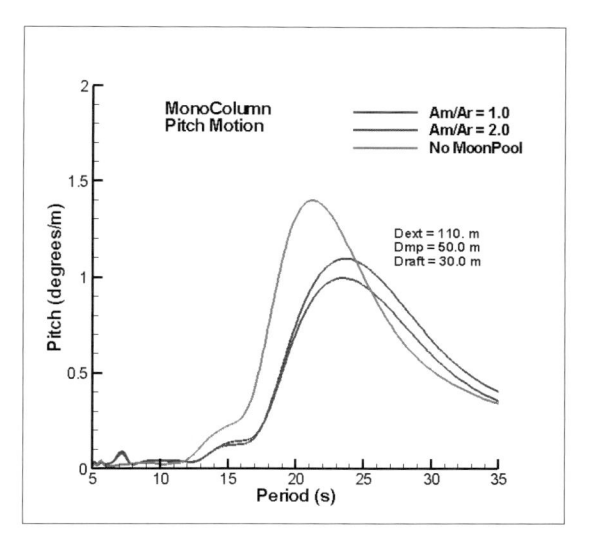

Fig. 11: Pitch motion of the monocolumn free-floating in waves

A Storage Monocolumn

An analysis based on results obtained with the mechanical model briefly described above, numerical calculations with WAMIT and experimental tests suggests that the effectiveness of the moonpool depends not only on the configuration of the entrance of the moonpool, on the relation between the volumes of the moonpool and the structure but also on the relation of the decoupled resonant periods of the structure and the moonpool. It seems like the resonant period of the structure mode should be higher than the resonant period of the moonpool. If we do not consider the added masses both periods would be equal and proportional to the square root of the draft. A way to increase the added mass of the structure is the use of a skirt along the external circumference on the structure at the bottom level. The added mass can also be increased changing the diameter of the structure bellow the waterline. These kinds of devices were used in a third set of tests presented here for a storage unit. The experimental results used here to explain the effects of the use of skirts and changes in the external diameter are part of a large experimental program developed at LabOceano, Masetti, Costa, Matter, Barreira and Sphaier (2007).

One premise imposed in the design of the storage structure presented here was a limitation of the external diameter. As a consequence of this premise the internal volume of the moonpool should be smaller than the structure volume. To account for an increase in the added mass different skirts and changes in the external diameter along the vertical have been used. Fig. 12 presents a scheme of a vertical plane cutting a half part of the storage monocolumn. The main dimensions of the structure are presented in Table 1. In Fig. 12 the skirt is 8 meters large. A second model was tested with a 10 meters large skirt. As shown in the figure, the change in the diameter is located at 23 m above the bottom line. The model with the different skirts was tested in the ballast and the loaded conditions.

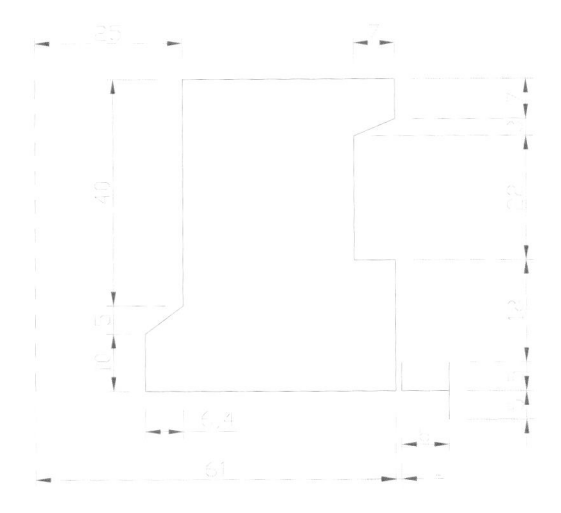

Fig. 12: Scheme of a vertical plane cutting a half part of the storage monocolumn.

Table 1:   Main Dimensions of the Structure

Main body external diameter	122.00 m
Internal diameter	50.00 m
Depth	55.00 m
Draft in full loaded condition	42.00 m
Draft in ballast condition	23.80 m
Diameter of the moonpool entrance	37.20 m
Position of change in the external diameter	23.00 m

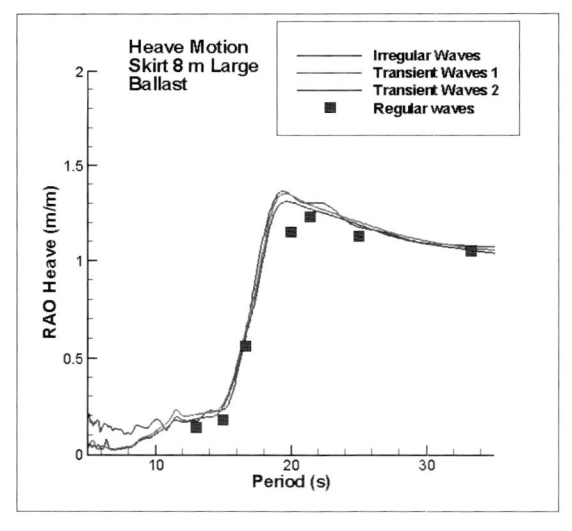

Fig. 13: Heave motion for the storage unit in ballast condition with the 8 m large skirt.

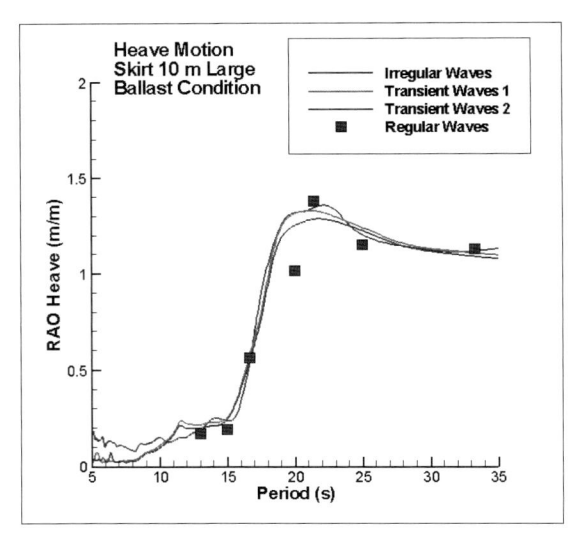

Fig. 14: Heave motion for the storage unit in ballast condition with the 10 m large skirt.

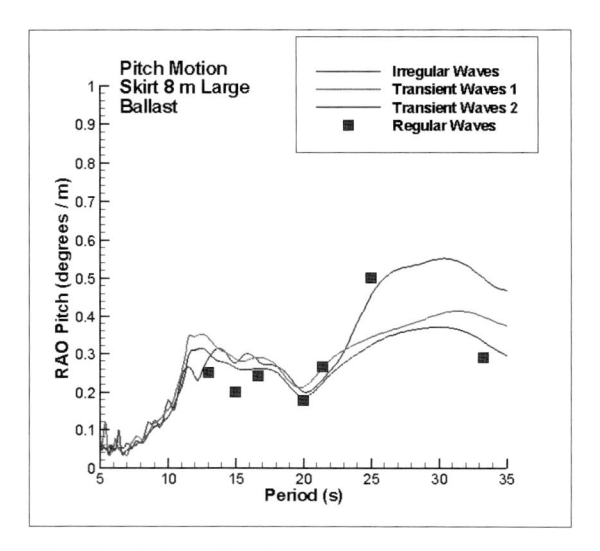

Fig. 15: Pitch motion for the storage unit in ballast condition with the 8 m large skirt.

Figs. 12~15 present the RAOs for pitch and heave motions of the storage unit in ballast condition with the two skirts. A Pierson-Moskowitz sea state and two transient waves have been used to obtain the RAO curves. The second transient wave is just 1.5 times the first one. For some regular waves the responses for heave and pitch were measured and are plotted in the figures. The results indicate that the period of heave is about 20 seconds. The pitch responses are very low.

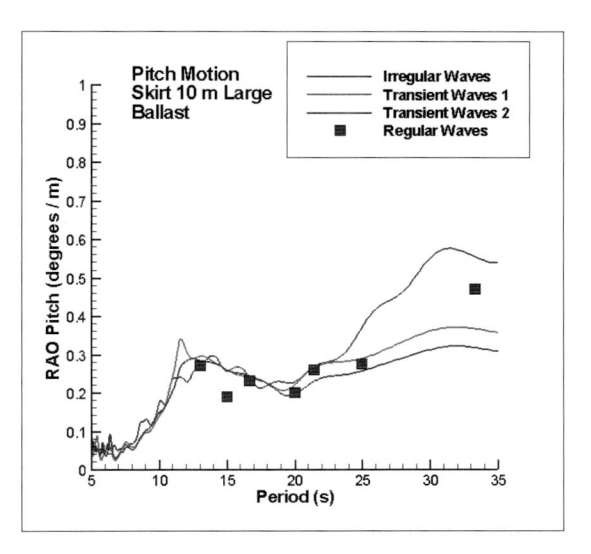

Fig. 16: Pitch motion for the storage unit in ballast condition with the 10 m large skirt.

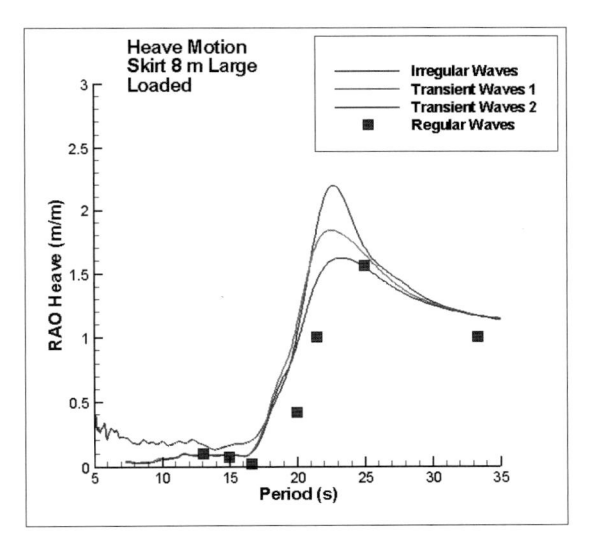

Fig. 17: Heave motion for the storage unit in loaded condition with the 8 m large skirt

A similar set of tests have been carried out for the loaded condition. The results are presented in Figs. 17~20. We can see that for both skirts the resonant periods are above 20 seconds for pitch and heave, and the pitch response is very low.

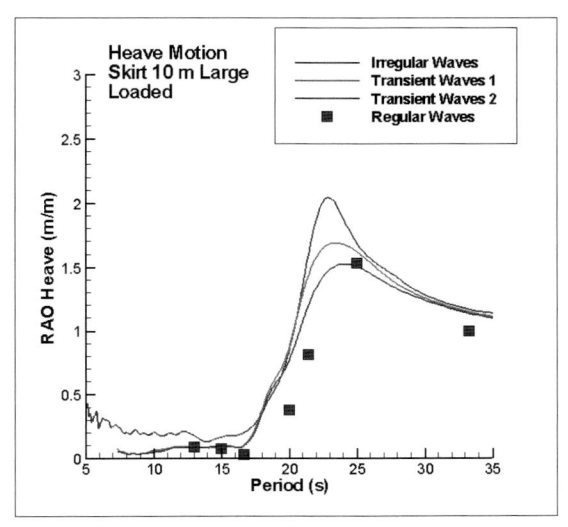

Fig. 18: Heave motion for the storage unit in loaded condition with the 10 m large skirt

Table 2: Damped Periods from Decay Tests

Case	Heave	Pitch
Ballast – Skirt 10 m Large	20.0	30.0
Ballast – Skirt 8 m Large	20.0	28.0
Loaded – Skirt 10 m Large	23.0	29.0
Loaded – Skirt 8 m Large	23.0	26.0

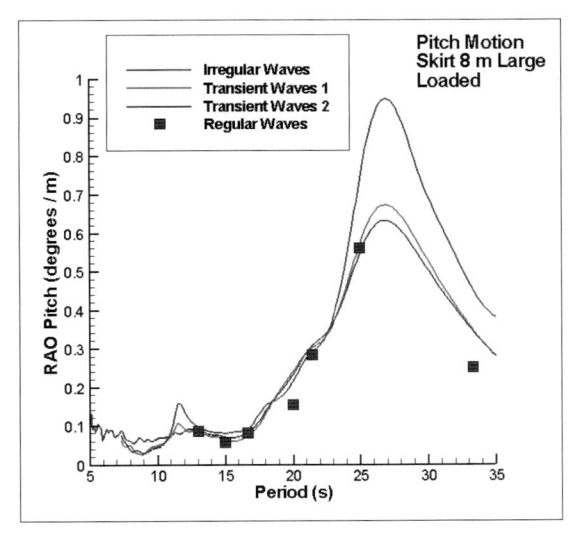

Fig. 19: Pitch motion for the storage unit in loaded condition with the 8 m large skirt

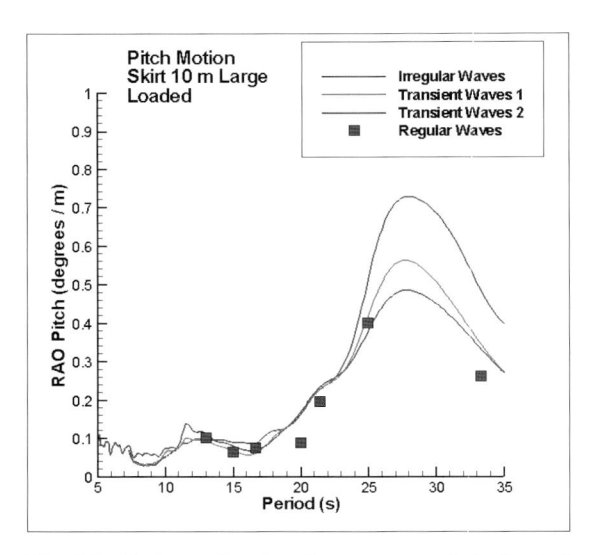

Fig. 20: Pitch motion for the storage unit in loaded condition with the 10 m large skirt

To determine more precisely the resonant period decay tests have been carried out. The results are presented in Table 2.

Mathieu Instabilities

The first and the third structures have changes in the area of the waterline section along the vertical axis, what can introduce some instabilities in heave for some wave frequencies. We did not observe any instabilities for the regular waves we tested, although a detailed set of waves have not been tested. The heave and the pitch periods are not in the relation 1 to 2, so that the heave motion does not induce pitch instabilities. Observing Table 2 one may expect possible instabilities for periods about 12~13 seconds (heave envelope or surge and pitch superposition). For 13 seconds regular waves instabilities were not observed. The transient tests present amplifications close to 12 seconds what may suggest that an investigation in regular waves for 12 seconds should be carried out. It should be mentioned that in irregular waves we could not identify any unstable behavior.

For the second structure tests with many regular waves has been carried out. When the periods of heave and pitch (roll) were set in the relation 1 to 2, resonant behavior in pitch (roll) was clearly observed.

Conclusions

Different sets of tests have been carried out to study the behavior of monocolumn structures provided with moonpool.

In an earlier work developed by the authors it was shown that the use of a plate at the bottom of the moonpool with a circular entrance could be investigate to determine the best diameter to minimize the vertical motion and change the resonant periods. The authors extended the study to observe the behavior of the structure when the volume of the structure increases with decrease of the moonpool volume, creating a structure like a tunnel at the moonpool entrance. The results indicate a loss of effectiveness.

A set of tests with a monocolum without skirt, with constant external diameter and lower relation of volume (volume of the moonpool to volume of the structure) indicate that the moonpool does not present an effective contribution. This suggests that the volume relationship and also the relation between the resonant periods of the moonpool mode and the structure mode play an important role in the responses.

A third structure was tested. In this case the structure was designed to have storage capacity with limitation on the external diameter. This means: low volume relationship and a tunnel effect at the moonpool entrance. From the experimental results we concluded that the use of a moonpool combined with skirts and changes in the external diameter bellow the free surface can increase the resonant period of heave and minimize the heave and the pitch motion in the range of periods of the waves in a sea state. These conclusions bring an important contribution to the design of floating structure with storage capacity.

Acknowledgement

The authors would like to acknowledge Petrobras, CNPq (Brazilian Agency for Research) and the Federal University of Rio de Janeiro to support this work.

References

Barreira, RA, Sphaier, SH, Masetti, IQ, Costa, AP and Levi, C (2005). "Behavior of a Mono-Column Structure (MONOBR) in Waves'', OMAE67512, Conference OMAE, 12-17, June, 2005, Halkidiki, Greece.

Haslum, HA and Faltinsen, (1999), "Alternative Shape of Spar Platform for Use in Hostile Areas" OTC10953, Offshore Technology Conference 1999, Houston, USA.

Hartog, JP den, (1957). "Mechanical Vibration", MacGraw-Hill Book Company.

Masetti, IQ, Costa, AP, Matter, GB, Barreira RA, and Sphaier, SH, (2007). "Effects of skirts on the behavior of a mono-column structure in waves", OMAE07-29024, Conference OMAE, 10-15, June, 2007, San Diego, USA.

Matos, V, Sales-Jr, J S and Sphaier, SH (2005). "Seakeeping Tests with Gaussian Wave Packets", OMAE05-67259, Conference OMAE, 12-17, June, 2005, Halkidiki, Greece.

Sphaier, SH, Torres, FGS, Masetti, IQ, Costa, AP and Levi, C. (2007). "Monocolumn Behavior in Waves: Experimental Analysis", Ocean Engineering, OE 1319.

WAMIT (1995). "A Radiation-Diffraction Panel Program for Wave-Body Interaction", Dept. of Ocean Engineering, Massachusetts Institute of Technology, USA.

Comparative Analysis of Design Criteria for Rigid Risers

Leile M. Froufe [1], Theodoro A. Netto [2]

[1] American Bureau of Shipping
Rio de Janeiro, Brazil
[2] COPPE / UFRJ
Rio de Janeiro, Brazil

Abstract

The risers systems are basically formed by tubular elements, which connect the floating unit to subsea wells, Christmas trees or manifolds, in order to transport oil, water, gas or mixtures. During the installation and operation phases, the risers are subject to different types of loads. Considering these loadings, the riser strength can be analyzed for different failure modes, such as bursting, buckling, buckle propagation and fatigue. There are different formulations in different codes for the evaluation of the risers' strength with respect to these failure modes. The objective of this paper is to evaluate the formulations and applicable requirements from the existing codes, comparing the obtained results with experimental ones, as well as, the analytical and/or numerical results available in the literature. Additionally, the estimation of some safety factors is made. Eventual discrepancies among each code are analyzed.

Keywords

Rigid risers; Design criteria; Buckling; Propagation buckling; Collapse; Fatigue.

Introduction

As mentioned above, considering all loads that the risers are subject to during the installation and operation, the burst, collapse, buckle propagation, and fatigue are the main failure modes to be analyzed. The main object of this paper is to provide a comprehensive comparison and analysis of the main Codes and Rules related to this subject. The main Codes/Rules used for this study are *"ABS Guide for Building and Classing Subsea Riser Systems"*[1], *"DnV Dynamic Risers, DNV-OS-F201"* [2], *"API Design, Construction, Operation, and Maintenance of Offshore Hydrocarbon Pipelines (Limit State Design), API RP 1111"*[3] and *"Manual for Determining the Remaining Strength of Corroded Pipelines, ASME B31G"*[4].

Burst

1. Proposed Theoretical Burst Pressure

The specified burst pressure for risers can be determined as follows:

ABS [1]:

$$p = 0.90(SMYS + SMTS)(\frac{t}{D-t}) \quad (1)$$

DnV [2]:

$$p = \left(\frac{2}{\sqrt{3}}\right)\left(\frac{2t}{D-t}\right).\min(f_y; f_u/1.15) \quad (2)$$

API [3]:

$$p = 0.90(S+U)(\frac{t}{D-t}) \quad (3)$$

ASME 31G [4]:

$$p = \left(\frac{2t}{D}\right).(1.1 SMYS) \quad (4)$$

Where:

D = nominal outside diameter of pipe

t = wall thickness

SMYS = S = specified minimum Yield Strength at design temperature

SMTS = U = specified minimum Tensile Strength at design temperature

f_y = (SMYS' – $f_{y,temp}$).α_u

f_u = (SMTS' – $f_{u,temp}$).α_u

$f_{y,temp}$ = temperature de-rating factor for the Yield stress

$f_{u,temp}$ = temperature de-rating factor for the Tensile strength

SMYS' = minimum Yield stress at room temperature

SMTS' = minimum Tensile strength at room temperature

α_u = material strength factor

2. Proposed Burst Design Criteria

A riser subject to an external pressure pe and an internal pressure pi shall satisfy the following, in order that no bursting occurs:

ABS [1]:

$$(pi - pe) \leq \frac{\eta.SMYS.k_T.2t}{(D-t)} \quad (5)$$

DnV [2]:

$$(pi - pe) \leq \frac{\left(\frac{2}{\sqrt{3}}\right)\left(\frac{2t}{D-t}\right).\min(fy; fu/1.15)}{\gamma_m.\gamma_{SC}} \quad (6)$$

API [3]:

$$(pi - pe) \leq 0.9 f_d f_e f_t p \quad (7)$$

Where:

SMYS, D, t, f_y, f_u and p = previously defined

η = utilization factor

k_T & f_t = temperature dependent material strength de-rating factor

γ_m = material resistance factor

γ_{sc} = safety class factor

f_d = internal pressure design factor

f_e = weld joint factor

The DnV safety classes can be taken from DNV-RP-F204 *Riser Fatigue* [5] and are defined below:

✓ Low safety class: Where failure implies low risk of human injury and minor environmental and economic consequences.

✓ Normal safety class: For conditions where failure implies risk of human injury, significant environmental pollution or very high economic or political consequences.

✓ High safety class: For operating conditions where failure implies high risk of human injury, significant environmental pollution or very high economic or political consequences.

3. Comparison Between Experimental, Analytical, Numerical and Rules Results

Considering the geometrical and material properties of the 6 models taken from reference [6] in the expressions (1) to (7) given above, the following ratios have been obtained and represent the intrinsic safety factor in the Rules.

Table 1: Ratio between the Rules and the experimental, analytical and numerical average values

Rule/Condition	(A)	(B)	(C)
ABS oil riser	1.68	2.21	1.32
ABS gas riser connected to unmanned platforms	2.01	2.65	1.32
ABS gas riser connected to manned platforms	2.42	3.18	1.32
DnV, low safety class	1.56	2.27	1.45
DnV, normal safety class	1.71	2.48	1.45
DnV, high safety class	1.89	2.75	1.45
API	1.48	1.95	1.32

Where:

(A) = Safety factor between the theoretical value (item 1) and the criteria value (item 2)

(B) = Safety factor between the criteria and the average between experimental, numerical and analytical values.

(C) = Safety factor between the Rules theoretical values and the average between experimental, numerical and analytical values.

4. Specified Burst Pressure and Criteria for API Standard Tubes

Figure 1 shows the results obtained for p x (D/t) for different pipes taken from [7], with D/t ratio between 15 and 35, considering expressions (1) to (4) above.

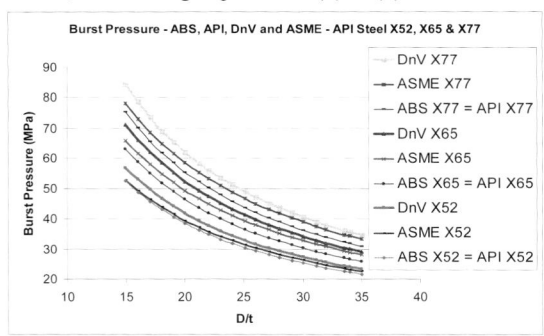

Fig.1: *p x (D/t)* – Burst theoretical values for pipes API X52, X65 e X77

From figure 1 above it can be noted that the DnV values are less conservative than those of ABS and API (10% difference). The ASME values are between ABS/API and DnV (5% between each one). These results indicate a good correlation between the Rules.

The apparent discrepancy between the values indicated in Table 1 and Figure 1, with respect to the conservativeness of the Rules, is due to the yield and tensile strength of the material and the ratio between these values (in Figure 1 DnV is less conservative and in Table 1 DnV is more conservative). For the standard API steels, the ratio between tensile and yield is about 1.20~1.25 and yield stresses are 52, 65 and 77 Ksi for the steel analyzed in this work. For the models used, the tensile to yield ratio is about 1.45 to 2.22 and yield is about 36 to 46 Ksi. These changes affect the conservativeness. Figure 2 shows the results obtained for p x (D/t) for a hypothetical steel with 40Ksi yield and tensile/yield ratio of 1.55, indicating the same behavior as Table 1.

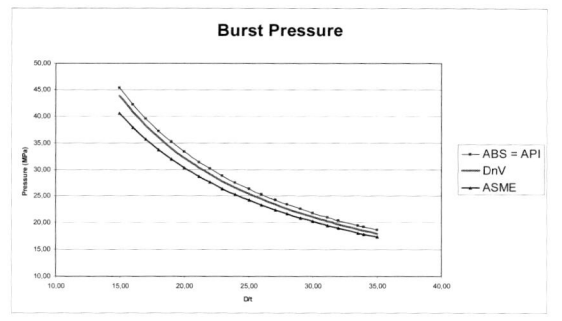

Fig. 2:- p x (D/t) – Theoretical burst pressure for a hypothetical steel

Figures 3, 4, and 5 show the results for $(pi - pe)$ x (D/t), according to Equations (5) to (7), for API X65 steel, for the different conditions described by the Rules (similar results were obtained for X52 and X77 steels).

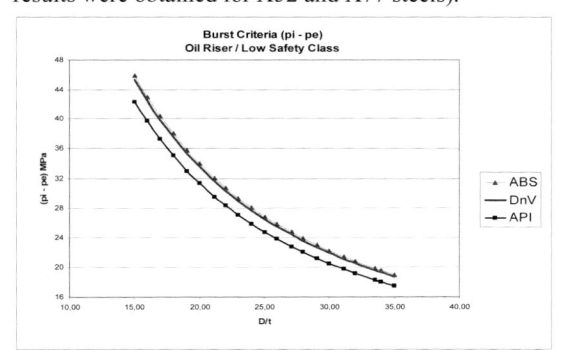

Fig.3: Burst criteria, oil riser / low safety class, API X65

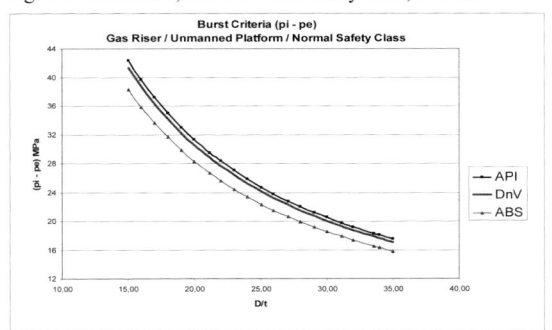

Fig. 4: Burst criteria, gas riser connected to unmanned platform / normal safety class, API X65

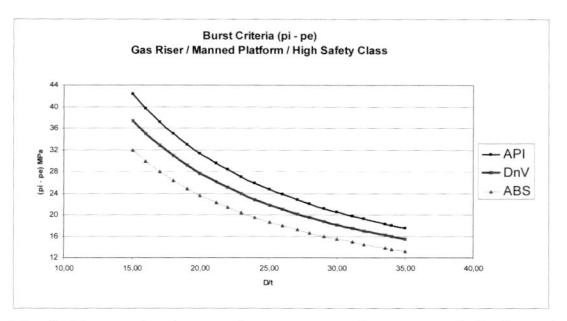

Fig. 5: Burst criteria, gas riser connected to manned platform / high safety class, API X65

We can note from Figures 3 to 5 that the conservativeness is dependent upon the safety class. However, we can note that for the higher safety classes (normal and high), the API criteria is less conservative compared to the Classification Societies criteria. As expected, the Classification Societies are more stringent where a high safety level is required.

Additionally, a comparison between the theoretical values and the criteria values, considering pe equal to zero, which gives the maximum allowable pi ($p_i - 0 = p_i$), has also been carried out. This comparison indicates an estimation of the safety factor contained in the Rules equations. Figures 6 to 8 show this comparison for API X65 steel.

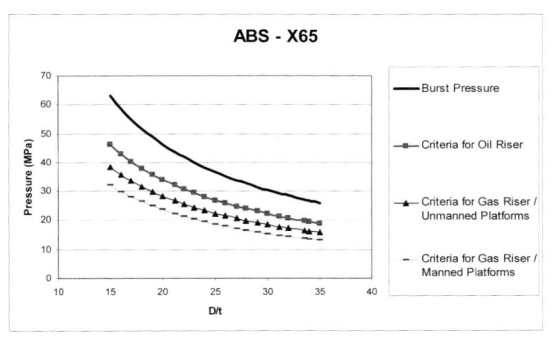

Fig. 6: Comparison between burst criteria and theoretical value, ABS, API X65 steel

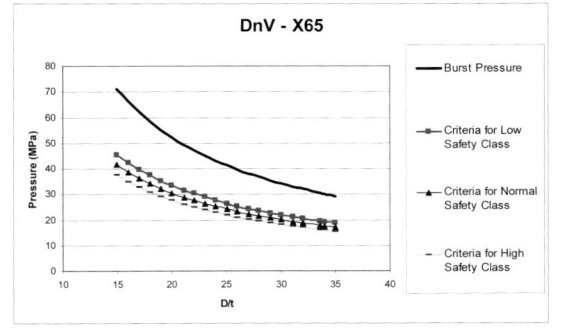

Fig. 7: Comparison between burst criteria and theoretical value, DnV, API X65 steel

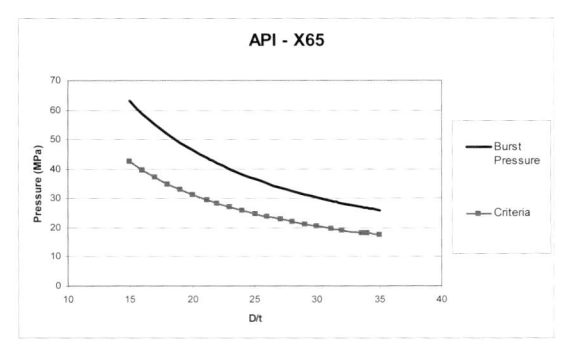

Fig. 8: Comparison between burst criteria and theoretical value, API, API X65 steel

The average ratio values between the theoretical values and the criteria values, obtained from Figures 6 to 8 are indicated on Table 2 below.

Table 2: Comparison between the criteria and the burst pressure

Rule/Condition	Theoretical / Criteria
ABS oil riser	1.43
ABS gas riser connected to unmanned platforms	1.67
ABS gas riser connected to manned platforms	2.00
DnV, low safety class	1.54
DnV, normal safety class	1.69
DnV, high safety class	1.89
API	1.47

4. Conclusions and Recommendations

The results obtained above show that with respect to the theoretical values proposed by the Rules, the DnV and ASME values are less conservative than the API and ABS for the standard API steels used in riser construction. With respect to the Rules dimensioning criteria, the conservativeness is dependent upon the safety level of the application.

Some safety factors have been estimated based on the burst pressure obtained from models found in the literature. However, only a few results have been found so these conclusions shall be limited to the geometries analyzed. Additionally, we noted that the conservativeness is dependent on the yield and tensile strengths of the material. In this regard, it is recommended that models with yield and tensile equivalent to the standard API steels are used.

Collapse

1. Proposed Theoretical Collapse Pressure

The specified collapse pressure for risers subject to external pressure only can be evaluated as follows:

ABS [1]:

$$p_c = \frac{p_{el} \cdot p_{p1}}{\sqrt{p_{el}^2 + p_{p1}^2}} \qquad (8)$$

DnV [2]:

$$p_c = y - \frac{1}{3}b \qquad (9)$$

API [3]:

$$p_c = \frac{p_{el} \cdot p_{p1}}{\sqrt{p_{el}^2 + p_{p1}^2}} \qquad (10)$$

Where:

$$p_{el} = \frac{2E}{1-v^2} \cdot \left(\frac{t}{D}\right)^3 \qquad (11)$$

$$p_{p1} = SMYS \cdot \frac{2t}{D} \qquad (12)$$

$$b = -p_{el} \qquad (13)$$

$$p_p = 2 \cdot fy \cdot \alpha_{fab} \cdot \frac{t}{D} \qquad (14)$$

$$c = -\left(p_p^2 + p_p \cdot p_{el} \cdot f_o \cdot \frac{D}{t}\right) \qquad (15)$$

$$d = p_{el} \cdot p_p^2 \qquad (16)$$

$$u = \frac{1}{3} \cdot \left(\frac{-1}{3} \cdot b^2 + c\right) \qquad (17)$$

$$z = \frac{1}{2} \cdot \left(\frac{2}{27}b^3 - \frac{1}{3}bc + d\right) \qquad (18)$$

$$\phi = \cos^{-1}\left(\frac{-z}{\sqrt{-u^3}}\right) \qquad (19)$$

$$y = -2 \cdot \sqrt{-u} \cdot \cos\left(\frac{\phi}{3} + \frac{60\pi}{180}\right) \qquad (20)$$

α_{fab} = fabrication factor

v = Poisson

E = Young's Modulus

f_o = initial out-of-roundness

SMYS and fy = previously defined

2. Proposed Collapse Design Criteria

A riser subject to an external pressure pe and an internal pressure pi shall satisfy the following, in order that no collapse occurs:

ABS [1]:
$$(pe - pi) \leq \eta_b \cdot p_c \qquad (21)$$

DnV [2]:
$$(pe - pi) \leq \frac{p_c}{\gamma_m \cdot \gamma_{SC}} \qquad (22)$$

API [3]:
$$(pe - pi) \leq \eta_b \cdot p_c \qquad (23)$$

Where:

η_b = design factor

p_c = collapse pressure (previously defined)

γ_m and γ_{sc} = previously defined

3. Comparison Between Experimental and Rules Results

Considering the geometrical and material properties of 21 experimental models taken from reference [6] in Equations (8) to (23) given above, the following ratios have been obtained and represent the estimated safety factor in the Rules, as shown on table 3.

Table 3: Ratio between the Rules and the experimental data

Rule/Condition	(A)	(B)	(C)
ABS & API, seamless pipe	1.44	1.57	1.09
ABS & API, cold expanded pipe	1.69	1.84	1.09
DnV, low safety class	1.57	1.72	1.10
DnV, normal safety class	1.72	1.89	1.10
DnV, high safety class	1.89	2.08	1.10

Where:

(A) = Safety factor between the theoretical and criteria value

(B) = Safety factor between the criteria value and the experimental results

(C) = Safety factor between the theoretical value and the experimental results

4. Specified Collapse Pressure and Criteria for API Standard Tubes

Figure 9 shows the results obtained for p_c x (D/t) for different pipes taken from [7], with D/t ratio between 15 and 35, considering Equations (8) to (20) above. For DnV equations, a minimum out-of-roundness of 0.5% has been considered.

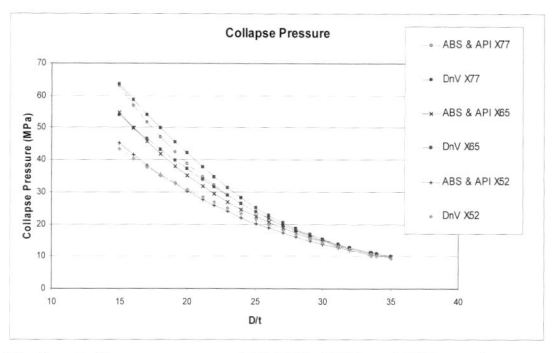

Fig.9 – Collapse pressure, API X52, X65 and X77 steels

Figure 9 shows a good correlation between the Rules and that DnV values are, in general, less conservative than those of ABS and API. It can be noted that DnV equations include the "out-of-roundness" value, not included in API and ABS equations. Due to this reason, it is expected that ABS and API are more conservative than DnV.

Similarly to the burst pressure, the discrepancy shown on the conservativeness (Figure 9, Table 3) is due to the material properties of the standard steels and material properties of the experimental models used.

Considering Equations (21) to (23), the results shown on Figure 10 have been obtained for $(pe - pi)$ x (D/t), for D/t between 15 and 35, for different tubes taken from [7], for API X65 steel (similar results were obtained for X52 and X77 steels).

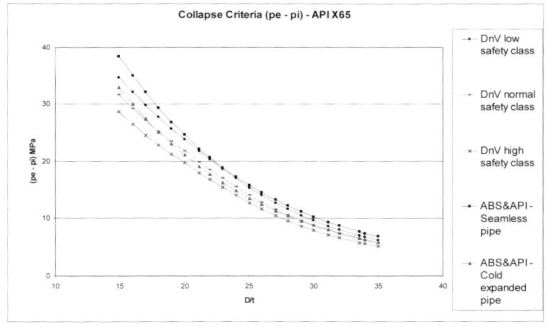

Fig.10: Collapse pressure criteria for API X65 steel

Figure 10 indicates that the difference between the Rules depends on the safety class and type of construction of the riser. As much as it it is lower in the safety class, the Rules results are similar.

Additionally, a comparison between the theoretical proposed collapse pressure values and the collapse criteria has been performed, considering p_i equal to zero ($p_e - 0 = p_e$). This comparison indicates an estimation of the Rules safety factor, estimating the maximum allowable value of p_e.

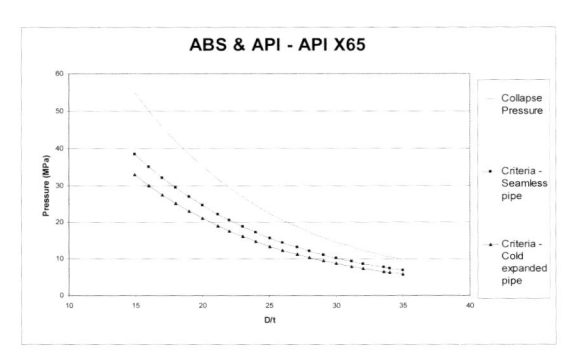

Fig. 11: Comparison between the criteria and the theoretical value, ABS and API, API X65 steel

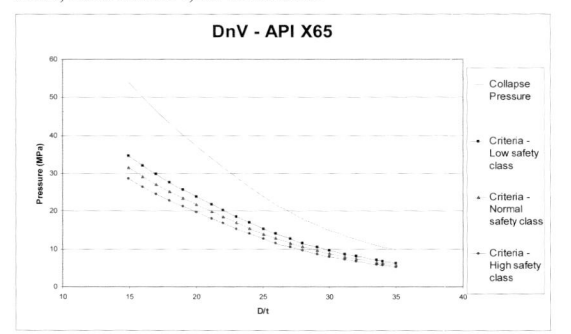

Fig. 12: Comparison between the criteria and the theoretical value, DnV, API X65 steel

From Figures 11 and 12, the following safety factors have been estimated (Table 4).

Table 4: Comparison between the criteria and the theoretical value

Rule/Condition	Theoretical / Criteria
ABS & API, seamless pipe	1.43
ABS & API, cold expanded pipe	1.67
DnV, low safety class	1.56
DnV, normal safety class	1.71
DnV, high safety class	1.89

4. Conclusions and Recommendations

Regarding the collapse pressure theoretical values, a good correlation between the Rules is noted. In addition, DnV values are less conservative for the usual D/t ratios used in the riser construction. Some safety factors have been estimated based on experimental models with no standard API material properties. However, it was also noted that there is a different behavior for the standard API steel material. In this regard, it is recommended that additional models with API standard steel material properties be used.

Additionally, it was noted that the collapse pressure for lower values of D/t have a higher discrepancy between the Rules. This is due to the fact that, for lower D/t values, some aspects in the collapse phenomena, such as the stress-strain behavior, although very significant, are not taken into account in the formulations.

It shall also be noted that the collapse phenomena is very dependent upon many factors (ovalization, defects) due to the "external pressure only" effect analyzed in this work., are due to the bending effect and the combination between bending and external pressure. These studies have not been included here but can be found on reference [6].

Buckle Propagation

1. Proposed Theoretical Propagation Buckle Pressure

The specified propagation buckle pressure for risers can be evaluated as follows:

ABS [1]:
$$p_p = 6.SMYS\left(\frac{2t}{D}\right)^{2.5} \qquad (26)$$

DnV [2]:
$$p_p = 35.f_y.\alpha_{fab}\cdot\left(\frac{t}{D}\right)^{2.5} \qquad (27)$$

API [3]:
$$p_p = 24.S\cdot\left(\frac{t}{D}\right)^{2.4} \qquad (28)$$

Where:
α_{fab} = fabrication factor
D, t, S, SMYS and fy = previously defined

2. Proposed Propagation Buckle Design Criteria

A riser subject to an external pressure *pe* and an internal pressure *pi* shall satisfy the following, in order to avoid propagation buckle:

ABS [1]:
$$(pe - pi) \leq 0.72.p_p \qquad (29)$$

DnV [2]:
$$(pe - pi) \leq \frac{p_p}{\gamma_m.\gamma_{SC}.\gamma_c} \qquad (30)$$

API [3]:
$$(pe - pi) \leq f_p.p_p \qquad (31)$$

Where:
γ_c = 1.0 if no buckle propagation is allowed. If buckle is allowed to travel a short distance, 0.9 can be used
f_p = propagation buckle factor
p_p = propagation buckle pressure (previously defined)
γ_m and γ_{sc} = previously defined

3. Comparison Between Experimental and Rules Results

Considering the geometrical and material properties of 96 experimental models taken from reference [6] in Equations (26) to (31) given above, the following ratios have been obtained and represent the estimated safety factor in the Rules, as shown on Table 5.

Table 5: Ratio between the Rules and the Experimental Data

Rules/Condition	(A)	(B)	(C)
ABS	1.39	1.65	1.19
DnV, low safety class	1.56	1.87	1.19
DnV, normal safety class	1.71	2.05	1.19
DnV, high safety class	1.89	2.26	1.19
API	1.25	1.53	1.22

Where:

(A), (B), (C) → previously defined on Table 3

4. Specified Propagation Buckle Pressure and Criteria for API Standard Tubes

Figure 17 shows the results obtained for p_p x (D/t) for different pipes taken from [7], with D/t ratio between 15 and 35, considering Equations (26) to (28) above.

A very good correlation can be noted between ABS/API and DnV. The largest difference, in the specified range, is about 8%, for lower values of D/t, where the expressions have not been calibrated.

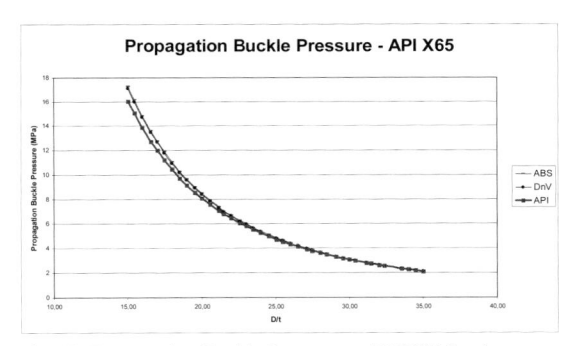

Fig. 17: Propagation Buckle Pressure – API X65 Steel

Considering Equations (29) to (31), the results shown on Figure 18 have been obtained for $(pe - pi)$ x (D/t), for D/t between 15 and 35, for different tubes taken from [7], for API X65 steel (similar results were obtained for X52 and X77 steels).

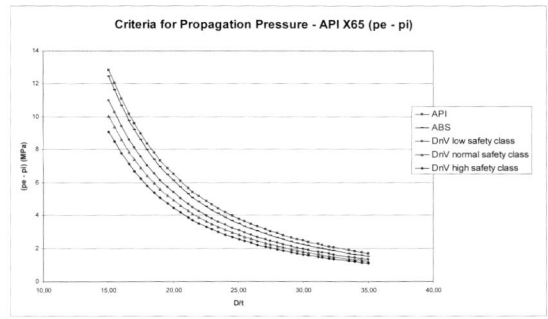

Fig. 18: Criteria for the propagation buckle - API X65 steel

From Figure 18, a good correlation is noted between ABS and API values, which are less conservative than DnV.

Additionally, a comparison between the theoretical proposed collapse pressure values and the propagation buckle criteria has been performed, considering p_i equal to zero ($p_e - 0 = p_e$). This comparison indicates an estimate of the Rules safety factor, estimating the maximum allowable value of p_e. Figures 19 to 21 show the comparison for API X65 steel (API X52 and API X77 are similar).

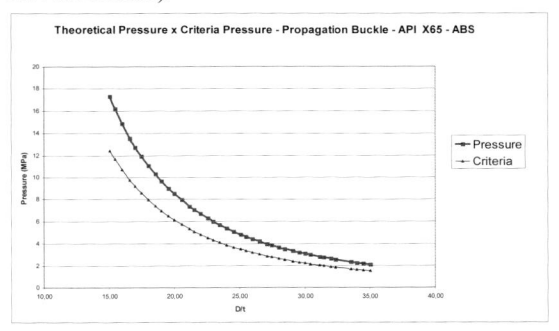

Fig. 19: Criteria and theoretical value, ABS, API X65 steel

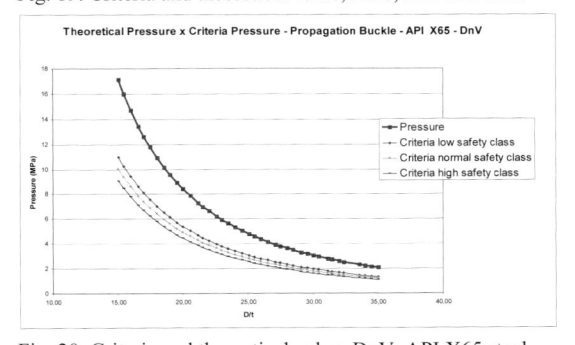

Fig. 20: Criteria and theoretical value, DnV, API X65 steel

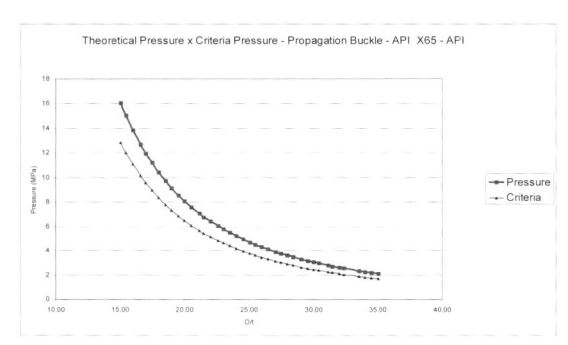

Fig. 21: Criteria and theoretical value, API, API X65 steel

The following estimated safety factors can be taken from Figures 19 to 21 above (Table 6).

Table 6: Comparison between the criteria and the theoretical Rules values

Rules/Condition	Theoretical / Criteria
ABS	1.40
DnV, low safety class	1.56
DnV, normal safety class	1.71
DnV, high safety class	1.89
API	1.25

4. Conclusions and Recommendations

A good correlation was noted among the Rules. ABS has been found to be the less conservative for the propagation pressure theoretical value and API the less conservative for the criteria evaluation (difference between the external and internal pressure).

It has been found that a large number of models and the results for the standard API steels are similar to the experimental results. In this regard, for the propagation buckle failure mode, we can be more confident in the results found.

Fatigue

1. Comparison Between the Rules Safety Factors

Regarding the safety factors proposed by the Rules, the following can be noticed:

- According to API [3]:

10 – shall be applied to all riser components

- According to ABS [1]:

10 – for non-inspected risers or where the risk of pollution or the safety requirement are high

3 – for inspected risers or where the risk of pollution or the safety requirement are low

- According to DnV [2]:

10 – for high safety classes;

6 – for normal safety class;

3 – for low safety calss.

With respect to the safety factors used in the fatigue evaluation, it is noted that the Rules have different values. The DnV safety factors are more related to a risk analysis than to the area inspection itself, as considered by API and ABS. However, for design purposes, considering all economical, social and environmental policies, and all the risks involved in a gas or oil leakage or in all the financial losses if a production plant has to be interrupted, in general a safety factor of 10 is applied.

2. Comparison Between the Rules S-N Curves

The following S-N curves, as indicated on Table 7, are recommended according to ABS ([1], [8]), DnV ([2], [5], [9]) and API ([3], [10]), depending on the welding construction detail.

Table 7: Fatigue curves for circumferential welding for ABS, DnV and API

Weld Detail	ABS	DnV	API
Bilateral circumferential welding, ground smoothly	C	C1	C
Bilateral circumferential welding	E	D	E
Unilateral circumferential welding with backing	F	F	F
Unilateral circumferential welding without backing	F2	F3	F2

Figures 22 to 25 show the comparison between the same welding details, considering cathodic protection, for all Rules. The S-N parameters were obtained in references [1], [2], [3], [5], [8], [9] and [10] above mentioned.

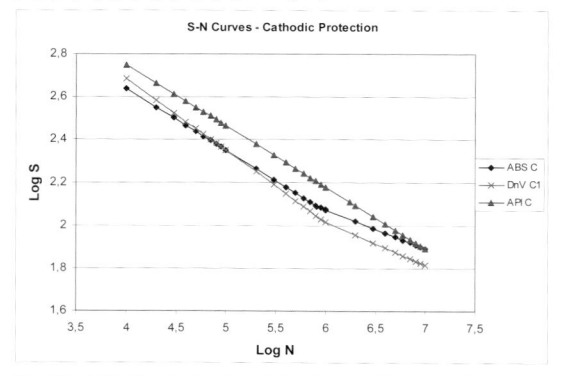

Fig. 22: ABS C x DnV C1 x API C, cathodic protection

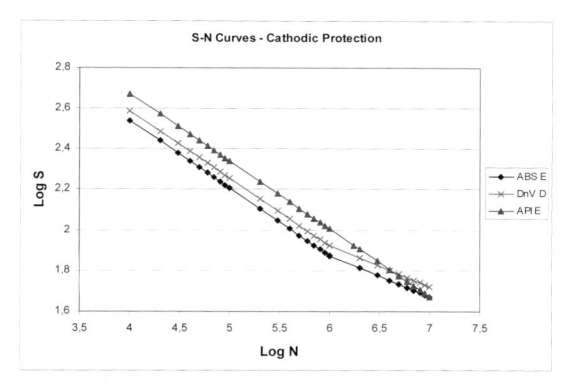

Fig. 23: ABS E x DnV D x API E, cathodic protection

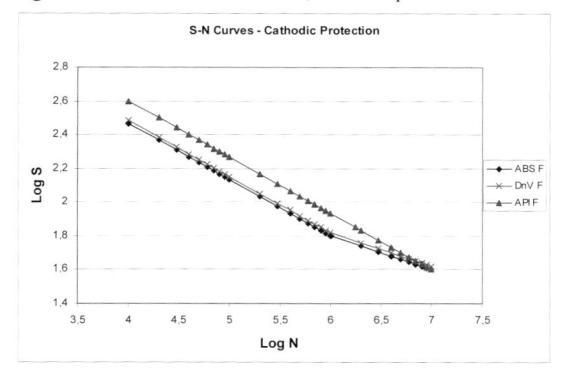

Fig. 24: ABS F x DnV F x API F, cathodic protection

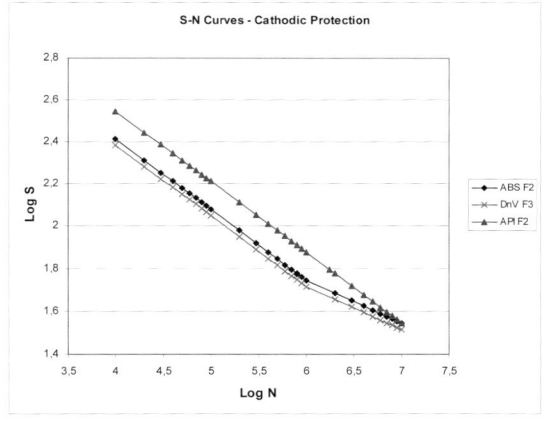

Fig. 25: ABS F2 x DnV F3 x API F2, cathodic protection

Based on Figures 22 to 25, it can be noted that:
- There is a good correlation between DnV and ABS.
- The API curves are less conservative for all cases.

Therefore, the curves proposed by the Classification Societies (ABS & DnV) are more conservative than those of the industry (API), as expected.

3. Comparison between the Rules S-N Curves and Numerical, Analytical and Experimental Data

The S-N curves have also been compared to numerical and experimental data found in literature, obtained from [6] and are shown on figures 26 to 28.

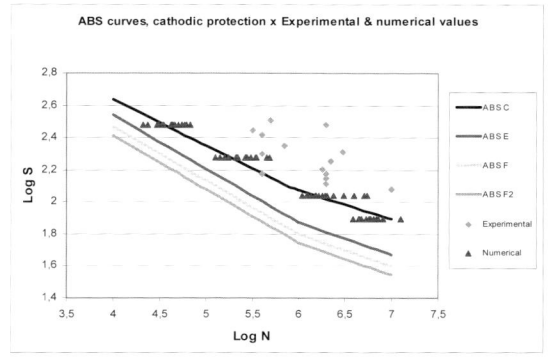

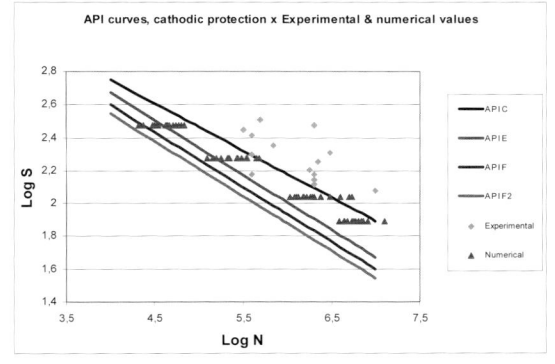

Fig. 26: S-N Curves, ABS with cathodic protection and experimental and numerical values

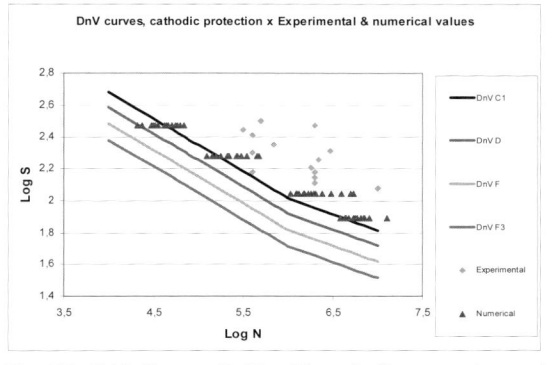

Fig. 27: S-N Curves, DnV with cathodic protection and experimental and numerical values

Fig. 28: S-N Curves, API with cathodic protection and experimental and numerical values

Based on Figures 26 to 28, it can be noted that:

• In general, except for some cases with the "best" welding procedure, it is noted that the experimental data is measuring above the Rules, indicating that the Rules are more conservative.

• Regarding the numerical data, in principle these appear to be more conservative than the Rules. However, it shall be noted that these values were obtained from models presenting different kinds of welding defects. Therefore, the number of cycles to initiate the failure is not accounted in the results. This can represent approximately 2/3 of the total number of cycles.

• It shall be noted that the comparison presented in this study is very simple. Some of the experimental data has been obtained from deformed tubes and the numerical data from tubes with welding defect. Both are not considered by the Rules and should not be directly compared.

• However, even considering all of the above, it is noted that the practical welding detail is the "unilateral welding, without backing." For these details, the Rules are always more conservative.

4. Conclusions and Recommendations

Regarding the safety factors, although different values are defined for each Rule, in general the same value of 10 is adopted for every design due to economical and environmental reasons.

Regarding the S-N curves, the ones from Classification Societies are more conservative that the ones from industry applications, as expected.

It was also noted that the S-N curves are conservative compared to experimental and numerical values found in the literature.

Final Conclusions and Final Recommendations

In addition to the conclusions indicated for each failure mode described above, recommendations and final notes are as follows:

1. General Comparison Between the Rules

The following can be noted with respect to the discrepancies found along this study:

• With respect to the discrepancies between the Rules and the literature data--

Development of a uniform standard needs to consider both the scientific basis and the industry experience. That is to say, data obtained from research, including theoretical derivations, FEM analyses, tests, etc., may not be adopted directly into the criteria in their original forms. One of the roles of industry experience in developing codes is to help reduce the possibility of engineering mistakes. In addition, a standard needs to be largely acceptable to the industry. For example, selections of some of the safety factors are based on industry experience and are difficult to justify scientifically. Therefore, discrepancies among available data and a given Rule are not uncommon. The formulation given in this work provides only minimum requirements for riser design. A design meeting every criteria stipulated in these formulations does not exempt the designer from performing required advanced engineering analyses of the riser system.

• Regarding the discrepancies between different rules

The fundamental difference between DnV standard and ABS & API standards in their basic design philosophies. ABS & API standards apply the Allowable Stress Design (ASD) while allowing for the application of the limit state format. DnV takes the limit state format as the basis for their standard. A limit state design code correlates each design equation with a failure mode. These two philosophies generally result in different representations of equations and different derivations of safety factors involved. This fact is the reason why some DnV results are sometimes singled out from ABS and API.

Even presenting different philosophies, it can be noted that the Rules are, in general, very similar.

2. Estimated Safety Factors

Considering experimental, numerical and analytical data found in the literature, some safety factors have been estimated for the burst, collapse and propagation buckle failure modes.

However, it shall be noted that this is only a simple estimate of the values. The Rules do not indicate the safety factors within the proposed equations.

Some Rules were found either less or more conservative for each failure mode. It is important to note that, the designer cannot mix all Rules for the design, taking advantage of the less conservative Rules for all design. Good engineering judgment and consistency should always be used.

Additionally, it shall be noted that all equations indicated in this work are used for the basic and primary design only. Structural static and dynamic analyses, taking into consideration all loads during installation and operation of the riser are to be carried out to confirm the proposed initial values of D and t (or D/t).

References

[1] ABS, *Guide for Building and Classing Subsea Riser Systems*, May 2006

[2] DNV-OS-F201, *Dynamic Risers*, 2001

[3] API RP 1111, *Design, Construction, Operation, and maintenance of Offshore Hydrocarbon Pipelines (Limit State Design)*, July 1999

[4] ASME B31G-1991, *Manual for Determining the Remaining Strength of Corroded Pipelines*, 1991

[5] DNV-RP-F204, *Riser Fatigue*, August 2004

[6] FROUFE, L.M., *Análise Comparativa de Critérios de Dimensionamento de Risers Rígidos* Tese de Mestrado, Rio de Janeiro, Junho, 2006

[7] API Specification 5L, *Specification for Line Pipe*, 1st July 2000

[8] AMERICAN BUREAU OF SHIPPING, *Guide for the Fatigue Assessment of Offshore Structures*, April 2003

[9] DNV-RP-C203, *Fatigue Strength Analysis of Offshore Steel Structures*, October 2001

[10] DEPARTMENT OF ENERGY, HSE, Health and Safety Executive, *Offshore Installations: Guidance on design, construction and certification*, Forth Edition, January 1990

Development of Overlapping Propellers for a Large LNG Carrier

Kazuyuki Ebira[1], Christian Johannsen[2], Yasunori Iwasaki[1]

[1] Kawasaki Shipbuilding Corporation, Kobe, Japan
[2] Hamburgische Schiffbau-Versuchsanstalt (HSVA), Hamburg, Germany

Abstract

The authors have developed an advanced propulsion system, Overlapping Propeller System (OLP), capable of obtaining high propulsive performance.
The OLP fully utilizes the rotational component of bilge vortices because the center of each propeller is close to that of the bilge vortex and the turning direction is outward, opposite to the rotational direction of the bilge vortices. In the OLP, the concept that the center of each propeller is close to the hull centerline and about half of each propeller closely overlaps, the added resistance by shaft bracket, etc. is negligibly small. The hydrodynamic characteristics of the OLP, in which the propellers are in the vicinity of each other, are especially important in designing a ship with the OLP.
The authors have designed the OLP for large liquefied natural gas carriers (LNG) with various propeller inflow improving devices. Energy saving by the OLP is proven to be up by 12% HP, compared with single screw ships. This paper describes the hydrodynamic characteristics and testing procedures of the propulsive performance, the cavitation behavior, the hull pressure pulses, and the shaft bearing force for the OLP.

Keywords

Overlapping propellers; LNG carriers; Wake improved fin; Bracket fin.

1. Introduction

Rapid growth in the East Asian economy, particularly in China, has led to dramatic growth in world energy consumption. In recent years, the image of natural gas as a clean energy source has resulted in a sharp demand growth, thereby resulting in the accelerated building of liquefied natural gas (LNG) carriers. The recent combination of expanding economies and political instability in energy-producing nations, continues to raise fuel costs. This fact in turn has led to calls from vessel operators to reduce fuel consumption by LNG carriers and to reduce transportation costs, often by increasing the vessel size and improving the propulsive performance.

However, as the size of the LNG carriers continue to grow, maximum draft restrictions imposed by ports have made it increasingly difficult to improve propulsive performance simply by increasing propeller diameter. For this reason the load of a propeller increases, which reduces propeller efficiency.

In response, the authors have developed the Kawasaki Overlapping Propeller System (Kawasaki OLP System, Photo 1). This system takes advantage of the bilge vortices to produce a high-efficiency propulsion system for large LNG carriers.

This paper describes the Kawasaki OLP System, focusing on propulsive performance, cavitation performance and bearing force performance.

Photo 1: Kawasaki OLP System for LNG Carriers

2. Feature of Kawasaki Overlapping Propeller System

The OLP System consists of fore and aft two propellers; their blades overlapping near the hull centerline to increase propulsive performance. The propulsion plant is assumed to consist of a single steam turbine or two electric motors.

2.1 Characteristics of Conventional Ship Design

On typical merchant ships, the pair of symmetrical bilge vortices that rotate inward arise on either side of the hull centerline, inflowing to the propeller. To increase propeller efficiency, propellers can be rotated in the direction opposite the rotational direction of the bilge vortices; that is inward turning.

As shown in Fig.1, single-propeller vessels do not take full advantage of bilge vortices, since the bilge vortex direction differs from the propeller rotation direction on either side of the hull centerline.

In conventional twin-propeller vessels, the load of each propeller is half of that for a comparable single-propeller vessel, resulting in higher propeller efficiency than single-propeller vessels. With conventional twin-propeller configurations, either inward or outward propeller rotation is selected to improve propulsion efficiency, since the propeller centerlines lie some distance from the bilge vortex centerlines. This condition prevents the use of the rotational component of the bilge vortices.

In addition to the differences described above, conventional twin-propeller vessels also require propeller support components in the form of shaft brackets and bossing. The components produce the added resistance and increase the water resistance of the vessels.

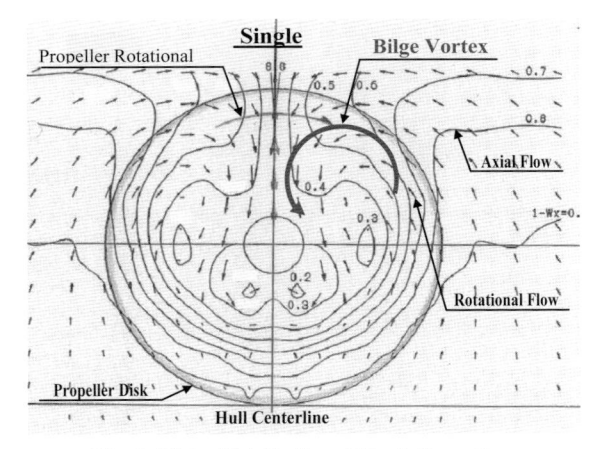

Fig. 1: Wake Distribution of Single Propeller

2.2 Feature of Kawasaki OLP System

As shown in Fig.2, the OLP System ensures that the centerlines of both propellers coincide with the approximate centerlines of the bilge vortices, with propellers rotating in the direction opposite to that of the vortices. This action makes it possible to take full advantage of the bilge vortex rotational components. Moreover, arranging the propellers so that their centerlines coincide with the approximate centerlines of the bilge vortices means the propellers overlap by nearly half their diameters. In addition the shaft supports are located in the low flow speed region close to the hull centerline, rendering the additional resistance of the propeller supports almost negligible as compared to conventional twin-propeller vessels.

The OLP System ensures that the two propellers are situated as close as possible to each other longitudinally to minimize lateral dynamic unbalances. The propeller blades are also raked (fore propeller raked forward, aft propeller raked back) to minimize the distance between them.

The overlapping arrangement of the propellers in the OLP System results in a complex wake flow environment. In particular, the aft propeller is partially subject to the periodically varying wake from the fore propeller in the region where the two propellers overlap – a factor that also increases the importance of flow studies involving the propeller exciting force.

Subsequent chapters outline the design of the hull, supports, and propellers for the OLP System, describing the respective hydrodynamic characteristics (propulsive performance, cavitation performance, and bearing force performance).

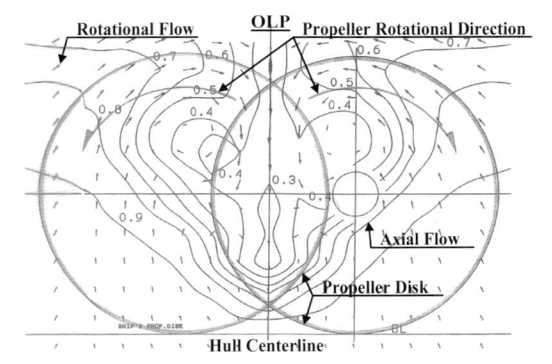

Fig. 2: Wake Distribution of OLP System

3. Kawasaki Overlapping System Design

3.1 Hull Configuration

The primary characteristic of the OLP System is the arrangement of two propellers in an overlapping configuration. This configuration makes it possible to reduce the length of the propeller shaft between the stern tube and the propellers, eliminating the need for the bulky supports (i.e., shaft brackets and bossing) used on conventional twin-propeller vessels. It also eliminates the need for the complex hull design seen with twin-skeg vessels.

Apart from the stern boss, the hull configuration used with the Kawasaki OLP System is identical to a conventional single-propeller hull. The short distance of the plane between the propeller shafts and the hull allows the use of a horizontal bracket fin, a very simple form.

The OLP System implies the risk to generate harmful cavitation, since the propellers generate high thrust when they cross the slow flow region close to the shaft centerline height of the hull centerline. For this reason, the water line form of the hull was made as sharp as possible near the plane of the propeller shafts to increase the flow speed near the hull centerline.

3.2 Bracket Fin (BF)

As shown in Photo 2, the bracket fin (BF) is located in the space between the propeller shaft and the hull. The BF can be tilted up or down longitudinally to control the propeller inflow.

The wake distribution without propellers (Fig. 2) shows the rotational flow in the same direction as the propellers of the OLP System below the propeller shafts and close to the hull centerline. However, the wake distribution with the fore propeller operating (Fig. 3) shows faster axial flow close to the hull centerline, due to it being affected by the fore propeller. Both factors reduce the incident flow angle on the propeller in the region in which the propellers overlap, which results in generating a larger bearing force than that for single-propeller configurations. To resolve this issue, the BF was swept downward, as shown in Photo 2, increasing the rotational flow component in the direction opposite propeller rotation of the OLP System near the hull centerline.

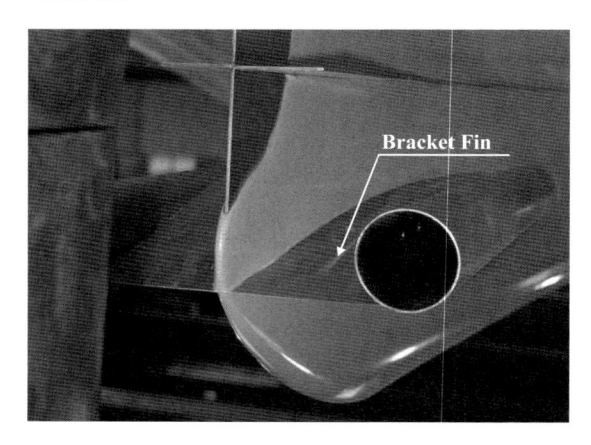

Photo 2: Bracket Fin

3.3 Wake Improved Fin (WIF)

The aft propeller in the OLP System is partially subject to the wake field generated by the fore propeller, and axial flow speed fluctuations are greatly increased near the hull centerline above the propeller shaft when the fore propeller is operating, as shown in Fig.3. This phenomenon may result in increasing fluctuating pressures due to propeller cavitation and increasing bearing forces.

To resolve this issue, a wake-improved fin (WIF) was added at the stern hull part above the propeller shaft, as shown in Photo 3, to moderate speed fluctuations in the wake. Fig. 4 shows the wake distribution measured with the WIF. Compared to the wake distribution generated in Fig. 3 by the fore propeller but without a WIF, the configuration with the WIF installed features lower speed fluctuations near the hull centerline and above the propeller shaft. The WIF is expected to help smaller bearing forces and smaller fluctuating pressures generated by propeller cavitation.

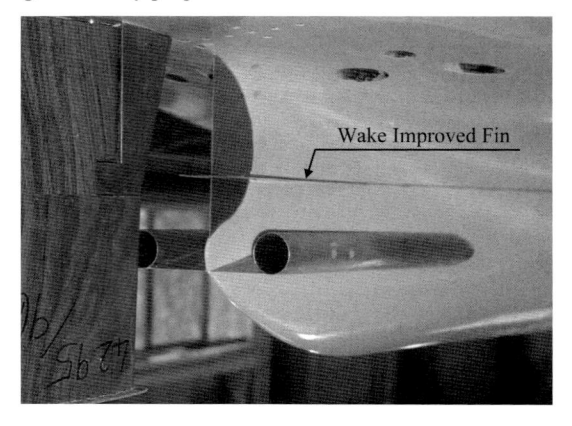

Photo 3: Wake Improved Fin

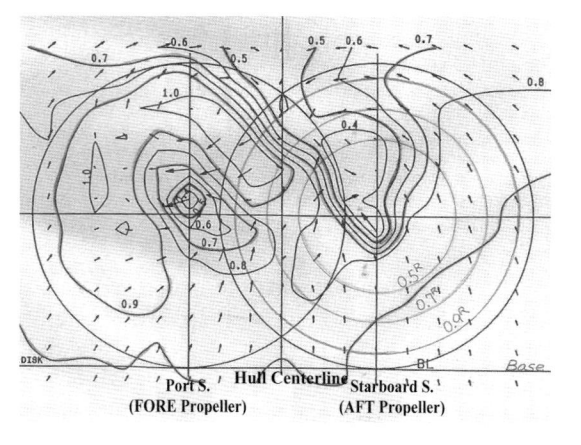

Fig. 3: Wake Distribution of Fore Propeller (P side) Rotating Without WIF

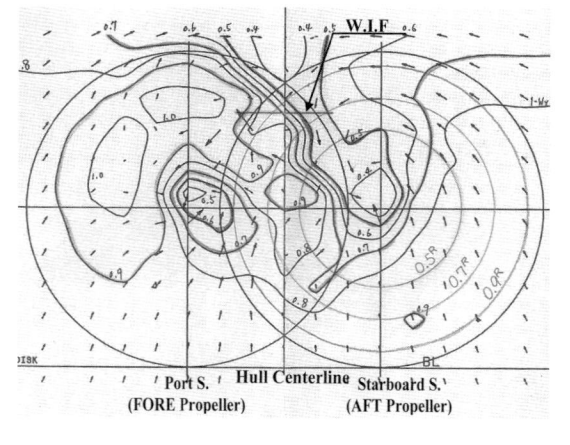

Fig. 4: Wake Distribution of Fore Propeller (P side) Rotating With WIF

3.4 Propeller Design

It is important to obtain wake distributions when designing propellers, since this data makes it possible to estimate cavitation and bearing forces. Particularly with the OLP System, the action of the fore propeller means that the aft propeller operates under extremely complex flow conditions to which the periodically fluctuating flows from the fore propeller operation.

The normal wake distribution without the use of propellers was used to design the fore propeller. Wake distributions with the fore propeller operating and affecting the aft propeller were used to design the aft propeller.

While cavitation performance and bearing forces must ultimately be confirmed by tank tests for propellers rotating in a flow environment as complex as that for the OLP System, wake distributions calculated from previous empirical measurements were applied at the design stage and incorporated into the theoretical studies of propeller performance.

Six-bladed propellers with a skew angle of 24 degrees were ultimately selected for use on the large LNG carrier fitted with the OLP System. Differing pitches were used for fore and aft propellers to ensure equal thrust, since the wake distributions differ for the two propellers.

4. Model Tests and Results

Resistance and self-propulsion tests of the large LNG carrier equipped with the OLP System was carried out at the Akashi Ship Model Basin (ASMB), using a 7.64 m long ship model.

4.1 Propulsive Performance

Fig.5 shows the results of resistance and self-propulsion tests. These results indicate dramatic power savings (12 to 13%) with the OLP System over a single-propeller vessel. While most of this is attributed to propeller efficiency, the results also indicate reductions in viscous drag attributable to the effects of the Bracket Fin.

The single-propeller vessel was equipped with Kawasaki RBS-F energy-saving devices, which reduce energy consumption by approximately 4%. The OLP System achieves power savings of 16 to 17% compared to vessels not fitted with energy-saving devices.

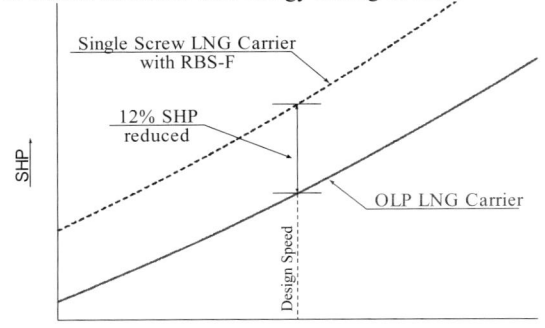

Fig. 5: Comparison of Estimated Power Curves

4.2 Tests in HSVA's HYKAT Cavitation Tunnel

As mentioned above, the aft propeller of the OLP System definitely operates in a very complex and nonstationary inflow. To investigate the influence of this fact on the cavitation behavior, the propeller induced hull pressure pulses as well as shaft bearing forces, special model tests were required, offering cavitation similarity of the complete system to the full scale situation. These tests were carried out in HYKAT, the large Hydrodynamics and Cavitation Tunnel of the Hamburg Ship Model Basin (HSVA)[1] in Germany.

The HYKAT (Fig. 6) is one of the world's largest cavitation tunnels with a test section of 11 m length, 2.8 m width and 1.6 m height, allowing installation of a complete ship model. Fig. 7 gives an impression on these large dimensions with a conventional container vessel being prepared for testing. The tunnel is operated without a free surface, this way allowing to deviation from Froude's scaling law and to run the cavitation test at tunnel water speeds around 6 to 7 m/s. Due to this technique a Reynolds number can be achieved, which is much higher than could be realized in a towing tank. The latter is essential for proper modeling of cavitation phenomena and consequently to achieve reliable results for propeller-induced hull pressure pulses.

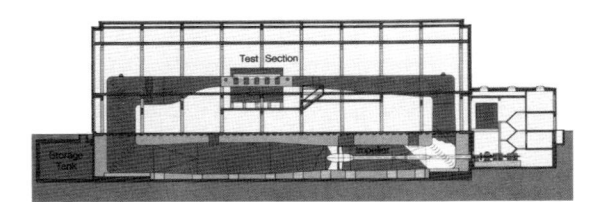

Fig. 6: HSVA's Cavitation Tunnel HYKAT

Fig. 7: Test Section of HYKAT Cavitation Tunnel

In the present case a second ship model was manufactured at HSVA just for cavitation observations, pressure pulse and bearing force measurements. The model was 8.3 m long, resulting in proper model propellers of 250 mm diameter.

The ship model was equipped with the complete OLP System, essential to model the complexity of the flow conditions properly. Various configurations comprising of different stern shapes and shaft brackets were tested. Tests with and without the above mentioned WIF were carried out as well as variations of the phase angle between fore and aft propeller. To allow the latter and to ensure a constant phase relation between the propellers, they were driven by the same motor via a gearbox inside the model. To avoid time-consuming model dismounting, the ship model was prepared with exchangeable stern parts that could be changed with the model remaining in the test section. Besides that, model tests were carried out additionally with a single screw variant of the LNG carrier as a comparator.

Five video cameras were used simultaneously to perform cavitation observations of both propellers. Four of these cameras were installed in watertight housings looking from inside the model. To measure propeller induced hull pressure pulses, 16 tiny pressure pick-ups, were installed in the model hull above the propellers.

A completely new measuring device was constructed at HSVA for the bearing force measurements. This device consisted of a special stern tube of 750 mm length. Behind the seal rings at both ends of this tube, special bearing rings for the measurement of horizontal and vertical force variations were supporting the propeller shaft as shown principally in Fig. 8. Each of these bearing rings consisted of a triple of load cells located in 120° spacing and supporting an inner bearing ring. To avoid any undesired coupling force, the propeller shaft was connected to the motor via a pair of cardanic joints. Due to the static bearing friction effects, the accuracy of the new device was not at its best with the use of the still standing shaft. Nevertheless, with the rotating shaft, the force and moment *variations*, which were of interest in this project, could be measured with an accuracy of about 5 %. This accuracy was determined prior to the real tests by means of well-defined excenter discs installed on the shafts instead of on the propellers and generating RPM-depending bending moments of predetermined magnitude. [2]

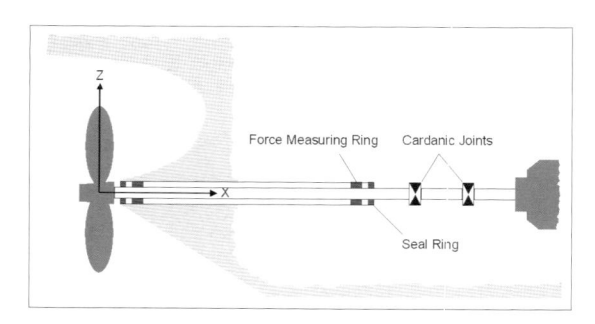

Fig. 8: New Measuring Equipment for Bearing Force Measurement

4.2.1 Cavitation Performance

Propeller cavitation was expected to be a critical issue with the OLP System, since the aft propeller encountered the cavitating tip vortex structure of the fore propeller. The different phase relations between the propellers were investigated to deal with this problem. As shown in Fig. 10, a very smooth cavitation behavior was finally achieved, which is comparable to a single screw arrangement with respect to aggressiveness of the cavitation phenomena as well as cavitation extent (Fig. 9). With optimized phase relation the fore propeller vortex structure did not negatively affect the aft propeller cavitation behavior. It is evident that this kind of investigation would be impossible in a conventional cavitation tunnel, where the nonuniform propeller inflow is generated by a wire screen or a dummy model.

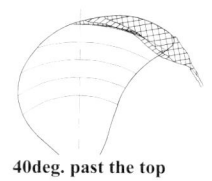

Fig. 9: Cavitation Phenomenon of Single Propeller

40deg. past the top

Aft Propeller: 10deg. before the Top

Fore Propeller: 20deg. before the Top

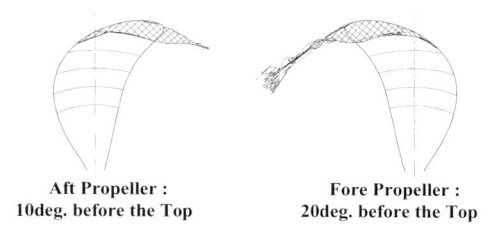

Fig.10: Cavitation Phenomenon of Kawasaki OLP System

4.2.2 Propeller Induced Hull Pressure Pulses

With the optimized OLP configuration the peak fluctuating pressure measured on stern surface was approximately 30% of that for single-propeller vessels for both the 1st blade frequency in Fig. 11 and the 2nd blade frequency in Fig. 12, reflecting the fact that cavitation with the OLP System is similar to that seen in single-propeller vessels, while the thrust per propeller is approximately halved. Fluctuation pressures on the stern surface should present no issues for installing the OLP System on large LNG carriers.

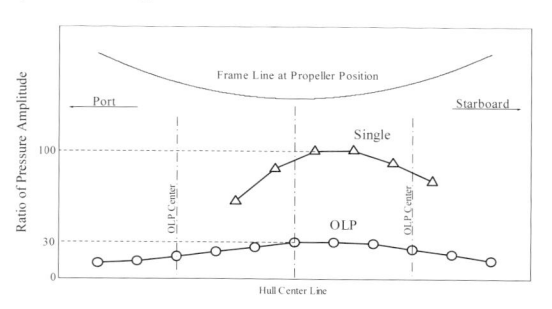

Fig.11: Comparison of Transverse Distribution of Fluctuating Pressure Amplitude (1st Blade Frequency)

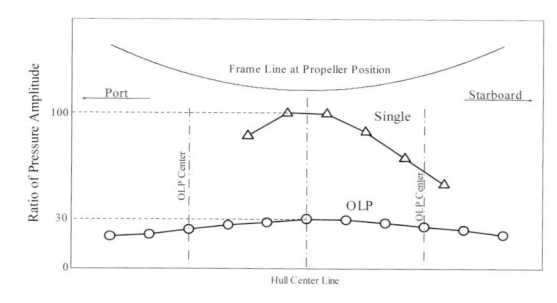

Fig.12: Comparison of Transverse Distribution of Fluctuating Pressure Amplitude (2nd Blade Frequency)

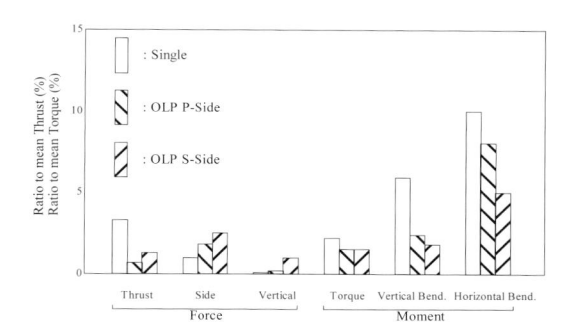

Fig. 14: Comparison of Bearing Forces (1st Blade Frequency)

4.3.3 Bearing Forces

Special emphasis was given to the shaft bearing forces, which were not at all encouraging at the beginning of the studies in HYKAT. Of particular note the vertical bending moment of the aft propeller, i.e. the moment around its vertical axis, was extremely high. Fig. 13 shows the development of these values during the optimization process in Hamburg. While starting with a bending moment of more than 60 % of the propellers mean torque on starboard side, the values finally achieved were even significantly lower than usual for a single screw arrangement (Fig. 14). The force components imposed on each propeller are similar to those seen with single-propeller installations.

Despite operating in a more complex flow environment, the OLP System vessels show lower moment components than do single-propeller vessels. This fact is believed to be attributable to the effects of the Wake Improved Fin in moderating flow rate fluctuations in the highly variable wake from the fore propeller, which affects the aft propeller, together with the significant advantages provided by the skewed propellers.

Comparison tests carried out to examine bearing forces on the aft propeller with and without the Wake Improved Fin confirmed that installing the Wake Improved Fin approximately cuts in half the moment component of the bearing forces.

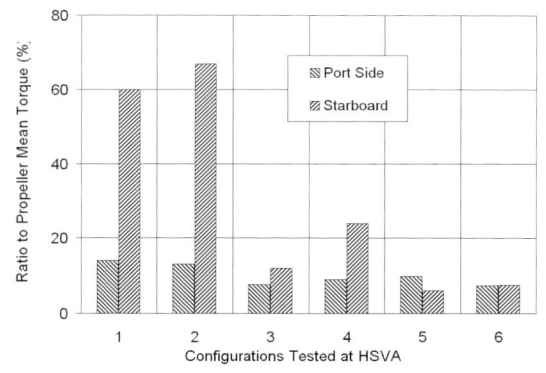

Fig. 13: Improvement Achieved During Model Tests (1st Blade Frequency of Vertical Bending Moment)

5. Conclusions

1) Ideal for large LNG carriers, the Kawasaki Overlapping Propeller System was developed as a high-efficiency propulsion system that takes advantage of bilge vortices.
2) Resistance and self-propulsion tests confirmed dramatic power savings of 12 to 13% with the Kawasaki OLP System compared to single-propeller vessels.
3) Cavitation tests confirmed extremely low fluctuating pressures for the OLP System – approximately 30% of that for single-propeller vessels – although the OLP System operates in a complex flow environment.
4) Bearing force measurements confirmed a force component comparable to that for single-propeller vessels, as well as significantly smaller moment component.
5) The results of these propeller vibratory force measurements are believed to be attributable to the combination of the propeller, Bracket Fin, Wake Improved Fin, and stern design developed during this research.
6) The nonstationary and complex flow conditions especially encountered by the aft propeller required highly sophisticated cavitation testing capabilities, comprised of tests with the whole ship model with its OLP arrangement in the test section as well as a new bearing force measuring equipment.

This study confirmed the Kawasaki OLP System as a propulsion system capable of resolving hydrodynamic problems and increasing the propulsive efficiency of LNG carriers. As an additional note, we hereby state that a patent has been granted for this OLP system.

6. Acknowledgment

We would like to express our sincere gratitude and appreciation to Dr. S. Yamasaki of NAKASHIMA Propeller CO., LTD. for the invaluable advice of the propeller design.

7. References

1) J. Friesch, "Ten years of Research in the Hydrodynamics and Cavitaion Tunnel HYKAT of HSVA", 50 International Conference on Propeller Cavitation, April 2000.

2) C. Johannsen, "New Equipment Allows 6D Bearing Force Measurement During Tests in HYKAT", The Hamburg Ship Model Basin Newsletter, January 2005.

3) G.Nilsson and K.Restad, "Problem in Full Scale Propulsion from a Shipbuilder's Viewpoint", 3rd Lips Symposium, Drunen, Netherlands, 1976

4) J.Strom-Tejsen and T.Roddy, "Performance of Containership with Overlapping Propeller Arrangement", David Taylor Model Basin Report 3750, Sept. 1972

5) H.Kerlen, et al., "Propulsions-, Kavitations- and Vibrationsverhalten von uber lappenden propellern fur ein Containerschiff", STG, Hamburg, Nov. 1970

6) T.Munk and C.W.Prohaska, "Tests with Interlocking and Overlapping Propellers", Hydro- and Aerodynamics Laboratory, Lyngby, Denmark, Report Hy-12, Jan 1969

7) T.Munk and C.W.Prohaska, "Unusual Two-Propeller Arrangements", 7th Symposium on Naval Hydrodynamics, Rome, Italy, Aug. 1968

Design of Marine Propellers Using Genetic Algorithm

Jaekwon Jung [1], Jae-Moon Han [1], Kyung Jun Lee [1] and In-Haeng Song [1]

[1] Marine Research Institute, Samsung Heavy Industries Co., Ltd., Daejeon, Korea

Abstract

This paper presents the automatic optimization design techniques with application of a genetic algorithm (GA). In order to perform a propeller design process automatically and to get the propeller blade shape with higher propeller efficiency, NSGA-II, which is a kind of the genetic algorithm, has been applied. NSGA-II is a compatible tool for both single-objective and multi-objective cases. Two different methods in using NSGA-II are proposed in this paper. One is to maximize the propeller open water efficiency at given ranges of thrust and torque coefficient, and the other is to maximize a speed of ship satisfying the target propeller rotational speed and limitation of cavitation volume. Two propellers have been designed using those methods. Through the numerical computations and model tests, both propellers have been confirmed to show the improved performances compared to the existing propellers.

Keywords

GA; NSGA-II; Optimization; Automatic design; Efficiency; Pressure fluctuations; Cavitation volume.

Nomenclature

J	Advance coefficient
K_T	Thrust coefficient
K_Q	Torque coefficient
η_O	Open water efficiency
η_D	Propulsive efficiency
P	Pitch
c	Chord length
f	Camber
D	Diameter of propeller
P/D_{mean}	Mean pitch
A_E/A_O	Expanded area ratio
N	Propeller rotational speed
V_S	Ship's speed
F	Objective function

Introduction

Marine propellers have to deliver the necessary thrust to maintain the ship's speed and to avoid cavitation-induced damage during operation. These two requirements should be fulfilled with the highest possible propeller efficiency and the lowest possible levels of pressure fluctuations. Since these are confronted with each other, the compromise between the propeller efficiency and the cavitation performance is essential in the design of marine propellers.

Most of the current propeller designs have usually been performed by applying a conventional lifting-surface analysis method in a *trial and error* manner. Several attempts to develop an optimization technique for marine propellers have been made in the last decade. Coney (1992) developed a design method for the optimal circulation distribution based on variational optimization. He represented propellers by concentrated lifting lines, which discretized into a finite number of horseshoe vortices and described the thrust and torque as functions of the vortex strengths which were solved for constrained optimization. Olsen (2001) also developed an optimization method applying the same variational approach as Coney to maximize the propulsive performance of propellers. Mishima and Kinnas (1997) developed a numerical method to determine the propeller blade geometry with the optimum efficiency for specified thrust and cavity size constraints. Unsteady cavitating propeller analysis method was coupled with a constrained nonlinear optimization in the design method.

Recently, a new optimization technique using the genetic algorithm such as the micro-GA was introduced for the process of marine propeller design by Karim et al (2004).

The objective of the present paper is to develop automatic optimization techniques for the design of marine propellers. A genetic algorithm is used to get optimal distributions of pitch, chord and camber with satisfaction to given constraint conditions. The propellers optimized by current method are evaluated by a conventional lifting-surface analysis method and compared with experimental results at Samsung Ship Model Basin (SSMB).

Genetic Algorithm (GA)

Concept of GA

The genetic algorithm is based on 'theory of evolution' of an ecosystem and has been introduced by Holland (1975). The genetic algorithm makes the engineering design process automatic using the evolution concept. This method produces individuals randomly in the initial generation, and then, lets the individuals evolve. The final objective of genetic algorithm is to find out the best individual from the point of view of fitness through the repeated and automatic evolution process. The evolution process of the genetic algorithm is made up of 'selection', 'crossover' and 'mutation'. These components are similar to that of the ecosystem's evolution process.

The basic concept of application of genetic algorithm is as following. The users set design variables to let each individual in a generation possess the information about propeller configuration. Then, the evaluation for each individual's configuration is conducted, and the fitness like the propeller open water efficiency is granted to each individual. After this evaluation stage, the generation evolves to the next generation through concept of 'selection', 'crossover' and 'mutation'. This process is repeated until the number of present generation is less than the maximum generations.

This genetic algorithm has been introduced to numerous fields of optimization design of configuration and has many branches such as NPGA, VEGA, NSGA and micro-GA.

Fitness, constraints and design variables

The fitness is called an objective function. It is used for discrimination whether each individual in a generation is superior or not, and the genetic algorithm has the generation evolve on the basis of these values. The important values like an open water efficiency that designers want to maximize or minimize during design process are selected as the fitness. There are cases in which two or more objective functions exist, and these cases are called multi-objective optimization. The 'Pareto' set is obtained by genetic algorithm for multi-objective case, and there are several branches of genetic algorithm for multi-objective optimization. For the general cases, the direction of evolutions by the genetic algorithm is to minimize the fitness. Therefore, if the designers want to maximize the fitness, the minus sign should be multiplied.

The concept of constraint conditions means that the penalty is imposed when the individual exceeds the range of limitation set by users. Although the fitness is high for an individual, the probability of inheritance is lessened if the individual exceeds the limitation range. In the usual cases, constraint conditions are set as an inequality form. These have the similar role as the objective functions in the evolution process.

The parts that the designers want to change in the optimization design process are called as design variables. Each individual has information about design variables, and the value of design variables is changed automatically by the genetic algorithm. Generally, in order to increase the possibility of finding out the whole field optimum solution, the bigger population size and the bigger number of the maximum generation are needed as the number of design variables increases. So, the efficient set of design variables is very important for the genetic algorithm to reduce the calculation time as well as to get the best optimum solution.

NSGA-II (Non-dominated Sorting Genetic Algorithm)

The NSGA has been introduced by Srinivas and Deb (1995) for multi-objective optimization design, and it has adopted the new selection process using a concept of 'non-dominated ranking' and 'fitness sharing'. The concept of the non-dominated ranking means that individuals are classified into several classes by their original fitness, and then new fitness value is granted to each individual by their classes. This ranking is elevated as the location of the individual in fitness diagram gets closer to the border.

The concept of fitness sharing means that the recalculated fitness value is granted to each individual after looking for the number of individual in a determined area in fitness diagram and dividing the original fitness value by this number. These concepts are able to prevent the solution converging to the local optimum point through dispersion of individual's location in a fitness diagram. These newly introduced concepts are able to make the optimization process find the whole field solution.

The NSGA-II has been proposed by the Deb et al (2000). This algorithm had been advanced from NSGA and has advantages about low computational requirements and elitist approach. So, it is able to find much better solutions in all problems.

Also, the NSGA-II is known as the compatible and efficient technique for both multi-objective and single-objective cases. Since the propeller design process would be either multi-objective or single-objective optimization, NSGA-II has been chosen as the suitable algorithm for the optimization of propeller design.

Application of Genetic Algorithm

Define of design variables

In order to represent propeller geometry with the minimum amount of distortion, NURBS (Non-Uniform Rational B-Spline) technique was used. Although the propeller offset has usually 11 ~ 13 input points in span-wise direction, the NURBS is able to make the expression possible with only 4 ~ 5 points in case of a pitch distribution. Fig. 1 shows an example of pitch distribution reproduced by NURBS technique. In Fig. 1, the square symbols indicate the input points of propeller offset, triangular symbols indicate the control points extracted from the propeller offset and circular points indicate the reproduction points by NURBS technique from the extracted control points. It is confirmed that the reproduction curve shows good agreement with the original offset curve.

The displacement of control points in y direction has been set as design variables in the present paper. Consequently, these control points were set to vary along the change of each individual's information, and the new configuration was obtained from changed control points. So, the number of the control points is similar to the number of the design variables. The limitation ranges of design variables have to be set before execution of the genetic algorithm. This process is separated from the setting of constraint conditions and affects the results of the genetic algorithm.

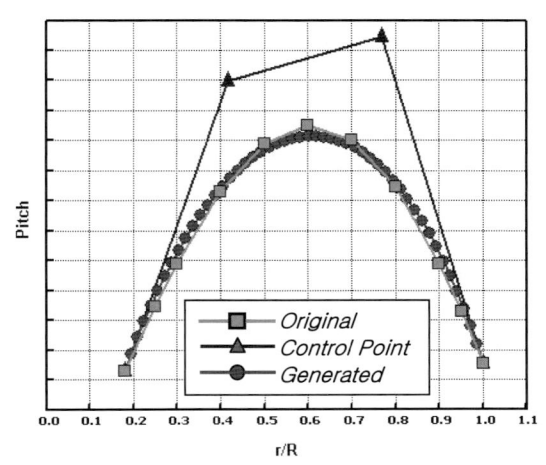

Fig. 1: Pitch distributions represented by NURBS technique

Methods of application

In this paper, two different methods with NSGA-II were applied for getting the optimal propeller shape. One is to maximize the propeller open water efficiency (η_O) with satisfaction of a designated thrust coefficient range (designated herein as *Method 1*) and the other is to maximize a ship's speed (*Vs*) with satisfaction of setting range of propeller rotational speed (*N*) and a limitation of cavitation volume (designated herein as *Method 2*). *Method 1* has been proposed to find out rapidly the propeller shape with the highest efficiency under the given operating condition such as the thrust and torque coefficients. *Method 2* is for the automation of the entire propeller design process, so it contains the processes to calculate propeller open water efficiency, corresponding ship's speed using the pre-described self-propulsion factor, and the cavitation behavior at the design point.

For both cases, the optimization processes have been treated as a single-objective function. It means that the factor such as the cavitation volume size is only considered as a constraint condition for *Method 2*. The objective functions for both methods are summarized in Table 1.

Table 1: Objective function, *F*

	F
Method 1	maximize η_O
Method 2	maximize *Vs*

The constraint conditions for *Method 1* were the range of the thrust coefficient and the torque coefficient. The allowable ranges of two coefficients for *Method 1* are expressed as follows:

$$0.99 \times K_{T\text{stock}} \leq K_{T\text{design}} \leq 1.02 \times K_{T\text{stock}} \quad (1)$$

$$0.98 \times K_{Q\text{stock}} \leq K_{Q\text{design}} \leq 1.01 \times K_{Q\text{stock}} \quad (2)$$

In the case of *Method 2*, the range of propeller rotational speed (*N*) and the maximum limitation of the cavitation volume were set as constraint conditions. The allowable difference of the propeller rotational speed between the stock and designed propeller was set as 0.5% of the value of stock propeller. In addition, the maximum value of cavitation volume ($Vol._{Max}$) should be less than that of stock propeller, which is one of the constraint conditions. All constraint conditions for *Method 2* are expressed as follows:

$$0.995 \times N_{\text{stock}} \leq N_{\text{design}} \leq 1.005 \times N_{\text{stock}} \quad (3)$$

$$Vol._{Max\,\text{design}} \leq Vol._{Max\,\text{stock}} \quad (4)$$

In order to predict the propeller open water efficiency of the designed propeller, the propeller boundary value problem is analyzed by the vortex lattice method of Kerwin & Lee (1978). The numerical procedure adopted in the present work for cavitating propellers is similar to that in Lee (1980). The nonlinear cavity flow problem is linearized by assuming the smallness of the cavity thickness. The cavity extents and shapes are determined by satisfying the kinematic and dynamic boundary conditions on the cavity surface. The predicted results from numerical computations were set as fitness or constraint conditions of the genetic algorithm.

Method 1 setting η_O as an objective function requires very short computing time as compared to *Method 2* which set the ship's speed as an objective function. In order to predict the ship's speed, it is necessary to have the propeller open water characteristics at several advance coefficients (at least 5 points). Therefore, *Method 2* takes more than 5 times compared to *Method 1* in the evaluation of the propeller open water performances. Furthermore, time-consuming process for the calculation of cavitation volume is followed for *Method 2*. Consequently, the required computing time for *Method 2* is significantly increased even for the same population size and maximum generation.

Fig. 2 shows a diagram of the design process for *Method 1*. As shown in Fig. 2, the entire process of the optimization is divided into two parts. One is the reformation of propeller blade shape through the production of a new generation. The other is the evaluation process. In the initial stage, all the individuals are produced randomly and have diverse kinds of configurations. Then, the evaluation for each individual is accomplished using a numerical solver. After this stage, the genetic algorithm reproduces the new generation on the basis of the evaluation results, which are set as the fitness or constraint conditions by designer. These two parts are repeated alternately until the number of maximum generation is reached. In the case of *Method 2*, the objective function is substituted as ship's speed with changing constraint conditions. For the simplicity of the problem, the variation of pitch, camber and chord distributions among many other geometrical variables are only allowed in the present paper.

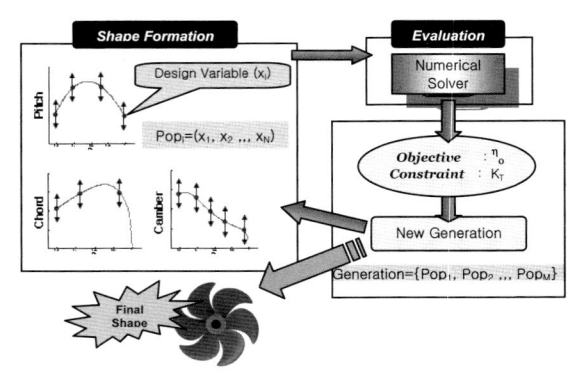

Fig. 2: Diagram showing the propeller design process using GA

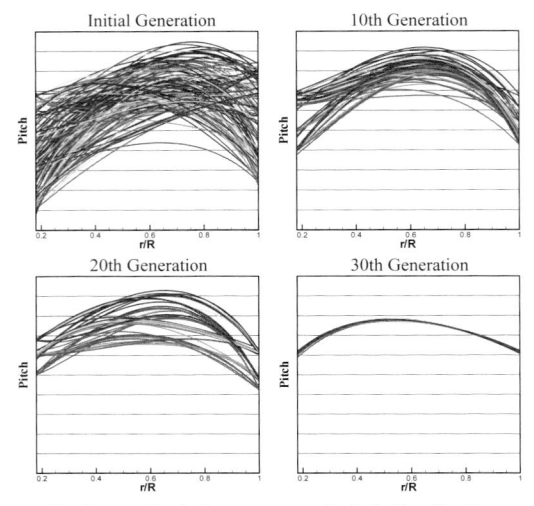

Fig. 3: Evolution process of pitch distribution

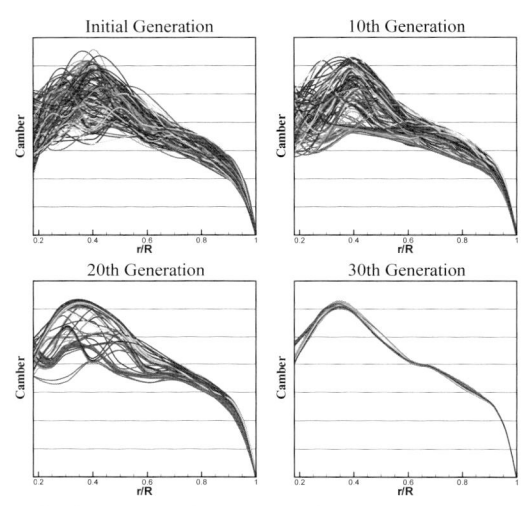

Fig. 4: Evolution process of camber distribution

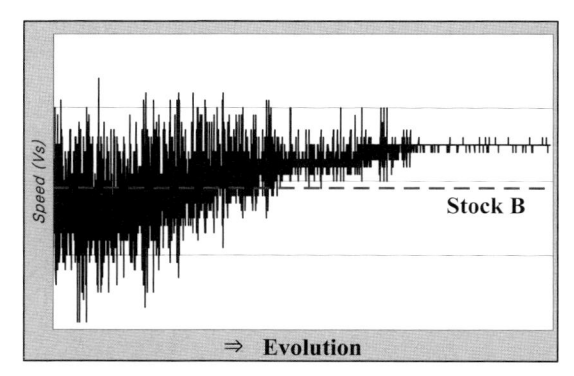

Fig. 5: Evolution process of ship's speed for Model B

Results

Process of evolution

The evolution processes of the pitch and camber distribution by *Method 1* are shown in Fig. 3 and 4, respectively. The number of design variables was set as 4 for the pitch distribution, whereas 11 for the camber distribution. Because the camber distribution is more complicated than the pitch or chord length distribution, the number of control points is increased to represent its shape correctly by NURBS. As mentioned before, the genetic algorithm was also applied to the chord distribution in the design process. The number of design variables was 4 for the chord distribution.

In Figs. 3 and 4, it is easily observed that the first generation had many diverse kinds of curves, and then the kinds of curves decreased as the evolution was progressed. In the first generation, the individuals were produced automatically in a random manner through the genetic algorithm. After a certain generation, the best superior individual remains with disappearance of recessive individuals. It means that the genetic algorithm has converged to a certain distribution.

Fig. 5 shows the variation of ship's speed for all individuals during the evolution process through the *Method 2*. The dashed line indicates the ship speed of the stock propeller, which is evaluated in the towing tank tests. As shown in Fig. 5, the ship speed of each individual converged to a certain value through the progress of the evolution. Some individuals showed higher values than a converged value, however, these individuals were considered as a trivial solution because they didn't satisfy the constraint conditions. From Fig. 5, it is well recognized that the developed automatic optimization method has been successfully applied to the design of the cavitating propellers.

Design of Propeller Blade

Method 1 has been applied to the design of 'Model A' propeller and *Method 2* has been applied to the design of 'Model B' propeller in this paper. Both propellers were 6-bladed and designed for container ships, but the sizes of the ships were different.

Fig. 6 shows the pitch distributions of the stock propeller as well as the designed propeller obtained by *Method 1* for Model A. Compared with the stock propeller, the pitch around the region of the propeller tip was increased. This is a similar trend of Kappel propeller (Olsen 2001). The camber distribution for Model A, which is not provided in the present paper, is also optimized to increase the propeller efficiency and to avoid the occurrence of an excessive cavitation at the tip region. It can be conjectured that the gradient of the span-wise loading for Model A may be reduced from the pitch distribution. Since the strength of the trailing vortex sheet may be reduced, the increase of the tip loading would result in the improvement of the propeller efficiency.

Fig. 7 shows the pitch distributions for both Stock B and Model B. Since the diameter of Model B was increased by 2.3%, the average level of pitch distribution is different. The expanded area ratio of Model B was reduced as much as possible to reduce viscous drag with the satisfaction of the constraint condition related to the cavity volume in the equation (4).

Principal particulars for the stock and designed propellers are given in Table 2.

In fact, the converged solution obtained by the genetic algorithm depends on the pre-described conditions such as the population size in a generation, the number of design variables and random seed to produce the initial individuals. Especially, it seemed that the random seed had considerably affected the results. Model A and Model B propellers have been selected through several trials with changing the pre-described conditions.

Table 2: Principal particulars of the propellers

	Stock A	Model A	Stock B	Model B
P/D_{mean}	1.010	1.020	1.017	0.989
A_E/A_O	0.798	0.776	0.895	0.779

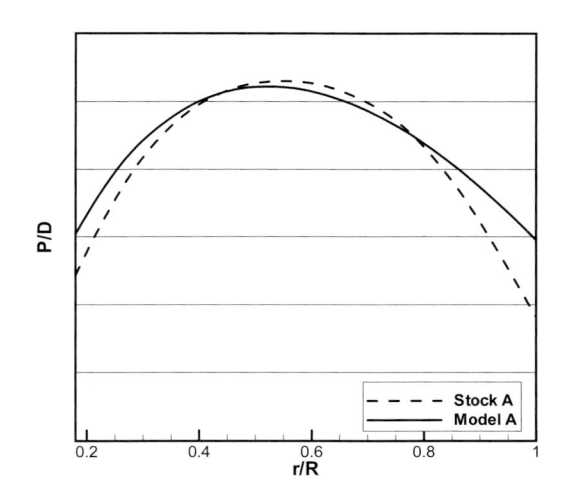

Fig. 6: Pitch distributions (Stock A & Model A)

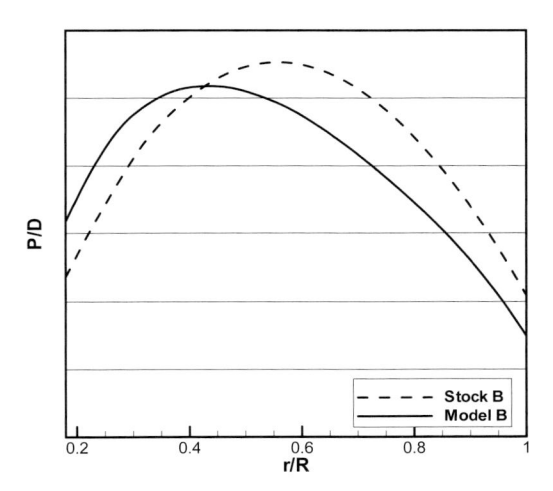

Fig. 7: Pitch distributions (Stock B & Model B)

Numerical evaluation

The prediction of the propellers performance using the numerical solver was conducted immediately after obtaining the propeller blade shape by the genetic algorithm. As shown in Table 3, the open water performances of newly designed propellers for both Model A and Model B were improved over 1% comparing to those of the stock propellers. Fig. 8 shows the calculated result of the cavity volume for Model B. As shown in Fig. 8, the maximum value of the cavity volume for Model B is slightly lower than that of the Stock B even though the expanded area ratio of Model B was considerably reduced. It implies that the constraint condition for the cavity volume in *Method 2* was satisfied.

Table 3: Predicted propeller open water efficiency by numerical computations

	Stock A	Model A	Stock B	Model B
J	0.730	0.730	0.740	0.740
η_O	0.666	0.673	0.661	0.672

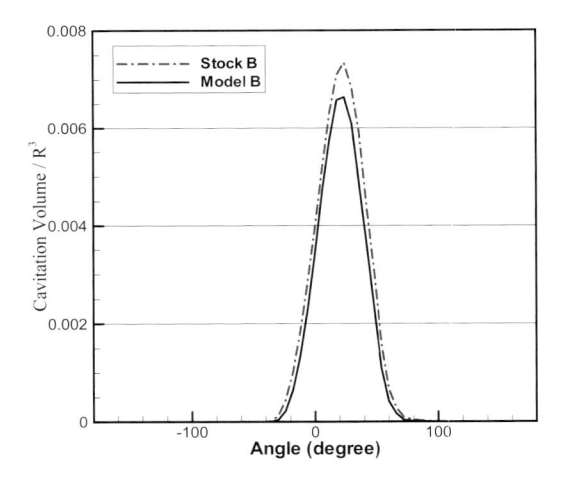

Fig. 8: Comparison of computed cavity volume (Stock B & Model B)

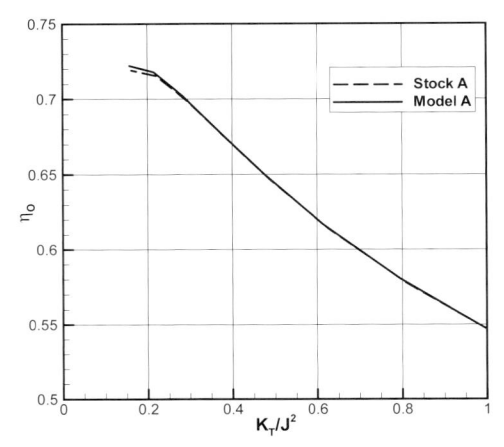

Fig. 9: Open water efficiency - K_T/J^2 vs. η_O (Stock A & Model A)

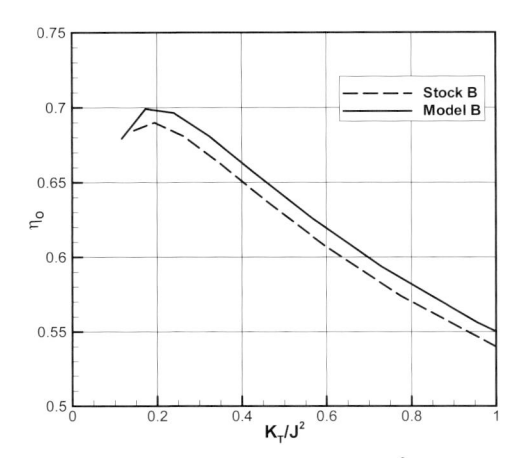

Fig. 10: Open water efficiency - K_T/J^2 vs. η_O (Stock B & Model B)

Model tests results

In order to verify the performance of the designed propeller, model tests were performed at the Samsung Ship Model Basin (SSMB). Resistance, open water and self-propulsion tests were performed in the towing tank and all investigations related to cavitation were carried out in the large cavitation tunnel. To improve the relative accuracy between the experiments, all propellers of each vessel were tested in the same experimental set-up.

Fig. 9 shows the results of propeller open water (POW) tests for Model A. Comparing with the stock propeller (Stock A), the increase of the propeller efficiency (η_O) of the designed propeller was very small whereas a considerable increase of the propeller efficiency was achieved in the numerical computations. However, the propulsive efficiency (η_D), which is the ultimate goal of the propeller optimization, in self-propulsion tests was increased by 1.1% as summarized in Table 4.

Fig. 10 shows the results of POW tests for Model B. Comparing with the stock propeller (Stock B), a considerable increase of the propeller open water efficiency (η_O) as well as the propulsive efficiency (η_D) could be obtained. The increases of η_O and η_D are 1.9% and 1.8%, respectively. This confirms the predicted result of the numerical computation in Table 3 which predicts the increase of 1.7%.

Table 4: Results of self-propulsion tests

	Stock A	Model A	Stock B	Model B
J	0.765	0.762	0.731	0.726
η_O	0.697	0.700	0.681	0.694
η_D	0.747	0.755	0.741	0.754

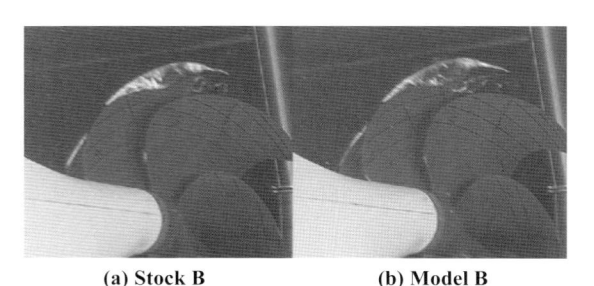

(a) Stock B (b) Model B

Fig. 11: Observed cavitation patterns

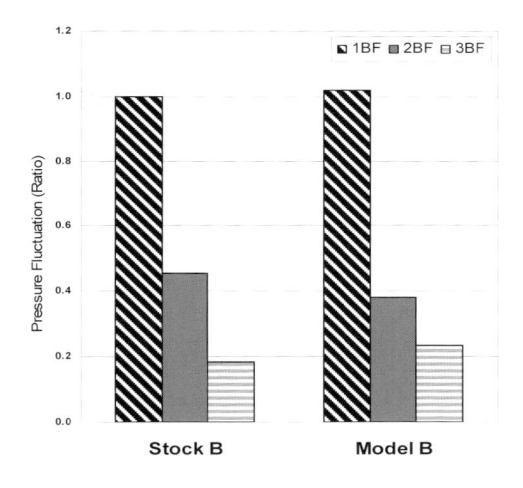

Fig. 12: Comparison of pressure amplitudes
(Stock B & Model B)

Fig. 11 shows the observed cavitation patterns for the stock and design propellers. It is observed that the cavitation extents and behaviors at the same angular position for both propellers are similar.

The results of pressure fluctuation measurements are shown in Fig. 12. All values shown in Fig. 12 are non-dimensionalized by the amplitude at the 1st blade frequency (1BF) of the Stock B. All the levels of the pressure fluctuations at each blade frequency for designed propeller are also similar to those of the stock propeller.

Conclusions

A numerical optimization method based on the genetic algorithm for the design of marine propellers has been successfully developed. Two different methods using NSGA-II has been applied in this paper. The first method is to maximize the propeller open water efficiency only, and the second method is to maximize the ship's speed within the designated cavitation performance. Although the second method requires more computing time, this method is able to evaluate all the processes automatically related to the propeller design. An experimental investigation for the designed propeller was carried out. Through systematic model tests, the designed propeller achieved a considerable increase in propeller efficiency coupled with a similar level of pressure fluctuations.

The optimization techniques proposed in this paper have been proven applicable to the design of marine propellers.

References

Coney, W.B. (1992) "Optimum Circulation Distributions for a Class of Marine Propulsors", Journal of Ship Research, Vol. 36, No. 3, pp. 210-222.

Deb, K., Agrawal, S., Pratap, A. and Meyariva, T. (2000) "A Fast Elitist Non-Dominated Sorting Genetic Algorithm for Multi-Objective Optimization: NSGA-II", Proceedings of the Parallel Problem Solving from Nature, Vol. VI, pp. 849–858.

Holland, J.H., (1975) "Adaptation in Natural and Artificial Systems", The University of Michigan Press, Michigan

Karim, M. M., Suzuki, K. and Kai, H. (2004) "Optimal Design of Hydrofoil and Marine Propeller Using Micoro-Genetic Algorithm", Journal of Naval Architecture and Marine Engineering. Vol. 1, pp. 45-58.

Kerwin, J.E. and Lee, C.-S. (1978) "Prediction of Steady and Unsteady Marine Propeller Performance by Numerical Lifting Surface Theory", Trans. SNAME Vol. 86, pp. 218-253.

Lee, C.-S. (1980) "Prediction of Steady and Unsteady Performance of Marine Propellers with or without Cavitation by Numerical Lifting Surface Theory", PhD Thesis, Dept. of Ocean Engineering, MIT.

Mishima, S. and Kinnas, S.A. (1997) "Application of A Numerical Optimization Technique to The Design of Cavitating Propellers in Nonuniform Flow", Journal of Ship Research. Vol. 41, pp. 93-107.

Olsen A.S. (2001) "Optimisation of Propellers Using The Vortex-lattice Method", Ph.D. Thesis, Technical Univ. of Denmark.

Srinivas, N. and Deb, K. (1995) "Multiobjective Optimization Using Nondominated Sorting in Genetic Algorithm", Evolutionary Computation, Vol. 2, No. 3, pp. 221-248.

10th International Symposium on Practical Design of Ships and Other Floating Structures
Houston, Texas, United States of America
© 2007 American Bureau of Shipping

Numerical Modeling of Propeller Tip Flow with Wake Sheet Roll-up by B-spline Higher-order Panel Method

G.-D. Kim[1], B.-K. Ahn[2], B.-G. Paik[1], W.-S. Lee[2] and C.-S. Lee[2]

[1]Maritime and Ocean Engineering Research Institute(MOERI), KORDI, Korea,
[2]Chungnam National University, Korea.

Abstract

A numerical model for the analysis of the marine propeller including wake alignment is presented. We apply a higher-order panel method, which is based on a B-spline representation for both generations of the propeller geometry and representing the hydrodynamic solutions, to make a modeling of the nonlinear wake including its alignment procedure to ultimately predict the flow around the propeller blades.

The present model is validated by comparison of the existing experimental results. Predicted forces, wake, and tip vortex trajectories show good agreement with the experimental measurements. The results indicate that the present method are well-able to predict the improved pressure distributions on the blade surface, especially close to the tip and trailing edge regions that are currently inaccessible with other methods.

Keywords

High order panel method; B-spline; Non-linear wake alignment; Wake roll-up; Propeller tip vortex.

Introduction

A large number of different panel methods have been developed and widely used in aerodynamic and hydro-dynamic design, since the pioneering work of Hess and Smith (1964). Until Morino(1974) introduced a panel method based on Green's formula in which the primary unknown is the potential, most of the previous works were based on the velocity-based formulation in which the boundary condition on the body surface is satisfied through the direct computation of the velocity. Morino's potential-based formulation is known to be more stable and hence more suitable to numerical computation than the velocity method, since the potential is one order less singular than the velocity.

The existing potential-based methods are based on the low-order model in which the potential is constant over a panel and the velocity distribution on the body surface is calculated using a finite difference scheme. However, this method inevitably introduces a truncation error that is most significant near the trailing edge and the tip of the lift-generating surface, and results in degradation of the accuracy.

Recently a B-spline based higher-order panel method has been developed and applied to the marine propeller analysis as an alternative way to reduce the error that can not be recovered by lower-order models. The order of B-splines to represent body geometries and potentials can be increased without limit, and hence solutions of any order can be obtained. The most detailed description of the higher-order panel method based on B-splines was first given by Hsin, Kerwin and Newman (1993) for the analysis of the flow around two-dimensional bodies.

Maniar (1995) extended it to three-dimensional cases. In his approach the integrals of the influence functions are expressed in terms of polynomials of a parametric coordinate, and the polynomial coefficients are derived from B-spline basis functions. Although the polynomial representation is sufficient for most bodies of interest, it is generally not appropriate to expand polynomials to non-uniform rational B-spline (NURBS) surfaces, which are the de-facto standard in industry to represent complex surfaces like ship hulls. Lee and Kerwin (2003) introduced a very general numerical procedure for the evaluation of influence coefficients for the analysis of lifting flows around two-dimensional and three-dimensional bodies including marine propellers. Pyo and Kinnas (1997) developed a wake roll-up model of the marine propeller in steady flow using a high-order panel method. Lee and Kinnas (2005) presented an algorithm for the unsteady wake alignment based on a low-order panel method in which they applied the tip vortex core size using the method developed by Lee and Kinnas (2004). Instead of following Maniar's method, we adopt a conventional numerical integration method such as Gauss-Legendre quadrature. This approach is very simple mathematically and numerically, yet there is no loss in evaluating induction integrals accurately. The coding requires far less efforts than that of Maniar.

In this work, the main focus is on applying the higher-order panel method in order to make a modeling of the nonlinear wake including its alignment procedure. Improved information on propeller tip flows is obtained. Pressure distributions on tip regions of DTRC 4119 propeller are compared with existing experimental data, and predicted wake roll-up of KP707 propeller is compared with experimental measurements conducted by the Maritime and Ocean Engineering Research Institute in Korea.

NUMERICAL FORMULATION

B-spline representations

The potential is represented as a weighted sum of tensor product B-spline basis functions in a similar form as for the geometry as $\phi(u,v)$ along the surface of the body. However, instead of treating the potential directly, we represent the potential as a weighted sum of tensor product B-spline basis functions in a similar form as for the geometry:

$$\phi(u,v) = \sum_{i=0}^{N^v-1} \sum_{j=0}^{M^v-1} \phi_{i,j}^v N_i(u) M_j(v) \quad (1)$$

where $N_i(u)$ and $M_j(v)$ are the B-spline basis functions, $\phi_{i,j}^v$ the potential control vertices, and N^v and M^v the numbers of potential control vertices in u,v directions respectively. The numbers of potential control vertices (N^v, M^v) and the basis functions $(N_i(u), M_j(v))$ may be different from the corresponding quantities for the geometry, but usable parametric spaces of the geometry and potentials should be identical. With the introduction of the potential vertices, the unknowns of the hydrodynamic problem are now values of the potential vertices $(\phi_{i,j}^v)$ that are not the potential in the physical sense. The potential knot vectors in (u,v) are defined:

$$\vec{U} = \{0, 0, 0, 0, 1/N^\phi, 2/N^\phi, \cdots, 1, 1, 1, 1\}^T$$
$$\vec{V} = \{0, 0, 0, 0, 1/M^\phi, 2/M^\phi, \cdots, 1, 1, 1, 1\}^T \quad (2)$$

The numbers of spans or panels in (u,v)-directions in usable parametric spaces for the potential are (N^ϕ, M^ϕ) and they are related with the number of potential control vertices in forms of $N^v = N^\phi + p$ and $M^v = M^\phi + q$.

Discretization of the integral equation

Discretization into a set of (N^ϕ, M^ϕ) panels on the blade and M^ϕ strips in wake yields

$$\frac{\phi}{2} + \sum_{v,\mu} \iint_{S_{v,\mu}} \phi \frac{\partial G}{\partial n} ds + \sum_{\mu} \iint_{S_\mu^w} (\Delta\phi)_\mu \frac{\partial G}{\partial n} ds$$
$$= \sum_{v,\mu} \iint_{S_{v,\mu}} \frac{\partial \phi}{\partial n} G dS \quad (3)$$

Noting that there are only $(p+1, q+1)$ nonzero basis functions at each span defined by the space between adjacent knots in (2), we may rewrite the potential (1) as a $(p+1, q+1)$ term summation:

$$\phi(u,v) = \sum_{a=0}^{p} \sum_{b=0}^{q} \phi_{\alpha,\beta}^v N_\alpha(u) M_\beta(v) \quad (4)$$

where subscripts (s,t) are span indices satisfying the relation $(u,v) \in ((u_s, u_{s+1}), (v_t, v_{t+1}))$ in the knot vectors (2), $\alpha = s - p + a$ and $\beta = t - q + b$. Substitution of the equation (4) into (3) gives the control point on (i,j)-th panel:

$$\frac{1}{2}\{\sum_{a,b} N_{\alpha_i}(u_i) M_{\beta_i}(v_i) \phi_{\alpha_i,\beta_i}^v\}$$
$$+ \sum_{v,\mu} \iint_{S_{v,\mu}} \{\sum_{a,b} N_\alpha(u) M_\beta(v) \phi_{\alpha,\beta}^v\} \frac{\partial G}{\partial n} dS \quad (5)$$
$$+ \sum_{\mu} \iint_{S_\mu^w} (\Delta\phi)_\mu \frac{\partial G}{\partial n} dS = \sum_{v,\mu} \iint_{S_{v,\mu}} \frac{\partial \phi}{\partial n} G dS$$

where $\alpha_i = s_i - p + a$, $\beta_i = t_i - q + b$, $\alpha = s_v - p + a$ and $\beta = t_\mu - q + b$. It should be noticed that the (v,μ) summation for the dipole over the panels in (5) includes cases $i = v$ and $j = \mu$. In the low order panel method, these terms are eliminated, since the effect is already considered by the subtended angle of the hemisphere surrounding the point where the potential is evaluated. In the higher-order panel method, there are additional effects from the curvature of the geometry and the higher order variation of the potential in addition to the subtended angle effect.

Induced potentials

Depending on the relative position of the control point to the singularity panel, induction integrals are divided into self-induction, near-field induction and far-field induction integrals. Self-inductions due to high order normal dipole and source distributions are evaluated by Gaussian quadrature through the desingularization. By adjusting the degree of the quadrature, induction integrals are able to reach any desired accuracy. When the control point falls very close to the panel, a continuous subdivision method can be applied to evaluate induction-integrals. Sub-divisions into smaller panels do not lose the accuracy of the geometry and the potential representations.

Kutta condition

Kutta condition is the zero pressure jump condition in the wake sheet. This fact is equivalent to the statement that magnitudes of the total velocity on both sides of the trailing edge should be identical in the steady flow, that is,

$$(\vec{U}_r + \nabla\phi^+)^2 = (\vec{U}_r + \nabla\phi^-)^2 \quad (6)$$

The simultaneous equation for determination of the potential is over-determined and may be solved by the least square approach with the dynamic Kutta condition equation as constraints.

Wake alignment

Applying the Green's theorem, the induced velocity can be expressed by;

$$\nabla_p \phi(p) = \iint_{S_B} \frac{\partial \phi}{\partial n_q} \nabla_p G - \phi(q) \nabla_p \left(\frac{\partial G}{\partial n_q} \right) dS \\ - \iint_{S_W} \Delta \phi(q) \nabla_p \left(\frac{\partial G}{\partial n_q} \right) dS \quad (7)$$

where q is a variable point in the integration and p is a fixed point which may be located anywhere in the space. S_B is the propeller blade surface and S_W the wake surface. Equation (7) represents that the induced velocity due to the body and the wake can be calculated by distributing dipoles and sources on the body and dipoles on the wake. The wake is aligned when the force-free condition is satisfied on each wake panel. Figure 1 shows the procedure of the wake alignment applied in this model.

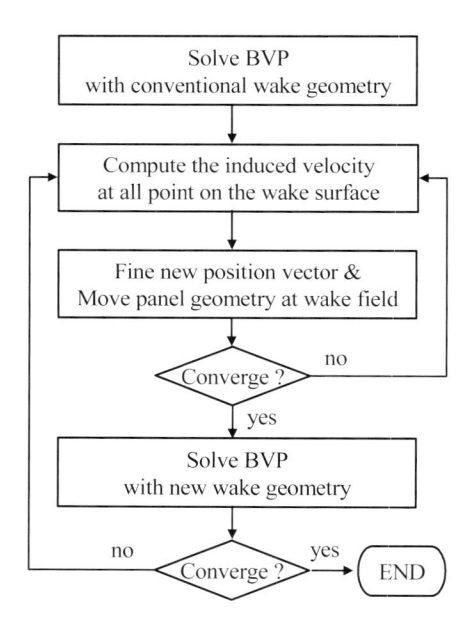

Figure 1: Procedure of the wake alignment.

RESULTS AND DISCUSSIONS

Convergence characteristics

To test the convergence of the new numerical method, numbers of chordwise and spanwise panels, N^ϕ and M^ϕ respectively, are varied for DTRC 4119 propeller at $J_s = 0.833$. Figure 2 shows the influence of the panel numbers on the circulation distribution. The figure shows generally good converged behavior with $N^\phi = 24$, $M^\phi = 16$ except a slight unstable behavior at the inner radii near the hub. This is considered caused by the change of the relative distance of the control points on the innermost strip to the hub panels. Although the influence is local, further study is necessary to improve the behavior in this region.

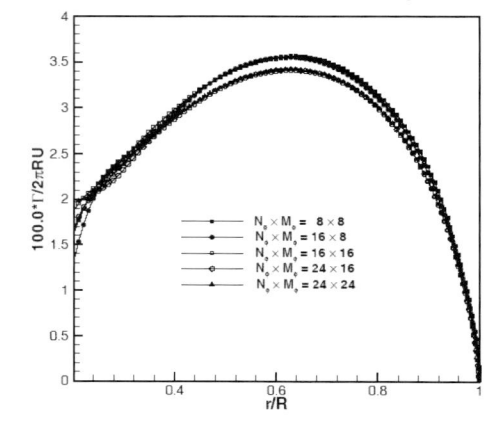

Figure 2: Convergence characteristics of radial circulation distribution for various number of panels (Js=0.833).

Comparison of model predictions with existing experimental measurements

Here the DTRC 4119 propeller that has abundant experimental data (Jessup 1989) is used for validations of the present model. Figure 3 shows blade and trailing wake surfaces represented by B-splines; wakes in (a) and (b) are generated with and without roll-up respectively.

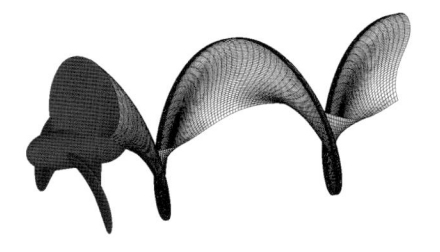

(a) Wake model without roll-up

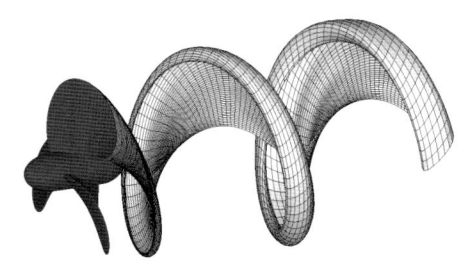

(b) Wake model with roll-up

Figure 3: Propeller and wake generated by B-splines

In Figure 4, the agreement in pressure distribution is generally good between the experiment and the theories. The most significant differences arise at the leading edge where the pressure varies drastically from the stagnation pressure to some finite value. In the present method, curvature effects appear at/near the leading edge, whereas in other methods, the low order method and the lifting surface method, do not detect these. Here the skin fraction coefficient, $C_f = 0.004$ is used. Pressure distributions at $r/R=0.9$ vary little from wake model with roll-up to without roll-up.

Figure 5 shows the pressure distributions at different locations, where the prediction at $r/R=0.99$ by the low order panel method has been practically impossible due to the abrupt change of both geometry and flow characteristics. The solution in this region may provide critical information for prediction of the tip vortex cavity flow. However, an unnatural behavior of the pressure distribution of the present method without wake roll-up occurs at the trailing edge, and it is likely to be influenced by the wake sheet location, which is fixed by a set of wake geometry parameters. By applying the roll-up model, it gives improved pressure distribution at the trailing edge. However, physical interpretations about increased pressure distributions around near trailing edge regions are still uncertain.

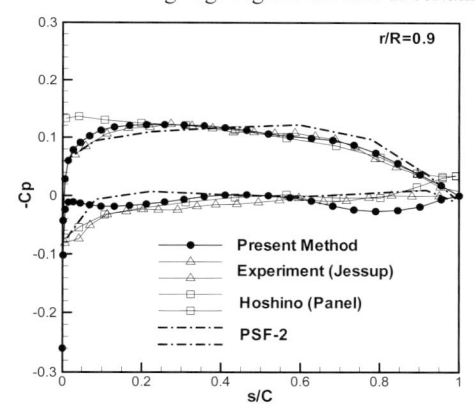

Figure 4: Comparison of the pressure distribution at $r/R=0.9$ of DTRC 4119 propeller (Js=0.833).

(a) r/R=0.3

(b) r/R=0.7

(c) r/R=0.9

(d) r/R=0.99

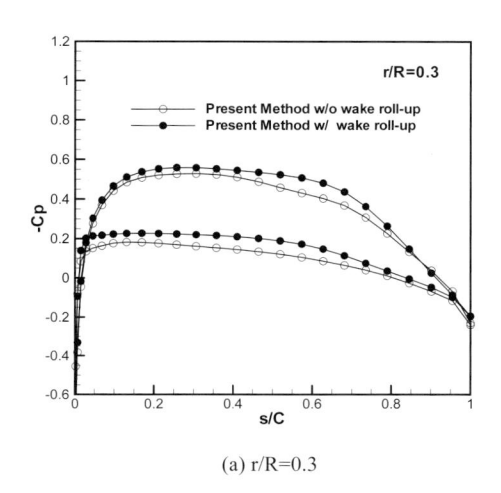

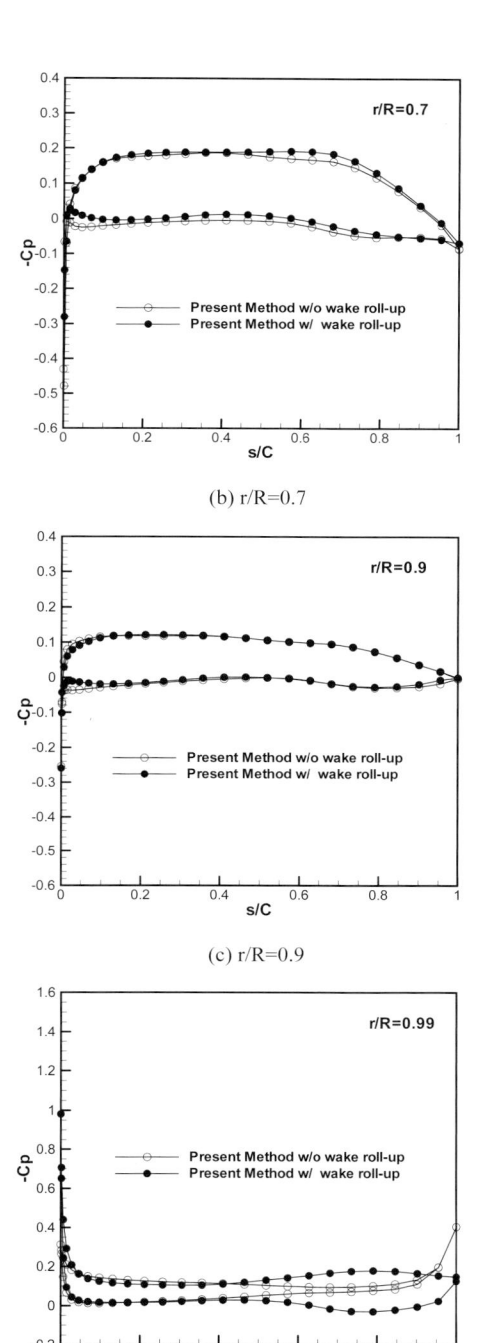

Figure 5: Pressure distribution at different locations of DTRC 4119 propeller (Js=0.833).

Figure 6 shows the performance of the objected model propeller. The present method using wake roll-up gives generally good predictions compared with experimental measurements even though it slightly under predicts.

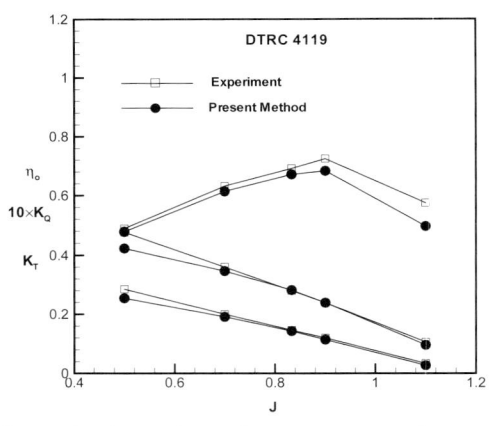

Figure 6: Comparison of open water performance of DTRC 4119 propeller

Comparison of model predictions with experimental measurements

Using a PIV technique, near wake fields of the KP707 propeller (see Figure 7) were investigated in the cavitation tunnel of the Maritime and Ocean Engineering Institute, Korea. Three hundred instantaneous velocity fields were measured at nine different phases of the propeller blade. Spatial evolutions of tip and trailing vortices of the propeller were estimated by phase-averaging velocity fields. Figure 8 (a) shows an instantaneous velocity field measured in the plane normal to the propeller plane at phase angle 10°. Figure 8 (b) shows a decomposed instantaneous velocity field. Tip vortices of the clockwise direction are clearly observed, and their numbers are the same with the number of propeller blades per an axial distance of a pitch.

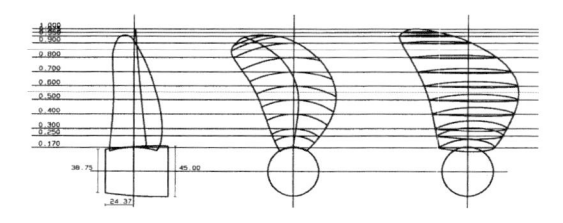

Propeller Principal Particulars	
Diameter (mm): 250	(P/D)mean: 0.969
No. of blades: 4	Ae/Ao : 0.570
Hub ratio: 0.175	Section: NACA66

Figure 7: KP707 propeller principal particulars.

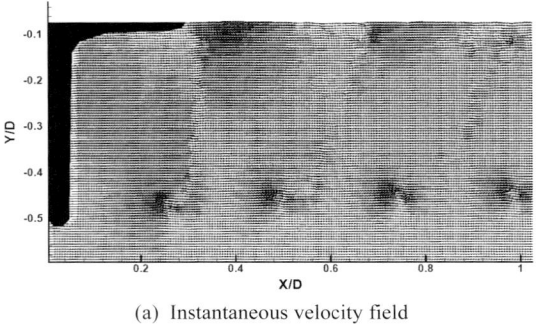

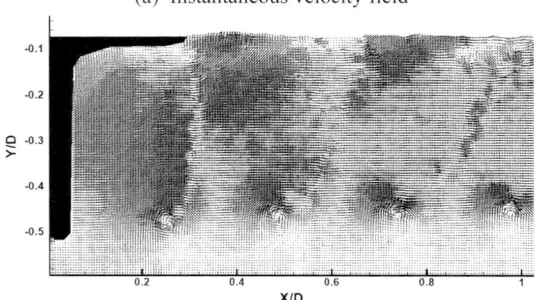

(a) Instantaneous velocity field

(b) Fluctuation velocity field ($U_C=0.95U_0$)

Figure 8: Instantaneous and fluctuation velocity fields at the phase angle 10° of J = 0.6.

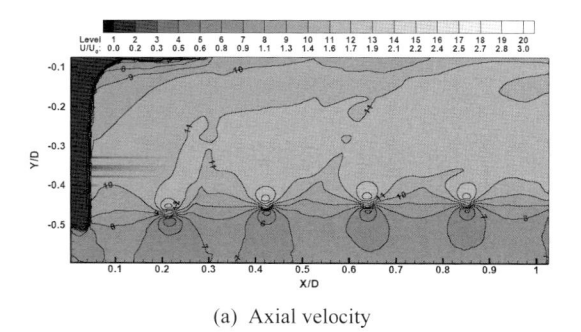

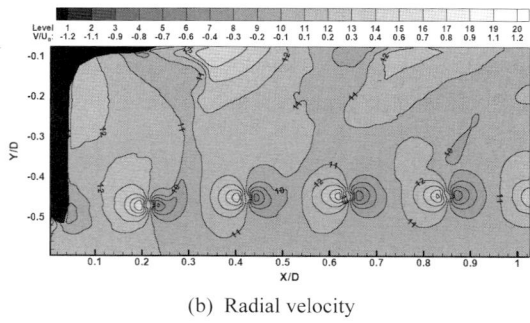

(a) Axial velocity

(b) Radial velocity

Figure 9: Contours of phase-averaged velocity components at the phase angle 10° of J = 0.6.

Figure 9 (a) and (b) show axial and radial velocity with the same condition of Figure 8. The axial velocity components are larger than that of near the regions of blade tip and propeller axis. It is expected that these results give good information on positions and contractions of tip vortices. Predictions that are now in progress will be validated later with these experimental measurements.

Conclusions

B-spline based high order panel method is developed for the analysis of the propeller performance. Both the geometry and the velocity potential are represented by B-splines, thus increasing the accuracy of geometry and flow representations. Numerical experiments show that the new B-spline based high order panel method is strong, can handle the flows of thin trailing edge and tip regions. A smaller number of panels may be used for practical purpose without sacrificing the accuracy. If the blades are represented by NURBS (Non-Uniform Rational B-Spline) surfaces, the panel method can be easily extended to adopt the NURBS surface.

In this study, wake roll-up model is applied to the present high order panel method and it improves the results at tip regions of the propeller. For more validations of the present method, additional computations are now going and the results will be presented later.

References

1) Greeley, D.S. and Kerwin, J.E., "Numerical Methods for Propeller Design and Analysis in Steady Flow," Transactions of SNAME, Vol. 90, 1982, pp. 415-453.
2) Hess, J.L., "Review of Integral-Equation Techniques for Solving Potential-Flow Problems with Emphasis in the Surface-Source Method," Computational Methods in Applied Mechanics and Engineering, Vol. 5, 1975, pp. 145-196.
3) Hess, J.L. and Smith A.M.O., "calculation of Nonlifting potential Flow About Arvitrary Three-Dimensional Bodies," journal of Ship Research, Vol. 8, No. 2, 1964, pp. 22-44.
4) Hess, J.L. and Valarezo, W.O., "Calculation of Steady Flow about Propellers by Means of a Surface Panel Method," 23-rd Aerospace Science Meeting, AIAA, January 14-17, 1985, Reno, Nevada.
5) Hoshino, T., : "Hydrodynamic Analysis of Propellers in Steady Flow using a Surface Panel Method," Journal of the Society of Naval Architects of Japan, Vol. 165, 1989, pp. 55-70.
6) Hsin, C,-Y., Kerwin, J.E and Newman, J.N., "HIPAN2: A Two-Dimensional Higher-Order panel Method Based on B-Splines, theory and program documentation," 1993, Department of Ocean Engineering, M.I.T.
7) Jessup, S.S., "An experimental investigation of viscous aspects of propeller blade flow," Ph.D. Thesis, The Catholic Uni. of America, 1989.
8) Kerwin, J.E., Kinnas, S.A, Lee, J.-T. and Shih, W.-Z., "A Surface Panel Method for the Hydro dynamic Analysis of Ducted Propellers," Transactions of SNAME, Vol. 95, 1987, pp. 93-122.
9) Lee, C.-S and Kerwin, J.E., "A B-Spline Higher Order Panel Method Applied to Two-Dimensional Lifting Problem," Journal of Ship Research, Vol.47, No. 4, 2003, pp. 290-298.
10) Lee, H. and Kinnas, S.A., "Application of BEM in the Prediction of Unsteady Blade Sheet and Developed Tip Vortex Cavitation on Marine Propellers," Journal of Ship Research, Vol. 48, No. 1, 2004, pp. 15-30.
11) Lee, H. and Kinnas, S.A., "Fully Unsteady Wake Alignment for Propellers in Non-axisymmetric Flows," Journal of Ship Research, Vol. 49, No. 3, 2005, pp. 176-190.
12) Maniar, H.D., "A three dimensional higher order panel method based on B-splines," PhD Thesis, Department of Ocean Engineering, M.I.T., 1995.
13) Pyo, S. and Kinnas, S.A., "Propeller Wake Sheet Roll-up Modeling in Three Dimensions," Journal of Ship Research, Vol. 41, 1997, pp. 81-92.

Measuring of Ice Induced Pressures and Loads on Ships in Model Scale

Janne Valkonen [1], Koh Izumiyama [2], Pentti Kujala [1]

[1] Ship Laboratory, Helsinki University of Technology
Espoo, Finland
[2] National Maritime Research Institute
Tokyo, Japan

Abstract

Ice load measurements are performed in the TKK ice tank to study ice load distribution along the ship hull in different operational scenarios. Two different types of models of ice going vessels are used in the tests. One is a conventional size tanker of 15700 dwt and the other is a larger general cargo carrier of 62000 dwt. Ice load is measured using I-Scan tactile sensor sheets installed on the ship hull at four locations along the hull. In the situation that the vessel is turning in the channel in level ice, the analysis of the measurement results show that the aft shoulder can experience high loading. These loads are higher than observed in the bow or midship area. The trend of the decreasing line load as a function of the load length is observed based on the analysis of the measured pressures by the tactile sensors. Local peak pressure analysis indicates that in the highest load cases, the total contact between the ice and the hull can be much wider than one frame spacing of a full-scale vessel.

Keywords

Ice load; Load distribution; Ice pressure; Model testing; Ship.

Introduction

Ships operating in ice covered waters experience loading on the hull due to the contact with ice. Ice load is located close to the waterline. Horizontally, the location of ice load depends on the operation of the vessel. Knowledge of ice load distribution along the ship hull in different operational conditions can give important background information for the development of design codes of the ice going ships.

Izumiyama,Wako and Uto (1999, 2001) have performed resistance tests in the ice tank in Japan with a straight going model to study ice load distribution along the ship hull in model scale. Experiments were conducted with a turning free running model by Izumiyama, Wako, Shimoda and Uto (2005). They noticed that the load distribution could be totally different in a turning ship from the ship going straight.. For this paper, model tests are performed in cooperation between TKK and NMRI in TKK's ice tank in Finland to extend the knowledge on the load distribution in turning mode and to study the effect of ship size on the load levels. Model tests performed are part of the European Union funded project, SAFEICE.

Tests include straight going runs in channel, breaking out of own channel and runs in the channel that corresponds to the turning circle of a Baltic Sea ice breaker.

The locations of the four pressure sensors are bow, bow shoulder, midship, and aft shoulder. Pressure sensors are installed on one side of the ship model. The test is performed in such a way that the load distribution on the outside and inside of the hull in turning can be measured. The free running model is used in the tests.

This paper presents the test set-up, main results and conclusions from the model tests.

Experiments

Test facility and ship models used

Model tests are performed in the TKK ice tank in Finland. The tank is 40 m x 40 m in area. These dimensions make it possible to make model scale tests in the turning mode. The model ice is granular ice that is frozen from the water containing ethanol injected spraying.

Two ship models are used in the tests. One is a conventional size tanker of 15700 dwt (MT Uikku) and the other is a larger general cargo carrier of 62000 dwt. MT Uikku represents a conventional narrow vessel with the breadth that is less than the breadth of the icebreaker. The general cargo carrier model presents a wide modern vessel. The model of MT Uikku is presented in Fig. 1. Uikku model has the ice-breaking bow and the general cargo vessel model has a bulbous bow. Both models are equipped with conventional propulsion and rudder for the free running tests. The main particulars of the model ships are presented in the Table 1. The models are scaled from the full-scale based on the scaling ratio 1:31. In this scale, the typical breadth of the Baltic icebreaker (25 m) is about 0.8 m.

Fig. 1: Uikku model going straight ahead in the channel.

Table 1: Main particulars of the ship models.

	MT Uikku	General cargo vessel
Length, overall [m]	5.21	7.36
Breadth [m]	0.70	1.15
Draught [m]	0.38	0.29
Model scale	31.56	31.56

Measurements of the model parameters during tests are as follows: location of the model, propeller speed, turning of the model, thrust of the propeller and rudder angle. Location of the model is measured as the location of the carriage in the ice tank. The speed of the vessel is calculated from the location data. A gyro is measuring the turning of the vessel.

Testing conditions

Several tests are performed in the ice sheet. The test set-up in the tank is presented in Fig. 2. Numbers in the figure refer to the order in which the different tests are performed. Tests 1 to 3 are straight going tests in a channel with different channel widths. Tests 4 and 5 are breaking out tests from channel to the port side and starboard side. Tests 6 and 7 are turning tests in a curved channel that has the radius of the turning circle of a typical Baltic Sea icebreaker.

In total 27 tests are performed, 15 using Uikku model and 12 using the model of the general cargo carrier. Both models are tested as straight going in channels of different widths. One of the channels for both vessels is 0.77 m wide, a typical width of a Baltic Sea icebreaker. Also, breaking out of their own channel is tested for both models. Uikku model is tested in two ice thicknesses of 20 mm and 25.2 mm thick ice, 0.63 m and 0.79 m in full-scale, respectively. The general cargo vessel model is tested but only in thinner 20 mm thick ice, 0.63 m in full-scale. Loads in turning in the curved channel are measured for both vessels. The curved channel is cut in ice sheet to present the turning circle of

a Baltic Sea icebreaker in width and diameter. All turning tests are performed in both port side and starboard side.

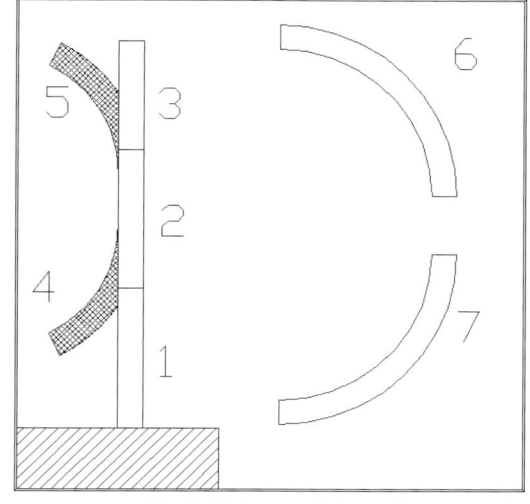

Fig. 2: Test set up in ice tank.

A new ice sheet is sprayed for each test day. Properties of model ice are measured every morning before the test. Ice properties for each test day are presented in Table 2. Properties of model ice are scaled to match ice properties in the Bay of Bothnia in the Baltic Sea. The smaller model is tested in two different ice thicknesses, 20 mm and 25 mm, which correspond to the ice thicknesses of 0.63 m and 0.79 m in full-scale, respectively. The larger model is tested only in 20 mm-thickness of ice. There is some scatter in the model ice properties, which is typical due to the complicated process to produce the model ice so that the scaling laws can be achieved.

Table 2 Model ice properties

Test day	Ice thickness [mm]	Bending strength [kPa]	Crushing strength [kPa]	Elastic modulus [MPa]
1 Test nos 1-8	20.0	20.4	51.3	7
2 Test nos 9-16	25.2	28.2	46.8	-
3 Test nos 17-22	20.8	29.2	51.3	48.5
4 Test nos 23-29	20.0	25.5	32.4	38.7

Pressure sensors

Pressure distribution along the ship hull is measured using tactile sensor sheets. Izumiyama (1999, 2001 and 2005) used similar sensors in the ice tank in the model scale measurements.

Tactile sensors, type I-SCAN 210, are used in the tests. The size of the sensor sheet is 238 mm x 238 mm, and the pressure range is from 20 kPa to 200 kPa. Sensing spots are arranged in a 44 x 44 grid. The area of one sensing spot is 5.4 mm x 5.4 mm. The I-Scan system was measuring 60 s periods in a 50 Hz frequency.

Tactile sensors are located in four locations on the port side of the model ship using thin tape. New sensor sheets are used for both models. Locations of the sensors for both models are presented in Table 3. There is some difference between locations of sensors between the two models. The shape of the bow of the general cargo carrier prevented the installation of a tactile sensor sheet at the bow area. Sensors are installed so that they cover the most interesting parts of the models.

Table 3: Location of the tactile sensors on the model ships given as a relative distance from the stern (frame 0 at stern, frame 10 at bow).

MT Uikku		General cargo vessel	
Sensor location	Frame	Sensor location	Frame
Bow	9.37	Bow shoulder	8.0
Bow shoulder	8.0	Midship	5.0
Midship	5.0	Aft shoulder	1.57
Aft shoulder	2.07	Aft	0.57

Analysis conducted

Calibration of the tactile sensors

Calibration of the I-SCAN sensor is not straightforward. This fact is due to the principle of pressure measurement and the structure of the sensor. The response of the sensor depends not only upon the load applied on it, but also on the local contact conditions between the sensor sheet and the ice. In the present test the sensor is calibrated using indentation tests. The sensor is pressed against a short beam cut in the ice sheet. The set-up is presented in Fig. 3. The total indentation force is measured using a load cell behind the tactile sensor as well as the raw numbers from the tactile sensor. Several indentation tests are performed in every ice sheet to get quantitatively good results for calibration purposes. Ice beams of different widths are cut out of the ice sheet and tested so that the sensor could be calibrated for a wide range of load. Fifteen beams are tested for the first to the fourth ice sheet and twelve beams for the fifth. In the fourth ice sheet the indenter is tilted by about 20 degrees from the vertical and five ice beams are tested in this bending mode.

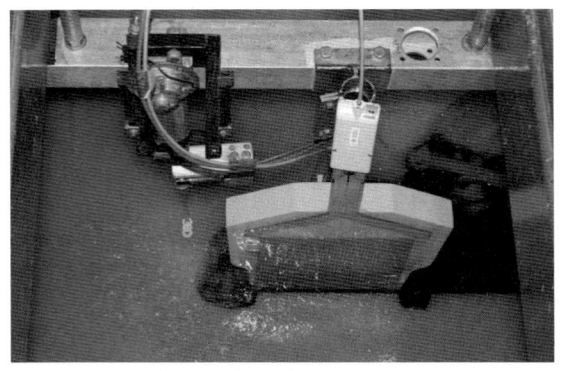

Fig. 3: Calibration test set up

Fig. 4 shows examples of data measured at a calibration test. The figure shows the load on the indenter measured by the load cell and Raw Sum from the tactile sensor in an indentation test. It should be noted that the two measurements are not exactly synchronized. It is shown that the tactile sensor gives the raw sum at the level of about 320 before the indenter actually touched the ice beam. Such an offset is often seen in the result of the I-SCAN measurement. In most of the cases the offset is due to "noise" in the data. The level of noise is low, usually lower than 10 Raws. However, the noise component may be comparable with the ice load component in the Raw Sum, since noise can takes place in a wide area of a sensor (at many numbers of sensing spots) while ice load concentrates in narrow areas. In the present calibration test, consistent noise is seen in sensing spots in a lower corner of the sensor sheet resulting in the offset as shown in Fig. 4. This situation seemed to be due to the stress in the sensor sheet caused by the sticky tape used to mount the sheet on the indenter. Analysis of the calibration data is performed so that the noise component is eliminated. Fig. 5 shows the result of the calibration tests of the tactile sensor.

(a) Time History of a Measured Load

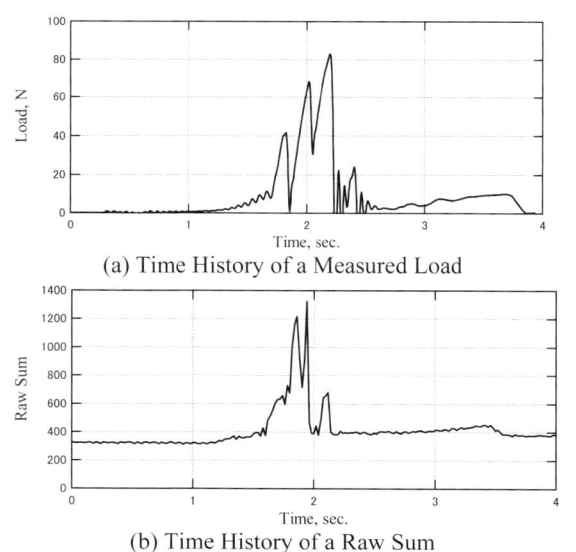

(b) Time History of a Raw Sum

Fig. 4: Comparison of measured load and Raw Sum (Test No.2)

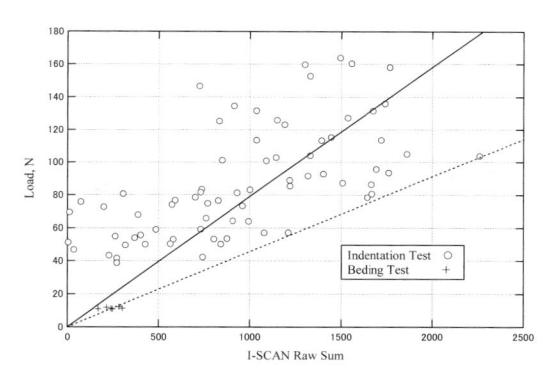

Fig. 5: Result of calibration tests

In Fig. 5, the maximum Raw Sum obtained at each test is plotted together with the peak load corresponding to the Raw Sum. Although there is a general trend of increasing Raw Sum with the increase of load, the plot also shows significant scatter. The scatter in Fig. 5 may be explained by the crystal structure of model ice. Fine-grained model ice (FG-ice) is used for the present test. This ice is formed by continuous spraying of tank water under the temperature of −15 °C. Sprayed water is cooled in the air and accumulated on the surface to form a layer of fine ice grains that is the main body of model ice. However, this ice also had a thin but very strong layer at the top. This top layer is about 1 mm in thickness and of a distinguished difference in strength from the ice below it. It is reasonable that this top layer took the most of the load from the indenter.

In the sensor sheet used in the present test there are sensing spots in a grid arrangement of 44 by 44. Each sensing spot is 3.9 mm by 3.9 mm in size and located at center-to-center intervals of 5.4 mm. This sensing spot arrangement leaves "insensitive" openings between spots. The width of the opening is 1.5 mm that is comparable with the thickness of the top layer of model ice. Taking this structure into account, it is easily guessed that the response of the sensor will be highly dependent on the relative location of the top layer in the sensor sheet. If the layer is in the middle of a sensing spot, there will be high Raw recorded. It is also possible that the top layer comes in contact with the insensitive opening with low or even practically no Raw recorded under the same load.

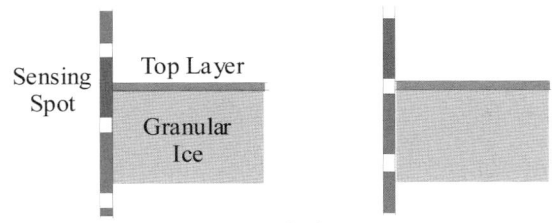

Fig. 6: Extreme cases for ice-sensor contact

Fig. 6 depicts the above-mentioned two extreme cases of ice-sensor contact. For example data from the calibration test on October 30 shows two different kinds of contacts between ice and the tactile sensor. In calibration test No. 13, very high Raws are measured, and some of them even reach the upper limit (255) of the sensor, while only low Raws were recorded in the calibration test No. 11. Despite differences on the load distribution, the load measured by the load cell for Test No. 11 is higher than that for Test No. 13 - 75.8 N and 53.0 N, respectively. It is deemed reasonable to attribute the scatter in Fig. 5 to different contact conditions in each indentation test.

Although the number of tests and the range of the measured load are limited, Fig. 5 shows the result of the bending test as well as those from the indentation test. The dotted line is the calibration line based on the results of this test. The line gives a lower bound for the data from the indentation test. This information may be explained by the difference of the ice failure mode between the two test types. In the indentation test, the location of the top layer is relatively stable during the load build-up phase until the failure. In the bending test, the ice-sensor contact (top layer) moves downwards during the load build-up phase as the beam bends down. Even if the failure takes place when the top layer happened to be at an insensitive area, the sensing spot above it has recorded the load before the ice failure, which can be comparable with the peak load at the failure.

It is difficult to say if the calibration factor can be determined from the Fig. 5 if the above-mentioned points related to the indentation test are considered. However, it will never be possible to have concrete information on the actual contact condition for the model test. It will be a mixture of the above-mentioned two extreme cases and the ones in-between them. Fig. 5 can be seen as a figure in which the load-Raw relations under various contact conditions are plotted. Taking this into account, it is proposed to take the linear regression line for the all indentation data as the calibration line to be used in the analysis of the local ice load measured in the present model test. This line, shown by the solid line in Fig. 5, gives a calibration factor of 0.0791 N/Raw. It should be kept in mind, however, that there always is some uncertainty in the calibrated load due to the unknown ice-sensor contact conditions.

Analysis of the tactile sensor data

Ice load data measured using the I-Scan tactile sensors is used for different kind of analysis. The most important concern is to study the load distribution along the ship hull in different operational scenarios. Data obtained is also used to study local peak pressures and the pressure distribution in the area of the sensor. Finally, the effect of the load width in the sensor area is studied.

The line load distribution along the ship hull is studied by finding the highest load value for each tactile sensor in each test. These values are plotted as a function of the sensor location on the ship's hull. The analysis gives a view as to how the load is distributed in different operation scenarios of ships.

The maximum load distribution is defined for both vessels. This definition presents the method of how the loading is distributed in all the tested operation scenarios. Such information can be used to define the design load distribution in ice class rules.

Local pressure peaks are calculated for time steps of 0.02 seconds. The test and time are selected for the analysis based on the maximum load distribution analysis. The distribution is plotted at the time when the maximum peak load occurred and some time steps before and after the time to see how the ice contact moves over the tactile sensor or that particular part of the hull. The analysis also gives a closer look to the ice-hull contact and especially to the load length at the time of the maximum loading event.

The effect of the load length is analyzed dividing the width of the sensor into the sections with different width. This feature makes possible the comparison of the load distribution with the full-scale measurements, where the load is measured on frame. The width of the strip can be made to equal to the area of the frame spacing in full-scale. It also gives information on the effect of the load length to the magnitude of the line load.

The area of the sensor is noted as "44 times 44" sensing spots. It can be divided in vertical strips that have widths of two, four, 11 and 22 sensing spots. That equals widths of 1.1 cm, 2.2 cm, 5.9 cm and 11.9 cm in model scale. Widths in full-scale, when the scale of models 31.56 is considered, are 0.34 m, 0.68 m, 1.87 m and 3.75 m, respectively. The line load on the strips, or "frames", is calculated for each time step of 0.02 s intervals. The maximum values for each "frame" in each time step are then plotted for selected tests for each panel to see how the line load behaves as a function of the load width.

Results of the analysis

Line load used to present the results is a load divided by the width of the tactile sensor 0.238 m. It could then be called as nominal line load over the sensor area. Load is calculated from the Raw values of the tactile sensor using the calibration factor 0.0791 N/Raw as previously described in this paper. Pressure in the local pressure plots is the load measured by one cell divided by the area of the sensing spot, 5.4 mm x 5.4 mm.

Load distribution

The distribution of the maximum ice load along the ship hull is determined from the tactile sensors. The time window of the test is extracted from the time history of the ice load. The I-Scan system is recording data for constant 60-seconds period for every test. The peak value for each sensor sheet is then picked for every test. The result presents the maximum measured ice load distribution in different operational scenarios. Also the maximum ice load distribution for both vessels is derived. It presents the highest load distribution in all the performed operational scenarios. This maximum load distribution gives a view to the maximum load distribution of merchant vessel in ice hull interaction scenarios that occurs in normal operation in ice. The distribution of the maximum line load along the model ship hull for the general cargo vessel model and the Uikku model are presented in Fig. 7~8, respectively.

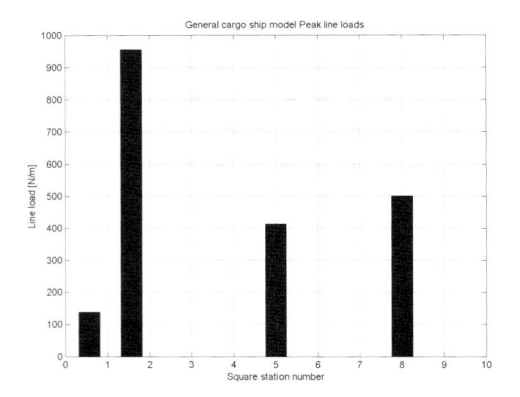

Fig. 7: Line load distribution along the hull. General cargo ship model (Include all the measured data)

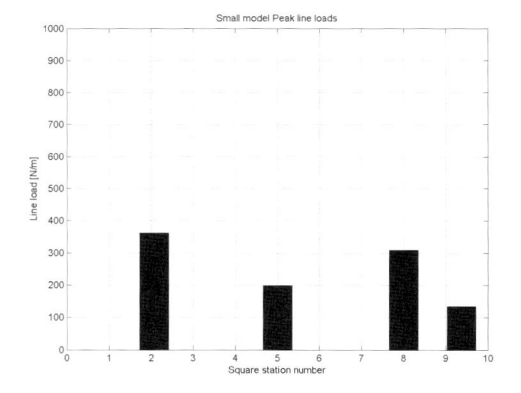

Fig. 8: Line load distribution along the hull for the Uikku model (Include all the measured data)

The general cargo ship model experienced the largest loading in bow shoulder and midship in test 17, the "straight ahead' test in 0.77 m wide channel (test types 1-3 in Fig. 2). The aft shoulder experienced the largest loading as it was breaking out of the channel to starboard side in test 21 (test type 4 in Fig. 2). The aft ship experienced the highest loading in test 26 when breaking out of the channel to starboard side (test type 4 in Fig. 2). The aft shoulder also experienced high loading in test 26 similar to test 21. Line load distribution in test 21 and in the test 17 are presented in Fig. 9~10, respectively.

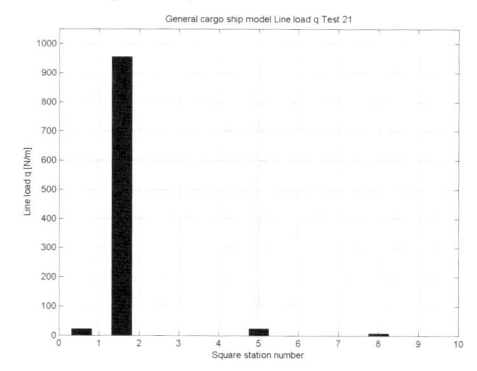

Fig. 9: Line load distribution in the test 21. General cargo ship model (test type 4 in Fig. 2)

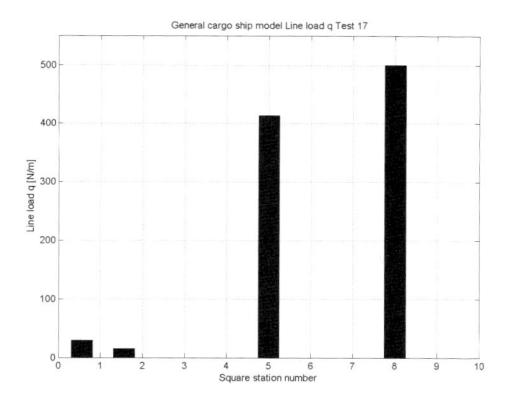

Fig. 10: Line load distribution in the test 17. General cargo ship model (test types 1-3 in Fig. 2)

The Uikku model experienced the largest line loads in bow and midship in test 11 that is straight ahead in level ice (test types 1-3 in Fig. 2). Bow shoulder experienced the largest line load in test 13 that is breaking out of the channel to port side (test type 5 in Fig. 2). The aft ship experienced the highest loading in test 16 that is test curved 0.77 m wide channel turning to starboard (test type 6 in Fig. 2). Line load distribution in the test 11 and in the test 16 are presented in Fig. 11~12, respectively.

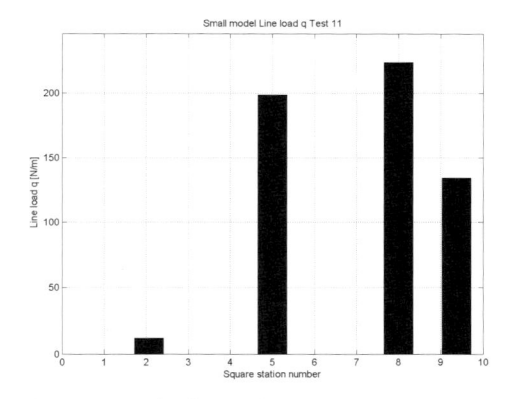

Fig. 11: Load distribution in the test 11 for the Uikku model (test types 1-3 in Fig. 2)

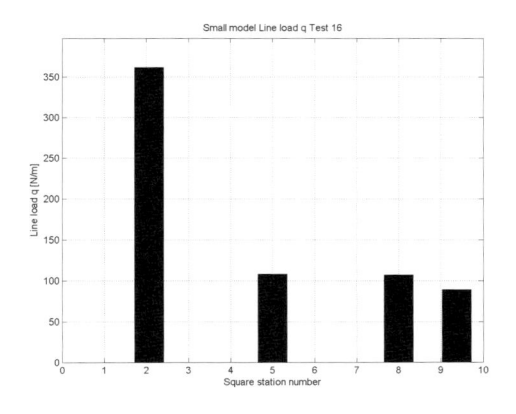

Fig. 12: Load distribution in the test 16 for the Uikku model (test type 6 in Fig. 2)

Effect of the load length

The effect of the load width to the line load at the bow shoulder of Uikku model in test 11 and at the aft shoulder of the general cargo carrier model in the test 21 are presented in Fig. 13~14, respectively. Results show significant scatter in small load width, whish is typical also in the measured ice load on one frame in full scale (Kujala and Vuorio, 1986). The scatter is smaller in wider load width. The trend of the decreasing line load as a function of increasing load width can still be seen in the figures and it seems to follow closely the exponential curve with -0.5 as the exponent. Similar trend was observed in other tests and in other sensor sheet locations. In the case lower loading there was less scatter in the line load was observed.

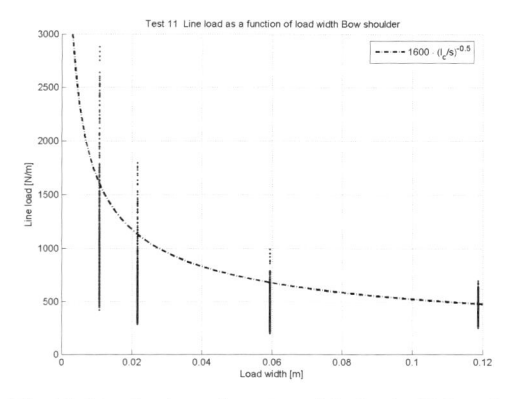

Fig. 13: Line load as a function of the load width at the bow shoulder of Uikku model in the test 11 (test types 1-3 in Fig. 2)

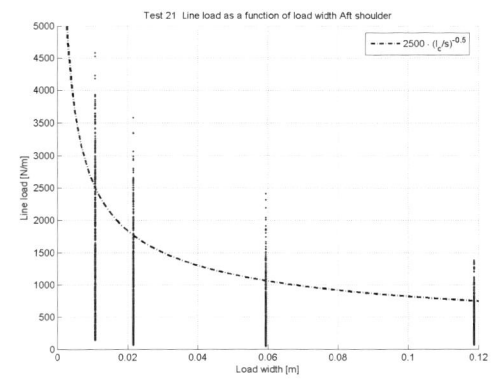

Fig. 14: Line load as a function of the load width in the aft shoulder of the general cargo carrier model in the test 21 (test type 4 in Fig. 2)

Local peak loads

Local peak pressures are analyzed for selected load events that produced the maximum loading on the tactile sensor. Pressure distributions on the tactile sensor at the different locations are presented in Fig. 15~16 for midship and the aft shoulder of Uikku model, respectively. At midship case the contact length is relatively small, five sensing spots wide or 0.85 m in full-scale. The contact is about three times longer in the case of the test 16, turning in the curved channel. In both cases variation on the magnitude of the pressure can be seen over the contact length. Contact is nice at the waterline.

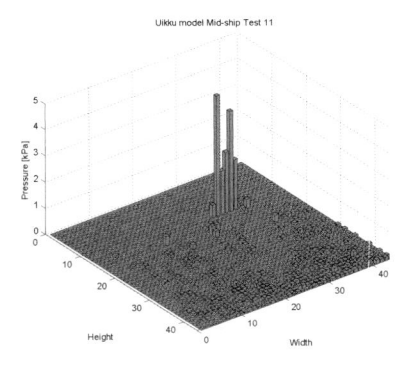

Fig. 15: Local pressure distribution at the time of maximum load at the midship area in the test 11 for the Uikku model (test types 1-3 in Fig. 2)

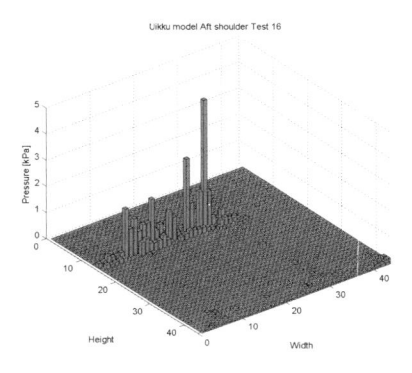

Fig. 16: Local pressure distribution at the time of maximum load at the aft shoulder area in the test 16 for the Uikku model (test type 6 in Fig. 2)

Pressure distribution in the two tests causing high loading at the aft shoulder of the general cargo carrier model are presented in 17~18. Contact length is very long at these events of extreme load. There can be seen two different contacts in both cases. The contact seems like a vertically narrow ridge of pressure mountains with some smaller hills and valleys in between.

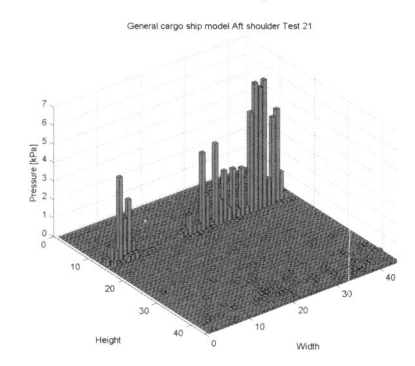

Fig. 17: Local pressure distribution at the time of maximum load at the aft shoulder in the test 21 for the general cargo ship model (test type 4 in Fig. 2)

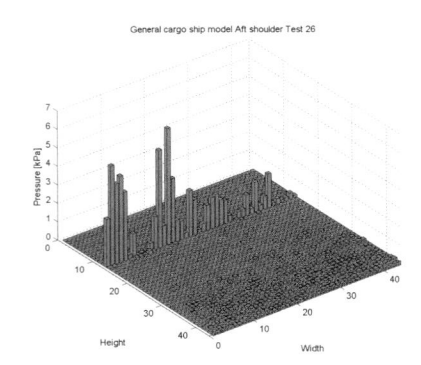

Fig. 18: Local pressure distribution at the time of maximum load at the aft shoulder area in the test 26 for the general cargo ship model (test type 4 in Fig. 2)

There is a dent in the channel edge that allows the rudder force to turn the aft ship. The dent in the channel edge and the contact at the time of high loading is presented in the Figure 18. The model moves 1.76 s without contact between the aft shoulder and the channel edge. After that, the model has momentum to turn starboard side and the new hard contact with ice edge causes the high peak in line load. The contact according to the tactile sensor is two times 12 sensing spots that equaling two times 2.05 m in full scale. The load is well-concentrated to the water line.

Conclusions

High loading in the bow and midship of the general cargo carrier model occurred with straight ahead test in the 0.77 m wide channel. In the breaking out of the channel test (to the starboard side) the aft shoulder experiences high loading for a long period of time. The contact is almost continuous between the channel edge and the hull of the model. There is not much bending of ice in the contact, but crushing is the dominating failure mode. The high peak in the bow shoulder in the breaking out of the channel test (to the starboard side) comes from the contact with the edge of the channel in high speed.

Ice load distribution along the ship hull shows that the aft shoulder can experience very high loading when the model was breaking out of the own channel or when operating in the curved channel. Bow shoulder area experiences high loading when going straight ahead in the narrow channel or in the level ice. These loads are still smaller than ice loads observed at the aft shoulder from the impact to channel edge. In the model scale the reaction force from the rudder and propeller might have been a bit extreme especially in the case of the general cargo carrier model. In full scale such turning force might occur in the ships equipped with pod propulsion. Ice loads when turning in the channel in full-scale might be surprisingly high on such vessels having high speed in the channel with consolidated edges.

The results obtained can open some new ways of thinking of the ice load distribution when developing new ice class rules. For larger ship the loads are about 40 % times higher than for the conventional tanker.

According to present Finnish-Swedish ice class rules the loads should be about 30 % higher for the larger ship based on the factor related to the ship displacement and horse power. The measured loads are higher at the bow shoulder area than at the bow and in the present rules the whole bow area have the same design load level. Loads can be high also at midship and aft shoulder area whereas according to the present rules the loads at mid/aft-ship should be about 50 % smaller than the ice load at the bow.

The trend of the decreasing line load as a function of increasing load width was observed when the load on the tactile sensor was divided into the narrower. Similar behavior was observed in full-scale by Frederking (1999) when analyzing ice load measurements in Arctic waters and by Kujala and Vuorio (1986) in the ice load measurements in the Baltic Sea.

Local peak pressure analysis showed that in the highest load cases the total contact between ice and the hull can be much wider than a frame spacing of a full-scale vessel. Ice load is concentrated close to the water line of the model. Analysis of the video recordings showed that in some cases ice pieces were rotated and pressed between the ice sheet and the model hull. That situation can cause high loading extent on vertical dimension. Similar behavior was indicated by Izumiyama, Wako and Uto (1999).

Acknowledgement

The authors would like to thank the European Union for making the model tests possible as a part of the SAFEICE-project. Special thanks go to the Finnish shipping company, ELS Shipping, as they loaned us their ship model for the ice tests.

References

Frederking, B, 1999: The Local Pressure-Area Relation in Ship Impact with Ice. In: Proceedings of the 15th International Conference on Port and Ocean Engineering under Arctic Conditions (POAC '99), volume 2, pp. 687–696. Helsinki, Finland.

Izumiayama, K., D. Wako and S. Uto, 1999: Ice force distribution around a ship hull. In: Proceedings of the 15th International Conference on Port and Ocean Engineering under Arctic Conditions (POAC '99), volume 2, pp. 707–716. Helsinki, Finland.

Izumiyama, K., D. Wako and S. Uto, 2001: Ice pressure acting over a model ship hull. In: Proceedings of the 16th International Conference on Port and Ocean Engineering under Arctic Conditions (POAC '01), volume 2, pp. 793–802.

Izumiyama, K., D. Wako, H. Shimoda and S. Uto, 2005: Ice load measurement on a model ship hull. In: Proceedings of the 18th International Conference on Port and Ocean Engineering under Arctic Conditions (POAC '05), volume 2, pp. 635–646. Potsdam, USA.

Kujala, P. and J. Vuorio, 1986: Results and statistical analysis of ice load measurements on board icebreaker Sisu in winters 1979 to 1985. Number 43. Winter Navigation Research Board, Espoo, Finland.

On Connection between Mesoscale Stress of Geophysical Sea Ice Models and Local Ship Load

Tarmo Kõuts[1], Kequang Wang[2] and Matti Leppäranta[2]

[1] Marine Systems Institute, Tallinn University of Technology, Tallinn, Estonia. Email: tarmo.kouts@sea.ee
[2] Department of Physical Sciences, University of Helsinki, Helsinki, Finland

Abstract

A numerical sea ice model has been applied to estimate the geophysical scale (1...10 km) compressive ice stresses in the Baltic Sea. Model equations to describe the evolution of ice mass and momentum, together with a categorization of the ice cover and a constitutive law for the mechanical behavior of ice on grid of one nautical mile. Compressive ice stresses represent mean stresses over the grid size length scale. Towards the local scale, such as ship's hull (10...100m), the compressive stress peaks increase remarkably. Ice thickness distribution and drift velocity are the main quantities determining the compressive ice stress. Computations of sea ice dynamics were performed in the Gulf of Riga and Gulf of Finland, both in the Baltic Sea. Model results were validated by satellite information and agreement was found to be good. In the Gulf of Riga case sea ice initially covered the northern part of the Gulf and was pushed to the south by the wind, compressed by about 40%. In order to link compressive stresses to the local scale ice loads, we need to obtain a typical size of ice floes in the concerned area, which can be done using satellite or aerial information. Results showed that compressive ice stress is extremely variable both in time and space ranging during this particular test case from 0 to 6 kN/m, which is generally in good agreement with ship borne measurements.

Keywords

Sea ice modeling; Ice compression; Baltic Sea; Ice loads.

Introduction

Sea ice covers polar and sub-polar basins and can be divided into the perennial polar ice pack and the seasonal sea ice zone (SSIZ). In the SSIZ there are several marginal and Mediterranean seas in which shipping is kept active year-round supported by icebreakers in winter or where the shipping is closed down in winter. The Baltic Sea, located in northeast Europe, is a freezing basin with heavy winter traffic. The region is densely populated for a cold climate region: there are nine coastal countries on the Baltic Sea and a population of 85 million is in the drainage basin.

For research on shipping in ice-covered seas, studies of the ice compressive situations are very important, as these conditions cause the highest ice loads on ship hulls. In the Baltic Sea, annually 45% of the sea area becomes ice-covered, with all the main harbors being kept active year-round based on the assistance provided by 20–25 icebreakers. In particular the Gulf of Finland has already become the main oil transportation corridor in the region with even greater growth projected for the future. The tanker traffic has increased tremendously during the last decade. The recently built Russian oil terminals in the eastern Gulf of Finland equipped with pipelines for oil transportation and modern loading equipment attract even bigger tankers to enter the basin. The oil transportation is mainly along the long axis of the basin (east – west). Very intensive passenger ship traffic between Finnish and Estonian harbors add crossing traffic in the Gulf of Finland, making the traffic system a very complicated one. The need for a year-round, unbreakable transportation service in the Gulf of Finland is obvious. In truth ice conditions along the Gulf are very dynamic, both in time and space. In the Gulf of Riga there are two major harbors, Pärnu in Estonia and Riga in Latvia, located in the northeastern and southeastern corners of the basin. Due to the intensive traffic and the largely variable ice season, the Gulf of Riga winter ship traffic becomes a very complicated system.

Ice forms in the Gulf of Finland and Riga annually, and the length of the ice season varies from one month up to 5 or 6 months, typically 2 to 3 months. The thickness of undeformed landfast ice reaches 80cm in closed coastal bays, but is typically still about 30 to 40cm in the open sea areas. This ice thickness in the open sea is not large enough to form stable ice cover and is broken and put into movement, as drift ice, by wind activity.

Drift ice is a granular, compressible, two-dimensional medium. These "grains" are individual ice floes, which form drift ice particles, and the resulting medium is approximated by a continuum. The necessary condition is that the length scales d, D and L_G of ice floes, drift ice particles, and gradients of drift ice properties, respectively, satisfy $d \ll D \ll L_G$ (Leppäranta, 2004). The motion of drift ice can be calculated by the use of dynamic models from the conservation laws of ice and momentum. Winds and currents drive the ice, and the response of the ice to the forcing comes from the internal stress and the adjustment of the ice mass distribution. High-resolution ice dynamics models for the sub-basins in the Baltic Sea, with grid length down to 1km produce realistic results, which can be validated against satellite data (Wang et al., 2006).

Thus, in mathematical modeling of sea ice dynamics, the spatial resolution of continuum models is cruder than the size of ice floes. On the other hand, in ice engineering the size of ships and fixed constructions have the magnitude 10–100 m, less than the size of ice floes normally. In consequence, the relationship between the ice stress on the geophysical scale and the ice engineering forces is highly complicated, and there is no easy method for downscaling or up scaling. This fact is presently one of the key problems in sea ice mechanics.

The purpose of this study is to investigate the applicability of this continuum model in fine resolution for estimation of compressive stress in ice fields and the possible relation with ship hull damages. Model simulations are performed for selected cases and the geophysical ice stress field is evaluated from the results. The model used in the study is the three-level sea ice dynamics model, which has been successfully applied in the investigation of the ice dynamics in the Gulf of Riga (Wang et al., 2003) and in Pärnu Bay (Wang et al., 2006). In the present study, two case studies were performed; one in the Gulf of Riga and the other in the Gulf of Finland.

1. Sea ice dynamics model

Sea ice is described in the model for its state and velocity. An ice state J is defined to include the relevant material properties of drift ice particles. In the present model a three-level ice state is used: $J = \{A, \bar{h}_u, \bar{h}_d\}$ where A is the total ice compactness, $\bar{h}_u = h_u A_u / A$ and $\bar{h}_d = h_d A_d / A$ the mean thickness of undeformed ice and deformed ice in the ice-covered region. The basic equations for sea ice dynamics are the conservation laws of momentum and ice (e.g., Leppäranta, 2004):

$$m\frac{dV}{dt} = -mf\mathbf{k} \times V + \tau_a + \tau_w - mg\nabla\xi + \nabla \cdot \sigma \quad (1)$$

$$\frac{\partial}{\partial t}\{A, \bar{h}_u, \bar{h}_d\} = -V \cdot \nabla\{A, \bar{h}_u, \bar{h}_d\} + \{\psi_A, \psi_u, \psi_d\} \quad (2)$$

where d/dt is the substantial time derivative, V the ice velocity, f the Coriolis parameter, $\mathbf{k}$ unit upward vector normal to the surface, τ_a and τ_w the air and water stresses, g the gravity acceleration, ξ the sea surface elevation, σ the internal ice stress, and ψ_A, ψ_u, ψ_d the ice redistribution functions due to mechanical deformation. Here short-term dynamic events are examined, and thermodynamic effects are neglected

The air and water stresses are determined by the bulk formula

$$\tau_a = \rho_a C_a |V_a|(V_a \cos\varphi + \mathbf{k} \times V_a \sin\varphi) \quad (3)$$

$$\tau_w = \rho_w C_w |V_w - V|[(V_w - V)\cos\theta + \mathbf{k} \times (V_w - V)\sin\theta] \quad (4)$$

where ρ_a, ρ_w are air and water densities, C_a, C_w are air and water drag coefficients, V_a, V_w are wind and current velocities, and φ, θ are boundary layer turning angles for air and water. The inertial time scale of thin ice, as represented here, is much less than one hour, and a quasi steady-state approach is taken. Also in the present study basins the pressure gradient due to the sea surface slope and momentum advection are small compared with the other terms and are ignored here.

The viscous-plastic ice rheology of Hibler (1979) gives a linear viscous law for very small strain rates and a plastic law with an elliptic yield curve for large strain rates. It is written as

$$\sigma_{ij} = 2\eta \dot{\varepsilon}_{ij} - [(\zeta - \eta)\dot{\varepsilon}_{kk} - P/2]\delta_{ij} \quad (5)$$

where σ_{ij} and $\dot{\varepsilon}_{ij}$ are two-dimensional stress and strain-rate tensors, ζ and η are non-linear bulk and shear viscosities, δ_{ij} is kronecker operator, $\dot{\varepsilon}_{kk}$ is the trace of $\dot{\varepsilon}_{ij}$, and P is the two-dimensional ice strength

$$P = P^* \bar{h} \exp[-C(1-A)] \quad (6)$$

where $\bar{h} = (\bar{h}_u + \bar{h}_d)A$ is the total mean ice thickness (ice volume per unit area), P^* is compressive strength of ice of unit thickness, and C is strength reduction constant for lead opening. The viscosity coefficients are functions of the strain-rate invariants and ice strength

$$\zeta = P/2\Delta, \quad \eta = \zeta/e^2 \quad (7)$$

where $\Delta = max\{\Delta_0, (\dot{\varepsilon}_I^2 + e^{-2}\dot{\varepsilon}_{II}^2)^{1/2}\}$, Δ_0 is maximum linear viscous creep rate, e is the ratio of compressive strength to shear strength or the aspect ratio of the yield ellipse, $\dot{\varepsilon}_I$ and $\dot{\varepsilon}_{II}$ are the sum and difference of the principal values of $\dot{\varepsilon}_{ij}$

Three cases of mechanical deformation arise (Leppäranta, 1981a): opening and closing of leads, rafting of thin ice ($\bar{h}_u \leq h_{cr}$), and ridging of thick ice ($\bar{h}_u > h_{cr}$), where h_{cr} is the maximum rafting ice thickness. In the case of opening and closing of leads, $A < 1$ or $\nabla \cdot \mathbf{V} \geq 0$, only concentration changes, hence $\psi_u = \psi_d = 0$ and $\psi_A = -A\nabla \cdot \mathbf{V}$. In the case of rafting, $A = 1$, $\nabla \cdot \mathbf{V} < 0$ and $\bar{h}_u \leq h_{cr}$, level ice thickness increases, therefore $\psi_A = \psi_d = 0$ and $\psi_u = -\bar{h}\nabla \cdot \mathbf{V}$ (rafted ice is treated as undeformed ice since it is more like layered undeformed ice in appearance and properties). In the case of Ridging, $A = 1$, $\nabla \cdot \mathbf{V} < 0$ and $\bar{h}_u > h_{cr}$, deformation only changes the ridge component, thus $\psi_A = \psi_u = 0$ and $\psi_d = -\bar{h}\nabla \cdot \mathbf{V}$.

The model uses an Arakawa-B grid, with the vectors and scalars staggered. To solve the momentum equation, first the viscosity ζ, current stress τ_w and ice strength P are calculated using the ice thickness, compactness and velocity from the previous time step; then the velocity is solved using the over-relaxation method. With the new velocity a new viscosity ζ and current stress τ_w, a new ice velocity consequently can be calculated. This process is repeated until a desired accuracy is achieved such that a plastic equilibrium is obtained or the system goes to a creep state to approximate the rigid flow in the case of very small strain rate (Wu et al., 1997; Wang et al., 2003). For land and fast ice boundaries a rigid boundary condition is applied, and for ice-open water boundary an open boundary condition is set, where the normal stress is zero. The equations of mass conservation are solved with the Lax-Wendroff scheme, using a two-step procedure. The redistribution processes are performed in the second step. To increase the computational stability, second- and fourth-order horizontal diffusion terms are also added in the second step.

The key parameters of the model are shown in Table 1. The model tuning is made first of all with the drag coefficients and strength constant P^*.

2. Case study in the Gulf of Riga, 16-21 March 2003

The winter of 2003 was severe in northern Europe. The Gulf of Riga froze over in January, and the ice melted at the end of April. In mid winter the whole basin was ice covered, apart from opening and closing of narrow leads .Consequently heavy pressures were built up in dynamical drift ice events.

The ice conditions during the period from March 16-21, 2003, are a typical case of compression (Fig. 1). As can be seen, the ice in the gulf, initially covered most of the northern part on March 16, was pushed toward the southern part. The northern edge showed a significant movement of about 15 km during the five days.

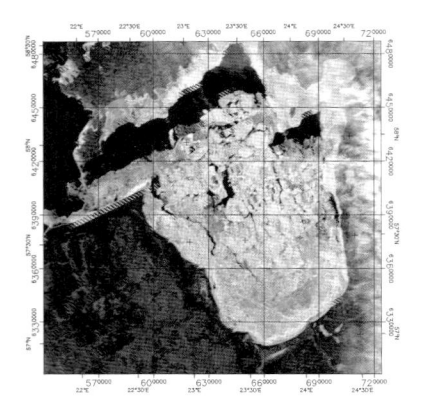

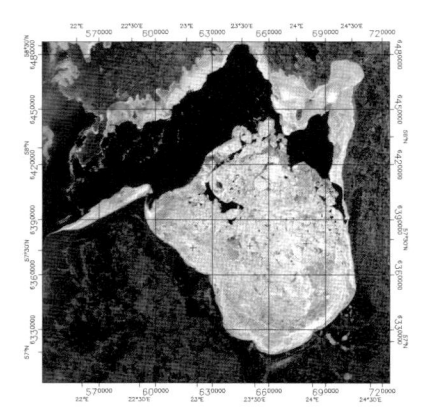

Fig. 1: Satellite imagery from MODIS, 16 March (upper) and 21 March (lower) 2003, showing ice compression event which was used as case study for basin scale ice stress calculations

The size of the Gulf of Riga is about 120 km across. The case showed a lead opening in the north and compression against the southeastern and southern coast (Figure 1). Pärnu Bay (size 15 km), on the northeastern corner, was covered by landfast ice in this case. This item is due to the condition that the ice was thick (50 cm), in mild winters much thinner ice (10–20 cm) in Pärnu Bay is still able to drift. Note that there is the small island of Ruhnu in the center of the Gulf of Riga that has a notable influence on the displacement of the ice field.

The model works well for the Gulf of Riga, with certain features of ice drift and compression as outcome from modeling well verified by satellite imagery. Figure 2 shows the modeled mean compressive ice stress, where the initial and final ice conditions are shown as the satellite images (Figure 1). The modeled ice stress is a vertically integrated line load. Typically it is estimated to range within $0 \sim 20$ kNm^{-1} in the Bay of Bothnia, the northernmost basin of the Baltic Sea where the ice is thicker, and within $0 \sim 10$ kNm^{-1} in the Gulf of Riga. Relevant measured values in Arctic first year ice range to $0 \sim 70$ kNm^{-1} (project SIMI), $0 \sim 80$ kNm^{-1} (project SHEBA). Local stress peaks go to ~ 1 MNm^{-1}, two orders of magnitude more than the mean geophysical stresses. Note that these stresses are two-dimensional stresses, three-dimensional stresses integrated over the thickness of the ice. Thus, e.g. 20 kNm^{-1} corresponds to three-dimensional stress of 100 kNm^{-2}, an order of magnitude less than the local (ship scale) strength of ice.

Table 1: The key parameters of the sea ice dynamics model.

Air	$C_a = 0.0018$
	$\varphi = 0°$
Water	$C_w = 0.0035$
	$\theta = 17°$
Ice	$P^* = 30$ kPa
	$C = 20$
	$e = 2$
	$\Delta_0 = 1.0 \times 10^{-9}$ s^{-1}
	$h_{cr} = 0.10$ m

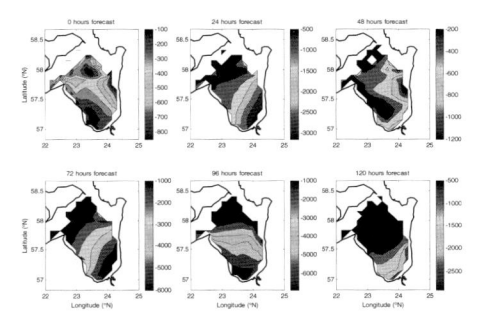

Fig.2: Modeled evolution of integrated over ice thickness mean compressive ice stress (Nm^{-1}) during case study period, 16-21 March 2003, in the Gulf of Riga

In order to link these geophysical stresses to the local scale ice loads acting on structures, such as ship or offshore structures, we need to obtain a typical size of ice floes in the concerned area. In the model scale, however, ice floe is not a drift state variable and stresses are independent of it. The floe size is best obtained from satellite observations. A mechanical analysis relating it to the typical ice thickness can also achieve this.

3. Ice compression estimates in the Gulf of Finland

In the Gulf of Finland ideal case studies have been performed. In normal winters the whole basin becomes ice-covered, and there is a remarkable gradient in ice thickness toward the east due to both thermodynamics and dynamics. The Gulf of Finland is a convenient basin for such studies, because it is an almost one-dimensional linear channel closed in one end.

One example of the ideal case studies in the Gulf of Finland is shown in Figure 3, showing the simulated evolution of compressive stress during a 5-day period, under the forcing of west wind of 10 m/s. The initial ice thickness was 20 cm and ice compactness was 99%. The Ekman angles in the atmospheric and oceanic boundary layers cause drift direction to deviate 20–25 degrees to the right from the wind direction. Therefore, open water appears in the northwest of the Gulf of Finland, and some ridged ice formed near the coastal areas and around the islands. The topography of the Gulf of Finland is more complicated than the topography of the Gulf of Riga, and therefore the contours show higher wave number features. Since the length scale of sea ice dynamics is proportional to ice thickness (e.g., Leppäranta, 2004), as well as with increasing ice thickness, high wave numbers disappear from the stress field. This feature has been well reproduced in simulations with variable ice thicknesses.

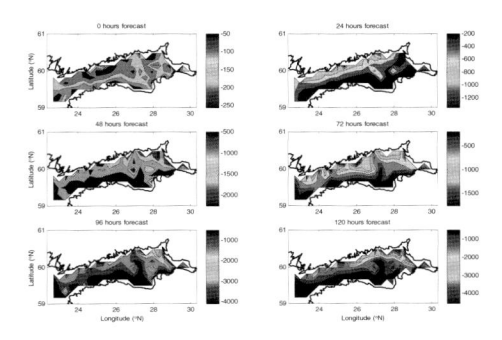

Fig.3: Modeled evolution of mean compressive stress (Nm^{-1}) in the ice field for the ideal case in the Gulf of Finland

As can be seen, the main region of high compressive stress level is on the northern coast, with the northeast coast reaching the maximum, being 4 kN m^{-1}. This situation is generally consistent with the ice thickness redistribution process. However, it is clear that the principal stress field with the principal axes orientations holds the whole truth. Therefore, Figure 4 shows more features of the stress field than just the mean compressive stress level.

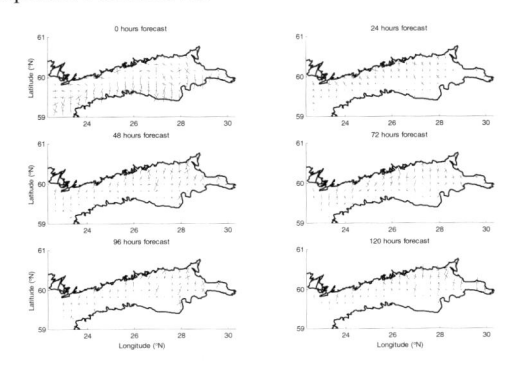

Fig 4: Modeled principal stresses in the Gulf of Finland for the ideal case

4. Discussion

A "sea ice landscape" consists of leads and ice floes with different morphological characteristics. Ice types have been defined originating from practical shipping activities in ice-covered waters, e.g., fast ice, undeformed ice or level ice, ridged ice, rafted ice, and brash barrier. They are based on the appearance, i.e. on how the ice looks to an observer on a ship or in an aircraft. The formation mechanism, aging and deformation influence the appearance, which therefore contain information of the ice thickness, seldom known from direct measurements. These processes give the ice top and bottom surfaces a relatively smooth appearance. Level ice, or undeformed ice, is the simplest ice type as it grows and decays by thermodynamic processes only, with the substructures of congelation ice, frazil ice and snow ice. Sea ice near the shore is in one sense an extension of land as it remains quasi-immobile during the winter, defined as fast ice.

The history of the evolution of the ice season can be approached using existing databases or utilizing a climatological sea ice model to generate the ice from proper forcing data. These forcing data include the time series of weather at daily time spacing or denser (air temperature, humidity, cloudiness, and wind speed and direction). Such histories are needed for statistical analyses of the ice conditions and ice loads along shipping routes. Models as such are presently good enough for such long-term simulations. In particular their use in the Baltic Sea functions as good databases to serve this purpose.

Sea ice grows and melts by thermal forcing and drifts under the influence of winds and currents. The dynamics and thermodynamics are coupled, and with the formation of leads, new ice starts to grow in them. Consequently, due to the dynamics, a sea ice field may contain a range of thicknesses of level ice, from thin sheets of nilas to maximum levels dictated by the regional climatology. A good estimate of the maximum thickness of level ice is the Stefan-thickness:

$$h^* = aS^{1/2} \tag{8}$$

where a = 2–3 cm/(°C d)$^{1/2}$ and S is the number of freezing-degree-days. In the Baltic Sea h^* = 130 cm in coldest winters.

Sea ice drift is caused mainly by the winds and then some extent on currents. The regime of the dynamics is divided into two basic categories: free drift and drift in the presence of internal friction. Free drift occurs when ice compactness is less than 70–80 per cent, and then the motion of ice could be described simply as:

$$\boldsymbol{u}_{\text{free}} = A\boldsymbol{u}_{\text{a}} + \boldsymbol{u}_{\text{w}} \tag{9}$$

where $\boldsymbol{u}_{\text{a}}$ is wind velocity, A is linear operator which contracts the wind speed to 2–3 % and rotates a counter clockwise direction (in the northern hemisphere) by θ = 20–30°, and $\boldsymbol{u}_{\text{w}}$ is the current velocity beneath the surface boundary layer. In these conditions, the compression of sea ice motion comes naturally as:

$$\text{div}(\boldsymbol{u}_{\text{free}}) = |A| \sin\theta \, \text{curl}_z(\boldsymbol{u}_{\text{a}}) \tag{10}$$

But since local fetches in open ice fields are small, the compression does not grow very large. It has also been shown using ice floe collision models that when compactness is less than about 70…80% compressive stresses are very small (Shen et al., 1987).

In compact ice, under compression ice the stresses become large, and ice mechanics show plastic behaviour. The yield curve is an ellipse, teardrop or diamond or alike in the compressive quadrant of the principal stress space, and it is specified by the compressive strength of the ice and the ratio between the shear strength and compressive strengths. The plasticity means that compression is rate independent. Consequently, in pure compression the average compressive stress of compact ice σ_c

$$\sigma_c = -P^*h \tag{11}$$

where P^* is the compressive strength of ice of unit thickness and h is the thickness of ice. The value of the parameter P^* is 10–50 kPa, and it represents the average compressive stress over drift ice continuum elements, which span over the length scale of 1–100 km depending on the model resolution. In pure shear the compressive stress is about one-half that of the stress under pure compression. In exact terms, the local peak stresses also depend on the mode of failure.

In the Baltic Sea the horizontal floe size magnitude normally ranges from 10 m to 1 km depending on the location and site, while in the Arctic Sea it is one order of magnitude larger. Therefore, the scale of the continuum models is much more than the size of ships. As in oceanography, mesoscale is understood as the range 10–100 km while large scale means 1000 km. Large-scale and mesoscale deformations are determined by external forces and internal forces. Floe-scale deformations are caused by interaction of individual ice floes (internal forces) and can be described in terms of a few basic deformation processes. During the passage of anomalous atmospheric-pressure fields, the internal forces in the sea ice field present one of the most hazardous conditions for constructions and ships in the sea-ice field.

With the drift driven by the three components of incompressible fluids, atmosphere, and ocean, the shear deformation part is usually much more than compressive deformation out from the coastline. But at the coastline, the geometry of the fast ice boundary plays a major role to determine the stress field.

On a large scale and mesoscale, ridging is the dominating factor causing the ice compression. Ridging in these cases can be treated statistically by the use of a redistribution process whereby thin ice is transferred to thick ice categories (Thorndike et al., 1975). The volume of ridges introduces a barrier to shipping due to its large potential energy. In first-year ridges the internal part of ridges is consolidated depending on the age of the ridge. The consolidation is much faster than the growth of undeformed ice. Consolidated layers of 1–2 m thick have been recorded in first-year ice ridges. These structures are the strongest solid ice features, well exceeding the Stefan-value of ice thickness. Beneath the consolidated layer the ice blocks are only partially frozen together, and they may be loose at very deep depths. As the ridge ages, erosion smoothes out the top and bottom surfaces, and the consolidated layer may reach the appearance of level ice, in particular after snow storms.

The ice dynamic model gives the state of drift ice in terms of the compactness and thicknesses of undeformed ice and deformed ice. Forced by the winds and currents, the model predicts the field of sea ice motion. The grid size has been 1…10 km in the Baltic Sea basins, depending on the governing floe size. Based on the plastic rheology taken to represent the mechanical behavior of the ice, the ice state and velocity fields can be used to evaluate the stress in the ice cover. This stress is a two-dimensional, horizontal tensor field. In the mathematical model the size and spatial density are transformed for one quantity, the thickness of deformed ice, which represents the volume of deformed ice per horizontal area. Since the mean thickness of ridges does not vary much in the Baltic Sea, the thickness of deformed ice can be inverted back to size and density information (Leppäranta, 1981b).

The mesoscale ice model is able to produce the strain rate tensor in the scale of the model resolution, from which point the kinematic compression and the compressive stress can be calculated. Model calculations were analyzed earlier for the stresses, and the outcome was considered good. However, with regards to the scale of the model grid, the stresses cannot be quantitatively validated against observations.

This compression field obtained from the mesoscale ice model is the starting point. Together with the local ice thickness distribution, the compression can be used to evaluate the compression in the scale of a ship. The algorithm to do this is additionally based on the hypotheses about the characteristics of the strain and stress fields, for which no known applicable solution exists to solve this problem. In general it is known that the mean stress level goes up by 1 –2 orders of magnitude when the spatial scale goes down from the mesoscale model grid size to the ship scale (Sanderson, 1988; Leppäranta, 2004). The model boundary for drift ice is the fast ice boundary. So, all ship channels within the fast ice zone are out from the model domain. In the drift ice, much ship traffic will help the mobility of the ice and in principle could be taken into account in the ice rheology parameters but so far it seems that this effect is within the noise. A critical are could be dense ship traffic at fast ice boundary, which could become critical and consequently should be accounted for in the boundary condition. Such approach has not yet done by us, neither it is known to us done elsewhere. A downscaling model is needed for the detail fine time and space scale prediction of the statistics of ship loads from the mesoscale model data. Although it is possible to establish reasonable and simple basic principles for this downscaling task, the lack of proper ship scale data has thus far prevented the quantification of the downscaling law.

Conclusions

A numerical model of sea ice dynamics has been presented and applied for the simulation and analysis of ice conditions in the Baltic Sea, and in particular for estimation of large-scale compressive ice stress field induced in ice cover by wind. The main equations describe the evolution of ice mass and ice momentum, together with a categorization of the ice cover and a constitutive law for the mechanical behaviour of ice.

The model has been applied to the Gulf of Riga and the Gulf of Finland in the Baltic Sea. the comparison between simulated and observed ice conditions shows that the model is generally capable of describing the evolution of dynamic processes in ice cover, i.e. the ice compactness, thickness of undeformed ice and ridged ice, and ice velocity. The model also calculates the model scale compressive ice stress field, which has been analyzed for the mean compressive stress and the principal stresses. Some basic studies have been performed to estimate the global ice load with ice pack during compression situations. Such studies are consistent to the field measurements in the Arctic Ocean.

The results for the stress investigations show a reasonable outlook. With a mesoscale model, at least risk regions of severe ice forcing are expected to be predictable for the shipping. This model will be useful, in our judgement, when analyzing the safety of navigation routes, both long term and operational planning.

The future plan is to continue model investigations. First of all, the downscaling scheme or hypotheses will be tested using statistical information and correlation analysis. Also a theoretical model of space–time variability of ice stress fluctuations has been constructed for testing with model calculations. The test basins are those previously noted, the Gulf of Finland and the Gulf of Riga. Yet, in order to obtain quantitative estimates of the ice forces, the need of good ship scale verification data to better understand the model scale stress field must be addressed. Only then it will possible to finally confirm the stress magnitudes and to relate the model scale stress to local or ship's scale stress.

Acknowledgement

This study was supported by the European Commission projects under contract FP6-PLT-506247 (SAFEICE).

References

Hibler III, W.D. (1979). A dynamic thermodynamic sea ice model. Journal of Physical Oceanography, vol .9, pp. 815-846.

Lepparanta, M. (1981a). An ice drift model for the Baltic Sea. Tellus 33(6), 583–596.

Lepparanta, M. (1981b). On the structure and mechanics of pack ice in the Bothnian Bay. Finnish Marine Research 248, pp. 3–86.

Lepparanta, M. (2004). The drift of sea ice. Springer-Praxis, Heidelberg, Germany.

Rothrock, D.A. (1975). The energetics of the plastic deformation of pack ice by ridging. Journal of Geophysical Research, vol.80, no. 33, pp. 4514-4519.

Sanderson, T.J.O. (1988). Ice mechanics - risks to offshore structures. Graham & Trotman, London.

Shen, H.H, W.D. Hibler III, and M. Lepparanta. (1987). The role of floe collisions in sea ice rheology. Journal of Geophysical Research, vol. 92, no. C17, pp. 7085-7096.

Thorndike, A.S., D.A. Rothrock, G.A. Maykut, and R. Colony. (1975). The thickness distribution of sea ice. Journal of Geophysical Research, vol. 80, no, 33, pp. 4501-4513.

Ueda, Y, and Rashed, SMH (1990). "Modern Method of Offshore Structures," Proc 1st Pacific/Asia Offshore Mech Symp, ISOPE, Seoul, Vol 3, pp 315-328.

Wang, K., M. Lepparanta and T. Kouts. (2003). A model for sea ice dynamics in the Gulf of Riga. Proc. Estonian Academy of Sciences. Engineering, 9(2). Pp. 107-125.

Wang, K., M. Lepparanta and T. Kouts (2006). A study of sea ice dynamic events in a small bay. Cold Regions Science and Technology 45, pp. 83–94.

Wu, H., S. Bai, Z Zhang, and G. Li, (1997). Numerical simulation for dynamical processes of sea ice, Acta Oceanologica Sinica, 16 (3), pp. 303–325.

A Comparison of Local Ice Pressure and Line Load Distributions from Ships Studied in the SAFEICE Project

Robert Frederking and Ivana Kubat

National Research Council, Canadian Hydraulics Centre
Ottawa, Ontario, Canada

Abstract

Within the SAFEICE Project a database of forces and local pressures has been compiled for icebreakers and commercial ships operating in ice. The areas of operation include the Arctic Ocean with multi-year ice and first year ice in the Baltic and Bering Seas. This ice type has the greatest effect on ice loading. The maximum local pressure measured in Arctic conditions was 8 MPa on an area of 0.7 m^2, and in first year sea ice 1.7 MPa on 0.6 m^2. At a probability of exceedance of 10^{-3}, local pressures on 0.7 m^2 were 4.5 MPa and 1.25 MPa for multi-year and first year ice, respectively. Comparable line loads were 4.5 MN/m and 1.4 MN/m for multi-year and first year ice, respectively. Average local pressure decreased with the inverse square root of the area. The landing craft bow form experienced line loads 25% lower than a conventional icebreaker.

Keywords

Ice pressure; Line loading; Ship response; Bow form.

Introduction

Local ice loading is required in the specification of design requirements for plating and framing of ship hull structures. The local loads may be specified in terms of pressure as a function of area or line load as a function of its length. This local loading is the underlying basis on which ship scantlings are specified in various ice class rules; e.g. International Association of Classification Society Polar Class (2007). The SAFEICE project addresses the safety of ships navigating in ice through establishing design requirements for ice impact loads in relation to ice conditions and managing the operations of ships in ice to reduce the risk of damage.

Detailed local ice load data from the five ships for which data were available are examined and compared in this paper, both in terms of pressure and line load.

Background

Local loading is examined in this paper. This term refers to the average pressure on a smaller area of a given size within a larger area which is subject to ice loading. It is sometimes referred to as the spatial pressure-area relation. Jordaan et al. (1993) referred to this pressure as the pressure on a local area within a global area. The spatial pressure-area relation describes the average pressure on a specified area and is applied to the local design of ship structure. Local loading may also be defined in terms of load per unit length longitudinally along the hull.

The five ships equipped with instruments for measuring local ice loading operated in various sea areas. Polar voyages in late summer were made by the Oden in 1991 and 1996, and the Louis S. St-Laurent in 1994. During these voyages they encountered both multi-year ice and first year ice. The Polar Sea made five measurement voyages to both the Arctic and Antarctic over the period 1982 to 1986. In some of the deployments both polar pack including multi-year ice and first year ice were encountered, while in others only first year ice was encountered. The Kemira and Uikku only encountered first year Baltic Sea ice. Ice condition information from these voyages and trials has been summarized in Table 1. The average ice thickness is the average of the reported maximum ice thickness for each ice loading event. The reported ice information did not allow for attributing an ice type to each loading event. Therefore, in order to get an appreciation of the amount of multi-year ice present, the percentage of ice greater than 2 m in thickness has been given. The 1983 Polar Sea trials in the North Chukchi Sea were in mostly first year ice; however, 15 multi-year floes with consolidated ridges 3 to 7 m thick were encountered in ramming trials and accounted for about 10 % of the ice encountered.

Table 1: Average and maximum ice thickness

Ship	Ice type	Ice thickness (m) Average	Ice thickness (m) Maximum	%> 2 m
Louis 94	my	3.7	7.6	85
Oden 91	my	3.2	6	88
Oden 96	my	3.3	6	96
Polar Sea 83	my	1.5	7	--
Polar Sea 86	fy	1.3	3.6	--
Kemira 87-88	fy	0.38	1	--
Uikku 03	fy	0.57	0.9	--

Ship particulars and hull angles of the centre of the bow instrumented area are presented in Table 2. Hull angles are defined in Fig.1.

Table 2: Ship particulars and hull angles of the centre of the bow instrumented area

Ship	Power MW	Displ. kt	α °	β °	γ °
Louis	29.4	11.4	18	35	--
Oden	18	12.8	90	--	20
Polar Sea	45	17	26	49	--
Kemira	4.1	8.2	19	20	--
Uikku	11.4	22.6	21	30	--

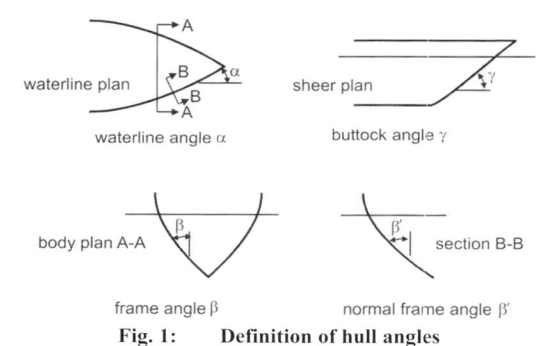

Fig. 1: Definition of hull angles

CCG Louis S. St-Laurent

The Louis S. St-Laurent trans-polar transit entered ice on July 26, 1994, reached the North Pole on August 22, and exited the ice August 30, 1994. Areas of the bow, shoulder and bottom were instrumented, but only bow data will be presented here. The bow instrumentation comprised strain gauges on frames from which the shear strain difference was used to determine loading. A more complete description of the instrumentation and voyage can be found in Ritch et al. (1999). The bow measurement area comprised 30 sub-panels, each 1.2 m wide by 0.6 m high arranged in an array 6 panels across by 5 high, for a total area of 21.6 m². The top of the measurement area was about 0.7 m below the DWL. Strain data were recorded whenever a threshold strain was exceeded, with a total of 1,730 events being recorded.

Oden

Measurement data are available from two polar transits of the Oden. Like the Louis S. St-Laurent, data were recorded whenever a threshold strain was exceeded. The 1991 voyage was in ice from August 1 until October 5. Strain gauges were used to measure shear difference on frames in order to obtain local ice loads (St. John and Minnick, 1993). The instrumented area of the bow had 40 sub-panels, each 0.85 m wide by 0.77 m high, arranged in an array 10 across by 4 down for an area of 26.2 m². The DWL was even with the top of the instrumented area. In 1991 there were 784 events recorded. Note that unlike the other ships which had conventional icebreaking bows, the Oden has a landing-craft type bow with a stem angle of only 20°. In 1996 the voyage made to the North Pole extended from July 12 to September 28. Both the bow and side were instrumented, but only the bow results are reported in this paper. In 1996 the bow instrumentation was comprised of 12 sub-panels of the same size as in the previous voyage arranged in an array 3 across by 4 down, for an area of 7.8 m². During this year 1,171 events were triggered on the bow.

USCG Polar Sea

The Polar Sea voyages tended to be more in the nature of trials in which particular ice was sought, rather than transits where the ship is primarily moving from A to B. Data from two of the five deployments will be presented, one from March to May, 1983 in the Bering and Chukchi Seas and the other into the Bering Sea in March, 1986. Data recording was triggered whenever a threshold strain was exceeded. In April, 1983, 513 events were triggered in the North Chukchi Sea where both first year and some multi-year ice were encountered. During the 1986 trials in first year ice in the Bering Sea, 653 triggered events were recorded. For the Polar Sea, gauges aligned to measure compressive strain in the webs were the means by which local ice loading was measured. The measurement array consisted of 60 sub-panels, each one 0.41 m wide by 0.38 m high, arranged in a matrix of 10 sub-panels across by 6 vertical, for an area of 9.3 m². Details of the measurement system may be seen in St. John and Daley (1984).

MS Kemira

Measurements on the Kemira were obtained during a number of commercial voyages in the Baltic during the period, 1985 to 1991. Strain gauges to measure shear difference were installed on three frames along the length of the ship, but only the results from the bow instrumentation will be presented here. The measurement width was 0.35 m and three sub-panels of height 0.58 m, 0.94 m and 0.84 m were arranged one above the other. Strain data were measured continuously, and in this case one-hour maxima were recorded for a total of 155 events for the winters of 1987 and 1988.

MT Uikku

The Uikku had been instrumented for a previous measurement program in the Arctic, but in 2003 it was available for a limited program in the Baltic. Again shear difference from strain gauges was used to determine local loads. Only two sub-panels on the bow were operational. One was 0.98 m high by 0.35 m wide and the other, directly beneath it, but separated by a gap of 0.96 m, was 1.31 m high by 0.35 m wide. Loads were measured continuously for 56 hours in three voyages and 10-minute maxima were recorded for a total of 336 events.

Measurement results

Both representative data on the distribution of pressures as well as statistical data on pressure and line loads will be presented in this section.

CCG Louis S. St-Laurent 1994

The distribution of local ice pressures on the bow of the Louis S. St-Laurent will be examined to demonstrate the nature of local loading. Local pressures at the time of maximum total load on the instrumented area for Event B3619001 are shown in Fig. 2. For this impact event the ship was traveling at 5 m/s and the maximum ice thickness was estimated to be 4.5 m of multi-year ice. It can be seen that the highest local pressures are concentrated in the two lowest rows (S4 and S5) of the measurement area, in a patch about 4.8 m long by 1.2 m high.

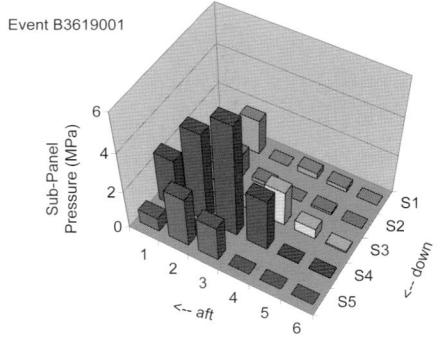

Fig. 2: Distribution of local pressure on bow at time of maximum force, Louis S. St-Laurent 1994

The local pressure can be looked at in terms of the spatial distribution of pressure. The following method is used. First, the highest pressure on one sub-panel is found, in this case frame 3 and row S4. Next, the average pressure on this sub-panel and any immediately adjacent sub-panel is determined, then the average pressure on this and any two immediately adjacent sub-panels, and so on. A plot of the spatial distribution of pressure with area at the instant of highest total force (same data as Fig. 2) is presented in Fig. 3. The average local pressure on an area within the measurement area is given by an expression of the nature

$$p = C (A/A_o)^e \qquad (1)$$

where
p = average pressure on a specific measurement area
C = pressure on area A_o
e = constant describing the shape of the curve.

The value of e in this case is -0.5. Values in the literature are in the range -0.4 to -0.6. Equation (1) describes the spatial pressure-area relation.

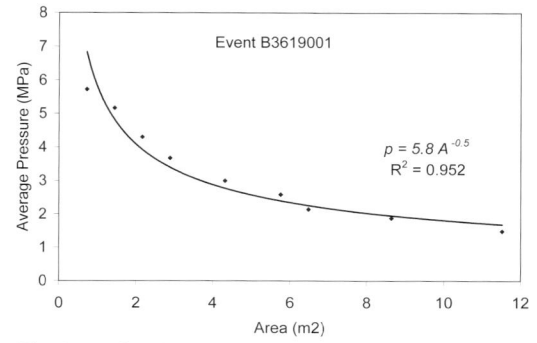

Fig. 3: Spatial distribution of pressure with area at time of maximum force, Louis S. St-Laurent

Ice loading is stochastic in nature so in order to obtain values useful for design, probability distributions have to be examined. The 1730 local ice pressures on a single sub-panel (0.72 m^2) and four sub-panels (2.88 m^2) have been plotted in Fig. 4. By comparing the two sets of plotted data, it can be seen that the pressure on a four sub-panel area is about half that on a single sub-panel, which follows the trend shown in Fig. 3 and the relation of Equation (1). This relation can be used to adjust pressures measured on various areas to a common area for comparison.

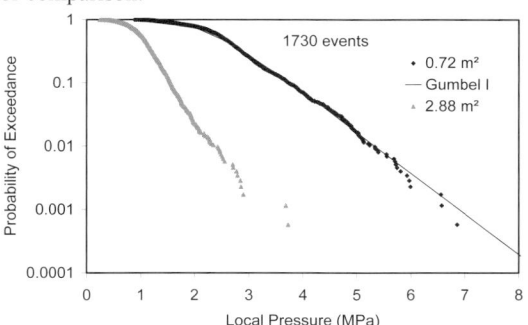

Fig. 4: Probability of exceedance of local pressure on 0.72 m^2 and 2.88 m^2, Louis S. St-Laurent, 1994

The data in Fig. 4 were drawn from the 1994 polar transit of the Louis S. St-Laurent which lasted about 35 days. Over the lifetime of a ship operating in ice, which would be much longer than 35 days, it is reasonable to expect it would encounter even higher local pressures than those plotted in Fig. 4. In extrapolating to longer service life it is necessary to fit some probability distribution to the data. A Gumbel 1 distribution was selected and fitted to the maximum pressure on one sub-panel (0.72 m^2). It defines the probability of exceedance $P(Y)$ of sub-panel pressure Y by

$$P(Y) = 1 - exp\{-exp[(Y-\varepsilon)/\theta]\} \qquad (2)$$

where
$\theta = \sigma/\sqrt{1.64}$
$\varepsilon = \mu - 0.577\,\theta$
σ = sample standard deviation
μ = sample mean

A Gumbel 1 distribution has been fitted to the local pressure data for a single sub-panel, and Fig. 4 shows it is a good representation. The data plotted in Fig. 4 and the Gumbel fit are for exposure on a 30-sub-panel area. The probability would be reduced by a factor of 30 for a single sub-panel. At the 10^{-3} exceedance level local pressure decreases from 7 MPa to 4.5 MPa.

Local loading can be examined in terms of pressure on a specified area or line load of a specified length. For thicker Arctic ice, average ice pressure over various sizes of patches seems to be most appropriate. This approach is the one taken in rules for Arctic Ships such as the Canadian Arctic Shipping Pollution Prevention Regulations (Transport Canada, 1995) and the International Association of Classification Societies' Polar Class Unified Requirements (2007).

Measurements from ships operating in the thinner ice of the Baltic Sea have generally been presented in the literature in terms of line load (Hanninen, 2003). In the case of line load, the issue is the magnitude of the line load and its dependence on the lengths over which it is averaged. Event B3619001 will be examined in terms of line load. The average line load at level S4 and the average line load over the full 3-m depth of the instrumented area are plotted as a function line load length over which they were averaged in Fig. 5. The line load intensity over the full depth of 3 m is not quite double the line load over level S4, which is 0.6 m deep, so that the effective height of the line load is probably about 1 m. Extending the line load length from 1 to 6 m results in about a 1/3 reduction in average line load as compared to a 5/6 reduction which would be expected if the line load was less than 1 m long.

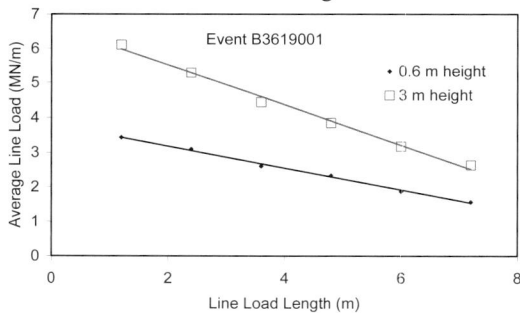

Fig. 5: Effect of line load length on average line load for two loading heights, Louis S. St-Laurent

Looking at the data from all 1,730 events in terms of average line load, the probability of exceedance of average line load over a length of 1.2 m for each individual level and combined for all five levels is plotted in Fig. 6. The line load for the total depth of 3 m is about twice that of a single level (0.6 m). A Gumbel I distribution has been fitted to the data, and is a good fit except for three extreme values in the tail.

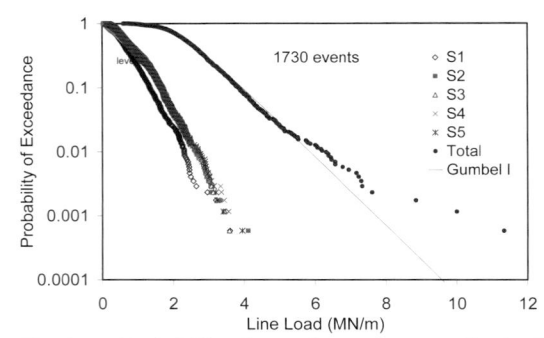

Fig. 6: Probability of exceedance of average line load over a length of 1.2 m for individual levels and combined over total depth, Louis S. St-Laurent

Oden 1991

The Oden has a very differently shaped bow from that of conventional icebreakers, so the distribution of local pressures and line loads on the bow is of considerable interest. The pressure distribution from one of the large impact events, O2420300 at 2 m/s on 3.5 m ice, at the instance of maximum load on the instrumented area is given in Fig. 7. In this case the local pressure is primarily distributed along one line, S3. A spatial pressure-area distribution was determined for this event, and it was very similar to the one for Event B3619001 the Louis S. St. Laurent.

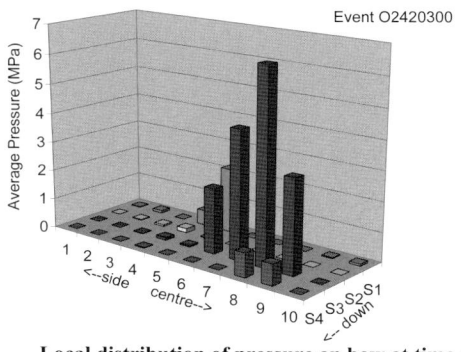

Fig. 7: Local distribution of pressure on bow at time of maximum force, Oden 1991

The local ice pressures on a single sub-panel (0.65 m^2) and four sub-panels (2.62 m^2) have been plotted in Fig. 8. Comparing the two sets of plotted data it can be seen that the pressure on a four sub-panel area is about half that on a single sub-panel, as described by Equation (1) with an exponent $e = -0.5$. Fig. 8 shows that a Gumbel 1 distribution describes the data. The distribution in Fig. 8 is for 40 sub-panels, adjusting it to one sub-panel reduces the local pressure at the 10^{-3} exceedance from about 7.5 MPa to 4 MPa, a value similar to that of the case of the Louis S. St-Laurent.

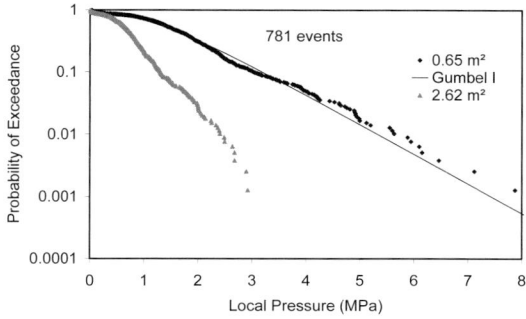

Fig. 8: Probability of exceedance of local pressure on two areas, 0.65 m² and 2.6 m² Oden 1991

Average line load over a length of 1.7 m has been plotted versus the probability of exceedance in Fig. 9. The average line load at each of the 4 levels (0.77 m) is quite comparable, and the total line over 3.08 m is less than twice the individual line load.

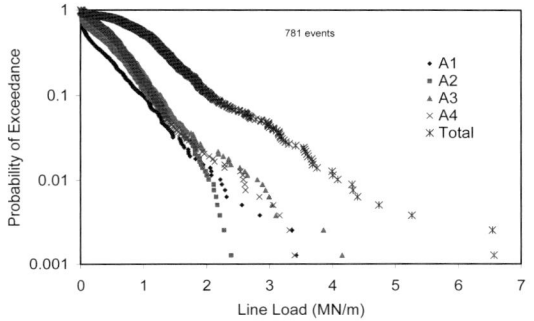

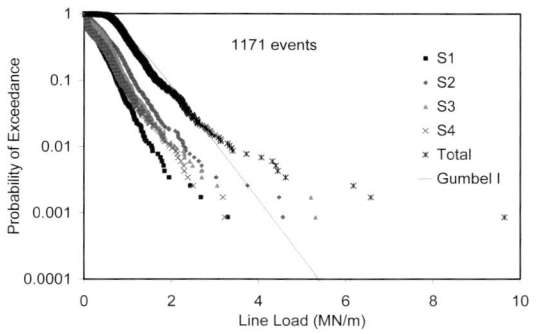

Fig. 9: Probability of exceedance of average line load over a length of 1.7 m, Oden 1991

Oden 1996

For the 1996 polar voyage of the Oden, only 12 sub-panels in a 3 by 4 array were being recorded. The local ice pressures on a single sub-panel (0.65 m²) and four sub-panels (2.6 m²) have been plotted in Fig. 10. By comparing the two sets of plotted data, it can be seen again that the pressure on a four sub-panel area is about half that on a single sub-panel. The fit of a Gumbel 1 distribution to the data is not good in this case. The distribution in Fig. 10 is for 12 sub-panels; reducing it to one sub-panel would put the 10^{-3} exceedance local pressure at about 3.5 MPa.

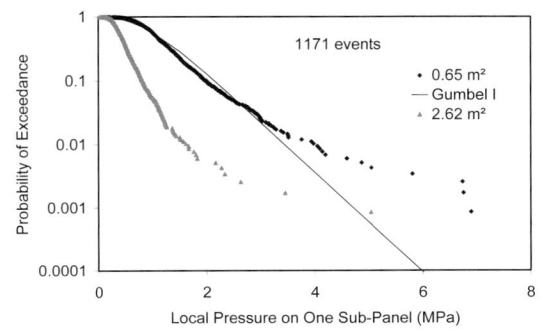

Fig. 10: Probability of exceedance of local pressure on two areas, 0.65 m² and 2.6 m² Oden 1996

Average line load over a length of 1.7 m has been plotted versus the probability of exceedance in Fig. 11. In this case the average line load for each individual level is more than half the line load for all four levels, inferring that the line load height is just a bit greater than the sub-panel height.

Fig. 11: Probability of exceedance of average line load over a length of 1.7 m Oden 1996

USCG Polar Sea 1983 and 1986

The Polar Sea was instrumented with smaller sub-panels than that of the Oden or Louis S. St-Laurent. Thus, results from this vessel can provide more detailed information on local pressures and line loads. Also, the Polar Sea did trials in areas where both multi-year ice was present and in areas where there was only first year ice making comparison of the effects of ice type easier.

The April 1983 trials in the North Chukchi Sea provide an opportunity for operations in pack ice where multi-year ice was present. The probability of exceedance of local pressures for six areas of approximately square shape is plotted in Fig. 12. Gumbel 1 distributions have been fitted to the 0.15 m² and 0.61 m² data and provide a good fit, except for the tails at low probabilities. The reduction in pressure from an area of 0.15 m² to 0.61 m² is greater than half, which indicates the exponent on the pressure-area relation of Equation (1) is less than -0.5 and is more like -0.6. The data plotted in Fig. 12 for an area of 0.61 m² represents 15 four-sub-panel groups, so adjusting for one 0.61 m² area. The pressure at the 10^{-3} exceedance level is reduced from 3.8 MPa to 2.7 MPa.

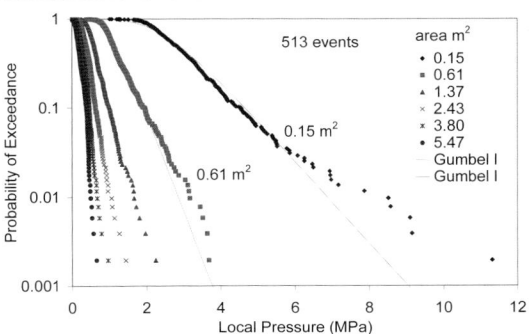

Fig. 12: Probability of exceedance of local pressure on six areas, 0.15 m², 0.61 m², and so on, Polar Sea 1983, North Chukchi Sea

The line loads over the full 2.28 m depth of the measurement area for the 1983 North Chukchi Sea trial are plotted in Fig. 13. A Gumbel 1 distribution is a reasonable fit to the data, with the exception of a couple outliers. The reduction in line load with increasing length from 0.41 m is small, suggesting that the line load is longer than 0.4 m. A systematic examination of this line load data, taking into account exposure showed a 20% reduction for a doubling of length from 0.41 m to 0.82 m and a 33% reduction for tripling the length. The function between line load, Q, and length, L, has the form

$$Q \propto L^{-0.4} \qquad (3)$$

where L is length over which line load is averaged.

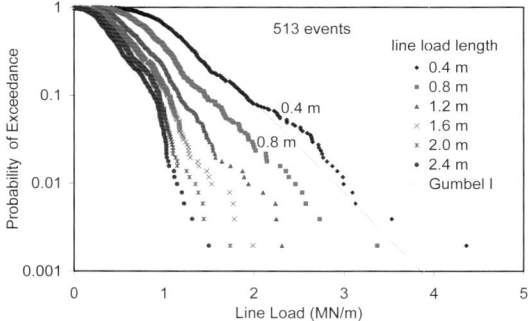

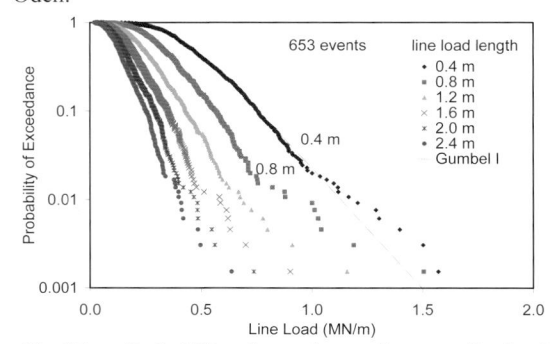

Fig. 13: Probability of exceedance of average line load for various line load lengths from 0.4 to 2.4 m, Polar Sea 1983, North Chukchi Sea

In March of 1986, the trials in the Bering Sea encountered primarily first year sea ice. The probability of exceedance of six different areas is presented in Figure 14. For the most part a Gumbel 1 distribution is a good fit, but there is some divergence in the tail at lower probabilities. Again, comparing pressure for areas 0.15 m² to 0.61 m² shows the pressure is less than half on the larger area, indicating the exponent in the pressure-area relation of Equation (1) is about -0.6. By comparing the pressures on an area of 0.15 m² in Fig. 14 with that in Fig. 12, it can be seen that they are much smaller for first year sea ice, being in the range of 3.5 MPa versus 9 MPa at an exceedance of 10^{-3}. For a single four-sub-panel area (0.61 m²) the pressure at the 10^{-3} exceedance level is reduced from 1.5 MPa to 1.1 MPa.

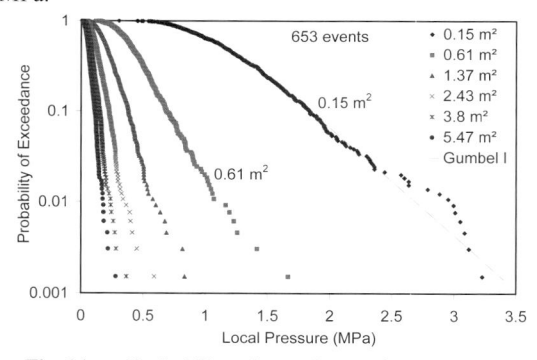

Fig. 14: Probability of exceedance of average local pressure on six areas, 0.15 m², 0.61 m², and so on, Polar Sea 1986, Bering Sea

Line loads averaged over various lengths for the full 2.3 m depth of the measurement area are presented in Fig 15 as a function of probability of exceedance. The line loads over lengths of 0.8 m and 1.2 m are much lower than those measured on the Louis S. St-Laurent or Oden.

Fig. 15: Probability of exceedance of average line load for various line load lengths from 0.4 to 2.4 m, Polar Sea 1986, Bering Sea

Kemira 1987 & 1988

Data gathering voyages were made with the Kemira for the winters of 1987 and 1988 when she operated in the first year sea ice of the Baltic. The ice conditions for both winters were comparable, so the data were grouped to provide one larger sample. The upper, middle and lower measurement areas on the bow were 0.17 m², 0.34 m² and 0.33 m² in area, respectively. The probability of exceedance of the local pressures is plotted in Fig. 16. These pressures are on smaller areas than for the Louis S. St. Laurent or Oden, so they have been adjusted to an area of 0.65 m² using Equation (1) with an exponent of -0.5 to facilitate comparison. Both the upper and middle areas give a local pressure of 1.25 MPa at the 10^{-3} exceedance level.

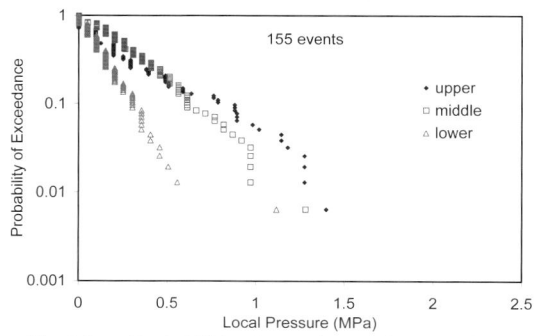

Fig. 16: Probability of exceedance of average local pressure on Kemira, winters 1987 and 1988

Line loads on the Kemira, which are for a single frame spacing of 0.35 m, are plotted in Fig. 17. Because of the long interval over which maxima were obtained, data from each level of instrumented area were treated independently.

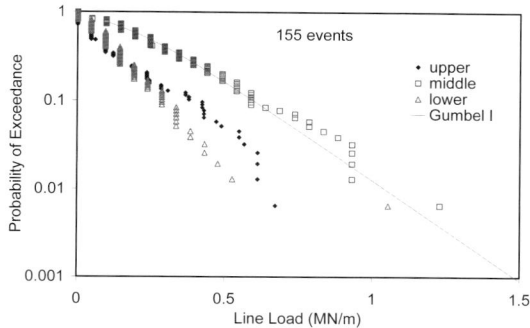

Fig. 17: Probability of exceedance of line load over 0.35 m on Kemira, winters 1987 and 1988

Uikku 2003

Data from 3 voyages of the Uikku were available from the winter of 2003. Local pressure results are presented in Fig. 18. Note that the data represent 10-minute maxima. There were two measurement areas, the upper at 0.34 m² and the lower one at 0.46 m². The two areas were separated by a vertical gap, which, when combined with the trim of the ship, resulted in a large number of time intervals when the lower area experienced no loading. By adjusting the actual measurement areas to 0.65 m², the local pressure at the 10^{-3} exceedance level was 1.2 MPa

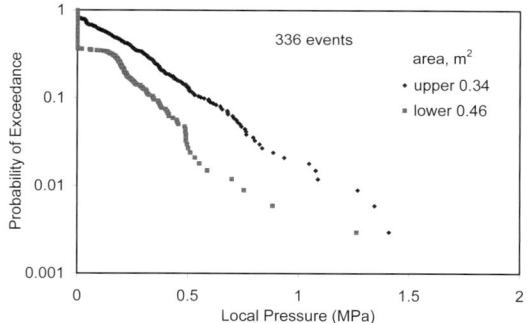

Fig. 18: Probability of exceedance of local pressure on Uikku, 2003

Line loads on the Uikku over the frame spacing length of 0.35 m are plotted in Fig. 19. They are similar but slightly greater than those on the Kemira.

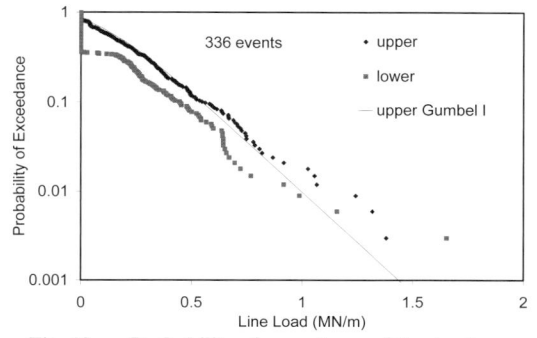

Fig. 19: Probability of exceedance of line load over length of 0.35 m on Uikku, 2003

Discussion of Results

The results from various ships and sea areas will be compared and discussed.

Comparison of Polar Sea with Louis S. S-Laurent and Oden in multi-year ice

A simpler and more direct comparison is to look at pressures on similar areas. Referring back to the single sub-panel plots in Figs. 4, 8 and 10 (areas 0.72 m² or 0.65 m² for the Louis S. St. Laurent and Oden respectively), and comparing it with the curve for an area of 0.61 m² in Fig. 12 for the Polar Sea, it can be seen that the local pressures for North Chukchi Sea pack ice are lower than those of the Louis S. St-Laurent and Oden 1991 voyages, but comparable to those of the Oden 1996 voyage. Note that the data plotted in these figures have not been adjusted for exposure in relation to the number of sub-panels in the measurement area. The Oden-1996 and Polar Sea North Chukchi Sea data were from a similar number of sub-panels (12 for the Oden 96 and 15 four-sub-panel groups for the Polar Sea), whereas the Louis S. St. Laurent and Oden 91 voyage data were from 30 and 40 sub-panels respectively. This difference in exposure would reduce the Louis S. St-Laurent and Oden local pressures by about 1.5 MPa at the 10^{-3} level, still leaving them with higher local pressures than the Polar Sea, as seen in Fig. 20.

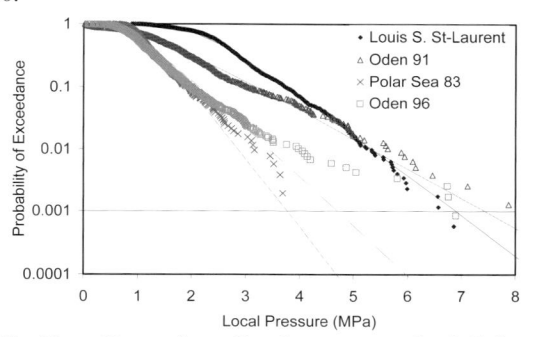

Fig. 20: Comparison of local pressures on Louis S. St-Laurent, Oden and Polar Sea in multi-year ice

The line load at the 10^{-3} probability level over a length of 1.2 m for the Louis S. St-Laurent was about 8 MN/m (see Fig 6), about 7 MN/m over a length of 1.7 m for the Oden in 1991 (see Fig. 9) and much lower, in the range 2 to 2.5 MN/m for the Polar Sea in multi-year ice in the North Chukchi Sea 1983 (see Fig. 13).

Comparison of pressures on all five ships

For comparative purposes, local pressures at the 10^{-3} exceedance level from all the data reviewed are compiled in Table 3. All these results have been adjusted to a common basis of exposure, one sub-panel (area noted in the table). Since the sub-panel areas for the Kemira and Uikku were smaller, the pressures have been adjusted to larger areas using Equation (1).

Table 3: Comparison of local pressures at 10^{-3} exceedance level

Ship	Multi-year ice Pressure (MPa)	Multi-year ice Area (m²)	First year sea ice Pressure (MPa)	First year sea ice Area (m²)
Louis 94	4.5	0.72	--	--
Oden 91	4	0.65	--	--
Oden 96	3.5	0.65	--	--
Polar Sea	2.7	0.61	1.1	0.61
Kemira	--	--	1.25	0.65
Uikku	--	--	1.2	0.65

Comparison of line loads on all five ships

All line loads results at the 10^{-3} exceedance level have been compiled in Table 4. As for the pressure, a common basis for comparison was established. Exposure on multiple columns was reduced to a single column. In the case of the Louis S. St. Laurent and Oden, this column was wider than the frame spacing of the Polar Sea, Kemira and Uikku. Therefore, the line load was adjusted to an equivalent width of L = 0.4 m using Equation (3).

Table 4: Comparison of line loads (MN/m) at 10^{-3} exceedance level

Ship	Height (m)	Multi-year ice L = 1.2	Multi-year ice L = 0.4	First-year L = 0.4
Louis	3.0	6.3	9.5	
	0.6	3.0	4.5	
		L = 0.85	L = 0.4	
Oden 91	3.08	5.2	6.9	
	0.77	2.7	3.6	
Oden 96	3.08	3.7	4.9	
	0.77	2.4	3.2	
Polar Sea 83	2.28			2.9
	0.38			1.5
Polar Sea 86	2.28			1.15
	0.38			0.75
Kemira	0.94			1.5
Uikku	0.98			1.45

Comparison of first year and multi-year ice pressures and line loads on Polar Sea

Polar Sea data can also be used for comparing the pressures and line loads from first year sea ice and multi-year ice. Pressure on an area of 0.15 m² is plotted in Fig. 21. Local pressures in first year ice are less than half those in multi-year ice. While not plotted here, line loads show a similar difference between first year and multi-year sea ice.

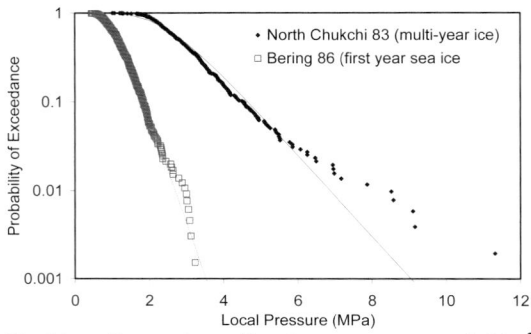

Fig. 21: Comparison of local pressures on area 0.15 m² on bow of Polar Sea

Conclusions

The results of these measurements quantitatively demonstrate that local pressures and line loads are three to four times higher in multi-year ice than in first year sea ice conditions. The shape of the bow of the Louis S. St-Laurent and Oden appeared to make no significant difference in terms of the local pressure. On the other hand, the line load on the Oden bow was about 25 % lower than on the Louis S. St-Laurent's bow. The local pressures for the Polar Sea, Kemira and Uikku in first year sea ice, in spite of being different ships (icebreaker versus tanker) and different ice thickness, are similar for comparable areas and exceedance level; 1.1 MPa to 1.25 MPa on an area of about 0.65 m² at the 10^{-3} exceedance level.

The spatial distribution of pressure with area follows a relation with the form

$$p = C\,(A/A_o)^e$$

where the exponent e is between -0.5 to -0.6, regardless of ice type, but the coefficient C is strongly dependent on ice type, being about 4 times greater for multi-year ice than first year ice.

Acknowledgement

This paper is a contribution within the EU Framework 6 project, SAFEICE. The authors very much appreciate the collaboration of the other partners in the project and gratefully acknowledge the technical interest and financial support of Transport Canada, which allowed their participation in the project.

References

Hanninen, S., 2003 Design Ice Load Level in the Baltic Sea, Proceedings 17th International Conference on Port and Ocean Engineering under Arctic Conditions, Trondheim, Norway, June 16-19, 2003, Vol. 1, pp.271-282.

International Association of Classification Societies, 2007. Requirements Concerning POLAR CLASS, Jan. 2007

Jordaan, I.J., Maes, M.A., Brown, P.A. and Hermans, I.P., 1993. Probabilistic analysis of local ice pressures, Journal of Offshore and Arctic Engineering, ASME Vol. 115, pp. 83-89.

Ritch, R., St. John, J., Browne, R. and Sheinberg, R., 1999. Ice load impact measurements on the CCGS Louis S. St. Laurent during the 1994 Arctic Ocean crossing, Proceedings of the 18th International Conference on Offshore Mechanics and Arctic Engineering, July 11-16, 1999, St. John's Newfoundland, paper OMAE99/P&A-1141.

St. John, J. and Daley, C., 1984. Shipboard Measurement of Ice Pressures in the Bering, Chukchi, and Beaufort Seas. Third International Offshore Mechanics and Arctic Engineering Symposium, Volume III, ASME, New Orleans, LA

St. John, J. and Minnick, P., 1993. Swedish icebreaker Oden ice impact load measurements during International Arctic Ocean Expedition 1991; Instrumentation and measurement summary, STC Technical Report 2682 to U.S Coast Guard Headquarters under contract DTCG23-91_D-ENM026, Delivery Order 92-0007, May 1993.

Transport Canada, 1995. Arctic Shipping Pollution Prevention Regulations, Equivalent Standards for the Construction of Arctic Class Ships, Transport Canada Publication TP12260.

Recent Design Advances in Ship-shaped Offshore Installations

Jeom Kee Paik

Department of Naval Architecture and Ocean Engineering, Pusan National University, Busan, Korea

Abstract

The present paper addresses current practices, recent advances and emerging trends as to core technologies for design of ship-shaped offshore units. Although a wide range of issues related to ship-shaped offshore installations do exist, the present paper will focus on the limit state design approaches in association with serviceability limit states, ultimate limit states, fatigue limit states, and accidental limit states. The paper will conclude that there are still a number of challenging issues to be resolved for more robust designing ship-shaped offshore installations.

Keywords

Ship-shaped offshore installations; FPSOs; Serviceability limit states (SLS); Ultimate limit states (ULS); Fatigue limit states (FLS); Accidental limit states (ALS); Risk assessment.

Introduction

Ship-shaped offshore units such as FPSOs (floating, production, storage, and offloading systems) have been recognized as perhaps one of the most economical systems for potential developments of offshore oil and gas, and are indeed often the preferred choice in marginal fields. These systems are becoming more attractive to develop oil and gas fields in deep and ultra-deep water areas (reaching more than 1,000m water depth) and remote locations from the existing pipeline infrastructures.

In the present paper, recent advances and future trends on core technologies for ship-shaped offshore installations (Paik and Thayamballi 2007) are presented, with the focus on limit states design (Paik and Thayamballi 2003).

Trading tankers versus ship-shaped offshore units

A ship-shaped offshore unit utilized for the offshore oil and gas development is similar to that of a trading tanker in terms of the hull structural arrangement. However, large differences between the two systems do of course exist in a variety of items, as indicated in Table 1.

A key difference between trading tankers and ship-shaped offshore units is in the consideration of design environmental conditions. For the design of trading tankers, the North Atlantic wave environment is typically considered as the design premise for an unrestricted vessel to make worldwide trade possible.

However, the design actions of ship-shaped offshore units will be based on the environmental phenomena specific to their operational sites, their transport to field before installation and mooring and the commencement of operations as the case may be.

For historical reasons, the return period of waves for the hull girder strength design of ship-shaped offshore units is typically taken as 100 years, although that of trading tankers for the same purpose is considered to be 20 to 25 years or so.

Winds and currents as well as waves among other factors may induce significant actions and action effects on offshore structures, whereas waves are often the primary source of environmental actions on trading ships at sea.

Trading tankers are typically loaded and unloaded at still water condition in harbor, but ship-shaped offshore units are subjected to significant environmental loads even during loading and unloading (or offloading). The number of loading / offloading cycles on ship-shaped offshore units is more frequent than that on trading tankers.

Ship-shaped offshore units are typically offshore for 100% time of their design life, while trading tankers are at open sea for perhaps 70% of the lifetime. Certainly, the fatigue failure characteristics of ship-shaped offshore structures may somewhat differ in comparison to trading tankers, e.g., in the need to consider low cycle fatigue related to loading and offloading. This can be important because large still water forces and moments can be created in ship-shaped offshore units due to loading patterns that may be very different from those of trading tankers, and also loading / unloading cycles are much more frequent.

In terms of operating conditions, trading tankers normally operate in either full load condition or ballast condition, but ship-shaped offshore units will be in varying states of loading and unloading. These characteristics in turn imply the possibility of frequent draft variations between the fully loaded and the minimally loaded and ballast conditions, compared to trading tankers. It follows that strength considerations must then address a number of loading conditions at varying drafts, and a number of environmental conditions with different return periods.

Trading tankers may avoid rough weather or alter their heading in operation by 'weather routing', but ship-shaped offshore units must be continuously located in the same area with site-specific environments.

Trading tankers are regularly dry-docked in 5 years intervals, while ship-shaped offshore units will not necessarily be dry-docked (and in any event are preferred not to be dry docked) during the entire production period in the field, possibly more than 10 years to even 20 years. This means that repairs in dry-dock are not economically realistic in many cases, primarily because of the potential production interruptions that must be dealt with. Also, welding or flame cutting which is common for traditional repairs of trading tankers in a dry-dock may not be as easily used for the repair work of offshore structures in situ for reasons of high fire and explosion risk.

Unlike trading tankers, ship-shaped offshore units have topsides, turret, flare towers, riser porches, drill tower, etc. which are items of large mass, high center of gravity and large windage area, which affect vessel motions and responses to environmental phenomena. Undesirable motion characteristics leading to green water, sloshing, slamming, mechanical downtime on equipments, crew discomfort, etc. are then very specific design considerations. For a turret moored ship-shaped offshore unit, the vessel may head into the weather and other differences can arise. For instance in comparative terms, the hull girder strength for FPSOs meant for turret moored operation in the North Sea must be significantly greater than that of trading tankers in unrestricted service. On the other hand, in some areas such as West Africa the wave environment can be considerably benign and this can be an advantage in terms of the strength required, whether turret moored or not.

In any event, the design considerations for ship-shaped offshore units may be more complex than those for trading tankers. This is not necessarily because ship design is any less complicated in principle, but because of the relative importance of site-specific conditions offshore and the need to consider many aspects in their design explicitly and specifically, unlike a trading ship wherein many of the same considerations may be implicitly considered by well-established rules and procedures.

New-build versus tanker conversion

Advantages and disadvantages do exist and need to be evaluated when deciding between a new build versus a tanker conversion option. The advantages of a new build option include the following, namely (Parker 1999):

- Design and fatigue lives for a field can be achieved easier;
- Technical, commercial and environmental risks can be more easily contained;
- System can be more easily designed to survive harsh environments;
- Resale and residual values can be maximized;
- Reusability opportunities can be improved.

On the other hand, the advantages of a tanker conversion option include the following, namely

- Capital costs can be reduced;
- Design and construction schedule can be less faster ad less extensive;
- Construction facility availability is increased;
- Overall project supervision requirements can be less.

The best option for a particular situation needs to be chosen taking their advantages and disadvantages into account. One of the key drivers for selection of either new build or conversion option may be the field life which corresponds in some manner to the economic depletion duration of the reservoir. When the design life for continuous operation on site is over 20 years, a new build will be invariably desirable. For marginal fields, the design life may often be 5, 10 or 15 years, and a conversion option may be more economical.

The building cost of new build FPSOs may of course vary depending on the many aspects including the capacity of production and storage. For instance, an FPSO operating in a marginal field may cost 60 million US dollars for a converted tanker with topsides plant installed, but an FPSO newly built for a large field may cost over 100 to 200 million US dollars or more depending on the size of the hull and size and complexity of the topsides installations.

The building project of an FPSO can be divided into different work packages, for example those related to hull, topsides, their integration, and of course project management. The related contracts are sometimes awarded separately or as a whole.

Front-end engineering and design (FEED)

Past projects of ship-shaped offshore installations certainly indicate that front-end engineering and design (FEED) involving substantial engineering capabilities and taking account of past lessons learned is very important for any new project; and this needs to be carried out to the necessary extent before the development of specifications, the invitation to tender package and in general the bidding phase (Adhia et al. 2004a, 2004b).

After award of contract, and before fabrication starts, the relevant parts of detailed engineering must of course be completed. Preliminary safety studies such as fire and explosion analyses and gas dispersion analyses for process facilities may significantly influence layout and design of the system, and they would have been carried out as part of the FEED, although detailed and specific studies of that nature will necessarily be part of the detailed design phase.

Engineering, whether FEED or detailed, will deal with many of the same aspects to different degrees of sophistication; aspects considered may include the following:

- Vessel principal particulars and general arrangement;
- Hull stability and strength analyses;
- Vessel motion analysis;
- Mooring system and station-keeping analyses;
- Riser system analysis;
- Turret system analysis and design where relevant;
- Process plant layout and determination of support loads;
- Operational and safety philosophies and plan development;
- Risk assessment and management planning.

Issues that must be resolved for design, building, and operation of ship-shaped offshore installations include:

- Site-specific metocean data
- Building material issues: yield stress, fracture toughness
- Hull structural scantling issues
- Action effect analysis issues
- Limit states design issues: serviceability limit states, ultimate limit states, fatigue limit states, accidental limit states
- Risk assessment issues
- Hydrodynamic impact-pressure action issues: sloshing, slamming, and green water
- Vessel motion and station-keeping issues
- Topsides design issues
- Mooring system design issues
- Export system design issues
- Corrosion issues
- Accommodation design issues
- Construction issues
- Equipment testing issues
- Towing issues
- Field installation and commissioning issues
- Inspection and maintenance issues
- Regulations and classing issues

Site-specific metocean data

Meteorological and oceanographic (metocean) data for the operational site is required for the development of an FPSO design. Wind, waves and current data for new fields must often be obtained by measurements, hindcasting or from comparable situations. For anchoring, piling and subsea construction design activities, bathymetric and geophysical data also need to be developed.

Based on the site-specific metocean data, various design parameters must be determined generally in terms of 1, 10, 50 and 100 years return periods, and stated in a design basis. Relevant information in the design basis document includes the following:

- Wind in terms of extreme speed and direction, vertical profile, gust speeds and spectra;
- Waves in terms of joint probability of significant wave height and period, extreme wave crest elevation, extreme wave height, direction and range of associated period, cumulative frequency distribution of individual wave heights and steepness, wave spectra and direction spreading;
- Water depth in terms of water depth below mean sea level, extreme still water level variations;
- Currents in terms of extreme current speed and direction, variations through the water depth, current speed for fatigue design, joint probability of wave, current occurrence and extremities;
- Temperatures in terms of extreme air temperatures (maximum and minimum), extreme sea temperatures (maximum and minimum);
- Snow and ice accretion in terms of maximum snow thickness, maximum ice thickness, densities of snow and ice;
- Marine growth in terms of type of growth, permitted thickness, terminal thickness profile.

The determination of the parameters noted above is very important for establishing the different environmental conditions for the different operational and extreme responses such as for mooring forces, hull bending moments, green water loading, bow slamming and steep wave impacts.

It is also important to note that FPSOs behave in much more complicated way than, say, fixed offshore platforms and that a much more detailed understanding of the environment is needed because of the much greater importance of wave period and joint probabilities of waves, current and wind which affect the responses to waves.

Serviceability limit state design

Serviceability limit states (SLS) for ship-shaped offshore structures address the following:

- Unacceptable deformations which affect the efficient use of structural or non-structural components or the functioning of equipment affected by them;
- Local damage (including corrosion, small dents, limited permanent set) which reduces the durability of the structure or affects the efficiency of structural or non-structural components;
- Intact vessel stability and watertight integrity;
- Vessel station-keeping;
- Vessel weathervaning or heading control;
- Vessel motions (or excursions) that exceed the limitations of equipment or mooring systems, risers, etc.;

- Vibration or noise which can injure or adversely affect the habitability of the unit and the performance of personnel or affect the proper functioning of equipment (especially if resonance occurs);
- Deformations which may spoil the aesthetic appearance of the structure.

The divisions are one of convenience, in that the limit state behaviors can be interlinked. For example, excessive deformation of a structure may also be accompanied by excessive vibration or noise as well as buckling. The acceptable SLS limits will be defined by the operator of a structure, the primary aim being efficient and economical in-service performance, usually together with a planned program of maintenance and upkeep for the unit. The SLS criterion is generally expressible as follows

$$\delta_{max} < \delta_a \tag{1a}$$

where δ_{max} = factored maximum value of the serviceability parameter in terms of actions effects (e.g., displacement, stress); δ_a = factored serviceability limit value of the consistent parameter.

The SLS criterion in Eq.(1a) is expressed in terms of action effects, and the same may be sometimes cast in terms of actions (e.g., forces, load-carrying capacity) and given in the following form,

$$F_{max} < F_a \tag{1b}$$

where F_{max} = factored maximum applied actions (loads); F_a = factored load-carrying capacity.

A 'factored' value indicates that an appropriate factor of safety associated with uncertainties is multiplied for loads or divided for strength. The acceptable limits necessarily depend on the type, mission and arrangement of the structure. Further, in defining such limits even for structural behavior, other disciplines such as machinery and equipment designers will also need to be consulted.

Ultimate limit state design

Ultimate limit states (ULS) for ship-shaped offshore structures include the following:

- Structural instability of part or all of the global structure resulting from buckling collapse of its structural components;
- Attainment of the maximum load-carrying capacity of the structure or its components by any combination of buckling, yielding, rupture or fracture;
- Significant in-flooding and loss of watertight integrity of the hull due to extreme actions under harsh environmental conditions;
- Loss of static equilibrium in part or for all of the global structure considered as a rigid body, i.e., capsizing or overturning.

The structural design criteria for the ULS are primarily based on buckling collapse or ultimate strength. To be safe in the ULS, the design criterion can be expressed as follows

$$C_d - D_d > 0 \tag{2a}$$

where C_d is design capacity (strength) and D_d is design demand (actions or action effects). The subscript d denotes the 'design' value which considers the uncertainties associated with capacity or demand. In ULS design, C_d indicates the ultimate strength and D_d is the extreme working load or stress in consistent units.

When the structure is subjected to multiple load components, C_d and D_d need to be expressed as the corresponding interaction functions taking into account the effect of combined actions.

Eq.(2a) may be rewritten in the form of a conventional structural safety check as follows

$$\eta = \frac{C_d}{D_d} > 1 \tag{2b}$$

where η = measure of structural adequacy which must be greater than unity to be safe.

Using the partial safety factor approach, Eqs.(2a) and (2b) can be rewritten, since $C_d = C_k / \gamma_C$ and $D_d = \gamma_D D_k$, as follows

$$\frac{C_k}{\gamma_C} - \gamma_D D_k > 0 \tag{2c}$$

$$\eta = \frac{1}{\gamma_C \gamma_D} \frac{C_k}{D_k} > 1 \tag{2d}$$

where C_k, D_k = characteristic values for capacity and demand, respectively; γ_C, γ_D = partial safety factors associated with capacity and demand, respectively, both of which are defined to be greater than unity. The partial safety factors must be obtained by probabilistic analysis involving associated uncertainties.

Similar to trading ships, the ULS design criterion of ship-shaped offshore unit hulls under vertical bending moments may be expressible as follows

$$\frac{M_u}{\gamma_u} \geq \gamma_{sw} M_{sw} + \gamma_w M_w \tag{2e}$$

where M_u = ultimate bending moment; M_{sw} = still water bending moment; M_w = wave induced bending moment; γ_u, γ_{sw}, γ_w = partial safety factors for M_u, M_{sw} and M_w, respectively.

For ULS calculations of ship-shaped offshore structures, gross thickness, i.e., as-built thickness is usually applied, although the net thickness (i.e., as-built thickness minus a nominal corrosion margin or allowance) is used for trading tanker structural design today in many cases (IACS 2006). This is often simply a matter of practice.

In usual operational condition of vessels, tensile strains of structural components at gross yielding may be small enough such that no fracture may occur. However, for offshore units operating in cold waters or for aged vessel structures, the structural material is more likely to become brittle and/or the fracture strain of the structural components may become smaller. In such cases, the structural components may experience brittle or ductile fracture and thus this type of failure must also be additionally considered.

Fatigue limit state design

Fatigue limit states (FLS) represent the fatigue crack occurrence of structural details due to stress concentration and damage accumulation under the action of repeated loading. In the relatively common context of use of S-N curves derived from small specimen fatigue test data, the related state of failure is often assumed to correspond roughly to the initiation of a through thickness crack at a particular location. It will be appreciated, however, that for practical purposes a crack that is even so initiated may not be visually observed until it is longer. In the same vein, surface cracks are even more difficult to observe without specialized means such as dye penetration or magnetic particle testing.

In any event, it is worth pointing out that there exists a certain amount of ambiguity as to what the FLS failure of the real structure physically correlates to the fatigue data used in design. For this and many other reasons, the FLS design in a particular case is carried out so that it is ensured that the structure has an adequate fatigue life which is longer than the design service life by an appropriate factor of safety. Also the predicted fatigue life is a required input for purposes of planning efficient inspection programs during the operation of the structure.

The design fatigue life for structural details of ship-shaped offshore units is normally specified by the operator or owner, while that of trading tankers is usually specified by bodies such as classification societies. For new build ship-shaped offshore structures, the fatigue life may often be taken anywhere from 20 to 60 years or longer (including safety factors), while it is typically taken as 20 to 25 years for trading tankers.

In new build ship-shaped offshore structures, the fatigue safety factors might vary from 1 to 3 or more, and occasionally even 10 depending on the maintenance philosophy to be employed in service and on the potential consequences of fatigue failure at a given location and the potential consequences of associated downtime. The shorter the design fatigue life, the smaller the inspection intervals need to be if a crack problem-free operation is to be assured. Table 2 indicates sample safety factors used for FLS design of ship-shaped offshore structures in practice.

The inability to dry-dock is also a factor in some owners specifying fatigue safety factors greater than those for trading tankers which are able to dry-dock every 5 years for extensive inspection and repairs. It will be appreciated that in the case of a tanker conversion to a ship-shaped offshore unit, fatigue safety factors closer to those for the trading tanker may usually be economically necessary; in such cases it is also common that an extensive structural integrity monitoring program will be employed in service, at least in harsh environments. Tanker conversions however are typically targeted for shorter times of on-site service than their new-build counterparts.

The FLS assessment and design should in principle be undertaken for every suspect location of fatigue cracking which includes welded joints and local areas of stress concentrations, and for all relevant loads. Although wave induced actions are primary sources of fatigue, the effects due to the following loads could also need to be considered depending on the design and circumstances, namely

- Functional loads including those related to loading and offtake of cargo;
- Wind actions, for example the effect of vortex induced vibrations and vortex shedding;
- Slamming actions;
- Sloshing actions;
- Local action effects arising from mooring and riser systems.

Procedures and criteria related to slamming and sloshing effects for FLS purposes are not generally well defined, and neither are these two load effects amenable to a closed form spectral fatigue method. In any event, it appears in practice that these conditions are primarily evaluated for strength, even if fatigue is sometimes said to be suspected in related failures.

While the dry-docking condition, any docking condition afloat, and any damage condition while relevant for strength assessment normally need not be considered for FLS, the calculations should address all transit conditions, e.g., tow to the field or to a shipyard for repair; and also all on-site operating conditions.

Accidental limit state design

Accidental limit states (ALS) potentially lead to a threat of serious injury or loss of life, pollution, damage and loss of property or significant financial exposure. The intention of ALS design is to ensure that the structure is able to tolerate specified accidental events and, when accidents occur, subsequently maintains structural integrity for a sufficient period under specified (usually reduced) environmental conditions to enable the following to take risk mitigation and recovery measures to take place, as relevant:

- Evacuation of personnel from the structure;
- Control of undesirable movement or motion of the structure;
- Temporary repairs;
- Safe refuge and firefighting in the case of fire and explosion;

- Minimizing outflow of cargo or other hazardous material.

Different types of accidental events may require different methodologies or different levels of refinement of the same methodology to analyze structural resistance or capacity during and following such events (demands). The ALS design is then necessarily an important part of design and operation risk assessment and management which consists of hazard identification, structural evaluation and mitigation measure development for specific types of accidents.

For ship-shaped offshore installations, accidental events such as unintended flooding (damage stability), collisions, dropped objects, fire, explosion and progressive accidental hull girder collapse must be considered.

The primary aim of the ALS design can be characterized by the following three broad objectives, namely

- To avoid loss of life in the structure or the surrounding area;
- To avoid pollution of the environment;
- To avoid loss of property or prevent significant financial exposure.

ALS considerations are necessary to achieve a design whose main safety functions are not impaired during any accidental event or within a certain time period after the accident to the necessary and acceptable degree. The ALS design criteria are normally based on limiting accidental consequences such as structural damage, health and environmental pollution. Risk mitigation for such events will take account of not only design features, but also operational measures including ceasing production; and also crew member training.

Since the structural damage characteristics and the behavior of damaged structures depend on the types of accidents, and risk perception is unique to individuals, societies and circumstances, it is not straightforward to establish universally applicable ALS design criteria. Typically, for a given type of structure, design accidental scenarios and associated acceptance criteria must be decided on the basis of particular risk assessment.

In selecting the design target ALS performance levels for such events, the approach is normally to tolerate a certain level of damage consistent with a greater aim such as survivability or minimized consequences; not to do so would result in an uneconomical structure. The main functions of the structure that should not be compromised during any accident event or within a certain time period after the accident may include the usability of escape ways; the integrity of shelter areas; and the integrity of global system structure and the environment.

For purposes of ALS design, the following three main aspects must be identified, namely

- Significant accident scenarios taking account of frequency of occurrence;
- Structural and other evaluation methods of the accident consequences;
- Relevant acceptance criteria.

Accident scenarios must reflect accidental phenomena which affect the safety of the installation and the surrounding environment in an unfavorable fashion, but must also be credible. The largest credible accident possible of a particular type is often of interest. The frequency of occurrence of the corresponding accident must fall within an acceptable range. The structural evaluation methods should be adopted so that the accident consequences can be analyzed to the needed accuracy.

While in some cases simplified approaches may often be enough, more sophisticated methodologies are in other cases necessary for analysis of the accident consequences which usually involve highly nonlinear aspects by their very nature. The acceptance criteria format depends on the accident situations to be avoided. Typical measures of the acceptance criteria include reserve stability, damage extent, quantity of oil outflow and residual load-carrying capacity for example. Required or limit values for accidental action effects (e.g., damage amount, material property change) and structural crashworthiness (e.g., energy absorption capability) are often used to represent the measure of safety level.

The ALS design format may hence be a set of deterministic rules representing acceptable safety level or some given limits to the probability of occurrence to adverse events or some specified bounds on the probability (likelihood) of consequences or some combination of these. A deterministic ALS design format may be expressible in terms of limits of deformation or energy absorption capability until the critical consequence occurs, as follows

$$w \leq w_a \quad (3a)$$

$$E_k \gamma_k \leq \frac{E_r}{\gamma_r} \quad (3b)$$

where w = factored accidental action effects (e.g., deformation, strain); w_a = allowable (factored) accidental action effects; E_k = characteristic value of kinetic energy loss due to accidental actions; E_r = characteristic value of energy absorption capability until a specified critical damage occurs; γ_k, γ_r = partial safety factors taking into account the uncertainties related to kinetic energy loss and energy absorption capability, respectively.

The partial safety factors used in Eq.(3b) may be chosen to represent one or more or perhaps even all of the following uncertainties, namely

- Natural variation of design variables;
- Modeling uncertainties of the assessment method;
- Return period of hazard event;

- Societal factors including risk perception;
- Consequences including economic factors.

In contrast to deterministic ALS design criteria, the risk based design format can be given, on the other hand, by

$$R \leq R_a \qquad (4)$$

where $R = \sum_i F_i C_i$ = risk; F_i = frequency (or likelihood) of the (i)th failure event resulting in the consequence C_i ; R_a = acceptable risk level.

Risk-based criteria are more general in nature, but usually more complex to apply than the prescriptive approaches. Risks to humans may be categorized into two main types, namely

- Individual fatality risks which are perhaps approximately the same as those typical for other occupational hazards;
- Societal fatality risks associated with frequency of accidents and hazards.

Any risk should not exceed a level defined as unconditionally intolerable, and the level of the consequences of any accident should be acceptable to the various stakeholders, primarily the owners, governments and the public. To achieve these aims within a risk based format to ALS, the well-known and general ALARP (As Low As Reasonably Practicable) technique can be applied for risk assessment.

Concluding remarks

Although the use of ship-shaped offshore units has been in existence since the late 1970s, the complexity and size of the units have been gradually increasing, and there are still many issues related to design, building and operation to be resolved for achieving the high integrity in terms of safety, health, the environment and economics / financial expenditures.

While ship-shaped offshore units are similar to trading tankers in structural geometry, they are different in a variety of ways. In particular, actions arising from environmental phenomena can be unique in each case, and subsequently their structural design concepts must be different to a large extent. Trading tankers may avoid rough weather or alter their heading in operation, but ship-shaped offshore units must be continuously located in the same area with site-specific environments; and without the ability to periodically dry-dock for the necessary inspection and maintenance. The latter is an aspect that must inevitably be reflected in some fashion in the design and long-term durability and reliability of the units concerned.

To continue further on the subject of differences from trading tankers, one should note that ship-shaped offshore units are likely to be subjected to significant environmental actions even during loading and unloading, while trading tankers are typically loaded and unloaded at still water condition in harbor. And for historical reasons, the design return period of ship-shaped offshore units is typically taken as 100 years, while that of trading tankers is considered to be 20 to 25 years or so, and so on.

The application of existing procedures, criteria and standards to the structural design of ship-shaped offshore units also requires additional thoughts and discussions. This can be particularly important for the many interface areas between the hull and topsides. Even for the hull part, shipbuilding industry standards may need to be selectively upgraded to ensure the long life and on-site reliability needed. Similarly, for the topsides part, it is often not straightforward to apply the relatively more economical shipbuilding industry standards, in part perhaps because of differences in the background, experience and culture of the operating personnel involved.

In any event, the complexities of the design are enormous, and there are many interface issues (such as those related to the interaction between hull and topsides facilities and related consistency in design information) that need to be identified up front and addressed / managed on a continuous basis.

In such a situation, direct analyses from first-principles, advanced engineering and practices are being increasingly desired for practicing engineers and academic researchers to resolve the issues that remain, reconcile differences in standards and practices, improve structural and other design procedures and criteria, in the never-ending quest for safe, reliable, yet economical structures and systems effectively designed and constructed the often demanding schedule and other constraints and challenges.

Also, many diverse international organizations in maritime industry such as IMO (International Maritime Organization), ISO (International Organization for Standardization), IACS (International Association of Classification Societies) and the industry in general are now increasingly applying the limit states design approach for both trading ships and ship-shaped offshore installations, making related knowledge and training even more relevant.

Another emerging and increasingly more important technology consists of risk-based approaches to design, operation, and human and environmental safety, with much of the same accompanying knowledge, training and familiarization needs.

Acknowledgements

The present study was undertaken at the Ship and Offshore Structural Mechanics Laboratory, Pusan National University, which is a National Research Laboratory funded by the Korea Science and Engineering Foundation (Grant No. ROA-2006-000-10239-0). The author is pleased to acknowledge their support.

References

Adhia, G.J., Pellegrino, S. and Ximenes, M.O. (2004a). "Practical considerations in the design and construction of FPSOs", Proceedings of OMAE FPSO 2004, OMAE Specialty Symposium on FPSO Integrity, OMAE FPSO'04-0090, August 30- September 2, Houston.

Adhia, G.J., Pellegrino, S., Ximenes, M.C., Awashima, Y., Kakimoto, M. and Ando, T. (2004b). "Owner and shipyard perspective on new-build FPSO contracting scheme, standards and lessons", Offshore Technology Conference, OTC 16706, Houston, May.

IACS (2006). "Common structural rules for double hull oil tankers", International Association of Classification Societies, London.

Paik, J.K., and Thayamballi, A.K. (2003). "Ultimate limit state design of steel-plated structures", John Wiley & Sons, Chichester, UK.

Paik, J.K., and Thayamballi, A.K. (2007). "Ship-shaped offshore installations: Design, building, and operation", Cambridge University Press, Cambridge, UK.

Parker, G. (1999). "The FPSO design and construction guidance manual", Reserve Technology Institute, Houston.

Table 1: Differences between trading tankers versus ship-shaped offshore units in terms of strength and fatigue design (Paik and Thayamballi 2007)

Trading tankers	Ship-shaped offshore units
Design condition – North Atlantic wave environment	Design condition – site- and tow route-specific environments
20 to 25-year return period	100-year return period
Predominantly wave actions	Currents as well as wind and wave actions
Limited number of loading/offloading cycles; loading occurs in sheltered situations	More frequent loading/offloading cycles; loading occurs with relatively more environmental effects present
Limited number of loading conditions	More number and variety of loading conditions
At open sea for about 70% time	Offshore for 100% time
Weather in any direction; rough weather avoidance possible	Highly directional weather and weathervaning; rough weather avoidance not possible once on site
Regular dry-docking every 5 years	Continuous operation usually without dry-docking
Without topsides	With topsides and associated interaction effects between hull and topsides

Table 2: Sample safety factors for fatigue limit state design of ship-shaped offshore structures

Structure	Hull			Topsides
Location	All structure excluding side connections	Side shell connections	Non-inspectable areas, e.g., off-vessel mooring components, I-tubes	Uniform throughout
Safety factor	1 for North Atlantic condition; 3 for combined transit and on-site condition	2 for North Atlantic condition; 4 for combined transit and on-site condition	10	2

Engineering Challenges in Offshore Construction Work in Conjunction with Offshore Fixed and Floating Platforms

Gengshen Liu

Aker Marine Contractors US Inc.
Houston, Texas, USA

Introduction

The increase of energy consumption and the gap between the supply and demand have driven up the price of oil and gas to an all time high. This fact leads to global increases in offshore activities, especially in the Gulf of Mexico (GOM). The trend is expected to continue for years to come. According to the Energy Information Administration (EIA), over the next 20 years Americans' demand for energy is expected to grow by 25 percent.

The offshore activities as mentioned above consist of mainly the following three categories:

1) Deepwater and ultra-deepwater field development
2) Shallow water field with deep oil and gas reserves and LNG terminals
3) Older marginal fields which become profitable

Among these activities, the importance of deepwater field development has been recognized globally. The GOM OCS (Outer Continental Shelf) plays an important role in America's domestic oil and gas production ---- 27% of domestic oil production and 20% of domestic natural gas production are from the GOM OCS. In the GOM, deepwater frontier expansion results from years of the joint industry efforts. New deepwater production systems and new deepwater field leasing activities are good proof. Deepwater projects in recent years and prospective projects in the near future are shown in Figure 1.1. According to Mineral Management Services (MMS), a total of 21 OCS lease sales are proposed in the 2007-2012 5-Year program. The leasing plan will be released in the middle of 2007.

According to MMS, within the next 5 years, offshore production will likely account for more than 40 percent of domestic oil and 25 percent of U.S. natural gas production, owing primarily to deepwater discoveries in the Gulf of Mexico.

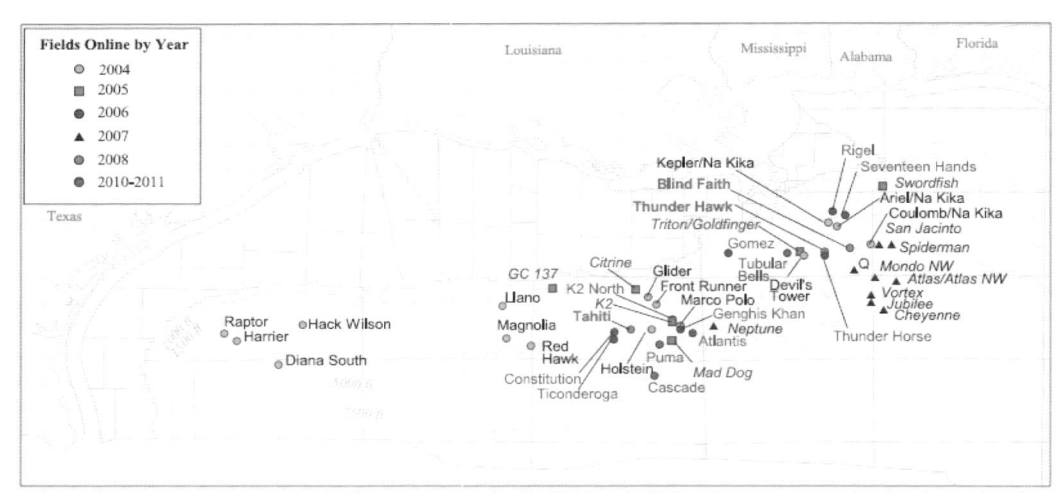

Figure 1.1 Deepwater projects that began production in 2004 and 2005 and those expected to begin production by year's end of 2011

The analysis completed for the proposed 5-year plan indicated that implementing the new program would result in the anticipated production of an additional 10 billion barrels of oil and 45 trillion cubic feet of gas, with $170 billion in net benefits for the nation over a 40-year time span.

When water depth increases and enters the ultra-deepwater range (> 5000 ft defined by MMS), various kinds of new challenges to the field development call for a step-change in new technology. The DeepStar program started 15 years ago, as the results of efforts by the oil and offshore industry, have contributed to deepwater technology development in the past years. New technology issues like deepwater riser VIV, floating platforms in 10,000 ft water depth, etc have been addressed. Now this effort is receiving a big boost from the Research Partnership to Secure Energy for America (RPSEA) organization. RPSEA contracted DeepStar to manage deepwater technology development projects — a research fund of $15 million for each year is provided.

Challenges to Offshore Industry Engineering

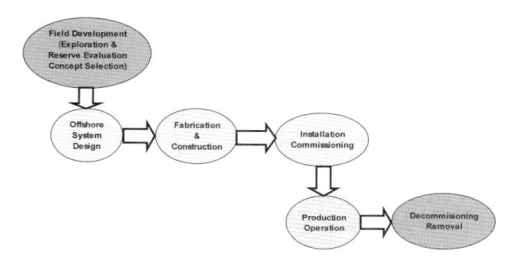

Figure 2.1 Main Stages of the Life Cycle of an Oil Field in Offshore

Figure 2.1 above shows the main stages in the life cycle of an offshore field. Strictly speaking, science and engineering of different disciplines are heavily involved at each stage for the sake of safety and cost-effectiveness. By disciplines, engineering includes geotechnical engineering, ocean engineering, naval architecture, mechanical engineering, marine engineering, structural engineering, etc.

During concept selection after the field reserve evaluation, intensive engineering activities will commence. The goal is to select and to design a new system to fit in the targeted environment and existing infrastructure to produce and transport oil and gas safely while keeping both the initial investment and operation costs at a minimum.

Challenges are more to the design of risers and station-keeping than to the hull

In the past few decades, experiences in design, construction and installation have been accumulated in making integration of platform, subsea system, risers and flow-lines. Floating production systems have conceptually become mature. Semi-submersible, Spar and TLP are well accepted by the industry and deployed in the GOM. According to MMS, in deepwater GOM (>1000 ft), there are 37 platforms and 184 subsea systems. The distribution between different offshore systems is shown in Figure 2.2.

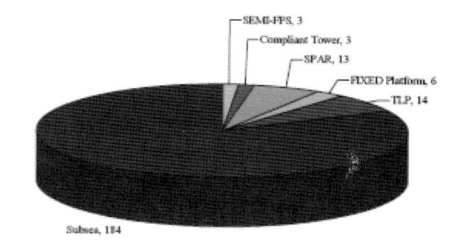

Figure 2.2 Distribution of different kinds of offshore systems

The FPSO concept may be new to GOM, but this technology has been in service in the North Sea, West Africa, Brazil area, Far East. With extremely high oil prices, early deployment of the floater becomes an important issue. Quick, conservative and robust design becomes the industry trend. It has been noticed that payload capacities for floaters to be developed for new deepwater fields are much higher.

The evolution in floater selection together with the change in environmental condition as water depth increases have more impact on the design of the risers as well as the station-keeping systems than the hull of the floaters. As the DeepStar studies show, for 10,000 ft floating platforms including semi-submersible, spar and TLP, challenges are the design of risers and mooring systems including tendons.

When water depth becomes greater or goes extremely shallow, challenges are also on the station-keeping and the riser design.

Subsea development leads to more complicated and heavier components.

The technology required to implement subsea production systems in deepwater evolved significantly in the past two decades. Subsea systems become a favorable concept in oil field development. When water depth increases at oil field, continuous efforts have been made on further technology improvement. For example, with water depth becoming greater, subsea tiebacks become longer. The longer subsea tiebacks for marginal deepwater fields pose the challenge in handling High-pressure High-temperature (HPHT) well's Shut-in Tubing Pressure (SITP). One of the new technologies under evaluation that provides alternate over-pressure protection is the High Integrity Pressure Protection System (HIPPS). It is safe to say that for deepwater and ultra-deepwater, subsea systems become more complicated, and the subsea components become larger and heavier.

Challenge to Installation is Huge

Looking at the field development trend for deepwater projects, the installation will be more difficult and expensive irrespective of the location or concept. Especially in the GOM, average time from oil discovery to production is quite short ---- less than ten years and as short as 5 years. For these kinds of fast track projects, the offshore construction issues need to be considered at the beginning of the field development and become one of the important links in the integrated efforts.

To meet the challenge, multi-dimensional efforts including step change technology, upgrading of equipment, optimization of management, etc. cannot be spared. Engineering efforts play an important role.

Engineering Plays a Very Important Role in Offshore Installation

It is commonly considered that offshore installation consists of a series of intensive operation activities. Therefore, planning, operational procedure development, coordinating and on site management are extremely important in order to accomplish the tasks in a safe and efficient manner.

During the intensive operations, which may only last a few weeks, the integrated efforts among the project managers, marine engineers, field engineers and crews are tremendous. To assure the offshore construction is safely and efficiently carried out, a thorough planning would start more than one year in advance prior to installation. Engineering involvement in supporting the planning is well recognized.

However, this is not the complete picture of the engineering involvement in offshore installation including transportation activities. The intensity of involvement of engineering design and analyses in an installation project as well as their importance may not be fully realized. Take the Blind Faith deep draft semi-submersible production platform project as an example, starting from pre-feed, engineering efforts on transportation and installation lasted more than eighteen (18) months in the following disciplines

- Naval architecture ---- stability analysis, weight management
- Hydrodynamic analysis and simulation ---- loads caused by environments and motions to structures and components to be installed and installation equipment including installation vessels
- Structural analysis and design — sea-fastening, design of temporary structure such as skid-way, sponson, local structural enhancement, etc
- Mechanical design to fit in the installation task requirements

It is evident for several reasons that offshore construction-related engineering work starts at the concept selection stage. Planning installation methodology, feasibility study, cost estimating are all involved with engineering analysis at certain levels. Some concepts may not be favored due to complexity and cost of the installation.

Installation issues need also to be addressed at the offshore system design stage. For example, if the topside of a fixed platform being installed by a single barge float-over in the future, the design of the jacket has to consider all the related requirements. Another example is the design of suction anchors ---- not only the extreme loads of the mooring legs but also the anchor loads of the installation conditions are important during the design. However the most intensive engineering activities supporting offshore transportation and installation are aimed at

- Methodology development
- Identification of weather window for various offshore operations
- Identification of capacity needs for installation equipment such as crane capacity, winch capacity, wire size, barge size, construction vessel capacity, etc
- Installation procedures for different transportation and installation tasks, such as load-out, topside and hull dry tow, deck installation, wet tow, anchor installation, mooring system hook-up, riser installation, etc
- HAZID and HAZOP interactively with risk assessment, to identify all the possible hazards **and** establish a contingency plan
- Design necessary installation equipment and supplemental structures
- Develop operation manuals to guide the in-field operation activities

For permanent offshore platforms and subsea system design, engineering work at the stage of system design focuses on safety and performance at in-place situation and fatigue life of the system. In contrast, quite often, the engineering work for installation activity needs to go through more cases to cover each step of the installation process. As will be shown later in the example of steel catenary riser (SCR) installation, analyses will not only cover the situation after the riser is hooked up to the floater, but also each step during the installation starting from pick up and then each step during the pull in and final hook up. The analyses will not only check the tension and bending stress on the riser, but will define the trajectory of the installation vessel and checking the clearance between risers, mooring lines and part of the hull structures. Simulation of the riser installation will also help in preparation of safely intermitting the installation and even laying back the riser to the sea bed for unexpected situations.

The challenges faced during installation of subsea piles, pumps, manifolds, PLET's, UTA's (umbilical termination assemblies) etc are related to the lifting and lowering operations and the met-ocean criteria. The steel wire ropes at large payout depths may well exceed the weight to be lowered. During the lowering, the harmonic excitations caused by the motions of the installation vessel can cause significant resonant amplification on the lowering systems, resulting in higher line tensions. High currents may also affect the lowering and positioning operations.

Probing by thorough engineering analyses and accurate simulations will help expose and identify all the potential problems. Transportation and installation can be carried out safely by either avoiding them or solving them through HAZID and HAZOP Safe operation is the most important aspect and is of utmost concern for the industry as any accident will be costly and lead to consequences including the damage to the installed offshore system, delay of production, risk of pollution to the environment and potential loss of lives.

At the same time, without good engineering support, one cannot expect solid installation planning and correct installation procedures. The direct consequences may include incorrect weather window defining, poor scheduling, and improper equipment identification. Once it happens, it will cause delay, repeat of work and so on leading to drastic increase in the costs. Of course, this might have safety related issues as well.

Meet Challenges in Offshore construction by Engineering Efforts

Challenges to offshore construction created by offshore frontier expanding to deeper water and activities in extreme shallow water include the following:

- Importance of loop currents and subsurface currents become greater with increasing water depth for installation operation
- Extreme shallow water at installation site
- More severe environmental conditions
- Offshore platform becomes larger and heavier
- More complicated subsea system and sea bed conditions

The new challenges result in the following:

- Tougher operation criteria such as
  - More severe operation weather conditions which will lead to narrower weather window
  - Tolerance of operation, especially clearance between structures, mating operations, etc.
  - The currents in the deep-water region cause increases in operation uncertainty. Floater behavior in extreme shallow water also brings in additional uncertain factors. These will lead to tougher operational criteria
- Reduction of operation capacity
  - Loop current and subsurface current will create difficulty to construction vessels' station-keeping capability
  - Extreme shallow water will reduce the availability of construction vessels for installation operation
  - With deepwater frontier expansion, the trip to more remote sites becomes longer
  - In ultra-deepwater, operations such as lowering will need longer wire that will reduce the construction vessel's buoyancy and also reduce the capacity of the winch in handling the lowering weight
  - Increase of offshore structure size and weight require increase of installation capacity

In summary, the new trend of the oil industry development brings about challenges that lead to an increase in the gap between the operation criteria and the existing installation capacity.

On the other hand, engineering efforts for installation operations can help:

- Create new technology or make new application of existing technology to establish new installation procedures and to increase the installation capacity. For example, for installation of heavy topside in deepwater or extreme water, availability of heavy lifting vessels (HLVs) is very low. However, applying float-over technology provides a cheaper alternate with an abundance of barges
- Equipment capacity can be increased through upgrading. For example, by careful design to replace wire by fiber rope in lowering operation, the winch capacity will be increased
- With intensive engineering simulations, loading during operation can be more accurately predicted and create opportunities of relaxing the operation weather limit
- Engineering analysis and design can help more efficiently use the existing equipment with supplementary structures or mechanical components. It may also help in creating an improved operation procedure

In summary, the engineering efforts can help in narrowing the gap between installation capacity and the operation criteria.

Success of engineering efforts heavily depends on the strength of the engineering team working on the projects. A strong engineering team is composed of engineers with strong backgrounds, intensive experiences and a unified spirit of co-operation.

Armed solely with solid engineering knowledge and accumulated practical experiences, he or she can execute more efficiently in meeting challenges. Engineers with strength in multi-disciplines are sorely needed. Therefore, it is critical for an offshore construction company to build up a capable engineering team facing various kinds of challenges.

New Challenges
- Deep / Ultra Deep Water
- Extreme Shallow Water
- Remote Location
- Loop Current / Subsurface Current Jet
- Severer Environmental Condition
- Structure with Increased Size and Weight
- More Complicated Sea Bed Conditions

Installation Capacity
- Vessel Availability
- Vessel Capacity
- On Board Equipment Capacity
- Plannning / Management
- Exacution Capability

Installation Criteria
- Minimum Operation Environment
- Safety Factor
- Tolerance
- Regulatory Codes

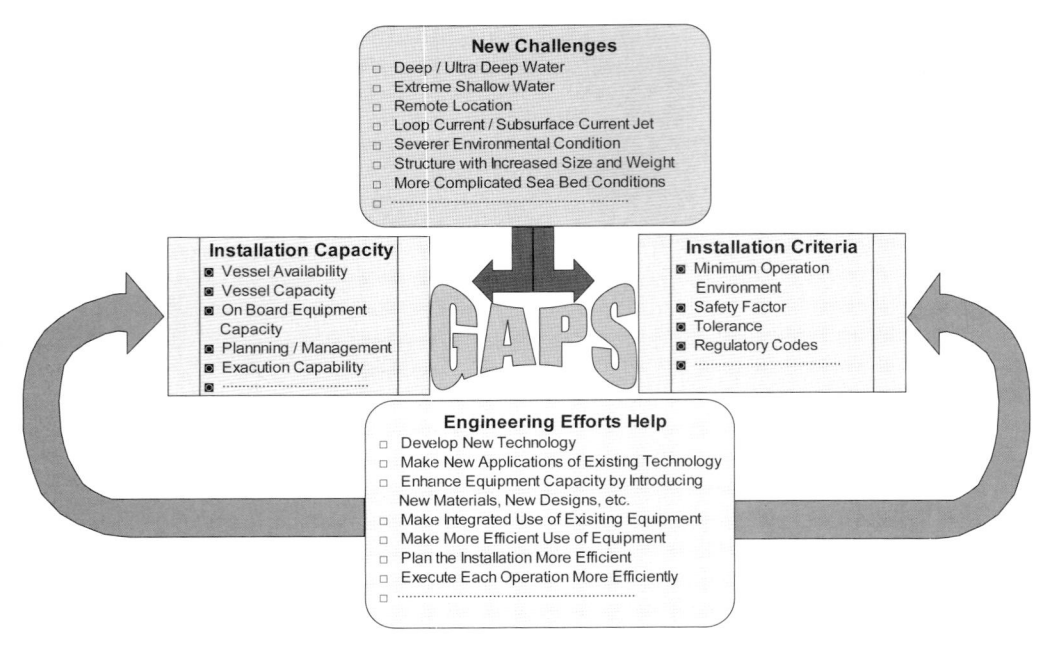

Engineering Efforts Help
- Develop New Technology
- Make New Applications of Existing Technology
- Enhance Equipment Capacity by Introducing New Materials, New Designs, etc.
- Make Integrated Use of Exisiting Equipment
- Make More Efficient Use of Equipment
- Plan the Installation More Efficient
- Execute Each Operation More Efficiently

Figure 4.1 Engineering Efforts Help Reduce Gaps between Installation Criteria and Installation Capacity

A Few Examples

In this section, a few examples are taken to show the importance of engineering efforts in offshore installation. Some of the tasks pose challenges to installation engineering. Both ultra-deepwater and extreme shallow water cases are covered.

Blind Faith Deep draft semi-submersible production platform mooring system installation

The Blind Faith deep draft semi-submersible is designed using as the anchor a chain-rope-chain system for mooring. The suction anchor is the heaviest and largest compared to the other suction piles installed in the GOM. Moreover, the installation has to be performed within the vessels crane-lifting capacity.

In order to install the eight (8) suction piles and hook up the mooring lines to the semi-submersible production platform, engineering analysis, design and model tests were conducted to help establish the following:

- Suction pile transportation and installation plan including the identification of the transportation barge, anchor layout on the deck of the barge, lifting consequence, sea fastening, anchor lowering, anchor installation, ROV operation, etc.

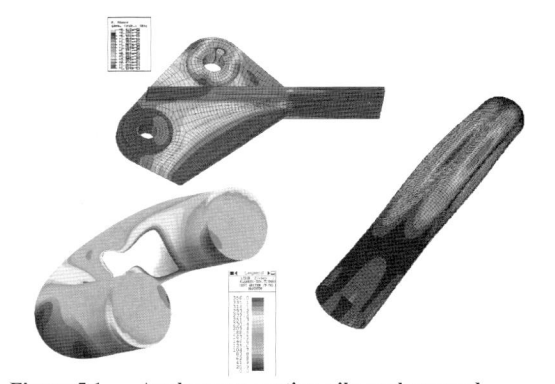

Figure 5.1   Analyses on suction pile, pad-eye and shackles for anchor installation

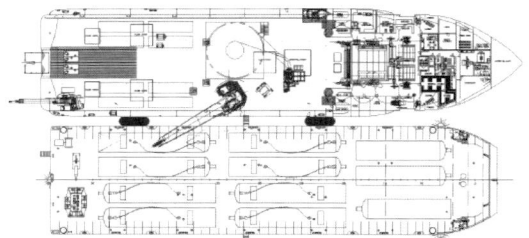

Figure 5.2   Anchor installation vessel and transportation barge

- Anchor installation contingency plan considering the tolerance on the verticality and the failure of reaching the designed penetration depth.

Geotechnical analysis and structural analyses of the suction pile were performed.

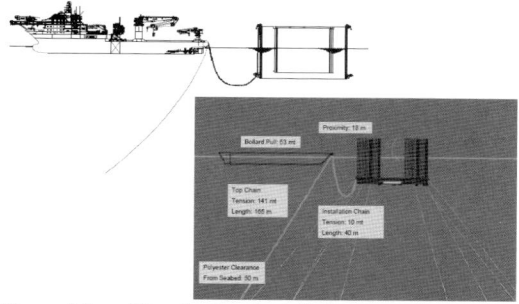

Figure 5.3 Mooring line installation procedure and simulation

- Mooring installation and hook-up method and plan including identification of the construction vessel, mooring line handling during the installation, connecting the subsea connector on the pre-installed suction piles, mooring line installation sequence, hook-up of the mooring lines, mooring line tensioning. Analyses were involved in the simulation of the mooring line loads at each step. Since the main section of each mooring line is polyester, engineers worked closely with the vendor on issues including the rope stiffness, rope fabrication length and installation length, etc. Two scenarios of rope installation – using carousel and using towing winch were evaluated.

- A mooring installation HAZID report identifying hazards and risks in mooring installation and hook-up.

- A mooring system installation manual functioning as the guide for Blind Faith mooring installation operation practices.

Without careful planning and dependable engineering analyses, successful installation cannot be guaranteed. There have been examples (in other projects) of crises of anchor installation failure, mooring line length inaccuracy and failure to meet proof loading, etc. Most of these events have been directly or indirectly related to engineering.

Blind Faith Steel Catenary Riser (SCR) Installation

In Blind Faith field, four (4) SCRs, two export pipelines and two flow lines, need to be connected to the deep draft semi-submersible platform. The SCRs are prelaid on the seabed at more than 6,000 ft water depth before the platform is towed in. How to safely pick up the pre-laid risers by the construction vessel, then pass them to the winches on the platform and hook them up to the platform becomes a challenge.

Combining past experiences, the SCR installation process is divided into several stages — picking up from the sea bed; transferring the load to the platform winch; pulling-up the riser and pulling-in the riser to the riser basket. Taking the pick-up analysis as an example, for each riser, the operation is simulated via multiple steps. The distance between the riser head and sea bottom as well as the length of the segment hanging in the water are different for each step. Correspondingly, the position of the construction vessel and the pulling load also vary. The simulation focuses on the following:

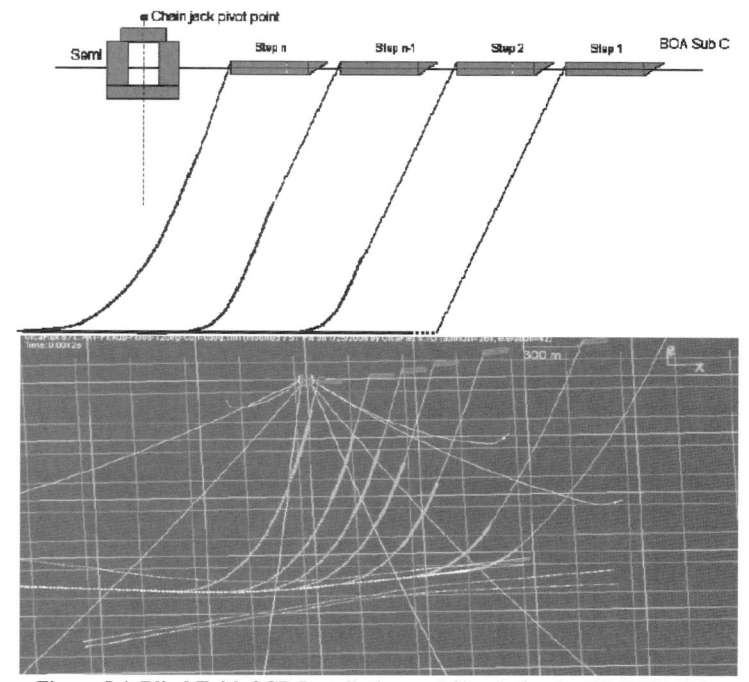

Figure 5.4 Blind Faith SCR Installation and Simulation by ORCAFLEX

- Installation equipment capacity (vessel DP system, vessel winch, pickup wire, pulling chain and chain jack, etc.)
- Safe clearance between the pickup wire and platform mooring lines / already installed risers
- Safe clearance between the pulling chain / riser and riser basket
- Safe clearance between the pulling chain / riser and topside deck cut-outs
- Integrity of risers (tension force, bending strain/stress, buckling, etc.)

Obviously, analysis corresponding to each step becomes an analysis case with specific modeling parameters. For each case there are several different combinations of the environmental conditions. Therefore, based on the steps defined an analysis case matrix is established.

In addition to the riser simulation, naval architectural work is also involved to set up the ballast procedure for the platform being tilted during the riser pull-in to make the installation safe and smooth.

The engineering efforts mentioned above help with the following:
- Identify installation capacity needs — riser pulling winch, pulling wire
- Riser installation plan — construction vessel motion trajectory and speed, ROV assistance, clearance tolerance, installation sequence, etc
- HAZID and HAZOP
- Riser installation manual

The riser pick-up and pull-in simulation also provided the load for the pull head design.

A Shallow Water Example ---- Offshore Lifting Using Strain Jack

It is an LNG terminal installation project ---- to install the LNG tank and topside module of offshore concrete GBS (gravity based structure) LNG terminal. Both the topside and the tank are built in an onshore yard. Since the towing channel is shallow, dredging is necessary if the topside is installed on the tank before towing. However, the cost impact due to the hard soil condition is significant if one chooses to dredge the GBS towing channel deeper (could be more than a million US$ per foot depth).

The better choice is to tow out the GBS tank without LNG tank and top-side module installed, and then mate them in the offshore site. However, a crane vessel is not available for the execution. In this case, strand jack lifting system as shown in figures below is a good option.

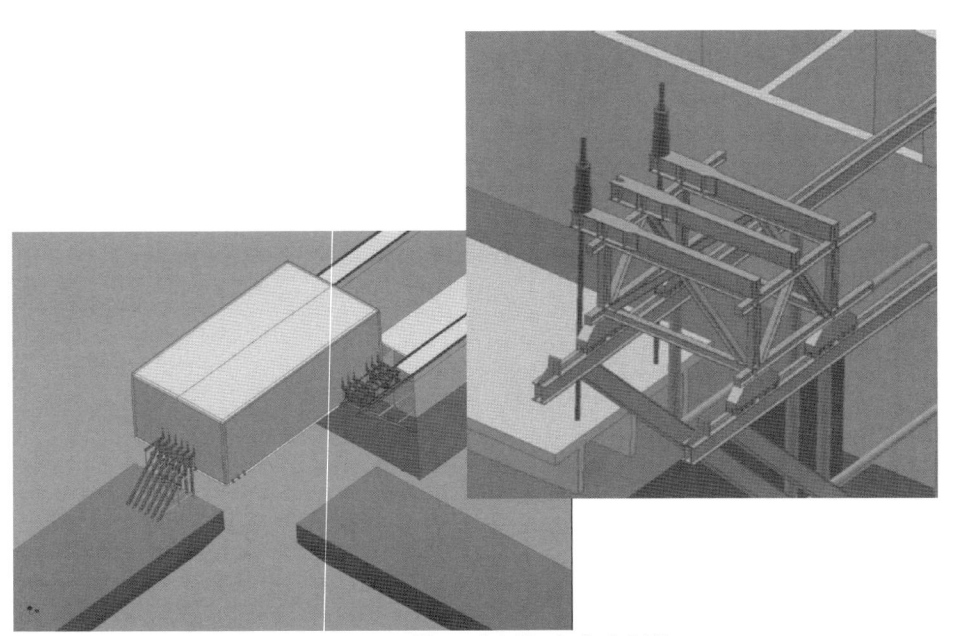

Figure 5.4 Strain Jack Lifting

This can be taken as new application of existing technology. To make the strain jack lifting work, the following engineering approach is necessary:

- Perform hydrodynamic analysis to predict the relative motion between barges and the barge motion at the moment of lifting commencement
- Perform structural analysis to predict impact loads at the moment of lifting commencement
- Design shock-cell to take impact loads
- Design the strain jack system based on the lifting needs

- Design the support structure of strain jack, including strain jack support frame and railway girder.

Of course, the analysis results will also help establish the plan for lifting operation using the designed strain jack system, identify the hazards and develop an operation manual correspondingly.

Sakhalin II Phase 2 Project Concrete Gravity Base Structure (CGBS) Installation

The construction of the CGBS ---- LunA and PA-B, each consists of a large concrete caisson base with four legs to support the topside facilities, was started in June 2004.

The Lunskoye CGBS, as an example, has a total weight of 103,000 tonnes. The base is 105 meters by 88 meters and 13.5 meters high. The diameter of each leg measures more than 20 meters at the base and they are some 56 meters high. Total height of the entire structure is 69.5 meters. The water depth is 48 meters.

The installation process was a delicate operation requiring skill from the engineers controlling the flooding of the base caisson of the structure, and the marine teams on the tugs that maintain the structure in position as it is lowered.

Figure 5.5 CGBS Lun-A Touch Down at the Site

During the installation, the structure is kept at its positive GM by having part of one side of the pontoon box above water during ballasting and tilting further until the other side of the pontoon reached the seafloor. The seafloor then supported the structure so that it was controlled during the critical pontoon submergence phase.

The pontoon was subdivided into several compartments. The ballast system and ballast procedure was prepared so that only sluicing was required to control the structure during the submergence operation. No pumps were installed for the purpose of installing the structure; hence the ballast sequences were pre-calculated so that no correction by pumping was necessary. The requirement to correct ballast and stability calculations and follow up of the actual operation was therefore crucial.

The piping system was, however, prepared for future installation of pumps for retrieval of the structure when it shall be removed some time in the far future.

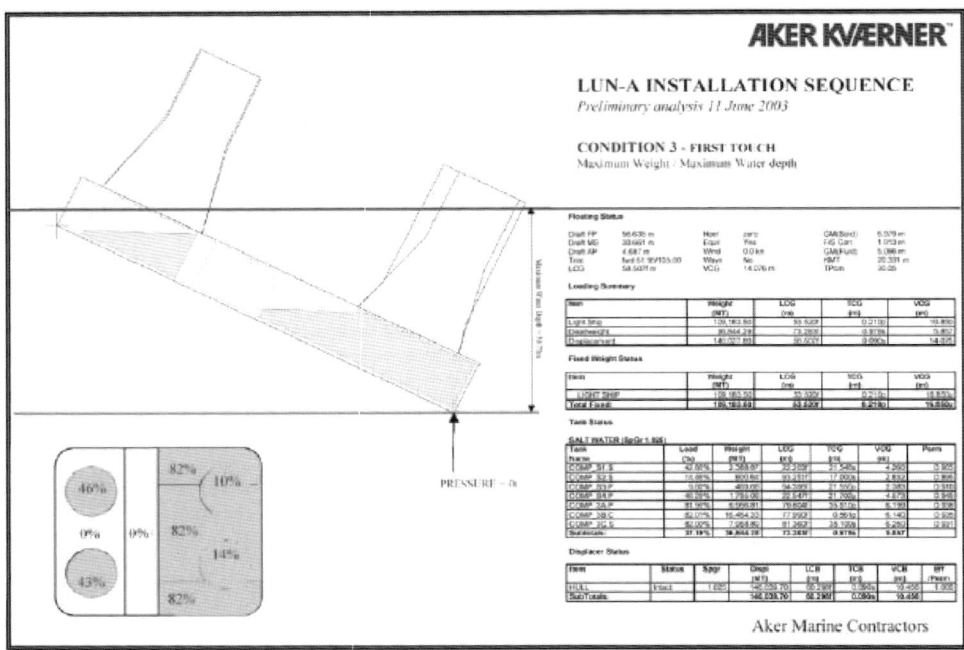

Figure 5.6　　Development of Installation Procedure by Engineering Simulation

The near-perfect operation lasted only 4 days. However, it can be seen that the engineering efforts by naval architects and operation engineers in preparing the flooding process are of tremendous importance.

Conclusion

The increases in offshore activities globally, especially in the Gulf of Mexico (GOM) lead to offshore industry expanding the frontier to deep and ultra-deepwater. At the same time the LNG terminals are often sited at extremely shallow water.

This industry trend brings about challenges to offshore field development as well as offshore installation. New challenges result in the increase of the gap between the operation criteria and the existing installation capacity. To meet the challenges, engineering efforts with intensive analyses and design will help reduce the gap by introducing new technology or making new application of existing technology as well as enhancing the installation capacity and improving operation efficiency.

References

[1] EIA, "Annual Energy Outlook 2007 With Projections to 2030", U.S. Department of Energy, Washington, DC 20585, 2007

[2] MMS, "OCS Five-Year Oil and Gas Leasing Program", www.mms.gov, February, 2007

[3] French, L, et al. (2006), "Deepwater Gulf of Mexico 2006: America's Expanding Frontier", OCS Report MMS 2006-022, New Orleans, May 2006

[4] Sakhalin Energy Investment Company Ltd., "Construction Site for Sakhalin II Phase 2 Concrete Gravity Base Structures Officially Opened", PRESS RELEASE, Yuzhno-Sakhalinsk, Sakhalin Island, June 2004:

[5] Sakhalin Energy Investment Company Ltd., "Russia's First Offshore Concrete Gravity Platform Begins Journey to Sakhalin", PRESS RELEASE, Yuzhno-Sakhalinsk, Sakhalin Island, June 2005:

[6] Sakhalin Energy Investment Company Ltd., "Russia's first concrete gravity base platform structure successfully installed in the Lunskoye gas field", PRESS RELEASE, Yuzhno-Sakhalinsk, Sakhalin Island, July 2005:

Extreme Load and Fatigue Damage on FPSO in Combined Waves and Swells

Booki Kim, Xiaozhi Wang, Yung-Sup Shin

Research and Product Development Department, Corporate Technology, American Bureau of Shipping
Houston, Texas, U.S.A.

Abstract

This paper provides information about the criteria to be used for predicting the extreme load and fatigue damage on an FPSO (Floating Production, Storage and Offloading) system in complicated wave conditions in areas such as those of West Africa and Offshore Brazil where both sea and swells exist and propagate in different directions. The analysis criteria for predicting the extreme response applicable to an FPSO at an intended site and in transit conditions are presented. More importantly, various stress cycle counting methods have been utilized for accurate fatigue damage prediction of the FPSO structural components under the combined waves and swells. The random loading due to the combined waves and swells is assumed to be a combination of two narrow-banded Gaussian processes. The resultant fatigue damage due to the waves and swells is then evaluated by introducing the appropriate stress cycle counting correction. Utilizing the environmental data, which include swells and waves propagating in different directions, the analysis results of extreme load response and fatigue damage calculations are presented. The background information about the analysis results is provided.

Keywords

Extreme load response; Fatigue damage; FPSO; Combined waves and swells; Stress cycle counting correction.

Introduction

In the design of offshore structures, a rational structural assessment is demanded to ensure necessary structural integrity throughout their service life. This process involves the evaluation of extreme loads and fatigue damages exerted from the environmentally-induced responses. In the design of FPSOs, the site-specific wave environment should be properly taken into account for each design analysis. The wave conditions in recent FPSO applications are very complicated, in noted area such as those of West Africa and Offshore Brazil where both waves and swells exist and propagate in different directions. Because of these conditions, the traditional approach cannot be directly applied. Therefore, the enhanced approach that can handle the complicated wave conditions has been demanded. This paper provides information about the criteria to be used for predicting the extreme load responses and fatigue damages on FPSOs in such complicated wave conditions.

Traditionally, there have been two approaches in predicting extreme load responses, the choice depending upon how the severity of the sea states is accounted for: a short-term approach based on the selected design sea state and a long-term approach based on various sea states during the design life. Ochi (1981) claimed that estimation through the long-term approach is superior to that through the short-term prediction approach because it deals with the accumulation of all responses. However, in reality, the relatively mild sea states that account for a considerable percentage in wave scatter diagrams do not contribute to the extreme value. In most situations, therefore, the extreme value obtained through the short-term approach is very close to that obtained through the long-term approach. We may apply these two classic approaches to predict the extreme response applicable to FPSOs. Then, the maximum response based on the extreme values obtained through the two approaches can be chosen for strength assessment.

For fatigue damage calculation of FPSO structural components under the combined waves and swells, it has been known that the simple summation of fatigue damages from each contribution gives non-conservative results. Therefore, it has been recommended to introduce an alternative approach, which requires introduction of appropriate stress cycle counting correction in fatigue damage accumulation. Under the assumption that the random loading due to the combined waves and swells is a combination of two narrow-banded Gaussian processes, the various stress cycle counting correction methods have been exploited in this paper. To name a few, these include Rice (1954), Wirsching and Light (1980), Dirlik (1985) and Jiao & Moan (1990). Utilizing the wave data that includes swells and waves propagating in different directions, the analysis results depending on the stress cycle counting correction methods are presented. Some sensitivity studies are conducted to examine the effect of the cycle counting correction on fatigue damage calculation.

Also, the influence of wave and swell directionality is further investigated.

Spectral Formulation

Knowledge of winds, waves, currents, tides and other environmental factors is crucial for the design of offshore structures, especially for a floating structure like an FPSO. There are numerous texts that provide information on ocean waves and its statistical parameters that are used to define the sea states. A sea state can be characterized with a spectral formulation that is comprised of numerous individual wave components.

The design sea state may come from intensification of the local wind-generated waves (sea) and/or swell propagating with different directions. In general, both are statistically independent. The wind seas are often characterized with the Bretschneider or the JONSWAP spectrum while the Gaussian distribution function can be used to describe swells. The spectral formulation for the swell in Guassian-swell spectrum is represented as follows:

$$S_\eta(\omega) = \frac{(H_s/4)^2}{\gamma\sqrt{2\pi}} \exp\left[-\frac{(\omega-\omega_p)^2}{2\gamma^2}\right] \quad (1)$$

where H_s is the significant wave height, γ ($= 2\pi\delta$) is the parameter for Gaussian spectral width, ω_p is the modal (peak) frequency corresponding to the highest peak of the spectrum, ω is the circular wave frequency.

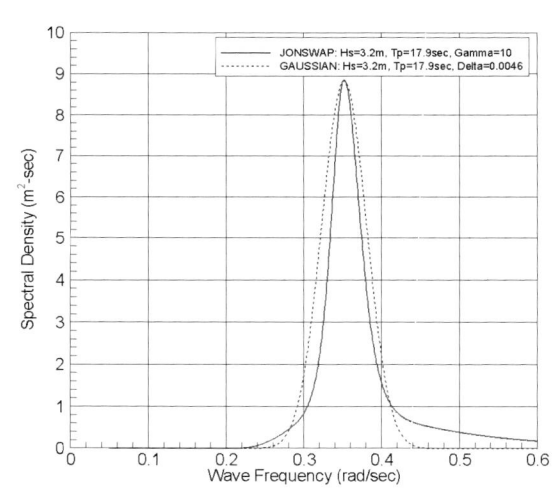

Fig. 1: JONSWAP and Gaussian-swell spectra

It is noted that the Gaussian-swell spectrum is symmetrical with respect to the modal frequency; therefore, the following relationship between the wave periods is valid:

$$T_1 = T_z = T_p \quad (2)$$

where T_1 is the mean wave period, T_z is the average zero up-crossing wave period, and T_p is the modal (peak) period corresponding to the highest peak of the spectrum. For comparison purposes, the spectral shapes of the JONSWAP and Gaussian-swell spectra have been computed, and the result is plotted in Fig. 1.

In order to cover a variety of shapes of wave spectra associated with the growth and decay of a storm, including the existence of swell, the Ochi-Hubble 6-parameter spectrum may be used.

Extreme Load Response

For a random process encountered in the field of ocean engineering, it is often necessary to predict the most probable extreme value of a random variable in the process. For example, prediction of the largest motions and wave-induced loads, etc., is essential for design of offshore structures. Preference is given to an extreme value method that follows the so-called long-term approach commonly used for ships and offshore structures. However, the use of a validated short-term extreme value approach, which is appropriate to the vessel type and installation site's environmental data, can also be considered. The supplementary use of such a short-term approach to confirm or test the sensitivity of the long-term based design values is encouraged. The procedure for calculating the value corresponding to a particular return period across a combined scatter-diagram-heading distribution of sea states is described below:

For each entry in the wave scatter diagram and each heading, we can determine the spectral moment of the response spectra. The variance (zeroth moment) of a response spectrum can be generalized to include the direction of vessel heading relative to the predominant wave direction and wave-spreading angle.

The other spectral moments can be also generalized in a similar manner over the wave-spreading angle. The average zero up-crossing rate for a Gaussian process is then given by

$$\bar{n} = \frac{1}{4\pi}\left(\frac{1+\sqrt{1-\varepsilon^2}}{\sqrt{1-\varepsilon^2}}\right)\sqrt{\frac{m_2}{m_0}} \quad (3)$$

where the bandwidth parameter ε is given by

$$\varepsilon = \sqrt{1 - \frac{m_2^2}{m_0 m_4}} \quad (4)$$

The spectral moments are calculated from the integration of the frequency components:

$$m_n = \int_0^\infty \omega^n |H_i(\omega)|^2 S_\eta(\omega) d\omega \quad n=0, 1, 2, 3 \quad (5)$$

where $|H_i(\omega)|$ is the transfer function of the load response. For any scatter-diagram-heading contribution, the number of response cycles will be calculated during the design lifetime. The contribution that any one scatter-diagram-heading contribution makes to the long-term exceedance distribution of the response is then the sum of Gaussian distributions multiplied by the normalized number of response cycles, so that the long-term probability that the response will exceed a particular value $\bar{x}$ is calculated from the equation

$$\frac{\sum_{m}\sum_{k}\bar{n}p_{m}p_{k}p_{\bar{x}}(\bar{x})}{\sum_{m}\sum_{k}\bar{n}p_{m}p_{k}} = \frac{1}{N} = Q \qquad (6)$$

where the sum over m and k is over the entire set of scatter diagram and wave heading contributions; $\bar{n}$ is the number of response cycles that will be experienced for each scatter-diagram entry at each heading; p_m is the probability of occurrence from the wave scatter table; and p_k is the weighing factor for heading to waves from the wave rosette in a given site area. The Gaussian (normal) distribution for probability of exceedance $p_{\bar{x}}(\bar{x})$ is given by

$$p_{\bar{x}}(\bar{x}) = 1 - \frac{2}{1+\sqrt{1-\varepsilon^2}}[-\frac{1}{2}(1-\sqrt{1-\varepsilon^2})$$
$$+ \Phi(\frac{\bar{x}}{\varepsilon\sqrt{m_0}}) - \sqrt{1-\varepsilon^2}\exp\{-\frac{1}{2}(\frac{\bar{x}}{\sqrt{m_0}})^2\} \qquad (7)$$
$$\times \{1 - \Phi(-\frac{\sqrt{1-\varepsilon^2}}{\varepsilon}\frac{\bar{x}}{\sqrt{m_0}})\}]$$

where

$$\Phi(u) = \frac{1}{\sqrt{2\pi}}\int_{-\infty}^{u}\exp(-\frac{u^2}{2})du \qquad (8)$$

For the narrow-banded case ($\varepsilon=0$), the exceedance distribution function for the peak values becomes a Rayleigh distribution. To determine the probability level corresponding to the design life time, the total number of response peaks N expected in the design lifetime T (years) is to be calculated from the following formula:

$$N = T \times 365 \times 24 \times 3600 \times \sum_{m}\sum_{k}\bar{n}p_{m}p_{k} \qquad (9)$$

where T is the total exposure time in years to seas. The values of $\bar{x}$ that satisfy Eq. (6) are those corresponding to this long-term probability of exceedance. For numerical implementation, we take log10 of both hand sides of Eq. (6) and then the Newton-Raphson method is applied to find the extreme value $\bar{x}$ at the corresponding probability level.

In the specific site, the environmental condition may be described as a combination of swell and wind seas (waves) as shown in Fig. 2. In this case, assuming waves and swells are statistically independent of each other, the two response spectra can be added to derive the equivalent spectra and then the root mean square value (or standard deviation) of the combined spectrum can be determined from

$$\sqrt{m_0} = \sigma_c = \sqrt{\sigma_{wave}^2 + \sigma_{swell}^2} \qquad (10)$$

This procedure is a so-called "combined spectrum method" and tends to be rational in evaluating the long-term extreme response calculation compared to the simple summation in which the long-term extreme values from the two processes are simply added.

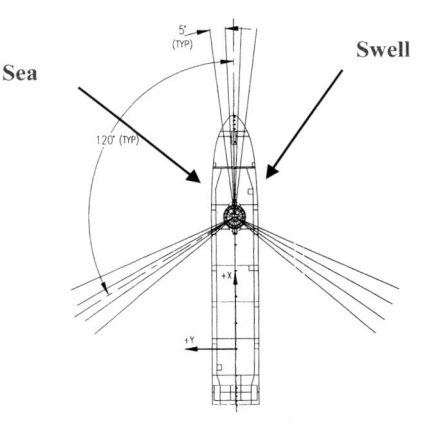

Fig. 2: FPSO under waves and swells with different directionality

Fatigue Damage

Stress Transfer Function

For fatigue damage calculation, the stress transfer function should be first determined from the load transfer function and its corresponding stress factor. The stress factor is defined as a conversion factor to obtain the stress transfer function from the load transfer function. The stress factor can be simply multiplied by the load transfer function to obtain the stress transfer function. The load transfer functions are the typical output of the seakeeping analysis program, and depend on hull form geometry, vessel speed, wave heading angle and frequency. The stress factor can be obtained through structural analysis techniques, which can be either a simple beam theory or finite element analysis procedures. The sophistication of the structural analysis needed depends on the physical system to be analyzed, the type of structural detail and the type of structural loading considered. For the application here, the stress factors are calculated by the simple beam theory, as described below:

The stress transfer function due to vertical bending moment can be calculated by

$$H_{VBM}^{\sigma}(\alpha,\omega) = \frac{H_{VBM}}{I_Y}(z-z_N) \qquad (11)$$

where H_{VBM} is the transfer function of wave-induced vertical bending moment; I_Y is the moment of inertia of hull cross section about transverse axis; and $(z-z_N)$ is the vertical distance from horizontal neutral axis of hull cross section to the structural member in consideration.

The stress transfer function due to horizontal bending moment is expressed by

$$H_{HBM}^{\sigma}(\alpha,\omega) = \frac{H_{HBM}}{I_Z}(y-y_N) \qquad (12)$$

where H_{HBM} is the transfer function of wave-induced horizontal bending moment; I_Z is the hull section moment of inertia about the vertical neutral axis; and (y-

y_N) is the horizontal distance from vertical neutral axis to the member in consideration.

The stress transfer function due to dynamic external wave pressure can be approximated by

$$H^\sigma_{PEX}(\alpha,\omega) = K_n \frac{H_{PEX}}{Z_S} \qquad (13)$$

where K_n is the stress concentration factor for an unsymmetrical stiffener on the laterally loaded panel; $H_{PEX} = f \cdot P_{ex} s l^2 / 12$; f is the factor for pressure corrections due to different pressure point compared to the hydrodynamic panel-location used in seakeeping calculation and stretching due to intermittent wetting if necessary; P_{ex} is the transfer function of external wave pressure; s is the stiffener spacing; l is the effective span of stiffener; and Z_S is the effective section modulus of the longitudinal stiffener.

The stress transfer function due to dynamic internal tank pressure can be approximated by

$$H^\sigma_{PIN}(\alpha,\omega) = K_n \frac{H_{PIN}}{Z_S} \qquad (14)$$

where $H_{PIN} = f \cdot P_{IN} s l^2 / 12$ and $P_{IN} = P_{INx} + P_{INy} + P_{INz} = \rho(a_l h_x + a_t h_y + a_v h_z)$ is the transfer function of internal tank pressure, where the accelerations are calculated at the center of gravity of the tank in consideration. The pressure heads, h_x, h_y and h_z, are the longitudinal, transverse and vertical distances from the structural location to the center of the free surface, respectively; ρ is the density of the liquid in the tank; and a_l, a_t and a_v are the longitudinal, horizontal and vertical accelerations of the tank calculated at the center of gravity of the tank, respectively.

The transfer function of the total stress in complex number notation can then be obtained by simply adding the transfer functions of the component stresses as described above. Therefore, a set of the stress transfer functions can be generated at the vessel speed, water depth, wave headings and frequencies under consideration. The response spectra for the stress transfer functions can then be determined by given wave spectra. Considering the stress distributions for the various sea states in the scatter diagram, the long-term extreme values of the total and component stresses can be obtained.

Closed-Form Damage Expression

In the "short-term closed form" approach, the stress range is normally expressed in terms of probability density functions for different short-term intervals corresponding to the individual cells (or bins) of the wave scatter diagram. These short-term probability density functions are derived by a spectral approach based on the Rayleigh distribution method whereby it is assumed that the variation of stress is a narrow-banded random Gaussian process. For all one-segment linear S-N curves, the closed form expression of damage, D is then given as follows (ABS, 2003):

$$D = \frac{T}{K}(2\sqrt{2})^m \Gamma(m/2+1) \sum_i \lambda(m,\varepsilon_i) f_{0i} p_i (\sigma_i)^m \qquad (15)$$

where T is total target fatigue life, K and m are physical parameters describing the S-N curve, $\sigma_i = \sigma_c$ is the root mean square value of the stress amplitude at the i-th sea state as in Eq. (10), f_{0i} is the zero up-crossing frequency of the stress amplitude at the i-th sea state, and p_i is the probability of the i-th sea state in the wave scatter diagram.

For bi-linear S-N curves where the negative slope changes at point $Q = (S_q, 10^6)$ from m to $m' = m + \Delta m$ ($\Delta m > 0$) and the constant K changes to K′, the expression for damage is as follows:

$$D = \frac{T}{K}(2\sqrt{2})^m \Gamma(m/2+1) \sum_i \lambda(m,\varepsilon_i) \mu_i f_{0i} p_i (\sigma_i)^m \qquad (16)$$

where μ_i is the endurance factor having its value between 0 and 1 and measuring the contribution of the lower branch to the damage. It is defined as:

$$\mu_i = 1 - \frac{\int_0^{S_q} S^m g_i ds - \left(\frac{K}{K'}\right)\int_0^{S_q} S^{m+\Delta m} g_i ds}{\int_0^\infty S^m g_i ds} \qquad (17)$$

If g(S) is a Rayleigh distribution, then μ_i is given by

$$\mu_i = 1 - \frac{\gamma(m/2+1, v_i) - (1/v_i)^{\Delta m/2} \gamma(m'/2+1, v_i)}{\Gamma(m/2+1)} \qquad (18)$$

where $v_i = (1/8)[S_q/\sigma_i]^2$, $\Gamma(.)$ and $\gamma(,)$ denote the gamma function and incomplete gamma function, respectively. Here, λ is a stress cycle correction factor that is applied when a narrow banded assumption is not valid for the stress process. In many situations, the counting correction factor proposed by Wirsching and Light (1980) has been widely used.

Combination of high frequency and low frequency responses

When the process that induces variable stresses in a structural detail contains wave-frequency (waves) and low-frequency (swells) components, the process is considered to be broad-banded. Although the Wirsching and Light's rainflow counting correction can be applied to account for a broad band process, the formulas are calibrated only to a wave frequency process.

When wave-frequency and low-frequency stress responses are obtained separately, simple summation of fatigue damage from the two frequency bands does not count the effects of simultaneous occurrence of the two frequency bands processes. This method is, therefore, non-conservative and should not be adopted.

There is an alternative method, which is both conservative and easy to use, that is known as the combined spectrum method. In this method the stress spectra for the two frequency bands are combined. The root mean square value and the mean up-crossing frequency of the combined stress process are given, respectively, as

$$\sigma_c = (\sigma_w^2 + \sigma_\ell^2)^{1/2} \tag{19}$$

$$f_{0c} = (f_{0w}^2 \sigma_w^2 + f_{0\ell}^2 \sigma_\ell^2)^{1/2} / \sigma_c \tag{20}$$

where σ_w is the root mean square value of the stress components due to waves, σ_ℓ is the root mean square value of the low-frequency stress components due to swells, f_{0w} is the mean up-crossing frequency of the wave-frequency (waves) stress components, and $f_{0\ell}$ is the mean up-crossing frequency of the low-frequency (swells) stress components

For each sea state, the fatigue damage for the combined wave-frequency and low-frequency process is obtained by substituting the above quantities for the combined process into the closed-form formula of spectral fatigue.

Cycle Counting Correction

It has been known that the Rayleigh stress distribution results in the conservative estimation of the fatigue damage when a random process is wide-banded. Therefore, the cycle correction factor in damage calculation should be introduced to reduce the conservatism due to the narrow-banded assumption. Some available theoretical approximations to calculate the correction factor are presented below:

Rice (1954)

For a general wide-banded Gaussian process, a theoretical approximation to the cycle correction factor can be found. According to Rice (1954) distribution, the correction factor can be derived as

$$\lambda(m,\alpha) = \frac{1+\alpha}{2}\left[1 + \frac{\sqrt{1-\alpha^2}-\alpha}{2\sqrt{\pi}\alpha}(1-\alpha^2)^{\frac{m+1}{2}}\frac{\Gamma(\frac{m+1}{2})}{\Gamma(\frac{m}{2}+1)}\right] \tag{21}$$

where the regularity factor α is defined as

$$\alpha = \sqrt{1-\varepsilon^2}$$

This formula may not be accurate for general cases because the regularity factor α is only considered to represent the random wide-banded process.

Wirsching and Light (1980)

Based on the results of the Monte Carlo simulation, Wirshing and Light (1980) proposed an empirical approximation for the damage correction factor as follows:

$$\lambda(m,\varepsilon) = a(m) + [1-a(m)][1-\varepsilon]^{b(m)} \tag{22}$$

where

$a(m) = 0.926 - 0.033m$

$b(m) = 1.587m - 2.323$

This formula is useful in obtaining less conservative results of fatigue damage calculation for a wide-banded random process. However, it may have its limitations for bimodal sea state applications since it is based on limited simulation with four types of spectra.

Dirlik (1985)

Based on extensive computer simulations, Dirlik (1985) suggested a combination of an exponential and two Rayleigh distributions for the stress range probability density function as follows:

$$f_{\Delta\sigma}(S) = \frac{1}{2\sqrt{m_0}}\left[\frac{D_1}{Q}\exp(-\frac{S}{2\sqrt{m_0}Q}) + \frac{D_2 S}{2\sqrt{m_0}R^2}\exp(-\frac{S^2}{8m_0 R^2})\right.$$
$$\left. + \frac{D_3 S}{2\sqrt{m_0}}\exp(-\frac{s}{8m_0})\right]$$

where

$$D_1 = \frac{2(x_m - \alpha^2)}{1+\alpha^2}, \quad D_2 = \frac{1-\alpha-D_1+D_1^2}{1-R}, \quad D_3 = 1 - D_1 - D_2$$

$$Q = \frac{1.25(\alpha - D_3 - D_2 R)}{D_1}, \quad R = \frac{\alpha - x_m - D_1^2}{1 - \alpha - D_1 + D_1^2}$$

$$x_m = \frac{m_1}{m_0}\sqrt{\frac{m_2}{m_4}}$$

Then, the correction factor can be derived as

$$\lambda(m,\alpha) = D_1\left(\frac{Q}{\sqrt{2}}\right)^m \frac{\Gamma(m+1)}{\Gamma(\frac{m}{2}+1)} + \left(\frac{R}{\sqrt{2}}\right)^m D_2 + D_3 \tag{23}$$

It is noted that this formula requires four spectral moment calculations.

Jiao and Moan (1990)

Jiao and Moan (1990) derived a formula for stress cycle correction factor for a combination of a high- and low-frequency narrow-banded Gaussian processes with assumption of well-separated spectra:

$$\lambda = \frac{v_p}{v_c}\left[\lambda_\ell^{m/2+2}\left(1-(\lambda_w/\lambda_\ell)^{1/2}\right) + (\pi\lambda_w\lambda_\ell)^{1/2}\frac{m\Gamma(m/2+1/2)}{\Gamma(m/2+1)}\right]$$
$$+ \frac{v_w}{v_c}\lambda_w^{m/2} \tag{24}$$

where

$$v_p = \lambda_\ell v_\ell[1 + \frac{\lambda_w}{\lambda_\ell}(\frac{v_w}{v_\ell}\delta_w)^2]^{1/2}$$

$$v_c = (\lambda_\ell v_\ell^2 + \lambda_w v_w^2)^{1/2}$$

$$\lambda_\ell = \sigma_\ell^2/\sigma_c^2$$

$$\lambda_w = \sigma_w^2/\sigma_c^2$$

$$v_\ell = \left(\frac{m_{2,\ell}}{m_{0,\ell}}\right)^{1/2}$$

$$v_w = \left(\frac{m_{2,w}}{m_{0,w}}\right)^{1/2}$$

$$\delta_w = \left(1 - \frac{m_{1,w}^2}{m_{0,w} m_{2,w}}\right)^{1/2}$$

Here, $m_{i,w}$ and $m_{i,\ell}$ are i-th-order spectral moment due to waves and swells, respectively.

It is noted that λ=1 for λ_l=1 or λ_w=1, which is the case for a narrow-banded spectrum. For small v_w/v_l values, it may lead to λ>1 for large λ_l, which is an incorrect result.

Results and Discussions

Subject Vessel

The seakeeping analysis was performed for a tanker-shaped FPSO of 316m in length. The full load condition was considered, and the load transfer functions were obtained from the seakeeping program PRECAL (MARIN, 2002), which is a three-dimensional panel code for analyzing the wave-induced rigid body motions and wave loads of a vessel in regular waves. The real and imaginary values of the transfer functions for vertical and horizontal bending moments, external wave pressure and acceleration components at the center of gravity of the tanks are obtained. To calculate the fatigue damage for the end longitudinal connections in midship cargo and ballast tanks, as shown in Fig. 2, the relevant stress factors were obtained from the beam theory, as described in the previous section, and then multiplied by the load transfer function to obtain the stress transfer function. The circles in Fig. 2 represent the locations of the longitudinals to be investigated for fatigue damage. The transfer function of the internal tank pressure was divided into three acceleration components with relevant pressure heads in each direction.

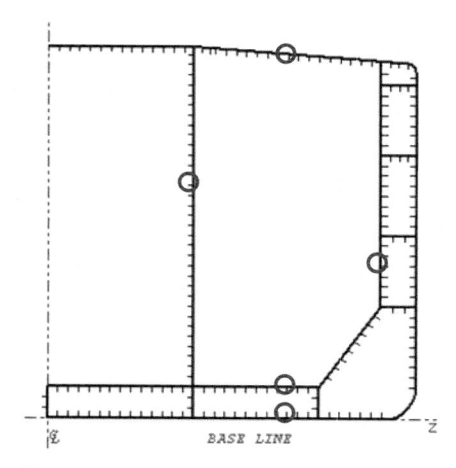

Fig. 2: Midship section with longitudinals

Sea States

In Table 1, the Gaussian-swell spectrum in combination with the JONSWAP spectrum is used to represent the bimodal sea states. This table is created to investigate the effect of bimodal sea sates on extreme loads and the stress cycle correction in the fatigue damage calculation. The subscripts 1 and 2 in the table denote individual wave components. One of the peaks is due to wind-driven seas (waves) and described with the JONSWAP spectrum. The other peak is "swells" and described with the Gaussian-swell spectra. For each component, H_s is the significant wave height, T_p is the peak period in the spectrum, γ is the JONSWAP spectral peakedness parameter, and θ is the wave/swell direction with respect to true North clockwise, and δ is the Gaussian-swell spectral width parameter. The cosine-squared (cos^2) spreading is used for the wave component while cos^4 spreading is used for the swell component. It is assumed that the subject FPSO on site is positioned towards the Northwest with 20 degrees off the true North.

Table 1: Wave scatter table to represent bimodal sea condition

Sea				Swell				%
H_{s1} (m)	T_{p1} (sec)	$θ_1$ (deg)	$γ_1$	H_{s2} (m)	T_{p2} (sec)	$θ_2$ (deg)	$δ_2$ (×10³)	
2.5	8.8	210	4.2	2.0	14.0	216	0.6	14
2.0	8.0	170	3.3	1.8	13.5	150	1.4	16
1.9	9.0	125	4.9	1.0	14.5	115	0.6	24
1.6	7.3	235	3.5	0.5	16.0	245	1.0	28
1.8	7.0	295	3.6	0.6	20.0	305	0.2	18

Basically, there are two ways to apply the combined spectrum method when the bimodal seas states exist. One is to apply the wave scatter table as given in Table 1 in a direct manner to calculate the extreme response. This approach is referred to as 'bimodal'. The other is to derive the 'equivalent' wave scatter table using the combined spectrum concept and then apply the derived table with single-peak (unimodal) spectra. For the latter approach, it is assumed that headings and peaked parameters for waves can be used to define the unimodal sea states. The 6 dynamic load parameters such as vertical bending moment (VBM) amidships, horizontal bending moment (HBM) amidships, external wave pressure port side amidships at waterline (EPP), pitch motion (PMO), roll motion (RMO), and wave height (WHT) are selected to investigate the difference of the analysis results between the two approaches. Fig.3 shows the environmental severity factors of β-type, which are defined as $β=L_S/L_U$ where L_S is the extreme value based on the intended environment (Table1) with a 100-year return period and L_U is the extreme value based on the unrestricted service in the North Atlantic with a 20-year return period. As can be seen in Table 3, the unimodal approach gives some conservatism in obtaining the extreme values of load responses.

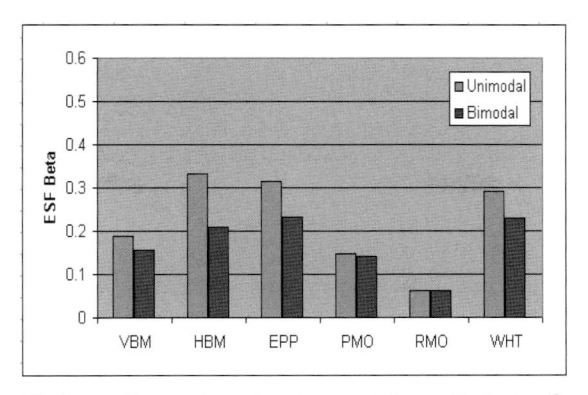

Fig. 3: Comparison of environmental severity factors β

Influence of Cycle Correction Method

To calculate the fatigue damage accurately, the appropriate stress cycle counting correction is important, especially for the multi-peak spectral case. To examine to what extent this correction would affect the fatigue damage result, a comparative study is carried out with the wave scatter table given in Table 1. The numerical results are presented in Fig. 4, which shows the environmental severity factors of α-type, which is defined as $\alpha=D_U/D_S$ where D_S is the annual fatigue damage value based on the intended environment (Table 2) and D_U is the annual fatigue damage based on the unrestricted service in the North Atlantic Ocean environment. The α values are based on the F2 S-N curve. As shown in Fig. 4, the deviations in the results are somewhat significant depending on the selected cycle correction method. It is noted that the α-factor obtained from the method of Jiao and Moan (1990) is on the conservative side compared to the other results. According to Jiao and Moan (1990), their formula is very close to the rainflow prediction in time domain and works inherently well for well-separated bimodal applications. However, it should be ensured that the calculated fatigue damage based on the method of Jiao and Moan (1990) does not exceed the one based on the Rayleigh approximation since the approximations are made within the assumption of a Gaussian process

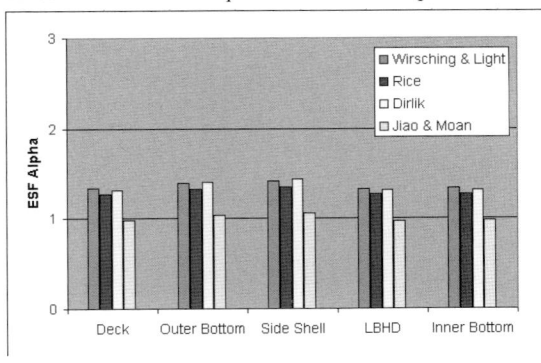

Fig. 4: Influence of cycle correction method on environmental severity factors α

Influence of Wave and Swell Directionality

The results obtained in Fig. 5 are based on the specific heading information in the corresponding wave scatter table in Table 1. To study the effect of wave directionality on the fatigue damage, the α-factor calculations with collinear heading assumption that waves and swells follow the same directionality are made. As shown in Fig. 5, the assumption of the collinear heading could overestimate the α-factors. In different situations such as a trimodal spectral case, based on our study, it could be underestimated at the same structural location. To ensure the accurate fatigue damage calculation, therefore, the accurate information of wave and swell heading directions should be properly used. The impact of wave and swell directionality could be significant in the critical structural locations.

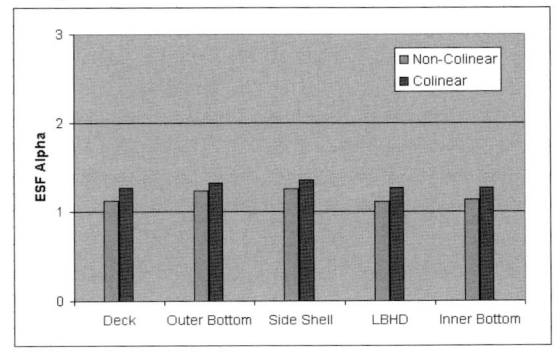

Fig. 5: Influence of wave and swell directionality on environmental severity factors α

Conclusions

The analysis criteria to be used for predicting the extreme load and fatigue damage on an FPSO in such complicated wave conditions where both waves and swells exist are presented. Several stress cycle counting correction methods available have been utilized for an accurate fatigue damage prediction of FPSO structural components under the combined waves and swells. The methodology presented in this paper can be readily extended to extreme load calculations in Dynamic Loading Approach (DLA) and fatigue damage calculations in Spectral Fatigue Analysis (SFA) for FPSO applications.

Acknowledgments

The authors wish to express their appreciation to the management of the American Bureau of Shipping for their support of this study. The authors also thank Mr. Jim Speed at ABS for proofreading the manuscript. The views expressed in this paper are those of the authors and are not necessarily those of the American Bureau of Shipping.

References

ABS (2003). *Guide for the Fatigue Assessment of Offshore Structures*, American Bureau of Shipping.

Dirlik, T. (1985). *Application of Computers in Fatigue*, Ph.D. Thesis, University of Warwick.

Jiao, G. and Moan, T. (1990). "Probabilistic Analysis of Fatigue due to Gaussian Load Processes," Probabilistic Eng Mechanics, 5(2), pp. 76-83.

PRECAL V5.0 User's Guide (2002), Maritime Research Institute (MARIN), Netherlands.

Ochi, M.K. (1981). "Principles of Extreme Value Statistics and their Application," Proc. Extreme Loads Response Symp., SNAME, pp. 15-30.

Rice, S.O. (1954). "Mathematical Analysis of Random Noise," *Selected Papers on Noise and Stochastic Processes*, Wax, ed., Dover, New York.

Wirsching, P.H. and Light, M.C. (1980). "Fatigue under Wide Band Random Stresses," Journal of Structural Division, ASCE.

10th International Symposium on Practical Design of Ships and Other Floating Structures
Houston, Texas, United States of America
© 2007 American Bureau of Shipping

Numerical Study on Horn Rudder Section to Reduce Gap Cavitation

Sunho Park, Jaekyung Heo, Byeongseok Yu

Hanjin Heavy Industries & Construction Co., Ltd.
Busan, Korea

Abstract

Flow around the gap of a horn rudder is investigated to minimize the gap cavitation. The RANSE(Reynolds-Averaged Navier-Stokes Equations) simulations are performed for various devices to control the gap flow in 2D and 3D domains. Flow characteristics with an emphasis on the pressure field near the gap are investigated. A significant difference in pressure field in 2D and 3D computations are compared. Also, the effect on the pressure field by the local flow through the gap and the main flow from the propeller is compared. Based on the comparison results, a modification is introduced to minimize the gap cavitation on the horn itself and the movable blade.

Keywords

Horn rudder; Gap cavitation; RANSE.

Introduction

Recently the capacity of container carriers increases above 10,000TEUs and even up to Malacamax of 18,000TEUs. On top of that, the shipping industry requires transportation of cargo at high speed. To meet the requirement, the engine power and the loading on the propeller increase. The trend of shipping market increases the concerns on the cavitation erosion on propeller and rudder.

Fig. 1:   Rudder Cavitation Erosion

The rudder is located in a very complex flow field which consists of the ship wake and the flow behind the rotating propeller. Therefore the accurate prediction of cavitation remains very difficult. Cavitation erosion is caused by the cavitation bubbles from the propeller and the local pressure at the rudder, called self cavitation(Kracht, 1995). The propeller induced cavitation is hardly unavoidable. The self cavitation of horn-type rudder occurs around discontinuous area, i.e. the sole edge and the gap between horn and blade. The gap cavitation is known to be induced by the geometric discontinuity and the flow through the gap(ITTC, 2005). Though the cavitation erosion on rudder can be predicted by model tests, many are found in service(Fig. 1) and require remedial measures such as round bar, horizontal plates, and use of stainless steel.

Shen et al.(1997) investigated a full spade twisted rudder which can reduce both propeller and geometry induced cavitation. The twisted rudder is now adopted for large container carriers. One of researches on cavitation is EROCAV project. The EU project dealt with fundamental mechanisms of cavitation, prediction methods and guidelines (Bark et al, 2004). Friesch(2006) and Carlton et al(2006) also summarized prediction methods, design guidance and remedial measures. Many Korean shipyards studied rudder cavitation to satisfy the market trend of large container carriers. Boo et al.(2003) and Hwang and Park(2004) numerically studied two dimensional gap flow. Both studies showed that the flow through the gap is an important factor on rudder cavitation which correlates with the same reason on the gap cavitation reported by ITTC (2005). Boo et al.(2004) and Park et al.(2006a) compared three-dimensional computations with small and large rudder cavitation tests, respectively. Park et al.(2006b) showed that the main flow by propeller has more effects than the gap flow on the gap cavitation.

Most of the previous researches conclude that the flow through the gap is one of primary sources of the gap cavitation. Thus, many devices and guidelines are introduced to reduce the gap flow rate. In this paper, the authors thoroughly investigate the gap flow effects on the gap cavitation of a 6,200TEUs container carrier by RANSE computation. First, a vertical round bar and the size of edge radius needed to reduce the gap flow rate are considered in two dimensional computations. The relationship of the minimum pressure to the flow rate is discussed. More devices, such as horizontal plates and guiding plates, are employed in three dimensional computations, including propeller effects by a simple body force treatment. The pressure distribution around the gap and streamlines inside the gap are investigated, especially comparing two- and three-dimensional results. The authors pay attention to the main flow from the propeller as well as the gap flow. The effects of both flows are compared and conclusions are drawn. Based on the results, the authors slightly modify the conventional section that significantly minimizes the gap cavitation.

Numerical Modeling

Flow field around the horn rudder of a 6,200 TEU container carrier was numerically simulated. To compare with model tests, all computations were performed at model scale. Fig. 2 shows the rudder section at the lower pintle. The deflection angle of 6° to starboard is considered.

In two-dimensional cases, inlet velocity distribution is uniform and the angle of attack is 0°. Reynolds number is 2.0×10^6. The computation domain has C-type topology and consists of about 36,000 hexahedral cells.

In three dimensional computations, propeller effect is considered by implementing body force (Hough and Ordway, 1965) as equations(1) and (2), which generate an angle of attack.

$$\iiint_v f_x \, dv = \frac{K_T}{J^2}\left(\frac{D_p}{L}\right)^2 \quad (1)$$

$$\iiint_v r f_Q \, dv = \frac{K_Q}{J^2}\left(\frac{D_p}{L}\right)^3 \quad (2)$$

Where, K_T, K_Q, J, n, and D_p are thrust coefficient, torque coefficient, advance number, rpm, and propeller diameter, respectively. f_x and f_Q are body forces in axial and rotational directions, respectively, which are defined as follows:

$$f_x = \frac{C_r}{\Delta x} \frac{105\, r^* \sqrt{1-r^*}}{16(4+3Y_h)(1-Y_h)} \rho U^2 \quad (3)$$

$$f_Q = \frac{K_\theta}{\Delta x J^2} \frac{105}{\pi(4+3Y_h)(1-Y_h)} \frac{r^*\sqrt{1-r^*}}{(1-Y_h)r^* - Y_h} \rho U^2 \quad (4)$$

Where, $r^* = (Y-Y_h)/(1-Y_h)$, $Y_h = r/r_p$, and r is hub radius.

Reynolds number based on the uniform inlet velocity is 1.2×10^6, which becomes almost double when the propeller body force term works. Structured grid system of 1.2 million cells is employed as shown in Fig. 3

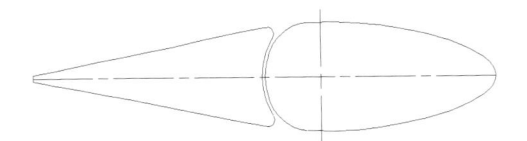

Fig. 2: Original Rudder Section at Lower Pintle

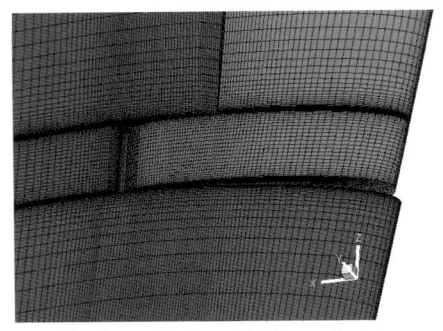

Fig. 3: Surface Grid near the Gap

The commercial CFD software, Fluent ver. 6.2, was used. The realizable k-ε turbulence model with wall function and 2nd order upwind scheme for the discretization of convection terms were used. For practical purposes, cavitation model was not considered and steady state computations were performed.

Two-Dimensional Computational Results

Fig. 4 shows pressure coefficient contours non-dimensionalized by $0.5*\rho U_\infty^2$, and a streamline for the original rudder section. The deflection angle generates pressure and suction sides. The streamline passes through the gap from the pressure side to the suction side. It can be regarded that the pressure field around the gap is affected by the geometry of the gap, neglecting the angle of attack by propeller flows.

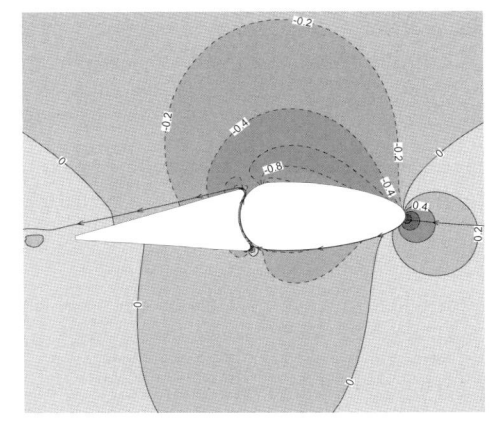

Fig. 4: Pressure Coefficient Contours and Streamline

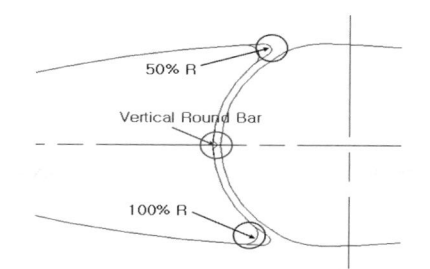

Fig. 5: Vertical Round Bar and Edge Radius

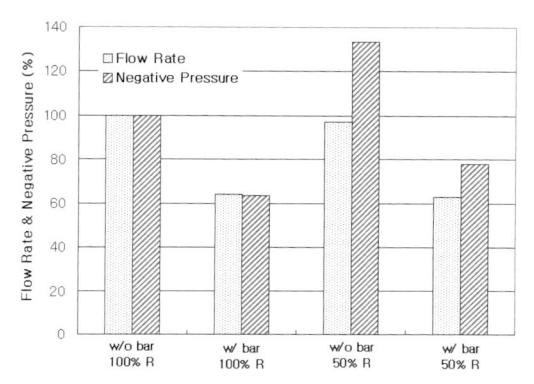

Fig. 6: Relative Flow Rate & Negative Pressure

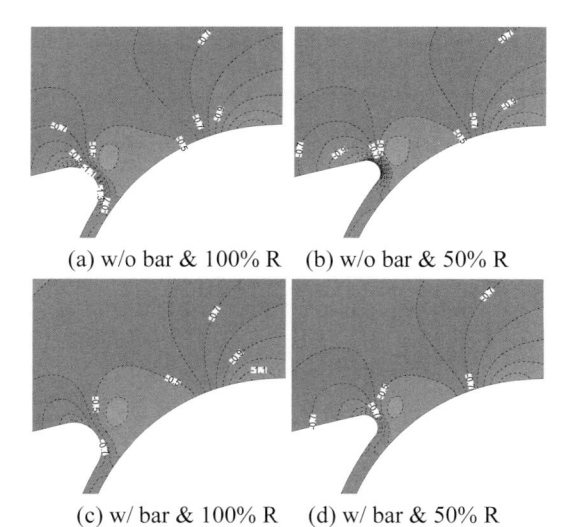

(a) w/o bar & 100% R
(b) w/o bar & 50% R
(c) w/ bar & 100% R
(d) w/ bar & 50% R

Fig. 7: Pressure Coefficient Contours around Suction Side Gap

To investigate the relationship between the flow rate through the gap and the pressure distribution, a vertical round bar and the change of the edge radius were considered. The height of the bar is 2/3 of the gap, and the small radius is 50% of the original radius as shown in Fig. 5.

Fig. 6 compares the relative flow rate and minimum negative pressure for each case. The edge radius has almost no effect on the flow rate, but the round bar reduces the flow rate by about 40%. The reduced flow rate results in the increase of the pressure. In addition, the radius of the edge changes the pressure for the same bar condition. The small radius shows higher negative pressure values.

The pressure contours of the above conditions are shown in Fig. 7. When the bar is absent, the pressure around the edge of the blade is lower. On top of that, the small radius decreases the pressure around the edge by accelerating the gap flow as it goes out the gap.

In the two-dimensional study, it is found that the flow rate has a strong relation with the pressure decrease. Thus, the flow control devices effectively control the gap cavitation.

Three-Dimensional Computational Results

The three-dimensional computations were carried out at model scale and at the same cavitation number of 0.18, which is non-dimensionalized by $0.5\rho(\pi nD)^2$. The cavitation tests were performed at HSVA, and Fig. 8 shows the observed rudder cavitation at deflection angle of 6° to starboard.

Vertical Round Bar

Fig. 9 compares the iso-Cp of 0.18 surfaces for the vertical bar application. Irrespective of the bar employment, the volume of the iso-surface is larger than the model tests. The neglect of wake field and the simple modeling of the propeller overestimate the negative pressure distribution. In addition, contrary to the two-dimensional results, the iso-Cp of 0.18 is larger when employing the vertical round bar. The reason could be found in Fig. 10. It is found in y-velocity contours that the vertical bar obstructs the gap flow. The y-velocity component plays a role of hindering the main flow. Thus, without applying the bar, the large magnitude of y-velocity reduces the x-velocity and increases the pressure around the gap.

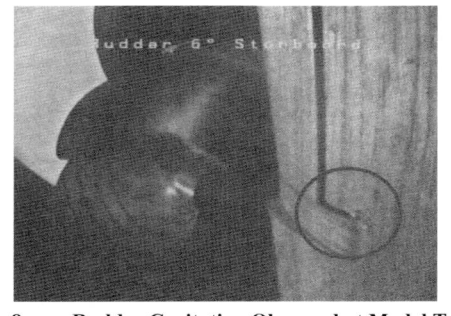

Fig. 8: Rudder Cavitation Observed at Model Tests

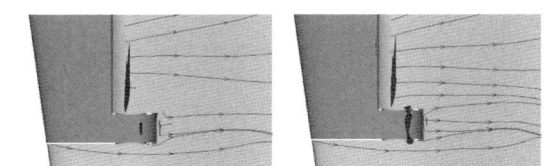

Fig. 9: Streamlines and Iso-Cp Surfaces (left: w/o bar & 100%R, right: w/bar & 100%R)

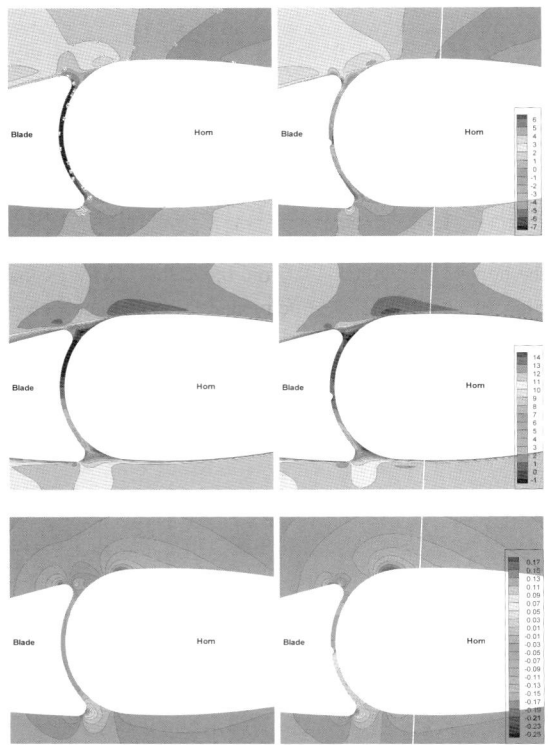

Fig. 10: Y-velocity(top), X-velocity(middle) and Pressure Coefficient(bottom) Contours(left: w/o bar & 100%R, right: w/bar & 100%R)

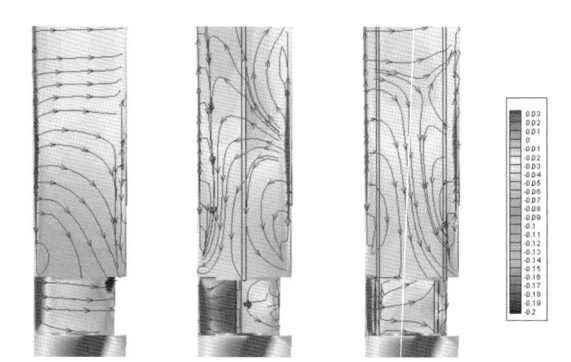

Fig. 11: Streamlines and Pressure Coefficient Contours inside the Gap (left: w/o bar, middle: w/ single bar, right: w/ twin bars)

Another difference from the two-dimensional cases is the location of the negative pressure on the movable blade. In the two-dimensional cases, the negative pressure was observed around the edge due to the acceleration of the gap flow. However, in the three-dimensional cases, the negative pressure appears only at the outside the gap. This fact means that the main flow has more effect on the pressure field than the gap flow.

The role of the vertical round bar is clearly shown in Fig. 11. Without the bar, the flow direction is the same as the two-dimensional cases, from the pressure side to the suction side. However, employing the bar totally changes the flow direction. It stagnates the flow from the pressure side and even makes the flow come from the suction side as well.

Edge Radius

Keeping the single round bar appended, the radius of the edge is reduced by 50%. Fig. 12 and Fig. 13 show the effectiveness of the edge size. The x-velocity and pressure fields are similar to large radius cases, as compared to the two-dimensional study. Also, the location of the negative pressure is outside the gap. Even the large curvature at the edge does not accelerate the gap flow. Thus, the volume of the iso-Cp surface for the small edge radius remains almost the same in Fig. 13.

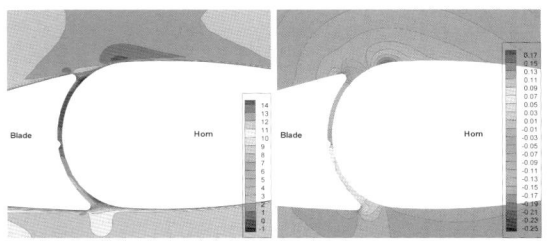

Fig. 12: X-velocity and Pressure Coefficient Contours for Small Edge Radius

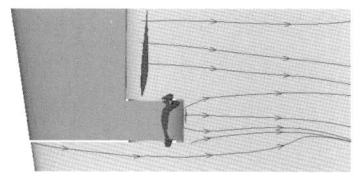

Fig. 13: Streamlines and Iso-Cp Surfaces for Small Edge Radius

Horizontal Plates

Horizontal plates are usually appended at the lower horizontal gap as shown in Fig. 14. Fig. 15 shows the pressure coefficient contours. It is shown that the pressure at the end of the horizontal plates increased locally. The horizontal plates can be used as a remedial measure to reduce the horizontal gap cavitation.

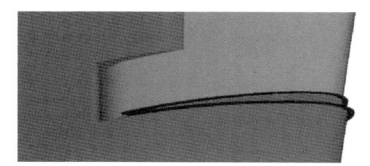

Fig. 14: Horizontal Plates

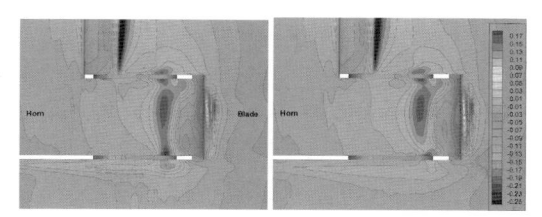

Fig. 15: Pressure Coefficient Contours(left: w/o horizontal plates, right: w/ horizontal plates)

Guiding Plates

Guiding plates are recommended by GL to reduce the gap size between rudder blade and horn (el Moctar, 2005). They also recommend that the guiding plates be in alignment with rudder profile to avoid flow separation.

Fig. 16 shows flow fields around the rudder with guiding plates. The axial velocity contours show that the boundary layer is almost continuous and aligned with the rudder profile. The continuous boundary layer develops along the chord and decreases the velocity at the gap. Thus, the pressure increases at this point and the volume of the iso-Cp surfaces reduces as shown in Fig. 17.

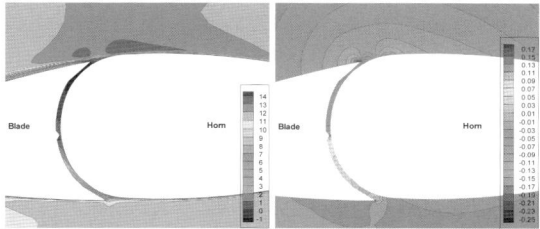

Fig. 16: X-velocity and Pressure Coefficient Contours of Guiding Plate Rudder

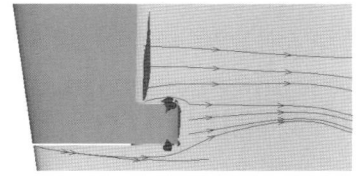

Fig. 17: Streamlines and Iso-Cp Surfaces of Guiding Plate Rudder

Modified Section

In the two-dimensional study, the flow rate through the gap has primary effects on the gap cavitation. The pressure remarkably decreases as the gap flow accelerates around the edge. However, in the three-dimensional study, the gap flow rate has little effect on the cavitation. Some cases showed that the flow direction into the gap is not consistent, whereas the direction is decided by the pressure difference between pressure and suction sides in two-dimensional computations. Moreover, the location of the negative pressure is quite different from the two-dimensional results. It tells that the pressure decrease is induced greatly by the main flow from the propeller rather than the gap flow.

Based on the investigation results, the original section was slightly modified as shown in Fig. 18. The length of the horn is increased along the section profile to the gap. This adjustment could reduce the curvature into the gap of the horn part, and increase the continuity of the horn and the blade. Besides, as the movable blade deflects, the horn protects the blade from the main flow.

Fig. 19 shows the x-velocity and pressure coefficient contours. The velocity on the suction side decreases and the boundary layer thickens due to the wake from the modified horn. Thus, the pressure on the blade significantly increases due to the velocity decrease. Also, the reduced curvature weakens the acceleration of the main flow around the rudder shaft area. Thus, the pressure on the horn increases.

Fig. 20 shows the effectiveness of the modification by removing the vertical round bar inside the gap. The x-velocity and pressure distribution are very similar to Fig. 19. It means that the gap flow has little effect in three-dimensional flows. Regardless of the gap flow, controlling the main flow is important to reduce the gap cavitation. The iso-Cp surface is shown in Fig. 21, where most of the iso-Cp surface disappeared.

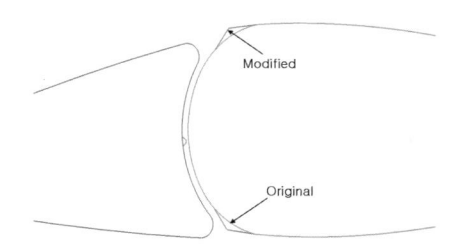

Fig. 18: Modification of Original Rudder

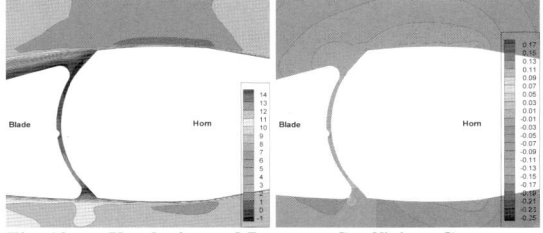

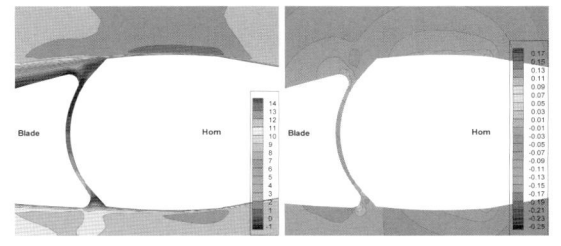

Fig. 19: X-velocity and Pressure Coefficient Contours of Modified Section Rudder(w/ bar)

Fig. 20: X-velocity and Pressure Coefficient Contours of Modified Section Rudder (w/o bar)

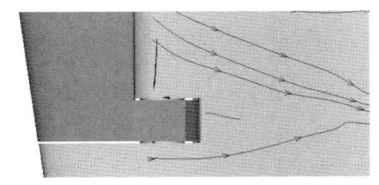

Fig. 21: Streamlines and Iso-Cp Surfaces of Modified Section Rudder(w/o bar)

Conclusions

This paper summarizes numerical analysis on the gap cavitation of a horn rudder.

In two-dimensional computations, a strong relation between pressure and flow rate exists. Thus, flow rate control devices are very effective in terms of gap cavitation. However, in three-dimensional study, the relation has less effect than controlling the main flow from the propeller. Various flow control devices are numerically tested and thoroughly investigated. Among the alternatives, the modified section to control the main flow shows the possibility to minimize the gap cavitation.

References

Bark, G, Friesch, J, Kuiper G, and Ligtelijn JT (2004). "Cavitation Erosion on Ship Propellers and Rudders," Proc 9th Symposium on Practical Design of Ships and Other Floating Structures, Germany.

Boo, K, Han, J, Song I, and Shin S (2003). "Viscous Flow Analysis for the Rudder Section Using FLUENT Code," Journal of the Society Naval Architects of Korea, Vol. 40, No. 4, pp 30-36. (in Korean).

Boo, K, Hong, C, and Lee, K (2004). "Simulation of Viscous Flow around the Ship Appended with the Propeller and the Rudder," Proc Annual Autumn Meeting of the Society of Naval Architects of Korea. (in Korean).

Carlton, J, Fitzsimmons, P, Radosavljevic, D, and Boorsma A (2006). "Factors Influencing Rudder Erosion: Experience of Computational Methods, Model Tests and Full Scale Observations," Proc International Conference on Ship and Shipping Research NAV 2006, Italy.

Friesch, J (2006). "Rudder Erosion Damages Caused by Cavitation," Proc 6th International Symposium on Cavitation CAV 2006, The Netherlands.

Hough, GR, and Ordway, DE (1965). "The Generalized Actuator Disc," Developments in Theoretical and Applied Mechanics, Vol. 2, Pergamon Press, pp 317-336.

Hwang, YS, and Park JJ (2004), "A Numerical Simulation of 2D Viscous Flows around Rudder Sections Considering Section Type and Gap Shape," Proc Annual Spring Meeting of the Society of Naval Architects of Korea. (in Korean)

ITTC (2005). "Report of the Specialist Committee on Cavitation Erosion on Propellers and Appendages on High Powered/High Speed Ships," Proc 24th ITTC, Edinburgh.

Kracht, AM (1995). "Cavitation on Rudders," Proc Cav '95, Newcastle upon Tyne.

el Moctar, O (2005). "Recommendations for Preventive Measures to Avoid or Minimize Rudder Cavitation," Paper No. 05-1, Germanischer Lloyd.

Park, J, Kim, S, Choi, Y, Kim, Y, Paik, B, Kim, K, and Ahn, J (2006a). "A Numerical Study of Viscous Flow around a Rudder with Gap," Proc Annual Spring Meeting of the Society of Naval Architects of Korea. (in Korean)

Park, S, Heo, J, and Yu, BS (2006b). "A Study on Rudder Section to Reduce Gap Cavitation of Horn Rudder," Proc Annual Spring Meeting of the Society of Naval Architects of Korea.(in Korean)

Shen, YT, Jiang, CW, and Remmers, KD (1997). "A Twisted Rudder for Reduced Cavitation," Journal of Ship Research, Vol. 41, No. 4, pp 260-272.

Development of Rudder Cavitation Suppression Devices and Its Concept Verification through Experimental and Numerical Studies

Shin Hyung Rhee [1], Jung-Keun Oh [1], Seung-Hee Lee [2], and Hyochul Kim [3]

[1] Dept. of Naval Architecure & Ocean Engineering, Seoul National University, Seoul, Korea
[2] Dept. of Naval Architecture & Ocean Engineering, Inha University, Incheon, Korea
[3] Jungseok Research Institute of International Logistics and Trade, Inha University, Incheon, Korea

Abstract

The development of a new rudder system aimed for lift augmentation and cavitation suppression is presented. In order to verify the design concept of the new devices, numerical simulations were conducted using a computational fluid dynamics code and model tests are carried out in a circulation water channel. The new rudder system is equipped with cam devices, which effectively close the gap between the horn/pintle and movable wing parts. The experimental and computational results suggest that the present concept for a cavitation suppressing rudder system is highly feasible and warrant further study for inclusion of the interactions with hull and mechanical design for manufacturing and operations.

Keywords

Rudder; Cavitation; CFD; Experiments.

Introduction

It is well known that the increased propeller loading to meet the needs for higher speed cargo ships results in increased rotational speed in the propeller slipstream. The higher rotational speed brings about increased angles of attack on the rudder system placed in the propeller slipstream. A sheet type cavitation occurs on the rudder system due to this high speed and low pressure flow field and its main impact is frequently observed around the leading edge and/or the gap region between the horn/pintle and movable wing parts, e.g., see Figure 1.

There have been several interesting studies on the suppression of this rudder cavitation with modified rudder shapes and/or various types of devices attached to the region inside or around the gap (Shen et al., 1997; Boo et al., 2003; Hwang and Park, 2004). However, many of them lack completeness in terms of suppressing the rudder cavitation and do not consider the additional devices to increase the rudder performance.

Fig. 1:   Erosion caused by rudder cavitation.

In the present study, a newly devised rudder system, which is recently proposed by the authors, is analyzed in terms of lift augmentation and cavitation suppression. The new rudder system differs from conventional ones in the cam devices, which effectively close the gap between the horn/pintle and movable wing parts. Results from both model tests and numerical simulations using a computational fluid dynamics (CFD) code are presented. Model tests are carried out in a circulation water channel at Inha University in Korea. The selected CFD code solves the Reynolds-averaged Navier-Stokes equations and was validated against existing experimental data (Rhee and Kim, 2006).

The present paper is organized as follows. The conceptual design of the new rudder system is presented in the next section. Then the computational method and results are presented, followed by the experimental method and results. Discussions on the computational and experimental results are also made in terms of the cavitation suppression and lift augmentation. Lastly, some concluding remarks are made.

Conceptual Design

The main difference of the new rudder system from the conventional one is found near the gap between the horn/pintle and movable wing parts. Two types of cam devices are placed in the gap and they effectively block the flow through the gap. By blocking this flow, (1) the pressure difference on the sides of horn part increases, which results in the lift augmentation, and (2) the negative pressure peaks are removed or mitigated, which eventually results in cavitation suppression. Figure 2 displays the conventional and new rudder systems with a deflection angle of *5 °*.

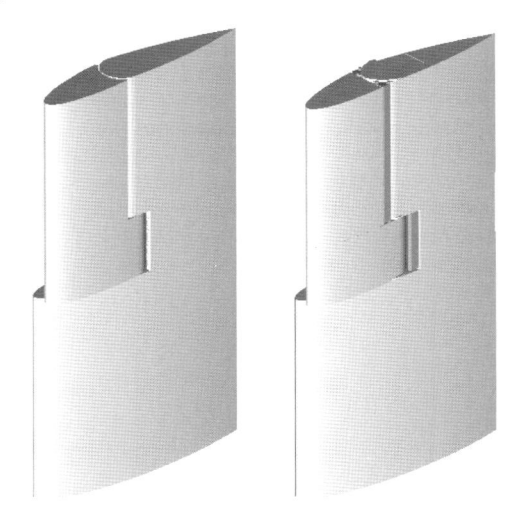

Fig. 2: Three-dimensional views of rudder system: conventional (left) and new (right).

For the present study, two different numerical simulations were carried out: (1) the design concept verification through 3D multiphase flow computation at a full scale condition, and; (2) the validation against experimental data through 2D sectional computations at a model scale condition. For the former, a representative foil section for conventional rudders with the chord length of *1 m* was selected. The span of the rudder system was *2 m*, and the pintle section was located between *0.7 m* and *1 m* from the top of the rudder. For the latter, the computational condition was set to match the experimental one as much as possible. The same foil section geometry was scaled by 0.2, so the chord length of the 2D section was 0.2 *m*. The corresponding two-dimensional (2D) shapes at the horn and pintle sections are shown in Figures 3 and 4, respectively. Note that two different cam devices were used for the horn and pintle section gaps.

In the experiments, the shape of the cam devices and of the leading edge of the moving part is slightly modified from that used for the numerical simulations. This is to improve the mechanism of the gap flow blocking. However, it is believed that, even with this difference, the overall characteristics of the flow do not change.

Obviously the flow around a rudder system is complex unsteady 3D flow, which involves not only the three-dimensionality of the rudder geometry, but also the transient 3D nature of the upstream propeller race. However, the main thrust of the present study lies in the verification of new design concept and validation against its experimental data, and thus it is believed that focusing on steady flow analysis is more beneficial at this stage of the development.

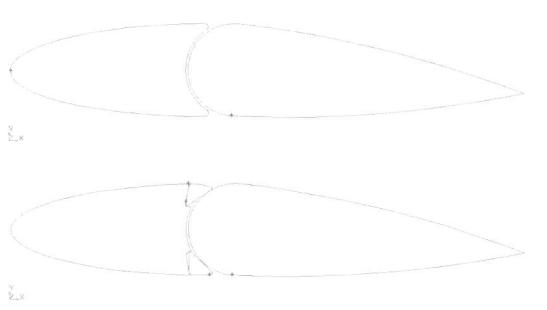

Fig. 3: 2D shapes at horn section: conventional (upper) and new (lower)

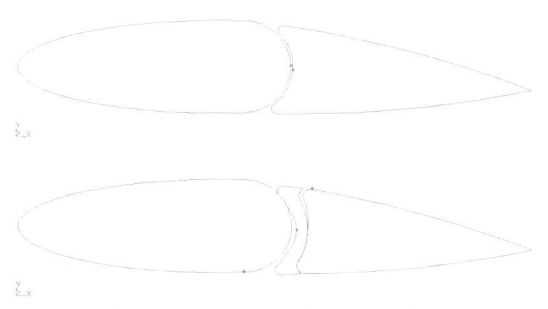

Fig. 4: 2D shapes at pintle section: conventional (upper) and new (lower)

Computational Method

The cavitation model employed in the present study is based on the so-called "full cavitation model" by Singhal et al. (2002). For the multi-phase flow solutions, the single-fluid mixture model is employed. The mixture model solves the continuity and momentum equations for the mixture, and the volume fraction equation for the secondary phases, as well as algebraic expressions for slip velocities. The governing equations are written for the mass and momentum conservation of the mixture fluid, such that

$$\frac{\partial}{\partial t}(\rho_m) + \nabla \cdot (\rho_m \vec{v}_m) = 0 \quad (1)$$

$$\frac{\partial}{\partial t}(\rho_m \vec{v}_m) + \nabla \cdot (\rho_m \vec{v}_m \vec{v}_m) \\ = -\nabla p + \nabla \cdot (\overline{\overline{\tau}}) + \nabla \cdot \left(\sum_{k=1}^{n} \alpha_k \rho_k \vec{v}_{dr,k} \vec{v}_{dr,k} \right) \quad (2)$$

where $\overline{\overline{\tau}}$ is the stress tensor. In the above equations, ρ_m is the mixture density, $\vec{v}_m$ the mass-averaged velocity, μ_m the mixture viscosity, I the unit tensor, and $\vec{v}_{dr,k}$ the drift velocity for the secondary phase k.

Once the Reynolds averaging approach for turbulence modeling is applied, the Reynolds stresses resulting from the process must be modeled to close Equation (2).

The so-called realizable k-ε turbulence model (Shih et al., 1995), which is based on the Boussinesq hypothesis with transport equations for the turbulent kinetic energy, k, and its dissipation rate, ε, was used for turbulence closure. The turbulent viscosity μ_t was computed by combining k and ε as $\mu_t = \rho C_\mu k^2/\varepsilon$, where C_μ is a function of the mean strain and rotation rates, the angular velocity of the system rotation, and k and ε. The realizable k-ε model is a variation of the standard k-ε model and has shown good performance for flows with strong streamline curvature, vortices, and rotation (Kim and Rhee, 2002; Rhee et al., 2005; Rhee and Makarov, 2005). For wall boundary conditions, the wall function approach based on the law of the wall was applied.

The mass transfer through cavitation is handled by the transport equation for the vapor mass fraction, $f_v \equiv \alpha_v \dfrac{\rho_v}{\rho_m}$, where α_v is the vapor volume fraction and ρ_v is the vapor density. The vapor transport equation is written as

$$\frac{\partial}{\partial t}(\rho_m f_v) + \nabla \cdot (\rho_m \vec{v}_v f_v) = \nabla \cdot \left(\frac{\mu_t}{\sigma_v} \nabla f_v\right) + R_e - R_c \quad (3)$$

where μ_t is the turbulent eddy viscosity, σ_v is the turbulent Prandtl number for the vapor, and R_e and R_c are the rates of vapor generation and condensation, respectively. The turbulent Prandtl number takes a value between *0.7* and *1.0* in most of the published studies, and is set to *1.0* in the present study.

To solve Equation (3), R_e and R_c need to be related to the bubble dynamics and volume fraction. To account for the bubble dynamics, the reduced Rayleigh-Plesset equation was employed, as for many other studies in the same modeling category. The approach used by Singhal et al. (2002) is followed in the present study.

The relationship between the mass fraction, f_ϕ, and the corresponding volume fraction, α_ϕ, is, for any given phase ϕ, is

$$\alpha_\phi = f_\phi \frac{\rho_m}{\rho_\phi} \quad (4)$$

The CFD code, FLUENT 6.2, employs a cell-centered finite-volume method that allows the use of computational elements with arbitrary polyhedral shape. Convective terms are discretized using the second order accurate upwind scheme, while diffusive terms are discretized using the second order accurate central differencing scheme. The velocity-pressure coupling and overall solution procedure are based on a SIMPLE type segregated algorithm adapted to unstructured grids. The discretized equations are solved using pointwise Gauss-Seidel iterations, and an algebraic multi-grid method accelerates the solution convergence. The convergence criteria in the present study were at least three orders of magnitude drop in the mass conservation imbalance and momentum equation residuals, which are deemed sufficient for most steady flow solutions.

Computational Results

As mentioned above, two different numerical simulations were carried out and their results are presented in this section: (1) 3D multiphase flow computation at a full scale condition, and; (2) 2D sectional computations at a model scale condition.

For the former simulation, computations were carried out in a simplified flow condition, i.e., the rudder system with a deflection angle of *5°* is placed in an unbounded uniform flow. The inflow velocity was *50 m/s* and the corresponding Reynolds number based on the chord length of the rudder, Re, was *50 million*. The cavitation number, σ, was set to *1.0*, based on the chord length and the inflow speed.

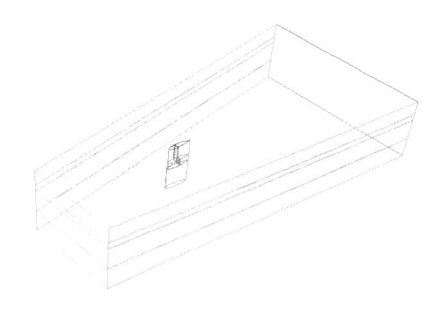

Fig. 5: 3D Computational domain.

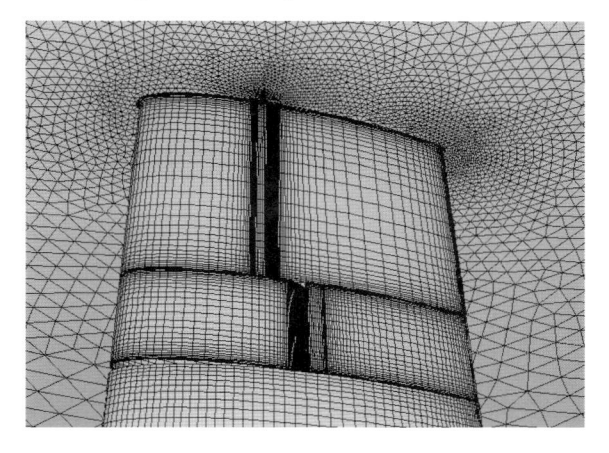

Fig. 6: Computational grid (partial view).

The computational domain with extent of $-5m \leq x \leq 10m$, $-4m \leq y \leq 4m$, and $-3m \leq z \leq 0m$ was constructed and is shown in Figure 5. Note that the shape of the domain resembles an expanding nozzle, so as to ensure pure inflow through the upstream and side inlet boundaries and pure outflow through the downstream exit boundary. The coordinate system origin is located at the mid-chord location of the rudder section on the top boundary. Note that the bottom boundary is located *1 m* below the bottom of the rudder configuration. For each rudder configuration, a hybrid unstructured grid was generated, i.e., ten layers of hexahedral cells on the rudder surface and prism cells in the remaining region. The first cell height off the solid surface was approximately *0.0005 m*, which ranges approximately *50* to *200* in terms of wall y^+ values. 3D grids were built by extruding the surface grid from one side to the other. Between each pair of blocks, a non-conformal interface was defined with a pair of collocated block surfaces. Figure 6 presents a partial view of the computational grid for the new rudder configuration. The grid refinement tests on the wall y^+ values and number of cells in the gap were conducted and reported in Rhee et al. (2003). The present grid design was based on the findings of the tests.

Table 1: Lift, drag, and moment coefficients

Configuration	C_L	C_D	C_M
Conventional	0.0879	0.00875	-.01604
New	0.126	0.00794	-.01605

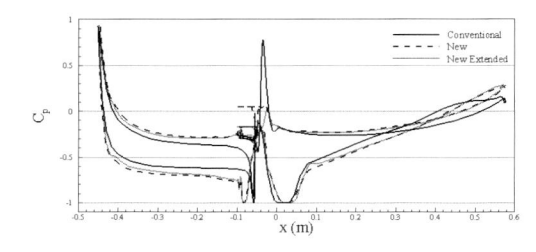

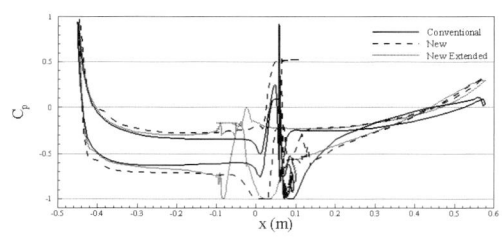

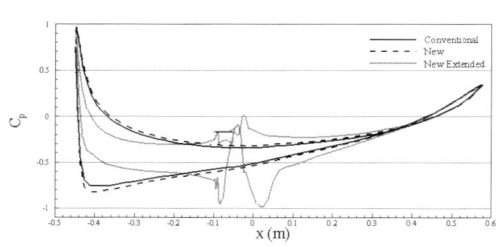

Fig. 7: Surface pressure coefficient comparison: $z = -0.35\ m$ (top); $z = -0.85\ m$ (middle); $z = -1.5\ m$ (bottom).

Table 1 presents the lift (C_L), drag (C_D), and moment (C_M) coefficients. Note that C_M is calculated with respect to the rudder stock axis in the spanwise direction. The new configuration produces increased lift by *43%*, as well as decreased drag by *9.3%*. By blocking the gap flow, the cam devices play a significant role in this lift augmentation and drag reduction. It is obvious from this observation that there are other advantages of employing the new devices, besides the cavitation suppression effect.

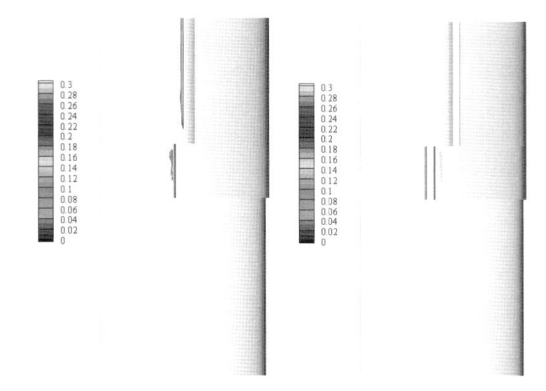

Fig. 8: Liquid volume fraction conours: conventional (left); new (right).

To examine the lift augmentation and cavitation suppression mechanism, the surface pressure coefficient (C_p) at the halfway location on the horn section, $z = -0.35\ m$, the halfway location on the pintle section, $z = -0.85\ m$, and the halfway location on the lower section, $z = -1.5\ m$, is plotted in Figure 7. C_p of the conventional configuration shows a plateau at *-1*, i.e., minimum possible C_p at the given condition of $\sigma = 1$, which suggests that there must be cavitation in that part of the rudder surface. C_p of the new configuration also approaches *-1*, but does not display a low pressure area of significant size. Another noteworthy is the increased pressure difference on the suction and pressure sides at all locations on the new and extended configurations, especially on the stationary parts, which leads to the lift augmentation discussed above.

Figure 8 shows the liquid volume fraction contours clipped at *0.3* on the suction side of the conventional and new configurations. With the liquid volume fraction above *0.3*, normally it is not considered that there is cavitation. As expected, sheet type cavitaion areas are observed on the conventional configuration, while only a very small area of relatively high liquid volume fraction, i.e., above *0.28*, is confirmed right upstream of the pintle gap on the new configuration.

Figures 9 and 10 present the detailed view of the gap area on the suction side, showing velocity vectors colored by C_p at $z = -0.35\ m$ and $z = -0.85\ m$, respectively. The cavity shape represented by the iso-surface line of liquid volume fraction equal to *0.2* is also shown. By blocking the gap flow, the suction side pressure distribution becomes more uniform and does not exhibit large pressure variations that often lead to structural damage near the exit of the gap. Furthermore, without the flow through the gap, the rudder can function with increased two-dimensionality, which certainly enhances the rudder performance. The location of the recirculating flow region on the conventional configuration is identified and it is one of the reasons of the relatively low lift produced by the conventional configuration. A further improvement is deemed necessary for the dead flow regions between cam devices and horn/pintle/movable wing parts of the new configuration: for example, make the flow along the rudder surface smoother; integrate a Coanda jet device to further augment the lift (Rhee et al., 2003; Choi et al., 2004).

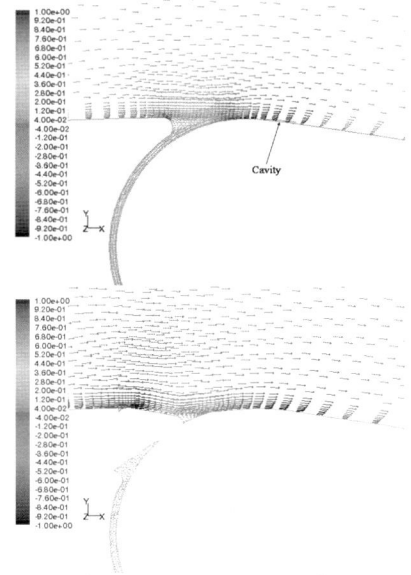

Fig. 9: Velocity vectors colored by C_p at $z = -0.35\ m$ – detailed view near the gap between horn and moving part on suction side: conventional (upper); new (lower).

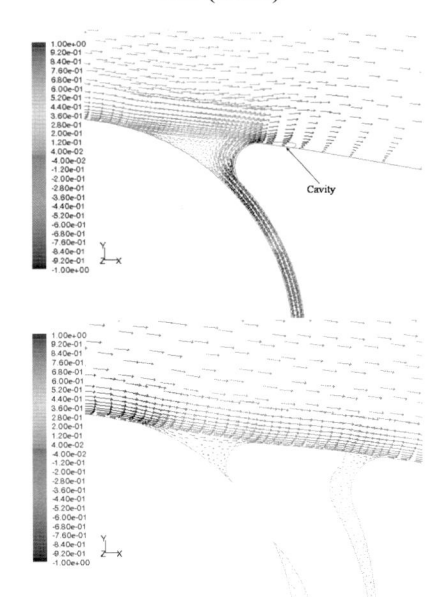

Fig. 10: Velocity vectors colored by C_p at $z = -0.85\ m$ – detailed view near the gap between pintle and moving part on suction side: conventional (upper); new (lower).

For the second simulation, i.e., 2D sectional computations at a model scale condition; computational condition was set to match that of experimental one. The rudder flap, i.e., the moving part, was deflected by $5°$ and the whole system was placed in an unbounded uniform flow. The inflow velocity was $2\ m/s$ and the corresponding Re was $0.4\ million$. Note that the ambient pressure was set sufficiently high and cavitation could not take place. Also the flow was turbulent owing to the high free stream turbulence level. Figure 11 shows the 2D computational domain, which is close to the experimental facility's test section. The computational grid near the rudder system is displayed in Figure 12.

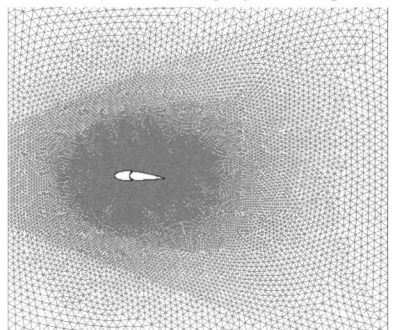

Fig. 11: 2D Computational domain (horn section).

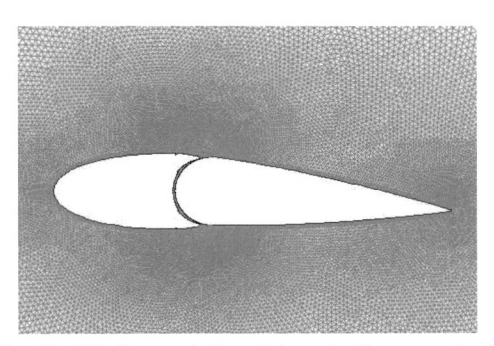

Fig. 12: 2D Computational domain (horn section).

Figure 13 shows the contours of pressure coefficient near the gap. As seen in Figure 7 for the 3D case, the pressure behind the gap, where the cavitation normally takes place, does not show low peak. Moreover, the wide and even distribution of lower pressure on the horn and pintle surface contributes to the lift augmentation, as discussed in Figure 7. Table 2 summarizes C_L and C_D computed from the simulation.

Table 2: Lift and drag coefficients

Section	C_L	C_D
Horn	0.373	0.0338
Pintle	0.362	0.0346

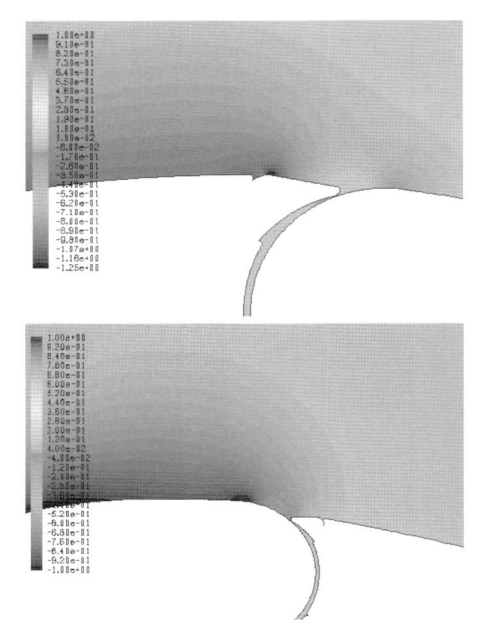

Fig. 13: Contours of pressure coefficient around the gap: horn section (upper); pintle section (lower).

Experimental Setup and Method

Model tests were carried out in the circulation water channel located at Inha University, Korea. The measurement section extends *5 m* long, *1.4 m* wide, and *0.02 – 0.84 m* deep, and can be depressurized by up to *10 kPa*. The maximum speed of the flow is *6 m/s*. Figure 14 shows the experimental facility used for the present study.

The rudder model was designed and manufactured for 2D experiments. It requires dummy parts in the upper and lower section of the model and was attached to circular cylinder-shaped strut to hold the model in the channel. The horn and pintle sections of the rudder system were made separately of aluminum alloy and inserted between the dummy parts for 2D forces and moment measurements. The chord length of the whole section is *0.2 m* and the span length is *0.17 m*. In the present paper, the experimental results for the horn section are presented, as the pintle section tests have yet to be carried out. Figure 15 shows the overview of the model. The test model consists of the middle measuring part and two dummy parts above and below. At the top and bottom of the model, end plates are attached to minimize the three-dimensional tip effect (Figure 16). Between the horn and moving part, the cam devices for blocking gap flow are inserted (Figure 17). Two three-component loadcells are inserted into the horn and moving part, respectively, and fixed at each upper dummy part. Figures 18 and Figure 19 show the calibration process of the model and the calibration results, respectively.

Fig. 14: Experimental facility: Circulation water channel at Inha University.

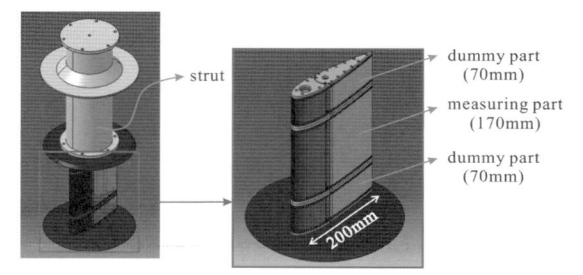

Fig. 15: Over view of the test model.

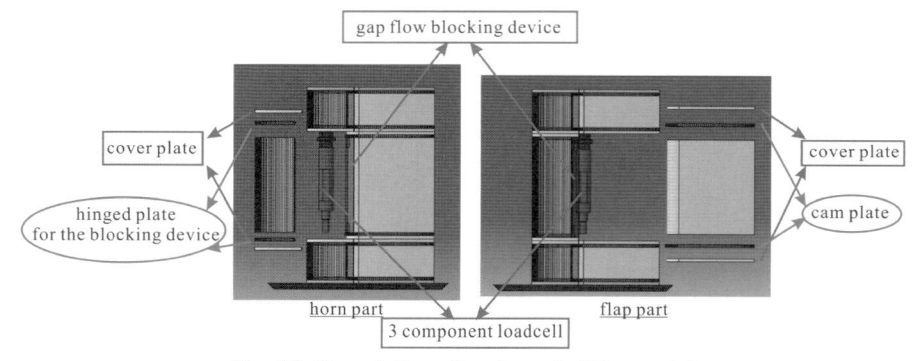

Fig. 16: Description of each part of the model

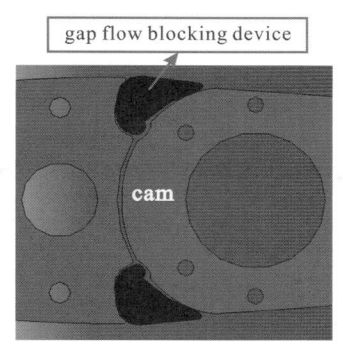

Fig. 17: Gap flow blocking device

Fig. 18: Test model rigged for calibration process.

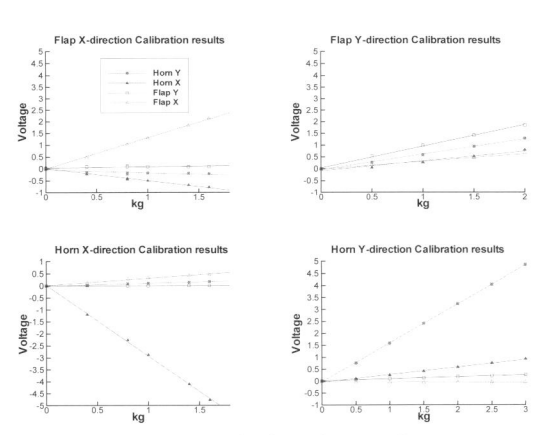

Fig. 19: Calibration results

Experimental Results

As mentioned in the previous section, the flap deflection angle was *5°* and the inflow velocity was *2 m/s*. Figure 20 shows the model test being conducted in the circulation water channel. With this test configuration, it was noticed that the cylindrical strut above the foil experienced vibration due to the shed vortices behind it. To avoid this, the free-surface location was changed from A to B in Figure 21.

For the horn section, C_L and C_D were measured *0.317* and *0.0350*, respectively. These values are *85%* and *104%* of the computed values, respectively. The possible causes of this discrepancy are (1) the not-so-fully turbulent flow around the model, (2) the three-dimensional flow effects, (3) the boundary layer effects from the end plates, and (4) the vortices from the juncture region of the foil and plates. Efforts are being made to get rid of these problems, as the experimental program is still underway. More results for the wider range of flow conditions and pintle section tests will be presented in the future, along with rigorous uncertainty assessment results.

Fig. 20: Model test in circulation water channel.

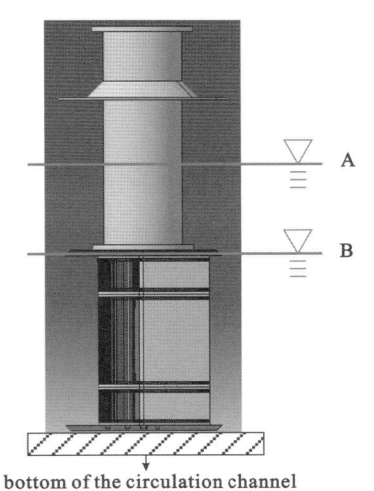

Fig. 21: Model configuration and free-surface location

Conclusions

A new rudder system configuration was devised and proposed with lift augmentation and cavitation suppression in mind. The new rudder system is equipped with cam devices, which effectively close the gap between the horn/pintle and movable wing parts. Simulations clearly display the mechanism of the lift augmentation and cavitation suppression. Model tests are conducted to verify the design concept of the new devices. The computational and experimental results also suggest that the present concept for a cavitation suppressing rudder system is highly feasible and warrant further study for inclusion of the interactions with hull and propellers, and mechanical design for manufacturing and operations.

Acknowledgment

It should be acknowledged that the present study was supported partly by the Korea Research Foundation Grant (KRF-2005-005-J10203) funded by the Korean Government (MOEHRD).

References

Boo, GT, Song, IH, and Shin, SC (2003). "Numerical Simulation for the Rudder in order to Control the Cavitation Phenomena," *Proc. International Workshop on Frontier Technology in Ship and Ocean Engineering*, Seoul, Korea.

Choi, B, Park, H, Kim, H, and Lee, S (2004). "An Experimental Evaluation on the Performance of High Lifting Rudder under Coanda Effect," *Proc. 9th International Symposium on Practical Design of Ships and Other Floating Structures*, Hamburg, Germany.

Han, JM, Kong, DS, Song, IH, and Lee, CS (2001). "Analysis of the Cavitating Flow around the Horn-Type Rudder in the Race of a Propeller," *Proc. 4th Int. Sympo. On Cavitation CAV2001*, Pasadena, CA.

Hinze, JO (1975). "Turbulence, 2nd Ed.," *McGraw Hill*, New York, NY.

Hough, G, and Ordway, DE (1965). "The Generalized Actuator Disk," *Developments in Theoretical and Applied Mechanics*, Vol. 2, Pergamon Press, Atlanta, GA, pp.317-336.

Hwang, Y-S, and Park, J-J (2004). "A Numerical Simulation of 2D Viscous Flows around Rudder Sections Considering Section Type and Gap Shape," *Proc. Annual Spring Meeting of the Society of Naval Architects of Korea*, Chungmu, Korea (In Korean).

Kim, S-E, Mathur, SR, Murthy, JY, and Choudhury, D (1998). "A Reynolds-Averaged Navier-Stokes Solver Using Unstructured Mesh Based Finite-Volume Scheme," *AIAA Paper 98-0231, Proc. 36th AIAA Aerospace Sciences Meeting and Exhibit*, Reno, NV

Kim, S-E, and Rhee, SH (2002). "Assessment of Eight Turbulence Models for a Three-Dimensional Boundary Layer Involving Crossflow and Streamwise Vortices," *AIAA Paper 2002-0852, Proc. 40th AIAA Aerospace Sciences Meeting and Exhibit*, Reno, NV, USA.

Rhee, SH, and Kim, H (2006). "Analysis of Rudder Cavitation in Propeller Slipstream and Development of its Suppression Devices," *Proc. 2006 SNAME Maritime Technology Conference & Expo*, Ft.Lauderdale, FL.

Rhee, SH, Kim, S-E, Ahn, H, Oh, J, and Kim, H (2003). "Analysis of a Jet-Controlled High-Lift Hydrofoil with a Flap," *Ocean Engineering*, Vol. 30, Issue 16, pp.2117-2136.

Rhee, SH, and Makarov, B (2005) "Validation Study for Free-Surface Wave Flows Around Surface-Piercing Cylindrical Structures," *Proc. 24th International Conference on Offshore Mechanics and Arctic Engineering*, Halkidiki, Greece.

Rhee, SH, Makarov, B, Krishnan, H, and Ivanov, V (2005). "Assessment of Volume of Fluid Method for Free-Surface Wave Flows," *Journal of Marine Science and Technology*, Vol. 10, No. 4, pp.173-180.

Shen, YT, Jiang, CW, and Remmers, KD (1997). "A Twisted Rudder for Reduced Cavitation," *J. Ship Research*, Vol. 41, No.4, pp.260-272.

Shih, T-H, Liou, WW, Shabbir, A, Yang, Z, and Zhu, Z (1995). "A New k-ε Eddy-Viscosity Model for High Reynolds Number Turbulent Flows - Model Development and Validation," *Computers Fluids*, Vol. 24, No. 3, pp. 227-238.

Singhal, AK, Vaidya, N, and Leonard, AD (1997). "Multi-Dimensional Simulation of Cavitating Flows Using a PDF Model of Phase Change," *ASME Paper FEDSM97-3272, Proc. ASME FED Meeting*, Vancouver, Canada.

Singhal, AK, Athavale, MM, Li, HY, and Jiang, Y (2002). "Mathematical Basis and Validation of the Full Cavitation Model," *ASME J. Fluids Engineering*, Vol. 124, No. 3, pp.617-624.

Stern, F, Kim, HT, Patel, VC, and Chen, HC (1988). "A Viscous-Flow Approach to the Computation of Propeller-Hull Interaction," *J. Ship Research*, Vol. 32, No. 4, pp.246-262.

Performance Prediction of Single or Multi-Component Propulsors using Coupled Viscous/Inviscid Methods

Spyros A. Kinnas[1], Hanseong Lee[2], Hong Sun[1], Lei He[1]

[1]Ocean Engineering Group; Department of Civil, Architectural, and Environmental Engineering,
The University of Texas at Austin, Austin, Texas, USA
[2]FloaTEC, LLC, Houston, Texas, USA

Abstract

This paper presents two different viscous/inviscid coupled methods that are used to predict the performance of single and multi-component propellers (podded or ducted propellers). In the first method, a vortex lattice method (named MPUF-3A) is coupled with a commercial Reynolds-Averaged Navier-Stokes (RANS) code (FLUENT). MPUF-3A solves for the potential flow around the propeller blades subject to an effective inflow, and FLUENT solves for the viscous flow field around the pod and the strut unit. The propeller effects are represented via time-averaged non-axisymmetric body force distributions over the volume swept by the propeller blades, and are included as source terms in the momentum equations in FLUENT. In the second method, a potential flow solver based on a boundary element method (named PROPCAV), which solves for the unsteady wetted or cavitating flow around propeller blades subject to non-axisymmetric inflows, is coupled with a two-dimensional integral boundary layer solver (XFOIL). In PROPCAV, the boundary layer is assumed to be two-dimensional along strips of constant radius on the propeller blades, and the effect of the boundary layer is included by distributing blowing sources on the blades, the cavity surface, and the trailing wake surface. Validation of the present methods is accomplished by comparing the predicted forces (or pressure distributions) with those measured in experiments or computed from other methods.

Keywords

Viscous/inviscid flow coupling; Podded propulsor; Ducted propulsor; Vortex lattice method; Boundary element method; RANS; Boundary layer.

Introduction

Potential flow methods, such as the vortex lattice method (VLM) or the boundary element method (BEM), have been used successfully in the past for the prediction of the flow (including the effects of sheet cavitation) and the resulting pressures and forces on blades of single or multi-component propulsors subject to non-axisymmetric inflows. To account for the effects of the boundary layers on the blades, traditionally, all potential flow methods have been using a uniformly applied friction coefficient over the blade surface (or the wetted part of it, in the presence of a sheet cavity) in order to account for the frictional part of the drag on the blades. In addition, the effects of the boundary layer on the pressure distribution (which contributes to the form drag on the blades) have been accounted for via an empirical reduction of the pitch of the blade. In the case of uniform inflows or inflows with zero vorticity, the effects of the other boundaries of the propulsor (e.g. hubs, pods, ducts, tunnel walls etc) have also been modeled via boundary element methods, with the effects of viscosity being accounted for in a similar way to those on the blades. In the case of inflows with vorticity in them (which is often the case since the propulsor is working inside the boundary layer at the stern of the hull) the inflow to the propeller must be the *effective wake*, which takes into account the interaction of the vorticity in the inflow with the flow around the blade. The effective wake is defined as the difference between the resultant total flow and the propeller induced flow. In order to evaluate the total flow we need to discretize the whole flow domain (as opposed to just the surfaces of the boundaries) and solve for either the (inviscid) Euler equations or the Reynolds-Averaged Navier-Stokes (RANS) equations in that domain. However, as the types of propulsors become more complicated, the accurate prediction of the flow field around the propulsor is becoming more difficult without considering the effects of viscosity. For example, in the case of a podded propulsor, the aft propeller operates within the boundary layer along the pod and the viscous wake field behind the strut, and thus the flow cannot be treated as accurately via inviscid flow methods. In recent years, with the help of high performance parallel computers, the use of Reynolds Averaged Navier-Stokes (RANS) solvers has been gradually increasing in the flow analysis around the blades and the other components of a marine propeller. Since a full RANS computation for marine propeller increases the computational time substantially and requires complicated grid generation due to moving propeller blades, the coupling of potential method (applied on the blades) with a RANS solver (applied to total flow) has been utilized as an efficient and useful method compromising the computational burden of full RANS simulation. In the viscous/inviscid coupling method, the flow field around the propeller is solved using a potential method, and a RANS calculation is performed for flows around the hull and propeller blades represented through body forces.

Various RANS/inviscid coupling methods have been developed for the flow analysis around the pod propulsors. Hsin et al. (2002) developed a blade design method for a pod propulsor using a coupled viscous/potential method. Then it was compared to the computed flow field around the pod with the results computed from a boundary element method. Ohashi and Hino (2004) applied the unstructured RANS solver to predict the performance of ship with a contra-rotating podded propeller. The propeller effects were represented through the body force distributions evaluated by a simplified propeller theory. Deniset et al. (2004) coupled a RANS flow solver with a potential code to perform the unsteady flow simulation around the whole pod and propeller. In their method, the pod/strut unit was modeled in RANS solver, and the propeller blades were modeled in potential solver. Later, their method was extended to reduce the computing time by separating the strut from viscous solver and solving it using a boundary element method (Deniset et al., 2006). Krasilnikov et al. (2006) also applied a viscous/potential coupling method that the panel method solved for the propeller flow and the RANS solver (FLUENT) simulated the axisymmetric flow around the pod with the effect of the propeller using an actuator disk scheme. Sanchez-Caja and Pylkkanen (2006) performed a full RANS simulation for the Compact Azipod unit at full and model scale at the design condition. However, their method was applied in the quasi-steady state, and the propeller was solved at a single blade position so that the memory effect was neglected. Kinnas et al. (2006) coupled a vortex lattice method with the FLUENT and an Euler solver (GBFLOW-3D) to predict the unsteady performance of pod propulsors.

Kerwin et al. (1994) initiated the application of the viscous/potential coupling method for ducted propeller. They coupled a lifting surface method with the axisymmetric viscous flow solver to design the flow adaptive ducted propeller. Warren et al. (2000) also coupled the unsteady lifting surface method with the time-averaged RANS solver for the prediction of propulsor induced maneuvering forces. In Sanchez-Caja et al. (2000), the RANS solver with $k - \varepsilon$ turbulence model was applied to analyze the viscous flow around a ducted propeller. Abdel-Maksoud and Heinke (2003) investigated the flow around the ducted propeller at different Reynolds numbers and loading conditions using the SST (Shear-Stress Transport) model. Recently, Hsiao and Chahine (2004) studied the cavitation inception in a ducted propeller using the Navier-Stokes computations and bubble dynamic models.

In the current paper, the potential methods (a boundary element method and a vortex lattice method) are coupled with the viscous analysis codes (XFOIL and FLUENT) to evaluate the viscous effects on pod and ducted propellers. Since Drela (1989) has successfully developed a strong coupling algorithm between the outer inviscid solution and the inner boundary layer, the XFOIL has been widely applied for the viscous analysis over propeller blades (Hufford et al. 1994). The coupling method has been extended to the 3-D hydrofoils (Nishida, 1996; Milewski, 1997; Mughal, 1998), and recently applied to the wetted and cavitating propellers by Sun and Kinnas (2006).

The first method solves for the flow around the pod propeller by coupling a vortex lattice method (MPUF-3A) with a RANS solver (FLUENT). MPUF-3A solves the potential flow around the propeller subject to effective velocities, and as a result determines the propeller forces and pressures. FULENT solves for the viscous flow field around the pod and the strut with body forces representing the propeller. Once MPUF-3A determines the pressure distributions on the propeller blade in a given effective inflow, FLUENT predicts the total velocity distributions within the fluid domain based on the body forces converted from the pressure distributions on propeller blades. The new effective inflow velocities are then determined by subtracting the propeller-induced velocities from the total velocities. This iteration procedure between MPUF-3A and FLUENT continues until the predicted forces are stabilized within the acceptable tolerance.

In the second method, a boundary element method (PROPCAV) is coupled with an integral boundary layer solver (XFOIL) to investigate the viscous effects on ducted propellers. PROPCAV solves for the flow around the ducted propellers, in which the propeller and duct are discretized with hyperboloidal panels. PROPCAV is a direct method and thus solves the integral equation for the duct/pod and the propeller simultaneously. The viscosity effects are included with coupling with XFOIL. The coupled method determines the friction on the blades and also evaluates the effects of viscosity on the pressure distributions over the blades.

Viscous flows around podded propulsors

The performance of a podded propulsor with the effect of viscosity was analyzed through the coupled vortex lattice method (MPUF-3A) and the commercial RANS code (FLUENT). Results are also presented from the coupling of MPUF-3A with our Euler solver, GBFLOW-3D.

Vortex lattice method (MPUF-3A)

The analysis of potential flow around the propeller was performed via a vortex lattice method (MPUF-3A), and the detailed information on the method can be found in Lee (1979). MPUF-3A solves for the potential flow around a pod propeller by placing the discrete vortices and sources on the blade mean camber surface and its trailing wake surface. The effects of a non-cylindrical pod was taken into account by employing a simplified image model in which the vortex and source segments of the blade and its trailing wake were imaged with respect to the pod.

In MPUF-3A, the discrete vortex segment forms a horseshoe with constant strength, Γ, and the line source segment represents the effect of the blade and cavity thickness. The unknown strengths of the singularities, Γ and cavity source strength (Q_C), can be determined by applying the kinematic and dynamic boundary conditions at control points.

The kinematic boundary condition requires the flow to be tangent to the mean camber surface, and can be written in discretized form as follows:

$$\sum_{\Gamma} \Gamma \vec{v}_{\Gamma} \cdot \vec{n} + \sum_{Q_B} Q_B \vec{v}_Q \cdot \vec{n} + \sum_{Q_C} Q_C \vec{v}_Q \cdot \vec{n} = \vec{q}_T \cdot \vec{n} \quad (1)$$

Where $\vec{q}_T$ is the inflow velocity, $\vec{n}$ is the unit normal vector, and Γ is the constant strength of bound vortex. Q_B and Q_C are the magnitude of line sources representing the blade and cavity thickness, respectively. $\vec{v}_Q$ and $\vec{v}_\Gamma$ are the velocity vectors induced by each unit strength of line source and vortex loop.

The dynamic boundary condition forces the pressures on the cavity surface to be equal to the cavity pressure.

$$P_\infty + \frac{1}{2}\rho |\vec{q}_T|^2 = P_C + \frac{1}{2}\rho |\vec{q}_C|^2 + \rho \frac{\partial \varphi}{\partial t} + \rho g y_s \quad (2)$$

Where P_C and P_∞ are the cavity pressure and the pressure far upstream along the axis of rotation. $\vec{q}_C$ is the total velocity on cavity surface. g is the gravitational constant, y_s is the vertical distance from the horizontal plane through the axis of rotation, and ρ is the fluid density. The boundary conditions and the modeling of blade and hub in MPUF-3A are shown in Fig. 1.

Once Eq. (1) is solved to satisfy the boundary conditions, the strengths of all the singularities are known. Then, the perturbation potential induced by the propeller can be computed as follows:

$$\phi(\vec{x}) = \sum_{\Gamma} \Gamma \phi_\Gamma + \sum_{Q_B} Q_B \phi_Q + \sum_{Q_C} Q_C \phi_Q \quad (3)$$

Where ϕ_Γ and ϕ_Q are the potential induced by the unit strength of vortex loop and line source, respectively. Based on the potential distribution obtained from Eq. 3, the propeller-induced velocity at the effective wake plane is then calculated by applying the central difference scheme between two planes adjacent to the effective wake plane in FLUENT grid.

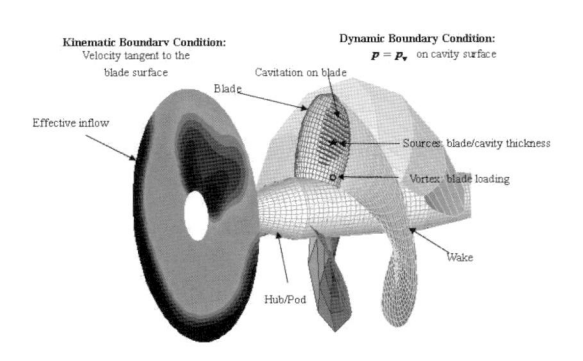

Fig.1: Modeling of propeller blade and hub in MPUF-3A, and the applied boundary conditions

RANS solver (FLUENT)

In the present work, the viscous flow field around the pod propeller was analyzed using FLUENT 6.3, which solved the continuity and the momentum equations by employing a cell-centered finite volume method. The realizable k-ε turbulence model was used to solve the RANS equations. Time derivative terms were discretized by the use of the second order implicit scheme. The SIMPLE algorithm was applied for pressure–velocity coupling, and the face pressures were interpolated by using the body-force-weighted scheme. The second order upwind scheme is applied to the other options in discretization. The boundary condition for the pod and the strut surfaces was set as a wall with a non-equilibrium wall function. In addition the tunnel walls were also modeled as walls on which the no-slip condtions were applied. The unsteady three-dimensional simulations were performed on the un-structured grid generated from GAMBIT with prismatic boundary layer elements attached on the pod and the strut surfaces so that $y^+ < 300$. In order to include the effects of the propeller, the momentum equations were modified to include the body force terms that were converted from blade pressures computed in MPUF-3A via User-Defined Functions. The convergence criteria were set so that the residuals were smaller than 10^{-6} at each time step, and the forces acting on the pod and the strut did not change at each iteration step.

MPUF-3A/ FLUENT coupling

Although the accurate prediction of inflow to the propeller is essential for the prediction of propeller performance, it is difficult to accurately evaluate the velocity due to the strong vorticity generated by the boundary layer along the ship hull, pod, and strut surfaces. In the present method, MPUF-3A is coupled with FLUENT to predict the inflow to the propeller, so called effective wake, and the coupling method requires an iterative procedure to archive the convergence.

First, MPUF-3A is applied by assuming that the effective is the same as the nominal wake (defined as the inflow wake in the absence of the propulsor). The pressure distributions on the blades and the blade forces are determined from the MPUF-3A run. In addition, the potential distributions are determined by using Eq. 3, and later those are used to evaluate the propeller-induced velocities at the effective wake plane in the FLUENT grid system. The determined pressure distributions are converted into the body force terms that represent the propeller blade in FLUENT. FLUENT solves for the viscous flow field with the strut and the pod. As a result of the FLUENT run, the total velocity and pressure distributions are determined in the fluid domain. The effective velocity is then calculated by subtracting the propeller-induced velocity from the total velocity at the effective wake plane. The updated effective velocity is used as a new inflow to the propeller in MPUF-3A. Iterations between MPUF-3A and FLUENT are repeated until the blade forces converge within a given tolerance.

MPUF-3A/GBFLOW-3D coupling

GBFLOW-3D is a finite volume method based three-dimensional Euler solver that was developed to solve the flow field around pod and strut. The method was initially developed to predict the effective wake of an open propeller by Choi (2000) and Choi and Kinnas (2001). Later, the method was extended by including the capability of flow analysis around multi-component propulsors via coupling with MPUF-3A. The details on the coupling method are aptly described in Kakar (2002), Kinnas et al. (2002, 2004, 2006), Gupta (2004) and Mishra (2005).

In the paper, the total force acting on the pod, strut and propeller system was calculated based on the method described in Gupta (2004) as follows:

$$F_{TOTAL} = F_{prop} - F_{GB} - F_{FR} - F_{NP}$$

where F_{prop} is the propeller force (or the sum of the propeller forces in the case of a twin podded propulsor) calculated from MPUF-3A, F_{GB} is the force obtained from GBFLOW-3D, and F_{NP} is the *tear force* evaluated without the effect of propeller on the pod and strut. F_{FR} is the frictional force calculated based on a constant frictional coefficient applied on the surfaces of the pod and the strut.

Results

This section describes the predicted performance of a twin-type podded propulsor by coupling MPUF-3A with FLUENT. The geometry of this podded propulsor is based on the experiment performed by Szantyr (2001). The numerical results are analyzed by comparing the experimental data (Szantyr 2001) with the results from MPUF-3A/GBFLOW-3D.

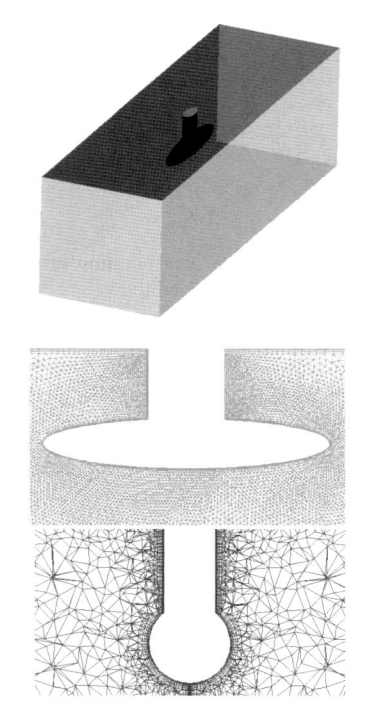

Fig. 2: Computational domain and grid in FLUENT

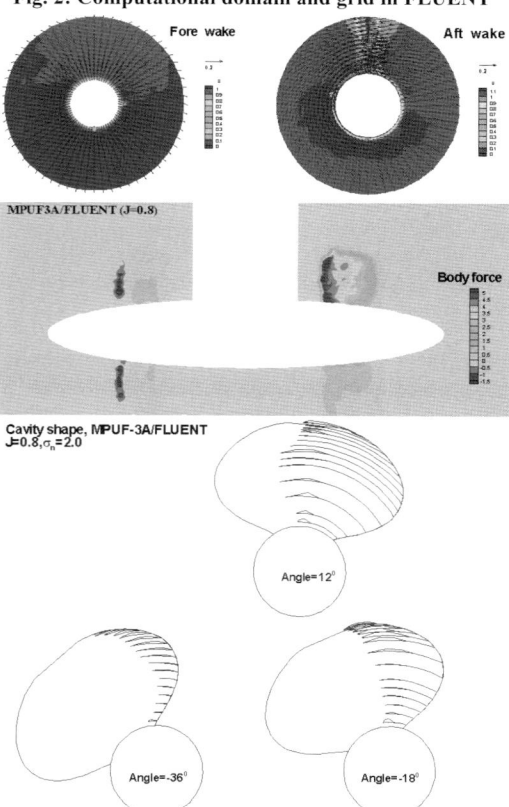

Fig. 3: Effective wakes for the fore and aft propeller (top), the corresponding axial body forces (middle), and the cavity patterns of the aft propeller (bottom); predicted by coupling MPUF-3A with FLUENT. Twin type podded propulsor (with left handed props), J=0.8 and σ_n=2.0.

In both FLUENT and GBFLOW-3D, the propellers are represented by the body force terms which are calculated from the results of MPUF-3A, as described in Choi and Kinnas (2001). The three components of the body forces are varying in the axial, radial and circumferential direction according to the time-averaged blade loading as the blade passes through a certain cell in the finite volume method. Figure 3 shows the (axial) body force distribution due to the presence of the propellers as well as the corresponding effective wakes for the fore and the aft propeller. Note the expected presence of the wake of the strut in the effective wake of the aft propeller, and the corresponding increase of the loading (body forces) at the 12 o'clock position of the aft propeller. At the bottom of Figure 3 the predicted cavity patterns from MPUF-3A are shown for the aft propeller at a cavitation number $\sigma_n = 2.0$, where $\sigma_n = \dfrac{p_0 - p_c}{0.5 \rho n^2 D^2}$; with p_0 being the absolute pressure at the shaft, p_c the vapor pressure, n the propeller RPS, and D the propeller diameter. The used cavitation number is hypothetical since only fully wetted conditions were reported in the experiment.

The convergence of the propeller thrust and torque for both fore- and aft- propellers with the number of iterations is shown in Figure 4. The convergence is obtained after three iterations between MPUF-3A and FLUENT.

Figure 5 shows the predicted forces compared with those from the MPUF-3A/GBFLOW-3D coupling and those measured in the experiment. Note that based on this case the predictions from the two approaches seem to agree very well with each other for higher advance ratios Js, but FLUENT seems to be lower for lower Js and actually closer to the measurements. However, more validations are needed before any general conclusions are drawn on the performance of either method.

A 16-node cluster with 2 CPUs (1.6GHz AMD Opteron) and 4GBs RAM per node was used in our numerical simulations. For 5 iterations between MPUF-3A and GBFLOW-3D, by using a single processor, it took about 10 hours of computational time. For 5 iterations between MPUF-3A and FLUENT, by using 10 processors, it took about 120 hours of computational time.

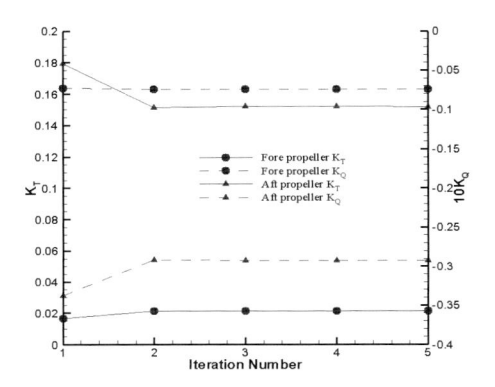

Fig. 4: Convergence of K_T and K_Q from MPUF-3A/FLUENT with number of iterations between the two methods. Twin type podded propulsor, J=0.8

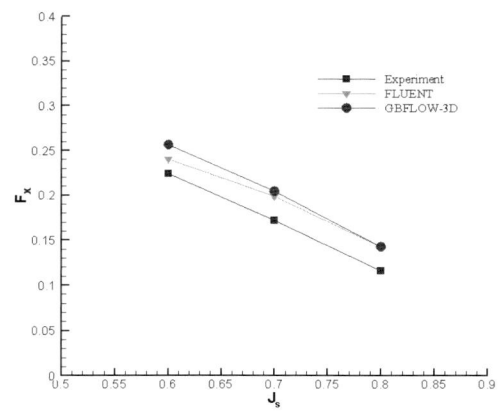

Fig. 5: Total axial force for twin type pod propulsor; predicted from coupling MPUF-3A with FLUENT or GBFLOW-3D, and measured in the experiment of Szantyr (2001).

Viscous flows around ducted propellers

Formulation

A viscous-inviscid interaction (VII) method is applied to investigate the effects of viscosity on flows around ducted propellers. The details of the viscous-inviscid interaction method applied for the conventional propellers in wetted condition are given in Sun and Kinnas (2006). The numerical techniques applied on the ducted propeller are similar to the previous authors' work (Sun and Kinnas 2006). However, the governing equations and the viscous-inviscid coupling procedure are summarized here for sake of completeness:

The governing equation for the inviscid flow around ducted propeller is the Green's equation, Eq. 4:

$$2\pi \phi_p(\vec{x}) = \iint_{S_{WB}+S_D+S_C}\left[\phi_q \frac{\partial G(p;q)}{\partial n_q} - G \frac{\partial \phi(p;q)}{\partial n_q}\right]ds \quad (4)$$
$$+ \iint_{S_W+S_{DW}} \Delta\phi_w(r_q,\theta_q)\frac{\partial G(p;q)}{\partial n_q}ds$$

where $p \in S_{WB} - S_D - S_C$

The subscripts p and q correspond to the field point and the variable point, respectively. $G(p;q) = 1/R(p;q)$ is the Green's function, with $R(p;q)$ being the distance between points p and q. $\vec{n}_q$ is the unit normal vector pointing into the flow domain. $\Delta\phi_w$ and $\Delta\phi_{DW}$ are the potential jump across the wake surfaces shedding from the blade and the duct trailing edge, respectively. S_{WB} is the wetted surface on the blade and the hub, S_D is the duct surface, and S_C is the partial- or super-cavity surface on the blade and its trailing wake.

In the viscous-inviscid interaction method, the effects of boundary layer are taken into account by distributing the "blowing" sources on the propeller blade, the sheet cavity and the wake surfaces. The strength of the "blowing" source is defined as:

$$\hat{\sigma} = \frac{d(U_e \delta^*)}{ds} \quad (5)$$

Then, the effects of the blowing sources can be included in the Green's formula given in Eq. 4 as follows:

$$2\pi\phi_p(\vec{x}) = \iint_{S_{WB}+S_D+S_C} \left[\phi_q \frac{\partial G(p;q)}{\partial n_q} - G\frac{\partial \phi(p;q)}{\partial n_q}\right]ds$$
$$+ \iint_{S_W+S_{DW}} \Delta\phi_w(r_q,\theta_q)\frac{\partial G(p;q)}{\partial n_q}ds \quad (6)$$
$$- \iint_{S_{WB}+S_D+S_C+S_W+S_{DW}} \hat{\sigma}(p;q)\frac{\partial \phi(p;q)}{\partial n_q}ds$$

where $p \in S_{WB}$ - S_D - S_C

The viscous solution is solved with coupling Eq. 6 with the boundary layer, Equations 7-10. The coupling is applied along each strip of the propeller blade and duct.

$$\frac{d\theta}{ds} + (2+H)\frac{\theta}{U_e}\frac{dU_e}{ds} = \frac{C_f}{2} \quad (7)$$

$$\theta\frac{H^*}{ds} + \left[2H^{**} + H^*(1-H)\right]\frac{\theta}{U_e}\frac{dU_e}{ds} = 2C_D - H^*\frac{C_f}{2} \quad (8)$$

$$\frac{d\tilde{n}}{ds} = \frac{d\tilde{n}}{dR_{e\theta}}\frac{dR_{e\theta}}{ds} \quad (9)$$

$$\frac{\delta}{C_\tau}\frac{dC_\tau}{ds} = 5.6\left[C_{\tau EQ}^{1/2} - C_\tau^{1/2}\right]$$
$$+ 2\delta \times \left\{\frac{4}{3\delta^*}\left[\frac{C_f}{2} - \left(\frac{H_k-1}{6.7H_k}\right)^2\right] - \frac{1}{U_e}\frac{dU_e}{ds}\right\} \quad (10)$$

The main coupling equation between the inviscid and viscous equations is given as:

$$U_e = U_e^{inv} + \varepsilon\left\{U_e \delta^*\right\} \quad (11)$$

Equation 8 implies that the edge velocity U_e along each blade strip can be expressed in terms of the inviscid edge velocity U_{inv}, and the mass defect term $m = U_e \delta^*$.

Results

Steady viscous flow around bare duct

The steady wetted flow around DTMB Duct II is investigated by using the viscous-inviscid coupling method (PROPCAV/XFOIL). Morgan and Caster (1965) provided the experimental measures to validate the numerical results. As shown in Fig. 6, the DTMB Duct II is an axisymmetric duct. The section of the DTMB Duct II is of a NACA66 modified thickness form, with the maximum thickness-chord ratio $t_{max}/C = 0.10$, and of a NACA $a = 0.8$ mean camber line, with the maximum camber-chord ratio $f_{max}/C = 0.04$. The chord-diameter ratio is $C/D = 0.8$, where C is the chord of the duct section and D is the diameter of the duct. The angle of the attack of the duct section is $\alpha = 0°$. The discretization on the duct is of 160 panels in the chordwise direction with cosine spacing, and 80 panels in the circumferential direction with uniform spacing.

The inflow wake of the duct is uniform, and the hydrostatic effect is neglected. The flow Reynolds number based on duct diameter is $R_{eD} = 2.06e+6$. The flow turbulence level is set as 1%. Forced transition at $5\%C$ from the leading edge is applied on both the inner and outer surfaces of the duct in the calculation. The convergence criterion for the integral boundary layer analysis is 1.0e−5. It takes less than 1 minute to finish both the inviscid and viscous analysis of the steady wetted flow on a SUN BLADE workstation.

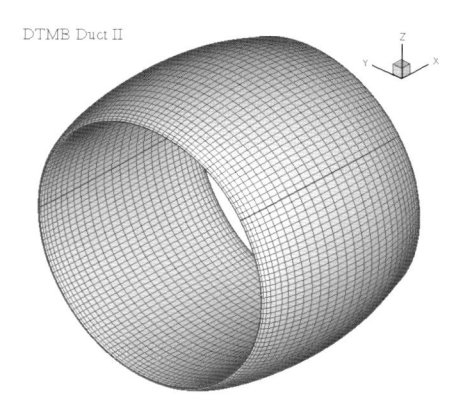

Fig. 6: Modeling of DTMB duct II in PROPCAV

Fig. 7 shows the comparison of the predicted inviscid and viscous pressure distributions with the measurements from the experiments. The definition of the pressure coefficient is shown as $C_p = (P - P_o)/(1/2\rho U_\infty^2)$, where P_o and U_∞ are the pressure and inflow far upstream. As shown in Fig. 7, the viscous effect decreases the pressure magnitude, and the viscous solution from the present method compares well with the measurement.

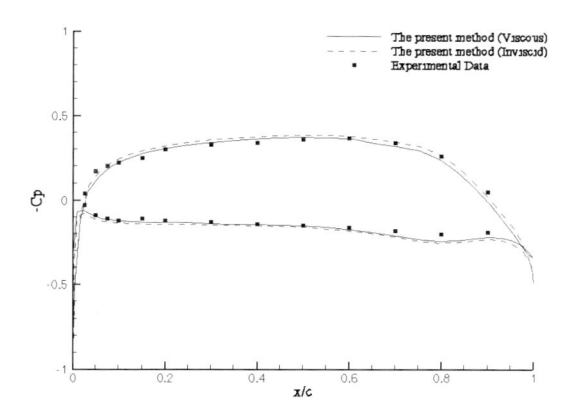

Fig. 7: Comparison of the predicted pressure distributions with the measured from experiment (Morgan and Caster, 1965) on DTMB duct II

Steady viscous flow around single propeller

In order to validate the method, PROPCAV/XFOIL is applied to predict the performance of a 3-bladed single propeller DTRC 4119 in steady wetted condition.

The propeller geometry is shown in Fig. 8. The discretization on the propeller blade is of 60 panels in the chordwise direction with cosine spacing, and 20 panels in the span-wise direction with uniform spacing. The propeller inflow is uniform, with $F_r = 9999.0$. For the viscous run, the Reynolds number based on the propeller diameter is $R_{eD} = 766,395$, and the flow turbulence level is 1%. Natural transition is applied on both the pressure and suction sides of the blade. The convergence criterion for the integral boundary layer analysis is $1.0e^{-5}$. It takes less than 1 minute to finish the viscous analysis of the steady wetted flow on a SUN BLADE workstation.

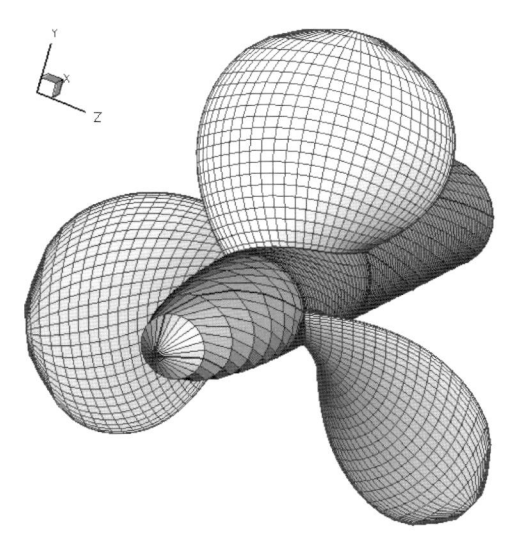

Fig. 8: Geometry of the propeller DTRC4119

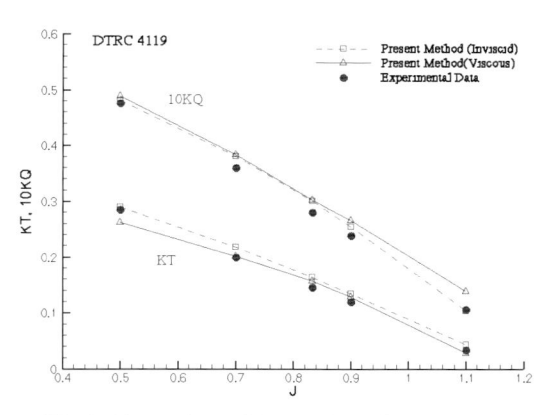

Fig. 9: Comparison of the predicted forces with the measured (Jessup, 1989) on propeller 4119

Fig. 9 compares the inviscid and viscous blade forces K_T and K_Q for different advance ratios with the measured blade forces of DTRC 4119 propeller by Jessup (1989). The viscosity effect decreases the thrust force and increases the drag force. As shown in the figure, the predicted viscous thrust and torque forces agree well with the measurement with the exception that the viscous torque forces are over-predicted at the highest advance ratio.

Steady viscous flow around ducted propeller

In this section, viscous wetted flow around a ducted propeller is presented. Propeller P1452 with D15 duct is chosen to compare the predicted forces with those measured in the experiments (Dyne, 1973).

Fig. 10 shows the geometries of the P1452 propeller and the D15 duct. P1452 is a 4-bladed propeller, with the hub ratio equal to 0.26. The propeller blade section is of NACA16 thickness distribution, and of NACA $a = 0.8$ mean line. For the duct D15, the profile angle is $9.2°$, and the maximum camber is 0.06. The gap size between the duct inner surface and the blade tip is 1.09% of the propeller radius.

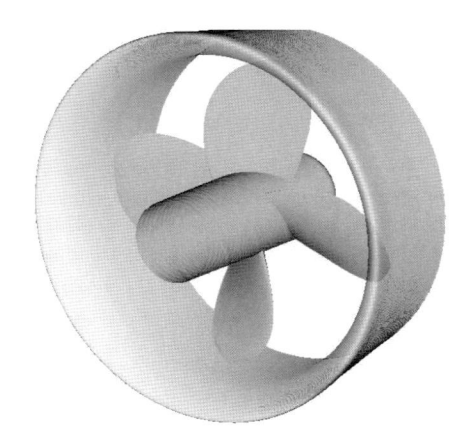

Fig. 10: Geometry of the P1452 propeller and D15 duct

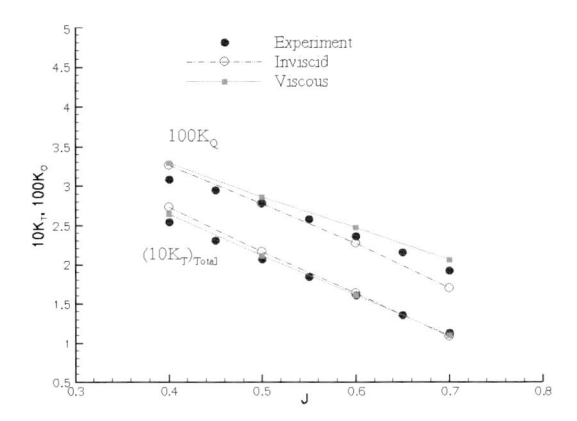

Fig.11: Comparison of the predicted blade forces with the measured from experiment (Dyne, 1973) on DYNE ducted propeller

The inflow wake is uniform, and the hydrostatic force is neglected. The flow Reynolds number based on propeller diameter is $R_{eD} = 1.15e+6$ for the high advance ratios and $R_{eD} = 0.67e+6$ for the low advance ratio. The flow turbulence level is also 1%. At $\sigma_v = 20$, the thrust and torque forces are compared with the measurements by Dyne (1973). σ_v is defined as:

$$\sigma_v = \frac{p_0 - p_c}{\frac{1}{2}\rho V_{ship}^2} \qquad (12)$$

where V_{ship} is the ship speed, p_0 is the far upstream pressure on the shaft axis, and ρ is the water density. For $\sigma_v = 20$, there is no cavity happening on the propeller blade, and the flow is actually fully wetted. The convergence criterion for the integral boundary layer analysis is $1.0e^{-5}$. It takes about 8 minutes to finish both the inviscid and viscous analysis for this case on a SUN BLADE workstation.

Fig. 11 compares the total inviscid and viscous thrust and torque forces K_T and K_Q for different advance ratios with the measured forces by (Dyne, 1973). The total thrust force is the sum of the thrust forces on the duct and the propeller. In this work, there are difficulties in obtaining converged results for the viscous analysis of the flow over the duct. Therefore, the total thrust force presented in the figure has excluded the viscosity analysis of flow over the duct. Instead, the viscosity effect is simulated with the use of the empirical formula. As shown in the figure, the predicted viscous thrust and the torque forces agree well with the measurement.

Conclusions

The coupled viscous/inviscid methods were developed to predict the performance of single or multi-components propellers in wetted or cavitating conditions. First, a vortex lattice method (MPUF-3A) was coupled with the commercial RANS code (FLUENT) in the case of a pod propulsor. The interaction between the two methods was taken into account through the effective wake computed from FLUENT, and the body forces evaluated from MPUF-3A. Second, an integral boundary layer solver (XFOIL) was incorporated into a boundary element method (PROPCAV) for the performance prediction of single and ducted propellers. The viscous effects were included in the potential solver by distributing the blowing sources on blade and cavity surfaces. Both coupling methods required the iteration procedure between viscous and inviscid methods to ensure the force convergence within specified criteria.

Both methods were validated through comparisons of the forces (thrust and torque) with those measured in experiments and/or calculated by other methods.

Acknowledgements

Support for this research was provided by Phase IV of the "Consortium on Cavitation Performance of High Speed Propulsors" with the following members: AB Volvo Penta, American Bureau of Shipping, Daewoo Shipbuilding and Marine Engineering Co. Ltd., Kawasaki Heavy Industry Ltd., Naval Surface Warfare Center Carderock Division through the Office of Naval Research (Contract N0001404-1-0287), Rolls-Royce Marine AB, Rolls-Royce Marine AS, VA Tech Escher Wyss GmbH, Wärtsilä Propulsion Netherlands B.V., Wärtsilä Propulsion Norway AS, and Wärtsilä CME Zhenjiang Propeller Co. Ltd.

References

Abdel-Maksoud, M, and Heinke, HJ (2002). "Scale Effects on Ducted Propellers," Twenty-Fourth Symposium on Naval Hydrodynamics, Fukuoka, Japan.

Choi, JK (2000). "Vortical inflow – Propeller Interaction using an Unsteady Three-Dimensional Euler Solver," Ph.D Thesis, Department of Civil Engineering, The Univ. of Texas at Austin.

Choi, JK, and Kinnas, SA (2001) "Prediction of Non-axisymmetric Effective Wake by a Three-Dimensional Euler Solver," Journal of Ship Research, Vol. 45, No 1, pp 13-33.

Deniset, F, Jaouen, R, Billard, JY, and Laurens, JM (2004). "Fluctuating Pressure Distribution on Pod," T-POD 2004, Newcastle, UK, April 14-16, pp 237-246.

Deniset, F, Laurens, JM, and Romon, S (2006). "Computation of the Fluctuating Pressure Distribution on the Pod Strut," T-POD 2006, Brest, France, October 3-5.

Drela, M (1989). "XFOIL: An Analysis and Design System for Low Reynolds Number Airfoils," Lecture Notes in Engineering (Vol. 54, Low Reynolds Number Aerodynamics), New York, Springer-Verlag.

Dyne, G (1973). "Systematic Studies of Accelerating Ducted Propellers in Axial and Incline Flows," Symposium on Ducted Propellers, RINA, pp 114-124.

Gupta, A (2004). "Numerical Prediction of Flows around Podded Propulsors," Master's Thesis, Department of Civil Engineering, The Univ. of Texas at Austin.

Hsiao, CT, and Chahine, GL (2004). "Numerical Study of Cavitation Inception due to Vortex/Vortex Interaction in a Ducted Propulsor," Twenty-Fifth Symposium on Naval Hydrodynamics, St. John's Newfoundland and Labrador, Canada.

Hsin, CY, Chou, SK, and Chen, WC (2002). "A New Propeller Design Method for the POD Propulsion System," Twenty –Fourth Symposium on Naval Hydrodynamics, Fukuoka, Japan.

Hufford, G, Drela, M, and Kerwin, JE (1994). "Viscous Flow around Marine Propellers using Boundary-Layer Strip Theory," Journal of Ship Research, Vol. 38, No 1, pp 52-62.

Jessup, SD (1989). "An Experimental Investigation of Viscous Aspects of Propeller Blade Flow," PhD Thesis, The Catholic University of America.

Kakar, K (2002). "Computational Modeling of FPSO Hull Roll Motion and Two-component Marine Propulsion Systems," Master's Thesis, Department of Civil Engineering, The Univ. of Texas at Austin.

Kerwin, JE, Keenan, DP, Black, SD, and Diggs, JG (1994). "A coupled Viscous/Potential Flow Design Method for Wake-Adaptive, Multi-Stage, Ducted Propulsors using Generalized Geometry," Trans. of SNAME, Vol. 102.

Kinnas, SA, Choi, JK, Lee, HS, Young, YL, Gu, H, Kakar, K, and Natarajan, S (2002). "Prediction of Cavitation Performance of Single or Multi-component Propulsors and their Interaction with the Hull," Transactions of Society of Naval Architects and Marine Engineers, Vol. 110, pp 215-244.

Kinnas, SA, Lee, HS, Gu, H, and Gupta, A (2004). "Prediction of Performance of Ducted and Podded Propellers," Proceeding of Twenty-Fifth Symposium on Naval Hydrodynamics, St. John's Newfoundland and Labrador, Canada, August 8-13.

Kinnas, SA, Lee, HS, Mishra, B, He, L, Rhee, SH, and Balasubramanyam, S (2006). "Hydrodynamic Analysis of Podded Propellers," Proceeding of Propellers/Shafting 2006 Symposium, The Society of Naval Architects and Marine Engineers, Williamsburg, VA, September 12-13, pp 1-13 (paper No. 1).

Sun, H, and Kinnas, SA (2006). "Simulation of Sheet Cavitation on Propulsor Blades using a Viscous/Inviscid Interaction Method," Sixth International Symposium on Cavitation (CAV2006), Wageningen, The Netherlands, September.

Krasilnikov, V, Ponkratov, D, Achkinadze, A., Berg, A., and Ying, SJ (2006). "Possibilities of a Viscous/Potential Coupled method to Study Scale Effects on Open-Water Characteristics of Podded Propulsors," T-POD 2006, Brest, France, October 3-5.

Lee, CS (1979). "Prediction of Steady and Unsteady Performance of Marine Propellers with or without Cavitation by Numerical Lifting Surface Theory," PhD Thesis, MIT, Department of Ocean Engineering.

Milewski, W (1997). "Three-Dimensional Viscous Flow Computations using the Integral Boundary Equations Simultaneously Coupled with a Low Order Panel Method," PhD Thesis, MIT, Department of Ocean Engineering.

Mishra, B (2005). "Prediction of Performance of Podded Propulsors via Coupling of a Vortex-Lattice Method with an Euler or a RANS solver," Master's Thesis, Department of Civil Engineering, The Univ. of Texas at Austin.

Morgan, W, and Caster, EB (1965). "Prediction of the Aerodynamic Characteristics of Annular Airfoils," Technical report 1830, DTMB.

Mughal, B (1998). "Integral Methods for Three Dimensional Boundary Layers," PhD Thesis, MIT, Department of Aeronautics and Astronautics.

Nishida, B (1996). "Fully Simultaneous Coupling of the Full Potential Equation and the Integral Boundary Layer Equations in Three Dimensions," PhD Thesis, MIT, Department of Aeronautics and Astronautics.

Ohashi, K, and Hino, T (2004). "Numerical Simulations of Flows around a Ship with Podded Propulsor," T-POD 2004, Newcastle, UK, April 14-16, pp 211-221.

Sanchez-Caja, A, and Pylkkanen, JV (2006). "RANS Predictions for Flow Patterns around a Compact Azipod," T-POD 2006, Brest, France, October 3-5.

Sanchez-Caja, A, Rautaheimo, P, and Siikonen, T (2000). "Simulation of Incompressible Viscous Flow around a Ducted Propeller using a RANS Equation Solver," Twenty-Third Symposium on Naval Hydrodynamics, Valde Reuil, France.

Szantyr, J. (2001). "Hydrodynamic model experiments with pod propulsors," Ocean Engineering International 5-2, pp 95-103.

Maximum Ice-Induced Loads on Ships in the Baltic Sea

Pentti Kujala, Janne Valkonen, Mikko Suominen

Ship Laboratory, Helsinki University of Technology
Espoo, Finland

Abstract

Ice-induced loads have a clear random nature with high scatter on the load level due to the varying ice conditions and ice operation situations. The maximum level of ice-induced loads on the shell structures of ships navigating in the Baltic Sea are analyzed in this paper. The approach used for life time maximum ice loads aims to relate the load level with the main ship parameters and the prevailing ice conditions on various parts of the Baltic Sea. A semi-empirical approach is used for estimation of long term ice loads, which relies partly on full scale measurements and partly on the analysis of the ice edge failure process. In addition damage statistics have been gathered and analyzed to obtain an additional verification for the calculated level of the extreme loads on ships navigating in the Baltic Sea. The conducted full scale measurements and related statistical analysis have given a fairly clear picture about the possible maximum load level at the bow of ice-strengthened vessels. The proper load level at midship and aftship is more complicated. The normal forward navigation of a ship causes a low basic load level at midship and aftship, but an extensive increase on the load level can take place due to the maneuvering activities of the ship. This results in the highly scattered load peaks on these parts of the ship hull.

Keywords

Ice load; Full scale measurements; Ice damages; Statistical analysis

Introduction

The maximum level of ice-induced loads on the shell structures of ships navigating in the Baltic Sea are analyzed in this paper. The scope of analyzing ice load statistics is wide. Ice conditions and ship operations in ice vary in the short term from voyage to voyage and in long term from winter to winter. It is important to determine the main parameters that can be used as a basis for reliable probabilistic ice load models.

The approach used for life time maximum ice loads aims to relate the load level with the main ship parameters and the prevailing ice conditions on various parts of the Baltic Sea. A semi-empirical approach is used for estimation of long term ice loads, which relies partly on full scale measurements and partly on the analysis of the ice edge failure process. The effect of ridges on the load level is included by specifying an equivalent level ice thickness for a ridged ice field. This approach yields results that can be used in the development of design codes for ice-strengthened ships. The models developed are subsequently verified using the results of extensive short term and long term ice load measurements onboard MS Kemira, MS Arcturus and MT Kashira.

In addition damage statistics have been gathered and analyzed to obtain an additional verification for the calculated level of the extreme loads on ships navigating in the Baltic Sea.

This paper presents the summary of the conducted full-scale measurements, developed statistical models to estimate long-term ice loads and compares finally the load level obtained by full scale measurements and by analyzing the damages occurred on ships in the Baltic Sea.

Ice conditions in the Baltic Sea

Ice formation in the Baltic Sea starts in the northernmost parts of the Bothnian Bay in late October or early November (Ice Atlas, 1982). The ice break-up starts in the southern parts in early March and the northern Bothnian Bay is usually open again in May. Only first year ice exists in the Baltic Sea. The ice conditions can be divided into fast ice and pack ice regions. Islands and grounded ice ridges hold the coastal ice motionless and cause the formation of stationary fast ice areas. All Finnish harbors are icebound every winter by this fast ice zone.

The ice outside the fast ice zone is pack ice, which can drift and collide to form open leads and ridged ice. The term ridged ice is used to cover all the deformed ice. Fig. 1 summarizes the annual frequency of ice occurrence on various parts of the Baltic Sea based on the statistics from the winters 1964 to 1979 (Ice Atlas, 1982).

Thickness of the solid ice cover is the main variable used in this work to describe the ice conditions. The thickness of the ice cover is strongly variable. These variations are caused by thermal and mechanical factors. The thermal factor is a continuous component and is related to the changes in air temperature and snow cover above the ice surface. The mechanical factors are discrete components caused by rafting, ridging, and opening of leads and polynyas. The development of fast ice thickness is mainly caused by the thermal factor, whereas for pack ice all the factors are important. The effect of ridging is included by analyzing the thickness of the consolidated layer inside a ridge. After the dynamic build-up of a ridge, contact joints form between ice blocks and a consolidated solid ice sheet forms down from the water surface level as illustrated in Fig. 2. The measurements conducted to study the thickness of this consolidated layer have indicated that on the average this thickness is about 1.4 times thicker than the surrounding level ice (Kujala, 1994). Naturally there is a big scatter also in this figure as it is affected by many factors such as the thermal history, age and height of the ridges.

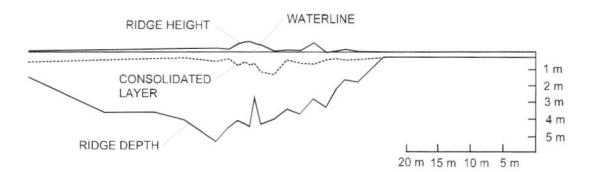

Fig. 2: An example of the shape of the measured ridge and thickness of the consolidated layer at the nothern Bay of Bothnia (Veitch et al., 1991).

The long term variation of level pack ice thickness can be obtained from the daily routine ice charts, in which the approximate upper and lower limits of the level ice thickness are given on various parts of the Baltic Sea. This thickness is obtained from observations onboard icebreakers and by conducting occasional thickness measurements. The thickness of ridged pack ice is not observed routinely. The measured winter maximum values of the level ice thickness observed continuously on four permanent stations (see Fig. 1) are, however, considered more accurate for presentation of the annual variation of the maximum level ice thickness on the various sea areas. Therefore, the long term data, given in Table 1, are used in this work when the long term ice loads are analyzed. The effect of ridges is included by multiplying the mean level ice thickness with a factor k shown also in Table 1. This factor is obtained by simulating the ice induced loads in an ice field with varying probability (P_r) of ridges and based on these calculations, a value for k_r is obtained so that the simulated load level is the same in the level ice field with ridges and in an ice field with equivalent level ice thickness (Kujala, 1994).

Table 1 Long term average and standard deviation for the level ice and equivalent thickness in various parts of the Baltic Sea (Kujala, 1994).

Sea area	Level ice				Equivalent ice thickness	
	Mean [m]	Std. [m]	P_r	k_r	Mean [m]	Std. [m]
Bothnian Bay	0,474	0,164	0,50	1,28	0,607	0,210
Bothnian Sea	0,414	0,153	0,25	1,21	0,501	0,185
Gulf of Finland	0,404	0,140	0,25	1,21	0,489	0,170
Baltic proper	0,336	0,136	0,10	1,12	0,376	0,152

Conducted full scale measurements

Extensive full-scale measurements have been conducted in the Baltic Sea especially during the 1980's as summarized e.g. by Hänninen (2002). In the following the measurements conducted onboard MS Kemira, MS Arcturus and MT Kashira is discussed in further detail.

MS Kemira was instrumented in autumn 1984 and the ice-induced loads were measured continuously during the winter 1985-1992, when the ship was navigating between Finnish harbors on the Bay of Bothnia (Kokkola), Bothnian Bay (Uusikaupunki) and Central Europe.

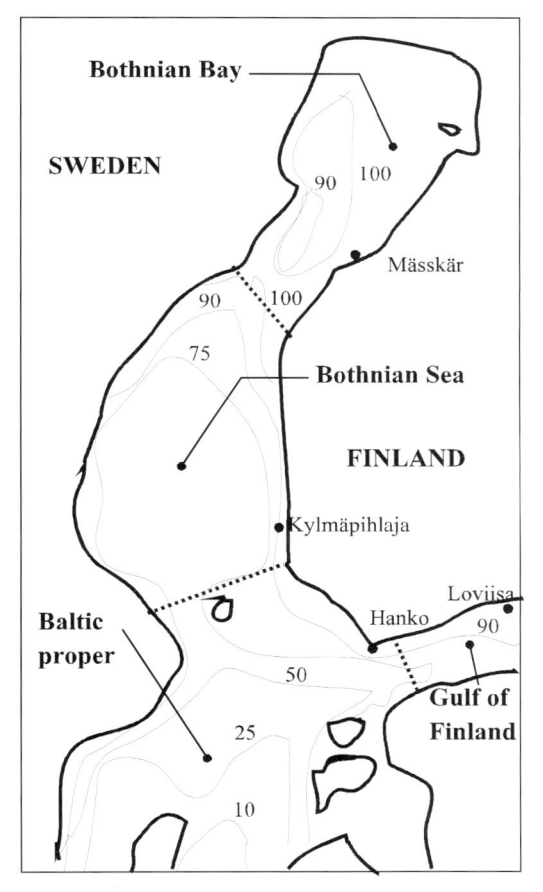

Fig. 1: The occurrence frequency of ice in the Baltic Sea. The frequency of ice is defined in percentage i.e. 100 % means that ice occurs every winter (Kujala, 1994).

Ro-Ro ship Arcturus was instrumented on 1982 and the ice-induced loads were measured during the winters 1983-1988, when the ship was navigating from South Finland (Helsinki, Kotka) to Central Europe.

Tanker Kashira was instrumented on 1983 and ice-induced loads were measured during 1984-1990, when the ship was navigating in the Russian Arctic and in the Gulf Finland. Table 2 summarizes the main particulars of the ships.

Table 2 Main particulars of the ship used for full scale measurements (Hänninen, 2002)

			Kemira	Kashira	Arcturus
Ice class			IAS	IAS/UL	IAS
Power	P	kW	4119	5000	13200
Displ.	Δ	ton	8250	9000	12000
Length	L_{max}	m	113	112	155
Breadth	B_{max}	m	17.5	18.5	25
Draught	T_{max}	m	8.23	7	8.3
Speed	v_{ow}	m/s	7.2	8	9.25
Frame sp	s	m	0,370	0.360	0,364
Waterline angle	α		19	20,0	16,5
Normal frame angle	β_n		21,3	20,6	27,2

In all the ships shown in Table 1, bow frames were instrumented to measure the loads on the frames. The instrumentation of MS Arcturus and MT Kashira included 5 frames and of MS Kemira 1 frame. Table 1 gives also the waterline angle and normal frame angle of the ship hull (measured from the vertical axis) on the instrumented area.

Determination of long-term ice loads

Background

The measured ice-induced load have always high scatter as indicated on Fig. 3.

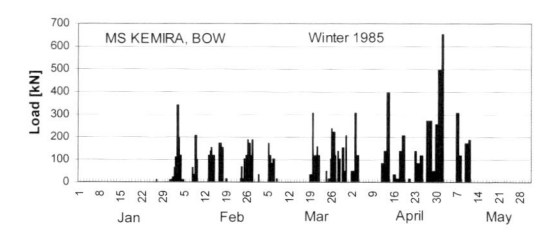

Fig. 3: An example of measured 12 hour maximum ice load values at the bow frame of MS Kemira (Kujala, 1994).

The statistical analysis of the ice-induced loads conducted (Kujala, 1994, Hänninen, 2002) have indicated that it is possible to relate the loads to the prevailing ice conditions and the ship's capability to move in ice. That approach can also be extended to calculation of the long term ice loads by summing to the cumulative ice load distribution the relative contribution of all the ice conditions encountered by a ship during its lifetime. In practice, however, some fundamental problems exist in the application of this type of approach.

The problems are related to the determination of a reliable lifetime ice condition profile for a ship, to the extension of ice load mechanics to cover other types of ice impacts than the continuous breaking of level or ridged ice, and to the incorporation of the ship's transit process to the formulations. To avoid these problems, another approach is used here for evaluation of the long term statistics of ice loads on ships navigating in the Baltic Sea.

The approach is semi-empirical, based on the analysis of the maximum ice load values measured during a specific time period, instead of an analysis of all the peak values during this period. Because the method is semi-empirical, the general application of the method requires a reliable and representative full scale database of the maximum load values. The long term measurements onboard MS Kemira are used to form the basic database and the general applicability of the method developed is tested by calculating long term loads for MS Arcturus and MT Kashira and comparing the obtained distribution with the measured long term results onboard these ships. The load on one frame at bow is studied throughout this analysis.

Description of the semi-empiric approach

The main question for determination of long term ice loads is how to relate the measured loads on the prevailing ice conditions and what are the main ship parameters to be used. The basic idea here is that the measured 12 hour maximum ice load values can be related to the maximum ice thickness during one winter on a specific sea area. Ice thickness is a good variable as it is well known fact that ice-induced loads are increasing with increasing ice thickness. The full-scale measurements have also indicated that ice-induced loads are higher in a ridged ice field than in a level ice (Kujala, 1989). This effect is included by using the equivalent ice thickness approach shown in Table 1 to describe the maximum ice thickness.

To describe the statistical characteristics of ice-induced load the measured mean value and standard deviation are chosen as the main statistical parameters. For evaluation of the long term ice loads, the Baltic Sea is divided into four sea areas as shown in Fig. 1. The empirical ice load database are gathered so that the maximum ice load values measured on each sea area during one winter form the basic sample of data. A number of these samples are then gathered by conducting measurements during several winters. The automatic measuring system onboard the studied ship is programmed to gather 12 hour maximum values, because this is about the average time required for a ship to pass each sea area. After each winter the measured maximum values are analyzed and divided into various sea areas based on the ship's time schedule and route in ice during each voyage.

The full scale measurements during the winters from 1985 to 1992 form the basic database. This is a good period because it includes hard, normal and mild winters. Fig. 4 illustrates the obtained mean value of the measured 12 hour maximum ice load on one frame plotted as a function of the maximum equivalent ice thickness of each sea areas on various winters. Similarly Fig.5 shows the coefficient of variation of the measured 12 hour maximum values.

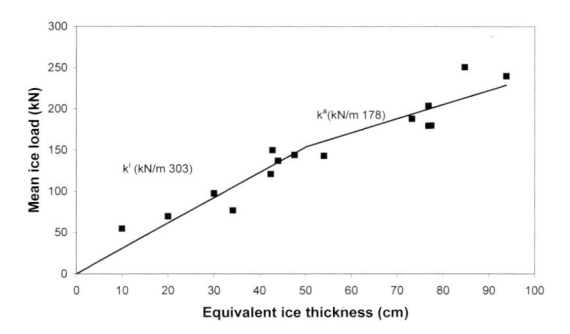

Fig. 4: The mean value of the measured 12- hour maxima at the bow frame as a function of the maximum equivalent level ice thickness (Kujala, 1994, Hänninen, 2002)

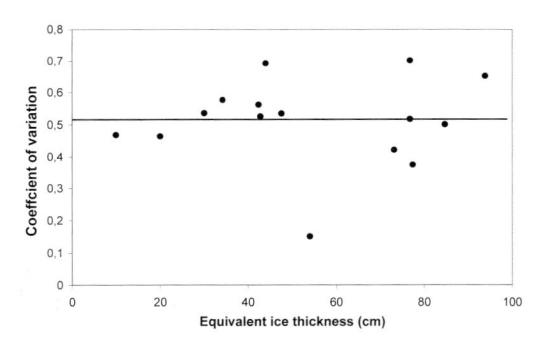

Fig. 5: The coefficient of variation of the measured 12-hour maxima at the bow frame as a function of the maximum equivalent level ice thickness (Kujala, 1994, Hänninen, 2002)

The scatter of the mean value is fairly high as can be seen in Fig. 5. This is understandable as the approach relies on the 12-hour maximum values and this 12 hour period typically includes a number various ice conditions and ship operations in ice. In addition the real time in ice varies from voyage to voyage.

The mean value line of Fig. 4 is divided in two parts. The idea is that the maximum ice-breaking capability divides the data in two parts: below this value the ship can navigate independently in ice and above this value the ship needs icebreaker assistance. With icebreaker assistance the increase of load level as a function of the equivalent ice thickness is slower than with independent navigation. For MS Kemira the maximum icebreaking capability is 0.5 m (Kujala, 1994).

Once the mean value and coefficient of variation is known statistical distributions can be fitted on the data. Gumbel 1 extereme value distribution is widely used to describe the statistical characteristics of ice loads and then cumulative distribution is (see e.g. Ochi, 1990) :

$$F_a(w_n/h_e) = e^{-e^{-\frac{1}{c_n}(w_n-u_n)}} \quad (1)$$

where w_n is used to describe the 12 hour maximum ice load, h_e is the maximum equivalent ice thickness, u_n and c_n are the Gumbel parameters, which can be related to the measured mean, m_{wn} and coefficient of variation, δ_{wn}:

$$c_n = \frac{m_{w_n}\delta_{w_n}}{\pi/\sqrt{6}} \quad (2)$$

$$u_n = m_{w_n} - \gamma c_n = m_{w_n}(1-\gamma\frac{\sqrt{6}}{\pi}\delta_{w_n}) \quad (3)$$

where γ is Euler's constant, 0.577.

The long term cumulative distribution function for each sea area can then be obtained by integrating over the long term statistics of h_e (see also Table 1):

$$F(w_n) = \int_0^\infty F_a(w_n/h_e)f(h_e)dh_e \quad (4)$$

The final lifetime cumulative distribution function for ice loads is then the weighted sum of the cumulative distributions on each sea area:

$$F_l(w_n) = \sum_{i=1}^4 a_i F_i(w_n) \quad (5)$$

where a_i is the relative distance of ice navigation in each sea area. The cumulative long term distributions are usually plotted as a function of return period, which is defined as the number of observations required to achieve a certain load level. The number of observations can be changed to a time scale by noting that the time between observations is a half day so that the return period in days $T(w_n)$ is:

$$T(w_n) = \frac{0.5}{1-F_l(w_n)} \quad (6)$$

To apply the relationship shown in Fig 4 for any other ship, two parameters are needed (Kujala, 1994): maximum ice breaking capability, h_{max} and normal frame angle, β_n, of the studied location at the bow ship. The maximum ice breaking capability defines the change of the slope of the line of Fig. 4 and the effect of normal frame angle is included using the equation:

$$k^i_p = (\frac{\beta_n}{\beta_{n_p}})^{b_1} k^i \quad (7)$$

where the subscript p is for definition of the coefficient for the new, project ship. The coefficient b_1 can be calculated by studying the ice edge failure mechanism when a ship is breaking ice and the following numerical value is found (Kujala, 1994): b_1=1.46.

Application of the semi-empiric approach

Using the equations (1) to (6), the long term load for MS Kemira is given in Fig. 6. It is assumed that the operation profile of MS Kemira include 57 % navigation in the Bay of Bothnia, 21% in the Bothnian Sea and 22% at the Baltic proper ice conditions (Kujala, 1994, Hänninen, 2002)). The long term statistics for ice conditions is given in Table 1. The load on Fig.6 is plotted as a lineload by dividing the frame load with the frame spacing as given in Table 2. Fig. 6 gives 2 long term curves for MS Kemira. The lower curve is obtained using the long term data of the ice thickness variation as given in Table 1 and the upper curve is obtained using the ice thickness variations during the years 1985-1991, which were somewhat harder than the long term average figures. Naturally the fit is better with the actual ice thickness statistics of the measured winters and the fit should be good as the approach developed is based on the Kemira data. The Gumbel 1 curve given in Fig. 6 for comparison purposes is obtained by fitting this distribution straight on the measured data.

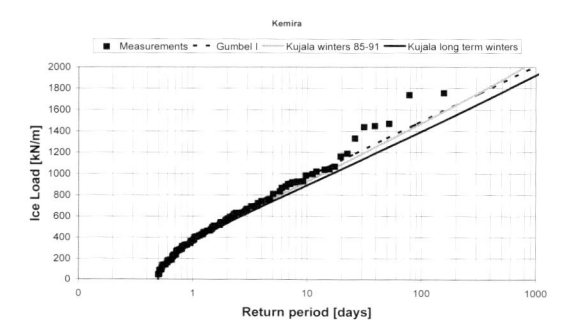

Fig. 6: The long term distribution of ice-induced load at the bow frame of MS Kemira compared with the measured values.

Using data in Table 2 and equation (7), the k-factors for MS Arcturus are 214 kN/m and 126 kN/m and the maximum icebreaking capability is estimated to be 0.9 m (Kujala, 1994). The operation profile of MS Arcturus include 88 % ice navigation in the Gulf of Finland and 12% on the Baltic proper (Hänninen, 2002). With these figures and the long term statistics of ice thickness of Table 1, the long term distribution shown in Fig. 7. is obtained.

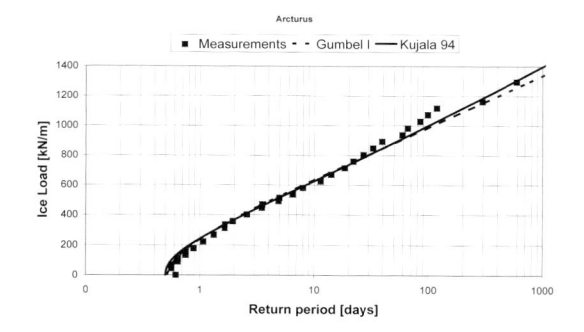

Fig. 7: The long term distribution of ice-induced load at the bow frame of MS Arcturus compared with the measured values.

Similarly for MT Kashira, the k-factors are 348 kN/m and 205 kN/m and the maximum icebreaking capability is estimated to be also 0.9 m. Assuming 100 % navigation in the Gulf of Finland, the curve shown in Fig. 8 is obtained. The exact operation profile for MT Kashira is not known and as the estimated curve is somewhat higher than measured, it can be due to the fact that MT Kashira has also navigated in the Baltic proper with somewhat lighter ice conditions than in the Gulf of Finland. In addition the database for MT Kashira is quite limited as the ship has been navigating mainly in the Russian Arctic.

Figs 6-8 show that the semi-empiric approach gives a good fit on the measured maximum values. As can be also seen from the Figs. 6-8, the measured maximum lineload values for the MS Kemira on one frame has been 1750 kN/m, for MS Arcturus 1300 kN/m and for MT Kashira 1290 kN/m.

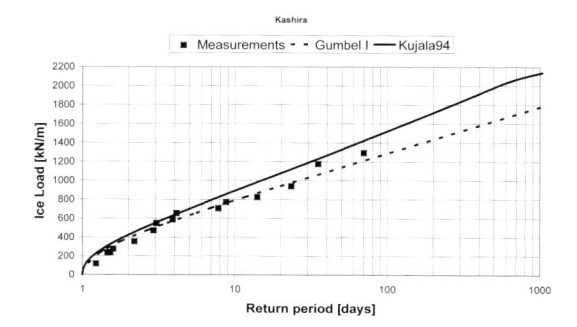

Fig. 8: The long term distribution of ice-induced load at the bow frame of MT Kashira compared with the measured values.

Analysis of ice-induced damages on the hull

Background

Analysis of damage statistics gives another approach to estimate the extreme ice-induced loads. The load level from damage statistics is considered in the following. The gathered damage statistics is described and the load level required to cause the damages is estimated. Fig. 9 shows typical ice damage on ships navigating in the Baltic Sea.

Fig. 9: Typical ice-induced damage on the shell structures of an ice-strengthened vessel (Kujala, 1991).

Damage is anyway quire a strong word here as typically the damages are small permanent dents on the shell plating of ice-strengthened vessel.

Gathered damage database

There have been a number of campaigns to gather ice damage statistics and to relate the design load level based on the analysis of ice damages (Johansson 1967, Kujala 1991, Hänninen 2005). Here the main focus is on the database given by Kujala (1991) as in that report the damage extent and damaged structures are specified detail enough. The damage data was gathered during the winters 1984 to 1987 from the ships navigating regularly in the Baltic Sea. The study included 61 ships of which 31 had ice class 1A Super, 28 ice class 1A, and 2 ice class 1C. The ships were examined visually during annual dry-docking, and the location, extent, and shape of the damages were recorded. Most of the damages were located at midship on the ice-strengthened region, especially at the aftend of the midship region. One sign of damage only was observed on the bow area and two on the aftship. From the observed damages, 56 % are known to have taken place in compressive ice, while the cause for the rest of the damages is unknown. Table 3 and 4 summarizes the observed plating damages on the longitudinally and transversely framed ships, which will be further analyzed in this paper.

Table 3: Observed maximum permanent deflection for longitudinally framed platings (values in mm)

Ship no.	Frame spacing	Frame span	Plate thickness	Maximum deflection
7	380	3040	20	10
13	350	2800	10	20
45	300	2800	14.5	24
45	300	2800	14.5	30
48-50	350	2100	15.5	15

Table 4: Observed maximum permanent deflection for transversely framed platings (values in mm)

Ship no.	Frame spacing	Frame span	Plate thickness	Maximum deflection
4	450	3000	19	20
7	380	3000	16.5	10
13	350	3200	16	20
	700	3200	10	15
14	350	2375	14	15
	700	2375	13	25
16	350	3500	10	25
21	400	2200	19.5	10
	800	2200	19.5	15
	400	2200	13.5	10
	800	2200	13.5	15
35	350	2500	15.5	15
43	400	1750	17	25
44	400	1750	9.5	30
51	350	2100	15.5	15

Analysis methods for the damage database

Hayward (2001) approach is used to calculate from the damages described in Table 3 and 4 the required ice-induced lineload for these damages. Hayward (2001) developed a regression formula to scale the yield line theory under uniform pressure (Jones, 1972) for the case of a patch load on the plating. The following formulation can be used to solve the upper bound line load q causing the deflection in the longitudinally framed plating when $w_p/t \leq 1$:

$$q = \frac{p_c h_c}{f_{DL}}\left[1 + \frac{w_p^2}{3t^2}\left(\frac{\zeta_0 + (3 - 2\zeta_0)^2}{3 - \zeta_0}\right)\right] \quad (8)$$

and when $w_p/t > 1$:

$$q = \frac{2 p_c h_c w_p}{t \cdot f_{DL}}\left[1 + \frac{\zeta_0(2 - \zeta_0)}{3 - \zeta_0}\left(\frac{t^2}{3w_p^2} - 1\right)\right] \quad (9)$$

Where t is the plate thickness, h_c is the load height, w_p is the permanent deflection in the plating, the threshold pressure p_c causing double Y-shaped yield line is:

$$p_c = \frac{48 M_p}{s^2\left(\sqrt{3 + \frac{s^2}{l^2}} - \frac{s}{l}\right)} \quad (10)$$

and

$$\zeta_0 = \frac{s}{l}\left(\sqrt{3 + \frac{s^2}{l^2}} - \frac{s}{l}\right) \quad (11)$$

where s is frame spacing, l is the frame span. The plastic moment M_p is:

$$M_P = \sigma_y \frac{t^2}{4} \quad (12)$$

where σ_y is the yield strength of the plate material.

In equations (8) and (9) f_{DL} is the average correction factor developed by Hayward (2001) applying extensive nonlinear FE-analysis for the studied structures. This correction factor for longitudinally framed plating is:

$$f_{DL} = -0.6263 \cdot x_L^2 + 1.5363 \cdot x_L \tag{13}$$

where

$$x_L = \frac{h_c}{s}\left(\frac{s}{t}\frac{s}{l}\right)^{0.1} \tag{14}$$

and for transversely framed plating:

$$f_{DT} = -0.1330 \cdot x_T^2 + 0.6701 \cdot x_T \tag{15}$$

where

$$x_T = \frac{h_c}{s}\left(\frac{s}{t}\right)^{0.2} \tag{16}$$

Detail analysis of one damage

One damage case has been studied in further detail by applying nonlinear FE-modeling (Valkonen, 2006). Fig.10 shows the damage which has been measured by applying stereo photography. The FE-model included about 10 frames in the vertical direction and 3 webframes in the horizontal direction. Eight node plate elements were used in the model. There were eight elements over the frame spacing, which makes the element height 37.5 mm. In the longitudinal direction, there were 75 elements over the web frame spacing, which makes the element length 37.33 mm. In the frame, there were eight elements height of 38.78 mm. The flange was described with 27.3 mm high element. Linear elastic - strain hardening material model was used in the finite element analysis. The steel with yield strength σ_y of 290 MPa, elastic modulus E of 206 GPa and Poisson's ratio ν of 0.3 were used in the analysis. The strain hardening continued until the stress value of 625 MPa with the strain ε of 0.5. Yield strength of 290 MPa was used because it is closer to the mean yield strength of normal construction steel than the nominal yield strength (Kujala 1991). Material was assumed to be isotropic. The program FEMAP v8.10 was used for modeling the structure. Finite element package ABAQUS version 6.5-1 was used in the analysis, Fig 11 shows the model.

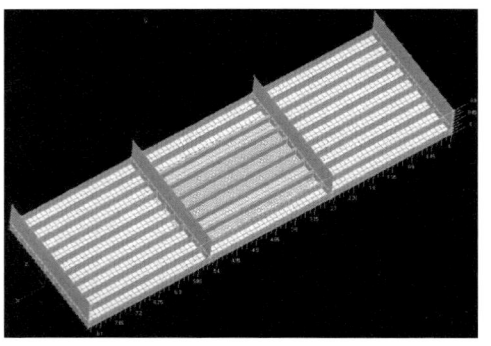

Fig. 11: The FE-model used in the analysis (Valkonen, 2006).

The idea was to calculate with varying load configurations (ice-induced pressure height and length) the structural response and then unload the pressure to find the load configuration causing exactly the same shape as measured onboard ship no 45.

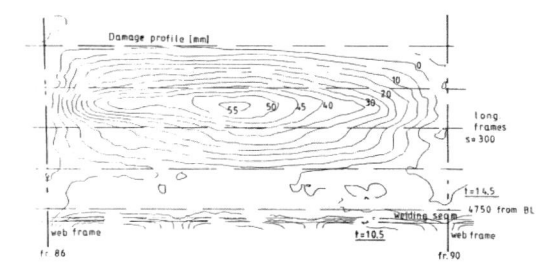

Fig. 10: The shape of damage on the ship no 45 (Kujala, 1991).

The finite element analysis of the side structure of ship 45 reveals that 2.358 m long, 1701 kN/m line load could have caused the original damage with close to 75 mm high loading.

Obtained load level from the damages

Fig. 12 summarizes the obtained line load values applying Hayward (2001) equations (8) to (16) on the damage database of Tables 3-4. The used yield strength of the plating was 290 MPa and load height h_c of 75 mm.

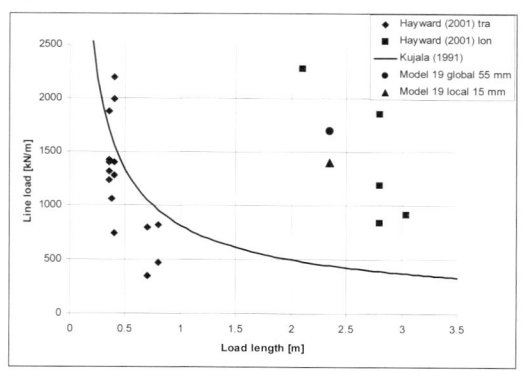

Fig. 12: Analysis of the plate damages using Hayward (2001) equation together with Kujala (1991) curve and finite element analysis results (Valkonen, 2006).

Fig. 12 gives also the load based on the detail FE-analysis of ship no. 45. In addition the line load curve obtained by previous damage analysis (Kujala, 1991) is given for comparison purposes. In that analysis a more simple approach was used to calculate the longitudinally framed plating damages. The curve includes also analysis of longitudinal frame and webframe damages, which typically take place earlier than extensive damages of the plating.

Discussion of the load level based on the full scale measurements and damage analysis

The conducted full scale measurements and related statistical analysis have given a fairly clear picture about the possible maximum load level at the bow of ice-strengthened vessels. The developed semi-empiric statistical ice load model connects the ice load level with ship maximum icebreaking capability and bow shape. The basic approach in the Finnish-Swedish ice rules have been to relate the load level with the factor $\sqrt{P\Delta}$ i.e. engine power times displacement as this describes basically the ship inertia when hitting ice. Maximum icebreaking capability is similar type of measure requiring though more detail analysis of e.g. the effect of hull shape.

The proper load level at midship and aftship is more complicated. During normal forward navigation of a ship in ice, the speed component normal to the ship's course is small at the midship and aftship area. This causes a low basic load level at midship and aftship, but an extensive increase on the load level can take place due to the maneuvering activities of the ship. This results in the highly scattered load peaks on these parts of the ship hull. However, the highest loads, especially at midship and aftship, are reported to have occurred when the ship has been stuck in ice and the moving ice has compressed the ship's side. The highest measured load on a frame at mid/aftship onboard MS Kemira has been 1140 kN/m (Kujala, 1989). This load level is well comparable with the load level based on the damage statistics of Fig. 12. The highest loads takes place in compressive ice, which is not the design case as the idea in the Baltic Sea is that there will be always icebreaker assistance available so that the compressive ice should be avoided.

The conducted analysis of the damages indicates surprisingly high load levels with nominal load lengths of 2.0-3.0 m as shown in Fig.12. These are naturally rare events but shows also that load level can be extremely high when ice is crushing against the straight midship shell structures. The recent model scale testing have shown similarly high load level when ice is crushed against the ship model (Valkonen et al., 2007).

Conclusions

This paper summarizes the main results of the extensive full scale measurements conducted in the Baltic Sea. In addition ice-induced damages are analyzed to evaluate the load level and load configurations required for these damages. A clear picture is obtained about the possible level of highest loads in the Baltic ice conditions.

A semi-empiric approach is developed to evaluate long term loads on ship navigating in ice in various parts of the Baltic Sea. The approach seems to give realistic estimates for the long term loading. Naturally the long term aim should be to evaluate the long term loads by simulating ice navigation and icebreaking process in various ice conditions and operation situation during the ship's lifetime.

One important question remains to be solved and this is the effect of ship size on the load level as the available databases are based on the measurements and observations of conventional size ships. Today the number of large tankers in the Baltic Sea is increasing to carry oil from the Russian ports. The best way to approach this problem is to instrument one large tanker to study whether the ice load models developed can be extended to large tankers as well.

Acknowledgement

Authors would like to thank European Union for making this analysis possible as a part of SAFEICE-project.

References

Hayward, R., 2001: Plastic response of ships shell plating subjected to loads of finite height. Master's Thesis, Memorial University of Newfoundland, St. John's, New Foundland, Canada.

Hänninen, S., 2002: The use of statistical methods in determination of design ice load on ship hull frame in the baltic sea. Master's Thesis, Helsinki University of Technology, Department of Mechanical Engineering, Ship Laboratory, Espoo, Finland, (in Finnish).

Hänninen, S., 2005: Incidents and Accidents in Winter Navigation in the Baltic Sea,Winter 2002-2003. Number 54.Winter Navigation Research Board, Espoo, Finland.

Ice Atlas, 1982. Climatological ice atlas for the Baltic Sea, Kattegat, Skagerrak and lake Vänern (1963-1979). Swedish Meteorological and Hydrological Institute & Institute of Marine Research, Finland. Norrköping. 220 p.

Johansson, B. M., 1967: On the ice strengthening of ship hulls. International Ship Building Progress, 14, 231 – 245.

Jones, N., 1976: Plastic behaviour of ship structures. SNAME transactions, 84, 115–145.

Kujala, P. 1989. Long term ice load measurements onboard chemical tanker Kemira during winters 1985 to 1988. Helsinki. Winter Navigation Research Board. Report No. 47. 55 p. + app. 139 p.

Kujala, P. 1991. Damage statistics of ice-strengthened ships in the Baltic Sea 1984-1987. Winter Navigation Research Board. Report. No. 50. 61 p. + app. 5 p.

Kujala, P., 1994. On the statistics of ice loads on ship hull in the Baltic. Dissertation. Acta Polytechina Scandinavica, Mechanical Engineering Series No. 116. Helsinki. 98 p.

Ochi, K.M., 1990. Applied probability and stochastic processes in engineering and physical sciences. John Wiley&Sons. New York. 499 p.

Valkonen, J., 2006, Determination of ship ice load from hull ice damages, Master's thesis, Helsinki University of Technology, Department of Mechanical Engineering, Ship Laboratory, Espoo, Finland,. p. 98.

Valkonen, J., Izumiyama, K., Kujala, P., 2007. Measuring of ice induced pressures and loads on ships in model scale. PRADS07, October 2007. Houston

Veitch, B., Kujala, P., Kosloff, P., Leppäranta, M. 1991. Field measurements of the thermodynamics of an ice ridge. Laboratory of Naval Architecture and Marine Engineering, report no. M-114. Helsinki University of Technology, Otaniemi. 24 p. + app. 28 p.

Length of Ice Load Patch on a Ship Bow in Level Ice

Koh Izumiyama, Tadanori Takimoto and Shotaro Uto

National Maritime Research Institute
Mitaka, Tokyo, Japan

Abstract

A series of ship model tests in level ice were performed at National Maritime Research Institute with a local ice load measurement by way of a tactile sensor system. It was observed that the ice load distribution in the bow region was of a broken-line-like fashion in which short load patches were aligned in a horizontal line. Field test results were analyzed to see if this could also be observed in the full-scale conditions. The analysis of the data measured on board PM *Teshio* of Japan Coast Guard showed that the ice load in the bow is also broken-line-like. More importantly, the data showed that the higher loads act on shorter load patches. The data from the US Coast Guard Cutter *Polar Star* also suggested that the higher load is the more concentrated. Discussions were conducted on the interpretation of these results from a viewpoint of the ice load model on ship hulls.

Keywords

Ice load, Load patch, Model test, Full-scale test.

Introduction

Ice loading on ship hulls is a complicated phenomenon. Field measurement is the method most commonly used to study the problem. Data obtained in field tests have broaden our knowledge of ice loading on ship hulls. In many cases, however, technical and often economical reasons limit the ice load measurement to narrow areas in a few locations of the ship hull. It is difficult to obtain information of the ice load behavior over wide areas of the ship hull in field tests.

To cope with the drawback associated with the field test, National Maritime Research Institute (NMRI) has performed model testing at their ice model basin as a tool to study ice loading on ship hulls. In the model test a tactile sensor system was used to measure local ice loads acting on the model ship hulls in level ice. This method enabled the measurement of the local ice loads over wide areas of the hull (Izumiyama et al, 2005).

The model test resulted in many valuable findings of the ice loads on ship hulls. One such finding was on the local ice load distribution in the bow region. The tactile sensor used in the model test had a very high spatial resolution. This point enabled detailed observations of ice load distribution on the model hull. It was shown that the ice load in the bow region was of a "broken-line-like" fashion in which short load patches were aligned in a horizontal line.

This paper focuses on the above finding of the ice load behavior in the bow region in level ice. Data obtained in field test was analyzed to show that the load distribution is also broken-line-like in the full-scale conditions. The analysis further showed that the load from the individual load patch is a function of the load patch length.

Model Test and Problem to be Studied

Model Test

A tactile sensor system called I-SCAN was used in the model test. The system is composed of sensor sheets, a PC and handles that connect the sensor sheets with the PC. The sensor sheet is 0.3 mm in thickness and also flexible. It has a square pressure sensing area of 238 mm by 238 mm. In the sensing area there are pressure-sensing spots in a grid arrangement of 44 by 44. Center-to-center spacing between the neighboring sensing spots is 5.4 mm that is the spatial resolution of the sensor.

Readings from all the sensing spots at a moment form a "frame" of pressure distribution on a sensor sheet. The PC records the data as a series of frames at given time intervals. The possible maximum data acquisition frequency was 100 frames per second.

Fig. 1   Sensor Sheets mounted on a Model Ship

In the model test eight sensor sheets were mounted on the model ship to cover wide areas of the hull from the bow to the stern. Fig. 1 shows sensor sheets mounted on a model ship hull. Two models of an icebreaker and a cargo vessel were tested. The models were tested in the free-running mode in level ice.

Ice Load Distribution Observed in Model Test

Fig. 2 shows a series of frames observed in the model test. These frames were from a sensor sheet mounted on the bow region of the cargo ship model. In this test the data acquisition frequency was 30 frames per second. Fig. 2 shows the ice load distribution on the sensor sheet for 0.5 second at time intervals of 0.033 second. In each frame loaded spots are shown by colored dots.

Fig. 2   Ice Load Distribution on a Model Ship Bow

Fig. 2 shows many loaded areas, often termed load patches, of short length are aligned in a horizontal line forming a broken-line-like pattern. Individual load patch is one- to five-spot width. The whole line moves downwards with time. The broken-line-like distribution of ice load as shown in the figure is observed in other tests in the bow regions of the cargo ship model and the icebreaker model as well.

Problem Identification

Both models tested had a conventional icebreaking bow with V-shaped frame lines. Fig. 3 schematically depicts the failure pattern of level ice around such a bow. Ice in contact with the bow is failed in bending due to the downward component of the icebreaking force from the inclined hull. A radial crack is formed in the ice at a distance away from the hull creating a crescent-shaped cusp. Although the size and form of the cusp can differ depending on the parameters such as ice thickness, hull form and ship speed, the ice failure depicted in Fig. 3 is the typical icebreaking pattern commonly observed both in the model- and full-scale conditions.

Izumiyama et al (1999) performed a series of resistance tests in level ice with a local ice load measurement by way of the same tactile sensor. They observed the similar ice load distribution as shown in Fig. 3. They explained it as a process in which the ice edge in contact with the hull is being deflected downward and failed in bending by the inclined bow, and then the cusp rotates on the hull. The ice load behavior observed in the present model test can also be interpreted in the same way.

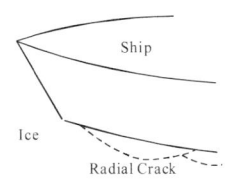

Fig. 3   Ice Failure around a Ship Bow

Fig. 4 schematically shows load components acting at the ice-hull interface. Note that ice-hull friction is ignored here. The downward component on the ice, F_V, is the load to break the ice in bending. In reaction to the icebreaking load, the ship hull receives load F_N, which is the ice load. This load is in equilibrium with the vector sum of the horizontal, F_H, and vertical load components exerted on the ice.

Ice load distribution observed in the model test indicates that the reaction load from the ice is transmitted to the hull through many sparsely distributed load patches. It is important to note here that the total load required to break the ice is in proportion to the sum of these local loads. This leads to an idea that the magnitude of individual local load can vary greatly depending on the local contact conditions under the same total load.

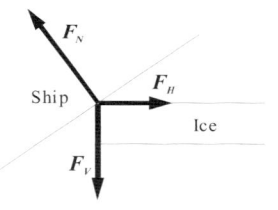

Fig. 4   Load Components at Ice-Hull Contact

Fig. 5 schematically explains the above idea of the effect of contact conditions on the local ice loads. It is of high importance and interest to study the local ice-hull contacts and ice loads in full-scale conditions. In the following of this paper, data obtained in field tests will be analyzed with objectives to estimate the load patch length and to correlate the load with it.

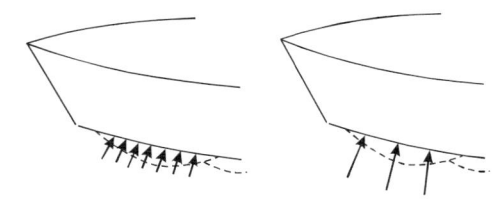

Fig. 5   Ice Loading on Ship Bow

Analysis of Full-scale Data

Broken-Line-Like Ice Load in Full-scale Conditions

The first and foremost question associated with the broken-line-like nature of ice load observed in the model test is if it is also seen in the full-scale conditions. Riska et al. (1990) used PVDF plates to measure ice load on icebreaker *Sampo*. They also made direct observations of the ice-hull contact through a window built in the ship hull. Unfortunately, however, the size of the PDVF-plate and window was about 20 cm, which was not large enough to obtain information of the ice load distribution as shown in Fig. 2. There is no full-scale data available to be directly compared with the data measured by the tactile sensor in the model test.

An indirect but possible way to examine the validity of the broken-line-like nature of ice load in full-scale conditions is to compare the ice load time curves obtained in field and model tests. Many ice-going ships, especially icebreakers, are built with transversely framed hull structures to withstand local ice loads. It is a common method in field tests to measure ice loads acting on the frames. In such measurement frames are instrumented with shear strain gauges. Ice load on a frame is calculated from the shear differences between two (sets of) shear gauges at different heights of the frame.

Fig. 6 schematically depicts the ice load measurement on transverse frames. In the analysis of the measured data each frame can be seen as a virtual "load panel." The width of the sensing area of the panel is a frame spacing. A frame may be segmented into several sub-panels if it is instrumented with more than two (sets of) strain gauges.

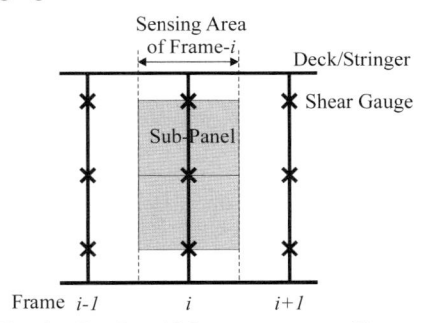

Fig. 6   Ice Load Measurement on Frames

From the model test result it is possible to have ice load data that is comparable with those measured on frames in field tests. The sensor sheet used in the model test had pressure-sensing spots in a grid arrangement of 44 by 44. The reading at each sensing spot is called "Raw" that is an integer between 0 (no pressure) and 255 (maximum pressure). In the analysis the whole sensor area was segmented into sub-areas in four different patterns as shown in Fig. 7. For each sub-area the "Raw Sum", which is the sum of Raws from the sensing spots within the sub-area, was calculated. The Raw Sum can be seen as a value corresponding to the total load acting on the sub-area. Segmentation (a) that divided the sensor area into vertically elongated eleven sub-areas.

Each sub-area is a four-sensing-spot, 21.6 mm in width. This sub-area can be comparable with the load panel of a transverse frame in field tests.

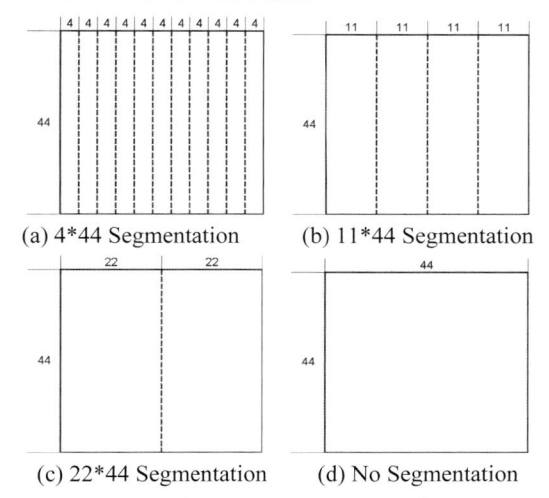

(a) 4*44 Segmentation   (b) 11*44 Segmentation

(c) 22*44 Segmentation   (d) No Segmentation

Fig. 7   Sensor Area Segmentations

Fig. 8 shows time curves of local ice loads measured in the model test and a field test. Model test results were scaled up to full-scale values. Fig. 8 (a) shows the time curve of ice load on a sub-area of 0.35 m in width on the icebreaker hull sailing in 0.5 m thick level ice. Fig. 8 (b) is the ice load measured by a frame of PM *Teshio* of Japan Coast Guard in a field test (Uto et al, 2005). This data will be further analyzed in the following section. In this test *Teshio* was sailing in a large ice floe of an average thickness of 0.49 m with a 0.1 m deep snow cover.

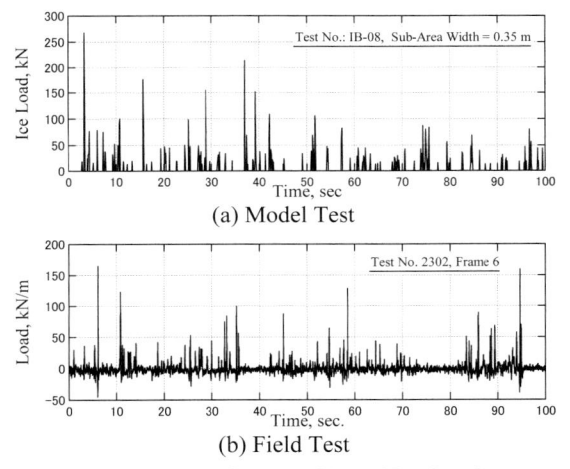

(a) Model Test

(b) Field Test

Fig. 8   Time Curves of Local Ice Loads

The load time curve of the model test shows many spike-like peaks with no load period in between. These peak loads occur when load patches passing over the sub-area analyzed. The broken-line-like nature of the ice load resulted in the intermittent occurrence of the peaks. The data measured in the field test also shows many spike-like peaks with very low load period in between. Similar results were obtained in many other field tests. From the similarity of the time curves of the two tests, it is deemed reasonable that the ice load in full-scale conditions is also of the broken-line-like nature.

Data from PM Teshio

The ice load data measured on frames of PM *Teshio* was further analyzed to estimate the length of load patches. Fig. 9 schematically shows the analysis method. The figure shows a loading event on a frame instrumented with strain gauges, and the load measured by the frame. At time $t=t_1$, the load patch comes in contact with the sensing area of the frame and the load starts to rise. The load increases with the load moving aft-ward ($t=t_2$). It reaches the maximum at $t=t_3$. The load then decreases ($t=t_4$) and vanishes at $t=t_5$ when the load passes out of the sensing area of the frame.

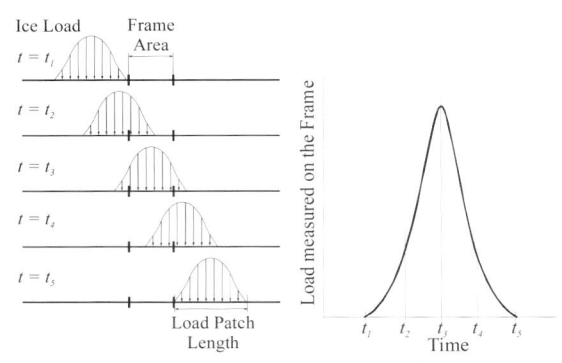

(a) Ice Loading on a Frame   (b) Ice Load of the Frame

Fig. 9   Ice Loading Model for Analysis

For the loading model shown in Fig. 9, we can write

$$V_L \Delta t = w + W \qquad (1)$$

where V_L is the moving speed of the load, $\Delta t = t_5 - t_1$ is the duration of the loading event, w and W are the lengths of the load patch and the sensing area of the frame, which is equal to the frame spacing, respectively. The moving speed of the load is given by

$$V_S = V_L \cos\alpha, \qquad (2)$$

where V_S and α are ship speed and the waterline angle at the location of the frame, respectively. Equations (1) and (2) give the load patch width as

$$w = \frac{V_S}{\cos\alpha}\Delta t - W. \qquad (3)$$

Ice load measured on frames No. 6 and No. 8 in the bow region of PM *Teshio* was analyzed using equation (3). The equation gives the load patch length of a loading event if the duration of the event is given. The duration of individual loading event was defined as follows from the load time curves measured by the frames.

Fig. 10 gives the definition of the duration, Δt, of a loading event. The figure is a close-up of a peak load in the ice load time history. It is seen that negative load is recorded before and after the peak. This occurrence will be due to the seesaw-like response of the plating as schematically shown in Fig. 11. When ice load acts on the plating fore or aft of the frame neighboring to the one analyzed, the loaded plating will bend. Riska et al. (1990) reported such bending of the plating. Because of the support by the frame adjacent to the ice load, this bending will cause the seesaw-like response of the plating that pulls the frame analyzed outward. This response results in the negative load on the frame. The duration of the peak load was defined as the time between the zero-up-cross point (the time when the load becomes from negative to positive) and the zero-down-cross point (positive to negative) as shown in Fig. 10.

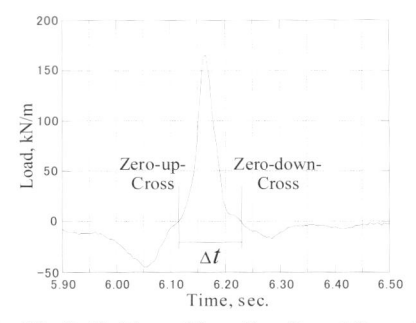

Fig. 10   Definition of Loading Event Duration

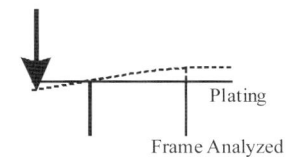

Fig. 11   Seesaw-like Response of Plating

The above definition of the loading duration gives many events with low peak loads. Such low peak loads are most likely due to noise in the signal or minor ice loading. Data from those low peak events are not of interest and may even confuse the interpretation of the analysis results. It was then decided that only events that had peak load values higher than 50 kN/m were taken in the analysis. In total there were 60 such loading events found in the data measured by the two frames for a period of 150 seconds.

Fig. 12 shows the histogram of the analyzed load patch length of the 60 loading events. In the figure the patch width, w, is normalized by the frame spacing, W. The figure shows that there are many loading events with short patch length. Most of the events (51 events out of 60, which is 85%) are with load patch length shorter than the two frame spacings, and more than a half of the events (37 events, 62 %) are shorter than the one frame spacing.

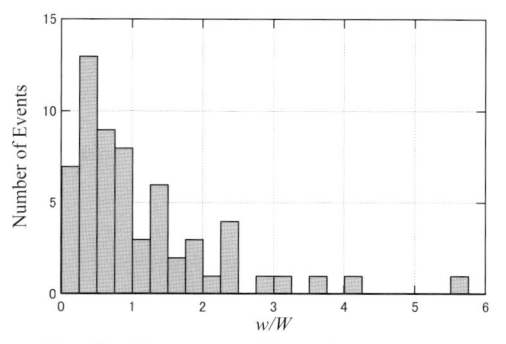

Fig. 12 Histogram of Load Patch Length

From the viewpoint of structure design, the peak load is of high interest. In the analysis the peak load values, as well as the load patch length, of each loading event was calculated from the load time curve. Fig. 13 shows the correlation of the peak ice load and the load patch length. There is a general trend of the peak load increasing with the decrease of the load patch length. The event that gave the highest load in the 60 events was of a load patch length of only about a half frame spacing.

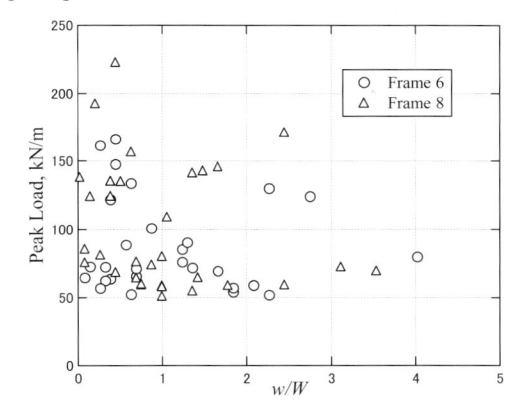

Fig. 13 Correlation of Peak Load and Patch Length

Data from USCGC Polar Sea

The method used in the analysis of the data from *Teshio* assumed the ice loading model that is consistent with time. The load patch length was assumed to be constant during the loading event. Equations (1) through (3) were derived based on this consistent load model.

However, the assumption may not always be relevant. Fig. 14 schematically shows a possible example of ice loading event that is inconsistent with time. In this loading event, ice load vanishes during its passing over the sensing area of the frame measured. Such a loading results in the load time curve that has shorter event duration than that by the consistent load. Naturally, there can also be reverse events in which the ice load breaks out over the frame measured and passes over it. The load patch length of such inconsistent loading events cannot correctly be calculated by equation (3).

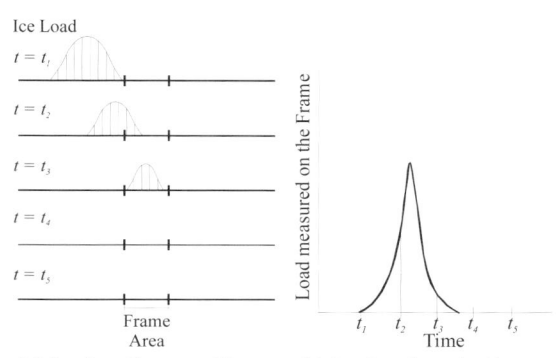

(a) Ice Loading on a Frame (b) Ice Load on the Frame

Fig. 14 Inconsistent Ice Loading

The average duration of the 60 events in the *Teshio* data was 0.177 second. Taking into account this relatively short event duration, the assumption of the consistent loading model may deem reasonable. However, at the interface between the ship hull and ice, there will be local ice failure taking place. Such local ice failure may change local hull-ice contact conditions rapidly. The 60 events found in the *Teshio* data may include such inconsistent loading events. In other words, the load patch length calculated from the *Teshio* data can include the effects not only of the patch length in space but also of the time-varying characteristics of the ice load.

To further examine the above point, ice load data measured on board the USCGC *Polar Sea*, which was compiled in SAFEICE project, was analyzed. In the measurement of *Polar Sea* ten consecutive cant frames in the bow region (frames No. 35 - 44) were instrumented with strain gauges (Frederking et al, 2005). Each frame was instrumented with eight strain gauges. The arrangement of the strain gauges formed a virtual load panel composed of sub-panels in the arrangement of 6 rows by 10 columns. In the measurement, 5-second-long segments were recorded whenever a threshold strain was exceeded on any sub-panel out of 60. The database gives the average ice pressure (ice load divided by the area) of sub-panels at a moment when the maximum pressure in the events was measured on one of the sub-panels. Therefore, the data of the *Polar Sea* can be seen as "snapshots", that are free of any time-varying effects, of ice load distribution over 60 sub-panels on the ship bow.

In the database there are several datasets for the *Polar Sea*. Among them the dataset measured in the Antarctic in 1984 was selected for the analysis, as this dataset gives local ice loads in level first-year ice. In the analysis the total load on each frame was calculated. This gives ten frame loads, F_{35} through F_{44}, for each event. From these ten frame loads, load values F_0, F_1 and F_2 were calculated as defined in Fig. 15. $F_0 = F_i$ is the maximum load, where i is the number of the frame that measured the load, of the ten frame loads. The average load of the neighboring frames, $F_1 = (F_{i+1} + F_{i-1})/2$, and the average load of the next neighboring frames, $F_2 = (F_{i+2} + F_{i-2})/2$ were also calculated. If the maximum load occurs in the end frames and one of the loads to calculate F_1 and/or F_2 is not available, only the load on the other frame was used to calculate the neighboring load value.

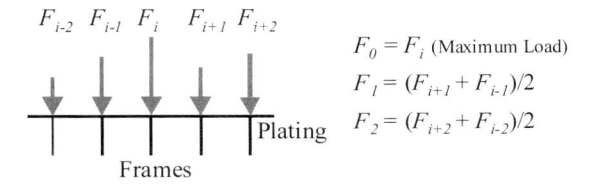

$F_0 = F_i$ (Maximum Load)
$F_1 = (F_{i+1} + F_{i-1})/2$
$F_2 = (F_{i+2} + F_{i-2})/2$

Fig. 15 Load Definition

Fig. 16 shows the results of the analysis. The figure shows the correlation of the load ratios, F_1/F_0 and F_2/F_0, and the maximum load, F_0. The load ratio can be seen as an index to the ice load distribution within the measurement area, which was 4.1 m in width, in the bow of the *Polar Sea*. If the load ratio is low, the load distribution is concentrated at the frame where the maximum load was measured. If the ratio is high, the maximum load is not remarkably high compared with those on the surrounding frames and the load distribution is relatively flat.

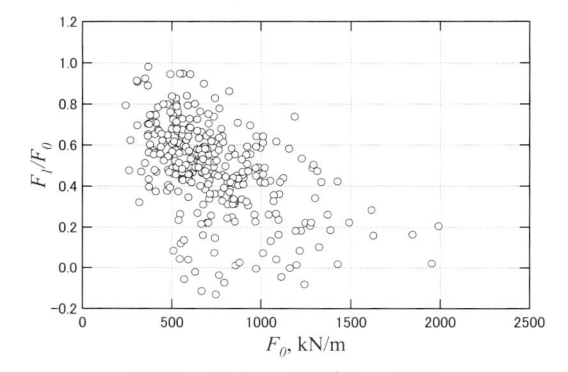

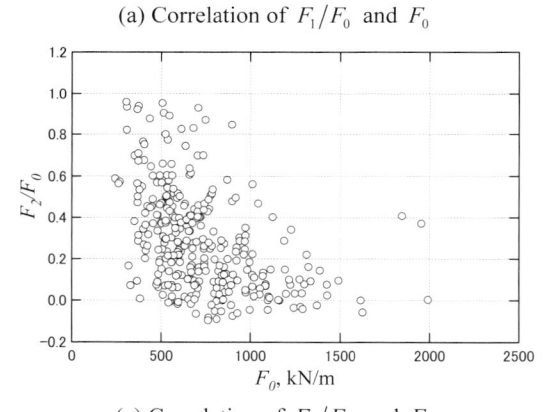

(a) Correlation of F_1/F_0 and F_0

(a) Correlation of F_2/F_0 and F_0

Fig. 16 Analysis Results of *Polar Sea* Data

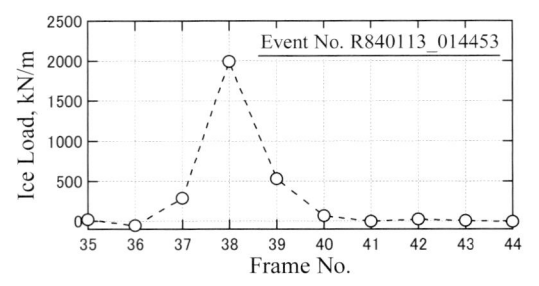

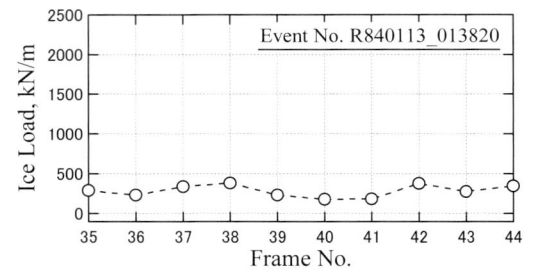

(a) Event with the Highest Load

(b) Event with Low Loads

Fig. 17 Ice Load Distribution over 10 Frames

In Fig. 16 there is a clear trend for the load ratios to decrease with the increase of the maximum load. This means that the higher the maximum load is the load distribution is the more concentrated. This condition is clearly evident as shown in Fig. 17. The figure shows ice load distributions over the ten frames in two events. Fig. 17 (a) is the ice load distribution in the event when the highest frame load of 1991 kN/m was measured in the dataset. The load distribution shows that frame No. 38 received this high load, while loads on other frames remained low. In this event the load ratios of F_1/F_0 and F_2/F_0 are 0.205 and 0.003, respectively. Fig. 17 (b) is the ice load distribution in an event when relatively low loads were measured. The load distribution is flat and all the frames received similar loads of about 300 – 400 kN/m.

The analysis of the *Polar Sea* data supports the results obtained by the analysis of the *Teshio* data. Although it is not possible to have detailed information of the load patch length from the *Polar Sea* data, both data show qualitatively the same result. The higher loads act on the shorter load patches, or in other words, the higher loads are the more concentrated.

Discussion

In this paper ice load data measured in two field tests was analyzed. It should be noted that in field tests ice loads were not directly measured but calculated from the shear strain measured on frames. To calculate ice load from strain measured, the line load model is usually applied. The line load model assumes a load distributed over a horizontal line or a horizontally elongated narrow area of some height over the frame to be analyzed. Ice load is calculated as the magnitude of line load from the measured strain based on the beam theories for relatively simple structures or finite element (FE) models for more complicated configurations.

The line load model may seem appropriate as the ice load model on ship bow in level ice. However, the present analysis showed that actual loads, especially high loads, are able to act upon load patches of short length. Kujara (1989) indicated that the line load model could give too small ice load if the load length was shorter than two frame spacings. It is of interest to check the validity of the line load model as a model to calculate ice load from the strain measurement.

An FE calculation was made to examine the effect of the load length on the calculated load (termed "ice load" here). In the calculation, loads of the same magnitude, 1 kN/m but of different lengths, were applied over a frame to be analyzed as depicted in Fig. 18. Shear strain in the frame was calculated for each loading case. The calculated strain was compared with that under a line load of a long length (four-frame spacing) to calculate the ice load magnitude under the load applied.

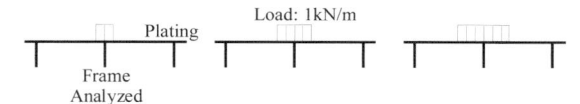

Fig. 18   Loads for FE Calculation

Fig. 19 shows the result of the FE calculation. In the figure, the ice load calculated from the shear strain of the loaded frame is plotted against the load width normalized by the frame spacing. The figure shows that the FE calculation correctly gives the ice load of 1 kN/m, which is the magnitude of the applied line load, when the load width is equal to or longer than the frame spacing. When the load length is shorter than the frame spacing, however, the calculation fails to give correct value. The calculated ice load is lower than the load applied and it decreases with the load length decreases.

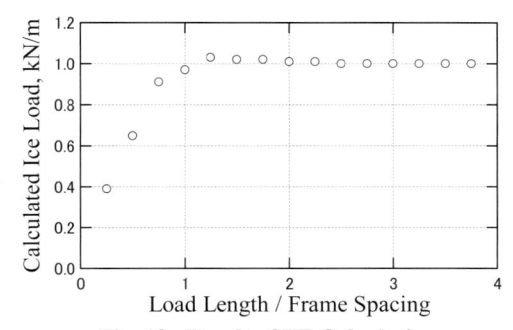

Fig. 19   Result of FE Calculation

The analysis of the data from the *Teshio* showed that the load patch length can be shorter than the one frame spacing (Fig. 12) and that higher loads can act on shorter load patches (Fig. 13). The data measured on the *Polar Sea* also showed that the higher loads can be the more concentrated (Fig. 16). Those findings in the analysis of the field data together with the result of the FE calculation shown in Fig. 19 will raise a question on the validity of the line load assumption as the model to calculate ice load from the frame strain measurement in field tests. There is a possibility that the calculation based on the line load assumption underestimates the actual loads. It is especially so for high loads. This means that high loads can actually be much higher.

At this stage, it is difficult to further discuss the results of the analysis presented in this paper. However, the analysis results certainly showed that the ice loading on the ship bow in level ice cannot be a line load but a broken-line-like load which is composed of a sequence of loads of short length or even point loads. The line load model has been applied to the interpretation of field test results as described above and to the ship hull design as well. Although it may seem reasonable to assume such a model for the load in level ice, the validity of the model should be re-examined.

At the same time, more studies, including reanalysis of existing field test results, are needed of the broken-line-like nature of the ice loads on ship hulls. There are many issues remaining to be studied associated with the problem. The following is a list of such issues.

- Mechanism that causes the broken-line-like ice loading,
- Physical explanation of the higher loads on shorter load patches, and
- Effects of parameters such as ice thickness and hull angles on the loading.

Summary

This paper presented the results of the study of the loading on ship bows in level ice. The study was originated to a finding in a model test. In the test detailed observations were made of the ice load distribution on the model by way of a tactile sensor system. It was shown that the ice load distribution was broken-line-like in which short load patches are aligned on a horizontal line.

Data obtained in field tests suggested that the ice load is broken-line-like also in full-scale conditions. Two sets of field data, one obtained on board PM *Teshio* in the Sea of Okhotsk and the other from USCGC *Polar Sea* in the Antarctic, were analyzed. The analysis showed that the load patch length of individual loading event might be short. Also, it was shown that the higher load might act on shorter load patches. These results suggest that the validity of the line load model should be re-examined as the ice load model for the interpretation of the field test results and for the structural design as well.

More studies are needed of the broken-line-like nature of the ice load on ship hulls. There are many issues remaining to be studied associated with the problem.

Acknowledgement

The authors are grateful to Japan Coast Guard for the support to the field test of PM *Teshio*. They also would like to thank European Union for having them participate in SAFEICE project.

References

Frederking, R. and Kubat, I., 2005. Database Structure, SAFEICE Deliverable 2-2, p. 23.

Izumiyama, K, Wako, D. and Uto, S. (1999). "Ice Force Distribution around a Ship Hull", Proceedings of the 15th International Conference on Port and Ocean Engineering under Arctic Conditions, POAC'99, Vol. 2, pp. 707-716.

Izumiyama, K. Wako, D. Shimoda, H. and Uto, S. (2005). "Ice load measurement on a model ship hull", Proceedings of the 18th International Conference on Port and Ocean Engineering under Arctic Conditions, POAC'05, Vol. 2, pp. 635–646.

Kujara, P. (1989) "Results of Long-term Ice Load Measurements on board Chemical Tanker Kemira in the Baltic Sea during the Winters 1985 to 1988", Winter Navigation Research Board, Research Report No. 47, p. 55 + App.

Riska, K., Rantala, H. and Joensuu, A. (1990). "Full scale Observations of Ship-Ice Contact. Results from Tests Series onboard IB Sampo, Winter 1989", Report M-97, Ship Laboratory, Helsinki University of Technology, Otaniemi 1990, p. 54 + App.

Uto, S., Oka, S., Murakami, C. Takimoto, T. and Izumiyama, K. (2005). "Ice Load exerted on the Hull of Icebreaker PM Teshio in the Southern Sea of Okhotsk", Proceedings of the 18th International Conference on Port and Ocean Engineering under Arctic Conditions, POAC'05, Vol. 2, pp. 683-692.

Strength and Vibration Multimode Control for Ship Moving in Ice Condition

V.Alexandrov[1], A.Matlakh[2], Yu.Nechaev[2], V.Polyakov[2]

[1] Admiralty Shipyards,
[2] State Marine Technical University –
Research and Production Association «Pole Star»,
St. Petersburg, Russia

Abstract

The problem of strength and vibration monitoring for the ship of active ice navigation is discussed. (The vibration while moving in ice is caused by impacts with pieces of broken ice.)

The principles of construction and peculiarities of operation of the strength and vibration monitoring intelligence system have been considered. Special attention is paid to higher efficiency in the monitoring of the ships' strength and vibration by the use of various methods for processing data measurements when faced with the conditions of uncertainty and incomplete data. Along with classical methods (theory of optimal control method of finite elements) the models developed on the basis of fuzzy logic and artificial neural networks can be used in the system. The operator interface is supported by applying simple and visual means of decision-making in the ship's maneuverability in icy conditions.

Keywords

Intelligence system; Ice field; Standard algorithm; Fuzzy logic; Neural network; Dynamic knowledge base.

Introduction

Steering the ship as a complex dynamic object (DO) in the Northern shelf region operation requires solving complicated problems of the information analysis and interpretation by applying adaptive algorithms. Defining these algorithms requires intense application of mathematical modeling. The use of these methods and modeling applications when designing intelligence systems (IS) of new generations provides necessary upgrades to functional efficiency, reliability and vitality. Implementing these systems with the use of algorithms and software is one of the most important conceptual elements of control and decision- making. It is this element that determines perfect qualities of the IS [1] – [11]. Below we discuss new approaches and technologies that will provide IS operation for monitoring ships' strength and vibration as well as technical facilities for the northern shelf exploration. Operational characteristics of these facilities were established by correcting methods to develop onboard IS by application of effective mathematical models developed on the principles of information processing discussed in [5], [6].

Architecture and the principles of the system operation

For decision-making transformation of information in onboard real-time, IS complex is used (Fig.1). The methods to upgrade the reliability of the IS operation during conditions of fuzzy and incompleteness of the initial information the mechanism of imitation modeling for information flows are provided in the knowledge base. This mechanism takes into consideration specifics of the situation under investigation as well as information about the ship's dynamics and the outside environment [1] – [3].

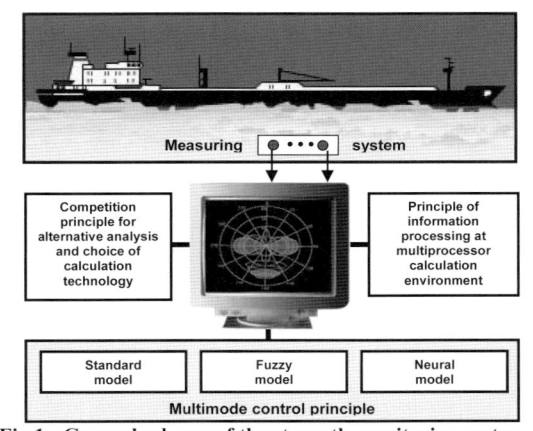

Fig.1: General scheme of the strength monitoring system operation

The onboard IS Hardware

Practical realization of information processing principles in the multiprocessing computer environment has been made on the high performance computer platforms. The soft – hardware system widely uses parallel programming and visual aids. The IS measuring unit consists of sensors mounted in the designated contact areas used for dynamic measuring parameters of the ship – environment interaction. . For upgrading IS performance, additional information from weather reconnaissance data, ice patrol, and air support are used. IS hardware is implemented by the use of standard components, software and hardware, and measuring devices suitable for real-time onboard systems.

Features of the System Operation

Real-time IS operates in the conditions of changing ship dynamics and environment. The concept of achieving optimum solutions using available resources (fuzzy objective and limitations) is the basis for constructing decision-making algorithmic procedures when said fuzzy conditions exist.

In order to check the practical accuracy of real-time IS, one can select certain time periods during which the system condition changes slightly (theory of fuzzy intervals). This practice allows the quasi-stationary hypothesis [1] to be tried along with the application of the well-developed "knowledge engineering" method. The adequate information representation is achieved by means of integrated models for the knowledge presentation that connects presentation schemes possibilities on various levels of abstraction. At this point the logical structure defines the object control model while the production one defines the decision making model.

Multimode Control Principle: The ship movement as a multimode dynamic system is described by the vector differential equation [4]:

$$x' = Ax + Bu, \qquad (1)$$

where $x=(x_1,\ldots,x_n)^T \in X \subset R^n$ is the phase vector of the dynamic system; $u=(u_1,\ldots,u_m)^T \in U \subset R^m$ – is the vector of controlling effects; $k=(k_1,\ldots,k_p)^T$ – is the vector of regulator parameters. Elements of the matrices A and B are functions of vector $\lambda=(\lambda_1,\ldots,\lambda_S)^T \in \Lambda \subset R^S$ and time $t \in [t_0,t_f]$. Here λ is the external vector of the discussed dynamic system, and the range of its values changing λ is the external set.

The multimode principle ensures the control system adjustment for different modes of the ship movement in ice conditions:

- standard mode when the ship overcomes the compact ice field without icebreaker assistance;
- mode of movement by "attacks" in complex ice conditions;
- mode of movement in broken ice after the icebreaker in different close ice conditions;
- mode of movement in drift ice which involves considerable impact loads.

The task is to reduce the system movement to the earlier prescribed movement considering uncertainty in parameters $\lambda \in \Lambda$. By changing the regulator parameter values $k \in K$, one can influence the regulation quality. Various values of k for different λ are used under complex situations with quite a great external set Λ. (This is especially true in movement in pack ice). Dependence of $k=k(\lambda)$, $\forall \lambda \in \Lambda$ is provided by the correction module (corrector) and the assembly of the regulator and corrector forms the controller [1], [4].

Control within the ship speed monitoring systems when moving in ice is connected with solving complex problems of information. Nonlinear transformation with different modes of movement resulted from environment and interaction of the ship and the close ice field of differing quality. Under these conditions the speed monitoring is reflects the use of the new approach for information analyzing and interpreting covered in [2], [3].

Information Processing Principles

By increasing the evaluation certainty and the situation, forecast is achieved by a new approach of information processing based on the concept development of "soft computing" [11]. This method uses theoretical principles allowing one to rationally organize computing technology of data measurements processing as well as formalize the information flow in realization of the fuzzy logic interface in multiprocessor computational environment [5],[6]. Implementation of these principles increases the IS effectiveness of operation with continuous changing of the object dynamics and the environment. The practice of testing the algorithms control correction along with decision-making is based on general requirements for the system algorithms. As to parallel algorithms of the logic control, the correct definition is connected to specific qualities of said algorithms: non-contradiction, stability and self-consistency.

The Alternatives Analysis

The choice of optimum solution by the competition principle is ensured by the subsystem of decision-making support. The basis of this statement refers to the hierarchy's analysis method [8]. With the multitude of alternatives every criterion is set according to corresponding linguistic variables (LV) L_i with the term-set $T_i=\{T_{i1},\ldots,T_{it}\}$. The LV basic set is the permissible set of C_i criterion values. For evaluating the alternative efficiency according to the separate criterion C_i, LV with the term-set $S = \{S_1,\ldots,S_l\}$ is introduced the rating of which coincides with the T_i term-set rating. The result is a cause-and-effect relationship between two LVs which is represented as a fuzzy implicit relationship:

$$\mu_{Rij}(x_i,y): X_i \times Y \to [0,1], \ x_i \in X_i, y \in Y, \qquad (2)$$

where X_i is the base set of i-criterion values; Y is the base set of values evaluation for the alternatives, efficiency.

For the direct contact between LV for implication the operation of taking minimum is used:

$(\forall i \in 1,...,m; \forall j \in 1,...,t)$

$$\mu_{Rij}(x_i,y) = \min(\mu_{Tij}(x_i), \mu_{Sk}(y)), k = j. \qquad (3)$$

The membership function (MF) of the alternative efficiency factor according to i-criterion considering (3) is written as follows:

$$\mu_{Sik}(y^d) = \sup xt \in Xt \min(\mu_{Rij}(x_i,y), \mu_{Tij}(x_{id})), \qquad (4)$$

where d=1,...,n is the alternative number.

The result of uniting MF efficiency factor in all the terms is represented by the relationship:

$$\cup_{k=1,...,t} \mu_{Sik'}(y^d) = \mu_{Si'}(y^d), \qquad (5)$$

The accurate factor value is calculated by defuzzyfication operation:

$$y_i^d = \int_T y\mu_{Si}(y)dy / \int_T \mu_{Si}(y)dy. \qquad (6)$$

Dynamic data base

The control system chooses the optimal ship speed according to the ice load intensity. The control process is made within the limits of "soft computing" concept [11]. The controlling algorithm is represented by a set of logic rules «IF – THEN» [1]-[3]. For the initial information we use the sensor (fitted in the contact area) readings about the hull strain. Information transformation algorithm determines the actual ice field characteristics (variables X_1 и X_2 and changing of these values dX_1/dt and dX_2/dt in time) and accordingly carries out the U control. The data about ice field and snow thickness are used respectively as variables X_1 and X_2. U control is provided as the speed changes V of the ship speed.

The Adaptive System of Fuzzy conclusion

The adaptive system of the fuzzy conclusion is used for producing controlling signals. The system is designed on the basis of "adaptive resonance" [10] and provides fuzzy rules and adjustment of MF parameters of the observed and controlled variables [6]. The system adjustment is performed in the training mode when the control is made by the operator. According to the current events analysis, the system develops the relative behavior rules.

The adaptive system operates on the basis of fuzzy conclusion rules. Each rule realizes the fuzzy model Sugeno [9]:

$$\text{«if x is } A_i \text{ \& y is } B_i, \text{ then } f_i = a_i x^2 + b_i y^2 + p_i\text{».} \qquad (7)$$

The system chooses the ship's speed according to the ice load intensity. The control is provided by the competition concept accompanied by the application of classical mathematics, fuzzy logic and artificial neural networks (ANN).

The Logic Conclusion Model in Complex Situations

In complex problems of data analysis and interpretation for dynamic measurements, the fuzzy logic conclusion model established by precedents is used. The generalized model conclusion by precedents is carried out as follows [2]:

$$<S_{PB}, M(W), M(W,V), M_{FD}>, \qquad (8)$$

where S_{PB} is the system of precedents-based neural network presentation; $M(W)$ – models of fuzzy conclusion by precedents; $M(W,V)$ – the fuzzy output complex model for the integrated processes set; M_{FD} – the model of alternatives analysis and the former solutions.

Neurocontroller

Realization of the information processing principles in multiprocessing calculation medium [5] is made by using multimode control principle which is applied in complex systems [4]. In this case the controller is represented by the cortege:

$$\Omega = (\Lambda, K, W, V, J), \qquad (9)$$

where $\Lambda \subset R^S$ – external set of the dynamic system which is the area of values changing for the neural network input vectors; $K \subset R^P$ – the area of values changing for the regulator coefficients to be found (neural network input vectors); $W=\{W_i\}, i=1,...,L+1$ – the matrices set of the neural network synaptic weights; L – the number of "hidden" layers in the neural network; $V=(v_1,...,v_q)^T \in V \subset R^q$ – the set of additional measured neural network parameters (parameters in activation functions); J – the error functional (of misalignment) between the required and realized movement, defining the way of the neural network training.

The multimode monitoring is achieved by realization of the neurocontrollers ensemble in the control system (Fig.2).

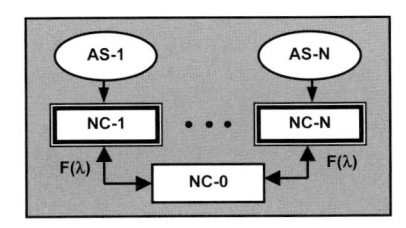

Fig.2: Functions carried out by the neurocontrollers ensemble: NC–1,...,NC–N – the neurocontrollers ensemble; F(·) – distribution function; AS–1,...,AS–N – areas of neurocontrollers specialization.

As you see in Fig. 2, the ensemble contains two kinds of controllers, each having its own specialization area AS_i. The first kind represents neurocontrollers NC_i (i=1,...,N), producing the controlling signal. The aim of the second kind of controller (NC–0) is to produce number i (1≤i≤N) for every current value $\lambda \in \Lambda$ in accordance with dependences $F(\lambda)$. This number shows which of the neurocontrollers NC_i is to control by the datum $\lambda \in \Lambda$. Changing of one neurocontroller for another is made by distribution function $F(\lambda)$ [4].

For evaluating the control quality realized by the neural network the efficiency index (neurocontroller optimum criterion) is used. This criterion takes into account the available varying neurocontroller parameters from areas W and V, and also the dynamic system multimode.

Ship dynamics monitoring models in ice conditions

For conducting experimental studies of dynamics for the ship – ice field interaction numerical algorithms operating in the competition principle were developed [5], [6]. On the basis of these algorithms we developed the program complex which allows us to carry out modeling processing and interpretation of the received data while the IS is in operation. The computing procedures are made by the multimode principle of monitoring and decision-making in the ship steering under various conditions of operation [4]. The main objectives for applying standard, fuzzy, and neural network models in the problem under discussion are as follows:

- find the operative forces determining the resulting strains and stresses caused by the ship movement;
- monitor the ship dynamics by the competition principle.

The vibration monitoring model operates in conjunction with the ship strength monitoring models on the basis of vibration measuring data in the most unfavorable hull structures.

Standard Model

Modeling the processes of the ship – ice field interaction was carried out on the basis of finite elements method and Stateflow procedure – the systems numerical modeling instrument characterized by the complex interaction of continuous and discrete components (Fig.3).

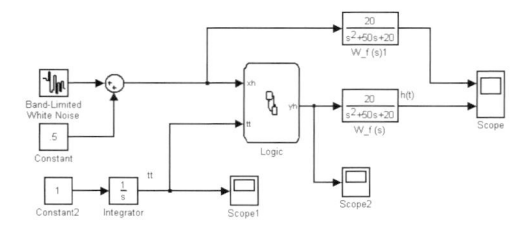

Fig.3: Simulink\Stateflow – the model of the effects simulator

The Fuzzy Model

The model of the ship – ice field interaction based on the fuzzy logic theory was presented as a set of production rules "if – then" describing interrelations of input and output variables [1],[9]:

R_l [k]: if ($x_1 = A_{11}^{[k]}$, $x_2 = A_{21}^{[k]}$, ..., $x_n = A_{nl}^{[k]}$);

then ($y_1 = B_{11}^{[k]}$, $y_2 = B_{21}^{[k]}$, ..., $y_m = B_{ml}^{[k]}$), $l = 1,...,N$;

$A_{il}^{[k]} \subseteq X_i \subset R$, $i=1,...,n$, $A_{il}^{[k]} \in \{A_i^p\}$, $p=1,...,P$;

$B_{jl}^{[k]} \subseteq Y_j \subset R$, $j=1,...,m$, $B_{jl}^{[k]} \in \{B_j^q\}$, $q=1,...,Q$, (10)

where $k \in \{1,...,K\}$ – model structure number; n,m – the number of input and output linguistic variables x_i, y_l, $i=1,...,n$, $j=1,...,m$; N – the total number of rules in the fuzzy model; $A_{il}^{[k]}$, $B_{jl}^{[k]}$ – fuzzy sets (concrete linguistic values of the relative input and output variables in l rule); $X_i, Y_j, (i=1,...,n, j=1,...,m)$ – areas of input and output variables.

The fuzzy model composition is presented in Fig.4. Fuzzyficator (F) transforms the exact set of the input data $x=(x_1,...,x_n)^T$ into the fuzzy set A' determined by the membership function $\mu_{A'}(x)$. In the output of the conclusion block the fuzzy set is formed on the basis of the extended rule modus ponens in the form of "condition – implication – output". Defuzzyficator (DF) solves the problem of representing the output fuzzy set $B^{[k]}$ into the single accurate value $y \in Y$, which is the model output signal. The centroid method is chosen from many defuzzyfication methods in this paper.

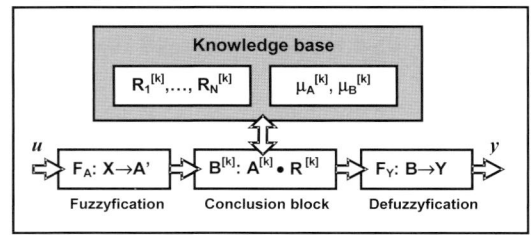

Fig.4: The fuzzy model scheme.

So, the initial data is evaluated to solve the problem of the fuzzy system synthesis. On the basis of prior information about possible interaction model structures, we give K fuzzy logic – linguistic models with the logic output form represented as fuzzy equations and control matrix. These data have been used in the problem of fuzzy modeling for the ship movement under ice conditions.

Neural Network Model

Neural network modeling has been discussed in the problem of ship dynamics monitoring not as a competitive computer technology, but also by the realization o measuring information processing algorithm in the real time mode. This approach is especially efficient in the problems where we need high certainty of the result and reliability of practical recommendations [1], [5]-[7], [10]. In the discussed system the neural networks are used in:

measuring information processing in functioning the ship dynamics evaluation system;

neural networks ensemble construction for conducting logic conclusion by precedent.

The general task for the neural network construction is connected with the selection of topology and network training (Fig.5) and consists of construction of continuous dependence with prescribed properties according to the discrete data set.

Formally, this problem is reduced to image finding F: $X^n \to Y^m$, defined foe every data discrete set as a vector in the coordinate space of n dimension, equal to the number of nodes – points of the data input set $x \in X^n \subset R^n$, and the point – vector in the m-measuring space of the model parameters $y \in Y^m \subset R^m$. This representation meets the generalized quality criterion of the approximation E: $Y^m \to R$, which includes the required approximation accuracy $\varepsilon > 0$ (error minimization) and additional requirements to the model appearance and behavior beyond the data area limits [3],[6],[10].

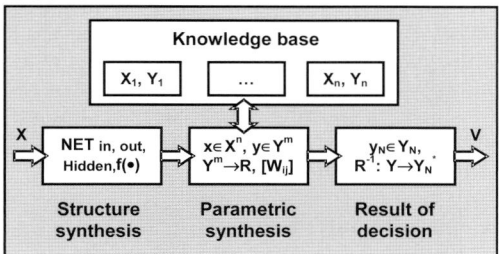

Fig.5: Scheme of the neural network model evaluating dynamics in the ice conditions

The normalized mean-square error is used as a numerical modulus of precision of the neural network

$$S_N = \left[\sum_{i=1}^{N} (y_i - y_i^*)^2 / (N-1) \right] / (y_{max}^* - y_{min}^*) \quad , \quad (11)$$

where $(y_{max}^* - y_{min}^*)$ – is the observation range of y* value.

The system operation in different movement modes

Let us consider the system construction for monitoring the ship strength and vibration which provides the making decision mechanism in ice condition. Different system structures are used depending on the ship – ice field interaction character estimated by the selected movement performance.

The simplest structure is made on the basis of fuzzy model considering the rules correction. This structure is shown in Fig.6 and represents the two-level system. It comprises blocks of preliminary information processing (calculation block, block of the situation analysis by methods of finite elements and the comparison block) and adaptation block on the basis of fuzzy logic rules matrix and neural network models. The operation principle of the system is as follows: Having analyzed the current value of the error vector [ε,dε/dt], ε=V(t)–V*(t), (where V(t) is the actual ship speed value, V*(t) the value which is the calculation block output) the adaptation block forms control effects which change the matrix right-hand parts of the linguistic rules. On this scheme screen there is the dynamic interaction picture for the prescribed movement mode.

In the adaptation block there is information about the desired system reaction as the logic rules matrix. The zero elements of this matrix correspond to conditions [ε,dε/dt] (ε is the fuzzy value of the control error) which do not require any correction. The non-zero elements show the rules correction necessity which is realized by the adaptive resonance principle [6], [10]. The adaptation procedure is the correction of a certain rule from the matrix of fuzzy logical rules. By correcting rules the system performance quality may be upgraded by repeating the situation [ε,dε/dt], that causes the correction, i.e. if the control is not satisfactory in the i-step, then it may be enhanced in the i+1 step. Thus, the discussed structure of the fuzzy control model requires the operations implementation for the system adaptation to ensure multimode movement principles.

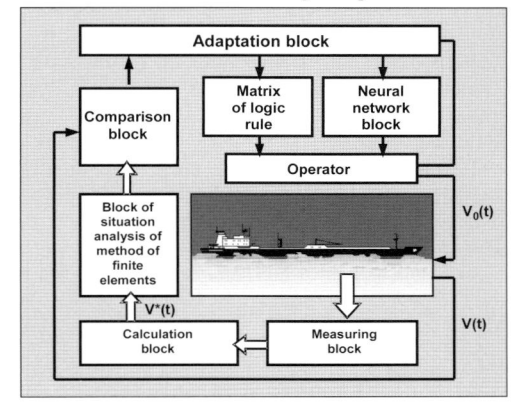

Fig.6: Ship dynamics monitoring system using the competition principle

The fuzzy logical rules adaptation in fulfilling the quasi-stationary hypothesis consists in selecting a suitable model from the logical rules matrices ensemble (or neural network models ensemble) corresponding to various ship movement modes. In this case the logical rules matrices may be constructed with respect to different interaction parameters determining the ship dynamics in ice conditions.

The expanded structure of the fuzzy multimode system for decision making to steer the ship in the complex ice conditions is shown in Fig.7. As you see on the figure, the system is supplemented by the correction block that adjusts the logical rules by applying identification methods, fuzzy adaptive model and neural network ensembles. The correction block operates on the basis of logic conclusion models by competition principle. The identification block uses traditional methods of current situation, and the fuzzy adaptive model was designed on the adaptive resonance principle [6],[10]. Neural network ensembles approximate the dynamics of interaction of the ship and hammocks of different forms and intensity. The correction block operation results in selecting the preferable computing technology for ensuring the ship's safety in moving under hard service conditions, especially in the pack ice. The correction block suppresses the signal from I fuzzy logical rule R_i, i={1,...,N}, which does not correspond to the current parameters of interaction and gives the solution for selecting the current speed by the alternatives analysis.

The operation algorithm of the fuzzy adaptive model is the sequence of steps determining the input image analysis procedure by the model of fuzzy output proposed by Sugeno [9]. If the procedures realized by the identification algorithm fail to give the result, then the modification of the logical rule is carried out. This has the largest "likeness" with the original information that entered on the fuzzy system input. This procedure is realized by re-adjustment of the initial values of the membership functions considering the continuous changing of the object and the environment dynamics. This is the way of dynamic self-organization of the fuzzy knowledge system by "supplementing" new rules and modifying the most "similar" ones. The discussed fuzzy system is efficient with quite high uncertainty, when the number of possible structures in the interaction model is not quite known. In this case the accumulated information in the operating system increases the number of fuzzy logical rules. In very complicated situations with the system troubles the logical conclusion is made by the precedent [7] realizing the dynamic picture of interaction accordingly (Fig.8).

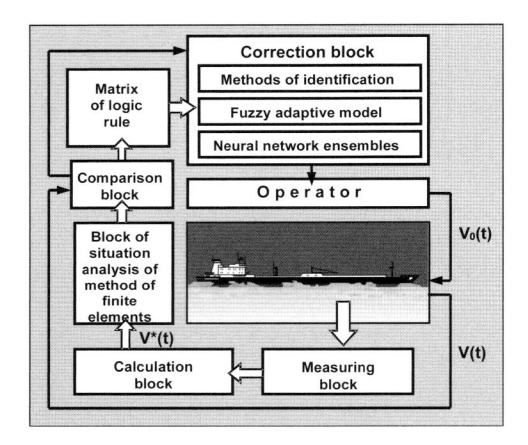

Fig.7: The dynamics monitoring system of the active ice navigation ship for moving in pack ice.

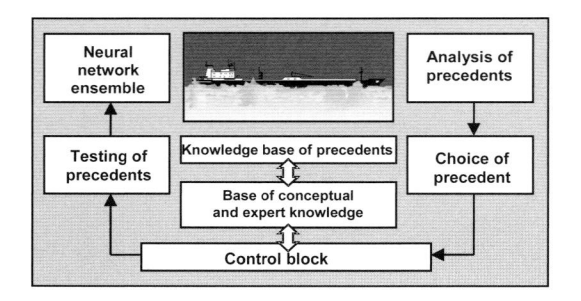

Fig.8: The scheme of correction block operation using the neural network ensemble

In some cases when the information about the possible structures of the object model is presented by the finite set of interaction models it is expedient to apply the fuzzy logical controlling system with slight adaptation. Such a system may be designed after accumulating sufficient data of full scale measurements by solving the identification problem of the current interaction model.

Thus, the main idea about applying the new information processing principles in the intelligence systems of the ship strength and vibration monitoring is in the rational organization of computing technology. Inclusion of fuzzy and neural networks into the information basis allows for the expansion of the system functionality and upgrades the reliability of the decisions made in complicated ice conditions. Matrices of the fuzzy logical models are able to be adapted to the changing environment, and the neural network ensembles can identify "patterns" (cause and effect relations) of every monitored process. Such continuous self-training process gives the possibility to accumulate information about the interaction dynamics and predict parameters deviation from rating (permissible) values.

The operation interface

The main IS feature as a system of new generation is the realization in it basic principles and procedures which makes it natural to communicate the operator and IS. The important principle of interface organization is also its operation in the conditions of uncertainty and incompleteness of the initial information. The safe operator support is determined by the control quality which is provided by the produced information. The safety criteria represented by the information monitor screen are defined by the dangerous situation according to the standard ratings and documents adopted in the home and international practice.

The operator is responsible for the ship steering on the basis of practical recommendations developed by IS in the standard conditions of service. In complicated (non-standard and extreme) situations the system needs adjustment and sometimes changing for corresponding strategies which make decisions for the ship steering by the principle of competition (the alternatives analysis is carried out by applying classic mathematics, fuzzy logic and the theory of neural networks). In these situations the output information on the display will instruct the operator to react quickly and effectively for the appearing events.

Because of complexity and uncertainty of situations when the ship is moving in the ice field, special attention must be paid to the making decisions system construction in the ship steering in the complicated weather situations. In the interface "Operator – IS" the following alternatives are specified:

- analysis and forecast of the situation;
- visualization of the interaction dynamics;
- running control.

The interface graphic window "Analysis and the situation forecast **Analysis – Forecast** (Fig.9) has three areas: the area of initial data – **Input Data**, The area of model tree – **Domain** and the scan window – **Results**. The initial data area contains the processed data of dynamic measurements and the forecast information from the coastal weather stations. The model tree area contains the following bookmarks: **Physics** is introducing the problem conditions, **Model** is the choice of the model (classical, fuzzy, neural network); **Simulation** – work with the model. The scan window **Results** contains the analysis results (the choice of preferable computing technology) and shows the corresponding curve of the speed changing due to the ice thickness, and the conclusions **Conclusion** is practical recommendations foe the ship speed selection.

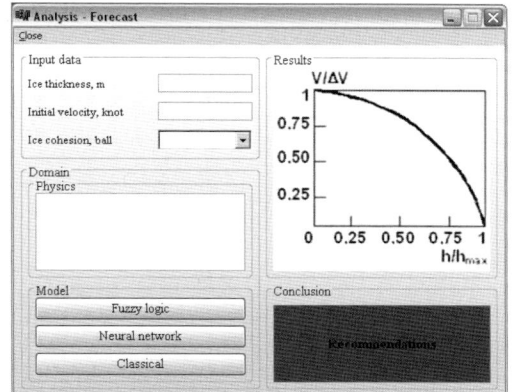

Fig.9: **The graphic window "Analysis and situation forecast": in the window "Results" you can see the predicted curve of the speed decreasing due to the relative ice thickness.**

The graphic window "Visualization of the dynamic interaction" **Visualization** (Fig.10) contains the results of the interaction dynamics modeling by the competition principle and displaying the corresponding dynamic picture on the screen. The window contains input information **Input Data** and current information **Current Data** about the ice field and ship speed characteristics. This window model is developed in detail considering the dynamic pictures of changing the ice thickness **Ice thickness, Change of ice thickness** and the ship velocity **Velocity**, estimated by the classic **Classic**, fuzzy **Fuzzy** and neural network **Neural Network** algorithms.

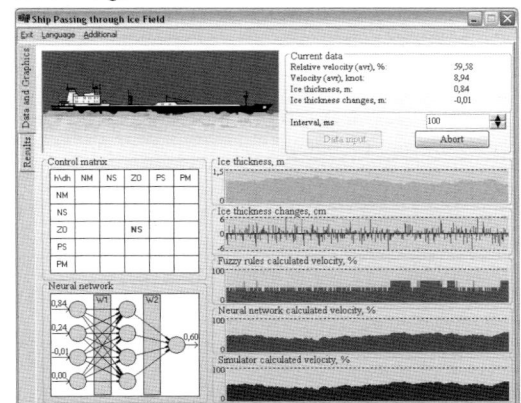

Fig.10: The graphic window "Visualization of the interaction dynamics"

The graphic window "The running control" Running Control (Fig.11) is the most responsible model in the operator intelligence support in the onboard real-time systems. Realization of this model is based on the cognitive paradigm usage. The main principle of the cognitive paradigm realization is the quick and reliable operator reaction to the represented information as various ways of the results presentation with the system operating in complicated ice conditions: moving in the consolidated ice field, broken ice and hammocks. The window is characterized by the simplicity of the information presentation and contains three bookmarks: the ice field characteristics Ice Field, the situation evaluation Situation and practical recommendations Recommendation. The current data about the ice condition characteristics (consolidated ice field, broken ice, hammocks) are given in the window Ice Field. The evaluation of ship strength, Strength, and ship vibration, Vibration, is given in the window Situation. And if these characteristics are satisfactory, the current values are displayed on the green display field. If these characteristics are approaching to the limiting value, the yellow display field is applied (the look out color). In cases of criteria distortions the data are presented on the red display field (threatening color). The window Recommendation contains proposals for the ship changing the speed Velocity considering the safe ship navigation in the current situation. If besides the current ice condition data the operator is interested in the forecast of the coastal weather stations, ice reconnaissance and air support, the corresponding information is given on the display screen Commentary.

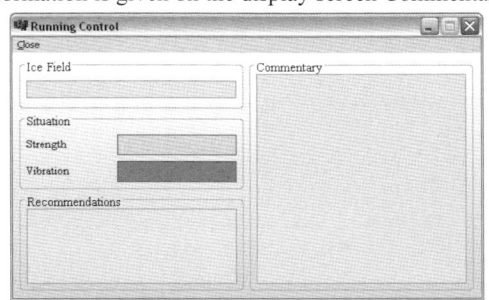

Fig.11: The graphic window "Running control"

Conclusion

Thus, the new paradigm for monitoring strength and vibration of the active ice navigation ships implemented by the intelligence support system has the following advantages:

1. Expansion of the traditional approaches for the information processing, supplementing them with new methods, models and algorithms for decision making support in the ship steering under complicated weather conditions.

2. Taking into consideration the uncertain and fuzzy initial information in interpreting and selecting complex solutions in steering the ship as a multimode dynamic system.

3. Developing the inner potential of the theory of control and decision making by the competition principle which gives the possibility by the preferable computing technology using the methods of classic mathematics, fuzzy and neural networks models.

The proposed technology for the information processing in the intelligence systems of new generations is essentially different from the existing traditional approaches for developing the systems of the ship strength and vibration monitoring. Expanding greatly the system functionality and upgrading the efficiency of solving the raised problems, the developed approach has a new quality, i.e. prediction and foreseeing of the critical and emergency situations in the service of ships of the active ice navigation.

References

[1]. ALEXANDROV V.L., MATLAKH A.P., NECHAEV Yu.I., POLYAKOV V.I., ROSTOVTSEV D.M. Intelligence systems in marine research and technology. – St.-Petersburg. SMTU, 2001.

[2]. ALEXANDROV V.L., MATLAKH A.P., NECHAEV Yu.I., POLYAKOV V.I..Ships safety navigation in conditions of the Arctic shelf // Proceedings of 2nd International Maritime Conference on DESIGN FOR SAFETY, Osaka Colloquium 2004, SAKAI, JAPAN, p. 231-237.

[3]. ALEXANDROV V.L., MATLAKH A.P., NECHAEV Yu.I., POLYAKOV V.I. Intelligence system for ship Dynamics monitoring in extreme situations // Proc. of International conference on marine research and transportation ICMRT-05. Naples – Italy. 2005, p.p.55 – 63.

[4]. BRUSOV V.S., TIUMENTSEV Yu.V. High performance aircraft flight controlbased on artificial neural networks // Proc. Of the RRDPAE-96. Warsaw.1997, p.p.97 – 100.

[5]. NECHAEV Yu.I. Mathematical modeling in real-time onboard intelligence systems // Proceedings of Russian conference «Neuroinformatics-2003». Moscow. MIFI. 2003. Lectures on Neuroinformatics. Part 2, p.119-179.

[6]. NECHAEV Yu.I. Principles of neural networks use in the onboard intelligence systems // Neurocomputers: development, application. №7-8. 2004. p.49-56.

[7]. NECHAEV Yu.I., TIKHONOV D.G. Neural forecast on basis of logical conclusion by precedents // Proceedings of Russian conference «Neuroinformatics-2005». Moskow. MIFI. 2005. Lectures on Neuroinformatics. Part 2, p.197-204.

[8]. SAATY T.L. A sealing method for priorities in hierarchical structures // J. Match. Psihology. 1977. Vol.15, №3.

[9]. TERANO T., ASAI K., SUGENO M. Applied fuzzy systems. – Moskow. Mir. 1993.

[10]. WASSERMAN F. Neurocomputer technics. – Moskow. MIR, 1992.

[11]. ZADEH L. Fuzzy logic, neural networks and soft computing» // Commutation on the ASM-1994. Vol.37. №3, p. 77-84.

Structural Analysis and Modifications – Two Tankers for Offshore FPSO and FSO Service

Lars Henriksen [1], Arata Kamishohara [2] Hiroyuki Hosokawa [2]

[1] Viking Systems, Inc.
Houston, Texas, U.S.A.
[2] MODEC International, LLC
Houston, Texas, U.S.A.

Abstract

This paper addresses the unique structural requirements for successful conversion of tankers for FPSO or FSO service. A description is given of the steps undertaken during two recent and very different conversions of a highly optimized 1980's VLCC to FPSO service, and a typical robust 1970's ULCC to FSO service. The paper describes the steps needed for ensuring the FPSO or FSO requirements are successfully met during conversion of the two tankers – each having its own history, e.g. date of build, original design, material choices, class society, voyage history, and repairs. First, the paper describes the procedure and results of an early initial structural assessment procedure based on an ABS Phase A analysis, past tanker voyage history, and a review of past survey records and thickness gauging data. Secondly, the paper describes the procedure and results of a detailed structural finite element analysis of the two vessels considering past tanker service and future FPSO or FSO service, including the effects of on and off loading of crude oil. Since the abstract was first written, a third FPSO, of similar configuration to the 1980's FPSO described in this paper has been analyzed with the same procedure.

Keywords

FPSO vessels; FSO vessels; Floating production storage and offloading; Conversion engineering; Structural design and assessment; Spectral fatigue assessment; Advanced finite element analysis; Classification calculations; Repair methods.

Nomenclature

ABS	American Bureau of Shipping
B	Moulded Breadth
BHD	Bulkhead
BT	Ballast Tank
CB	Block Coefficient
CL	Centerline
CT	Cargo Tank
D	Hull Depth
DNV	Det Norske Veritas, FPSO Package
FEA	Finite Element Analysis
FEMAP	Finite Element Pre/Post Processor by UGS
FPSO	Floating Production Storage and Offloading
FSO	Floating Storage and Offloading
HGSA	ABS Hull Girder Strength Program
HHI	Hyundai Heavy Industries
HTS	High Tensile Steel
LBP	Length Between Perpendiculars
LOA	Length Overall
LR	Lloyd's Register of Shipping
NKK	Nippon Kaiji Kyokai
NX	NX Nastran Finite Element Solver by UGS
PHASEA	ABS SafeHull Program, Version 10.0
SAGA	Structural Assessment Graphical Assessment program developed by Viking Software, Inc.
SEAS	ABS Environmental Loading Program
SH	Single Hull
t	Metric tonnes
VT	Void Tank
WT	Wing Tank

Introduction

MODEC International, LLC has recently converted two tankers to operate as FPSO or FSO offshore Brazil, both projects supported concurrently with structural conversion engineering by Viking Systems, Inc. The FPSO vessel was converted from an existing single hull VLCC built at a Japanese shipyard in 1986, and the FSO vessel was converted from a single hull ULCC built at a US shipyard in 1979. As is evident in the next sections of this paper, the results of the conversion analysis procedures are vastly different for the two vessels, primarily due to the differences in design and build histories. The impact on the shipyard conversion process is also vastly different for the two vessels, however, as is seen in the paper a suitable tanker from each of the tanker generations of the 1970's and 1980's can be converted successfully by taking proper detailed care during the inspection, structural analysis, and conversion process. An important lesson learned is that for optimized designs, analysis work should be started as early as possible, and must include feedback from close up inspections.

Description of Conversions

Tanker Vessel Principal Characteristics

The two original tanker vessels are described in Table 1. The VLCC (see Fig. 1) is a typical mid 1980's tanker employing a larger amount of high tensile steel for the longitudinal structure as well as portions of the transverse structure. The tank arrangement uses a typical 5 tank layout in the length direction and three tanks across the breadth. See Fig. 2 for a view of the tanker and converted FPSO tank arrangements.

Table 1: Tanker Basic As Built Data

Tanker	VLCC SH	ULCC SH
Conversion	FPSO	FSO
LOA	322 m	362 m
LBP	310 m	348 m
B	58 m	69.5 m
D	29.5 m	29 m
CB	0.81	0.84
Displacement	300,000 t	460,000 t
Frame Spacing	5.950 m	5.461 m
Longest Tank (CT/WT)	47.6 /59.5m	21.8 /43.6m
Year built	1986	1979
HTS (approximate)	75%	45%
Original Class	NKK	ABS
Yard	Japan	US

The ULCC tanker (see Fig. 3) is of a typical late 1970's type employing high-tensile steel only for the deck and bottom structure and the upper and lower portions of the longitudinal bulkhead and side shell, whereas the transverse structure is built from mild steel of heavy construction.

Fig 1: Spreadmoored FPSO

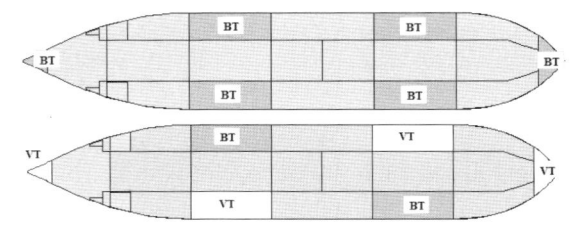

Fig 2: Tank Arrangement (Tanker / FPSO)

In addition, the tank arrangement as shown in Fig. 4 uses 13 short wing tanks in the length direction, and three tanks across the breadth.

FPSO or FSO Vessels Principal Characteristics

The principal characteristics of the two vessels, as converted, are summarized in Table 2.

Table 2: FPSO or FSO Basic Conversion Data

	FPSO	FSO
LOA	322 m	409 m
Topsides	10,000 t	2,750 t
Mooring	Spreadmoored	External Bow Turret
Design Life (years)	12	25
Fatigue Safety Factor	1.0	2.2
Class	ABS	ABS
Year Re-delivered	2006	2007

The FSO was fitted with a large SOFEC external turret. See fig. 4 for a photo of the FSO.

Fig. 3: FSO with External Turret

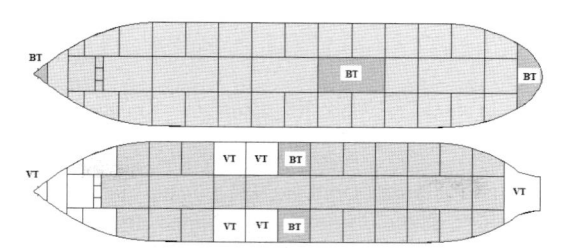

Fig 4: Tank Arrangement (Tanker / FSO)

The FPSO was converted from a tanker with 75% of its construction steel in HTS grades including 100% of the longitudinal structure constructed from HTS. As a contrast, the FSO was converted from a tanker with 45% of its construction steel as HTS with all transverse material of mild steel.

Conversion Engineering Approach

Initial Scantling Assessment Method

Both vessels were initially analyzed using the ABS Phase A program with its supporting environmental loading program SEAS. Phase A was used to assess global and local strength, using the design still water bending moment and the site environmental loads as calculated by the program SEAS. The resulting FPSO scantling requirements are used to develop the renewal scantling at conversion incorporating the future corrosion values expected during the FPSO service life.

The longitudinal strength was assessed with the ABS program HGSA to develop the FPSO allowable shear force and bending moments curves. Generally, the tanker allowable values for still water shear force and bending moment are maintained for FPSO service, except at locations where the ABS rules required a reduction, or where FPSO service required an increase.

In addition, the fatigue strength of longitudinal stiffener end connections is verified by using the Phase A program to calculate the damage expected during the tanker phase of the vessel life as well as the fatigue damage predicted by using the site loads as calculated by the ABS SEAS program. The outcome of the fatigue calculation is a value representing the remaining fatigue life for each longitudinal stiffener.

The Phase A analysis can typically be completed in about a month which allows evaluation of candidate tankers and development of repair and modification plans at an early stage of the projects

Survey Report Data Collection

The authors have used a method to visualize damage reported via class survey reports. Each damage situation is plotted electronically onto a schematic drawing using symbols corresponding to the type of damage (crack in web, crack on bracket, corrosion, buckling, denting, etc). This set of drawings of each major structure group, e.g. bottom, side shell, longitudinal bulkhead, deck and transverse bulkhead proves very useful to ensure that the shipyard conversion team is aware of past damage, and it becomes an invaluable tool for the design and analysis as an easy-to-access visual collection. The engineering team is then able to determine the locations of damage, the type of repair, and whether a repair has been successful. See Fig. 15 as an example.

The survey data is used to correlate the results of both the fatigue screening analysis and the detailed fine mesh FEA based spectral fatigue analysis (see later in this paper for description of fatigue assessment).

FEA Direct Analysis Assessment Method

Both vessels were assessed using a series of advanced FEA based analysis tools consisting of the DNV FPSO Package, Viking Software's computer program SAGA, FEMAP, and NX Nastran.

For each vessel, two Nastran finite element models are constructed using SAGA to represent the tanker vessel in its original configuration using as-built scantlings, and a model representing the FPSO configuration with scantlings equal to those expected at the end of the service life. It is recommended that the entire cargo block is modeled in order to capture the complete effects resulting from FPSO loading cases. This is especially true in the case of the FPSO conversion described in this paper due to the use of non-symmetric loading of ballast tanks. We believe the transition between the cargo block and the end structures are proven in tanker service, so that a full length model is not required for a conversion. The authors develop highly accurate coarse mesh style models using one element between longitudinal stiffeners and approximately five to six elements between transverse frames in order to accurately model web frame tripping brackets, docking brackets, and bilge brackets and to be able to maintain aspect ratios near unity. The models are made with SAGA's shell meshing capability to rapidly and accurately model the entire bottom, side shell and deck structure as defined by the shell expansion and main deck drawings.

Each model is loaded with loading cases representing the tanker's full and ballast loading cases, as well as approximately seven operating cases specific for the FPSO design agreed with class. Unlike tankers, converted FPSO's may have minimum drafts less than those resulting from IMO segregated ballast, and significantly less than the load line draft. See examples, Table 3

Table 3: Tanker vs. FPSO/FSO Drafts

Tanker	VLCC / FPSO	VLCC / FPSO	ULCC / FSO
Min Draft, Tanker (m)	10.090	9.980	13.128
Min. Draft, FPSO (m)	7.876	7.582	6.393
Max. Draft, Tanker (m)	19.880	19.290	22.860
Max. Draft, FPSO (m)	20.242	13.420	20.365

The FPSO design cases are constructed so as to stress each structural member to the maximum 100-year return value of its dynamic loading component at the location of interest by using DNV's frequency domain program WADAM. The loads are obtained by determining the wave height, wave period and wave heading that maximizes the dynamic component. The corresponding loads are applied as pressures for external sea and internal tank loads, as well as six degrees of freedom accelerations. The locations of interest are defined as the locations where the still water loading and the dynamic loading add to produce a maximum design value. Since the model consists of the cargo block only, additional global shear forces and bending moments are applied to the cut sections of the model in both the vertical and horizontal directions. Alternatively, the entire vessel can be modeled with a slight impact to schedule.

For the vessels described in this document, the resulting stresses are assessed against the ABS Steel Vessel Rules for yielding and buckling. This otherwise laborious task has been automated by using the features of SAGA to determine extents of all panels of the model, irrespective of mesh size, to carry out both plate buckling and stiffener buckling calculations. An advanced method to orient the stress tensor in the direction of the panel dimensions allows for an accurate assessment of transverse structure where the majority of the structure is made up from panels that are at angles with the orthogonal coordinate system defined by the length, breadth, and depth dimensions of the vessel. The rules used for the FPSO and FSO are referenced below:

- Plate and Beam Yielding Checks per ABS SVR 5-1-5/3
- Plate and Beam buckling Checks per ABS SVR 5-1-5/5

On other projects, code checks using SAGA's built-in buckling and yielding rules of Bureau Veritas, Lloyds, and DNV have been used.

The fatigue assessment is carried out using the stochastic (e.g. spectral) assessment capabilities of the DNV FPSO package as represented by the STOFAT program. For the two vessels described in this paper, dynamic loads have been developed for four representative FPSO loading cases, each corresponding to four equally spread drafts including and between the full and light displacement cases. Each of the four cases is solved by the DNV FPSO Package for a number of heading and wave periods to be able to allow the use of subsequent STOFAT analysis using heading probabilities and a wave scatter (Hs-Tp) diagram corresponding to each wave heading. The outcome is a calculation of the FPSO damage ratio for the intended design life.

The same procedure is used for the tanker phase of the vessel while trading on its routes. A combined wave scatter diagram is created for the past routes and the fatigue damage ratios are calculated for the tanker phase. The results of the fatigue analysis are correlated with the tanker class survey damage report as produced in graphical format. Correlations are made to ensure that the damage predicted matches the damage recorded.

The on and offloading of the crude is accounted for by using the FPSO strength cases. SAGA is used to determine the maximum principal stress range by subtracting each of the still water cases from one another to obtain the maximum stress range obtained during one on and offloading cycle. We have found low cycle, high stress on and offloading to affect mainly the transverse structure such as cutouts in transverse bulkhead horizontal girder web to allow for vertical bulkhead stiffeners.

The FEA direct analysis assessment method requires a four to six months effort, including iterations to develop practical solutions to problems identified.

Analysis Results

The two ships are built based on very different design methods in place at the time of construction. The results of the initial analysis indicated early that the two vessels have very different structural response against the current ABS class rules in effect in 2005. As such, the two vessels required very different structural modifications for FSO and FPSO service

Tables 4~5 show the modifications implemented during the conversion phase of the FSO and the FPSO, using ABS Rules for screening, FEA to assess response due to site-specific environment loading on operational loading cases, and detailed fine-mesh FEA to site-specific loads and on and offloading to determine requirements for reinforcement in way of structural details.

FPSO Results

The initial screening analysis showed that the wing tank deck transverses required reinforcement for FPSO service. The reinforcement was accomplished by installing on-deck transverse deck beams incorporating the topside stool design. In addition, transverse bulkhead horizontal girder flanges were replaced with stronger members to be acceptable for class.

For the FEA phase six FPSO loading cases were used to ensure that all structure types are loaded to their maximum values considering both static and dynamic loads.

Fig. 5 shows an example of the maximum sagging load case with a maximum wave-induced sagging moment.

Table 4. FPSO Design Modifications

Method	Class Rules	FEA Strength	FEA Fatigue
Deck Transverse Frames	57 t (in way of module supports)	-	-
Deck Longitudinal Reinforcement	-	10 t / 27 locations	-
Transverse Frames	-	35 t / 232 locations	23 t / 1132 locations
Transverse Bulkhead Horizontal Girders	9.8 t	20 t	5 t / 510 locations
Web Frame Cutouts	-	-	7 t / 220 locations
Longitudinal Bulkhead / Side Shell Longitudinal Stiffeners	Reduced corrosion margins	8 t / 4 locations	-
Panel Breakers, Brackets	22 t	45 t 7 t / 54 locations	-
Total	89 t	125 t / 317 loc.	35 t / 1862 locations

Each structure in the cargo block was analyzed for conformance with the ABS Part 5 Rules. For the FPSO, 24 design load cases are processed for conformance to the ABS Rules

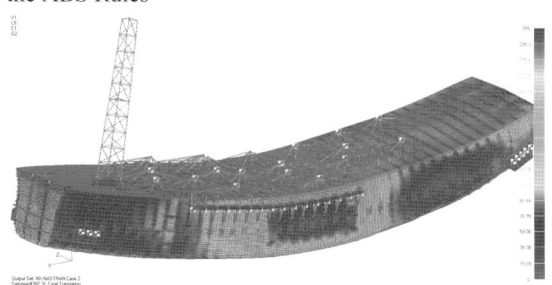

Fig 5: Global Ship Response due to Maximum Sagging

Fig. 6 shows a view of the internal tank structures with empty wing tanks and full center tank during a maximum heave acceleration load.

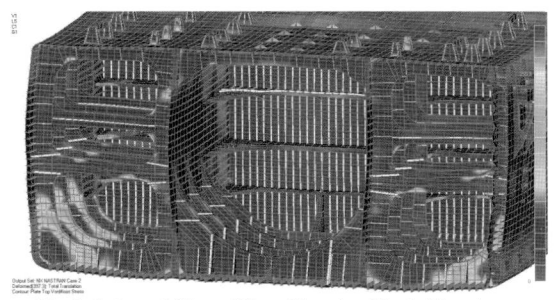

Fig 6: Internal Stress View Showing Tank Structures

As an example, Fig. 7 shows the buckling results obtained for a transverse web frame expressed as a buckling ratio, defined such that a value of 1.0 or less indicates an acceptable structure, and a value greater than 1.0 indicates a structure requiring reinforcement. Several panel breakers were installed as a result of the buckling calculations.

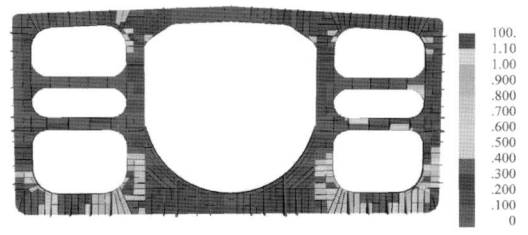

Fig 7: Transverse Frame Buckling Assessment

The FEA strength assessment showed the need for under deck reinforcement in way of a transverse bulkhead that was installed in the center tank only for the tanker.

In addition, a total of 35t of steel at 1862 locations was installed as collar plate modifications to prevent fatigue cracking in way of web frame cutouts for longitudinal stiffeners and at horizontal girder cutouts for vertical bulkhead stiffeners.

The original tanker had experienced cracking in the cutouts for the longitudinal structure as documented by the NKK survey reports. The reason for the cracking is attributed to the extensive use of high tensile steel and the large frame spacing, introducing increased deflection of the web frames in relation to their surrounding bulkheads. The NKK survey reports were very detailed and proved valuable in the correlation of fatigue calculations for the tanker. A lug plate repair as shown in Fig. 8 had been installed during tanker service to prevent further cracking. This repair was shown to be insufficient for FPSO service required and a full collar plate was installed as shown in Fig. 9.

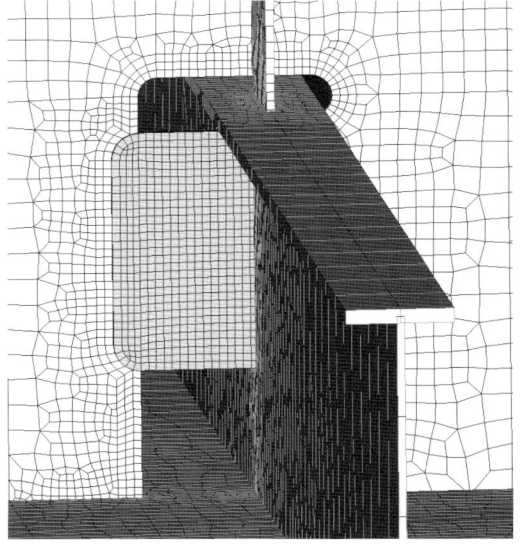

Fig 8: Lug Plate Reinforcement

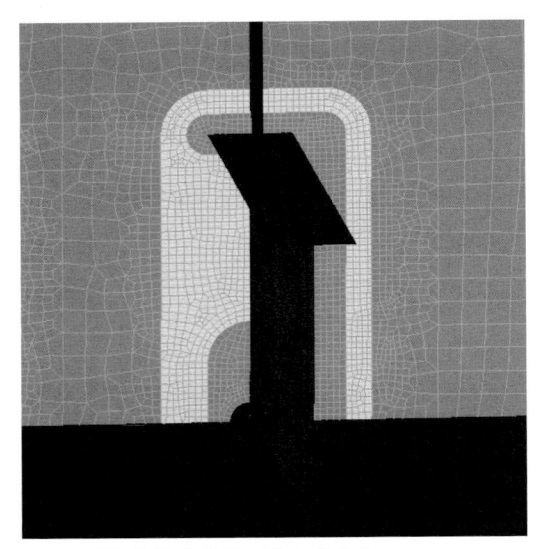

Fig 9: Full Collar Plate Reinforcement

FSO Results

As seen in Table 4, the FSO required significant steel modifications due to strength-related issues, and nearly no modifications due to fatigue strength.

Steel modifications were made to the longitudinal bulkhead, swash bulkhead reinforcements and centerline brackets, in order to provide sufficient strength for the FPSO operation, as required by the 2005 ABS Rules. Two strakes were replaced with HTS steel. The swash bulkheads were converted to oil-tight bulkheads.

Table 5: FSO Design Modifications

Method	Class Rules	FEA Strength	FEA Fatigue
Transverse Frames Reinforcement	-	27 t / 24 locations	11 t / 40 locations
Transverse Bulkhead Horizontal Girders	-	19 t / 16 locations	-
Longitudinal Bulkhead Plating	240 t / 2 strakes	-	-
Panel Breakers, Brackets	100 t / 60 locations	24 t / 68 locations	-
Swash Bulkhead Reinforcement	98 t	-	-
Side and Center Bottom Girder Reinforcement	-	67 t / 20 locations	-
Total	438 t	137 t / 128 locations	11 t / 40 locations

The FEA strength analysis (Fig. 10) showed the need for additional stiffeners to be installed on the longitudinal bulkhead to increase the buckling strength.

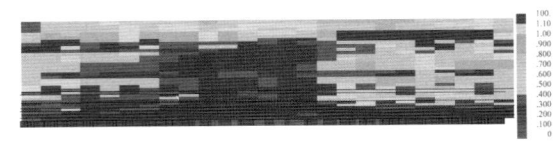

Fig 10: Longitudinal Bulkhead Before Adding Stiffeners

In addition, the FEA strength analysis showed the need for reinforcement on the transverse frames in ballast tanks.

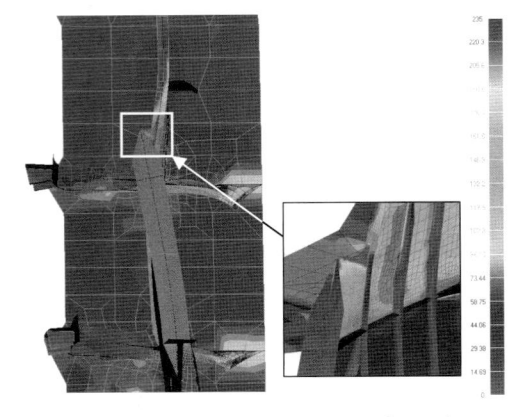

Fig 11: Transverse Frame Bracket Deformation

The original structure was designed with a soft toe and a sniped flange, introducing a highly stressed toe connection. Fig. 11 shows the out-of-plane deformation of the transverse frame bracket and the resulting high stress in the toe of the web. Fig 12 shows the reinforcement installed to prevent overstressing in way of the side shell transverse bracket connection.

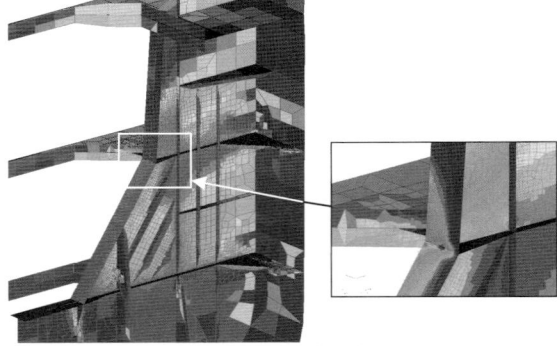

Fig 12: Reinforcement Solution for FSO BT Web Frames

In addition, the transverse bulkhead horizontal girders and the side and center bottom girder structures required reinforcement to reduce stresses below allowable stress levels.

The FEA fatigue analysis showed the need for a smaller reinforcement in the same area show in Fig 12, in way of the cargo tanks.

Stress and Deflection Screening

The authors have been using a longitudinal stiffener end connection fatigue screening method developed by LR

(Reference 1) as a method to predict fatigue cracking of longitudinal stiffener end connections before detailed FEA, and as a method to determine the extent of required repair to longitudinal stiffener brackets. This is established by correlating the deflection screening results and the results of a detailed finite element analysis using spectral fatigue methods.

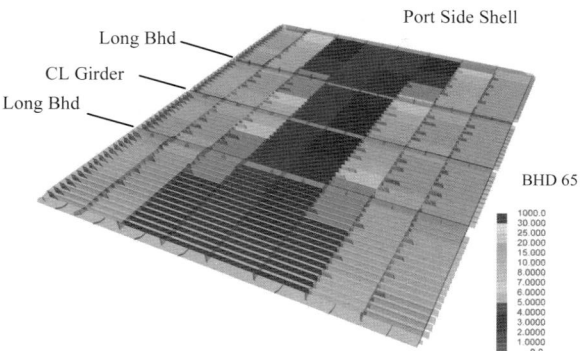

Fig 13: Relative Deflection Plot for Bottom Stiffeners for Predicting Bracket Cracking (mm)

The LR method uses a relative deflection method where the relative deflection of any two neighboring web frames is used to determine whether the end connections of a longitudinal stiffener require special attention during the detailed finite element based spectral fatigue method. The results of this method are shown in pictorial form in Fig 13. As seen in the figure the longitudinals near the transverse bulkheads experience the largest relative deflection matching what is typically experienced in service.

In addition, a web frame cutout cracking prediction procedure has been used similar to the approach used by Mr. D. D. Lee of HHI. This method is used as a tool to determine the required extent of repair by correlating the deflection screening results and the results of a detailed finite element analysis using spectral fatigue methods. The web cracking prediction method is used by determining the actual (as opposed to relative) deflection of web frames as projected to a straight line between the deflected locations of the two neighboring transverse bulkheads.

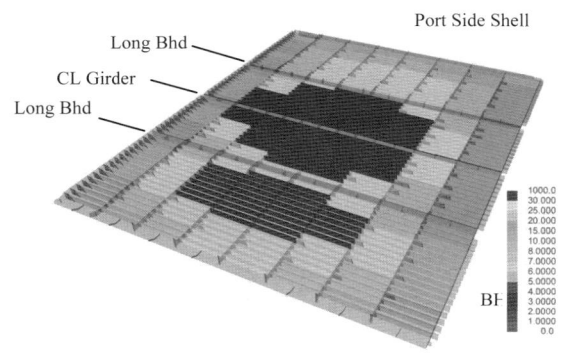

Fig 14: Deflection between Bulkheads for Bottom Stiffeners for prediction of Web Frame cracking (mm)

The outcome is a graphical plot of each stiffener segment (Figs. 13 and 14) as well as a table of deflection values for the relative and actual deflections, which are used in subsequent engineering calculations to determine the extent of repair or reinforcement required to longitudinal brackets and web cutouts, respectively.

As seen in Figure 13 there is strong correlation between the actual cracking seen in the bottom cutouts and the prediction made by the screening procedure (Fig 14).

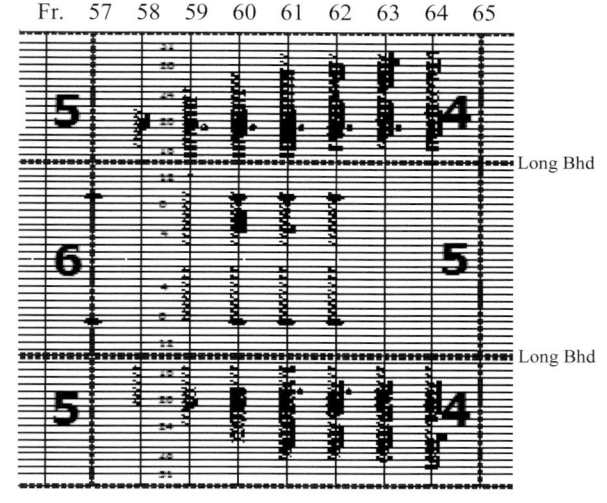

Fig. 15: NKK Survey Data Plotted (Typical)

In addition to deflection based fatigue screening, a stress based fatigue screening is also used to correlate the results of the detailed FEA based spectral fatigue analysis to determine the extent of repair required.

Conclusions

Reliable Initial Scantling Assessment Method

It was found that the Phase A program accurately identified areas requiring FPSO modifications due to strength deficiencies in the original tanker structure, allowing for accurate budget estimation for major steel early in the project. It is especially required that the Phase A program be used with great care to ensure that stiffener end connections and effective length calculations for transverse main supporting members are accurately defined. It was also found that the Phase A program (this is also true for most other class screening programs) was not able to identify cracking in web frame cutouts. It is therefore recommended that alternative methods are employed early in any project to facilitate awareness to problems related to fatigue damage, see next sections. Methods include deflection screening (LR, Ref. 1 and bulkhead-to-bulkhead deflection) and survey data collection.

Survey Report Data Collection

Typically there are accurate class survey damage reports available for the tanker to be converted. It is imperative, but often overlooked, that this data be processed properly to allow the entire conversion team to learn from the past use of the tanker as the FPSO loading will stress the steel in similar ways. The development of a procedure to plot the damage data graphically as early as possible in the project, gave the conversion team the ability to address the structural solutions at all levels of budgeting, shipyard scheduling, and development of adequate conversion engineering solutions.

Strong Value of Direct Strength and Fatigue Analysis

The authors consider the use of an advanced analysis tool set mandatory for FPSO conversion to be able to find adequate solutions to structural deficiencies. This is simply due to the level of detail required to find adequate solutions to problems identified in the early stages by Phase A or by damage reports and inspections. This will become even truer as the trend continues of increasing FPSO design life requirements, and the use of design safety factors. There are no substitutes for the solutions provided by an advanced, accurate, direct analysis of fatigue damage.

Tanker Pool for Future FPSO and FSO Candidates

The pool of candidate tanker have changed away from strong robust mild steel tankers of the early 1970's to 1980's highly optimized tankers using extensive amounts of HT steel, up to 70 to 80% of the steel weight. Compared to the cost of a double hull candidate the 1980's single skin candidates offer a significant savings in cost, and will likely remain an attractive alternative to conversion of double hull tankers and new-built hulls. The conversion of the 1980's tankers will continue to require extensive modifications to structural connections, and it is considered extremely important that powerful tools such as the ones described in this paper be used as early as possible in the project.

Acknowledgement

The authors wish to thank Mr. Boyden Williams, Viking Systems, Inc, for his analysis work during project execution on the two vessels described, and for his input to the paper. Our thanks also to Mr. Clive Badger, LR for explaining the LR deflection method, and to Messrs. Shashank Karve and Tom Koster, Modec, for the encouragement to write this paper.

References

1. Lloyds Register, SDA, Primary Structure of Tankers, May 2004, "Section 7: Deflection of primary members", Chapter 2, Section 7.

Damping and Stiffness from the Taut-Leg Mooring Lines in FPSOs Model Testing

Antonio C. Fernandes[1], Fabio P. S. Mineiro[2], André L. Rosa[1], Joel S. Sales[1], André Ramiro[1],

[1] LabOceano, COPPE/UFRJ
[2] Petrobras
Rio de Janeiro, RJ, Brazil

Abstract

This work describes a methodology to design mooring taut-leg lines for model testing of a FPSO. It describes how to use a nonlinear time domain program for that matter. Model testing validates the method.

Keywords

Mooring line; Damping; Stiffness; Model testing; FPSO.

Introduction

The design of mooring lines for model testing is a difficult problem probably because it is ill posed. A difficulty is that the main dimensions of the lines used to hold a FPSO vessel are very different from the vessel dimensions themselves.

Before the testing, it is necessary to define whether or not the MLD (Mooring Line Damping) is significant for both the longitudinal and the transversal direction. The correct representation of the damping is essential not only due to the resonant slow drift behavior second order effect in the horizontal plane, but also for the behavior in the vertical plane for the roll mode.

This one may also have a second effect with responses away from the usual wave frequencies. On the other hand, the restoring force representation is also essential due to the frequency response. Moreover due to the usual necessary truncation, extra care should be taken. These considerations were made in the design of the FPSO model testing in waves. This task was done with the help of a time domain nonlinear computer program.

A preliminary numerical assessment was then performed before the model testing to get an idea about the MLD. A comparison with the HDD (Hull Drift Damping) was made. Subsequently, decaying tests were performed allowing a frame work for discussion of the MLD (and HDD) relative importance also in full-scale. It became clear that the mild truncation can be performed without compromising the testing.

Preliminary numerical stiffness and damping

The work used in all of the numerical analyses the nonlinear time domain is the commercial code ORCAFLEX (Orcina 2006). The reference case is the design of the model testing of an FPSO taut-leg moored with 20 lines in full-scale. This case is shown in Fig. 1. The FPSO and mooring lines characteristics are described in Tables 1 to 3.

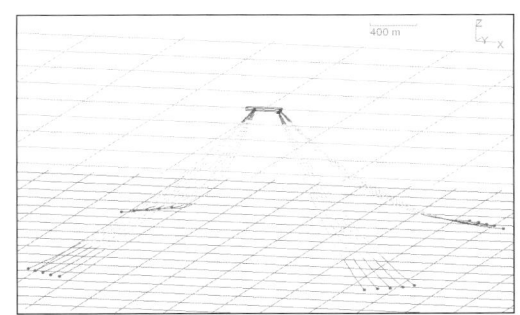

Fig. 1: Taut-leg moored FPSO with 20 lines

Table 1: FPSO main characteristics

Length - L(m)	322,38
Beam - B(m)	54,52
Depth – D(m)	33,45
Draft – T(m)	23,78
Displacement (ton)	371243,3
LCG (m)	5,01
TCG (m)	0,00
VCG (m)	18,41
Rxx (m)	20,03
Ryy (m)	77,95
Rzz (m)	78,12
Ixx (ton.m2)	148900127
Iyy (ton.m2)	2255983470
Izz (ton.m2)	22655820058

Table 2: Mooring lines characteristics

Segment (m)	Ønom (mm)	Material	Weight in water (kN/m)
1	114	R4chain	2,218
2	225	Polyester	0,086
3	114	R4chain	2,218
4	225	Polyester	0,086
5	114	R4chain	2,218
6	225	Polyester	0,086
7	120	R4chain	2,458

Segment (m)	EA (kN)	Length (m)	MBL (kN)
1	919077	550	12420
2	206010	600	13734
3	919077	10	12420
4	206010	600	13734
5	919077	10	12420
6	206010	600	13734
7	982080	150	13573

Table 3: Fairlead coordinates e Azimuth angle.

Line n°	X (m)	Y (m)	Z (m)	Angle (dg)
1	133,85	-28,39	6,80	316
2	131,30	-28,39	6,80	313
3	128,48	-28,39	6,80	310
4	126,20	-28,39	6,80	307
5	123,65	-28,39	6,80	304
6	-88,83	-28,39	6,80	236
7	-91,38	-28,39	6,80	233
8	-93,93	-28,39	6,80	230
9	-96,48	-28,39	6,80	227
10	-99,03	28,39	6,80	224
11	-99,03	28,39	6,80	136
12	-96,48	28,39	6,80	133
13	-93,93	28,39	6,80	130
14	-91,38	28,39	6,80	127
15	-88,83	28,39	6,80	124
16	123,65	28,39	6,80	56
17	126,20	28,39	6,80	53
18	128,75	28,39	6,80	50
19	131,30	28,39	6,80	47
20	133,85	28,39	6,80	43

The water depth in the site is 1246 m. The fairlead coordinates for each line are in Table 3.

For the configuration in Fig.1, the restoring force was obtained for several horizontal displacements for both X (corresponding to surge) and Y (corresponding to sway) direction. The results are in Table 4 and Figs. 2 and 3.

Table 4: Mooring line Stiffness assessment

Fx (KN)	X (m)	Fy (KN)	Y (m)
21145,70	-96,95	31375,70	-95,36
18215,20	-87,31	26999,40	-86,38
15537,30	-78,27	22962,20	-77,94
13111,50	-69,89	19295,30	-70,17
10919,50	-62,10	15993,90	-63,06
8929,11	-54,82	13018,30	-46,57
7087,16	-42,90	10305,80	-40,45
5307,24	-31,06	7707,78	-34,30
3536,58	-24,00	5116,16	-27,77
1770,76	-16,34	2527,77	-10,56
8,18	-0,80	-59,05	5,15
-1753,00	19,61	-2646,09	18,35
-3514,28	28,40	-5228,00	25,61
-5276,50	35,66	-7795,91	32,25
-7054,00	42,64	-10443,20	48,86
-8907,24	51,49	-13327,40	55,79
-10902,90	61,61	-16525,20	63,24
-13091,80	74,26	-20102,00	71,35
-15503,40	82,49	-24069,80	80,13
-18152,70	91,28	-28396,40	89,51
-21038,90	100,55	-33023,60	99,35

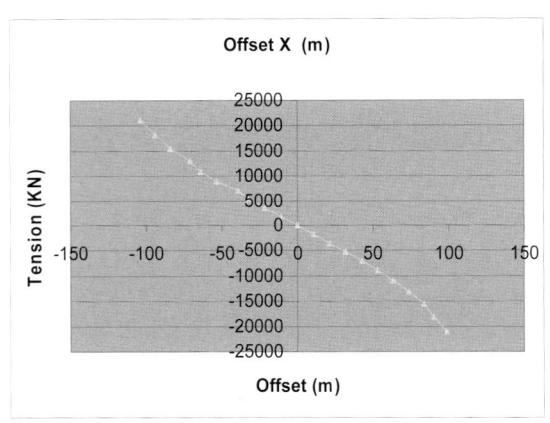

Fig. 2: X direction restoring force.

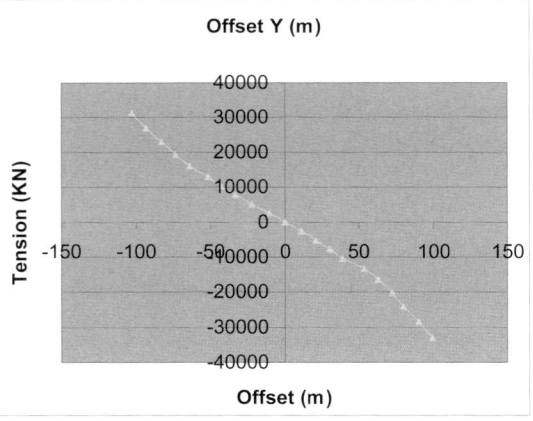

Fig. 3: Y direction restoring force.

Once the static analysis is finished, several dynamic analyses were performed to obtain an estimate of the mooring line damping for X and Y directions. The results are in Figs. 4 and 5, such that Fig. 4 is solely for the FPSO hull and the mooring lines together. Fig. 5 is just for the hull, obtained by setting the lines drag coefficients to zero.

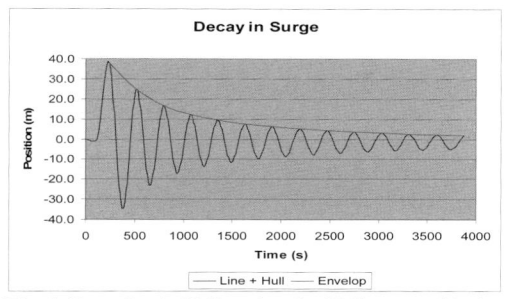

Fig. 4: Decaying in X direction for 20 lines considering both the lines and the FPSO hull.

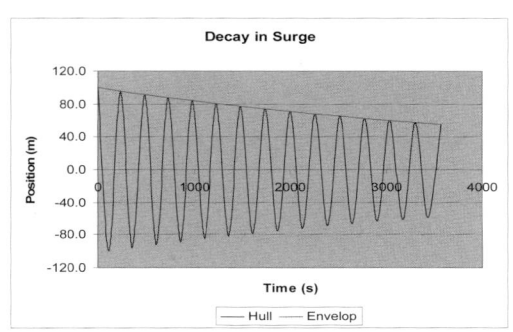

Fig. 5: Decaying in X direction for 20 lines considering only the FPSO hull.

The estimated linear damping coefficient (ς) is obtained by fitting an envelope such that

$$x = x_0 e^{-\varsigma \omega_n t} \quad (1)$$

where ω_n is the natural frequency. For the case with hull and lines the result was $\varsigma_{H+L} = 0.05$ and for the hull only $\varsigma_H = 0.007$. As expected, in the X direction the mooring line damping is much higher. In fact the last one was estimated with the well known ITTC 1957 flat plate line (Lewis, 1988).

For the Y direction an analogous path was followed. The results are in Figs. 6 and 7. The values are now $\varsigma_{H+L} = 0.138$ and $\varsigma_H = 0.092$. Now the hull effect is much lager as expected. For the last one a cross flow principle-type approach was followed.

In the absence of full-scale data, the reduced model test should repeat the same characteristics for both the stiffness and the damping and for both for the hull and the 20 mooring lines.

It is important to say that the drag coefficients used for the lines were 1.0, which is adequate for the estimated Reynolds numbers for the cases here that are between 5×10^2 and 2×10^5.

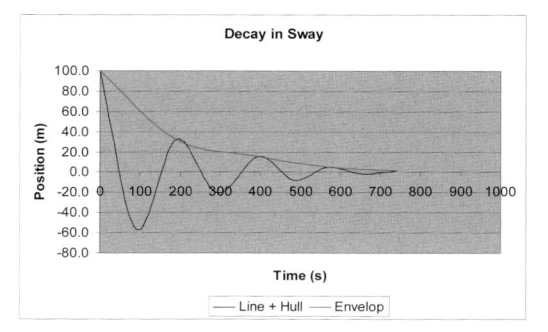

Fig. 6: Decaying in Y direction for 20 lines considering both the lines and the FPSO hull.

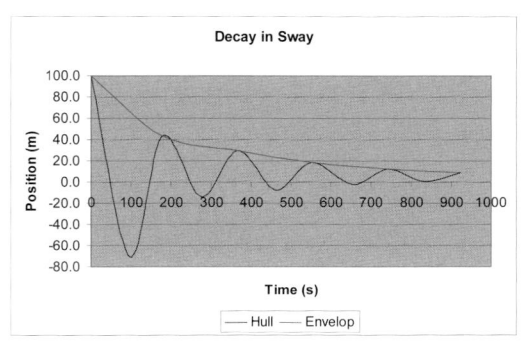

Fig. 7: Decaying in Y direction for 20 lines considering only the FPSO hull.

Model Design

The design of the model does not necessarily have to follow the construction of all 20 lines. This task would prove to be quite cumbersome. Hence, another route was tried by using equivalent lines. The requirement would have to have the same restoring effect and damping.

Even for a wave basin as in the LabOceano from COPPE/UFRJ, it also usually necessary to cut the lines due to either the depth or the vertical wall proximity. Therefore, usually truncation is needed.

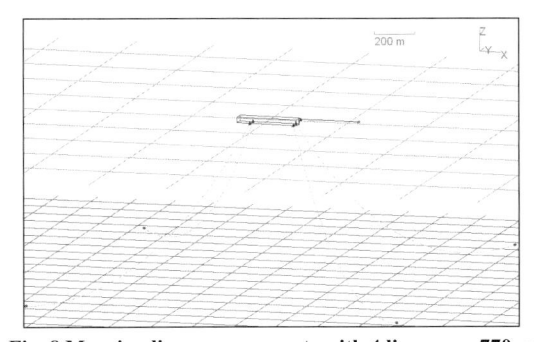

Fig. 8 Mooring line arrangements with 4 lines over 770 m depth.

For the 20 lines cases under study, the number of lines was reduced to 4, and the depth was reduced to 770 m. The last would fit the model with its 4 lines in the LabOceano model basin using a scale of 1:70. The wave basin of the last one is 15 m, but the test was made over 11 m due to the walls. Fig. 8 illustrates the scenario.

For the truncated system of Fig.8 the stiffness was made to match the original one (20 lines over 1246 m).

For the truncated modeling again forces were applied at the vessel's CG on both X and Y directions.

The matchings are shown in Fig. 9 and 10 in X and Y direction respectively.

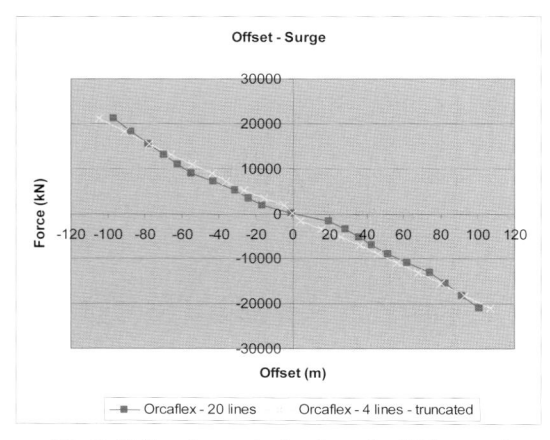

Fig. 9: X direction restoring force for 20 lines and truncated 4 lines over 770 m.

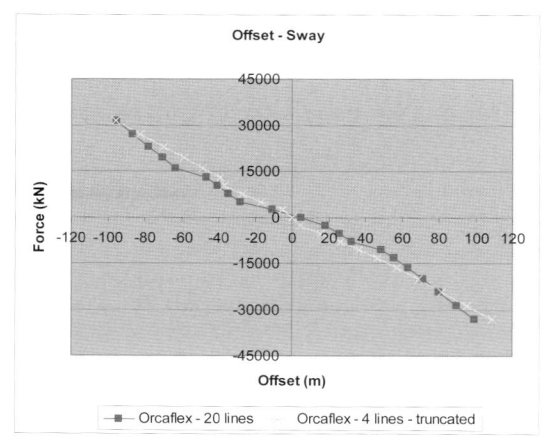

Fig. 10: Y direction restoring force for 20 lines and truncated 4 lines over 770 m.

As an important contribution of the present work in addition to the stiffness, it is also possible to distort the truncated line diameter to get the same damping as predicted by the numerical model. The final diameter after parametric simulations was 1,45 m in full-scale.

Considering both the hull and the lines damping, Fig. 11 shows the numeric decaying in X direction for the cases with truncation. Fig 12 shows only the hull case.

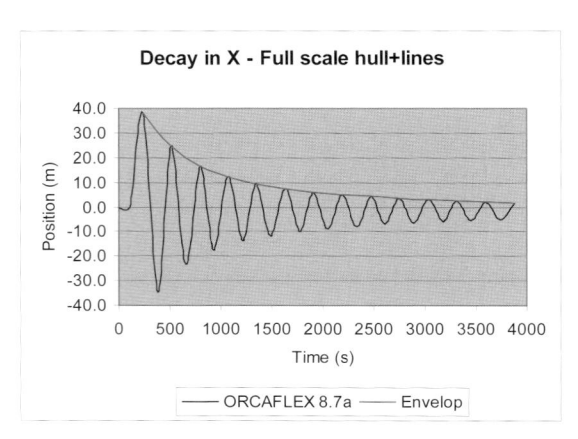

Fig. 11: Decaying in X direction for 4 truncated lines (with 1,45 m diameter) considering both the lines and the FPSO hull.

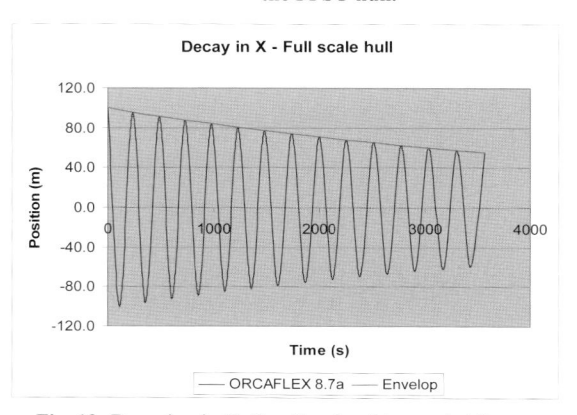

Fig. 12: Decaying in X direction for 4 truncated lines considering only the FPSO hull.

The linear matching in X direction for the envelopes with the truncated 4 lines case leads to $\varsigma_{H+L} = 0.05$ (with the 1.45 m diameter) and for the hull only $\varsigma_H = 0.007$.

Fortunately, the same compatible results arise from the Y direction with the same diameter. (See Figs. 13 and 14).

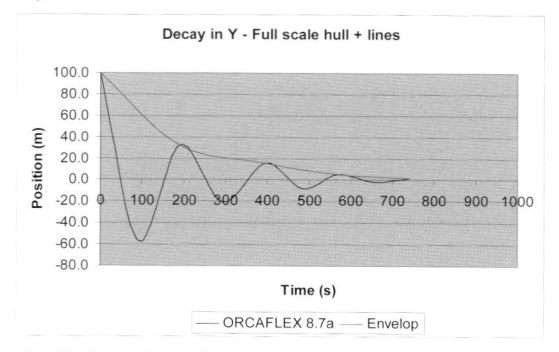

Fig. 13: Decaying in Y direction for 4 truncated lines (with 1,45 m diameter) considering both the lines and the FPSO hull.

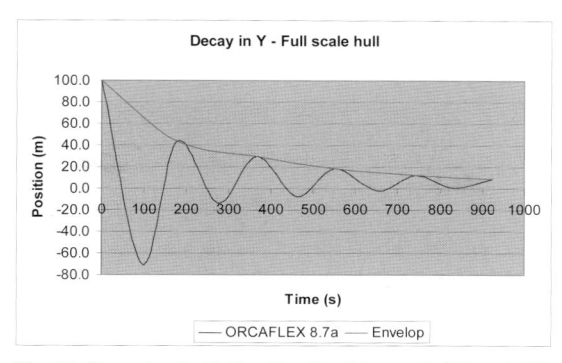

Fig. 14: Decaying in Y direction for 4 truncated lines (with 1,45 m diameter) considering only the FPSO hull.

The linear matching in Y direction for the envelopes with the truncated 4 lines case leads to $\varsigma_{H+L} = 0.138$ (with the 1.45 m diameter) and for the hull only $\varsigma_H = 0.046$.

Table 5: Damping coefficients

Prototype	ζH+L (%)	ζH (%)	ζL (%)
X 20 lines	5,0	0,7	4,3
X 4 (trunc.) lines	5,0	0,7	4,3
Y 20 lines	13,8	4,6	9,2
Y 4 (trunc.) lines	13,8	4,6	9,2

Model Construction

Fig. 14 shows the system at the LabOceano model basin. Table 6 shows the pretensions at each line.

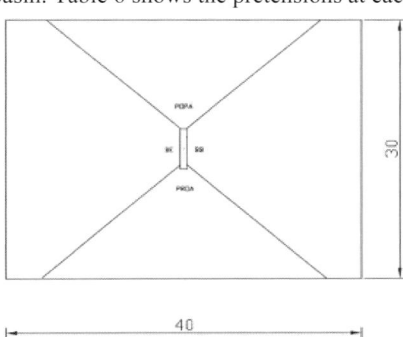

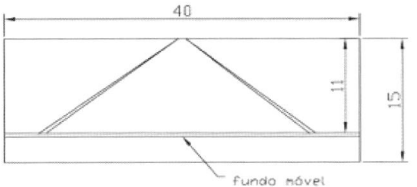

Fig. 15: Truncated lines at the LabOceano model basin (dimension in m).

Table 6: Pre-tension for the truncated and truncated mooring line systems.

Line	Pretension (KN)	Equivalent Line	Equivalent Pretension (KN)	Model Pretension (gf)
1	2106	Line 1	10431	2991.2
2	2110			
3	2112			
4	2116			
5	2120			
6	2198	Line 2	10431	2991.2
7	2196			
8	2194			
9	2191			
10	2188			
11	2031	Line 3	10431	2991.2
12	2027			
13	2021			
14	2017			
15	2014			
16	2015	Line 4	10431	2991.2
17	2016			
18	2017			
19	2018			
20	2018			

For the model diameter this work concluded that there is no need to resort to distortion. Hence, the model diameter was taken as 21 mm, just reducing the 1.45 m to the 1:70 model.

For the line tension elasticity, a spring was designed to represent the full-scale polyester.

Fig. 16 illustrates the main characteristics of the model line parts.

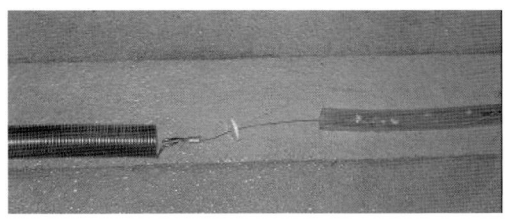

Fig. 16: Equivalent line; picture shows spring, steel cable and hose with 21 mm.

Decaying Model Tests

The decaying model tests in the model scale were then performed. The positive results are shown in comparison with the numerical prediction in Figs. 17 and 18.

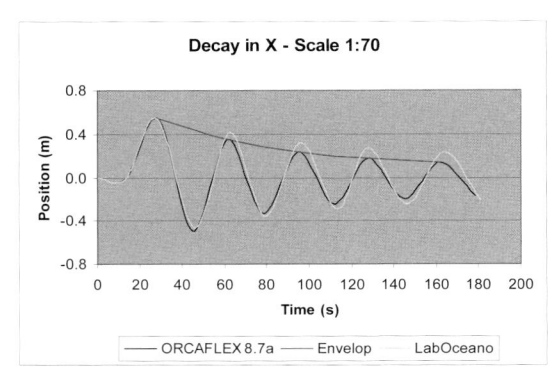

Fig. 17: Decaying test comparison numeric and experimental results, X direction.

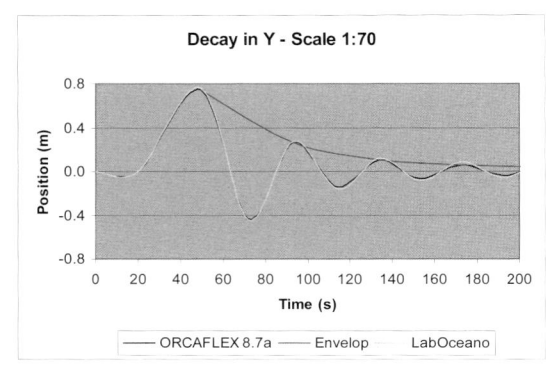

Fig. 18: Decaying test comparison numeric and experimental results, Y direction.

It is clear from Figs. 17 and 18 that the two methods match well. Table 7 summarizes the results.

Table 7: Numerical and experimental damping coefficients

Model – 1:70	ζ H+L (%)
4 Lines – X Numerical	4,7
4 Lines – X Ocean basin	4,0
4 Lines – Y Numerical	13,4
4 Lines – Y Ocean basin	12,7

Conclusions

Following are some of the conclusions of the experience:

- The work shows that it is possible to reproduce the model test result with the numerical code. For that, it was necessary to use adequate coefficients such as the drag for the hull in model scale, the diameter for the mooring lines (no diameter distortion was necessary), etc.
- This is significant since if one could **not** reproduce the model test results one would have a useless numerical code.
- On the other hand, the problem is still open since one needs correct correlation with full scale. For that, there are few results in the literature. But the present work leads to conclusions that with appropriate full-scale coefficients, the use of the numerical code is recommendable.
- Another important aspect of the work is that the mild mooring line truncation may be absorbed with distortion both for the stiffness and damping behavior reproduction in the model scale.
- The same may not be true for a radical truncation say in a case with a 5 m depth. This last figure is an average depth of the ocean basins around the world. However, this is still open since a more broader research would be necessary to reach conclusive results and the applicable limits.
- The combination of the numerical analysis with the experimental analysis yields rewarding results. This method is being called the CONCOMINTAT model testing approach (Fernandes et all, 2007);
- It is wise, when possible, to reduce the number of lines at least when the hull is dominant, typically in first order responses.
- Both the processing time and the experimental work are reduced because of that.
- Future work should address second order phenomena.

Acknowledgement

Positive acknowledgements go to PETROBRAS and ANP for allowing the present studies and scholarship support respectively.

References

Fernandes, A.C. e Sales, J.S., Private communication, 2006.

Fernandes, A. C., Neves, C.R. Sales, J.S, "The Concomitant Model Test Approach for the Development of the Pendulous Installation Method of Heavy Devices", Proceedings OMAE 2007, 26th International Conference on Offshore Mechanics and Arctic Engineering, June 10-15, 2007, San Diego, California USA.

Lewis, E.V., "Principles of Naval Architecture", Second Revision, Vol. II, The Society of Naval Architects and Marine Engineers, NJ, USA, 1988.

MATLAB, "MATLAB Manual Version 6.5", The MathWorks, Inc., 2002.

Orcina, "OrcaFlex Manual Version 8.7a", Orcina Ltd, 2005.

Neves, C.R., Fernandes, A.C. e Sales, J.S., "Análise da Instalação de Manifold Através do Método Pendular Através da Combinação de Testes com Modelos Reduzidos e Ferramentas Numéricas", XXVII CILAMCE - Iberian Latin American Congress on Computational Methods in Engineering; Belém; Brazil, September, 2006.

The Propulsion and Maneuvering Concept of the BCF- Super C- Class Double End Ferries

Stefan Krüger [1], Heike Billerbeck, Tobias Haack [2]

[1] Hamburg University of Technology (TUHH), Institute of Ship Design and Ship Safety
Hamburg, Germany
[2] Flensburger Schiffbau Gesellschaft mbh & Co. KG
Flensburg, Germany

Abstract

One important milestone of British Columbia Ferries (BC Ferries) during their Major Fleet Replacement Program was the development of a new Double Ended Ferry class to replace their existing C-Class vessels. The final design of the ships called the BCF Super Class Ferries, which are actually the world's largest double end ferries, was finally carried out by Flensburger Schiffbau- Gesellschaft (FSG), Germany.

Some of the Design requirements put forward by BCF had been very hard to fulfill in the final concept. Most challenging was the demand for extremely low fuel consumption, low wake wash, and very good steering performance that had to be combined with the requirement for a diesel electric power plant. Furthermore, the operational profile of the vessel required a very short acceleration time of the vessel from zero up to full design speed, which is quite high with 21 knots. These requirements lead to an unconventional propulsion concept with bow and stern CPP- Propellers which are operated in constant rpm mode where the bow propeller feathers with the trailing edge. This propulsion concept is embedded into a completely new hull form that was developed on the basis of numerical flow simulations.

The concept was finally derived from the numerical and experimental evaluation of many alternative concepts.

With respect to the maneuvering demands, most challenging was the fulfillment of the Active Pass Route operation, which was demonstrated by a full mission maneuvering simulation carried out during the initial design phase. The harbor approach procedure requires a mode shift which includes the de-feathering of the bow propeller at full speed and the starting procedure of the bow drive motor into the constant shaft speed mode using a soft starter. To do so, the automation system of the propulsion plant was combined with the maneuvering model that allowed for the determining of all important interactions of the complex systems; thus finally leading to the design of the propulsion control system. The paper shows that the technological challenges of such a complex kind of ship can only be tackled in close cooperation between the owner, the shipyard, the main suppliers, and the research institutions, as many design tasks require scientific simulations on a high level.

Keywords

Double-ended ferry; Super C-Class; Wake wash; Diesel electric propulsion; Active Pass, Product development.

Introduction and Initial Considerations

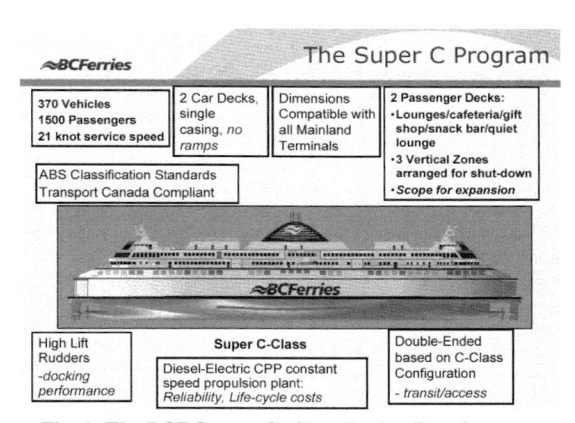

Fig. 1: The BCF Super- C- Class Design Requirements

When BC- Ferries quoted for the new design of the so called SUPER- C- Class Ferries, the following main design requirements were demanded by BCF with respect to the existing C- Class vessels which are to be replaced by the new designs:

- 370 vehicles, 1500 day passengers on 2 car decks
- Dimensions and deck strake compatible with all mainland terminals
- 21 knot service speed, 20 knots w/o one prime mover, 18 knots w/o two prime movers

- Double-ended configuration based on C- class experience
- Diesel electric propulsion
- High lift rudders for optimum docking performance
- Fast acceleration to service speed
- Significant turning rate > 90 Deg/min

Based on the initial requirements, the following propulsion variants should be considered:

- Podded propulsion with either for or two prime movers
- Conventional propulsion with bow/stern propeller and power sharing
- CPP bow/stern propulsion with either trailing or leading edge feathering

BC-Ferries itself initiated a detailed model test program at the OCEANIC model basin to get a clearer picture of the most efficient propulsion configuration, where a model of the existing C- class vessels was used. To most efficiently exploit the results of these tests for our concept development, detailed numerical investigations of some double-ender hulls (see e.g. Fig. 3) were carried out prior to the experiments in order to figure out the most important design drivers of a double-ended ferry. This concern was also considered of major importance to validate our numerical codes with respect to the specific problems related to double-ended ferries and to get an initial impression of numerical problems which might become relevant later during the hot product development phase.

When the hull form of the C- class vessels was developed in 1973, it was pointed out by the model basin that the displacement should be shifted from the ends to the main frame to allow for lower entrance angles of the waterlines at the end(s). The other lesson to be learned from these experiments was that the design of the propeller for a double-ended ferry has much greater impact on the total power requirement as for single-enders due to the fact that the forward propeller may generate excessive resistance if not properly designed. To cope with this design task, basic computations were carried out to roughly estimate the effect of parasitic resistance of the bow propulsion unit and its effect on the propulsion. The calculations have shown that large excessive power demands can be generated if the whole system was not optimized in total for the following reasons:

Even for a fully optimized hull with minimum resistance, the thrust loading of the stern propeller is still quite high resulting in reduced propulsion efficiency and demanding a large propeller diameter which the hull must be capable of accommodating.

The large propeller (if acting as the forward propeller) might generate excessive additional parasitic resistance if not properly designed which generates additional thrust loading on the aft propeller, reducing its efficiency further. This coupling makes the design as well as the speed- power prognosis quite complex. In this respect, a fundamental principle was found that is generally valid for all types of double-ender propulsions:

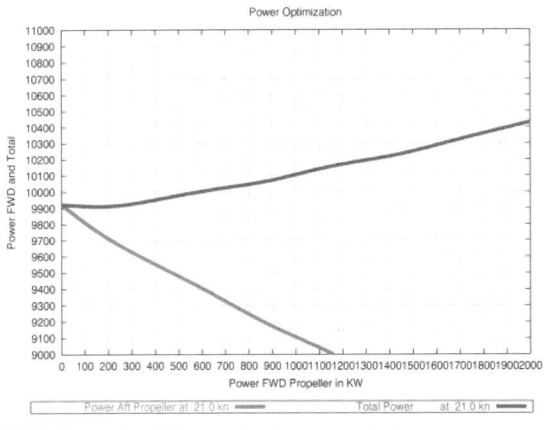

Fig2: Example of Power sharing computations

If the thrust loading of the stern propeller exceeds a certain limit, then power sharing might be an option (see Fig. 2). This condition is due to the fact that the power absorbed by the forward propeller even at a low efficiency unloads the stern propeller in such a way that the efficiency of the stern propeller increases significantly due to the reduced loading. This circumstance would then demand podded propulsion, as the efficiency of the forward unit is then larger as compared to a conventional propeller in reversed operation. It was further found that four podded units were not a competitive option, as the parasitic increase in thrust deduction for the forward unit was too high, even if optimum power sharing was considered.

On the other hand, if the thrust loading can be kept low enough, power sharing has an adverse effect on the propulsion efficiency as it most usefully spent to work on the stern propeller. Low thrust loadings can be achieved by minimum hull form resistance and a large propeller diameter. But if the propeller is not designed for minimum resistance as bow unit as well, the parasitic resistance of this large bow propeller then leads again to a high stern thrust loading with then reduced propulsion efficiency. These basic considerations have to be taken into account when formulating the governing requirements of the hull form development.

Basic Hull Form Requirements

The sections of the fore- and aft body have to combine both minimum resistance and maximum propulsion efficiency. As the propulsion concept converged to either bow- and stern propeller or bow-and stern pod, the hull form must allow for the installation of a large propeller diameter to keep the thrust loading at an absolute minimum. In order to avoid large amplitudes of propeller induced fluctuations, it is also important to have sufficient clearance to the hull. Thus, the profile was clearly determined by the propulsion requirements. As the thrust loading is quite high due to the double-end ferry concept, the pressure pulses can hardly be reduced to extremely low levels. This concern was a further problem as BCF insisted on having ice strengthening for the propeller design to cope with objects floating in the water. Therefore, the area exposed to the pressure fluctuations must be kept at a minimum in order to keep the exciting forces low. In this case, some fluctuations bearing higher pressure measurements can be accepted.

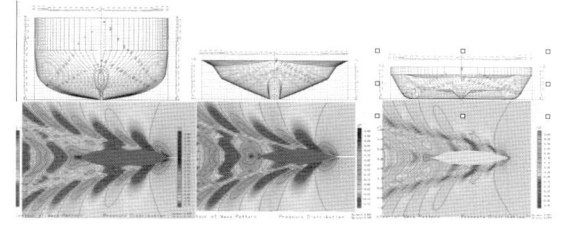

Fig. 3: Some Double-Ender Concepts and their wave patterns

As the resistance (mainly wave making) is influenced by the waterline shape of the end(s), slim waterlines have to be designed into the profile determined by the propulsion requirements. This feature includes dynamic effects such as trim and bow wave generation, so also the hull above the DWL also had to be designed for minimum wave making. The analysis of several hull form alternatives generated during the design process clearly indicated that MARIN's proposal in 1973 to shift buoyancy from the ends towards the main frame during the evaluation of the C-Class is clearly beneficial for the wave making resistance.

The hull form must further generate a propeller inflow as uniform as possible to increase the propulsion efficiency and to reduce propeller fluctuations.

As the propulsion concept resulted in propellers installed at the centerline of the ship it was absolutely crucial not to have a center skeg. Because such a sharp center skeg would result in a local wake peak at the 6 o'clock position (keel) which results in very low propulsion efficiency, as the relative rotation efficiency drops. Then, care must be taken that the hull is able to generate sufficient cross- force for good course stability. For this reason it was decided to replace the center skeg by a hydro- dynamically efficient gondola. This concept can in principle be used for both conventional and podded propulsion if designed properly.

The hull form must further have a minimum thrust deduction fraction. This action is important for the following reasons:

If podded propulsion should be favored, then the forward propeller will generate a large additional resistance if the axial clearance is not large enough. The benefit from having an additional propulsion unit at the bow is compensated to a certain degree by the amount of additional thrust deduction.

If conventional propellers are used, the forward propeller can be operated in two different modes: It can turn freely at some rpm which correspond to zero torque (or close to zero torque) or it can be turned by the engine at some revs which lead to a total propulsion optimum. (Braking the propeller is not an option,

because the resistance is excessive at this point.). Alternatively, the forward propeller could be used as booster if desired. In such cases, the system will benefit from high axial clearance like the podded variant. Low thrust deduction for the stern propeller has the same effect as reducing the resistance and decreases thrust loading.

For low thrust deduction fraction a large axial clearance to the hull and small waterline angles at the gondola were realized. To minimize the wave resistance, the optimum interference between bow and stern waves is important as well as the interference between bow wave and main section (more or less the position of the shoulder). Therefore, the bow wave was shifted to a position where the wetted length leads to an optimal interference of the wave pattern components. With respect to maneuvering, especially keeping course, there is a problem from the main dimensions: a course stable ship can hardly be expected at the relatively high speed. Therefore, it is beneficial to shift as much displacement towards the main section as possible and to reduce the buoyancy at the ends. This action will lead to a longitudinal distribution of section added masses that supports course keeping ability. Besides, care has to be taken that the hull is able to produce sufficient cross force. The rudders had to be integrated into the hull without creating too much additional resistance due to the forward rudder. The head box of the forward rudder is part of the waterline and was carefully integrated into the hull. The rudder type chosen is of FSG- TWIST FLOW high lift type that is beneficial for high steering forces at low resistance. Care was further taken to fully integrate the Costa Bulb into the appendage concept to avoid additional resistance from the propeller hub. Based on these considerations, an initial hull form was designed by intense use of numerical flow computations. The results that are presented in Fig. 4 show the significant decrease of wave resistance of the new design, although the displacement is about 60 % larger than for the existing C- class vessels.

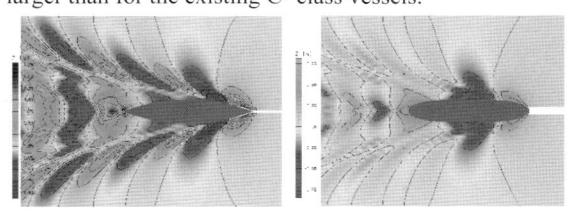

Fig. 4: Wave Pattern of existing C- Class (left) and new initial design at 21 knots.

The Results of the BCF OCEANIC Model Tests

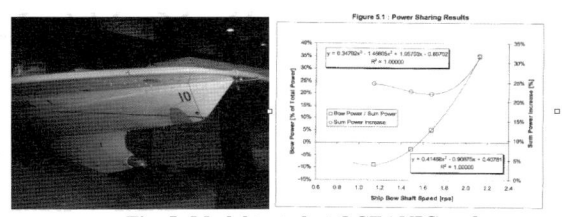

Fig. 5: Model tested at OCEANIC and power sharing results

Based on the model test results performed at the OCEANIC model basin, where the original C-Class-Vessel has been thoroughly tested at a higher draft of 5.90 m, the following conclusions could be drawn for the new building project: The wave pattern (see also Fig. 4, left) is characterized by a significant bow wave which causes a large trough in its wake. Although the dynamic trim was consequently down by stern during all tests, it was found beneficial for the overall resistance if the model was pre- trimmed down by stern, which increases dynamic trim. This behavior is quite unusual, because typically, a pre- trim in the opposite direction is more favorable, because the vessel is dynamically more on even keel. It can clearly be concluded that the vessel suffers from the large bow wave. Therefore, the trim by stern reduces overall resistance due to the fact that the bow wave is decreased, although the dynamic trim is so large that the stern balcony knuckle was fully wetted. These findings are in line with the conclusions that the buoyancy should have been removed from the end part of the hull and shifted into the main section.

The additional resistance of the two rudders was quite large. This resistance is due to the fact that the hollow profile type chosen with an indication of a fish-type trailing edge is not very favorable for the bow rudder in reverse flow. The rudders clearly needed to be optimized for both conditions. The results of the power sharing tests showed that there was a small benefit only when putting additional power into the forward propeller. Also, the additional power requirement of the forward propeller was quite large, although the forward propeller was running at a very favorable pitch ratio. This action was in line with our theoretical considerations: To minimize its additional resistance, the bow propeller must have a large P/D-Ratio. On the other hand, the stern propeller can benefit from a large P/D-ratio only if the thrust loading is so low that the stern propeller still runs at a favorable J-Value. In this respect, a CPP should further be considered as a useful option. In general, all numerical predictions that were performed before the model tests were conducted were validated by the OCEANIC model tests. These tests gave proof that these codes could usefully support the product development. Most important was the finding that the wave pattern could be predicted correctly, as we did not have experience in applying the code to double-ended ferries, and the interaction of the bow wave with our hull form resulted in significant numerical problems. Now we were in a position to finally optimize the hull form and the propulsion concept based fully on numerical predictions.

The advantages of CPP propulsion

The most important finding from the OCEANIC model tests with respect to the final configuration of the propulsion concept was the fact that regardless of the optimum power sharing, roughly 25% of the total propulsive power were required simply to compensate for the existence of the forward propulsor, if this unit is designed as a fixed pitch propeller (see Fig. 5, right).

Therefore, it was a straightforward consequence to go for CPP propulsion and to feather the bow propeller into a position where the additional resistance of the bow propeller was a minimum. From theoretical considerations based on 2 quadrant experimental results of a CPP operating freely without torque, the optimum feathering angle of the propeller was determined to be about 88 Degrees, trailing edge forward. A special hub was considered which allowed for a blade turning range of beyond 115 degrees. It was possible to fully feather the CPP into the desired position and at the same time operate the stern propeller at a reasonable design pitch. At the same time, the CPP also offers a big economical advantage, as the design requirements put forward by BCF clearly demanded a diesel electric configuration. In case a CPP is used, this allows for constant rpm operation and there is no need for any cycle or syncro converters, which significantly reduced the initial building costs. However, this decision makes the final automation concept, especially the starting procedure of the drive motor, a little more complex with respect to the BCF acceleration and stopping requirements. The propulsion plant then consisted mainly of the four MaK 8M32 prime movers, the electric drive motors, gearbox, shaft line and the CPP. From this propulsion train design, the important feedback to the bow propeller is the fact that in case the bow propeller would not be feathered to a zero torque condition, it would have to turn the complete shaft line, gear box and drive motor, which is obviously not a zero torque condition. From initial calculations, it was suspected that the additional resistance of the bow propeller would be significant in case it was not set to a close to zero torque condition. In this respect, large care was taken to perfectly meet this condition. Based on the maximum draft of 5.75m, a propeller diameter as large as reasonably possible was selected, which resulted in a 5.00m propeller diameter. If the stern wave height and the dynamic sinkage at the A.P. were taken into account, the dynamic immersion of the propeller was large enough to fully absorb all required power without any hint on air drawing. Fig. 6 shows the aft body outline and the towing tank model of the final hull form design that was thoroughly tested in the Hamburg Model Basin (HSVA).

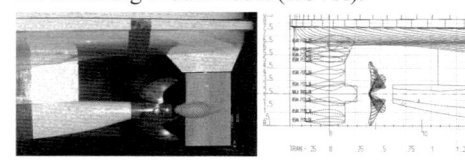

Fig. 6: Propulsion arrangement and feathering concept

The HSVA resistance and propulsion tests

Systematic model tests were carried out at the Hamburg model basin. Both during resistance and propulsion tests, the bow propeller rpm as well as the bow propeller torque and thrust were measured. During the resistance tests, the model was equipped with all appendages including the bow propeller in the pre-calculated feathering position. The stern propeller was replaced with a dummy hub. Together with the measurement of the resistance, the bow propeller thrust measurements gave a clear picture of the effect of the feathered bow propeller on both the resistance and propulsion behavior. The resistance tests confirmed the pre-calculated wave pattern as well as the dynamic sinkage characteristics of the hull, which was always down by stern. The bow wave was smooth, and a little spray could be observed only at the 23 knot testing condition.

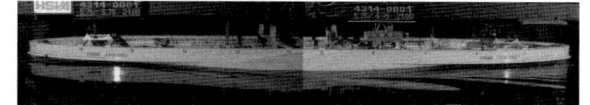

Fig. 7: Model test at design speed of 21 knots at HSVA

During the resistance tests, it was found that the bow propeller was slightly turning at about 0.5 revs/s, an indication for the fact that the optimum feathering condition was not fully met, which could have also been a consequence of the wake of the asymmetrically-shaped rudder. An additional run where the bow propeller was fixed confirmed the fact that the influence of the bow propeller on the performance was significant, as the required effective power increased for about 500 kW (see Fig. 8). The propulsion tests showed an extremely large propulsive efficiency that was determined to be about 0.80. This fact was mainly a result of the high propeller efficiency and the low thrust deduction fraction. In total, the power demand was more or less as expected and took the very low value of about 9200 kW for the full-scale ship. As the tests were governed by the scale effect of the appendages, a form factor evaluation was additionally performed, which resulted in a prognosis of about 500 kW less than the conventional method. Therefore, the design target was fully met, even if the standard evaluation method was used, and it can be expected from the form factor results that the full-scale vessel will perform slightly better. During all tests, there was no indication of air drawing. To check for the influence of air drawing on the station keeping, additional bollard pull tests were performed. These tests showed that without stern wave, some slight air drawing could be noted. Yet the measured power under these conditions was still larger than the maximum output of the drive motor, which resulted in more than sufficient thrust for the station keeping requirements. The wake field measurements have shown smooth gradients in the 12 o'clock position. Although the hull was fully symmetric, the wake field (see Fig. 9) is slightly asymmetric, a result of the bow propeller and the twisted bow rudder.

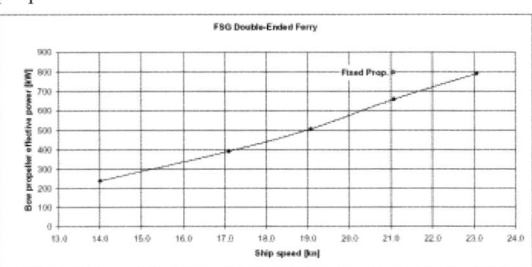

Fig. 8: Effective power and effect of fixed bow propeller

Wake Wash Requirements

As the new SUPER C-class vessels will operate in a protected environment, special requirements put forward by the Canadian Administrations with respect to wake wash had to be fulfilled. Reference is made to the BCFERRIES report "British Columbia Corporation, Fast Ferry Program - Wake and Wash Project - Final Report, August 2000." In this report, wave heights in the near and far field of the existing C- Class which have been measured in full scale are documented, and the wave heights generated by the existing ships have been found to be to be uncritical for the environment. For the wake wash analysis, the computations were also validated against the wave patterns obtained by the model basin OCEANIC, St. John's, where model tests for the existing C- Class ships were carried out. These tests were performed at a larger draft, which was also evaluated by our CFD method, and the agreement between model experiment and calculation was found to be good. Fig. 9 gives an overview about the results, which compares the existing C- Class vessels (left) with the new design (right). The report by British Columbia Ferries states the following permissible wave heights in wave cuts perpendicular to CL of the vessel:

- 0.90 m in the range of 0.00 - 0.10 nm
- 0.72 m in the range of 0.10 - 0.25 nm
- 0.56 m in the range of 0.25 - 0.60 nm
- 0.46 m in the range of 0.50 - 1.00 nm

From the near field calculation, there is good agreement between calculation and measurement: Close to the ship in the stern wave pattern, the maximum wave height was calculated to about 1.00m, (We calculated the intended speed of 21 knots instead of 20 kn, as in the report.), and in a distance of about. 0.05 nm a wave trough of about 0.80 m is found. The far field calculations show wave heights of slightly above 0.40 m. The results are roughly in line with the values stated in the BCF report. The same calculations carried out for the FSG design show that the wave heights generated are significantly lower, especially in the wake, although the local trough at L/2 is somewhat larger. In the near-field, a maximum wave trough of about 0.80 m is generated very close to the hull at L/2. Due to interference effects, at a distance of about 0.05 nm from the CL of the ship, a maximum wave height of about 0.3m can be found. The far field calculations show maximum wave heights of about 0.2- 0.3m. In general, the whole wave pattern is characterized by lower wave heights compared to the existing C- Class ships. Again, this view is valid proof that the chosen concept is competitive, as the wave making is significant although the displacement is far higher.

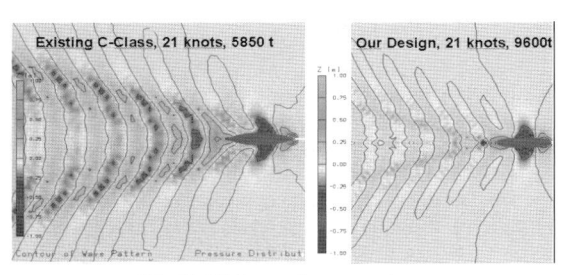

Fig. 9: Wake wash comparison

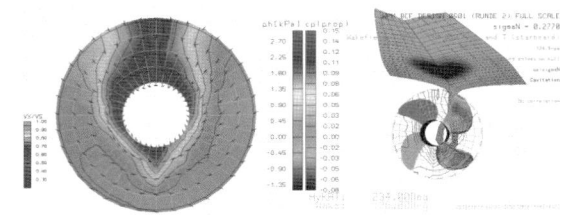

Fig. 10: Wake field and propeller excited fluctuations

Propeller design and pressure fluctuations

Regarding the propeller design, BCF required a very high comfort class, which resulted in low acceptable vibration levels. At the same time, the ice strengthening for the propeller was a main driver for the propeller design, because the ice strengthening resulted in thicker blades, which increases blade rate. Due to demands of the classification society, the ice class requirements restricted the skew that limited the possibilities of the propeller design. Further, the operational profile of BCF required a significant amount of time where both propellers were idling in harbor during loading/unloading, resulting in an off- design condition that had to be regarded for the propeller design with respect to erosive cavitation. This condition was considered a problem as the propellers were always operated in the constant rpm mode.

To check how these demands fitted to the hull form concept as such, fully unsteady VLM-cavitation calculation was performed to judge both upon the cavitation behavior and the propeller excited pressure fluctuations. For the calculations, the wake field measurements that were taken at HSVA were adopted to the full-scale ship applying Yazaki's approach. Also, deformation of the wavy surface and the sinkage at the A.P. were taken into account. Based on these calculations, the propeller-excited pressure fluctuations were calculated for various propeller alternatives as well as for the final propeller design prior to the cavitation tests. The clearance to the propeller is about 30% of the propeller diameter, and the area exposed to the propeller fluctuation was kept to a minimum during the design of the hull. The forced vibration analyses of the steel structure have brought the result that the BCF requirements could be fulfilled if blade rate was below 2 kPa, higher harmonics steadily decreasing. Due to the design restrictions with respect to the limited skew, the first propeller did not meet the requirements, and it was then agreed upon with ABS and the propeller maker that the propeller design should be evaluated according to acceptable blade stresses instead of simply limiting the skew. This decision allowed them to modify the propeller, and the final propeller design met the target of both according to the numerical simulations as well as during the final tests in HSVA's HYKAT. The propeller development clearly showed that without assistance by scientific numerical simulations, competitive design tasks could hardly be performed.

Maneuvering performance

The most important maneuvering criterion to be achieved was a good course keeping ability of the vessel, because sufficient turning is not a problem for this type of ship. It is extremely important for such kinds of vessels to have excellent course keeping ability, because low yaw checking ability will result in permanent rudder action resulting in higher fuel demand and larger wear of the steering components. Course keeping ability is a problem for this type of ship due to the unfavorable main dimensions (with respect to maneuvering) combined with the double-end ferry restrictions. There are only a few ways to influence the hull yawing moment due to the fact that both the fore- and aft body are the same. Furthermore, the bow rudder is problematic because it decreases course stability drastically even if fixed at the neutral rudder angle. Maneuverability was achieved by a highly efficient twist flow rudder of FSG type (see e.g. Fig. 6) that was designed for both the maximum lift and quick rudder actions due to good balancing. The rudder was designed by the application of a nonlinear panel method for rudders in the propeller slipstream. The numerical simulations of the standard IMO maneuvers, such as turning circles or zig/zags, have shown that the related maneuvering data such as turning circles and overshoots is far better than the IMO data. Even the turning rate demanded by BCF for the full rudder turning circle, which was more than 90 degree/min, could be achieved without major problems. Since the numerical prediction of the standard maneuvers by the TUHH/FSG code is sufficiently validated, there seemed to be no critical points in the standard maneuvering behavior. The challenging part of the maneuvering requirements put forward by BCF was the prescribed acceleration time and stopping distance. To obtain information on the acceleration time, a full simulation model of the vessel was required which included the dynamic behavior of the propulsion plant and the system automation. The available propeller torque during a time step of the acceleration maneuver depends on the ability of the diesel engines to increase their dynamic load, which then influences the pitch control of the CPPs. The hydraulic system of the CPPs was designed for blade turning rated of about 1.2 Deg/s, and the automation system had to be designed to cope with this high value. On the other hand, the stopping procedure of the vessel as it approached the berth required a so-called mode shift: The bow propeller needs to be de-feathered, and during this de-feathering phase, a wind-milling control module must control the pitch setting to prevent the propulsion train from over-speed. Due to the trailing edge feathering, the propeller turns in the wrong direction. When the wind-milling limit is passed, the propeller must be set to negative pitch settings to get the rpm down to zero. Then, the drive motor can be started, and the mode shift is completed, as both propulsion trains are now active. Due to the trailing edge feathering, the procedure is of course more complex. It was a clear demand of the BCF that the mode shift procedure should not be limited by the de-feathering process, as longer times required to berth the vessel were not accepted. The simulation model that was set up was tested on other FSG new building during the trial trip. It is here that such kinds of maneuvers were performed to validate the computations. With respect to acceleration, stopping times, and distances, the model was then used to verify that the whole system was able to cope with the BCF demands. The propulsion system, especially the CPP pitch setting command procedure, was then designed and finalized based on the simulation results. Fig. 11, at left, shows the system behavior during the simulated acceleration maneuver, and Fig. 11, at right, the stopping procedure with de feathered bow propeller.

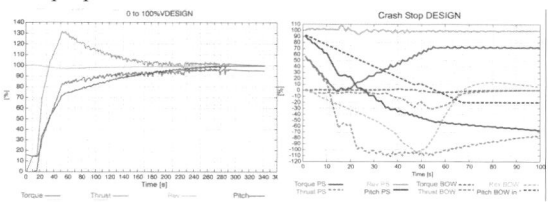

Fig. 11: System behavior during acceleration and stopping

Active Pass requirement

During the development of the new Super- C- Class vessel, an additional requirement that was not initially planned by the BCF was put forward. The BCF also intended to use the vessels on the so-called Active Pass route, characterized by narrow navigation space and significant and dangerous currents (up to 8 knots) due to tide effects (see Fig. 12, left). At this point it was required to demonstrate that the vessel could navigate safely through the Active Pass, which was a TC requirement. Together with the BCF, it was decided that the most efficient way to demonstrate the Active Pass capability of the new SUPER C- Class design was to carry out full mission simulations in a nautical training simulator. As both TUHH and FSG use the SIMFLEX simulator developed by FORCE technology, it was decided to model the Active Pass in the SIMFLEX environment and to transform the mathematical maneuvering model from our design environment into the SIMFLEX. This task was done by FORCE Technology, Copenhagen, and the SIMFLEX model was benchmarked against our existing design maneuvering model. As both models converged in the principle response of the vessel, the BCF was in the position to operate the vessel in the virtual Active Pass. In several training sessions, the virtual SUPER C- class vessels were successfully maneuvered through the virtual Active Pass, and it was found that the vessel was fully able to operate in the Active Pass even under the most critical weather condition. So the numerical simulation was again a useful tool that enabled the BCF to check their requirements long before the actual delivery of the vessel.

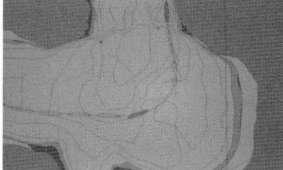

Fig. 12: Active Pass (left) and Transit Simulation (right) in the SIMFLEX environment

Conclusions

A new hull form and propulsion concept for the new BCF SUPER C- Class double-ended ferries was developed totally from scratch. As the design requirements for the new building tackled completely new design aspects such as detailed maneuvering requirements and Active Pass transit, many different design alternatives had to be systematically investigated to find the best solution that could cope with the requirements. It was found that the majority of the design tasks could only be handled with numerical simulations, where the simulation models had to be generated on time during the hot product development phase. As for many design tasks, no reference data was found. Therefore, validation data had to be generated by either model tests or full-scale trials that had to be carefully evaluated. The simulations helped to figure out critical design drivers or design risks that could then be rationally judged. All of these investigations assisted the design process and ended in a competitive product. Finally the BC ferries chose the FSG design for their replacement program of the existing C- Class vessels. This selection process is proof for the fact that competitive solutions must be assisted by state of the art design tools and methods, which consequently have to be applied during the product development phase.

References

Abels, W.: "Reliable Prediction of Propeller Induced Pulses on the Aftbody by Correlation Direct Calculation". Proc. CAV2006, Wageningen, The Netherlands.

Haack, T., Krüger, S.: "A new concept for the simulation of extreme manoeuvres in an early design stage." Proc. MANOEVRERING 2005, Gdansk-Ostroda, 2005

Haack, T., Krüger, S.: "Design of propulsion control systems based on the numerical simulation of nautical manoeuvres." Proc. PRADS 2004, Travemünde, Germany.

Krüger S., Stoye, T.: "First Principle Applications in RoRo- Ship Design." Proc. PRADS 2004, Travemünde. Germany.

Correction of Current Effects from Maneuvering Trials

Young Jae Sung, Kyoung-soo Ahn, Tae-il Lee

Ship Performance Research Department, Hyundai Heavy Industries Co. Ltd.
Ulsan, Korea

Abstract

New method for the correction of current effects not only from the turning circle test but also from the zigzag tests was suggested. Digital smoothing polynomial filter was used to estimate kinematical information from the position measurements. The filtered ground speed and water track speed were used to estimate current speeds. Then multiple regression analysis was applied to estimate the maneuvering coefficients. The estimated coefficients were used to obtain the calm sea maneuvering performances or the corrected trial results. The corrected trajectory and heading angles show reasonable agreement with the calm sea results.

Keywords

Correction; Current; Turning; Zigzag; Polynomial filter; Regression; Maneuvering; Coefficients.

Introduction

Ship maneuverability can be significantly affected by the immediate environments such as wind, wave and current. Hence, the maneuvering trials should be performed in the calmest possible weather conditions. The IMO standards for ship maneuverability (2002) state that maneuvering trials should be conducted in conditions within the following limits:

1. Deep unrestricted water: more than 4 times the mean draught

2. Wind: not to exceed Beaufort 5

3. Waves: not to exceed sea state 4

4. Current: uniform only

In case of HHI, most of the trials are carried out on the east coast of Korean Peninsula. Trial waters are about 30~50 km off the coast and the depth requirement has been well satisfied. But the conditions on wind and wave are not always satisfied. Table 1 summarizes the Beaufort scale and sea state during the maneuvering trials of recently built 138 ships. About 10% of the ships did not satisfy the IMO requirements.

In the case that the minimum weather conditions for the criteria requirement are not applied, the Explanatory note for the IMO standards (2002) states that trial results should be corrected. But how can we correct the effects of environmental loads from maneuvering trials? This is the subject of our research, and we would like to make some discussion on this subject.

Table 1: Beaufort scale and sea state for the recently built ships during maneuvering trials

Beaufort scale	No. of ships (%)	Sea state No.	No. of ships (%)
0	1 (0.7)	0	4 (2.9)
1	3 (2.2)	1	0 (0.0)
2	12 (8.7)	2	12 (8.9)
3	36 (26.1)	3	36 (26.1)
4	46 (33.3)	4	73 (52.9)
5	27 (19.6)	5	10 (7.2)
6	10 (7.2)	6	3 (2.2)
7	3 (2.2)	-	-

Effects of environmental load on maneuvering trials

Before the correction of environmental load effects, we tried to check what effects can happen when the environmental loads exist. Numerical simulations were performed for this purpose.

The maneuvering motions under wind, wave and current have been modeled as follows: (Kobyahsi et.al. 1995)

$$\left. \begin{array}{rcl} m \cdot (\dot{u} - vr) &=& X_H + X_R + X_P + X_W + X_{Wave}, \\ m \cdot (\dot{v} + ur) &=& Y_H + Y_R + Y_W + Y_{Wave}, \\ I_{zz} \cdot \dot{r} &=& N_H + N_R + N_W + N_{Wave} \end{array} \right\} \quad (1)$$

The subscripts H, P, R and W represent hull, propeller, rudder and wind respectively.

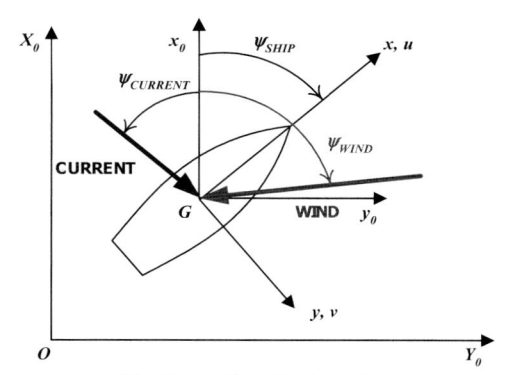

Fig. 1: Coordinate system

Hull, propeller and rudder

$$\left.\begin{aligned} X_H &= -m_x \cdot \dot{u} + (m_y + X_{vr}) \cdot vr + X(u), \\ Y_H &= -m_y \cdot \dot{v} - m_x \cdot ur + Y_{H0}(v, r), \\ N_H &= -J_{zz} \cdot \dot{r} + N_{H0}(v, r) - x_G \cdot Y_{H0}(v, r) \end{aligned}\right\} \quad (2)$$

$$\left.\begin{aligned} Y_{H0} &= Y_v v + Y_r r + Y_{vvv} v^3 + Y_{rrr} r^3 + (Y_{vvr} v + Y_{vrr} r) \cdot vr, \\ N_{H0} &= N_v v + N_r r + N_{vvv} v^3 + N_{rrr} r^3 + (N_{vvr} v + N_{vrr} r) \cdot vr \end{aligned}\right\}$$

$$X_P = (1-t)T = (1-t)\rho n^2 D_P^4 K_T(J_P)$$

$$\left.\begin{aligned} X_R &= -(1-t_R) F_N \sin\delta, \\ Y_R &= -(1+a_H) F_N \cos\delta, \\ N_R &= -(x_R + a_H x_H) F_N \cos\delta \end{aligned}\right\}$$

Wind

$$\left.\begin{aligned} X_W &= C_{X_W}(\theta_W) \cdot \frac{1}{2} \rho_A A_{AT} V_W^2, \\ Y_W &= C_{Y_W}(\theta_W) \cdot \frac{1}{2} \rho_A A_{AL} V_W^2, \\ N_W &= C_{N_W}(\theta_W) \cdot \frac{1}{2} \rho_A A_{AL} L_{OA} V_W^2 \end{aligned}\right\} \quad (3)$$

where

C_{XA}, C_{YA}, C_{NA} : wind load coefficients
ρ_A : density of air
θ_A, V_W : relative wind angle and velocity
A_{AT}, A_{AL} : frontal and lateral projected area above free surface

Wind load coefficients can be obtained from the wind tunnel experiments or the empirical formulae.

Current

Local surface currents in the open sea are generally modest and close to constant in the horizontal plane, hence, the space-time changes of current speed, V_C and direction, ψ_C can be neglected for practical purpose. Effects of constant current are usually treated by using the relative velocity between the ship and the water. If a ship navigates with u, v, r, and ψ (surge, sway, yaw velocities and heading angle respectively), relative speeds and accelerations can be described as follows:

$$\left.\begin{aligned} u_r &= u + V_c \cdot \cos(\psi - \psi_c), \\ v_r &= v - V_c \cdot \sin(\psi - \psi_c), \\ \dot{u}_r &= \dot{u} - V_c \cdot r \cdot \sin(\psi - \psi_c), \\ \dot{v}_r &= \dot{v} - V_c \cdot r \cdot \cos(\psi - \psi_c) \end{aligned}\right\} \quad (4)$$

By substituting these relative components for u, v, $\dot{u}$, $\dot{v}$ in the Eq. 2, current effects can be considered.

Wave

Researches on the wave loads, especially the second order forces, are under steady development since early 1960s. In spite of some encouraging results, the theory of second order forces still requires plenty of model tests for validation, particularly in the whole range of wave incidence angle. Furthermore, the calculated second order sway forces are comparatively less validated than in surge direction. The situation is more and more critical in the case of the second order yaw moment, actually constituting the arm of the sway force and being very sensitive to the hull forms under the free surface. (Jaroslaw Artyszuk, 2003) For design purpose, both the theoretical method as relating to the rather simple shape and the numerical methods which provide a qualitative adequacy may be sufficient. However, for the precise maneuvering analysis and control, more model tests and improvements to the theory are required. Hence, we remain the effects of wave loads for the future study.

Simulation result

Turning and zigzag motions of three ships are simulated. Principal dimensions of the ships are summarized in Table 2. Figs. 2~3 show the sea trial measurements and the simulation results. Sea trials are marked by red delta symbols. Simulations are made for eight environmental conditions: calm sea, trial wind condition, three winds and three currents. Maximum wind speed is 30 knots which corresponds to Beaufort scale 7.

Table 2: Principal dimensions of ships

	COT	Gas	Container
Loading	Full load	Ballast	Ballast
L/B	5.317	5.975	7.300
B/T	2.782	4.944	1.498
C_B	0.816	0.656	0.546
$C_B\,B/L$	0.153	0.110	0.075
A_{AL} [m²]	3401	8417	6538
A_{AT} [m²]	1132	1677	1493

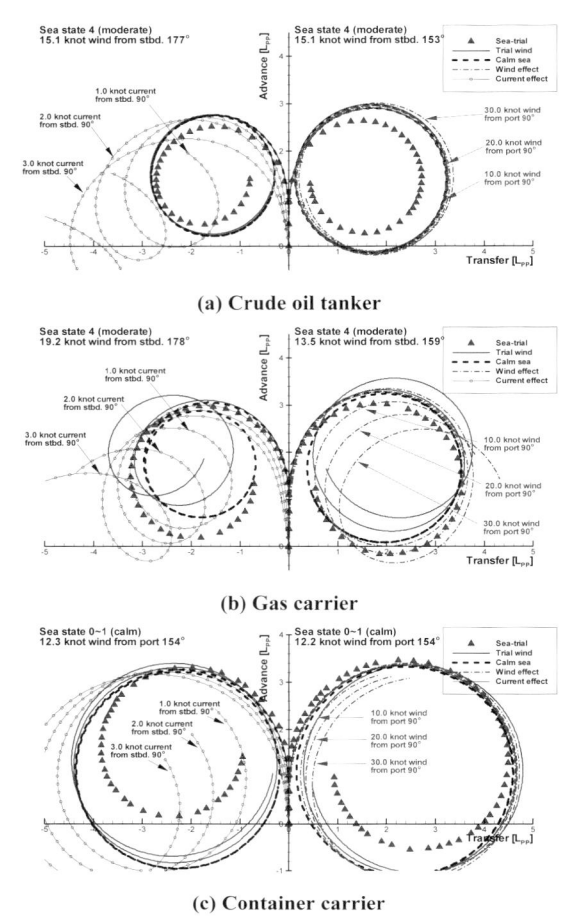

Fig. 2: Sea-trial and simulation results of 35° rudder turning maneuvers

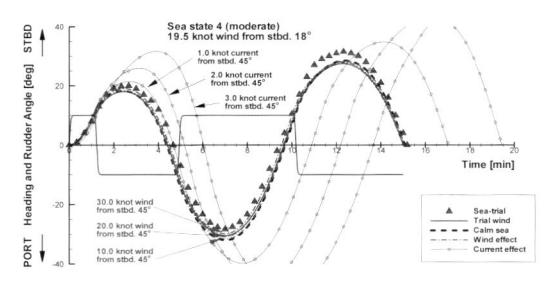

(a) Crude oil tanker
(b) Gas carrier
(c) Container carrier

Fig. 3: Sea-trial and simulation results zigzag maneuvers

(a) 10°/10° zigzag maneuver of crude oil tanker
(b) 10°/10° zigzag maneuver of gas carrier 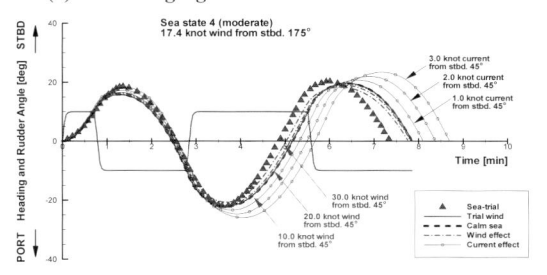
(c) 20°/20° zigzag maneuver of container carrier 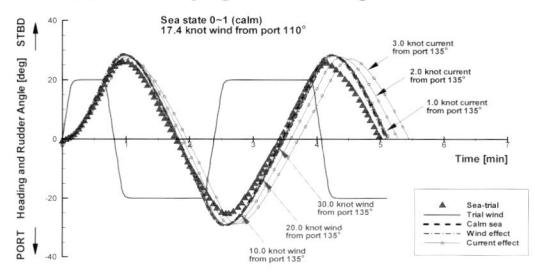

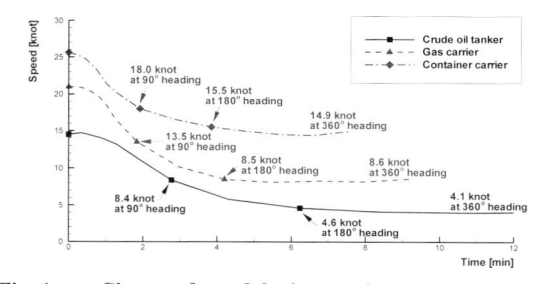

Fig. 4: Change of speed during turning maneuver

Wind load coefficients are calculated by Fujiwara's empirical formulae. (Fujiwara et.al., 1998) Current speed at our trial site varies with the seasons between 0.5 and 2.0 knots. Sea states are noted on the figure, but the wave loads are not considered.

Fig. 2 shows the turning trajectories. In case of crude oil tanker, whose above water projected areas are smaller than others, wind does not make clear differences, but current makes obvious drift on the trajectories. When current comes from starboard direction during port turning maneuver, trajectories are drifted about 30 ~ 40° to the left of current direction. This reduces advances and increases tactical diameter. Similar current effects can be found in gas carrier and container carrier. In case of these ships, wind effects also can be found. For gas carrier, whose above water lateral area is about 2.5 times larger than crude oil tanker, even the 10 knot wind generates obvious drift on the trajectories. But the progress of drift is somewhat different from that by current. Drift by current can be seen from the early stage of turning, but drift by wind doesn't clear until 180° change of heading angle.

This can be explained by the ratio of aerodynamic forces to hydrodynamic forces. IMO standards specify that the approach speed of maneuvering trial is more than 90% of ship's speed corresponding to 85% of the maximum engine output. This corresponds to about 15 knots for oil tanker, 20 knots for gas carrier and 25 knots for container carrier. At these high speeds, hydrodynamic forces dominate the ship motions. However, during the turning maneuver, ship experiences large change of speed as Fig. 4. Until the 180° change of heading angle, ship speed is decreased by 40 ~ 70% of approach condition. Considering that the hydrodynamic forces and the aerodynamic forces are proportional to $[\rho_{water}LTU^2]$ and $[\rho_{air}A_{AL}U_w^2]$ respectively, the relative magnitude of aerodynamic components gradually increases as turning proceeds. Hence wind can make an appreciable effect only on the latter stage of turning.

Similar analysis can be applied to the heading angles of zigzag maneuvers. During the zigzag test, rudder deflection is smaller and shorter than that of turning circle test. Hence, the speed drop during zigzag test is less than 30%, and a ship maintains at least 70% of its approach speed until the end of test. This explains why wind effects can not be obviously found on the heading angles of zigzag maneuvers.

Through simulation analysis, we can see that not only current but also wind can affect the ship maneuverability. But wind effects become appreciable only when the ratio of wind velocity to ship speed is large, hence it is not always necessary to correct wind effects from the maneuvering sea trials.

Correction of current load

IMO MSC/Circ.1053

The only officially ratified correction method for environmental load is correction of constant current effect from turning circle test. The IMO MSC Circular 1053 (2002) suggests that, after performing turning circle test of 720° change of heading, the data obtained after ship's heading change 180° are used to estimated magnitude and direction of the current. Position (x_{1i}, y_{1i}, t_{1i}) and (x_{2i}, y_{2i}, t_{2i}) are the positions at the start of and the completion of a heading rotation of 360°. By definition of local current velocity $\underline{v}_i$ for any two corresponding positions, the estimated current velocity can be obtained from the following equation:

$$\underline{v}_i = (x_{2i} - x_{1i}, y_{2i} - y_{1i})/(t_{2i} - t_{1i}) \quad (4)$$

The averaged current velocity can be obtained from the following equation:

$$\underline{v}_c = \frac{1}{n}\sum_{i=1}^{n}(\underline{v}_i) = \frac{1}{n}\sum_{i=1}^{n}\{(x_{2i} - x_{1i}, y_{2i} - y_{1i})/(t_{2i} - t_{1i})\} \quad (5)$$

The vector $\underline{v}_c$ obtained from a 720° turning test will also include the effect of wind and waves. All the trajectories obtained from the sea trials should be corrected as follows:

$$\underline{x}'(t) = \underline{x}(t) - \underline{v}_c \cdot t \quad (6)$$

Where $\underline{x}(t)$ is the measured position vector and $\underline{x}'(t)$ is the corrected one of the ship and $\underline{x}(0) = \underline{x}'(0)$.

Table 3 is the application results of the IMO method on the cases of Fig. 2. The estimated speed and direction of current are quite different from true values. The disagreement is due to the assumption that the direction of drifted trajectory is the same current direction. If a ship was a point mass system, this assumption might be applicable. But ship has a large underwater volume, and it acts as a lifting body with small aspect ratio during the maneuvering motions. Hence the direction of hydrodynamic forces is not always aligned with flow or current direction. In spite of these errors, IMO method has some advantages; it surely makes the drifted trajectory into a circle, the corrected advance and tactical diameter show reasonable agreement with calm sea values and it is easy for application. These merits make it possible to keep its position as the only one officially ratified correction method for many years.

Table 3: Application of IMO MSC/Circ.1053 correction method on the port turning data of Fig. 2

	COT	Gas	Container
Calm sea	-	-	-
Advance	2.69 L	2.92 L	3.23 L
Tactical dia.	2.74 L	2.86 L	4.34 L
1.0kts s.90°	0.9kts s.71°	0.6kts s.50°	0.9kts s.75°
Advance	2.73 L	2.98 L	3.30 L
Tactical dia.	2.80 L	2.90 L	4.38 L
2.0kts s.90°	1.9kts s.70°	1.4kts s.56°	1.9kts s.75°
Advance	2.80 L	2.98 L	3.29 L
Tactical dia.	2.85 L	2.84 L	4.39 L
3.0kts s.90°	3.2kts s.72°	2.4kts s.61°	2.8kts s.75°
Advance	2.49 L	2.97 L	3.29 L
Tactical dia.	2.66 L	2.75 L	4.44 L

Estimation of current

One of the problems of IMO correction method is the disagreement of estimated current with true one. This is caused by the algorithm which estimates the current from the trajectory alone. Nowadays ships are equipped with various navigation systems and they can measure not only ship's position but also its water track speed (u_r, v_r), gyro heading angle ψ and etc. With position and gyro heading angle, we can filter out the body fixed speeds (u, v). Digital smoothing polynomial filter or Savitzky-Golay smoothing filter can be used for this purpose. (William et.al., 1992) As the dynamics of a ship is slow, second order polynomial approximation with 15 data points is sufficient to estimate the kinematical information. With these filtered information and water track speeds, current speed, V_C and direction φ_C can be easily estimated as follows:

$$\begin{Bmatrix} V_c \cdot \cos\psi_c \\ V_c \cdot \sin\psi_c \end{Bmatrix} = \begin{bmatrix} \cos\psi & -\sin\psi \\ \sin\psi & \cos\psi \end{bmatrix} \cdot \begin{Bmatrix} u_r - u \\ v_r - v \end{Bmatrix} \quad (7)$$

Table 4: Application of Eq. 7 on the estimation of current from the cases of Fig. 2 and Fig. 3

	COT	Gas	Container
Port turning			
1.0kts s.90°	1.0kts s.90°	1.0kts s.90°	1.0kts s.90°
2.0kts s.90°	2.0kts s.91°	2.0kts s.91°	2.0kts s.90°
3.0kts s.90°	3.1kts s.91°	3.0kts s.91°	3.0kts s.90°
10/10 zigzag			
1.0kts s.45°	1.0kts s.48°	1.0kts s.47°	-
2.0kts s.45°	2.0kts s.50°	2.0kts s.49°	-
3.0kts s.45°	3.0kts s.52°	3.0kts s.51°	-
20/20 zigzag			
1.0kts p.135°	-	-	1.0kts p.136°
2.0kts p.135°	-	-	2.0kts p.138°
3.0kts p.135°	-	-	3.0kts p.139°

Table 4 shows the application results of previously mentioned algorithm to the cases of Fig. 2 and Fig. 3. Estimated current from turning data are almost the same as true value. Current speeds estimated from the zigzag data also show good agreement but the directions have about 2~7° error. For practical purpose, however, this amount of error seems to be acceptable.

Two disadvantages of our estimation of current are that it needs more measurements and filtering of kinematical information and the estimation of current does not mean the correction of trial data. Fig. 5 compares the corrected turning trajectories by the estimated currents. The IMO method, which combines inexact physics and wrong current, gives reasonably looking trajectory. But the combination of inexact physics and right current generates another drifted trajectory. Hence we need a new method which can make reasonable correction with the reasonably estimated current.

Correction of trial data

For the physically appropriate correction of current effects, analysis based on the dynamics of motion is necessary. Mathematical model on the dynamics of maneuvering motions are Eqs. 1~4. If we consider only current effects, these can be rewritten as follows:

$$\left.\begin{array}{l} m \cdot (\dot{u} - vr) = -m_x \cdot \dot{u}_r + (m_y + X_{vr}) \cdot v_r r + X(u_r) + X_R + X_P \\ m \cdot (\dot{v} + ur) = -m_y \cdot \dot{v}_r - m_x \cdot u_r r + Y_{H0}(v_r, r) + Y_R \\ I_{zz} \cdot \dot{r} = -J_{zz} \cdot \dot{r} + N_{H0}(v_r, r) - x_G \cdot Y_{H0}(v_r, r) + N_R \end{array}\right\}$$

With these given equations of motion, we can think of two problems of ship Maneuvering. One is the prediction of ship responses u, v, r under the specific combination of rudder angle, propeller rpm and current with the known maneuvering coefficients and initial condition. It can be solved by the time marching or integration of the given coupled 1st order differential equation. The other is the estimation of maneuvering coefficients from the known ship motions under the given rudder angle, propeller rpm and current.

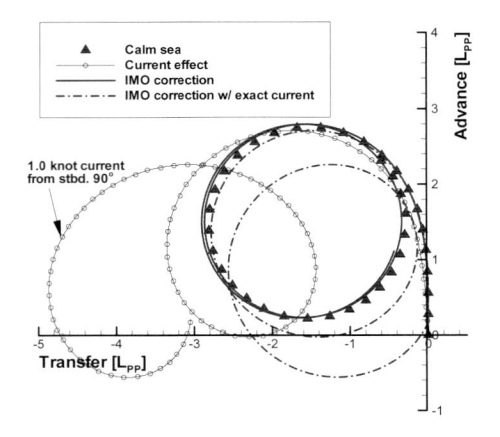

(a) Crude oil tanker, 1.0 knots from starboard 90°

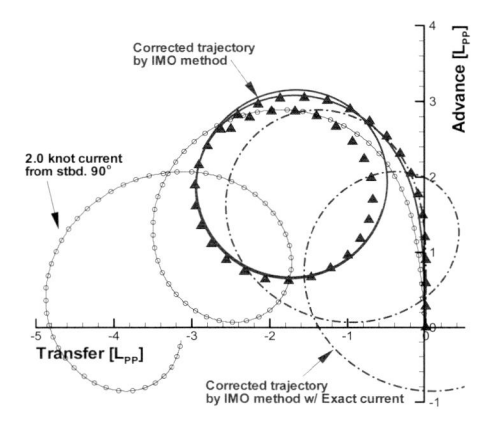

(b) Gas carrier, 2.0 knots from starboard 90°

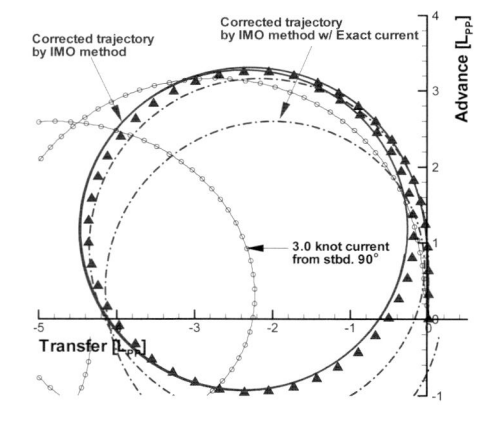

(c) Container carrier, 3.0 knots from starboard 90°

Fig. 5: Application of IMO correction method

As the unknown coefficients are linearly combined with the known motion variables, it can be solved by multiple regression analysis. Weighted least square estimator has been used to calculate the linear parameters or maneuvering coefficients. Table 5 shows the percentage error of estimated coefficients.

Table 5: Percentage error of estimated maneuvering coefficients

	COT	Gas	Container
Maneuver	Port turning	10/10 zigzag	20/20 zigzag
Current	1.0kts s.90°	2.0kts s.90°	3.0kts s.90°
(m_y+X_{vr})	76.1	86.9	142.2
X_{vv}	−108.3	121.6	−4956.2
X_{rr}	−8.0	337.2	127.9
$(1-t_R)$	101.6	123.1	103.1
$R^2_{adj.}$ for X	1.000	0.997	0.975
Y_v	115.7	104.6	76.3
Y_r	102.0	112.1	57.5
Y_{vvv}	799.2	77.3	−824.1
Y_{rrr}	−4025.2	682.6	690.4
Y_{vvr}	−1039.0	958.0	−1020.8
Y_{vrr}	770.7	−407.3	508.3
$(1+a_H)$	100.0	100.9	108.2
$R^2_{adj.}$ for Y	1.000	0.999	0.998
N_v	96.5	103.7	79.3
N_r	97.9	106.6	81.3
N_{vvv}	960.5	652.5	2909.4
N_{rrr}	1034.1	6339.2	446.8
N_{vvr}	−74.2	18.2	763.6
N_{vrr}	232.4	−536.3	3573.7
$(x_R+a_H \cdot x_H)$	100.0	98.1	99.0
$R^2_{adj.}$ for N	1.000	0.999	0.999
(m_y+X_{vr})	81.6	116.1	100.6
X_{vv}	-	45.3	-
X_{rr}	-	-	108.2
$(1-t_R)$	101.1	122.8	98.6
$R^2_{adj.}$ for X	0.999	0.999	0.972
Y_v	122.1	112.0	75.8
Y_r	103.3	114.0	67.4
Y_{vvv}	-	-	-
Y_{rrr}	−3338.2	-	87.6
Y_{vvr}	-	812.6	-
Y_{vrr}	435.3	-	125.7
$(1+a_H)$	99.8	95.6	107.9
$R^2_{adj.}$ for Y	1.000	0.999	0.998
N_v	93.9	104.7	95.8
N_r	96.7	107.3	93.7
N_{vvv}	-	-	-
N_{rrr}	1829.8	5912.1	116.0
N_{vvr}	-	-	88.6
N_{vrr}	296.1	−536.3	-
$(x_R+a_H \cdot x_H)$	100.0	98.6	102.3
$R^2_{adj.}$ for N	1.000	0.999	0.999

Two sets of error are given in Table 5. The upper set is the error when the whole set of coefficients are estimated from the given full model. The lower set is the error when the coefficients are estimated from the reduced model. Given equations are developed to cope with various situations of maneuvering motions. But the motion ranges of turning and zigzag motion are not so much various that every motion variables can not be sufficiently excited. This is related to the adequacy of regression model and the significance of regression coefficients. The significance of coefficients has been checked by the t-statistics of estimated coefficients. If the t-statistics was less than a specified level, corresponding coefficient will be eliminated from the model without loss of adequacy or adjusted coefficient of determination, R^2_{adj}. We can see that the difference between R^2_{adj} of full and reduced model are negligible, and the hydrodynamics forces during turning and zigzag test can be sufficiently modeled by the reduced model.

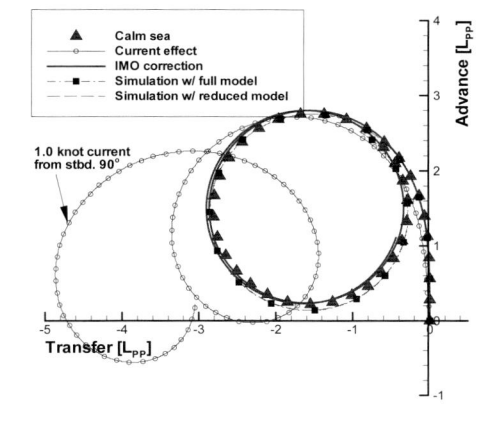

(a) Crude oil tanker, port turning

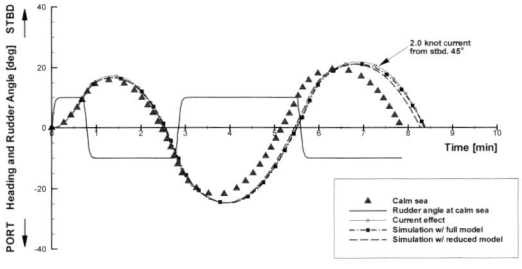

(b) Gas carrier, 10°/10° starboard zigzag

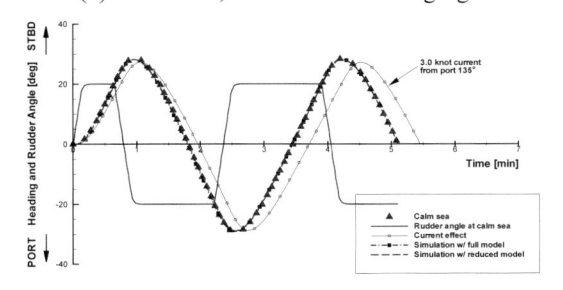

(c) Container carrier, 20°/20° starboard zigzag

Fig. 6: Corrected trajectories and heading angles

Linear coefficients and rudder coefficients are estimated within 20% error but nonlinear coefficient show large error. With these estimated coefficients, calm sea maneuvering performances were simulated. Fig. 6 shows the calm sea, current affected and corrected turning trajectories and zigzag heading angles. Although the corrected heading angle of gas carrier's 10°/10° zigzag maneuver shows some discrepancy with calm sea results, the corrected port turning trajectory of crude oil tanker and the heading angle of container carriers 20°/20° zigzag maneuver show good agreement with those of calm sea results. This shows the possibility of our method on the correction of turning and zigzag sea trial results.

Conclusion

In this study, we tried to develop a new method for the correction of maneuvering trial data, especially turning and zigzag data affected by constant current.

We first checked what effects can happen on the trial results when the environmental loads exist. Numerical simulations were executed for this purpose and we can see that not only current but also wind can severely affect the ship maneuverability. But wind effects become appreciable only when the ratio of wind velocity to ship speed is large, and it is not always necessary to correct wind effects from the maneuvering sea trial data.

As a second step, the IMO correction of constant current effect from turning circle test was reviewed. Although this method is based on a physically inexact assumption and the estimated current is different from the true one, it has many advantages; it is easy, it can surely make the drifted trajectory into a circle; the corrected advance and tactical diameter show reasonable agreement with those of calm sea results.

For the more accurate estimation on current, a digital smoothing polynomial filter was used to estimate the body fixed velocities from the position measurement. Current speed and direction can be easily estimated by using the kinematical relationship between the water track speed and ground speed. Estimated current from turning data are almost the same as true value but the current direction from the zigzag data have about 2~7° error. For practical purpose, however, this amount of error seems to be negligible.

Maneuvering coefficients in the equations of motion were estimated by multiple regression analysis. Both the whole set of coefficients in the given full model and the selected set of coefficients in the reduced model were estimated. The reduction of model was determined by the elimination of motion variables whose significance level of estimated coefficient is less than specified level. Adequacy of reduced model was checked by the adjusted coefficient of determination and it can be confirmed that the hydrodynamics forces during turning and zigzag test can be sufficiently modeled by the reduced model.

Calm sea maneuvering performance is predicted by both full model and reduced model. Although the corrected heading angle of gas carrier's 10°/10° zigzag maneuver show a little disagreement with calm sea results, the corrected turning trajectory of crude oil tanker and the heading angle of container carriers 20°/20° zigzag maneuver show reasonable agreement with those of calm sea results. This shows the possibility of proposed method on the correction of turning and zigzag sea trial results.

For the new method to be more practically useful correction tool, more research is needed. The first one is the modeling and correction of wave loads. Especially the second order forces by wave in irregular sea should be considered. The second one is consideration on the simultaneous action of environmental loads. In real sea, wind, wave and current do not affect the ship maneuverability separately. The third is the more validation of the new method by free running model test and sea trials.

References

IMO Resolution MSC.137(76) (2002). "Standards for Ship Manoeuvrability".

IMO MSC/Circ.1053 (2002). "Explanatory Notes to the Standards for Ship Manoeuvrability".

Jaroslaw Artyszuk (2003). "Wave Effects in Ship Maneuvering Motion – A Review Analysis", Proceedings of MARSIM'03, RC-12.

Kobayashi Eiichi, Kagemoto Hiroshi and Furukawa Yashitaka (1995). "Mathematical Models of Ship Maneuvering Motion", MMG Report No.12, Ch.2 (Japanese).

T. Fujiwara, M. Ueno, T. Nimura (1998). "Estimation of Wind Forces and Moments acting on Ships", Journal of Society of Naval Architecture of Japan, Vol. 183, pp.77~90 (Japanese).

William H. Press, Saul A. Teukosky, William T. Vetterling, Brian P. Flannery (1992). "*Numerical Recipes in C*", 2nd edition, Cambridge University Press, pp.650~655.

Concept Basis of On-board Intelligent Systems Development

Alexander B. Degtyarev[1], Yury I. Nechaev[2]

[1] Applied Mathematics and Control Processes Faculty, St. Petersburg State University, Professor
St. Petersburg, Russia
[2] Naval Architecture and Ocean Engineering Faculty, State Marine Technical University, Professor
St. Petersburg, Russia

Abstract

The concept and principles used in the basic design of the onboard intelligence systems (IS) functioning in real-time regime with conditions of fuzzy input information are considered for study in this work. The concept provides parallel processing of the information in multiprocessor computing environment. The principles of processing the information are based on the use of adaptive algorithms and competing computing technologies within the framework of the soft computing concept. Dynamic knowledge base (KB) is focused on the functioning of the system in conditions of continuous change of the dynamics object and external environment.

Keywords

Intelligent system; Safety seagoing; Soft computing; Competition principle.

Introduction

Information technology of the onboard IS development provides conditions of onboard computer system design and knowledge formalization about the interaction dynamics "ship – environment". Features of information analysis and interpretation problems define the concept of such systems engineering (Intelligence systems, 2001; On-board intelligence systems, 2006):

1. Alternatives analysis, forecast of situation development and decision-making are carried out on the basis of the dynamic measurements data, mathematical models and knowledge base.
2. Algorithms and software are realized in view of the real-time system functioning. Estimation and forecast of dynamic characteristics of the ship are based on an effective combination of traditional methods of ship behavior analysis with fuzzy and neural network algorithms for measuring and processing information in conditions of uncertainty and incomplete data.
3. IS knowledge base in the maximal degree is adapted for perception of the actual information about ship behavior. Interpretation of complex processes and phenomena determining ship behavior on waves is carried out on the basis of principles of information processing in multiprocessor computing environment (Degtyarev, 2003, 2003a).

Thus, the models and control objects used in the new generation of onboard IS represent the class of dynamic systems that are changing in time. The features of ship behavior in a continuously changing environment make it necessary to determine the use of various approaches, such as combining traditional methods and models of analysis and forecast of dynamic situations with new mathematical tools, including fuzzy models, artificial neural networks (ANN) and genetic algorithms (GA).

Conceptual model

The fundamental idea of the use of IS for solving complex problems of dynamic object interaction with the environment is connected to the application of the measuring means and methods of analyzing the original information and supercomputer technology.

The invariant kernel of the system includes the problem field, KB and database of IS. For creation of this set, the conceptual model of IC is formed. The consideration of the system in its functional aspect allows it to select the following components (Bogdanov, 2001):

$$<S_F, S_M, S_W> \quad (1)$$

where $S_F = \{S_{F1}, ..., S_{FN}\}$ is the set of functional subsystems; S_M is structural scheme of the system; S_W are conditions of formation of complete system;

$$S_F = <X, Y, A, P_F, T_F>, S_M = <E, C, \Phi, P_M, T_M>,$$
$$S_W = <G, R, U_R, K_R, E_f>$$

where $X = X^{;j}$ ($j = 1,..., n$) is the vector-set of input signals; $Y = Y^{;i}$ ($i = 1,..., m$) is the vector-set of output signals; $A : \{X \rightarrow Y\}$ is the operator determining process of functioning of system S; $P^{;F} = \{P^{x;F}, P^{y;F}, P^{A;F}\}$ is the full set of functional parameters; $P^{x;F} = \{\pi^{x;F}\}$; $P^{y;F} = \{\pi^{y;F}\}$; $P^{A;F} = \{\pi^{A;F}\}$ are the parameters for considered subsets; $T^{;F}$ is the set of the time moments, invariant to object of modeling; $E = E^{;v}$ ($v = 1,…, N^{;v}$) is the set of system components; $C = C^{;q}$ ($q = 1,…, Q^{;c}$) is the set determining relations between elements; $P^{;M} = \{P^{E;M}, P^{C;M}, P^{\Phi;M}\}$ is the set of morphological parameters. $\Phi = \{\Phi_\lambda\}$ ($\lambda = 1,…,r$) is the configuration set determining way of S_F formation. $P^{E;M} = \{\pi^{E;M}\}$; $P^{C;M} = \{\pi^{C;M}\}$; $P^{\Phi;M} = \{\pi^{\Phi;M}\}$ are the parameters for considered subsets; $T^{;M} = \{t^{M;k}\}$ is the set of the time moments of dynamic structures; G are the purposes of functioning of object in realization of a task R; U_R are the principles and algorithms of management of object; K_R is an execution result quality; E_f is the efficiency determining at what price the purpose G is achieved.

The problem of selection of optimal requirements to quality operation index Q_l (l=1,…,L) and of characteristics of IC tools C_s (s=1,…,N) in conditions of incomplete and indefinite initial data is formulated on the basis on Zadeh' generalization principle (Zadeh, 1976). In accordance with this principle, the possibilities of considered indices realizations are defined by the following:

for IC characteristics

$$\mu_S(C_S) = \max_{C_{S1},…,C_{Sh}:C_S=f_S(C_{S1},…C_{Sh})} \mu_{S1}(C_{S1}) \wedge … \wedge \mu_{Sh}(C_{Sh}), \quad C_S \in R^1 \quad (2)$$

and for quality indexes

$$\mu_{\Pi Q}(q_l) = \max_{C_{u1},…,C_{up}:q_l=Q_l(C_{u1},…C_{up})} \mu_{u1}(C_{u1}) \wedge … \wedge \mu_{up}(C_{up}), \quad q_l \in R^1 \quad (3)$$

with fuzzy sets

$$\mathbf{C}_S = \{C_s, \mu_s(C_s)\}; \quad PQ_l = \{q_l, \mu_{\Pi q l}(q_l)\}.$$

It is possible to present optimal solution of problem for fuzzy goals Q and fuzzy possibilities PQ having in view conditions (2) and (3) as

$$\mu_{\Pi Q l}(q_l) \wedge \mu_{Q l}(q_l) \rightarrow \max \quad (4)$$

During IS functioning each of the subsystems works according to the accepted collective strategy determining ship behavior in permitted state space. Thus, subsets of permitted and forbidden ship states are assigned:

$$\{R_A(t)\}_k^\beta = F_\beta(\{R_A(t)\}, R_A(t)_k, k);$$

$$\{R_A(t)\}^\beta = U_{k=1,…,q} \{R_A(t)\}_k^\beta; \quad (5)$$

$$\{P_A(t)\}_l^\alpha = \{P_A(t)\} \setminus \{R_A(t)\}^\beta, (k=1,…,q, l=1,…,p).$$

Here $\{R_A(t)\}_k^\beta$ и $\{R_A(t)\}^\beta$ are subsets of forbidden states for IS and for separate subsystems; $\{P_A(t)\}l^\alpha$ is a subset of permitted conditions.

Principles of data processing

The conceptual basis of onboard IS development is based on the theoretical principles defining architecture of system and levels of its control (Intelligence systems, 2001; On-board intelligence systems, 2006). The knowledge of highly skilled experts in the considered fields with the use of the vast array of methods and means of knowledge analysis and interpretation are used during the decision-making phase. Traditional mathematical methods achievements of an artificial intellect (AI) are widely applied in conjunction with new principles of real-time IS functioning. The most important role among them belongs to the principle of openness, which allows for the provision of the most complex levels of hierarchical structure of system – self-organizing and self-training. Use of these principles allows IS "to understand" complex processes of "dynamic object – environment" interaction, "to model" its actions and "to be trained" in the experience.

Soft computing concept

The theoretical base of IS development is formed on the basis of the effective combination of the collected knowledge system with new approaches and paradigms of AI. Methods and models assume a very important role in providing knowledge formalization and integration, inferential mechanism, search of decisions and delivery of practical recommendations. In conjunction with the traditional methods of knowledge engineering soft computing concept (Zadeh, 1994) (fig.1), cognitive paradigm, multimedia and virtual reality are also used. This action provides for a raise in the efficiency of the interaction of the operator with IS.

Features of mathematical modeling methods application in new generations of IS require that we obtain approximation error during model construction. It also emphasizes the importance of reliable measuring information use at adaptive components of the knowledge base realization in problems of algorithmic and IS software perfection.

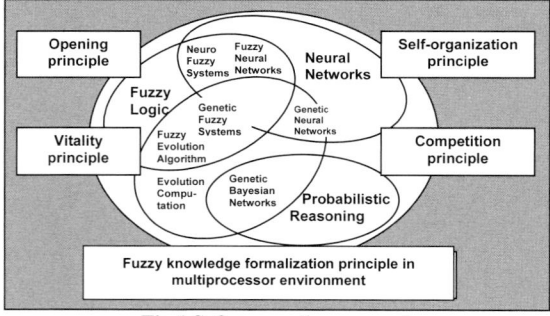

Fig.1 Soft computing concept

Competition concept

We propose a new approach to data processing based on the development of the soft computing concept. It makes possible the opportunity to improve the reliability of assessment and situation forecast. This approach applies two theoretical principles (Fig. 2 and 3) towards the provision of rational organization of computing technology of measurement data processing in analysis and forecast problems. Such an approach is especially important for information flow formalization at fuzzy logical inference realization in multiprocessor computing environment (Degtyarev, 2003, 2003a).

The competition principle (Fig. 2) as a choice of computing technology provides the comparative analysis of the results of the situation estimation using traditional algorithms and neural network models.

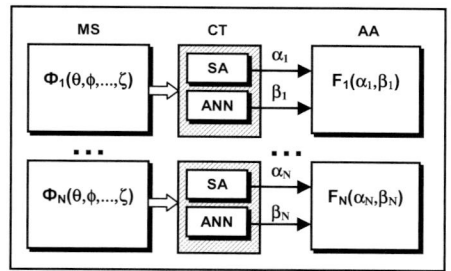

Fig. 2. Information flow in multiprocessor computing environment: MS – measuring system; CT – competing technologies; AA – analysis of alternatives; $\Phi1(\cdot)$,..., $\Phi(\alpha)$ - measurement data (standard (SA) and artificial neural network (ANN) algorithms); $\alpha_1\beta_1$,...,$\alpha_N \beta_N$ – output data for SA and ANN; $F_1(\cdot),...,F_N(\cdot)$ – situations determined as a result of alternatives analysis.

Fuzzy information formalization

The use of the principle of fuzzy information formalization in multiprocessor environment makes possible the ability to carry out parallel fuzzy derivation sequence in continuously changing conditions of object dynamics and environment (Fig.3). The use of the principle identifies the following possibilities:

• to develop software for complex models of representation and processing of fuzzy knowledge system;

• to provide real-time system functioning and to reduce consumptions on hardware for fuzzy inferential mechanism;

• to remove problem solution difficulties that we have in computation process parallelization with essential irregularity of calculations characterized for complex systems.

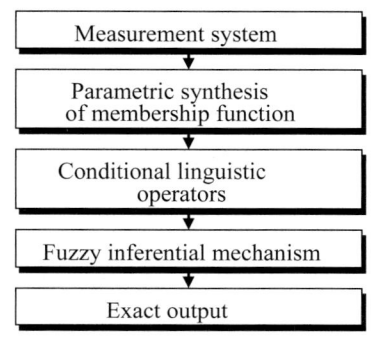

Fig. 3 Information flow

In order to enable the raise of the level of the efficiency of IS functioning at continuous change of object dynamics and environment, realization of the noted principles must be made. The practical importance of information streams processing in real-time is caused by aspirations to heighten the speed of computer calculations by algorithms parallelization and their realization on high performance computers. The task of checking the accuracy of control algorithms and decision-making is carried out in a formal process on the basis of general requirements to algorithms of the system.

Alternative analysis

The problem of decision-making in fuzzy environment is connected with various constructions (choices of alternatives) in order to satisfy the restriction set. The problem is presented by the tuple:

$$< A, W, S, U > \qquad (6)$$

where A is alternative set; W is environment characteristics; S is system of preferences; U is action. So it is necessary to carry out an operation over the alternative set having determined the most preferred among them.

The process of decision support system synthesis is a sequence of hierarchical structure analysis operations. The elementary subtasks in this structure are analyzed preliminarily by method of hierarchies (Nechaev, 2001). Realization of this method is connected to the allocation of priorities (weights) of attributes with a view of choice of the best of them with the use of algebraic theory of matrixes and expert procedures:

$$W\pi = \lambda_{max}\pi; \quad \Pi = \begin{bmatrix} \pi_{11} & \cdots & \pi_{1m} \\ \vdots & \pi_{ij} & \vdots \\ \pi_{n1} & \cdots & \pi_{nm} \end{bmatrix} \times \begin{bmatrix} g_1 \\ \vdots \\ g_m \end{bmatrix}, \qquad (7)$$

where W is the inverse symmetric matrix of values of paired comparisons of attributes concerning the given attribute; π is the normalized vector of attributes weights; λ_{max} is the greatest eigenvalue of matrix W; Π is the result of determination of global priorities of attributes $\Pi_1,..., \Pi_N$; N is the number of attributes; π_{ij} (i=1,..., n, j=1,...,m) is the relative weight of i-th attribute on j-th attribute; g_j is the relative weight of j-th attribute.

On set of alternatives linguistic variables with term-set $T_i = \{T_{i1}, ..., T_{it}\}$ which characterize personal preferences of navigator are put in correspondence to each criterion. Admissible set of criterion values is base set of linguistic variable. Estimation of alternative efficiency by separate criterion is carried out with the help of additional linguistic variable characterized by term-set $S = \{S_1, ..., S_t\}$. Cardinal number coincides with T_i. Such linguistic variable is invariant in relation to each CR_i criteria. Cause-and-effect relation is between two linguistic variables. It could be represented in the form of fuzzy implicative relation:

$$\mu_{Rij}(x_i,y): X_i \times Y \to [0,1], x_i \in X_i, y \in Y \qquad (8)$$

where X_i is base set of i-th criterion values; Y is base set of alternatives efficiency assessment.

Distinguish forward and backward associations between linguistic variables. Forward association characterizes alternative efficiency by criterion "reliability", and backward association characterizes time interval of decision-making (the more this interval, the less efficiency of algorithm).

Dynamic knowledge base

Development of software for onboard IS was based on the following features of IT. Dynamic knowledge base is the main element of informational model for problem domain:

$$< P, F, S, I >, \qquad (9)$$

where P is product rules base; F is base of formal procedures for measurement data processing; S is statistical models base; I is base of simulation models and models utilizing untraditional methods for data processing.

Algorithms of information transformation at inferential mechanism realization in IS are presented on the basis of production-rule system.

$$<\text{if } X, \text{then } Y, \text{else } Z> \qquad (X \rightarrow Y(Z)) \qquad (10)$$

where X,Y,Z are fuzzy sets defined on universes U,V,W; sets X,Y,Z are interpreted as fuzzy input and fuzzy output of some system where relationships between them are determined by the fuzzy model.

At the interpretation of model (10) various built-in procedures based on application of statistical analysis, methods of mathematical modeling, methods of qualitative research of the differential equations on a phase plane are used. Methods of traditional mathematics and fuzzy logic are used alongside wide application of artificial neural networks theory and genetic algorithms.

Mechanism providing logic of functioning and development of decisions in the processing of information income about dynamics of ship and environment is based on decisions concluded with the help of the formal procedure:

$$F_i : S_k(t_i) \rightarrow U_j (k = 1,...,n; j = 1,...,J; i = 1,...,N), \qquad (11)$$

where $S_k(t_i)$ is a situation in time moment t_i; U_j is a decision; F_i is a rules set.

The development of operating influences at IS knowledge base functioning is carried out on the basis of the results of dynamic measurements of external excitations parameters after certain computing and logic operations. Quality of onboard IS operation at collective strategy realization is determined by a mismatch function characterizing divergence of technical conditions of the ship for decision $T_S(P)$ (forecast) and actual condition $F_S(t)$ in the considered time moment:

$$\Phi(R,t) = \Phi(T_S(P), F_S(t)) \qquad (12)$$

The value of mismatch function $\Phi(R, t)$ is determined by reliability of the algorithms incorporated in the formalized knowledge system. Analysis of available information allows the establishment of an actual condition of vessel and parameters of external excitations. Methods of experiment planning are used for increase of measurements reliability in normal operation conditions.

Principle of nonlinear self-organization

Onboard IS functioning is connected to the operative control of situation and forecasting of its development. Maintenance of such control is reached on the basis of adaptive algorithms, capable of reconstructing the structure at ship behavior change on the waves. Deterministic and stochastic approaches, as well as approaches based on self-organizing principle, are used for algorithms synthesis. This principle is most effective in problems of extreme situations control and forecasting connected with sudden (spasmodic) changes in ship behavior. On the basis of forecast data IS develops practical recommendations in order to avoid this danger. Realization of nonlinear self-organization principle in such cases demands greater calculation volume connected with a tentative object dynamics estimation on the basis of mathematical modeling of extreme situations with subsequent formulation corresponding criterial estimations.

Synergetic approach

One of the important directions of systems investigation based on knowledge is the use of new approaches realizing modern applications of information technologies and systems theory. Among those put forward are applications connected with development synergetic control theory. (Fig. 4).

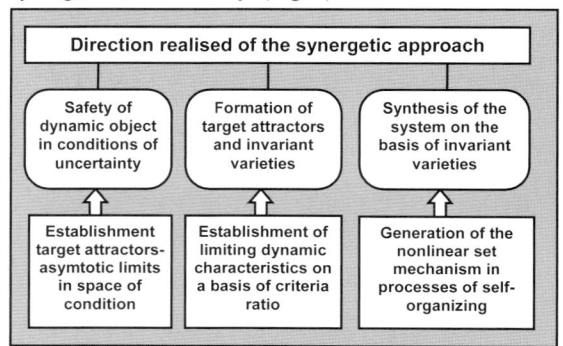

Fig. 4. Features of the synergetic approach

Realization of synergetic approach is connected not only with performance of requirements to process character describing object dynamics, but also necessity of required asymptotic system behavior on point of attraction or in its relative closeness (Kapitsa, 1977). Such an approach leads to a stricter, more refined decision of analytical synthesis problem of decision support system for vessel safety in extreme situations.

IS structure

Development of IS for ship safety is connected with the decision of actual problems of control and diagnosing. These problems characterize ship functioning as a dynamic system with high probability of non-failure operation. The basis for such a system is control of technical condition by results of forecasting of object and environment dynamic parameters values. The multiprocessing computer system (Fig.5) processes the information stream from measuring system and functions in real-time.

Behavior of the considered dynamic system is described by state vector $x = \{x_i\}$ (i=1, ..., n). External excitation characterized by vector $W = \{W_k\}$ (k=1, ..., K) influences on the system. Target coordinates of system $y = \{y_j\}$ (j=1, ..., m) represent controllable values. They depend on operating influences $U = \{u_q\}$ (q=1, ..., Q) which are understood as practical recommendations on safety navigation. IS functioning carrying out the operative control and delivery of practical recommendations $R_1, ..., R_n$ in conditions of uncertainty $U_1, ..., U_Q$ is provided on the basis of data processing in real-time.

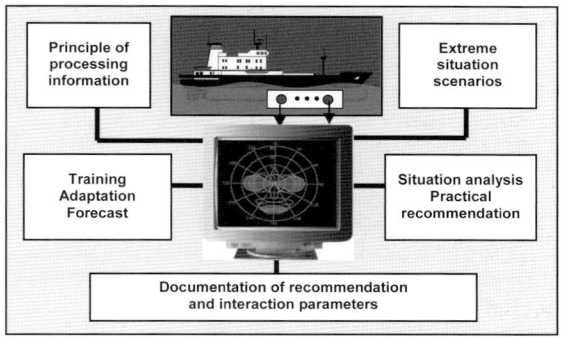

Fig.5 Architecture of onboard IS

Initial information comes from gauges of the measuring system. Observations are fixed in discrete time moments 1, 2, ..., t and characterize information vector.

$$I = (\theta, \psi, ..., \xi, t \in [t_0, T]), \quad (13)$$

where $\theta, \psi, ..., \xi$ are parameters determining dynamic object state.

Measurement system

The block of initial information gauges includes sensors for angular and linear motion control, velocities and accelerations, level of liquid in ship's compartments, wind speed and direction. Types of gauges and features of their installation are determined during the decision of optimization problem. Each gauge registers continuous process (measurement of dynamic characteristics in time).

The system of information transfer is organized depending on conditions of measuring system gauges installation. Information preprocessing is carried out in the special block, which is located in wheelhouse together with onboard computer system providing functioning of the system in real-time. Environmental characteristics and features of ship dynamics are determined during information processing.

The control system carries out a choice of optimum ship speed and course angle depending on environmental features. The control process is organized on the basis of soft computing concept. Fuzzy logic rules realization is reached with the help of the control matrix constructed for membership functions appearing in the inferential mechanism. The control algorithm provides useful information processing in multiprocessor computers. Membership functions construction is carried out on the basis of ANN. ANN training is carried out with the help of «error back propagation » procedure and GA (Anderson, 1988).

Thus, IS provides an opportunity of purposeful control change. The operator accepts the decision depending on changing conditions. Active inclusion of navigational intelligence in the vessel control process, optimum functions of distribution between crew and onboard system, development of the new human-machine interface are all major contributions in the direction of new generations of onboard IS development.

Software & Hardware

The concept of onboard IS development provides the use of multilevel organization models of the multiprocessor integrated computing environment. The top level represented by the control computer carrying out communications with onboard subsystems and information input. The bottom level consists of a set of parallel operating nodes (processors) providing the decision of separate functional problems in accordance to loading determining by control computer. Parallelization and multithreading in investigated problems resulted in the speed up of the calculation process. Principles of "openness" and "clarity" are very important at IS functioning. These features make it possible to provide open scalable IS architecture.

IS testing

The complexity of the considered problem and the formal tool for its solution demand resource-intensive experimental investigations providing IS functioning. The problem of testing and IS knowledge-based diagnostics is represented in the form of set of hypotheses, symptoms and problems (Fig. 6). Initial data for testing and diagnostics provide conformity between the problem and symptoms. Procedures of knowledge testing and diagnostics are based on application of mechanisms of decision-making in IS (Nechaev, 2001).

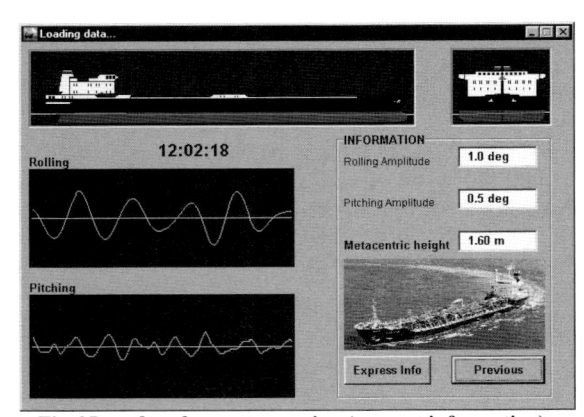

Fig.6 Interface for system testing (current information)

The testing problem is represented by the tuple:

$$<H_i, S_j, T_k>; (i=1,...,n; j=1,...,m; k=1,...,l) \quad (14)$$

where H, S, T are sets of hypotheses, symptoms and tasks.

Initial data (14) characterize matrixes:

$$G = \begin{matrix} & H_1 & \cdots & H_n \\ S_1 \\ \vdots \\ S_m \end{matrix} \begin{bmatrix} w_{11} & \cdots & w_{n1} \\ \vdots & w_{ij} & \vdots \\ w_{1m} & \cdots & w_{nm} \end{bmatrix} ; \quad R = \begin{matrix} T_1 \\ \vdots \\ T_\ell \end{matrix} \begin{bmatrix} v_{11} & \cdots & v_{1m} \\ \vdots & v_{kj} & \vdots \\ v_{\ell 1} & \cdots & v_{\ell m} \end{bmatrix} \begin{matrix} C_1 \\ \vdots \\ C_\ell \end{matrix}$$
$$\quad E_1 \cdots E_n$$

Here E_i (i=1, _, n) are estimations; C_k (k=1, _, l) are expenses; w_{ij} (i=1,...,n; j=1,...,m) is weight of a symptom in the given hypothesis; v_{kj} (k=1,...,l; j=1,...,m) is characteristic vector specifying correspondence between a problem and symptoms.

In that specific case, at unequivocal correspondence between symptoms and problems matrix R is identity. Then the initial data can be described by replacement of appropriate tasks in matrix R and adding a vector-column of expenses on the right. The procedures of the IS testing and diagnostics are based on application of acceptance decisions mechanisms with use of KB fuzzy models.

Conclusion

Thus, development of methodological bases and formal constructions for structural knowledge, models and methods for decision-making determine the real-time IS development concept:

1. Theoretical IT basis of integrated IS assumes use of multiprocessor computing platforms and wide parallelization in conditions of uncertainty and incompleteness of initial information.

2. Practical parallel action IS realization is connected with solution of the problem of semantic correctness of knowledge representation models and inference performance in high performance computer systems functioning in the dynamic problem area.

3. Rules of inference are interpreted as a condition of problem area transformation. Model of knowledge representation is interpreted as mapping on set of acceptable states. Such mapping is focused on measuring information, perception and transformation in frameworks of self-organizing systems.

References

Anderson J., Rosenfeld E. (1988) Neurocomputing: foundation of research. MIT Press. Cambridge. MAAS. 1988

Asai K., Sugeno M., Terano T. (1994) Applied fuzzy system, Academic Press, New York, 1994.

Bogdanov A., Degtyarev A., Nechaev Yu. (2001) Fuzzy Logic Basis in High Performance Decision Support Systems. //in book "Computational Science - ICCS 2001", LNCS 2074, Springer, part II, pp.965-975.

Degtyarev A. (2003) High performance computer technologies in shipbuilding. //in book "Optimistic. Optimization in Marine Design", Mensch & Buch Verlag, Berlin, 2003, pp.245-258

Degtyarev A. (2003a) Use of high performance computer technologies at the organization of onboard computing system // Proc. of the International conference STAB'2003, Madrid, 2003, pp.485-494

Intelligence systems (2001) in marine research and technology/ Ed. Yu. I.Nechaev. St.-Petersburg, SMTU, 2001 (in Russian)

Kapitsa S.P., Kurdumov S.P., Malinetsky G.G. (1977) Synergetic and future forecast. – Moscow, Science, 1977 (in Russian).

Kosko B. (1986) Fuzzy cognitive maps // International Journal of Man-Machine Studies. 1986. Vol.24, p.p.65 – 75.

Nechaev Yu., Degtyarev A., Boukhanovsky A. (2001a) Complex situations simulation when testing intelligence system knowledge base // Proceedings of International conference «Computational Science-ICCS 2001». San Francisco. CA.USA. Part.1. Springer 2001, pp.453-462.

On-board intelligence systems. (2006) Part 2. Ship systems. – Moscow: Radiotechnik, 2006 (in Russian)

Winston P.N. (1993) Artificial intelligence. – Addison Wesley Publishing Company. USA.1993.

Zadeh L. (1976) Concept of linguistic variable and its application for acceptance approximate decision. – Moskow: World, 1976

Zadeh L. (1994) Fuzzy logic, neural networks and soft computing // Commutation on the ASM-1994. Vol.37. №3, p.p.77-84.

Engineering Practice on Ice Propeller Strength Assessment Based on IACS Polar Ice Rule – URI3

Sing-Kwan Lee

Research and Product Development, Technology, American Bureau of Shipping
Houston, USA

Abstract

The "Machinery Requirements for Polar Class Ships" IACS URI3 has been released and is to be uniformly applied by IACS Societies on ships contracted for construction on and after 1 March 2008. Unlike the pervious ice class rule, URI3 relies more on direct calculations for propeller strength assessment. In this paper, some concerns on general practice on finite element analysis according to the URI3 Rule will be discussed based on our current experiences.

Keywords

Ice propeller strength; Polar ice class; IACS URI3; Plastic FEM.

Introduction

In propeller strength assessment, the current IACS URI3, "Machinery Requirements for Polar Class Ships" (IACS), requests finite element stress analyses to be performed based on ice loads. The propeller design ice loads given in URI3 are different from the ice torque traditionally used in the past and are the results of extensive research activities. Included in the activities, there were analyses of service history of propeller damages, propeller and shaft load measurements on full-scale trials, laboratory investigations and numerical simulation of propeller-ice interaction. It was found through these activities the traditional ice torque was not adequate to the ice propeller strength assessment task. Rather than the in-plane ice torque, the out-of-plane blade bending moments due to the backward and forward ice forces were found to be the main attribution to the causes of major blade deformation and breakage.

In the development of the IACS URI3 Rule, finite element analyses based on the aforementioned out-of-plane ice load were carried out by classification societies. The results were compared with the measured stresses from the icebreakers, Polar Star and Gudingen. Based on these analyses, it was found the simplified cantilever beam method cannot predict the blade stresses with reasonable accuracy, especially for a highly skewed blade. It was then concluded FEM-based analyses are necessary to ice propeller strength assessment.

To assess the blade strength based on the FEM results, a less restricted reference stress criterion is proposed in URI3. This reference stress has originally been developed to reflect the real capability of the blade to carry loads aimed to in particular for extreme ice loads that can cause plastic bending of the blade.

In FEM analysis for non-ice propeller, since the stress criteria are based on elastic stress criteria such as yielding or fatigue limits, linear stress analysis is regarded to be accurate enough for blade strength review. For ice propeller, however, slight plastic deformation on blade is common and almost unavoidable. In order to consider the plastic deformation situation, the reference stress criterion is more rational. In light of the reference stress criterion, it is natural the FE stress analysis should be extended to the plastic stress analysis level so that the stress due to the plastic deformation can be taken into account more appropriately. In fact, in ABS experience, it was found that linear FE stress analysis could be too conservative for some safe designs proven by their service history. In such cases, plastic FEM analysis should be adopted for correctly assessing the blade strength.

In this paper, some concerns on general practice on ice propeller strength assessment according to IACS URI3 Rule will be discussed based on our current experiences.

Ice rule on propeller strength

In URI3 document, the design forces on the propeller blade resulting from propeller-ice interaction, including hydrodynamic loads are provided. These forces are the expected ice loads for the whole services life of the ship under normal operational conditions, including loads resulting from the changing rotational direction of fixed pitch propellers. The Rules cover open- and ducted-type propellers with fixed or controllable pitch designs for the following Polar ice classes defined in URI1 (IACS).

Table 1: Ice class defined in URI1

Polar Class	Ice Description (based on WMO Sea Ice Nomenclature)
PC 1	Year-round operation in all Polar waters
PC 2	Year-round operation in moderate multi-year ice conditions
PC 3	Year-round operation in second-year ice, which may include multi-year ice inclusions
PC 4	Year-round operation in thick first-year ice which may include old ice inclusions
PC 5	Year-round operation in medium first-year ice which may include old ice inclusions
PC 6	Summer/autumn operation in medium first-year ice which may include old ice inclusions
PC 7	Summer/autumn operation in thin first-year ice which may include old ice inclusions

Design ice loads

For the sake of briefness, only the ice loads formulae for open propeller are briefed here. For ducted propeller, the details can be referred to the original URI3.

Maximum backward blade force F_b in [kN] unit

$$F_b = 27 \cdot S_{ice} [nD]^{0.7} \left[\frac{EAR}{Z}\right]^{0.3} D^2 \quad \text{when } D \leq D_{limit}$$

$$F_b = 23 \cdot S_{ice} [nD]^{0.7} \left[\frac{EAR}{Z}\right]^{0.3} DH_{ice}^{1.4} \quad \text{when } D > D_{limit}$$

where $D_{limit} = 0.85 \cdot H_{ice}^{1.4}$ [m]
H_{ice} = design ice thickness (see Table 2)
S_{ice} = ice strength index (see Table 2)
D = propeller diameter [m]
EAR = expanded blade area ratio
Z = blade numbers
n = propeller rps [1/s]
For CPP, n = nominal rotational speed at MCR in free running condition
For FPP, n = 85% of the nominal rotational speed at MCR in free running condition

Maximum forward blade force F_f in [kN] unit

$$F_f = 250 \cdot S_{ice} \left[\frac{EAR}{Z}\right] D^2 \quad \text{when } D \leq D_{limit}$$

$$F_f = 500 \cdot S_{ice} \left[\frac{EAR}{Z}\right] D \frac{1}{\left(1-\frac{d}{D}\right)} H_{ice} \quad \text{when } D > D_{limit}$$

where $D_{limit} = \dfrac{2}{\left(1-\dfrac{d}{D}\right)} \cdot H_{ice}$ [m]

d = propeller hub diameter [m]

Table 2: Values of H_{ice} and S_{ice} for different PC ice class

Ice class	PC1	PC2	PC3	PC4	PC5	PC6	PC7
H_{ice}[m]	4.0	3.5	3.0	2.5	2.0	1.75	1.5
S_{ice}	1.2	1.1	1.1	1.1	1.1	1.0	1.0

Load cases

In ice blade strength assessment, according to URI3 load cases 1 - 4 have to be covered, as given in Table 3 below, for CP and FP open propellers. In order to obtain blade ice loads for a reverse rotating propeller, load case 5 also needs to be considered for FP propellers.

Table 3: Load cases defined in URI3

	Force	Loaded area (refer to Figure 1)
case 1	F_b	Uniform pressure applied on the back of the blade (suction side) to an area from 0.6R to the tip and from the leading edge to 0.2 times the chord length.
case 2	$0.5 F_b$	Uniform pressure applied on the back of the blade (suction side) on the propeller tip area outside 0.9R radius.
case 3	F_f	Uniform pressure applied on the blade face (pressure side) to an area from 0.6R to the tip and from the leading edge to 0.2 times the chord length.
case 4	$0.5 F_f$	Uniform pressure applied on propeller face (pressure side) on the propeller tip area outside 0.9R radius.
case 5	$0.6 \times \min\{F_b, F_f\}$	Uniform pressure applied on propeller face (pressure side) to an area from 0.6R to the tip and from the trailing edge to 0.2 times the chord length

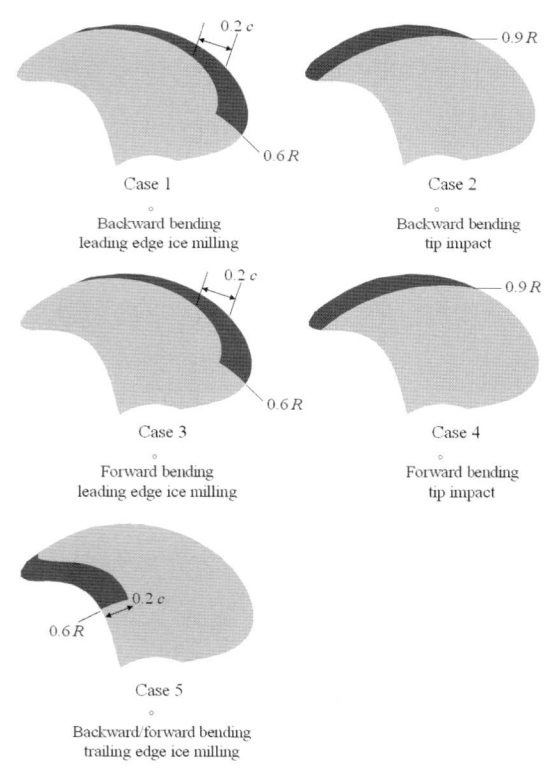

Case 1
Backward bending
leading edge ice milling

Case 2
Backward bending
tip impact

Case 3
Forward bending
leading edge ice milling

Case 4
Forward bending
tip impact

Case 5
Backward/forward bending
trailing edge ice milling

Fig. 1: Loaded area for different cases

Stress criterion

For propeller strength, URI3 uses the following plastic stress criterion.

$$\frac{c_{ref}}{c} \geq 1.5$$

where σ = calculated stress for the design loads; if FE analysis is used in estimating the stresses, von Mises stresses shall be used

σ_{ref} = reference stress defined as min{$0.7\sigma_u$, 0.6σ +$0.4\sigma_{0.2}$}; σ_u is ultimate tensile strength, $\sigma_{0.2}$ is proof strength

Loads on propeller

As known, there are contact (ice) and non-contact (hydrodynamic) loads on ice propellers. Non-contact load considered here is the hydrodynamic load on blade for propulsion under open water condition. For contact load, it is mainly the ice load due to the ice milling and impact processes. The difference between these contact and non-contact loads is significant. To illustrate this, a four blade PC7 polar ice class CP propeller is selected, and its hydrodynamic loads on the blade at MCR conditions (ahead and crash-stop operations) are compared to the different ice load scenarios defined in IACS URI3. This PC7 propeller is a highly skewed design with a diameter 5400 mm. The details of the propeller geometry are given in Table 4 and Figure 2 as follows.

Table 4: Propeller particulars

r/R [-]	Pitch [mm]	Camber [mm]	Tmax [mm]	Chord [mm]	Skew [mm]	Rake [mm]
.270	4311.5	24.5	244.7	876.7	-0.0	-0.0
.300	4345.5	27.6	228.0	966.2	-43.3	-7.0
.350	4396.7	32.7	202.0	1113.8	-123.5	-18.7
.400	4440.0	37.5	178.9	1256.6	-207.2	-30.5
.450	4475.4	41.8	158.6	1393.5	-287.8	-42.3
.500	4503.0	44.9	141.2	1523.5	-358.8	-54.0
.550	4522.7	46.3	126.7	1644.9	-413.7	-65.8
.600	4534.5	45.8	115.0	1755.6	-445.9	-77.6
.650	4538.4	43.7	104.8	1852.8	-448.9	-89.3
.700	4529.1	40.5	94.5	1932.4	-416.2	-101.1
.750	4501.4	36.8	84.2	1988.0	-341.3	-112.9
.800	4455.0	33.1	74.0	2009.9	-217.6	-124.6
.850	4390.2	30.2	63.8	1980.3	-38.7	-136.4
.900	4306.9	27.8	53.5	1863.6	202.2	-148.2
.950	4205.0	23.0	43.3	1563.3	511.3	-159.9
.990	4110.1	12.5	35.1	861.3	812.2	-169.3
1.000	4084.6	9.9	33.0	0.0	895.4	-171.7

Fig. 2: Blade expanded outline and section profile

Hydrodynamic load

The hydrodynamic loads are calculated by ABS PropS2 software, which can handle ahead and crash-stop for CP propeller (ABS, 2005). Calculated thrust, torque, power, and pressure difference are summarized in Table 5 for the ahead condition. The calculated propeller absorbed power shown in the table is matched with the engine MCR power. The calculated hydrodynamic pressure difference (net pressure) distribution on blade is plotted in Figure 3. As seen, high net pressure occurs near the leading edge area. This net pressure distribution can generate not only the moment to bend the blade forward but also the spindle torque to twist the blade.

Table 5: Propeller performance and load at ahead MCR

Thrust	Torque	Absorbed Power	Max. pressure difference
kN	kN-m	kW	N/mm2
626.35	529.65	6300.0	0.135

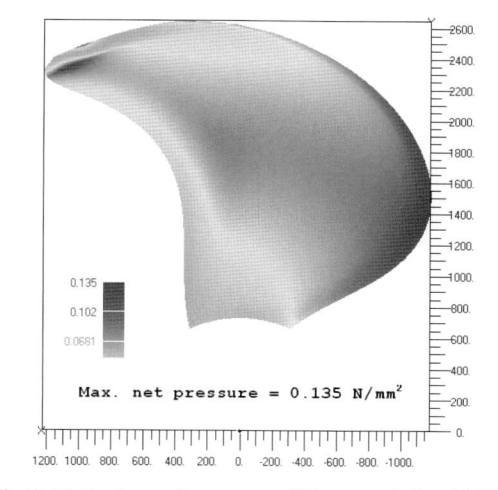

Max. net pressure = 0.135 N/mm^2

Fig. 3: Hydrodynamic pressure difference at ahead MCR

For crash-stop operation of CP propeller, propeller is turned along the spindle axis with $\Delta\theta$ to a position with "negative" pitches (Figure 4). Usually, $\Delta\theta$ should be selected to absorb the engine power as much as possible to generate maximum backward thrust. It should be noted after $\Delta\theta$ turning, the original pressure side in ahead operation becomes the suction side in crash-stop operation. Also as is well-known, the section profiles are distorted (Figure 5). This geometry changing affects a lot the propeller hydrodynamics. As shown in Table 6, same absorbed power (6300 kW) cannot generate same thrust force (626.35 kN) as the ahead condition in crash stop operation. Only 47% of the ahead thrust can be generated in crash stop operation.

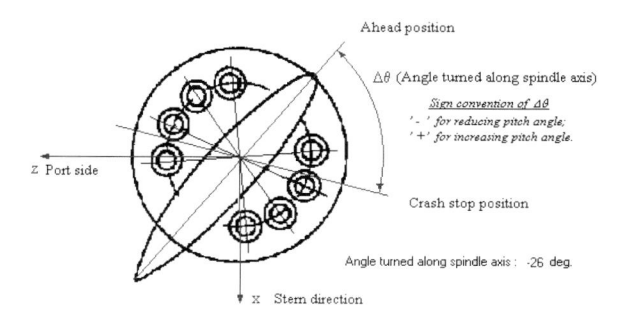

Fig. 4: Ahead vs. crash stop position

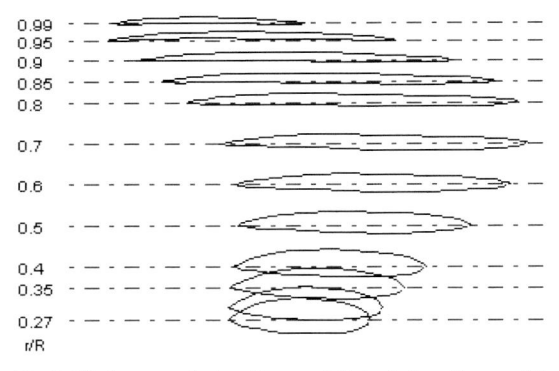

Fig 5: Blade expanded outline and distorted section profile

The pressure difference for the crash stop is plotted in Figure 6. As seen in the figure, quite a different pattern occurs as compared to the ahead condition. Basically, the highest net pressure is localized around the trailing edge at outer radius area (>0.7R). As the total backward thrust reduces compared to the ahead thrust, the maximum net pressure also shows smaller value compared to ahead condition (see the values in Table 5 and 6).

Table 6: Propeller performance and load under crash stop

Thrust	Torque	Absorbed Power	Max. pressure difference
kN	kN-m	kW	N/mm2
-297.0	537.29	6300.0	0.128

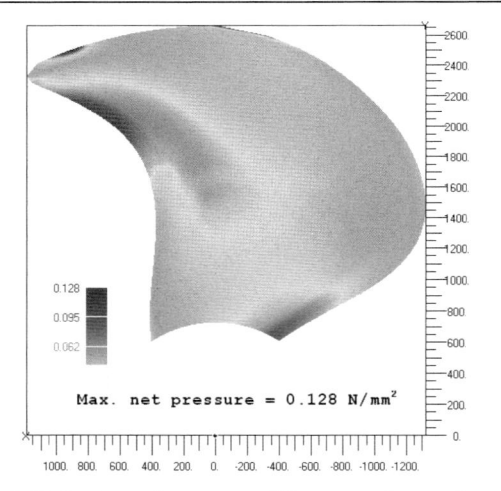

Fig. 6: Hydrodynamic pressure difference under crash-stop

Ice load

Backward and forward ice forces, F_b and F_f, are calculated based on IACS URI3 formulae mentioned earlier. Table 7 below summarizes the results of ice and hydrodynamic loads resulting in backward and forward blade bending. Also included in the table are the ice and hydrodynamic torques. For hydrodynamic loads, it should be noted that the values in the table are for the whole propeller. For each blade, dividing the loads by 4 should be done. It is found that the ice loads per blade are much higher than the hydrodynamic loads.

Table 7: Comparison of ice and hydrodynamic loads

	Forward force	Backward force	Torque
	kN	kN	kN-m
Ice load per blade	762.84	-609.68	721.51
Hydrodynamic load whole propeller	Ahead 626.35	Crash stop -297.00	Ahead 529.65 Crash stop 537.29

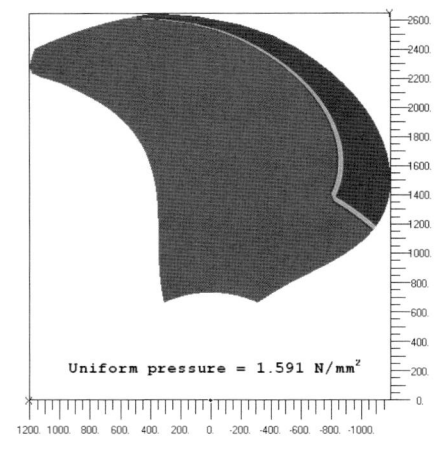

Fig. 7: Ice pressure distribution – URI3 case 1 & 3

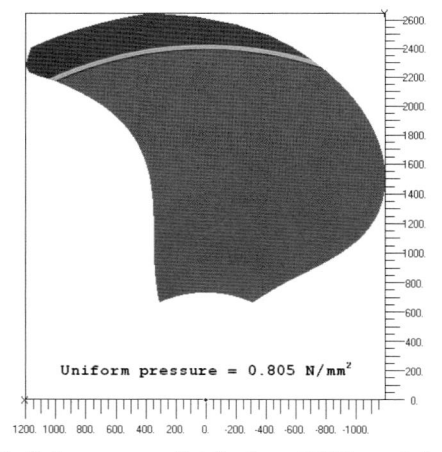

(Uniform pressure = 1.591 N/mm²)

Fig. 8: Ice pressure distribution – URI3 case 2 & 4

(Uniform pressure = 0.805 N/mm²)

For ice load cases 1 and 3 defined in URI3, the ice pressure distribution on blade (Figure 7) is more or less similar to the hydrodynamic pressure in open water ahead condition. They are both concentrated in the leading edge area, although ice pressure is much higher than hydrodynamic pressure. For ice load case 2 and 4, the ice pressures (Figure 8) are totally different from the hydrodynamic pressure distribution and will cause totally different stress distribution on blade. However, in any cases the ice load induced stresses are expected to be much higher than the hydrodynamic load induced stresses, as ice loads are much higher than hydrodynamic loads (see Table 8).

Table 8: Calculated ice loads based on URI3

```
          ice/hydro force      ice/hydro pressure
           per blade              max. value
              kN                    N/mm2
Case 1     609.684                 1.591
Case 2     304.842                 0.805
Case 3     763.230                 1.992
Case 4     381.615                 1.008
Ahead      156.588                 0.185
Crash       74.250                 0.128
```

Strength assessment

Based on the calculated ice loads, FE analyses were performed for the propeller. In this section, some experiences of propeller strength assessment are reported.

Elastic vs. plastic stress analysis

As mentioned earlier, stress criterion for blade strength is based on reference stress σ_{ref} that is beyond yielding strength. It is natural to ask what the difference between elastic and plastic FE analyses will be when ice load causes the blade stress beyond the yielding limit. To investigate this, both the elastic and plastic stress analyses are performed for the PC7 ice class propeller. The results are summarized in Table 9 and 10. Since the propeller is a CPP, load case 5 is not requested according to URI3 rule.

Table 9: Elastic stress analysis results

```
Ultimate tensile strength: 590. N/mm2
0.2% proof strength: 245. N/mm2

        Reference       Calculated        S.F.
         stress       (Von Mises)stress
-------------------------------------------------
         N/mm2           N/mm2           >=1.5
Case 1   383.000         246.120         1.556
Case 2   383.000         380.950         1.005
Case 3   383.000         283.900         1.349
Case 4   383.000         475.920         0.804
-------------------------------------------------
```

Table 10: Plastic stress analysis results

```
Ultimate tensile strength: 590. N/mm2
0.2% proof strength: 245. N/mm2

        Reference       Calculated        S.F.
         stress       (Von Mises)stress
-------------------------------------------------
         N/mm2           N/mm2           >=1.5
Case 1   383.000         245.100         1.563
Case 2   383.000         248.870         1.538
Case 3   383.000         245.440         1.560
Case 4   383.000         253.790         1.509
```

In elastic FE analyses, it is found the blade strength cannot pass the safety factor > 1.5 reference stress criterion for case 2, 3, and 4. Also, it is noted that although the case 1 pass the safety criterion, the calculated stress is already beyond the yielding limit (yielding strength = 245 N/mm^2). In plastic FE analyses (Table 10), the results show that once the stress excesses yielding limit, the increasing rate of the stress to the ice loads is largely reduced compared to elastic FE analyses. Accordingly, the final stresses for case 2, 3, and 4 are still within the reference stress criterion safety limit.

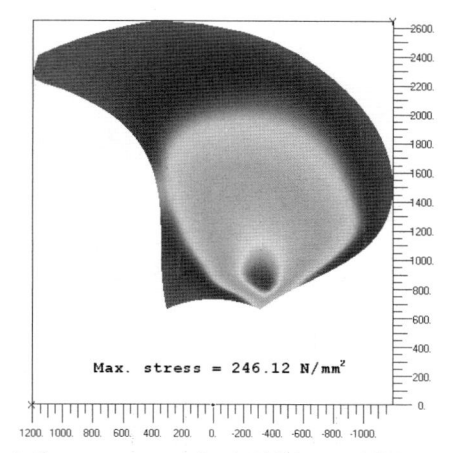

Fig. 9: Stress contour – elastic FEM, case 1 F$_b$ load

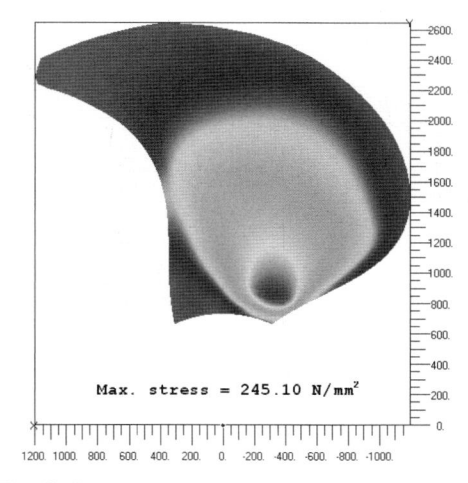

Fig. 10: Stress contour – plastic FEM, case 1 F$_b$ load

To have better idea of the stress distributions on elastic and plastic FE results, stress contours of ice load case 1 are plotted in Figure 9 and 10 for elastic and plastic FE analyses. For this case is not much far off the stress beyond the yielding limit, the stress contours in elastic and plastic analyses does not appear too much different, although it does find in plastic FE result (Figure 10) the high stress area is slightly expanded compared to the elastic FE analyses due to the material yielding.

For ice load case 2, again the stress contours are plotted in Figure 11 and 12. In this case, since the ice load causes the blade stress (380.95 N/mm² in elastic analysis) far beyond the blade yielding strength, the plastic FE analysis shows obvious difference from the elastic FE result. Basically, the high stress in plastic FE analysis is extended greatly indicating that large area is under yielding. As is well-known, once the stress passes the yielding point, the stress-strain relation will follow a material curve with less slope, and this causes the plastic stress becomes lower than the elastic stress. This is the main reason behind for plastic FE analyses come up lower stress values.

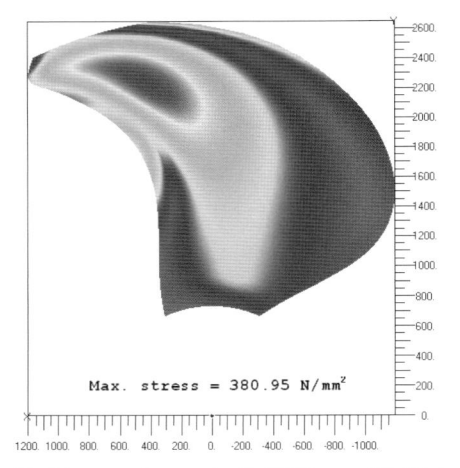

Fig. 11: Stress contour – elastic FEM, case 2 0.5F_b load

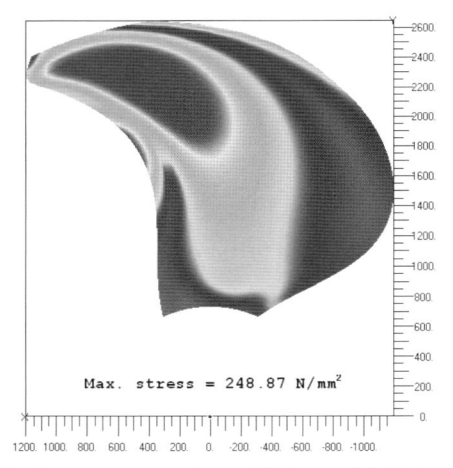

Fig. 12: Stress contour – plastic FEM, case 2 0.5F_b load

Blade edge strength

In ice operation, experience shows edge area damage is the most frequent damage on the blade. Unlike the whole blade damage caused by the pervious forward and backward ice forces, edge damage is the result of highly concentrated ice impact pressure. In IACS URI3, this is treated with a simplified model – a cantilever beam subjected to a uniform pressure load. For the convenience of later discussions and FEM comparisons, the blade edge rule formula is re-derived here. According to URI3 method, when the propeller blade hits ice block, ice impact pressure will concentrate in a small area (typical area used in URI3 is an area of 2.5% chord length by 2.5% chord length around edge). Uniform pressure p_{ice} 16 MPa is taken as the ice impact pressure in URI3. As shown in Figure 13, a cantilever beam model (with length x, thickness t and width B) is used to evaluate the stress in a narrow strip of the ice impact area. This results in the stress at x as follows:

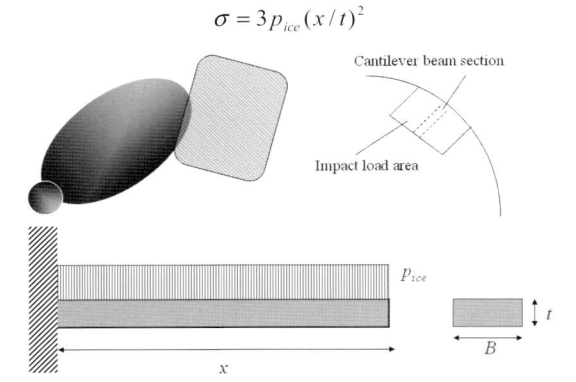

$$\sigma = 3 p_{ice} (x/t)^2$$

Fig. 13: Simple beam model for edge strength URI3 rule

Comparing the above stress formula with URI3 blade edge thickness t_{edge} formula (section I3.5.3.2 in URI3), the actual safety factor SF_σ based on stress value used in URI3 is obtained as follows:

$$SF_\sigma = \frac{c_{ref}}{3 p_{ice}(x/t_{edge})^2} = (SS_{ice})^2 / 3$$

where S = safety factor defined in URI3
= 2.5 for trailing edges
= 3.5 for leading edges
= 5 for tip

S_{ice} = ice strength index; 1. for PC6 – PC7; 1.1 for PC2-PC5; 1.2 for PC1

t_{edge} = thickness at x

p_{ice} = ice pressure; 16MPa

x = min{2.5% chord, 45mm}; for radius < 0.975R propeller radius, it is measured from edge along cylindrical sections; for radius > 0.975R propeller radius (tip area), it is measured perpendicularly from the edge

For the seven polar ice classes, the actual edge safety factors based on stress values are calculated using the above SF_σ formula and summarized as follows:

Table 11: Stress based safety factors for Polar ice class

Ice class	S_{ice}	Leading edge S = 3.5 SF_σ	Trailing edge S = 2.5	Tip S = 5.0
PC1	1.2	5.88	3.00	12.00
PC2-PC5	1.1	4.94	2.52	10.08
PC6-PC7	1.0	4.08	2.08	8.33

To evaluate the validity of simplified beam approach, FE analyses are performed for the previously selected skewed propeller. In the FE analyses a 16MPa uniform pressure with 2.5% chord by 2.5% chord loaded area is applied in a different radius from 0.5R to 0.9R around edge and mid-chord at tip. The comparisons of FE analyses and Rule calculations for edge/tip stress are summarized in the following table.

Table 12: Comparison of Rule and FE results for edge stress

Location	Leading edge FEM calculated σ N/mm2	Leading edge URI3 calculated σ N/mm2	Trailing edge FEM calculated σ N/mm2	Trailing edge URI3 calculated σ N/mm2
0.5R	18.53	36.94	52.58	138.68
0.6R	40.34	73.82	104.01	238.36
0.7R	53.56	130.44	152.91	341.80
0.8R	49.89	219.47	183.10	511.06
0.9R	45.19	314.68	489.53	1425.87
Tip*	17.65	142.32		

* Tip at mid-chord

As seen in the table, simplified beam approach tends to over-predict a lot the edge/tip stresses. The over-prediction of the stress in URI3 simplified model becomes more serious at outer radius and also the trailing edge area. It should be noted that for this CP propeller, there is no need to have this safety check for the trailing edge, although this is done here for completeness. Safety factors (σ_{ref}/σ, here σ_{ref} = 383 N/mm^2) based on FEM and simplified beam approach are calculated. Summarized in Table 13, the URI3 required safety factor for edge strength from Table 11 are also listed.

Table 13: Safety factor comparison of Rule and FE results

Location	Leading edge S.F. based on FEM σ	Leading edge S.F. based on URI3 σ > 4.08	Trailing edge S.F. based on FEM σ	Trailing edge S.F. based on URI3 σ > 2.08
0.5R	20.66	10.37	7.283	2.76
0.6R	9.49	5.19	3.68	1.61
0.7R	7.15	2.94	2.50	1.12
0.8R	7.68	1.75	2.09	0.75
0.9R	8.47	1.22	0.78	0.27
Tip*	21.70	2.69		

* S.F. > 8.33 for tip

For this PC7 ice class propeller, URI3 simplified model concludes the propeller has inadequate edge strength to sustain ice impact load. However, if the same required stress based safety factors derived from URI3 (Table 11) are used, the FEM analyses conclude the leading edge and tip are safe for 16 MPa ice impact load. For trailing edge area, FEM results predict the trailing edge could be a failure at 0.9R. This is consistent with the fact that CP propeller can be designed with weaker trailing edge strength, as no reverse rotation is needed in CPP operation. Trailing edge safety check is only requested for FP propeller in URI3.

To obtain a general picture of the ice impact induced stress, stress contours are plotted for the cases with ice load at 0.5R areas for leading and trailing edges (Figure 14 and 15). As seen, since the ice pressure is highly concentrated in a small area, the stress also shows a highly localized pattern. However, for tip load case, the highly localized stress pattern doesn't appear at tip. Instead, a relatively large area with high stress is found in the inner middle area around 0.8R (see Figure 16).

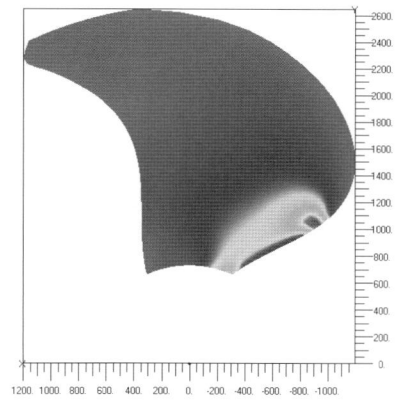

Fig. 14: Stress contour – 16MPa ice pressure at 0.5 R L.E.

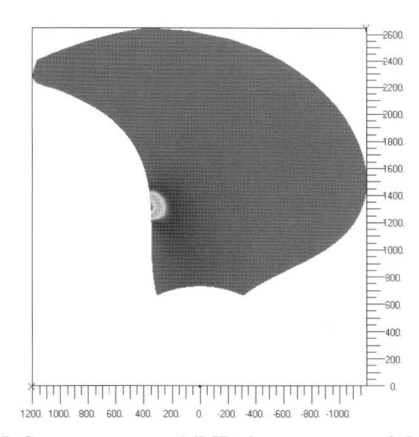

Fig. 15: Stress contour – 16MPa ice pressure at 0.5 R T.E.

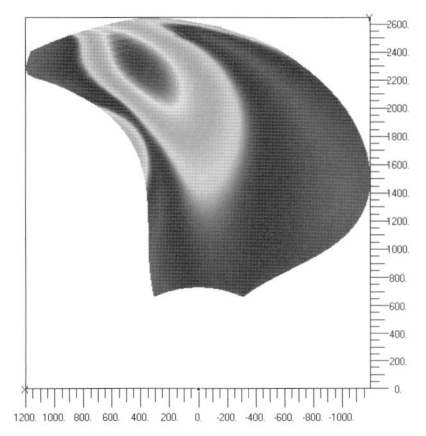

Fig. 16: Stress contour – 16MPa ice pressure at tip

To further investigate what causes stress pattern to diverge from the tip concentrated pattern for the tip concentrated load case, the original skewed blade is changed to a zero skewed blade. With the same ice load applied as before on the blade, FEM analysis is performed. The stress contours obtained are plotted in Figures 17, 18, and 19. As seen, all stress patterns are highly concentrated pattern. This concludes blade skewness is the main cause for the non-concentrated stress pattern before and the highest stress 'shifting'. This fact also implies simplified URI3 approach for edge strength assessment is not appropriate for highly skewed propeller even for the approximate location of the highest stress.

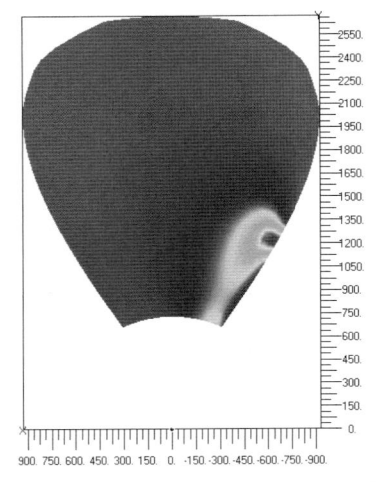

Fig. 17: Stress contour – 16MPa ice pressure at 0.5 R L.E.

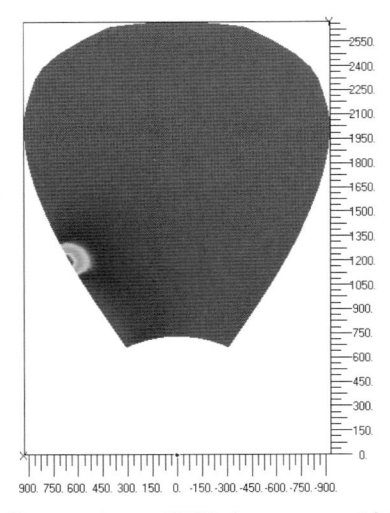

Fig. 18: Stress contour – 16MPa ice pressure at 0.5 R T.E.

Finally, to further investigate the propeller skew geometry effect on the blade edge stress due to ice impact loads, FEM analyses are performed for the zero skew propeller blades under the ice impact load (16 MPa) at different radius at leading and trailing edges. The calculated stresses are summarized in Table 14. As shown in the table, the skewness of the propeller does have significant effect on the blade edge stress. This implies although impact ice pressure is localized in a small area, its induced stress is not only affected by the local propeller geometry but also by the propeller global geometry parameter.

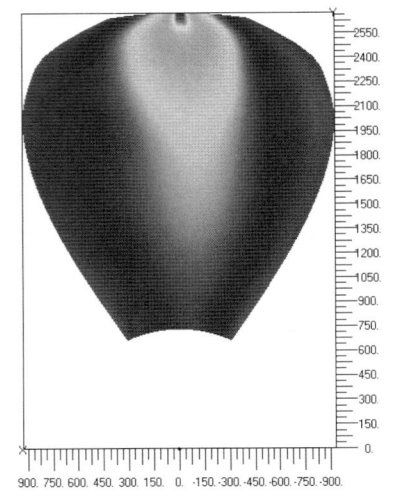

Fig. 19: Stress contour – 16MPa ice pressure at Tip

Table 14: Edge stress comparison between skewed and non-skewed propellers

Location	Leading edge FEM calculated σ N/mm2		Trailing edge FEM calculated σ N/mm2	
	Non-skewed	Skewed	Non-skewed	Skewed
0.5R	18.74	18.53	58.36	52.58
0.6R	42.56	40.34	115.18	104.01
0.7R	76.83	53.56	176.10	152.91
0.8R	104.36	49.89	212.20	183.10
0.9R	123.72	45.19	409.60	489.53

To further illustrate the stress distribution difference of the skewed and non-skewed propellers from the ice impact load, the stress contours for the case with the load applied at 0.9R are plotted in Figure 20 and 21. As seen, there is an obvious difference of the stress pattern due to the propeller skewness. For skewed propeller, the localized impact pressure has larger influence area than the non-skewed propeller.

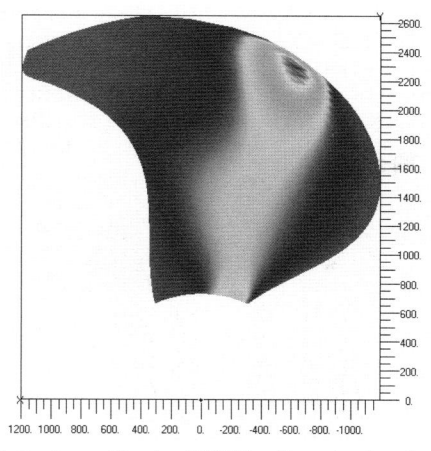

Fig. 20: Ice impact loads at 0.9R leading edge for skewed propeller

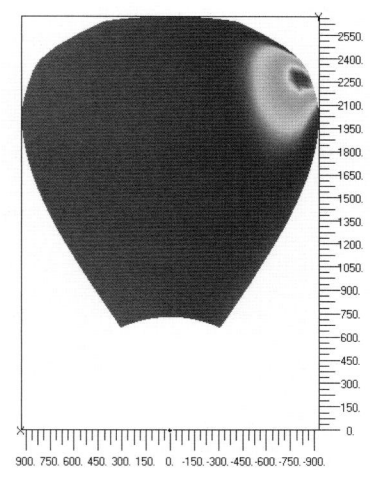

Fig. 21: Ice impact loads at 0.9R leading edge for non-skewed propeller

Concluding Remarks

In this paper, the general practice on ice propeller strength assessment based on the IACS polar ice rule – URI3 are discussed. The findings of our FE analysis practices through a PC7 ice class highly skewed CP propeller are summarized as follows:

- Compared to ice load hydrodynamic load is small. For an ice class propeller, ultimate strength of blade should be controlled by ice force. However, for fatigue failure, hydrodynamic load could still be the dominated source (although the fatigue analyses are not presented here because of the length limit of the paper, the results do show the ice induced fatigue stress is much lower than the hydrodynamic stress).

- In the viewpoint of the blade strength safety, crash-stop for the propeller concerned is not a critical operation condition. This is mainly because under the crash stop operation the propeller cannot generate a large backward force (restricted by the engine power) to endanger the blade.

- It is found the net pressure distribution on blade under normal MCR ahead operation is similar to ice load case 1 and 3 in URI3. Basically, the high pressures are localized around the leading edge area. These loads can generate not only the moment to bend the blade forward (backward also for ice load) but also the spindle torque to twist the blade. Due to the twisted torque, the maximum stress is found to be shifted to near the leading edge at the root area (see Figure 9), instead of at the mid-chord at root section as expected in conventional blade propeller.

- For ice loads, both elastic and plastic FE analyses were performed. In elastic FE analysis, it is found that the calculated stresses are beyond the yielding limit and cannot pass the reference stress criterion in URI3. As the stresses on the blade already are in plastic stress region, the stress analysis based on elastic FE may not be appropriate for this ice propeller strength assessment. By using plastic FE analyses, it is found the calculated stresses are reduced and satisfy the reference stress criterion. This result is consistent with the service experience of this propeller. In general, we tend to agree if the calculated stress is beyond yielding limit, plastic stress analysis needs to perform.

- Blade edge strength is studied by using URI3 Rule simplified calculation and FEM analysis. 16 MPa ice pressure proposed in URI3 is used in the analyses. It is found that the simplified URI3 rule calculation tends to over-predict the stress a lot compared to FEM analysis.

- In the blade edge strength study, it also finds although the ice impact pressure is localized in a small area around the load applied location, the stress is influenced by the global geometry. This is proven by the large change of stress due to the propeller skewness changing. In other words, in the edge strength assessment, the 3D effect of the blade geometry should be considered.

References

ABS (2005) "PropS2 User's Guide & Manual"
IACS (2006) "URI1 Polar Class Descriptions and Application"
IACS (2006) "URI3 Machinery Requirements for Polar Class Ships"

Structural Risk Analysis of a NO96 Membrane Type LNG Carrier in the Baltic Ice Operation

Sungkon Han[1], Jae-Yeol Lee[1], Young-Il Park[1], Jungsin Che[2]

[1] Structure R&D Team, Daewoo Shipbuilding & Marine Engineering Co., Ltd.
Koje, Kyungnam, Korea
[2] Innoqual Co. Ltd. Busan, Kyungnam, Korea

Abstract

The present study addresses results of a structural risk analysis for a 170K m^3 with Ice Class 1A for the operation from the Baltic Sea to Quebec, Canada. The target vessel is characterized by GTT NO 96 containment system for LNG cargo. Capacity of the double hull structure has been assessed considering inner hull deflection as the critical factor of the safety of the containment system. This capacity is compared with accidental ice load, as 'Demand' to the LNG carrier, from ice hazards that can take place in the Baltic Sea operation in winter or in the East Canadian Coast. Risk analysis has been performed to evaluate the risks of considered ice features in the operation route based on the study of Capacity and Demand.

Keywords

Risk analysis; Ice; Hazard; GTT NO96; LNG carrier; Ice Class IA; Ice collision.

Introduction

The objective of the present paper is to study safety of GTT NO96 Membrane Type LNG carriers in the context of the Baltic operation in winter. A DSME 170K CBM LNG carrier with Finnish Maritime Administration (FMA) Ice Class IA was used as the object of structural risk analysis. The developed vessel has a trade route from the Baltic to Quebec, Canada, which will be subjected to ice field operation and iceberg hazard.

This paper deals with risks induced only by ice hazards of the Baltic and the ice belly located near the East Canadian Coast. In the Baltic operation, FMA IA class is imposed to a vessel operating with the escort of an icebreaker. Therefore, additional hazards exist in actual operation with the escorting icebreaker. However, the present study is focused on hull-ice interactions alone in order to highlight ice operating features of membrane type LNG carriers.

Fig. 1 shows general elevation view with ice belt.

The most critical risk of LNG carriers is LNG leakage from damages of the tank boundary wall, where the cargo containment system is erected. Ice hazards will directly affect the outer hull and the hull damages extend into inner hull depending on the magnitude of applied force or energy of the considered hazards. The present structural risk analysis involves quantification of ice load, definition of critical condition of the containment system with evaluation of occurrence probability of the hazards.

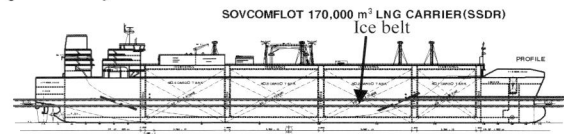

Fig. 1 Target Vessel and Ice Belt for Ice Class 1A

The quantification of ice load is termed by 'DEMAND' and the strength of the double hull is termed by 'CAPACITY' in the present work. Determination of the capacity is made with the consideration that a possible critical damage that will eventually lead to LNG leak or other significant disasters. The quantity used for the comparison between demand and capacity is strain energy.

The forebody is mainly exposed to ice interaction but it is not a unique feature of the membrane type LNG carrier. All ice-infested sea going vessels have the same risk at the forebody area; hence, the present study does not cover the forebody area. Tank No.1 can be said to be most critical area in the present context with the exception of the forebody area, ice interactions and LNG containment system.

A risk analysis form composed of four consequence levels (C1 ~ C4) and four probability levels (P1 ~ P4) has been used. Definition of the levels are given as follows:

PROBABILITIES:

P1: less than one time > 50 years
P2: 10 year < one time < 50 years
P3: 1 year < one time < 10 years
P4: several times per winter

CONSEQUENCES:
C1: minor damage to outer hull
C2: moderate damage to outer hull
C3: remarkable damage to small plastic strain at inner hull
C4: LNG leakage due to damages at inner hull or invar membrane plate

Capacity Assessment

Allowable inner hull deflection is to be determined first since the term of capacity is used to denote the energy that hull structure can absorb before LNG leakage. Regarding this limit state, general review of the GTT NO96 Containment System is made in the following subsection.

GTT NO96 Containment System

The features detailing the method of attachment of the insulation boxes to the hull are characteristics of the GTT NO96 containment system. The insulation boxes are placed on the hull boundary and fixed by four couplers at its four corners rather than being glued to the hull. The coupler base is known to provide flexibility and allowance to absorb local deflection from ballast pressure. Schematic drawings of the containment system are given in Fig. 2.

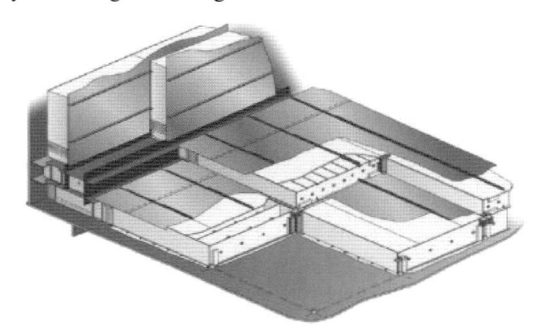

Fig. 2   Configuration of No96 Containment System - Double Barrier

The insulation boxes are covered with two layered invar membranes. This feature provides a gas-proof role to the whole cargo containment system. This invar membrane plate is welded at the transverse edge using the tongue configuration as shown in Fig. 3 and at the longitudinal end using anchoring flat bar. The welding details at the transverse and longitudinal ends are thought to be one of the critical factors governing elongation of inner hull and the membrane itself.

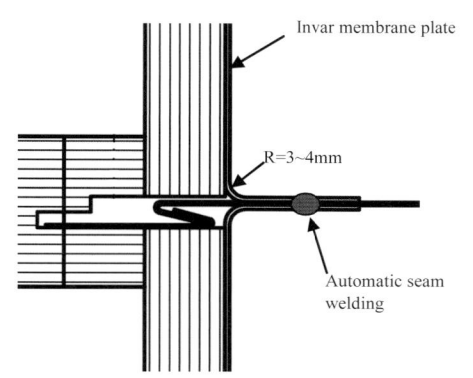

Fig. 3   Invar membrane welding at tongue

Allowable Inner Hull Deflection

Operational Limit: The operational limit of inner hull deflection for the containment system, in actual design, governs the scantling of the plates of the tank boundary. This fact explains the reason that the inner bottom plate thickness is the main target to which the operational limit is applied in actual design practices. A local fine-meshed FE model is used in design practice to calculate deflection between adjacent two longitudinal stiffeners, while the calculated deflection is being compared with the operational limit.

The operational limit is defined with the statement that a maximum 4.6mm on a 1 meter length or breadth will be accommodated by the containment system.

Much care should be taken to determine an operational limit state from ice interactions, because ice loading will mainly induce global deflection rather than local deflection at the inner hull area. In hull-ice interactions ice loads are transmitted through primary members between external and inner hulls, not applied to inner hull plates directly like ballast pressure. Therefore, it is expected that the operational limit case will not be easily violated by ice interactions due to the overall deflection feature.

Survival Limit: The worst disaster of LNG carriers will be LNG leakage through damages of the membrane barriers. The invar membrane is well known for its excellent performance in elongation. An example of mechanical properties of invar membrane is given in Table 1. The elongation limits are seen to be 35.8 ~ 42.3% depending on rolling direction and temperature.

Table 1   Mechanical properties of invar membrane from tensile test

Annealed at	23 °C		-196 °C	
Direction	Longitudinal	Transverse	Longitudinal	Transverse
Yield Stress (MPa)	377	376	720	716
Tensile Stress (MPa)	534	527	985	972
Elongation Limit (%)	36.1	35.8	42.3	41.9

However, the elongation limit cannot be used as a survival limit. The most critical factor for the functionality function of the invar regards the stresses applied at the welded joints of transverse edges and longitudinal ends at the tongue and the anchoring flat bar, respectively. The welded joint at the tongue is found to afford lager elongation than in the longitudinal direction involving the welded joints at the anchoring flat bar. This feature is from the flexibility of the geometry of the tongue as shown in Fig. 3. GTT provides the following survival limits:

Table 2 Survival limits in the longitudinal and vertical directions

	Elongation in the longitudinal direction	Elongation in the vertical direction
Survival limit	40mm/m (between fore and aft bulkheads)	55mm/m (from hopper to upper chamfer)

These survival elongation limits at side structure can be simulated using a sinusoidal deflection shape. A theoretical deflection model shows that the maximum deflection at the center of the considered hold can amount to the lateral deflection of 6,417mm for the 40mm/m longitudinal elongation limit. This magnitude of membrane deflection will not occur in real situation because the supporting hull structure will collapse before it is reached.

The criteria based on the elongation limit of the invar membrane provide a guide to a survival limit state; however, its practical application appears to be rather difficult because collapse of the hull structure is expected before the invar membrane reaches the tensile limit state. In another sense this observation can be used to vindicate the safety of No.96 containment system against ice hazards. Even though it may be premature to say there is the absolute integrity of the membrane type LNGC against the ice hazards from the Baltic Sea, the membrane containment system can be said to be sufficiently strong from the view point of the elongation limit, as long as the double hull structure is performing its supporting role without failure.

In the present study, from the practical reason, a grounding damage case is highlighted to provide a rough survival criterion without information of involved safety level. The grounding damage case of El Paso PAUL KAYSER in June 1979 is selected, which resulted in about 30cm warping of the inner hull. The invar membrane was able to accommodate without any loss of tightness in that grounding accident. Thanks to their flexibility, the membrane containment systems can withstand very sharp or important inner hull deformation without loss of tightness.

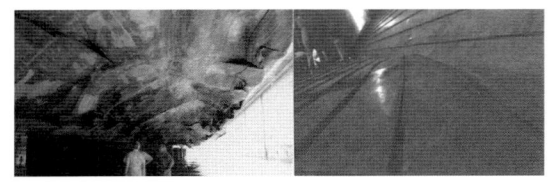

Fig. 4 Grounding near Gibraltar of El Paso Paul Kayser LNGC in June 1979 and its deformation of the invar membrane inside tank

The reported deformation should be interpreted as a permanent one rather than sum of elastic and plastic deformations. This permanent deformation can be simulated in a numerical structural analysis where geometric and material nonlinearities should be taken into account. Increasing external load is applied to the FE model up to a certain point where plastic deformation occurs and subsequently unloading is made to check permanent deformation at the state without external loading. Therefore loading and unloading iterations are required to find a target permanent deflection.

Another alternative survival limit condition can be proposed by checking integrity of tank boundary structure, in addition to the GTT-provided limit state and the reported permanent deflection from Paul Kayser LNGC. Applied stress and plastic strain of the hull structure are to be investigated carefully to check whether the tank boundary is performing its mission without damages, through which ballast water can permeate and corrupt contaminate the containment system.

The following candidates can be postulated for survival condition of the membrane type LNG carriers:

a) Tension failure of the membrane overlap welds caused by stretching when the inner hull is deformed including "A possible localized dent".

b) Failure of the membrane due to deformation of the inner hull structure based on the experience from the LNGC Paul Kayser.

c) Failure of the inner hull structure causing leakage of ballast water into the insulation space and subsequent damage to the membranes.

Design Condition

Design conditions for the evaluation of capacity and demand are defined for the operations in the Baltic Sea and Canadian East Coast. Finish-Swedish Ice Class Rules specifies 0.8m for IA and 1.0m for IA Super. The design thickness of level ice in open sea conditions, for the subject vessel with Ice Class IA, is determined as 0.8m according to the rule. However, 1.0m thick level ice is considered in the present study as conservative measures.

The Russia Maritime Register of Shipping (RMRS) rule of 8 knots is considered in order to determine the design speed in the present study. For reference FMA rule specifies a minimum speed in ice channel by 5 knots to maximize use of icebreakers.

For a special consideration, operation in Canadian east coast is also taken into account for iceberg collision scenario. The Canadian east coast is known for frequent infestation of icebergs and there is a zone called 'Iceberg Alley', considered to be the most dangerous area in terms of iceberg collision. Fig. 5 shows the location of the area of 'Iceberg Alley' and iceberg observations.

It is expected that the subject vessel may not reduce its forwarding speed and small size of icebergs have a possibility not to be detected even with iceberg detecting systems. It is widely accepted that ice features less than 2m high above sea level will not be easily detected and can be most dangerous in ice-ship collision.

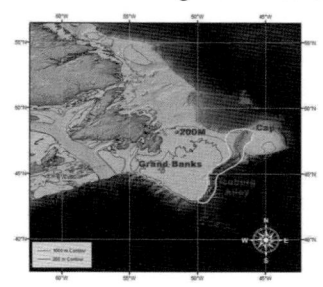

Fig. 5   **Iceberg Alley near East Canadian coast and iceberg drift observations**

Considering the factors mentioned above, the design condition for ice-ship collision is determined as follows:

a) Ice classification: Icebergy bit
b) Ice height above sea level: 2m
c) Ship speed: 19.5 knots (forward) with various incident angles

Capacity Calculation

The membrane LNG carriers have a double hull structure, in which cargo tanks are protected by outer hull. Ice hazard sources have interactions with the outer hull and the applied loading or energy transmits through longitudinal stiffeners and transverse web frames to the inner hull.

To calculate capacity, pressure load is applied to a certain area of outer hull and increased to a significant level in inner hull deflection. Absorbed energy in the hull structure is investigated as the function of inner hull deflection, since the safety of inner hull is of main concern in the present context. The loaded areas are determined by ice hazard types – such as level ice, ice ridge, ice floe collision, ice stuck and icebergy bit collision. The size of ice features and contact areas are determined in postulated scenarios and these data are used to determine the load areas.

Tank No.1 and Cofferdam BHD (Transverse Bulkhead between Tank Nos. 1 and 2) are the main target area. In ice stuck scenario, the area from the center of Tank No.1 to the center of Tank No.3 is investigated. The loaded area varies vertically at design draft and ballast draft, and bilge and bottom areas are also considered for the ice floe collision scenario.

Calculation is made using MSC.DYTRAN, which is a general-purpose, three-dimensional explicit finite element analysis software program. The capacity assessment involves geometric and material nonlinearities because it deals with plasticity and large displacement. Ice features are idealized as rigid body to exert pressure on the hull in the capacity assessment.

Various ice features have been investigated with the information of hull location and contact area. Table 3 shows details of capacity calculation for various ice features.

Table 3 Specification of capacity assessment

Ice hazard	Longitudinal location	Draft level	Contact area ($w \times h$)[+]
Level ice collision	Tank No.1 / Cofferdam BHD No.2[‡]	design / ballast	6.72m x 1.0m
Ice ridge collision	Tank No.1 / Cofferdam BHD No.2	design	6.72m x 6.5m
Ice floe collision	Tank No.1 / Cofferdam BHD No.2	bilge / bottom	6.72m x 1.0m
Icebergy bit collision	Tank No.1 / Cofferdam BHD No.2	design	6.72m x 6.5m
Ice stuck in level ice	The middle of Tank No.1 to the middle of Tank No.3	design	100m x 1.0m

Note: [‡] - T. BHD between Tank Nos.1 and 2
    [+] - w: width, h: height

Level ice and ice ridge are estimated to have possibility to interact at fore part during the turning of the vessel following an icebreaker in a narrow and sharply curved ice channel. In the present study Tank No.1 and Cofferdam BHD No.2 are the main targets on which safety assessments are made. Level ice contact is made at design and ballast drafts; ice ridge contact is made at design draft. Capacity calculation for icebergy bit collision is estimated to be similar to ice ridge collision since the same location and contact area are postulated. This fact is true only for capacity calculation and separate evaluation should be performed in demand assessment.

Pressure loading is applied incrementally to the predefined contact area until a maximum deflection of inner hull becomes 1.0m. The internal energy stored in the hull structure for the considered ice features are given graphically in Fig. 6 thru Fig. 7. Energy storing capacity can be compared between the middle of Tank No.1 and Cofferdam BHD No.2. At initial stage with small hull deflection, the bulkhead area shows significantly high capacity for most ice contact conditions. This observation supports common understanding that T.BHD area is stiff and can afford higher external loading than the middle part of tank. It is to be noted in Fig. 7 that the strain energy curve of the Ice stuck condition is plotted against inner hull displacement at the amidships area rather than T.BHD.

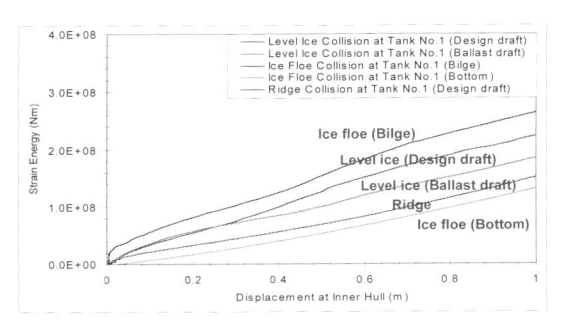

Fig. 6 Strain energy – inner hull displacement curve as capacity at Tank No.1

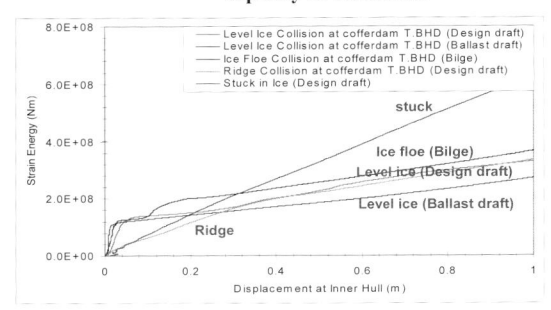

Fig. 7 Strain energy – inner hull displacement curve at Cofferdam BHD No.2 and for the case of ice stuck

It is observed from the deflection contours shown in Fig. 8 that deflection changes in the vertical direction more rapidly than in the longitudinal direction. Therefore elongation of the invar is checked in the vertical direction. Fig. 9 shows the deflection of inner hull (No.1 Tank) at 40cm-deflection-load step of the level ice contact.

a) Deflection contour   b) Plastic strain

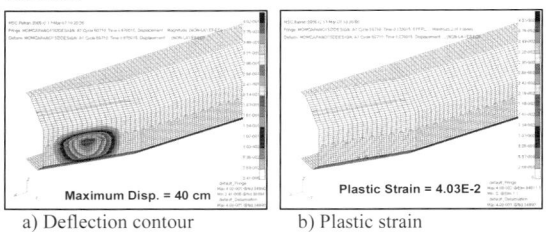

Fig. 8 Deflection contour of inner hull (No.1 Tank) at 40cm-deflection-load step of level ice contact

The boxed area shows the most rapid changes in deflection and the elongation of invar membrane is calculated as 1.89mm/1m, which is very low compared to the survival limit (55mm/m) in the vertical direction

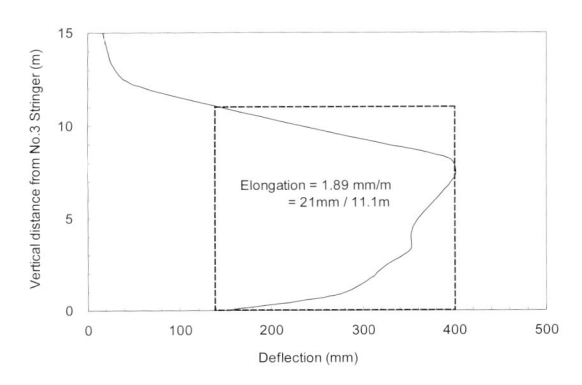

Fig. 9 Deflection of inner hull (No.1 Tank) at 40cm-deflection-load step of the level ice contact

The integrity of the hull should also be checked. It is found from the results that the plastic strains at 40cm and 70cm-deflection-load steps of the level ice collision are 4% or 6% acceptable even in the sense of hull integrity.

The example of Paul Kayser LNGC can be investigated using these calculations and observations. A calculation involving unloading of applied pressure shows that the amount of the spring-back deflection is about 10 cm for the deflection at the inner hull. Therefore the total deflection of 40cmm at the inner hull can be said to induce about 30cmm of permanent deflection at the inner hull. It can be said from the plastic strain given in Fig. 8 that the inner hull was in intact condition as well as invar membrane structure.

The following conclusion can be drawn from the above investigation of the application of three criteria as a survival limit condition:

a) The invar membrane can afford very large inner hull deflection before the survival criteria given in Table 2.
b) The integrity of inner hull structure is to be checked before the invar limit condition since any damage to the hull will lead to leakage of ballast water into the containment layer.
c) Determination of a survival condition based on the grounding accident case of Paul Kayser LNGC will lead to a very conservative limit.

In the present study 70cm of inner hull deflection is selected as a survival condition, considering the above aspects. Uncertainties coming from material properties, ice-loading scenarios, the adopted methodology, etc can be compensated by the conservatism practiced in this decision.

Demand Evaluation

The shape of a target structure and involved failure modes significantly affect ice loads. In simple terms, ice will fail in bending on sloping structures, in crushing on narrow vertical structures, and sometimes in mixed mode failures against wide structures. The ability to predict ice loads requires that these failure modes be understood and can be predicted as a function of ice feature geometry, ice type and structure shape and stiffness. The load magnitudes are also a function of the ice strength at the appropriate ice temperature, salinity, strain rate and size of failure zone; as well as other factors such as friction and clearing processes.

There are three basic mechanisms by which ice loads can be exerted on a structure:

a) limit stress: the maximum load for an event is governed by the failure of the ice immediately adjacent to the structure
b) limit energy: the maximum load for an event is limited by the kinetic energy of the impacting feature
c) limit force: the maximum load for an event is limited by force applied by or to the ice feature

All these mechanisms can interact simultaneously to produce the maximum load associated with a particular event. It is observed that ice failure is a complex process that can involve crushing, fracture, lifting, and rotation of the impacting ice features. In nature, the ice inhomogeneities, flaws, finite feature size, etc., are all integrated into the loading process.

In the present study, the limit stress and the limit energy mechanisms are applied depending on ice hazard types and analysis methodology. The limit stress mechanism can be dealt with using controlled applied pressure loading because it involves design ice crushing pressure as a function of ice contact area. The limit energy mechanism should be dealt with using a numerical tool to simulate the energy transmitted to the hull structure by a colliding ice feature with initial speed, where complexity of ice mechanical properties is to be idealized considering practicability, design conservatism and affordability by used software.

Ice Crushing Pressure

Ice failure by crushing usually occurs while moving ice hits against a vertical structure and fails mainly under compressive stresses. Ice cover can also fail by buckling in case of wide structures.

Ice fails in crushing in a multi-axial state of stress that is too complicated to be accurately used in a design code. Therefore, ice-crushing strength is adopted as reference strength. It has a complicated relation to uniaxial ice compressive strength that can be measured. Crushing strength is dependent on the geometry of ice-structure interaction, ice thickness, loading rate, size, etc.

In the present work, two approaches have been adopted for definition of ice crushing strength. For the application of limit stress mechanism, where pressure loading is applied to the FE model in order to represent ice interaction to the hull in scenarios such as ice collision and ice stuck, pressure-area relationship is used to define ice crushing pressure because scale effect significantly affects ice load.

Ice features, however, are directly idealized by FE elements in the application of limit energy mechanism. In this case modeled ice features – icebergy bit, level ice, ice ridge and ice floe – are moving toward to the hull structure with a particular design speed. In this case, the collapse mechanism of each ice features is to be carefully implemented to define yield condition of ice models. As previously noted, ice mechanical properties are complex phenomenon and one of the most important design factors is its dependency on strain rate. In general ice-operating ships can be assumed in a moving speed and brittle collapse will be involved in most situations.

Fig. 10 shows an example of compress strength as a function of strain rate. Transition from ductile to brittle modes takes place at strain rate of 10^{-3} s^{-1}. Ice-ship interaction is known to involve the strain rate of 10^{-2} s^{-1} or larger value. Brittle behavior is characterized by its decreasing failure stress as loading speed becomes higher. The present study adopts compressive strength at strain rate of 5×10^{-3} s^{-1} using the curve given in Fig. 10 and used it to idealize ice feature FE model in the application of limit energy mechanism.

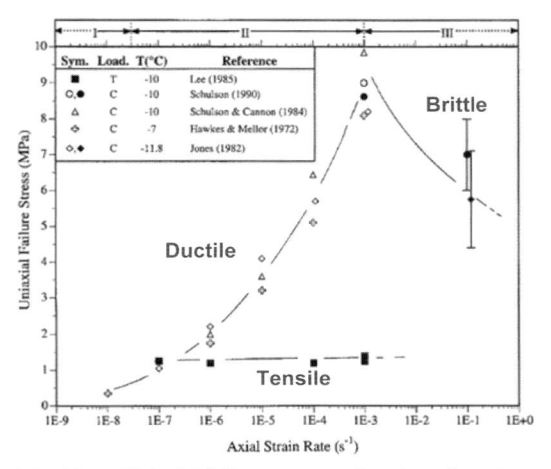

Fig. 10 Uniaxial failure stress as function of strain rate (Erland M. Schulson, 1999)

In the application of limit stress mechanism, crushing strength is applied to the ice contact area projection in the direction of ice movement. The ice load on the hull structure is given in the simple way: $F = p_e A$, where p_e is the effective ice crushing pressure and A is the nominal contact area. The ice crushing pressure is determined in many ways and many ice codes provide details with a large dispersal. The present study adopts the guide by Canadian Standard Association (CSA) in CSA S471-04, 2005. Masterson and Spencer have derived the crushing pressure as a function of contact area based on experimental database. The ice crushing pressure is determined by $p_e = C_p A^{D_p}$, where C_p is a ice coefficient and D_p is a negative exponent.

Masterson and Frederking (CSA, 2005) extracted a design curve with two-standard deviation of the measured data. Based on their work, CSA S471-04 specifies the coefficient C_p and exponent D_p as a function of the nominal contact area and geometrical region. The coefficients are given in Table 4.

Table 4 Ice pressure coefficients for low aspect ratios ($W/h < 10$): W- width, h- thickness

Nominal contact area	C_p	D_p
$A \leq 0.1$ m^2	26.9	0
0.1 m$^2 < A \leq 30$ m^2	8.5	-0.5
30 m$^2 \leq A$	2.7	-0.165

Note: The coefficients are for Zone I of Canadian waters, which has a number of freezing-degree days annually of temperature of 3000 to 4000 °C-days. The data used to derive the coefficients were based primarily on multi-year sea ice data from Zone I. See CSA S471-04, E.6.2.2 for more details about the Zone I.

A large degree of uncertainty lies in the mechanical properties of ice ridge, of which the conceptual structure is plotted in Fig. 11. Ice ridge, therefore, needs to be idealized considering various observation reports.

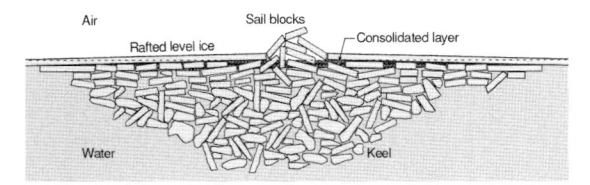

Fig. 11   Principal cross section of an ice ridge (Jensen et al., 2001)

The depth of design contact area is 6.5 m, which is assumed to consist of sail, consolidated layer and keel as shown in Fig. 11. Sail blocks are observed to contain a large amount of cavity – filled with snow and air, which inevitably reduces its strength to a great extent. A number of researches have been done regarding the strength of the consolidated layer, where ice blocks freeze together with the level ice or with rafted ice layers, revealing that the strength decreases by 30% to 64% with spherical voids or irregular voids respectively (Rogachko et al., 1997). Cavities in the rubble of the keel are filled with water and slush. The failure mechanism of the keel is represented by cohesive-frictional material behavior describing its shear strength. From a few number of full-scale tests for pressure mechanical properties providing reliable results, the maximum strength of the keel was found to be 12.8 kPa and the average 8.5 kPa (Timco et al., 2000).

These strength details depending on layers are idealized with simplification. The strength of the sail can be almost negligible due to its cavity filled with snow and air; the consolidated layer should be fully appreciated in its strength; and the strength of the keel is also expected to be insignificant compared to the consolidated layer. Considering all of this data, the present study adopted 50% of the strength of level ice, which is determined from the pressure-area curve proposed by the CSA requirement. Hence half of 1.5MPa (=0.75MPa) is used as the design crushing pressure for ice ridge collision in the application of limit stress mechanism.

Calculation of Demand in the Baltic Operation

Winter operation in the Baltic has ice hazards from ice channels or ice ridge near shores or ports. Level ice, ice ridge, small ice floe, and ice stuck have been studied in terms of 'Demand', which is the energy exerted on the hull structure.

Calculation of energy induced by ice features involves dynamic loading. The application of limit energy mechanism is carried out with moving ice features; therefore, no difficulty arises in the calculation of exerted energy on the hull.

The application of limit stress mechanism, which uses the ice crushing pressure, seems to indirectly involve dynamic loading; however, the background of the CSR pressure-area curve provides justification on the scheme involving dynamic feature. The crushing pressure data given in Table 4 was obtained from field measurements carried out in dynamic condition. Full-scale ice breaking ships were deployed to perform the tests, from which the measure data was obtained. This means that the pressure value given by Table 4 intrinsically involves the dynamic feature. This understanding can justify that design pressure load is applied incrementally within a short time to the hull, causing kinetic energy induced in the load hull. This load application scheme can be easily implemented using commercial software and for this purpose ABAQUS has been used.

Application of Limit Stress Mechanism: Strain energy that the hull absorbs until the hull-ice interaction pressure reaches the ice crushing pressure level can be used as an indicator to 'Demand' of a considered ice hazard. The calculation of the strain energy of the hull should take into account material nonlinearity of steel and the loaded area, which is the same concept used in the calculation of 'Capacity'.

This methodology needs to be justified in order that it can be applied to the case of ship in compressive ice – in other word, ice stuck condition. Ice stuck conditions should be simulated carefully considering given trade routes. In Arctic zones, the vessel should survive considerably long period in ice stuck. However, in the Baltic Sea the requirement can be mitigated in terms of ice stuck duration. An icebreaker should be accompanied by the subject vessel in the considered design ice condition (1m thick ice is considered in this report). When the situation of ice stuck takes place, the leading icebreaker will be used to break surrounding ice for escape and ice load will be exerted on the hull at the instance of ice breaking. The ice collapse mode in this escape practice will include buckling, bending and crushing of the surrounding ice field and the collapse load is estimated to be less than normal ice crushing pressure. Ice bending and buckling occurs at load level less than ice crushing pressure.

Therefore, the use of the ice crushing pressure to calculate 'Demand' for ice stuck hazard is justified in two senses. One is from the expectation that the vessel will not be stuck in ice for long time; the other from the normal practice that the icebreaker will be used to break the surrounding ice which will involve, as collapse mode, bending, buckling and ice crushing. It can be said therefore that the application of ice crushing pressure to the ice stuck in the Baltic Sea operation yields a conservative result.

Ice contact area is determined according to hazard scenarios as in the capacity calculation. Strain energies are calculated using nonlinear elasto-plastic analysis by ABAQUS for each ice hazard. Pressure load is applied incrementally up to Ice Load (p_e) and any plasticity involved in the hull structure is investigated. Strain energies stored in the structure are calculated at the final stage of loading (p_e). Pressure loading to the contact areas are increased up to p_e within a short time and then unloaded to zero. This loading speed is adequately treated in the numerical analysis so as not to involve any strength increase from the dependency of steel material on strain rate. The only comparison to be made of strain energy is between 'Capacity' and 'Demand'. As demand, strain energies of each hazard scenario are given in Table 5 with detailed calculation conditions and maximum deflection at inner hull.

Table 5 Calculation conditions and strain energy as 'Demand' with deflection information for various ice hazards at design draft

Target	Hazard type	‡p_e (MPa)	Demand: Max. Strain Energy (MJ) Total	Elastic	Plastic	Max. deflection at Inner hull (mm)
Tank No.1	Level ice	3.28	1.505	0.998	0.512	15.37
	Ice ridge	0.75	0.283	0.270	0.020	12.96
Tank No.2	Level ice	3.28	1.667	0.478	1.180	16.86
	Ice ridge	0.75	0.373	0.331	0.043	19.38
Tank No.1-3	Ice stuck	1.5	1.707	1.400	0.303	15.03
Coff. BHD No.2	Level ice	3.28	1.829	0.410	1.411	4.94
	Ice ridge	0.75	0.143	0.111	0.031	3.704

Note: ‡: Ice crushing pressure is determined by Table 4.

The calculated demand – strain energy absorbed in the hull structure – is to be interpreted in line with maximum deflection at inner hull that can be used as one of indicators to the consequence level in the risk form. The severity of resultant deflection can be checked using the case of ice ridge at Tank No.2 giving 19.38mm at inner hull. The operational limit of inner hull deflection considering integrity of NO96 containment system is given by 4.6mm/m. The lateral deflection plotted in Fig. 12 proves that the inner hull with maximum lateral deflection of 0.23mm/m remains intact under the most critical hazard – ice ridge at Tank No.2 - in the sense of the operability of the containment system.

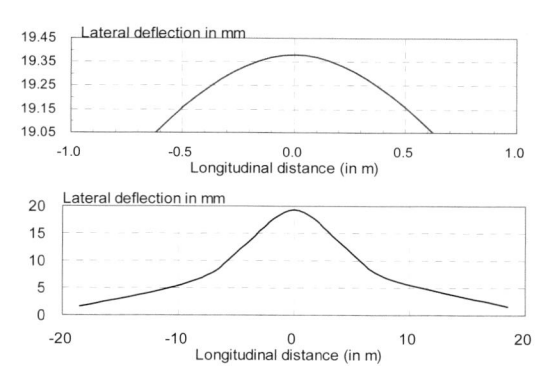

Fig. 12 Maximum deflection along ship length to check the operational limit (4.6mm/m)

The integrity of outer hull can also be confirmed using the case of ice ridge collision to Tank Nos.1 and 2. Applied stress at the instance of maximum pressure is found to be below 200MPa, which is not high enough to make a hole at the outer hull

Application of Limit Energy Mechanism: Hull-ice interactions have been simulated using a numerical analysis tool, MSC.DYTRAN an explicit solver mainly for collision. Ice features are idealized into the FE model with appropriate failure conditions. Modeled ice features are set to move into the hull and its kinetic energy is transmitted to the hull structure. The hull absorbs the external energy by deforming itself. All these complicated processes are simulated in numerical analysis.

Table 6 Strain energy as 'Demand' with deflection information for various ice hazards

Hazard type	Draft	Colliding location[1]	Internal Energy[2] [J]	Inner hull Stress[3] [MPa]	Disp.[4] [mm]
Level ice	Design[5]	Tank[6]	8.98E5	108	5.2
		T.BHD[7]	3.91E5	37	2.8
Ice floe	Bilge	Tank	3.51E3	16	1.1
		T.BHD	1.05E4	16	0.9
	Bottom	Tank	5.86E4	72	7.4
Ice Ridge	Design	Tank	1.26E6	101	6.8
		T.BHD	1.02E6	38	4.9
Stuck in ice	Design		1.50E6	98	8.2

1 Initial contact location
2 Internal energy of LNGC
3 Maximum stress
4 Total displacement of elasticity and plasticity
5 Design draft
6 Tank No.1
7 Cofferdam BHD No.2

The Baltic Sea involves collision with ice floes, ice ridge, and level ice. Special considerations are made for ice ridge and ice stuck conditions regarding the failure definition. Ice ridge is characterized by its complex composition – sail, consolidated layer, and keel – and low shear strength. By giving initial speed to the ice field surrounding the hull, even the condition of ice stuck may be simulated. Ice stuck condition is characterized by the escape methodology in which a convoying icebreaker navigates around the stuck vessel to break the ice field. In this escape practice dynamic load is applied to the surrounding ice field from the ice break and ice failure occurs in bending and buckling modes by being compressed between the icebreaker and stuck vessel.

Application of the limit energy mechanism has been carried out to level ice, ice ridge, small ice floes and ice stuck condition. Failure criteria for compression and tension are imposed to the level ice and small ice floes. Shear yield criteria is additionally imposed to ice ridge collision according to details given by Jaakko Heinonen (2004). Especially in the simulation of ice stuck condition, the characteristic length is used in ice modeling to allow bending failure to occur at the joints of each level ice block.

The results of these simulations are summarized in Table 6 listing internal energy as 'Demand' and the maximum applied stress and displacement at inner hull. The stress level and displacement levels are found to fall below the allowable levels such as yield stress and operational deflection limit. The maximum deflection levels at inner hull shown in Table 6 are found to be small, even compared to the application example in Fig. 12, where 19.38mm deflection at inner hull is only corresponding to 0.23mm/m. The maximum deflection calculated using the limit energy mechanism is found to be less than those of the limit stress mechanism.

Calculation of Demand in the Canadian East Coast Operation

A special consideration should be made regarding iceberg collision since the target vessel has been developed for the Baltic to Quebec, Canada. DNV (2006) has carried out a risk analysis for LNG carriers trading near the Iceberg Belly and specified the most dangerous ice size in the context of collision to ships. It concluded that ice features of 2m high above water line would not be easily detected by deployed ice monitoring systems of ships and should be fully investigated with the possibility of collision to ships voyaging in their full speed.

The calculation of demand from iceberg, hereafter referred to as *icebergy bits*, is used considering its size and ice nomenclature practices – has been made in collision simulation using MSC.DYTRAN. Icebergy bits are idealized into FE model and postulated to move into ship in a combined speed with ship and tide.

Collision Scenario: Various sizes and shapes of icebergy bits have been investigated based on the DNV suggestion (DNV, 2006) and the hull form of the target vessel. Fig. 13 shows the considered icebergy bit shapes and size.

Cubic, conical and spherical type icebergy bits are selected from pure geometrical consideration and bell types are devised to maximize the contact area between ice and the ship's side.

Two locations, middle of Tank No.1 and Cofferdam BHD No.2, have been investigated in the collision scenario. The attack angle of icebergy bits is determined considering hull form shape, vessel speed and tide. Icebergy bits are postulated to move toward to the ship in 19.5 knots with the attack angle of $15°$ to the ship longitudinal direction. The attack angle of $15°$ corresponds to tide in 2.6m/s to the normal direction to the ship.

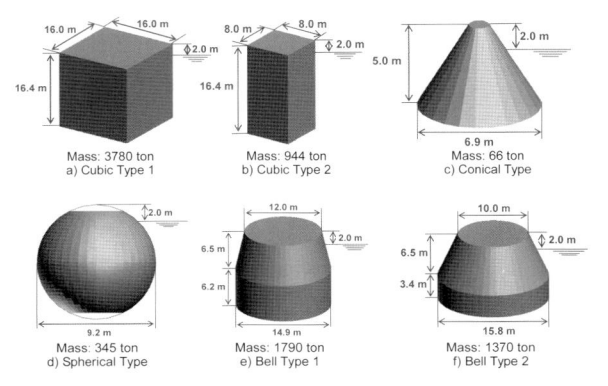

Fig. 13 Icebergy bit shapes and sizes used for the collision simulation

Demand Summary from Collision Scenario: Demand is defined by the maximum strain energy absorbed in the struck ship and the calculated details are summarized in Table 7 and Table 8 for the collision at Tank No.1 and Cofferdam BHD No.2, respectively. The shape of icebergy bits is found to have a significant effect on absorbed energy. Bell Type 1 is observed to impose the maximum energy (Demand), among the considered different shapes, to the hull. Even though Cubic Type 1 has the maximum in the initial kinetic energy due to its heavy weight, the contact with the struck ship is not made as well as Bell Type 1. Bell type icebergy bits have a large absorption rate (definition is given in Table 7) compared to other shapes since it has a good contact with the hull side shell.

Table 7 Strain energy as 'Demand' of Icebergy bit collision at Tank No.1

Icebergy Bit Collision		Initial Kinetic Energy of Ice [Nm]	Struck ship (LNGC) Strain Energy: [Nm]	Kinetic Energy [Nm]	Absorption rate[+]
Cubic	Type 1	1.90E+8	8.40E+6	1.34E+6	*4.4%*
	Type 2	4.74E+7	1.63E+6	7.66E+5	*3.4%*
Conical		3.31E+6	9.71E+4	8.27E+4	*2.9%*
Spherical		1.73E+7	8.66E+5	3.56E+5	*5.0%*
Bell	Type 1	8.99E+7	1.51E+7	6.12E+5	*16.8%*
	Type 2	6.89E+7	7.53E+6	8.86E+5	*10.9%*

Note-[+] : (LNGC strain energy) / (Ice Initial Kinetic Energy)

Table 8 Strain energy as 'Demand' of Icebergy bit collision at Cofferdam BHD No.2

Icebergy Bit Collision		Initial Kinetic Energy of Ice [Nm]	Struck ship (LNGC) Strain Energy: [Nm]	Kinetic Energy [Nm]	Absorption rate[+]
Cubic	Type 1	1.90E+8	6.77E+6	1.41E+6	3.6%
	Type 2	4.74E+7	1.55E+6	7.45E+5	3.3%
Conical		3.31E+6	8.47E+4	6.77E+4	2.4%
Spherical		1.73E+7	7.96E+5	2.16E+5	4.6%
Bell	Type 1	8.99E+7	1.02E+7	3.56E+5	11.4%
	Type 2	6.89E+7	4.66E+6	6.03E+5	6.8%

Table 9 summarizes the effects of the collision events on the hull structures. Bell Type 1 to Tank No.1 is found to induce the highest stress at side shell and web frames. It is estimated from these results that damage, if any, will take place confined to outer hull and transverse web frames. The integrity of the inner hull can be checked from the applied maximum stress and displacement. Applied stress level is found to be low compared to the design criteria and deflection at the inner hull is within the operational limit defined for the containment system operability.

Table 9 Maximum responses in icebergy bit collision at Tank No.1 (unit: MPa, mm)

Icebergy Bit Collision		Side shell Max. Stress	Plastic strain	Web frames Max. Stress	Plastic strain	Inner hull Max. Stress	Max. Disp.
Cubic	1	237	0.011	253	0.027	89	6.0
	2	237	0.003	239	0.007	61	4.2
Conical		136	-	142	-	18	1.6
Spherical		237	0.002	236	0.008	36	2.5
Bell	1	248	0.026	356	0.15	92	8.8
	2	241	0.015	289	0.088	85	8.0

Results

Summary of Capacity

The survival criterion of GTT NO96 containment system is defined as the state where inner hull deflection is 70cm. This limit condition is determined from the following three aspects:

a) GTT-provided limit state of the invar membrane
b) Limit state by the deformation from the grounding accident of Paul Kayser LNGC
c) Limit state of the hull structure as tank boundary

Capacity of the subject vessel is defined as internal strain energy that the hull structure absorbs until the critical limit. Ice collision location and area are to be predefined in order to calculate the capacity using an FE model, where incremental loading is applied until the limit state. Therefore the capacity of the hull structure should be defined as function of contact location and area.

Table 10 Summary of Capacity of the subject vessel against ice hazards

Hazard type	Draft	Colliding location	Capacity[+] (MJ)
Level ice	Design	Tank No.1	171.43
		Coff. BHD No.2	279.32
	Ballast	Tank No.1	136.84
		Coff. BHD No.2	215.56
Ice Ridge	Design	Tank No.1	98.50
		Coff. BHD No.2	267.17
Ice floe	Bilge	Tank No.1	209.02
		Coff. BHD No.2	299.05
	Bottom	Tank No.1	82.71
Icebergy Bit	Design	Tank No.1	98.50
		Coff. BHD No.2	267.17
Stuck in ice		Design	452.37

Note - [+]: Energy at 70cm inner deflection is read from Fig. 6 and Fig. 7.

Summary of Demand

Demand is defined, in the present study, as internal strain energy that the hull structure will absorb under interactions with ice features. The interaction types are classified into the following categories:

a) Limit stress mechanism
b) Limit energy mechanism

The limit stress mechanism defines ice load by pressure applied at the instance when ice collapse with a particular or combined failure mode. Similar to the scheme used in the capacity calculation, pressure load is incrementally applied to predefined contact area within a short time and the energy stored until after the design pressure is reached becomes 'Demand'. The failure mode is assumed to be mainly ice crushing pressure. The ice crushing pressure is given as a function of nominal contact area and CSA S-471-04 is used to determine the crushing pressure. The demand calculation has been performed, using ABAQUS, in a nonlinear elasto-plastic analysis considering plasticity occurred inside the hull structure.

The limit energy mechanism is rather straightforward compared to the limit stress mechanism. Considered ice features are idealized into FE model with relevant limit conditions and the ice models are set moving toward to the hull FE model with an initial speed. The kinetic energy of the ice models is transmitted to hull structure and some part of the kinetic energy is stored in the hull as the form of strain and kinetic energies. The strain energy stored in the hull structure is used as 'Demand'. MSC/DYTRAN is used as a numerical tool.

Comparison between Capacity and Demand

Simple comparison of Capacity and Demand given by Table 5 thru Table 10 gives an idea on how much safer the subject vessel will be in the proposed operational conditions.

The demands from level ice and ice floe collision are found to be very small. It seems that a direct comparison with the capacity in Table 10 is not necessary. From the fact that ice regulations require the outer hull to be designed against loads from commonly encountered ice hazards, these demands from level ice contact and ice floe collision can be considered to be operational requirement rather than accidental load. It can be said from the present study results that the membrane type LNG carriers have sufficient strength resulting in deflection response within the operation limit against the working loads from the commonly encountered ice hazards in the Baltic Sea winter operation.

Structural Risk Assessment

A simple risk analysis form has been used, where occurrence level appears vertically from rare to occasional frequency. Consequence levels are defined considering the severity of impact on the LNG containment system. LNG leak is grouped to C4 as a catastrophe and minor damage to outer shell to C1 acceptable on the maintenance basis.

The following details are proposed to fill out the risk analysis form:

PROBABILITIES:
P1:
P2: ice stuck (the Baltic Sea), icebergy bit collision (Canadian East Coast)
P3: ice ridge contact (the Baltic Sea)
P4: level ice contact, ice floe collision (the Baltic Sea)

CONSEQUENCES:
C1: Scratches or minor dents at outer shell
C2: Small dents at outer shell
C3: Small plastic strain at inner hull
C4: Leak due to damages at inner hull or invar membrane plate

Application of the guides for consequences to the demands given in the preceding subsection can lead to the following clarification:

a) The level ice and ice floe collisions with low energy demand can be said to correspond to Consequence C1;
b) In the same sense, the ice ridge collision and ice stuck can be Consequence C1;
c) The icebergy bit collision can be said to cause damages at transverse web frame corresponding to Consequence C2.

Conclusion

The main objective of the present study is to evaluate structural integrity of a 170K m³ LNG Carrier with Ice Class IA for the Baltic Sea Winter Operation and the trading route between the Baltic Sea and Quebec, Canada. The study has been carried out through the following steps:

a) to investigate collapse modes of GTT NO96 containment system (Limit state)
b) to assess the capacity of a membrane type LNG carrier (Capacity)
c) to quantify risks from the Baltic Sea operation (Demand)
d) to quantify risks from the Canadian East Coast operation (Demand)
e) to compare the capacity with the demand for the proposed ice hazards
f) to carry out structural risk analysis

Table 11 Risk Analysis Form for membrane type LNG Carrier from the Baltic Sea Operation

		CONSEQUENCES			
PROBABILITY	P4	Level ice contact Ice floe collision			High risk
	P3	Ice ridge contact			
	P2	Ice stuck	Icebergy bit collision		
	P1	Low risk			
		C1	C2	C3	C4
		Minor	Moderate	Remarkable	Catastrophic
Hull		Minor damage to outer hull	Small damage to outer hull	Small damage to inner hull	Large damage to inner hull
CCS		No damage	No damage	Small damage to containment system	LNG Leak

Accidental hull-ice interactions considered in the present study includes:

a) level ice collision (the Baltic Sea)
b) ice ridge collision (the Baltic Sea)
c) ice floe collision (the Baltic Sea)
d) ice stuck (the Baltic Sea)
e) icebergy bit collision (Canadian East Coast)

The limit states of the membrane type LNG carrier with GTT NO96 containment system has been investigated from the following aspects:

a) GTT-provided limit state of the invar membrane
b) Limit state by the deformation from the grounding accident of Paul Kayser LNGC
c) Limit state of the hull structure as tank boundary

The present study adopts the 70cm-deflection at inner hull as a survival criterion, based on which Capacities are calculated for the purpose of hull-ice interactions. The capacity of the double structure is calculated from nonlinear numerical analyses using MSC.DYTRAN.

The Demand of the hazards scenarios are calculated from the following two aspects:
a) Limit stress mechanism
b) Limit energy mechanism

In the application of limit stress mechanism, the regulation of CSA S-471-04 was used to calculate ice-crushing pressure given as a function of normal contact area. Elasto-plastic FE analysis was used to calculate internal strain energy stored in the hull structure as ice features collapse due to compression. This internal strain energy is used as Demand from the considered ice hazards. For this analysis ABAQUS has been used.

In the application of limit energy mechanism, ice features are modeled into FE model and a comprehensive numerical simulation has been done for postulated collision scenarios to calculate 'Demand'. For this analysis, MSC.DYTRAN has been used.

In the calculation of Demand by the limit stress and energy mechanisms, the deflections at inner hull have been checked and compared with the GTT operational limit (4.6mm relative lateral deflection on 1m). The maximum deflection from the most severe scenario is found to be less than the operational limit, which means that the consequence levels in the risk form should be less than or equal to, at most, C2 for all the considered scenarios.

Comparison of the Demands with the Capacities shows that the subject vessel can operate in the Baltic Sea without serious damage at inner hull and the containment system by accidental ice loads. The Demand levels are found to be very small compared to the Capacity levels.

It can be concluded from this risk analysis that the target vessel – GTT NO96 type 170K CBM LNGC with Ice Class 1A – can operate in the proposed areas with a low risk and a sufficient capability of reliable performance.

References

Canadian Standard Association (2005). CSA S471-04.

Det Norske Veritas(2006). DNV Rules for Ships, January 2006, Pt.5 Ch.1 Sec.4 D400.

Det Norske Veritas(2006). "Iceberg Collision Scenario," March. 2006-0672.

Erland M.Schulson (1999). "The Structure and Mechanical Behavior of Ice," In the journal JOM. 51 (2), pp. 21-27.

Finish Maritime Administration(2002). Finish Maritime Administration Regulations on the Structural Design and Engine Output required of Ships for Navigation in Ice, September 2002.

Jaakko Heinonen (2004), "Constitutive Modeling of Ice Rubble in First-Year Ridge Keel", VTT Publication 536, Espoo/2004.

Jensen, A., Løset, S., Høyland, K.V., Liferov, P., Heinonen, J. and Evers, K.-U(2001). "Physical Modelling of First-Year Ice Ridges-Part ii: Mechanical Properties," The 16th International Conference on Port and Ocean Engineering under Arctic Conditions (POAC), Ottawa, Canada, pp. 1493-1502.

Rogachko S., Evdokimov, G., Melnikov, M., Kärnä, T. and Lehmus, E(1997). "The Influence of Porosity on Mechanical Strength of Hummocks," Proc. 16th Int. Conf. Offshore Mechanics and Artic Engineering (OMAE'97 & POAC'97). Yokohama, April 13-18, 1997, Vol. IV, pp. 151-157.

Russia Maritime Registration of Ships (2003), Rules for the Classification and Construction of Sea-Going Ships.

Timco, G.W. Croasdale, K. and Wright, B (2000). "An Overview of First-Year Sea Ice Ridges," Technical Report HYD-TR-047, PERD/CHC Report 5-112, August 2000, p. 157.

Authors Index

Abdel Naby, Maged M 1126
Abt, Claus 1041
Ahn, B.-K. 1200
Ahn, Kyoung-soo 1324
Alexandrov, V. 1295
Alford, Laura K. 477
Alsos, Hagbart S. 622, 631
Amdahl, Jørgen 622, 631
Ando, Jun 1050
Andric, Jerolim 468
Andrieu, Celine 865
Antão, Pedro 82
Ashcroft, Frederick H. 165
Ashe, Glenn 19
Asokumar, G. 808
Awal, Zobair Ibn 275
Ayaz, Zafer 588

Bacicchi, Giorgio 428
Baker, Clifford C. 749
Banawan, Adel A 1126
Bay, M. 758
Beadling, Robert G. 741
Belenky, Vadim 309, 510
Berggreen, Christian 1086
Besnier, F. 57
Bi, Naipei P. 10
Bian, Rugang 1064
Bigler, Christopher 97
Billerbeck, Heike 1317
Blanchet, A. 57
Bøe, Åge 677, 1003
Bogaert, Hannes 35
Boon, Bart 855
Branchereau, S. 57
Brennan, Feargal P. 617
Breuer, Andrew 510
Brizzolara, Stefano 205
Bronsart, Robert 461
Bruhns, Hendrik 191
Bruzzone, Dario 205
Buannic, N. 57
Bulian, Gabriele 275
Byklum, E. 437

Calix St. Pierre, Jessica 97
Caprace, J.-D. 758
Carapellotti, Daniele 527
Cerruti, M. 149
Che, Jungsin 1346
Chen, Qiaofeng 336
Chen, Shunhuai 661
Chen, X.B. 224
Chen, Yingqiu 776
Cho, Minsu 674
Cho, S.-R. 453
Choi, Jae-Woong 330
Choi, Yun We 799
Chua, Kie Hian 588

Chung, Hyun 242
Chung, S.H. 981
Chung, Y.K. 981
Cojeen, H. Paul 865
Collette, Matthew 105, 944, 1107
Costa, Ana Paula dos Santos 1167
Cui, Weicheng 1064
Cusano, Giovanni 428
Cyrino, Julio C. R. 639

Daley, Claude 953, 1016
Daliakopoulos, D. 823
Dam Nielsen, Ulrik 284
Davidson, Andrew 165
de Bruijn, Arnold 855
de Jager, A. 968
de Kat, Jan Otto 309
De Luca, Michele 527
Degtyarev, Alexander B. 1331
Del Castillo de Comas, Francisco 82
Dessi, Daniele 527
Dhinesh, G. 808, 1057
Djie, Hien T. 373
Donkov, Ivica 724
Dow, R.S. 379
Downes, Jonathan 1025
Drummen, Ingo 322

Ebira, Kazuyuki 1186
Egorov, Gennadiy V. 73
Elhewy, Ahmed A. 1126
Endresen, Øyvind 266
Engle, Allen 105
Estefen, Segen F. 731
Estefen, Tiago P. 731

Farinetti, V. 847
Fernandes, Antonio C. 1311
Ferraris, S. 847
Fonseca, N. 141
Fournier, J.R. 224
Francescutto, Alberto 487
Fréchou, Didier 790
Frederking, Robert 1221
Fricke, Wolfgang 1071
Froufe, Leile M. 1175
Fukasawa, Toichi 716

Garbatov, Yordan 543
Godin, Philippe G. 989
Grashorn, Henning 1117
Grevink, Jasper 158
Guadalupi, D. 149
Guedes Soares, C. 141, 354, 543, 935

Ha, Mun-Keun 44, 330
Ha, Woo Il 601

Ha, Yun-Sok 250
Haack, Tobias 1317
Hackett, John P. 97
Han, Jae-Moon 1193
Han, Kyeong-Hee 250
Han, Sungkon 674, 1346
Harada, Minoru 345
Hasegawa, Kazuhiko 275
Hashimoto, Hirotada 693
Hashimoto, Kiyoshi 1142
Hayman, Brian 1086
He, Lei 1269
Hendrikse, Jr., E. Johan 749
Henriksen, Lars 1303
Heo, Hee-Young 250
Heo, Jaekyung 1255
Heo, Joo-Ho 1150
Hermanski, Greg 953
Hirayama, Akihito 1050
Hochkirch, Karsten 903
Hollenbach, Uwe 580, 1117
Hong, Lin 622
Hong, Sam Kwon 799
Hong, Sung Hyun 44
Hørte, Torfinn 553, 677
Hosokawa, Hiroyuki 1303
Hovem, Liv 677
Hu, Changhong 894
Hughes, Owen F. 445, 764
Hussein, Amghad 953
Hussein, Arwa W. 354
Hutchison, Bruce L. 903
Huther, I. 257

Ibrahim, Ahmed 212
Incecik, Atilla 1025
Inoue, Yoshiyuki 196
Iqbal, Kho Shahriar 275
Ivanov, Lyuben D 565
Iwasaki, Yasunori 1186
Izumiyama, Koh 1206, 1287

Jang, Chang Doo 889
Jang, Hyun-Sook 330
Jang, Tae-Won 250
Jang, Young-Hun 114
Jensen, Jørgen J. 1158
Jenstrup, Claus 1086
Jeong, Han Koo 831
Jessup, Stuart 1107
Ji, Chunyan 784
Jian, L. 57
Jo, Young Chun 889
Joensen, Sunvard 1158
Joh, Ki Hun 44
Johannsen, Christian 1186
Jung, Jaekwon 1193

Kahl, Adrian 1071
Kaminski, Mirek 35
Kamishohara, Arata 1303
Kamruzzaman, Md. 196
Kang, Joong-Kyoo 1150
Kang, Kuk Jin 831
Kang, Sung Won 601, 1134
Karlsen, Kasper 1086
Karr, Dale G. 242, 815
Kashiwagi, Masashi 894
Kawabata, K. 44
Kawabe, Hiroshi 217
Kehren, Felix-Ingo 174
Kendrick, Andrew 1016
Kery, Sean M. 1
Khalid, Muhammed S. 477
Kim, Hyochul 1261
Kim Sung, ManSoo 674
Kim, Bong Ju 445, 764
Kim, Booki 1247
Kim, Chun-Gon 831
Kim, DaeHyun 477
Kim, G.-D. 1200
Kim, Gyeong Rae 1134
Kim, H.-S. 453
Kim, Hyun-Soo 330
Kim, Ki-Jung 330
Kim, Kukbin 997
Kim, Kyung-Su 1150
Kim, M. G. 981
Kim, Myung Hyun 601, 1134
Kim, Pan Young 997
Kim, Seong Min 1134
Kim, SeongKi 674
Kim, Sung Geun 1134
Kim, Wha Soo 601, 997
Kim, Won Beom 1012
Kim, Yong Tae 889
Kim, Young Nam 1134
Kinnas, Spyros A. 1269
Kippenes, J 437
Klæbo, Frank 622
Klanac, Alan 839
Klug, Hilmar 580
Kluwe, Florian 396
Kobayashi, E. 574
Konovessis, Dimitris 588
Kontovas, Christos A. 182
Kortenoeven, Jeroen 855
Kõuts, Tarmo 1214
Krüger, Stefan 174, 396, 1317
Kubat, Ivana 1221
Kuhn, John 1107
Kujala, Pentti 1206, 1278
Kumar, Manoj 412
Kusumoto, Hiroki 50

Lavis, David 1107
Lebaillif, D. 257
Lee, C.-S. 1200
Lee, Ai-Kuo 565
Lee, Bok Won 831

Lee, Dong Yeon 799
Lee, H.H. 518
Lee, Hanseong 1269
Lee, I. H. 518
Lee, Jae Myung 1134
Lee, Jae-Yeol 1346
Lee, Joong Nam 44
Lee, Kyoung Eon 1134
Lee, Kyung Jun 1193
Lee, Sang-Heon 250
Lee, Seung-Hee 1261
Lee, Sing-Kwan 1337
Lee, Tae-il 1324
Lee, Tai Yong 44
Lee, W.-S. 1200
Lee, Y.W. 518
Lee, Young Jin 799
Leguen, Jean-François 790
Leheta, Heba W. 1126
Leppäranta, Matti 1214
Li, Dongqin 661
Li, Jun 105
Li, Lin 234
Li, Y.N. 815
Lin, Woei-Min 1, 105, 1107
Lindemark, Torbjørn 1003
Liu, Xiangchun 1064
Liu, Gengshen 1238
Losseau, N. 758
Lotsberg, Inge 1003
Luís, Rui M. 354
Lundsgaard-Larsen, Christian 1086
Luo, Hanbing 535

Maki, Kevin 477
Malenica, S. 224
Mansour, Alaa E. 1158
Mariani, Riccardo 527
Masetti, Isaias Q. 1167
Mashud Karim, Md. 275
Matlakh, A. 1295
Matsuda, Akihiko 693
Mauro, S. 149
McCafferty, Denise B. 749
McClure, Scott C. 373
McCue, Leigh 10
McGregor, Jon 1025
McSweeney, Kevin P. 749
Melchers, Robert E. 919
Menna, A. 149
Menon, Balji 212
Mewis, Friedrich 580
Milgram, Judah 10
Minegaki, Shohei 693
Mineiro, Fabio P. S. 1311
Miyake, Ryuji 894
Miyazaki, Satoshi 716
Miyazaki, Keiko 91
Moan, Torgeir 217, 322, 336, 419, 881
Moe, Erlend 64
Moon, Song-Soo 250

Moore, Colin 1025
Murali, K. 1057

Nakai, Tohei 1142
Nakamura, Tetsuya 687
Narayan, T.K. 250
Nechaev, Yury I. 1295, 1331
Neki, Isao 50
Netto, Theodoro A. 1175
Neves, Marcelo A S 699
Ngiam, Shi Song 617
Ni, Qi-Jun 911
Nick, Eleanor 666
Nienhuis, Ubald 650
Nieuwenhuis, Jan Jaap 650
Novak, Derek 19, 212

Ogawa, Yoshitaka 132, 404
Oh, Jung-Keun 1261
Okada, T. 574
Osawa, Naoki 1080, 1142
Ota, Susumu 91

Paik, B.-G. 1200
Paik, Jeom Kee 445, 764, 823, 865, 1012, 1230
Papanikolaou, Apostolos D. 497
Park, Je-Jun 114
Park, D.W. 981
Park, Gun-Il 330
Park, H.-Z. 453
Park, J.H. 27
Park, Jinsoo 997
Park, Jung-Goo 250
Park, Mi Young 831
Park, Sunho 1255
Park, T.H. 518
Park, Young-Il 1346
Parsons, Michael G. 666, 758
Parunov, Joško 724
Pascoal, R. 141
Patay, S. 758
Patel, Harish N. 363
Paulling, J. Randolph 707
Pavic, Mihailo 953, 1016
Penrose, Justin 989
Podenzana Bonvino, C. 149
Polyakov, V. 1295
Prebeg, Pero 468
Psaraftis, Harilaos N. 182

Qiu, Qiang 535
Quadvlieg, Frans 97
Queutey, P. 968

Ramiro, André 1311
Rana, I. 379
Remes, H. 609
Rezende, F. 224
Rhee, Shin Hyung 989, 1261
Richir, T. 758
Rigo, P. 758

Rodríguez, Claudio A. 699
Roemen, Rik 158
Romanoff, Jani 839
Rosa, André L. 1311
Rundhaug, Trond A. 1003
Rynn, Phillip G. 363
Ryu, Hong Ryeul 601
Ryu, Hyun Su 889

Sales Jr., Joel S. 1167
Sales, Joel S. 1311
Sames, Pierre C. 293
Samuelides, M.S. 823
Saraiva, Alexandre P. 639
Sawamura, Junji 1142
Schellenberger, Gregor 1041
Sebastiani, Luca 428
Sedat, Robert D. 1096
Sen, Debabrata 122
Senjanovic, Ivo 724
Seo, J.-S. 453
Seo, Jung Kwan 445, 764
Serratella, Chris 363
Serror, M. 257
Sherman, Brook 10
Shigemi, Toshiyuki 345
Shin, Yung-Sup 1247
Sielski, Robert A. 960
Singh, S.P. 412
Skjong, Rolf 82, 266
Smith, Craig B. 1033
Soles, Julian 595
Song, In-Haeng 1193
Sphaier, Sergio H. 1167
Spyrou, Kostas J. 388
Srinivasan, Nagan 122
Steen, E. 437
Storhaug, Gaute 64, 419

Streckwall, Heinrich 114
Stumpf, Estelle 1025
Subramanian, Rahul 1057
Subramanian, V. Anantha 808
Sumi, Yoichi 928
Sun, Hong 1269
Sung, Young Jae 1324
Suominen, Mikko 1278
Suzuki, Shota 1142

Takeda, Yu 50
Takimoto, Tadanori 1287
Tanwar, Ravinder 234
Teixeira, A.P. 935
Temarel, P. 27
Terai, Koji 1080
Thoresson, A. 968
Thorkildsen, Harald 1003
Thunes, Ragnar 677
Tian, Chao 911
Tigkas, Ioannis G. 388
Torres, Fernando G. S. 1167
Toyoda, M. 574
Troesch, Armin W. 477
Trovoado, Leandro C. 731

Umeda, Naoya 309, 693
Urm, Hang-Sub 1150
Uto, Shotaro 1287

Valkonen, Janne 1206, 1278
Vanem, Erik 82, 266
Varsta, P. 609
Vassalos, Dracos 299, 588
Visonneau, M. 968
Viviani, M. 149
Voogt, Arjan 595
Vorus, William S. 1096

Wada, Yojiro 799
Wan, Zheng-quan 535
Wang, G. 815
Wang, Chengfang 661
Wang, Ge 553, 565
Wang, Kequang 1214
Wang, Lizheng 661
Wang, Xiaozhi 1247
Weems, Kenneth M. 1
White, Nigel 553
White, Charles N. 373
Windt, J. 968
Wu, Qiang 911
Wu, You-Sheng 911

Xie, Wei 911

Yamamoto, Satoshi 687
Yamamoto, Norio 1080
Yang, S.H. 518
Ye, Naiquan 881
Yoon, Ho Byung 44
You, Guo-Hong 911
Yu, Byeongseok 1255
Yu, Han 105
Yum, Jae-Seon 242

Zachariadis, Panos 182
Zanic, Vedran 468
Zhan, Zhihu 776
Zhang, Sheguang 1
Zhang, Yan 911
Zhou, Sa-Ya 911
Zhu, Tingyao 894
Zimmermann, Michael 461
Zwart, Philip J. 989

Keywords Index

ABIC 284
Abnormal waves 141
Accidental damage 1025
Accidental limit states (ALS) 1230
Active fin control 808
Active pass 1317
Added resistance 894
Advanced finite element analysis 1303
Aluminum 847, 881, 944
Aluminum high-speed vessels 960
Aluminum panels 336
Aluminum ship structures 960
Aluminum stiffened plate structures 865
Anti-rolling tank 693
Artificial neural networks 1126
Asphalt carrier 724
Automatic design 1193

Baltic Sea 1214
Bangladesh water transport 275
Bayesian Modeling 284
Beam winds and waves 404
Benchmark study 437
Bending response 527
Bifurcation 388, 815
Blended method 477
Body forces 114
Boil-off gas (BOG) 44
Bottom damage 174
Boundary element method 1269
Boundary layer 1269
Bow and stern slamming 527
Bow form 1221
Bow-flare slamming 428
Bracket 1071
Bracket fin 1186
Broad band 57
B-spline 1200
B-spline finite element 242
Buckling 437, 1175
Buckling analysis 731
Buckling strength 776
Bulbous bow 1057
Bulk carrier fleets 661
Business transformation 741
Butt joint 609

CAD 741
CAE (Computer-Aided Engineering) 250
Capsizing 388, 396
Capsizing probability 404
Cargo tank pressure 44
Casualty threshold 299
Catamaran 196, 1096
Cathodic protection 1012
Cavitation 114, 1261
Cavitation volume 1193
CFD 518, 808, 894, 903, 968, 981, 1041, 1057, 1261
CIP 894

Classification 1016
Classification calculations 1303
CNG 373
Code calibration 553
Collapse 1175
Collapse strength 354
Collapse strength of plates 935
Combined loads 445
Combined waves and swells 1247
Common Structural Rules (CSR) 674, 677, 776
Competition principle 1331
Composite structure 831
Composition 919
Conditional stochastic processes 1158
Container ship 64, 322, 453, 580, 693, 716, 799
Continuation method 388
Contribution rate analysis 217
Conversion engineering 1303
Core inserts 1086
Correlation of winds and waves 404
Corroded plate 928
Corrosion 919
Corrosion fatigue crack propagation 1012
Corrugated bulkhead 437
Coupled motions 699
Coupling analysis 1142
Course keeping 97
Crack 257
Crack box 257
Crack growth analysis 997
Crack initiation 601
Crack propagation 601
Crack shape control 617
Critical wave episodes 1158
Cruise ships 428
Crushing 631
Cubic spline interpolation 1126
Current 1324
Curvature effect 453
Curved stiffened plates 453, 889
Cylinders 373

Damage 257
Damage combination 1150
Damage safety 174
Damage stability 174
Damping 1311
Damping ratio 50
Data management 105
Dead ship 404
Debond 1086
Decision support 468, 650
Deformability 928
Degree of restraint 889
Design and operation 82
Design criteria 1175
Design for production 250
Design format 677
Design irregular wave 716

Design optimization 911
Design philosophy 35
Design short-term sea state 716
Diesel electric propulsion 1317
Digital manufacturing 741
Direct loading analysis method 716
Distortion prediction 250
Double hull tanker 354, 764
Double-ended ferry 1317
Dredging ship structure 855
Ducted propulsor 1269
Ductile fracture 815
Dynamic knowledge base 1295
Dynamic material properties 823
Dynamics 388

Effect of ship operational intervention 217
Efficiency 1193
Elasto-plastic structural response 823
Energy saving device 580
Environment 165, 919
Ergonomics 749
Evacuation analyses 91
Experiment 322, 419, 453, 953, 1167, 1261
Extreme load response 1247
Extreme responses 477
Extreme waves 1033
Extremely nonlinear 894

Fabrication related initial imperfections 865
Fatigue 1071, 1080, 1142, 1175
Fatigue crack propagation theory 1064
Fatigue damage 1247
Fatigue design 1134
Fatigue life 601, 1134
Fatigue limit states (FLS) 1230
Fatigue strength 609, 776
Fatigue strength evaluation 1134
Fatigue test 601
Fender 1
Fiber bridging 1086
Finite element analysis (FEA) 50, 250, 437, 687, 831, 953, 1003, 1080
Finite element method 724, 889
Finite element simulation of structural response 823
Fishing vessels 699
Flat-stern slamming 428
Floating body 122
Floating offshore structures 588
Floating production storage and offloading 1303
Fluid-structure interaction 35
Force-deformation curve 622
FORM 1158
Formal safety assessment 82
FPSO 622, 1230, 1247
FPSO platform 141
FPSO vessels 1303
Fracture 631
Freak waves 141
Free surface elevation 1057
Free surface 989
Freight capacity 661

FSO vessels 1303
Full QTF 224
Full scale measurements 284, 1278, 1287
Fuzzy logic 1295
Fuzzy optimization 666

GA 1193
Gap cavitation 1255
Gas combustion unit(GCU) 44
General arrangements 666
Genetic algorithm 574, 666, 839
Geometric properties 565
Geometrical correlation 242
Global response 631
Grounding 631
GTT NO96 574, 1346

Habitability 749
Hatch opening deflectionRisk analysis 574
Hazard 574, 1346
Hazard identification 275
Head and bow seas 132
Heat-affected zone (HAZ) 944
Heat-affected zone (HAZ) effect 336
HiCASS 1
High cycle fatigue 1150
High order panel method 1200
High speed craft 97, 847
Highest temperature 889
High speed 1107
High-speed ocean-going vessels 865
Hogging/sagging bending moment 428
Horn rudder 1255
Hotspot stress 997, 1003, 1080, 1134, 1142
HSSL 1107
Hull design 968
Hull form 903
Hull form optimization 1050
Hull girder 553
Hull girder cross-section 565
Hull lines 580
Hull resistance 631
Human fatigue management 749
Humidity 749
Hybrid SWATH 205
Hydrodynamic design 1041
Hydrodynamic performance 911
Hydrodynamic resonance 224
Hydrodynamic stability 234
Hydrodynamic standards 981
Hydrodynamics 149, 205, 1096, 1107
Hydroelasticity 27, 35, 428, 790, 911
Hydrostatic properties 234

IACS CSR (Common Structural Rules) 764
IACS requirements 758
IACS URI3 1337
Ice 574, 1346
Ice Class IA 574, 1346
Ice collision 574, 1346
Ice compression 1214
Ice damages 1278

Ice field 1295
Ice load 1206, 1214, 1278, 1287
Ice pressure 1206, 1221
Ice propeller strength 1337
Identification 50
Impact 639
Impact loads 412
Impact pressure loads 823
Impact pressures 518
Inherent strain 889
Initial design 574
Inland transportation 275
Inland water units 1126
Instrumentation 165
Intact stability 234, 309, 396
Intact stability assessment 275
Intact stability code 404
Intelligent system 1295, 1331
Interaction equation 354
Interface capturing method 894
International Maritime Organization 91
ISO 15016 165
Isogeometric structural analysis 242

JTP rule 784

Knowledge-based engineering 461

Large container carrier 132
Laser hybrid welding 609
Laser-weld 839
LBR-5 software 758
Life cycle value 693
Lifting body technology 97
Limits of stability 699
Line loading 1221
Line-spring 257
LNG 44
LNG carriers 82, 574, 1186, 1346
LNG terminals 224
Load distribution 1206
Load patch 1287
Load scenarios 677
Local stress 1071
Long-duration simulation 122
Longitudinal stiffeners 687
Longitudinal strength 354
Longitudinal waves 799
Long-term 322
Long-term distribution 217
Long-term loading 105
Low cycle fatigue 1150

Maintenance 847
Maneuvering 149, 1324
Maneuvering sea trial 330
Marine structures 1064
Mariner comfort 749
Maritime platform 639
Maritime safety 82
MARPOL 174
Mathematical models 919

Maximum stress 716
Mean stress effect 1016
Measured ship responses 284
Measurement 64, 419
Mechanical collapse testing 865
Midship section 354
Miner's rule 997
Modal analysis 790
Model test at towing tank 981
Model tests 1107, 1117, 1206, 1287, 1311
Model uncertainty 345
Modern containerships 518
Monocolumn platform 1167
Monte Carlo simulation 174
Moonpool 1167
Mooring line 1311
Motion control 799
Multibody interaction 224
Multicriterial optimization 468, 758, 1041
Multi-deck ship 468
Multi-hull 196
Multiobjective optimization 1050
Multiple load conditions 1050

Natural gas 373
Neural network 1295
NLFEA 622
Noise 57, 749
Nonlinear 27, 132, 322, 437, 477, 953
Nonlinear finite element analysis 865
Nonlinear finite element method 345, 445, 764
Nonlinear responses 911
Nonlinear seakeeping 141
Nonlinear wake alignment 1200
Nonlinear wave loads 595
Nonuniform corrosion 935
Notch stress approach 609
NSGA-II 1193
Numerical analysis 453, 639
Numerical ship motion simulation methods 497
Numerical simulation 510
Numerical wave tank 122

Offshore 373, 741
Offshore patrol vessel 1158
Offshore wind turbines 1158
Oil tanker 784
Onboard measurement 574
Open-source software 105
Operability 595
Operation and regulation 497
Optimal design 784
Optimization 205, 574, 580, 903, 1193
Optimized hull form 981
Out-crossing rate 1158
Overlapping propellers 1186

Parametric design 1041
Parametric geometry 903
Parametric roll 396, 693, 699, 799
Pareto optimal solution 1050
Passenger ship 91

Passenger ship safety 299
Passenger submersible 234
Passenger vessel 275, 758
Penetration 622, 631
Performance-based criteria 309
Plastic FEM 1337
Plastic limit states 953
Plastic response 1016
Plates 445
PLM 741
Podded propulsor 1269
Polar ice class 1337
Polynomial filter 1324
POSS 1050
Post-buckling 437
Potential flow 1
Potential flow calculations 1117
Prediction 661
Pre-processing system 250
Pressure dynamic 44
Pressure fluctuation 57
Pressure fluctuations 1193
Pressure pulse 823
Pressure-area relationship 622
Probabilistic assessment 497
Probabilistic damage calculation 174
Probabilistic interpretation 510
Probabilistic methods, ship strength calculation 565
Probabilistic stability 588
Probabilistic viewpoint 284
Probability of failure 1025
Product data management 741
Product development 1317
Product lifecycle management 741
Product platform 650
Production cost 855
Progressive collapse analysis 764
Propagation buckling 1175
Propeller design 968
Propeller excitation 57
Propeller tip vortex 1200
Propulsion 149
Pseudo hotspot stress 1016

Quasi-static analysis 35

Rainflow 105, 419
Random fields 935
RANS 114, 1269
RANSE 412, 1255
Real-coded genetic algorithm 1050
Reduced yield strength of material in HAZ 336
Regression 1324
Regulations 1016
Relative wave height 196
Relief valve 44
Repair methods 1303
Replica specimen 928
Residual resistance estimation 1126
Residual strength of a ship's hull 1025
Residual stress 617
Resistance 1057, 1096

Resistance prediction 1117
Response conditioned waves 322
Response of marine structure 35
Response time distributions 91
RIAM-CMEN 894
Ride control system 97
Rigid risers 1175
Risk 293
Risk analysis 82, 1346
Risk assessment 1230
Risk-based approval 293
Risk-based design 293, 497, 588
Risk-based rule development 677
Risk control option 693
Road test 330
Rogue waves 141, 1033
Roll 388
Roll motions 595, 699
Roll stabilization 808
Rough seas 132
Rudder 799, 1261

Safe return to port 299
Safety seagoing 1331
Sandwich panel 855, 1086
Scale effects 968
Scantling design 758
Sea ice modeling 1214
Sea trial measurement system 330
Sea trials 149
Seabasing 1
Seakeeping 1, 196, 412, 790, 1096
Seakeeping performance 396
Seakeeping with liquid motion in tanks 224
Sealift 1107
Seawater 919
Seawater ballast tank 1012
Segmented model experiments 535
Segmented models 527
Semi-balanced rudder 114
Semi-submersible 595
Serviceability limit states (SLS) 1230
Shell elements 1003
Ship collision 622, 639
Ship damage stability 497
Ship design 650, 666, 953, 1016, 1033
Ship design optimization 1126
Ship detailed design 461
Ship hull 989
Ship loads and vibrations 527
Ship losses 1033
Ship motions 894
Ship operation 580
Ship responses 477, 1221
Ship safety 275, 293, 396
Ship structural design 716
Ship structural detail 1071
Ship structure 953, 1016
Shipbuilding 741
Ship-shaped offshore installations 1230
Shot peening 617
Similarity 928

Simulation 1, 815, 1107
Sinking 1033
Size effects 815, 928
Slamming 27, 35, 412
Sloshing 35
S-N curves 601, 1003
Soft computing 1331
Solid boundary factor 57
Spectral fatigue assessment 1303
Speed-power prediction 1117
Sponson 693
Springing 64, 419
Stability 388
Stability criteria 396
Stability failure 510
Stability in waves 699
Stability of offshore installations 510
Stability of ships 510
Standard algorithm 1295
Standardization 650
Standardization of ship structural parts 461
Stationary test 330
Statistical analysis 217, 1278
Statistical B-spline curve 242
Statistical B-spline surface 242
Steel 847, 919
Stern flow 981
Stern slamming 518, 535
Stiffened panels 731
Stiffened plate structures 445
Stiffness 1311
Stochastic simulations 284
Storm loading 997
Strain concentration 944
Stranded 373
Stranding 631
Strength design 622
Stress 790
Stress concentration 687, 881
Stress cycle counting correction 1247
Structural analysis 724, 839
Structural design 574, 674, 911
Structural design and assessment 1303
Structural hotspot stress 1071
Structural modeling 50
Structural profiles 565
Structural reliability 553, 1025
Structural reliability analysis 345
Structural responses 831
Structural stress 1134
Super C-Class 1317
Superstructure 50
Supply vessel 622, 639
Surface crack 617
SWATH 911, 1158
Symmetric response 27
Symmetric wedge 518
Synthetic seawater 1012

Task lighting 749
Taylor series expansion 565
Temperature 749

Tensile strength 928
Thickness effect 687
Thickness measurement patterns 935
Three-dimensional Green function method 196
Three-dimensional hydro-model 234
Time domain simulation 27
Time-to-flood 299
Time-variant reliability 565
TLP 1158
TMCP steel 1012
Toe grinding 601, 881
Towing tank 790
Transverse compression 336
Trials 165
Turbulence 1057
Turning 1324
Twin-skeg ship 981
Twisted nose 114
Two-parameter unified approach 1064
Two phase flow 114

Ultimate bending moment 731
Ultimate capacity 437, 553
Ultimate limit state design 865
Ultimate limit states (ULS) 445, 764, 1230
Ultimate longitudinal strength 345
Ultimate strength 336, 354, 453, 731, 944
Unconventional fast hull 205
UNDX 1050
Uniform safety level 677

Validation 1107
Variable-amplitude fatigue test 997
Variational analysis 242
Variational simulation 242
VBM amidships 535
VDR (Voyage Data Record) 330
Vectorization 839
Vertical bending moment 141, 322
Very large crude oil carrier 50
Vibration 57
Virtual instrumentation 808
Viscous/inviscid flow coupling 1269
VLCC 165, 674
VOF 989, 1057
Vortex lattice method 1269

Wake improved fin 1186
Wake roll-up 1200
Wake wash 1317
Warping 64
Water entry 518
Water impact loads 831
Wave condition 217
Wave-induced vibration 64
Wave loads 27, 132
Wave records 141
Wave resistance 205
Wave spectra 284
Wave-induced load 217
Wave-making resistance 903, 1050
Waves 234

Wave-structure interaction 122
Weather criterion 275
Web stiffened cruciform connections 1003
Web-core 839
Weibull distribution 105
Weight 674, 855
Weight vector 661
Weighted support vector regression 661
Weld 881, 944
Weld distortion 250
Weld notch 609
Weld profile 1071
Weld size 1003
Weld toe 687

Welded joint 687, 1016, 1071
Welded structures 1134
Welding deformation 889
Wet drop test 518
Whipping 64, 419, 527, 535
Whipping vibrations 428
Whole-body vibration 749
WIG craft 831

X-joint 1086

Yield strength 776

Zigzag 1324